T0402095

European Yearbook of International Economic Law

Christoph Herrmann · Jörg Philipp Terhechte
Editors

European Yearbook
of International
Economic Law 2012

 Springer

Editors
Professor Dr. Christoph Herrmann, LL.M.
Chair for Constitutional
and Administrative, European Law
European and International Economic Law
University of Passau
Innstraße 39
94030 Passau
Germany
christoph.herrmann@eui.eu

Dr. Jörg Philipp Terhechte
Assistant Professor of Law
Chair of Public Law and European Law
University of Siegen
Hölderlinstr. 3
57068 Siegen
Germany
terhechte@techt.wiwi.uni-siegen.de

ISBN 978-3-642-23308-1   e-ISBN 978-3-642-23309-8
DOI 10.1007/978-3-642-23309-8
Springer Heidelberg Dordrecht London New York

Library of Congress Control Number: 2009932417

Printed on acid-free paper

Springer is part of Springer Science+Business Media (www.springer.com)

Editorial

"All good things go by three", the saying goes. As editors, we hope, firstly that readers will consider EYIEL to be "a good thing", and secondly that EYIEL will not go by after this third volume.

Like volume two, Part I of EYIEL 3 (2012) focuses on two topics we considered to be of particular relevance for International Economic Law: 10 years of membership of the People's Republic of China (PRC) in the WTO; and Global Energy Markets and their legal regulation under International Economic Law.

China's accession to the WTO marked a milestone in the development of the WTO as a truly global institution, for many reasons. It expanded its territorial reach significantly and it brought the economy, which will pretty soon – presumably – not only be the world's largest exporter but also the largest economy in the world, under the disciplines of the world trade regime. Whether the relationship between the traditional and remaining trade powers, in particular the US and the EU, on the one hand, and the PRC on the other hand will develop smoothly or will become more bumpy with tensions rising, remains to be seen. It will be a dominant factor for the overall development of International Economic Law at any rate. The contributions in Part I devoted to China's tenth WTO birthday shed light on different aspects of China's membership and of its trading relations – and conflicts – with other major WTO members, and they treat the problems from different perspectives.

Energy is one of the sources of life which is absolutely indispensable and at the same time potentially devastating. Long before the nuclear catastrophe of Fukujima and the re-assessment of nuclear energy, it was already clear that the regionally asymmetric availability of energy sources and their similarly asymmetric consumption patterns bring about particular difficulties for the regulation of trade in energy. The second thematic focus of Part I tries to give an overview of the quite diverse regulatory approaches being used to deal with energy trade, globally in the WTO, bi- or tri-regionally in the Energy Charter Treaty, regionally in the newly established Energy Community of the Balcan and – of course – in the European Union. It clearly demonstrates that the regulation of international energy markets touches upon much more than just trade restrictions, namely investment protection, transfer of technology, competition law and network regulation.

The contributions in Part II deal with dispute resolution developments under NAFTA, with the Rule of Law in the regional integration process in sub-Saharan Africa and with the trends in the recent trade agreement practice of the European Union. The institutional reports in Part III treat the activities of the G8/G20, dispute settlement practice of the WTO, the WTO Doha negotiations, the new IMF financial structure and – as a novelty – the activities of the World Customs Organization (WCO). Customs law is the legitimate mother of International Economic Law but is often neglected by its offspring. We are very happy to re-unite "the family" by covering the WCO in the Institutions' Part of EYIEL.

The publication calendar of EYIEL allows directing the attention already to the next volume. Vol. 4 (2013) will focus mainly on Global Competition law. With Vol. 4, Markus Krajewski will join us and complement the then editorial team with his particular competencies in the fields of WTO law, competition law and regulation of services of general interest.

Again, we would like to express our gratefulness to a great number of people without whom EYIEL could never be published. Firstly, we thank our reliable and cooperative contributors. EYIEL is first and foremost their work! Secondly, we are thankful for the support by our Editorial Advisory Board's members. Dr. Brigitte Reschke of Springer was the extremely professional and supportive contact at the publisher we have got used to over the last years. Finally, we thank our academic and student assistant teams at the Universities of Passau and Hamburg respectively for their professional handling of the manuscripts. A particular gratitude goes to Christoph's secretary, Ms. Liane Dobler for the formatting of most of EYIEL Vol. 3 (2012). All remaining omissions and errors are – of course – our sole editorial responsibility. We can only hope for having minimised their number.

Passau/Hamburg   Christoph Herrmann
                                                                   Jörg Philipp Terhechte

Contents

Special Focus II: Global Energy Markets and International Economic Law

Part II   Regional Integration

Part III   Institutions

Part IV   Book Reviews

Contributors

Wolfgang Bergthaler is counsel at the International Monetary Fund's Legal Department, where he works on legal aspects of IMF financing operations, governance and financial issues, exchange system issues, financial sector issues, and corporate insolvency issues. Before joining the IMF in 2006, he practiced as an attorney in Vienna and Brussels. Wolfgang is a graduate of Karl-Franzens University Graz, Austria (Magister iuris and Doctor iuris), Georgetown University Law Center (LL.M.) and the Université Robert Schuman, Strasbourg (Certificate Erasmus). Wolfgang is admitted to practice in the State of New York and the District of Columbia and was admitted to practice in Vienna. He lectures on international financial law matters and publishes in the area of financial regulation.

Colin Brown is a lawyer in Unit F.2 (Legal Aspects of Trade Policy) of the Directorate General for Trade of the European Commission where he works on trade and energy and trade and environment issues as well as international procurement issues. He advises on bilateral trade negotiations and co-ordinates DG TRADE's legal work on bilateral negotiations. Colin is also responsible for institutional issues, including the roll-out of the changes to EU trade policy brought about by the Lisbon Treaty. Before joining DG Trade in October 2006 he served for 6 years for the Legal Service of the European Commission. Previously, he worked on trade law issues in private practice in Brussels. Colin has been chair of the Legal Advisory Committee of the Energy Charter Treaty since January 2004. He is visiting lecturer in WTO law at the Université Catholique de Louvain, Belgium. He holds an LL.B. (first class Honours) from the Faculty of Law of the University of Edinburgh, Scotland (1996), a Diploma in International Relations from the Bologna Center of the School of Advanced International Studies (SAIS), Johns Hopkins University, Bologna, Italy (1997) and an LL.M. in European Law from the College of Europe, Bruges (1998). He is a member of the New York Bar.

Julien Chaisse is Assistant Professor (Research) at the Faculty of Law, Centre for Financial Regulation and Economic Development, Chinese University of Hong

Kong (CUHK). He is the co-editor of the book entitled Asia Expansion of Trade and Foreign Direct Investment (Routledge: London 2009), and the author of several journal articles on international trade law and investment law such as 'Sovereign Wealth Funds in the Making - Assessing the Economic Feasibility and Regulatory Strategies' (Journal of World Trade, 2011). The article in this volume is part of the research entitled "the evolving international investment regime" led by Julien at the Faculty of Law of the Chinese University of Hong Kong and which aims to investigate the evolution of investment law across relevant agreements and to discern patterns of congruence and divergence across key issue areas, substantive disciplines and countries and regions.

Mireille Cossy is a Counsellor in the Trade in Services Division of the World Trade Organization (WTO) in Geneva. Her main areas of interest include the legal aspects of international trade in services, as well as the interface between the multilateral trading system and other policy areas, in particular environment, energy and public health. Since joining the WTO in 1995, she acted as a Secretary to various WTO bodies and dispute panels. Mireille regularly publishes on various WTO-related topics. Before joining the WTO, she carried out humanitarian missions with the International Committee of the Red Cross and worked for the Swiss Ministry of Economic Affairs. Mireille graduated in Law at the Universities of Lausanne and Geneva (Switzerland).

Christopher Dallimore is Senior Researcher in the Department of Customs and Excise at the University of Münster. He specializes in the legal implications of supply chain security measures as well as customs-related problems under European and international law. Christopher is also the Head of Studies of the Master of Customs Administration programme offered by the University of Münster and sub-editor of the World Customs Journal.

Katharina Gnath is a Ph.D.-student at the Berlin Graduate School for Transnational Studies, a joint programme of the Free University Berlin, the Hertie School of Governance and the Social Science Research Center Berlin (WZB). She holds a B.A. in Philosophy, Politics and Economics from the University of Oxford and an M.Sc. in European Politics and Governance from the London School of Economics. Katharina is an Associate Fellow of the German Council on Foreign Relations' (DGAP) Globalization and World Economy Programme.

Ludwig Gramlich is Professor for Public Law and Public Economic Law at Chemnitz University of Technology since 1992. He received his doctorate in law (1978) and his Habilitation from the University of Würzburg (1983). His main fields of research are legal issues of networks and infrastructure (in particular telecommunications, postal affairs, banking and monetary law).

Adeline Hinderer has been working on trade relations between the EU and China in the European Commission since 2008. Prior to that, she was a negotiator for investment and services, which included WTO multilateral and bilateral negotiations as well as OECD and G8 work. Before joining the European Commission, she worked for a federation of multinational companies. Adeline holds a Master Degree in European affairs from the College of Europe in Bruges and graduated from the Institut d'Etudes Politiques in Strasbourg. She also studied international relations at Georgetown University in Washington, D.C.

Gary Clyde Hufbauer has been the Reginald Jones Senior Fellow since 1992, was the Maurice Greenberg Chair and Director of Studies at the Council on Foreign Relations (1996–1998), the Marcus Wallenberg Professor of International Finance Diplomacy at Georgetown University (1985–1992), senior fellow at the Institute (1981–1985), deputy director of the International Law Institute at Georgetown University (1979–1981), deputy assistant secretary for international trade and investment policy of the US Treasury (1977–1979), and director of the international tax staff at the Treasury (1974–1976). Gary has written numerous books on international trade, investment, and tax issues, including Figuring Out the Doha Round (2010) and US Taxation of Foreign Income (2007).

Roland Ismer holds the chair for tax law and public law at the University of Erlangen, Germany. He has master's degrees in law from the University of Munich and in economics from the London School of Economics as well as a PhD and a habilitation in law, both from the University of Munich. His research focuses on (international) tax law, legal aspects of climate change and economic analysis of law.

Claudia Kemfert is Professor of Energy Economics and Sustainability at the Hertie School of Governance in Berlin and Head of the department of Energy, Transportation, Environment at the German Institute of Economic Research (DIW Berlin) since April 2004. Her research activities concentrate on the evaluation of climate and energy policy strategies. She studied economics at Oldenburg, Bielefeld (Germany) and Stanford University (USA). Claudia worked for the Fondazione Eni Enrico Mattei (FEEM) (Italy) and Stuttgart University (Institute for Rational Energy Use). She gave lectures at the universities of St. Petersburg (2003/04), Moscow (2000/01) und Siena (1998, 2002/03). Claudia was Associate Professor and headed a PhD research group at Oldenburg University. She has been awarded the most prestigious prize from the German Science Foundation ("Elf der Wissenschaft 2006"). Claudia advised EU president José Manuel Barroso in a "High level Group on Energy", and is member of the advisory group on energy of the European Commission (DG Research). She acts as scientific advisor of the Austrian Institute of Economics (WIFO), the EUREF Institute and of the Energy Institute at University of Linz.

Edwini Kessie is Regional Coordinator for African Countries in the Institute for Training and Technical Cooperation, WTO. Previously, he was Counsellor in the Council & Trade Negotiations Committee Division of the WTO. He holds a Doctorate Degree in Law from the University of Technology, Sydney, Australia,

Masters' Degrees in Law from the University of Toronto, Canada and the University of Brussels and a Bachelor's Degree in Law from the University of Ghana. He is admitted as a solicitor to the Supreme Courts of England & Wales, New South Wales, Australia and Ghana. He is also a part-time lecturer in international trade law at the World Trade Institute (Berne), the University of Lausanne, the University of Technology (Sydney) and at the Universities of Pretoria and Western Cape in South Africa. His principal areas of interest are dispute settlement, trade and development, regional integration and legal aspects of international trade.

Markus Krajewski is Professor of public and international law at the University of Erlangen-Nuremberg (Germany) and a visiting professor at the World Trade Institute in Berne. Previously he held positions at the universities of Bremen and Potsdam and at King's College London. His research interests include international and European law, in particular constitutional and institutional issues of WTO law, trade in services, external relations of the EU and the treatment of public services under European and international law. He is a regular consultant on international trade law for governmental institutions and non-governmental organisations. In the academic year 2009/2010 he directed a capacity building project at the Faculty of Law of Addis Ababa University in support of Ethiopia's accession to the WTO. Since 2011 he is a member of the Committee on International Trade Law of the International Law Association (ILA).

Andreas Krallmann is a First Secretary in the WTO unit of the Permanent Mission of Germany to the Office of the United Nations and other International Organisations in Geneva, Switzerland. Andreas studied law at the Free University Berlin, where he graduated in 2000. In 2001, he obtained an LL.M. in International Commercial Law from the University of Nottingham, UK. After taking his bar exam in Germany (Berlin, 2003), he worked in the European departments of the German Federal Ministry of Finance (2004–2006) and the Federal Ministry of the Economy and Technology (2006–2007). In 2007, the latter seconded him to his current posting in Geneva. Andreas is currently chairing the WTO Committee on Subsidies and Countervailing Measures.

Robert MacLean is a partner at Squire Sanders Brussels office (Competition, Trade & EU Regulatory) and his particular expertise covers international and EU trade law and customs law. He has been involved in a large number of the EU's trade defence investigations initiated by the European Commission. Many of these investigations have been high-profile ones raising novel aspects of EU trade policy and, in some instances, have involved litigation in the European Courts. He is also recognised as a leading international trade practitioner by many of the publications ranking lawyers including Chambers Global, the Legal 500 EMEA and European Legal Experts. Robert received his legal education at the University of Glasgow (LL.B. (Hons., 1985), Diploma (1986), Ph.D. (1995)) and the University of Alberta (LL.M., 1988).

Bryan Mercurio is a Professor of Law and Associate Dean (Research) at the Chinese University of Hong Kong. His expertise is in international economic law, focusing primarily on the interaction between international trade law and intellectual property as well as the public policy aspects of trade negotiations and agreements. Professor Mercurio is the author of a leading WTO law textbook, 'World Trade Law: Text, Materials and Commentary' (Hart, 2008), as well as numerous other books and articles. A consultant to industry and legal firms, he has also advised Members of both the Australian and New Zealand parliament on international trade law and intellectual property matters and been a consultant on, among other issues, the Australia-United States Free Trade Agreement.

Carsten Nowak is Professor of Public Law, especially European Law, at the Europa-University Viadrina Frankfurt (Oder) and Director of the new Frankfurt Institute for the Law of the European Union (FIREU). He studied law at the University of Hamburg, where he received his doctorate in law and his Habilitation. His main fields of research are German and international public law and European law (especially European economic law, fundamental freedoms, competition law, judicial protection and fundamental rights).

Christoph Ohler is Professor for Public Law, European Law, Public International Law and International Economic Law at the Friedrich-Schiller-University of Jena, Germany. Since August 2008 he is also speaker of the graduate progamme "Global Financial Markets", funded by the German "Foundation Money and Currency". He graduated in law at the University of Bayreuth (1993) and the College of Europe, Bruges (LL.M., 1994). Christoph received his doctorate in law from the University of Bayreuth (1997) and his Habilitation (2005) from the Ludwig-Maximilians-University of Munich, Germany.

Mauro Petriccione is Director in the EU Commission, DG Trade, in charge of bilateral trade relations with the Americas (both North America and Latin America); the Far East (China and Japan), Australia and New Zealand; trade in services and investment. Born in Italy (1957), he graduated in Law from the University of Bari (1982). After a brief spell doing research at the same University and performing military service in the Italian Navy (officer of the Coast Guard), Mauro moved to London in 1984, first as a Visiting Research Scholar at the Institute of Advanced Legal Studies and then as postgraduate student at the London School of Economics, where he obtained an LL.M. (1986). After working as in-house Attorney for IBM Italy in Milan for a little less than a year, he joined the European Commission in September 1987. He has worked in trade policy ever since, covering a wide range of activities, negotiations (both multilateral and bilateral) and areas: from trade defence to standards, investment, competition, WTO, dispute settlement, relations with Member States and the other European Institutions.

Patrick C. Reed is a member of the New York and District of Columbia Bars and a lawyer with the firm of Simons & Wiskin in New York City. His law practice concentrates on customs, international trade, and import-export regulatory law, including the World Trade Organization agreements and other international trade and investment agreements. He is an adjunct professor in the Center for Global Affairs, New York University, and an adjunct assistant professor in the Law Department, Baruch College, City University of New York. He holds a J.D. degree from Columbia University School of Law and a master's degree and a Ph.D. in international relations from The Fletcher School of Law and Diplomacy, Tufts University, with concentrations in international law and international economic relations.

August Reinisch is Professor of international and European law at the University of Vienna and Adjunct Professor at the Bologna Center/SAIS of Johns Hopkins University. He holds Master's degrees in philosophy (1990) and in law (1988) as well as a doctorate in law (1991) from the University of Vienna and an LL.M. (1989) from NYU Law School. He has widely published on international Law, with a recent focus on investment law and the law of International Organizations. He currently serves as arbitrator on the In Rem Restitution Panel according to the Austrian General Settlement Fund Law 2001, dealing with Holocaust-related property claims, as president of an UNCITRAL investment arbitration tribunal and as arbitrator and expert in other investment cases.

Raymond Ritter is senior economist in the International Policy Analysis Division of the European Central Bank. Prior to joining the ECB in 2000, he was economist at the German Ministry of Economics. He studied economics at the Universities of Passau, Pennsylvania and Hamburg, where he earned a master's degree. He holds a doctorate degree in economics from the University of the Bundeswehr, Hamburg. From 1996 to 1999, Raymond served as research assistant at the Europa-Kolleg Hamburg. He has been lecturer in international relations at the Frankfurt School of Finance and Management since 2009 and has published on international and European policy issues.

Claudia Schmucker is head of the Globalization and World Economy Program at the German Council on Foreign Relations (DGAP) in Berlin. Before joining the institute in 2002, she was a project manager at the Center for International Cooperation (CIC) in Bonn. She started her studies at the University of Bonn and Elmira, NY, and holds a Master in North American Studies and a Ph.D. in economics from the Free University of Berlin. Claudia attended the Yale Center for International and Area Studies (YCIAS) of the Yale University, conducting research on transatlantic trade relations between the EU and the U.S. and the WTO.

Yulia Selivanova is a trade expert in the Energy Charter Secretariat in Brussels. She holds a Doctorate degree from the University of Berne (Switzerland). Her thesis focused on energy dual pricing under WTO law. Yulia graduated from the Master of International Law and Economics program at the World Trade Institute in Berne and worked for 5 years in Geneva – first as a consultant in the Rules Division in the WTO, and then in the global WTO & International Trade Practice Group of Baker & McKenzie, an international law firm. Previously, Yulia worked as a lawyer in an international law firm and an international bank in Moscow, Russia. She published on a range of trade and WTO issues, in particular trade in energy and Russian trade policies.

Bernhard Steinki is Senior Counsel in the Legal Department of the International Monetary Fund where he focuses on Fund financial and budget issues. Before joining the IMF in 1999, he was Counsel in the Legal Department of Deutsche Bundesbank working on European Monetary Union issues. Bernhard is a graduate of Freiburg University and holds Master of Laws degrees from the University of London (King's College) and George Washington University. He is a member of the Frankfurt bar.

Christian J. Tams is Professor of international Law at the University of Glasgow. He is a qualified German lawyer and holds LL.M. and Ph.D. degrees from the University of Cambridge. His research focuses on the law of State responsibility, international investment law and questions of dispute settlement. In addition to his academic work, he has advised States in proceedings before the International Court of Justice and the International Tribunal for the Law of the Sea. He is a member, inter alia, of the German Court of Arbitration for Sports, the ILA Committee on Non-State Actors, and the scientific council of the United Nations Association (Germany).

Teresa Thorp is a director of Insight International, an international trade and development advisory association. Her practice supports private sector clients, governments, Law Commissions and Attorney General Offices on matters of WTO Law, investment, regional integration, environmental law and sustainable development worldwide. Within an African context, Teresa has been engaged by Member States of COMESA, EAC, ECOWAS and SADC. From 2008 to 2009, she worked in the SADC Secretariat as Services and Investment Law Advisor and facilitated EPA negotiations. In 2007, as Chief Technical Advisor to Zanzibar's Ministry of Tourism, Trade and Investment, Teresa participated in trade negotiations on EAC integration. She was an Associate in International Economic Law with Bizclim (the ACP/EC private sector facility) during its 3-year lifespan. Teresa has qualifications in business, economics and law (BCM, LL.B. (Hons), PGDip Com (Econ.), PGDip Legal Practice, MBA, LL.M., DEA international law).

Mitali Tyagi is a Senior Legal Officer at the Australian Attorney-General's Department, Office of International Law, working primarily on issues relating to international trade law. Previous work experience has included acting as a lawyer in litigation and mergers & acquisitions at Mallesons Stephen Jaques; working on technical assistance and legal institution building projects in the Sydney and Banda Aceh offices of the International Development Law Organisation; researching constitutional aspects of sentencing for federal crimes at the Australian Law Reform Commission; and on native title issues at the Cape York Land Council. She holds a Master of Laws (International Legal Studies) from New York

University, a Bachelor of Laws (Hons I) and Bachelor of Commerce from the University of Sydney. Her research focuses on issues relating to public international law and international trade law.

Andrea Wechsler M.A. (Oxon), LL.M. (Columbia), LL.M. (Munich) is both a Research Fellow at the Max Planck Institute for Intellectual Property and Competition Law and Coordinator of the International Max Planck Research School for Competition and Innovation (IMPRS-CI), Munich, Germany. Further work experience includes management consulting with McKinsey & Company, Inc., court clerking at the European Court of Justice in the Chambers of Judge Ninon Colneric, and lecturing at the Ludwig Maximilians University Munich and the China-EU School of Law, Beijing, China. Andrea Wechsler received her education at the University of Oxford (M.A.), Columbia University School of Law (LL.M.), Ludwig Maximilians University (LL.M.), Munich, and Beijing University (Chinese language diploma). Presently, Andrea is a Max-Weberportdoc-Fellow at the European University Institute, Florence, Italy.

Hans-Michael Wolffgang is Professor of International Trade and Tax Law and Head of the Department of Customs and Excise which forms part of the Institute of Tax Law at the University of Münster, Germany. He is director of the Münster Master studies in Customs Administration, Law and Policy and has written extensively on international trade law, customs law and export controls in Europe.

Jared Woollacott is an economic geography Ph.D. candidate at Boston University focusing on energy. Prior to his Ph.D. work, Jared earned Master's Degrees in Public Policy and Environmental Management from Duke University. Jared has worked as an economic research analyst in various capacities. For 4 years, he worked in economic consulting at Analysis Group, Inc. During the summer of 2009, he worked in the Economic Research and Statistics division at the World Trade Organization. Since early 2010, he has conducted international trade research on a part-time basis for the Peterson Institute for International Economics.

Chien-Huei Wu is Assistant Research Fellow in Academia Sinica, Taipei, Taiwan. He received his Ph.D. degree from the European University Institute, Florence, Italy, in 2009. Since then, he worked for a short period as an Assistant Professor at National Chung Cheng University, Chiayi, Taiwan. Prior to his doctoral studies, he worked for the Ministry of Justice of Taiwan as a district attorney. Chien-Hueis research interests cover international economic law and EU external relations law. He pays particular attention to Asian regionalism and WTO-IMF linkage and he also follows closely EU-China and EU-ASEAN relations.

Part I
Topics

China–EU Trade Relations: A View from Brussels

Mauro Petriccione and Adeline Hinderer

Introduction

China's trading relationship with the EU and Western economies has evolved dramatically since Deng Xiaoping initiated reforms in China more than 30 years ago, from a situation in which almost nothing was traded to the establishment of a major trading relationship with the EU as well as the US. This rapid growth in trade has been observed since the beginning of the 1980s. In 1980, China was only the 22nd largest source for EU imports and the 25th largest destination for EU exports.[1] In 2004, the EU surpassed Japan and the US to become China's largest trading partner. It is now also the EU's first source of imports and its fastest growing export market, and is widely predicted to become soon the EU's first trading partner altogether. China also drew much attention worldwide by surpassing Germany as the world's largest exporter in value in 2009 and Japan as the second largest national economy in 2010 after the US (or the third economy in the world counting the EU as one). Significant developments have taken place since China acceded to the WTO in 2001, after 15 years of negotiations. The WTO accession was seen as historic and the result of strong political will in China and its key trading partners. It did generate hope that China would follow a path of further reforms and progress towards a rules based economy firmly anchored in the multilateral system.

---

[1] At that time the EU had 15 Member States.

Disclaimer: This article reflects the views of its authors only, and in no way can be taken to represent the position of the European Commission. It attempts to sketch out a view – perhaps a very subjective one – of trade relations between Europe and China and how these are rooted in China's own economic policies. The article does not attempt to explain the vastly more complex political and strategic relationship between the European Union and China.

M. Petriccione (✉) • A. Hinderer
Directorate General for Trade, European Commission, Charlemagne Building, 1049 Brussels, Belgium
e-mail: mauro.petriccione@ec.europa.eu; adeline.hinderer@ec.europa.eu

C. Herrmann and J.P. Terhechte (eds.), *European Yearbook of International Economic Law (EYIEL), Vol. 3 (2012)*, European Yearbook of International Economic Law 3, DOI 10.1007/978-3-642-23309-8_1, © Springer-Verlag Berlin Heidelberg 2012

Ten years later, while a number of substantial reforms have taken place, many of the expectations – probably at least somewhat excessive – formed in the West at the time of accession remain unmet. In a number of sectors, the Chinese leadership has shown little appetite for liberalisation beyond what it considers it has accepted as a result of its WTO commitments. And following the financial crisis, China seems more than ever determined to follow its own development path and economic model, at its own pace, regardless of the West's views and pressure. As a result, trade and economic irritants regularly make headlines and cast a cloud on the relationships between China and its trading partners, notably the EU, the US and Japan. Recent examples include China's policies on 'indigenous innovation' and raw materials as well as difficulties encountered by Western operators to access the Chinese market in sectors ranging from wind power to information technology.

Yet, regardless of bilateral tensions, the EU's engagement with China in multi-lateral and plurilateral settings has become more than ever an obvious necessity, as no major global economic challenge can be resolved today without China's involvement. In the WTO context, China is now systematically included in all configurations tasked with finding possible compromises, such as the so-called G7 that emerged in 2008 as a core group of Members with a shared interest in finding a deal that could then be presented to the wider membership. China has also been an active participant in the G20, which emerged as a key platform for discussions on international economic and financial issues in the wake of the financial crisis. Although the status of the G20 and its relationship with global institutions such as the IMF and the UN remain unclear, it is a potentially promising avenue for international economic governance and Beijing's overall engagement in the G20 is an encouraging signal that this may indeed be the right format for macroeconomic coordination and shaping of global economic rules in the future, which is of key importance for the EU. At the same time, interrogations remain as to Beijing's readiness to assume responsibilities commensurate with China's growing weight in the global economy.

Other trends are likely to shape relationships with China over the coming years, including China's increased role as an outward investor as envisioned by its 'Go Global' policy. In 2009 China was the world's fifth largest outward investor[2] and indications pointing towards increased Chinese investment in Europe (bond but also non bond-investment) are another key element to factor in when looking at the EU–China relationship in the coming years.

The picture becomes even more complex if one takes political and geopolitical aspects into account. It is worth mentioning briefly that political considerations have often been entangled with economic and trade aspects in the development of the relationship between China and its partners. For instance, tensions over what China has labelled its 'core interests' (Tibet, Taiwan in particular) have at times

---

[2] Sauvant/Davies, What will an appreciation of China's currency do to inward and outward FDI?, Issues in International Investment, Vale Columbia Centre on Sustainable International Investment, January 2011.

generated trade tensions with the EU or with some EU Member States. Likewise, the EU's 'arms embargo' towards China is regularly quoted by China as a major irritant in the bilateral relationship, whose removal would contribute to better ties, including in the economic sphere. The same applies to the US, although the US–China relationship also comprises a military and security dimension that is much less present in the EU–China relationship. More generally, US military involvement in the region, the US pledge to defend Taiwan against aggression, its stated interest in the peaceful resolution of territorial disputes over the South China Sea, and its stance towards North Korea have been colliding with what many analysts perceive as a more assertive stance of China towards its neighbours. For instance, the territorial dimension and geographic proximity is an important factor for the relationship between China and Japan – in addition to historic grievances and mistrust. The relationships between China and India and other South East Asian neighbours also encompass multiple economic and political dimensions, making for both conflicting and converging interests: despite growing trade and investment ties, uncertainties and tensions remain, due notably to territorial disputes, concerns over Chinese competition and hegemony across the region, relationships and alliances with other parts of the world, etc.

Another noteworthy development for the economic relationship between China and its partners is the evolution of China's ties with Hong Kong and Taiwan. These two economies have greatly contributed to Mainland China's economic transformation, providing capital at a time when China needed it (and Western investors where still shy) and, even more importantly, technology and know-how, as well as access to global financial and trade circuits. Close cultural ties facilitated this process, as did the prospect of Hong Kong's 're-absorption' and – somewhat paradoxically – the complex Taiwan-Mainland China relationship, since the strengthening of economic ties was largely seen by Beijing as a tool to demonstrate the benefits of reunification and by Taipei as an insurance policy against rash moves by Beijing. These relationships have now evolved, but remain strong: economic ties have been reinforced with the 2003 Mainland-Hong Kong Closer Economic Partnership Arrangement (CEPA), in particular its provisions facilitating access to the Chinese market for Hong Kong services suppliers, as well as various measures to allow Hong Kong banks to undertake operations in RMB. Despite Shanghai's ambitions to become a leading financial centre, Hong Kong will remain for years to come China's key international financial centre and a main source of investment to Mainland China – in addition to being a model and the study ground for the impact and benefits of reforms and liberalisation and the internationalisation of the RMB.[3] Cross-Strait *rapprochement* led to the signature of the China-Taiwan Economic Cooperation

---

[3] Chen/Peng, "The Potential of the Renminbi as an International Currency", China Economic Issues, November 2007; Speech by Martin Wheatley, Chief Executive Officer of the Securities and Futures Commission at the Fourth Annual Conference of the Hong Kong Investment Funds Association, October 2010, available at: http://www.sfc.hk/sfc/doc/EN/speeches/speeches/10/Martin_20101004.pdf.

Framework Agreement (ECFA) in June 2010, a significant development that would have been unthinkable a few years before. ECFA and the related ongoing economic cooperation in a range of areas may lead to increased competitiveness resulting from the fostering of bilateral investment, technology transfer to the mainland and closer integration of the Chinese and Taiwanese economies.

The evolution of relationships between China and its neighbours will undoubtedly also impact the relationship between China and the West, and in particular the US–China but also the EU–China relationship. Some analysts believe it will even "shape our next decade".[4] And the future of the region will be influenced both by the increasing integration between the economies of these Asian countries and by conflicting national interests between the three local powers – China, India and Japan.

Against this background, to understand better the foundations and the evolution of the economic relationship between China and the EU, including some of the difficulties and misunderstandings that have emerged over the past years, we first examine the rationale for China's economic objectives and the contradictions in the EU and China's attitudes and policies towards each other. We then review China's economic policies, especially those that have a major influence on the business climate in China, and pause on the possible emergence of a 'rule of law with Chinese characteristics', before offering thoughts on convergence and conflicts between Western and Chinese interests. The conclusion looks at possible ways forward and lessons that could be drawn for the EU's economic and trade policy vis-à-vis China in the coming years.

China's Economic Objectives: Development or Hegemony?

China's 11th Five-Year Plan first outlined 'scientific development' and the construction of a 'harmonious society' as national objectives, and the 12th Five-Year Plan continues in the same vein. The Chinese leadership has frequently underlined some of the implications for China's relations with the world: China does not aim at world dominance, whether in the economic or geopolitical sense, and its priority is its economic development and its impact on welfare and employment of the Chinese people. These are, in turn, the key to the stability of the country (and of the CPC leadership), as well as, indirectly, to its territorial integrity. In this perspective, economic growth, through the modernisation of the economy, is of paramount importance, but as a means to an end. The end is the development of China and the welfare of its citizen. This 'growth *uber alles*' scenario finds its roots in Deng Xiaoping's revolution, the factual acknowledgment that Mao's Communist doctrine had not delivered this outcome, and the advent of a far reaching pragmatism, exemplified by Deng's aphorisms that "it doesn't matter if a cat is black or

---

[4] Emmot, Rivals – How the power struggle between China, India and Japan will shape our next decade, 2008–2009.

white, so long as it catches mice", and that "poverty is not socialism; to be rich is glorious". This scenario has obviously benign implications for the rest of the world, and it is not surprising that it is a recurrent theme in the rhetorical armoury of Chinese leaders and officials.[5] Regardless of any other aim the Chinese leadership may have, those objectives in themselves are genuine, are being pursued with great energy and are working. China's poverty rate is expected to fall to around 5% of the population by 2015,[6] and there are now 420 million Chinese in the nine Eastern provinces having a *per capita* income on a par with some EU Member States. However, there is an alternative scenario that many in the West have begun to fear: China does not aim at world dominance – yet, but in 2050? China's national power and the projection of power are evolving, and not always in a comfortable direction,[7] in particular for China's neighbours: world domination maybe not, but regional hegemony? Western and Chinese analysts alike debate whether Deng's "lying low" advice is still appropriate, but one usually forgets to listen to the entirety of Deng's words: "Keep a cool head and maintain a low profile. Never take the lead – but aim to do something big". China is certainly doing "something big", and its motivations are bound to be complex. Nor would it be wise to underestimate more profound philosophical differences between China and the West. Alongside the desire for economic development for its own sake, China is also motivated by a desire for economic emancipation – with strong echoes of the Unequal Treaties and of the political and economic troubles of the post-Imperial era – and by a complex attraction to/rejection of Western models. The US, in particular, more than Europe, appears as much of a Western benchmark as China would (implicitly) admit. This is so for a number of reasons, whose undertones are positive or negative, and sometimes frankly ambiguous: the US involvement in East Asia, and in China in particular, since before WWII; the Taiwan question; the legacy of the Cold War; but also the fact that, much as China appreciates Europe's economy and technological base, the US remains today the only national power combining military, geopolitical, economic and technological reach worth aspiring to if a country aspires to world status.

Finally, it would be a mistake to underestimate the perception in China that the West is naturally critical, if not clearly distrustful of China because of its regime, as well as – why not – its growing power. In the more radical version of this view, strongly reminiscent of Cold War rivalry, the West – and the US in particular – is not prepared to accept competition from China, and either does little to help, or

---

[5] For recent examples, see Chinese Vice-Premier Li Keqiang's speech in Davos emphasising that China's development is peaceful and that peace is "the essence of China's 5,000-year culture and the ideal constantly pursued by the Chinese nation" or Li Keqiang's editorial "The world should not fear a growing China", Financial Times, 10th January, 2011.

[6] Millenium Goals Development Report 2010, http://www.un.org/millenniumgoals/pdf/MDG%20Report%202010%20En%20r15%20-low%20res%2020100615%20-.pdf.

[7] Glaser, Ensuring that China Rises Peacefully, Clingendael Asia Forum Publication, December 2010.

even actively undermines China's "peaceful rise". However, even those who do not subscribe to this view are often persuaded that the West applies a double standard.[8] This perception, which the Chinese find profoundly irritating, is often compounded by Western contradictory attitudes: for instance, at the same time wanting China to exert global responsibilities that match its economic development, yet also very wary of China using all the attributes of a major power (developments of its military, economic diplomacy in Africa, etc.).

China, Europe, 'Double Standards' and Other Contradictions

These contradictory attitudes also increasingly pervade European attitudes to China. A very pertinent example in the economic field concerns technology transfers. There is a growing perception in Europe that Chinese firms copy and 'steal' technology[9]; that this is unfair; and that Chinese firms should really acquire the technologies they want on commercial terms. Likewise, inadequate intellectual property protection, including in respect of patents, continues to be a major problem for European firms who invest in China or licence their technologies there.[10] In fact, the problem of patent protection in China is not limited to insufficient enforcement of otherwise adequate or at least sufficient rules: there are worrying indications that China may be moving towards a system of patent protection that would not be entirely in line with international practices and would be aimed primarily, instead, at the 'absorption' of foreign technologies and at encouraging 'indigenous innovation', as well as tolerating or facilitating technology 'theft'.[11] This not only fosters insecurity in European investors, leading them not to deploy their best technologies in China,

---

[8] See for instance Pei, outlining the far more sceptical and distrustful prisms the West applies to China because of its authoritarian regime, "What China needs to learn", The Diplomat, 1st October, 2010, and "Why the West should not demonise China", Financial Times, 25th November, 2010.

[9] The debate is clearly reminiscent of that about Japan until the 1980s. As to China today, only 22% of European businesses feel that the enforcement of IPR laws and regulations is adequate, and 48% consider local protectionism to be one of the key risks for their business in China (European Chamber Business Confidence Survey, EU Chamber of Commerce in China in partnership with Roland Berger, 2010). A number of policies and legislation aimed at maximising disclosure of technical developments by foreigners inside China contribute to these perceptions, for instance: joint venture requirements in a number of industrial and high tech sectors; local content requirements, which were in place for the wind-turbine sector notably (70% domestic content); requirements to file payments first in China to increase the number of locally owned IPRs; regulation on Commercial Encryption that requires disclosure of source codes for certain IT products, etc.

[10] The issue of intellectual property rights (IPRs) protection and its enforcement is dealt with in greater detail in section V.

[11] The OECD in a report on China's IP environment noted that "national pride often gives legitimacy to behaviours that are at the border of IP laws", OECD report TAD/TC/WP(2010)12/ANN/FINAL.

but it also gives strength to those voices that argue that European firms should be actively discouraged from transferring technology to China. Yet, European firms are China's most important source of technology transfer[12] and, even though for some companies the technology and intellectual property risk in China is indeed too high to take, the economic attraction of a presence in the Chinese market means that most of them are unlikely to stay away, even if European public authorities had the means and the inclination to suggest that they should do so. Europeans, therefore, feel that they have the high moral ground on the question of technology transfer to China: we do contribute, more than anyone else, to China's technological development, and we are not repaid with the kind of fair and safe legal and administrative environment that we believe is the essential condition for innovators to flourish and be justly rewarded. However, a growing number of Chinese firms are coming of age, especially in the information technology sector, but also in mature industries like motor vehicles, and appear to be acting on the basis of commercial considerations: flush with cash from China stellar economic growth performance, as well as with access to easy and low cost finance (largely because of the policies of state-owned banks and the scarcity of suitable investment instruments in China) they go abroad and buy the technologies they need, on the market and at market prices. Better than that, they buy the firms who have that technology: executives at Geely (the Chinese automaker) are reported to have quipped that Geely does not need an R&D centre after its acquisition of Volvo. This also raises more than passing concerns in Europe – just like the Japanese acquisition spree in the 1980s did. Is our economy in danger of being hollowed out? At present these are isolated cases, but surely they are destined to multiply? Is it fair that companies that have grown rich on unfair trade – too cheap labour; too cheap financing by state-owned banks; state-owned firms need not reward shareholders, etc. – buy our technologies, take them back to China and use them to compete with us even more effectively, including on third markets, as well as in Europe and in China?[13] Again, reality is more complex, and more complicated: at least some Chinese firms are successful because they have the right recipe and

---

The transfer of patents or patent applications to foreigners requires registration and approval before being valid, both by the State Intellectual Property Office (SIPO) and the Ministries of Science and Technology (MOST) and of Commerce (MofCOM) (Art 10 Patent Law). Foreigners are encouraged to file first in China (Art. 20 Patent Law) and need approval if they want to file first abroad; approval requires full disclosure of their invention to SIPO and related ministries for each industry.

[12] MofCOM, China-EU Economic and Trade Cooperation is Increasingly Enhanced, 10th May, 2010. see http://english.mofcom.gov.cn/article/newsrelease/significantnews/201005/201005069 10123.html.

[13] Such concerns can be found in a number of recent articles and opinion pieces touching upon Chinese investments in Europe. See for instance comments relayed by Vice President Tajani in the article "Europa fürchtet Technikklau aus China", Handelsblatt, 27th December, 2010 or "Les emplettes européennes de la Chine", L'Expansion, December 2010, as well as the article co-signed by Ministers from Poland, Germany, Spain, Portugal, Italy and France in Le Monde and Il Sole 24 Ore, "L'Europe doit défendre ses intérêts tout en restant fidèle à son ouverture au monde", Le Monde, 9th February, 2011.

they may also invest in Europe to stay. Issues related to subsidies, cheap financing, state ownership, are real concerns, and cannot be ignored by Europe or China. At the same time, it is hard for the Chinese not to feel that double standards are being applied to them.

In parallel, China's own attitude and behaviour towards the outside world, and the West in particular, are equally riddled with contradictions and a degree of duality, if not outright double standards. Two examples of such dualities are what one could call the 'Great Power vs. Developing Country complex', and the 'Multi-polar World vs. Middle Kingdom syndrome'. Of course, these two labels cover a number of factors that interact with each other in many ways, and are often exacerbated by the rhetorical needs of any given occasion. This notwithstanding, the resulting picture is one of deep-seated uncertainty as to where exactly China is today, where it is – or where it ought to be – going, and how it should relate to the rest of the world. This uncertainty may at times be a healthy anchor to the very complex reality of today's China, for both China itself and its foreign partners. Yet, if mishandled, it equally has the potential to seriously damage China's relations with the world.

To begin with, to say that China is still a developing country may not be very popular among the growing ranks of those who feel threatened by its economic reach but remains nevertheless partly true. On the one hand, it is striking that China accounts for nearly all the world's reduction in poverty, reached its Millennium Development Goal of halving poverty compared to 1990 14 years ahead of the 2015 target date,[14] with some analysts predicting that China could nearly eradicate extreme poverty by 2015.[15] On the other hand, the overall level of wealth of most ordinary Chinese remains well below developed countries' standards. China is usually ranked halfway in various GDP *per capita* rankings[16] but this doesn't account for growing income inequalities and large disparities between the various provinces: nine Eastern provinces on a par with developed countries, nine provinces with a GDP *per capita* comparable to lower middle-income countries and thirteen provinces with less than USD 1,000 GDP *per capita*.

China's economic growth rates ranged between 8.3 and 14.2% over the last decade, and were still above 9% in 2008 and 2009,[17] in the middle of the worst

---

[14] Chen/Ravallion, "The developing world is poorer than we thought, but no less successful in the fight against poverty", World Bank, August 2008.

[15] Chandy/Gertz, Poverty in Numbers: The Changing State of Global Poverty from 2005 to 2015, The Brookings Institution, January 2011.

[16] IMF World Economic Outlook database, October 2010 update. China was ranked 93 out of 181 countries in terms of GDP per capita at purchasing power parity. Other sources such as World Bank and CIA World Fact Book have different rankings, for instance the CIA Worldfactbook ranks China 127 out of 229 countries in February 2010, see www.cia.gov/library/publications/the-world-factbook/rankorder/2004rank.html.

[17] GDP variation at constant prices, IMF World Economic Outlook database, visited in February 2010. Looking at quarter-to-quarter growth rates however, the economy slowed almost to a halt at the end of 2008 and the beginning of 2009 and rebounded sharply after. See Naughton, "The Turning Point: First Steps toward a Post-Crisis Economy", China Leadership Monitor, N°31.

economic crisis since the Great Depression, thanks in no small part to a massive economic stimulus package and lending by state-owned banks. Nor are Chinese leaders slow to point out how China's financial resources have propped up the US economy at the height of the recent financial crisis, or that they are ready to support the Euro.[18]

It is not surprising, therefore, to hear growing objections to China still being a beneficiary of trade preferences under the EU's Generalised System of Preferences (GSP), or to the fact that Europe still has a budget for development assistance, albeit shrinking,[19] for a country that possesses nuclear weapons and can put an astronaut in orbit. Nor should China be surprised at the impatience of many of its partners as to the increasingly slow and erratic pace of implementation of legal and economic reform even though it is generally acknowledged that China's record in drafting new laws and regulations is one of continuous improvement, in terms of identification of objectives, increasing opportunities for consultation of stakeholders and the general public, quality of the legislative work, especially if confronted with the enormity of the task of transformation of the Chinese society in the past three decades. As it is often the case, implementation is by far the weaker side, in terms of administrative resources devoted to it, of uniformity across provinces, of ability of the judicial system to cope with legislative innovation (for instance, in the intellectual property field). China usually ascribes its struggle with implementation of modern laws and regulations to the extraordinary speed of this modernisation, and pleads its status as a developing country to ask its partners for more patience. While the point is undoubtedly valid, China should hardly be surprised that the equation "China is a developing country, hence it cannot be held to the same standards as a developed country, or not yet at least; but China is still a Great Power and its standards of behaviour are as good as anyone else's" does not necessarily carry the day.

China is also a staunch champion of a multi-polar world. Partly, this has historical and geopolitical roots. Already after the 1911 revolution, 'balance of power'

---

[18] See for instance (1) Chinese President Hu Jintao at Summer Davos 2010: "At a time of negative economic growth for major developed countries, the fast economic stabilization and rapid economic growth of China and other major developing countries greatly boosted international confidence in overcoming the financial crisis and provided a strong impetus to the world economic growth", http://www.china-embassy.org/eng/zt/768675/xw/t752077.htm; (2) Premier Wen Jiabao's pledge to support the Euro and buy Greek bonds on his October 2010 European visit. "China's Premier, Wen Jiabao, pledges support to the Euro", http://www.guardian.co.uk/world/2010/oct/04/china-wen-jiabao-euro. Similar support to the Euro and promises to buy Spanish bonds were made by Vice Premier Li Keqiang during his January 2011 trip to Spain; (3) Vice Premier Wang Qishan at the 3rd EU-China High Level Economic and Trade Dialogue also said his nation had taken "concrete action" to help the European Union with its debt problems, http://www.bloomberg.com/news/2010-12-21/euro-rises-as-china-s-wang-pledges-to-help-eu-with-debt-crisis-yen-gains.html.

[19] €128 m was set aside for the Multiannual Indicative Programme (MIP) for 2007–2010. In the MIP for 2011–2013, the amount is €45 m, with more emphasis on the poorer provinces in Middle and Western China and a focus on two areas: 1) support to reforms in areas covered by sectoral dialogues; 2) assistance related to environment, energy, and climate change.

politics appeared as the only way in which China could escape the isolation – and the failures – of the late Imperial era, find its place in the world, and resist Japanese hegemonic ambitions in Asia. After the Communist revolution, and especially after the break with the Soviet Union, again, a multi-polar world felt a much safer place for China. Today, after the end of the Cold War and of the Soviet Union, and faced with the prospect of the US as the single dominant superpower, multi-polarity remains the safest choice for China. This is true in the economic sphere too. In the 1980s and 1990s the choice of GATT and then WTO membership, which became a true national priority for China and was pursued with great determination, was motivated by China's economic vulnerability. Trade with and investment from the West was perceived as taking place on the West's terms, and China felt that its fledgling export economy could be exploited, or simply shut down, for either economic or other reasons – although perceptions in the West differed dramatically. More recently, it is the vulnerability to an interdependent global economy that motivates China multi-polar and multilateral choice. Given that the same applies to Europe, albeit as a result from different historical roots, and that even in the US the recurrent isolationist or unilateralist temptations permeating segments of society and the political apparatus remain a minority view, China and Europe, and the West more generally, ought to be on the same page in maintaining and strengthening multilateral economic governance.

Yet, one could be forgiven for thinking that the legacy of the Middle Kingdom still permeates China's attitudes to the rest of the World. This is perhaps more palpable in the economic sphere, given the astounding economic success of modern China. China's efforts to modernise its economy have long ceased to be the by-product of the need to attract Western investment – if they ever truly were so – and have acquired the same aims as everywhere else: a stable economy, the elimination of poverty, the welfare of citizens, a sustainable economy, national prestige, etc. The switch from dismantling soviet-style regulation to re-regulating the economy along modern lines poses two distinct challenges to the Chinese leadership. The first one is how to reconcile a modern market economy with the kind of highly discretionary political control that the Chinese regime is not prepared to abandon. The second – very relevant to the 'Middle Kingdom syndrome' – relates to the model to be followed for this regulation. No Western model provides a complete answer, or one that can be readily and easily adapted to China's reality, and neither do international norms, where they exist. Like their counterparts in Europe, the US or Japan, Chinese regulators and policy-makers borrow, copy, adapt, transform and sometimes subvert foreign models. This trend is of course far from linear, especially given the magnitude of the task and the speed at which change is taking place. Yet, there is a growing perception in Western business and economic policy circles that China is slowly but steadily moving towards an alternative model of economic regulation and that China is less concerned with integration and compatibility with the standards in its main foreign markets (as one would expect), and more inspired by economic nationalism: China's economic performance should benefit – or should be made to benefit – primarily the Chinese themselves, and this means essentially Chinese firms. Observers also note with concern how nationalism as such – the belief that China is now important enough to stop catering to the 'special needs' of foreign business and that foreigners should fully adapt to Chinese norms if they wish to do business in and with China – increasingly seems to shape China's economic policies.

Of course, none of this is exclusively Chinese, and this is not China's overt official position. Indeed, Chinese leaders have gone out of their way to reassure foreign business.[20] Nevertheless, if one looks at developments in the field of product standards, conformity assessment, investment, construction services, public procurement or renewable energies to name a few examples,[21] it is increasingly difficult to draw a line between rules and regulations aimed at serving China above all, and rules and regulations aimed at serving Chinese firms to the disadvantage of their foreign competitors.

Whenever contradictory attitudes like this emerge in relations between countries allegations of 'double standards', unfairness, excessive selfishness, veiled or explicit, become common currency. While everyone realistically expects everyone else to protect and pursue their self-interest, the notion that this is somehow 'unfair' always lurks just beneath the surface. Still, most countries have a basic understanding of where the acceptable limits of this tension are in their relations with another country, as well as ways to signal that those limits are in danger of being stretched, before tensions explode, for instance in a full blown trade war. There appears to be a much greater uncertainty as to where those limits are in the bilateral economic relations between China and Europe – or, for that matter, China and the US or Japan – than there is in the relations between the other world economic powers. Instead, this knowledge of where the 'acceptability benchmark' lies appears to have been replaced by the awareness that a trade war with China could have disastrous consequences and would almost certainly prove impossible to contain, which has made both China and its foreign partners exercise caution and restraint – so far. So, why this uneasy truce, rather than peace?

As far as Europe and the West are concerned, size and speed are probably the main reason. China has always loomed large in the European imaginary, but for a long time it was far away and difficult to reach. When China became more easily reachable as of the 1800s, it remained technologically backward and

---

[20] Examples include statements made by Premier Wen Jiabao on the occasion of European Commission's President Barroso visit to Beijing in April 2010 as well as his speech at the October 2010 EU-China Business Summit. "I do not want to read the prepared speech, I want to talk about the issues that are of interest to European business leaders (..) and remove some misunderstandings to work more closely together (. . .) China offers a broad market for international companies (. . .) China will press ahead with reforms and opening up. All multinationals registered in China enjoy equal treatment as Chinese national enterprises (. . .) We will not only protect your intellectual property but also accord you equal national treatment as enjoyed by Chinese enterprises. If there is a problem in this regard you can directly call Premier Wen and I will take my responsibilities to solve your problem", http://tvnewsroom.consilium.europa.eu/story/index/story_id/15261/media_id/34997.

[21] See section V for more details on some of these aspects.

non-threatening in any sense, including economic. As a result it was easy to put it safely away in the mental box of the 'sleeping giant', who would "make the world tremble when awaken" – maybe, one day. The same applies to Communist China until Deng Xiaoping and the 'opening up' policy. Today, however, China is everywhere: in our wardrobes, on our tables, in our children's toy box, in our pockets, offices and homes in the form of electronic and ICT appliances, in our factories in the form of parts and components, increasingly in our public and private budgets as a result of purchases of government bonds and of portfolio and foreign direct investments. Is the giant now awake and getting ready to swallow us? The reality is that there is a growing sense in Europe that this economic relationship is growing so fast that it could become unmanageable, with those 'acceptability benchmarks' being exceeded well before the EU could notice and signal to China that a mutual adjustment was needed. If we look back at our contradictory attitude to technology transfer, the problem is not so much that technology is one of our last competitive advantages and we do not wish to give it away. Technology is rather like working capital: its value lies in being deployed, in being 'spent', but it needs an adequate return. Can we get an adequate return from investing in China's future? This is not only about the ability of our firms trading with and investing in China to make profits today or tomorrow, but also and perhaps primarily about our competitiveness and therefore our future. Can our competitiveness be enhanced, or at least not be diminished, by this investment in China? These are very much the same gripes we had towards Japan in the 1980s. Those went away for a number of reasons, not all of them good: Japan could leverage its scarce resources way beyond what anyone would have believed possible, but those resources were still limited; Japan reached the limits of its growth 'at our expenses', as many in Europe saw it, before it could do irrecoverable damage to our industrial fabric, so we could stop wringing our hands; moreover, Japanese investment in Europe and elsewhere had the intelligence of eventually integrating and bringing growth and jobs, and indeed spurred more innovation in Europe and elsewhere. That being said, the closure of the Japanese economy to EU imports and investment remains a cause of concern, so that we still complain that we have contributed to Japan's wealth without an adequate return, something which still hangs over our bilateral relations with that country.

As far as China is concerned, while the causes may be different, the resulting feeling of uneasiness seems to be reciprocal. And the list of causes, real, perceived or somehow re-constructed, is long. It starts with distant memories of the Unequal Treaties and with the superficial comparison between the foreign commercial presence then and now in places like Shanghai. It feeds itself on lingering communist mistrust of capitalism and consumerism, as well as, more importantly, on the growing complexity of controlling a modern and increasingly affluent society. Above all, the question that seems to be constantly at the back of the mind of Chinese officials is "how good is this for China?" "How can these foreigners be useful to China?" "How do we ensure that China is not exploited unfairly – again?" For all the talk of mutual benefit, there seems to be many who believe – or fear – that trade and investment is a zero-sum game: a view dangerously mirroring

European fears of a Great Chinese Takeover. And if all this sounds slightly paranoid, it is because it may well be so. Yet we should not underestimate how harmful this kind of mutual paranoia can be for what has become an essential trade and investment relationship for both Europe and China.

China's Economic Policies

The 'official' view of China's economic policies, relayed by Chinese official sources but also endorsed by the more optimistic observers in Europe and elsewhere, is one of continuous adaptation over the past three decades, from the communist, centrally planned economy to a vibrant capitalist market economy in the twenty-first century. In this view, while it is true that the state has a much bigger role than in the West, there are good reasons for it, and these are partly transitory, since the private sector of the economy is still developing, and partly structural, because only the state can take care of the social, welfare, employment considerations that make for a 'harmonious society'. The same view admits that there are of course weaknesses, due to the fact that China is after all still a developing country and that certain reforms and their implementation take time, but they will be corrected in due course: overall, however, the Chinese system today is effective, solid and delivers the goods, as attested by many years of double-digit economic growth as well as good performance, well beyond 'coping', in both the 1997 Asian financial crisis and the recent global one. Finally, this view holds that there is still much to learn from the West, but less than one may think, as shown by the fact that the much vaunted western financial system not only does not work well when exported to other parts of the world, but is capable of sudden collapse on its home turf.

Given this worldview, the real concerns of Chinese economic policy makers have to do primarily with the efficiency of the economy and its autonomy: the debate about re-balancing the Chinese economy away from exports as the main motor of economic growth and towards domestic consumption is not new, but only with the recent global financial and economic crisis it seems to have acquired real political urgency in Beijing,[22] as outlined in the 12th Five-Year Plan, which puts

---

[22] Indications of increased focus include: (1) the Health Reform plan issued in January 2009 with plans to spend RMB 850 billion by 2011 to provide universal medical service to the whole population and make health care more accessible and affordable. (2) The 2009 National People Congress Work Report from March 2009, http://www.npc.gov.cn/englishnpc/news/Events/2009-03/14/content_1493265.htm. (3) China Economic Policy Guidelines for 2010 as outlined by the Central Economic Work Conference in December 2009, that stress the need for transforming China's economic model notably by improving social security, pension, income subsidies to the poor and access to low cost housing as a way to support domestic consumption. (4) The low-cost housing policy that was operationalised in the April 2010 State Council "New 10 Articles" designed to cool off the property market – a remarkable change of policy from stimulating growth in the housing sector. Naughton, "The turning point in housing", China Leadership Monitor, No. 32.

forward 're-balancing' as one of the key objectives,[23] with an undertone of serious concern as to how much China's growth and economic development depend on growth elsewhere and how much more fragile than expected the world economy really is.

As it is often the case, a closer look shows a much more complex picture, with elements of vulnerability that are sometimes in themselves not good for China, whereas in other cases the harm for China may come from the reactions that certain policies may eventually generate among China's foreign partners or investors. In particular, it is true that, thanks to its massive stimulus package China still managed to achieve 9% growth in 2009; however, much of this came from investment in fixed infrastructure, mainly railways, which had already been planned. More came from the instruction given to the domestic, especially state-owned, banking system to relax credit conditions. This reversed part of a decade of efforts to clear those same banks of bad debts accumulated since the 1997 crisis, and fuelled once again real estate speculation, which the Chinese government had been trying to dampen. Moreover, China could only lessen the impact of the crisis on its export-oriented sector, so that the weight of the adjustment fell on internal migrant workers: semi-official figures spoke of about 30 million workers being at least temporarily laid off, but given the notorious unreliability of any estimates on the real number of internal migrant workers in China, this is likely to be a conservative figure. Needless to say, few other countries in the world could politically afford proportional unemployment of this size, even temporary, without the adjustment mechanisms (unemployment compensation as well as various forms of safety nets) that have added very substantially to the cost of the crisis in Europe and elsewhere. Even in China, prolonged unemployment on this scale could have caused serious social and political unrest, given that most of these workers had to return to their home provinces, already the poorer in China, with little hope of finding alternative sources of support. Thus, there must be question marks on whether the Chinese economic system was truly better equipped or whether the Chinese leadership 'simply' made intelligent use of whatever favourable circumstances happened to be present. The much talked-about 're-balancing' of the economy towards a domestic market that is largely yet to be built is not a very close prospect, especially if one looks at the relatively small financial resources that are being devoted to it.[24] It has become apparent, by now, that investment (mostly domestic, or channelled via Hong Kong, or the usual low tax jurisdictions such as the Virgin or Cayman Islands, or Taiwan),

---

[23] The 12th Five Year Plan adopted by the Chinese National People's Congress in March 2011 outlines a broad programme of domestic growth and rebalancing, combined with more income distribution and state provision of social and public services. Expanding domestic demand is explicitly referred to as a long term objective and gradual process.

[24] In fact, the choice not to deploy massive resources towards this goal before the instruments to ensure their adequate use (health care schemes, medical infrastructure and personnel, pension schemes, etc.) have been set up and received a minimum of testing on the ground may well be a wise one. All the same, this put the issue of re-balancing at best in a medium-term perspective.

is the main driver of China's economic growth. Nevertheless, exports remain important, as earner of foreign reserves and as provider of employment: while it is probably true that China does not deliberately pursue a trade surplus, neither does the Chinese government worry too much about it.[25] In the end, there are important similarities with Japan in the 1980s: imbalances between investment, exports and domestic consumption, currency undervaluation, etc. While there are also important differences between the two cases,[26] they do not seem sufficient to reassure that a potential 'China threat' will go away naturally, the way the 'Japan threat' did, primarily because at a given point Japan seemed to reach the limits of its growth potential and there is no sign of the same happening to China.

From a more structural point of view, important elements of China's trade and industrial policies betray a mercantilist orientation, with more than a trace of Communist belief in planned industrialisation at all cost. The process of privatisation of state-owned enterprises has virtually halted, replaced by a process of consolidation and efficiency-seeking that sees SOEs not as burdensome relics of the centrally planned economy, whose main residual value was the employment they provided, but rather as the core of new national champions, to be provided with the resources (financial, human and technological) and the know-how to succeed both in China and eventually abroad. Nor are SOEs the only national champions: 'private' firms are sometimes equally nurtured, supported and encouraged, including in their forays abroad (also thanks to close links between management, the Communist Party, and the Army). Foreign direct investment remains restricted, by the 'catalogue' of prohibited, allowed and encouraged investment managed by the National Development and Reform Commission (NDRC)[27] and the Ministry of Commerce,[28] as well as by a complex array of ad hoc restrictions (ownership limitations and equity caps, joint venture requirements, choice of partner restrictions, etc.). Easy access to cheap financing is one of the strengths of Chinese firms nowadays, as well as one of the key concerns of its foreign partners. Although China does not lack capital these days, investment opportunities for it remain relatively undeveloped. Moreover, both bank lending and the use of the high rate of savings by SOEs can be controlled by public authorities, and not only at central government level. The result has been the

---

[25] True, the Chinese government does try to assuage the growing concerns of its foreign partners – primarily the US, but increasingly a number of European countries as well, and therefore the EU – but so far it has employed mostly political statements (including complaining about western restrictions on the export of "high tech products" – code for dual-use technologies – whose removal would miraculously redress the trade imbalance between China and the US or the EU) or deployed "buying missions", without taking any structural action aimed at facilitating imports.

[26] If anything, China's economy is much more open to the world than Japan was (or arguably still is).

[27] The former State Planning Commission and now the "super-ministry" in charge of economic planning and industrial policies.

[28] Catalogue for the Guidance of Foreign Investment Industries (amended in 2007), Decree No. 57 of the National Development and Reform Commission and the Ministry of Commerce of the People's Republic of China.

proliferation of 'productive' investment, making China a producer of capital intensive goods with massive overcapacity in sectors such as steel and chemicals, rather than fit its traditional image of source of labour intensive goods.

China's external trade regime, at least as far as trade in goods is concerned, is more open than those of many developing countries, including other emerging economies, largely because of the terms of its WTO accession. Still, restrictions remain, and even more so in services sectors. While China is not actively promoting import substitution policies in general, it does so regularly in public procurement,[29] along with local content requirements and other restrictions.

As usual, there are different readings of these policies. One view is that they are a relic of an outdated attitude, or the preference of a 'conservative faction' of the Chinese leadership, and that in fact China is somewhat 'betrayed' by these 'weaknesses' in policy-making, which do not serve well its goals of economic efficiency. China's policies, therefore, can be changed through persuasion and appealing to China's self-interest. Another view, however, is that these policy choices are deliberate – or even that they serve the 'hegemony' scenario. In this case too, China would be 'betrayed' by the same 'weaknesses' in policy-making, because those policies are 'objectively' not effective. In this view, China's policies can only be changed through a combination of outside pressure and – again – appeal to China's self-interest.

One common element that underpins all scenarios, however, is the relative lack of efficiency of China's economy and the need for China to up its game in terms of economic policies if the goal of economic development is to be maintained – whatever broader goals it is pursuing. With all respect undoubtedly due to China's economic achievements so far, a number of analysts (and not only from the West) believe that an adjustment will be necessary and possibly painful, and others believe that the days of double-digit growth are coming to an end.[30] Thus, the common thread towards nudging China into changing its policies is persuading China's leadership that changes are in China's own interest. This ought to be axiomatic, yet it is striking how much this is neglected, in practice, by Western analysts and practitioners alike. It is fair to say, however, that China's leadership has gained in self-confidence and self-assurance very rapidly (with the handling of the financial and economic crisis giving them an additional, substantial boost) and that lessons from any source in running a successful economy are less and less

---

[29] China is not yet a party to the WTO plurilateral Government Procurement Agreement. In its WTO accession protocol China undertook to negotiate its accession to the GPA too: it is now in the process of doing so, but negotiations are taking their time, with few indications of any great level of ambition as to access to procurement contracts that China is prepared to guarantee to its partners.

[30] For instance, Pettis, "China Faces a Difficult Economic Transition", Carnegie Commentary, 25TH August, 2010, or Yu Yongding, President of the China Society of World Economics, "China going forward", New Europe, special edition, January 2011, and in China Daily, 23rd December, 2010.

appreciated. Likewise, the increasingly loud arguments from Europe (and even more so from the US) that trade tensions will eventually 'force' the West into a trade war with China, which would benefit no-one, do not appear to have too much impact either.

Business Climate and 'Rule of Law with Chinese Characteristics'

While in private conversations European companies have been voicing for several years serious concerns about the difficulties encountered in the Chinese market, 2009–2010 saw the international business community become much more vocal in public about the evolution of China's business climate. The European Chamber of Commerce in China, on the occasion of the launch of its annual position paper in 2009, emphasised the slowdown in the pace of reforms, and the worsening of the situation in some sectors due to an increase of industrial policy interventions and foreign investment restrictions.[31] That year the wind-turbines industry made the headlines when it appeared that no foreign wind-turbine manufacturers (including leading global manufacturers from the EU, US and India that had undertaken significant investments in China) were selected for a package of 5 billion Euro tendering procedures for wind turbines. Initial reactions from Chinese authorities recalling existing procurement rules and calling for a tougher application of 'Buy Chinese' policies at local level only increased concerns further.[32] A significant number of articles relayed businesses concerns on China's business environment[33] and some statements from disappointed CEOs of multinational companies were quoted in the press. A Financial Times article by the then European Chamber's President tellingly entitled 'China is beginning to frustrate foreign business'[34] attracted significant attention internationally and among Chinese leaders. Following these public displays of anxiety and concerns over China, the Chinese leadership began to go to great lengths to offer public reassurances on the occasion of many high level meetings with European policy makers and companies. One case in point is the speech delivered by Premier Wen Jiabao on the occasion of the October 2010 EU–China Business Summit.[35] Some of the developments and trends that

---

[31] Press release on the occasion of the release of the European Business, European Chamber Calls for Further Opening up and Fundamental Reforms to Build a Sustainable Economic Recovery in China, China Position Paper 2009/2010, 2nd September, 2009.

[32] See for instance "Foreign companies blowing in the wind", Asia Times, 11th June, 2009; "Foreigners favoured in some deals, says NDRC", South China Morning Post, 16th June, 2009.

[33] Roberts, "China: Closing for Business? Western companies are finding themselves shut out as Beijing promotes homegrown rivals", Business Week, 25th March, 2010.

[34] Wuttke, President, European Chamber of Commerce in China, "China is beginning to frustrate foreign business", Financial Times, 4th April, 2010.

[35] Available at: http://tvnewsroom.consilium.europa.eu/story/index/story_id/15261.

have caught the attention of Western businesses and policy makers alike relate to intellectual property and technology, procurement and standards.

Technology and know-how are priorities for the Chinese government. Chinese figures indicate that China spent 1.7% of its GDP in research and development in 2009, and aims to increase this figure further. The massive investments and government incentives that the Chinese leadership is putting in place are likely to turn China into a global leader for research in some areas, for instance life sciences.[36] Another policy aimed at increasing China's research capability are the schemes and incentives that try to lure Chinese scientists abroad back to China. For instance, it is estimated that at least 80,000 Western-trained PhD experts in life sciences have already returned to China to work in the industry or in academic institutes since the mid-1980s.[37] Some of the policies and means deployed with a view to increase China's innovation and technology capabilities have led to tensions with the West for many years but irritation seems to have increased as the technology gap between China and the EU or other developed economies has diminished substantially over the past few years. Chinese authorities have often been reported to be involved in (or turning a blind eye to) various forms of pressure on foreign companies to transfer technology, and this phenomenon has grown – for instance when technology transfer is set as a condition for participating in a government procurement contract, obtaining an investment authorisation, licence, product approval/certification or is part of a joint venture requirement. While Western businesses may accept such terms in order to obtain a stake in the Chinese market, they appear to be more and more careful and reluctant to do so. Some have had painful experiences, with promises for market access in some of the deals proving of a limited duration with new market restrictions appearing as soon as the Chinese partners had acquired the technology. In addition, the capacity of Chinese companies in certain sectors increased dramatically, and some companies came to the conclusion that financial benefits obtained in the short term were insufficient to compensate for future losses linked to increased competition based on the trans-ferred technology, not only on the Chinese market but also on third markets or even in Europe.

A more recent noteworthy development related to technology and innovation has been the growth of the Chinese patent system. Double-digit growth rates for filing of all types of patents have been observed – for instance a 20% increase in 2008 in applications in 2008.[38] In 2009, almost one million patents applications were filed in China alone largely exceeding the number of patents filed with the European Patent Office. These filings are made mostly by Chinese companies. As a result, at the end of 2008, out of the 2.5 million patents that had been granted in China, more than 2.1 millions were given to Chinese companies. In many cases, in

---

[36] Baeder/Zielenzige, "China, the Life Sciences Leader of 2020", The Monitor Group, 17th November, 2010.

[37] Ibid.

[38] 2008 SIPO Annual Report.

particular for utility models and designs, patents have been granted to copies of existing technologies already patented elsewhere, with slight modifications whose innovative effect seems limited – the so-called copy patents or 'junk patents'. Abuses may also occur when a company files a multitude of utility models and designs with only minor modifications of existing technologies, creating a number of rights (a 'wall of patents') which cannot be all invalidated as the costs for invalidation are prohibitive.

Attention turned to the Chinese patent and litigation system and alarm bells started to ring in corporate headquarters worldwide when Chint Corporation, China's biggest maker of low-voltage electrical products, successfully sued Schneider Electric on the basis of its utility model patent and obtained very significant damages in front of local courts from Chint's hometown in 2007. The case was eventually settled by Schneider with a very large financial compensation paid to Chint despite the fact that the Chinese utility model of Chint was a slight modification of a technology patented by Schneider both in France and China, and already made readily available in China. The Schneider court case is now a textbook example for law firms advising foreign companies on "navigating the Chinese patent litigation minefield". More generally, a series of other cases have generated fears that invalidation and enforcement procedures in China do not offer a level playing field for foreign companies. Foreign companies' patents get more frequently invalidated than domestic ones, the burden of proof is set at higher level for foreign rights holders and the scope for protection for foreign patents is reduced allowing domestic companies to use foreign patented technology. Litigation is also substantially longer for foreign than domestic litigants and preliminary injunctions are very hard to obtain.

Some observers may contend that these are the normal woes of a new, overwhelmed system that will mature – as patent systems have done in developed nations in the past. However, the National Patent Development Strategy (2011–2020) published by the State Intellectual Property Office of China in November 2010 remains ambiguous and in some respect alarming on the directions pursued. Some of the goals set would lead to improvements of the system, for instance increasing the capacity and training of the patents examiners, increasing international exchanges and cooperation, or further research on regulation dealing with substantial and procedural abuse of patent rights. At the same time, the strategy forecasts two million patents applications in China a year by 2015. Far from recognising the pernicious nature of the current system of incentives at central, provincial and local level that rewards Chinese companies for filing patents regardless of their innovative value, which has driven the exponential growth in patent applications by Chinese companies, it supports further incentives and rewards for patent filing. It also describes the progressive development of a "Chinese patent administration and mechanism with Chinese characteristics" that would be "guided by national strategic demands" to "master the patent rights in core technologies and support the development of some emerging industries in China" as well as to foster exports of patented products. Whether or not China will take a path towards developing an environment that encourages real innovation by all economic operators, based on consistency, transparency and non discrimination in the way patent applications and patent litigation are handled remains therefore an open question.

Discrimination with regards to access to procurement has been another prominent issue for concern in the West. Policy makers have long lamented the difficulties for Western companies to enjoy a fair access to tenders, because of the rules set by the existing procurement law or various restrictions specific to certain sectors such as construction services or wind energy. Tensions ran high with the publication of the draft circular on Indigenous innovation in November 2009.[39] The prospect of China using 'indigenous innovation catalogues' creating preferences for procurement based on where the intellectual property was owned or developed raised fears among Western businesses and policy makers alike and generated a host of diplomatic contacts at all levels. Concerns put forward included the fact that foreign companies would not be able to meet the criteria set, would no longer be able to pursue a global R&D strategy and worldwide branding and use of patents, and would need to review their investment policies in China and reveal sensitive IPR information in order to benefit from access to procurement.

Yet another issue where Western business and policy makers had assumed – perhaps hastily – that China's economic development and economic reform would inevitably lead to the adoption of international models is that of product standards. As always, reality has proven at the same time more complex and more disturbing. To begin with, Western countries themselves still have a sizeable problem of standards compatibility, as well as more than slightly different attitudes in this respect.[40] Thus, China was not offered a single working model to follow in its drive to modernise product standards and raise product safety and quality, but slightly different and competing models, albeit all variants of the same basic philosophy: high levels of protection for public interests such as health and safety of workers and consumers and the environment, as well as high quality products; and the lightest instruments possible, compatibly with the need to achieve these aims limitation of regulation to actual needs, resort to voluntary standards rather than mandatory technical regulations when possible, standards and regulations written in terms of performance requirements rather than product specifications; a risk-based approach to conformity and certification.[41] While at the beginning of the 'opening

---

[39] Circular 618 by the Ministry of Science and Technology, the National Development and Reform Commission and the Ministry of Finance.

[40] Suffice it here to mention the US preference for proprietary standards competing in the market, as compared with the European increasingly sophisticated mechanism of creation of common standards to allow and facilitate competition among products and producers in the single market; or the – related – different attitudes to what constitutes an international standard or an international standardisation body.

[41] For instance, resort to supplier's declaration of conformity rather than mandatory third party certification, or use of Good Manufacturing Practices and Quality Assurance Systems rather than sampling and final product inspection, whenever the risk linked to the manufacturing or use of a product is low enough.

up' policy Western products were accepted almost regardless of applicable standards, the modernisation of China's economy and society has inevitably – and rightly – entailed a major drive to revise old and adopt new product standards aimed at attaining, in China too, higher levels of health and safety for workers and consumers, of protection of the environment, as well as higher quality products. As a result, in 2008 China promulgated more than 10,000 new standards – probably more than the rest of the world combined. A slight slowdown was observed in 2009, although the figures are still very high. When these standards diverge from international norms, the costs and complexity for global operators can become significant. Yet, the question remains for China, of what are the international norms that China could usefully follow. At the same time, it is also clear that Chinese policy makers also ask themselves whether international norms are desirable for China. The situation on the ground, therefore, is increasingly confused – and confusing – for foreign and Chinese business alike. While Chinese authorities seem in certain areas to go to great lengths to favour some domestic standards, this is not systematic. There are instances – arguably more frequently in sectors that are not considered strategic – where possible incompatibilities with Western standards resulted from lack of knowledge and expertise, and have been resolved at technical level. Yet, the 'strategic' use of standards is common enough to be a very serious cause of concern, whether it stems from national pride or – more worrying – from a deliberate policy of technology 'appropriation' and support of domestic 'technology champions'.

Two examples illustrate the nature of these concerns. The first concerns mobile telephony. China carried out an in-depth restructuring of its telecom sector in 2008, which resulted in several SOEs being re-combined into three major entities, all possessed of a fixed telephony network and a mobile telephony network, though of varying sizes: China Telecom, China Unicom and China Mobile. The three entities were then instructed to adopt three different technologies for third generation mobile telephony: the European/Japanese standard WCDMA (UMTS), the North American CDMA2000 as well as the interface TD-SCDMA which is only offered in China. Even though the Chinese technology was generally deemed inferior to both the European and the American standard, it was clearly developed and supported by Chinese policy makers in order not to depend on Western technologies and patents. It was clear, therefore, that Chinese policy makers were not ready to abandon the quest for an indigenous technological capability for mobile voice and data transmission, independent from Western technologies and patents, even at the cost of some loss of 'quality'.

The second example concerns the certification of conformity with applicable standards. Not only do Chinese authorities impose mandatory third party certification of conformity almost regardless of the level of risk of a product, which in itself already creates a considerable and largely unnecessary burden for business; there are also serious concerns that this could be used as a means to obtain confidential and proprietary data for the products to be certified, as a means of 'technology appropriation'. For instance, the Chinese Compulsory Certification system involves notably type testing by an accredited Chinese laboratory according to Chinese mandatory standards, an initial factory inspection as well as a follow-up inspection once per year. One of the EU request in this respect is for China to accept testing by internationally accredited foreign laboratories and exempt companies that an ISO-9001 certifying the quality of their management from factory inspections. Such concerns came to the fore in 2010 notably, when China decided to extend the scheme initially dealing with safety aspects, to the new area of information security (13 categories of products among which smartcards, routers, firewalls, etc.).

Having offered a glimpse of what Western business worries about, it is also fair to say that there are many in China (and a few elsewhere) who have raised the question of how legitimate really are the West's concerns about China's business climate and how different are China's practices from those followed by other countries seeking to develop innovation, given that seeking to protect procurement markets for domestic operators and encourage technology transfer has historically been tried and tested by many. Without going back to the nineteenth century or to the pre-World War II part of the twentieth century, it is easy to think of post-war Japan or – much closer – of US 'Buy America' policies, never discontinued and which have raised their ugly head again in the recent crisis. And in Europe, while the development of a single market for public procurement has effectively open this market to everyone, the temptation to leverage public funds for other purposes than procuring the best and cheapest goods and services remains present. Standards are another area where the US and the EU in particular have also at times sought to use their market power to have their preferred technologies prevail.

Why is China different from the West then? To begin with, the sheer challenge of implementing rules in China is also a factor that should be counted in. While rhetoric over China as a developing country having difficulties to implement policies and control what is happening on the ground at provincial and local level may sometimes appear as an easy excuse, there is truth in it. More generally, the differences in business cultures may also explain some of the difficulties encountered and the perception of China's business climate as a difficult one. Business executives are often warned before entering negotiations with Chinese partners that a contract does not have the same value in the West and in China. Trainings on doing business in China recall that in China the signature of a contract marks the beginning of the real negotiations: in other words, the contract sets out the shared objectives of the parties and lays down the frame of reference for their relationship, but does not define in precise detail the rights and obligations of the parties, which can change according to circumstances. Some of the business disputes among joint ventures where Chinese partners are accused of lack of loyalty and side deals also seem to be partly cultural, and linked to factors such as the role of *guanxi*.[42]

More generally, however, and perhaps more fundamentally, this also begs the question of what 'rule of law' means in China. One could also wonder whether 'rule of law' the way it is seen in the West is even possible in China in view of the complex links between the state and corporate apparatus, the major role played by

---

[42] A notion that is defined in various ways, roughly encompassing the concept of personal networks of influence.

the Communist Party in directing the economy and the importance attached to personal relationships for individuals' careers as well as companies' success. What is certain is that the opacity of the Chinese system and the ability of the Chinese system to exert influence on all key economic levers only fuel suspicions and general mistrust in the West about China's policies or corporate activities. In conjunction with the sheer size of the Chinese economy, the standards used to judge China may not always be the same as those used to judge policies in other countries. At the same time the Chinese economy is like no other economy in the world, and China at times seems ready to move forward with drastic policies – such as 'indigenous innovation' preferences for procurement – that do not seem to have been tested anywhere else in the world. As a result, Western business and policy makers cannot help wondering whether the problem is simply one of cultural differences that need to be explained and understood, as well as one of waiting for – and encouraging and supporting – further development of both business and administrative culture in China, or whether there is something more fundamental, more long lasting, as to how laws and regulations are understood and applied in China, which poses an irreducible difference with the way they are in the West: the question of a 'rule of law with Chinese characteristics', precisely.

Do Western and Chinese Fundamental Interests Coincide or Conflict?

Questions like the real meaning of 'rule of law' in China or the deep reasons for the peculiar difficulties of the business climate in China raise the broader issue of whether China's increasing integration in the world economy is accompanied or not by a growing coincidence of interests with other major players. It can be argued that the interest of the West is for China to become like the West, or at least to buy into the Western system of economic governance[43] to a sufficient degree to make conflict management predictable. In fact, the West possesses elaborated and effective in-built conflict resolution mechanisms: they include not only formal mechanisms to arbitrate and adjudicate the substance of a disputed matter, but also the political mechanisms that make adjudication possible, or replace adjudication altogether, in order to reduce the conflict to an outcome that is acceptable and accepted. If – and as long as – this does not happen there is at least the risk of an irreducible conflict. This is true both in the economic and in the political sphere, but there are enough differences between the governance mechanisms in the two spheres that the analysis done for one of them would not necessarily hold true for the other. For present purposes suffice it to say that until the fall of the Soviet Union

---

[43] Both international economic governance and domestic governance, that is, the way economic activity is regulated within the country.

and the emergence of China as a major player in world trade there seemed to be little reason to think that international economic governance would develop otherwise than in a linear fashion. Trade meant essentially trade in goods and international trade rules (including the GATT[44] and then the WTO) had been shaped essentially by the West; the Soviet Union and other Communist countries played a very small role in international trade and other countries adapted easily, inter alia because those rules mostly stopped at the border and did not imply that a country should change the way it run its economy to play by those rules; as to financial flows, they involved mainly the West, hence the absence of a challenge to institutions like the IMF. The changes brought about by the 1990s are not yet fully understood – also because they are still happening – but there are a few observations concerning China that may help understand better some of the tensions between China and Europe (and the US, for that matter).

The basic problem is that China does not appear to want to become the West. China does want many of the things that make the West what it is today: essentially, wealth, technology and welfare – and, for an increasing number of Chinese citizens, lifestyle. But neither China's leadership, nor many of its citizens, wish to actually be the West. This is not simply due to a rejection of Western-style democracy as a threat to the leadership's own power, but to deeper roots. After all, in China's millenary history, its economic interaction with the outside world on anything than its own (rather limited) terms only began less than two centuries ago, and much of this latter period is associated with bad news for China, from the humiliations of the nineteenth century, to the turmoil, civil war and foreign occupation of the first half of the twentieth century, to the isolation and poverty of the first 30 years of Communist China. Given the importance China has now attained in world economic affairs (which means, first and foremost, how important trade with China has become for the welfare of much of the rest of the world), it should not be surprising to see not only the Chinese leadership, but Chinese economic elites too ask themselves how much they really wish to play by rules they did not write, especially when playing by those rules has very deep implications for domestic regulation of the economy and, inevitably, for domestic political governance.

The question of China 'buying into' international economic rules was crucial to its accession to the WTO, beyond its practical advantages in terms of trade privileges, and there is little evidence that China was – or is – in anything than good faith in its quest for membership. However anyone who thought that China was also accepting the spirit of WTO rules and that it would *ipso facto* follow that spirit in how to regulate economic activity within China must have been sadly disappointed. By the same token, one can wonder whether the Chinese leadership had rightly measured how many expectations WTO membership carries, beyond

---

[44] General Agreement on Tariffs and Trade agreed "provisionally" in 1947, after the US Congress refused to ratify the Havana Charter for the International Trade Organisation, meant to be a sister institution to the IMF and the World Bank. See, WTO, The Results of the Uruguay Round of Multilateral Trade Negotiations: The Legal Texts, 2007.

the letter of the rules, and how much disappointing those expectation could be the source of serious conflict with its foreign partners. It is perhaps symptomatic that WTO disputes involving China so far, more than with other WTO Members, have involved question of interpretation of where exactly the limits of China's obligations were; that once those limits have been clarified China has moved reasonably quickly to comply[45]; that most of the complaints that are raised by European business also involve issues where the extent of China's WTO obligations are not entirely clear and that China is clearly not prepared to go beyond the exact scope of its obligations.

That China's participation in international economic governance mechanisms, whether formal ones like the IMF or the WTO, or the more political ones like the G20, is likely to change them is rather obvious (while it is unlikely that this change could turn those mechanisms upside down).[46] The more difficult question is whether China will develop a model of domestic regulation of the economy different from those prevailing in the West, which delivers comparable results in terms of citizens' welfare, and which is still compatible with those international economic rules and ensures reasonably smooth economic relations with the rest of the world. This question is far from being an abstract one. It would have an immediate, practical and quantifiable impact, as we have tried to show in preceding sections, on the treatment of foreign investors in China, on the actual degree of protection of intellectual property, on how much China is prepared to subscribe to international standards, etc. We are not saying that China would not be prepared to follow European or American-style models of domestic economic regulation: indeed, it has done so and is continuing to do so in earnest. However, it is certainly not prepared to do so uncritically, and assuming that any 'Chinese adaptations' would be always manageable, or that it is only a matter of time and resources before European business could find in China a business environment fully comparable to what they find at home, would be a serious mistake. This, in turn, begs the question of how hard the possible emergence of an alternative Chinese development model would be for the West to accept (recalling, for instance, the contradictions we have underlined as to technology transfers and protection of intellectual property), not only in economic terms, but also in terms of political sustainability of a relationship that is perceived by the voting public in the West as "unfair" and unbalanced.

---

[45] See for instance, Measures Affecting Imports of Automobile Parts, DS339, for which China appealed the Panel report but ultimately complied with the ruling once this was confirmed by the Appellate Body; Measures Affecting Financial Information Services and Foreign Financial Information Suppliers (Xinhua case), DS372, which was settled with a Memorandum of Understanding without a panel. Grants, Loans and Other Incentives, DS387, which was also resolved through a settlement.

[46] Assuming, that is, that China would have an interest in doing so, which is very unlikely, given the built-in bias towards stability in Chinese leaders of any time: even the Communist Revolution won in large part because of the ability of the PLA and the Party to ensure greater stability to the "liberated" areas than the Kuomintang government could, or indeed than what they had experienced for decades.

Conclusion

Seen from the West, China's future path remains very uncertain and therefore a source of concern. Worse, that uncertainty now includes the long-term outlook of the Chinese economic system. The Millennium closed with the perspective of a rising China, yes, but one that sooner or later would join the ranks of the developed free market economies – and perhaps of Western-style democracies. WTO accession in 2001 was to be the first international recognition of this 'inevitable' trend. Ten years on, the only certainty of the new Millennium is the centrality of China's role, while everything else is assorted of a question mark: will China continue to rise? Probably – and in any event we join the many who have said that the world should worry a lot more at the prospect of an unsuccessful China than at the prospect of its success. Will it be peaceful? Possibly – and hopefully; perhaps probably. Will it make China 'like us'? Based on current trends, not really, or at least not necessarily.

The Chinese leadership itself is very clearly conscious of the uncertainties and challenges it will have to grapple with over the next years, from rebalancing of growth to environmental concerns or access to resources. The overall goal is equally clear: the full economic, social and technological development of China and the assumption of its 'proper' role on the world scene. What is less clear, at least to Western observers, is what the Chinese leadership think this future China will look like – or even whether there is a single such vision in Beijing. The Chinese Communist Party is not a monolith, and a lively political debate is taking place around precisely these questions. However, even though China-watchers have long since surpassed Kremlinologists in numbers and importance, the walls of the Forbidden City remain more opaque than those of the Moscow fortress ever were. Obviously, decisions taken in Beijing will continue to be under intense scrutiny from China's trading partners – developed and developing countries alike. Various journalists and experts have used the phrase "joined at the hip" to describe the US and Chinese economies. This is also true for Europe, when one considers trade flows, or the estimate that already in 2010 China was holding 7.3% of the Euro zone public debt (and more than 28% of public debt detained by non-residents).[47] At the same time, in view of China's interdependency with the rest of the world in terms of natural resources, export markets or investments, 'going it alone' does not seem a viable option for the Chinese leadership, which will need to pay more attention in the pursuit of its own domestic interests to possible consequence and reactions in the rest of the world. A scenario where China would pursue dominance or a mercantilist orientation is indeed bound to engender very strong reactions, leading to a reduction of welfare for both China and its partners. While this has not

---

[47] See for instance estimates of China's public debt holding, "La Chine contrôle plus de 7% de la dette publique totale de la zone euro", La Tribune, 5th January, 2011.

happened yet, both sides should be aware that the string is taut and may well snap should more tensions arise.

The best insurance against this remains the anchoring of China in international rules and strengthening of China's own preferences for multilateral solutions. WTO membership was a key element in this respect, and remains relevant. China's increased use of WTO dispute settlement mechanism, its firmer support to the Doha Round and signals that it may at last be ready to play a more proactive role in the negotiations reflecting its trading giant status go in the right direction. Beyond the WTO, the G20 and a reformed IMF with more participatory decision making offer opportunities to ensure China becomes a real stakeholder in the development of global governance in the years to come. This is why the EU should pursue its efforts to increase China's engagement in these *fora*. Yet, the uncertainty we just outlined as to how much this is really consonant with the long-term vision of Beijing will persist, heightened by the upcoming change in leadership in 2012 – the obvious time for any course correction that the Chinese leadership might be mulling over.

As far as the bilateral Europe-China angle is concerned, economic and trade aspects are discussed between the EU and China in a multiplicity of working groups and dialogues ranging from technical to political level. While maintaining communication channels between Ministries and Commission Directorate-Generals is important in itself, there has often been frustration on the EU side that pressure on various issues would only lead to inconclusive talking shops. It clearly 'takes two to tango', and the EU will not be able to resolve pressing issues without some good-will and opening on the Chinese side. That being said, changes and improvements can also take place on the EU side. While it may be convenient for China to point to the different priorities relayed by the European institutions and the Member States as an excuse for not addressing the EU's demands in the economic sphere, more efforts to speak to Chinese interlocutors with one voice can only improve the communication and exchanges between the EU and China. Based on our experience, another factor to keep in mind in view of the lingering lack of trust between China and the West is that dialogue and negotiations between the EU and China are more likely to succeed if they appeal to China's self-interest and offer scope to accommodate China's legitimate aspirations.

Peer pressure is another avenue that has worked in some instances in the past when a number of China's trading partners are affected by decisions taken by the Chinese leadership. The efforts deployed in the context of the 2008 Beijing Olympics and the 2010 Shanghai Expo are reminders that Chinese leaders want to project a positive image of their country internationally, and may be increasingly aware that China's image abroad needs to be polished. This is possibly one factor in the recent renewal of China's 'panda diplomacy' and public relations efforts such as the large China campaign shown on Times Square in January-February 2011. The US and EU and on occasion a few other developed economies have traditionally been those ready to voice public concerns about some of the policies pursued by China. There are signs that other emerging economies, such as Brazil and India, that are affected by China's rise and increasing competition, may now also ready to resort to critical public statements. The Chinese leadership has also at times reacted quickly to reverse controversial measures that had been criticised both by domestic actors and its trading partners.[48] More generally, when European business interest coincide with some domestic interests, for instance on standards or new rules and requirements, it is important for European business and EU authorities to reach out to and join forces with affected Chinese companies. While this frequently occurs with many of the EU's trading partners, it remains relatively rare in China, partly because Chinese companies hesitate both to criticise government policies and to associate themselves with foreign interests.

Finally, as we have highlighted earlier on, 'China Inc.' will continue to generate fears – rational or not – as an opaque engine of economic globalisation doubled with an emerging military power, or a "Wal-Mart with an army"[49], unless it is able to address the concerns of its trading partners. By developing systems and guarantees ensuring more transparency with regards to decision-making and linkages between companies and the state apparatus in China, Chinese leaders would go a long way to address some of the suspicions regarding Chinese corporate activities in Europe and the rest of the world. In this context, the involvement of China Investment Corporation (CIC) in the work of the International Forum of Sovereign Wealth Funds that led to the Santiago Principles on Generally Accepted Principles and Practices for Sovereign Wealth Funds provides one example of how an international initiative played a significant role to overcome fears over takeover of assets and economies by opaque and unaccountable state actors.

Beyond that, tensions with the West would certainly diminish if the new Chinese leadership in 2012 would decide put in place credible measures generating more equitable market opportunities for foreign companies. Doing so would also imply a genuine recognition that, beyond origin and ownership, foreign companies continue to make a significant contribution to generate employment, innovation and create value all across China.

In conclusion, we should perhaps apologise to the reader for putting this paper under the sign of uncertainty. Yet, uncertainty is the red thread we have found in our experience of working with Western (and Chinese!) lawyers, businessmen, academics, Government officials. However, we hope this paper has offered at least some modestly useful tools to read that uncertainty better.

---

[48] One can think of the example of the "Green Dam" content-control software that was made mandatory for all personal computers sold in China by a notice from May 2009. In August 2009 this was restricted only to schools, internet cafes and other public use computers.

[49] Expression used by Lohr, "Who's Afraid of China Inc.?", New York Times, 24th July, 2005 http://www.nytimes.com/2005/07/24/business/yourmoney/24oil.html.

Trade Disputes Between China and the United States: Growing Pains so Far, Worse Ahead?

Gary Clyde Hufbauer and Jared C. Woollacott

Introduction

Sino-US trade flows have exploded in the years since the Peoples' Republic of China (PRC or China) made its first bid for GATT/WTO accession in 1986. In 1985, one year before China's accession bid, US merchandise imports and exports with China were nearly equal ($4.2 billion imported by the United States and $3.8 billion exported). As of 2009, both the volume and imbalance of US merchandise trade with China had increased dramatically. The United States imported $310 billion and exported $70 billion, a ratio of $4.50 of merchandise imports from China for every dollar of exports to China. However, expressed in ratio terms, the imbalance peaked in 1999: that year the US import-export ratio reached $6.70 of imports for every dollar of exports. Since 1999, the ratio has declined, while the absolute dollar gap between merchandise imports and exports has widened from $94.1 billion in 1999 to $240.0 billion in 2009 (see Table 1). Trade in services has followed a similar pattern, but on a much smaller scale. Services trade between the countries has increased substantially over the past several years in percentage terms, but from a tiny base, and the US trade deficit has continued to widen; however, US services imports from China account for under 3% of total US services imports from the world (see Table 1; Fig. 1).[1]

---

[1] Note that the total services trade share occupied by China is not presented in Table 1 for economy. All dollar adjustments are made using data from the U.S. Department of Commerce, Bureau of Economic Analysis, Gross Domestic Product: Implicit Price Deflator, retrieved 30th June, 2010, from Federal Reserve Bank of St. Louis, Economic Research, http://research.stlouisfed.org/fred2/series/GDPDEF/downloaddata?cid=21.

G.C. Hufbauer • J.C. Woollacott (✉)
Peterson Institute for International Economics, 1750 Massachusetts Avenue NW, Washington, DC 20036-1903, USA
e-mail: ghufbauer@piie.com; jcw16@bu.edu

C. Herrmann and J.P. Terhechte (eds.), *European Yearbook of International Economic Law (EYIEL), Vol. 3 (2012)*, European Yearbook of International Economic Law 3, DOI 10.1007/978-3-642-23309-8_2, © Springer-Verlag Berlin Heidelberg 2012

Table 1 US-China Trade, 1999–2009

US Trade with China, 1999–2009 (2009 $US Billion)

	US-China Trade									
	Merchandise						Services			
	Imports		Exports		Total		Imports		Exports	
Year	Value ($)	China / World	Value ($)	China / World	Value ($)	China / World	Value ($)	China / World	Value ($)	China / World
1999	110.6	8.3%	16.5	1.9%	127.1	5.8%	n/a	n/a	n/a	n/a
2000	132.4	8.6%	20.0	2.1%	152.3	6.1%	n/a	n/a	n/a	n/a
2001	131.9	9.3%	23.2	2.6%	155.1	6.7%	n/a	n/a	n/a	n/a
2002	158.1	11.1%	26.1	3.2%	184.2	8.2%	n/a	n/a	n/a	n/a
2003	189.3	12.5%	32.9	3.9%	222.2	9.4%	2.7	1.3%	2.8	1.0%
2004	236.5	13.8%	39.0	4.2%	275.5	10.5%	6.5	3.1%	5.8	2.2%
2005	281.9	15.0%	45.4	4.6%	327.3	11.4%	7.2	3.5%	6.4	2.3%
2006	322.5	15.9%	58.2	5.3%	380.8	12.2%	8.9	4.3%	6.7	2.5%
2007	349.2	16.9%	67.0	5.6%	416.1	12.7%	10.4	5.0%	7.1	2.6%
2008	358.7	16.5%	71.9	5.5%	430.7	12.3%	n/a	n/a	n/a	n/a
2009	309.5	19.3%	69.6	6.6%	379.1	14.3%	n/a	n/a	n/a	n/a
Total	2,581	13.8%	470	4.3%	3,050	10.3%	36	2.3%	29	1.5%

Sources: UN Comtrade; UN Service Trade; Bureau of Economic Analysis GDP Implicit Price Deflator

Notes: Data are as reported by the United States. Dollar values are 2009 USD. Services data for 2009 are as yet unavailable. Dollar value totals represent the cumulative trade flows with China for reported years; percentage totals are calculated only for the years of available data in the case of services trade

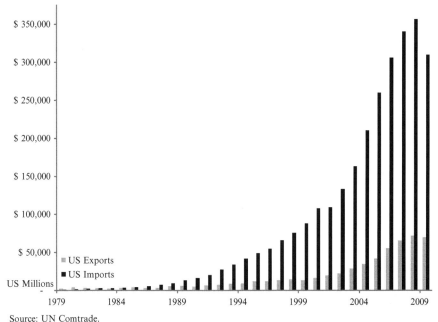

Source: UN Comtrade.

Fig. 1 30 Years of US merchandise trade with China, 1979–2009

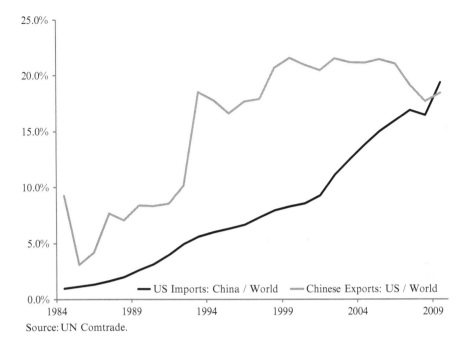

Source: UN Comtrade.

Fig. 2 Sino-US merchandise trade dependence, 1984–2009

Each country has grown to occupy a greater portion of the other's trade portfolio. In 2003, China overtook Mexico as the second largest provider of US merchandise imports. Four years later, it overtook Canada as the largest provider. The United States was China's number one export destination through 2007, when it was overtaken by the European Union (according to PRC-reported data).[2] However, the United States is still by far the largest single-country destination for PRC merchandise. In 2009, the United States relied on China to supply 19.3% of its merchandise imports, and China relied on the United States to purchase 18.4% of its merchandise exports (see Fig. 2). In the same year, China purchased 6.6% of US exports, while 7.7% of Chinese imports came from the United States.[3]

The growth in Sino-US trade has been rapid. Expressed in percentage growth terms, US merchandise imports from China since 1984 have been impressive (21.0% average annual growth). Each year over the past quarter century, China has supplied an additional $11.8 billion of imports to the US economy on average, some 23.1% of average US import growth over the period 1984–2009. Canada has supplied the second largest share of import growth over this period, with an average of $6.7 billion additional imports per year, some 13.1% of average US import

---

[2] UN Comtrade (2010), http://comtrade.un.org/db. According to US-reported data, PRC exports to the United States were $310 billion (19.3%) in 2009, versus $287 billion (17.9%) for the EU-27.

[3] UN Comtrade (2010), http://comtrade.un.org/db.

Table 2 Growth in Sino-US merchandise trade

Top ten sources of average annual merchandise trade growth, 1984–2009

US imports			PRC exports		
Source country	Annual per cent growth	Annual value growth ($ billion)	Destination country	Annual per cent growth	Annual value growth ($ billion)
1. China	21.0%	11.8	United States	22.6%	9.1
2. Canada	6.4%	6.7	Hong Kong	16.6%	6.7
3. Mexico	9.9%	6.2	Japan	14.1%	3.9
4. Germany	7.4%	2.3	Korea (Rep. of)	186.3%	2.6
5. Japan	3.9%	2.1	Germany	20.3%	2.0
6. UK	5.5%	1.4	Netherlands	23.1%	1.5
7. Korea (Rep. of)	7.6%	1.3	UK	31.4%	1.3
8. France	7.2%	1.1	India	36.1%	1.2
9. Russia	27.2%	1.1	Singapore	15.9%	1.2
10. Ireland	17.0%	1.1	Russia	18.2%	0.9
Total	7.5%	51.2	**Total**	18.3%	49.0

Source: UN Comtrade

Note: The annual dollar amounts and percentage growth rates are reported by the respective countries. While the figures in the first row differ, in principle they represent the same flows

growth.[4] PRC figures differ somewhat from US statistics. According to PRC reported data, the United States has purchased an annual average of $9.1 billion in additional exports from China over the 1984–2009 period, not $11.8 billion (indicating annual growth of 22.6%, not 21.0). These flows have supported average annual growth of 18.3% in total PRC export volume (see Table 2).

During this remarkable growth period in two-way trade, the United States and China have also invested directly in each other's economies. Between 2000 and 2008 US capital provided 5.8% of foreign direct investment (FDI) in China. On average, total foreign investment in the United States has been much greater than that in China: $180 billion per year in the United States and $69 billion per year in China. The trends in FDI into the two countries also differ. China has enjoyed a steady rise in inward FDI, while inflows to the US economy have been more volatile (see Table 3).

The ripple effect of rapid shifts in the intensity of the economic relationship, particularly with respect to trade flows between a developed and developing country, can create political friction. Rising US imports from China have been much debated over the past two decades. Major news and business press in the United States gave frequent coverage to the US trade deficit with China during the years of the East Asian Financial crisis (1997–1999) and the years just prior to the Great Recession (2005–2007). The US media have offered considerable

---

[4] UN Comtrade (2010), see: http://comtrade.un.org/db. Amounts given are in nominal terms.

Table 3 FDI flows between China and the United States

Foreign Direct Investment between the United States, China, and the World, 2000–2009 ($US Millions)

	United States				China		Outward
	Inward	Outward			Inward		Outward
Year	Total ($)	Total ($)	To China ($)		Total ($)	From US	Total ($)
2000	313,997	142,626	4,400	3.1%	40,715	10.8%	916
2001	159,478	124,873	4,900	3.9%	46,878	10.5%	6,885
2002	74,501	134,946	5,400	4.0%	52,743	10.2%	2,518
2003	53,141	129,352	4,200	3.2%	53,505	7.8%	2,855
2004	135,850	294,905	3,900	1.3%	60,630	6.4%	5,498
2005	104,809	15,369	3,100	20.2%	72,406	4.3%	12,261
2006	237,136	224,220	3,000	1.3%	72,715	4.1%	21,160
2007	265,957	393,518	2,600	0.7%	83,521	3.1%	22,469
2008	324,560	330,491	2,900	0.9%	108,312	2.7%	52,150
2009	129,883	248,074	N/A	N/A	95,000	N/A	48,000
Cumulative	1,799,311	2,038,374	34,400	1.9%	686,424	5.8%	174,712
Average	179,931	203,837	3,822	4.3%	68,642	6.7%	17,471

Sources: Total inward and outward FDI data are from UNCTAD Stat (www.unctadstat.unctad.org). FDI from the United States to China are as reported by the US-China Business Council (http://www.uschina.org/statistics/fdi_cumulative.html)

Notes: All amounts are in millions of current US dollars. The anomaly in US outward FDI in 2005 is attributable in part to corporate tax code changes. The "to China" per cent column is US FDI to China as a per cent of total US outward FDI. The per cents in the "from US" column are total US outward FDI into China as a per cent of all PRC inward FDI

coverage of the Sino-US trade relationship in 2010 and 2011 as well. In 2010, the number of articles mentioning the trade deficit was 55% higher than in 2006 and 2007, the prior high water mark years (see Fig. 3).

Extrapolating coverage intensity from the first quarter of 2011 indicates that it too will be a heavy press year in the United States.[5] Alongside considerable growth in media coverage of the trade relationship, US public opinion has remained largely steady, with approximately half of US residents holding an unfavourable opinion of China (see Fig. 4).

While deepening its bilateral trade and investment relationship with the United States over the past 25 years, China has also integrated itself more fully into the world economy and multilateral institutions. Of the cumulated historical trade flows between China and the United States, the great majority have been governed by the terms of the WTO legal framework. The increasing interdependence between the United States and China, and the conflicts interdependence has sparked, make the history of the relationship an interesting object of study. This chapter pays

---

[5] Articles were identified from the Dow Jones Factiva database with the search terms "(China or Chinese) w/2 (trade or import*) and (trade deficit or trade surplus)" in the headline or lead paragraph of articles published by US "Major News and Business Publications," excluding duplicates, republished news, market data, and obituaries.

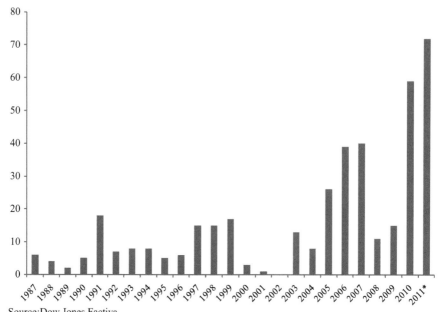

Source:Dow Jones Factiva.
Note: Count for 2011 is projected by quadrupling the count from quarter one 2011.

Fig. 3 US major news articles on the US trade deficit with China, 1987–2010

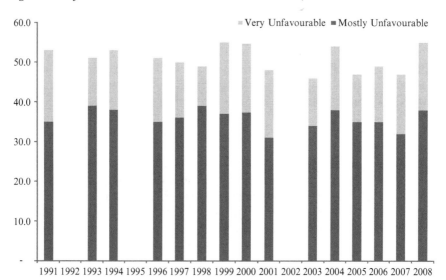

Source: Gallup opinion polls provided by www.WorldPublicOpinion.org

Note: China, Regional Issues Poll. Americans and the World Digest, World Public Opinion.org,
retrieved 29th July, 2010, from http://www.americans-world.org/PDF/china_data_update-8_2008.pdf.
No Gallup polls were available in the years without a column (1992, 1995, 2002)

Fig. 4 Per cent of US public with an unfavourable opinion of China

particular attention to the ten years of China's WTO membership and the bilateral trade conflicts that have occurred and those that are likely to occur.

We begin with a brief account of modern Sino-US economic relations in three sub-periods: Pre-GATT, GATT to PRC Accession Process, and the PRC Accession Process. We then address the trade disputes between the United States and China that have been mediated through the WTO since China's accession in late 2001. Section "Sino-US Disputes Adjudicated Within the WTO Framework" identifies current protectionist measures that could lead to future conflicts and examines patterns of past conflicts that may colour future Sino-US trade relations. Section "Dispute History" summarizes the themes of Sino-US protectionism and highlights the most likely flashpoints for future disputes. The final section concludes with recommendations for how the trading partners can best cope with future conflicts.

Sketch of Commercial History

Pre-GATT

The beginning of Sino-US trade relations coincided approximately with US independence in 1783. The opening of trade was marked by the arrival of the US ship "Empress of China" in Canton (Guangzhou) China in 1784.[6] The following sixty years, known as "The Old China Trade," saw a substantial expansion in Sino-US commerce. In 1839, however, Sino-US trade suffered setbacks during the First Opium War (1839–1842), which pitted China against Britain, France and the United States. Sino-US relations were restored by the Treaty of Wangxia in 1844, which opened several additional ports, granted the United States most favoured nation status, and established official Sino-US diplomatic relations. Trading ports (e.g., Shanghai) and privileges (notably, legalization of the opium trade) were further expanded by the Treaty of Tianjin in 1858 following the Second Opium War (1856–1860).

Fearing political obstacles that would hinder US access to the Chinese economy, Secretary of State John Hay issued the "Open Door Notes" at the turn of the twentieth century, advocating the US position of "perfect equality of treatment" among foreign economic interests in China. A wave of Chinese nationalism erupted shortly after, threatening all foreign economic interests in China. In 1915, Japan encroached severely on Chinese economic sovereignty with its "21 demands" for trade and territorial privileges. The most intrusive of these demands were resisted by China with the encouragement of the US government. The United States

---

[6] A Guide to the United States' History of Recognition, Diplomatic, and Consular Relations, by Country, since 1776: China, retrieved 24th May, 2010, from http://history.state.gov/countries/china.

supported China against Japanese aggression some years later in the prelude to the Second World War, principally by lending money for military supplies. US aid to China, which expanded throughout the war and the immediate post-war period, ended with the Communist victory and founding of the Peoples' Republic of China in 1949. Sino-US relations then deteriorated as a casualty of the Cold War.[7]

GATT to PRC Accession Process

In 1947, China and the United States signed the General Agreement on Tariffs and Trade (GATT) along with 21 other countries.[8] Three years later, the Kuomintang nationalist government, from its perch on the island of Taiwan, withdrew China from the GATT. In the same year, the US Congress refused to ratify the International Trade Organization, leaving the provisional GATT to govern world trade for the following 44 years. After 1950, the Peoples' Republic of China, under Mao Zedong, had minimal relations with the world economic system and the United States. For its part, the United States enforced certain trade restrictions through the Coordinating Committee for Multilateral Export Controls (CoCom), a multilateral agreement between most NATO members and Japan with the primary goal of controlling exports of certain merchandise (e.g., military equipment) to Communist states. While the role of the CoCom embargo in suppressing Sino-US trade flows in the nearly thirty years following the Second World War should not be overstated, it is emblematic of the generally frosty diplomatic and economic relationships between the United States and communist countries. Relations with China began to thaw in 1972 following President Nixon's landmark visit to mainland China. The visit yielded the Shanghai Communiqué, which vaguely committed both countries to the normalization of relations. Economic relations began to improve thereafter, furthered by President Ford's visit in 1975.

In 1978, Deng Xiaoping assumed leadership of a massive and remarkably successful economic transformation, leading to a market-oriented and capitalist-flavoured PRC economy. China and the United States signed a Trade Relations Agreement the following year, according each other most-favoured nation status. The Deng leadership ushered in a period of PRC rapprochement with the international economic community. In 1980, China occupied the erstwhile Taiwanese seat within the IMF and the World Bank and requested observer status within the GATT

---

[7] Chronology of US-China Relations, 1784–2000, retrieved 24th May, 2010, from http://history.state.gov/countries/china/china-us-relations.

[8] The General Agreement on Tariffs and Trade, 1947 and as incorporated in Annex 1A to the Marrakesh Agreement Establishing the World Trade Organization, 15th April, 1994, retrieved 29th July, 2010, from http://www.wto.org/english/docs_e/legal_e/legal_e.htm#gatt47.

(granted in 1982). In 1983, China signed the Multi-Fibre Agreement and in 1986 it asked to rejoin the GATT, starting a 15 year long process toward WTO accession.[9]

PRC Accession Process

Diplomatic efforts by China toward GATT membership were frustrated early on by the PRC government's response to the Tiananmen Square protests of 1989, which roused political resistance to China among many GATT member states. At the time, China's MFN status with the United States was subject to annual congressional review and approval under the Jackson-Vanik Amendment.[10] This gave critics of China in the United States a regular forum to air grievances, both political (primarily on human rights and environment) and economic (notably, US job displacement). There were broader challenges to integrating China's external trade into the WTO legal framework as well. China's strict quotas, high tariffs, poor intellectual property rights, restrictions on foreign investment, and other forms of market intervention all had to be reconciled with the GATT and the interests of WTO members. Setting parameters for China's transition to WTO membership was a central challenge of the accession process, and this challenge proved even greater since China was not granted Special and Differential Treatment, which was the norm for other developing country members.

China's willingness to expose its domestic industries to foreign competition faltered during the East Asian financial crisis of 1997–1998. In 1999, Chinese premier Zhu Rongji emerged from the crisis with an appealing, though domestically controversial, set of liberalization offers to the United States and other WTO members. However, the Clinton administration, beset by scandals and unified Republican Party opposition, was not then in a position to accept the Chinese offers.

Sino-US relations deteriorated in the late spring and summer of 1999. The concessions China offered in April were summarized and published electronically by the United States Trade Representative (USTR) without China's consent. The summary was vehemently denied by Chinese officials, who then proceeded to back away from prior commitments. In early May 1999, a NATO plane with an American pilot accidentally bombed the PRC embassy in Belgrade, inciting anti-US protests and boycotts in China. Sino-US trade negotiations recovered quickly,

---

[9] The Chinese Nationalist Party government in Taiwan rejoined the GATT with observer status in 1965 after withdrawing in 1950. In 1971, the China seat in the United Nations was transferred from Taiwan to the PRC government and Taiwanese observer status in the GATT was subsequently revoked. Taiwan applied to rejoin the GATT/WTO in 1990. It acceded immediately following the PRC accession under the label of the Separate Customs Territory of Taiwan, Penghu, Kinmen and Matsu (the TPKM customs territory).

[10] The Jackson-Vanik Amendment prohibited normal trade relations with non-market economies that restricted emigration or otherwise infringed on human rights; however, it did allow for an annual presidential waiver.

however, culminating in an agreement in November 1999, just before the controversial WTO Seattle ministerial. A Sino-EU agreement followed six months later in May 2000.[11] China had already reached agreement with many other WTO members, but the US and the EU bilateral pacts were the most comprehensive and most difficult to conclude. After fifteen years of negotiation, China acceded to the WTO on December 11, 2001.

Sino-US Disputes Adjudicated Within the WTO Framework

Introduction

Through the first quarter of 2011, China and the United States have filed a combined total of seventeen disputes against each other through the WTO Dispute Settlement Body (DSB); eleven filed by the United States and six filed by China. Fourteen of the seventeen cases have been filed since 2007. Since China's accession in 2001, it has filed a total of eight disputes against all WTO members (see Table 4) and the United States has filed 28 (see Table 5). Three quarters of PRC complaints have therefore been filed against the United States and two fifths of US disputes (since China's accession) have been filed against China.

This section provides an overview of the WTO disputes between China and the United States. We then summarize the seventeen Sino-US disputes, explaining the measures in question, the alleged violations of WTO rules, and how, if at all, the disputes have been resolved.

Dispute History

Overview

Since 2002, the United States has requested consultations on eleven occasions with China, the most with any WTO member. In fact, the United States has requested consultations on more than one occasion with only four WTO members since 2002:

---

[11] See Bhala, Enter the Dragon: An Essay on China's WTPO Accession Saga, American University International Law Review 15 (2000), p. 1469, for a comprehensive review of China's "Accession Saga".

Table 4 WTO DSB consultations involving China, 2002–2011:Q1

Consultations requested by China

Respondent	2002	2003	2004	2005	2006	2007	2008	2009	2010	2011-Q1	ALL	Cumulative two-way trade flow ($US billion)	Disputes per $US trillion trade flow
1. United States of America	1					1	1	2		1	6	1,837	3.3
2. European Communities								1	1		2	2,068	1.0
ALL:	1	0	0	0	0	1	1	3	1	1	8	12,832	0.6

Consultations requested with China

Complainant	2002	2003	2004	2005	2006	2007	2008	2009	2010	2011-Q1	ALL	Cumulative two-way trade flow ($US billion)	Disputes per $US trillion trade flow
1. United States of America			1		1	3	2	1	3		11	1,837	6.0
2. European Communities					1		1	1	1		4	2,068	1.9
3. Mexico						1	1	1			3	83	36.3
4. Canada					1		1				2	179	11.2
5. Guatemala								1			1	5	208.5
ALL:	0	0	1	0	3	4	5	4	4	0	21	12,832	1.6

Source: WTO Secretariat, IMF DOTS

Notes: Cases with more than one complainant are counted multiple times (once for each complainant). Dispute data are current to March 31, 2011. Trade flows are as reported by China for merchandise trade only and represent the cumulative two-way flows between China and the respondent/complainant for the years 2002–2009 only. No consultations were sought involving China in 2001 (it acceded December 11, 2001). Trade flows in the "ALL" row are cumulative flows with the world

Table 5 WTO DSB consultations involving the United States, 2002–2011:Q1

Consultations requested by the United States

Respondent	2002	2003	2004	2005	2006	2007	2008	2009	2010	2011:Q1	ALL	Cumulative two-way trade flow ($US billion)	Disputes per $US trillion trade flow
1. China	1				1	3	2	1	3		11	2,467	4.5
2. European Communities		1	2		1	1	1	1			7	4,106	1.7
3. Mexico	1		1								2	2,393	0.8
4. Canada		1	1								2	3,861	0.5
5. Philippines									1		1	136	7.4
6. Venezuela	1										1	316	3.2
7. Turkey				1							1	82	12.2
8. Japan	1										1	1,518	0.7
9. Egypt		1									1	49	20.6
10. India					1						1	246	4.1
ALL:	4	3	4	1	3	4	3	2	4	0	28	21,168	1.3

Consultations requested by the United States

Complainant	2002	2003	2004	2005	2006	2007	2008	2009	2010	2011:Q1	ALL	Cumulative two-way trade flow ($US billion)	Disputes per $US trillion trade flow
1. European Communities	2	1	3	1	1						8	4,106	1.9
2. Canada	4		2			1	1				8	3,861	2.1
3. Mexico		3			1	1	2				7	2,393	2.9
4. China	1					1	1	2		1	6	2,467	2.4
5. Brazil	3					1	1				5	349	14.3
6. Thailand				1	1			1			3	220	13.6
7. Korea (Republic of)	1	1					1				3	587	5.1
8. Japan	2		1								3	1,518	2.0
9. Argentina	1			1							2	71	28.4

10. India	1									2	246	8.1
11. Viet Nam	1					1				1	81	12.3
12. Switzerland	1									1	219	4.6
13. Norway	1									1	72	13.9
14. Chinese Taipei	1									1	N/A	N/A
15. Indonesia	1					1				1	134	7.4
16. Antigua and Barbuda		1								1	1	738.4
17. Ecuador	1					1				1	65	15.3
18. New Zealand	1									1	43	23.2
ALL:	19	6	7	3	5	3	6	3	2	55	21,168	2.6

Source: WTO Secretariat (disputes), IMF DOTS (trade flows)

Notes: Cases with more than one complainant are counted multiple times (once for each complainant). Dispute data are current to March 31, 2011. Trade flows are as reported by the United States for merchandise trade only and represent the cumulative two-way flows between the United States and the respondent/complainant for the years 2002–2009 only. No consultations were sought involving China in 2001 (it acceded December 11, 2001). IMF DOTS trade data are unavailable for Chinese Taipei. Trade flows in the "ALL" row are cumulative flows with the world. Trade flows are as reported by the United States

Canada, China, the European Communities, and Mexico.[12] Relative to two-way merchandise trade, US requests for consultations with China were the highest among these four members (See Table 5 for a summary of all disputes involving the United States).[13] Since 2002, the United States requested 4.5 consultations for every trillion dollars of two-way merchandise trade flow with China.[14] By contrast, over this same period, the United States requested just 1.3 consultations for every trillion dollars of merchandise trade flow with the world.

Since 2002, the United States has requested 28 consultations with ten WTO members, or 2.8 consultations per respondent.[15] In the same period, eighteen WTO members requested 55 consultations with the United States, an average of 3.1 consultations per complainant. China's complaint intensity (2.4 complaints per trillion dollars of cumulative two-way trade flow with the United States) is below the aggregate intensity (2.6 complaints received by the United States per trillion dollars of cumulative two-way US trade flow with the world) and well below the median intensity of those members lodging multiple complaints against the United States (4.0 complaints per trillion dollars of cumulative two-way trade flow).

China has only requested consultations with two WTO members: the United States (on six occasions) and the European Communities (on two occasions). On the basis of PRC-reported merchandise trade data, China requested 3.3 consultations for every trillion dollars of cumulative two-way merchandise trade flow with the United States and 0.6 consultations for every trillion dollars of cumulative two-way merchandise trade flow with the world (less than half the US complaint intensity for trade with the world; see Tables 4 and 5).[16]

Among WTO members requesting consultations with China on more than one occasion, Mexico, with three complaints, had the highest dispute intensity of trade (36.3 complaints for every trillion dollars in cumulative bilateral merchandise trade flow). The European Communities lodged four complaints against China, approximately one third of the number lodged by the United States. The EC complaint

---

[12] Prior to December 2009, the legal name of the European Union in the WTO was the European Communities.

[13] The United States has a dispute resolution alternative with Canada and Mexico, the North American Free Trade Agreement (NAFTA). The NAFTA alternative biases downward the overall intensity of US trade disputes within the WTO for these two countries.

[14] Note that the intensity figure is biased upward as bilateral trade data for 2010 and 2011 are unavailable from UN Comtrade as of the time of this writing. Dispute counts are current to the first quarter of 2011.

[15] For the majority of WTO members with which the United States requested consultations, it did so on only one occasion. Among these members, Egypt, Turkey, and the Philippines had higher dispute intensities than China, calculated relative to trade. Trade flows of these countries are significantly smaller than the bilateral trade flow between the United States and the four members with multiple consultations (see Table 5).

[16] Merchandise trade flow data in Table 5 are as reported by the United States. Data in Table 4 are as reported by China. US and PRC trade data differ, giving different dispute intensities in Table 5 and Table 4.

intensity with China is proportionate (1.9 versus 6.0 for the United States using trade flows reported by China).[17]

The following paragraphs cover the seventeen complaints lodged between the United States and China (see Table 6). Six of the eleven consultations requested by the United States have been concluded. Four of the six consultations requested by China have been concluded by WTO proceedings or bilateral agreement. Five of the six consultations requested by China are related to anti-dumping and countervailing duties measures (these measures are covered more generally in the next section). Where feasible, we have approximated the dollar value of the import or export flows at issue and the share of total exports or imports connected with the partner country in the year of the dispute. With respect to these calculations, it is worth noting that trade flows in 2009 were significantly dampened by the Great Recession.

US Complaints

Value-Added Tax on Integrated Circuits: March 2004

The United States alleged that China had been offering a partial rebate on the value-added tax (VAT) for integrated circuits (ICs) produced or designed domestically, but discriminated against ICs designed abroad and most ICs produced abroad.[18] According to the US complaint, this not only violated national treatment for both goods and services, but afforded preferential treatment to certain imports (i.e., those ICs designed domestically but produced abroad), thereby violating the MFN principle.[19] China and the United States notified the WTO's Dispute Settlement Body (DSB) of a settlement in July 2004, under which China agreed to revoke the preferential VAT treatment. In October 2004, the United States and China notified the DSB that China had complied with the terms of the settlement and that both parties considered the dispute resolved.[20]

---

[17] The intensities are calculated on the basis of PRC-reported trade flows.

[18] Dispute settlement number 309, retrieved 2nd June, 2010, from http://www.wto.org/english/tratop_e/dispu_e/cases_e/ds309_e.htm.

[19] The European Communities, Japan, Mexico and the TPKM customs territory requested to join the consultations. China accepted only the requests of the European Communities, Japan and Mexico.

[20] Case summaries are available on the WTO website. See Dispute Settlement: The Disputes, retrieved 7th June, 2010, from http://www.wto.org/english/tratop_e/dispu_e/find_dispu_cases_e.htm#results.

Table 6 WTO disputes between China and the United States

Request date	Summary	Trade flow at issue ($ billion)	Current status
Complainant: United States			
1. Mar-04	Value-added tax on integrated circuits	$2.6	Settled by parties, agreement implemented
2. Mar-06	Measures affecting imports of automobile parts	0.5	DSB recommendations to be implemented
3. Feb-07	Measures granting refunds, reductions or exemptions from taxes and other payments	N/A	Settled by MOU
4. Apr-07	Measures affecting trading rights and distribution services for certain publications and audiovisual entertainment products	0.4	DSB recommendations to be implemented
5. Apr-07	Measures affecting the protection and enforcement of IP rights	N/A	DSB recommendations to be implemented
6. Mar-08	Measures affecting financial information services and foreign suppliers	0.9	Settled by MOU
7. Dec-08	Grants, loans and other incentives	N/A	In consultations
8. Jun-09	Measures related to the exportation of various raw materials	0.1	Panel composed
9. Sep-10	Countervailing and anti-dumping duties on grain oriented flat-rolled electrical steel from the United States	0.3	Panel composed
10. Sep-10	Certain measures affecting electronic payment services	N/A	Panel composed
11. Dec-10	Measures concerning wind power equipment	N/A	Request for consultations
Total trade flow at issue:		$ 4.8	
Complainant: China			
1. Mar-02	Safeguard duties imposed on imports of certain steel products	$ 0.3	DSB recommendations implemented
2. Sep-07	Anti-dumping duties imposed on coated free-sheet paper from China	0.4	In consultations
3. Sep-08	Anti-dumping duties imposed on certain products from China	2.9	Appellate body reports issued
4. Apr-09	Measures affecting imports of poultry from China	N/A	DSB reports issued
5. Sep-09	Safeguard measure imposed on certain tyres from China	1.9	DSB reports issued
6. Feb-11	Anti-dumping measures on certain frozen warmwater shrimp from China	0.1	Request for consultations
Total trade flow at issue:		$ 5.5	

Note: Trade flows represent the dollar value of one-way trade in the product(s) alleged to be impacted by the contested measures in the year of the dispute. It was not possible to estimate the flows at issue for all cases. See text for additional detail

In 2004, the United States exported $2.6 billion in integrated circuits to China, 6.2% of the $43.0 billion total IC exports by the United States.[21]

Measures Affecting Imports of Automobile Parts: March 2006

The United States, the European Communities and Canada requested consultations on certain PRC measures targeting the automobile sector in 2004 and 2005.[22] The EC and US requests were lodged simultaneously and alleged that imports of automobile parts were subject to higher completed-vehicle tariffs if the imported parts exceeded a given threshold, or if the parts were incorporated in a completed vehicle with domestic parts content below a given threshold. Canada requested consultations two weeks later, adding that China's measures adversely impacted foreign investment and that the application of completed-vehicle tariffs to semi-knocked-down and completely-knocked-down (SKD and CKD) vehicle kits was inconsistent with the Working Party Report on the Accession of China.[23] Canada also alleged that domestic PRC automobile manufacturers were subsidized as a consequence of domestic content and export performance thresholds, violating the Agreement on Subsidies and Countervailing Measures (ASCM).

All three complaining parties subsequently requested to join each other's consultations and were accepted by China.[24] A single panel was composed in October 2006.[25] The panel circulated its reports in July 2008, largely finding in favour of the complainants. The panel held that the measures implemented with respect to auto parts in general were inconsistent with GATT Article III (national treatment) and were not justified under Article XX(d), the defence argued by China.[26] The panel also held that the measures were inconsistent with GATT

---

[21] Data are from UN Comtrade (2010), http://comtrade.un.org/db. Integrated Circuits are covered under the 2002 Harmonized System (HS 2002) code 8542, "Electronic integrated circuits and microassemblies." Many exports from the United States bound for, for example, China "detour" through other countries where the goods are minimally processed before continuing to their final destination. For all intents and purposes, one might consider this an effective export from the United States to China. Such exports are not captured in our estimates and we do not attempt to control for the downward bias this activity could induce.

[22] China – Measures Affecting Imports of Automobile Parts, DS340, retrieved 30th July, 2010, from http://www.wto.org/english/tratop_e/dispu_e/cases_e/ds340_e.htm.

[23] Report of the Working Party on the Accession of China, WT/ACC/CHN/49, 1st October, 2001, retrieved 29th July, 2010, from http://unpan1.un.org/intradoc/groups/public/documents/apcity/unpan002144.pdf.

[24] Australia, Japan and Mexico also requested to join the consultations. China accepted all requests.

[25] Argentina, Australia, Brazil, Japan, Mexico, the TPKM customs territory and Thailand reserved third-party rights.

[26] Art. XX provides for exceptions to the general provisions of GATT. Art. XX(d) provides exceptions for measures "necessary to secure compliance with laws or regulations which are not inconsistent with the provisions of this Agreement . . .".

Article II since treatment of the imports did not accord with the appropriate entries in China's Schedule of Concessions (i.e., bound tariffs). The panel exercised "judicial economy" and did not rule on the consistency of the measures with the Agreement on Trade-Related Investment Measures ("TRIMS"). With respect to the SKD and CKD kits, the panel held that the measures in question were consistent with the general provisions of GATT, but were *inconsistent* with the specific commitments in Paragraph 93 of China's Working Party Report.[27]

China appealed the panel's findings to the Appellate Body with limited success. In December 2008, the Appellate Body overturned the finding of the panel with respect to the treatment of SKD and CKD kits under Paragraph 93 of the Working Party Report, but upheld all other findings and affirmed the recommendation that China should bring its measures into conformity. China stated that it would do so by September 2009; however, the United States has yet to agree that conformity has been reached.

In 2006, the United States exported $0.5 billion in auto parts to China, 1.6% of the $33.5 billion total auto parts exports by the United States.[28]

Measures Granting Refunds, Reductions or Exemptions from Taxes and Other Payments: February 2007

The United States alleged that certain provisions of Chinese law allowed for preferential tax treatment to Chinese enterprises that favour domestic over imported goods.[29] Preferential treatment was alleged to be conferred by reducing monies otherwise owed to the Chinese government, thereby violating the national treatment principle. The United States requested supplemental consultations in April 2007 following the passage of new Chinese income tax legislation.[30] In December 2007, China and the United States informed the DSB that they had agreed to a memorandum of understanding (MOU) on the dispute. In the MOU, China agreed to apply its revised income tax legislation in a manner consistent with its obligations under GATT. China confirmed that the measures in question with respect to refunds, reductions or exemptions for monies owed the Chinese government were no longer

---

[27] Paragraph 93 of China's Working Party Report stipulates that if China were to create tariff lines for CKD and SKD kits, that the "rates would be no more than 10 per cent".

[28] Data are from UN Comtrade (2010), http://comtrade.un.org/db. Auto parts are covered under HS (2002) code 8708, "Parts and accessories of the motor vehicles of headings 87.01 to 87.05".

[29] China – Certain Measures Granting Refunds, Reductions or Exemptions from Taxes and Other Payments, DS358, retrieved 30th July, 2010, from http://www.wto.org/english/tratop_e/dispu_e/cases_e/ds358_e.htm. Australia, the European Communities, Japan and Mexico asked to join the consultations. China accepted all requests.

[30] Australia, the European Communities, Japan, Mexico and Canada requested the join the supplemental consultations. China accepted all requests but Canada's. Australia, Canada, Chile, the European Communities, Japan, the TPKM customs territory, Turkey, and subsequently Argentina, Colombia and Egypt reserved third-party rights.

in effect and could not be used to confer preferential treatment. China further agreed to ensure that imported equipment receives no less favourable treatment than domestically-produced equipment.[31]

Measures Affecting Trading Rights and Distribution Services for Certain Publications and Audiovisual Entertainment Products: April 2007

The United States alleged that China had implemented measures that restrict distribution rights and market access for various audio visual and print media.[32] The United States requested supplemental consultations in July 2007. The European Communities requested to join both consultations and was accepted by China. The panel was composed in March 2008.[33] In August 2009, the panel held that many, but not all, of the measures at issue were inconsistent with China's Accession Protocol in that they restricted the trading rights of other WTO members. The panel held that there was at least one other reasonably available alternative to the implemented measures and therefore did not rule whether the measures were permissible under the Article XX(a) exception to the general provisions of the GATT (exceptions to "protect public morals"). With respect to the distribution services at issue, the panel ruled that China's measures were inconsistent with national treatment under the GATS and further that measures limiting foreign investment to Chinese majority-owned joint-ventures were inconsistent with China's obligations under Articles XVI and XVII of GATS. With respect to the content review of hard-copy sound recordings and restrictions on the distribution of films, the panel concluded that the United States failed to demonstrate that the measures violated China's obligations under the GATT.

Both countries appealed the panel decision in fall 2009. The panel's conclusions were largely upheld by the Appellate Body. The Appellate Body clarified that China's Article XX(a) defence was invalid in that the measures at issue could not be characterized as "necessary to protect public morals." The Appellate Body report was adopted by the DSB in January 2010 with the recommendation that

---

[31] We are unable to give an approximate dollar value of the trade flows affected by the PRC tax rebates.

[32] China – Measures Affecting Trading Rights and Distribution Services for Certain Publications and Audiovisual Entertainment Products, DS363, retrieved 30th July, 2010, from http://www.wto.org/english/tratop_e/dispu_e/cases_e/ds363_e.htm. The affected media include films for theatrical release, audiovisual home entertainment products (e.g. video cassettes and DVDs), sound recordings and publications (e.g. books, magazines, newspapers and electronic publications) and distribution services for publications and foreign suppliers of audiovisual services (including distribution services) for audiovisual home entertainment products. The European Communities requested to join the consultations. China accepted the request.

[33] The European Communities and Japan and subsequently Australia, Korea and the TPKM customs territory reserved third-party rights.

China bring its policies into conformity. China has yet to notify the DSB that corrective policy measures have been implemented.

In 2007, the United States exported $0.1 billion of optical media and $0.1 billion of print media to China, 3.3% of the $3.3 billion total optical media and 1.6% of the $5.9 billion print media exports by the United States.[34] In 2007, the United States exported $0.2 billion of audiovisual and related services to China, 1.1% of the $15.1 billion total audiovisual and related services exports by the United States.[35]

Measures Affecting the Protection and Enforcement of IP Rights: April 2007

The United States alleged that Chinese measures to protect intellectual property rights were insufficient relative to China's obligations under the Trade-Related aspects of Intellectual Property Rights Agreement (TRIPS). Specifically, the United States challenged PRC policy with respect to the minimum extent of infringement necessary to initiate a prosecution, the manner of disposing confiscated goods, and the fact that copyright protection did not extend to works not authorized for publication or distribution.[36] The panel was composed in December 2007.[37]

In January 2009 the panel circulated its report finding that China's copyright law was inconsistent with Articles 9.1 and 41.1 of the TRIPS Agreement.[38] The panel held that the United States had not demonstrated that the customs measures were

---

[34] Data are from UN Comtrade (2010), http://comtrade.un.org/db. Optical media are covered under HS (2007) code 8523.40, "Discs, tapes, solid-state non-volatile storage devices, 'smart cards' and other media for the recording of sound or of other phenomena, whether or not recorded, including matrices and masters for the production of discs, but excluding products of Chapter 37: Optical media." The 8523.40 code did not exist prior to HS 2007. Print media are covered under HS (2007) code 49, "Printed books, newspapers, pictures and other products of the printing industry; manuscripts, typescripts and plans". Total US optical and print media exports were $3.59 and $6.17 billion in 2008, respectively.

[35] Data are from UN Service Trade (2010), http://comtrade.un.org/db. Audiovisual and related services are covered under service code 288.

[36] China – Measures Affecting the Protection and Enforcement of Intellectual Property Rights, DS362, retrieved 30th July, 2010, from http://www.wto.org/english/tratop_e/dispu_e/cases_e/ds362_e.htm.

Canada, the European Communities, Japan and Mexico requested to join the consultations. China accepted all requests.

[37] Argentina, the European Communities, Japan, Mexico and the TPKM customs territory and subsequently Australia, Brazil, Canada, India, Korea, Thailand and Turkey reserved third-party rights.

[38] Art. 9.1 of the TRIPS agreement incorporates the rights and obligations of the Berne Convention for the Protection of Literary and Artistic Works (exclusive of Art. 6bis). Art. 41.1 of the TRIPS agreement requires "... enforcement procedures as specified in this Part are available under their law so as to permit effective action against any act of infringement of intellectual property rights...".

inconsistent with sentence one of Article 46 of the TRIPS agreement[39]; however, the measures were inconsistent with sentence four of Article 46 (both sentences one and four were incorporated by Article 59).[40] It further held that the United States had not demonstrated that the criminal thresholds were inconsistent with Article 61 of the TRIPS agreement.[41] The panel's recommendation that China bring the offending measures into conformity was issued in March 2009. China notified the DSB that it had achieved conformity as of March 2010, and the United States concurred one month later.[42]

Measures Affecting Financial Information Services and Foreign Suppliers: March 2008

The United States requested consultations over measures allegedly restricting the ability of foreign firms to solicit customers and supply financial information services.[43] The United States alleged that foreign firms were required to both supply and solicit through an entity designated by the Xinhua News Agency, and that Chinese consumers were prohibited from contracting financial information services directly from foreign suppliers. The United States claimed that Xinhua designated only one agent through which foreign firms could do business, a subsidiary of Xinhua, and that foreign firms were required to provide extensive information, including confidential customer information, to the Chinese Foreign Information Administration Centre, another entity within the Xinhua framework. Finally, the United States alleged that the Chinese government was preventing foreign financial information services providers from establishing a substantive commercial presence within China.

Nine months after the US request for consultation, China and the United States reached agreement under an MOU. The MOU included a Chinese commitment to

---

[39] Sentence one of Art. 46 stipulates that goods "... found to be infringing be, without compensation of any sort, disposed of outside the channels of commerce in such a manner as to avoid any harm caused to the right holder, or, unless this would be contrary to existing constitutional requirements, destroyed".

[40] Sentence four of Art. 46 stipulates that "... the simple removal of the trademark unlawfully affixed shall not be sufficient, other than in exceptional cases, to permit release of the goods into the channels of commerce".

[41] Art. 61 of the TRIPS agreement stipulates that "... members shall provide for criminal procedures and penalties to be applied at least in cases of wilful trademark counterfeiting or copyright piracy on a commercial scale. Remedies available shall ... [be] sufficient to provide a deterrent...".

[42] We are unable to give an approximate dollar value of the trade flows affected by the PRC IP system. For summary coverage of IP issues with coarse proxies of the overall magnitude of IP infringement in China, see the US section of "US Intellectual Property-Related " under "Sino-US Trade Measures Outside the WTO Framework" below.

[43] China – Measures Affecting Financial Information Services and Foreign Financial Information Suppliers, DS373. The European Communities requested to join the consultations. China accepted the request.

establish a new regulator of financial information services without a commercial interest on the part of Xinhua; in other words, a regulator no longer within the Xinhua framework. The MOU stipulated that the new regulator could request "only information that is relevant to matters under the license," taking "all necessary steps to protect the information provided" and to "only use such information for the specific regulatory purpose for which it is provided."[44] China agreed to revise its licensing process to ensure conformity with Paragraph 308 of its WTO Accession Protocol Working Party Report, which states "that China's licensing procedures and conditions would not act as barriers to market access and would not be more trade restrictive than necessary." China further agreed not to impose any interme-diation requirements on foreign suppliers and to allow consumers to contract financial information services freely and directly.

In 2007, the United States exported $0.9 billion of financial services to China, 1.6% of the $58.3 billion total financial services exports by the United States.[45]

Grants, Loans and Other Incentives: December 2008

The United States alleged that grants, loans and other incentives being offered to Chinese enterprises that meet certain export criteria violated Article 3 of the Agreement on Subsidies and Countervailing Measures (ASCM).[46] The United States also alleged that the measures were potentially inconsistent with Articles 3, 9 and 10 of the Agreement on Agriculture, with Article III of the GATT, and with Sections 5, 8 and 11 of Part I of China's Accession Protocol.[47] No further action has been taken on the case to date.[48]

---

[44] The text of the MOU is available online, retrieved 23rd July, 2010, from http://www.wto.org/english/tratop_e/dispu_e/cases_e/ds373_e.htm (follow the "all documents" link on the right).

[45] Data are from UN Service Trade (2010), http://unstats.un.org/unsd/ServiceTrade. Financial services are covered under service code 260. Data on financial services exports to China are not available for 2008 from UN Service Trade.

[46] China – Grants, Loans and Other Incentives, DS387, retrieved 30th July, 2010, from http://www.wto.org/english/tratop_e/dispu_e/cases_e/ds387_e.htm. Art. 3 of the ASCM prohibits subsidies contingent upon export performance and the use of domestic over imported goods.

Canada, the European Communities, Mexico and Turkey, subsequently Australia and Colombia, and subsequently Ecuador, Guatemala and New Zealand requested to join the consultations. China accepted all requests.

[47] Agreement on Agriculture, Art. 3, "Incorporation of Concessions and Commitments," Art. 9, "Export Subsidy Commitments," and Art. 10, "Prevention of Circumvention of Export Subsidy Commitments", retrieved 29th July, 2010, from http://www.wto.org/english/docs_e/legal_e/14-ag.pdf. GATT Art. III, "National Treatment on Internal Taxation and Regulation." Part I of China's Accession Protocol: Section 5, "Right to Trade," Section 8, "Import and Export Licens-ing," and Section 11, "Taxes and Charges Levied on Imports and Exports."

Canada, the European Communities, Mexico and Turkey and subsequently Australia and Colombia and finally Ecuador, Guatemala and New Zealand requested to join the consultations. China accepted all requests.

[48] We are unable to give an approximate dollar value of trade flows affected by the PRC incentive system.

Measures Related to the Exportation of Various Raw Materials: June 2009

The United States requested consultation over some 32 measures it identified as restricting Chinese exports of raw materials.[49] The United States also suggested that additional unpublished restrictive measures might also be in force. The United States argued that such measures are inconsistent with Articles VIII, X and XI of GATT and several paragraphs of Part I of China's Accession Protocol.[50] A single panel was composed in March 2010.[51]

In 2008, the United States imported $1.7 billion of the raw materials at issue from China, 46.4% of the $3.6 billion total US imports of the raw materials at issue. However, in 2009, the United States imported only $0.1 billion of the raw materials at issue from China.[52]

Countervailing and Anti-Dumping Duties on Grain Oriented Flat-Rolled Electrical Steel from the United States: September 2010

The United States requested consultations with China over countervailing and anti-dumping duties China imposed on grain-oriented, flat-rolled, electrical steel from the United States.[53] The countervailing measures implemented by China were a response to certain "Buy American" provisions in the American Recovery and Reinvestment Act (ARRA, also "stimulus").

---

[49] China – Measures Related to the Exportation of Various Raw Materials, DS394, retrieved 30th July, 2010, from http://www.wto.org/english/tratop_e/dispu_e/cases_e/ds394_e.htm. The raw materials at issue were bauxite, coke, fluorspar, magnesium, manganese, silicon carbide, silicon metal, yellow phosphorus, and zinc.

[50] GATT Art. VIII, "Fees and Formalities connected with Importation and Exportation," Art. X, "Publication and Administration of Trade Regulations," and Art. XI, "General Elimination of Quantitative Restrictions."

[51] The European Communities and subsequently Canada, Mexico and Turkey requested to join the consultations. China accepted all requests. Argentina, Brazil, Canada, Chile, Colombia, Ecuador, the European Union, India, Japan, Korea, Mexico, Norway, the TPKM customs territory and Turkey and subsequently Saudi Arabia reserved third-party rights.

[52] Trade in 2009 was adversely affected by the Great Recession, as well as PRC export restrictions.
Data are from UN Comtrade (2010), http://comtrade.un.org/db. The identified raw materials are covered under HS (2007) codes: 2606, aluminium ores and concentrates; 2704, coke and semicoke of coal, of lignite or of peat; 2529.21 fluorspar; 8104, magnesium and articles thereof, including waste and scrap; 2602, manganese ores and concentrates; 2849.20, carbides, whether or not chemically defined of silicon; 2804.61, silicon; 2804.70, phosphorus; 2608, zinc ores and concentrates.

[53] China – Countervailing and Anti-Dumping Duties on Grain Oriented Flat-rolled Electrical Steel from the United States, DS414, retrieved 4th April, 2011, from http://www.wto.org/english/tratop_e/dispu_e/cases_e/ds414_e.htm.

In 2008, the United States exported \$0.3 billion of the steel at issue to China, 33.1% of the \$0.8 billion of total US exports of the steel at issue.[54] However, in 2009, the United States exported \$0.1 billion of the steel at issue to China, only 15.5% of the \$0.5 billion of total US exports of the steel at issue.

Certain Measures Affecting Electronic Payment Services: September 2010

The United States requested consultations with China over its alleged restriction of credit card payment processing of purchases made in Renminbi to a single PRC entity (China UnionPay), and the requirement that all other payment services carry China UnionPay's logo and be compatible with its technologies.[55] The United States further alleged that China UnionPay was guaranteed preferential access to merchants over foreign payment service providers.[56]

Measures Concerning Wind Power Equipment: December 2010

The United States requested consultations with China over certain grants, loans, and subsidies to domestic producers of wind power equipment it alleged were contingent on use of domestic materials, an apparent violation of the Agreement on Subsidies and Countervailing Measures.[57] The US request also argued that China had not fulfilled its transparency obligations by not translating the PRC legislative measures at issue.[58]

---

[54] US and PRC reports of grain-oriented, flat-rolled, steel approximately agree for 2008, but do not agree for 2009. In 2008, the United States reports \$270 million of exports of the steel at issue to China and China reports \$271 million of imports from the United States. In 2009, the United States reports \$81 million of exports of the steel at issue to China and China reports \$125 million of imports from the United States.

   Data are from UN Comtrade (2010), http://comtrade.un.org/db. Grain-oriented, flat-rolled, electrical steel is covered under HS (2007) codes 7225.11, "Flat-rolled products of other alloy steel, of a width of 600 mm or more: grain-oriented," and 7226.11 "Flat-rolled products of other alloy steel, of a width of 600 mm or less: grain-oriented".

[55] China – Certain Measures Affecting Electronic Payment Services, DS413, retrieved 3rd April, 2011, from http://www.wto.org/english/tratop_e/dispu_e/cases_e/ds413_e.htm.

[56] We are unable to give an approximate dollar value of trade flows affected by the payment services policies.

[57] China – Measures Concerning Wind Power Equipment, DS419, retrieved 2nd April, 2011, from http://www.wto.org/english/tratop_e/dispu_e/cases_e/ds419_e.htm. The European Union and Japan requested to join the consultations.

[58] We are unable to give an approximate dollar value of trade flows affected by the wind power incentive program.

PRC Complaints

Safeguard Duties Imposed on Imports of Certain Steel Products: March 2002

China alleged that certain definitive safeguard measures taken by the United States that increased the import duties on various steel products were unjustified.[59] In all, eight WTO members submitted independent requests for consultation regarding these measures.[60] The DSB composed a single panel for all eight requests in July 2002.[61]

The panel published its reports in July 2003, holding that the United States had not justified the measures at issue by showing the pre-requisite conditions for the imposition of safeguards (namely, unforeseen developments, increased imports, causation and parallelism).[62] The United States appealed the decision one month later. In November 2003, the Appellate Body upheld the conclusions that the ten measures at issue were inconsistent with US obligations under the GATT; however, for two of the measures, it reversed the finding that the United States had not demonstrated a causal link. This reversal did not, however, change the ultimate finding that the measures were inconsistent with US obligations under the GATT. In December 2003, the United States informed the DSB that President Bush had issued an order repealing all of the safeguard measures. During the period of the dispute, China imposed a safeguard measure on US steel, which was abolished in December 2003 following President Bush's repeal order.

In 2002, the United States imported $0.3 billion of steel products from China, 2.2% of the $12.4 billion total US steel imports, and 10.4% of total PRC steel products exports.[63]

---

[59] United States – Definitive Safeguard Measures on Imports of Certain Steel Products, DS252. China identified the following steel products in its request for consultation: "flat steel, hot-rolled bar, cold-finished bar, rebar, certain welded tubular products, carbon and alloy fittings, stainless steel bar, stainless steel rod, tin mill products and stainless steel wire." China's request for consultation is available online. Retrieved 23rd July, 2010, from http://www.wto.org/english/tratop_e/dispu_e/cases_e/ds252_e.htm (follow the "all documents" link on the right).

[60] Brazil, China, the European Communities, Japan, Korea, New Zealand, Norway and Switzerland filed independent requests. Japan and New Zealand also requested to join the consultations. The United States accepted all requests. Many of these members joined each other's consultations. China joined the consultations of Brazil, the European Communities, and New Zealand.

[61] Canada, the TPKM customs territory, Cuba, Malaysia, Mexico, Thailand, Turkey and Venezuela reserved third-party rights.

[62] Despite having a single panel, the US requested that the panel issue eight individual reports so as not to jeopardise its right to settle the claims independently with each member. The panel complied, issuing "one document constituting eight Panel Reports," each of which is particularised to the individual complainants in its conclusions and recommendations, but not in its findings.

[63] Steel products are covered under HS (2002) code 72, "Iron and Steel."
Data are from UN Comtrade (2010), http://comtrade.un.org/db. US and PRC reports of steel trade flows nearly agree. In 2002, China reported $0.24 billion of steel exports to the United States, not $0.27 billion. The PRC amounts are used to calculate the per cent of total PRC steel exports purchased by the United States.

Anti-Dumping Duties Imposed on Coated Free-Sheet Paper
from China: September 2007

China alleged that the International Trade Administration (ITA), a unit of the US Department of Commerce, had wrongly entered a finding of dumping for Chinese, Korean (Rep. of) and Indonesian manufacturers of coated, free-sheet paper.[64] China alleged that the ITA finding was inconsistent with US obligations under GATT Article VI, the Agreement on Subsidies and Countervailing Measures (ASCM) Articles 1, 2, 10, 14, 17 and 32, and Anti-Dumping Agreement Articles 1, 2, 7, 9 and 18.[65] China has not requested the establishment of a panel and no further action has been taken on this case to date.

In 2007, the United States imported $0.4 billion of coated, free-sheet paper from China, 10.7% of the $3.4 billion total US imports of coated, free-sheet paper and 19.0% of the $1.5 billion total PRC coated, free-sheet paper exports.[66]

Anti-Dumping Duties Imposed on Certain Products
from China: September 2008

China challenged the US identification of several instances of dumping by the International Trade Administration.[67] The determinations were made with respect to steel, off-the-road tyres, light-walled rectangular pipe and tube, and laminated woven sacks. China alleged violations of GATT Articles I and VI; ASCM Articles 1, 2, 10, 12, 13, 14, 19 and 32; Anti-Dumping Agreement Articles 1, 2, 6, 9 and 18;

---

[64] United States – Preliminary Anti-Dumping and Countervailing Duty Determinations on Coated Free Sheet Paper from China, DS368, retrieved 30th July, 2010, from http://www.wto.org/english/tratop_e/dispu_e/cases_e/ds368_e.htm.

[65] Art. VI GATT, "Anti-dumping and Countervailing Duties"; ASCM, Art. 1," Definition of a Subsidy," Art. 2, "Specificity," Art. 7, "Remedies," Art. 9, "Consultations and Authorized Remedies," and Art. 18, "Undertakings"; Anti-Dumping Agreement, Art. 1, "Principles," Art. 2, "Determination of Dumping," Art. 7, "Provisional Measures," Art. 9, "Imposition and Collection of Anti-Dumping Duties," and Art. 18, "Final Provisions."

[66] Coated, free-sheet paper is covered under HS (2007) code 4810, "Paper and paperboard, coated on one or both sides."

US and PRC reports of free-sheet paper trade flows do not agree. In 2007, China reported $0.29 billion of free-sheet paper exports to the United States, lower than the US import figure of $0.36 billion. The PRC amounts are used to calculate the per cent of total PRC free-sheet paper exports purchased by the United States.

[67] United States – Definitive Anti-Dumping and Countervailing Duties on Certain Products from China, DS379, retrieved 23rd July, 2010, from http://www.wto.org/english/tratop_e/dispu_e/cases_e/ds379_e.htm.

and Article 15 of China's Accession Protocol.[68] A panel was composed in March 2009.[69]

In October 2010, the panel found that the US imposition of anti-dumping and countervailing duties on the same goods could constitute a "double remedy," which is inconsistent with US WTO obligations, but that China had failed to substantiate this inconsistency in US practice and obligation in its complaint. The panel held that, counter to China's complaint, the United States had correctly identified the source of the countervailed subsidies as "public bodies" (i.e. supported by the PRC government). The Panel rejected the benchmark prices and interest rates used by the United States in its duty determinations and those proposed by China as appropriate for the benefit (subsidy) calculation. The Panel did affirm other aspects China's complaint against the US Department of Commerce's method for benefit calculation (e.g. period average instead of daily interest rates). As for the specificity of the subsidies countervailed by the Department of Commerce, the panel was mixed, upholding China's claim against regional specificity and rejecting its claim against the DOC's identification of the tyre industry.

China appealed the finding in December 2010. In March 2011, the Appellate Body (AB) overturned the initial ruling in important respects.[70] The AB held that the panel had failed to provide an objective assessment of the appropriate benchmark for benefit calculations and had therefore erred in rejecting PRC claims against the US calculation. More critically, the Appellate Body overturned the panel finding with respect to "double remedy," holding that the United States failed to show that its application of countervailing and antidumping duties on the same goods was consistent with US obligations under Articles 10, 19.3, and 32.1 of the Agreement on Subsidies and Countervailing Measures.[71] Finally, and perhaps most importantly, the AB held that a state owned enterprise (SOE) cannot be equated with "public body" (to use the terminology of the Agreement on Subsidies and Countervailing Measures, ASCM) carrying out government functions merely by virtue of majority government ownership in the SOE. Instead, the United States would need to submit additional evidence (which in most instances it did not) that the SOE acted as an arm of the government. Failing this additional evidence, subsidies expended by the SOE to promote its own exports, to sell more inputs to downstream Chinese firms that in turn exported more highly finished products, were held not to violate the ASCM.

---

[68] GATT, Art. I, "General Most-Favoured-Nation Treatment," and Art. VI, "Anti-dumping and Countervailing Duties"; ASCM, Art. 1, "Definition of a Subsidy," Art. 2, "Specificity," Art. 10, "Application of Article VI of GATT 1994," Art. 12, "Evidence," Art. 13, "Consultations," Art. 14, "Calculation of the Amount of a Subsidy in Terms of the Benefit to the Recipient," Art. 19, "Imposition and Collection of Countervailing Duties," and Art. 32, "Other Final Provisions"; Art. 15 of China's Accession Protocol, "Price Comparability in Determining Subsidies and Dumping."

[69] Argentina, Australia, Bahrain, Canada, the European Communities, Kuwait, Saudi Arabia and Turkey reserved third-party rights.

[70] Report of the Appellate Body and Report of the Panel, WT/DS379/9, Document Number 11–1580, retrieved 23rd July, 2010, from http://www.wto.org/english/tratop_e/dispu_e/cases_e/ds379_e.htm (follow "all documents" link on the right).

[71] Art. 10, "Application of Article VI of GATT 1994" (agreement on antidumping), Art. 19, "Imposition and Collection of Countervailing Duties," Art. 32, "Other Final Provisions".

Table 7 Sino-US trade flows in certain products

Summary of Sino-US trade flows in steel, tyres, pipe and woven sacks in 2008 ($US million)

Product	US imports			PRC exports		
	China ($)	World ($)	Share	US ($)	World ($)	Share
Steel pipe	103	722	14.3%	107	594	18.0%
Off-the-road tyres	2,728	9,974	27.4%	2,468	8,060	30.6%
Rectangular pipe and tube	5	724	0.7%	3	317	1.0%
Woven sacks	84	206	40.7%	117	813	14.4%
Total	$2,920	$11,626	25.1%	$2,694	$9,784	27.5%

Source: UN Comtrade

Notes: US imports are as reported by the United States. PRC exports are as reported by China. China and US columns do not agree, but in principle represent the same trade flows

The trade flows of the four products at issue are summarized in Table 7.[72]

Measures Affecting Imports of Poultry from China: April 2009

China alleged that the effective ban on any imports of Chinese poultry by the Omnibus Appropriations Act of 2009 (Public Law 111–8) was an unjustified sanitary and phytosanitary measure.[73] The House of Representatives' Appropriations Committee cited concerns about contaminated foods from China when writing in the ban. China alleged that the measures in the Appropriations Act violate GATT Articles I and XI and the Agriculture Agreement Article 4.[74] China also alleged that the measures violate various provisions of the SPS Agreement. Subsequently, the US Appropriations Act for 2010 was revised so as not to include an outright ban on

---

[72] The PRC complaint identified the following products: "Circular Welded Carbon Quality Steel Pipe," covered under HS (2007) code 7306.19, "Other tubes, pipes and hollow profiles ... of iron or steel: other,"; "Off-the-Road Tires," covered under HS (2007) code 4011, "New pneumatic tires, of rubber"; "Light-Walled Rectangular Pipe and Tube," covered under HS (2007) code 7306.61, "Other tubes, pipes and hollow profiles of iron or steel ... of square or rectangular cross section"; and "Laminated Woven Sacks," covered under HS (2007) code 6305.33, "Sacks and bags, of a kind used for the packing of goods: other, of polyethylene or polypropylene strip."

Off-the-road tires were identified by the ITA report as falling under the US HTS headings: 4011.20.10.25, 4011.20.10.35, 4011.20.50.30, 4011.20.50.50, 4011.61.00.00, 4011.62.00.00, 4011.63.00.00, 4011.69.00.00, 4011.92.00.00, 4011.93.40.00, 4011.93.80.00, 4011.94.40.00, and 4011.94.80.00. See ITA Fact Sheet, retrieved 23rd July, 2010, from http://ia.ita.doc.gov/download/factsheets/factsheet-prc-tires-prelim-020608.pdf.

The PRC complaint is available online, retrieved 23rd July, 2010, from http://www.wto.org/english/tratop_e/dispu_e/cases_e/ds379_e.htm (follow "all documents" link on the right).

[73] United States – Certain Measures Affecting Imports of Poultry from China, DS392, retrieved 30th July, 2010, from http://www.wto.org/english/tratop_e/dispu_e/cases_e/ds392_e.htm.

[74] GATT, Art. I, "General Most-Favoured-Nation Treatment," and Art. XI, "General Elimination of Quantitative Restrictions." Art. 4 of the Agriculture Agreement, "Market Access", retrieved 29th July, 2010, from http://www.wto.org/english/docs_e/legal_e/14-ag.pdf.

Chinese poultry; rather it provides funds to establish sanitary and phytosanitary standards for imported Chinese poultry products.

A panel was composed in September 2009 and circulated reports in September 2010.[75] The panel found that the appropriations bill's provisions against PRC poultry were inconsistent with US obligations under certain sections of Articles 2, 5, and 8 of the SPS agreement in that they were not based on a risk assessment, lacked sufficient scientific evidence, did not justify the isolation of PRC imports in the measure, and had not avoided undue delays in food safety inspection.[76] The relevant section of the appropriations bill (727) had expired by the time the panel circulated its reports, so no recommendation on conformity was issued.

Neither the United States nor China reported any US imports of chicken products from China in 2008 or 2009. In 2009, the United States imported $0.2 billion total and China exported $0.3 billion total of chicken products.[77]

Safeguard Duties Imposed on Certain Tyres from China: September 2009

China objected to the imposition of safeguard tariffs imposed by the Obama Administration in September 2009.[78] The tariffs followed the finding of a threat of "market disruption" in the US tyre market by the US International Trade Commission (ITC).[79] The tyre products identified in this case were fewer than, and distinct from, those identified in the dispute China brought in September 2008.[80] The safeguard was imposed as a three-year descending tariff. China argued that a safeguard is not justified by the conditions of the US industry and that the measures imposed are both more restrictive and longer-lived than would be

---

[75] The European Communities, Guatemala, Korea and Turkey and subsequently, Brazil and the TPKM customs territory reserved third-party rights.

[76] Art. 2, "Basic Rights and Obligations", and Art. 5, "Assessment of Risk and Determination of the Appropriate Level of Sanitary or Phytosanitary Protection".

[77] Data are from UN Comtrade (2010), http://comtrade.un.org/db. Chicken products are covered under HS (2007) codes: 0207, "meat and edible offal, of the poultry heading 0105, fresh, chilled or frozen"; 0105.11, "Live poultry of the following kinds: Chickens".

[78] United States – Measures Affecting Imports of Certain Passenger Vehicle and Light Truck Tyres from China, DS399, retrieved 30th July, 2010, from http://www.wto.org/english/tratop_e/dispu_e/cases_e/ds399_e.htm.

[79] Fact Sheet: Commerce Preliminarily Finds Unfair Dumping of New Pneumatic Off-The-Road Tires from the People's Republic of China, International Trade Administration, United States Department of Commerce, retrieved 29th July, 2010, from http://ia.ita.doc.gov/download/factsheets/factsheet-prc-tires-prelim-020608.pdf.

[80] The US ITC identified the following US HTS codes in its finding: 4011.10.10, 4011.10.50, 4011.20.10, and 4011.20.50. The investigation (Number TA-421-7) report is available online, retrieved 23rd July, 2010, from http://www.usitc.gov/publications/safeguards/pub4085.pdf.

necessary to remedy any potential damage from increased Chinese imports. A panel was composed in March 2010.[81]

In November 2010, the panel circulated its report finding that the United States had established a rapid increase in imports, had satisfied that the imports "contribute significantly" to the disruption of the US tyre market, and had applied a remedy consistent with its findings. Both the United States and China requested that the report adoption be delayed and the DSB agreed. Neither party has appealed the findings as yet.

In 2009, the United States imported $1.9 billion of tyres from China, 26.1% of the $7.3 billion total US tyre imports and 27.7% of the $6.7 billion total PRC tyre exports.[82]

Anti-Dumping Measures on Certain Frozen Warmwater Shrimp from China: February 2011

China requested consultations with the United States over its calculation method for establishing its dumping duties on frozen shrimp imports from China.[83] Specifically, the PRC complaint questions the United States' use of "zeroing" in its calculation, a broadly controversial practice that has been contested by other WTO members.

In 2009, China exported $0.1 billion of frozen shrimp to the United States, 11.2% of China's total shrimp exports.[84]

---

[81] The European Union (formerly the European Communities), Japan, the TPKM customs territory, Turkey and Viet Nam reserved third-party rights in January 2010.

[82] US and PRC reports of tyre trade flows nearly agree. In 2009, China reported $1.86 billion of tyre exports to the United States, not $1.89 billion. The PRC amounts are used to calculate the per cent of total PRC tyre exports purchased by the United States.

Data are from UN Comtrade (2010), http://comtrade.un.org/db. Tyres are covered under HS (2007) codes 4011.10, "New pneumatic tires, of rubber: of a kind used on motor cars," and 4011.20, "New pneumatic tires, of rubber: of a kind used on buses or trucks."

[83] United States – Anti-Dumping Measures on Certain Frozen Warmwater Shrimp from China, DS422, retrieved 3rd April, 2011, from http://www.wto.org/english/tratop_e/dispu_e/cases_e/ds422_e.htm

Japan requested to join the consultations.

[84] US and PRC reports of frozen shrimp trade flows nearly agree. The United States reports $70 million of frozen shrimp imports from China and China reports $82 million of frozen shrimp exports to the United States.

Data are from UN Comtrade (2010), http://comtrade.un.org/db. Frozen shrimp are covered under HS (2007) 0306.13, "shrimps and prawns, frozen".

Other Consultations Joined by China

In addition to requesting consultations with the United States on eight occasions, China has also joined other members' consultations with the United States. In 2004 and 2006, Thailand sought consultations with the United States the use of the controversial "zeroing" practice in determining whether Thai exporters were dumping shrimp in the US market.[85] (In anti-dumping investigations, the United States maintains a practice of not counting, or zeroing, imports when prices are above fair value.) The dispute panel upheld Thailand's claims that the US practice of zeroing with respect to Thai shrimp was inconsistent with the Anti-Dumping Agreement. The decision was appealed by both parties; however, the Appellate Body upheld the panel's findings. Although the United States notified the DSB that it has reached conformity in April 2009, Thailand has yet to agree.

In 2006, China also joined India's consultations with the United States over the enhanced bond requirements on US imports of shrimp from India as implemented under the Amended Bond Directive (ABD).[86] While the panel did not find the ABD itself in violation of US obligations under the Anti-Dumping Agreement, it did find that the US application of the law in the case of shrimp from India was inconsistent with US obligations under the ASCM and Anti-Dumping Agreement. Both parties appealed the findings, but they were upheld by the Appellate Body. In April 2009, the United States informed the DSB that it had reached conformity. India informed the DSB that it would need to wait to observe how the modifications made by the United States would be practiced.

---

[85] Japan and Brazil, subsequently the European Communities, and subsequently, with China, India requested to join the consultations with the United States in the 2004 episode (United States – Provisional Anti-Dumping Measures on Shrimp from Thailand, DS324, retrieved 30th July, 2010, from http://www.wto.org/english/tratop_e/dispu_e/cases_e/ds324_e.htm). No requests were accepted. In the 2006 consultations (United States – Measures Relating to Shrimp from Thailand, DS343, retrieved 30th July, 2010, from http://www.wto.org/english/tratop_e/dispu_e/cases_e/ds343_e.htm), India, subsequently Japan, and subsequently Brazil requested to join the consultations. The United States accepted all requests but Japan's.

[86] Brazil and Thailand also requested to join India's consultations (United States – Customs Bond Directive for Merchandise Subject to Anti-Dumping/Countervailing Duties, DS345, retrieved 30th July, 2010, from http://www.wto.org/english/tratop_e/dispu_e/cases_e/ds345_e.htm). The United States accepted all requests.

Sino-US Trade Measures Outside the WTO Framework

Administrative Law Remedies

Overview of WTO Codes

WTO law provides for several administrative law remedies that members can pursue independently when they believe other WTO members are maintaining trade practices that are inconsistent with the obligations of WTO law. The sections below discuss how the United States and China have utilized their rights and obligations under the various agreements to implement trade remedies. Of course, the trade remedies taken under these agreements have often been contested by other members. First we provide some background on the agreements.

The Agreement on Subsidies and Countervailing Measures (ASCM) provides a framework by which members can identify subsidies of various types provided by other members that are inconsistent with WTO obligations.[87] The agreement provides substantive and procedural requirements that must be met by a member in order to implement a countervailing measure on an identified subsidy. In addition to finding a subsidy, the member must show that the imports in question are causing, or threaten to cause, material injury to a domestic industry. Countervailing duties can be implemented for a maximum initial term of five years; after that, the CVDs must be reviewed. The ASCM provides for special and differential treatment for developing countries.

The Anti-Dumping Agreement (ADA) provides another mechanism through which countries may seek relief from unfair trade practices of foreign firms.[88] Dumping occurs when firms sell products at prices below their "normal value" in an attempt to capture a larger market share in the importing country. To justify the implementation of an anti-dumping duty, members must both show that a product is being sold below its normal value and that these sales are causing material injury to a domestic industry. Anti-dumping duties, like CVDs, can be implemented for a maximum initial term of five years before they must be reviewed.

---

[87] Agreement on Subsidies and Countervailing Measures (ASCM), Annex 1A to the Marrakesh Agreement Establishing the World Trade Organization, 15th April, 1994, retrieved 29th July, 2010, from http://www.wto.org/english/docs_e/legal_e/24-scm.pdf.

[88] Agreement on the Implementation of Article IV of the General Agreement on Tariffs and Trade 1994 (Anti-Dumping), Annex 1A to the Marrakesh Agreement Establishing the World Trade Organization, 15th April, 1994, retrieved 29th July, 2010, from http://www.wto.org/english/docs_e/legal_e/19-adp.pdf.

Safeguard measures allow for the implementation of duties in circumstances where, without any behaviour inconsistent with WTO obligations by other members, a member determines that imports are rising so rapidly, relatively or absolutely, as to cause or threaten to cause serious injury to the domestic industry. The Agreement on Safeguards prohibits "grey area" measures, such as voluntary export restraints. As with the ASCM and ADA, the Agreement on Safeguards sets out procedures by which a government many authorize a safeguard measure. Unlike the ASCM and ADA, safeguard measures are to be implemented for an initial period of only four years, with the possibility of extension. Safeguard measures are, in principle, general measures, although some allowance is made for differential trade restrictions as between WTO members. Another key difference is that the exporting country has the right to seek compensation for the safeguard measure implemented against it. Barring an agreement on compensation, the affected member may retaliate.

The Agreement on Trade Related Aspects of Intellectual Property Rights (TRIPS) establishes a minimum standard of intellectual property rights (IPR) protections that members must uphold.[89] The agreement covers seven substantive areas: copyright and related rights; trademarks and service marks; geographical indications and appellations of origin; industrial designs; patents, including genetically modified organisms; the layout-designs of integrated circuits; and trade secrets and test data. The agreement incorporates the standards set out by the Paris and Berne conventions, which are administered by the World Intellectual Property Organization (WIPO). While the TRIPS Agreement does not specifically authorize retaliatory measures by member countries, the United States engages in "self-help," under Section 337 of the Tariff Act of 1930, to confiscate counterfeit imports and address other intellectual property violations. Many of these cases are against China, as detailed below.

US Measures

US Administrative Law

Four types of US trade remedy measures are intended to offset foreign trade practices that are determined by national authorities to harm domestic firms. While the WTO framework contemplates remedial action, the remedies are applied by national trade authorities. The manner of application may be later deemed by the WTO Dispute Settlement Body to be inconsistent with WTO law. The four

---

[89] Agreement on Trade-Related Aspects of Intellectual Property Rights (TRIPS), Annex 1C to the Marrakesh Agreement Establishing the World Trade Organization, 15th April, 1994, retrieved 29th July, 2010, from http://www.wto.org/english/docs_e/legal_e/27-trips.pdf.

measures discussed below relate to: dumping; subsidies and other government support; rapid rises in import volumes; and intellectual property rights.[90]

Anti-dumping and countervailing duty determinations under US law follow proceedings outlined by Section 731 of the Tariff Act of 1930, as amended. The imposition of duties is authorized either by Section 701 (AD) or Section 303 (CVD) of the Tariff Act of 1930 (the Smoot-Hawley Tariff Act) or Section 753 of the Act (so-called "black hole" cases where no prior injury determination has been made). Cases begin with petitions by domestic firms that believe they are being injured by foreign subsidies or dumping activity. The petitioner decides whether to seek a trade remedy in the form of anti-dumping duty (ADD) or countervailing duty (CVD) remedies, or perhaps both. The International Trade Administration (ITA), a division of the Department of Commerce, and the International Trade Commission (ITC), an independent body, investigate different aspects of the case. The ITA examines trade and production data to determine whether export sales are made at "less than fair value" in a dumping case ("normal value" in WTO parlance), or whether they are subsidized in a countervailing duty case. The ITC determines whether the exports sales in question cause or threaten material injury to the domestic industry. If the ITA and the ITC both make affirmative findings, then penalty duties are imposed. Duties are typically imposed for a period of five years followed by a sunset review to determine whether to continue the duty for a further period. Both countervailing and anti-dumping duties are recognized as valid trade remedies under the GATT. However, the investigations leading to the duties are often challenged.

WTO members may also impose safeguard measures when imports of a certain product are rising so rapidly (absolutely or relatively) as to cause or threaten to cause serious injury to the member's domestic industry. In the United States, safeguard cases are investigated by the ITC pursuant to Section 201 of the Trade Act of 1974 (Section 203 for safeguard review cases). If it makes a positive finding, the ITC issues a recommendation to the President, who must then decide whether to take action.

Under Section 421 of the Trade Act of 1974, the ITC can also recommend China-specific safeguards if imports cause or threaten material injury. These investigations follow slightly different procedures. China's Protocol of Accession to the WTO allows Section 421 safeguard actions until 2013.

Under US law, trade remedies related to intellectual property rights (IPR) violations are sought through proceedings authorized by Section 337 of the Tariff Act of 1930. Section 337 cases are investigated by the International Trade Commission.[91]

---

[90] For additional background on US trade measures see, United States International Trade Commission, Import Injury Investigations Case Statistics (FY 1980–2008), February 2010, retrieved 29th July, 2010, from http://www.usitc.gov/trade_remedy/documents/historical_case_stats.pdf.

[91] The data on administrative law remedies in the following sections cover the first half of 2010 only.

Table 8 US anti-dumping cases

US anti-dumping investigations resulting in imposed duties, 2002–2010

Respondent location	Annual									Overall	
	2002	2003	2004	2005	2006	2007	2008	2009	2010	2002–2010	Per Cent of all investigations
China	8	7	6	3	3	12	10	11	1	61	85.9%
Korea (Rep. of)	1	2	1	1	1	2	1	–	–	9	90.0%
India	–	2	2	1	–	1	2	–	–	8	57.1%
Japan	1	3	1	2	–	1	–	–	–	8	88.9%
Mexico	–	2	2	–	1	1	–	2	–	8	100.0%
All Other	7	13	13	2	2	10	3	5	–	55	74.3%
Total	17	29	25	9	7	27	16	18	1	149	77.6%
Total (Ex. China)	9	22	19	6	4	15	6	7	–	88	76.5%

Source: Bown, Chad P. (2010) "Global Antidumping Database," available at http://econ. worldbank.org/ttbd/gad/

US Anti-Dumping Actions Against China

Since China joined the WTO, the United States has conducted 71 AD investigations against PRC exporters, covering 83 product sectors.[92] The United States has imposed anti-dumping duties in 86%, or 61 of the 71 AD investigations. Among targets outside of China, 77% of investigations led to the imposition of duties. China is by far the most frequent target of AD investigations, and Korea (Rep. of) is second, with just 9 cases. In fact, PRC firms were the target in 40% of US cases leading to AD duties (see Table 8). Sectors that are prominently subject to AD investigations are oil country tubular goods and paper and paperboard.[93] China has challenged just three of the anti-dumping duties through WTO proceedings (discussed above).

US anti-dumping remedies have been applied to a significant volume of Sino-US trade. Anti-dumping measured covered an average of 6.5% of US imports from China by dollar volume (see Table 9). The highest anti-dumping duty import coverage during the period 2002 to 2009 (16.5% average) was in the stone, glass, and metals categories (HS categories 68 through 83), followed by chemicals and mineral products (12.4%; HS categories 25 through 38).

---

[92] Data are from Bown, Global Antidumping Database, 2010, available online at: http://econ. worldbank.org/ttbd/gad. Sectors are counted at the four-digit HS code level. Note that goods are cited in AD investigations at the six and eight digit level. Where multiple sub-classified products within a four-digit code are cited by a given case, the 4-digit parent code is counted only once.

[93] The HS (2007) 4-digit codes were 7306, 7304 (oil country tubular goods), and 4811 (paper and paperboard). Code 7306 was cited by seven cases, codes 7304 and 4811 were cited by four cases. China disputed one of the paper cases through the WTO DSB in September 2007.

Table 9 Summary of US anti-dumping duty trade coverage

US anti-dumping duty coverage of imports from China ($US million and percent of trade flow)

Code	Description	2002	2003	2004	2005	2006	2007	2008	2009	Average
01-24	Agricultural Products	$352	$556	$461	$267	$415	$247	$267	$245	$351
		17.2%	20.9%	14.6%	7.3%	8.9%	4.6%	4.4%	4.7%	10.4%
25-38	Chemical and mineral products	$349	$409	$1,092	$925	$1,011	$734	$2,022	$769	$914
		10.8%	10.3%	19.7%	13.5%	12.3%	8.7%	15.2%	8.9%	12.4%
39-49	Plastics, Rubbers, Wood	$977	$1,285	$1,704	$2,319	$2,670	$2,919	$2,489	$1,930	$2,037
		7.6%	8.5%	9.1%	10.2%	10.3%	10.2%	8.4%	7.7%	9.0%
50-67	Textiles, footwear, and headgear	$25	$50	$78	$176	$210	$195	$263	$172	$146
		0.1%	0.2%	0.3%	0.4%	0.5%	0.4%	0.5%	0.4%	0.3%
68-83	Stone, glass, and metals	$1,555	$1,908	$2,632	$3,701	$4,768	$5,703	$7,154	$2,704	$3,766
		14.8%	15.2%	15.5%	17.4%	17.3%	18.7%	21.3%	11.9%	16.5%
84-85	Machinery and/or electrical	$1,372	$1,828	$2,531	$4,239	$6,606	$3,086	$3,434	$2,735	$3,229
		3.0%	3.0%	2.9%	3.9%	5.0%	2.1%	2.3%	2.0%	3.0%
86-89	Transportation	$154	$217	$309	$407	$477	$495	$515	$392	$371
		6.8%	7.3%	7.6%	8.0%	7.7%	6.8%	6.8%	6.6%	7.2%
90-97	Miscellaneous	$3,955	$4,923	$5,805	$6,736	$7,404	$7,813	$5,207	$3,959	$5,725
		12.4%	13.3%	13.7%	14.0%	14.0%	13.0%	8.6%	7.8%	12.1%
	Total	$8,740	$11,177	$14,612	$18,770	$23,562	$21,193	$21,350	$12,905	$16,539
		6.5%	6.8%	6.9%	7.2%	7.7%	6.2%	6.0%	4.2%	6.5%

Sources: Bown, Chad P. (2010) "Global Antidumping Database," available at http://econ.wordlbank.org/ttbd/gad/; UN Comtrade

Notes: Code ranges refer to all 2-digit SITC codes within the indicated range. For example, 01–24 (agricultural products) refers to goods in 2-digit SITC codes starting with 01 and including all subsequent 2-digit codes to 24. Dollar amounts represent the US import trade flows from China for the given trade category covered by an anti-dumping duty in the given year. Anti-dumping duties are assumed to be initially implemented and renewed for five year periods. Categories are analyzed at the 6-digit HS code level and summarized at the 2-digit level. Only categories with AD duties are shown. Per cents represent the fraction of US import trade flow from China in the given category covered by an anti-dumping duty in the given period. Totals are the sum of all import trade flows from China covered by an anti-dumping duty. Total per cents are total import trade flow from China covered by a duty divided by the total import trade flow from China of all goods

Table 10 US countervailing duty cases

US countervailing duty investigations resulting in imposed duties, 2002–2010

	Annual									Overall	
Respondent location	2002	2003	2004	2005	2006	2007	2008	2009	2010	2002–2010	Per cent of all investigations
China	–	–	–	–	1	7	5	8	–	21	84.0%
India	–	2	1	1	–	–	1	–	–	5	55.6%
Indonesia	–	–	–	1	1	–	–	1	–	3	100.0%
All other	3	–	–	–	1	–	–	2	–	6	46.2%
Total	3	2	1	2	3	7	6	11	–	35	70.0%
Total (Ex. China)	3	2	1	2	2	–	1	3	–	14	56.0%

Source: Bown, Chad P. (2010) "Global Antidumping Database," available at http://econ.worldband.org/ttbd/gad/

US Countervailing Duty Actions Against China

Countervailing duty investigations have been less frequent than AD cases over the past decade. The United States has investigated 50 CVD cases and 192 AD cases worldwide in the years since China's WTO accession. Of the 50 CVD cases, the United States imposed duties in 35 instances. Again, the United States has imposed countervailing duties most frequently by far on PRC exporters (21 instances out of 25 investigations). India is a distant second with 5 instances of imposed duties out of 9 investigations (see Table 10).[94]

US countervailing duties have covered an average of 1.5% of imports from China by dollar volume over the period 2002 to 2009 (see Table 11). Countervailing duties have impacted the stone, glass, and metals industries (HS codes 68–83) to the greatest extent (6.4%), followed by the plastics, rubbers and wood industries (4.2%; HS codes 39–49).[95]

US Safeguard Actions Against China

Since 2001, the United States has implemented only one global safeguard. The Bush administration implemented the safeguard following the ITC's affirmative finding of injury to US steel manufacturers in 2002. The measure was subsequently challenged in the WTO by several WTO members, including China, and ruled inconsistent (see PRC Complaints above). The United States subsequently dropped the safeguard measures.

---

[94] Bown, Global Countervailing Duties Database, 2010, available at: http://econ.worldbank.org/ttbd/gcvd.

[95] HS Codes can be identified from the Archive Pages of the Harmonized Tariff Schedule, retrieved 18th June, 2010, from http://www.usitc.gov/tata/hts/archive/index.htm.

Table 11 Summary of US countervailing duty trade coverage

US countervailing duty coverage of imports from China ($US million and percent of trade flow)

Code	Description	2002	2003	2004	2005	2006	2007	2008	2009	Average
25-38	Chemical and Mineral Products	$79	$103	$131	$161	$198	$209	$322	$139	$168
		2.4%	2.6%	2.4%	2.3%	2.4%	2.5%	2.4%	1.6%	2.3%
39-49	Plastics, Rubbers, Wood	$511	$704	$981	$1,432	$1,600	$1,709	$1,521	$1,169	$1,202
		4.0%	3.8%	4.3%	5.1%	4.9%	4.6%	3.9%	3.4%	4.2%
50-67	Textiles, footwear, and headgear	$5	$15	$34	$51	$69	$89	$84	$56	$50
		0.0%	0.1%	0.1%	0.1%	0.2%	0.2%	0.2%	0.1%	0.1%
68-83	Stone, glass, and metals	$273	$357	$673	$1,290	$1,908	$2,691	$4,366	$1,612	$1,646
		2.6%	2.9%	4.0%	6.1%	6.9%	8.8%	13.0%	7.1%	6.4%
84-85	Machinery and/or electrical	$205	$290	$424	$552	$615	$760	$822	$666	$542
		0.4%	0.5%	0.5%	0.5%	0.5%	0.5%	0.5%	0.5%	0.5%
90-97	Miscellaneous	$425	$433	$532	$645	$763	$830	$860	$587	$634
		1.3%	1.2%	1.3%	1.3%	1.4%	1.4%	1.4%	1.2%	1.3%
	Total	$1,497	$1,901	$2,774	$4,122	$5,153	$6,290	$7,974	$4,228	$4,242
		1.1%	1.2%	1.3%	1.6%	1.7%	1.8%	2.2%	1.4%	1.5%

Sources: Bown, Chad P. (2010) "Global Antidumping Database," available at http://econ.worldbank.org/ttbd/gad/; UN Comtrade
Notes: Code ranges refer to all 2-digit SITC codes within the indicated range. For example, 25-38 (chemical and mineral products) refers to goods in 2-digit SITC codes starting with 25 and including all subsequent 2-digit codes to 38. Dollar amounts represent the US import trade flows from China for the given trade category covered by a countervailing duty in the given year. Countervailing duties are assumed to be initially implemented and renewed for five year periods. Categories are analyzed at the 6-digit HS code level and summarized at the 2-digit level. Only categories with countervailing duties are shown. Per cents represent the fraction of US import trade flow from China in the given category covered by a countervailing duty in the given period. Totals are the sum of all import trade flows from China covered by a countervailing duty. Total per cents are total import trade flow from China covered by a duty divided by the total import trade flow from China of all goods

In the same time period, the ITC has conducted 7 China-specific safeguard investigations under Section 421, finding affirmatively in 5 instances. In only one case, PRC tyre imports, was action taken by the President, under the Obama Administration in 2009. China subsequently brought the case to the WTO DSB (see PRC Complaints above).

US Intellectual Property-Related Actions Against China

Between January 2002 and June 2010, 255 investigations were initiated, 43 of which were pending as of mid 2010. China was by far the most frequently cited respondent in these investigations (104 investigations), followed by Taiwan (60), Japan (48) and the Republic of Korea (36). PRC respondents were cited in 40.8% of the investigations initiated since 2002. Of these 104 investigations of PRC respondents, 21 remained pending as of mid 2010. Of the 83 completed investigations involving a PRC respondent, in 26 cases (31.3%) the ITC issued a finding of violation or a cease and desist order (see Table 12).[96]

These investigations address only a small fraction of losses allegedly caused by IP infringement. As discussed above (under US Complaints), the United States has also attempted to redress IP violations through the WTO DSB. However, the total losses from intellectual property violations faced by US firms are extremely difficult to measure. Guesstimates are plagued by poor data, and rely on dicey assumptions. A recent US Government Accountability Office (GAO) report indicated that many unsubstantiated estimates of the cost of IPR violations are widely cited even though it is "difficult, if not impossible, to quantify the net effect of counterfeiting and piracy on the economy as a whole."[97] However, some proxy measures indicate the magnitude of IPR offenses in China relative to other countries. For example, in 2009, 79% ($205 million) of the total dollar value of goods seized by US Customs and Border Protection (CBP) for IPR violations were from China. Another 10% ($27 million) were from Hong Kong and 1% ($3 million) from India.[98] Seizures of PRC goods were disproportionate to its share of US merchandise imports (19.3%) by a factor of four.[99] The US CBP seized $1 in

---

[96] All 337 Investigations. Office of Unfair Import Investigation, United States International Trade Commission, retrieved 30th June, 2010, from http://info.usitc.gov/ouii/public/337inv.nsf/All? OpenView.

[97] Government Accountability Office Washington, D. C., Intellectual Property – Observations on Efforts to Quantify the Economic Effects of Counterfeit and Pirated Goods, April 2010, GAO-10-423, p. 16.

[98] US Customs and Border Protection, Top IPR Seizures 2009, retrieved 26th July, 2010, from http://www.cbp.gov/linkhandler/cgov/trade/priority_trade/ipr/pubs/seizure/fy09_stats.ctt/ fy09_stats.pdf.

These percentages undoubtedly reflect, at least in part, US CBP policy, which may or may not be consistent with the actual prevalence of infringement.

[99] UN Comtrade (2010), http://comtrade.un.org/db.

Table 12 US intellectual property-related unfair import investigations

Section 337 intellectual property investigations by respondent country and year

Respondent location	2002	2003	2004	2005	2006	2007	2008	2009	2010	Total	Per cent of total investigations	Violations Cited in country-cases	Per number of completed investigations
1. China	5	8	10	8	13	20	14	15	11	104	40.8%	26	31.3%
2. Taiwan	4	3	7	7	4	5	13	8	9	60	23.5%	13	29.5%
3. Japan	2	2	4	3	5	6	10	10	6	48	18.8%	4	11.1%
4. Korea (Rep. of)	1	1	3	5	7	4	9	4	2	36	14.1%	5	16.1%
5. Hong Kong	5	3	2	1	4	4	5	4	4	32	12.5%	5	20.8%
6. Canada	1	4	1	4	2	1	4	5	4	26	10.2%	5	25.0%
7. Germany	1	2	2	3	6	3	1	2	–	20	7.8%	5	27.8%
8. Mexico	2	–	2	4	1	1	1	3	2	16	6.3%	1	8.3%
9. Singapore	–	2	2	1	1	1	6	1	2	16	6.3%	5	38.5%
10. Malaysia	–	2	2	1	3	3	3	–	3	15	5.9%	4	44.4%
All other	4	11	11	10	10	11	17	10	4	88	34.5%	26	29.5%
Total	17	18	26	29	33	35	41	31	25	225	100.0%	44	20.8%
Pending	–	1	–	–	3	1	3	14	21	43	16.9%		
Complete	17	17	26	29	30	34	38	17	4	212	83.1%		

Source: US International Trade Commission, Office of Unfair Import Investigations

Notes: Counts by country do not sum to total. A single investigation will be identified more than once over that total row if it identifies multiple respondent countries. Only countries who are respondents in ten or more investigations are shown. The row counts in the "Total," "pending," and "complete" rows represent the number of investigations for all countries (shown and not shown) without double counting investigations that identify more than one respondent country. Violations are terminated investigations where a violation was found and/or a cease and desist order was issued against the respondent or a co-respondent. The final column indicates the per cent of completed investigations against the given country where a violation was cited. For example, in 26 cases against China a violation was cited, this is 31.3% of the 83 cases that have been completed against China. China has had 104 investigations initiated against it, indicating that (104 − 83 =) 21 investigations against China are pending

goods for every $1,874 worth of goods imported from China and $1 of goods for every $1,174 imported from Hong Kong. In a recent study by the Organisation for Economic Co-operation and Development (OECD), Hong Kong was identified as the leading source of global counterfeited goods trade relative to the volume of exports.[100] The study placed China as the fifteenth highest source of counterfeited goods relative to the volume of exports. The OECD also estimated that the maximum amount of global trade in counterfeited and pirated goods was $250 billion in 2007. This amount, however, does not include IP infringing goods that do not cross borders. As mentioned above, these estimates should be read with caution.

The PRC government has handled an increasing number of IPR infringement disputes over the past 15 years. IPR holders that suspect violations in China typically seek recourse through an administrative process that is not used in other countries. The process does not award damages to the plaintiff, but can fine the defendant. Although the great majority of IP infringement complainants are pursued via administrative procedures, IPR violations are also litigated in the PRC courts, and the number of cases has grown considerably over the past 15 years. The number of cases filed in PRC courts in 2006 was four times the average annual number of cases filed in the mid-1990s.[101] According to sampling conducted by Sepetys and Cox (2009), the vast majority of cases are filed in lower-level courts and more cases are filed by China-based plaintiffs (38%) than US plaintiffs (26%). Japan and France filed 9% of the sampled cases each. However, the share of cases filed is not proportionate to the number of patents held by firms in these countries. While US firms held 18.7% of valid foreign-origin patents in China in 2008, Japanese firms held 43.0%, and French firms held 3.7%.[102] The highest damage awards for these cases, based on the Sepetys and Cox (2009) sample, were for plaintiffs headquartered in China (top 3 awards) and Japan (fourth and fifth largest awards). Ninety per cent of the awards were for $100,000 or less and most awards were a small fraction of the damages claimed.[103]

PRC Measures

Trade remedies under PRC law are governed chiefly by the Foreign Trade Law of the PRC. Foreign Trade Remedies, an article within this law, deals specifically with

---

[100] OECD, Magnitude of Counterfeiting and Piracy of Tangible Products: An Update, 2009, retrieved 26th July, 2010, from http://www.oecd.org/dataoecd/57/27/44088872.pdf.

[101] Sepetys/Cox, *Intellectual Property Rights Protection in China: Trends in Litigation and Economic Damages*, 2009, p. 8.

[102] State Intellectual Property Organisation (SIPO) of the People's Republic of China, 2008 Annual Report, retrieved 3rd April, 2011, from http://www.sipo.gov.cn/sipo_English/laws/annualreports.

[103] Sepetys/Cox, *Intellectual Property Rights Protection in China: Trends in Litigation and Economic Damages*, 2009, pp. 8, 11 (Table 6), 13 (Table 10).

countervailing duties and anti-dumping duties. PRC trade remedy law was further articulated in 1997 with the Anti-Dumping and Anti-Subsidy Regulations. To comply with its WTO accession protocol, China revised its trade remedy rules effective January 2002 by separating anti-dumping and anti-subsidy measures, giving each distinct regulations. Until 2003, PRC trade remedy proceedings were administered by the Ministry of Foreign Trade and Economic Cooperation (MOFTEC) and the State Economics and Trade Commission (SETC). MOFCOM subsumed both MOFTEC and the SETC in March 2003, and anti-dumping and anti-subsidy measures were revised once more in mid-2004. MOFCOM generally initiates investigations in response to a petition from the domestic industry; however, in exceptional circumstances, MOFCOM may initiate its own investigation. Anti-dumping and anti-subsidy duties are initially imposed for a period of five years; a sunset review then determines whether they should be extended.[104]

MOFCOM also administers proceedings for safeguard measures under Decree Number 330. The decree initially promulgated the regulations in November 2001, just prior to PRC accession to the WTO. It was subsequently revised in 2004, placing safeguards under the newly created MOFCOM and modifying some of the language in the decree. Similar to anti-dumping and anti-subsidy investigations, MOFCOM may initiate safeguard investigations independently.[105]

PRC Anti-Dumping Duty Actions Against the United States

In the period since its accession to the WTO, China has initiated 24 AD investigations against the United States covering 24 product sectors.[106] China imposed AD duties in 22 of these cases. China imposed a similar number of AD duties on Japan (22) and the Republic of Korea (20); however, the investigations of US exporters had the highest yield (92% of investigations led to imposed duties). Among targets not including the United States, 83% of PRC AD investigations led to the imposition of AD duties (see Table 13). The sectors cited by the most PRC cases were those related to hydrocarbons, phenols, polyamides, synthetic rubber, and uncoated paper.[107] The United States has not challenged any of the AD duties imposed by China in WTO proceedings.

---

[104] Choi/Gao, Procedural Issues in the Anti-Dumping Regulations of China: A Critical Review under the WTO Rules, Chinese Journal of International Law 5 (2006) 3, p. 663.

[105] China Safeguard Measures Regulations (Revised), retrieved 27th September, 2010, from http://tradeinservices.mofcom.gov.cn/en/b/2004-03-31/27907.shtml.

[106] Data are from Bown, Global Antidumping Database, 2010, available online at: http://econ.worldbank.org/ttbd/gad. Sectors are counted at the four-digit HS code level. Note that goods are cited in AD investigations at the six and eight digit level. Where multiple sub-classified products within a four-digit code are cited by a given case, the 4-digit parent code is counted only once.

[107] The HS (2007) 4-digit codes were 2903 (hydrocarbons), 2907 (phenols), 3908 (polyamides), 4002 (synthetic rubber), and 4804 (uncoated paper). Each was cited in two AD investigations.

Table 13 PRC anti-dumping investigations

PRC anti-dumping investigations resulting in imposed duties, 2002–2010

Respondent location	Annual									Overall	
	2002	2003	2004	2005	2006	2007	2008	2009	2010	2002–2010	Per cent of all investigations
USA	4	5	5	3	–	–	2	3	–	22	91.7%
Japan	6	4	5	3	3	1	–	–	–	22	81.5%
Korea (Rep. of)	7	3	4	1	1	1	2	1	–	20	87.0%
Taiwan	3	2	1	3	2	1	2	1	–	15	93.8%
EU	1	2	1	1	1	–	2	1	–	9	75.0%
Russia	3	–	2	–	–	–	–	2	–	7	77.8%
All other	3	5	4	2	3	1	5	3	–	26	78.8%
Total	27	21	22	13	10	4	13	11	–	121	82.3%
Total (Ex. US)	23	16	17	10	10	4	11	8	–	99	82.5%

Source: Bown, Chad P. (2010) "Global Antidumping Database," available at http://econ.worldbank.org/ttbd/gad/

Table 14 PRC anti-dumping duty coverage of US imports

PRC anti-dumping duty coverage of ARC imports from the United States ($US million and percent of trade flow)

Code	Description	2002	2003	2004	2005	2006	2007	2008	2009	Average
25-38	Chemical and mineral products	$1	$95	$234	$248	$748	$695	$795	$624	$430
		0.0%	2.0%	4.0%	3.8%	10.7%	7.6%	7.4%	6.3%	5.2%
39-49	Plastics, rubbers, wood	$0	$54	$41	$166	$188	$196	$238	$395	$160
		0.0%	1.2%	0.7%	2.5%	2.4%	1.9%	2.0%	3.7%	1.8%
50-67	Textiles, footwear, and headgear	$0	$0	$0	$0	$5	$5	$9	$5	$3
		0.0%	0.0%	0.0%	0.0%	0.2%	0.2%	0.3%	0.3%	0.1%
	Total	$2	$149	$275	$414	$941	$895	$1,042	$1,024	$593
		0.0%	0.4%	0.6%	0.8%	1.6%	1.3%	1.3%	1.3%	0.9%

Sources: Bown, Chad P. (2010) "Global Antidumping Database," available at http://econ.worldbank.org/ttbd/gad/; UN Comtrade

Notes: Code ranges refer to all 2-digit SITC codes within the indicated range. For example, 25–38 (chemical and mineral products) refers to goods in 2-digit SITC codes starting with 25 and including all subsequent 2-digit codes to 38. Dollar amounts represent the PRC import trade flows from the United States as reported by China for the given trade category covered by an anti-dumping duty in the given year. Anti-dumping duties are assumed to be initially implemented and renewed for five year periods. Categories are analyzed at the 6-digit HS code level and summarized at the 2-digit level. Only categories with AD duties are shown. Per cents represent the fraction of PRC import trade flow from the United States in the given category covered by an anti-dumping duty in the given period. Totals are the sum of all import trade flows from the United States covered by an anti-dumping duty. Total per cents are total import trade flow from the United States covered by a duty divided by the total import trade flow from the United States

PRC Countervailing Duty Actions Against the United States

China has used almost exclusively AD actions to protect its industries from foreign competition. In the period since it acceded to the WTO, China has investigated only three CVD cases and imposed duties in two. All three cases were launched in 2009. China investigated US exports of steel and chicken products, both of which led to the imposition of duties. China also investigated certain cars, but MOFCOM has yet to issue a final determination.

PRC Safeguard Actions Against the United States

China has imposed only one safeguard measure, on steel in 2002, following the US steel safeguard (disputed in the WTO, see the first case under PRC Complaints above). The China safeguard was revoked in December 2003, when the United States removed its own steel safeguard duties.

Legislative Measures

This section covers instances of protectionism embedded within recent PRC and US proposed or implemented legislation. None of the measures has yet landed on the doorstep of the WTO. The measures discussed here are identified primarily from the Global Trade Alert (GTA) project, supplemented with additional research.[108] We cover six US measures and five PRC measures (see Table 15). All these measures have been proposed or implemented within the past two years. The majority of the US measures arose in response to the "Great Recession" of 2008–2009, whereas the PRC measures appear more broadly motivated. Where possible, we approximate the dollar value of the affected import or export market and the share of the total export or import market occupied by the trading partner in the year of the dispute. Again, it is important to note that trade in 2009 was significantly impacted by the Great Recession, so the reported trade values are depressed.

---

[108] See www.globaltradealert.org. Measures addressed in this Chapter are those that, according to the GTA, have been proposed or implemented and, if enacted, "almost certainly" discriminate against foreign commercial interests.

Table 15 Protectionist measures that affect Sino-US trade

Inception date	Summary	Trade flow at issue ($ billion)
US measures		
1. Dec-08/09	Support for GMAC, general motors, and Chrysler	$5.2
2. Jan-09	Solar Panel Tariff Schedule Reclassification	0.1
3. Feb-09	American Recovery and Reinvestment Act and Buy American Provision	N/A
4. Feb-09	Employ American Workers Act	N/A
5. May-09	Dairy Export Incentive Program	0.1
6. Mar-09	Currency Exchange Rate Oversight Reform Act	N/A
Total trade flow at issue		$5.4
Chinese measures		
1. Apr-09	Export Tax Rebates	$224.0
2. Apr-09	Ban or Foreign Investment in Express Postal Services	2.0
3. Sep-09	Adjustment of Import Tariffs Policy on Key Technical Equipment	N/A
4. Nov-09	National Indigenous Innovation Products Accreditation Program	10.0
5. Feb-10	Temporary Increase of Fuel and Jet Oil Import Tariffs	0.2
Total trade flow at issue		$236.2

US Legislative Measures

Support for GMAC, General Motors and Chrysler: December 2008-December 2009

In November 2008, US auto industry executives appeared before a congressional hearing and requested $25 billion in public aid.[109] Just prior to this hearing, European Commission President Barroso warned of potential WTO action against US subsidies to domestic automakers. However, in mid-December 2008, President Bush authorized $17.4 billion in loans to GM and Chrysler, half of what the industry ultimately requested, but on terms far more favourable than commercially available at the time. The stimulus package offered automakers additional support with electric-drive vehicle and battery technology provisions that contained "Buy American" requirements.

In May 2009, the Treasury Department purchased a $7.5 billion stake in GMAC, LLC (formerly known as, General Motors Acceptance Corp.). In its May 21 press release, the Treasury Department indicated that $4 billion of the investment was

---

[109] United States of America: Support for General Motors and Chrysler, retrieved 8th June, 2010, from http://www.globaltradealert.org/measure/united-states-america-support-general-motors-and-chrysler.

intended to "support GMAC's ability to originate new loans to Chrysler dealers and consumers and help address GMAC's capital needs."[110] The Treasury Department also declared its intention to convert $884 million in convertible GM securities to GMAC common equity, giving it a 35.4% stake in GMAC common equity. In December 2009, the Treasury Department expanded its investment in GMAC, adding an additional $3.8 billion in total capital. Following the December transactions, the Treasury had $14.1 billion in capital invested in GMAC, holding 56% of its common equity.[111]

Following the 2009 bankruptcy filings by Chrysler (April) and GM (June), coupled with additional government financing in the context of both proceedings, the US House of Representatives passed a provision that would have limited new cars eligible for purchase incentives to those produced by the "big three" US auto firms. However, this provision was eliminated in the September 2009 reconciliation with the Senate.

In March 2009, the US and Canadian governments invested nearly $40 billion in General Motors in exchange for debt, preferred stock and 72% of GM's common equity. While no explicit border measures were enacted to favour GM or Chrysler, government control of GM and GMAC, and the absence of similar support for the operations of competing foreign auto and auto financing firms, almost certainly affected trade and investment patterns in the auto industry.

In 2009, China exported $5.2 billion of vehicles and vehicle parts to the United States, some 18.7% of China's total $27.9 billion exports in the categories and 4.0% of total US imports of vehicles and vehicle parts.[112]

Solar Panel Tariff Schedule Reclassification: January 2009

In January 2009, the U.S. Customs and Border Protection agency ruled that certain solar panels equipped with a particular diode fall under the U.S. Harmonized Tariff Schedule classification of "electric motors and generators" (HTS 8501.31), rather than "Diodes, transistors and similar semiconductor devices" (HTS 8541.40). Reclassification subjected the panels to a 2.5% tariff as opposed to zero under the former classification. This decision cuts against US calls within Doha Round talks for free trade in environmental goods and services.

---

[110] See Treasury Department Press Release TG-154, 21st May, 2009, retrieved 23rd July, 2010, from http://www.treas.gov/press/releases/tg154.htm.

[111] See Treasury Department Press Release TG-501, 30th December, 2009, retrieved 23rd July, 2010, from http://www.treas.gov/press/releases/tg501.htm.

[112] Data are from UN Comtrade (2010), http://comtrade.un.org/db. Vehicles are covered under HS (2007) code 87, "Vehicles other than railway or tramway rolling stock, and parts and accessories thereof." Note that US and PRC reports of US imports are slightly different. The United States reported $5,336 million in vehicle and vehicle parts imports from China in 2009, not $5,235.

In 2009, the United States imported $0.1 billion of electric motors and generators (HTS 8501.31) from China, 17.9% of the $0.8 billion total US electric motors and generators imports and 21.1% of the $0.7 billion PRC exports of electric motors and generators.[113]

American Recovery and Reinvestment Act and Buy American Provisions: February 2009

By far the leading piece of US protectionist legislation was the Buy American amendment inserted in the American Reinvestment and Recovery Act (ARRA).[114] Following the original $787 billion stimulus bill that was enacted in February 2009 (Public Law 111–5), several additional applications of the Buy American provision have been proposed and some have been enacted. The ARRA requires domestic procurement in two sections. First, with certain exceptions, all covered items[115] procured by the Department of Homeland Security with stimulus funds must be "grown, reprocessed, reused, or produced in the United States."[116] Next, and much bigger, the ARRA requires that "all of the iron, steel, and manufactured goods used in [an ARRA] project [must be] produced in the United States."[117] A minor exception is allowed when the cost of the overall project would be increased by more than 25% to meet the Buy American provision.[118] After strong objections were voiced both domestically and internationally, the Buy American amendment was further amended to stipulate that the provisions "shall be applied in a manner consistent with United States obligations under international agreements."[119] The term "international agreements" most notably includes the WTO Government Procurement Agreement (GPA) and bilateral free trade agreements (FTAs). A certain amount of compliance guidance has been issued by federal agencies (e.g., OMB, DHS, FHA), but rather little has been said about the key phrase, "in a manner consistent with international agreements."[120]

---

[113] Data are from UN Comtrade (2010), http://comtrade.un.org/db. PRC and US reports of electric motors and generators trade flows are in close agreement for 2009, within half a per cent.

[114] United States of America: Buy American provisions and set-asides in the Fiscal Year 2010 defense appropriations bill, retrieved 8th June, 2010, from http://www.globaltradealert.org/measure/united-states-america-buy-american-provisions-and-set-asides-fiscal-year-2010-defense-approp. Note that not all Buy American measures discussed have been implemented or are clearly trade distortive.

[115] Covered items include, e.g., clothing, tents, tarps and other utility goods, and fabrics.

[116] § 604 ARRA (2009). Note that certain DHS purchases may be exempted under the Government Procurement Agreement.

[117] § 1605 ARRA (2009).

[118] § 1605(b.3) ARRA (2009).

[119] § 604, 1605(d) ARRA (2009).

[120] See the Global Trade Alert pages: http://www.globaltradealert.org/measure/united-states-america-buy-american-provisions-stimulus-package, and http://www.globaltradealert.org/measure/united-states-america-expanded-buy-american-provisions-public-projects.

Since the ARRA was enacted, additional legislation has incorporated Buy American provisions in funding for: construction, renovation and maintenance projects; Amtrak assistance; electric car and battery manufacturing incentives; school construction; and defence appropriations.

The Hiring Incentives to Restore Employment (HIRE) Act (Public Law 111–147) was enacted in March 2010. The HIRE Act carries a House amendment, H.Res. 947, which includes a general Buy American provision under the "Jobs for Main Street Act." The provision cites Section 1605 of the ARRA (the Buy American provision). The Jobs for Main Street Act redirects $75 billion dollars under the TARP program. Of the redirected funds, $45 billion is allocated for construction and renovation projects: highway infrastructure ($27.5 billion), public transit and Amtrak ($9.2 billion), school renovation ($4.1 billion), drinking water provision ($2.1 billion), public housing ($1.0 billion), Corps of Engineers ($0.7 billion).[121] The Buy American provision subjects the allocated funds to the requirement that all "construction, alteration, maintenance, or repair" ensure that "all of the iron, steel, and manufactured goods used in the project are produced in the United States." The Jobs for Main Street Act imposes additional requirements on the procedure for waiving the Buy American obligations. In particular, senior officials responsible for highway and public transportation projects must analyze the impact on domestic employment before issuing a waiver and give advance public notice of the waiver.[122]

The ARRA's Buy American provision was expanded with the Appropriations Act of 2010 (Public Law 111–117), which forbids Amtrak from issuing "contracts [for] . . . services provided at or from any location outside the United States."[123] The penalty for violating this provision is a complete loss of the funding, which totals $563 million.[124]

The 21st Century Green High-Performing Public School Facilities Act (H.R. 2187) has passed the House and awaits Senate approval.[125] The bill would authorize $6.4 billion for school renovation, subject to the same Buy American provisions set forth in the ARRA.[126]

---

[121] See Jobs for Main Street Act of 2010 summary, retrieved 29th July, 2010, from http://www. speaker.gov/newsroom/legislation?id=0351.

[122] Buy American Provisions in Jobs Bill Could Complicate Canada Talks, Inside U.S. Trade 27 (2009) 50; see also Global Trade Alert page, retrieved 29th July, 2010, from http://www. globaltradealert.org/measure/united-states-america-expanded-buy-american-provisions-public-projects.

[123] See Global Trade Alert page, retrieved 29th July, 2010, from http://www.globaltradealert.org/ measure/united-states-america-buy-american-provisions-amtrak.

[124] § 149 Consolidated Appropriations Act of 2010.

[125] See Library of Congress Bill Summary & Status, retrieved 29th July, 2010, from http://thomas. loc.gov/cgi-bin/bdquery/z?d111:HR02187; see also, United States of America: Buy American provisions in school construction bill, retrieved 8th June, 2010, from http://www.globaltradealert. org/measure/united-states-america-buy-american-provisions-school-construction-bill.

[126] § 306 of the 21st Century Green High-Performing Public School Facilities Act.

The National Defence Authorization Act for Fiscal Year 2010 (Public Law 111–84) initially required components of military uniforms to be produced within the United States.[127] Exceptions could only be made by the Secretary of Defense. The explicit Buy American provisions were struck from the enacted legislation; however, the Act does expand the definition of small arms and gives the Secretary of Defense the authority to redefine the list of firms in the small arms production industrial base. Finally, the Act restricts the amount of work that can be done on certain construction projects in Guam by persons holding temporary H-2B work visas.[128]

The American Clean Energy and Security Act (H.R. 2454), better known as the Waxman-Markey climate and energy bill, barely passed the House in 2009 during the 111th Congress, and has no future in the 112th Congress which opened in January 2011 under Republican control. While the central disputes are far removed from Buy American provisions, the bill would enable the Secretary of Energy to "provide financial assistance to automobile manufacturers [in the United States] to facilitate the manufacture of plug-in electric drive vehicles" (§123). Financial assistance is also available for manufacturers investing capital toward "qualifying advanced technology vehicles . . . [or] components." This includes manufacturers of new technology batteries for such vehicles. No explicit appropriations are made for financial assistance; rather funding is at the discretion of the Secretary of Energy. The bill contains a competitive grant process similar to the Energy Independence and Security Act of 2007 (Public Law 110–140).[129]

Employ American Workers Act (EAWA): February 2009

The Employ American Workers Act (EAWA) restricted Troubled Asset Relief Program (TARP) fund recipients from hiring certain foreign workers. The EAWA, which became Section 1611 of the ARRA (Public Law 111–5), was scheduled to sunset two years from enactment (February 17, 2011). While EAWA was in force, TARP fund recipients were prohibited from hiring H-1B workers unless the firm first tried to recruit US workers. This procedure was originally reserved for firms employing a large number of H-1B workers; however, the EAWA applied the requirement to all TARP fund recipients.[130] The *New York Times* identified more than 650 firms that received $400 billion in TARP funds;

---

[127] § 2834(a)(6)(F) of the National Defense Authorization Act, 2010 : public law 111–84, official text.

[128] § 2834(a)(6)(F) of the National Defence Authorization Act of 2010.

[129] United States of America: Subsidies and Buy American provisions for electric cars and batteries, retrieved 8th June, 2010, from http://www.globaltradealert.org/measure/united-states-america-subsidies-and-buy-american-provisions-electric-cars-and-batteries.

[130] United States of America: Employ American Workers Act, retrieved 8th June, 2010, from http://www.globaltradealert.org/measure/united-states-america-employ-american-workers-act.

these firms clearly had to observe the EAWA restrictions.[131] The provision is mainly symbolic, and probably affects very few Chinese H-1B workers.

Dairy Export Incentive Program: May 2009

The Dairy Export Incentive Program (DEIP) was revived by Secretary of Agriculture Vilsack in May 2009.[132] The program itself is over twenty years old, but has not been utilized to the extent permitted under the Uruguay Round accord. Revival of the DEIP was triggered by higher European dairy subsidies implemented in January 2009. The new DEIP allocations provide export support for "68,201 metric tons of non-fat dry milk; 21,097 metric tons of butterfat; 3,030 metric tons of various cheeses and 34 metric tons of other dairy products, as well as individual product and country allocations."[133] The ultimate DEIP program allocations are determined by the USDA in a bidding process, the results of which are posted on its website. As of February 2010, the DEIP program had approved 99 submitted bids.[134] The program subsidies are not expected to exceed 1% of the US dairy market according to the Congressional Research Service. Despite being within the WTO subsidy limits and its negligible impact, the program attracted an international backlash given its dissonance from the commitment to restrain protectionist measures pledged at the London G-20 summit just two months prior.[135]

In 2009, the United States exported $95 million of dairy products to China, 4.9% of the $1,949 million total US exports of dairy products and 9.9% of the $1,046 million total PRC imports of dairy products.[136]

Legislation Targeting Currency Manipulation: 2010

Senator Charles Schumer (Democrat, New York) introduced a bill (S.3134) in March 2010 to counter currency manipulation by foreign governments. The bill

---

[131] Ericson/He/Schoenfeld, "Tracking the $700 Billion Bailout", New York Times, retrieved 11th February, 2010, from http://projects.nytimes.com/creditcrisis/recipients/table.

[132] United States of America: Dairy Export Incentive Program, retrieved 8th June, 2010, from http://www.globaltradealert.org/measure/united-states-america-dairy-export-incentive-program.

[133] USDA 2008–2009 DEIP Allocations Announcement, retrieved 26th July, 2010, from http://www.fas.usda.gov/scriptsw/PressRelease/pressrel_dout.asp?Entry=valid&PrNum=0081-09.

[134] US Department of Agriculture DEIP website, retrieved 23rd July, 2010, from http://www.fas.usda.gov/excredits/deip/deip-new.asp.

[135] U.S. Revival of Dairy Subsidies Sparks Global Outrage, but Effect Minimal, Inside U.S. Trade 27 (2009) 21.

[136] Data are from UN Comtrade (2010), http://comtrade.un.org/db. Dairy products are as covered under HS (2007) code 04, "Dairy Produce." US and PRC reports of US dairy products exports to China in 2009 are close. China reported $103 million of dairy products imports from the United States, not $95 million.

would authorize the deployment of several counter measures. Notably, it would require that the Department of Commerce consider currency undervaluation in its anti-dumping investigations and it would disqualify suppliers from currency manipulating countries from US government procurement. The measures authorized by the bill would be contingent on the bi-annual "International Economic and Exchange Rate Policies" (IEERP) Report of the Treasury Department, which identifies countries it determines are manipulating their currency regimes in such a fashion as to prevent balance of payments adjustments. No edition of the IEERP report has yet identified China as a country that engages in exchange rate manipulation; however, recent issues of the report have expressed concern over undervaluation. In June 2010, China announced that it would allow some degree of exchange rate flexibility, and indeed the RMB was allowed to appreciation by about 5% against the dollar over the following nine months (from 6.83 to 6.53 RMB to the dollar). But this extent of RMB appreciation is not viewed as adequate by most members of Congress.

In addition to authorizing counter measures following the finding of currency manipulation by the Treasury Department, the bill would limit Treasury Department discretion in identifying a "manipulated" currency and limit executive discretion in responding to an affirmative finding of manipulation. The Treasury Secretary would be further constrained by a requirement to oppose any governance changes in the international financial institutions (the IMF, World Bank, and others) that would increase the voting share of identified currency manipulators. This is particularly relevant given recently proposed changes in IMF voting shares.[137]

Despite China's decision to allow a degree of exchange rate flexibility, the core concepts of the Schumer bill remain popular in the Senate and have gained overwhelming support in the House. In March 2010, 130 representatives signed a letter to the Secretary of the Department of Commerce, Gary Locke, calling for countervailing duties in response to PRC currency manipulation.[138]

At the end of September 2010, the House passed the Currency Reform for Fair Trade Act (CRFTA; HR 2378) by a bipartisan margin of 348–79. CRFTA permits, but does not require, the Commerce Department to identify unfair subsidies resulting from currency manipulation. CRFTA differs from the Schumer bill (S.3134), which offers a range of sanctions, in that CRFTA only specifies countervailing duties as a possible retaliatory measure. Under the bill, a currency will be considered "fundamentally undervalued" if the currency and the country

---

[137] Bill Summary & Status: 111th Congress (2009–2010), S.3134, retrieved 14th July, 2010, from http://thomas.loc.gov/cgi-bin/bdquery/z?d111:SN03134:@@@D&summ2=m&.

[138] Sino-US relations have been strained in the past over the RMB. One year after failed diplomatic attempts by the Bush administration in 2004–2005, Treasury Secretary John Snow criticized the lack of progress China had made with respect to RMB exchange rate flexibility. Several bills were tabled in congress to address the issue, but none passed. See Report to Congress on International Economic and Exchange Rate Policies. (2006): US Department of the Treasury, retrieved 29th July, 2010, from http://www.ustreas.gov/offices/international-affairs/economic-exchange-rates/pdf/international_econ_exchange_rate.pdf.

meet four criteria during an 18-month period: substantial government intervention in the exchange market; undervaluation by an average of 5% for 18 months; large and persistent current account surpluses; foreign asset reserves beyond certain thresholds.[139] The same bill, or one very similar, would probably sail through the House in the 112th Congress (January 2011 – January 2013) – provided the reluctant Republican leadership allows a floor vote. If that happens it will be up to the Senate whether to endorse the legislation and send a bill to President Obama.

Any currency bill imposing trade sanctions would face a difficult test within the WTO if China brought a case. While CRFTA is limited to authorizing CVDs, it is not clear how the WTO Appellate Body would rule on their legality. The precise language of the Agreement on Subsidies and Countervailing Measures (ASCM) would be parsed to argue for and against the concept of a CVD to offset an alleged currency subsidy.[140] However, other provisions of the GATT cede pre-eminence to the International Monetary Fund (IMF) in the realm of exchange rate relations. For example, GATT Article XV(9)(a) allows members the explicit right to utilize "exchange controls or exchange restrictions in accordance with the Articles of Agreement of the [IMF]." Clearly the IMF has primary responsibility for establishing currency norms, which explains why past efforts by Congress have sought to pressure the IMF (using the Treasury Department as the messenger) to voice strong disapproval of the Chinese RMB regime. The CRFTA bill, however, makes no mention of Treasury Department communication with the IMF on currency issues. This twist reflects Congressional frustration with the Treasury Department's caution and the tepid force of IMF action.

PRC Legislative Measures

Export Tax Rebates: April 2009

In April 2009, the PRC Ministry of Finance announced an increased rebate on value-added tax (VAT) for exporters of various products.[141] China notified the WTO Trade Policy Review Body (TPRB) in March of its intention to increase the VAT rebates.

---

[139] The thresholds include any of the following three: the amount necessary to repay all debt obligations of the government due within 12 months; 20% of the country's M2 money supply; or the value of the country's imports during the previous four months.

[140] See Hufbauer/Wong/Sheth, *US-China trade disputes: rising tide, rising stakes*, 2006, and Staiger/Sykes, Currency Manipulation and World Trade, World Trade Review 9 (2010), p. 583, for expositions of the potential legal debate over the application of the ASCM to an alleged currency subsidy.

[141] China identified the following products in its communication with the WTO Trade Policy Review Body in March 2009: "textiles and clothing; ceramic; plastic; furniture; pharmaceutical, household appliances; books; rubber; moulds, dies; glassware; suitcases; bags; footwear; watches; chemicals; machinery; and electrical products." See China: Export tax rebates, retrieved 29th July, 2010, from http://www.globaltradealert.org/measure/china-export-tax-rebates.

It simultaneously notified the TPRB that it had or would soon reduce or eliminate export duties on over 100 products and increase export duties on five products.[142]

Due to the broad and general nature of the products identified by the PRC government in its communication to the WTO Trade Policy Review Body, the estimated coverage of the program is extensive.[143] Under the proposed export tax rebate program, 72.4% of US imported products, or $224 billion worth, would have been eligible for larger tax rebates in 2009.

Ban on Foreign Investment in Express Postal Services: April 2009

China Post issued a law in April 2009 banning foreign investment in business express postal services, effective October 2009.[144] The law bans foreign firms from providing domestic delivery of express letters by foreign firms, but allows foreign delivery. The law bans foreign firms from providing international delivery of packages, but allows domestic delivery. The law also introduced a new licensing system for express delivery services.

Service trade data are not sufficiently disaggregated to identify trade in postal services; however, China State Post Bureau data indicate that express postal services revenue was $1.46 billion in the first quarter of 2009 alone, nearly 40% of total Post Bureau revenue in that period.[145] As a conservative guess, perhaps one-third of the annualized Post Bureau express revenue represents the services of US express post firms adversely impacted, around $2 billion annually.

Adjustment of Import Tariffs Policy on Key Technical Equipment: September 2009

Several PRC ministries jointly issued a policy revision exempting imports by domestic enterprises of key components of "major technical equipment" and

---

[142] Report to the TPRB from the Director-General on the Financial and Economic Crisis and Trade-Related Developments, (JOB(09)/62), 2009, retrieved 29th July, 2010, from http://www.wto.org/english/news_e/news09_e/trdev_dg_report_14apr09_e.doc.

[143] China identified the following products in its communication with the WTO TPRB: "textiles and clothing; ceramic; plastic; furniture; pharmaceutical, household appliances; books; rubber; moulds, dies; glassware; suitcases; bags; footwear; watches; chemicals; machinery; and electrical products." See WTO document JOB(09)/62, p. 29.

[144] China: Ban on foreign investment in express postal services, retrieved 29th July, 2010, from http://www.globaltradealert.org/measure/china-ban-foreign-investment-express-postal-services.

[145] Li, "2nd UPDATE: China Bans Foreign Invest In Local Express Mail Op", Dow Jones Newswires, 24th April, 2009.
   Revenue amount of CNY10 billion converted to USD as of the 31st March, 2009 rate of 6.8329 Yuan per USD reported by the Federal Reserve Statistical Release H.10, Historical Rates for China, retrieved 26th July, 2010, from http://www.federalreserve.gov/releases/h10/Hist/dat00_ch.htm.

select other products from import duties and import-related value-added taxes.[146] The policy revision simultaneously abolished a duty exemption on imports of whole machines. Enterprises must apply for accreditation annually in order to receive the VAT exemption on their imports. Duty exemptions are subject to quotas for the eligible enterprises.[147]

National Indigenous Innovation Products Accreditation Program: November 2009

In November 2009, China's Ministry of Science and Technology, National Development and Reform Commission, and Ministry of Finance jointly issued Directive 618, known as the National Indigenous Innovation Products Accreditation Program (NIIPA). NIIPA establishes a subscribed directory of products whose manufacturers are screened based on several criteria: general legality and approved product licensing (when applicable); possession of undisputed intellectual property rights[148]; advanced technology, especially those improving resource efficiency; reliable quality; existing sales or "potential economic benefits and bright market prospects."[149] NIIPA is part of China's Medium and Long-Term National Plan for Science and Technology Development, which aims to promote indigenous innovation by facilitating government purchase of indigenous innovation products.[150] China's Evaluation Measures on Indigenous Innovation Products, issued in 2007, offers explicit preferential treatment in government procurement, allowing for preference at a margin of 5–10% if price is the sole determinant, a preference of 4–8% for technical and price metrics in

---

[146] China: Adjustment of import tariffs policy on key technical equipments, retrieved 29th July, 2010, from http://www.globaltradealert.org/measure/china-adjustment-import-tariffs-policy-key-technical-equipments.

[147] Six Government Authorities Jointly Adjust Import Duties on Major Technical Equipment, 2009, retrieved 26th July, 2010, from http://www.chinatax.gov.cn/n6669073/n6669118/9291788.html. We are unable to give an estimate of the approximate dollar value of imports affected.

[148] The applicant may also license the IP. The NIIPA program conditions for IP require that "the applying unit owns the intellectual property (IP) rights in China or licensed IP usage rights in China of products it has researched and developed, by means of either technological innovation or transfer, and the IP does not have any disputes or controversies with other products' IP".

[149] PRC Notice Regarding the Launch of the National Indigenous Innovation Product Accreditation Work for 2010, Draft for Public Comment (Unofficial translation by the US-China Business Council), retrieved 26th July, 2010, from http://www.uschina.org/public/documents/2010/04/ii_asccreditation_translation.pdf.

[150] The Plan specifically targets certain innovation sectors, including the following identified by Global Trade Alert: "Computers and application equipment; Communications products; Modern Office Equipment; Software; New Energy and new energy devices; and High-efficiency and energy-saving products", retrieved 26th July, 2010, from http://www.globaltradealert.org/measure/china-accreditation-suppliers-certain-high-tech-products.

comprehensive evaluations, and support for initial purchases of new-to-market domestic innovation products.[151]

The accreditation program follows the announcement of explicit preference for local content in procurement decisions by the PRC National Development and Reform Commission (NDRC) in May 2009. The NDRC announced the preferential procurement policy jointly with several other government ministries including Industry and Information Technology, Commerce, and Housing and Urban-Rural Development. Exceptions to local procurement must be approved by the appropriate ministry.

While it is unclear to what extent foreign suppliers will be disadvantaged by the new procurement policy, the market for sales to the PRC government is quite large and much is at stake. One estimate puts PRC government procurement at $70-130 billion per year.[152] Based on this figure, a conservative impact on the potential US exporters might be $10 billion per year.

Temporary Increase of Fuel and Jet Oil Import Tariffs: February 2010

In February 2010, China notified the WTO that it was increasing its tariffs on fuel oil and jet fuel to 3% and 6%, respectively.[153] Both tariffs had previously been set at 1%. Neither tariff exceeds its bound rate.

In 2009, the United States exported $156 million of petroleum oils to China, 0.4% of total US exports of petroleum oil.[154]

Protective Themes and Future Disputes

Protective Themes

US and PRC complaints within the WTO differ in several respects. While US complaints have focused entirely on "behind the border" measures, PRC complaints have been entirely lodged against US border measures. The broad scope of PRC

---

[151] Issue Brief: New Developments in China's Domestic Innovation and Procurement Policies, January 2010, retrieved 26th July, 2010, from http://www.uschina.org/public/documents/2010/domestic_innovation_policies.pdf.

[152] Grams/Epstein, China Advisory: What Next in China's Indigenous Innovation Program?, 2010, retrieved 29th July, 2010, from http://www.troutmansanders.com/chinaadvisory07122010.

[153] China: Temporary increase of import tariffs on fuel, retrieved 29th July, 2010, from http://www.globaltradealert.org/measure/china-temporary-increase-import-tariffs-fuel.

[154] Data are from UN Comtrade (2010), http://comtrade.un.org/db. Petroleum oil is covered under HS (2007) code 2710, "Petroleum oils and oils obtained from bituminous minerals, other than crude; preparations not elsewhere specified or included".

measures targeted by US complaints has attracted support from many other WTO members. Nine of the eleven US consultations with China engendered requests from other members to join the consultations. Five of the six US measures targeted by PRC complaints have been China-specific, and PRC consultations with the US have been joined by other members only in the US steel safeguards case.

PRC measures challenged by the United States are best characterized as offensively protectionist in that they reflect legislation designed to selectively support the development of domestic industries using behind the border measures (see Table 14 above). Nearly all the cases brought against China through the DSB have questioned legislation, particularly with respect to high value-add industries in which the United States, and other advanced WTO members, have specialised and China has yet to fully develop (e.g., financial services, integrated circuit design).

US measures challenged by China are best characterized as defensively protectionist. They are generally motivated more by a desire to guard mature domestic industries (e.g., steel, tyres) from further erosion than to support the growth of nascent industries. This is evident in the heavy reliance of the United States on border protection. Well over half of the 111 consultations sought with the United States by China and other WTO members through the DSB have questioned classic border measures – anti-dumping and countervailing duties, and safeguards.

These patterns are broadly consistent with the nature of each country's economy, but in common, each country is protecting its domestic industries from foreign competition: China is sheltering space for high value-add industries, while the United States is guarding the sunset sectors of its economy.

Future Disputes

Since PRC protective measures implement a broader economic development strategy, fresh examples are likely to spark future disputes. While PRC growth has been remarkable, the share of high value-add industry in the economy remains low, and this ensures considerable scope for intensive development efforts. The NIIPA program in particular illustrates future prospects. The same can be said of inadequate PRC efforts (from a US perspective) to enforce intellectual property rights.

Similarly, as the US economy continues to grow and mature, additional industries will lose their competitive edge, and seek shelter from imports. PRC exporters will thus continue to face numerous anti-dumping investigations in the US market (see Table 9 above). From time to time, these will be accompanied by market disruption, countervailing duty and safeguard actions, and occasional administrative law measures, such as the solar panel reclassification decision. Even the Buy American legislation can be interpreted as a defence of mature sectors of the US economy.

The pending currency bill, if enacted in the 112th Congress, could place considerable strain on the Sino-US relationship. Perhaps the bill passed by the

House, in September 2010, will serve as the warning shot that prompts Beijing to allow the RMB to appreciate quite significantly – by 20% or more. However, if China stands fast at an exchange rate near RMB 6.53 to the dollar (April 2011 rate), and if several US industries then seek CVD protection under the new law, the stage will be set for a trade war with significant political and legal ramifications. The PRC would very likely challenge the CVDs within the WTO. Beyond that, the PRC might well engage in retaliatory self help that could span across both finance and trade. The dispute could easily become the centrepiece of US-Sino relations for a protracted period.

Conclusion

The Sino-US economic relationship has grown in intensity over the past two decades and has now become highly contentious. It is not surprising that the sheer magnitude of the increased flow of goods and services between the economies has generated political friction. The way leaders and their officials in China and the United States manage that friction has been the story in this chapter. Trade frictions are unlikely to subside in the near future, particularly as the United States tries to double exports as part of its growth strategy after the Great Recession. Unless China allows the RMB to appreciate, by a substantial amount, against the dollar and other currencies, the exchange rate will be a flash point in the bilateral relationship. Equally troublesome to many US-based multinational corporations is the Chinese emphasis on indigenous innovation and the panoply of preferences and subsidies to purely domestic firms.

Global economic imbalances require huge adjustments in the trajectories of the PRC and US economies. The world economic community is looking to the United States and China for specific structural changes that will narrow both the US current account deficit and the Chinese current account surplus. In the United States, this means reducing consumption and increasing savings. The converse is true for China. Small and tentative steps have been taken in each country. President Obama set the goal of doubling US exports by 2015, and China announced it will allow its currency to appreciate. Much needs to be done to implement these aspirations.

Moreover, with its huge stake as a global exporter, China needs to take proactive measures to foster the multilateral trading system. After joining the WTO in 2001, China has strongly resisted taking additional policy measures that would relax its border barriers and open its domestic markets to foreign imports. China has also taken a more nationalistic attitude towards inward foreign direct investment by multinational corporations.

If cooperative approaches are not sufficiently bold, the United States may reach for protectionist measures to narrow its trade deficit. The PRC could respond by building a trade bloc, with exclusionary walls, in Asia and by taking measures to undermine the role of the dollar as the world's reserve currency. A path of destructive responses would not only damage the Sino-US relationship, but would also disrupt commerce on a global scale.

In our view, the run of cases illustrated in our account by WTO disputes and national administrative law decisions (anti-dumping, market disruption, and similar trade remedies) are a normal part of rapidly growing commerce between the United States and China. Frictions must be expected. Adding the potential trade coverage of all the cases enumerated in Tables 6, 9, 11, 14 and 15, the figure is only $45.7 billion, around 12% of two-way trade in 2009.[155]

Trade disputes of this sort can be managed if each country respects adverse decisions handed down by the WTO, whether the decisions entail zeroing, intellectual property rights, or other targeted measures.

More troublesome are broad-gauged measures that threaten to isolate whole swaths of the economy from foreign competition. Leading examples are China's National Indigenous Innovation Products Accreditation Program (NIIPA), Buy American, and the currency legislation now debated in Congress. In our view, the challenge facing US and PRC political leaders is two-fold: first, to implement the broad macroeconomic policies necessary to reduce their current account imbalances; second, to channel broad-gauged measures into targeted policies that can be reversed if they are judged to violate WTO norms.

---

[155] Table 6. WTO Disputes between China and the United States; Table 9. Summary of US Anti-Dumping Duty Trade Coverage; Table 11. Summary of US Countervailing Duty Trade Coverage; Table 14. PRC Anti-Dumping Duty Coverage of US Imports; and Table 15. Protectionist Measures that Affect Sino-US Trade. Note that trade in 2009 was significantly dampened by the Great Recession. Total two-way trade in 2009 was $379.1 billion. The $45.7 billion coverage figure gives a coarse approximation as the amounts summed come from the years of dispute, not 2009. The $45.7 billion figure excludes the $224 billion of PRC exports covered under the China's 2009 export tax rebate plan.

China's Evolving Role in WTO Dispute Settlement: Acceptance, Consolidation and Activation

Bryan Mercurio and Mitali Tyagi

Introduction

The establishment of the World Trade Organization (WTO) in 1995 marked a watershed in the history of international trade relations. Most notably, the WTO expanded sectoral coverage to include services and intellectual property (IP), allowed for an increased role for developing countries and created of a binding and enforceable dispute settlement system.[1] Since that time, however, the WTO has been the subject of numerous public criticisms and delivered few tangible and substantial achievements. Perhaps the greatest WTO-era achievement is the completion of China's accession into the WTO.[2] While China had already become a major trading nation prior to its accession to the WTO, its membership in the multilateral trading regime is significant for a host of reasons. Foremost, not only is China now an active participant in the system but it is also disciplined by the system. China undertook wholesale legal changes in order to reach the point of

---

[1] See Lester/Mercurio, *World Trade Law: Text, Materials and Commentary*, 2008, Chapters 3 and 6.

[2] See Pascal Lamy's speech 'China's WTO membership is "win-win" of 22nd July, 2010, to inaugurate WTO Day at the Shanghai 2010 World Expo on 22 July 2010, available at: http://www.wto.org/english/news_e/sppl_e/sppl162_e.htm ('China's historic accession to the WTO in November 2001 is among the most important events in the history of the WTO and the multilateral trading system'). See generally, Martin/Ianchovichina, Implications of China's Accession to the World Trade Organisation for China and the WTO, The World Economy 24 (2001) 9, p. 1205.

B. Mercurio (✉)
The Chinese University of Hong Kong, 5/F, Teaching Complex at Western Campus, Shatin, NT, Hong Kong, China
e-mail: Bryan.mercurio@cuhk.edu.hk

M. Tyagi
Attorney-General's Department, Central Office, 3-5 National Circuit, Barton ACT 2600, Australia
e-mail: mitali.tyagi@gmail.com

C. Herrmann and J.P. Terhechte (eds.), *European Yearbook of International Economic Law (EYIEL), Vol. 3 (2012)*, European Yearbook of International Economic Law 3, DOI 10.1007/978-3-642-23309-8_3, © Springer-Verlag Berlin Heidelberg 2012

accession and has continued to do so in the decade since accession.[3] In short, China's accession to the WTO has increased the 'security' and 'predictability' of trade with China while at the same time levelling the playing field for Chinese exporters.[4] Without accession to the WTO, China's total percentage of world trade would not have more than doubled since 2001 and in 2009 it would not have become the world's largest exporter.[5]

China's accession to the WTO also brought many uncertainties, such as whether China would be a positive or obstructionist presence, whether China would meaningfully engage with the Doha Round, and whether China would utilize the dispute settlement system and comply with DSB reports and recommendations.[6] Only some of these (and many other) uncertainties have been fully answered in the first 10 years of Chinese membership in the WTO. In some cases, perceptions of China's expected course of behaviour have in many instances proved wrong. In other instances, China has behaved as expected. Chinese behaviour in the WTO and its positioning and negotiating strategies relating to the Doha Round has been much discussed in the literature. To date, however, there has been little reflective scholarly analysis of the changing pattern of China's participation in the WTO, and more specifically in the dispute settlement process. While scholars have analysed at length each particular dispute involving China as a party, there is a dearth of scholarly literature examining or attempting to understand the why and how China's participation and contribution has so radically shifted throughout the last decade. This article seeks to fill the gap by not only demonstrating that there has in fact been a shift in China's engagement with the dispute settlement process (and more broadly the WTO) during its 10 years of membership but also by assessing and analysing why the shift has taken place.

More specifically, Part II of this article will evaluate China's participation in the WTO dispute settlement process since its admission into the organization in 2001 to present. The aim of the article is to demonstrate China's changing attitude towards

---

[3] See Lardy, *Integrating China into the Global Economy*, 2002.

[4] See, e.g., Lardy, Issues in China's WTO Accession: The U.S.-China Security Review Commission, 2001, available at: http://www.brookings.edu/views/testimony/lardy/20010509.htm; Ji/ Huang, China's Path to the Center Stage of WTO Dispute Settlement: Challenges and Responses, Global Trade and Customs Journal 5 (2010) 9, pp. 365, 369 ("[T]he dispute settlement system was regarded as a great benefit from China's WTO accession since this device operated well with strong legal characteristics and China could use it to safeguard its own interests under a rule-based system.").

[5] For statistics and analysis, see Rumbaugh/Blanche, China: International Trade and WTO Accession, 2004 IMF Working Paper WP/04/36; WTO, Trade Profiles, available at: http://stat.wto.org/Home/WSDBHome.aspx?Language=; United Nations Statistics Division, Trade Statistics Branch, available at: http://unstats.un.org/unsd/trade/default.htm; WTO, International Trade and Tariff Data, available at: http://www.wto.org/english/res_e/statis_e/statis_e.htm. For information on China's membership in the WTO, see http://www.wto.org/english/thewto_e/countries_e/china_e.htm.

[6] For a useful review, see Gao, Elephant in the Room: Challenges of Integrating China into the WTO System, Asian Journal of WTO and International Health Law and Policy 6 (2011), p. 137.

its role in the multilateral trading system by focussing on China's engagement with the WTO dispute settlement process as both a complainant and respondent. Through analysing China's participation in the dispute settlement system one can see that three distinct phases emerge, namely an Acceptance, Consolidation and Activation. The first phase is one of 'Acceptance', whereby China dutifully accepted the rules of the multilateral trading regime and quickly resolved any potential disputes with other Members. The second phase of membership is one of "Consolidation", whereby China became more secure of its place in the organisation and began defending certain select measures (i.e. laws and regulations). Simply stated, China consolidated its position in the organisation. Finally, in the "Activation" phase, China began defending all of its measures and even actively seeking to challenge the measures of other large and powerful Members of the WTO (most notably, of course, are the United States (US) and European Union (EU)).[7] Taken further, China has begun appearing in a leadership role in the organisation and, as such, now desires not only to accept existing rules but to be at the forefront of amending existing rules and making new rules.[8]

Through three distinct phases, the article describes how China has transitioned from a timid new Member lacking the confidence and understanding to fully utilise the dispute settlement system to become on the most prolific users of the system – in short, China now fully embraces the 'aggressive legalism' model of using the multilateral dispute settlement process as a 'shield' and a 'sword' to defend and promote its trade interests.[9] In this regard, China's path

---

[7] This is not to suggest that problems involving the 'conflict of ideological attitudes toward the WTO dispute settlement mechanism' or the 'significant capacity constraints' have been completely rectified, but only that China is now becoming a more confident and assertive Member of the WTO. See Ji/Huang, China's Path to the Center Stage of WTO Dispute Settlement: Challenges and Responses, Global Trade and Customs Journal 5 (2010) 9, p. 368.

[8] Marcia Don Harpaz makes the broader point that China's participation in the WTO demonstrates a new willingness to accept western legal norms and binding adjudication: "WTO dispute settlement system is part of a social environment that serves as a site and means for socialization, in this case, bringing about a change in China's attitude toward international third party adjudication. China's profile of avoiding third party adjudication is being transformed into a willingness to participate in it, a process which entails continuous social interaction. Through interaction, China is not only becoming accustomed to new norms and rules but it is increasingly conforming to them in a more automatic manner", Harpaz, Sense and Sensibilities of China and WTO Dispute Settlement, International Law Forum of the Hebrew University of Jerusalem Law Faculty, Research Paper No. 02-10, available at: http://papers.ssrn.com/sol3/papers.cfm?abstract_id=1599563.

[9] The term "aggressive legalism" was first used by Saadia M. Pekkanen in a 2001 article analysing Japan's trade strategy and use of the multilateral dispute settlement mechanism. See Pekkanen, Aggressive Legalism: The Rules of the WTO and Japan's Emerging Trade Strategy, The World Economy 24 (2001), p. 707. Pekkanen originally defined "aggressive legalism" as "a conscious strategy where a substantive set of international legal rules can be made to serve as both "shield" and "sword" in trade disputes among sovereign states", ibid, p. 708. Pekkanen later clarified the meaning of "aggressive legalism" to mean: "the use or invocation of legal rules in consultations, negotiations, agreements, and administrative and dispute settlement procedures to counter what

towards aggressive legalism is similar to the experience of both Japan and Korea.[10]

Section "Concluding Analysis: Aggressive Legalism or Plain Aggressive?" concludes that this newfound path will be beneficial not only to China but also to the world trading system as a whole. China's experience in the WTO and through its use of the dispute settlement mechanism demonstrates that it not only accepts international rules but also is willing to abide by the rules and accept international arbitral decisions enforcing the rules.

China's Role in WTO Dispute Settlement Process: Ten Years, Three Phases

Acceptance

From accession in 2001 until the beginning of 2006 China was in the first stage, the "Acceptance" phase, of its WTO membership. Having undertaken extensive review and amendments to its laws and regulations in order to facilitate its accession to the WTO the Chinese were simply not in any position to challenge existing institutional norms, influence debate within the WTO and in the course of the Doha Round or meaningfully participate in the dispute settlement process.[11] Put simply, China lacked the understanding, experience and confidence to significantly engage with or in the WTO operating framework. Realising this, China's approach was very pragmatic as it made use of the Acceptance phase by learning through watching; in the context of dispute settlement, this meant at least from mid-2003 by participating

---

trade-related actors deem to be the unreasonable an economically harmful acts, requests, and practices of their major trade partners", Pekkanen, *Japan's Aggressive Legalism – Law and Foreign Trade Politics Beyond the WTO*, 2008, p. 5.

[10] For analysis of Japan's evolving role with multilateral dispute settlement, see ibid.; Araki, Beyond Aggressive Legalism: Japan and the GATT/WTO Dispute, in: Matsushita/Ahn (eds.), *WTO and East Asia: New Perspectives*, 2004, pp. 149–175 (disputing Pekkanen's evidential substantiation for the theory but not the theory per se). For analysis of Korea's evolving role with dispute settlement, see Ahn, Korea on the GATT/WTO Dispute Settlement System: Legal Battles for Economic Development, *Journal of International Economic Law* 6 (2003), pp. 598 et seq. (598–626). For a useful review, see Gao, Aggressive Legalism: The East Asian Experience and Lessons for China, in: Gao/Lewis (eds.), *China's Participation in the WTO*, 2005, pp. 315–322.

[11] Ji and Huang state: "In the authors view, what China thought to do and was asked to do were limited mostly to how to follow and comply with the WTO rules rather than how to change the WTO rules...", Ji/Huang, China's Path to the Center Stage of WTO Dispute Settlement: Challenges and Responses, Global Trade and Customs Journal 5 (2010) 9, p. 368. China has always, however, been active in making written proposals in WTO committees and working groups (although such activity increased markedly in 2003), including the Trade Negotiations Committee, the DSU Review and in the course of the Doha Round. Publicly available submissions are available at: www.wto.org.

as a third party in almost every case[12] and by attempting to participate in the ongoing Review of the WTO Dispute Settlement Understanding ('DSU Review').[13] Coupled with this pragmatism and lack of understanding and confidence was the fact that China was accumulating massive trade surpluses with major industrialised countries, most notably the US, and it simply did not want to provoke these nations into taking action to balance their accounts.[14]

With this background in mind, it is not surprising that in the Acceptance phase China chose to avoid active participation in the panel phase of the dispute settlement process.[15] During the Acceptance phase, China was subject to three separate claims and potential disputes.[16] In every instance, China hurriedly reached a mutually agreeable solution with the complainant. In every case, the agreed solution was essentially that China would amend its measure as desired by the complainant. There is, however, one exception to this general statement on China actively avoiding the formal dispute settlement procedures of the WTO – in 2002, China joined seven other Members in challenging US safeguards on steel imposed in the lead up to the US elections. Commentators are united in viewing China's participation not as a sign of its movement towards a policy of 'aggressive

---

[12] From accession to July 2003, China reserved third party rights in only three of 26 disputes; from August 2003 – January 2007, however, China reserved third party rights in every dispute. Since February 2007, China has only selectively reserved third party rights. This change is likely at least partly due to the increased number of disputes initiated against China and correspondingly the substantial amount of resources needed to handle these cases, see Ji/Huang, China's Path to the Center Stage of WTO Dispute Settlement: Challenges and Responses, Global Trade and Customs Journal 5 (2010) 9, p. 367.

[13] See Ji/Huang, China's Experience in Dealing with WTO Dispute Settlement: A Chinese Perspective, *Journal of World Trade* 45 (2011) 1, pp. 28–29. For a brief but useful description of China's institutional capacity building in the area of WTO law, see Ji/Huang, China's Path to the Center Stage of WTO Dispute Settlement: Challenges and Responses, Global Trade and Customs Journal 5 (2010) 9, pp. 370–374.

[14] For analysis of China's trade surplus, see International Monetary Fund, People's Republic of China: 2005 Article IV Consultation, available at: http://www.imf.org/external/pubs/ft/scr/2005/cr05411.pdf; Organization for Economic Cooperation and Development, OECD Economic Surveys: China, Volume 2005/13, available at: www.oecd.org/.../0,3343, en_2649_34111_35331797_1_1_1_1,00.html; Lum/Nanto, China's Trade with the United States and the World, CRS Report for Congress, 2007, available at: http://www.fas.org/sgp/crs/row/RL31403.pdf.

[15] See generally Harpaz, Sense and Sensibilities of China and WTO Dispute Settlement, International Law Forum of the Hebrew University of Jerusalem Law Faculty, Research Paper No. 02-10, pp. 24–28. China's behaviour was in contrast to that predicted by some scholars, who believed China would quickly adopt a strategy of "aggressive legalism". See, e.g., Pekkanen, Aggressive Legalism: The Rules of the WTO and Japan's Emerging Trade Strategy, The World Economy 24 (2001), p. 735; Araki, Beyond Aggressive Legalism: Japan and the GATT/WTO Dispute, in: Matsushita/Ahn (eds.), *WTO and East Asia: New Perspectives*, 2004, p. 171.

[16] It should be noted that in this "honeymoon" phase of China's WTO membership potential complainants such as the US and EU showed significant restraint in bringing cases against China so as not to overburdening the new, inexperienced member as well as to avoid upsetting the rising trading giant.

legalism' but more so 'the result of a combination of ... unique features of [the] case',[17] including the fact that a number of active users of the dispute settlement system had initiated the case and would undoubtedly take primary responsibility for the case, the fact that the case against the US was very strong (and that every safeguard measure challenged at the WTO had been successful), the negative publicity the case generated against the US position and the threat of unilateral retaliatory measures.[18]

China's general policy of avoiding formal dispute settlement at the WTO can best be illustrated by its reaction and corresponding action to the three complaints it faced in the Acceptance phase. For instance, in 2004 China became a respondent in a WTO dispute for the first time when the US challenged its value-added tax (VAT) rebate on integrated circuits (ICs) produced or designed in China.[19] As various Chinese ministries issued regulations provided the VAT rebate for domestically produced or designed ICs,[20] it seemed clear the US complaint (*China – Value-Added Tax on Integrated Circuits*), alleging violations of Article I and III of the General Agreement on Tariffs and Trade (GATT) and Article XVII of the General Agreement on Trade in Services (GATS) would be successful.[21] According to media reports and academic accounts, China was genuinely 'confused' and 'embarrassed' by the US Request for Consultation, as the two countries had already been negotiating over the issue.[22] Less than 4 months after the Request for Consultation, China agreed to amend its measures and immediately end the VAT refund scheme.[23]

---

[17] Gao, Aggressive Legalism: The East Asian Experience and Lessons for China, in: Gao/Lewis (eds.), *China's Participation in the WTO*, 2005.

[18] See, e.g., Gao, Aggressive Legalism: The East Asian Experience and Lessons for China, in: Gao/Lewis (eds.), *China's Participation in the WTO*, 2005, pp. 324–329. On the last point, see Regulation (EC) No. 1031/2002, OJ [2002] L 157/8. Gao makes the point that while the EC moved to suspend concessions against the US in retaliation for the safeguards China made no such move despite its longstanding propensity for unilateral retaliatory measures. Gao, Taming the Dragon: China's Experience in the WTO Dispute Settlement System, Legal Issues of Economic Integration 34 (2007) 4, pp. 369 et seq. (373–374). For analysis of China's trade barrier investigation measures, see Gao, Taking Justice into Your Own Hand: The TBI Mechanism in China, Journal of World Trade 44 (2010) 3, pp. 633–659.

[19] Request for Consultations by the United States, China – Value-Added Tax on Integrated Circuits, WT/DS309/1.

[20] The most significant document in this regard is Document 18 of 24th June, 2000, Notice of the State Council Regarding Issuance of Certain Policies Concerning the Development of the Software Industry and Integrated Circuit Industry, and specifically Art. 41 and 48.

[21] The US also claimed the measures violated China's Protocol of Accession (WT/L/432).

[22] Gao, Taming the Dragon: China's Experience in the WTO Dispute Settlement System, Legal Issues of Economic Integration 34 (2007) 4, p. 376.

[23] Joint Communication from China and the United States – Memorandum of Understanding Between China and the United States Regarding China's Value-Added Tax on Integrated Circuits, China – Value-Added Tax on Integrated Circuits, WT/DS309/7.

While it would be easy to simply state that China's initial reaction and obvious aversion to dispute settlement were caused by its difficulties separating the legal issues from the political issues resulting from, *inter alia*, its Confucian traditions and post-1949 style of management and governance, such a view is perhaps too naïve to fully explain China's behaviour. Some two years earlier, China joined seven other members in successfully challenging US safeguards on steel – it therefore could not have been too averse to settling disputes through a formal dispute settlement mechanism rather relying solely on negotiation. Thus, while it certainly seems the case that China did misread the nature of the WTO dispute settlement process and truly believed that the dispute would have 'great political and diplomatic significance'[24] this is not the only reason that China quickly capitulated. As stated above, the complainants' case appeared to be very strong and plausible arguments in defence of the measure are not immediately apparent given existing WTO jurisprudence.[25] Moreover, due to the design of the rebate system, which required certain export and gross profit levels in order to be eligible for the rebates, foreign companies with significant investments in China actually claimed the majority of the rebates.[26] Realising this to be the case, China had little reason to resist US pressure to end the rebate scheme.[27]

At the same time China was responding to the US complaint in *China–Value-Added Tax on Integrated Circuits*, it also had to deal with a complaint filed by the EC concerning measures taken to limit the export of coke ostensibly both for environmental reasons and to ensure adequate domestic supply (so-called *China–Measures Affecting the Export of Coke*). Like the previous dispute, China moved quickly to settle the dispute (and thus guarantee the availability of sufficient quantities of coke to the EC) even though it could have possibly defended the reduced export quota as a measure taken to protect human life and the environment from the harmful effects of pollution resulting from the production of coke.[28] The

---

[24] Gao, Taming the Dragon: China's Experience in the WTO Dispute Settlement System, Legal Issues of Economic Integration 34 (2007) 4, p. 378.

[25] See in particular Report of the Appellate Body, Canada – Certain Measures Concerning Periodicals, WT/DS31/AB/R, adopted on 30th July, 1997, DSR 1997:I, 449, para. 34; Report of the Appellate Body, Canada – Certain Measures Affecting the Automotive Industry, WT/DS139/AB/R, WT/DS142/AB/R, adopted on 19th June, 2000, DSR 2000:VI, 2985, para. 78.

[26] See Gao, Aggressive Legalism: The East Asian Experience and Lessons for China, in: Gao/Lewis (eds.), *China's Participation in the WTO*, 2005, pp. 333–334.

[27] Gao also claims that as a result of China not accepting Taiwan as a third party, it hurriedly capitulated in order to avoid the threat of Taiwan bringing its own claim to the DSB. Gao, Taming the Dragon: China's Experience in the WTO Dispute Settlement System, Legal Issues of Economic Integration 34 (2007) 4, pp. 378–380. Others disagree and do not feel that the issue impacted upon China's decision-making process. See, e.g., Ji/Huang, above n 13, 15 Fn 40. Interviews conducted by Bryan Mercurio with PRC scholars and Taiwanese scholars and government officials also did not believe the Taiwan issue impacted China's decision to settle.

[28] See Gao, Aggressive Legalism: The East Asian Experience and Lessons for China, in: Gao/Lewis (eds.), *China's Participation in the WTO*, 2005, pp. 337–348.

EC would likely have made out its prima facie claim of a violation of Article XI:1 of the GATT, which prohibits quotas on the importation or exportation of goods, but China could have argued the measures were justified under Article XI:2 or Article XX of the GATT. While success would not have been assured, the point is merely that China could have raised a plausible argument in defence of its measures. Again, the main reason for China's willingness – indeed, eagerness – to settle the dispute seemed to be its desire to avoid formal dispute settlement proceedings at the DSB. Gao states:

> [The most] important reason for China's eagerness to settle is its fear of the WTO dispute settlement system. As the VAT Rebate case was brought only two weeks before the EC threatened WTO action, if China had not settled the coke case, China would have had to fight two legal battles against two of the most powerful WTO Members. As China lacks expertise and resource on WTO dispute settlement, China would have a very hard time defending itself in the WTO.[29]

In November 2005, China again faced the possibility of WTO dispute settlement when US producers of kraft linerboard petitioned MOFCOM to reconsider its earlier decision to issue positive preliminary and then final determinations and the imposition of anti-dumping measures against US producers.[30] In addition, on 6th January 2006 the USTR informed MOFCOM that it would bring a dispute over the positive determinations and duties if they were not removed by 9th January 2006 (*China–Antidumping Duties on Kraft Linerboard*).[31] Despite the short time frame, China undertook a quick administrative reconsideration of the issue and removed the duties on 9 January 2006.[32]

As China's anti-dumping proceedings had long been viewed by many to be inconsistent with WTO rules[33] and the current case appeared to be exceedingly

---

[29] Gao, Taming the Dragon: China's Experience in the WTO Dispute Settlement System, Legal Issues of Economic Integration 34 (2007) 4, p. 384. Gao also suggests that China's attempt to persuade the EC to recognize it as a market economy also factored into the decision to quickly settle the case. See ibid., pp. 382–383. Interviews conducted by Bryan Mercurio with PRC scholars and EU government officials do not believe this issue had much, if any, impact on China's decision to settle the dispute.

[30] USTR Press Release of 10th January, 2006, China Terminates Antidumping Duty Order on Kraft Linerboard, available at: http://ustraderep.gov/Document_Library/Press_Releases/2006/January/China_Terminates_Antidumping_Duty_Order_on_Kraft_Linerboard.html.

[31] Gao, Taming the Dragon: China's Experience in the WTO Dispute Settlement System, Legal Issues of Economic Integration 34 (2007) 4, p. 384. See also Wang, Rule of Law *and* Rule of Officials: Explaining the Different Roles Played by Law in Shareholders' Litigation and Anti-dumping Investigation in China, in: Peerenboom (ed.), *Dispute Resolution in China*, 2008.

[32] USTR Press Release of 10th January, 2006, China Terminates Antidumping Duty Order on Kraft Linerboard, available at: http://ustraderep.gov/Document_Library/Press_Releases/2006/January/China_Terminates_Antidumping_Duty_Order_on_Kraft_Linerboard.html; International Trade Reporter, China Lifts Dumping Duties on Linerboard in Face of US Threat of WTO Proceedings, 11th January, 2006.

[33] See, e.g., Working Party Report, para. 147; USTR, 2005 Report to Congress on China's WTO Compliance, p. 29 (cited in Gao, Taming the Dragon: China's Experience in the WTO Dispute

strong,[34] it is unsurprising that China quickly moved to settle this dispute. That being the case, MOFCOM rather strategically overturned the decision not on substantive grounds but on more limited procedural grounds (i.e. the failure to disclose all relevant facts relied upon in making its determination, which is in contravention of Article 25 of the Antidumping Regulations). Such a decision allows the Chinese to avoid having the core provisions of its Antidumping Regulations challenged in a WTO dispute and, more likely than not, being found to be inconsistent with the WTO Anti-dumping Agreement. In doing so, agreeing to overturn the decision and remove the duties also delays the inevitable restructuring of the relevant laws and regulations.

China's response to these three potential disputes characterises its course of action in the "Acceptance" phase of its WTO membership. By 2006, however, China dramatically modified its reactions to threats of dispute settlement and its ultimate response to such threats. This change marked the end of the Acceptance phase and the transition to the 'Consolidation' phase of membership.

Consolidation

Two months after China's retreat in *China–Antidumping Duties on Kraft Linerboard*, the US, EC and Canada brought a dispute against Chinese measures relating to the automobile industry. With the quick Chinese concessions in the previous disputes and a relatively strong case at hand, the complainants likely were expecting another rapid surrender; but this time China decided to defend its measures and engage with the dispute settlement process.

Evident in the three disputes discussed in this section is the fact that China began consolidating its learning from the Acceptance stage such that it began to no longer view participation in WTO dispute settlement as a failure in its membership.[35] Although still reluctant to go before a panel and remaining open to negotiation and

---

Settlement System, Legal Issues of Economic Integration 34 (2007) 4, pp. 385–386. For academic analysis, see Choi/Gao, Procedural Issues in the Anti-Dumping Regulations of China: A Critical Review under the WTO Rules, *Chinese Journal Of International Law* 5 (2006) 3, p. 663.

[34] See Gao, Taming the Dragon: China's Experience in the WTO Dispute Settlement System, Legal Issues of Economic Integration 34 (2007) 4, pp. 386–387.

[35] Interviews conducted by Bryan Mercurio with PRC academics and government officials substantiate the fact that initially the Chinese government, media and citizenry viewed every claim against China as an embarrassing failure of the nation to adequately implement its obligations. See also Gao, China's Participation in the WTO: A Lawyer's Perspective, Singapore Year Book of International Law 11 (2007), p. 1. For additional evidence of China's transition towards "aggressive legalism", see Nakagawa, No More Negotiated Deals?: Settlement of Trade and Investment Disputes in East Asia, Journal of International Economic Law 10 (2007) 4, pp. 837–867.

mutually agreed solutions,[36] it is clear that in 2006 China took its first public steps towards actively defending itself in WTO dispute settlement. Although on the defensive and seemingly insufficiently skilled to successfully manage the complex disputes and sophisticated issues of law at play,[37] in what we term the 'Consolidation' stage China begins to test the dispute settlement system and defend some of its measures.[38] In short, China began to see disputes at the WTO not as an aggressive act of diplomacy but instead as part of the usual course of business at the multilateral trading regime.[39]

The change in attitude, to a less conciliatory and more confident one, was also evident at the 4th October 2006 meeting of the Transitional Review Mechanism. At accession, China agreed to allow WTO members to periodically review its implementation of WTO commitments until 2011. At the October 2006 meeting, both the EC and US representatives reportedly expressed 'concern' about 'China's belligerent' attitude, which they considered a reversal from previous years.[40] For its part, China complained about the 'excessive' nature of questions and because there was nothing specifically obliging it under the Accession Protocol to provide written answers to questions it refused requests to do so.[41]

Importantly, the Consolidation stage marks a shift not only in the posture of China but also that of the key WTO Members. In particular, the EC and the US began treating China as a 'mature trading partner' who should now be held accountable for its actions.[42] For instance, in 2006 the then-EU Trade Commissioner, Peter Mandelson, argued:

---

[36] See, e.g., China – Measures Affecting Financial Information Services and Foreign Financial Information Suppliers 2008, DS372, DS373, DS378; China – Certain Measures Granting Refunds, Reductions or Exemptions from Taxes and Other Payments 2007, DS358, DS359.

[37] For instance, the Panel in China–Autos delayed its report citing the "complexity of issues presented in the case"; China–AV involved a contentious invocation of the "public morals" exception contained in GATT XX(a); and China–IPRs involved detailed issues of IP enforcement and censorship issues. See "WTO Panel Announces Delay in Ruling On Auto Parts Tariff Imposed by China", International Trade Reporter 24 (2007), p. 1080; Report of the Appellate Body, China–AV, paras. 205–415; Report of the Panel, China–IPRs, paras. 7.1–7.192 (copyright), 7.193–7.395 (customs measures), 7.396–7.669 (criminal thresholds).

[38] For Harpaz, this is the beginning of the "socialisation" of China process. See Harpaz, Sense and Sensibilities of China and WTO Dispute Settlement, International Law Forum of the Hebrew University of Jerusalem Law Faculty, Research Paper No. 02-10, pp. 28–33.

[39] Qin, China, India and the World Trade Organization, Asian Journal of Comparative Law 3 (2008) 1, pp. 21–24, available at: http://www.bepress.com/asjcl/vol3/iss1/art8.

[40] "Latest China Review at WTO Begins on a Sour Note, as China Refutes U.S, EU", International Trade Reporter 23 (2006), p. 1467.

[41] Ibid.

[42] USTR Press Release, "United States Files WTO Case Against China Over Treatment of U.S. Auto Parts", 30th March, 2006, available at: http://www.uspolicy.be/Article.asp?ID=83CBA7B7-2BF5-4276-8764-73F270C8BF5B (last visited on 15th January, 2011). In both cases, the rising trade deficit played a role in the altered treatment and demands for a tougher stance against China – in 2005 the US trade deficit vis-à-vis China surpassed US\$200 billion while the EU's trade deficit

China has reached a stage in its development when it is legitimate to point to China's growing responsibilities: to maintain an open global trading system, to help deliver a global trade deal in the WTO, and to remove barriers to further trade.[43]

Likewise, the USTR's 2006 Top-to-Bottom Review of the US-China trade relations marked 2006 as the beginning of 'Phase-3' of that relationship[44]: China had established a track record as a new WTO Member and would now be expected to demonstrate compliance with more substantial membership obligations.

A month after the release of the aforementioned USTR Review, the US, EC and Canada requested WTO consultations regarding the imposition of measures affecting exports of automobile parts to China. As *The Economist* noted, 'on a symbolic and practical level, the case would be a turning point for many industries in China: the start of a new era in which they are attacked by litigation.'[45]

China – Auto Parts[46]

This complaint, which has been termed the end of China's "honeymoon period" as a WTO Member,[47] was only the second complaint to be formally filed against China and the first to make it to the panel stage of the dispute settlement process. Moreover, not only was this the first dispute that China did not settle, China appealed the Panel Report and sought review by the Appellate Body.

While no doubt China initially debated whether to settle the dispute with the complainants, the sheer size of China's contribution as both producers and

---

with China exceeded €100 billion. Trade in Goods (Imports, Exports and Trade Balance) with China, see http://www.census.gov/foreign-trade/balance/c5700.html#2006; EU-China Trade: Questions and Answers – Strasbourg, 24th October, 2006, see http://trade.ec.europa.eu/doclib/docs/2006/october/tradoc_130788.pdf.

[43] Press Release of 24th October, 2006, Mandelson: "Europe has to accept fierce competition. China has to ensure it is fair competition", available at: http://www.delcan.ec.europa.eu/en/press_and_information/press_releases/2006/06PR035.shtml (last visited on 23rd February, 2011)

[44] United States Trade Representative, "U.S.-China Trade Relations: Entering a New Phase of Greater Accountability and Enforcement, Top-to-Bottom Review," February 2006, available at: http://www.ustr.gov/sites/default/files/Top-to-Bottom%20Review%20FINAL.pdf. See also Ikenson, Growing Pains: The Evolving U.S.-China Trade Relationship, CATO Institute Free Trade Bulletin No. 28, 7th May, 2007, available at: http://www.cato.org/pub_display.php?pub_id=10660 (last visited on 15th January, 2011).

[45] "Inevitable Collision", The Economist, 23rd February, 2008, pp. 82-83. Of course, as discussed in the "Acceptance" stage above, China had previously been subject to WTO dispute settlement but this phase marks the first time China actively challenged the complainant.

[46] China – Measures Affecting Imports of Automobile Parts 2008, DS339, 340, 342.

[47] "WTO Sets up Panel to Rule on Complaints by U.S., EU, Canada on China Car Parts Duty", International Trade Reporter 23 (2006), p. 1559: "[This dispute] marks the formal end of the 'honeymoon' period for China, when Beijing's major trading partners were willing to give China some leeway to bring its practices in line with WTO requirements because of its recent accession".

consumers to the global automobile market[48] meant that the case attracted considerable interest and made it hard to compromise.[49] In fact there is no evidence that China genuinely offered to settle the case with the complainants. Based on the relative unsophistication of the case presented by China, this litigation and recourse to the Appellate Body appears to be more a result of the high stakes rather than a confident grasp on WTO legalities.[50]

Briefly, the complaint concerned a tax imposed on automobile parts imported into China. If imported auto parts were used in a vehicle manufactured in China such that the imports exceeded a specified threshold (set by volume or value, roughly 60%) then the charge levied on each imported auto part equalled the tariff placed on a *complete* imported automobile (approximately 25%). The tariff thus applied was significantly *higher* (25%) than the maximum agreed by China for auto parts (10%). Furthermore, the Chinese laws and regulations at issue placed administrative burdens, including registration and detailed recordkeeping, on manufacturers in China using imported auto parts. The complainants alleged violations under Article III of the GATT (national treatment); Articles 3.1(b) & 3.2 of the Agreement on Subsidies and Countervailing Measures (SCM Agreement); Articles 2.1, 2.2 and paragraph 1(a) & 2(a) of Annex 1 of the Agreement on Trade Related Investment Measures (TRIMs) relating to local content requirements[51]; and China's pledge to keep tariffs on auto parts below 10% under its Accession Protocol to the WTO and Article II:1(a) of the GATT.[52]

China's initial response to the claims bore the emotive signs of a young WTO member in the Acceptance stage as China expressed 'great disappointment' at the

---

[48] "China to become 3rd biggest car producer", Xinhua, 20th September, 2006, available at: http://www.chinadaily.com.cn/china/2006-09/20/content_692770.htm (last visited on 19th January, 2011); "China car firms gear up for booming sales", BBC News, 25th March, 2007, available at: http://news.bbc.co.uk/2/hi/business/6364195.stm (last visited on 19th January, 2011): "The Chinese car market has just overtaken Japan and is now the second largest market in the world, after the United States."

[49] In addition to local interest, the dispute attracted the attention of the international media. Argentina, Australia, Brazil, Japan, Mexico and Thailand joined as the dispute as third parties.

[50] See Bhala, Teaching China GATT, Trade L. & Dev. 1 (2009), pp. 1 et seq. (8): "The historic Auto-Parts case is a multi-layered story in an environment of colossal challenges for China and the world. The case is about the development of legal capacity in the one developing country about which every other country cares. It is about a sector on which the fortunes of tens of millions of Chinese and foreigners ride. It is about the structure of the Chinese economy and the role the CCP plays in directing domestic and foreign factors of production. The Auto Parts case may even be about – in a tiny way – the beginning of the end of six decades of political dominance by the CCP."

[51] Agreement on Trade-Related Investment Measures, 15th April, 1994, Marrakesh Agreement Establishing the World Trade Organisation, Annex 1A, Legal Instruments – Results of the Uruguay Round, 1868 U.N.T.S. 186.

[52] Accession of the People's Republic of China to the World Trade Organisation, 11th December, 2001, WT/L/432; GATT Article II:1(a).

request for consultations, labelled the action 'unproductive to finding a solution'[53] and refused to allow the public view the panel hearings.[54] However, this time China also showed some of the boldness of adolescence as it advanced several arguments to counter the claim. China's key argument was that to achieve a 'substance-over-form' implementation of the *permitted* 25% tariff on complete imported vehicles, General Interpretive Rule 2(a) of the Harmonised System allowed it to classify any group of parts as a complete article if they have the essential character of that article, regardless of the state of assembly or disassembly at the time of importation.[55]

Amongst the myriad of issues raised in this dispute, the national treatment requirement under Article III of GATT and the prohibition against local content requirements in Article 2 of TRIMs are of particular interest. More specifically, the dispute demonstrates China's unfamiliarity with dispute settlement in the WTO because of the poor judgement it showed with respect to the principle of national treatment – one of the cornerstone principles of international trade law.

China's construction of the problem *presumed* that the challenged duty was a border charge under GATT Article II (2), and therefore defended the *level* of the duty under its Schedule of Commitments as its primary argument. However, the key question brought before the Panel was whether the excess tariff rate, applied to auto parts assessed to have the character of complete vehicles, was a discriminatory internal charge/tax under Article III. As the EC bitingly noted,

> [I]n its first written submission China has decided to largely ignore [the European Communities and its co-complainants prima facie case of inconsistency with Article 2 of the TRIMs Agreement and Article III, paragraphs 2, 4 and 5 of the GATT 1994] and insists that the Panel must first decide as a "threshold issue" whether the measures are "border measures" or not. We wonder if and when China will address our main claims.[56]

Being a seasoned participant in WTO dispute settlement, the EC began its presentation to the Panel by reminding the Panel and China that the burden of proof was on China to disprove the prima facie case of Article III.2 GATT and

---

[53] "WTO Sets up Panel to Rule on Complaints by U.S., EU, Canada on China Car Parts Duty", International Trade Reporter 23 (2006).

[54] "WTO Panel Chairman Sets Dates for Decision on China Auto Tariffs", International Trade Reporter 24 (2007), p. 308.

[55] Report of the Panel, China — Measures Affecting Imports of Automobile Parts, WT/DS339/R, WT/DS340/R and WT/DS342/R, 18th July, 2008, paras. 4.137–4.138: "This case concerns the relationship between substance and form in the administration of national customs laws. The European Communities, the United States, and Canada submit that the GATT 1994 does not permit China to look beyond the form of how an auto manufacturer imports and assemble auto parts into complete motor vehicles. China considers that, on the contrary, its authority to give effect to the substance of how an auto manufacturer imports and assembles auto parts is entirely supported by Article II of the GATT 1994."

[56] Report of the Panel, China – Measures Affecting Imports of Automobile Parts, WT/DS339/R, WT/DS340/R WT/DS342/R, 18th July, 2008, Oral Statement By The European Communities At The First Substantive Meeting of the Panel, paras. 4.200–4.201.

Article 2 TRIMs. It also highlighted that China's analysis of the issues in the dispute was "remarkable" since the TRIMs Agreement 'very clearly requires no preliminary assessment as to whether a measure is a a "border measure" or an "internal measure".[57]'The US drew further attention to China's inadequate identification of legal issues:

> [A]lthough China's first submission contains a considerable amount of material, very little of that material is relevant to the issues in this dispute. Most notably, China presents an extensive discussion of the complainants' practices with regard to circumvention of antidumping duties, but this dispute has nothing to do with dumping. And conversely, aside from the threshold issue, China does not even dispute the inconsistency of its measures with core obligations of Article III.[58]

In addition to bypassing the main concern of the complainants during the panel stage, China's attempts before the Appellate Body remained problematic as it sought to use an interpretive rule in the Harmonised System as a panacea against its core GATT obligations. In a confused argument China asked the Appellate Body to find that the Panel had erred in its analysis of the threshold question (i.e. did the impugned measure fall within Art II or Art III of GATT) because the Panel had not adequately applied a General Interpretive Rule of the Harmonised System to the Schedule of Commitments that Article II required members to uphold. Essentially, China wanted the Panel to analyse the application of Article II *before* it had determined that Article II was the properly applicable rule. Secondly, China was asking the Appellate Body to use the Harmonised System as interpretive context over core obligations of GATT.

To the first issue, the Appellate Body rejected China's appeal on the basis of the logical problems in its request. It pointed out that 'fundamental structure and logic' of the agreements here required the Panel to first decide which of these two provisions is applicable to the charge under China's measures.[59]

> [T]his issue (whether a duty applied to a product by virtue of its classification is consistent with Article II:1(b)) **is separate from** the issue of whether a charge falls under the first sentence of Article II:1(b) **at all** (as opposed to under Article III:2). It is not evident to us how classification rules are relevant to the latter issue. While it is true, as China argues, that the "classification of the product necessarily precedes the determination of which 'ordinary customs duty' applies", it is not the case that classification of the product (even if properly done) necessarily **precedes** a determination of whether the charge that applies is an ordinary customs duty.[60]

---

[57] Ibid, para. 4.202.

[58] Report of the Panel, China – Measures Affecting Imports of Automobile Parts, WT/DS339/R, WT/DS340/R and WT/DS342/R, 18th July, 2008, Oral Statement by the United States at The First Substantive Meeting of the Panel, para. 4.261; See also Reports of the Panel, China — Measures Affecting Imports of Automobile Parts, WT/DS339/R, WT/DS340/R and WT/DS342/R, 18th July, 2008, Oral Statement by Canada at The First Substantive Meeting of the Panel, para. 4.306 ("China mischaracterizes its measures as consistent with its Schedule of Concessions and thereby consistent with Article II of the GATT 1994, which China does in place of dealing squarely with its violation of Article III.").

[59] Reports of the Appellate Body, China – Measures Affecting Imports of Automobile Parts, WT/DS339/AB/R, WT/DS340/AB/R, WT/DS342/AB/R, 15th December, 2008, pp. 139–142.

[60] Ibid., p. 155 (emphasis added).

On the second issue, the Appellate Body essentially lectured China as to the hierarchy of its obligations as a Member of the WTO:

> [W]e see the Harmonized System as context that is most relevant to issues of classification of products. The Harmonized System complements Members' Schedules and confirms the general principle that it is "the 'objective characteristics' of the product in question when presented for classification at the border" that determine their classification and, consequently, the applicable customs duty. The Harmonized System, and the product categories that it contains, cannot trump the criteria contained in Article II:1(b) and Article III:2, which distinguish a border measure from an internal charge under the GATT 1994. **Among WTO Members, it is these GATT provisions that prevail**, and that define the relevant characteristics of ordinary customs duties for WTO purposes. Thus, even if the Harmonized System and GIR 2(a) would allow auto parts imported in multiple shipments to be classified as complete vehicles based on subsequent common assembly, as China suggests, this would not per se affect the criteria that define an ordinary customs duty under Article II:1(b).[61]

At the appellate stage, China lost on all but one count (the alleged violation of its Protocol of Accession). Interestingly, it did not even raise a defence against allegations of violating national treatment obligations under Article III and it did not pursue its Article XX(d) defence raised during the panel stage at the Appellate Body.

It would be easy to argue that China defended its measures and took the Panel's decision to the Appellate Body simply to buy time for its automotive industry. Given that there is no retrospective compensation at the WTO, the delay in removing the offending provisions ostensibly would continue benefitting the automotive industry until the dispute was completed and decision fully implemented. However, this argument fails to appreciate the insight available in China's attempt to assuage the complainants after consultations were requested.

In July 2006, Chinese customs authorities announced that they would suspend the surcharge on imported auto parts making up more than 60% of the final vehicle for a period of 2 years.[62] The suspension did not cover all the discriminatory provisions as imported auto parts used in certain combinations would still attract the surcharge. If the dispute settlement proceedings were merely a ploy to buy time, then China would not have any incentive to forego benefits under its scheme over 2 years. A plausible explanation, especially given the discussion above, may be that China just did not understand the significance of its national treatment obligation. Put simply, we contend that China genuinely believed that the General Interpretive Rule of the Harmonised System gave it the right to treat certain auto parts as complete vehicles, and this right was not to be analysed against the national treatment obligation.

---

[61] Ibid., p. 164 (emphasis added).

[62] "China Blocks U.S, EU, Canadian Requests for WTO Panel Review of Auto Parts Tariffs", International Trade Reporter 23 (2006), p. 1436; "U.S., EU, Canada Request Panel to Rule on Chinese Auto Parts Tariffs", International Trade Reporter 23 (2006), p. 1350.

China – AV[63]

On 10th April 2010, and prior to the Panel *China-Autos* releasing the Panel Report, China received two additional requests for consultations from the US[64]: the disputes concerned the protection of intellectual property rights in China (*China – IPR*) and China's barriers on the importation and sale of books, music, videos, and movies (*China – AV*).

In *China-AV*, the US again assailed Chinese laws for providing preferential treatment to Chinese-sourced products over foreign publications and entertainment products (allegedly in violation of national treatment) and added that Chinese laws restricted market access to foreign material (against 'right to trade' commitments in its Accession Protocol, GATS and the GATT). Under Chinese law, the import and distribution of publications and audio-visual products was limited to government appointed agencies or entities with a controlling Chinese stake. Further, books, music, videos or movies had to go through a stringent content review process if they were from outside China. Essentially, the US complaint took aim at the central control and censorship of media in China.[65] A Chinese concession would have led to grave ideological and political ramifications for the Chinese Communist Party. Accordingly, China had little choice but to mount a strong, public defence.

Despite its weak legal positioning, China's response relied on creative arguments to justify its measures. In particular, China questioned the Panel's jurisdiction over issues which were not raised in the panel request for consultations and challenged the DSB to make a determination about "public morality" under Article XX (a). Even arguments raised in China's response and appeal that suffered from a weaker basis in law and adverse Appellate Body jurisprudence (e.g. the

---

[63] China – Measures Affecting Trading Rights and Distribution Services for Certain Publications and Audiovisual Entertainment Products 2007, DS363. For deeper case analysis, see Voon, International Decisions – China – Publications and Audiovisual Entertainment Products, American Journal of International Law 103 (2009), p. 710; Wu, Case Note: China – Measures Affecting Trading Rights and Distribution Services for Certain Publications and Audiovisual Entertainment Products 2007 (WT/DS363/AB/R), Chinese Journal of International Law 9 (2010), pp. 415–432.

[64] US Trade Representative Susan Schwab stated on the China-AV complaint and its connection with China-IPR: "That means our exporters can't shop around for the best way to get their products into China. Instead state-run import companies can impose high costs and build in delays that give IPR pirates and counterfeiters a leg up in the marketplace, all to the detriment of our exporters and China's consumers", quoted in "U.S. Initiates Two New WTO Complaints Against China Over IPR Protection, Barriers", International Trade Reporter 24 (2007), p. 505.

[65] See Pauwelyn, Case Note – Squaring Free Trade in Culture with Chinese Censorship: The WTO Appellate Body Report on *China-Audiovisuals*, Melbourne Journal of International Law 11 (2010), p. 119.

argument that GATT and Accession Protocol requirements do not apply to certain products such as motion pictures for theatrical release because they are services as opposed to goods)[66] demonstrate China's increasing grasp of WTO law and ability to argue on a level that warranted a considered rebuttal.[67] Thus, although a defensive stance born out of necessity, we see growth from *China-Autos* as China uses the vocabulary of WTO dispute settlement to defend itself in *China-AV*, rather than using the WTO Panel or Appellate Body as another forum for diplomatic wrangling and political point-scoring.

Notably, China succeeded in narrowing the terms of the complaint filed by the US by noting discrepancies between the panel request and content of consultations. Despite the broad victory granted to the US in *China-AV*, China's careful argument ensured that it limited its loss.

---

[66] Report of the Panel, China – Measures Affecting Trading Rights and Distribution Services for Certain Publications and Audiovisual Entertainment Products, 12th August, 2009, WT/DS363/R, paras. 4.96, 4.105. The Appellate Body rejected China's argument: "We do not see the clear distinction drawn by China between 'content' and 'goods'. Neither do we consider that content and goods and the regulation thereof, are mutually exclusive. Content can be embodies in a physical carrier, and the content and carrier together can form a good." Report of the Appellate Body, China – Measures Affecting Trading Rights and Distribution Services for Certain Publications and Audiovisual Entertainment Products, 21st December, 2009, WT/DS363/AB/R, p. 195; With respect to previous adverse jurisprudence, the Appellate Body stated: "In EC – Bananas III, the Appellate Body observed that, although the subject matter of the GATT 1994 and that of the GATS are different, particular measures "could be found to fall within the scope of both the GATT 1994 and the GATS", and that such measures include those "that involve a service relating to a particular good or a service supplied in conjunction with a particular good." These findings specifically concern the relationship between the GATS and the GATT 1994, and thus do not directly address the relationship between China's trading rights commitments and its commitments on trade in services. Yet, these findings provide assistance in analyzing the issue of whether a measure can be simultaneously subject to obligations relating to trade in goods and those relating to trade in services. Given that China's trading rights commitments apply to trade in goods, the Appellate Body findings in these earlier disputes are also relevant to resolving the issue of whether measures regulating services may be subject to China's trading rights commitments." Report of the Appellate Body, China–Measures Affecting Trading Rights and Distribution Services for Certain Publications and Audiovisual Entertainment Products, 21st December, 2009, WT/DS363/AB/R, para. 193.

[67] See Report of the Panel, China – Measures Affecting Trading Rights and Distribution Services for Certain Publications and Audiovisual Entertainment Products, 12th August, 2009, WT/DS363/R, para. 4.184, First Written Submission of China: "[M]otion pictures for theatrical release cannot be qualified as goods, and their distribution does not consist in the distribution of a good, but in the distribution of an intangible work through the organisation of public shows on the basis of licensing agreements allowing their exploitation. The only goods involved in theatrical distribution services, the film reels, are mere accessories to such services. Even though a film reel is initially imported, the materials actually being distributed within China are copies produced after various transformations of the motion pictures (dubbing, subtitling, etc.). Therefore, the challenged measures cannot be scrutinized under Article III:4 of the GATT and paragraphs 5.1 and 5.2 of China's Accession Protocol."

The United States did not inform China that it was challenging every possible discriminatory requirement in its measures, but rather the specific ones described in the narratives.
Just as the European Communities did in *US – Carbon Steel*, the United States has,
through its description of its claim in the panel request, only notified China that its claim
concerned the specific requirements set forth in the panel request. Therefore, we find that
these additional requirements (pre-establishment legal compliance, approval process
requirements, and decision-making criteria) are outside our terms of reference.[68]

More significantly, China convinced the Appellate Body to apply Article XX of
the GATT to the Chinese Accession Protocol, thus allowing it to limit the right to
trade, required of it under Paragraph 5.1 of the Accession Protocol, in a manner
consistent with the WTO Agreement, including Article XX of the GATT.[69]
Although, the Appellate Body ultimately upheld the Panel's decision that China's
measures restricting market access did not satisfy the 'necessity' threshold in
Article XX(a), this is the first time that the general exceptions have been applied
outside of the GATT. In fact the Appellate Body rejected the Panel's *arguendo*
analysis[70] and cemented the application of GATT Article XX to the Accession
Protocol. As Pauwelyn notes, the impact of this extension of Article XX beyond the
GATT could be – however unlikely – the justification under GATT Article XX of
a health or environmental regulation, anti-dumping duty, safeguard or subsidy that
violates the SPS Agreement, Safeguards Agreement, BT Agreement, Anti-Dumping
Agreement or SCM Agreement.[71]

China – IPRs[72]

Despite substantial amendments to intellectual property (IP) laws in the years
leading up to its WTO accession critics (including several prominent US IP
industries) nevertheless continue to question China's conformity with the multilateral

---

[68] Report of the Panel, China – Measures Affecting Trading Rights and Distribution Services for
Certain Publications and Audiovisual Entertainment Products, 12th August, 2009, WT/DS363/
R, para. 7.104.

[69] Ibid, para. 4.112: "Paragraph 5.1's right to regulate trade is the expression of the WTO general
exception to Members' obligations, which leaves room for the implementation of public policies
and is crucial for the preservation of China's sovereignty".

[70] Report of the Appellate Body, China–Measures Affecting Trading Rights and Distribution
Services for Certain Publications and Audiovisual Entertainment Products, 21st December,
2009, WT/DS363/AB/R, p. 215.

[71] Pauwelyn, Case Note – Squaring Free Trade in Culture with Chinese Censorship: The WTO
Appellate Body Report on *China-Audiovisuals*, Melbourne Journal of International Law 11
(2010), p. 123.

[72] China – Measures Affecting the Protection and Enforcement of Intellectual Property Rights,
2010 (DS362). For deeper analysis, see Yu, The TRIPS Enforcement Dispute, Nebraska Law
Review 89 (2011), forthcoming, available at: http://papers.ssrn.com/sol3/papers.cfm?
abstract_id=1676558.

agreement. China's well-known spotty record of enforcing its IP laws continued following accession and served to intensify the demands for US action. Given this background, as well as China's large-scale manufacturing of counterfeit goods and piracy of intellectual property rights (IPRs), it is not surprising that the US challenged China's compliance with the TRIPs Agreement.

On its face, China's decision to cease negotiations and defend the measures rather than settle to dispute appears somewhat surprising. Upon deeper inspection, however, China's reaction to the complaint are not only in line with its development during the Consolidation phase of its WTO membership but also entirely pragmatic for at least two reasons. First, throughout several years of IP negotiations, it became clear to the Chinese leadership that the US did not appreciate the significant advance it had already made in protecting and enforcing IPRs.[73] As a consequence, any additional Chinese concession would result not in a lessoning of the pressure but merely in yet another demand. Second, China simply did not believe the US case was very strong, and was filed more as a result of political pressure (from both Congress and the IP industry) rather than legal merit.[74]

The US complaint in *China–IPRs* focussed on three specific Chinese measures: (1) the denial of copyright and related rights protection and enforcement to works that have not been authorised for publication or distribution within China; (2) the disposal of goods confiscated by customs authorities that infringe intellectual property rights; and (3) thresholds triggering criminal procedures and penalties relating to wilful trademark counterfeiting and copyright piracy on a commercial scale[75];

The first claim challenged China's denial of copyright protection to works containing prohibited content such as content that is deemed to be 'against the fundamental principles established in the Constitution', 'disrupt public order and undermine social stability' or "jeopardize social ethics or fine national cultural traditions."[76] Here, the US claimed violations of Article 5(1) of the Berne

---

[73] See Ji/Huang, China's Experience in Dealing with WTO Dispute Settlement: A Chinese Perspective, *Journal of World Trade* 45 (2011) 1, p. 18.

[74] See ibid.

[75] Request for Consultations by the United States, China – Measures Affecting the Protection and Enforcement of Intellectual Property Rights, G/L/819, IP/D/26, WT/DS362/1, 16th April, 2007.

[76] See Report of the Panel, China – Measures Affecting the Protection and Enforcement of Intellectual Property Rights, WT/DS362R, adopted on 20th March, 2009, para. 7.79. The relevant laws and regulations include Criminal Law; Regulation on the Administration of Publishing Industry; Regulation on the Administration of Broadcasting; Regulation on the Administration of Audiovisual Products; Regulation on the Administration of Films; Regulations on the Administration of Telecommunication. See, e.g., Art. 4 of the PRC Copyright Law sates: "Works the publication or distribution of which is prohibited by law shall not be protected by this Law. Copyright owners, in exercising their copyright, shall not violate the Constitution or laws or prejudice the public interests ... Works the publication and/or dissemination of which is prohibited by law shall not be protected by this Law. Copyright owners, in exercising their copyright, shall not violate the Constitution or laws or prejudice the public interests."

Convention (incorporated into the TRIPs Agreement via Article 2.2),[77] which it claimed mandated protection, and of Article 41.1 of the TRIPs Agreement, which oblige Members to adopt IP enforcement procedures.[78] More specifically, the US claimed that in denying copyright protection to prohibited works, China precluded such procedures from being available or otherwise utilized. Despite several attempts at justifying the measures under WTO law,[79] the panel agreed with the US and found China's measures inconsistent with the TRIPs Agreement.

In the second claim, the US argued that China's customs regulations were inconsistent with Article 59 of the TRIPS Agreement, which states that competent authorities "shall have the authority to order the destruction or disposal of infringing goods in accordance with the principles set out in Article 46."[80] By contrast, China's customs regulations give customs authorities several options for disposing of IPR-infringing goods seized at the border: (i) Customs may hand the goods over to public welfare bodies for public welfare undertakings; (ii) if the holder of the intellectual property wishes to buy the goods, Customs may sell them; (iii) if the first two options are not possible, and if Customs can eradicate the infringing features, then the goods may be auctioned; or (iv) when eradication is impossible, Customs may destroy the goods.[81] The US argued that China's regulations created a "compulsory scheme" that mandated Customs to follow the order listed – in other

---

[77] Art. 5(1) of the Berne Convention reads: Authors shall enjoy, in respect of works for which they are protected under this Convention, in countries of the Union other than the country of origin, the rights which their respective laws do now or may hereafter grant to their nationals, as well as the rights specially granted by this Convention."

[78] Art. 41 reads: "Members shall ensure that enforcement procedures as specified in this Part are available under their law so as to permit effective action against any act of infringement of intellectual property rights covered by this Agreement, including expeditious remedies to prevent infringements and remedies which constitute a deterrent to further infringements. . .".

[79] China's mainly argued there is a difference between a denial of authority to publish from a denial of copyright. It further drew a distinction between "copyright" and "copyright protection"., stating that Art. 4(1) did not remove copyright, but simply denied the particularized rights of private copyright enforcement. China further stated that copyright would attach (and be enforceable) to works edited to pass content review – the edited version of the work would be protected, but copyright in the unedited, prohibited work would not be enforced. See Report of the Panel, China–IPRs, paras. 7.17–7.21.

[80] Art. 46 reads: "In order to create an effective deterrent to infringement, the judicial authorities shall have the authority to order that goods that they have found to be infringing be, without compensation of any sort, disposed of outside the channels of commerce in such a manner as to avoid any harm caused to the right holder, or, unless this would be contrary to existing constitutional requirements, destroyed ... In considering such requests, the need for proportionality between the seriousness of the infringement and the remedies ordered as well as the interests of third parties shall be taken into account. In regard to counterfeit trademark goods, the simple removal of the trademark unlawfully affixed shall not be sufficient, other than in exceptional cases, to permit release of the goods into the channels of commerce." (emphasis added).

[81] Report of the Panel, China–IPRs, paras. 7.193–7.196. See Chinese Regulations on Customs Protection of Intellectual Property Rights; Measures for the Implementation of the Customs IPR Regulations; Public Notice No. 16/2007 as notified by the General Administration of Customs.

words, China's scheme precluded destruction or proper disposal of infringing goods if it were possible to either provide the goods to public welfare bodies or sell the goods to the IP owner.[82] The panel rejected the US claims that customs authorities were not authorized to destroy or properly dispose of infringing goods,[83] as Article 59 does not mandate that domestic agencies must have the absolute power to order destruction of infringing goods in any circumstance.[84] The panel did, however, accept the claim that the third option is inconsistent with Article 46 (as referenced in Article 59); the panel concluded: 'China's Customs measures provide that the simple removal of the trademark unlawfully affixed is sufficient to permit release of the goods into the channels of commerce in more than just "exceptional cases".'[85]

In relation to the third issue, China showed its increasing grasp of WTO law in defending the consistency of its criminal thresholds (500 copies of a DVD or 50,000 yuan worth of counterfeit goods)[86] with Article 61 of the TRIPS Agreement, which requires the criminalization of 'wilful trademark counterfeiting or copyright piracy on a commercial scale'.[87] In the complaint, the US alleged that significant retail sales of infringing product take place at levels below the thresholds and, correspondingly, that the numerical thresholds provide a 'safe harbour' for those engaged in commercial activities (such as distribution of infringing products).[88] The US further argued that the term 'commercial scale' should equate with

---

[82] Ibid, para. 7.197.

[83] Customs destroyed 58 percent of the total value of infringing goods between 2005 and 2007. Ibid., para. 7.198.

[84] Ibid., para. 7.236. The panel stated: "the obligation that competent authorities 'shall have the authority' to make certain orders is not an obligation that competent authorities shall exercise that authority in a particular way, unless otherwise specified." Ibid., para. 7.238.

[85] Ibid., para. 7.393.

[86] See Art. 213 of the Chinese Criminal Code, which must be read together with Art. 1 of Judicial Interpretation No. 19 and Art. 1 of Judicial Interpretation No. 6. Art. 213 reads: "Whoever, without permission from the owner of a registered trademark, uses a trademark which is identical with the registered trademark on the same kind of commodities shall, if the circumstances are serious, be sentenced to fixed-term imprisonment of not more than three years or criminal detention and shall also, or shall only, be fined; if the circumstances are especially serious, the offender shall be sentenced to fixed-term imprisonment of not less than three years but not more than seven years and shall also be fined." Art. 1 of Judicial Interpretation No. 19 provide monetary fines and Art. 1 of Judicial Interpretation No. 6 reads: "Whoever, for the purpose of making profits, reproduces [/] distributes, without permission of the copyright owner, a written work, musical work, cinematographic work, television or video works, computer software and other works of not less than 500 张(份) in total, [the offence] shall be deemed as 'there are other serious circumstances' under Article 217 of the Criminal Law...." (emphasis added).

[87] See Report of the Panel, China–IPRs, paras. 7.399–7.414. Art. 61 reads: "Members shall provide for criminal procedures and penalties to be applied at least in cases of wilful trademark counterfeiting or copyright piracy on a commercial scale. Remedies available shall include imprisonment and/or monetary fines sufficient to provide a deterrent, consistently with the level of penalties applied for crimes of a corresponding gravity... Members may provide for criminal procedures and penalties to be applied in other cases of infringement of intellectual property rights, in particular where they are committed wilfully and on a commercial scale."

[88] Ibid, para 7.622.

expected financial return or sufficient extent or motive regardless of expected financial return.[89] Importantly, the US challenged the Chinese measures 'as such', meaning that the law itself is inconsistent with the TRIPs Agreement, not as the laws applied on the ground (and thus widespread reports and common knowledge regarding lack of enforcement of IPRs in China were irrelevant to this issue). China's wholeheartedly defended its measures, broadly arguing that 'commercial scale' relates to a 'significant magnitude of infringement activity, subject to national discretion and local conditions',[90] and more specifically arguing that (1) it sets thresholds across a range of commercial crimes; (2) that its thresholds reflect the significance of various illegal acts for public and economic order and its preference to prioritise criminal enforcement, prosecution and judicial resources; (3) that criminal thresholds for counterfeiting and piracy are reasonable and appropriate in the context of its legal structure and the other laws on commercial crimes; and (4) that its system of administrative enforcement of IP infringement operates separately from criminal enforcement system.[91]

In deciding the issue, the panel refused to equate 'commercial scale' with 'commercial' activity[92] – while also refusing to label all activity as 'commercial' – instead stating it results from 'the magnitude or extent of typical or usual commercial activity'. Thus, in the view of the panel, 'counterfeiting or piracy "on a commercial scale" refers to counterfeiting or piracy carried on at the magnitude or extent of typical or usual commercial activity' with respect to a given product in a given market.'[93] Under the panel's interpretation of Article 61, the key question becomes whether the infringing activity is equal to or larger than the usual size of a commercial operation concerning a given product or market. Here, the US evidence failed to prove its case and the panel, while nevertheless stating that China's measures 'exclude certain commercial activity from criminal procedures and penalties', held there was insufficient evidence to prove that the measures are inconsistent with Article 61.[94]

---

[89] Ibid, para 7.480. The US is negotiating such a definition into its free trade agreements. See, e.g., Art. 17.1.26 (a) US-Australia FTA: "... Wilful copyright piracy on a commercial scale includes: (i) significant willful infringements of copyright, that have no direct or indirect motivation of financial gain; and (ii) willful infringements for the purposes of <u>commercial advantage or financial gain</u>." (emphasis added).

[90] Report of the Panel, China–IPRs, para 7.481.

[91] Ibid, paras. 7.425–7.429.

[92] The panel defined the term "commerce" as "buying and selling; the exchange of merchandise or services, especially on a large scale." The panel found the word scale is a quantitative concept whilst commercial is qualitative.

[93] Ibid, para. 7.577.

[94] The US provided industry reports, newspaper articles and other anecdotal evidence in support of its claim. See ibid, para. 7.622. The panel heavily criticised the US in this regards. See, e.g., ibid., para 7.614. ("[T]he United States did not provide data regarding products and markets or other factors that would demonstrate what constituted 'a commercial' scale in the specific situation in China's marketplace."). Unfortunately, the panel did not recognise the difficulties experienced by the US in obtaining such evidence or cooperation from China in this matter.

While the US technically 'won' this dispute, the decision allowed both sides to claim victory. Academic commentary generally viewed the result as a Chinese victory,[95] but the reality of the situation is more complicated. For instance, the US' success in regards to the copyright claim is merely a pyrrhic victory since even if protected by copyright the censored products will garner little to no economic value. Given this, the political (rather than legal) situation seems to have driven both the US' pursuance of the issue as well as China's vigorous defence. With politics at the forefront of this dispute, it is therefore somewhat of a surprise that neither party appealed the report.[96]

Activation

In the Consolidation period (2006–07), China defended itself against trade complaints that attacked core Chinese economic and ideological interests (i.e. media control, intellectual property, automobiles). The level of complaints against China further intensified from 2008, but for the first time China became a complainant as well as respondent. It became an active player in the dispute settlement process, involved in half of the 14 disputes initiated in 2009 and almost 40% of those initiated in 2010.[97] With these statistics in mind, it is unsurprising to see that

---

[95] See, e.g., the blog of Michael Geist (University of Ottawa) entitled, "Why the U.S. Lost Its WTO IP Complaint Against China. Badly.", available at: **http://www.michaelgeist.ca/content/view/ 3645/125/**.

[96] See, e.g., USTR Press Release of 26th January, 2009, United States Wins WTO Dispute Over Deficiencies in China's Intellectual Property Rights Laws, available at: http://www.ustr.gov/ about-us/press-office/press-releases/2009/january/united-states-wins-wto-dispute-over-deficiencies-c; "China expresses mixed feelings over WTO ruling on IPR protection", Xinhua, 27th January, 2009, available at: http://news.xinhuanet.com/english/2009-01/27/content_10726209.htm. On 20th April, 2010, China reported to the DSB that it had complied with the panel report. See WTO, Minutes of the DSB meeting on 20th April, 2010, WT/DSB/M/282, p. 12.

[97] China – Measures concerning wind power equipment (Complainant: United States of America), DS419, 22nd December, 2010; China – Countervailing and Anti-Dumping Duties on Grain Oriented Flat-rolled Electrical Steel from the United States (Complainant: United States of America), DS414, 15th September, 2010; China – Certain Measures Affecting Electronic Payment Services (Complainant: United States of America), DS413, 15th September, 2010; China – Provisional Anti-Dumping Duties on Certain Iron and Steel Fasteners from the European Union (Complainant: European Union), DS407, 7th May, 2010; China – Measures Related to the Exportation of Various Raw Materials (Complainant: Mexico), DS398, 21st August, 2009; China – Measures Related to the Exportation of Various Raw Materials (Complainant: European Communities), DS395, 23rd June, 2009; China – Measures Related to the Exportation of Various Raw Materials (Complainant: United States of America), DS394, 23rd June, 2009; China – Grants, Loans and Other Incentives (Complainant: Mexico), DS388, 19th December, 2008; China – Grants, Loans and Other Incentives (Complainant: United States of America), DS387, 19thDecember, 2008; China – Measures Affecting Financial Information Services and Foreign Financial Information Suppliers (Complainant: Canada), DS378, 20thJune, 2008; China –

China's mannerisms and behaviour shifted again to become more aggressive, active and vocal, both within the dispute settlement process and in the wider WTO system.

For instance, from late 2007 onwards China has taken an offensive stance towards dispute settlement and now appears at ease as a complainant and in using the DSB to promote its trade interests. Likewise, China's growing confidence can also be seen from its shifting posture at the Doha negotiations in Geneva in 2008. In short, the Activation phase is a period which has overseen China complete its transition to 'aggressive legalism' – China now feels sufficiently integrated into the international trade regime to negotiate as an insider with the protection of its domestic interests as a legitimate aim and to adopt "a conscious strategy where a substantive set of international legal rules can be made to serve as both 'shield' and 'sword' in trade disputes among sovereign states".[98] China's changing stance in the Doha negotiations and its evolving role in the formal dispute settlement process will now be discussed in turn.

Doha Negotiations 2008

In July 2008 during the 'mini-ministerial' conference held in Geneva, China received an invitation to the 'big-kids' table'[99] and the G-7 (Australia, Brazil, China, EC, Japan and the US) unquestionably replaced the 'Quad' (US, EC, Japan and Canada) as the dominant negotiating group. China's rise to prominence was not unexpected, and in fact it was in line with the expectations that China would take on a greater leadership role in negotiations to finalise this protracted round,[100] but it did signify a changed attitude within the Chinese government who up until this point showed little interest in leading (much less fully engaging with)

Measures Affecting Financial Information Services and Foreign Financial Information Suppliers (Complainant: European Communities), DS372, 3rd March, 2008; China – Measures Affecting Financial Information Services and Foreign Financial Information Suppliers (Complainant: United States of America), DS373, 3rd March, 2008. For a statistical analysis of 2009, see Leitner/Lester, WTO Dispute Settlement 1995–2009 – A Statistical Analysis, Journal of International Economic Law 13 (2010) 1, pp. 205, 217 (calling 2009 "the rise of China in WTO dispute settlement").

[98] Pekkanen, Aggressive Legalism: The Rules of the WTO and Japan's Emerging Trade Strategy, The World Economy 24 (2001), p. 708.

[99] As Paul Blustein of the Brookings Institute reports in "The Nine-Day Misadventure of the Most Favored Nations How the WTO's Doha Round Negotiations Went Awry in July 2008": "'China wanted a seat at the big kids' table,'" the New York Times quoted one anonymous member of the U.S. delegation as saying. 'They got it...'" available at: http://www.brookings.edu/~/media/Files/rc/articles/2008/1205_trade_blustein/1205_trade_blustein.pdf (last visited on 22nd February, 2011).

[100] "China urged to play a bigger role", AFP Newswire, 7th November, 2006: "[China must] assume a level of global responsibility that matches the huge impact it is having on global trade, security and the environment." See also Lim/Wang, China and the Doha Development Agenda, Journal of World Trade 44 (2010) 6, pp. 1309, 1310.

the negotiations.[101] In fact, while in 2006 then-USTR Susan Schwab "expressed surprise that China was willing to allow other developing countries to represent their interest in the Doha talks,"[102] the situation had dramatically changed in 2008 and the balance of power in global trade negotiations had firmly shifted to China.[103]

By 2008, it was clear to all involved that China's participation, combined with the collective influence of the 'BICs' (Brazil, India and China as advanced developing countries), demanded some show of leadership.[104] Although China officially remains reluctant to 'lead',[105] given its interests as a major exporter and a developing country means that it is not always aligned with the same 'friends',[106] it realises it can no longer be a passive bystander as the trade rules are further negotiated and it must actively protect its interests. Economist C. Fred Bergsten of the Council on Foreign Relations captured the change by noting that '[i]n the past, China never

---

[101] Gao argues that China still "lacks familiarity with the rules of the game and cannot participate effectively", despite its now-10 years in the WTO. Gao, Elephant in the Room: Challenges of Integrating China into the WTO System, Asian Journal of WTO and International Health Law and Policy 6 (2011), pp. 145–147.

[102] "US presses China to take Doha role", Financial Times, 30th August, 2006, quoted by Gu/ Humphrey/Messner, Global Governance and Developing Countries: The Implications of the Rise of China, World Development 36 (2006) 2, pp. 274, 282. See also Schwab, Remarks at the 40th Anniversary Gala Dinner of the National Committee on US–China Relations, 12th October, 2006, available at: http://www.ncuscr.org/files/2006Gala_SusanSchwab.pdf.

[103] Castle, "Balance of power shifts to China at global trade talks", The New York Times, 28th July, 2008, available at: http://www.nytimes.com/2008/07/28/business/worldbusiness/28iht-wto.3.14835752.html (last visited on 21st February, 2011).

[104] US Trade Representative Ron Kirk stated: "The success or failure of the Doha round depends on whether advanced developing countries like China, India and Brazil will accept the responsibility that goes along with their growing roles in the global economy." Remarks by US Trade Representative Ron Kirk, 18th May, 2010, "Next Steps on World Trade" Conference, Washington, DC, available at: http://www.ustr.gov/about-us/press-office/speeches/transcripts/2010/may/remarks-ambassador-ron-kirk-us-chamber-commerce (last visited on 21st February, 2011). See also Grammling, Major setback for WTO's Doha Round: "Mini-Ministerial" failed and future looks dim – a chance for reclaiming its "development dimension"?, FES Geneva, August 2008, available at: http://library.fes.de/pdf-files/bueros/genf/05597.pdf (last visited on 22nd February, 2011): "The meeting made clear that developing countries, such as India, China and Brazil, had emerged as coequal powers and irrevocably changed negotiation dynamics. They showed that no deal will be possible against their development interests, which gives hope that a real "development outcome" might be possible sometime in the future".

[105] See Administration Likely to Be Frustrated By China's Leadership on WTO, Other Issues, International Trade Reporter 26 (2009), p. 750 (Reportedly, "[e]very time the word leadership was used [in the initial drafts of documents from the G-20 financial summit in London], China struck it out").

[106] See Lim/Wang, China and the Doha Development Agenda, Journal of World Trade 44 (2010) 6, p. 1312: "China wants a reduction of subsidies in developed countries, which brings China in line with many developing countries. On the other hand, as a major exporting country for agricultural products, China would also like to see lower barriers in developing countries. Meanwhile, China insists on special and special and differential treatment for all developing countries."

played an active role in the Doha talks, but it is now aggressively challenging the system.'[107]

This shift was most visible in the Agriculture negotiations, where China challenged the duplicity of protectionism practiced by the US and refused to agree with the EC and US proposal to link agricultural negotiations with non-agricultural market access (lower tariffs on machinery, electronics and chemicals, where developed countries have export interests).[108] The failure to reach agreement on this issue played a large role in the collapse of the talks. As a result, US trade official David Shark accused China, along with India, of placing the Doha round into the "gravest jeopardy".[109] As to the situation, the *Washington Post* reported:

> India and China essentially torpedoed the talks, asserting a broad right to raise tariffs to protect their poor farmers from "import surges," price drops and other vicissitudes of the world market. China, which had been relatively quiet throughout most of the talks, was particularly vituperative, blasting U.S. arguments as "absurd," even though Brazil and several other developing countries agreed with Washington. China's role in the demise of the Doha Round is particularly dismaying, considering China has reaped huge benefits from global trade in the seven years since it joined the organization – with strong U.S. support. Chinese exports have quadrupled from $300 billion in 2002 to $1.2 trillion in 2007, thanks in large part to free access to the U.S. market. U.S. supporters of Chinese inclusion in the WTO argued that drawing China into a system of multilateral give-and-take would mute its nationalistic tendencies. Evidently, the Chinese see the matter differently. They, and the world, will be poorer because of it.[110]

In response, China reacted aggressively, labelling the US as hypocritical for heavily subsidising its areas of vulnerability – its cotton farmers – while asking

---

[107] Bergsten, "China and The Collapse of Doha", Foreign Affairs, 27th August, 2008, available at: http://www.foreignaffairs.com/print/64911 (last visited on 21st February, 2011).

[108] For example, the EC sought to create "new market access for European exporters in the markets of the 'emerging economies' like Brazil, China and India, who have benefitted hugely from the open global trading system and now have a responsibility to contribute to it by lowering their border protection. The emerging economies need to cut and bind some of their applied tariffs, bind the remaining existing tariffs at applied levels, bind most of the tariffs that are not currently bound and reduce their tariff peaks.", http://trade.ec.europa.eu/doclib/docs/2008/july/tradoc_139792.pdf.

[109] See "Deal still elusive at trade talks", BBC News, 28th July, 2008, available at: http://news.bbc. co.uk/go/pr/fr/-/2/hi/business/7528067.stm (last visited on 22nd February, 2011). See also Blustein, "The Nine-Day Misadventure of the Most Favored Nations How the WTO's Doha Round Negotiations Went Awry in July 2008": "To make the deal attractive for U.S. exporters of manufactured goods, Schwab and her team had been pressing hard for the inclusion of sectoral negotiations – that is, talks leading to very low tariffs in specific sectors, with chemicals and machinery being the main items of interest. But developing countries had been stiffly resisting that idea, and it was far from clear from the language in the Lamy paper that big developing countries – China, in particular – would participate in the sectorals Washington wanted".

[110] "Doha's Demise", The Washington Post, 29th July, 2008, available at: http://www. washingtonpost.com/wp-dyn/content/article/2008/07/29/AR2008072902110.html (last visited on 22nd February, 2011). See also "Administration Likely to Be Frustrated By China's Leadership on WTO, Other Issues", International Trade Reporter 26 (2009), p. 750.

other countries to expose their farmers to increased competition.[111] Although China had previously been reticent to draw attention to its extensive commitment at accession, some still unfulfilled, at the Doha 2008 negotiations, now China lauded them over the US and EC as the high 'price' of entry into the WTO *already* paid by China.[112] In a related response to the contention that China was failing to bring enough to the table, Chinese WTO Ambassador Sun Zhenyu pointed out that China's average farm tariff was lower than that of EU or Canada's, and that its average manufacturing tariff was only 9%, due to the strict liberalisation commitments that the country accepted at accession.[113] Ambassador Sun went further by noting the expansion of US 'sensitive' farm products tariff rate quotas which paled in comparison to the size of China's tariff rate quotas, often by more than a factor of ten: "Where is the access to the developed countries?", he asked.[114] As Lim and Wang note, Sun's response came as a surprise given China's previous mild and passive approach to the Doha negotiations.[115]

Essentially, the US had hoped that China would 'lead' the developing countries bloc to temper demands (from India in particular) with respect to the Special Safeguard Mechanism in the WTO Agreement on Agriculture (which allow developing countries to impose tariffs above the bound rates in the event that a surge in cheap imports threatens domestic farmers, food supplies or rural development).[116] However, on this point China maintained its alliances with the G-33 developing

---

[111] See Statement by H. E. Ambassador Sun Zhenyu At the Informal Trade Negotiations Committee Meeting, available at: http://wto2.mofcom.gov.cn/aarticle/aboutchina/custom/200807/20080705700132.html (last visited on 22nd February, 2011), posted on 31st July, 2008; "Negotiators Sift Debris" Financial Times Online, 28th July, 2008, quoted by Lim/Wang, China and the Doha Development Agenda, Journal of World Trade 44 (2010) 6, p. 1310.

[112] James, Plenty of Blame for All on Doha Collapse, CATO Institute, 31st July, 2008, available at: http://www.cato.org/pub_display.php?pub_id=9579 (last visited on 22nd February, 2011): "Further intransigence followed from China, which expressed a belief that it had cut its own tariffs by more than enough when it joined the WTO."

[113] See Statement by H. E. Ambassador Sun Zhenyu At the Informal Trade Negotiations Committee Meeting; "G-7 Talks on Special Safeguard Mechanism Inconclusive as Blame Game Heats Up", Bridges Daily Update, International Centre for Trade and Sustainable Development, 29th July, 2008, available at: http://ictsd.org/downloads/2008/07/daily-update-issue-9-template.pdf (last visited on 22nd February, 2011).

[114] "G-7 Talks on Special Safeguard Mechanism Inconclusive as Blame Game Heats Up", Bridges Daily Update, International Centre for Trade and Sustainable Development, 29th July, 2008, available at: http://ictsd.org/downloads/2008/07/daily-update-issue-9-template.pdf (last visited on 22nd February, 2011).

[115] Lim/Wang, China and the Doha Development Agenda, Journal of World Trade 44 (2010) 6, p. 1310.

[116] The two sides of the SSM argument are well summarised by Bhala, Resurrecting the Doha Round: Devilish Details, Grand Themes, and China Too, Texas International Law Journal 45 (2009–2010), pp. 1 et seq. (63): "About one hundred developing countries, led by China and India, continued to demand an SSM remedy they could use with reasonable ease to protect the livelihood of subsistence farmers, with upwards of 700 million of them in China, and 600 million in India. China and India were concerned not only with surges of agricultural products from developed (and even some developing) countries, but also with surges of farm goods subsidized by the United States and EU. Developed countries, led by the United States, rejected that position as an

countries. At the end of the day it is generally believed the inability of the US and India to find common ground on the Special Safeguard Mechanism that brought the 2008 Geneva negotiations to ruin.[117]

Thus, even though China was included at the table, it was not regarded as an equal.[118] It was asked to act as a counter to the representation of India's strong developing country interests. This expectation underestimated China's allegiance to the G-33, and the determined will of the developing countries who have a substantial interest in the result of the trade negotiations.[119]

As the world's largest holder of foreign reserves[120] and the world's second largest economy,[121] China's active stance in the 2008 Doha negotiations is not an isolated incident. China realises the importance of trade to its economy and the stability of its 'harmonious society', and as such has elevated the status of trade relations.[122] With

---

opportunity to scupper all market access gains won through other rules. They also saw the SSM as a device to impede normal trade growth by mischaracterizing such growth as a surge".

[117] "Day 9: Talks collapse despite progress on a list of issues", WTO 2008 News Item, 29th July, 2008, available at: http://www.wto.org/english/news_e/news08_e/meet08_summary_29july_e. htm (last visited on 22nd February, 2011); Grammling, Major setback for WTO's Doha Round: "Mini-Ministerial" failed and future looks dim – a chance for reclaiming its "development dimension"?, FES Geneva, August 2008, available at: http://library.fes.de/pdf-files/bueros/genf/ 05597.pdf (last visited on 22nd February, 2011); Steward, "Tariffs: WTO talks collapse after India and China clash with America over farm products", The Guardian, 30th July, 2008, available at: http://www.guardian.co.uk/world/2008/jul/30/wto.india (last visited on 22nd February, 2011); Parry, "Dismayed powers plea to salvage WTO talks", The Age, 30th July, 2008, available at: http://news.theage.com.au/world/dismayed-powers-plea-to-salvage-wto-talks-20080730-3myb. html (last visited on 22nd February, 2011).

[118] Gao also questions whether China has been elevated to a key player in the WTO. See Gao, Elephant in the Room: Challenges of Integrating China into the WTO System, Asian Journal of WTO and International Health Law and Policy 6 (2011), pp. 141–142.

[119] Statement by H. E. Ambassador Sun Zhenyu At the Informal Trade Negotiations Committee Meeting Sun, stating: "This is a Development Round. They have to remember that this is a Development Round. If [the major developed players] cover all their sensitivities for themselves, and keeping on putting pressures on developing countries, I think we are going nowhere". See also, Statement by H. E. Ambassador Sun Zhenyu at the General Council Meeting, 15th October, 2008, available at: http://wto2.mofcom.gov.cn/aarticle/aboutus/mission/200810/20081005830306.html (last visited on 2nd March, 2011).

[120] "China's Foreign Reserves Top $2tn", BBC News, 15th July, 2009, available at: http://news. bbc.co.uk/2/hi/8151223.stm (last visited on 23rd February, 2011).

[121] "China overtakes Japan as world's second-biggest economy", BBC News, 14th February, 2011, available at: http://www.bbc.co.uk/news/business-12427321 (last visited on 23rd February, 2011).

[122] China has even unveiled an imposing building in Geneva to house its WTO mission. In terms of monetary policy, China has increased efforts to have more power at both the IMF and World Bank. See Miller, "EU Dealt Setback on China at WTO", Wall Street Journal Online, 4th December, 2010, available at: http://online.wsj.com/article/SB1000142405274870398900457565287045 2563284.html (last visited on 23rd February, 2011); for an exploration of China's steps in developing its own capacity in WTO law and disputes, see Hsieh, China's Development of International Economic Law and WTO Legal Capacity Building, Journal of International Economic Law 13 (2010) 4, pp. 997, 1005.

the global financial crisis and ensuing recessions causing tensions in the developed world, some partly blame China's exchange rate policies which allegedly keep the yuan artificially low.

The frequency and retaliatory characteristics of the disputes canvassed below and others have led to murmurs of a trade-war between China and the US.[123] There are also hints that the WTO dispute settlement mechanism is being used to place pressure on China with respect to currency undervaluation. In 2010, President Obama fuelled such sentiment:

> We've got to make sure that countries we're trading with are being fair. I believe in free trade...For example, if China has a currency that's undervalued, that makes our exports more expensive. It makes their imports cheaper. So we've been putting pressure on them to say, you know what, let's make sure that we're not favoring one side or the other in this trade deal.[124]

Importantly, for the thesis of this article, China's reaction has been swift, aggressive (perhaps overly so) and uncompromising. However, some may consider it heartening that, as a salute to western conceptions of the rule of law (a lesson learnt at last by the Chinese?),[125] in economically stressful times, the three key players on the international economic arena are fighting inside WTO "courts" using the vocabulary of a common law as opposed to other less desirable, but only too imaginable, alternatives.

Dispute Settlement

Anti-dumping and countervailing duties – attacking where hardest hit

> On March 30, 2007, the [US] Commerce Department preliminarily decided to apply [anti-dumping and countervailing duties] to coated free-sheet paper imported from China. The

---

[123] See for example, "The Makings of a Trade War With China", Newsweek, 27th September, 2010, available at: http://www.newsweek.com/2010/09/27/the-makings-of-a-trade-war-with-china.html (last visited on 23rd February, 2011); "US rejects 'trade war' with China", Financial Times, 30th September, 2010, available at: http://www.ft.com/cms/s/0/5ebfd848-cc8b-11df-a6c7-00144feab49a.html#axzz1EosihdKL (last visited on 23rd February, 2011); "China's commerce minister: U.S. has the most to lose in a trade war", Washington Post, 22nd March, 2010, available at: http://www.washingtonpost.com/wp-dyn/content/article/2010/03/21/AR2010032101111.html (last visited on 23rd February, 2011).

[124] The White House, Office of the Press Secretary, Remarks by the President at a Town Hall Meeting on the Economy in Racine, Wisconsin, 30th June, 2010, available at: http://www.whitehouse.gov/the-press-office/remarks-president-a-town-hall-meeting-economy-racine-wisconsin.

[125] See generally, Wang, The Rule of Law in China: A Realistic View of the Jurisprudence, the Impact of the WTO, and the Prospects for Future Development, Singapore Journal of Legal Studies 2004, p. 347; Peerenboom, *China's long march toward rule of law*, 2002; M. Mushkat/ R. Mushkat, Economic Growth, Democracy, The Rule Of Law and China's Future, Fordham Journal of International Law 29 (2006), p. 229.

decision altered a 23-year-old policy of not applying the CVD law to NMEs, and it reflects China's economic development.[126]

With this momentous announcement, the US government triggered the Activation phase and final step of China's membership of the WTO. This was certainly not the first time China anti-dumping duties were imposed on China (being a leading target for such duties),[127] but this was the first time it used the WTO dispute settlement forum to challenge the measures. With this move, China completed its transition to 'aggressive legalism'.[128]

In fact, China's recent steps in activating its membership have been largely focused, in the dispute settlement arena, to anti-dumping and countervailing duties. This is not surprising given the profile of China in the WTO: briefly, it is still characterised as a 'non-market economy'[129] by most Members and importing Members are well aware of the continued presence of government subsidies in industry (a reminder of centrally planned policies of the recent past). Further, through its Accession Protocol to the WTO, China accepted that investigating authorities in other WTO Members can apply non-market methodologies in anti-dumping and subsidy-countervail investigations, if 'producers under investigation cannot clearly show that market economy conditions prevail in the industry

---

[126] Truman, "Commerce Department Targets Chinese Subsidies on Coated Free-Sheet Paper", International Trade Update, April 2007, International Trade Administration, available at: http://trade.gov/press/publications/newsletters/ita_0407/china_paper_0407.asp (last visited on 23rd February, 2011).

[127] See Li, Why Is China The World's Number One Anti-Dumping Target?, 2005 United Nations Conference On Trade And Development, China in a Globalizing World, available at: http://www.worldeconomy.org.cn/UploadFiles/200621311594413.pdf#page=89 (last visited on 24th February, 2011); Messerlin, China in the World Trade Organization: Antidumping and Safeguards, World Bank Economic Review 18 (2004) 1, p. 105.

[128] Ji and Huang state the prevailing view in China: "with respect to challenges to Chinese measures, China shall not compromise any more and shall exhaust all possible DSU procedures and thus protect [its] interests; with respect to foreign measures, if there is no change China shall not hesitate to sue the member concerned", Ji/Huang, China's Path to the Center Stage of WTO Dispute Settlement: Challenges and Responses, Global Trade and Customs Journal 5 (2010) 9, p. 370.

[129] This finds its basis in Ad Art. VI:1 para. 2 of GATT 1994. WTO Members recognize that non-market economy countries may need to be treated differently to market economies in anti-dumping cases. Authorities administering antidumping legislation and investigations have generally taken advantage of this provision to reject information provided on costs and prices in countries considered to be non-market economies. See Stoler, Treatment Of China As A Non-Market Economy: Implications For Antidumping And Countervailing Measures And Impact On Chinese Company Operations In The WTO Framework, Presentation to Forum on WTO System & Protectionism: Challenges China Faces After WTO Accession Shanghai WTO Affairs Consultation Center, 1st and 2nd December, 2003, available at: http://www.iit.adelaide.edu.au/docs/Shanghai%20Speech.pdf (last visited on 24th February, 2011).

producing the like product with regard to manufacture, production and sale of that product.'[130]

A few months after the above announcement by the US, and not long before its vocal appearance at the 2008 Doha negotiations, China initiated its second complaint before the DSB: *United States-Preliminary Anti-Dumping and Countervailing Duty Determinations on Coated Free Sheet Paper from China*.[131] This time, unlike its first complaint in 2002,[132] China was not sheltered by numerous well-positioned co-complaints or certainty of outcome. Further, unlike *China-Autos*, *China-IPRs*, *China-AV*, action in the dispute settlement forum was not necessitated by the strategic importance of the industry. The decision to actively defend its coated free sheet paper exports came from the pervasiveness of subsidies in China and the dangers it associated with the trend in countervailing duties.[133]

Before the *US–Paper* dispute went further (it is still under consultation) China broadened the scope of its complaint by challenging the imposition of anti-dumping and countervailing duties on a range of Chinese products.[134] Both these complaints primarily challenged the 'non-market economy' designation of China and the evaluation of domestic prices based on this characterisation. A Panel report on the later, broader complaint, found against China on most counts.[135] However, in line with the bold postures of China in recent years, before the release of the Panel Report, it imposed its own countervailing and anti-dumping duties on grain oriented flat-rolled electrical steel from the US, arguing that the "Buy America" provisions of the *American Recovery and Reinvestment Act* of 2009 and State government procurement laws effectively granted a subsidy.[136] Upon release of the panel report in *US-Certain Products from China*, China immediately announced its intentions to appeal the panel's findings.

In an example of the tit-for-tat behaviour (see disputes with EC on steel fasteners below) that has become familiar in China's trade relations with the EC and US, the

---

[130] See Art. 15(a)(ii) Protocol on the Accession of the People's Republic of China to the WTO, WT/L/432, 23rd November 2001.

[131] United States – Preliminary Anti-Dumping and Countervailing Duty Determinations on Coated Free Sheet Paper from China, 14th September, 2007, DS368.

[132] United States – Definitive Safeguard Measures on Imports of Certain Steel Products, 26th March, 2002, DS252.

[133] Hufbauer, Three US-China Trade Disputes, Peterson Institute for International Economics, 2nd May, 2007, Note prepared for "The China Balance Sheet in 2007 and Beyond Conference" (Center for Strategic and International Studies and Peterson Institute for International Economics), available at: http://www.iie.com/publications/papers/paper.cfm?ResearchID=749 (last visited on 23rd February, 2011).

[134] United States – Definitive Anti-Dumping and Countervailing Duties on Certain Products from China, 19th September, 2008, DS379.

[135] Ibid.

[136] "China levies anti-dumping tariffs on US and Russian electric steel", China People's Daily, 13th April, 2010, available at: http://english.peopledaily.com.cn/90001/90778/90861/6949178.html (last visited on 23rd February, 2011).

US initiated dispute settlement proceedings challenging the Chinese duties on US steel.[137] In response, China immediately launched another complaint against the US safeguard measure raising tariffs on tyres imported from China.[138] What is startling is that China's request for consultations occurred a mere 3 days after the US announced the imposition of the safeguard measures.

The *US–Tyres* dispute concerned substantial tariff hikes applied to imports from China of certain passenger vehicle and light truck tyres into the US. The complaint focused on the provisions in the Chinese Accession Protocol to the WTO and, in particular, put the operation of the Accession Protocol's 'Transitional Product Specific Safeguard Mechanism' before the Panel for the first time. This mechanism allows WTO Members to impose safeguard measures on imports from China alone, with less stringent requirements than those applicable to safeguards measures under the WTO Agreement on Safeguards. Although the Panel ruled in favour of the US, the Chinese complaint showed a willingness to challenge a seemingly permissible use of the WTO-plus obligations accepted by China at accession. In its case, China exposed the political pressures that had led to the Obama administration's decision to apply the measures. The request for these measures came not from the US tyre industry (which had voluntarily shifted its manufacturing operations to China) but from a powerful labour union, the United Steelworkers.

Interestingly, even if ultimately unsuccessfully, China argued that the measures, which were included into Accession Protocol to protect 'domestic producers from market disruption', were in fact not being applied to protect US tyre manufactures, but rather to be *seen* to protect jobs in a recession. The questions of domestic politics, globalisation and business concerns that faced the Panel's ultimate finding are worth setting out here:

> 7.9. ....[T]his case involved the invocation of a mechanism designed to protect a domestic industry that did not want that protection and by its own actions had precipitated the events that were now being invoked to justify the application of the transitional product-specific safeguard mechanism of China's Protocol of Accession. Arguably, it explained too why the investigation had been initiated by a labour union, a body that was concerned with job losses resulting from this transfer of manufacturing capacity to China, and not by the domestic producers themselves. Thus, the Panel was aware that this aspect of the case raised the question of the suitability or relevance of safeguard mechanisms in the context of "outsourcing" and "globalization", matters of considerable systemic interest to WTO Members.
>
> 7.10. Having stated this important contextual background, the Panel was also aware that the issues before it involved the interpretation of the provisions of the transitional product-specific safeguard mechanism and that it was the task of the Panel to do that. It was not for the Panel to seek to recalibrate what the WTO Members had agreed to in the negotiations that led to the accession of China to the WTO in the light of what the Panel might perceive as changing economic circumstances that perhaps had not been considered when the

---

[137] China – Countervailing and Anti-Dumping Duties on Grain Oriented Flat-rolled Electrical Steel from the United States, DS414, 15th September, 2010.

[138] United States – Measures Affecting Imports of Certain Passenger Vehicle and Light Truck Tyres from China, DS399, 14th September, 2009.

Protocol was negotiated. That remains the prerogative of the WTO Members themselves. Nevertheless, the Panel felt that it was important to set this background out as it informed the understanding of the Panel of the arguments made before it in this case.

7.320. The Panel was confronted with the fact that the majority of the USITC and the dissenting commissioners drew precisely the opposite conclusions on the issue of business strategy. The majority took the view that the strategy to reduce U.S. production and locate production in China was itself a response to increased imports and thus it was not an alternative cause that prevented the increasing imports from China to be a significant cause. The dissenting commissioners took the view that the business strategy of relocating production to China was an independent business strategy that began before imports were increasing.[139]

The series of complaints and appeals that Chinas has undertaken in the last 3 years certainly dismisses any complacence that a trading partner may have had in acting undesirably towards Chinese trade interests. As commentators have noticed, and the ever ready litigation arm of the Chinese has confirmed, 'the big message from China to the United States is think twice, think three times before repeating this kind of relief because if you do this again, we are going to hit you again.'[140]

Unsurprisingly, China has already announced its intention to appeal the panel report in *US–Tyres*. Such bravado was not displayed by the US, in its loss over poultry imports from China. In *US–Certain Measures Affecting Imports of Poultry from China*, China challenged Section 727 of the US *Omnibus Appropriation Act 2009* which banned the importation of Chinese poultry on the basis of health and safety concerns under the SPS Agreement (in the aftermath of the avian flu), even though the measure was due to expire 5 months after the request for consultations.[141] Therefore, by the time the panel report found in China's favour in September 2010, the offending provision had already expired. However, China strategically imposed countervailing duties on US chicken imports, ostensibly as retaliation for the US maintaining the ban on its poultry despite the health threat no longer being valid.

A few months later, China successfully challenged the EC's improper application of anti-dumping duties in *EC–Definitive Anti-Dumping Measures on Certain Iron or Steel Fasteners from China*.[142] In a case that required China to argue against minute details of the procedural application of anti-dumping duties, China demonstrated that it had indeed learned its lesson from previous cases dealing with similar subject matter.

---

[139] United States – Measures Affecting Imports of Certain Passenger Vehicle and Light Truck Tyres from China, WT/DS399/R, 13th December, 2010.

[140] Hufbauer, Peterson Institute, quoted in McDonald, "China: U.S. Tire Tariffs Violate WTO Rules", Huffington Post, 14th September, 2009.

[141] United States – Certain Measures Affecting Imports of Poultry from China, DS392, 17th April, 2009.

[142] EC – Definitive Anti-Dumping Measures on Certain Iron or Steel Fasteners from China, DS397, 31st July, 2009.

However, perhaps in a display of over-aggressiveness, before the Panel gave its verdict, China imposed provisional anti-dumping duties on certain iron or steel fasteners imports from the EC, through a regulation that applied "where a country (region) discriminatorily imposes anti-dumping measures on the exports from the People's Republic of China, China may, on the basis of actual situations, take corresponding measures against that country (region)".[143] Although wisely origin-neutral, the Chinese Notice was clearly aimed at the EC's Council Regulation No. 91/2009 (contested in China's *EC–Steel Fasteners* complaint of July 2009), which imposed a definitive anti-dumping duty on imports of certain iron or steel fasteners originating in China. The result is another tit-for-tat dispute launched by the EC against this Chinese duty.[144]

As all sides are flexing their litigation muscles, China had already launched another complaint on anti-dumping duties imposed by the EC, regarding foot-wear,[145] before the EC had a chance to complain about the Chinese countervailing duty on steel fasteners. Both (DS407, DS 405) are currently before a WTO Panel. While it is unclear for how long the tit-for-tat filing of complaints will continue, there can be no doubt that 'China has transformed itself from being a reluctant player into an aggressive litigant in WTO dispute settlement activities.'[146]

Concluding Analysis: Aggressive Legalism or Plain Aggressive?

...observe developments soberly, maintain our position, meet challenges calmly, hide our capacities, and bide our time.[147]

This oft-quoted Deng Xiaoping principle from 1989 may offer some insight into the gradient of activity that has characterised China's WTO membership as canvassed above. It appears that China has strategically mapped its participation in interna-tional trade to fit this guidance. China's recent behaviour indicates its belief that its time has now come, and that it is now embarking on a path of aggressive legalism.

After initially appearing mistrustful and even frightened of the WTO dispute settlement process, China eventually used the next few years to watch and learn

---

[143] Ministry of Commerce of the People's Republic of China, Notice No. 115, 2009, see Request for Consultations by the European Union, China – Provisional Anti-Dumping Duties on Certain Iron and Steel Fasteners from the European Union, WT/DS407/1, May 2010.

[144] China – Provisional Anti-Dumping Duties on Certain Iron and Steel Fasteners from the European Union, DS407, 7th May, 2010.

[145] EC – Anti-Dumping Measures on Certain Footwear from China, DS405, 4th February, 2010.

[146] Gao, Elephant in the Room: Challenges of Integrating China into the WTO System, Asian Journal of WTO and International Health Law and Policy 6 (2011), p. 153.

[147] Foot, Chinese strategies in a US-hegemonic global order, International Affairs 82 (2006), pp. 77, 84.

before gaining 'substantial experience and knowledge' in allowing claims to reach the panel and appellate stage of dispute settlement.[148]

China has a good track-record of compliance,[149] and perhaps even more importantly, after decades of intransigence China has demonstrated a willingness to abide by international law and to the decisions of neutral international arbitrators. However, its recent tit-for-tat disputes with the US and EU, display aggression more so than legalism. Undoubtedly, there is a growing element of technical maturity in China's use WTO law and the dispute settlement process in the Activation stage, compared to its initial attempts at the Consolidation stage, but there appears to be a lack of diplomatic restraint.

That being the case, one cannot be certain that China's use of aggressive legalism will morph into mere aggression. In fact, it is unlikely as the Chinese government must realise that such a change would damage not only their political standing in the multilateral trading system but also (and perhaps more importantly) their own economic prospects. With that in mind, the likely course of action is for China to increasingly assert itself at the diplomatic level and throughout the Doha negotiations while wholeheartedly defending its interests both as a shield and a sword in WTO dispute settlement. China learned many lessons over the course of its 15 years of accession negotiations and tough first decade of WTO membership, including that the WTO, a self-proclaimed 'member driven organisation' will accommodate politics, domestic interests and strong stances by its more powerful Members – it has done so with the EU and US, and it can do the same for China.

---

[148] Ji/Huang, China's Path to the Center Stage of WTO Dispute Settlement: Challenges and Responses, Global Trade and Customs Journal 5 (2010) 9, p. 367.

[149] See, e.g., China–Auto Parts and China–IPRs, discussed above.

China's WTO Accession Revisited: Achievements and Challenges in Chinese Intellectual Property Law Reform

Andrea Wechsler

Introduction: China's Long March Toward Intellectual Property Protection[1]

The Long March[2] represents one of the most significant turning points in modern Chinese history.[3] Building upon this significance, the Long March-metaphor has found its way into the assessment of Chinese law reform efforts and achievements.[4]

The accession of the People's Republic of China (China) to the World Trade Organisation (WTO) in 2001 is often regarded as the culmination of China's "open door"-policy[5] and, thus, China's Long March towards its legal, political and economic integration into the international trade community.[6] This integration is closely linked with China's Long March towards intellectual property (IP) protection in the larger framework of Chinese reform efforts towards a law-based order. Recent years have seen countless legislative efforts to improve intellectual property rights (IPR) protection, adjudication and enforcement. Together with bilateral and multilateral pressures on China and the external impetus provided by WTO accession, it is the economic objectives of the Chinese government and the commercial imperatives of its domestic knowledge industry which have motivated Chinese IP law reform.

---

[1] All online resources were last visited on 20th February, 2011.

[2] 长征, chángzhēng.

[3] Sun, *The Long March: The True History of Communist China's Founding Myth*, 2008.

[4] See Peerenboom, *China's Long March Toward Rule of Law*, 2002.

[5] 门户开放政策, ménhù kāifàng zhèngcè.

[6] Hutschenreiter/Zhang, China's Quest for Innovation-Driven Growth – the Policy Dimension, Journal of Industry, Competition and Trade 7 (2007), pp. 245 et seq. (245–246).

A. Wechsler (✉)
Max Weber Fellow, European University Institute, Florence, Italy, and Affiliated Research Fellow, Max Planck Institute for Intellectual Property and Competition Law, Munich, Germany
e-mail: andrea.wechsler@ip.mpg.de

C. Herrmann and J.P. Terhechte (eds.), *European Yearbook of International Economic Law (EYIEL), Vol. 3 (2012)*, European Yearbook of International Economic Law 3, DOI 10.1007/978-3-642-23309-8_4, © Springer-Verlag Berlin Heidelberg 2012

With 10 years having passed since WTO accession, the time is ripe for an assessment of China's Long March towards a modern IP law regime. The following research therefore discusses the role of WTO accession as driver for IP law reform in China with reference to historical determinants of IP reform, to the role of further bilateral and multilateral external pressures, and with reference to China's larger innovation agenda. It further assesses achievements and challenges of 30 years of Chinese IP law reform before providing concluding remarks on China's Long March Forward towards IP policy, law and enforcement.

Drivers of Chinese Intellectual Property Law Reform

Chinese IP law reform was influenced by a variety of determinants: social, cultural and historical attitudes, bilateral and multilateral external pressures, the prospect of WTO accession and China's larger innovation agenda. The following section discusses the role of WTO accession as driver of Chinese IP law reform in the light of alternative reform determinants. It will further demonstrate that recent policy shifts in China are the first omens of China's larger innovation agenda and, thus, of the Chinese emergence as potent force in reshaping the global IP landscape according to their own political, economic and social interests.

Historical Perspectives

Social, cultural and historical attitudes have consistently been cited as explanation for the deficiencies of IP protection in modern China.[7] In recent years, however, the number of voices has increased which have pointed to a long history of familiarity of China's culture with copyright and trademarks.[8] In the light of these divergent views, the question arises as to the role and relevance of Chinese IP history for the present state of IP protection in China.

IP regulation in China does not have as long a history as IP regulation in Western societies.[9] For the most part of its history, China has not actively promoted patent law or any other intellectual property right.[10] Even though Chinese technological

---

[7] Alford, *To Steal a Book is an Elegant Offense. Intellectual Property Law in Chinese Civilization*, 1995.

[8] Shao, The Global Debates on Intellectual Property: What if China is not a Born Pirate?, Intellectual Property Quarterly (2010) 4, pp. 341 et seq. (354).

[9] First records of a copyright case dates back to the year AD 567, cf. Bainbridge, *Intellectual Property*, (7th ed.) 2009, p. 29.

[10] It has been argued that Chinese tradition – though insisting on Confucian traditions – has ignored science and technology while stressing humanities and politics which has proven inimical to the development of patent law, see Wang, The Chinese Tradition Inimical to the Patent Law, Northwestern Journal of International Law and Business 14 (1993) 15, pp. 15 et seq. (16).

discoveries and inventions had been far more advanced than those in Europe in the fifteenth century,[11] China has not been a major instigator to any revolution in science ever since. It was only in the Maoist era that a strong commitment to the development of science and technology (S&T)[12] led to discussions about the need for patent legislation with socialist rationales.[13] However, due to the ideological grounding of the Chinese Communist Party (CCP) in Marxism-Leninism, this commitment to S&T has never translated into endeavours to enact a modern patent law system.[14] Rather, commercial profits were scorned by socialist tradition and Confucian morality so that patent legislation degenerated into an instrument for state control over patents without providing adequate non-material or financial rewards to inventors.[15]

Comparably in copyright law, it was only the desire of Chinese emperors to control the dissemination of information from the fourth century onwards that may be compared to the origin of copyright law in Western society.[16] After the invention of the printing press, for instance, Chinese emperors required private printers to submit works to government officials for prepublication review.[17] However, apart from this parallel in the development of Chinese and Western copyright law the concept of having a property in one's work had very little counterpart in China.[18] The first formal copyright law in China was only enacted in 1910 just one year before the overthrow of the Qing Dynasty[19] with the consequence that it was never fully implemented.[20] Even though both the warlords government and the subsequent

---

[11] Needham, *Science and Civilization in China*, 1965, p. 4.

[12] Goldman/Simon, *Science and Technology in Post-Maoist China*, 1989, p. 7.

[13] Sidel, Copyright, Trademark and Patent Law in the People's Republic of China, Texas International Law Journal 21 (1986), pp. 259 et seq. (259).

[14] Sidel, Copyright, Trademark and Patent Law in the People's Republic of China, Texas International Law Journal 21 (1986), pp. 259 et seq. (278).

[15] Wang/Zhang, *Introduction to Chinese Law*, 1997, p. 448; Hsia/Haun, Laws of the People's Republic of China on Industrial and Intellectual Property, Law and Contemporary Problems 38 (1973), p. 276.

[16] Zheng/Pendleton, *Chinese Intellectual Property and Technology Transfer Law*, 1987, p. 89; Zheng/Pendleton, *Copyright Law in China*, 1991, p. 17, discussing the enactment of China's first official copyright law in 1910; see also Alford, Don't Stop Thinking about Yesterday: Why There Was No Indigenous Counterpart to Intellectual Property Law in Imperial China, Journal of Chinese Law 7 (1993) 3, pp. 3 et seq. (7–34) on the development of China's system of copyright through its imperial history.

[17] See Alford, *To Steal a Book is an Elegant Offense. Intellectual Property Law in Chinese Civilization*, 1995, pp. 13–17, see also Wei, Der Urheberrechtsschutz in China mit Hinweisen auf das Deutsche Recht, 1994, pp. 1–2, for a historical account of copyright and the invention of the printing press in China.

[18] See, however, counter-argument by Shao, The Global Debates on Intellectual Property: What if China is not a Born Pirate?, Intellectual Property Quarterly (2010) 4, pp. 341 et seq. (354).

[19] 清朝 (qīng cháo).

[20] Zheng/Pendleton, *Chinese Intellectual Property and Technology Transfer Law*, 1987, p. 17; Schulze/Xu, Das Urheberrecht in der Volksrepublik China, Gewerblicher Rechtsschutz und Urheberrecht Internationaler Teil (1995) 7, p. 548 (548), see Wei Shi, *Intellectual Property in the Global Trading System, EU-China Perspective*, 2008, pp. 4–5.

Guomindang government reinstated the statute in 1915 and 1928, respectively, said statute never sufficed to induce Chinese domestic awareness for copyright law issues.[21] Thereafter, awareness-building for copyright issues happened through the lens of Maoism. The CCP overturned all existing copyright and publication laws[22] with Mao stipulating that the creation of cultural expression was to serve the overall interest of society.[23] This overturn culminated eventually in the abolition of all administrative orders and internal regulations governing plagiarism and remuneration in the Cultural Revolution.[24]

While Chinese rationales of IP protection were, thus, at most rudimentary or ideology-driven until the 1980s, foreign pressures on China to provide for effective IP protection took their inception with the introduction of IPR provisions into a series of unequal treaties at the beginning of the twentieth century.[25] The *Treaty of 1901*, the *Renewed Treaty of Commerce and Navigation between Britain and China of 1902*, the *Treaty of Commerce and Navigation between the United States and China of 1902* and later the *Treaty of Amity, Commerce and Navigation between the United States and China* all required the Qing and the Nationalist Governments to adopt and transplant Western-style IP laws into China.[26] The enactment of IP law in China has therefore been heavily influenced by Western concepts of IP protection. It was only from 1949 onwards, that China has increasingly explored how to "localize" its IP laws, first, in support of Maoist thinking and, subsequently, in supports of its transition from a planned economy to a Socialist market economy.[27]

In conclusion, occurrences of IP concepts in China were at most rudimentary when external pressures for the adoption of a Western-style IP protection system began to be exerted in the last years of the Qing Dynasty.[28] And they were not any more prominent when Maoist thinking left its imprint on IP protection in China. In

---

[21] Lazar, Protecting Ideas and Ideals: Copyright Law in the People's Republic of China, Law and Policy in International Business 27 (1996), p. 1185.

[22] Löber, Urheberrecht und Verlagswesen in der Volksrepublik China, Gewerblicher Rechtsschutz und Urheberrecht Internationaler Teil (1976) 8, p. 388; see also Guo, Entwicklung und Perspektiven des geistigen Eigentums in der Volksrepublik China, Gewerblicher Rechtsschutz und Urheberrecht Internationaler Teil (1997) 12, pp. 949 et seq. (955).

[23] Mao, *Quotations from Chairman Mao Tse-Tung*, 1967, p. 23.

[24] 无产阶级文化大革命 (wúchǎnjiējí wénhuàdàgémìng, Cultural Revolution). See Lazar, Protecting Ideas and Ideals: Copyright Law in the People's Republic of China, Law and Policy in International Business 27 (1996), pp. 1185 et seq. (1187).

[25] Zhong, 版权法浅谈 (bǎnquán fǎ qiǎn tán, *A Basic Discussion of Copyright*), 1982, pp. 103–104.

[26] Ling, 中美知识产权冲突与合作的影响 (zhōngměi zhīshi chǎnquán chōngtū yǔ hézuò de yǐngxiǎng, The Impact of Conflicts and Co-Operations Concerning Intellectual Property Rights between China and the United States), 2005, p. 215.

[27] Wu, Intellectual Property Law as China Moves Toward an Innovation-Oriented Society, in: Cai/Wang, *China's Journey toward the Rule of Law. Legal Reform 1978–2008*, 2010, pp. 339 et seq. (444).

[28] 清朝 (qīng cháo) from 1644 to 1912; Ganea/Pattloch/Heath et al. (eds.), *Intellectual Property Law in China*, 2005, p. 205.

consequence, Chinese tradition and its social, cultural and historical attitudes can hardly be held responsible for deficiencies in modern Chinese IP law and enforcement. History has rather created dogmatic and conceptual tensions through the transplantation of Western-style IPRs – both common law and civil law – into the Chinese legal system[29] and through the ideological distortions of Western IP rationales under Maoist rule. History has further stirred an inherently deep Chinese scepticism about the further adoption of Western IP laws in China which has had a noticeable influence on Chinese IP cooperation until today.[30]

External Pressures

External pressures have not only influenced Chinese IP law development in the early twentieth century but also from the early post-Maoist reform period to the present day.

The first phase of post-Maoist IP law reform was essentially triggered by the *1979 Agreement on Trade Relations*[31] between China and the United States (U.S.), which provided for equivalent treatment of copyright, patent, and trademark protection in both countries. Furthermore, the Agreement entailed provisions relating to the acknowledgement of the importance of IP protection and provisions containing a pledge to enforce or enact patent, trademark and copyright laws for their respective countries.[32]

Thirteen years later, in 1992, the U.S. and China signed their first bilateral trade-related IP agreement, the *Memorandum of Understanding on the Protection of Intellectual Property* (*Memorandum of Understanding*),[33] which required China to revise its patent law, to accede to the *Berne Convention*[34] and the *Geneva Phonograms Convention,*[35] and to enact a law against unfair competition as

---

[29] Zhu, 从麻将规则的本土性看中国知识产权法移植, (cóng májiàng guīzé de běntǔ xìng kàn zhōngguó zhīshi chǎnquán fǎ yízhí, Legal Transplant of Intellectual Property Law in China: Reflections from the Indigenous Nature of the Rule of Majang), Legal Daily, 2nd December, 2004.

[30] Liu, The Tough Reality of Copyright Piracy: A Case Study of the Music Industry in China, Cardozo Arts and Entertainment Law Journal 27 (2010), pp. 621 et seq. (623).

[31] Agreement on Trade Relations, 7th July, 1979, U.S.-P.R.C., 31 U.S.T. 4651.

[32] See Art. VI of the Agreement on Trade Relations, 7th July, 1979, U.S.-P.R.C., 31 U.S.T. 4651.

[33] U.S.-P.R.C. 34 I.L.M. 676 (1995), see also Zhang, Intellectual Property Law Enforcement in China: Trade Issues; Policies and Practices, Fordham Intellectual Property, Media & Entertainment Law Journal 8 (1997), pp. 63 et seq. (73).

[34] The Berne Convention for the Protection of Literary and Artistic Works, 1886, 331 U.N.T.S. 217.

[35] Convention for the Protection of Producers of Phonograms against unauthorized Duplication of Their Phonograms, adopted on 29th October, 1971, 25 U.S.T. 309.

provided for in Article 10bis of the *Paris Convention*.[36] China fully complied with the requirements of the *Memorandum of Understanding* by passing the 1992 Revision of the *Patent Law of the P.R. China*,[37] the 1992 *Implementing International Copyright Treaties Provisions*,[38] and in 1993 the *Law Against Unfair Competition*.[39]

However, these reform steps did not suffice to satisfy the U.S. expectations in the field of IP enforcement. Thus, the U.S. further resorted to the threat of trade sanctions pursuant to the Special 301 provisions of the U.S. trade law in 1994 and 1995.[40] It threatened China with the imposition of a 100% duty on Chinese imports,[41] with the revocation of China's most-favored nation status and it dispatched a U.S. carrier group in response to the Chinese military manoeuvres during the 1996 Taiwan Straits crisis.[42] The conflicts were resolved in the *1995 Agreement Regarding Intellectual Property Rights*[43] and the *1996 Agreement* that included a *Report on Chinese Enforcement Actions* and an *Annex on Intellectual Property Rights Enforcement and Market Access Accord*.[44]

---

[36] The Paris Convention for the Protection of Industrial Property, 1883, 21 U.S.T. 1583, 828 U.N. T.S. 305.

[37] 中华人民共和国专利法 (zhōnghuá rénmín gòng hé guó zhuānlì fǎ), 1984, 1992, 2000, 2008, Gazette of the State Council (国务院公报 (guówùyuàn gōngbào)), 2000, No. 30, p. 9, 2008 revision: China Law & Practice (February 2009), pp. 60–74; English translation, CCH Business Regulation 11-600 (English-Chinese); 2008 revision: China Law & Practice (February 2009), pp. 60–74. See also Steinmann, *Grundzüge des chinesischen Patentrechts*, 1992.

[38] 实施国际著作权条约的规定 (shíshī guójì zhùzuò quán tiáoyuē de guīdìng), Gazette of the State Council (国务院公报 (guówùyuàn gōngbào)) 1992, No. 105; English translation, China L. Foreign Bus. (CCH) P 11-703 (1992).

[39] 中华人民共和国反不正当竞争法 (zhōnghuá rénmín gòng hé guó fǎn bù zhèngdāng jìngzhēng fǎ), adopted at the 3rd Session of the Standing Committee of the 8th NPC on 2nd September, 1993, Gazette of the State Council (国务院公报 (guówùyuàn gōngbào)), 1993, p. 986; English translation, CCH Business Regulation 16-640 (English-Chinese).

[40] Special 301 – based on Special 301 of the 1974 Trade Act, enacted 3rd January, 1975, Pub. L. No. 98-618, § 182, as added by Omnibus Trade and Competitiveness Act of 1988, Pub. L. No. 100-418, § 1303(b), 102 Stat. 1107 (23rd August, 1988 (codified as amended at 19 U.S.C.A. § 2242) – requires the United States Trade Representative to notify Congress of priority foreign countries that fail to adequately protect US intellectual property rights and to undertake all required remedial measures within a mandated period, available at: http://www.access.gpo.gov/uscode/title19/chapter12_.html.

[41] Zhang, Intellectual Property Law Enforcement in China: Trade Issues; Policies and Practices, Fordham Intellectual Property, Media & Entertainment Law Journal 8 (1997), pp. 63 et seq. (74).

[42] Mertha, *The Politics of Piracy*, 2005, p. 6.

[43] Agreement Regarding Intellectual Property Rights, 26th February, 1995, U.S.-P.R.C., 34 I.L.M. (1995).

[44] Li, Evaluation of the Sino-American Intellectual Property Agreements: A Judicial Approach to Solving the Local Protectionism Problem, Columbia Journal of Asian Law 10 (1996), pp. 391 et seq. (424) on the Evaluation of the Sino-American IP Agreements.

Despite 30 years of noticeable achievements of Chinese IP law reform, these external pressures have continued to the present day. Recent examples are evident in China's appearance on the Priority Watchlist of the 2010 Special 301 Report[45] and the filing of a WTO complaint by the U.S. which was to become WTO case 362 *China – Measures Affecting the Protection and Enforcement of Intellectual Property Rights* (DS362).[46] This gradual shift of U.S. IPR policy from the utilization of Special 301 reviews to enforcement efforts in WTO dispute resolution panels[47] testifies to the changing nature of these external pressures in recent years. The filing of the WTO complaint DS362 is widely considered to represent the "mounting domestic dissatisfaction with China's role in the global trading system and China's staunch resistance to U.S. pressure to reform its legal regime."[48] Thus, the latest drumbeat of U.S. pressures on China signals a turning point in U.S.–Chinese IP relations: China has reached such a powerful position in the global trading regime that it could, for the first time in history, put equal or even greater economic pressure on the U.S.

However, external pressures have not been limited to the U.S.. This first WTO litigation on IP enforcement must be considered against the backdrop of the ongoing global trends in TRIPS-plus IP enforcement[49] and, in particular, against the backdrop of G8 statements and the 2007 announcement of the U.S., the European Union (EU) and Japan to negotiate an *Anti-Counterfeiting Trade Agreement* (ACTA).[50] In consequence, external pressure on China is continuing albeit changing in strategy, focus, and emphasis.

In conclusion, the Sino-U.S. IP battles of the 1980s and early 1990s – and the still ongoing external pressures – demonstrate the extent to which external pressure and coercion have contributed to the reinstitution of IP protection as part of the new legal system.[51] At the same time, however, it is widely recognized that external

---

[45] 2010 Special 301 Report, 30th April, 2010, p. 19, available at: http://www.ustr.gov/webfm_send/1906.

[46] Report of the Panel, WT/DS362/R, 26th January, 2009; Harris, The Honeymoon is Over: The U.S.-China WTO Intellectual Property Complaint, Fordham International Law Journal 32 (2008), pp. 96 et seq. (99).

[47] As of August 2008, the U.S. has brought nineteen IPR cases to WTO panels and prevailed (or settled without litigation) in all cases, cf. LaCroix/Konan, Intellectual Property Rights in China: The Changing Political Economy of Chinese-American Interests, Working Paper (2002) 02-1, p. 31.

[48] Harris, The Honeymoon is Over: The U.S.-China WTO Intellectual Property Complaint, Fordham International Law Journal 32 (2008), pp. 96 et seq. (98).

[49] Li, The Agreement on Trade-Related Aspects of Intellectual Property Rights Flexibilities on Intellectual Property Enforcement: The World Trade Organization Panel Interpretation of China-Intellectual Property Enforcement of Criminal Measures and Its Implications, The Journal of World Intellectual Property 13 (2010) 4, pp. 639 et seq. (640).

[50] See for the final ACTA text http://trade.ec.europa.eu/doclib/docs/2010/december/tradoc_147079.pdf.

[51] Feng, *Intellectual Property in Chinua*, (2nd ed.) 2003, pp. 3–4.

pressures are not and should not be the key to continued development of Chinese IP policies.[52]

WTO-Accession

Alongside external pressures it was the prospect of joining the international trade circle through membership in the WTO with its associated *Agreement on Trade-Related Aspects of Intellectual Property Rights* (TRIPS)[53] which constituted one of the strongest forces shaping Chinese IP policy to adopt Western legal rules.[54]

As early as the 1970s, Western countries had sought to revise the existing IP conventions while gradually shifting the efforts to the *General Agreement on Tariffs and Trade* (GATT) and Uruguay Round negotiations when negotiations at the *World Intellectual Property Organization* (WIPO) had come to a standstill.[55] On 20 December 1991, the *Draft Final Act Embodying the Results of the Uruguay Round of Multilateral Trade Negotiations*[56] including the text of the TRIPS Agreement was presented.[57] On 1 January 1995 the WTO began its operation and the TRIPS Agreement went into effect with the objective to *"promote effective and adequate protection of intellectual property rights, and to ensure that measures and procedures to enforce intellectual property rights do not themselves become barriers to legitimate trade."*[58] TRIPS not only established minimum protection levels but also provided for the application of other international IP agreements, the enforcement of such internationally recognized IPRs, the settlement of disputes over IPRs between WTO members, and special transition arrangements for selected countries.[59]

The *TRIPS Agreement* entailed a number of obligations that had not yet been met by Chinese IP protection at that time. Chinese law had, for instance, not yet

---

[52] Yu, From Pirates to Partners (Episode II): Protecting Intellectual Property in Post-WTO China, American University Law Review 55 (2006), pp. 901 et seq. (905).

[53] *The Agreement on Trade-Related Aspects of Intellectual Property Rights* (TRIPS), adopted in Marrakesh on April 15, 1994, 33 ILM 81 (1994).

[54] Bird, Defending Intellectual Property Rights in the Bric Economies, Am. Bus. L.J. 43 (2006), p. 317 (317).

[55] Dessler, China's Intellectual Property Protection: Prospects for Achieving International Standards, Fordham Int'l L.J. 19 (1995), p. 181 (185).

[56] Gatt Doc. No. MTN.TNC/W/FA (1991).

[57] Dessler, China's Intellectual Property Protection: Prospects for Achieving International Standards, Fordham Int'l L.J. 19 (1995), p. 181 (186).

[58] Preamble, *The Agreement on Trade-Related Aspects of Intellectual Property Rights* (TRIPS), adopted in Marrakesh on April 15, 1994, 33 ILM 81 (1994).

[59] KIM, The World Trade Organization Dispute Settlement System: China – Measures Affecting the Protection and Enforcement of Intellectual Property Rights, 23 N.Y. Int'l L. Rev. 83 (2010), p. 83 (103).

extended the *Berne Convention*[60] protection to computer software, Chinese laws were silent on the protection of trade secrets,[61] and Chinese enforcement standards were not yet TRIPS-compatible.[62] Even though the adoption of the *TRIPS Agreement*, thus, imposed numerous obligations on Chinese IP law reform, the Chinese government recognized the benefits from WTO membership: the opportunity to disable trade sanctions and the annual renewals of most-favored-nation status as U. S. policy levers, the gradual reduction of country quotas on textiles, the prospect of secure markets, and the appropriate political leverage for the Chinese government to continue its reform and privatization program.[63] These benefits acted as indirect pressure on the Chinese government to sign up to the *TRIPS Agreement* even though it was widely recognized that the establishment of TRIPS standards at that time were not perfectly suited to the level of economic development in China.[64] Eventually, however, China's accession to the WTO in 2001, and thus the *TRIPS Agreement*, marked one of the most important milestones along the IP reform path of the country.

This period of accession to the WTO is, however, also marked by a rising awareness of Chinese politicians and businessmen about the benefits of IP protection.[65] Chinese officials even argue that the development of the Chinese legal IP system occurred entirely independently of external pressures.[66] Support for this view is provided by Maskus and Dougherty who reported that, in the 1990s, piracy caused larger losses in the Chinese entertainment, publishing and consumer goods industries than in prominent Western firms such as Microsoft or Disney.[67] It was then argued that additional pressure from Chinese enterprises on the Chinese government together with the high per capita income growth in the creative

---

[60] The Berne Convention for the Protection of Literary and Artistic Works, 1886, 331 U.N.T.S. 217.

[61] Dessler, China's Intellectual Property Protection: Prospects for Achieving International Standards, Fordham Int'l L.J. 19 (1995), p. 181 (233).

[62] Especially relating to procedures for remedying acts of infringement, written decisions and evidence, damages and injunctive relief, cf. Dessler, China's Intellectual Property Protection: Prospects for Achieving International Standards, Fordham Int'l L.J. 19 (1995), p. 181 (233).

[63] Reichman, Intellectual Property in the Twenty-First Century: Will the Developing Countries Lead or Follow?, 46 Hous. L. Rev. 1115 (2009), 26, p. 1116 (1119).

[64] Wu, Intellectual Property Right System: Under the Background of International Change and Chinese Development. 法学研究 (fǎxué yánjiū), (2009) 2, pp. 1 et seq. (3); Wu, 后TRIPs时代知识产权制度的变革与中国的应对方略. 法商研究 (hòu TRIPS shídài zhīshi chǎnquán zhìdù de biàngé yǔ zhōngguó de yìngduì fāng lvè. fǎ shāng yánjiū) (2005) 5, pp. 3 et seq. (20).

[65] LaCroix/Konan, Intellectual Property Rights in China: The Changing Political Economy of Chinese-American Interests, Working Paper (2002) 02-1.

[66] Mertha, *The Politics of Piracy*, 2005, p. 3

[67] Maskus/Dougherty, Intellectual Property Rights and Economic Development in China, NBR Regional Studies (1998), p. 1 (1–30), see also LaCroix/Konan, Intellectual Property Rights in China: The Changing Political Economy of Chinese-American Interests, Working Paper (2002) 02-1, for an account that Chinese products, such as Hongtashan cigarettes and Maotai liquor, have repeatedly been prominent targets of counterfeiting.

industries somewhat replaced the external U.S. pressures on the Chinese government and, therefore, partly explained the cooling down of the U.S.–Chinese IPR disputes in the 1990s.[68]

A final conclusion on the force of external pressures as compared to intrinsically motivated IP law reform is rather difficult to draw as IPR policy processes in China are highly complex.[69] It has nevertheless been shown that, in this period of WTO accession, the U.S. and China have moved closer "from conflict to cooperation over intellectual property rights."[70] This cooperation entailed not only the proliferation and improvement of formal legal protection for intellectual property but also the creation of a political, organization and social foundation for the effective enforcement of IPRs on the Chinese part.

The Chinese Move Toward an Innovation Economy

In recent years, the Chinese dragon has awakened to the realization that globalization requires the protection of its own national interests in transnational and national IP policies. Therefore, recent years have exposed a very specific Chinese approach to IPR regime-building which has been termed "gradualism"[71] by KONG, meaning the adaptation of the standards for IP protection to the level of economic development and their use in furtherance of the Chinese national innovation system.[72]

From the very outset of Chinese modernization in the late 1970s, it was one of China's top priorities to formulate its own IPR regime.[73] However, contrary to some of the rationales of Western IP protection systems that involved a commitment to

---

[68] Yang, The Development of Intellectual Property in China, World Patent Information 25 (2003) 2, pp. 131 et seq. (136–142); The Creative Industries in China, 2010, IVCA Report, available at: http://www.ivca.org/ivca/live/news/2010/develop-your-business-in-china-join-the-ivca-trade-mission-to-shanghai/IVCA_Report_-_The_Creative_Industries_in_China.pdf.

[69] Mertha, *The Politics of Piracy*, 2005, p. 4.

[70] LaCroix/Konan, Intellectual Property Rights in China: The Changing Political Economy of Chinese-American Interests, Working Paper (2002) 02-1.

[71] Kong, The Political Economy of the Intellectual Property Regime-Building in China: Evidence from the Evolution of the Chinese Patent Regime, Pac. McGeorge Global Bus. & Dev. L.J. 21 (2008), p. 111 (112).

[72] Head, Feeling the Stones When Crossing the River: The Rule of Law in China, Santa Clara Journal of International Law 7 (2005) 7, pp. 25 et seq. (81); Holbig/Gilley, In Search of Legitimacy in Post-revolutionary China: Bringing Ideology and Governance Back, GIGA Working Paper Series (2010) 127, available at: http://repec.giga-hamburg.de/pdf/giga_10_wp127_holbig-gilley.pdf.

[73] Extracts of Deng's speech are available in Chinese at: http://www.cas.cn/html/cas50/bns/1977.html; see also Kong, The Political Economy of the Intellectual Property Regime-Building in China: Evidence from the Evolution of the Chinese Patent Regime, Pacific McGeorge Global Business & Development Law Journal 21 (2008), pp. 111 et seq. (113).

markets, the foremost motivation for IP protection was the promotion of inventions rather than the protection of the rights of inventors.[74] As Clarke rightly observed, this first phase of economic and legal reform in China from 1979 to 1984 "did not involve a commitment to markets"[75] but was "essentially an attempt to make the planning system work better."[76] In line with this observation, the *Regulations on Awards for Inventions* were adopted in 1978.[77]

In addition to improvements of the Chinese planning system, the promulgation of new IP laws in the 1980s was also directed at the promotion of foreign investment.[78] As developing country, China expected trade and foreign direct investment (FDI) to function as important channels of technology transfer (TT), learning, and competition yielding thereby higher growth rates.[79] Support for this expectation was provided by academicians demonstrating the positive impact of IPRs on technology diffusion and economic development.[80] A positive relationship was also shown between strong IP protection regimes and economic growth in open

---

[74] Palmer, An Identity Crisis: Regime Legitimacy and Politics of Intellectual Property Rights in China, Indiana Journal of Global Legal Studies 8 (2000), pp. 449 et seq. (450).

[75] Clarke, China: Creating a Legal System for a Market Economy, The George Washington University Law School Legal Studies Research Paper No. 396, 2007, p. 5.

[76] Clarke, China: Creating a Legal System for a Market Economy, The George Washington University Law School Legal Studies Research Paper No. 396, 2007, p. 5, citing the Economic Contract Law adopted in 1981 (中华人民共和国经济合同法) (zhōnghuá rénmín gòng hé guó) and the Law on Sino-Foreign Equity Joint Ventures of 1979 (中华人民共和国中外合资经营企业法, zhōnghuá rénmín gòng hé guó zhōngwài hézī jīngyíng qǐyè fǎ) as examples.

[77] Adopted 28th December, 1978, available in English at: http://preview.english.mofcom.gov.cn/aarticle/lawsdata/chineselaw/200211/20021100050646.html; see also Kong, The Political Economy of the Intellectual Property Regime-Building in China: Evidence from the Evolution of the Chinese Patent Regime, Pacific McGeorge Global Business & Development Law Journal 21 (2008), pp. 111 et seq. (114).

[78] Maskus, The Relationship between Intellectual Property Rights and Direct Investment, Duke Journal of Comparative & International Law 9 (1998), pp. 163–186.

[79] See Schiappacasse, Intellectual Property Rights in China: Technology Transfers and Economic Development, Buffalo Intellectual Property Law Journal 2 (2004), pp. 164 et seq. (170) on the interrelationship of IP protection and TT and economic development in China; more generally see Maskus/Dougherty, Intellectual Property Rights and Economic Development in China, NBR Regional Studies, Chongqing, 1998; Haug, The International Transfer of Technology: Lessons that East Europe can learn from the failed Third World Experience, Harvard Journal of Law & Technology 5 (1992), pp. 209 et seq. (217–218).

[80] See in particular Maskus, *Intellectual Property Rights in the Global Economy*, 2000; see also: Maskus, The Role of Intellectual Property Rights in Encouraging Foreign Direct Investment and Technology Transfer, in: Fink/Maskus (eds.), *Intellectual Property and Development, Lessons from Recent Economic Research*, 2004, p. 54; Maskus, Intellectual Property Rights and Foreign Direct Investment, Policy Discussion Paper (2000) 0022, p. 1; Maskus, Intellectual Property Rights and Economic Development, Case Western Reserve Journal of International Law 32 (2000), p. 47; Branstetter, Intellectual Property Rights, Imitation, and Foreign Direct Investment: Theory and Evidence, NBER Working Paper (2007) 13033; IIPA International Intellectual Property Alliance, *Initial Survey of the Contribution of Copyright Industries to Economic Development*, 2005, p. 1.

economies[81] and the creation of frameworks for enhanced IP protection and economic growth in developing countries.[82] Yet, there were also studies that questioned the causal relationship between IP protection and inventive activity or economic development.[83] They demonstrated that strong IPR regimes were only really effective once economies had become sufficiently developed to adopt stronger regimes themselves[84] and when countries disposed of both a strong imitation capacity and a sufficiently large market to enable foreign firms to capture economies of scale.[85] In addition, it was argued that it would be difficult to foster attitudes of creativity, invention, and risk-taking in an environment of weak protection.[86] Despite these concerns, it is unquestionable that the strength of IPRs affects decisions by multinational firms on where to invest, how much to invest, in what forms, and whether to transfer advanced technologies.[87] It follows that simply waiting for the Chinese economy to reach a certain level of development, was not

---

[81] Gould/Gruben, The Role of Intellectual Property Rights in Economic Growth, Journal of Development Economics 48 (1996), p. 323 (estimation of the relationship between patent regimes and growth among open economies).

[82] Braga/Fink/Sepulveda, Intellectual Property Rights and Economic Development, Worldbank, TechNet Working Paper, 1998, pp. 1–21. Mansfield, Intellectual Property Rights, Technological Change, and Economic Growth, in: Walker/Bloomfield (eds.), *Intellectual Property Rights and Capital Formation in the Next Decade*, 1988; Smarzynska, The Composition of Foreign Direct Investment and Protection of Intellectual Property Rights: Evidence from Transition Economies, in: Fink/Maskus (eds.), *Intellectual Property and Development, Lessons from Recent Economic Research*, 2005, p. 159; see also: Smarzynska/Spatareanu, Do Foreign Investors Care About Labour Market Regulations?, Discussion Paper 4839, 2005.

[83] See Maskus/Reichman, The Globalization of Private Knowledge Goods and the Privatization of Global Public Goods, Duke Law Faculty Scholarship Paper 1195, 2004; Musungu/Dutfield, Multilateral Agreements and a TRIPS-plus World: The World Intellectual Property Organization (WIPO), 2003, p. 3, TRIPS Issues Paper, available at: http://www.geneva.quno.info/pdf/WIPO (A4)final0304.pdf; Boyle, A Manifesto on WIPO and the Future of Intellectual Property, Duke Law & Technology Review 9 (2004), p. 9; Khan, *The Democratization of Invention, Patents and Copyrights in American Economic Development, 1790-1920*, 2005, pp. 1–3.

[84] Liebig, *Geistige Eigentumsrechte: Motor oder Bremse wirtschaftlicher Entwicklung? Entwicklungsländer und das TRIPS-Abkommen*, 2001, p. 22; Qian, Do Additional National Patent Laws Stimulate Domestic Innovation in a Global Patenting Environment? A Cross-Country Analysis of Pharmaceutical Patent Protection: 1978–1999, The Review of Economics and Statistics 89 (2009) 3, pp. 436 et seq. (437); see also Maskus, *Intellectual Property Rights in the Global Economy*, 2000, for an extensive overview over existing critical studies in this area.

[85] See Maskus, *Intellectual Property Rights in the Global Economy*, 2000; Braga/Fink, The Relationship between Intellectual Property Rights and Foreign Direct Investment, Duke Journal of Comparative & International Law 9 (1998), pp. 163 et seq. (164); Heald, Mowing the Playing Field: Addressing Information Distortion and Asymmetry in the TRIPS Game, Minnesota Law Review 88 (2003), pp. 249 et seq. (255).

[86] Liebig, *Geistige Eigentumsrechte: Motor oder Bremse wirtschaftlicher Entwicklung? Entwicklungsländer und das TRIPS-Abkommen*, 2001, p. 8.

[87] Cf. Maskus/Dougherty, Intellectual Property Rights and Economic Development in China, NBR Regional Studies, 1998, pp. 1 et seq. (7-10), for a detailed discussion of how IPRs stimulate economic development.

an option for the Chinese government. Rather it relied on preliminary assessments of the impact of IP protection on the Chinese market[88] and took a very proactive stance on IP policy since the early 1980s.[89]

An analysis of Chinese industrial policy in support of a slow transition from a socialist system, in which property was expropriated by the state, to a socialist market economy[90] shows this proactive stance on IP policy.

On a small scale, annual action plans on IPR Protection[91] were launched together with White Papers[92] and IPR campaigns to allow for better protection of IPRs.[93] On a larger scale, however, the most important effort in Chinese IP policy was the adoption of a *National IPR Strategy*[94] that comprehensively addresses issues of IP protection improvements, enforcement, fostering of IP talents, and enhancement of public awareness which was adopted on June 5, 2008.[95] For the first time, it elevated IP issues on the policy level of the State Council thereby signalling its highest priority to the ministries and constituted the culmination of all IP policy efforts in one single policy document.

---

[88] Samuelson, Intellectual Property and Economic Development: Opportunities for China in the Information Age, International Symposium on the Protection of Intellectual Property for the 21st Century, 1998; Straus, The Impact of the New World Order in Economic Development: The Role of Intellectual Property Rights Systems, John Marshall Review of Intellectual Property Law 6 (2006), pp. 1 et seq. (7).

[89] See Dietz, *Die Neuregelung des gewerblichen Rechtsschutzes in China, Texte und Einführungen zum Patent-, Warenzeichen-, Wettbewerbs- und Kartellrecht*, 1988, for an account of and regulations from the earlier periods of IP law reform in China; Kueh, The Maoist Legacy and China's New Industrialization Strategy, The China Quarterly 119 (1989), Special Issue: The People's Republic of China after 40 Years, p. 420.

[90] See the 1993关于建立社会主义市场经济体制若干问题的决定 (guānyú jiànlì shèhuì zhǔyì shìchǎng jīngjì tǐzhì ruògān wèntí de juédìng, *Decisions on Some Issues Concerning the Building of a Socialist Market Economy*), adopted on 14th November, 1993, at the 3rd Session of the 14th Central Committee of the Chinese Communist Party.

[91] 中国保护知识产权行动计划 (zhōngguó bǎohù zhīshi chǎnquán xíngdòng jìhuà), for the 2007 Action Plan see: Wechsler, Volksrepublik China – Verabschiedung des „Aktionsplans 2007 zum Schutz geistigen Eigentums", Gewerblicher Rechtsschutz und Urheberrecht Internationaler Teil 56 (2007) 6, p. 554.

[92] E.g. the 1994 White Paper 中国知识产权保护状况 (zhōngguó zhīshi chǎnquán bǎohù zhuàng kuàng), and the 2005 White Paper 中国知识产权保护的新进展 (zhōngguó zhīshi chǎnquán bǎohù de xīn jìnzhǎn).

[93] Wechsler, Volksrepublik China – Verabschiedung des „Aktionsplans 2007 zum Schutz geistigen Eigentums", Gewerblicher Rechtsschutz und Urheberrecht Internationaler Teil 56 (2007) 6, p. 554.

[94] 国家知识产权战略纲要的通知 (guójiā zhīshi chǎnquán zhàn lu:e4 gāngyào de tōngzhī), Gazette of the State Council (国务院公报 (guówùyuàn gōngbào)) 2008, No. 17, pp. 12–18.

[95] See Wechsler, *Intellectual Property Law in the P.R. China: A Powerful Economic Tool for Innovation and Development*, forthcoming in 2011 (copy on file with author); cf. News on the Chinese IPR strategy http://english.ipr.gov.cn/en/iprspecials/IPRStrategy/index.htm.

The National IPR Strategy has to be seen in conjunction with the *Medium and Long-Term Plan on Scientific and Technological Development* (MLP) of 2006[96] which proposes the full implementation of an IPR strategy and a technical standardization strategy for safeguarding the advancement of S&T. It has further to be seen in conjunction with Chinese standardization strategies which are yet to cumulate in a National Standardization Strategy.[97] While being aware of its obligations under the *Technical Barriers to Trade (TBT) Agreement*[98] whereby it accepted the *Code of Good Practice for the Preparation, Adoption and Application of Standards*,[99] China is now well on its way towards a standardization policy that fosters the representation of Chinese indigenous innovations in national and international standardization.[100]

Indigenous innovation has also become the core of China's overall pro-innovation industrial policy. The MLP defines as its major objectives the enhancement of China's indigenous innovation capability, the leapfrogging in key scientific disciplines, and the utilization of S&T to support and lead future economic growth.[101] Government procurement, for instance, serves these objectives as set out in a number of policies issued by the State Council, the Ministries of Foreign Trade and Science and Technology (MOST) and the National Development and Reform Commission (NDRC).[102] Yet, Chinese government pro-indigenous innovation procurement processes have so far been without sanctions as China

---

[96] 国家中长期科学和技术发展规划纲要 (2006–2020年) (guójiā zhōng chángqī kēxué hé jìshù fāzhǎn guīhuà gāngyào), issued by the State Council on 9th February, 2006, http://www.gov.cn/jrzg/2006-02/09/content_183787.htm.

[97] Wang et al., Standardization Strategy of China – Achievements and Challenges, East-West Center Working Paper 107, 2010, p. 7, available at: http://www.eastwestcenter.org/fileadmin/stored/pdfs/econwp107.pdf; See also SAC (2006) Outline of Eleventh Five-Year Plan on the Development of Standardization (国家"十一五"科学技术发展规划, guójiā shíyī wǔ kēxué jìshù fāzhǎn guīhuà), available at: http://www.most.gov.cn/kjgh/kjfzgh/200610/t20061031_55485.htm. See also Suttmeier, A New Technonationalism? China and the Development of Technical Standards, Communications of the ACM 48 (2006) 4, pp. 35 et seq. (36).

[98] Available at: http://www.wto.org/english/docs_e/legal_e/17-tbt.pdf.

[99] See Annex 3 to the TBT, available at: http://www.wto.org/english/docs_e/legal_e/17-tbt.pdf.

[100] Wang/Wang/Hill, Standardization Strategy of China – Achievements and Challenges, East-West Center Working Paper 107 (2010), p. 5, available at: http://www.eastwestcenter.org/fileadmin/stored/pdfs/econwp107.pdf; See also SAC (2006) Outline of Eleventh Five-Year Plan on the Development of Standardization (国家"十一五"科学技术发展规划 (guójiā shíyī wǔ kēxué jìshù fāzhǎn guīhuà), available at: http://www.most.gov.cn/kjgh/kjfzgh/200610/t20061031_55485.htm.

[101] Cao/Simon/Suttmeier, Commentary: China's Innovation Challenge, Innovation: Management, Policy & Practice (2009) 11, p. 253.

[102] See 2009 年申报说明 (nián shēnbào shuōmíng, *Explanatory Report Regarding National Indigenous Innovation Products*), available at: http://www.most.gov.cn/tztg/200911/t20091115_74197.htm.

has not yet acceded to the *WTO Agreement on Government Procurement* (GPA).[103] Nevertheless, these processes and policies have stirred concern on the part of foreign entities and policy-makers about China's technonationalism[104] which is seen as an emanation of a government-directed innovation policy.[105]

The government direction of innovation is further evident in a number of recent legislative initiatives in China. The *Chinese Science and Technology Progress Law*[106] puts enormous emphasis on the role of IP policies in the promotion of S&T in China while considering S&T as the primary productive force in socialist modernization.[107] The 2008 passage of the *Chinese Anti-Monopoly Law*[108] does not represent the outcome of external pressures on Chinese lawmakers but was intended to provide for the optimal policy level to allow China's domestic firms to compete effectively with their foreign counterparts.[109] Likewise, the 2008 patent law reform marks a clear departure from previous patent law amendments in that it was neither external coercion nor an international treaty that pressurized China into this reform. Rather it was intrinsically motivated by the Chinese interest to safeguard China's economic security and national interest.[110] The substance of the new patent law reflects the Chinese determination to promote domestic innovation and to reduce its reliance on foreign-controlled patents by providing for a confidentiality examinations

---

[103] See http://www.wto.org/english/tratop_e/gproc_e/gp_gpa_e.htm; See also the concerns voiced on behalf of foreign businesses, Lubman, "China's "Indigenous Innovation" Policy Creates Obstacles for Foreign Business", The Wall Street Journal, 7th April, 2010.

[104] For an extensive argument on China's technonationalism see Suttmeier/Yao/Tan, *China's Post-WTO Technology Policy: Standards, Software, and the Changing Nature of Techno-Nationalism*, NBR Reports, 2004.

[105] Linton, China's R&D Policy for the 21st Century: Government Direction of Innovation, 2008, p. 1, available at: http://ssrn.com/abstract=1126651.

[106] 中华人民共和国科学技术进步法 (zhōnghuá rénmín gòng hé guó kēxué jìshù jìnbù fǎ), Law of the P.R. China on Science and Technology Progress), adopted at the 2nd Meeting of the Standing Committee of the 8th NPC on 2nd July, 1993, promulgated by Order No. 4 of the President of the P.R. China, and effective as of 1st October, 1993; revised on 29th December, 2007; Gazette of the State Council (国务院公报 (guówùyuàn gōngbào)) 2008, No. 2, English translation available at: http://www.most.gov.cn/eng/policies/regulations/200412/t20041228_18309.htm.

[107] See Art. 3 of the 中华人民共和国科学技术进步法 (zhōnghuá rénmín gòng hé guó kēxué jìshù jìnbù fǎ, Law of the P.R. China on Science and Technology Progress), 1993, 2007; Gazette of the State Council (国务院公报 (guówùyuàn gōngbào)) 2008, No. 2.

[108] 中华人民共和国反垄断法, (zhōnghuá rénmín gòng hé guó fǎn lǒngduàn fǎ, Anti-Monopoly Law of the P.R. China), adopted at the 29th Session of the Standing Committee of the Tenth NPC on 30th August, 2007 and effective as of 1st August, 2008, Gazette of the State Council (国务院公报 (guówùyuàn gōngbào)) 2008, No. 58; see also: Student, China's New Anti-Monopoly Law: Addressing Foreign Competitors and Commentators, Minnesota Journal of International Law 17 (2008), pp. 503 et seq. (503).

[109] Student, China's New Anti-Monopoly Law: Addressing Foreign Competitors and Commentators, Minnesota Journal of International Law 17 (2008), pp. 503 et seq. (503).

[110] Ollier, China's Controversial Amendment Plans, Managing Intellectual Property (2007) 12, pp. 3 et seq. (5).

requirement in Article 20, by providing that inventions made in China must first be filed in China, by providing enhanced protection for genetic resources which goes beyond the *Convention on Biological Diversity*[111] and by providing more efficient and convenient channels in application, acquisition, and enforcement of patent rights.[112] It follows that China is increasingly taking into account its own domestic interests to further its national economic development.

In summary, the times have passed in which China's motivation for implementing IP laws was to gain favourable trading partnerships with Western countries.[113] Recent developments in Chinese IP policy and reform have shown the Chinese drive to excel in S&T and to become the world's innovation leader with the help of its IP protection regime. The extensive use of IP policy space for the promotion of indigenous innovation is widely supported by emerging Chinese IP industries which – in recent years – have moved from unprecedented success in competition within an imitation paradigm towards a competitive paradigm in which creation is central.[114] In almost all industry branches, Chinese companies are increasingly adopting proactive IP protection strategies by not only proactively filing and registering IPRs but also by proactively taking international companies to Chinese courts.[115] In consequence, this functional approach to IP policy together with its ever-increasing economic and political power puts China into a position whereby it could take a leadership role in developing IP policies which constitute a viable alternative to Western-style IPRs.

---

[111] E.g., invalidation grounds, definition of genetic resources including human factors; see International Chamber of Commerce, Comments on the Draft Amendment of the Patent Law in China, dated 27th December, 2006, Comments on the Draft Amendment of the Patent Law in China; Convention on Biological Diversity (Biodiversity Convention) adopted in Rio de Janeiro in June 1992, http://www.cbd.int; note also that genetic resources includes traditional knowledge, like Traditional Chinese Medicine (TCM).

[112] Ollier, China's Controversial Amendment Plans, Managing Intellectual Property (2007) 12, pp. 3 et seq. (5).

[113] Crane, Riding the Tiger: A Comparison of Intellectual Property Rights in the United States and the People's Republic of China, Chicago-Kent Journal of Intellectual Property 7 (2007), pp. 95 et seq. (97).

[114] Xie/White, From Imitation to Creation? The Critical and Uncertain Paradigm Shift for Chinese Firms, Journal of Technology Management in China 1 (2006) 3, pp. 1 et seq. (2). See especially the following Chinese firms: 海尔 (hǎiěr), 华为 (huáwèi), 影视库 (yǐngshìkù, Legend), TCL, and长城汽车 (chángchéng qìchē, Greatwall).

[115] Lerer, Special Report, China, Chinese Tech Companies are growing Patent Savy, and Shenzhen-based Netac leads the Charge. This Year the Company sued Sony – the first foreign corporation sued for patent violations in China, IP Law & Business (2005) 12, pp. 28 et seq. (28).

Achievements and Challenges of Chinese Intellectual Property Law Reform

Ever since the 1978 Third Plenary Session of the 11th Central Committee of the CCP which re-oriented the Party towards a socialist rule of law and an opening-up of China to the outside world[116] China has worked towards IP regime adoption, towards a full embrace of international IP norms and towards the improvement of the climate of its IP law regime.[117] In the light of these developments, the following section provides an account of the present state of Chinese IP law reform with reference to the black-letter law, its administration and its enforcement.

The Law

From 1978 onwards, Chinese IP protection was firmly embedded into a larger constitutional, civil, criminal and administrative law framework through recognition in and application of, for instance, the *Civil Procedure Law*,[118] the *Criminal Law*,[119] the *Criminal Procedure Law*,[120] the *Administrative Procedure Law*,[121] and the *Property Law*.[122] However, the dogmatic treatment of IPRs in China is as of yet contentious as the strong reliance on the administrative system is seen as distorting

---

[116] Hutschenreiter/Zhang, China's Quest for Innovation-Driven Growth – the Policy Dimension, Journal of Industry, Competition and Trade 2007, pp. 245 et seq. (246).

[117] Ganea, China, in: Goldstein/Straus (eds.), *Intellectual Property in Asia. Law, Economics, History and Politics*, 2009, pp. 17 et seq. (54).

[118] 中华人民共和国民事诉讼法 (zhōnghuá rénmín gòng hé guó mín shì sù song fǎ, The Civil Procedure Law of the P.R. China), 1993, 2004, 2007, Gazette of the State Council (国务院公报 (guówùyuàn gōngbào)) 2007, No. 35, p. 1250; available in English and Chinese, China Law and Practice 22 (2008) 1, pp. 22–72.

[119] 中华人民共和国刑法 (zhōnghuá rénmín gòng hé guó xíngfǎ, Criminal Law of the P.R. China), 1979, 1997, 2009, Gazette of the State Council (国务院公报 (guówùyuàn gōngbào)) 2009, No. 4, p. 8.

[120] 中华人民共和国刑事诉讼法 (zhōnghuá rénmín gòng hé guó xíng shì sù song fǎ, Criminal Procedure Law of the People's Republic of China), 1979, 1996, Gazette of the State Council (国务院公报) 1996, No. 10, p. 356.

[121] 中华人民共和国行政诉讼法 (zhōnghuá rénmín gòng hé guó, Administrative Procedure Law of the P.R. China), 1989, Gazette of the State Council (国务院公报) 1989, No. 7, p. 297.

[122] 中华人民共和国物权法 (zhōnghuá rénmín gòng hé guó wùquán fǎ, Property Law of the P.R. China), 2007, Gazette of the State Council (国务院公报 (guówùyuàn gōngbào)) 2007, No. 14, p. 4; available in English and Chinese, China Law and Practice, 21 (2007) 4, pp. 31–66.

the nature of IPRs as private rights[123] as, inter alia, envisaged by the *TRIPS Agreement*.[124]

Regardless of these conceptual difficulties, IPRs are regarded as being rights expressly created by the 1982 *Constitution of the P.R. China*.[125] In particular, Articles 13 and 47 of the *Constitution*[126] do not only protect IPRs and guarantee the freedom to create intellectual property, they are also indicative of the increasing internalization of concepts of IP and their importance for the Chinese policy-maker.[127]

In 1986, the *General Principles of Civil Law*[128] formally recognized IPRs as civil rights[129] rendering civil liabilities the most important remedies for IPRs.[130] Section 3 of the *General Principles of Civil Law* is entitled "Intellectual Property Rights" and is, thus, devoted to IPRs only. More specifically, Article 94 guarantees the rights of authorship, moral rights and the right to remuneration; Article 95 establishes the protection of lawfully obtained patents; Article 96 protects the exclusive use of trademarks while Article 97 establishes the right of discoveries. However, the *General Principles of Civil Law* fail to specify different types and contents of property rights and contracts as a result of which separate laws – such as the *Contract Law*[131] – were enacted to address these deficiencies.

Alongside this embedding of IPRs into a larger reform framework, China has engaged in numerous legislative initiatives to build and improve a comprehensive IP law system. A detailed overview of major Chinese IP legislation and IP-related events since 1979 is provided in Table 1.

---

[123] Sun/Yang, The Division of Public Law and Private Law and the Internal Structure of La, 度国家社科基金重点项目 (dù guójiā shèkē jījīn zhòngdiǎn xiàngmù) (2003) 3; Chen, *Chinese Law: Context and Transformation*, 2008, p. 332.

[124] See Preamble of *The Agreement on Trade-Related Aspects of Intellectual Property Rights* (TRIPS), adopted in Marrakesh on 15th April, 1994, 33 ILM 81 (1994).

[125] 中华人民共和国宪法 (zhōnghuá rénmín gòng hé guó xiànfǎ, Constitution of the People's Republic of China), 1982, revisions 1988, 1993, 1999, 2004, Gazette of the State Council 30 (国务院公报 (guówùyuàn gōngbào)) (2000), p. 9, English translation, CCH Business Regulation 4-500 (English-Chinese).

[126] 中华人民共和国宪法 (zhōnghuá rénmín gòng hé guó xiànfǎ, Constitution of the People's Republic of China), 1982, revisions 1988, 2004, Gazette of the State Council 30 (国务院公报 (guówùyuàn gōngbào)) (2000), p. 9.

[127] See also Long, Intellectual Property in China, St. Mary's Law Journal 31 (2001), pp. 63 et seq. (71).

[128] 中华人民共和国民法通则 (zhōnghuá rénmín gòng hé guó mínfǎ tōngzé, General Principles of Civil Law of the P.R. China), 1986, Gazette of the State Council (国务院公报 (guówùyuàn gōngbào)) 1996, p. 388; English translation, CCH Business Regulation pp. 19–150 (English-Chinese).

[129] Chen, *Chinese Law: Context and Transformation*, 2008, p. 567.

[130] Jianqiang Nie, *The Enforcement of Intellectual Property Rights in China*, 2006, p. 193.

[131] 中华人民共和国合同法 (zhōnghuá rénmín gòng hé guó hétong fǎ, Contract Law of the P.R. China), 1999, Gazette of the State Council (国务院公报 (guówùyuàn gōngbào)) 1999, No. 11, p. 388.

Table 1 Timeline of major IP-related legislation and events

Time	Legislation/events
1979	US-China Agreement on Trade Relations
1979	Criminal Law, revised in 1997
1980	Accession to WIPO Convention
1982	Trademark Law, revised in 1993 and 2001
1984	Patent Law, revised in 1992, 2000 and 2009
	Accession to the Paris Convention
1986	General Principles of Civil Law
1987	Customs Law
1989	Accession to the Madrid Agreement
1990	Copyright Law, revised in 2001
1991	Civil Procedure Law
	Regulations on Computer Software Protection, revised in 2001
1992	Sino-U.S. Memorandum of Understanding on IPRs
	1st Patent Law Reform
	Accession to the Berne Convention
	Accession to the Universal Copyright Convention (UCC)
1993	Trade Secret Law/Anti-Unfair Competition Law
	1st Trademark Law Reform
	Accession to the Geneva Phonograms Convention
1994	Accession to the Patent Cooperation Treaty
	Accession to the Nice Agreement
1995	Sino-US Agreement on IPRs
	Accession to the Madrid Protocol
	Customs IP Protection Rules, revised in 2004
	Accession to Budapest Treaty
1996	Criminal Procedure Law
	Accession to the Strasbourg Agreement
1997	Regulations on New Varieties of Plants Protection
1999	Contract Law
	Accession to UPOV
2000	2nd Patent Law Reform
	2nd Trademark Law Reform
2001	Regulation on the Protection of Layout Designs of Integrated Circuits
	1st Copyright Law Reform
	Accession to the WTO
	Technology Import and Export Administrative Regulations
2004	Company Law
	Customs Protection of Intellectual Property Rights Regulations
2006	Medium and Long-Term Plan on Scientific and Technological Development
	Accession to WCT and WPPT
2007	Property Law
2008	Anti-Monopoly Law
	National IP Strategy
2009	3rd Patent Law Reform
	WT/DS362/R Report of the Panel, China – Measures Affecting the Protection and Enforcement of Intellectual Property Rights

Adapted from Feng, *Intellectual Property in China*, (2nd ed.) 2003, pp. lvii–lviii

In terms of legislative initiatives, the *Trademark Law*[132] and its implementing regulations[133] were adopted in 1982 and 1983, respectively, closely followed in 1984 and 1985 by the adoption of the *Patent Law*[134] and its implementing regulations,[135] and in 1990 and 1991 the *Copyright Law*[136] and its implementing regulations.[137] The enactment of these cornerstones of IP protection were complemented by the ongoing revision of these laws, on the one hand, and the enactment of further laws, on the other hand, such as the enactment of the *Anti-Unfair Competition Law*[138] in 1993, the *Chinese National IPR Strategy*,[139] and the *Chinese Anti-Monopoly Law* in 2008.[140]

These legislative initiatives were intertwined with a great number of accessions of China to international IP treaties as well as bilateral agreements. Most noticeably, in 1980 China acceded to the *WIPO Convention*[141] and in 2001 to the WTO.

---

[132] 中华人民共和国商标法 (zhōnghuá rénmín gòng hé guó shāngbiāo fǎ), 1982, revisions 1993, 2001, Gazette of the State Council (国务院公报 (guówùyuàn gōngbào)) 2002, No. 59; English translation, CCH Business Regulation 11-500 (English-Chinese).

[133] 中华人民共和国商标法实施条例 (zhōnghuá rénmín gòng hé guó shāngbiāo fǎ shíshī tiáolì), 2002, revisions 1988, 1993, Gazette of the State Council (国务院公报 (guówùyuàn gōngbào)) 2002, No. 358; English translation, CCH Business Regulation 11-505 (English-Chinese).

[134] 中华人民共和国专利法 (zhōnghuá rénmín gòng hé guó zhuānlì fǎ), 1984, 1992, 2000, 2008, Gazette of the State Council (国务院公报 (guówùyuàn gōngbào)) 2000, No. 30, p.9; 2008 revision: China Law & Practice 23 (2009), pp. 60–74.

[135] 中华人民共和国专利法实施细则 (zhōnghuá rénmín gòng hé guó zhuānlì fǎ shíshī xìzé), 2001, revision 1992, Gazette of the State Council (国务院公报 (guówùyuàn gōngbào)) 2001, No. 23, p7; English translation, CCH Business Regulation 11-603 (English-Chinese).

[136] 中华人民共和国著作权法 (zhōnghuá rénmín gòng hé guó zhùzuò quán fǎ), 1990, revisions 2001, Gazette of the State Council (国务院公报 (guówùyuàn gōngbào)) 2001, No. 33, p. 10; English translation, China Patents and Trademarks (Hong Kong) No. 1, 83 (2002); German Translation, Gewerblicher Rechtsschutz und Urheberrecht Internationaler Teil (2002) 1, pp. 23–30; This section corresponds to Art. 51 of the first Chinese Copyright Law of 1990, see Wei, *Der Urheberrechtsschutz in China mit Hinweisen auf das Deutsche Recht*, 1994, pp. 14–18.

[137] 中华人民共和国著作权法实施条例 (zhōnghuá rénmín gòng hé guó zhùzuò quán fǎ shíshī tiáolì), 1991, revision 2002, Gazette of the State Council (国务院公报 (guówùyuàn gōngbào)) 1991, p. 745; English translation, CCH Business Regulation pp. 11-702 (English-Chinese).

[138] 中华人民 共和国反不正当竞争法 (zhōnghuá rénmín gòng hé guó fǎn bù zhèngdāng jìngzhēng fǎ), 1993, Gazette of the State Council (国务院公报 (guówùyuàn gōngbào)) 1993, No. 33, p. 27.

[139] 国家知识产权战略纲要的通知 (guójiā zhīshi chǎnquán zhàn lu:e4 gāngyào de tōngzhī), 2008, Gazette of the State Council (国务院公报 (guówùyuàn gōngbào)) 2008, No. 17, pp. 12–18.

[140] 中华人民共和国反垄断法, (zhōnghuá rénmín gòng hé guó fǎn lǒngduàn fǎ, Anti-Monopoly Law of the P.R. China), 2007, Gazette of the State Council (国务院公报 (guówùyuàn gōngbào)) 2008, No. 58; see also: Student, China's New Anti-Monopoly Law: Addressing Foreign Competitors and Commentators, Minnesota Journal of International Law 17 (2008), pp. 503 et seq. (503).

[141] Convention Establishing the World Intellectual Property Organization, 1967, 21 U.S.T. 1749, 828 U.N.T.S. 3.

Furthermore, China joined the *Paris Convention*,[142] the *Madrid Protocol*[143] and the *Washington Treaty*[144] in 1984, the *Berne Convention*[145] and the *Universal Copyright Convention*[146] in 1992, the *Geneva Phonograms Convention*[147] in 1993, and the *Patent Cooperation Treaty* (PCT)[148] in 1994. By now, China is also a member of a number of other international agreements relating to patents, trademarks, and copyrights as well as other kinds of IPRs.[149]

However, despite Chinese accession to international IP treaties and despite extensive legislative initiatives, there still remain issues with Chinese black-letter laws. First of all, Chinese IP law is torn between a dogmatic grounding in civil law and common law rationales as is evident, for instance, in the unsystematic distribution of trade secret protection in both general civil laws and IP laws.[150] Second, Chinese IP regulation is in selected instances still ambiguous and overly general.[151] Third, selected IP regulation – such as its trademark regulation – is either insufficient or outdated in the light of digital and Internet technologies.[152] Fourth, China will still have to incorporate into its laws the latest legislative developments such as, for instance, in the area of diversity of cultural contents and artistic expressions.[153]

In conclusion, over the last 30 years, China has established a relatively comprehensive system of IP protection and acceded to major international IP conventions. The comprehensive enactment of largely TRIPS-compliant IP legislation has won

---

[142] The Paris Convention for the Protection of Industrial Property, 1883, 21 U.S.T. 1583, 828 U.N. T.S. 305.

[143] The Protocol Relating to the Madrid Agreement Concerning the International Registration of Marks (Madrid Protocol), 1989, 2006, 1161 U.N.T.S. 3.

[144] Treaty on Intellectual Property in Respect of Integrated Circuits (Washington Treaty), 1989, 28 I.L.M. 1477 (1989).

[145] The Berne Convention for the Protection of Literary and Artistic Works, 1886, 331 U.N.T.S. 217.

[146] Universal Copyright Convention, 1952, 1971, 25 U.S.T. 1341.

[147] Convention for the Protection of Producers of Phonograms against unauthorized Duplication of Their Phonograms, 1971, 25 U.S.T. 309.

[148] Patent Cooperation Treaty (PCT), 1970, 1979, 1984, 2001, 28 U.S.T. 7645.

[149] E.g. of the Strasbourg Agreement Concerning the International Patent Classification. See Wechsler, *Intellectual Property Law in the P.R. China: A Powerful Economic Tool for Innovation and Development*, forthcoming in 2011 (copy on file with author).

[150] Wu, Intellectual Property Law as China Moves Toward an Innovation-Oriented Society, in: Cai/Wang, *China's Journey toward the Rule of Law. Legal Reform 1978–2008*, 2010, pp. 349 et seq. (474).

[151] Zheng, Special Features, Merits and Shortcomings of China's Laws for Intellectual Property Protection (Part II), China Patents & Trademarks 1994, pp. 16 et seq. (16).

[152] Alexander, The Starbucks Decision of the Shanghai No. 2 Intermediate People's Court: A Victory Limited to Lattés?, Case Western Reserve Law Review 58 (2008), pp. 881 et seq. (896).

[153] See the Convention on the Protection and Promotion of the Diversity of Cultural Expressions 2005, available at: http://portal.unesco.org/en/ev.php-URL_ID=31038&URL_DO=DO_TOPIC &URL_SECTION=201.html.

acclaim around the world.[154] At the same time, however, there still remains urgent need for revision of overly general, dispersed, unsystematic or outdated laws.[155]

Administration

As China established a comprehensive legal IP regime, it also made great strides towards the establishment of an effective administration for IPRs. The following section discusses achievements and challenges in Chinese IP administration, on the one hand, and statistics relating to the administration of IPRs in China, on the other hand.

Administrative Authorities

Administrative authorities do not only enforce IPRs in accordance with a system of "dual enforcement" by courts and administration. They are also responsible for managing IPRs for the acceleration of IP progress in China.

Numerous government agencies are responsible for the administration of IPRs in China: the State Intellectual Property Office (SIPO),[156] the State Administration for Industry and Commerce (SAIC),[157] the National Copyright Administration of China (NCAC)[158] and the General Administration of Press and Publication (GAPP).[159] Several ministries – such as the Ministry of Culture, the Ministry of Agriculture, the State Forestry Administration and the Ministry of Public Security – are further involved in the administration of IPRs as are the following enforcement agencies: the General Administration of Customs (GAC),[160] the Supreme People's Court (SPC)[161] and the Supreme People's Procuratorate.[162]

---

[154] E.g. Duan, China's Intellectual Property Rights Protection Towards the 21st Century, Duke Journal of Comparative & International Law 9 (1998), pp. 215–218.

[155] See, e.g. the unsatisfactory protection of trade names, Xue, Domain Name Dispute Resolution in China: A Comprehensive Review, Temple International and Comparative Law Journal 18 (2004), pp. 1 et seq. (19).

[156] 中华人民共和国国家知识产权局 (zhōnghuá rénmín gònghéguó guójiā zhīshi chǎnquán jú).

[157] 国家工商行政管理总局 (guójiā gōnghāng xíngzhèng guǎnlǐ zǒng jú).

[158] 国家版权局 (guójiā bǎnquán jú).

[159] 中华人民共和国新闻出版总署 (zhōnghuá rénmín gònghéguó xīnwén chūbǎn zǒngshǔ).

[160] 中华人民共和国海关总署 (zhōnghuá rénmín gònghéguó hǎiguān zǒngshǔ).

[161] 中华人民共和国最高人民法院 (zhōnghuá rénmín gònghéguó zuìgāo rénmín fǎyuàn, Supreme People's Court), available at: http://en.court.gov.cn/, specifically authorized by the Art. 127 of the 中华人民共和国宪法 (zhōnghuá rénmín gòng hé guó xiànfǎ, Constitution of the People's Republic of China), Gazette of the State Council (国务院公报 (guówùyuàn gōngbào)) 2000, No. 30, p. 9.

[162] 中华人民共和国最高人民检察院 (zhōnghuá rénmín gònghéguó zuìgāo rénmín jiǎncháyuàn).

A fine division of duties and responsibilities of each of these respective agencies is intended to ensure the effective administration of IPRs.[163] SAIC, for instance, is responsible for the administration of the filing, grant and renewal of trademarks.[164] Patents, by contrast, must be filed with SIPO.[165] Nevertheless, the multitude of offices responsible for IPRs has extensively been criticized as being overly costly, as causing lack of uniformity, as causing conflict between the respective agencies and as impeding China's international IP cooperation.[166] Addressing the weaknesses of this division of responsibilities, the government established the *National IP Leading Group* in 2004 as coordination mechanisms between the different departments and ministries while strengthening the role of SIPO as frontrunner in IP administration.[167] In addition, several joint declarations have been issued by a number of departments for the better coordination of administration and enforcement of IPRs.[168]

Despite increasing cooperation, the dispersed administration of IPRs is certainly one of the bigger challenges of the Chinese IP law regime. The future will tell whether and when the government will opt for a model of lean administration of IPRs.

Statistics

Chinese IP administration has considerably been challenged by an enormous increase of reliance on IP protection as is evident from statistics about rising numbers of patent and trademark applications and grants as well as copyright and software registrations.[169]

---

[163] Chen, Administrative Management and Enforcement of Copyright in China, Duke Journal of Comparative & International Law 9 (1998), pp. 249–252.

[164] Alexander, The Starbucks Decision of the Shanghai No. 2 Intermediate People's Court: A Victory Limited to Lattés?, Case Western Reserve Law Review 58 (2008), pp. 881 et seq. (887).

[165] Crane, Riding the Tiger: A Comparison of Intellectual Property Rights in the United States and the People's Republic of China, Chicago-Kent Journal of Intellectual Property 7 (2007), pp. 95 et seq. (113).

[166] Wu, Intellectual Property Law as China Moves Toward an Innovation-Oriented Society, in: Cai/Wang, *China's Journey toward the Rule of Law. Legal Reform 1978--2008*, 2010, pp. 349 et seq. (473).

[167] SIPO Press Release, IP Achievements During 10th Five-Year Plan, 2008.

[168] See, for instance, the 2001 Notice on Strengthening the Coordination and Collaboration in Investigation of Criminal Cases Involving Infringement of Intellectual Property Rights; Wu, Intellectual Property Law as China Moves Toward an Innovation-Oriented Society, in: Cai/ Wang, *China's Journey toward the Rule of Law. Legal Reform 1978–2008*, 2010, pp. 349 et seq. (459).

[169] Wechsler, Chinese, Japanese, Korean, and Indian Patent Information in Comparison: Asia's Rising Role in Technology Disclosure through the Patent System, Tsinghua China Law Review (2009) 2, pp. 101–158.

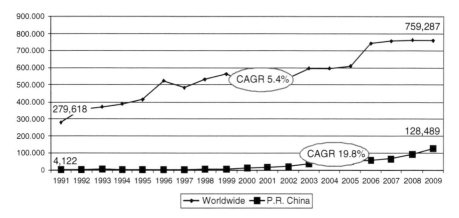

Fig. 1 Chinese and worldwide patent grants in comparison, 1991–2009. WIPO Patent Statistics Database, available at: http://www.wipo.int/ipstats/en/statistics/patents

Over the last 30 years, China has in particular experienced a tremendous increase in the demand for patents. While there were only 44 patents in force in 1985, there were already 337,215 patents in force in 2009 corresponding to a Compound Annual Growth Rate (CAGR) of 43.0%.[170] The 2009 figure amounts to 25.5% of Japanese patents in force (1,270,367) and 5.0% of worldwide patents in force (about 6.7 million).[171] Thus, China still has a Long March ahead towards the same significance as patenting location as Japan. However, a look at the number of patent applications by the language of filing is promising: the number of PCT international patent applications in the Chinese language demonstrates that Chinese is the fourth often used language of filing with 5,009 applications in 2007.[172]

Further analyses of Chinese patent grant data become, in particular, instructive when considered with reference to worldwide patent grant data. The comparison of Chinese and worldwide patent grants in Fig. 1 shows not only that Chinese patent grants have increased from 4,122 in 1991 to 128,489 in 2009 but also that its growth has substantially exceeded the worldwide growth of patent grants with a CAGR of 19.8% as compared to a CAGR of 5.4%. In consequence, China is predicted to assume a leading role for patenting and the provision of technological information through the patent system.

The comparison of resident and non-resident patent grants in Fig. 2 shows that non-resident patent grants have increased with a CAGR of 17.8% from 2,811 in 1991 to 63,098 in 2009. In the same period of time, resident patent grants have

---

[170] WIPO Patent Statistics Database, available at: http://www.wipo.int/ipstats/en/statistics/patents.

[171] Patents in force in 2008, Wallace, IP growth data shows 2008, 2009 slowdown with China exception, 16th September, 2010, available at: http://www.genevalunch.com.

[172] Wechsler, Chinese, Japanese, Korean, and Indian Patent Information in Comparison: Asia's Rising Role in Technology Disclosure through the Patent System, Tsinghua China Law Review (2009) 2, pp. 101–158 (133).

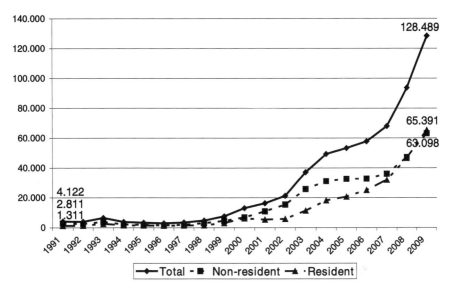

Fig. 2 Number of resident versus non-resident patent grants, 1991–2009. WIPO Patent Statistics Database, available at: http://www.wipo.int/ipstats/en/statistics/patents

increased with a CAGR of 22.9% from 1,311 to 65,391. Thus, 2009 marks the first year in Chinese history in which there were more resident patent grants than non-resident patent grants with 63,098 and, thus, a growing ability of Chinese residents to take advantage of IP law by obtaining legitimate IPRs.

China is also gaining ground in terms of trademark applications and is held out to account for 90% of the worldwide increase in trademark registration.[173] Looking at the applicants under the Madrid system, there were already four Chinese companies amongst the top 50 applicants in 2009.[174] With 625,969 trademark applications filed in 2008, China has become the leading trademark application filer worldwide, followed by the U.S. with 396,856 applications.[175] Likewise, Chinese residents were issued the highest number of registrations worldwide in 2008 with 371,898 registrations, followed by the U.S. with 285,489 registrations.[176] As of yet, however, only 6% – and thus relatively few – of all Chinese applications have been filed abroad.[177] Nevertheless, the 35,444 applications designated for protection outside

---

[173] WIPO, *World Intellectual Property Indicators*, 2010, p. 11.

[174] 浙江好梦来集团有限公司 (Zhejiang Province Haomenglai Group Co., Ltd.), 北京万金岛商贸有限公司 (Beijing Wanjindao Shangmao Youxian Gongsi), 宁波远东照明有限公司 (Ningbo Far East Lighting Co., Ltd.), 杭州中策橡胶有限公司 (Hangzhou Zhongce Rubber Co., Ltd.), see WIPO, *World Intellectual Property Indicators*, 2010, p. 90.

[175] WIPO, *World Intellectual Property Indicators*, 2010, p. 84.

[176] Ibid.

[177] Ibid, p. 83.

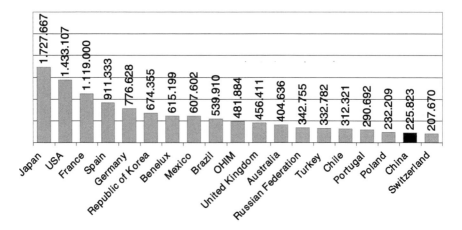

Fig. 3 Trademarks in force by destination, 2008. WIPO Patent Statistics Database, available at: http://www.wipo.int/ipstats/en/statistics/patents

China, place the country in eighth position in terms of applications filed abroad.[178] Comparably, only 8% of registrations of trademarks by Chinese residents were issued by IP offices abroad.[179] Despite the tremendous increase of trademark applications and registrations, however, China is still not leading the list of countries with numbers of trademarks in force but is placed 18th with 225,823 trademarks in force in 2008 as Fig. 3 demonstrates.[180]

Before concluding, several words of caution are warranted in the assessment of IP statistics.

First, IP statistics are often cited as proof for a growing capacity for inventive activity and technological change.[181] However, the causal relationship between an increase of IP applications and grants – in particular patents – and a capacity for innovation is most difficult to prove due to the lack of information on the technical and economic significance of the intellectual property concerned.[182] Since no procedure has as of yet been developed for the appropriate weighting of IP documents,[183] IP statistics have their limitations in terms of information about

---

[178] Ibid.

[179] Ibid, p. 84.

[180] WIPO, *World Intellectual Property Indicators*, 2010, p. 95.

[181] Wu, Intellectual Property Law as China Moves Toward an Innovation-Oriented Society, in: Cai/Wang, *China's Journey toward the Rule of Law. Legal Reform 1978–2008*, 2010, pp. 349 et seq. (464).

[182] Bhattacharya, Mapping Inventive Activity and Technological Change Through Patent Analysis: A Case Study of India and China, Scientometrics 61 (2004) 3, pp. 361–362.

[183] Griliches, Patent Statistics as Economic Indicators: A Survey, Journal of Economic Literature, Vol. XXVIII, December 1990, pp. 1661 et seq. (1679).

innovative activities but remain instructive as to general application, registration or grant trends.

Second, the ever-larger increase of the volume of Chinese-held IPRs and IPRs registered and granted in China has repeatedly been explained with reference to abusive behaviour – such as patent trolling – and thus strategic behaviour to extract excessive license fees by non-practicing Chinese companies.[184] More importantly, however, IPR quality remains one of the biggest challenges for Chinese IPRs.[185] While there is no quality check on design and utility models due to the lack of substantive examination, even the rise in invention patents can be traced back to domestic companies having been incentivized by subsidies, tax breaks and cash bonuses to file patents.[186] The distortion of application and grant statistics through such incentives for local companies should therefore be considered when assessing Chinese IP statistics.

In conclusion, China is not only well on its way to becoming one of the most important locations for IP registration but Chinese residents are also becoming the most important group of applicants and filers for IP protection in China and abroad.[187] However, the quality of IPRs in China remains one of the biggest challenges.

Enforcement

A major pillar of Chinese IP law reform has been the establishment and improvement of an effective and efficient enforcement system[188] with enforcement still being, however, the weakest element in the modern Chinese IP law regime.[189] One of the peculiarities of the Chinese IP law regime has thereby been a system of "dual

---

[184] See also "Don't Feed the Patent Trolls in China and Start Your Own IP Team", Discussion on IP Dragon, 18th May, 2010, available at: http://ipdragon.blogspot.com/2010/05/dont-feed-patent-trolls-in-china-and.html. Patent trolls are known as 蟑螂 (cockroach) in China.

[185] "The Patent Quality Challenge Facing China and Its Businesses", IAM Magazine, 20th January, 2011. Also: "Innovation in China: Patents, yes; Ideas, maybe", The Economist, 14th October, 2010, available at: http://www.economist.com/node/17257940.

[186] "Quality is China's Biggest Patent/IP Challenge", The Lowdown, 27th January, 2011, http://thelowdownblog.blogspot.com/2011/01/quality-is-chinas-biggest-patentip.html.

[187] Chinese growth of utility model applications is also unbroken. With an increase in industrial design applications in China of 45,472 in 2008, China also explains the 5.7% rise in global industrial design applications; see WIPO, *World Intellectual Property Indicators*, 2010, pp. 9, 98.

[188] E.g. Cao, *Die Durchsetzung von Patenten in China. Verletzungstatbestände, Gerichtsbarkeit, Gerichtsverfahren und die Durchsetzung durch Patentverwaltungsbehörden*, 2010.

[189] Crane, Riding the Tiger: A Comparison of Intellectual Property Rights in the United States and the People's Republic of China, Chicago-Kent Journal of Intellectual Property 7 (2007), pp. 95 et seq. (115).

enforcement" by both administrative agencies and the courts.[190] In the light of this peculiarity, the following section discusses both administrative and judicial enforcement systems and analyses enforcement statistics.

Judicial Enforcement

In China, the court system comprises four levels with a basic level[191] of about 3,000 courts, an Intermediate Court level [192] of about 400 courts, and a High Court level [193] of about 30 courts,[194] and the SPC. In general, each court consists of civil, criminal, economic and administrative divisions.[195] Out of all courts, it is the SPC which plays a key role in facilitating the interpretation of IP law as it issues comprehensive guidelines on matters such as the strengthening of the IPR trial work or adjudication openness.[196]

IP-related lawsuits are generally grouped into, first, civil law suits, such as patent infringement suits, second, criminal law suits, which play an only minor role in the Chinese court system[197] and, third, administrative suits. Due to their complexity, IP-related civil disputes are usually brought in the first instance of Intermediate Courts which are situated in the capital city of the provinces because, by 2005, the Intermediate Courts at the provincial level in all capital and major Chinese cities and all Higher Courts had established specialized IPR trial divisions.[198] This establishment of IPR trial divisions – also in the SPC itself in 1996[199] – has gone hand in hand with an improved quality of IPR judges which are now considered by some observers among the most educated of civil law judges in China.[200]

---

[190] Nie, *The Enforcement of Intellectual Property Rights in China*, 2006, p. 10.

[191] 基层人民法院 (jīcéng rénmín fǎyuàn).

[192] 中级人民法院 (zhōngjí rénmín fǎyuàn).

[193] 高级人民法院 (gāojí rénmín fǎyuàn).

[194] See Bachner, *Intellectual Property Rights and China. The Modernization of Traditional Knowledge*, 2009, p. 39.

[195] See Zimmermann, China Law Deskbook. A Legal Guide for Foreign-Invested Enterprises, 2004, p. 64.

[196] E.g. 关于加强人民法院审判公开工作的若干意见 (guānyú jiāqiáng rénmín fǎyuàn shěnpàn gòngkāi gòngzuò de ruògān yìjiàn, Several Opinions on Enhancing Adjudication Openness in the People's Courts (2009)).

[197] Lin/Connor, An Overview of the Judicial Protection of Patents in China, Journal of Intellectual Property Law & Practice 3 (2008), pp. 163 et seq. (172–173).

[198] See Bachner, *Intellectual Property Rights and China. The Modernization of Traditional Knowledge*, 2009, p. 55.

[199] Zhang, Intellectual Property Law Enforcement in China: Trade Issues; Policies and Practices, Fordham Intellectual Property, Media & Entertainment Law Journal 8 (1997), pp. 63 et seq. (67).

[200] For contrary opinions see Natividad, Stepping it up and taking it to the streets: Changing Civil & Criminal Copyright Enforcement Tactics, Berkeley Technology Law Journal 23 (2008), pp. 469 et seq. (475).

Improvements of the Chinese judicial enforcement system have not only been widely acknowledged but also celebrated by the system itself as evident by the 2009 publication *Intellectual Property Protection by Chinese Courts.*[201] Efficiency, speed and transparency of the Chinese court system have considerably improved. The clearance rate of first civil IP cases has increased from 75% in 2003 to 85% in 2009 with appeals having dropped from 59% to 49%.[202] The reversal of decisions at second instance has fallen from 15% in 2003 to 6% in 2009.[203] Furthermore, the international reputation of the Chinese court system is increasing with the improvement of its transparency. Thus, the SPC is entertaining a website which contains a database of judgments and decisions of IP-related cases at all court levels since 2006.[204]

Turning to the question of remedies, Chinese law now provides for the remedies as stipulated in the *TRIPS Agreement.* The *General Principles of Civil Law* provide for injunctions, seizures and disposal of infringing goods and related tools and materials, public apology, and damages.[205] The *Civil Procedural Law*[206] further provides for the regulatory principles integral to the *TRIPS Agreement,* such as the entitlement of all parties to a hearing to substantiate their claims and to present all relevant evidence and that this evidence should be heard before the rendering of a judgment.

However, an analysis of trends in litigation and damages awards shows that damages awards are still based upon rather simple calculations based on unjust enrichment disregarding how a market would have evolved in the absence of an infringement.[207] In consequence, economic damages claimed and awarded in Chinese courts are still comparatively low even though there is no upper limit on the damages that could be awarded under the law.[208] Recent IP damages awards

---

[201] SPC, 中国法院知识产权司法保护状况 (2009)年 (zhōngguó fǎyuàn zhīshi chǎnquáns īfǎ bǎohù zhuàngkuàng, Intellectual Property Protection by Chinese Courts in 2009), available at: http://ip.people.com.cn/mediafile/201004/23/P201004230952441589443251.doc.

[202] SPC, 中国法院知识产权司法保护状况 (2009)年 (zhōngguó fǎyuàn zhīshi chǎnquáns īfǎ bǎohù zhuàngkuàng), p. 31.

[203] SPC, 中国法院知识产权司法保护状况 (2009)年 (zhōngguó fǎyuàn zhīshi chǎnquáns īfǎ bǎohù zhuàngkuàng), p. 31.

[204] 中国知识产权裁判文书网 (zhōngguó zhīshi chǎnquán cáipàn wénshū wǎng, China IPR Judgments and Decisions), available at: http://ipr.chinacourt.org/.

[205] Art. 134 of the 中华人民共和国民法通则 (zhōnghuá rénmín gòng hé guó mínfǎ tōngzé, General Principles of Civil Law of the P.R. China), 1986, Gazette of the State Council (国务院公报) 1996, p. 388.

[206] 中华人民共和国民事诉讼法 (修正) (zhōnghuá rénmín gòng hé guó mín shì sù song fǎ, Civil Procedure Law of the People's Republic of China), 1993, revisions 2004, 2007, Gazette of the State Council (国务院公报 (guówùyuàn gōngbào)) 2007, No. 35, p. 1250.

[207] Sepetys/Cox, *Intellectual Property Rights Protection in China: Trends in Litigation and Economic Damages,* 2009, p. 5.

[208] E.g. Art. 58 of *Implementing Regulations of the Patent Law,* 中华人民共和国专利法实施细则 (zhōnghuá rénmín gòng hé guó zhuānlì fǎ shíshī xìzé), Gazette of the State Council (国务院公

show that more than 90% of all IPR damages awards were below 70,000 Euros, that the median damages award across all IP-related cases from 2006 to 2007 was about 10,000 Euros and, thus, constituted about 15% of the original damages claim of IP owners[209] and that the highest damages award ever in Chinese courts to Schneider stood at about 35 million Euros in 2010.[210]

As a results of these insufficient damages awards and despite improvements in Chinese judicial enforcement more generally, foreign entities have remained sceptical in terms of litigation prospect, of the quality of judgments and of chances of actual enforcement of judgments.[211] Local protectionism, poor coordination and agency rivalries are amongst the reasons given for enforcement issues in China.[212] This scepticism is also an emanation of the helplessness of businesses faced with piracy not only being rampant but an accepted and large industry in China.[213] Yet, an excellent preparation of cases through, for instance, the preparation of documentary evidence in support of infringement allegations and in support of the proof of actual losses suffered is known to vastly improve chances of success in Chinese courts.[214]

In conclusion, progress in enforcing IPRs in China has been slow[215] and enforcement is still considered to be the most problematic area in Chinese IP law. However, recent initiatives have led to widespread hopes that the improvement of China's enforcement system will accelerate in upcoming years as a result of the internalization of top-level IP instructions at lower levels of IP administration. Yet, the development of an effective enforcement system will also depend on the

---

报 (guówùyuàn gōngbào)) 2001, No. 23, p. 7. Art. 36 of the *Implementing Regulations of the Copyright Law,* 中华人民共和国著作权法实施条例 (zhōnghuá rénmín gòng hé guó zhùzuò quán fǎ shíshī tiáolì), Gazette of the State Council (国务院公报 (guówùyuàn gōngbào)) 1991, p. 745.

[209] Sepetys/Cox, *Intellectual Property Rights Protection in China: Trends in Litigation and Economic Damages,* 2009, p. 8.

[210] Duncan/Sherwood/Shen, A Comparison Between the Judicial and Administrative Routes to Enforce Intellectual Property Rights in China, John Marshall Review of Intellectual Property Law 7 (2008), pp. 529 et seq. (537).

[211] Zhang, International Civil Litigation in China: A Practical Analysis of the Chinese Judicial System, Boston College International & Comparative Law Review 25 (2002), pp. 59 et seq. (63).

[212] Natividad, Stepping it up and taking it to the streets: Changing Civil & Criminal Copyright Enforcement Tactics, Berkeley Technology Law Journal 23 (2008), pp. 469 et seq. (494).

[213] Creemers, The Effects of World Trade Organisation Case DS362 on Audiovisual Media Piracy in China, European Intellectual Property Review 31 (2009) 11, pp. 568 et seq. (569).

[214] Clark, Intellectual Property Litigation in China, China Business Review 31 (2004) 6, pp. 25 et seq. (28).

[215] Clark, Intellectual Property Litigation in China, China Business Review 31 (2004) 6, pp. 25 et seq. (27).

cultivation of a legal consciousness about the value of intellectual property amongst the common man in China.[216]

Administrative Enforcement

Administrative procedure is a frequently used method for the enforcement of IPRs – and in particular copyrights and trademarks – in China.[217] It constitutes a cost- and time-efficient avenue for IP enforcement albeit not offering financial compensation for the prevailing party. Instead, administrative enforcement allows for the fining of IP infringers and for the seizure of goods or equipment used for manufacturing the respective products.[218]

The evaluation of administrative enforcement procedures is difficult due to the lack of obligation upon administrative agencies to publish information relating to their administrative actions.[219] From a private law perspective, however, administrative proceedings – as a public matter – are to be heavily criticized.[220] Even though the quasi-judicial competences of administrative authorities were considerably curtailed in 2000 and 2001, the administration still has wide-ranging powers to intervene into private rights and, thus, into the market.

Customs protection in China, however, deserves an outright positive evaluation.[221] Numerous laws and regulations have been adopted by the Chinese government requiring Chinese customs authorities to enforce IP laws in relation to the import and export of goods.[222] Recognizing not only legislative but also implementation achievements, the *Quality Brands Protection Committee – China Association*

---

[216] Li, Copyright Reform in China, Intellectual Property Journal 22 (2010), pp. 203 et seq. (221).

[217] Sepetys/Cox, *Intellectual Property Rights Protection in China: Trends in Litigation and Economic Damages, 2009*, p. 4.

[218] Sepetys/Cox, *Intellectual Property Rights Protection in China: Trends in Litigation and Economic Damages, 2009*, p. 5.

[219] Sepetys/Cox, *Intellectual Property Rights Protection in China: Trends in Litigation and Economic Damages, 2009*, p. 5.

[220] For criticism see also Ganea, China, in: Goldstein/Straus (eds.), *Intellectual Property in Asia. Law, Economics, History and Politics*, 2009, pp. 17 et seq. (31).

[221] Jiang, Customs Border Enforcement of IP Rights, China Law & Practice 2009, p. 27.

[222] 中华人民共和国知识产权海关保护条例 (zhōnghuá rénmín gòng hé guó zhīshi chǎnquán hǎiguān bǎohù tiáolì, Rules of the P.R. China on Customs Protection of Intellectual Property Rights), 1995, Gazette of the State Council (国务院公报 (guówùyuàn gōngbào)) 2005, No. 5 (20 February 2004), p. 5. 中华人民共和国知识产权海关保护条例 (zhōnghuá rénmín gòng hé guó zhīshi chǎnquán, Implementing Regulations for the Rules of the People's Republic of China on Customs Protection of Intellectual Property Rights), 2003, Gazette of the State Council (国务院公报) 2005, No. 6 (28 February 2005), pp. 40–46. 关于实施专利权海关保护问题的若干规定 (guānyú shíshī zhuānlìquán hǎiguān bǎohù wèntí de ruògān guīdìng, Circular on Issues Related to the Implementation of Customs Protection of Patent Rights), 1997, Gazette of the State Council (国务院公报 (guówùyuàn gōngbào)) 1997, No. 0 (6 May 1997), pp. 765–766.

of Enterprises with Foreign Investment (QBPC)[223] selected China's Customs Office as the most efficient administrative agency for IP protection in 2007. In the same year, the World Customs Organization (WCO) awarded the "2007 Achievement Award of the WCO for Cracking Down on Counterfeits and Piracies" to China's Customs Office.[224]

In conclusion, administrative channels have long been viewed as the quickest and least expensive way to combat IPR infringement. Until today, they have remained a rather popular option for dealing with violations. However, in the light of the ongoing improvement of enforcement in the courts and in the light of criticism of the quasi-public nature of administrative enforcement, the future will tell which system will prevail. It is hoped that the improvement of customs protection of IPRs will be unaffected by these developments.

Statistics

Although judicial resolution was historically not favoured among the Chinese business community, China has increasingly become a most litigious country.[225] This – together with improvements of the Chinese enforcement system and a growing number of successfully litigated cases in Chinese courts[226] – has also led to foreign companies having been encouraged to proactively litigate their IPRs in China. In consequence, IP-related case numbers have seen a rapid overall increase.

As Fig. 4 demonstrates, the number of concluded IP-related civil cases has increased from 8,332 in 2004 to 24,406 in 2009. In the same period of time, the number of criminal cases has remained largely constant at around 3,000 cases. Administrative cases have doubled from 549 to 1074 cases. Case filings, however, were considerably higher as 50% of IP cases are generally resolved through mediation in China.[227]

These figures are even more striking when compared with the 2,797 trademark cases, the 2,192 copyright cases and the 1,674 patent cases filed in the U.S. in

---

[223] 中国外商投资协会 (zhōngguó wàishāng tóuzī xiéhuì), http://www.qbpc.org.cn.

[224] Wu, Intellectual Property Law as China Moves Toward an Innovation-Oriented Society, in: Cai/Wang, *China's Journey toward the Rule of Law. Legal Reform 1978–2008*, 2010, pp. 349 et seq. (462).

[225] "Real and Present Danger: Patent Litigation in China", Law360 (2009).

[226] See the Schneider case with a 44.3 million U.S. dollar damages award, Duncan/Sherwood/ Shen, A Comparison Between the Judicial and Administrative Routes to Enforce Intellectual Property Rights in China, John Marshall Review of Intellectual Property Law 7 (2008), pp. 529 et seq. (535).

[227] McCabe, Enforcing Intellectual Property Rights: A Methodology for Understanding the Enforcement Problem in China, Pierce Law Review 8 (2009), pp. 1 et seq. (25); Wu, Intellectual Property Law as China Moves Toward an Innovation-Oriented Society, in: Cai/Wang, *China's Journey toward the Rule of Law. Legal Reform 1978–2008*, 2010, pp. 349 et seq. (457).

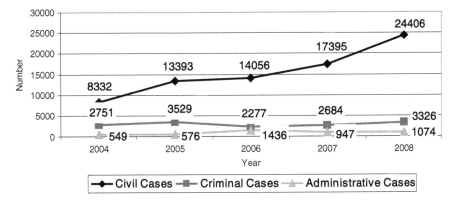

Fig. 4 Number of concluded IPR cases. 2004–2007 figures Wu, Intellectual Property Law as China Moves Toward an Innovation-Oriented Society, in: Cai/Wang, *China's Journey toward the Rule of Law. Legal Reform 1978–2008*, 2010, pp. 349 et seq. (457–458). 2008 figures Cao, *Die Durchsetzung von Patenten in China. Verletzungstatbestände, Gerichtsbarkeit, Gerichtsverfahren und die Durchsetzung durch Patentverwaltungsbehörden*, 2010, p. 11. 2009 figures by Cohen, IP Challenges for Tech Companies in China, Presentation, December 2012, p. 32

2009.[228] The comparatively high number of IP-related cases in China as compared to the U.S. was taken as indicator of an ever-more effective IP system with the caveat, however, that the vast majority of cases are between Chinese parties and involve very small sums of money.[229]

The percentage of cases with matters relating to foreign IPRs confirms this explanation. Out of the 30,626 civil IP cases that were decided in Chinese courts in 2009 only 1,361 cases dealt with matters relating to foreign IPRs.[230] Thus, contrary to Western intuition, an overwhelming majority of 96% of Chinese civil IPR cases were brought by Chinese right holders against Chinese infringers.

Looking more specifically at the types of IPRs litigated, statistics show that – unlike in the U.S. – copyrights are most litigated with 51% of IPR civil cases brought at first instance in 2009.[231] Copyrights are followed by trademarks with 23% of cases, patents with 14% of cases, unfair competition law cases with 4% of cases, technology contracts with 2% of cases, and others with 6% of cases.[232]

Yet, even though there was a clear increase in IP cases in recent years, intellectual property matters are not yet extensively litigated in Chinese court as opposed to civil law matters at large. Out of the 22,145,000 civil cases accepted by the first

---

[228] PWC, 2010 Patent Litigation Study. The Continued Evolution of Patent Damages Law, 2010, available at: http://www.pwc.com/us/en/forensic-services/publications/assets/2010-patent-litigation-study.pdf.

[229] Ian, "IP Litigation Statistics from China: But What Do They Tell Us?", IP Prospective, 9th March, 2010.

[230] Cohen, IP Challenges for Tech Companies in China, Presentation, December 2012, p. 32.

[231] Ibid., p. 34.

[232] Ibid., p. 34.

instance courts in China from 2002 to 2007, only 64,625 cases related to IPR matters thereby accounting merely for 0.29% of the total civil cases.[233]

In summary, Chinese IP statistics reflect the growing sophistication of the Chinese enforcement system and the consequent reliance of right holders on the system. The numbers further reflect a growing tendency to chose the judicial over the administrative avenue of enforcement as it allows not only for the enjoining of the infringer's activity but the recovery of adequate damages.[234]

Concluding Remarks: China's Long March Forward

Over the last 30 years, China has gone a Long March towards the establishment of a modern IP law regime – ranging from policy, law to enforcement. This Long March was influenced not only by social, cultural and historical attitudes but by bilateral and multilateral external pressures and, in particular, the prospect of WTO accession. More recently, Chinese IP policy shift towards a larger innovation agenda was the first omens of China's increasingly functional use of IP policy, law and enforcement for the furtherance of its national innovation system.

China's Long March towards IP protection has led to China's accession to major international IP conventions and the establishment of a relatively comprehensive IP framework. It has further led to an improved administration and enforcement of IP protection through ambitious institutional reforms. The achievements of Chinese IP law reform are reflected in China's enforcement system having gained considerably in sophistication but also in China having become one of the most important locations for IP registration and enforcement.

Nevertheless, China's Long March towards IP protection still requires revision of those laws which are overly general, dispersed, unsystematic or outdated. It also requires institutional solutions to the issue of tattered administration of IPRs and an improvement of the still insufficient and dual enforcement mechanisms. Finally, it requires a further curbing of widespread piracy in conjunction with promoting the IP consciousness of the common man.

In conclusion, the extent of resoluteness and stringency of China's Long March towards IP protection is unknown in the history of IP protection. Soon enough, Chinese pro-innovation IP policy might serve as an example for Western industrialized countries on how to foster scientific, technological and societal innovation. Soon enough, China's Long March forward in IP policy might reach policy-formation processes at the international level and thereby underline the emergence of China as potent force in reshaping the global intellectual property landscape.

---

[233] Ibid., p. 32.

[234] Duncan/Sherwood/Shen, A Comparison Between the Judicial and Administrative Routes to Enforce Intellectual Property Rights in China, John Marshall Review of Intellectual Property Law 7 (2008), pp. 529 et seq. (544).

The Regulation of Trade-Distorting Restrictions in Foreign Investment Law

An Investigation of China's TRIMs Compliance

Julien Chaisse

Introduction: The Regime of International Investment and the WTO Rules

Capital-exporting countries use international rules to seek investment opportunities abroad[1] and to protect their investments in foreign jurisdictions. Capital-importing economies wish to promote inward investment by ensuring that foreign investors have a stable business environment which is in accordances with high international standards. A selected group of developing countries stands on both sides of that road. As developing countries, they wish to benefit from foreign investment. As vigorous and growing economies, it is in their interests to expand their businesses into other markets. The People's Republic of China stands in this particular position.[2] Mainland China has for the last decade been the primary developing

---

[1] However, the extent to which BITs actually attract increased flows of foreign direct investment remains disputed. See Salacuse/Sullivan, Do BITs Really Work?: An Evaluation of Bilateral Investment Treaties and Their Grand Bargain, Harvard International Law Journal 46 (2005), pp. 67–127 (111).

[2] From this dual perspective, China's interests were on providing substantive protection for its investors abroad as well as opening new investment opportunities, while simultaneously consolidating through the undertaking of international obligations internal reforms conducive to promoting domestic market openings and a stable business environment. Given these interests, it may not come as a surprise that China also ranks high in the conclusion of bilateral investment agreements: China has signed 117 such treaties, outclassed only by Germany, which has a world-high of 133 BITs. These agreements negotiated outside of the WTO system, however, demonstrate China's willingness to complement the commitments taken under the WTO in order to improve investment climate for foreign investors.

J. Chaisse (✉)
The Chinese University of Hong Kong, 5/F, Teaching Complex at Western Campus, Shatin, NT, Hong Kong, China
e-mail: Julien.chaisse@cuhk.edu.hk

C. Herrmann and J.P. Terhechte (eds.), *European Yearbook of International Economic Law (EYIEL), Vol. 3 (2012)*, European Yearbook of International Economic Law 3, DOI 10.1007/978-3-642-23309-8_5, © Springer-Verlag Berlin Heidelberg 2012

country receiving foreign direct investment.[3] As a capital-exporting developing country, China also ranks amongst the world highest – it is in the third position.[4]

The current legal framework for foreign investors in China consists of a wide variety of national and international rules and principles that differ in form, strength, and coverage.[5] The result is an increasingly complex international setting for international investment in which governments must ensure consistency between differing sets of obligations. An important advantage of bilateral investment treaties and regional agreements is that they can be tailored to the specific circumstances of the parties concerned, such as their development issues.[6] Comprehensive multilateral rules governing international economics are currently limited to trade issues. Even though the WTO agreements contain major loopholes, multilateral rules on trade constitute a broad umbrella of rights and obligations under which regional, plurilateral and bilateral agreements as well as national laws all regulate trade issues.[7] Although foreign direct investment (FDI) has increased significantly over the last two decades, outpacing the already significant expansion of trade during the same period, the current international legal framework for FDI is highly fragmented.

The WTO and its predecessor organization, GATT, have not directly tackled the broad issue of foreign investment rules. Instead, GATT and the WTO have dealt with a narrow set of very specific issues, which has left nations to formulate their own policies, or through BITs. The WTO handles two major agreements that

---

[3] Bungenberg, Going Global? The EU Common Commercial Policy After Lisbon, in: Herrmann/Terhechte (eds.), *European Yearbook of International Economic Law (2010)*, 2010, p. 125.

[4] On economic data, see e.g., Gugler/Chaisse, Patterns and dynamics of Asia's growing share of FDI, in: Chaisse/Gugler (eds.), *Expansion of Trade and FDI in Asia: Strategic and Policy Challenges*, pp. 4–7.

[5] International investment regulation is an example *par excellence* for fragmentation in an important area of international economic law. See Boie/Chaisse/Gugler, The International Investment Framework – Regulatory Fragmentation Challenge in a Changing World Economy, in: Cottier/Delimatsis (eds.), *The Prospects of International Trade Regulation – From Fragmentation to Coherence*, 2011.

[6] The "treatification" of international investment law shows the significant and quick recalibration of the law of international investment law over the last 20 years. Whereas in 1990 there were approximately 400 BITs negotiated worldwide, by 2010 the number of BITs negotiated globally stood at a staggering 2,740. However, as the number of bilateral investment treaties and regional agreements continues to expand, different standards and disciplines are beginning to be exerted over foreign investments. This might create confusion for MNEs operating on a global scale. See Salacuse, The Treatification of International Investment Law, Law and Business Review of the Americas 13 (2007), pp. 155–166.

[7] Contemporary international of foreign direct investment is one of the fastest-growing areas of international economic regulation. Although national laws and policies still constitute the most concrete and detailed part of the legal framework of FDI, the current system has become increasingly dependent upon international treaties. Predictability may be enhanced when domestic policies and regulations are enshrined or locked into regional and bilateral treaties and agreements. See Xiao, Chinese Bilateral Investment Treaties in the 21st Century, in: Chaisse/Gugler (eds), *Expansion of Trade and FDI in Asia: Strategic and Policy Challenges*, 2009, pp. 4–7.

address investment directly: the General Agreement on Trade in Services (GATS) and the Agreement on Trade-Related Investment Measures (TRIMs).[8] Among the issues addressed, GATT and the WTO have dealt with specific aspects of the relationship between trade and investment through (GATS,[9] which concerns the supply of services by foreign companies, and through TRIMs. Additionally, under WTO rules, investment measures, such as local content rules or trade-balancing requirements, would be prohibited, to the extent that they impact upon trade and violate the GATT rules on national treatment and quantitative restrictions.

Upon China's accession to the WTO, China made comprehensive commitments in areas of international trade and foreign investment, and China has made serious efforts to implement those commitments.[10] It is an important case study because

---

[8] Three further agreements (the Agreement on Trade-Related Aspects of Intellectual Property Rights (TRIPs), the Government Procurement Agreement (GPA), and the Agreement on Subsidies and Countervailing Measures (ASCM)) have only indirect effects on investment. The Agreement on Government Procurement deals with public procurements and services because GATS excludes public procurement services. The GPA requirements deal with investment once they apply to procurement of foreign products or services as well as to goods or services produced by locally established foreign suppliers. The Agreement on Subsidies and Countervailing Measures deals with subsidies. Because the Agreement includes in its definition of subsidies a number of commonly used investment incentives, it does not address this subject in terms of discrimination between foreign and domestic investment. For this reason, this Agreement tackles investment directly but it does not build up any significant incompatibility between foreign and domestic investment. Among them the TRIPs is the most interesting. It provides protection for intangible assets that form the basis of the activities of multinational corporations. It further requires that Members provide effective legal procedures and remedies for the enforcement of such rights.

[9] To the extent that trade in services may require a commercial presence by a foreign service-provider in the territory of another state, the provider may enjoy certain investment rights under the GATS. In the GATS, China made specific commitments in nine out of the 12 large sectors contained in the classification list generally used by Members for GATS scheduling purposes. There are comprehensive commitments related to market access through commercial presence. China has passed laws and regulations which implement those commitments. For example, with regard to value-added, basic mobile voice and data services, Foreign Service providers were permitted to establish joint ventures with the foreign equity restricted to 30%, and the geographic restrictions of providing services were gradually eliminated. To regulate foreign investments in this sector, the 'Provisions on Administration of Telecommunications Enterprises with Foreign Investment' have been promulgated by the State Council in December 2001 and amended in September 2008 (Laws and regulations indicated in this article are available at: http://www.fdi.gov.cn/pub/FDI_EN/Laws/default.jsp?type=530). In April 2004, MOFCOM approved "Measure for the Administration on Foreign Investment in Commercial Field", which permitted the establishment of foreign-funded commercial enterprises and cancelled the geographic restrictions as from 11th December, 2004. Similar foreign investment guidelines were issued by MOFCOM and other Ministries in service sectors, such as international maritime transportation (Provisions on the Administration of Foreign Investment in International Maritime Transportation, on 25th February, 2004) and advertising (Provisions on the Administration of Foreign-invested Advertising Enterprises, on 2nd March, 2004, amended on 22nd August, 2008).

[10] As underscored by Pasha Hsieh, China "has become increasingly active in WTO rule-making by submitting proposals to revise WTO rules and by appointing Chinese nationals to WTO bodies". But this movement has been reinforced by a significant shift "from having a passive attitude to

foreign investment is a crucial parameter of China's development, albeit the TRIMs is certainly not the most commented agreement of the WTO. The TRIMs remains however a frequent origin of trade dispute and is fundamentally the only multilateral agreement addressing investment in the field of goods (the major sector of export for China).[11] China's compliance with the TRIMs Agreement is the main focus of this article and it will be discussed in the following sections. We present the WTO contribution to disciplining China's investment policies (section "WTO Contribution to Disciplining Investment Policies"). The multilateral framework is logically followed by a presentation of the relevant Chinese domestic rules before and after accession (section "China Evolving Regulation of FDI: The Accession Effect"). This effort of compliance by China will be assessed in the light of WTO litigation over the past decade (section "Lessons and Prospects of TRIMs Litigation"). We conclude by drawing key lessons as to the enforcement of the TRIMs in China and its consequences for Chinese investments (section "In Lieu of Conclusion: The TRIMs, the WTO and Beyond").

WTO Contribution to Disciplining Investment Policies

In the Uruguay Round the Agreement on Trade-Related Investment Measures, which prohibits performance requirements involving quantitative restrictions, was adopted. Developing countries are frequent users (but by no means the only users) of TRIMs. The TRIMs Agreement has constituted a next step forward in the investment area at the multilateral level, firstly from the substantive point of view, but it also 'unambiguously and explicitly put investment policies on the multilateral agenda'.[12] It addresses investment measures that are trade-related and which violate Article III (National Treatment) or Article XI (general elimination of quantitative restrictions).

Basically, it prohibits member countries from making the approval of investment conditional on compliance with laws, policies or administrative regulations that

---

acting preemptively in its litigation approach, as demonstrated by a series of complaints that China filed against the US and the European Union from 2007 to 2010". See Hsieh, China's Development of International Economic Law and WTO Legal Capacity Building, Journal of International Economic Law 13 (2010) 4, p. 999.

[11] China amended the Foreign Trade Law in 2004, which replaced the examination and approval procedures by a registration requirement for the right to trade in goods and technology. China has made efforts to improve transparency, e.g., publication of all foreign trade-related laws, regulations, and rules in the China Foreign Trade and Economic Cooperation Gazette, establishment of enquiry points and enquiry websites under the Ministry of Commerce (MOFCOM) and the General Administration of Quality Supervision, Inspection and Quarantine (AQSIQ), and regular notifications to the WTO (See also Trade Policy Review, Report by the Secretariat, People's Republic of China, WT/TPR/S/161, 28th February, 2006).

[12] Brewer/Young: Investment issues at the WTO: the architecture of rules and the settlement of disputes, Journal of International Economic Law 1 (1998) 3, p. 462.

favoured domestic products. The scope of TRIMs regulation is pretty narrow. As an agreement that is based on existing GATT rules on trade in goods, the TRIMs Agreement is not concerned with the regulation of foreign investment. The disciplines of the TRIMs Agreement focus on the discriminatory treatment of imported and exported products and do not govern the issue of entry and treatment of foreign investment. Even if commentators frequently pointed out the shortcomings of this agreement, the TRIMs agreement adds value to the WTO system by describing types of trade-related investment measures that are considered to be inconsistent with GATT Article III or XI.

Prohibition of Trade-Distorting Restrictions

Governments often tend to impose trade-related investment measures (performance requirements) to achieve certain national priorities. These measures relate to trade-distorting restrictions imposed by the host country on multinational enterprises, which negatively influence trade as well as investment development. According to John Dunning,[13] performance-related measures may embrace the whole gamut of operating practice. They can notably include behavioural guidelines or requirements in respect of local purchases of capital goods, raw materials, intermediate goods and services, the proportion of output exported, the type of value added (e.g., R&D) undertaken by affiliates, information provided on intra-firm pricing practices, conditions attached by MNEs on the use of technology transferred.

The TRIMs Agreement, however, does not attempt to regulate the entry and treatment of foreign investment, but it applies only to those measures that impose discriminatory treatment on imported and exported goods. This Agreement recognizes that certain national practices, such as local content requirements, can restrict and distort trade and, therefore, supports the concept of 'national treatment'. As a result, the Agreement outlaws investment measures that restrict quantities, and it discourages measures which limit a company's imports or which set targets for the company in relation to exporting. Among the measures not covered by the Agreement are export performance requirements, technology transfer requirements, and subsidies to attract investments in specific industries or projects.

The Agreement did not define TRIMs, but provided an illustrative list (Annex 1). The lack of a precise definition means that the issue is not always clear-cut, and there has been disagreement as to whether or not certain measures are covered by the Agreement. Yet, the WTO has recognized that some of the TRIMs violate the principles of the GATT and it has required countries to abandon the TRIMs that have been identified as being inconsistent with the GATT rules.

---

[13] Dunning, Multinational Enterprises and the Globalization of Innovatory Capacity, Research Policy 23 (1994) 1, pp. 67–88.

A few things should be mentioned at this stage on the question of the relationship between TRIMs and GATT. The issue of the legal relationship between the GATT and the TRIMs Agreement arises when a measure is challenged under both agreements. Several panels have dealt with measures which have been challenged under both provisions of the GATT and Article 2.1 of the TRIMs agreement. Panels have analysed whether measures should be examined under the TRIMs Agreement before being examined under the GATT, based on the principle that, where two agreements apply, the more specific agreement should be examined before the more general agreement.[14] In another case, the panel analysed the measures in question under the GATT first, partly because India, the responding party, encouraged the panel to refrain from analysing the measures under the TRIMs Agreement. The panel then stated that 'for the purposes of this case, therefore, there appears to be, in that respect, no particular reason to start our examination on any particular order. Nor does it find that the end result would be affected by either determination of order of analysis'.[15] The order of analysis should not affect the outcome but may have an impact on the potential for panels to apply the principle of judicial economy.[16] WTO jurisprudence suggests that panels finding a violation of one of the agreements will consider that the action taken to remedy the inconsistencies under one agreement would necessarily remedy any inconsistencies under the other agreement.[17]

---

[14] "As to which claims, those under Article III:4 of GATT or Article 2 of the TRIMs Agreement, to examine first, we consider that we should firstly examine the claims under the TRIMs Agreement because the TRIMs Agreement is more specific than Article III:4 as far as the claims under consideration are concerned. A similar issue was presented in *Bananas III*, where the Appellate Body discussed the relationship between Article X of GATT and Article 1.3 of the Licensing Agreement and concluded that the Licensing Agreement being more specific it should have been applied first. This is also in line with the approach of the panel and the Appellate Body in the *Hormones* dispute, where the measure at issue was examined first under the SPS Agreement since the measure was alleged to be an SPS measure" (footnotes omitted). Report of the Panel, Indonesia – Certain Measures Affecting the Automobile Industry, WT/DS54/R, WT/DS55/R, WT/DS59/R, WT/DS64/R, 2nd July, 1998, para. 14.63.

[15] Report of the Panel, India – Measures Affecting the Automotive Sector, WT/DS146/R, WT/DS175/R, 21st December, 2001, para. 7.158.

[16] See Report of the Panel, India – Measures Affecting the Automotive Sector, WT/DS146/R, WT/DS175/R, 21st December, 2001, paras. 7.158–7.161. See Matsushita/Mavroidis/Schoenbaum, *The World Trade Organization – Law, Practice and Policy*, 2003, pp. 527–529.

[17] "Under the principle of judicial economy, a panel only has to address the claims that must be addressed to resolve a dispute or which may help a losing party in bringing its measures into conformity with the WTO Agreement. The local content requirement aspects of the measures at issue have been addressed pursuant to the claims of the complainants under the TRIMs Agreement. We consider therefore that action to remedy the inconsistencies that we have found with Indonesia's obligations under the TRIMs Agreement would necessarily remedy any inconsistency that we might find with the provisions of Article III:4 of GATT". Report of the Panel, Indonesia – Certain Measures Affecting the Automobile Industry, WT/DS54/R, WT/DS55/R, WT/DS59/R, WT/DS64/R, 2nd July, 1998, para. 14.93.

Scope of TRIMs Regulation

TRIMs may be understood to be any measure taken by a government to discriminate between a domestically produced good and a good produced overseas. This includes:

- Local content requirements: where governments require a corporation to use or purchase domestic products in order to avoid a penalty or to benefit from an incentive.
- Trade-balancing measures where governments impose restrictions on the import of inputs by a corporation or limit the import of inputs in accordance with its level of exports.
- Foreign exchange balancing requirements where an enterprise has the level of imports linked to the value of its exports in order to maintain a net foreign exchange earning.

Article III:4 and Article XI:1 of the GATT are worded broadly enough to cover investment-related measures. Article III:4 of the GATT applies to 'all laws, regulations and requirements affecting ... internal sale, offering for sale, purchase, transportation, distribution or use'. Article III:4 has been found to apply to investment-related measures that require the investor to use a certain amount of 'domestic content' in manufacturing operations.[18] Article XI:1 applies to 'prohibitions or restrictions' other than duties, taxes or other charges on the importation, exportation or sale for export of any product. By definition, we must emphasize that any measure that conditions investment upon export performance operated as a restriction.

The Illustrative List is annexed to the TRIMs Agreement and it 'provides additional guidance as to the identification of certain measures considered to be inconsistent with Article III:4 and XI:1 of the GATT 1994'.[19] As the *Indonesia – Automobiles* panel observed: 'An examination of whether the measures [in question] are covered by Item (1) of the Illustrative List ... will not only indicate whether they are trade-related but also whether they are inconsistent with Article III:4 and thus in violation of Article 2.1 of the TRIMs agreement'.[20]

This List cites the following as examples of host-country investment measures that either restrict imports or exports or require imports or exports: local content requirement; export performance requirements; trade-balancing requirements; foreign exchange balancing restrictions; and restrictions on an enterprise's export or sale for export of products. Such measures are prohibited.

---

[18] Report of the Panel, Canada – Administration of the Foreign Investment Review Act (FIRA), L/5504 - 30 S/140, 7th February, 1984, p. 140.

[19] Report of the Panel, India – Measures Affecting the Automotive Sector, WT/DS146/R, WT/DS175/R, 21st December, 2001, para. 7.157.

[20] Report of the Panel, Indonesia – Certain Measures Affecting the Automobile Industry, WT/DS54/R, WT/DS55/R, WT/DS59/R, WT/DS64/R, 2nd July, 1998, para. 14.83.

Member states were then given a 'transition period' during which their notified TRIMs were to be eliminated. The TRIMs agreement provided for three different transition periods during which WTO Members, according to their level of development, must phase out WTO- inconsistent TRIMs that were notified to the Council on Trade in Goods.[21] A transition period allowed WTO Members to phase out WTO-inconsistent measures that were notified to the WTO under the TRIMs Agreement. If a government does *not* notify the WTO of an existing TRIM, then it is open to legal action by other WTO members. The length of time was based on a state's level of development: developed countries were given 2 years; developing countries were given 5 years; and least-developed countries were given 7 years. Therefore all developing countries should have implemented the TRIMs agreement and eliminated their regulations by 1st January, 2000. The problem with this notification provision is that failure to notify can be largely left unpunished because WTO remedies are always prospective.

The general WTO dispute settlement procedure, as laid down in the Dispute Settlement Understanding, also applies to disputes arising under the TRIMs Agreement (Article 8). Issues relating to the alleged inconsistency of particular measures with the TRIMs Agreement have been raised in a dispute settlement proceeding in which a panel was established in 1997 concerning measures applied by Indonesia in the automotive sector. We will detail this case and subsequent ones to examine in which circumstances the TRIMs Agreement has been used to regulate investment domestic regulations.

TRIMs Shortcomings: Issues and Options

The TRIMs Agreement bans a limited number of performance requirements insofar as they are inconsistent with GATT provisions on national treatment and quantitative restrictions. All Members needed to notify and phase out contravening measures, although developing and least-developed countries were granted transitive periods. The Agreement has considerably enhanced the transparency of investment policies around the world. To promote business and investment, it is very important to emphasize transparency. The TRIMs Agreement greatly relies on transparency because it requires each Member to notify of the publications in which TRIMs may be found, including those applied by regional and local governments and authorities.

But beyond these beneficial aspects, the TRIMs Agreement has several drawbacks.

---

[21] Art. 5.2 TRIMs: "Each Member shall eliminate all TRIMs which are notified under paragraph 1 within two years of the date of entry into force of the WTO Agreement in the case of a developed country Member, within five years in the case of a developing country Member, and within seven years in the case of a least-developed country Member".

Firstly, the Agreement is limited only to measures affecting trade in goods.

Secondly, the Agreement is notable for its lack of any reference to most-favoured-nation treatment, for the lack of a specific definition of investment; also fair and equitable treatment is also not mentioned in the Agreement.

Above all, whereas the Agreement prohibits a category of performance requirements that impact negatively upon trade (e.g., requirements to export a given percentage of goods), governments generally remain free to impose a broad range of other requirements on foreign investors including requirements to establish joint ventures, hire local employees (including from minority or disadvantaged groups), or invest in local research and development. In contrast to this, Article 1106 of NAFTA contains an extensive list of prohibited policies concerning export percentages, domestic content percentages, domestic purchase requirements or preferences, relationships between imports and exports or foreign exchange flows, relationships of domestic sales and exports or foreign earnings, technology transfer requirements, or exclusive supplier arrangements. Thus, NAFTA represents a significant advance in attempts to limit performance requirements. To the same extent, whereas the Agreement is only applicable to local content requirements and trade-balancing requirements, the Multilateral Agreement for Investment would have regulated the use of the following performance requirements: trade-related performance requirements such as the ratio of exports to total sales; the domestic content; local purchases; the ratio of imports to exports; and the ratio of local sales to exports.

Technically, TRIMs could be expanded by adding more examples to the Illustrative List.[22] This adds to the uncertainty about which aspects of a national industrial policy can or will be challenged in the WTO – either through a loose interpretation of TRIMs or additions to the Illustrative List.

China Evolving Regulation of FDI: The Accession Effect

All WTO Members, and therefore China, are bound by the obligation to adapt their legal systems to WTO law. This obligation must be seen from the point of view of the international organization for two reasons.[23] The first reason is the willingness to find tools that can ensure that international trade laws are enforced effectively on behalf of those who have undertaken to implement them. In this sense, the provision in Article XVI:4 does not contain anything original because that is the aim of every international organisation or of any entity that lays down rules intended to be

---

[22] See Edwards/Lester, Towards a More Comprehensive World Trade Organization Agreement on Trade Related Investment Measures, Stanford Journal of International Law 33 (1997), p. 169.

[23] See Chaisse/Chakraborty, Implementing WTO Rules through Negotiations and Sanction: The Role of Trade Policy Review Mechanism and Dispute Settlement System, University of Pennsylvania Journal of International Economic Law 28 (2007) 1, pp. 153–186.

enforced by a particular social body. At the same time, the obligation to conform is justified only insofar as its immediate object is to avoid any risk of conflict between two legal systems (the WTO system and Members' internal systems) as well as serious disputes between various Members of the organization.

China's national regulation of trade-distorting restrictions in foreign investment law had to in compliance with WTO law at the time of its accession to the organisation. China's national regulation of trade-distorting restrictions in foreign investment law is a three-tiered legal system,[24] consisting of constitutional rules, national laws, and sub-national laws. As a result, the current domestic legal framework for foreign investments which has been constructed as a result of the reforms and open policy as from 1978, has also experienced a major transformation in the years 2000 in order to comply with TRIMs. The Chinese efforts to comply will be interpreted.

China's Regulation of FDI: An Overview

Several law, regulations and measures apply to foreign investment in China.[25] The first piece of national legislation in this respect was the *Law on Chinese-Foreign Equity Joint Venture* (EJVL),[26] passed by the National People's Congress in 1979. In 1982, a new Article 18 was added to the Constitution. It requires all foreign enterprises and EJVL in China to abide by Chinese law, and it promises that their rights and interests are protected by Chinese law; the protection of foreign investments has thereby been granted in the Chinese Constitution.

A few years later, the *Law on Wholly Foreign-owned Enterprises* (WFEL, 1986)[27] and the *Law on Chinese-Foreign Contractual Joint Venture* (CJVL, 1988)[28] were promulgated. The EJVL, CJVL and WFEL, with their respective

---

[24] Chinese laws mentioned in this article are available at: http://www.fdi.gov.cn/pub/FDI_EN/ Laws/ default.jsp?type = 530 (last visited on 15th March, 2011), most of which is also in an English version.

[25] The comprehensive list of norms reviewed in this paper is provided in Annex 1: List of Chinese norms with Trade-distorting Restrictions in Foreign Investment Law. For an overview, see Wolff, *Mergers and Acquisitions in China: Law and Practice*, (3rd ed.) 2009, pp. 5–24.

[26] The EJIL was adopted at the Second Session of the Fifth National People's Congress on 1st July, 1979. Under the Equity Joint Venture, the rights and obligations of the partners are divided in accordance with the equity/shares they possess.

[27] The WFEL was adopted at the Fourth Session of the Sixth National People's Congress on 12th April, 1986.

[28] The CJVL was adopted at the First Session of the Seventh National People's Congress on 13th April, 1988. Under the Contractual Joint Venture, everything, e.g., the investment or conditions for cooperation, the distribution of earnings, is defined by the joint venture contract between the partners.

implementing regulations,[29] constitute the basic legal framework for foreign investments in China. Besides, China has issued rules and regulations concerning some specific foreign investment forms, including: *Regulations on the Exploitation of Offshore Petroleum Resources in Cooperation with Foreign Enterprises* (REOFF, 1982); *Regulations on the Exploitation of Onshore Petroleum Resources in Cooperation with Foreign Enterprises* (REON, 1993); *Interim Provisions Concerning Some Issues on the Establishment of Joint Stock Limited Companies with Foreign Investment* (1995); *Interim Provisions on the Establishment of Investment Companies with Foreign Investment* (1995), replaced by *Provisions on the Establishment of Investment Companies with Foreign Investment* (2003); *Interim Provisions on Mergers and Acquisitions of Domestic Enterprises by Foreign Investors* (2003), replaced by *Provisions on Mergers and Acquisitions of Domestic Enterprises by Foreign Investors* (2006).

With respect to investment admission, the *Provisions on Guiding the Orientation of Foreign Investment* (hereafter the Guidance) was promulgated in 2002. The Guidance provides that the *Catalogue for the Guidance of Foreign Investment Industries* (hereafter the Catalogue) shall be formulated and revised in a timely way.[30] Projects with foreign investment are thereby classified into four categories, namely, encouraged, permitted, restricted and prohibited. The encouraged, restricted and prohibited industries are listed in the catalogue whereas all the others are classified as permitted by default. In addition, in order to encourage foreign investment into the underdeveloped Central-Western Region, a *Catalogue of Advantaged Industries for Foreign Investment in the Central-Western Region* was adopted,[31] and the industries listed therein may enjoy the preferential policies for the encouraged projects.

Prior to its accession to the WTO, as with many other developing countries, China believed that the imposition of performance requirements would enhance the value of the foreign investment,[32] and many such requirements were incorporated into the Chinese investment laws.

---

[29] They are the Regulations for the Implementation the Law on Chinese-Foreign Equity Joint Venture (hereafter the Implementation Regulations of the EJVL), promulgated by the State Council on 20th September, 1983; the Detailed Rules for the Implementation of the Law on Wholly Foreign-owned Enterprises (hereafter the Implementation Regulations of the WFEL), approved by the State Council on 28th October, 1990 and promulgated by the Ministery of Foreign Trade and Economic Cooperation (MOFTEC) on 12th December, 1990; and the Rules for the Implementation of the Law on Chinese–Foreign Contractual Joint Venture (hereafter the Implementation Regulations of the CJVL), approved by the State Council on 7th August, 1995 and promulgated by the MOFTEC on 4th September, 1995.

[30] Accordingly, the Catalogue was promulgated in 2002, and the latest revision took place in 2007.

[31] The latest revision in 2008.

[32] To the point of view of the developing countries in this respect, see Sornarajah, *The International Law on Foreign Investment*, 2004, p. 237.

- Local content: The local content requirement was incorporated into all Chinese basic laws on foreign investment. Article 9(2) of the EJVL (1990),[33] Article 57 of the Implementation Regulations of the EJVL (1983), Article 19 of the CJVL (1988), Article 15 of the WFEL (1986), as well as Articles 19 and 20 of the REOFF (1982), stipulated 'purchasing in China as far as possible'.
- Foreign exchange balancing: The foreign exchange balancing was another performance requirement, like the local content, which could be found in Chinese basic foreign investment laws. With respect to the EJVs, Article 75 of the Implementation Regulations of the EJVL (1983) explicitly provided for that a EJV shall in general maintain a balance between its foreign exchange receipts and expenditures. To this end, Article 14 required a statement in the joint venture contract relating to the arrangement for receipts and expenditures in a foreign currency. It is likely that Article 20 of the CJVL (1988), Article 18(3) of the WFEL (1986), Article 3, and Article 56 of the Implementation Regulations of the WFEL (1990) contained a foreign exchange balancing requirement.
- Export performance: There are several provisions in the Implementation of the EJVL (1983), which stipulated the export performance requirement:
- Article 4 set out the export performance as one of those selective requirements to be complied with when an EJV applied for the establishment;
- Article 14 provided for a statement in the joint venture contract relating to the ratio of products sold within China to those sold abroad;
- Article 28 required industrial property rights contributed as investment by the foreign investor to be capable of producing exports.

Export performance played an important role in the admission of the establishing a WFE in China. According to the Article 3 (1) WFEL (1986), the establishment of a WFE would be permitted only if it was export-oriented or technologically advanced. Therefore, in the Implementation Regulations of the WFEL (1990):

- Articles 10 and 15 required a statement relating to the ratio of products sold within China to those sold abroad for the application for establishment of a WFE, and, according to Article 45, the domestic sales should in general not exceed this ratio;
- Article 28 provided that industrial property rights contributed as investment by the foreign investor had to be capable of producing exports.

Complying with TRIMs

WTO allows its Members considerable room for manoeuvre as far as the formal conditions of conformity are concerned. In fact, it is not obligatory for WTO

---

[33] The EJIL from 1979 was revised in 1990 and adopted at the Third Session of the Seventh National People's Congress on 4th April, 1990.

members to comply in a determined, homogeneous and formal manner following the enactment of law incorporating these rules in their internal legal systems. "Conformity can be ensured in different ways in different legal systems. [...] Only by understanding and respecting the specificities of each Member's legal system, can a correct evaluation of conformity be established."[34] Hence the statement claiming that "it is the end result that counts, not the manner in which it is achieved".[35]

As the prospect of WTO accession had been cleared, China began with the revision of its investment laws to comply with the obligations of the TRIMs Agreement as well as the Accession Protocol by using different instruments such as laws, regulations and measures. It has to be noted that China had undertaken some TRIMs-plus obligations in its Accession Protocol.[36]

- Firstly, China committed itself to immediate compliance with TRIMs Agreement, without recourse to the provisions of Article 5, which provides for a transition period for the elimination of TRIMs.
- Secondly, China shall not only eliminate trade-balancing and foreign exchange balancing requirements, local content, and domestic sales requirements, which are explicitly mentioned in the Illustrative List, but also the export performance, which might be regarded as not included in the Illustrative List. Moreover, China undertook not to enforce the provisions of contracts imposing such requirements.
- Thirdly, China shall ensure that the distribution of import licences, quotas, tariff-rate quotas, or any other means of approval for importation, the right of importation or investment by national and sub-national authorities, are not conditional on performance requirements of *any kind*, including offsets, the transfer of technology, export performance, or the conduct of research and development in China.[37]

---

[34] The AB further affirms that "frequently the Legislator itself does not seek to control, through statute, all covered conduct. Instead it delegates to pre-existing or specially created administrative agencies or other public authorities, regulatory and supervisory tasks which are to be administered according to certain criteria and within discretionary limits set out by the Legislator. The discretion can be wide or narrow according to the will of the Legislator". Report of the Panel, United States – Sections 301–310 of the Trade Act of 1974, WT/DS152/R, 22nd December, 1999, para. 7.25.

[35] Report of the Panel, United States – Sections 301–310 of the Trade Act of 1974, WT/DS152/R, 22nd December, 1999, para. 7.24.

[36] Paragraph 7.3 of the Accession of the People's Republic of China, WT/L/432, 23rd November, 2001. China's major impact on WTO law stems from the special terms of the accession of this "gigantic transition economy", many of which depart from the basic norms and principles of the WTO law, see: Qin, China, India, and the Law of the World Trade Organization, in: Sornarajah/ Wang (eds.), *China, India and the International Economic Order*, 2010, p. 182.

[37] It could be an interesting question whether the structure of those China's commitments to TRIMs could contribute to the interpretation of the TRIMs Agreement, e.g., that export performance would be prohibited by the Agreement also, whereas technology transfers are not.

The results of China's efforts to comply with TRIMs requirements are synthesized in Table 1.

On 31st October, 2000, the State Council revised the CJVL[38] and the WFEL. A few months later, on 15th March, 2001, the EJVL was revised. Subsquently, the revision of the Implementation Regulations of the WFEL, on 12th April, 2001, and of the Implementation Regulations of the EJVL, on 22nd July, 2001, took place. Finally, the REOFF and the REON were revised on 23rd September, 2001.

By this revision,[39] the above-listed provisions of the respective laws were either deleted or amended.

- Article 9(2) of the EJVL (1990) was amended, and the new provision[40] read as follows: 'The joint venture may purchase the materials [...] either on the domestic or international market according to the principle of fairness and reasonableness.' Article 19 of the CJVL (1988) and Article 15 of the WFEL (1986) were amended in the same way. The local content requirement in Article 57 of the Implementation Regulations of the EJVL (1983) and Articles 19 and 20 of the REOFF (1982) were simply deleted.
- With respect to the foreign exchange balancing, Article 75 of the Implementation Regulations of the EJVL (1983), Article 20 of the CJVL (1988), Article 18 (3) of the WFEL (1986) and Article 56 of the Implementation Regulations of the WFEL (1990) were deleted. The 'arrangement for receipts and expenditures in foreign currency' in the Article 14 of the Implementation Regulations of the EJVL (1983) was moved away from the required content of joint venture contract. Article 3 of the Implementation Regulations of the WFEL (1990) was revised. Instead of the explicit foreign exchange balancing requirement, the new version of this provision provided that the State 'encourages the establishment of export-oriented wholly foreign-owned enterprises'.
- The export performance requirements in the Implementation Regulations of the EJVL (1983) were deleted, including: Article 4; the phrase 'the ratio of products sold within China to those sold abroad' in Article 14; and the requirement in Article 28 that industrial property rights contributed as investment by the foreign investor must be capable of producing exports. Likely, in the Implementation Regulations of the WFEL (2001), the phrase 'the ratio of products sold within China to those sold abroad' in Articles 10 and 15, and the requirement relating to

---

[38] The Implementation Regulations of the CJVL were not subject to this revision, probably because they were promulgated in 1995, later than were the other basic investment laws, and they did not contain the prohibited TRIMs.

[39] For a brief notification of this revision of the WTO by China, see Communication From China, G/TRIMS/W/27, 22nd October, 2002. Since then, China has made annual Communications, as follows: G/TRIMS/W/34 from 2003, G/TRIMS/W/40 from 2004, G/TRIMS/W/45 from 2005, G/TRIMS/W/51 from 2006, G/TRIMS/W/56 from 2007, G/TRIMS/W/59 from 2008, and G/TRIMS/W/64 from 2009. Except the Communication from 2008, other Communications did contain little, if any, new information.

[40] Renumbered as Art. 10 of the EJVL (2001).

Table 1 China's Compliance with TRIMs

Piece of legislation	Key provisions	Year of entry into force	Content of revision
Revision of the EJVL		2001	
	Article 9 (2)		Deleted the phrase 'purchasing in China as far as possible'
Revision of the Implementation Regulations of the EJVL		2001	
	Article 57		Deleted the phrase 'purchasing in China as far as possible'
	Article 14		Deleted foreign exchange balancing and export performance requirement
	Article 75		Deleted
	Article 4		Deleted
	Article 28		Deleted export performance requirement
Revision of the REOFF		2001	
	Articles 19 and 20		Deleted
Revision of the WFEL		2000	
	Article 15		Deleted the phrase 'purchasing in China as far as possible'
	Article 18 (3)		Deleted
	Article 3 (1)		Substituted by the encouragement of export
Revision of the Implementation Regulations of the WFEL		2001	
	Article 3		Substituted by the encouragement of export
	Article 56		Deleted
	Article 10		Deleted the phrase 'the ratio of products sold within China to those sold abroad'
	Article 15		Deleted the phrase 'the ratio of products sold within China to those sold abroad'
	Article 28		Deleted the requirement that industrial property rights contributed as foreign investment to be capable of producing exports
Revision of the CJVL		2000	
	Article 19		Deleted the phrase 'purchasing in China as far as possible'
	Article 20		Deleted

Source: Constructed by the author from China's national law

the industrial property rights in Article 28 were also abolished. Moreover, the compulsory condition for WFEs to be export-oriented or technologically advanced was deleted. Instead, the new Article 3 of the WFEL (2001) provides that the State 'may encourage' the establishment of WFEs of that kind. Accordingly, Article 45 of the Implementation Regulations of the WFEL was changed to read: 'A wholly foreign-owned enterprise may sell its products in Chinese market. The State encourages wholly foreign-owned enterprises to export their products.'

Hence, the revision of Chinese basic investment laws to comply with the TRIMs Agreement took place prior to the WTO accession. Provisions obviously in contradiction with the obligations in the TRIMs Agreement and those in the Accession Protocol were deleted. On the other hand, it has to be noted that this revision was extensive.[41] Its most important objective was perhaps the compliance with the WTO obligations. Nevertheless, some provisions which were not covered by the WTO rules were amended too, because they were unsuitable to new circumstances in reform and development.[42]

Interpreting China's TRIMs Compliance

With respect to this revision, one may make some interesting observations.

Firstly, the deletion of TRIMs in the EJVL was thorough and neat, but not in the WFEL. The latter still explicitly *encourages* the WFEs to export their products. Whether this is consistent with the TRIMs Agreement or not will be discussed below. The possible considerations underpinning such differences are noteworthy. In an EJV, Chinese partners play a part in the decision of the enterprise, and they may still learn something from the foreign partners. Thus, the State may consider it as sufficient to benefit domestic industries and development. This is not the case in a WFE. Therefore, the State would encourage the WFEs to be export-oriented and technologically advanced, in order to make foreign investment beneficial to development.

Secondly, the extensiveness of the revision could imply that it was not only the compliance with the WTO obligations, but also a part of the autonomous reform of the legal framework on foreign investment. From the Chinese point of view, the progressive reform of the legal system in accordance with its development level would be as important as the compliance with the international law obligations. China's attitude towards the performance requirements in general seems to be unchanged, namely, as mentioned above, that they would consider the value of

---

[41] For a comprehensive description of this revision, see Shan, Towards a Level Playing Field of Foreign Investment in China, Journal of World Investment 3 (2002) 2, p. 327.
[42] Ibid, p. 334.

the foreign investment. Logically, China would impose those performance requirements, which were deemed necessary for development, but not, at least not obviously, in contradiction with the TRIMs Agreement.

The willingness of China to maintain certain performance requirements can be proved by its practice of BITs and investment chapters in the FTAs. The US Model BIT[43] and FTAs, for example the US–Singapore FTA,[44] explicitly prohibit an extended list of performance requirements which go beyond the TRIMs Agreement. Although the ASEAN Comprehensive Investment Agreement, an agreement among developing countries, does not provide for the prohibition of performance requirements as do the US BITs, it is open to further development in this respect, as the Member States shall undertake assessment to consider the need for additional commitment.[45] On the other hand, Chinese BITs and FTAs have not dealt with the issue of performance requirements until now. The only exception is the China–New Zealand FTA (2008), which provides that the TRIMs Agreement shall be incorporated *mutatis mutandis* into the FTA (Article 140). Because both states are WTO Members such a provision does not have practical significance.

Lessons and Prospects of TRIMs Litigation

A given law, independently of its application in a precise case (and comparatively without any actual damage), can be incompatible with the WTO law as reaffirmed on several occasions in jurisprudence.[46] This is what the Panel means when it states that Article XVI:4 "though not expanding the material obligations under WTO agreements, expands the type of measures made subject to these obligations",[47] without, however, claiming that it does not induce a widening of the range of the obligations. The three types of measures explicitly made subject to the obligations imposed in the WTO Agreements (*"laws, regulations and administrative*

---

[43] Art. 8 of the 2005 Model BIT of the USA, available at: http://www.state.gov/documents/organization/ 117601.pdf (last visited on 20th January, 2011).

[44] Art. 15.8 of the United States – Singapore Free Trade Agreement, available at: http://www.ustr.gov/trade-agreements/free-trade-agreements (last visited on 20th January, 2011).

[45] Art. 7 of the ASEAN Comprehensive Investment Agreement, available at: http://www.aseansec.org/ documents/FINAL-SIGNED-ACIA.pdf (last visited on 20th January, 2011).

[46] Report of the Panel, Argentina – Measures Affecting Imports of Footwear, Textiles, Apparel and other Items, WT/DS56/R, 25th November, 1997, paras. 6.45–6.47. Regarding the same case, Report of the Appellate Body, Argentina – Measures Affecting Imports of Footwear, Textiles, Apparel and other items, WT/DS56/AB/R, 27th March, 1998, paras. 48–55. Also see Report of the Panel, Canada – Export Credits and Loan Guarantees for Regional Aircraft, WT/DS222/R, 28th January, 2002, paras. 9.124 and 9.208, Report of the Panel, Turkey – Restrictions on Imports of Textile and Clothing Products, WT/DS34/R, 31st May 1999, para. 9.37.

[47] Report of the Panel, United States – Sections 301–310 of the Trade Act of 1974, WT/DS152/R, 22nd December, 1999, para. 7.41.

procedures") are measures that are applicable generally; not measures taken necessarily in a specific case or dispute.

Basically, the TRIMs Agreement prohibits Member Countries from making the approval of investment conditional on compliance with laws, policies or administrative regulations that favour domestic products. The Agreement did not define TRIMs, but it provided an illustrative list (Annex 1). The lack of a precise definition means that the issue is not always clear-cut and there has been considerable disagreement as to whether or not certain measures are covered by the Agreement.

The TRIMs Agreement prohibits WTO Members from applying TRIMs that are inconsistent with Article III of the GATT. The TRIMs Agreement prohibits WTO Members from applying TRIMs that are inconsistent with Article XI of the GATT. We will the see the potential for TRIMs disputes which involve China. In 2007, the case *China – Measures Granting Refunds, Reductions or Exemptions from Taxes* stopped at the consultation stage, whereas the case *China – Measures Affecting Imports of Automobile Parts* reached the Appelate Body in 2008. None of these two cases offer significant lessons but we can anticipate further disputes by looking at the current Chinese legislation.

Inconsistency with GATT Article III:4

Article III:1 of the GATT 1994 establishes a general principle according to which internal regulations and taxes should not be applied 'so as to afford protection to domestic production'. It informs, as a chapeau, the following paragraphs of the provision. Paragraph 2 stipulates national treatment in relation to internal taxes and other internal charges, whereas Paragraph 4 sets out the general obligation to accord imported products treatment no less favourable than that accorded to like products of national origin in respect of internal laws and regulations affecting the sale and use of such products. The second notion of equal treatment and mainstay of the world trading system under the WTO is the principle of national treatment prohibiting discrimination between products (goods and services) produced domestically and those imported from other member countries. Together with the MFN obligation, it forms the fundamental principle of non-discrimination in WTO law in the limit of existing exceptions.[48]

In regulations explicitly treating domestic and imported products differently, a violation of the national treatment obligation is obvious because an internal law affecting the sale of products, or a tax, on its face has discriminatory effect. Most regulations, however, are designed in a neutral and *de jure* non-discriminatory

---

[48] National treatment is subject to a number of important exceptions, thus permitting differential treatment for various policy reasons. In the GATT 1994, the most common exceptions are stipulated in Art. III:8 (subsidisation and government procurement), Art. XVI (subsidies), Art. XIX (safeguard measures), Art. XX (general exceptions) and Art. XXI (security exceptions).

manner but nonetheless result in *de facto* discriminatory treatment of imported products. The distinction between *de jure* and *de facto* discrimination is often difficult to draw and blurred in practice. The problem is related to the scope of protection under national treatment. Since the early days of the GATT 1947, the scope of national treatment has been read in broad terms and thus has traditionally covered *de facto* discriminations extensively.

The Illustrative List annexed to the TRIMs Agreement sets out two categories of 'TRIMs that are inconsistent with the obligation of national treatment provided for in [Article III:4 of the GATT]'[49] TRIMs that are inconsistent with Article III:4 include TRIMs that are:

> 'mandatory or enforceable under domestic law or under administrative rulings, or compliance with which is necessary to obtain an advantage, and which require:
> - the purchase or use by an enterprise of products of domestic origin or from any domestic source [...]' or
> - 'that an enterprise's purchases or use of imported products be limited to an amount related to the volume or value of local products that it exports'.[50]

For example, it is a violation of the requirement of national treatment for an investment measure to require the purchase of local products by foreign enterprises to be tied in with its exports. In *Indonesia – Certain Measures Affecting the Automobile Industry*, the panel ruled on the legality of an Indonesian car programme linking tax benefits for cars manufactured in Indonesia to domestic content requirements and linking customs duty benefits for imported components of cars manufactured in Indonesia to similar domestic content requirements. The panel found that these local requirements were 'investment measures' because they had a significant impact on investment in the automotive sector[51] and that they were 'trade-related' because they affected trade.[52] The panel also found that compliance with the requirements for the purchase and use of products of domestic origin was necessary in order to obtain the tax and customs duty benefits and that such benefits were 'advantages' within the meaning of the Illustrative List.[53] As a result, the panel ruled that the local content requirements violated the TRIMs Agreement.[54]

---

[49] TRIMs Annex, para. 1.

[50] TRIMs Annex, para. 1.

[51] Report of the Panel, Indonesia – Certain Measures Affecting the Automobile Industry, WT/DS54/R, WT/DS55/R, WT/DS59/R, WT/DS64/R, 2nd July, 1998, para. 14.80.

[52] Report of the Panel, Indonesia – Certain Measures Affecting the Automobile Industry, WT/DS54/R, WT/DS55/R, WT/DS59/R, WT/DS64/R, 2nd July, 1998, para. 14.82.

[53] Report of the Panel, Indonesia – Certain Measures Affecting the Automobile Industry, WT/DS54/R, WT/DS55/R, WT/DS59/R, WT/DS64/R, 2nd July, 1998, paras. 14.89–14.91.

[54] Report of the Panel, Indonesia – Certain Measures Affecting the Automobile Industry, WT/DS54/R, WT/DS55/R, WT/DS59/R, WT/DS64/R, 2nd July, 1998, para. 14.91.

Inconsistency with GATT Article XI:1

Article XI of the GATT 1994 stipulates the general elimination of quantitative restrictions. Article XI of the GATT 1994 prohibits any measure other than duties, taxes or other charges 'or other measures having equivalent effect'. Therefore, it is not the legal form of the measure but its effect on trade which is important.

The GATT regulation on quantitative restrictions, however, has a limited effect because of the many exceptions. Article XI allows for the following exceptions to this prohibition:

- Temporary export restrictions of foodstuffs or other 'essential' products when there is a shortage of such products on the national market;
- Import restrictions on agricultural and fishery products when these restrictions are part of a national policy of subsidising agricultural prices;
- Restrictions on basic products which follow from an international agreement on basic products.

Moreover, Article XIII:1 prohibits any form of discrimination in the establishment or application of import or export restrictions; quantitative restrictions must apply equally to all third countries (thus, not only to the other GATT members).

Furthermore, quantitative restrictions are also permitted on the basis of other exceptions, particularly for the protection of the balance of payments and the currency reserves of contracting states and for the protection of domestic industries against serious injury. Quantitative restrictions are mainly lifted within regional unions or on the basis of other co-operation agreements.

The Illustrative List annexed to the TRIMs Agreement sets out three categories of 'TRIMs that are inconsistent with the obligation of general elimination of quantitative restrictions provided for in [Article XI:1 of the GATT]'.[55] TRIMs that are inconsistent with Article XI:1 include TRIMs that are:

Mandatory or enforceable under domestic law or under administrative rulings, or compliance with which is necessary to obtain an advantage, and which restrict:

the importation by an enterprise of products used in or related to its local production, generally or to an amount related to the volume or value of local production that it exports;
(b) the importation by an enterprise of products used in or related to its local production by restricting its access to foreign exchange to an amount related to the foreign exchange inflows attributable to the enterprise; or
(c) the exportation or sale for export by an enterprise of products.

For instance, it is a violation of prohibitions of quantitative restrictions when investment measures require an enterprise to use its own foreign exchange reserve to import products. The prohibition of quantitative restriction is similarly violated if export is tied in in any way with the local production. In 2001, the *India – Measures Affecting the Automotive Sector* case involved a TRIM requiring 'trade balancing'.

---

[55] TRIMs Annex, para. 2.

In May 1999 the government of the United States of America lodged a complaint against the Indian government for the auto industry measures it introduced in November 1997. Under the 1997 law, the Indian government required all new foreign auto manufacturing investments to sign a standard Memorandum of Understanding (MoU) with the government establishing:

- A minimum US$50 million investment in joint ventures with majority foreign ownership;
- A waiver of import licences if local content exceeds 50%;
- And the obligation to export within 3 years, with possible restrictions on imports for CKD and SKD if export requirements are not met.

According to the Panel, as of the date of the establishment of the trade-alancing condition, 'there would necessarily have been a practical threshold to the amount of exports that each manufacturer could expect to make, which in turn would determine the amount of imports that could be made. This amounts to an import restriction. The degree of effective restriction which would result from this condition may vary from signatory to signatory depending on its own projections, its output, or specific market conditions, but a manufacturer is in no instance free to import, without commercial constraint, as many kits and components as it wishes without regard to its export opportunities and obligations'.[56] The Panel therefore found that the 'trade balancing condition contained in Public Notice No. 60 and in the MoUs signed thereunder, by limiting the amount of imports through linking them to an export commitment, acts as a restriction on importation, contrary to the terms of Article XI:1'.[57]

After finding that the trade-balancing requirements violate GATT Article XI:1, the India – Measures Affecting the Automotive *Sector* panel invoked the principle of judicial economy and concluded that it was not necessary to analyse the measures under the TRIMs Agreement.[58]

The TRIMs Agreement has an indirect impact on national policies, which may affect the activities of foreign firms.[59] Indeed, as stated above, this agreement relates to local-content requirements and incentives such as tax concessions tied to exports. Domestic regulations in these areas violate the principle of national treatment (Article III GATT) and the prohibition of quantitative restrictions (Article XI GATT). These restrictions are therefore forbidden under the TRIMs Agreement.

---

[56] Report of the Panel, India – Measures Affecting the Automotive Sector, WT/DS146/R, WT/DS175/R, 21st December, 2001, para. 7.277.

[57] Report of the Panel, India – Measures Affecting the Automotive Sector, WT/DS146/R, WT/DS175/R, 21st December, 2001, para. 7.278.

[58] Report of the Panel, India – Measures Affecting the Automotive Sector, WT/DS146/R, WT/DS175/R, 21st December, 2001, paras. 7.323–7.324.

[59] Edwards/Lester, Towards a More Comprehensive World Trade Organization Agreement on Trade Related Investment Measures, Stanford Journal of International Law 33 (1997), pp. 169 et seq.

The TRIMs Agreement also prohibits other measures that violate Articles III and IV of the GATT 1994, such as trade-balancing requirements, foreign exchange restrictions related to foreign exchange inflows, and export controls.

The TRIMs Agreement has also been referred to in the disputes concerning the European Community's import regime for bananas; however, the panels established in those disputes did not make any findings under the TRIMs Agreement. Besides, measures taken by Brazil and the Philippines have been the subject of bilateral consultations pursuant to the TRIMs Agreement.[60]

China as a Defending Party? Some Prospects

The TRIMs firstly appeared as a possible cause of violation in 2007 in the case *China – Measures Granting Refunds, Reductions or Exemptions from Taxes* initiated by the USA.[61] The main issue was about Chinese measures providing refunds, reductions or exemptions to enterprises in China on the condition that those enterprises purchase domestic over imported goods, or on the condition that those enterprises meet certain export performance criteria. To the extent the measures accord imported products treatment less favourable than that accorded 'like' domestic products, they were alleged to be inconsistent with Article III:4 of the GATT 1994 and Article 2 of the TRIMs Agreement. However, China and USA reached an agreement in relation to this dispute, in the form of a memorandum of understanding. However, in terms of practice the main candidates for litigation are the Chinese laws and regulations addressing export performance, technology transfer, and industrial policies.

As discussed above, the compulsory local content, foreign exchange balancing, and export performance requirements were deleted from Chinese basic investment laws by their revision prior to the WTO accession. Nevertheless, the WFEL still explicitly encourages the WFEs to export their products. Besides, according to Article 10 of the Guidance from 2002, the permitted projects with foreign investment of which the products are all directly exported shall be regarded as the encouraged projects. Consequently, such projects would enjoy preferential treatments according to relevant laws and administrative regulations (Article 9 of the Guidance), which would not be granted to 'normal' permitted projects. Accordingly, the Catalogue from 2004 explicitly listed permitted projects with foreign investment, and which export all of their production, as encouraged projects. The consistency of such kind of encouragement of export performance with the China's WTO obligations is questionable. This is because the TRIMs Agreement clearly

---

[60] Kennedy, A WTO Agreement on Investment: A Solution in Search of a Problem?, University of Pennsylvania Journal of International Economic Law 24 (2003), p. 145.

[61] China – Certain Measures Granting Refunds, Reductions or Exemptions from Taxes and Other Payments – Request for Consultations by the United States, WT/DS358/1, 7th February, 2007.

provides that it prohibits not only those TRIMs which are mandatory or enforceable under domestic law or under administrative rulings, but also those the compliance with which is necessary to obtain an advantage. Although the Guidance does not require a permitted foreign investment project to export, it would 'obtain an advantage', i.e. being upgraded to encouraged projects and accordingly enjoying certain preferential treatments, if it export all its products. Hence, it should be quite certain that this kind of upgrade constitute a TRIMs, which is inconsistent with China's WTO obligations. China should be aware of that and abolished this upgrade from the Catalogue 2007.[62] However, the Guidance has not been revised, and Article 10 of the Guidance remains unchanged. Soon after the 2000 revision, the encouragement provision of the WFEL was questioned by commentators.[63] Nevertheless, the consistency of that provision with WTO obligations seems to be not as sceptical as that of the Guidance and the Catalogue 2004. Because the WFEL does not clearly provide whether the State should encourage export performance in all cases and how it would be encouraged. In other words, the consistency depends on the practical implementation of that encouragement provision. Hence, it is not at all unexpected that the USTR Report laid stress on the questionable practice when it referred to such encouragement.[64]

China has been actively exploring international collaboration for technology transfer. Some doubts also concern the Regulations for the Implementation of the Law on Sino–Foreign Equity Joint Ventures.[65] The Sino–Foreign Equity Joint Ventures was amended several times since the accession with a view to removing all articles that were in contradiction with the TRIMs Agreement. However, some doubts have been expressed that Articles 41 and 43 of this Law still imposed requirements on technology transfer agreements concluded by Joint Ventures. In reference to Article 41, technology has to be 'appropriate and advanced'. The question is to know whether Article 43 contains a compulsory requirement that foreign investors must include a technology transfer agreement in their contract.[66] Should this be the case, there is a rick of a TRIMs violation.

Last but not least, China industrial policies are other types of measures which could be a problem in connection with China's WTO obligations. The most famous one was the *Measures on the Importation of Parts for Entire Automobiles*, which

---

[62] See also 2010 USTR Report to Congress on China's WTO Compliance (hereafter the USTR Report), available at: http://www.ustr.gov/webfm_send/2460 (last visited on 20th January, 2011), p. 68. The questionable Chinese measures discussed in this article are also noted by the USTR Report.

[63] See for example Shan, Towards a Level Playing Field of Foreign Investment in China, Journal of World Investment 3 (2002) 2, p. 338.

[64] See USTR Report, p. 67.

[65] On this see Wolff, *Mergers and Acquisitions in China: Law and Practice*, (3rd ed.) 2009, p. 1.113.

[66] Doubts have been expressed in 2008 by the EU delegation, see Committee on Trade-Related Investment Measures, Minutes of the Meeting Held on 23rd October, 2008, G/TRIMS/M/27, 29th October, 2008.

had triggered a WTO case, i.e., China – Measures Affecting Imports of Automobile Parts.[67] This case concerns China's measures on imports of automobile parts. The measures impose a 25% charge on imported auto parts used in the manufacture of motor vehicles in China, if the imported auto parts are 'characterized as complete vehicles' according to specified criteria prescribed under the measures. The complainants notably challenged the consistency of the measures with China's obligations under Article 2 of the TRIMs Agreement and paragraph 1(a) of Annex 1. China's measures were considered by the EU, the USA and Canada as being inconsistent with Article 2 of the TRIMs Agreement. In essence, these measures fall within the types of measures covered in the Illustrative List in the Annex to the TRIMs Agreement. The Chinese measures at issue provide an advantage, i.e., an exemption from paying the internal charge and related burdensome administrative requirements, for auto manufacturers that decide to purchase or use domestic auto parts. Thus, the measures require 'the purchase or use by an enterprise of products of domestic origin or from any domestic source' so as 'to obtain an advantage'; they fall squarely within the Illustrative List of measures covered by the TRIMs Agreement.[68] Although the measure did not formally require the use of domestic auto parts, it would bring about in practice. The panel firstly decided to address the claims under GATT Article III, then, because it found that the measure is inconsistent with Article III, the Panel exercised judicial economy with respect to the claims under the TRIMs Agreement[69] and, as a result, the Appellate Body did not have to re-examine the measures in the light of the TRIMs agreement. Nevertheless, it is clear from the decisions of that case that the measure is inconsistent with the TRIMs Agreement, too. In September 2009, China abolished this inconsistent measure.

In Lieu of Conclusion: The TRIMs, the WTO and Beyond

The present paper analyses the Chinese regulations and successive reforms of foreign investment. Following the failure to install a multilateral framework on foreign investment within the OECD as well as within the WTO, opinions diverge as to whether approaches to regulate FDI through multilateral regulations should

---

[67] Report of the Panel, China – Measures Affecting Imports of Automobile Parts, WT/DS339/R, WT/DS340/R, WT/DS342/R, 18th July, 2008.

[68] Report of the Panel, China – Measures Affecting Imports of Automobile Parts, WT/DS339/R, WT/DS340/R, WT/DS342/R, 18th July, 2008, paras. 3.1(a), 3.4(c), and 3.7(d). In addition, the United States claimed that the measures fell within paragraph 2(a) of the Illustrative List in Annex 1 to the *TRIMs Agreement*. (Report of the Panel, para. 3.4(c)).

[69] Report of the Panel, China – Measures Affecting Imports of Automobile Parts, WT/DS339/R, WT/DS340/R, WT/DS342/R, 18th July, 2008, paras. 8.2, 8.5, and 8.8. See also, Report of the Appellate Body, China – Measures Affecting Imports of Automobile Parts, WT/DS339/AB/R, WT/DS340/AB/R, WT/DS342/AB/R, 15th December, 2008.

continue. This paper does not intend to give an answer, but it can be observed that the Chinese experience reflects current regulatory uncertainities because it firstly concludes that the TRIMs compliance by China is satisfactory as demonstrated by recent litigation.

At the WTO, China has been pro-active in amending its internal laws and no dispute had ended before the DSB with a determination of TRIMs violations by China. The experience of China to date in the WTO, when it comes to investment measures, can be described as a successful one. The TRIMs Agreement prohibits certain measures that violate the national treatment and quantitative restrictions requirements of the GATT. Prohibited TRIMs may include requirements to: achieve a certain level of local content; produce locally; export a given level/ percentage of goods; balance the amount/percentage of imports with the amount/ percentage of exports; transfer technology or proprietary business information to local persons; or balance foreign exchange inflows and outflows. These requirements may be mandatory conditions for investment, or can be attached to fiscal or other incentives. As is suggested by the case law, China has been doing well because only a small number of disputes with China as the defending party have included TRIMs measures. The absence of disputes does not however mean that all regulations are being fully complied with and we identified a few of them which are good candidates for a prompt clarification. Despite the relative lack of WTO coverage on investment, many WTO Members have seized on the WTO accession process as a lever to encourage prospective Members to go beyond the WTO agreements on investment and investment-related issues, and China is a very good case in point. They believe, with some justification, that they will never have more leverage as long as a State wants to join the WTO. As a result, investment-related issues have become an important aspect of WTO accession: prompt compliance with the requirements of TRIMs industrial policy, including subsidies under the SCM Agreement market for access for certain types of investment, including financial services and telecom.

International investment law fragmentation is also reflected in the fact that the accession to the WTO did contribute to the development of the new generation of Chinese BITs in several aspects. Because of the market access and national treatment commitments in the GATS, China has made further liberalization of investment regime in its service sectors. The acceptance of the national treatment standard in China was pushed forward by the WTO accession. The trade liberalization has promoted China's economic development, which has resulted in the rapid increase of Chinese outward investment and a growing interest in the protection of Chinese investments in foreign countries. With respect to the performance requirements, the WTO accession and the undertaking of obligations of the TRIMs Agreement has had little influence on China's BITs and FTAs. There are still some performance requirements in the Chinese investment regime; their consistency with the TRIMs Agreement and China's Accession Protocol is at least questionable.

Beyond the WTO commitments related to foreign investments, China has undertaken obligations to protect foreign investments in a large number of BITs and Free Trade Agreements (FTAs). Following the reforms and open policy from 1978, and beginning with the first Chinese BIT between China and Sweden (1982), China has signed more than 120 BITs, second in number only to Germany.[70] In accordance with the progressive integration of China's economy into that of the rest of the world, Chinese BITs have reflected the gradual acceptance of high-level investment protection in China, especially with respect to the national treatment standard and the investor-state arbitration mechanism. In the Chinese BITs signed in the 1980s and 1990s, only a fraction of them contained a provision of national treatment, whereas the fair and equitable treatment and the most-favoured-nation treatment had usually been provided for. The absence of a national treatment provision had been seen as a speciality of Chinese BITs in comparison with BITs signed by other countries.[71] But since 2000, the post-establishment national treatment obligation has been stipulated in most of the new Chinese BITs. With regard to the investor-state arbitration provisions, the access of foreign investors to international arbitration was restricted to disputes concerning an amount of compensation by the former Chinese BITs. The China–Barbados BIT from 1998 is the first Chinese BIT, in which the contracting parties have granted a far-reaching consent to international arbitration for 'any dispute concerning investments'.[72] Since then, similar investor-state arbitration consent has been given by most of the Chinese BITs conducted in the 21st century. Because these new Chinese BITs contain substantial improvements both with respect to investor's substantive rights (national treatment) and procedural rights (investor-state arbitration),[73] they constitute a new generation of Chinese BITs.

There are many reasons for this development. The first two directly derive from the WTO experience and they are the understanding and accepted practice of national treatment and international litigation. The third reason is a consequence of a globalised world into which China is fully integrated and needs now to protect its (growing) investment abroad. The accession to WTO has generally contributed to the acceptance of granting national treatment to foreigners. The WTO accession and 'culture' has also played a role in a better understanding of international litigation. China has changed its perception of the international judge role[74] and accepted international investment arbitration which has witnessed an exponential

---

[70] UNCTAD, Recent Developments in International Investment Agreements (2008 – June 2009), IIA Monitor (2009) 3, available at: http://www.unctad.org/en/docs/webdiaeia20098_en.pdf.

[71] WTO, The Development Provisions, WT/WGT/W/119, available at: http://docsonline.wto.org.

[72] But it did not provide for national treatment.

[73] It is in the 1998 Sino-Barbadian BIT that for the first time China agreed to allow foreign investors to resort to international arbitral tribunals without specific consent from the Chinese government. See Hsieh, China's Development of International Economic Law and WTO Legal Capacity Building, Journal of International Economic Law, 13 (2010) 4, p. 1005.

[74] China tended for many years to employ strategies of "dispute avoidance", see Hsu, China, India and Dispute Settlement in the WTO and RTAs, in: Sornarajah/Wang (eds.), *China, India and the International Economic Order*, 2010, pp. 255–259.

surge of investment disputes between foreign investors and host country governments. Traditionally, China has restricted unilateral consent to arbitration to disputes on the amount of compensation to be granted in cases of expropriation. Controversies on other matters, such as the existence of expropriation itself, or breaches of treatment obligations, were to be settled in domestic courts, or could be submitted to arbitration by mutual consent of the investors and national authorities.[75] The new generation of Sino–Foreign BITs have instead eliminated this substantial restriction, granting unilateral consent to disputes concerning all disciplines of the agreement. Finally, a number of investment agreements require the foreign investor to fulfil certain procedural requirements prior to filing the arbitration claim.[76] Last but not least, there is surely a desire to attract more foreign investment into China, but the growing interest in the protection of Chinese investors in foreign countries by means of BITs should also underpin the acceptance of high-level investment protection in BITs.[77]

Acknowledgements The present article is part of the research entitled "the evolving international investment regime" led by Dr. Julien Chaisse at the Faculty of Law of the Chinese University of Hong Kong and which aims to investigate the evolution of investment law across relevant agreements and to discern patterns of congruence and divergence across key issue areas, substantive disciplines and countries and regions (See: www.law.cuhk.edu.hk). The author would like to thank Christian BELLAK, Ming DU, Pasha HSIEH, Xinjie LUAN and Jun XIAO for helpful comments. Different elements of this paper were presented at the Annual Conference of the Asian Law and Economics Association (AsLEA), Beijing, 23–24 August 2010. The author would also like to thank the conference participants for their discussion regarding the theoretical and policy

---

[75] See, for instance, China-Korea BIT, Art. 9.3. for a discussion, see Xiao, Chinese Bilateral Investment Treaties in the 21st Century: Protecting Chinese Investment, in: Chaisse/Gugler (eds), *Expansion of Trade and FDI in Asia: Strategic and Policy Challenges*, 2009, pp. 122–130.

[76] The most usual procedural restrictions pertain to waiting periods and the exhaustion of local remedies. Both of these types of requirement are commonly found in Sino-Foreign BITs. Prior to the launch of the arbitration, foreign investors must hold negotiations with the host country's authorities with a view to reaching an amicable settlement. Should these negotiations fail to bring the parties to a commonly agreed solution within a 6-month period, the investor may bring the claim to international arbitration. Whereas the great majority of Sino-Foreign BITs require a 6-month waiting period, a few agreements require somewhat shorter periods – i.e., 3 months: BITs with the Netherlands (2001), Germany (2003), and Finland (2004) – or, exceptionally, no waiting period at all – i.e., Ghana (1989).

[77] For a detailed discussion to the new generation of Chinese BITs, see Xiao, Chinese Bilateral Investment Treaties in the 21st Century: Protecting Chinese Investment, in: Chaisse/Gugler (eds.), *Expansion of Trade and FDI in Asia*, 2009, p. 122. There are views that Chinese BITs should be divided into three generations, yet in different periods, see Cai, China-US BIT Negotiations and the Future of Investment Treaty Regime: A Grand Bilateral Bargain with Multilateral Implications, Journal of International Economic Law 12 (2009) 2, pp. 457 et seq. (462); Gallagher/Shan, *Chinese Investment Treaties: Policies and Practice*, 2009, pp. 35–43. Indeed, those changes which lead to the differentiation of three generations are also important. Nevertheless, the two-generations-analysis would be simpler and properly reflect the more significant and consistent improvements mentioned here.

implications of this research. Thanks also are due to Ms Yaling ZHANG from CUHK Faculty of Law for the background research and for producing the information synthesized in Table 1 and Annex 1.

Annex 1: List of Chinese Norms with Trade-Distorting Restrictions in Foreign Investment Law[78]

Law

Law on Chinese-Foreign Equity Joint Venture, 2001; (PRC Sino-Foreign Equity Joint Venture Law, Second Revision) Adopted in 1979, first amended in 1990

PRC Sino-Foreign Equity Joint Venture Law Implementing Rules, adopted in 1983, revised in 1986, 1987 and 2001

PRC Sino-Foreign Cooperative Joint Venture Law, adopted in 1988, revised in 2000

PRC Sino-Foreign Cooperative Joint Venture Law Implementing Rules, adopted in 1988, revised in 2000

PRC Wholly Foreign-Owned Enterprises Law, adopted in 1986, revised in 2000

PRC Wholly Foreign-Owned Enterprises Law Implementing Rules, adopted in 1990, revised in 2001

Regulations on the Implementation of Enterprise Income Tax Law of the People's Republic of China, 2008

Rules for the Implementation of the Income Tax Law of the People's Republic of China for Enterprises with Foreign Investment and Foreign Enterprises, adopted in 1991. repealed

Regulations and Measures

Changes in Equity Interest of investors in Foreign-Invested Enterprises Several Provisions, 1997

Asset Reorganization by State-Owned Enterprises Using Foreign Investment Tentative Provisions, 1998

Investment within China by Foreign-Invested Enterprises Tentative Provisions, 2000

Merger and Division of Foreign-Invested Enterprises Provisions (Revised), 2001

---

[78] Available at: http://www.fdi.gov.cn/pub/FDI_EN/Laws/ default.jsp?type = 530 (last visited on 15th March, 2011).

Issues Relevant to the Transfer of State-Owned Shares and Legal Person Shares in Listed Companies to Foreign Investor Circular, 2002

Using Foreign Investment to Reorganize State-Owned Enterprises Tentative Provisions, 2003

Decision of the State Council on Reforming Foreign Investment System, 2004

Administration of Equity Investment of Overseas Financial Institutions in Chinese-Funded Financial Institutions Procedures, 2004

Measures for the Administration on Foreign Investment in Commercial Fields, 2004

Supplementary Provisions on the Establishment of Companies with an Investment Nature by Foreign Investors Provisions (or Supplementary Provisions on the Establishment of Investment Companies by Foreign Investors), 2006

Establishment of Companies with an Investment Nature by Foreign Investors Provisions, 2004

Supplementary Provisions to the Establishment of Companies with an Investment Nature by Foreign Investors Tentative Provisions, 1999

Establishment of Companies with an Investment Nature by Foreign Investors Tentative Provisions, 1995

Administration of Strategic Investment in Listed Companies by Foreign Investors Procedures, 2005

Foreign Investment Industrial Guidance Catalogue (Amended in 2007)

The Foreign Investment Industrial Guidance Catalogue (Amended in 2004)

Administration of the Takeover of listed Companies Procedures, 2007

Guidelines for the Administration of Entry of Foreign Investments, 2008

Provisions of State Council on Declaration Threshold for Concentration of Business Operators, 2009

Catalogue of Dominant Industries for Foreign Investments in Central and Western China, 2009

Provisions on Merger and Acquisiton of Domestic Enterprises by Foreign Investors, adopted in 2003, revised in 2006, 2009

Notice of the General Office of the State Council on Launching the Security Review System for Mergers and Acquisitions of Domestic Enterprises by Foreign Investors, 2011

Interim Provisions on Issues Related to the Implementation of the Security Review System for Mergers and Acquisitions of Domestic Enterprises by Foreign Investors, 2011

Adored and Despised in Equal Measure: An Assessment of the EU's Principle of Market Economy Treatment in Anti-Dumping Investigations Against China

Robert M. MacLean

In simple terms, the European Union's anti-dumping policy and laws are designed to offer protection to EU industries facing unfair competition in the form of "dumping" from foreign suppliers of goods and merchandise. All Members of the World Trade Organisation (the WTO) are entitled to take such action and, in doing so, the EU is no different from any of its trading partners who have similar laws. However, given the size of the EU internal market, comprising some 500 million consumers, and the fact that the adoption of anti-dumping measures can drastically impede effective access to such a large market for the EU's trading partners, the use by the European Union of such trade defence measures attracts widespread attention as well as both fair and unfair criticism.

In the case of the EU's policy towards China, there is a further perceived inequity which serves as a constant source of friction between the two colossal trading partners. This is the general status of China as a non-market economy

In the interests of assessing objectivity and impartiality, the author declares that he has been engaged in material representations of interested parties in the following EU administrative and judicial proceedings involving cases mentioned in this Article. Administrative procedures: Coated Fine Paper from China (AD and AS); Certain Seamless Pipes of Iron and Steel from China (AD); Certain Iron and Steel Fasteners from China (AD); Stainless Steel Rolled-Cold Flat Products from China, Korea and Taiwan (AD); Sodium Metal from the USA (AD and AS); Monosodium Glutamate from China (AD); Citric Acid from China (AD); Canned Mandarins from China (AD); Certain Compressors from China (AD); Compact Recordable Disks (CD-Rs) from Malaysia, Hong Kong and China (AD); Candles from China (AD); Ironing Boards from China (AD); PSC Wires and Strands from China (AD); Certain Leather Footwear from China (AD); Plastic Bags and Sacks from China (AD); Compact Recordable Disks (CD-Rs) from India. Court procedures: ECJ/GC Cases T-300/04 and C-535/06 P, *Moser Baer India* vs. *Council of the European Union*; GC Case T-299/05, *Shanghai Excell Precision Limited* vs. *Council of the European Union*; GC Case T-274/07, *Zhejiang Harmonic Hardware Products* vs. *Council of the European Union*.

R.M. MacLean (✉)
Squire, Sanders & Dempsey (UK) LLP, Avenue Lloyd George, 7, 1000 Brussels, Belgium
e-mail: robert.maclean@ssd.com

C. Herrmann and J.P. Terhechte (eds.), *European Yearbook of International Economic Law (EYIEL), Vol. 3 (2012)*, European Yearbook of International Economic Law 3, DOI 10.1007/978-3-642-23309-8_6, © Springer-Verlag Berlin Heidelberg 2012

country and, at the same time, the use of a special set of rules to allow individual Chinese producers to escape from this situation if certain conditions are shown to exist in relation to their specific commercial circumstances. Collectively, these special rules are known as conditional Market Economy Treatment (MET) in EU anti-dumping parlance. To qualify for MET, a Chinese manufacturer must demonstrate to the satisfaction of the European Commission that its business activities are conducted in a kind of market economy "oasis" where the forces of supply and demand operate free of distortions caused by the kinds of state interference that typically characterise a non-market economy country. If this can be established, then the European Commission resorts to the "normal" rules of EU anti-dumping law for that specific applicant enterprise, thereby treating it as a special case. It effectively becomes the exception to the rule and other Chinese manufacturers of the same products that cannot show they operate under the same market conditions remain stranded in the desert of the non-market economy system.

So, why is this issue important and why is the conditional MET principle loved and despised in equal measure? The answer stems from two basic principles that the EU has consistently applied for some time now. First, "dumping" is essentially defined as the difference between the price of a certain kind of merchandise in the country where it is produced (known as the "normal value") measured against the price of the same merchandise when sold for export to the European Union (known as the "EU export price").[1] This price difference, or "dumping margin", is ascertained for individual exporters in the country concerned in the investigation and, when expressed as a percentage of the EU CIF price, becomes the applicable individual dumping duty rate for the exporters. After anti-dumping duties have been imposed, each time an import transaction involving goods from a particular exporter occurs, an assessment of anti-dumping duties is made on the value or volume of the imported goods in more or less the same way as happens when normal EU customs duties are levied. So, the EU customer of the exporter receives a bill from the EU customs authorities that includes three taxes namely conventional EU customs duties, the EU anti-dumping duties and Value Added Tax (VAT). Until these charges are paid, the goods cannot be released for free circulation in the European Union. The anti-dumping duties are therefore effectively a way to return the EU export price to the same level as the domestic price or normal value via a taxation mechanism.

Second, in the case of all countries deemed by the European Union to be non-market economy counties - not just China - domestic prices are deemed to be an unreliable indication of real prices. Why? Because in the case of classical centrally

---

[1] This explanation is a simplification of the way the system applies and there are special rules where actual domestic prices are not used because the sales in question are not profitable, not representative, etc. In such a case, the EU constructs a normal value or domestic prices based on costs of production plus Selling, General and Administrative (SG&A) expenses plus a reasonable margin for profit. For the purposes of the present discussion, these special techniques are not particularly relevant.

controlled economies this is completely logical. Real economic market forces are suspended through centrally controlled decision-making processes. Central, local or regional governments decide what volume of production should happen and these volumes are manufactured using inputs (i.e. components, raw materials, energy, etc.) that have their prices determined in the same way. Leaving aside for a moment the question whether the economic reforms in China over the last two decades or so have moved the country as a whole out of the category of a non-market country into the market economy one, in classical non-market economies, this is indeed a valid proposition. Final prices to industries or consumers are unreliable where state interference in the economy is the chosen means of running the country's affairs.

In the absence of reliable Chinese domestic prices, the EU (in common with many other WTO members) uses prices from other countries, known as the "analogue country prices" as a surrogate for establishing reliable normal values. In the case of Chinese exporters, this regularly means that domestic prices charged by totally unrelated manufacturers are inserted into their calculation and these enterprises can be located in the United States, Canada, Japan, Indonesia, Taiwan and even, somewhat bizarrely, the European Union.[2] As a general proposition, it is true that domestic prices in analogue countries tend to be higher, in some cases substantially so, than in China. If substitute normal values from an analogue country are used which are higher than actual Chinese domestic prices, then of course any final dumping margin is increased since dumping is determined by comparing normal values to EU export prices. In contrast, when the conditional MET principle is applied, actual Chinese domestic prices are used in the dumping margin calculations for eligible Chinese manufacturers, and final dumping duty rates are normally significantly lower when calculated in this basis. But successful MET applications by Chinese enterprises are relatively infrequent. This is the principal source of inequity of the system from the Chinese perspective and, as illustrated later, empirical evidence indicates that, generally speaking, their point is valid.

Returning to the central question of the emotional response to the conditional MET principle, for obvious reasons outlined above, China and its manufacturers and exporters despise the EU's approach toward the application of the MET criteria because they perceive that the European Commission applies the principle too rigidly, harshly and with excessive vigour meaning that far too few Chinese enterprises qualify for MET treatment and escape from the prism of a non-market economy. As a result, their individual anti-dumping duty rates are set, in their view, at far too high levels because foreign and unrealistic prices are used in the dumping calculations. If, so the argument runs, the European Commission was more liberal in its application of MET, more Chinese exporters would have dumping margins set on the basis of their own pricing practices – both domestic

---

[2] In Regulation (EC) No. 1355/2008, OJ [2008] L 350/35, the European Commission used Spain as the analogue country for the purpose of establishing normal values in the absence of any other country in the world making these products except Spain and China.

and export – and these would be lower, preventing the total market foreclosure that accompanies higher anti-dumping duty levels. Indeed there is a direct correlation between the levels of the EU dumping duty rates for those Chinese companies qualifying for MET – and the application of the "normal rules" of EU anti-dumping policy – against those that do not.

In contrast, EU industries are ardent supporters of a strict approach towards the practical application of the rules established in the EU's Basic Anti-Dumping Regulation for MET evaluation. From the perspective of EU industries, the higher the EU dumping rates, the more effective the exclusion of Chinese competition from the EU market. For this reason, European Union industries have waged a sustained and effective campaign against any reform of the EU's approach towards conditional MET as it applies to China, especially as contemplated by the former EU Commissioner for Trade, Lord Mandelson. Allegations of unfair commercial advantages are commonly made including claims that Chinese producers are able to benefit from government subsidies, unfairly low costs of production and predatory intentions. In short, from their perspective, and understandably, a strict application of the principle of MET towards China means higher numbers in terms of EU anti-dumping duty rates and more effective level of protection. A more liberal and relaxed approach would have the opposite effect. For this reason alone, the policy, administration and legal tenants of the conditional MET principle in EU law should remain unchanged for as long as possible.

In theory at least, the administration and application of the EU's conditional MET principle attempts to strike a balance between these fiercely opposing perspectives. Since the policy itself is a middle ground compromise, it is not surprising that the policy has attracted criticism from both sides. The debate on where the proper balance lies seems largely to ignore that the EU's MET approach is essentially a legal one since the principles behind the concepts of MET are framed largely in legal and fact finding terminology. On the one side, EU industries and enterprises facing fierce competition from Chinese producers vigorously argue that the policy is too liberal and the conditions are too easily satisfied by Chinese companies that are not functioning under true market economy conditions. The opposing side claims that the way MET conditions are being applied by the EU result in the protectionist exclusion of those Chinese producers operating in market economy conditions because these companies face unjustifiably high anti-dumping duty rates for their exports.

The purpose of this article is to contribute to this debate. It is primarily intended to assess where the current EU approach lies in terms of its declared objective, namely to distinguish between Chinese producers who operate under market economy conditions from those that do not. This involves assessment of criteria such as objectiveness, impartiality, legal certainty, quality of assessment and ultimately where the current balance lies. It is also important to address the consistency of this approach with the applicable international trade standards, given that China is now a member of the WTO. The procedural conditions and substantive criteria applied by the EU in this regards should also be consistent with these standards.

Impact Assessment of the EU's Conditional MET Principle Towards Chinese Exports

Compared to the scale of the volume of trade generally between the EU and China, EU anti-dumping duties should be only a minor irritant in the trading relationship between the two sides. In theory, only a small volume of imports from China are covered by EU anti-dumping measures. Yet, despite this situation, the issue of recognition of China as a market economy country as a whole, and specifically the application of MET in EU anti-dumping actions directed against it, raises passions that seem quite disproportionate. It is therefore useful to try to empirically assess what is the real economic impact of the EU's anti-dumping approach towards China in light of the use of the conditional MET principle.

The Big Picture – Profile and Trends in EU Anti-Dumping Actions Against China

The EU's anti-dumping instrument is a complaints-driven one meaning that it is not the EU itself who decides which countries and products should be targeted for action under the instrument. Rather, the onus is on EU industries to prepare, lodge and pursue anti-dumping complaints against the EU's trading partners if the necessary evidence points towards the existence of dumping, injury to the EU industry and a casual link between these two elements as well as an overarching requirement that the adoption of such protective measures should be in the interests of the EU as a whole. The European Commission investigates these allegations and decides if the allegations are substantiated based on a thorough analysis of the facts and circumstances in each case and in line with the requirements set out in the EU's Basic Anti-Dumping Regulation[3] which itself is modelled generally on the WTO Anti-Dumping Agreement. Accused exporters also have rights under the Basic Anti-Dumping Regulation which are intended to allow them to defend themselves against these allegations and express their views on the subject to the European Commission.

The complaint-driven character of the EU anti-dumping process largely explains why the profile of the use of the instrument is unpredictable. Other factors include the internal economic climate inside the European Union, the character of the political appointee who heads up DG-Trade of the European Commission at any given time, the metrics of comparative advantage and sector-specific issues for particular EU industries. The figure below summarises this profile for the last 5 years (Fig. 1).

---

[3] The currently applicable EU Basic Anti-Dumping Regulation is Regulation (EC) No. 1225/2009, OJ [2009] L 343/51.

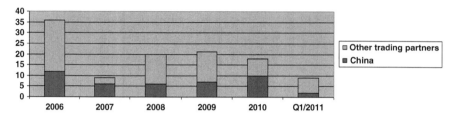

Fig. 1 Profile of the EU's use of its trade defence instruments (2006–2011). Figures also include a comparatively small number of EU trade defence actions under the EU's Basic Anti-Subsidy Regulation. Figures refer to the initiation of new investigations each year. Source: European Commission Report to the European Parliament on Trade Defence Activities 2010 and European Commission Statistical Report for Q1/2011

Although EU trade defence activity increased during the period of the global financial crisis compared to the immediately preceding period, these levels of activity are not particularly high compared to those between 2003 and 2006 when more than 30 cases on average were being initiated each year with more than 40 being started in 2003 alone. On the other hand, with the exception of Q1/2011 (for which the data is too premature to evaluate), the percentage of cases initiated against China does indicate an increasing trend. From 2007 until 2009, anti-dumping action against China accounted for around a third of all new cases and then exceeded more than half in 2010. Therefore, both in absolute and relative terms, activity against Chinese exporters under the EU's anti-dumping instrument does indeed appear to be on the increase.

What does this mean in financial terms? According to the most recent information available, approximately 0.6% of total imports into the EU were covered by EU trade defence measures in 2009. In the same year a total of 135 EU anti-dumping orders were in place with 54 orders against various kinds of Chinese merchandise.[4] Although this figure seems modest, it should be borne in mind that, in 2009, the total value of imports into the EU stood at €1,199.7 billion[5] meaning that around €7.20 billion in imported merchandise is impacted by EU trade defence measures. Since around 40% of the EU trade defence orders were against Chinese imports, it is clear that a substantial part of this trade involves Chinese-made products. Yet this is only part of the story. While it may be true that only 0.6% of total EU imports were affected by these measures, what is not included in this assessment is the value of the trade that was lost because of the commercial impact of the duties applied. Where the anti-dumping duties are relatively low (say below 10%), in the experience of the writer, trade does continue at levels approximately equal to those before

---

[4] European Commission, 28th Annual Report to the European Parliament on Trade Defence Activities 2009, COM(2010) 558 Final, p. 5.

[5] Eurostat, available at: http://epp.eurostat.ec.europa.eu/statistics_explained/index.php/Extra-EU_trade_in_goods.

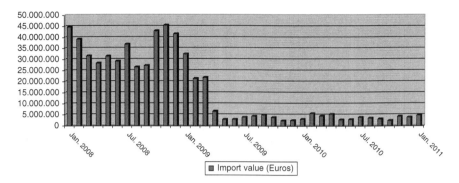

Fig. 2 Impact of EU anti-dumping measures on seamless pipes and tubes from China. Source: Eurostat using same CN Codes as used in definitive regulation

the measures. This is because the EU market gradually absorbs the cost of these duties in final pricing to EU end-users and consumers especially when Chinese-made goods are competitively priced. At higher levels, trade is curtailed and at levels above 20%, the EU market is effectively foreclosed to non-EU suppliers subject to the EU duties. Three recent cases illustrate this point given that sufficient time has now passed to make the assessment.

Case 1: Certain Seamless Pipes and Tubes from China from China[6] This investigation resulted in the introduction of EU provisional anti-dumping duties in April 2009 and definitive measures in September of the same year. Duty rates were established at rates between 17.7% and 39.2% (Fig. 2).

In 2008, being the last full year before the EU provisional anti-dumping duties came into effect, the total import value for the product concerned imported from China was €426 million. In the 12 months period immediately after the provisional duties were imposed, namely April 2009 to March 2010, the total value of imports of the same products plummeted to €48 million. In other words, lost sales for Chinese exporters because of the EU anti-dumping duties, with the lowest rate being 17.7%, was around €378 million or around 88% of the value prior to the imposition of the duties. No significant recovery in value levels subsequently occurred in the course of 2010 and is unlikely for the remaining period of validity of the measures, namely until April 2014.

Case 2: Certain Iron and Steel Fasteners from China[7]: Definitive EU anti-dumping measures were imposed against Chinese fasteners (which are in fact screws and bolts) in January 2009 at the rate of 0% (for two Chinese companies owned and controlled by two EU fastener enterprises) up to 85% for indigenous

---

[6] Regulation (EC) No. 289/2009, OJ [2009] L 94/48; and Regulation (EC) No. 926/2009, OJ [2009] L 262/19.

[7] Regulation (EC) No. 91/2009, OJ [2009] L 29/1.

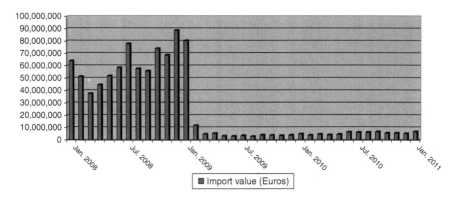

Fig. 3 Impact of EU anti-dumping measures on iron and steel fasteners from China. Source: Eurostat using same CN Codes as used in definitive regulation

Chinese manufacturers. In this case, no provisional EU anti-dumping duties were applied and instead the European Commission moved directly towards final measures (Fig. 3).

This import profile, much resembling a cliff's edge, also illustrates the typical impact on imports of the application of anti-dumping duties by the EU. Prior to the imposition of definitive measures, Chinese import value for these products in 2008 was €731 million. In the subsequent 12 months period following the introduction of the duties, namely February 2009 to January 2010, the relevant value was €56 million. On the basis of this comparison, lost sales were around €675 million or 92% compared to the value of imports in the year prior to the introduction of the measures.

Case 3: Monosodium Glutamate (MSG) from China[8]: Provisional EU anti-dumping duties were imposed in June 2008 followed by definitive measures in December of the same year. The definitive duty rates ranged between 33.8% to 39.7%, being the same rates applied at the provisional stage. The result of the introduction of the provisional duties reflects much the same as the previous two illustrations and is typical of the profile of the impact of provisional and definitive EU anti-dumping measures on Chinese imports. Import values between the 6 months prior to the introduction of the duties versus those in the following 6 months indicate a collapse in import value of around 85% (Fig. 4).

Assessing the scale of the imports covered by EU anti-dumping measures at 0.6% completely ignores the point that this calculation is based on already extremely depressed import values that are the almost inevitable consequence of the imposition of anti-dumping measures. This "after the fact" approach downplays to a large extent the import value suppression impact that is part and parcel of the

---

[8] Regulation (EC) No. 492/2008, OJ [2008] L 144/14; and Regulation (EC) No. 1187/2008, OJ [2008] L 322/1.

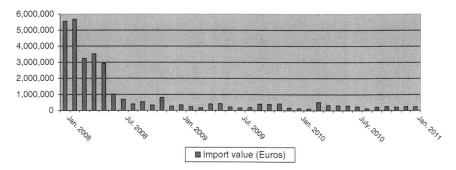

Fig. 4 Impact of EU anti-dumping measures on monosodium glutamate (MSG) from China.
Source: Eurostat using same CN Codes as used in definitive regulation

whole scheme of trade protective measures. The financial impact of this impairment and/or market foreclosure is invisible in the figure of 0.6% presented above. Assessed in terms of import volumes and values prior to the application of each set of measures, the total value of imports covered by such measures would be considerably magnified by a factor that is almost impossible to calculate but could easily be five or six times the assessment made by the EU. Since a considerable portion of the EU's anti-dumping measures in force apply to China, it becomes more obvious why China and its exporting producers hold a very negative opinion of the EU's approach towards China in anti-dumping cases. The EU market is often completely foreclosed to them when high duty rates are put in place, export volumes rapidly decline and, of course, profits are lost.

On the other side, EU industries and manufacturers welcome the adjustment to an apparently fair and level playing field when such action is taken. This provides a shield to price competition from Chinese manufacturers. In large measure, this shield is underpinned by the EU's conditional MET principle. The removal of this concept from the EU's arsenal of trade defence measures, and recognition of China as a market economy country, would likely drastically reduce these levels of protection. The considerable decline in anti-dumping cases against the Russian Federation after full MET was granted to that country fully supports this hypothesis.[9] Over the course of the last 5 years, only three EU anti-dumping investigations have been initiated against Russian exports and no new case has been started in the last 3 years. This compares very favourably with the significant number of anti-dumping investigations that were triggered against Russia prior to its recognition as a market economy country.

---

[9] Russia was granted full MET Status in 2002 on the authority of Regulation (EC) 1972/2002, OJ [2002] L 305/1.

Assessment of the Impact of the Application of the Conditional MET Principle on a Micro-Economic Level

There are two ways to attempt to make a quantitative assessment of the impact of a successful MET application by a Chinese manufacturer or exporter against the application of the default approach used by the European Commission which is to treat Chinese exporters as part and parcel of the non-market economy. The first is an assessment of the different individual anti-dumping duty margins that Chinese producers have obtained in the same investigation where some Chinese enterprises were granted MET in contrast to others. It is true that individual dumping margin determinations are highly dependant on the historical sales records and data profiles, both domestically and for export, for the individual enterprises involved. However, the purpose of this assessment is to assess the scale of the differences involved and therefore this exercise has validity. The second, more accurate, metric is to examine those relatively rare cases in which the European Commission has made a provisional determination without granting MET and then changed its mind at the definitive stage of the investigation. Both approaches offer a way, albeit at a somewhat general level, to measure the effect of a successful MET application by Chinese enterprises.

Comparing Different Dumping Methodologies in the Same Investigations

In most EU anti-dumping investigations against China, three different categories of results are produced. First, using the conditional MET approach, the actual EU export prices for individual companies are compared to actual or constructed normal values (Chinese domestic sales prices) to arrive at a dumping determination. Second, there is the principle of individual treatment (IT) which involves determining the actual EU export prices for each individual Chinese company and then comparing these to the domestic prices in an analogue country market. Third, there is the determination of the non-market economy rate which is applied to those companies unable to obtain either MET or Individual Treatment. This means that, broadly speaking, the results of the three different methodologies can be compared in the context of precisely the same investigation into the same product concerned.

To carry out this exercise objectively, it is logical to select a sufficiently representative number of investigative results. For this purpose, the 15 most recent investigations have been selected where determinations were made in all three categories i.e. MET, individual treatment or IT, and non-market economy treatment. A large number of EU investigations against Chinese products during this period have been excluded for the simple reason that separate determinations for the three different baskets do not always emerge in the results of each investigation

Table 1 Fifteen most recent decisions rendered in Chinese Anti-Dumping Investigations (2004–2011)

Product concerned	MET lowest rate	MET highest rate	IT lowest rate	IT highest rate	Residual duty rate
Iron castings	0%	0%	19%	38%	48%
Polyester filament fabrics	14%	14%	27%	56%	56%
Trichlorisocyanuric acid	7%	14%	40%	40%	43%
Magnesia bricks	3%	8%	15%	28%	40%
Tungsten electrodes	26%	26%	35%	47%	87%
Ironing boards	0%	0%	18%	37%	38%
Candles, tapers and the like	0 €/ton	0 €/ton	0 €/ton	367 €/ton	549 €/ton
Frozen strawberries	0%	0%	63 €/ton	63 €/ton	170 €/ton
Sodium gluconate	6%	6%	27%	27%	53%
Polyester high tenacity filament yarn	0%	0%	8%	9%	9%
Citric acid	7%	8%	33%	43%	43%
Ferro-silicon	16%	16%	29%	29%	31%
Tungsten electrodes	17%	17%	39%	41%	64%
Air compressors	11%	14%	52%	78%	78%
High tenacity yarn of polyester fibres	0%	0%	0%	5%	10%

Source: EU Official Journal

which makes the comparison impossible to make.[10] Based on the results of this reasonable sample of the most recent cases, a comparison of the various determinations is set out in the table above (Table 1).

The indisputable conclusion to be derived from this exercise is that in all of these instances, Chinese companies awarded MET obtained significantly lower individual dumping duty rates compared with those obtaining individual treatment and NME treatment. Where Individual Treatment is applied, but domestic prices are disregarded in favour of those from an analogue country producer, the difference in most cases is also significant. This is because, even when the analogue country is selected on a reasonably objective basis, the local domestic prices in the analogue country are very often higher than comparable Chinese ones. What can be said without doubt is that there is a consistent pattern, over the course of a reasonable range of separate investigations into different products carried out by the European Commission, of Chinese enterprises obtaining MET achieving a lower dumping margin.

---

[10] These investigations include: Regulation (EU) No. 1035/2010, OJ [2010] L 298/10; Regulation (EU) No. 248/2011, OJ [2011] L 67/1; Regulation (EU) No. 964/2010, OJ [2010] L 282/1; Regulation (EC) 1355/2008, OJ [2008] L 350/35; Regulation (EC) No. 1187/2008, OJ [2008] L 322/1; Regulation (EC) No. 91/2009, OJ [2009] L 29/1; Regulation (EC) No. 926/2009, OJ [2009] L 262/19; Regulation (EC) No. 925/2009, OJ [2009] L 262/1; Regulation (EC) No. 703/2009, OJ [2009] L 203/1; Regulation (EC) No. 691/2007, OJ [2007] L 160/1; Regulation (EC) 383/2009, OJ [2009] L 118/1; Regulation (EC) No. 1338/2006, OJ [2006] L 251/1; Regulation (EC) No. 1136/2006, OJ [2006] L 205/1; Regulation (EC) No. 1472/2006, OJ [2006] L 275/1; Regulation (EC) No. 1425/2006, OJ [2006] L 270/4; and Regulation (EC) No. 1987/2005, OJ [2005] L 320/1.

Comparison of Different Dumping Methodologies for the Same Chinese Enterprise Inside the Same Investigation

As a cross-check to determine whether or not the application of the MET methodology results in a lower individual dumping margin than the other non-MET approaches, it is useful to empirically examine those instances in which a change in the methodology has occurred towards the same company in the course of an anti-dumping investigation. In principle, Article 2.7(c) of the EU's Basic Anti-Dumping Regulation requires the European Commission to render a definitive determination of MET status within 3 months of the initiation of the investigation and that determination is meant to remain in force throughout the whole investigation. In other words, there should be no change in MET status between the provisional and definitive determination. For this reason, there are few cases where such a comparison is possible but three examples provide some guidance.

One instance of such a change of heart is *Hand Pallet Trucks and Parts from China*[11] where one Chinese producing company was denied MET at the provisional stage of the investigation and given Individual Treatment leading to an individual dumping duty rate of 36%. Subsequently, the European Commission decided that the company was eligible for MET and calculated its dumping margin based on its actual Chinese domestic prices compared to its EU export prices. As a result, its individual dumping margin dropped to 8% even although there appear to be no other factors or adjustments introduced in the intervening period that influenced this calculation other than the switch from individual treatment to MET.

In another case, *Leather Shoes from China and Vietnam*,[12] again a negative MET determination was changed to a positive one in the intervening period between provisional measures and the definitive stage of the investigation. The result was a reduction in the applicable duty rate from 21.4% to 9.7%. It should be pointed out that the provisional determination of the individual dumping duty rate for this specific company was made on a China-wide basis since no Chinese company qualified for either MET or Individual Treatment at the provisional stage of this investigation. Hence, the change in methodology was a leap from a negative determination for MET and individual treatment into a positive one for MET status. Regardless of the unusual circumstances of this case, the change in status still resulted in a meaningful reduction of the individual dumping rate even although no material change in the data on which the calculations were based appears to have occurred.

The third example is *Ironing Boards from China* which corroborates the conclusion that changing methodology mid-stream in an EU anti-dumping investigation, in which there are no other significant changes in the relevant data, results in a

---

[11] Regulation (EC) No. 128/2005, OJ [2005] L 25/16; Regulation (EC) No. 1174/2005, OJ [2005] L 189/1.

[12] Regulation (EC) No. 553/2006, OJ [2006] L 98/3, Recital 143; Regulation (EC) No. 1472/2006, OJ [2006] L 275/1, Recital 146.

substantial reduction in the company-specific anti-dumping duty rate. The European Commission imposed provisional anti-dumping duties on Chinese ironing board producers ranging from 0% to 38%. After representations were made by Chinese producers, the European Commission subsequently granted MET to three Chinese producers that were not initially granted conditional MET status. For one, the duty rate dropped from 36% to 3.5%, another dropped from 26% to 3% and for yet another no dumping margin was found.[13] It should be emphasised that nothing changed in the intervening period except a re-appraisal of the consistency of the companies' audited accounts for compliance with the International Accounting Standards (IAS). Subsequently, the European Commission again reversed its decision to grant conditional MET to these three companies and, in the definitive regulation, the rates returned to their original provisional levels. Two of the Chinese exporting producers filed applications for annulment at the European General Court to challenge the last minute reversal of their MET status and one of them succeeded on appeal to the European Court of Justice to have the anti-dumping measures annulled.[14]

Conclusions from the Empirical Analysis of the Most Recent Chinese Anti-Dumping Cases

Both empirical approaches appear to lead to the same conclusion which is that, all elements being as reasonably comparable as possible, conditional MET treatment leads to a significantly better individual dumping margin for Chinese co-operating enterprises than the alternatives. This confirms that a liberal approach to the application of the EU's MET criteria would likely lead to significantly lower individual dumping margin for Chinese exporting producers. Conversely, a restrictive approach would result in a larger number of co-operating Chinese exporting producers being able to successfully achieve lower duty rates. The balance between these two extremes is determined by many factors, the most obvious being the five MET criteria themselves but, crucially, the practical application of these principles to the facts and circumstances of each individual Chinese enterprise claiming such status. This in turn depends on the approach taken by each individual investigation team dispatched by the European Commission to carry out the verification exercise and the analysis of their findings. This has led to a very high degree of variation in final results. For example, in *Plastic Bags and Sacks from China*,[15] eight co-operating producers obtained conditional MET status which equates to a very

---

[13] *Ironing Boards from China*, European Commission – Final General Disclosure Document dated 20th February 2007.

[14] GC Case T-206/07, *Foshan Shunde Yongjian Housewares & Hardware* vs. *EC Council*, [2008] ECR II-1; ECJ Case C-141/08 P, *Foshan Shunde Yongjian Housewares & Hardware* vs. *EC Council*, [2009] ECR I-9147; and GC T-274/07, *Zhejiang Harmonic Hardware Products Co. Ltd* vs. *EC Council*, application on 19th July, 2007, case still pending, summary in OJ [2007] C 223/15.

[15] Regulation (EC) No. 1425/2006, OJ [2006] L 270/4, Recitals 83–131.

high success rate while in *Tartaric Acid from China*, all three co-operating Chinese enterprises achieved a similar result.[16] On the other hand, in *Certain Iron and Steel Fasteners from China, Certain Seamless Pipes of Iron and Steel from China*, and *Monosodium Glutamate (MSG) from China*, no Chinese enterprise was successful in establishing MET status.[17]

China's General Status in the Progress Towards Market Economy Status

Before moving to the subject of the legal and practical criteria for granting conditional MET status to individual Chinese enterprises, a number of questions merit attention. These are the following: (a) why does China's membership of the WTO not automatically mean that it is a member of the club of market economy countries?; (b) why is China not treated like the Russian Federation and the Ukraine since economic progress in China appears to be far more rapid and tangible than in these countries as China moves up to the world's second largest economy?; and (c) why is it that China will inevitably prevail despite the apparent delays, blockages and disputes between the parties in this assessment? Each of these issues raises valid questions and answers to them are merited to clear the clouds of confusion that circle around the discussion of MET for China in EU anti-dumping investigations.

Why Does China's Membership of the WTO Not Automatically Mean That It Is a Member of the Club of Market Economy Countries?

The question is frequently asked why China's membership of the WTO does not automatically entail full MET status? When China acceded to the WTO,[18] this step did not create an obligation on the part of any WTO Member to extend recognition of comprehensive market economy status to China. Simply put, the determination that China satisfied the conditions for membership of the WTO did not mean that it automatically became a recognised market economy country. More specifically, Section 15 of China's Accession Protocol to the WTO sets out how Chinese exports

---

[16] Regulation (EC) No. 1259/2005, OJ [2005] L 200/73, Recitals 14–47.

[17] Regulation (EC) No. 91/2009, OJ [2009] L 29/1, Recitals 58–111; Regulation (EC) No. 289/2009, OJ [2009] L 94/48, Recitals 20–52; and Regulation (EC) No. 492/2008, OJ [2008] L 144/14, Recitals 15–43.

[18] Decision of the WTO Ministerial Conference of 10th November, 2001 Concerning the Accession of the People's Republic of China, WTO Doc WT/L/432, 23rd November, 2001.

may be treated in anti-dumping proceedings.[19] WTO members – including for this purpose the EU – are permitted to use this approach. The material parts of this provision are as follows:

> Article VI of the GATT 1994 [and] the Agreement on Implementation of Article VI of the General Agreement on Tariffs and Trade 1994 ("Anti-Dumping Agreement") shall apply in proceedings involving imports of Chinese origin into a WTO Member consistent with the following:
>
> (a) In determining price comparability under Article VI of the GATT 1994 and the Anti-Dumping Agreement, the importing WTO Member shall use either Chinese prices or costs for the industry under investigation or a methodology that is not based on a strict comparison with domestic prices or costs in China based on the following rules:
>
> (i) If the producers under investigation can clearly show that market economy conditions prevail in the industry producing the like product with regard to the manufacture, production and sale of that product, the importing WTO Member shall use Chinese prices or costs for the industry under investigation in determining price comparability;
>
> (ii) The importing WTO Member may use a methodology that is not based on a strict comparison with domestic prices or costs in China if the producers under investigation cannot clearly show that market economy conditions prevail in the industry producing the like product with regard to manufacture, production and sale of that product. . ...

The requirement to "clearly show" the existence of these conditions in the particular circumstances of a Chinese exporting producer illustrates that the onus of demonstrating that this is on the Chinese producer asserting that these conditions exist. Nor is there any elaboration of what the term "market economy conditions" means for this purpose. The lack of specification for identifying these conditions has led to different WTO member countries applying their own rules for making this assessment and each saying that their own individual standards are consistent with this obligation. That said, the terms of the Accession Protocol are not in themselves a justification for rendering MET status virtually unachievable through the excessively rigorous application of the relevant criteria or indeed the setting of the goal posts beyond the reach of Chinese producers who are in reality effectively subject to the market economy forces of supply and demand.

It is interesting to note that the relevant criteria set out in Article 2.7.(c) of the EU's Basic Anti-Dumping Regulation towards the conditional MET treatment of Chinese exporters did not change in any material respect after this commitment was entered into by WTO members. Presumably, the EU took the position that the criteria of the conditional MET test were sufficient when compared to the rubric of this provision and consequently no significant changes were required. In any event, the actual terms of Section 15 remain vague as far as the practical and investigative requirements of examining MET for Chinese exporting producers are concerned. As a result, considerable latitude is given to the EU in the way that it applies the MET principle towards exports from China and this space for manoeuvre was not seriously attacked by China in the recent WTO panel review of the EU's anti-dumping

---

[19] For an EU anti-dumping ruling applying this interpretation see Regulation (EC) No. 1472/2006, OJ [2006] L 275/1, Recital 75.

measures on *Certain Iron and Steel Fasteners from China.*[20] On the other hand, the EU's approach to the granting of Individual Treatment for Chinese exporters was heavily criticised by the WTO panel which found that Article 9(5) of the EU's Basic Anti-Dumping Regulation conflicted with Article 6.10 of the WTO Anti-Dumping Agreement because it fails to allow each known exporter the opportunity to establish an individual dumping duty margin.[21]

Why Is China Not Treated Like Other Former Non-Market Countries Since Economic Progress in China Appears to Be Far More Tangible?

The European Union has consistently expressed the view that the application of full MET towards China in its anti-dumping laws is largely a technical issue.[22] In other words, if China can satisfy the EU that its technical progress towards a fully-developed market economy is largely achieved for most of its industrial sectors and the necessary underpinning laws and regulations adopted then the country as a whole can be treated as a market economy and thus the whole issue of conditional MET automatically disappears. For this reason, the EU has been working with the Chinese government at a technical level to move forward the issue of full recognition of China as a market economy country for the purpose of the EU's anti-dumping laws.

What has never been convincingly explained by the EU is why the granting of full MET status towards China is predominantly a technical issue while the award of such status to other neighbouring EU countries has been a blatant political decision. The reality is that, although clothed in the form of a technical process, in fact the exercise is mainly a political one. Its political character is apparent from the history of the EU's approach towards this issue for other trading partners. In 1998, the EU originally introduced the concept of conditional market economy treatment initially to exports of goods originating in China and Russia and then subsequently extended its application to other countries including Kazakhstan, the Ukraine and Vietnam. The political forces in the decision-making processes manifested themselves openly when the EU subsequently allowed certain countries to pass from non-market economy country status, through conditional MET, and eventually to full MET status at an indecently rapid rate. Both Russia and the

---

[20] Report of the Panel, EC – Definitive Anti-Dumping Measures on Certain Iron and Steel Fasteners from China, WT/DS 397/R.

[21] For a discussion of this case, see Healy/Azau, The EU's Practice Relating to Imports from NME Countries: An Examination of the WTO Panel's Report in the Chinese Iron and Steel Fasteners Case", International Trade Law and Regulation 17 (2011) 2, p. 70.

[22] Commission Communication "Treatment of Former Non-Market Economies in Anti-Dumping Proceedings", COM(97) 677 Final, pp. 1–2.

Ukraine were allowed to leap-frog China to achieve full market economy status in EU anti-dumping cases.[23] In both instances, there is no doubt that these decisions were made for geopolitical reasons and technical consideration of progress towards full market economy status was conveniently forgotten.

China, on the other hand, has not been the recipient of such political favours. Instead, China currently remains entangled in technical discussions with the EU over whether or not sufficient progress has been made towards full market economy recognition. Clearly, the European Union is not yet ready to make the significant step towards granting China full MET status as a political decision and hence the current limbo whereby conditional MET applies on an individual company-by-company basis. The EU's claim that the grant of full MET towards China in EU anti-dumping investigations could therefore be easily construed as a strategic tactic to forestall as long as possible the inevitable day of judgment which would also explain the snail's pace of the discussions with no apparent finalisation in sight. In the meantime, China has charged on to become the world's second largest economy and a global work-shop for the international community. Both domestic and foreign investment has been ploughed into the country, boosting its technical know-how and expertise, and leaving both Russia and the Ukraine behind in the race towards economic progress and prosperity. All of this points towards a worrying reluctance on the part of the EU to plan for the inevitable day when Chinese exporters are treated in the same way as almost all their competitors in the world for the purposes of EU anti-dumping law.

The "Two Track Approach" Explains Why China Will Inevitably Prevail

Patience and resilience, two of the main attributes of the Chinese character and psyche, combined with ample forward planning, explain why China will eventually prevail in this process.

The Formal Terms of China's Protocol of Accession to the WTO

The Chinese government intelligently negotiated an expiry of the country's treat-ment as a non-market economy status as part and parcel of its accession to the WTO. Under the terms of China's Protocol of Accession to the WTO, Section 15(d) provides:

> Once China has established, under the national law of the importing WTO Member, that it is a market economy, the provisions of subparagraph (a) shall be terminated provided that the importing Member's national law contains market economy criteria as of the date of accession. In any event, the provisions of subparagraph (a)(ii) shall expire 15 years after the

---

[23] Regulation (EC) No. 1972/2002, OJ [2002] L 305/2, and Regulation (EC) No. 2117/2005, OJ [2005] L 340/17.

date of accession. In addition, should China establish, pursuant to the national law of the importing WTO Member, that market economy conditions prevail in a particular industry or sector, the non-market economy provisions of subparagraph (a) shall no longer apply to that industry or sector.

It does not take a genius to work out that, regardless of whether any WTO Member holds aspirations to delay recognition of China as a market economy country indefinitely, this is not an achievable long-term strategy in light of the terminology deployed in this provision. The EU can, of course, unilaterally recognise China as a market economy before November 2016 but, if it chooses not do so, China will ascend to such status anyway. In other words, either before or in November 2016, the whole discussion about conditional MET in EU anti-dumping law will become moot unless, of course, the European Union can conjure up some kind of pretext to either completely or partially alleviate the impact of full market economy treatment for Chinese exports. In the absence for such a conjuring trick, no amount of lobbying on the part of EU industry can – legally speaking – prevent this event from happening.

So, the value of market economy recognition for China in EU dumping cases is a currency that is progressing devaluing especially as a bargaining chip for negotiations on other key issues between the EU and China. This begs the question of whether or not it is better to use this bargaining chip in EU trade policy towards China especially in a bilateral negotiations context to achieve appropriate advantages before it has no meaningful value. Holding out the possibility of this concession remains significant, although increasingly weak, leverage for example in the EU's attempts to negotiate a new Partnership and Cooperation Agreement with China and an updated set of agreements on trade and investment. Sooner or later, and probably sooner, China will simply decide that, having waited a decade to persuade the EU to grant full market economy status, the better strategy is to wait another five or so years until the EU is forced to make the concession to it.

Of course, there is no appetite inside the EU for taking such an approach. The lobbying faction supporting giving up the principle of conditional MET in favour of full recognition is simply non-existent among EU industries or indeed the majority of the EU's member states, especially those where the manufacturing base remains significant. This effectively ties the hands of the European Commission in any effort to make such a gesture in return for future advantages and concessions on the part of China. Consequently the possibility of a concession for MET towards China is destined to become an asset with almost no residual value within a couple of years.

Going Through the Motions of Technical Discussions Towards MET

In 2003, China made its first formal request towards the EU to grant it market economy status for the purpose of EU trade defence investigations.[24] An MES

---

[24] European Commission, Staff Working Document on Progress by the PRC Towards Graduation to Market Economy Status in Trade Defence Investigations, SEC(2008) 2508 Final, p. 5.

Working Group was established between the parties in 2004 with the mandate of exchanging information and views between the Chinese authorities and the services of the European Commission to facilitate an evaluation on the EU's side of China's progress towards market economy status. The terms of reference of the MES Working Group mirror those set out in Article 2.7.(c) of the EU's Basic Anti-Dumping Regulation and the assessment is framed in the context of whether or not China as a whole satisfies these criteria.

Since then, progress has been made at what can only be described as a snail's pace compared to the rapid advancement of the Russian Federation and subsequently the Ukraine, towards this goal. Although little publicly-available information is issued regarding these discussions, it seems reasonably clear that the goal posts are constantly being changed by the EU's side even although these discussions are typically conducted, according to the EU, "in a good and constructive atmosphere".[25] The latest publicly-available assessment of the situation indicates that the European Union has moved far from the quite basic rubric provided in Article 2.7.(c) and is delving deep into issues not initially contemplated when the original five criteria were established.[26] Reference is now being made in this evaluation to substantive criteria that are difficult to fathom in the criteria as originally postulated. For example, legitimate focus is given to China's relatively recent wholesale reforms of its bankruptcy, property and tax laws which were adopted at a level and for reasons mostly unrelated to its assessment for market economy status. Equally true, the reform of the Chinese accounting laws and practices are given proper attention which directly relates to one of the five MET criteria established in the EU's Basic Anti-Dumping Regulation and indeed one that is very problematic for reasons explored later. The proper enforcement of these laws and regulations is equally worthy of the European Commission's attentions in this context.

At same time, new elements have clearly entered the equation. These include assessment of the following Chinese laws and their implementation: (i) the Anti-Monopoly law and its effective enforcement; (ii) adoption and effective enforcement of the protection of intellectual property rights; (iii) privatisation activities relating to former state-owned assets; (iv) the pricing of energy and related utilities; (v) price intervention on commodity and raw material prices generally; (vi) reform of the Chinese financial sector; (vii) the provision of credit for private sector operators; (viii) corporate governance issues; (ix) policies designed to promote research and development as well as industrial policy goals; and (x) restrictions on exports and imports under customs law. The impression of the most recent publicly-available report is that the list of compliance requirements is expanding in terms of both coverage and depth. Certainly, it is a struggle to see why the assessment being

---

[25] European Commission, 28th Annual Report to the European Parliament on Trade Defence Activities 2009, COM(2010) 558 Final, p. 3.

[26] European Commission, Staff Working Document on Progress by the PRC Towards Graduation to Market Economy Status in Trade Defence Investigations, SEC(2008) 2508 Final.

applied to China is now far more rigorous than contemplated earlier when the MET criteria for EU trade defence measures were established.[27] Precisely how profound this exercise should be has a direct correlation to how high the hurdles should be for China to jump towards the achievement of market economy status. Since China perceives the conferment of market economy status by the EU as a key offensive trade policy objective, no doubt these discussions will continue in parallel to the ticking down of the clock towards November 2016.

These negotiations are therefore a parallel course for China to achieve this objective within a sooner timeframe but so far, despite China being acknowledged as a "modern and increasingly market-based system", only one criterion has been closed off from further discussions, namely the absence of state-induced distortions in the operation of enterprises linked to privatisation and the use of non-market trading or compensation systems. As at May 2011, further substantial progress on the other four criteria is, however, still reported to be required leaving the final conclusion of this exercise on a far from clear and certain time track.

The General Architecture of the MET Principle

At the heart of the conditional MET policy being applied towards Chinese producers and exporters is the notion that, in certain circumstances and under particular conditions, the influence of the state is curtailed vis-à-vis the activities of specific Chinese commercial enterprises. This independence, or freedom of commercial decision-making, allows the production activities of these enterprises to be viewed in isolation from the distortions that are otherwise caused in the larger national economy as a consequence of state or governmental influence. In order to make this assessment, indisputably certain criteria need to be applied to the facts and circumstances of each individual Chinese enterprises co-operating in an investigation and requesting MET status.

There are three aspects that comprise the overall architecture of the EU's conditional MET approach towards China, namely: (i) the five criteria themselves; (ii) the procedural framework within which they function; and (iii) their practical application by the European Commission's Trade Defence services. The last of these subjects is handled comprehensively in the next section. However, it is prudent to explain the other two at this stage in the process.

---

[27] See Commission Communication, Treatment of Former Non-market Economies in Anti-Dumping Proceedings, COM(97) 677 Final, pp. 4–11; and European Commission, Review of the Anti-Dumping Regime Applicable to Russia and China, COM(2000) 363 Final, pp. 5–9.

The Five MET Criteria for Conditional MET Status

The origins of the five MET criteria date back to the *European Commission's Communication on the Treatment of Former Non-Market Economies in EU Anti-Dumping Proceedings*, a document conceived and finalised in 1997.[28] The essential premise of the proposition was that because China (and also Russia at that time) had made "remarkable advances" towards reforming its economy some form of gesture was appropriate from the EU's side through revisions to the EU's anti-dumping legislation. The "carrot and stick" approach that has now come to characterise the EU's approach to this issue was already evident in this reform package. For example, it is expressly mentioned that:

> [T]he proposed changes will be a recognition of the efforts made so far by China and Russia to transform their economies. They will also act as an important incentive for continued and accelerated reform in those enterprises in Russia and China which do not yet operate in a market economy environment and will bolster the efforts of the Russian and Chinese governments to advance reform at a micro-economic level.

Although seeming somewhat patronising now, the fundamental idea and intention of the EU to contribute towards economic reform in China, and recognise the advances that had already been made by that point in time, were well intended. The idea of a unilateral reward being made for progress was well-received at the time by China.

These revisions took the form of amendments to the EU's Basic Regulation which allowed Chinese manufacturers to apply for MET in EU anti-dumping investigations and, if accepted, the European Commission would use their actual (or constructed) domestic prices for making its dumping calculations. The criteria themselves, set out in Article 2.7.(c) of the EU's Basic Anti-Dumping Regulation, as they apply to Chinese manufacturers and enterprises, are the following:

- Decisions of firms regarding prices, costs and inputs, including for instance raw materials, cost of technology and labour, output, sales and investment, are made in response to market signals reflecting supply and demand, and without significant State interference in this regard, and costs of major inputs substantially reflect market values;
- Firms have one clear set of basic accounting records which are independently audited in line with international accounting standards and are applied for all purposes;
- The production costs and financial situation of firms are not subject to significant distortions carried over from the former non-market economy system, in particular in relation to depreciation of assets, other write-offs, barter trade and payment via compensation of debts;

---

[28] See fn. 26, supra.

– The firms concerned are subject to bankruptcy and property laws which guarantee legal certainty and stability for the operation of firms; and
– Exchange rate conversions are carried out at the market rate.[29]

Thirteen years later, the original MET criteria, as postulated in the EU's Anti-Dumping Regulation, have changed little despite the changes in the geopolitical, financial and commercial structure of the global economy. While there is little doubt that these five criteria collectively establish a high threshold that must be met before MET status is approved, they constitute the general parameters within which a Chinese enterprise operating under market economy conditions can be distinguished from others that do not. The critical factor that essentially shapes the detailed contours of the policy in reality is, of course, how these basic elements are applied by the European Commission in practice.

Under EU law the onus is placed on individual Chinese exporters to establish that they meet the criteria for special treatment because this is an exception to the general principle. It should be mentioned that the five conditions have to be met cumulatively. In other words all must be satisfied before market economy treatment can be granted. This means that there is no trade-off among the respective strengths and weakness of the specific assessments made under each of these criteria.[30] So, for example, an exporter who establishes beyond doubt that it operates completely independently from the influence of the Chinese government, and which takes commercial decisions solely in accordance with market forces, may still find its MET application rejected if it fails to maintain accounting records in accordance with the required standards. Indeed precisely this situation is a relatively regular occurrence in practice.

As a final point, it should be mentioned that prior to the introduction of the conditional MET regime, Chinese exporting producers could benefit from Individual Treatment which allowed Chinese enterprises to make use of their actual EU export prices (as opposed to their domestic sales values) if certain conditions were satisfied. This facilitated a determination of dumping margins through a comparison of actual EU export sales prices against analogue country prices and was the alternative to simply establishing a single so-called "China wide" dumping margin being the rate applied to all Chinese exporters. This concept was initially created through administrative practice on the part of the European Commission but was subsequently codified in Article 9(5) of the EU's Basic Anti-Dumping Regulation.

---

[29] The amendments were originally made by Regulation (EC) No. 905/98, OJ L 128/18; and Decision 1000/1999/ECSC, OJ [1999] L 122/35, amending Art. 2(7) of Regulation (EC) No. 384/96.

[30] This has been confirmed by the EU General Court in case in GC Case T-299/05, *Shanghai Excell M&E Enterprise Co. Ltd and Shanghai Adeptech Precision Co. Ltd vs. EC Council*, [2009] ECR II-573, para. 76; and GC Case T-35/01, *Shanghai Teraoka Electronic vs. EC Council*, [2004] ECR II-3663, para. 54.

In terms of order of application, the assessment of conditional MET is made first and, if not obtained, the default assessment is one of Individual Treatment. If a Chinese company fails to satisfy either of these standards, the residual duty rate normally applies to its exports on a "China wide" basis.

Procedural Integration of the MET Assessment

Administrative procedures have been put in place to facilitate the examination of MET applications at an early stage in anti-dumping investigations. A special claim must be made by a Chinese enterprise applying for market economy treatment and extensive supporting certified documentation together with English language translations must be submitted, i.e. articles of association and memorandum, joint venture agreements, business licences, approvals for the establishment of the business, minutes of the board of directors and shareholder meetings, most recent audited accounts, organisational and hierarchical charts, lease or land ownership certificates, sample labour contracts, utility invoices, loan agreements, bank account contracts, asset appraisals and depreciation schedules, R&D agreements, etc. Details are also required for raw material purchases and suppliers, production and sales volumes, diagrams of the production process, auditor details and customer lists.

A period of 15 days from the publication of the Notice of Initiation was, until recently imposed by the European Commission for the completion of the MET Form, the submission of all supporting documentation, certifications and translations. True the European Commission, in special cases, did illustrate a flexible approach towards this deadline (i.e. by normally giving up to seven additional days for the submissions to be filed), but this task was, and still remains, highly onerous. Even when sampling was clearly indicated in the Notice of Initiation, all Chinese exporters wishing to claim MET had to file this documentation in time. Failure to comply in full, and furnish all relevant information and documentation, resulted in non co-operation and exclusion from the list of non-sampled co-operating companies entitled to the benefit of the average rate found in the course of the investigation.[31] This meant that dozens, and in some cases over a hundred,[32] Chinese exporters were required to file MET Forms and supporting documentation that was never any real part of the formal investigation examination process.

This excessive burden, for no real purpose, but with a high price to pay for non-compliance, has been heavily criticised although the European General Court

---

[31] Footwear with Protective Toecaps from China and India [Termination Decision], OJ [2006] L 234/3.

[32] See, for example, Regulation (EC) No. 91/2009, OJ [2009] L 29/1, Annex I (110 Co-operating Exporting Producers Not Included in the Sample); and Regulation (EC) No. 1472/2006, OJ [2006] L 275/1, Annex I (141 Co-operating Exporting Producers Not Included in the Sample).

endorsed the process and saw nothing wrong in law with this approach.[33] As regards the tight deadline imposed for completion, the WTO Panel in *Certain Iron and Steel Fasteners from China* ruled that the MET form and its completion did not constitute an anti-dumping questionnaire and therefore was not subject to the minimum completion times for such documents specified in the WTO Anti-Dumping Agreement.[34] However, since the issuing of this report, the European Commission has changed its practice and now does not require Chinese exporters to submit completed MET forms until a sampling determination has been made, meaning that Chinese exporters are now considered co-operating non-sampled companies as long as they offer themselves for inclusion in the sample.[35]

The European Commission also requires that each subsidiary in corporate group submits an individual MET form for review and verification. This requirement applies to all related companies located in China and involved in the production, sale or marking of the product concerned, including joint venture entities where the control exercised by the main applicant is a minority one. This means that, for some large Chinese corporate groups, a high volume of MET Forms have to be filed on behalf of each entity. In one recent investigation, one applicant was an exporting producer group and was required to submit 33 MET claim forms referring to its four related exporting producers and a series of other related companies involved in the product concerned i.e. pulp mills, chemical companies, forestry companies (upstream producers) and domestic trading companies.[36] Where MET applications are not submitted by all related parties in a group involved in the production, marketing and sale of the product concerned, the European Commission rejects the application in total on the grounds of inadequate co-operation and the impossibility of subsequent verification of all material data and information.[37] Equally onerously, all subsidiaries within a corporate group are required to satisfy all five criteria and if one related company does not qualify, MET cannot be granted to the group.[38]

Thereafter this information is normally verified by the European Commission by way of an on-the-spot investigation at the companies' premises. In the course of this verification, the European Commission is allowed to exercise the normal powers conferred by the EU's Basic Anti-Dumping Regulation to require the

---

[33] GC Case T-401/06, Brosmann Footwear (HK) Limited and Others vs. EC Council, [2010] ECR II-00000, Paras. 59–98.

[34] Report of the Panel, EC – Definitive Anti-Dumping Measures on Certain Iron and Steel Fasteners from China, WT/DS 397/R, 3rd December, 2010, paras. 7.566–7.579.

[35] The first instance of this revised practice occurred in Regulation (EU) No. 404/2010, OJ [2010] L 117/64, Recitals 5–9. See also Regulation (EU) No. 138/2011, OJ [2011] L 43/9; and Commission Notice of Initiation 2010/C 343/18, OJ [2010] C 343/24.

[36] Regulation (EU) No. 1042/2010, OJ L [2010] 299/7, Recital 33.

[37] Regulation (EU) No. 1035/2010, OJ [2010] L 298/10, Recital 28.

[38] See, for example, Regulation (EU) No. 1042/2010, OJ L [2010] 299/7, Recital 51.

production of evidence, explanations and data.[39] The European Commission may decline to carry out an MET determination, and therefore provide an individual dumping duty rate where a first analysis of the MET claim form fails to show that all the criteria were met. For example, in *Polyethylene Terephthalate (PET) From Australia, China and Pakistan,*[40] the applicant companies were all entirely or predominantly state-owned and allegedly failed to demonstrate that appropriate measures have been taken to prevent state interference in their business decisions. It is difficult to criticise this approach since verification visits are not compulsory but shall be carried out, where it is considered appropriate, the onus is on the Chinese exporter to prove its claim for MET and, of course, for reasons relating to the consumption of the EU's financial resources.

Article 2.7.(c) of the EU's Basic Anti-Dumping Regulation purportedly imposes on the European Commission an obligation to determine whether the criteria for market economy treatment are satisfied by applicant Chinese enterprises within 3 months of the initiation of the investigation.[41] The European Commission regularly – if not constantly – fails to meet these deadlines. The European Commission justifies this practice on the ground that non-compliance with the deadline has no prejudicial effect on the outcome of the MET determination. It is claimed only to be an internal guidelines with no external impact that would affect – beneficially or adversely – the treatment of the MET determination.[42] The General Court has declined to annul definitive anti-dumping measures when this occurs.[43] Although initially the European Commission carried out two separate verification exercises – one for MET and the other for the verification of the full questionnaire – its practice has changed in this respect. Commonly now one and the same verification is carried out for both purposes.

The same provision also stipulates that the MET determination – whether positive or negative – shall remain in force for the remainder of the investigation. The rationale for this stipulation has been explained by the European General Court in the following terms:

> Since it governs the choice of the method to be used to calculate normal value, the answer to the question whether the producer concerned operates under market economy conditions affects the calculation of the dumping margin and, therefore, the amount of the definitive anti-dumping duty imposed by the Council. Furthermore, the grant of market economy treatment also entails consequences as regards the manner in which the investigation will be

---

[39] Art. 16 EU Basic Anti-Dumping Regulation.

[40] Regulation (EC) No. 306/2004, OJ [2004] L 52/5, Recital 53.

[41] The European Commission originally proposed that this assessment should be made within month of initiation but this was changed to 3 months in the final version of the amendments made to the EU's Basic Anti-dumping Regulation – see Commission Communication, Treatment of Former Non-Market Economies in Anti-Dumping Proceedings, COM(97) 677 Final, 12th December, 1997, p. 12.

[42] Regulation (EC) No. 128/2005, OJ [2005] L 25/16, Recitals 27–29.

[43] GC Case T-299/05, *Shanghai Excell M&E Enterprise Co. Ltd and Shanghai Adeptech Precision Co. Ltd vs. EC Council*, [2009] ECR II-573, paras. 113–146.

conducted, since, if Article 2(1) to (6) of the basic regulation is applied, the Commission is to determine normal value on the basis of the information provided by the exporter in question and may, for that purpose, check its correctness. That is not so, on the other hand, if normal value is to be determined in accordance with Article 2(7)(a) of the basic regulation.

That is why the final indent of Article 2(7)(c) of the Basic [Anti-Dumping] Regulation provides that the determination whether the producer concerned operates under market economy conditions must be made within three months of the initiation of the investigation and that the determination is to remain in force throughout it. That provision is intended, in particular, to ensure that the question is not decided on the basis of its effect on the calculation of the dumping margin. Thus, the last sentence of Article 2(7)(c) of the basic regulation prohibits the institutions from re-evaluating information which was already available to them at the time of the initial determination as to market economy treatment.[44]

Yet, in the same case, the General Court ruled that, where new facts and evidence emerge after an affirmative MET determination has been made, and these occurred after the determination was made and only came to light at a later point in time, the European Commission was entitled to reverse its original affirmative determination and withdraw MET status from the applicant Chinese enterprise. Therefore, these protections are not at all cast in stone. On the other hand, it is clear that the General Court acknowledged that the purpose and structure of this requirement was designed to be a protection against the European Commission withdrawing MET when the results are clearly more favourable – in terms of a final dumping margin for the applicant – than would otherwise be the case if MET was denied. In reality, both positive and negative MET determinations have been reversed later in the course of the investigation.[45] True, this is not a frequent occurrence but it happens despite the terminology employed in the relevant provision of the EU Basic Anti-Dumping Regulation.

Finally, the award of MET in an original investigation does not ensure that the European Commission will reach the same conclusion in a subsequent review or refund relating to the exports of the same Chinese exporter. For example, in *Certain Ironing Boards from China*,[46] one Chinese exporter was awarded MET and a zero anti-dumping duty rate effectively taking it out of the scope of the EU anti-dumping measures. Following a complaint lodged by the EU industry under Article 5 of the EU's Basic Anti-Dumping Regulation, exports from this Chinese producer were reinvestigated and, although passing all five MET criteria the first time around, it was deemed to have failed two of the five criteria for the purposes of the second investigation.[47] Similarly, it is common practice for the European Commission to require Chinese exporters to re-establish their MET eligibility in any EU

---

[44] GC Case T-138/02, *Nanjing Metalink International Co. Ltd vs. EC Council,* [2006] ECR II-4347, paras. 43–44.

[45] See Section 1.B.2 above.

[46] Regulation (EC) No. 452/2007, OJ [2007] L 109/12, Recital 9.

[47] Regulation (EU) No. 1243/2010, OJ [2010] L 338/22. This case is now under appeal to the EU General Court, GC Case T-156/11, *Since Hardware (Guangzhou) Co. Ltd vs. EU Council,* application submitted on 15th March, 2011, OJ [2011] C 120/18.

anti-dumping refunds requested by their EU customers under the Basic Anti-Dumping Regulation.

The Practical Application of the Five MET Criteria

The basic legislative structure for the extension of the conditional MET principle to China has remained unchanged and it has been the European Commission that has been the principal driving force for developing the principle through its administrative and investigative practices. In other words, it has been the European Commission that has put the flesh onto the bones of the basic framework and, as a result, shaped the practical application of the regime. It has been both criticised and praised for its role in this context, depending on the perspective from which a judgment is made and the specific cases in question. Before passing another judgment on this question, it seems more appropriate to make a holistic review of the way the European Commission has carried out this task in light of the relevant principles themselves.

Criterion 1: Commercial Decisions Must Be Taken Without Significant State Interference

General Observations

This criterion requires the European Commission to examine whether:

> decisions of firms regarding prices, costs and inputs, including for instance raw materials, cost of technology and labour, output, sales and investment, are made in response to market signals reflecting supply and demand, and without significant State interference in this regard, and costs of major inputs substantially reflect market values.

No serious commentator or critique of the MET principles could refute the paramount need for the inclusion of this requirement in the MET criteria. Material interference by the state authorities as regards costs, prices, raw material requirements and sales policy suggests that a producer or exporter is not functioning on the basis of genuine market economy principles. In the most simple terms, the application of this concept allows for the separation of those Chinese enterprises operating under market economy conditions from those that do not by requiring successful enterprises to establish their independence from the influence of governmental interference – national, regional and local – in their basic commercial decision-making processes. Underpinning this requirement is also the fundamental need for the effective enforcement of the EU's anti-dumping laws. If two Chinese enterprises were to be granted individual dumping duty rates, one on the basis of MET and the other not, but in reality both were controlled by the Chinese state, then by exercising government control, it would be possible to circumvent any EU anti-dumping measures by increasing the EU exports through the one granted MET (and which normally would have the lower duty rate) while decreasing those by the other enterprise.[48]

Specific Comments

It should be noted that this criterion requires state interference to be "significant" before the European Commission determines that the assessment of the specific factors involved disqualify a Chinese enterprise from obtaining MET status. Restrictions of these kinds commonly appear in corporate constitutional documents (i.e. pre-establishment permits, company memorandum and articles of association, joint venture agreements, shareholder and management agreements and board and shareholder resolutions), business licences, export and import licensing agreements as well as audit reports. Practical assessments of these factors are also assessed in terms of prices (for raw materials, cost of production, labour and the price of finished goods), external setting of prices (i.e. price controls) and stock valuations. The degree of control exercised by the state is measured through an examination of the corporate governance of the enterprise in question, the origin of the capital, the extent of participation of the state in the company's share capital and control as well as national or local state approvals for otherwise normal commercial activities.

Demand Side Issues

Practice indicates that the European Commission gives considerable weight to the ability of a Chinese enterprise to decide, on its own account, what the prices for its products should be, where these goods should be sold and in what volumes, according to the forces of supply and demand.

Control over Domestic Pricing

The pricing policy of companies are scrutinised to ensure that prices are set in response to the forces of supply and demand and the competitive environment in which the company in question operates. A clear example of when this is not happening is when Chinese producers are either required, or in practice do, price their products by reference to centrally imposed price controls. This happened in *Electronic Weighing Scales from China*[49] where MET applications by two Chinese

---

[48] This "channelling" of exports through related companies with different duty rates is something that the EU prevents at all costs against all non-EU enterprises, not only those located in China.

[49] Regulation (EC) No. 2605/2000, OJ [2000] L 301/42, Recital 46.

companies were rejected on the grounds that internal price control regulations set prices in the domestic market. Apparently, this was evidenced by the fact that there was little, if any, price variations between Chinese domestic customers over a prolonged period of time. It was also found that domestic sales at loss-making levels, especially for a number of years, corroborated the determination that the companies' price setting policies were not sufficiently independent from state control. Another example was when MET was denied to a Chinese company because high quality (okoumé) plywood, which would normally command a price premium, was being sold at the same price as plain plywood.[50] This lack of price differentiation on the grounds of quality caused the European Commission to conclude that demand was somehow being distorted by state interference. It is also reasonable to conclude such controls impair the credibility of domestic prices as a means of determining genuine dumping margins since the overall effect of decreasing domestic prices is to decrease dumping margins.

Prohibitions on Domestic Sales

Prohibitions and restrictions on the ability to make domestic sales is also a significant impediment to obtaining market economy treatment, for both domestic producers and foreign investors alike. Although these kinds of restrictions are less and less common, especially since the Chinese local authorities changed their practice around 4 years ago to refrain from imposing such restrictions on Chinese business licences, earlier cases illustrate this point. In both *Glycine from China*[51] and *Leather Shoes from China and Vietnam*,[52] the Commission decided that the restrictions imposed by the Chinese authorities prohibiting domestic sales of products meant that the manufacturing and sales activities were not taking place under market economy conditions. Considerable flexibility has recently been shown by the Commission where domestic sales are not legally restricted but simply have not taken place within the relevant investigation period. The justification for an absence of such sales would, of course, have to be market forces such as, for example, the absence of sufficient price levels being achieved from domestic consumers or the possibility of realising comparatively higher profitability levels through export sales.

---

[50] Regulation (EC) No. 988/2004, OJ [2004] L 181/5, Recital 29.

[51] Regulation (EC) No. 1043/2000, OJ [2000] L 118/6, Recital 13.

[52] Regulation (EC) No. 1472/2006, OJ [2006] L 275/1, Recitals 71–72.

Restrictions on Freedom to Make Export Sales

It is equally logical that such intervention in relation to the setting of export prices
or volumes would also justify a conclusion that a particular exporting producer is
not operating in true market economy conditions for more or less the same reasons.
For this reason, the Commission has also taken a consistent line on companies that
either required to export through state-owned intermediaries or, alternatively,
through related entities which are licensed to export. For example, in *Cathode-
Ray Colour TV Picture Tubes from China*,[53] a Chinese manufacturer who could
only sell for export through a related entity was not entitled to market economy
treatment for this reason. Another example is another company that did not have an
export licence and had to export exclusively via State-owned Chinese traders
against an agency fee, which equalled the net profit on turnover during the same
period.[54] Again, these kinds of restrictions are increasingly less common-place.

Supply Side Issues

Freedom to control production volumes and output is equally critical to proving that
an enterprise operates under market economy conditions. The use of raw materials
and other costs of production, including labour, that are priced themselves
according to the forces of supply and demand is also a critical issue.

Prices and Supply of Raw Materials

Where prices and supplies of major raw materials are influenced through state
invention measures, the Commission has refused to grant market economy treatment on the grounds that the prices of these materials are either artificially high or
low. This has been a particularly controversial issue since such a finding can rule
out all players in an industry from obtaining MET if the raw materials in question
are important cost elements and the prices are distorted. This is even although this
element of state interference in the upstream raw material supply market is beyond
the control of the producers of finished merchandise. In *Certain Iron and Steel
Fasteners from China*,[55] no Chinese producer was granted MET because the
domestic Chinese price for the principal input merchandise – iron and steel wire
rod – was considered below the market prices charged in Europe, India, North
America and Japan. Since China had no significant natural resources of the raw
material to make iron and steel wire rod, which is iron ore, the European

---

[53] Regulation (EC) No. 837/2000, OJ [2000] L 102/15, Recital 28.

[54] Commission Decision No. 1238/2000/ECSC, OJ [2000] L 141/9, Recital 27.

[55] Certain Iron and Steel Fasteners from China [Definitive Measures], supra fn. 13, Recitals 63–69.

Commission concluded that the abnormally low price of this raw material in China could only be explained through state interference in pricing. This distortion of raw material costs permeated throughout all Chinese industries using this raw material and therefore tainted them with the effects of the non-market economy.

A similar conclusion was reached in *Aluminium Foil from Armenia, Brazil and China*,[56] where the European Commission concluded that the internal price setting system for primary aluminium in China, being open only to Chinese traders, contributed to depressed domestic prices as did an external export tax on export sales. The effect of the export tax was to create an artificial surplus of primary aluminium in the Chinese market which in turn translated into a cost advantage for Chinese manufacturers using primary aluminium to fabricate other finished products. Similarly, where purchase prices of fresh strawberries, i.e. the major raw material input to produce and process frozen strawberries, were fixed for the whole season irrespective of quality and seasonal fluctuations, the European Commission declined to grant MET to applicant companies subject to such artificial market forces.[57]

Energy Supplies

The supply of electricity prices at rates below material costs has also been a reason to reject MET application.[58] In *Melamine from China*, the European Commission went one step further in applying a pass on liability for Chinese exporters by determining that the use of natural gas, the price of which was controlled by the Chinese government, to manufacture an intermediate product, namely urea, prevented Chinese manufacturers of a further stage processed product, melamine, from obtaining MET status.[59] This "reverse engineering" of costs back all the way to energy inputs appears to be one step too much in the MET evaluation process and is likely to be challenged at some future point in time.

Labour Costs

As regards labour costs, the fact that the salaries for workers are set by state agencies, compounded by the existence of tax rebates for employers, has allowed the European Commission to conclude that a company is not eligible for market economy treatment.[60]

---

[56] Regulation (EC) No. 287/2009, OJ [2009] L 94/17, Recital 32.

[57] Regulation (EC) No. 1551/2006, OJ [2006] L 287/3, Recital 23.

[58] Regulation (EC) No. 1331/2007, OJ [2007] L 296/1, Recital 23; and Regulation (EC) No. 862/2005, OJ [2005] L 144/11, Recital 33.

[59] Regulation (EU) No. 1035/2010, OJ [2010] L 298/10, Recitals 20–24.

[60] Decision No. 1238/2000/ECSC, OJ [2000] L 141/9, Recital 27.

State Control over the Running of Business Operations

Participation in the Board of Directors and State Interest in Shareholdings

The fact that the state partly or fully owns an enterprise, or its representatives sit on the board of such an undertaking, suggests that undue influence could be exercised over decisions that would otherwise be determined purely by market forces. However, this assessment must be made on a case-by-case basis and does not justify an automatic assumption that such participation can justify an automatic denial of MET. This was made clear by the EU General Court in *Zhejiang Xinan Chemical Industrial Group v EC Council*.[61] In the investigative phase of the procedure, the European Commission ascertained that a majority of the shares of the applicant company were owned by private persons but due to the wide dispersion of the non-State-owned shares, together with the fact that the State owned by far the biggest individual block of shares, the company was under State control. Moreover, the board of directors was appointed by the State shareholders and the majority of the directors of the board were either State officials or officials of State-owned enterprises.

The Court first observed that state 'control' or 'influence' is not a criterion expressly laid down in the first indent of Article 2(7)(c) of the basic regulation. It was therefore to be determined whether state control, as found in this case, necessarily entailed 'significant state interference', within the meaning of this criterion. The Court then pointed out that the concept of 'significant state interference' could not be assimilated to just any influence on the activities of an undertaking or involvement in its decision-making process but must be understood as meaning action by the state which is such as to render the undertaking's decisions incompatible with market economy conditions. This criterion, according to the Court, was intended to determine whether the relevant decisions of the exporting producers concerned were based on purely commercial considerations, appropriate for an undertaking operating under market economy conditions or whether they were distorted by other considerations appropriate to State-run economies. However, State control, as established in this particular case, was not, as such, incompatible with the taking of commercial decisions by the undertaking concerned in keeping with market economy conditions and, in particular, did not mean that its decisions on prices, costs and inputs were based on considerations unrelated to an undertaking operating under such conditions.

Making these assessments on a case-by-case basis, the European Commission has determined that the presence of state representatives on the boards of Chinese companies poses problems when the majority of the posts on the Board of Directors are held by such individuals and there were no effective right for minority

---

[61] GC Case T-498/04, *Zhejiang Xinan Chemical Industrial Group vs. EC Council*, [2009] ECR II-1969, summary report in OJ [2009] C 180/42.

protection.[62] Even when a Chinese enterprise is listed on a Chinese Stock Exchange and the Board of Shareholders can appoint 'independent directors' (i.e. individuals that do not represent the shareholders and that have professional qualification relevant to the operations of the company), the listing may not sufficiently safeguard against undue state interference, especially if there are no voting restrictions in force that could prohibit the state-appointed majority of the directors taking decisions against the will of the independent directors who are a minority.[63]

Similarly, a substantial direct and/or indirect shareholding of the Chinese government in a company's share capital has been considered sufficient to exclude the possibility of a company gaining market economy treatment.[64] In another case, because the State-owned shareholder owned the majority of the company's shares, and consequently nominated the majority of the members of the board, this precluded MET because the Articles of Association regarding share ownership were not respected and could be easily changed by the company itself. Hence, the decision was reached that provisions of such Articles of Association, seeking to ensure that the State cannot significantly influence the company's decision, may be unreliable and cannot provide any guarantee in that respect.[65]

Investment Issues

Where a Chinese enterprise is unable to establish to the satisfaction of the European Commission who or which legal entity injected either the original capital or subsequent capital contributions, MET status will not be granted.[66] In some instances, where no independent evaluation was made as to whether the investments in the company reflect fair market prices, neither when the company was established nor when additional capital was subsequently injected later into the company, this has compromised MET status.[67] Similarly, uncertainty about the businesses' future, mirrored by shareholders' reluctance to provide the companies with sufficient capital, can constitute a major problem in capital-intensive businesses.[68]

---

[62] Regulation (EC) No. 289/2009, OJ [2009] L 94/48, Recital 27.

[63] Regulation (EC) No. 538/2005, OJ [2005] L 89/4, Recitals 46–49.

[64] Regulation (EC) No. 306/2004, OJ [2004] L 52/5, Recitals 60–64.

[65] Regulation (EC) No. 862/2005, OJ [2005] L 144/11, Recitals 33–34.

[66] Regulation (EU) No. 258/2011, OJ [2011] L 70/5, Recital 38.

[67] Regulation (EC) No. 552/2005, OJ [2005] L 93/6, Recital 25.

[68] *Frozen Strawberries from China*, supra fn. 67, Recital 23.

Criterion 2: Maintaining Accounting Records That Are Consistent With International Standards

General Observations

This criterion requires the European Commission to examine whether or not:

> firms have one clear set of basic accounting records which are independently audited in line with international accounting standards and are applied for all purposes.

The obligation imposes three separate requirements (a) that the company must have a clear set of basic accounting records; (b) these records must be independently audited; and (c) they must comply with international accounting standards. The justification for the insertion of this requirement into the MET criteria is often said to be the fact that the backbone or keystone point of reference for any EU anti-dumping investigation is the audited accounts. The fact that an external and independent expert has examined the companies' records and prepared the audited accounts accordingly provides the European Commission with a reliable starting point for carrying out its verification. The apparent lack of enforcement of the internationally recognised accounting standards and the accounting rules applicable in the PRC can be a form of State interference in the normal operation of a market economy.[69] In reality the European Commission has deviated from this reference point in a number of cases not involving Chinese exporters and this deviation has been endorsed by both the European General Court and the European Court of Justice: For example, in *CD-Rs from India*, the European Commission disregarded information contained in the company's audited accounts relating to depreciation periods in favour of information contained in the company's tax records.[70] Furthermore, the ability of the EU institutions to do so was confirmed by the European Court of First Instance and the European Court of Justice.[71]

The application of this criterion in practice is the single most common reason explaining the high failure rate for Chinese producing exporters seeking MET status. This is because the requirement is interpreted by the European Commission to mean that the audit reports have to meet international accounting standards (not national Chinese ones) and that they are complete, virtually flawless and totally accurate as are the underlying internal accounting records. This creates question-marks over the permissibility of applying this criterion in the rigorous way that it does for a number of reasons.

First, the European Commission frequently applies the International Accounting Standards (IAS) developed by the International Accounting Standards Board

---

[69] Regulation (EC) No. 128/2005, OJ [2005] L 25/16, Recital 26.

[70] Regulation (EC) No. 960/2003, OJ [2003] L 138/1, Recitals 38–44.

[71] GC Case T-300/03, *Moser Baer India Limited vs. Council of the European Union*, [2006] ECR II-3911, paras. 65–70, and on appeal, ECJ Case C-535/06 P, *Moser Baer India Limited vs. Council of the European Union*, [2009] ECR I-7051, paras. 28–43.

(IASB) which have not been adopted in China. Indeed, these standards are only applied in the EU towards certain large EU enterprises.[72] This practice has been accepted unconditionally by the European General Court which has explained:

> It must be pointed out that the fact that Chinese undertakings are not subject under their domestic law to compliance with certain accounting standards has no bearing on whether their accounts may be assessed in the light of those standards. The second criterion laid down in Article 2(7)(c) of the basic regulation clearly states that the accounts of any undertaking which comes from a country without a market economy and wishes to obtain MES must be audited in line with International Accounting Standards and it is irrelevant whether the application of those standards is mandatory in its state of origin. Furthermore, it is precisely because that state does not have a market economy that the Basic [Anti-Dumping] Regulation requires the undertakings concerned to comply with accounting standards which are not necessarily national standards.
>
> Secondly, the fact that the international accounting standards applied in the present case are not mandatory for all Community undertakings under a Community act does not necessarily imply that those standards, or even other accounting standards which pursue the same objectives and implement them just as strictly, if not more so, are not mandatory for those undertakings under their domestic laws. Nor does it imply that those standards are not widely accepted at international level or that they might not embody accounting principles common to the majority of countries with market economies, including the Member States.[73]

As regards the argument that few EU companies are required to comply with these standards, the European Commission itself has also directly addressed this issue at a very early stage in its practice. In one early investigation, Chinese companies argued that by imposing the obligation to apply the IAS to foreign exporters while they are not imposed on the domestic industry, meant that the EU applies its trade laws not in an 'impartial' way. Thus, it was claimed that the Community industry was put in a more favourable position than exporters. However, the European Commission noted that the analysis of whether Chinese companies fulfil the criteria for obtaining market economy treatment was carried out on the basis of Article 2(7)(c) of the Basic Anti-Dumping Regulation. Since this evaluation is never done for the EU industry it decided that it could not be accused of being impartial in its analysis.[74]

Second, the question that then arises is whether the EU imposes these three requirements standards (i.e. (a) to (c) above) upon exporting producers from other WTO member countries in anti-dumping investigations. As far as the need to maintain basic accounting records and/or audited accounts, the answer is probably affirmative. It is unlikely that the European Commission would be prepared to

---

[72] Since 2005 only listed EU companies must prepare their consolidated financial statements in accordance with the IFRS. Member States may also permit or require EU-listed companies to use this standard for their annual accounts and non EU-listed companies for their annual and/or consolidated accounts.

[73] GC Case T-299/05, *Shanghai Excell M&E Enterprise Co. Ltd and Shanghai Adeptech Precision Co. Ltd vs. EC Council*, [2009] ECR II-573, paras. 86, 87.

[74] Regulation (EC) No. 552/2005, OJ [2005] L 93/6, Recital 27.

establish a dumping margin where no accounting records were maintained by an exporting producer even from Less-Developed Countries (LDC). It is far less likely, however, that the audited accounts of a non-Chinese company involved in an EU anti-dumping investigation would have to be maintained in line with "international accounting standards" and not national ones. It seems to be the European Commission's standard practice that the accounts under examination need only be in line with national accounting standards. For example, in *Cotton-Type Bed-Linen from Pakistan*,[75] the European Commission expressly commented on the failure of the audited accounts to meet Pakistani Generally Accepted Accounting Principles (GAAP). Furthermore, assessments of financial and cost information is regularly made based on local accounting principles which is why Article 2(5) of the EU's Basic Anti-Dumping Regulation allows allocation of costs "provided that such records are in accordance with the generally accepted accounting principles of the country concerned."

Precisely why the standard applied to Chinese exporting producers should be "international accounting standards" and not national or local ones probably has political origins rather than legal ones. The question is whether this requirement remains permitted after Chinese accession to the WTO This is doubtful. The rationale for imposing a requirement that a higher (or unattainable) standard of accounting principles than those which are applied inside a particular country leads to the obvious result that this requirement will only be met in exceptional cases (for example by multinational and EU corporations established in China). It is the exception rather than the rule that locally qualified Chinese accountants are applying these extraneous standards when they are trained and instructed to prepare accounts based on the local and/or national Chinese standards.

Specific Comments

Companies Must Have One Clear Set of Basic Accounting Records

If a Chinese company's accounts are incomplete or contain significant errors this requirement is not satisfied.[76] An English version of the complete financial statements including the auditor's notes must also be provided to the European Commission in addition to the Chinese original versions. Practically speaking, this requirement also raises two difficulties. First, in situations where an exporting producer is not a legal entity, and is therefore not legally obliged to main basic audited accounting records, the European Commission will not allow the entity to successfully apply for MET.[77] Second, for companies in a start-up phase and which

---

[75] Regulation (EC) No. 397/2004, OJ [2004] L 66/1, Recital 38.

[76] Regulation (EC) No. 862/2005, OJ [2005] L 144/11, Recital 36.

[77] Regulation (EC) No. 837/2000, OJ [2000] L 102/15, Recitals 28, 29.

does not have either audited or any other sort of financial accounts again no MET investigation will be undertaken.[78]

Accounting Records Must be Independently Audited in Line With International Accounting Standards

If companies' accounts are not independently audited, they cannot get MET.[79] Even if the accounts have been audited by independent external auditors, numerous problems persist. The importance of qualifying opinions expressed by auditors (i. e. accounts approved with qualifications or refusals to approve) depends on the significance of the defects founding the course of the audits. The fact that an auditor does not issue an 'adverse opinion' but mentions deficiencies in its report does not mean in itself that the accounts are not correct.[80] When an audit does point at severe accounting inconsistencies or towards a severe financial situation, issues become acute and shed doubts on the reliability and independence of the audits.[81]

In one case, the company's own auditors made reservations with regard to, amongst others, the booked sales figures, assets valuation and depreciation. However, no corrections were made to rectify the shortcomings identified by the auditors and no action was taken towards the reservations expressed by the auditors to explain under which conditions some of the company's assets were transferred from the collectively-owned pre-existing company.[82]

The Company's Accounting Records Must Be Applied for All Purposes

The existence of reliable audited accounts for a Chinese enterprise is only part of the requirement. The final audited accounts must accurately reflect the underlying accounting records maintained by the company in question and must reconcile with those records. Frequently, the European Commission denies MET because Chinese companies maintain diverging versions of their accounts which contained significant errors such as closing and opening balances of consecutive financial years that do not correspond to each other or changes in accounting policy that were not properly substantiated by any kind of disclosure in the accounts. This means that it is not possible to reconcile important figures such as sales turnover with the company's internal accounting records.[83] In other instances, the audited balance sheets did not reflect the fair and true value of assets and liabilities at all times because they were not booked at the moment they were incurred (i.e. at the time of purchase) but when payments were made.[84]

Findings of major breaches of the IAS are replete in the European Commission's practice because of inaccurate reflections of Chinese companies underlying records

---

[78] Regulation (EC) No. 771/2005, OJ [2005] L 128/19, Recital 35.

[79] Regulation (EC) No. 449/2000, OJ [2000] L 55/3, Recital 114.

[80] Regulation (EC) No. 306/2004, OJ [2004] L 52/5, Recitals 67, 68.

[81] Regulation (EC) No. 1551/2006, OJ [2006] L 287/3, Recital 25.

[82] Regulation (EC) No. 145/2005, OJ [2005] L 27/4, Recital 22.

[83] Regulation (EC) No. 771/2005, OJ [2005] L 128/19, Recital 37.

[84] Regulation (EC) No. 452/2007, OJ [2007] L 109/12, Recital 25.

compared to their audited financial statements (i.e. the accrual basis of accounting, prudence and substance over form, valuation of inventories, buildings not recognised and properly depreciated, land use rights not properly amortised, failure to properly account for foreign exchange movements and the impairment of assets).[85] It is also true that some failures on the part of Chinese enterprises strike at the heart of normal commercial practices. In one instance, a Chinese enterprise borrowed money from a bank and lent it to one of its state-controlled shareholders notwithstanding all other legal aspects such as the protection of the interest of other minority shareholders and other creditors. However, the European Commission only observed that this transaction had not been accounted for in accordance with the appropriate accounting standards although it also criticised the fact that, taking into account the significant amount involved, the auditors did not react on this item.[86] In another case, the auditors had not made the comments on the loss of almost all of the paid-in capital.[87]

Other shortcomings appear petty for the purposes of the MET assessment. In some cases, the financial records of the companies involved are simply unclear, for example, because sales or purchase vouchers were incomplete,[88] the depreciation of fixed assets was found to be inconsistently applied[89] or some transactions were booked on an accrual basis whereas others were not,[90] and non-compliance with normal stock valuation method for raw materials.[91] In other instances companies rented warehouses from third parties but the rent charged did not itemise electricity costs. Irregular depreciation practices were observed for the same company. Land-use rights were rented at favourable conditions and depreciation inconsistencies were also found.[92]

Criterion 3: Production Costs and Financial Performance Must Not Be Affected by Distortions Carried Over from the Former Non-Market Economy

General Observations

This criterion specifies that, to be successful for MET status:

---

[85] Regulation (EC) No. 692/2005, OJ [2005] L 112/1, Recital 16.

[86] Regulation (EC) No. 538/2005, OJ [2005] L 89/4, Recital 56.

[87] Regulation (EC) No. 988/2004, OJ [2004] L 181/5, Recital 30.

[88] Regulation (EC) No. 1472/2006, OJ [2006] L 275/1, Recital 74.

[89] Regulation (EC) No. 862/2005, OJ [2005] L 144/11, Recital 37.

[90] Regulation (EC) No. 1350/2006, OJ [2006] L 250/10, Recital 19.

[91] Regulation (EC) No. 781/2003, OJ [2003] L 114/16, Recital 25.

[92] Regulation (EC) No. 1551/2006, OJ [2006] L 287/3, Recital 26.

the production costs and financial situation of firms are not subject to significant distortions carried over from the former non-market economy system, in particular in relation to depreciation of assets, other write-offs, barter trade and payment via compensation of assets.

In common with Criterion 1 (Commercial Decisions Must be Taken Without Significant State Interference) this criterion justifiably distinguishes Chinese enterprises operating under market economy conditions from those that do not. In other words, it constitutes a clear barrier from state interference and the commercial operations of an individual Chinese enterprise. This requirement is measured, in particular, by reference, inter alia, to the availability of subsidies and other forms of state support, undervalued loans, the purchase of land use rights for below market value, the unjustified depreciation of assets, other write-offs, barter trade and payments via compensation for debt. These elements are measured by reference to the activities of individual enterprises. In other words, it is how these companies are affected by these factors that is critical and not the fact that they function in the context of the wider economy of China as a whole.

Specific Comments

Transfer of Assets from State-Owned Companies

For the purposes of establishing MET for former state-owned enterprises, it is necessary to establish that the former State-owned shares or assets have been sold freely and at a market price during the transfer of the company into private ownership.[93] The classic illustration of non-compliance is the purchase of production facilities from a State-owned company, however, at a substantial discount relative to the value determined by independent evaluators.[94] Distortions caused by both low valuations and excessive deprecations ruled out two exporting producers in *Integrated Electronic Compact Fluorescent Lamps from China,*[95] because their financial situation and production costs were significantly distorted because of the arbitrary valuation of assets. These distortions meant that neither producer could demonstrate the "absence of distortions" resulting from the existence of the former market economy system. Similarly, in another case, the production costs and the financial situation were considered distorted due to the arbitrary evaluation of assets of one company.[96]

---

[93] Regulation (EC) No. 781/2003, OJ [2003] L 114/16, Recital 21.

[94] Regulation (EU) No. 1042/2010, OJ [2010] L 299/7, Recital 37.

[95] Regulation (EC) No. 255/2001, OJ [2001] L 38/8, Recital 18.

[96] Regulation (EC) No. 1612/2001, OJ [2001] L 214/3, Recital 21.

Purchase of Land Use Rights and Fixed Assets

The purchase of land-use rights or machinery that has not been passed on at market conditions to Chinese manufacturers will also constitute distortions of costs and financial situations carried over from the non market economy system.[97] Where decisions on matters involving the lease of land were explicitly determined by the state in the company's business investment licence or, for example, a company enjoyed a waiver on the payment of land lease until its basic construction plans were completed, market economy status was declined.[98] Similarly, in another case, a Chinese company denied MET received their land use right certificate before paying in full for it and used this certificate to obtain a mortgage from a State-owned bank.[99]

A frequently cited reason for denying MET is when Chinese enterprises are able to obtain or acquire land use rights that are below market rates for property in the same or neighbouring areas or regions. This often occurs when the companies in question are established in special industrial zones which offer cheap land as an incentive for attracting investment to their locations. The European Commission considers that the acquisition of land use rights at rates below those in similar vicinities constitutes a distortion carried over from the former non-market economy situation.[100] Questions do arise, however, as to how this assessment is made. In one case, the European Commission asserted that the land price in a region quite far from Shanghai should be compared to prices in that city. Obviously this is not an apples-to-apples comparison and the European Commission's margin for discretion in making such comparisons has not been successfully challenged through an appeal. Even comparisons with the land use right prices paid by other enterprises in the same general vicinity have been rejected on the basis of the argument that such evidence only shows that prices in the whole area in general may be artificially depressed. Owing to the absence of readily available comparative information, frequently this issue becomes heated in the course of verification visits conducted by the European Commission.

The purchase of land use rights and fixed assets which subsequently become much more valuable raises suspicions that assets were purchased at unreasonably low values reflecting state interference in the purchase principle. In one case, two companies purchased land use rights and the value of land use right and fixed assets increased substantially over a relatively short period of time between the moment when they were acquired or brought into the company as a capital contribution and between 1 and 5 years later when they were re-evaluated. According to the European Commission, this indicated that the respective assets were acquired at a

[97] Regulation (EC) No. 1472/2006, OJ [2006] L 275/1, Recital 75.

[98] Regulation (EC) No. 771/2005, OJ [2005] L 128/19, Recital 39.

[99] Regulation (EC) No. 287/2009, OJ [2009] L 94/17, Recital 36.

[100] Regulation (EC) No. 390/2007, OJ [2007] L 97/6, Recital 75.

value below market price which represented a hidden subsidy. Both companies claimed that the increase had actually not been so substantial and was in line with the increase normally observed in China for comparable assets but no evidence was provided to support their proposition. Given the significant advantage that these companies received by obtaining assets for prices substantially below market value, compliance with this criterion was deemed not satisfied.[101]

Loans

The use of loans that are granted at below normal market interest rates and on terms and conditions that are abnormal from the perspective of a prudent lender can give rise to a negative MET determination.[102] As far as borrowings from external sources are concerned, where significant amounts of interest-free borrowings were found to exist, resulting in a significant amount of negative working capital and in potential high financial costs not reflected in the records of the individual companies or the Group, MET has been denied on this ground.[103] In another instance, when six out of seven loans held by a company were not secured by any guarantees, this led to a denial of MET status.[104] The European Commission applies much the same approach in the case of inter-group loans as well and in one example, a Chinese company was discovered that it received bank loan guarantees from its State-owned shareholder and operated a settlement account in such a way that it was not possible to link invoices and payments.[105]

As far as the use of guarantees for obtaining loans and mortgages is concerned, this practice was analysed in some detail in *Citric Acid from China*.[106] Three companies or groups of companies mortgaged most of their assets in order to receive loans. Despite having mortgaged most of their assets, they were still in a position to guarantee loans that were granted to other companies. As compensation, they received similar guarantees for their own loans from the same companies for which they had acted as a guarantor. The companies used these guarantees to obtain further loans amounting to 25–50% of their total assets. The companies argued that such a system is also applied in market economy countries and explicitly provided for under Chinese banking legislation. However, the information collected by the European Commission during the investigation showed that the banks' policy should normally be to grant loans only for a fraction of the value of the assets used as a guarantee and not for an amount which exceeds such value. Moreover, the

---

[101] Regulation (EC) No. 488/2008, OJ [2008] L 143/13, Recital 26.

[102] Regulation (EU) No. 1042/2010, OJ [2010] L 299/7, Recital 39.

[103] Regulation (EC) No. 492/2008, OJ [2008] L 144/14, Recital 24.

[104] Regulation (EC) No. 1551/2006, OJ [2006] L 287/3, Recital 26.

[105] Regulation (EC) No. 862/2005, OJ [2005] L 144/11, Recital 39.

[106] Regulation (EC) No. 488/2008, OJ [2008] L 143/13, Recital 25.

banks from which the loans were obtained, and the financial system as a whole, were under substantial State influence. Therefore, it was concluded that the three companies did not meet the relevant MET criterion.

Benefit of Subsidies

Perhaps the most controversial aspect of this criterion is the question of subsidies. The conferment of subsidies and other forms of financial assistance, especially for production and export-promotion purposes, represent a pure form of state intervention. Yet all countries, and specifically all WTO members, engage in these activities for the purposes of economic stimulation and the promotion of particular economic sectors. For this reason, the WTO has its own Subsidies Agreement to regulate both the amounts of subsidies that can be granted by WTO member in specific sectors and the actions that other trading partners can take against actionable and/or prohibited subsidies. This practice is not exclusive by any means to China.

Generally speaking, the granting of subsidies and/or financial assistance to Chinese enterprises is considered by the EU as a justification for denying MET status. However, there is no real pattern of consistency in practice on this issue. In some case, the European Commission has considered the grant of subsidies as a bar to obtaining MET status[107], but in others has been prepared to accept that the subsidies in question are relatively insignificant or that the return of the financial benefits granted can wipe the slate clean of this infraction.[108] For example, in *Frozen Strawberries from the PRC*, five companies benefited from subsidies. These companies were found to have purchased fresh strawberries from local farmers but the farmers did not pay any VAT on these strawberry sales. In turn, however, the producers of the product concerned deducted an 'implied VAT' on these purchases from the VAT liable on their sales of frozen strawberries. While the companies may have benefited from lower costs as a result of this mechanism, the effect on overall costs remained limited and any benefit to the companies from these lower costs could be corrected by a normal value adjustment.[109]

On the other hand, the European Commission has not been prepared to accept the argument or supporting evidence that subsidies that comply with the WTO Subsidies Agreement prevent the rejection on an application for MET status. In other words, there is a disconnect between the issue of MET, on the one hand, and legitimate subsidies under the WTO Subsidies Agreement on the other hand. This is clear from the European Commission's assessment in *Coated Fine from China*[110]

---

[107] Regulation (EC) No. 289/2009, OJ [2009] L 94/48, Recital 25; and Regulation (EU) No. 404/2010, OJ [2010] L 117/64, Recital 44.

[108] Regulation (EC) No. 488/2008, OJ [2008] L 143/13, Recital 28 and Regulation (EC) No. 1425/2006, OJ [2006] L 270/4, Recital 104.

[109] Regulation (EC) No. 1551/2006, OJ [2006] L 287/3, Recital 24.

[110] Regulation (EU) No. 1042/2010, OJ L [2010] 299/7, Recitals 47–49.

where the Chinese exporter argued that its ability to obtain preferential financial facilities should be considered as subsidies and not distortions carried over from the former non-market economy system. Since there was a parallel anti-subsidy investigation into the same products, it was argued that these alleged subsidies cannot be a ground for rejecting MET and should be evaluated as being, or not, countervailable subsidies. This line of argumentation was dismissed by the European Commission who insisted that the financing arrangements were indeed a distortion carried over from the non-market economy system and had no link with whether or not the impact of such acts could be considered as countervailable subsidies. It stressed that the criteria on MET are clearly set out in the EU's Basic Anti-Dumping Regulation and the fact that there was also an anti-subsidy investigation in progress did not deprive the European Commission, as the investigating authority, from its "obligation" to ensure that the conditions for granting MET were fulfilled.

In the same procedure, the claim was made that the Chinese exporting producers group must be granted MET so as to avoid "double counting" or "double remedies" in the context of the parallel anti-subsidy. The WTO Panel in *US – Definitive Anti-Dumping and Countervailing Duties on Certain Products From China*[111] accepted, "without difficulty", the general proposition that the use of a non-market economy methodology in an anti-dumping investigation likely provides some form of remedy against subsidisation and therefore that the simultaneous imposition of anti-dumping duties calculated on such a basis methodology, and the application of countervailing duties on the same products likely results in any subsidy granted in respect of the merchandise at issue being offset more than once. But the European Commission also rejected this argument for two reasons. First, as mentioned above, the European Commission was obliged to respect and apply the provisions of the EU's Basic Anti-Dumping Regulation. Second, according to the Commission, the issue of 'double counting' of anti-dumping and countervailing duties is regulated by the provisions of the relevant EU legislation, notably Article 14(1) of the EU's Basic Anti-Dumping Regulation and 24(1) of its Basic Anti-Subsidy Regulation. In the final anti-dumping and anti-subsidy measures adopted by the EU in these investigations, the European Commission adopted a more robust line of defence consisting of three parts although the effective thrust of its position was to deny that the theory had any relevance in EU MET assessments.[112] First, in this specific procedure, the EU was applying its so-called "lesser duty rule" meaning that the trade protective measures are applied at the lower of the dumping/subsidisation margins found to exist and the injury margin. Since the latter was lower, this meant that the lower level of duty rates in final measures adopted effectively eliminated any possible double counting. Second, it was the EU's consistent practice to apply the duty amount resulting from the anti-subsidy investigation first and, if there was

---

[111] Report of the Panel, US – Definitive Anti-Dumping and Countervailing Duties on Certain Products From China, WT/DS 379/R, 22nd December, 2010, paras. 14.67–14.76.

[112] Regulation (EU) No. 452/2011, OJ [2011] L 128/18, Recitals 269–274.

a "gap" between the duty level and the injury margin, this "gap can be filled" with the duty resulting from the anti-dumping investigation.[113] Third, not all Chinese exporters requested MET in the parallel anti-dumping investigation and therefore the automatic granting MET because of the findings in the investigation into the issue of subsidisation in the countervailing duty investigation, as put forward by the Chinese government, would create a remedy that is not permitted in EU law. Whether or not these assertions are correct, it is clear that the EU intends to maintain hard-line position in this matter.

Barter Trade and Payment via Compensation of Debts

The alleged existence of barter trade, on the other hand, has played only a marginal role in the rejection of a number of MET applications. In *Ferro Molybdenum from China*[114] for example, the fact that one of the applicants was found to have engaged in barter trade was considered an important element in rejecting their applications. Adverse findings for MET status are, however, relatively rare especially in the most recent decisions made by the European Commission probably because this form of commerce is no longer widespread in the Chinese economy.

Criterion 4: Companies Must Be Subject to Bankruptcy and Property Laws

General Observations

This requirement specifies that:

> the firms concerned are subject to bankruptcy and property laws which guarantees legal certainty and stability for the operation of firms.

It should be stressed at the outset that the adoption by China of a wide-ranging series of reforms to its bankruptcy system, culminating in the enactment of the Chinese Bankruptcy Law in 2006, although perceived by the European Commission as a significant advance, is not viewed as sufficient to render this criterion non-applicable any longer in anti-dumping investigations into China.[115] This is mainly for two reasons. The first is that the Bankruptcy Law is not comprehensive in its

---

[113] The results of the EU anti-dumping investigation can be found in Regulation (EU) No. 452/2011, OJ [2011] L 128/18.

[114] Regulation (EC) No. 1612/2001, OJ [2001] L 214/3, Recital 22.

[115] Commission, Staff Working Document on Progress by the PRC Towards Graduation to Market Economy Status in Trade Defence Investigations, SEC(2008) 2508 Final, 19th September, 2008, pp. 16–17.

coverage meaning that a significant number of Chinese state-owned enterprises are excluded from its scope. Second, the European Commission takes the view that the law is not efficiently or effectively enforced for a variety of reasons including a lack of trained specialists in bankruptcy proceedings and the low rate of actual bankruptcy and liquidation procedures compared to the size of the Chinese economy as a whole.

Hence, the individual facts and circumstances of an applicant Chinese company's situation is the main parameter used to conduct this evaluation rather than the macro-economic situation. In the past, when China did not have an advanced bankruptcy law in place, this allowed many Chinese companies to prevail under this criterion even although the underlying statutory framework was questionable in terms of both content and enforcement.

Specific Comments

In the first notable case concerning the rejection of MET on the basis of this criterion, namely *Okoumé Plywood From the PRC*,[116] the European Commission ascertained that during the verification visit at that company's premises, for certain financial years, the company's losses were higher than its capital meaning that it was effectively and technically insolvent Therefore, it was found that, whilst the company may in theory be subject to the bankruptcy laws, these de facto did not apply to it, since under those circumstances a proceeding for bankruptcy should have been launched. Furthermore, the company's auditors made no comments in this respect suggesting that proper accounting disciplines were not being properly applied in breach of Criterion 2. Hence, the company failed to demonstrate that it operated under a legal framework which guaranteed legal certainty and its claim for MET was rejected.

In another instance, a Chinese company was found to face significant financial difficulties having been loss-making for a number of consecutive years, and was bailed out by its State-owned shareholder. Although the company argued that such significant financial difficulties may not necessarily result in bankruptcy, the fact that the State-owned shareholder rescued the company (including through debt write-off), in a situation where under normal market conditions a shareholder would not have done this, indicated that the application of the Chinese bankruptcy laws in this particular case was doubtful. It was therefore concluded that, in the absence of evidence that the bankruptcy law was being applied in practice to the company, the criterion was considered as not being fulfilled.[117]

Clearly, sustained losses over a prolonged period, and the erosion of a company's capital in a significant matter, point towards its insolvency. The

---

[116] Regulation (EC) No. 988/2004, OJ [2004] L 181/5, Recital 32.

[117] Regulation (EC) No. 862/2005, OJ [2005] L 144/11, Recital 39.

question is whether or not its insolvency remains only theoretical in the absence of the company's creditors or the company's directors themselves seeking insolvency. Another possibility is the prospect of mandatory liquidation of the company at the request of government agencies such as the tax bureau. While a company's auditors should issue an adverse or qualified opinion on the status of the company as a going concern in its financial statements this does not compel a company to seek liquidation. On the other hand, where the European Commission can clearly establish that a company's debts exceed its capital, it is not unreasonable to make the assumption that the continued operation of a company means the possible exclusion of the company from the impact of Chinese bankruptcy rules unless material elements justify its continued functioning such as commitments on the part of its parent company to support these operations.

Non-compliance with this criterion has not extensively featured as a common basis for denying MET and in most investigations, especially in recent years, little if any reference is made in investigative results to Chinese companies failing to satisfy this requirement. In other words, meeting this requirement has not emerged as a major stumbling block in proving eligibility for MET status.

Criterion 5: Exchange Rate Conversations Must Be Carried Out at Market Rates

General Observations

This criterion requires simply that:

> exchange rate conversions to be carried out at the market rates.

At the time of the adoption of the original MET criteria in 1997, it was widely speculated that this criterion would play a significant role in deciding the outcome of MET determinations since the Chinese currency was not easily convertible into other currencies, officially at least, restrictions applied to the import and export of capital into China and the currency itself was pegged in value relative to a foreign currency, namely the US dollar. Precisely how this condition could be satisfied by individual Chinese exporters was therefore difficult to predict at the time.

However, from the outset, the European Commission also took a practical approach to the examination of this attribute and whether or not it is satisfied turns on the individual facts and circumstances of each applicant company, in much the same way as was taken towards the application of Criterion 4. As a result, fulfilling this requirement not been the obstacle perceived at the time. For example, when the EU industry attacked the European Commission for granting positive determinations under this criterion, despite the fact that the Chinese currency was pegged to the USD by a decision of its government and the currencies had allegedly not been exchanged at market rates by any of the co-operating exporters, the Commission response was that:

The fact that the Chinese currency RMB is pegged to the USD is a decision by the Chinese government, against which an applicant for MET cannot be held responsible. Similar decisions have in the past also been taken by other countries, notably in Latin America...Indeed, all of the co-operating exporters in this investigation were found to be able to purchase and sell foreign currencies obtained in their business operations, despite the fact that the exchange rate RMB/USD was pegged.[118]

In addition, over the course of time, this criterion has become less and less relevant in MET appraisals.

Specific Comments

At a relatively early state in its practice, the European Commission adopted a consistent practice to consider this criterion as fulfilled if the company used the official exchange rate for all its transactions involving foreign currencies. This meant that the European Commission was applying this criterion in reality as a way mainly to ensure that no "black market" exchange practices were being used in the applicant companies' commercial activities.[119]

Practices which have the potential to violate this criterion include: restrictions on the ability to repatriate capital and profits; limits on liquidation of fixed assets, limits on the amounts held in foreign currency accounts and restrictions on remissions of amounts outside China. In reality only one practice has been considered as impinging on this condition and that is failure to properly account for foreign currency conversions in accounting records although this has been frequently been treated as a violation of the obligation to maintain proper accounting records under Criterion 2.[120]

Looking to the Not Too Distant Future

The use by the EU of its anti-dumping procedures against China is, despite protestations to the contrary, an important aspect of the trade relationship between the two trading partners. If volume and value suppression is taken into account because of the introduction and maintenance of anti-dumping duties, then a far larger amount of bilateral trade between the parties is adversely impacted by such trade protective measures than the figures provided by the EU would otherwise suggest. Measured in terms of shares of imports into the EU, China is also targeted on a more frequent basis than exporters from other non-EU countries and especially

---

[118] Regulation (EC) No. 538/2005, OJ [2005] L 89/4, Recital 62.

[119] Ibid.

[120] Regulation (EC) No. 128/2005, OJ [2005] L 25/16, Recital 32; Regulation (EC) No. 692/2005, OJ [2005] L 112/1, Recital 17.

the United States, Japan, Brazil, India and Russia. Both these conclusions are difficult to dispute and together explain why China views the attainment of full Market Economy Treatment as a key offensive trade objective in its interactions with the EU. Granting full MET would at least partially offset the negative impact of such measures by lowering average dumping duty rates to levels more in line with those established in investigations into exports from the EU's other main trading partners.

The functioning of the conditional MET principle only goes part of the way towards achieving this goal and, given the limited number of successful MET applications in most EU anti-dumping cases, and the relatively high non-MET rates applied even when Individual Treatment is used, from the Chinese perspective, the situation is unsatisfactory given the rapid progress made in terms of economic development. There is also little doubt that because China inhabits the twilight space between a non-market economy country and full status as such, EU industries are encouraged to see Chinese exporters as a soft target for EU anti-dumping actions. Given that EU anti-dumping rates against Chinese exporters who fail to satisfy the five MET criteria can be four or five times higher than if actual or constructed Chinese domestic prices were used in the calculations, there is unquestionably an additional incentive to file complaints against Chinese exporters that does not exist relative to exporters in other non-EU countries.

The riposte from the EU industry side is to point out that competition from China is increasingly intense in the EU market in a number of capital intensive sectors where EU industries have made substantial investments, notably chemicals, iron and steel merchandise, consumer products and mechanical goods. The rise in import volumes from China in many of these sectors are a clear indication of this intensification in competition. In many EU anti-dumping complaints, EU industries accurately point out that they are unable to compete with Chinese manufacturers because the final price of Chinese goods does not even cover their costs of production in the EU for the same merchandise. This is more likely to be a combination of two factors rather than dumping. The first is the clear comparative advantage that China enjoys in terms of significantly reduced labour costs. This rationale, of course, also explains that attractiveness of China as a location for foreign investment by EU enterprises. The second is distortions in costs that are more likely to be considered as specific subsidies liable to countervailing duty action. Now that the EU has broken its own taboo on initiating anti-subsidy actions in parallel with anti-dumping ones against China,[121] and recently imposed anti-subsidy duties of up to 12% against Chinese exports,[122] there is no reason at all why these distortions cannot be tackled on this basis. Overall, the final combined duty rates might be lower but they would be a more accurate and precise form of redress

---

[121] Commission Notice of Initiation 2010/C 99/13, OJ [2010] C 99/30; and Commission Notice of Initiation 2010/C 249/08, OJ [2010] C 249/7.

[122] Regulation (EU) No. 452/2011, OJ [2011] L 128/18, Art. 2(2).

against Chinese unfair competition than is currently dispensed under the present conditional MET system used by the EU.

In fact, EU industries have little choice in this matter given that the clock is progressively ticking down towards November 2016 when the WTO Accession Agreement for China mandates recognition as a market economy country for the purposes of applying EU anti-dumping measures. To renege on this international obligation would be inconceivable. While it is well known that the European Commission is examining ways to soften the impact of full market economy recognition for China, a wholesale step back from this commitment seems an unrealistic objective. In much the same way as other reforms on EU anti-dumping practices were compelled by the WTO, for example the elimination of the practice of "zeroing" and the accompanying overall reduction in average dumping margin determinations, compliance with its commitments towards the WTO will be a game changing event with the direct effect of considerably reducing anti-dumping margin assessments for Chinese exporters. Chinese exporters view this eventuality as the establishment of a level playing field while EU industries take a diametrically opposite position.

It is unlikely that the EU will recognise that granting MET in the intervening period is an asset at the negotiating table with China, albeit with constantly diminishing value. The alternative is to adjust the application of the conditional MET principle, and indeed the EU's approach to trade defence instruments as a whole vis-a-vis China, to face the future challenges that will face EU industries from "unfair" Chinese competition. Such a progressive relaxation of the conditional MET principle is in the overall interests of EU industry if supported by the right flanking action and would prevent the sudden shock that will otherwise occur. If anything, the European Commission's practice towards applying the five MET criteria illustrates the flexible latitude available to it within the legislative parameters that have been established. Possible reforms, and aspects that should remain unchanged in principle, could include the following elements.

First, Criterion 1 (commercial decisions should be taken without significant state interference) in principle remains reasonably fair in its application with the exception of the approach taken towards raw material costs as a justification for denying MET. This treatment is excessive because it penalises exporters with no control over upstream pricing of raw materials (especially when the upstream distortions are not directly relevant raw materials or inputs but instead basic commodities such as, for example, natural gas). The issue of "state control" requires close examination on a case-by-case basis and assessment of de facto operations of Chinese enterprises seems a more appropriate focus rather than the theoretical possibility of state interference through decision-makers that are simply appointed by the state, especially when these individuals in question have actual sector-specific experience (e.g. in the Chinese steel-making sector).

Similarly, Criterion 3 (production costs and financial performance must not be affected by distortions carried over from the former non-market economy) is a fundamental parameter for the application of conditional MET. The assessment of the relative market value of land-based assets, however, requires re-evaluation since this is simply too frequently an apparent pretext for denying MET. The difficulties of being able to make an apples-to-apples comparison undermines the legitimacy of the European Commission's approach towards this assessment although, of course, where the evidence of undervaluation is probative rather than based on mere assumption, it is justified to arrive at a different conclusion. The assessment of loan commitments requires additional reflection especially when the Chinese company is able to adduce external evidence of high (i.e. AAA) credit worthiness from institutional sources.

Second, the approach taken by the European Commission towards the application of Criteria 4 and 5 should remain unchanged. In both instances, the approach taken is practical and objectively fair. While there will always be exceptions, especially in cases where companies have been overwhelmed by debt in comparison to their capital base, the reality of the situation is that the European Commission has already adapted its administrative and investigative practices to recognise the steps taken by China towards both these objectives.

Third, the European Commission's approach towards the application of Criterion 2 (maintaining accounting records that are consistent with international standards) requires significant adjustments. At the outset, it is questionable, despite the support of the European General Court on this point, that, if tested in the WTO, the European Union could establish that compliance with the International Accounting Standards (IAS) is a reasonable requirement. This is especially so since these standards are not applicable to all enterprises in the EU and conflict with the normal rules and practice to require that financial reports and accounting records are maintained in accordance with the standards applied in the country where the exporting producer is located. This requirement is unduly onerous and has resulted in a disproportionate number of Chinese exporters being denied MET. Instead, the European Commission such adopt a more practical approach and assess whether the accounting record and financial reports of individual enterprises are reasonably reliable and accurate for the purposes of corroborating the integrity of the information and data required for the purposes of establishing a reliable dumping margin calculation. This is simply a mirror reflection of its practice in other non-Chinese anti-dumping investigations.

Minor instances of deviation from accounting standards should also be disregarded if the overall result is that the financial reports of a Chinese enterprise are, overall, reliable. Requiring absolutely rigorous compliance with accounting standards implies that the European Commission is prepared to put form over substance when accurate dumping calculation are possible. It should be borne in mind that the European Commission does not require the same degree of robust compliance with accounting standards when it examines the financial records of EU enterprises in the context of its material injury and causation analysis. In itself, relaxation of some of the most arduous, and arguably unjustified, requirements under this criterion would result in a marked improvement in the success rate for Chinese enterprises who otherwise are able to demonstrate that they operate in real market economy conditions in conformity with criteria 1 and 3, being the main tests for making a genuine distinction between companies operating under market economy conditions from those that do not.

Fourth, it is regrettable that the European Commission has consistently refused from the outset to comply with the EU Council's recommendations that it should give special consideration to the specific situations of Chinese Small and Medium Sized Enterprises (SMEs) when applying the MET criteria."[123] Especially in relation to the preparation of audited accounts complying with international accounting standards, the European Commission has refused to make exceptions of the rigorous application of the MET criteria for Chinese SMEs.[124] This is despite the case that Chinese SME's, in virtually all instances, do not have sufficient resources to prepare their accounts in accordance with these standards.[125] Reflections on the part of the European Commission whether or nor this remains a reasonable approach seem prudent.

Lastly, as the *quid pro quo*, China has to accept the proposition that the EU will be more muscular in its use of another trade defence instrument, namely the Basic Anti-Subsidy Regulation towards exports from China. This is an inevitable consequence of China's march towards full market economy status and cannot be construed in any way as discrimination because the EU makes full use of this instrument against other trade partners.[126] It is also the correct approach to addressing the fundamental issue whether, holistically, Chinese imports are fair or unfair within the context of the complete prism of the EU's trade defence instruments.

Acknowledgment The author wishes to thank Haiya Wo at Squire Sanders Dempsey (UK) LLP for her assistance in providing research support for this project.

---

[123] In the Council's minutes attached to the 2000 Proposed Council Regulation to amend the EU Basic Anti-Dumping Regulation, COM(2000) 363 final, Annex 1), the Council called on the European Commission "to implement this Regulation in such a way that firms of all sizes have equivalent opportunities to make use of its provisions if they fulfil all the necessary criteria".

[124] Ironing Boards from China [Provisional Disclosure Document dated 26th February, 2007], not public.

[125] The EU General Court has supported the Commission's policy on this issue – see GC Case T-299/05, *Shanghai Excell M&E Enterprise Co. Ltd and Shanghai Adeptech Precision Co. Ltd vs. EC Council*, [2009] ECR II-573, paras. 72 and 88.

[126] See, for example, Decision 2009/452/EC, OJ [2009] L 149/74.

A New Landscape in the WTO: Economic Integration Among China, Taiwan, Hong Kong and Macau

Chien-Huei Wu

Introduction

At the World Trade Organisation (the WTO) Ministerial Conference held in Doha in 2001, two events were under the spotlight: the launch of Doha Round of negotiation and the People's Republic of China's accession.[1] In addition to these two events, a less-noticed event was that, in parallel to China's successful bid for the WTO membership, Taiwan, acting as a "separate customs territory possessing full autonomy in the conduct of its external commercial relations and of other matters provided for" in the WTO Agreement under the title of "Separate Customs Territory of Taiwan, Penghu, Kinmen and Matsu"[2] instead of its official title of "Republic of China",[3]

Part of this contribution was previously published in *Global Jurist*, http://www.bepress.com/gj/vol7/iss3/art7.

[1] In this contribution, China refers to the People's Republic of China (the PRC); while Republic of China (ROC) will be referred to as Taiwan, which is generally known.

[2] John H. Jackson observes that Taiwan crafted its application for the GATT (and then the WTO) as a separate customs territory so as not to offend China. He also mentions that Hong Kong, China, through the sponsorship of the United Kingdom, became a Contracting Party to the GATT, and continues as an original member of the WTO. However, it seems that Jackson fails to differentiate the accession procedures employed by these two members. See Jackson, *Sovereignty, the WTO, and Changing Fundamentals of International Law*, 2006, p. 109.

[3] Since this contribution focuses on the economic integration between these four WTO members and their interaction with the WTO forum, the official title of Taiwan, namely, Republic of China will not be used. For the benefit of convenience and comprehension, I will use the term of "Taiwan" instead of its full title of "Separate Customs Territory of Taiwan, Penghu, Kinmen and Matsu" in the WTO or its abbreviation "Chinese Taipei".

C.-H. Wu (✉)
Institute of European and American Studies, Academia Sinica, Taipei, Taiwan
e-mail: wch@gate.sinica.edu.tw

C. Herrmann and J.P. Terhechte (eds.), *European Yearbook of International Economic Law (EYIEL), Vol. 3 (2012)*, European Yearbook of International Economic Law 3, DOI 10.1007/978-3-642-23309-8_7, © Springer-Verlag Berlin Heidelberg 2012

joined the WTO 1 day after China.[4] The WTO has thus become one of the very few international organisations where both China and Taiwan enjoy full membership. The story does not end here. Prior to the accession to the WTO of China and Taiwan, Hong Kong and Macau had long participated in the General Agreement on Tariffs and Trade (the GATT) under the sponsorship of the United Kingdom and Portugal. Being Contracting Parties to the GATT, Hong Kong and Macau had thus become two of the founding members of the WTO organisation came into being in 1994. With China resuming its sovereignty over Hong Kong and Macau in 1997 and 1999 respectively, they began to participate in the WTO using the official title of "Hong Kong, China" and "Macau, China".[5]

Counting Taiwan's official title, Republic of China, altogether, the situation then turns out to be that there are four Chinas in the WTO, which presents a unique legal landscape and has much to explore.[6] This contribution thus aims to examine economic integration among these four WTO members that may be characterised as "hub and spark" in nature: China being the hub and the other three members the sparks. Since (in fact, even earlier before) their return back to China, Hong Kong and Macau have heavily relied on Chinese economy. It is also generally shared that aid from China was one of the important weapons to shield Hong Kong to go through the Asian financial crisis bursting off in 1997, immediately after China's resumption of its sovereignty over Hong Kong. One of the major instruments to boost the economies of Hong Kong and Macau is the Closer Economic Partnership Arrangements [hereinafter CEPAs] signed between China and Hong Kong and Macau on 29 September and 17 October 2003 respectively.[7]

The speed of economic integration varies depending on the political climate. It is especially so in relations to China and Taiwan. During 2000 to 2008 when the Democratic Progress Party which is in favour of dependence, was the ruling party in

---

[4] Regarding Taiwan's application for the GATT and WTO, see generally, Cho, *Taiwan's Application to GATT/WTO: Significance of Multilateralism for an Unrecognized State*, 2002; see also Hsieh, Facing China: Taiwan's Status as a Separate Customs Territory in the World Trade Organization, JWT 39 (2005) 6, pp. 1195 et seq. (1199–1200).

[5] When referring to the WTO-related activities or their positions therein, I will use the official title of "Hong Kong, China" and "Macau, China". When special reference to Chinese domestic legal status as a special administrative region [hereinafter SAR] is made, I will use the terms of Hong Kong Special Administrative Region, or the HKSAR and the Macau Special Administrative Region, the MASAR. Nevertheless, I will mostly use the term of Hong Kong and Macau for geographic indications.

[6] For a background knowledge of China's accession to the WTO and its relationship to the Chinese Taipei accession and to Hong Kong, China, and Macau, China, see the WTO document, available at: http://www.wto.org/english/thewto_e/acc_e/chinabknot_feb01.doc (last visited on 5th March, 2011).

[7] The China-Hong Kong CEPA and its supplements are available at the website of the Trade and Development Department of the HKSAR, http://www.tid.gov.hk/english/cepa/ (last visited on 5th March, 2011); the China-Macau CEPA and supplements are also available at the website of the MASAR government, http://www.cepa.gov.mo/cepaweb/front/eng/index_en.htm (last visited on 5th March, 2011).

Taiwan, the political interaction between China and Taiwan remained lukewarm and economic integration stagnant. Until the entry into force of direct-transportation agreements on 15 December 2008,[8] direct transportation between China and Taiwan had been prohibited. Goods shipping and passengers travelling between China and Taiwan had had to transit via a third country or area, normally Hong Kong and Macau. However, since 20 May 2008, when the Ma administration that is more sympathetic toward China came into power, the speed of economic integration between China and Taiwan has sharply increased. Among those measures adopted by the Ma administration, the landmark Economic Cooperation Framework Agreement [hereinafter the ECFA][9] between China and Taiwan signed on 29 June 2010 attracts the most attention.[10]

In observing the economic integration among these four WTO members, there are some important historical points to highlight: the accession to the WTO of China and Taiwan at the Doha Ministerial Conference; the direct transportation between China and Taiwan; and the ink of the CEPAs and ECFA. This contribution is thus organised in chronological order while examining the economic integration between China and Hong Kong and Macau first and then that between China and Taiwan. Following this introductory section, this contribution, in Section "Economic Integration Between China and Hong Kong and Macau", will examine economic integration between China and Hong Kong and Macau with a brief note on trade policy and practice of Hong Kong and Macau at the first place and particular emphasis on the CEPAs. Section "Economic Integration Between China and Hong Kong and Macau" then explores the economic integration between China and Taiwan under the Ma administration with an introductory background on the cross-Taiwan strait trade relations and special focuses on direct-transportation agreements and the ECFA. Section "Dispute Settlement Mechanisms in CEPAs and ECFA" then compares the dispute settlement mechanisms contained in the CEPAs and ECFA. This contribution then concludes with a short summary of its main findings and major arguments.

---

[8] The legal text of the direct-transportation agreements between China and Taiwan is available at the website of the Strait Exchange Foundation of Taiwan [hereinafter the SEF], http://www.sef. org.tw (last visited on 5th March, 2011). See infra, fn. 54, et seq.

[9] The legal text of the ECFA is available at: http://www.ecfa.org.tw/RelatedDoc.aspx (last visited on 5th March, 2011). This website is launched by the Taiwanese government for the promotion for the public support and understanding of the ECFA.

[10] During the Trade Policy Reviews conducted within the WTO, both the Secretariat Reports on China and on Taiwan mention the negotiations of the ECFA. See, Trade Policy Review Report by the Secretariat on China, WT/TPR/S/230, 26th April, 2010, para. 42; Trade Policy Review Report by the Secretariat on Separate Customs Territory of Taiwan, Penghu, Kinmen and Matsu, WT/TPR/S/232, 31st May, 2010, para. 35.

Economic Integration Between China and Hong Kong and Macau

Trade Policy and Practice of Hong Kong and Macau Before CEPAs

In terms of the economic developments in Hong Kong and Macau, three events are of great significance: the GATT and subsequent WTO memberships; the handover to China; and the signatures of the CEPAs. Prior to its formal accession to the GATT, Hong Kong had participated in some GATT activities. The Hong Kong Office in the Mission of United Kingdom had sought recourse to Article XXIII:2 of the GATT to request the establishment of the panel by the Contracting Parties.

In *Norway – Restrictions on Imports of Certain Textile Products* [hereinafter *Norway – Textiles*], the United Kingdom, acting on behalf of Hong Kong, requested a panel to be established. The subsequently established panel found that Norway's Article XIV action was inconsistent with Article XIII, and should be immediately terminated or be brought in accordance with the provisions of Article XIII.[11] Besides, in the Panel report on *EEC – Quantitative Restriction on Certain Products from Hong Kong* [hereinafter *EEC – Import Restrictions*], France was found to infringe its obligations assumed in Article XI of the GATT and to, prima facie, nullify and impair the benefits of Hong Kong accruing from the Agreement after a complaint was brought against EEC by the United Kingdom on behalf of Hong Kong.[12]

Compared to Hong Kong, Macau's experiences in participating in the GATT prior to its accession were much more limited. Even since its accession to the GATT and, later on, to the WTO, Macau has not been as active a member as Hong Kong has. It was partly because the UK had constantly helped Hong Kong to develop its capacity in participating in the international trading system with the aim to ensuring its market economy and political autonomy, since China's resumption of its sovereignty over Hong Kong was inevitable. Macau was not able to benefit from this.

Hong Kong and Macau experienced a significant constitutional change when they were returned to China and Hong Kong Basic Law [hereinafter the HKBL] and Macau Basic Law [hereinafter the MABL] became their mini-constitution. As certified by China, these two SARs of China could be qualified as separate customs territories "possessing full autonomy in the conduct of its external commercial

---

[11] Report of the Panel, Norway – Restrictions on Imports of Certain Textile Products, L/4959, adopted 18th June, 1980, BISD 27S/119, paras. 16–18.

[12] Report of the Panel, EEC – Quantitative Restrictions Against Imports of Certain Products from Hong Kong, L/5511, adopted 12th July, 1983, BISD 30S/129, para. 34. This case is extremely interesting in that, the United Kingdom, being a member of EEC, initiated a complaint on behalf of Hong Kong, against France, also an EEC member. It turned out to be the United Kingdom, acting on behalf of Hong Kong against EEC in the panel proceedings. It is also usual in terms of the internal/external liberalisation of EEC. While the United Kingdom did not maintain a quota system, it was forced to "de-liberalise" as EEC had the exclusive competence in external trade.

relations and of the other matters provided for the WTO Agreement". Their memberships in the WTO would thus remain unchanged and would still be able to participate in the international trading system. The two Basic Laws also guarantee their economic autonomy and enable Hong Kong and Macau to continue to participate in the international trading system.

After the WTO came into being, Hong Kong had once acted as a complaining member. In *Turkey – Restrictions on Imports of Textile and Clothing Products* [hereinafter *Turkey – Textile*],[13] Hong Kong requested for a consultation with regard to Turkey's quantitative restrictions on imports of textile and clothing products. This consultation request addressed the same issue as the famous *Turkey – Textile*,[14] complained by India because of the customs union agreement between European Community and Turkey. Although Hong Kong did not request for the establishment of a panel, it intervened as a third party in the complaint brought about against Turkey by India. Overall, Hong Kong's participation in the WTO is very active, let alone to mention its hosting 2005 Hong Kong Ministerial Conference.

Trade policies of Hong Kong and Macau have some important and distinctive characteristics. As claimed in the government report during the 1998 trade policy review, Hong Kong's import and export system was characterised by "(a) zero tariffs; (b) minimum controls; and (c) no subsidies or assistance to export".[15] With regard to its role as a middleman to China, while some argues that it will soon come to an end with the full opening of China's economic and the emergence of rival hubs, such as Shanghai and Shenzhen, it is also argued that Hong Kong is still comparatively competitive, especially in the area of financing and professional services.[16] In respect of Macau, it is characterised by its free-port status and zero-tariff policy, as mandated by article 110 of the MABL. Macau's economy also relies much on services trade, where the gambling service plays a pivotal role.

However, the Asian financial crisis exploded immediately after the handover. These two economies, especially Hong Kong, had suffered from a great depression of their economic development. The gradual recovery was challenged again when the Severe Acute Respiratory Syndrome burst off. The situation in Macau was no better. The stagnating development and the growing crime rate had long plagued Macau. Against this background, some efforts must be made with the aim to boost the economic development of these two SARs. The CEPAs are designated to meet this need.

---

[13] WT/DS29/1, 15th February 1996. As this submission was dated on 15th February, 1996, the official name in the WTO was still "Hong Kong", instead of "Hong Kong, China". Nevertheless, when it intervened as third party in the complaint brought by India, the official name was switched to "Hong Kong, China", as it was already returned to China.

[14] Report of the Appellate Body, Turkey – Restrictions on Imports of Textile and Clothing Products, WT/DS34/AB/R, adopted 19th November, 1999, DSR 1999:VI, 2345.

[15] WTO Document, Trade Policy Review Report of Hong Kong, China by Government of Hong Kong, China, WT/TPR/G/52, 11th November, 1998, para. 46.

[16] Sung, The Evolving Role of Hong Kong as China's Middleman, in: Ho/Ash (eds.), *China, Hong Kong and the World Economy: Studies on Globalization*, 2006, pp. 152 et seq. (152–169).

Closer Economic Partnership Arrangements Between China and Hong Kong and Macau

The Negotiation History

The China-Hong Kong CEPA "establishes a free-trade area within the meaning of Article XXIV of the GATT 1994 and provides for the liberalization of trade in services within the meaning of Article V of General Agreement on Trade in Services (the GATS)".[17] It is the first free trade agreement [hereinafter FTA] signed both by China and by Hong Kong.[18] This model was soon copied by Macau. The China-Macau CEPA was consequently signed on 17 October 2003, entering into effect on 1 January 2004,[19] and the first FTA ever signed by Macau.[20]

The idea for proposing an FTA within the same country sounds odd at the first glance. The motive for this was out for the fear that Hong Kong's economic growth would be undermined after China's accession to the WTO since China's preferential treatment to Hong Kong would be inconsistent with the WTO rules. A WTO-compatible FTA was thus proposed by Hong Kong General Chamber of Commerce [hereinafter the HKGCC] through a written request to and a meeting with the Chief Executive of the HKSAR on 22 November 2001. With consensus reached between the HKSAR and China's Central Authority, consultations in relation to the coverage of this FTA and its form were initiated which led to the final agreement on the main parts of the CEPA in late June 2003.[21] The Parties also carefully employed the term of "arrangement" to differentiate from other FTAs which carry sovereignty implications as they are normally signed by two states.

After the China-Hong Kong CEPA was successfully concluded, this model was introduced to Macau; most provisions in the China-Macau CEPA are nearly identical with those provided in China-Hong Kong CEPA. Since the signatures of the original CEPAs, seven supplements have so far been signed between China

---

[17] WT/REG162/N1, S/C/N/264, 12th January, 2004.

[18] WT/REG162/M/1, 21st March, 2005, paras. 4, 6.

[19] WT/REG163/N1, S/C/N/265, 12th January, 2004.

[20] WT/REG162/M/1, 21st March, 2005, para. 6.

[21] Gao, The Closer Economic Partnership Arrangement (CEPA) Between Mainland China and Hong Kong? Legal and Economic Analyses, in: Davidson (ed.), *Trading Arrangements in the Pacific Rim: ASEAN and APEC*, 2004, 10, available at: http://ssrn.com/paper=752785 (last visited on 5th March, 2011). See also, Wang, Regional Integration: Comparative Experiences: A Lawful Free Trade Agreement under "One Country, Two Customs Territories?", Law & Business Review of the Americas 10 (2004), p. 647.

and Hong Kong and Macau. These seven supplements relate mainly to further liberalisation and market access in Chinese market. Besides, the definition of service suppliers and rules of origin are also amended.

As claimed, since 1 January 2006 with the entering into force of Supplement II, China applied zero tariffs to all imported goods from Hong Kong and Macau as long as the requirements of rules of origin laid down in the CEPAs were satisfied. In 2004, when the CEPAs firstly came into force, 95 and 94 per cent of imported goods, in value terms, into China from Hong Kong and Macao respectively enjoyed zero tariffs.[22] It was also claimed by Parties to these two CEPAs that, those imported goods which did not enjoyed zero-tariff treatment are mainly due to the exclusion of "imported goods" under the CEPA because of China's laws/regulations and its international obligations, and the unavailability of rules of origin under the existent tariff lines.[23]

One Main Text, Six Annexes, and Seven Supplements

In both CEPAs, there are 23 articles in the main text, accompanied by six annexes. Annex 1 provides the schedule for the zero-tariff treatment on imported goods from Hong Kong and Macau. The procedures for the producers in Hong Kong and Macau to include their products into the zero-tariff schedules are also therein dealt with. Annex 2 governs the rules of origin in respect of trade in goods. Apart from goods wholly obtained in either Party, goods undergone "substantial transformation" can also be qualified as goods originating from the Parties, as set out by rules of origin laid down in this annex. Article 3 and 5 of Annex 2 define, respectively the term of "wholly obtained" in either Party, and of "substantial transformation". Annex 3 lays down the procedures for the issuing and verification of certificates of origin. Annex 4 provides specific commitments with regard to the liberalisation of trade in services; Annex 5 defines the term "service supplier" as set out in the CEPAs, and clarifies who is entitled to the benefit of market access in services trade. As the services professions constitute the major element of Hong Kong's economy, Hong Kong thus attached more importance to the services trade during the negotiation. The China-Hong Kong CEPA responds this concern by laying down detailed rules governing the eligibility of being a service supplier. Lastly, Annex 6 stipulates scope and measures to be taken in the field of trade and investment facilitation.

With regard to the coverage, as indicated above, the CEPAs cover three elements, trade in goods, trade in services, and trade and investment facilitation, to which the six annexes duly correspond. As Hong Kong and Macau are both free ports, only China has to adjust for the zero-tariff treatment on imported goods, while Hong Kong and Macau are merely required to remain their zero-tariff policy.

---

[22] WT/REG162/M/1, 21st March, 2005, para. 9; WT/REG163/M/1, 21st March, 2005, para. 10.
[23] WT/REG162-3/7, 30th May, 2006.

Contracting Parties to the two CEPAs undertake not to take anti-dumping and anti-subsidy measures.[24] However, since Hong Kong and Macau have never taken any of these two measures, and Hong Kong even does not have anti-dumping and anti-subsidy legislation, it is thus clear that this obligation is designated only to China. Nevertheless, due to the small trade volume of imported goods from Hong Kong and Macau, this article is of more symbolic significance than economic importance.

Both Article 9 of the two CEPAs deal with safeguard measures which exclude the application of transitional product-specific safeguard measures, and safeguard measures in textile products between these Contracting Parties. When taking safeguard measures, China, Hong Kong and Macau should therefore, refer back to the existing Agreement on Subsidies and Countervailing Measures [hereinafter SCM Agreement]. Nevertheless, the safeguard provisions in the CEPAs lay down different rules, which, according to some members deviate from the existing SCM Agreement.[25] The safeguard provisions also refer to the consultation mechanism as provide in Article 19 of the two CEPAs. When preferential treatments or concessions are suspended due to the "sharp increase" of imported products, the affected Party should, upon request, promptly commence the consultations mechanisms as provided in Article 19 with the aim to reaching a mutually satisfactory agreement. This is the sole provision in the CEPA which explicitly refers to the consultation procedures in case of trade disputes. Article 10 governs general rules of origin, which are further elaborated in the afore-mentioned Annex 2, in order to determine whether imported goods are eligible for the preferential treatments.

In respect of trade in services, Article 11 deals the market access, which is supported by Annex 4. Another key issue in services trade, the scope and requirement of "service suppliers" is defined in the subsequent article, and further elaborated in Annex 5. The following three articles govern the cooperation in financial sector in tourism, and mutual recognition of professional qualifications. Chinese tourists to Hong Kong and especially to Macau contribute a lot to the economic growth in these two separate customs territories. The cooperation in financial sectors, namely, banking, insurance and securities, is of great importance in the policy aspect, as financial professions in Hong Kong may be of great help to Chinese financial reform, and contribute to the competitiveness of financial sectors in China. On the other hand, funding coming from China may also contribute to the prosperity of the financial market in Hong Kong. With regard to the qualification, the Parties opt to "mutual recognition" approach, and it is too unpractical to

---

[24] The CEPA, Art. 7, 8.

[25] Concerns have been voiced during the process of the examination in the CRTA. It is pointed out that the safeguard provision as set out in the China – Hong Kong CEPA derogates considerably from the WTO Safeguard Agreement. However, in response to these doubts, Hong Kong, China reiterates its long-established free trade policy and states that there are no rules governing global safeguard measure in Hong Kong, China, and that it has never adopted any safeguard measures in the past. Therefore, this safeguard measure provided in the China – Hong Kong CEPA appears to design mainly for China, which is nevertheless unlikely to use it. See WT/REG162/6, 13th March, 2006, p. 3.

imagine such a thing as "common rules on professional qualifications" due to their disparity of development and quality in these three areas.

Article 16 and 17 govern the trade and investment facilitation. Greater transparency, standard conformity and enhanced information exchange are "measures" to be taken for this end. The scope of cooperation is defined in Article 17, namely "trade and investment promotion; customs clearance facilitation; commodities inspection, inspection and quarantine of animals and plants, food safety, sanitary quarantine, certification, accreditation and standardization management; Electronic business; transparency in laws and regulations; cooperation of small and medium sized enterprises; and industries cooperation". However, other fields not covered can be included through consultations between the Parties.

Regarding the institutional arrangement, both CEPAs, in Article 19, provide nearly identical provisions regulating this issue. It is provided that a joint Steering Committee, comprising senior representatives or officials of both China and Hong Kong and Macau should be established. Under this Steering Committee, liaison offices should be established in both the Central Authority and the governments of these two SARs. Working groups may also be set up under this joint Steering Committee. Subsequently, three working groups, Working Groups on Trade in Goods, Trade in Service, Trade and Investments Facilitation were established at the first Steering Meeting.

Paragraph 3 of this Article provides the functions of the Steering Committee, which reads:

The functions of the Steering Committee include:

1. *Supervising the implementation of the "CEPA";*
2. *Interpreting the provisions of the "CEPA";*
3. *Resolving disputes that may arise during the implementation of the "CEPA";*
4. *Drafting additions and amendments to the content of the "CEPA";*
5. *Providing steer on the work of the working groups;*
6. *Dealing with any other business relating to the implementation of the "CEPA."*

This provision aims to define the competence of the Steering Committee. It covers the interpretation and implementation, further additions and amendments, the supervision of the working groups. The Steering Committee is also responsible for the disputes resolution. However, the legal text is far from clear in this aspect. As indicated by the submission of the HKGCC on 25 July 2003, where it presented 51 questions related to the CEPA, the functions of the Steering Committee were questioned in terms of its working procedures, private participation in this Steering Committee, and the substantive content of the dispute resolution mechanism, such as enforcement and appeal.[26] In August 2003, the government of HKSAR released a preliminary response with regard to other aspects of the implementation of the

---

[26] CEPA Questions I, submitted by the General Chamber of Commerce of Hong Kong, available at: http://www.chamber.org.hk/en/information/policy_comments.aspx?ID=119 (last visited on 5th March, 2011).

China – Hong Kong CEPA. However, those questions related to the competence, working procedures and substantial content of the dispute resolution have so far not been answered.[27]

The Compatibility of CEPAs with WTO Rules on FTA

Procedural and Substantial requirements governing the compatibility of FTAs with WTO rules are laid down in Article XXIV of GATT 1994 and Article V of GATS. The Appellate Body has also dealt with this issue in *Turkey – Textile*,[28] where Hong Kong, China intervened as a third party. Apart from the so-called "neutrality" requirement, which requires that the effects of FTAs not to be more trade restrictive, overall, than were previous trade policies of the Contracting Parties.[29] Two elements should be further elaborated here: the procedural requirement; and "substantially all the trade"/"substantial sectoral coverage".

With regard to the procedural requirement, as mentioned above, both CEPAs have been notified to the Committee on Regional Trade Agreements (the CRTA), and examination has been conducted in the Committee. Although substantial decision with regard to the compatibility of these two CEPAs with Article XXIV of GATT 1994 and Article V of GATS has not been made, the procedural requirements have been duly fulfilled with.

In respect of the coverage of the trade in goods/services, the Appellate Body slightly addresses this issue. According to the Appellate Body, "substantially all the trade" is not the same as *all* the trade and a "substantially all the trade" is something considerably more than merely "*some*" of the trade".[30] This ruling seems not to offer too much guidance as the line between "some", "substantially all", and "all" has never been clear. As argued, the main text of CEPA and its six annexes have already

---

[27] Chamber's Question on CEPA: A Preliminary Update, available at: http://www.chamber.org. hk/FileUpload/201007081540052496/Answer_CEPA_Q.pdf (last visited on 5th March, 2011).

[28] Report of the Appellate Body, Turkey – Restrictions on Imports of Textile and Clothing Products, WT/DS34/AB/R, adopted 19th November, 1999, DSR 1999:VI, 2345.

[29] The Report of the Appellate Body addresses this requirement in para. 58, and lays down two conditions, which should be fulfilled, so that the regional trade agreement can pass the scrutiny. In the words of the Appellate Body, "[F]irst, the party claiming the benefit of this defence must demonstrate that the measure at issue is introduced upon the formation of a customs union that fully meets the requirements of sub-paragraphs 8(a) and 5(a) of Article XXIV. And, second, that party must demonstrate that the formation of that customs union would be prevented if it were not allowed to introduce the measure at issue". Report of the Appellate Body, Turkey – Restrictions on Imports of Textile and Clothing Products, WT/DS34/AB/R, adopted 19th November, 1999, DSR 1999:VI, 2345, para. 58. Another relevant issue here is whether the rules of origin as set out in the CEPA constitute "more trade restrictive" measures.

[30] Report of the Appellate Body, Turkey – Restrictions on Imports of Textile and Clothing Products, WT/DS34/AB/R, adopted 19th November, 1999, DSR 1999:VI, 2345, para. 48 (emphasis origional).

covered 90% of total exported trade to China from Hong Kong, and has fully liberalised five sectors (construction and related engineering service; distribution services; financial services; tourism and travel related services; and transport services), and partially liberalised two sectors (business services and communication services). Besides, no mode of service supply is *a priori* excluded. Consequently, those commitments made in the China – Hong Kong CEPA, read together with China's accession commitments, cover "substantially all the trade" and have "substantial sectoral coverage".[31] However, this view is not shared by some members of the WTO. For example, the European Union has repeatedly emphasised on its position that the China – Hong Kong CEPA cannot be qualified as covering "substantial all the trade". As claimed, the CEPA is "more as a framework agreement to provide future liberalization than an actual liberalization agreement".[32]

The Political and Economic Implication of CEPAs

The CEPAs may be read in a broader context. This arrangement of closer economic partnership was actually proposed with the aim of resolving the legitimacy crisis that Hong Kong had encountered. The judicial autonomy had been undermined, since the judgment of the Court of Final Appeal regarding the right to abode was "overruled" by the interpretation of the Standing Committee of the National People's Congress. Hong Kong people had gradually lost their patience with the long-awaited suffrage election. Resentment of the Chief Executive surged with the continuous economy depression and higher unemployment rate. The China – Hong Kong CEPA thus serves a means not only to boost the economic development in Hong Kong, but also to prevent the 'One China, Two Systems' from collapsing.

As is pointed out by an author, the China-Hong Kong CEPA is unique in various ways. First, it is the first "FTA" signed by two members of the WTO, but at the same time, of the same state. It is also peculiar in terms of rights and obligations of two Parties: while China offers so much "concessions", Hong Kong offers almost nothing. Besides, the size, openness, and economic developments of these two parties draw a sharp contrast: while Hong Kong is small, highly developed and very open, China is large, less developed, and relatively closed.[33] As the China – Hong Kong CEPA provides Hong Kong preferential market access in some services

---

[31] Gao, The Closer Economic Partnership Arrangement (CEPA) Between Mainland China and Hong Kong? Legal and Economic Analyses, in: Davidson (ed.), *Trading Arrangements in the Pacific Rim: ASEAN and APEC*, 2004, pp. 1 et seq. (4–5), available at: http://ssrn.com/paper=752785 (last visited on 28th February, 2011).

[32] WT/REG162/M3, 15th May, 2006, para. 12.

[33] Sung, *The Emergence of Greater China: The Economic Integration of Mainland China, Taiwan and Hong Kong*, 2005, pp. 199–200.

areas, it is believed that Hong Kong will much benefit from the China's opening in services trade. With regard to Macau, as the gambling service is the key element of its economy, with the signature of China-Macau CEPA, tourists from China is believed to contribute a lot to the recovery of the economy of Macau.

Another interesting question is why China bothers to sign an "FTA" with Hong Kong and Macau, which are both free port and adopt zero-tariff policy. It is not difficult to understand that Hong Kong wishes to take advantage of the "open-up" of China and to contribute to its economic growth, as the economic policy of Hong Kong has long emphasised on its role as an "intermediary". Hong Kong also wanted to locate its services industries in China before China's commitments in respect of trade in services are fully liberalised to all other WTO members.[34] It is nevertheless confusing and difficult to figure out why China would agree to enter into an "FTA" with Hong Kong. As is a free port, Hong Kong seems to have no concessions to offer.

In economic terms, it may be arguably true that China hardly benefits from entering into an "FTA" with Hong Kong. However, a further thought contradicts this easy supposition. In the national context, as noted above, this arrangement of closer economic partnership was precisely proposed with the objective to resolving the legitimacy crisis that Hong Kong had been faced with. China has significant interests in preventing the "One Country, Two Systems" from collapsing. What is of the equal, if not more, importance is the implication of the CEPAs in international economic context. As prescribed in Article 4 of both CEPAs, specific provisions in China's Accession Protocol and its Working Party Report will not be applicable between these Contracting Parties. The legal text reads as follows:

> The two sides recognize that through over 20 years of reform and opening up, the market economy system of the Mainland has been continuously improving, and the mode of production and operation of Mainland enterprises is in line with the requirements of a market economy. The two sides agree that Articles 15 and 16 of the "Protocol on the Accession of the People's Republic of China to the WTO" and paragraph 242 of the 'Report of the Working Party on the Accession of China' will not be applicable to trade between the Mainland and Hong Kong (Macao).[35]

Article 15 of China's Accession Protocol governs the method in determining price comparability in anti-subsidy and anti-dumping investigations. In anti-dumping procedures, members are entitled to adopt "a methodology that is not based on a strict comparison with domestic prices or costs in China". Besides, other methodologies may be employed in identifying and measuring subsidy benefit, in

---

[34] As for the case of Macau, zero-tariffs in trade in goods seem not very beneficial since its economy relies much on services trade, in particular gambling service. What is of great significance to the economy of Macau is its tourism services to Chinese visitors, which is limited in scope in the main text of the CEPA and its annexes. This exposed one of the weaknesses of mirroring the China-Macau CEPA to China-Hong Kong CEPA, in spite of the fact that the scope of tourism services was expanded in later stage.

[35] The CEPAs, Art. 4.

anti-subsidy proceedings, to take into account the "prevailing terms and conditions in China" and thus to establish appropriate benchmarks. Article 16 lays down a transitional product-specific safeguard measure, to which members may opt for the prevention of and remedy for market disruption. Paragraph 242 of China's Working Party Report deals with the potential market disruption with the expiry of the Agreement on Textile and Clothing, as China's textile exports have amounted to a tremendous market share. As China included Hong Kong's recognition of China as a market economy in the China – Hong Kong CEPA, it has successfully made a step forward toward its market economy status. Even though this practice has only symbolic significance, it paves the way for China to negotiate with other trading partners with regard to its market economy status. Besides, the non-application of Article 15, 16 of China's Accession Protocol and paragraph 242 in the China – Hong Kong CEPA helps China to negotiate with its trading partners by following the same pattern, and consequently reduces the impacts of these "WTO-plus" obligations.[36] Needless to say, the same provisions can be found in the China – Macau CEPA.

Economic Integration Between China and Taiwan

Economic Relations Between China and Taiwan Before 2008

In terms of economic relations between China and Taiwan, 2008 marked a new era. Since then, restrictive measures against China trade have been greatly liberalised. In view of the changing political economy between China and Taiwan, it is feasible to briefly illustrate the evolution of Taiwan's trade policy toward China which corresponds to Taiwan's political change.

Taiwan, in 2000, experienced its historic political change. The long-ruling Kuomintang (the KMT) lost the presidential election and became the opposition

---

[36] This approach has proved itself very successful. According to the Trade Policy Review Report conducted in 2006, China has included the recognition of its market economy status into every regional and bilateral FTA, or economic partnership agreement. See Secretariat's Trade Policy Report on People's Republic of China, WT/TPR/S/161, 28th February, 2006, para. 46. See also Secretariat's Trade Policy Review Report, WT/TPR/S/199/rev.1, 12th August, 2008, para. 53. So far, A Framework Agreement on Comprehensive Economic Cooperation between China and ASEAN, Chile-China FTA, China-Pakistan Preferential Trade Agreement, China-Australia Trade and Economic Framework Agreement (aiming to establish an FTA), China-New Zealand Trade and Economic Cooperation Framework, China and the Southern African Customs Union (SACU) Joint Declaration (with the aim to establishing an FTA), China – Gulf Cooperation Council Framework Agreement on Economic, Trade, Investment and Technology Cooperation, as well as the accompanying talks and negotiations have recognised China as a market economy. Besides, before commencing the negotiation of an FTA, Iceland and Switzerland have also recognised China as a market economy.

party; whereas the DPP became the ruling party. Before the KMT stepped down, the former President, Lee Teng-huei, dominated trade policy toward China.[37] Restrictions on trade and investment with China was adopted and maintained according to the "No Haste, Be Patient" policy due to the fear of hollowing-out Taiwan' industry into China. Besides, in order to reduce Taiwan's economic dependence on China, he also proposed to diversify Taiwan's exporting market to Southeast Asian countries, the so-called "Go South" policy.[38] Due to the regulatory policy of "No Haste, Be Patient", followed by "Positive Openness with Effective Management" adopted and maintained by the DPP, there existed an imbalance between political dialogue and economic exchange between Taiwan and China. It was normally referred to as "political chill/economic zeal", a contradiction between economic interdependence and political hostility.

This situation thus raised concerns to some WTO members. When pursuing its membership in the WTO, it was hoped that the WTO memberships of Taiwan and China would help to normalise the cross-Taiwan-strait trade relations. As both Taiwan and China opted not to take the non-application approach toward each other, it was believed that trade relations between Taiwan and could channel more smoothly through the WTO. Nevertheless, even after its accession to the WTO in 2002, Taiwan's external trade with China is still subject to many restrictions, and has not yet to be fully liberalised. It ranges from the implementation of the market access commitments, the infringement of Most-Favoured-Nation Treatment, National Treatment, and to various restrictions on outbound investments toward China.

Such concerns were strongly voiced by many other members, as illustrated in Taiwan's first Trade Policy Review conducted on 20 and 22 June 2006. Many WTO members voiced their concerns about the cross-Taiwan-strait trade relations.[39] The response of Chinese representative when hearing Taiwan's replies referring to the cross-strait relations as "special and complex", "unique and complicated", "not a simple trade issue" drew a vivid picture of this issue. He commented that Taiwan could not excuse itself from running counter to the fundamental principles of

---

[37] It is also President Lee Teng-huei who, in an interview by Deutsche Welle radio station on 7th July, 1999, defines the relation between Taiwan and China as "a special relationship between State and State".

[38] On Taiwan's "Go South" policy, see Peng, Economic Relations between Taiwan and Southeast Asia: A Review of Taiwan's "Go South" Policy, Wisconsin International Law Journal 16 (1998), p. 639.

[39] Apart from China, which had indicated Taiwan's violation of many WTO rules, notably non-discriminatory principle, Switzerland, Japan, EC, and among other members had questioned about Taiwan's restrictions on the cross-strait trade. The discussant also expressed similar concerns about this issue, see WTO Document, Minute of Trade Policy Review on Separate Customs Territory of Taiwan, Penghu, Kinmen and Matsu, WT/TPR/M/165, 22nd September, 2006, paras. 33–35, 47, 53, 65.

non-discrimination. It would be difficult to justify this argument in terms of the fact that 4 years had passed, and various restrictions persisted.[40]

It should be however, noted that, notwithstanding various restrictions, the economic interdependence between Taiwan and China has been becoming closer and closer. According to the official statistics of Taiwan, the export volume in 2010 was 2,746.4 billion US dollars while China's share amounted to 769.4, i.e. 28%; the import volume was 2514 billion US dollars while China's share reached 359.5 billion US dollars and 14.29%. The trade volume with China was 1128.9 US dollars and constituted 21.46% of its total trade.[41] In 2003, total trade with China exceeded trade with the United States or Japan, and since then China has become the largest trading partner of Taiwan. Since 2003, Taiwan has ranked steadily China's 7th trading partner.

However, with the enormous trade volume and high degree of economic interdependence, trade frictions, and subsequently trade disputes, seem inevitable. There are numerous good examples of such frictions, followed by trade remedies measures, in China and Taiwan against each other. Although China and Taiwan have not officially sought recourse to the WTO dispute settlement mechanism, Taiwan has intervened as a third party in a number of complaints brought about by and against China.

With regard to trade remedies measures in domestic level, various examples can be found. As in the area of anti-dumping measures, since its accession to the WTO, China has initiated many investigations procedures against Taiwanese products, including unbleached kraft liner/linerboard, polyurethane, polybutylene, terphthalate resin, nonyl phenol, phenol, bisphenol-A (BPA), cold rolled steel products, nylon 6,66 filament yarn.[42] As of 30 June 2010, definite anti-dumping duties were imposed upon polyvinyl chloride, phenol, ethanolamine (monoethanolamine diethanolamine), polybutylene terphthalate resin, polyurethane, nonyl phenol, bisphenol-A, methyl ethyl ketone, acetone, 1,4-butanediol, polyamide-6, and polyamide-6, 6. On the other hand, Taiwan has also taken several anti-dumping measures against Chinese products. It has so far initiated three investigations procedures against towelling products, footwear, uncoated printing and writing paper since its accession to the WTO.[43] As of 25 February 2011, definite anti-dumping duties were imposed upon benzoyl peroxide (BPO) and sodium formaldehyde sulfoxylate (SFS).[44]

---

[40] WTO Document, Minute of Trade Policy Review on Separate Customs Territory of Taiwan, Penghu, Kinmen and Matsu, WT/TPR/M/165, 22nd September 2006, para. 138.

[41] Department of Statistics, Ministry of Economic Affairs, available at: http://2k3dmz2.moea.gov.tw/gnweb/Indicator/wFrmIndicator.aspx (last visited on 5th March, 2010, in Chinese).

[42] WTO document, G/ADP/N/202/CHN, 1st October 2010, p. 12; see *also* other previous semi-annual reports of Anti-dumping committee.

[43] International Trade Commission, Ministry of Economic Affairs of Taiwan, available at http://portal.moeaitc.gov.tw/icweb/default.aspx (last visited on 28th February, 2011, in Chinese).

[44] WTO Document, G/ADP/N209/TPKM/rev.1, 25th February, 2011.

Economic Integration Between China and Taiwan Under Ma Administration

Direct-Transportation Agreements Between China and Taiwan

Before the entry into force of the direct-transportation agreements, goods imported from and exported to China should be shipped via a third port, normally Hong Kong. A direct flight or direct shipment, except some occasional arrangements, between Taiwan and China was not possible. Article 95.1 of the *Statute Governing Relations between People of the Taiwan Area and Mainland Area* (the *Statute*, last amended 3 September 2010)[45] dictates the competent authorities to acquire the approval of the Legislative Yuan (the Congress of Taiwan) prior their decision to engage direct transportation with China. A trial mini-three-link is carried out between Kinmen, Matsu and Penghu[46] in Taiwan and several coastal cities of China, including Xiamen, Quanzhou, and Fuzhou. The Executive Yuan (the administrative branch of Taiwan's government), coordinating all relevant ministries and agencies, publishes its *Impact Assessment on the Direct Transportation between Taiwan and China*,[47] but little progress had been made except the aforementioned mini-three links prior to the Ma administration.

However, there has been a significant regulatory change in this regard since the President Ma came to power on 20 May 2008. After the suspension for almost 15 years, the President of the Strait Exchange Foundation [hereinafter the SEF], Chiang Pin-Kung and the President of the Association for the Relations across the Taiwan Strait [hereinafter the ARATS], Chen Yunlin met again in Beijing on 12 June 2008, and subsequently in Taipei on 4 November 2008. The Chiang-Chen meeting in Beijing resulted in an agreement on the Chinese tourists travelling to Taiwan[48] and minutes on charter flights between Taiwan and China.[49] The agreement and the minutes of the Chiang-Chen talks effectuated the liberalisation of

---

[45] An English version of the legal text is available at the Mainland Affairs Council (the MAC) website, http://www.mac.gov.tw/ct.asp?xItem = 63756&CtNode = 6447&mp = 3 (last visited on 5th March, 2011).

[46] This trial mini-three-link was firstly applied to Kinmen and Matsu in 2001 and subsequently extended to Penhu in 2007.

[47] The Executive Yuan of Taiwan, Impact Assessment on the Direct Transportation Between Taiwan and China, 15th August, 2003.

[48] Cross-Strait Agreement Signed between SEF and the Association for the Relations across the Taiwan Strait [hereinafter the ARATS] Concerning Mainland Tourists Travelling to Taiwan, Beijing, 23rd June, 2008 [hereinafter the Chinese Tourists Agreement], an official English translation version is available at http://www.sef.org.tw/ (last visited on 5th March, 2011).

[49] SEF-ARATS Minutes of Talks on Cross-Strait Charter Flights, Beijing, 23rd June, 2008 [hereinafter the Charter Flights Minutes]; an official English translation version is available at http://www.sef.org.tw/ (last visited on 5th March, 2011).

Chinese tourists to Taiwan up to a quota of 3,000 persons per day.[50] The travelling should be conducted through group tourism.[51] Besides, the minutes on the charter flights provide the legal basis for charter flights for passengers between Taiwan and China during the weekends, as defined as from Friday afternoon to Monday morning.[52]

During the meeting in Taipei on 4 November 2008, four agreements were signed in relation to the cooperation of food safety,[53] direct air transport,[54] sea transport,[55] and postal service.[56] With the effectuation of the Sea Transport Agreement and Air Transport Agreement, direct sea and air transportation between Taiwan and China can be conducted. The requirement of transshipment through a third-port is thus lifted. Direct passenger and cargo charter flights can be conducted by airline companies capitalised and registered on either side of Taiwan Strait, namely, Taiwan and China.[57] In order to implement this direct air transport agreement, air traffic control agencies in Taiwan and in China should establish the procedure for the direct handover of air traffic control.[58] Direct cross-strait air transport path is opened through a northern line across the Taiwan Strait, from Taipei to Shanghai Flight Information Regions. The Air Transport Agreement also provides a very primitive dispute resolution mechanism. According to Article 11 of this agreement, any dispute arising from its application shall be resolved by prompt negotiation. Nothing else is offered with regard to this "prompt negotiation".[59]

In respect of the direct sea transport, vessels owned and registered on either side of Taiwan Strait, i.e. Taiwan and China can engage in direct cross-strait transport of

---

[50] Special Arrangements Concerning Cross-Strait Tourism, Annex I to the Chinese Tourists Agreement, Art. 1.

[51] Chinese Tourists Agreement, Art. 2.1

[52] Annex to the Charter Flights Minutes, Time, Destination, and Flights of Cross-Strait Charter Flights, Art. 1.

[53] Cross-Strait Food Safety Agreement, Taipei, 4th November, 2008 [hereinafter the Food Safety Agreement]; an official English translation version is available at http://www.sef.org.tw/ (last visited on 5th March, 2011).

[54] Cross-Strait Air Transport Agreement, Taipei, 4th November, 2008 [hereinafter the Air Transport Agreement]; an official English translation version is available at http://www.sef.org.tw/ (last visited on 5th March, 2011).

[55] Cross-Strait Sea Transport Agreement, Taipei, 4th November, 2008 [hereinafter the Sea Transport Agreement]; an official English translation version is available at http://www.sef.org.tw/ (last visited on 5th March, 2011).

[56] Cross-Strait Postal Service Agreement, Taipei, 4th November, 2008 [hereinafter the Postal Service Agreement]; an official English translation version is available at http://www.sef.org.tw/ (last visited on 5th March, 2011).

[57] The Air Transport Agreement, Art. 2.

[58] The Air Transport Agreement, Art. 1.1.

[59] The same "prompt negotiation" provision is included in all these four agreements. While this 'prompt negotiation' does not necessarily prevent Taiwan or China from referring to the WTO Dispute Settlement Mechanism, it nevertheless signals their intent not to.

passengers and cargo.[60] With regard to the controversial flag-flying issue, it is agreed that, "vessels registered on either side of the Taiwan Strait shall not fly their flag on the stern or mainmast of the vessel between entering and leaving the other side's port, but shall fly their company flag for vessel identificator".[61] The sovereignty controversies are avoided but unresolved. Another issue relating great economic interests is the flag-of-convenience flags owned by the shipping companies of Taiwan and China may undertake direct cross-strait sea transport if they have already been engaging in offshore shipping centre transport ("testing point for direct shipping"), cross-strait third-territory container line transport, and sand and gravel transport before the signature of this agreement.[62] This has the effect to limiting the scope of application to Taiwanese capitalised flag-in-convenience vessels. As reported, only 16 out of 477 or 3% of Taiwanese flag-in-convenience vessels can benefit from this direct transport agreement.[63] By contrast, vessels capitalised by Taiwan or China that are registered in Hong Kong may benefit from this direct air transport agreement.[64] In total, China has liberalised 63 ports, including 48 seaports and 15 river ports while Taiwan has liberalised 11 ports, including the five 'mini-three-link' ports.[65] This sea transport agreement includes the same dispute resolution mechanism as contained in the Air Transport Agreement.

Nevertheless, the prompt negotiation virtually provides no legal/judicial protection for international economic actors. The prompt negotiation relies mainly upon the attitude of the government, especially that of Chinese government. Two cases reveal the weakness or the uselessness of this mechanism. After the signature of the Sea Transport Agreement, Taiwanese enterprises, which previously operated between Taiwan and China for gravel shipment, were not able to acquire the permit from China to continue their business. In the absence of a thicker form of dispute resolution mechanism in the Sea Transport Agreement, the operators were forced to stage a protest in front of Taiwan Democracy Memorial Hall.[66] The second case related to the allocation of flights during the Lunar New Year 2009 – Taiwanese airlines were not able to obtain the approval from Chinese authorities on their scheduled 36 flights while the tickets had already been sold out. Due the weak dispute settlement mechanism provided in the Air Transport Agreement, all the

---

[60] The Sea Transport Agreement, Art. 1.

[61] The Sea Transport Agreement, Art. 3.

[62] Annex to the Sea Transport Agreement, Art. 2.

[63] Shan, "Shipping Industry Representatives are Mixed on Result of Cross-strait Talks", Taipei News, 17th November, 2008, available at http://www.taipeitimes.com/News/taiwan/archives/2008/11/17/200342 8837 (last visited on 5th March, 2011).

[64] Annex to the Sea Transport Agreement, Art. 1.

[65] Annex to the Sea Transport Agreement, Art. 3.

[66] Ko, "Gravel Shippers to Stage Protest", Taipei News, 19th January, 2009, p. 3, available at http://www. taipeitimes.com/News/taiwan/archives/2009/01/19/2003434117 (last visited on 5th March, 2011).

SEF could do was to ask the ARATS to look into the possibilities to increase the charter flights.[67] These two examples expose the ineffectiveness of the dispute settlement mechanisms provided in these agreements. The fatal point nevertheless lies in the state-centred approach. Under these agreements, private individuals and enterprises have no enforceable rights. In case of any dispute, they have to refer to the governments to negotiate on the subject matter concerned. Whether the governments are willing to negotiate for the interests of these injured private economic actors depends solely on their discretionary power. Therefore, the protection provided in these agreements is extremely insufficient.

Finally, as dictated by Article 95 of the *Statute*, the Air Transport Agreement and the Air Transport Agreement shall refer to the Legislative Yuan for resolution, while the Food Safety Agreement and the Postal Agreement shall only notify the Legislative Yuan. With the entering into effect of the Air Transport Agreement, Sea Transport Agreement and Postal Service Agreement, the three direct links between Taiwan and China are finally realised. Nevertheless, it should be noted that serious demonstration was taking place when the agreement were signed. Besides, the entry into force of the direct-transportation is effectuated without any legislative approval by virtue of Article 95 of the *Statute* which provides that if the legislature does not reach any resolution within 1 month, it is deemed to be approved. This then points to the legitimacy and constitutionalisation deficit of Taiwan's trade relations toward China, which unfortunately tend to be regarded as the sole realm of executive branch. Legislative oversight and judicial scrutiny are absent.

Economic Cooperation Framework Agreement Between China and Taiwan

The Negotiation History

Overall, the ECFA oscillates between the two models of CEPAs and the China-ASEAN Framework Agreement on Comprehensive Economic Co-Operation (China-ASEAN FTA). Whereas Taiwan tried to inject contours of the China-ASEAN FTA into the ECFA, China made great efforts to couple the ECFA and the CEPAs. In other words, while Taiwan may refer to the WTO rules on FTA, China prefers the ECFA an "internal" arrangement carrying no international implications.

The first point to note about its formality is that the ECFA is signed in Chinese with both simplified and tradition versions, two versions being authentic and carrying the same meaning. It is understandable given that Taiwan uses traditional

---

[67] "China Asked to Boost direct Flights for Lunar New Year Holiday", China Post, 10th January, 2009, available at: http://www.chinapost.com.tw/taiwan/china-taiwan-relations/2009/01/10/191357/China-asked.htm (last visited on 5th March, 2011).

Chinese language and China uses simplified Chinese as their official languages. This practice may also have political implication since China has clear preference not to internationalise the ECFA and would not happy to see the text of the ECFA in English. Apart from political implications, the usage of Chinese has practical and legal implications. The interpretation of the commitments and obligations as contained in the ECFA will greatly depend on the translation efforts, if a judicialised dispute settlement mechanism is to be included in the future agreements and a panel composed of non-nationals of either Party established. This difficulty has been visible in those WTO complaints brought about against China.

In terms of the format of the agreement, following the pattern of direct-transportation agreements, the ECFA was signed by the President of the SEF, Chiang Pin-Kung and the President of the ARATS, Chen Yunlin. Namely, the Ma administration, notably the Mainland Affairs Council [hereinafter the MAC] that is in charge of China affairs, delegated the negotiating mandate to the SEF to initiate and conclude ECFA negotiations. The ECFA was finally inked on 29 June 2010 by the SEF and ARATS and becomes the first FTA signed by private organisations delegated with public authority by governments. After the ECFA was signed on 29 June 2010, it was subsequently referred to the Legislative Yuan for deliberation. It was finally approved by the Legislative Yuan on 17 August 2010 with the withdrawal of the opposition party (the DPP) from the deliberation process,[68] and entered into forced on 12 September 2010 after being notified to each other in accordance with Article 15 of the ECFA.[69]

One Main Text and Five Annexes

The ECFA comprises one main legal text and five annexes regulating products list and tariffs reduction;[70] provisional rules of origin;[71] safeguard measures;[72] sectors and liberalisation measures;[73] and the definition of services supplier.[74] Similar to the CEPAs concluded between China and Hong Kong and Macau, the main text of the ECFA is relatively short and premature. There are five chapters as contained in the main text covering general principles;[75] trade and investment;[76] economic

---

[68] "Taiwan-China Trade Deal Passed by Taipei Legislators", BBC News, 18th August, 2010, available at: http://www.bbc.co.uk/news/world-asia-pacific-11008076 (last visited on 5th March, 2011).

[69] "ECFA Becomes Effective on September 12", see http://www.chinaipr.gov.cn/newsarticle/news/governme nt/201009/947875_1.html (last visited on 5th March, 2011).

[70] Annex I to the ECFA.

[71] Annex II to the ECFA.

[72] Annex III to the ECFA.

[73] Annex IV to the ECFA.

[74] Annex V to the ECFA.

[75] The ECFA, Chap. 1.

[76] The ECFA, Chap. 2.

cooperation;[77] early harvest programme;[78] and other provisions relating to the institutional arrangement and dispute settlement.[79]

Article 1 speaks of the objective of the ECFA, aiming to "strengthen and advance the economic, trade and investment cooperation";[80] "promote further liberalization of trade in goods and services"[81] and "gradually establish fair, transparent and facilitative investment and investment protection mechanisms"; and to "expand areas of economic cooperation and establish a cooperation mechanism".[82] In view of its objectives, the scope that the ECFA envisages in contrast to other FTAs or partnership and cooperation agreements is rather limited. The objectives as set out in the ECFA are purely economic which does not even touch upon sustainable development. During the course of negotiation, some scholars advocated the inclusion of human rights clause.[83] Doubtlessly, their efforts are in vain.

Article 2 then specifies a number of cooperation measures including gradually reducing "tariff and non-tariff barriers to trade in a substantial majority of goods"[84] and "restrictions on a large number of sectors in trade in services"[85]; providing investment protection and promoting and facilitating trade and investment and industry cooperation.[86] The pertinent point here is the terms of "in a substantial majority of goods" and "a large number of sectors in trade in services" which clearly deviate from the requirement of "substantially all the trade"/"substantial sectoral coverage". The terminology may pose the question of WTO-compatibility of the ECFA.

Chap. 2 of the ECFA then regulates trade in goods, trade in services and investment. The common feature of these three articles is that the Parties are instructed to initiate negotiations with the aim to conclude agreements on trade in goods, trade in services and investment within 6 months after the entry into force of the ECFA.[87] In addition, the ECFA then provides a list of issues to be dealt with in the envisaged negotiations.[88] The negotiations of trade in goods and trade in

---

[77] The ECFA, Chap. 3.

[78] The ECFA, Chap. 4.

[79] The ECFA, Chap. 5.

[80] The ECFA, Art. 1.1.

[81] The ECFA, Art. 1.2.

[82] The ECFA, Art. 1.2.

[83] Tseng/Wu, ECFA Should Benefit Human Rights, Taipei Times, 17th July, 2010, available at: http://www.taipeitimes.com/News/editorials/archives/2010/07/17/2003478124 (last visited on 5th March, 2011).

[84] The ECFA, Art. 2.1.

[85] The ECFA, Art. 2.2.

[86] The ECFA, Art. 2.3–2.4.

[87] The ECFA, Art. 3.1, 4.1, 5.1.

[88] The ECFA, Art. 3.2, 4.2, 5.2.

services should step on the basis of Early Harvest Programmes.[89] On the basis of the commitments to be made under the envisaged agreements on trade in goods and trade in services, the Parties may also at its own discretion accelerate the tariff reduction or liberalisation of restrictive measures on services trade.[90] Regarding the tariff reduction, the ECFA categorises goods trade as goods subject to immediate tariff elimination, goods subject to phased tariff reduction, and exceptions or others. This implies that, under the envisaged agreement on trade in goods, the speed of liberalisation varies depending on sensitivity of products.[91] Some categories of products may be *a priori* excluded from the liberalisation schedules.

The Early Harvest Programmes are provided in Chap. 4 which contains two articles regulating trade in goods[92] and trade in services respectively.[93] This Early Harvest Programme, modelled from the China-ASEAN FTA, aims at the fast realisation of the objectives of the ECFA. The Early Harvest Programme for goods trade should be implemented within 6 months after the entry into force of the ECFA whereas there is no specific timeframe for the Early Harvest for services trade. The ECFA simply directs the Parties to implement the services trade Early Harvest Programme expeditiously.[94]

The ECFA, in Article 7.2, then directs the Parties to implement the Early Harvest Programme in goods trade in accordance with the tariff reduction schedules as set out in Annex I,[95] applying provisional rules of origin as set out in Annex II and subject to trade remedy measures as set out in Annex III.[96] Products satisfying the requirements as set out in the Provisional Rule of Origin should be accordingly conferred preferential treatment.[97] The provisional rules of origin and trade remedy measures regulation cease to apply when the envisaged agreement on trade in goods comes into force.[98] With respect to services trade, the Parties agree to reduce or eliminate restrictive measures in force affecting services and services suppliers of the other Party.[99] The definition of a service supplier is then provided in Annex V which ceases to apply with the entry into force of the envisaged agreement on trade in services.[100] Article 8.2(3) then regulates the safeguard measures of services trade. In case of "a material adverse impact on the services sectors" arising from

---

[89] The ECFA, Art. 3.1, 4.1.

[90] The ECFA, Art. 3.4, 4.3.

[91] The ECFA, Art. 3.3.

[92] The ECFA, Art. 7.

[93] The ECFA, Art. 8.

[94] The ECFA, Art. 8.1.

[95] The ECFA, Art. 7.2(1).

[96] The ECFA, Art. 7.2(2), (3).

[97] The ECFA, Art. 7.2(2).

[98] The ECFA, Art. 7.3.

[99] The ECFA, Art. 8.2(1).

[100] The ECFA, Art. 8.2(2),(3).

the implementation of the Early Harvest Programme for trade in services, the affected Party may request consultations with the other Party to seek a solution. The solution here referred to seems to be mutually-agreed or mutually-satisfactory in nature since no further guidance on unilateral measures is provided for either under the Early Harvest Programme or institutional arrangement. In the same spirit, the dispute settlement as provided in the ECFA is also consensus-based without litigating features.[101]

Regarding the institutional arrangement, a Cross-Straits Economic Cooperation Committee [hereinafter, the ECFA Committee] composed of representatives from both Parties is established under the ECFA. The tasks of this ECFA Committee are to conclude negotiations necessary for the attainment of the objectives of the ECFA; monitor and evaluate its implementation; interpret the ECFA and resolve any dispute arising therefrom; and to notify each other important trade and economic information.[102] The ECFA Committee should convene regularly on semi-annual basis with the possibility of *ad hoc* meeting if agreed by both Parties.[103] It may also establish working groups on specific subject-matters under its supervision.[104]

The Compatibility of ECFA with WTO Rules on FTA

In determining the compatibility of the ECFA with the WTO rules, there are several questions to answer at the first place, namely, the nature and the legal basis of the ECFA. In other words, the first question is: whether the ECFA is an FTA in itself or merely an interim agreement leading to the formation of a free trade area under Article XXIV:5(b) of the GATT1994. The second question then relates as to, in addition to XXIV:5 and Article V of the GATS, whether the Enabling Clause can also provide a legal basis for the ECFA. A question relevant to these two questions would then be: if the ECFA is an interim agreement, does Article V o the GATS envisage such interim agreement? Regardless of the nature and legal basis of the ECFA, an FTA in itself or an interim agreement, Enabling Clause relevant or not, the same procedural notification requirement applies. Article XXIV:7 of the GATT 1994 obliges the Parties to an FTA or interim agreement to promptly notify the WTO and make available relevant information. Similarly, paragraph 4 of the Enabling Clause also dictates the Parties to differential and more favourable arrangements to notify the GATT Contracting Parties, furnish relevant information and to offer opportunities for consultation upon request.

---

[101] See infra, text to note 124, et seq.

[102] The ECFA, Art. 11.1.

[103] The ECFA, Art. 11.3.

[104] The ECFA, Art. 11.2.

Regarding the procedural requirement, since its ink on 29 June 2010, the ECFA has not yet been notified to the WTO. Whether and when the Parties intend to fulfil their WTO obligation remains unclear. Nonetheless, the opposition party has continued to press the Ma administration to abide by the WTO rules and duly notify the WTO. One may wonder why the Parties hesitate to fulfil this mere procedural requirement and risk of the WTO-compatibility of the ECFA and subsequently their reputation within the WTO. This again comes from the domestic politics concerns: both Parties, in particular China, may prefer to keep the ECFA within the realm of "internal affairs" instead of internationalising it.

With respect to the nature of the ECFA, it seems clear that the ECFA is only an interim agreement leading to the formation of a free trade area for the following reasons. Firstly, the first preambular and Article 1.1 the ECFA speaks of its aim to strengthen trade and economic relations between China and Taiwan.[105] The ECFA then further clarifies its objective to promote further liberalisation of trade in goods and services between the Parties,[106] which implies that the liberalisation processes would be implemented in accordance with further developments. The ECFA then in Chap. 2 explicitly instructs the Parties, within 6 months after the entry into force of the ECFA, to enter into negotiations with the aim to conclude agreements on trade in goods and services.[107] In addition, these two provisions include Early Harvest Programmes which means the major obligations and commitments of tariff-reduction and liberalisation should be based upon the envisaged agreements on trade in goods and services. Tariff-reduction and liberalisation measures under the Early Harvest Programmes are those merely adopted prior to the entry into force of these two envisaged agreements. Consequently, the ECFA is an interim agreement leading to the formation of a free trade area and, consequently, those measures on tariff-reduction and other liberalisation measures under the Early Harvest Programmes on goods trade may rely upon Article XXIV:5(b) for its legal basis. However, it remains unclear whether the Enabling Clause is relevant here.

The advantage for the WTO member referring to the Enabling Clause as the legal basis is mainly the less stringent requirements as laid down therein. Parties to an agreement concluded on the basis of the Enabling Clause are not obliged to eliminate duties or other restrictive regulations on commerce on the basis of "substantially all the trade". At the same time, the Parties are not required to provide a plan or schedule for the formation of a free trade area "with a reasonable length time". While the agreement concluded under the Enabling Clause should also be notified to the WTO; the review and consultation process is conducted under the Committee on the Trade and Development which tends to be more lenient than the CRTA. Nonetheless, the Enabling Clause applies only to trade in goods but not to trade in services and can only be relied upon by two or more developing countries

---

[105] The ECFA, 1st preambular & Art. 1.1.

[106] The ECFA, Art. 1.2.

[107] The ECFA, Art. 3.1, 4.1.

members. The pertinent point here is thus whether Taiwan, in acceding to the WTO, has renounced its rights stemming from the status of developing countries. Paragraph 6 of the Taiwan's Working Party Report reads that "[t]he representative of Chinese Taipei stated that his government would not claim any right granted under WTO Agreements to developing country Members".[108] At the same time, some members of the Working Party also noted that "Chinese Taipei should assume a level of obligations commensurate to that of the developed economy original Members of the WTO".[109] One may tend to argue that Taiwan acceded to the WTO as a developed country and therefore cannot refer to the Enabling Clause for the legal basis of the ECFA. Nonetheless, a closer look may find this argument groundless given that these two paragraphs are not referred to in paragraph 224 of Taiwan's Working Party Report and do not constitute a part of the obligations or commitments under Taiwan's Accession Protocol. As a consequence, from a legal perspective, Taiwan and China may rely upon the Enabling Clause as the legal basis for the ECFA; whether this is a good policy choice remains to be seen. Nevertheless, even if Taiwan and China refer to the Enabling Clause for the legal basis for the ECFA, the Enabling Clause does not cover trade in services of which the recourse should be eventually sought to from Article V of the GATS.

In the context of Article V of the GATS, similar controversies arise as to Taiwan's development country status, given that Article V:3(a) of provides some flexibility for an FTA to which developing countries are Parties. According to Article V:1 of the GATS, WTO members are not prevented from being a party to or entering to agreement liberalising services trade provided that such agreement has "substantial sectoral coverage"[110] and contains no discrimination, in the sense of Article XVII, or eliminates substantially all discrimination through "the elimination of existing discriminatory measures"[111] and/or "the prohibition of new or more discriminatory measures".[112] Article V:3(a) of the GATS then provides some flexibility to developing countries when they wish to enter into such agreement. In addition to the leniency on "substantial sectoral coverage", this subparagraph also lessen the stringency of the elimination of discriminatory measures in accordance with the level of the development of the countries concerned, both overall or in individual sectors or subsectors.[113] Therefore, if Taiwan may avail its status of a developing country, the ECFA and the envisaged agreement on services trade does not necessarily have to cover "substantial sectoral coverage"; it may also not be obliged to eliminate all discriminatory measures on the basis of a reasonable time-frame.

---

[108] Report of the Working Party on the Accession of the Separate Customs Territory of Taiwan, Penghu, Kinmen and Matsu, WT/ACC/TPKM/18, 5th October, 2001, para. 6.

[109] Report of the Working Party on the Accession of the Separate Customs Territory of Taiwan, Penghu, Kinmen and Matsu, WT/ACC/TPKM/18, 5th October, 2001, para. 7.

[110] The GATS, Art. V:1(a).

[111] The GATS, Art. V:1(b)(i).

[112] The GATS, Art. V:1(b)(ii).

[113] The GATS, Art. V:III(a).

However, one issue remains unsettled even if the Parties to the ECFA refer to V:3(a) of the GATS for the flexibility provided therein: the WTO-compatibility of the Early Harvest Programme on trade in services. As noted above, the ECFA is an interim agreement leading to the formation of a free trade area. The Early Harvest Programme for trade in goods, depending on whether Taiwan avails itself to the developing country status within the WTO, may rely upon Article XXIV:5(b) of the GATT 1994 or the Enabling Clause for its legal basis neither of which extends to trade in services. However, in contrast to the designation XXIV:5 of the GATT 1994, there is no explicit reference to interim agreement under the GATS. Controversies then arise as to whether such an Early Harvest Programme is permissible under the WTO law. In reading provisions governing economic integration within the context of Article V of the GATS, Article XXIV of the GATT 1994 and subsequent practice of the WTO, as guided by Article 31 of Vienna Convention on the Law of Treaties, Chang-fa Lo is of the view that a transitional arrangement under a free trade area and an interim agreement leading to the formation of a free trade area should be differentiated and the latter is not permissible under the GATS. Consequently, the WTO-compatibility of the Early Harvest Programme on services trade under the ECFA containing only a plan or schedule to liberalise services trade but not completing of the services trade negotiations, may be questionable.[114]

The Political Implications of the ECFA

The ink of the ECFA has a number of political implications. According to a commentator, the ECFA has the international nature from treaty perspective and of being subject to the WTO review.[115] Besides, the ECFA implies China's recognition of Taiwan's legal capacity to enter into FTA talks and to conclude an FTA.[116] Legally, as a WTO member, Taiwan has its own right to initiate FTA negotiations with other WTO members. In practice, Taiwan has already concluded several FTAs with those countries who maintain diplomatic with it. However, the economic interests covered by these FTAs are quite limited.[117] Taiwan's major

---

[114] Lo, Can There Be an Interim Agreement for Economic Integration in GATS, Paper presented in Conference on Trade Remedy, Financial Crisis and the Challenge to the WTO, held in Taipei on 29th October, 2010, pp. 17–21.

[115] Lo, Can There Be an Interim Agreement for Economic Integration in GATS, Paper presented in EMC 2010–2011 Asia-Pacific Round Academic Conference on Conference on Economic Integration of the Asian-Pacific Region and Beyond, held in Taipei on 4th March, 2011, p. 6–7.

[116] Lo, Can There Be an Interim Agreement for Economic Integration in GATS, Paper presented in EMC 2010–2011 Asia-Pacific Round Academic Conference on Conference on Economic Integration of the Asian-Pacific Region and Beyond, held in Taipei on 4th March, 2011, p. 9.

[117] Even in the case of Hong Kong and Macau, they also conclude FTAs which have been notified to the WTO. In addition to the CEPA, Hong Kong has also concluded an FTA with New Zealand.

trading partners remain reluctant to enter into FTA negotiations with Taiwan due to political concerns. The conclusion of the ECFA may thus contribute to the expansion of the Asian economic integration from which Taiwan can benefit.[118] Since China itself enters into an FTA with Taiwan, other WTO members may feel more confident to initiate FTA negotiations with Taiwan.

From the geopolitics perspective, the ECFA has to ease the potential conflicts between China and Taiwan as the ECFA is not a single instrument in itself. It is a framework agreement aiming to further conclusion of agreements on trade in goods, services, investments and dispute settlement mechanisms. With closer economic integration, it is reasonable to believe the possibility of military conflicts between China and Taiwan would be substantially lessened. Finally, from the domestic politics perspective, in Taiwan, whether accelerated economic integration with China is desirable is highly debated. There are some attempts to present the ECFA for a referendum, but eventually, they failed due to the block of the ruling party. Whether it is feasible to decide such a major and highly controversial issue through referendum remains contested, it nevertheless again points to the great divide within domestic politics and exposes the legitimacy crisis in Taiwan's trade policy toward China.

Dispute Settlement Mechanisms in CEPAs and ECFA

This section aims to compare the dispute settlement mechanisms as contained in the CEPAs and the ECFA. As noted above, Article 19 of the two CEPAs regulates the institutional arrangement by setting up a Steering Committee. In the fifth paragraph, it lays down procedural rules governing the interpretation and implementation of the CEPAs.[119] As prescribed, with regard to problems resulting from the interpretation and implementation of the CEPAs, the two sides (China and Hong Kong, or China and Macau) shall resolve these problems "through consultation in the spirit of friendship and cooperation". Based on this spirit, the Steering Committee shall thus make its decisions by consensus. In the notification to the CRTA, a passage by Parties in respect of the dispute resolution procedures is particularly telling:

> The two sides have set up a Joint Steering Committee to, among others, supervise the implementation of the CEPA, interpret the provisions of the CEPA, and resolve disputes that may arise during the implementation of the CEPA. The two sides will resolve any problems arising from the interpretation or implementation of the CEPA through consultation in the spirit of friendship and cooperation. The Joint Steering Committee will make its decisions by consensus.[120]

---

[118] Lo, Can There Be an Interim Agreement for Economic Integration in GATS, Paper presented in EMC 2010–2011 Asia-Pacific Round Academic Conference on Conference on Economic Integration of the Asian-Pacific Region and Beyond, held in Taipei on 4th March, 2011, p. 9.

[119] China-Hong Kong CEPA, Art. 19.5.

[120] WT/REG/162/3, 25th January 2005, p. 5; WT/REG163/3, 28th January 2005, p. 5.

This passage clarifies the Parties' perception and characterisation of the dispute resolution mechanism provided in the CEPA. It is indeed very primitive. As pointed out by a commentator, the dispute resolution mechanism provided in the CEPA is too simple: it does not follow practices generally employed in bilateral or regional FTAs; neither does it provide formalities and working procedures to settle disputes. It is thus argued that these characteristics suggest that these CEPAs differ from FTAs. The CEPAs are more an arrangement within a country to facilitate internal trade than bilateral or regional FTAs.[121] These two CEPAs may be deemed as policy instruments in nature, which aim to provide preferential treatments to Hong Kong and Macau. It is thus understandable that the dispute resolution mechanism set out in these two CEPAs is essentially political and diplomatic.[122]

While this argument may be true, to some degree, this informal dispute resolution mechanism constitutes one of the major defects of these two CEPAs. Although China and Hong Kong and Macau are politically of the same sovereignty, there certainly exist conflicts of economic interests among these three areas. The dispute resolution mechanism set out in the CEPAs cannot offer a secured protection of their interests, as the commercial disputes between China and Hong Kong and Macau, in light of the conflicting economic interests, are inevitable.[123] The unavailability of private participation in this dispute resolution mechanism is another major defect. As this dispute resolution mechanism is solely dealt with through the channel of governmental consultation, no opportunity is provided for private economic actors to participate. Private actors can only influence their governmental decision-making through lobbying and various informal petitions. The same concern has also been voiced, as previously noted, in the submission of the HKGCC.

Strictly speaking, this consensual consultation in the spirit of friendship and cooperation is a trade dispute resolution mechanism in its very thin form. It nevertheless, to some extent, reflects the real perception between China and its two SARs on this issue. Disputes, if any, between China and Hong Kong and Macau should not be resolved in an adversary manner, where one side complains against the other, since it does not fit China's understanding of "One Country, Two Systems", with "One China" being emphasised. This informal dispute resolution mechanism seems the best alternative. So far, to the author's understanding, no case has been referred to this Steering Committee. One might be tempted to argue that

---

[121] Fan et al. (eds.), *Commentary on the Mainland and Macau Closer Economic Partnership Arrangement (CEPA)*, 2005, p. 240.

[122] Chen/Zhao, A Study on the Dispute Resolution Mechanism in Region Trade Agreements: Article 19 of CEPA, in: Wang (ed.), *A Research on the Economic Arrangement among the Cross-Strait Four Areas*, 2006, p. 253 (in Chinese).

[123] Chen/Zhao, A Study on the Dispute Resolution Mechanism in Region Trade Agreements: Article 19 of CEPA, in: Wang (ed.), *A Research on the Economic Arrangement among the Cross-Strait Four Areas*, 2006, pp. 253–254 (in Chinese).

this suggests a more formalised trade dispute resolution mechanism is unnecessary. However, a better interpretation of this is: this ill-designated dispute resolution mechanism has been discouraging disputes from being referred to it and preventing efficient resolution of commercial disputes between China and Hong Kong and Macau and effective protection of economic interests of private economic actors. However, there is no sign for further reform for this dispute resolution mechanism.

With respect to the ECFA, the Parties to the ECFA like a judicialised form of dispute settlement mechanism no better than those to the CEPAs. Firstly, the ECFA directs the Parties to enter into negotiations with a view to establishing an appropriate dispute settlement mechanism within 6 months after the entry into force of the ECFA.[124] At the same time, it also instructs the Parties to reach an agreement expeditiously in case of any dispute resulting from its interpretation, implementation and application.[125] The second paragraph then provides that, where a dispute arises prior to the entry into force of the envisaged agreement on dispute settlement mechanisms, it should be resolved through consultations or by the ECFA Committee in an appropriate manner.[126]

Although the ECFA directs the Parties to enter into negotiations with the aim to concluding an agreement on dispute settlement mechanisms, it is not completely clear whether the Parties may successfully conclude such agreement. Judging from the legal text of the ECFA, one may tend to say that the dispute settlement mechanism as provided in the ECFA is even more primitive than those as provided in the CEPAs. The only pertinent element as contained in the ECFA relating to dispute settlement is to resolve the dispute "in an appropriate manner" which does not speak of anything. It suffers from all the weaknesses relating to the dispute settlement mechanism as provided in the CEPAs; while it remains yet to be seen as to whether the political negotiations can make up these pitfalls. Furthermore, given that the conflict of economic interests between China and Taiwan is even stronger than that between China and Hong Kong or Macau, the capacity of this premature dispute settlement mechanism as contained in the ECFA in resolving disputes between the Parties may cast more concerns.

Conclusion

In the wake of the 10th anniversary of China's and Taiwan's accession to the WTO, this contribution examines the peculiar interaction and integration among the four WTO members of China, Taiwan, Hong Kong, China and Macau, China. This contribution focuses on three major instruments: the CEPAs, direct-transportation

---

[124] The ECFA, Art. 10.1.

[125] The ECFA, Art. 10.1.

[126] The ECFA, Art. 10.2.

agreements and ECFA. It also compares the dispute settlement mechanisms as contained in the CEPAs and ECFA. This contribution argues that the CEPAs serve both economic and political functions. Economically, it aims to booster the economic growth of Hong Kong and Macau and political confidence of these two SARs on the "One Country, Two Systems" regime. At the same time, the CEPAs have some international political economic implications. It is the first step that China moves toward its FTA talks which China soon becomes zealous of. It also poses some new challenges to existent WTO rules on FTA since the CEPAs are the first FTA concluded by two WTO members but of the same sovereignty. In terms of the ECFA, it also carries a number of political implications. Firstly, it signifies the warming up of the political climate between China and Taiwan. At the same time, the ink of the ECFA also implies China's recognition of Taiwan's legal capacity to enter into FTA talks and to conclude an FTA. It may also helps to the expansion of economic integration in the Asian-Pacific region since Taiwan's other trading partners may feel more confident to initiate FTA negotiations with Taiwan in view of the fact that China, itself, signed an FTA with Taiwan. This contribution nevertheless argues that dispute settlement mechanisms as provided in the CEPAs and ECFA are all too primitive to resolve the resultant trade disputes efficiently or effectively. One of the major weaknesses shared by the CEPAs and ECFA is the state-centred approach on dispute resolution which excludes possible venues for private economic actors. Relying solely on the prompt consultations between the Parties in the spirit of friendship and cooperation is not sufficient to ensure the full implementation of the obligations and commitments stemming from the CEPAs and ECFA and to protect rights and interests of private economic actors.

Global Energy Markets: Challenges and Opportunities – Energy Vision for 2050

Claudia Kemfert

The Challenge

Increasing energy prices – especially for oil and gas – and recent geopolitical conflicts have reminded us of the essential role affordable energy plays in economic growth and human development and of the vulnerability of the global energy system to supply disruptions. To secure energy supplies is once again at the top of the international policy agenda. Yet the current pattern of energy supply carries the threat of severe and irreversible environmental damage – including changes in global climate. Reconciling the goals of energy security and environmental protection requires strong and coordinated government action and public support. As a consequence, the decoupling of energy use and economic growth, a diversification of energy supply, and the mitigation of climate change causing emissions are more urgent than ever.

The major share of primary energy demand today comes from fossil fuels, oil, gas, and coal. The main suppliers of oil are the OPEC region, Russia, and the USA. If the oil demand continues to grow as fast as in the past decades, the demand for oil will be higher than supply 15 years from now (depletion point). Although the oil price would also rise with increasing demand and other oil reserves such as oil shale or tar sands would be financially attractive to exploit further, oil still remains the scarcest fossil resource on earth, followed by gas. The world's largest gas reserves are in Russia, followed by Qatar and Iran. The supply of coal is more widely spread in many countries of the world, and the coal reserves will last for over 200 years (Fig. 1).

C. Kemfert (✉)
Head of Department of Energy, Transportation, and Environment, German Institute of Economic Research (DIW), Mohrenstrasse 58, 10117 Berlin, Germany
e-mail: ckemfert@diw.de

C. Herrmann and J.P. Terhechte (eds.), *European Yearbook of International Economic Law (EYIEL), Vol. 3 (2012)*, European Yearbook of International Economic Law 3, DOI 10.1007/978-3-642-23309-8_8, © Springer-Verlag Berlin Heidelberg 2012

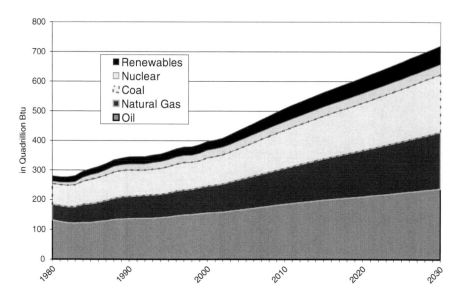

Fig. 1 World energy use by fuel type, 1980–2030, in quadrillion BTU (Source: IEA 2010)

Energy forecasts demonstrate that the share of fossil fuel supply would remain high if no policy to reach a sustainable energy future takes place.[1] As major OECD countries have successfully decoupled their energy consumption from economic growth – primarily by increased energy efficiency – developing countries continue to grow fast. The enormous economic and fuel consumption growth in developing countries – especially China, followed by India – leads to higher energy supply scarcity and energy prices, but also to higher CO_2 emissions. If no sustainable policy would take place, global energy-related carbon dioxide (CO_2) emissions would increase by 55% between 2004 and 2030, as developing countries account for over three-quarters of the increase in global CO_2 emissions (Fig. 2).[2]

Because of high economic and energy growth, OECD and developing Asian countries are becoming increasingly dependent on imports, as their indigenous production fails to keep pace with demand. By 2030, the OECD as a whole would import two-thirds of its oil needs, compared with 56% today. Much of the additional imports come from the Middle East, along vulnerable maritime routes. The concentration of oil production in a small group of countries with large reserves – notably Middle East OPEC members and Russia – will increase their market dominance and their ability to impose higher prices. An increasing share of gas demand is also expected to be met by imports, via pipeline or in the form of liquefied natural gas from increasingly distant suppliers.

---

[1] See International Energy Agency (IEA), *The World Energy Outlook*, 2010.

[2] See Stern, *The Global Deal: Climate Change and the Creation of a New Era of Progress and Prosperity*, 2009.

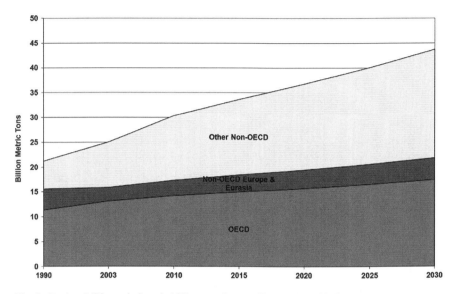

Fig. 2 Regional CO_2 emissions in billion metric tons (Source: IEA 2010)

Meeting the world's growing hunger for energy requires massive investment in energy-supply infrastructure. The International Energy Agency (IEA) estimates cumulative investments of around 20 trillion USD (2005) within the next 25 years. However, if these investments would not be made, a secure energy supply could no longer be guaranteed.

The – Almost – Oil Crisis 3.0

In April 2010, the global community once again was reminded that our energy supply is largely dirty, expensive, and unstable. The spill on the deep-sea oil platform in the Gulf of Mexico startled society, resulting in calls for an immediate halt to deep-sea drilling. Oil-covered pelicans in the Gulf made a daily appearance on the evening news and briefly reminded us just how dirty oil production really is and how dangerous and unsustainable our way of life is. Everyone is seemingly of the impression that we can completely do without oil all of a sudden. Yet it's not that simple. It would be nice if it were.

Industrial nations should have begun to earnestly bid farewell to oil 20 years ago. Then, the current global demand for oil could decrease instead of increase.[3] The

---

[3] See McKay, *Sustainable Energy – Without the Hot Air*, 2008; Kemfert/von Hirschhausen/Holz/ Huppmann, World Crude Oil Markets: OPEC's Supplier Power Remains Unchallenged, Weekly Report 5 (2009) 22, p. 154.

global political economy is still based on cheap oil; it's the "blood of our political economy". The first and second oil price crises in the 1970s and 1980s did lead to a short-term wave of outrage and a passing rethinking; however, as soon as the price of oil fell, everything returned to normal. When oil becomes affordable, problems are gladly forgotten. Global oil supplies have so far been sufficient to meet demand. Although supporters of various theories argue as to when global oil production will reach maximum levels, all agree: Oil is and will remain finite. And the era of sufficient oil supply is coming to an end. The question is as to how much longer sufficient oil will remain available. Global oil production currently lies at 85 million barrels a day, and the demand was roughly as high before the global economic crisis. Booming and especially fast-growing political economies have an enormous thirst for oil. This means that we clearly have to increase global oil supplies in order to even be able to meet the demand. It is safe to assume that the global demand for oil will rise to 100 million barrels a day in the next decade. Traditional oil fields have mostly already exceeded their production capacity. For this reason, it will be necessary – unfortunately! – to also conduct deep-sea drilling in order to avoid shortages.

A trend reversal beforehand is as good as impossible, as mobility technologies almost completely rely on oil. Without oil, the economy would come to a halt. However, especially now it is necessary for us to stem the energy tide away from oil, so that the economy can continue to thrive in the long term.

Unfortunately, many nations waste vast quantities of valuable oil, as they often don't increase the price. In fact, many artificially keep the cost of oil low. The United States is one of the countries that need to take a look in the mirror: It uses more than double the amount of Europe and Germany. The US wastes an unimaginable amount of energy, whereas it could easily conserve energy in the areas of building energy and mobility. As opposed to Europe, the US levies virtually no energy tax, and mobility is regarded as a symbol of freedom and prosperity – one that must remain untouched. And that is exactly where the problem lies: Artificially raising the price of oil is an extremely unpopular political move. In order to introduce new technologies, it takes far-sightedness, and intelligent political and correct decisions need to be made.

Recently, news reached us that China's energy consumption has surpassed that of the USA in absolute quantity. Immediately, an American newspaper opined that China's energy consumption is also partially responsible for oil problems in the USA – this is hardly true. Per capita, China's energy consumption lies drastically below that of the US or Europe. Of course, enormous economic growth in Asia not only brings positive economic advantages – German exports are once again booming – but also challenges, especially for secure and climate-friendly energy supply. The energy supply in China still is largely based on coal, as it is affordable. And China's mobility is growing – and, with it, oil consumption. As we so far have not been able to switch to new mobility technologies, we need to continue to conduct deep-sea drilling in order to avoid an economic crisis. In order to really reduce greenhouse gases by the middle of this century, we need to explore environmentally-friendly coal technologies and especially employ these in China. China is catching up and has understood that economic opportunities in the energy effi-ciency sector, intelligent networks, and a decentralised energy production, as well as electromobility and solar energy are tremendous. We won't be able to connect with China by means of mandatory climate protection goals, but by means of market leadership in these technologies.

In order to expand oil supplies to 100 million barrels in the next decade, we unfortunately need to exploit all oil production sites. Traditional and easily-sourced field are increasingly disappearing, while supplies need to be expanded globally and not remain unchanged. This is why we need deep-sea drilling, not only in the US, but, for example, also off Brazilian and African coasts. We also – with a tremen-dous expenditure of energy and widespread pollution – need to gain oil from sands and minerals, such as is the case in Canada. As much as we would like to believe that we no longer need to do any of this, we need to realise that we should have begun to say goodbye to oil in a serious manner 20 years ago if we want current global demand for oil to decrease and not increase. Deep-sea drilling is risky, without a doubt. Especially when drilling at depths of over 1500 metres, as the oil catastrophe in the Gulf of Mexico has shown us. However, we can control the technology, and risks need to me minimised both on the technical side and the political side. And we especially need to do everything to prepare, much better than in the past, for damage repair and accident minimisation.

A majority of global oil resources is in the hands of state-controlled systems, such as in Arabic states, in Russia, or in Venezuela. Private companies who are able to conduct such costly and capital-intensive drilling only actually have access to ca. 20% of global oil resources. This is why we shouldn't underestimate the fact that we will have to diversify oil fields. This especially means deep-sea drilling.

Goodbye to Oil – But How?

The majority of oil utilised globally is used for mobility, followed by building energy and other uses, such as for pharmaceuticals, the chemical industry, and other product manufacturing. So, in order for us to be noticeably less dependent on oil, we would need to employ alternative propulsion technologies and materials in mobility as quickly as possible. This would not only require new technologies such as, for example, electromobility and associated storage technologies, but also especially a new infrastructure. Using natural gas or liquefied gas as propulsion materials, this would be possible within a short term, thanks to an existing petrol station and automobile system; with hydrogen, this already becomes more difficult. Hydrogen must be produced, stored, and transported, therefore requiring new technology and infrastructure. We could especially employ renewable energies in order to produce hydrogen. Renewable energies require storage capacities in order to balance out volatilities. Fuel could be a possible form of storage and a way to kill two birds with one stone, as we would create a valuable storage method for renewable energies while facilitating a departure from oil. Hydrogen could be used as an important means of storage. Just like, for example, methane or biomethane or other fuels that need to be manufactured energetically could be used as storage for volatile renewable energies. However, we need to be aware that enormous investments in exploring these technologies would be necessary, and new vehicles and infrastructure would need to be built. Biofuels are, for example, already being added to traditional fuels. In some countries, such as Brazil, a high percentage of ethanol, manufactured from sugarcane, is already being used. Sustainable manufacturing is important when using renewable resources for fuel production, as this should not compete with foodstuffs and not result in environmental destruction.

All in all, it will take wide-ranging, consistent, and especially global efforts in order to explore innovative technologies like this and to introduce them on the market.[4] However, this development needs to be introduced today, as it will take at least 20 years to witness noticeable success and change. At the same time, everything should be done to conserve energy, such as making energy processes more efficient or dramatically improving the efficiency of building energy. All of this requires wide-ranging political regulation and intelligent corporate decision-making. "Green" markets – in other words, energy efficiency technologies, sustainable mobility, but also an intelligent infrastructure – are the markets of the future. More and more, corporations are discovering the enormous business opportunities. Politicians shouldn't let environmental catastrophes result in hectic and uncontrolled political decisions. They must especially take long-term measures. These must include, aside from unpopular decisions concerning oil prices, measures and parameters for the improvement of energy efficiency and the encouragement of a sustainable energy turnaround and mobility. This is something that can't be solved in a single afternoon by way of a television address to the nation or a short discussion with oil companies; this calls for far-reaching and, most of all, long-term global political decision-making.

The accident in the Gulf of Mexico has almost been forgotten by now, since the leak has been blocked. The pelicans covered in oil have also disappeared from view. However, we can't afford to relax. We mustn't lose valuable time and start the energy turnaround now.

The Energy Challenge

More than any other before it, today's society is facing great challenges. Fossil fuels such as oil, gas, and coal are finite and expel environmentally-damaging greenhouse gases when burned. Three quarters of global greenhouse emissions are caused by industrial nations such as the US, Europe, and Japan. The concentration

---

[4] See Kemfert, How to Resolve Market Failures: A Sustainable Energy Mix Needs to Be Clean, Clever and Competitive, Baltic Development Forum Magazine 2008, p. 28.

of greenhouse gases in the atmosphere has almost reached a level that should not be exceeded without irreversibly damaging the climate.

In order to reduce climate change, modern, developed political economies need to succeed in dramatically reducing emissions and also replace fossil energies with alternative ones. Global demand for fossil resources continues to rise dramatically. Emerging economies such as China, but also Russia and India, have an enormous need for energy. Especially the continually-growing consumption of coal leads to an ever-increasing output of greenhouse gases. Often, the use of fossil energy is subsidised, resulting in energy waste.

A sustainable energy future must be CO_2-free, environmentally-friendly, and secure. A future energy system cannot only rely on one energy source, but must be as broad as possible. Energy security also means that energy imports are reduced and diversified from many different supply countries and that domestic energy sources should have a major contribution. Many domestic energy sources are not sustainable, as coal emits climate-harming carbon dioxide emissions and nuclear energy causes high environmental risks. Conventional nuclear energy can therefore only be a technology that bridges the gap between the fossil fuel and carbon-free technology area. The main aim is to make a future energy system sustainable by, on the one hand, increasing energy efficiency and, on the other hand, establishing innovative, carbon-free, and environmentally-friendly technologies. In 100 years, the share of renewable energy can increase up to 80%. In between these areas, the carbon capture and storage technology can play a dominant role. By promoting innovative technologies for a sustainable energy future, new branches and sectors grow and become more competitive. Especially because a strengthening of renewable energy improves the competitiveness of small business firms, a promotion of renewable energy creates growth machines and increases competitiveness.

The possibilities of expanding renewable energies are great. Depending on how global demand for renewable energy develops, export potential can greatly be heightened. If, in addition to Germany, many other countries greatly advance the development of renewable energies, not only is the export potential increased for German firms, but market share of German companies will decrease on a global scale. More and more countries are recognising the sign of the times and betting on renewable energies. Even the American president has said that the dependency of importing fossil resources makes countries unnecessarily vulnerable and that environmental protection must play a bigger role. That is why it is very safe to assume that the global potential for developing renewable energies is big and that individual countries will continue to spearhead this movement by a multitude of concepts and instruments.

Without a doubt, the financial crisis changed the world. And yet we should see the crisis as an opportunity. Climate protection is the way out of the crisis. Climate protection powers the economy and creates jobs, whether in the area of low-emission energy technologies, energy production (as the area of renewable energies has shown), but also sustainable mobility, climate protection technologies, energy, and financial services. All will profit – or already profit – from climate protection. We can't afford to say "not now", but must say "now more than ever".

However, it is important that politicians pave the way to an energy-efficient, sustainable, and climate-friendly business world. Renewable energies must continue to be cultivated, and financial incentives to conserve energy must be created.[5] Especially within the area of building energy there lies an unimaginable amount of energy conservation potential. The right signals can be given by way of targeted financial incentives, tax breaks, and improved ways of shifting costs for property owners. There is also great room for improvement when it comes to mobility: Train transport and public transportation must be strongly supported, while air traffic should be placed under emissions trading and the German automobile industry be geared up for the future. Instead of car scrapping schemes for old automobiles, car companies should be better supported financially when it comes to introducing innovative and climate-friendly products and fuels to the market.

Climate protection and a secure energy supply can be combined. Climate protection creates jobs. Climate protection will drive the economy in the next decades. Instead of falling into a climate depression, we should look to the future optimistically if we take action. Climate protection isn't a burden, but the engine to tomorrow's economy. Climate protection is the way out of the crisis, and we can solve the crises all at once: the economic crisis, the energy crisis, and the environmental crisis.

What will the future of energy look like? Will we go back to living by candlelight and without electricity and warm water, using a horse and cart as a means of transport? Hardly. As downtrodden some futurists and visionaries like to be: The future will neither take place in outer space aboard the USS Enterprise nor will humanity be determined by intelligent machines in breeding colonies in a matrix. Sure, technological advances have changed a lot in the past century, but the future will be far less spectacular on earth than in certain science fiction dreams. Just like 150 years ago, when the Industrial Revolution got a jolt with the invention of the steam engine, we are now at a similar crossroads. Climate change continues to march on, as the share of fossil energies and energy consumption continues to rise. However, fossil fuels – especially oil – are starting to dry up and become more expensive. Coal will continue to be available in ample quantities, but burning it leads to dangerous greenhouse emissions. This is why we need a climate-friendly, secure, and affordable energy supply, but also innovative fuels and techniques and sustainable mobility concepts. Germany can explore these technologies and offer them to the world.

Prices for fossil fuels will rise sharply in the next few years. Renewable energies are already clearly the more affordable alternative. Many people make the mistake of regarding the development of renewable energies as strictly a climate protection measure. However, expanding these domestic energy sources decreases the need to import from politically-unstable countries, thereby securing a supply; it also strengthens Germany's economy and international competitiveness. Whoever

---

[5] See Giddens, *Politics of Climate Change*, 2009.

suggests it would be nonsense to encourage the development of solar energy in Germany – due to the comparatively small amount of average sunshine – ignores the fact that renewable energy has (also backed up by multiple domestic examples) turned out to be a huge export hit internationally. Already in the last 10 years, wind energy costs have been cut in half, while and photovoltaics cost a third less. Renewable energy costs continue to drop thanks to serial production and technological optimisation, while the costs of traditional energies continue to rise.

The Energy Vision 2050

The future of energy will be free of CO_2, secure, and affordable. Mobility will be sustainable and will no longer be based on oil, but on alternative propulsion fuels and techniques. Electromobility will be used in conurbations. In 2050, many more people will live in cities than today, while the logistical interconnectedness will remain fundamental. Houses in the future will produce more energy than they use, will themselves be small power plants that produce electricity and building energy, fill up the electric car, as well as produce fuel for the car. Oil will no longer be used, and coal will be used far less than now for energy production. Traditional coal-fired power stations will funnel CO_2 into the Earth, coal from biomass will replace traditional coal. Gas will be the only resource of importance in 2050. Large energy production facilities – using sun, wind, and water to produce large amounts of energy – will be used, as will decentralised plants that supply buildings and mobility with energy. Europe will also be able to transport energy long-distance, thanks to data and energy highways. Solar power plants in Southern Europe and wind and water power plants in Northern Europe will ensure Europe's basic energy supply. People will also not sacrifice flying; instead, the globally connected world will be maintained by way of alternative propulsion fuels. Energy will definitely be used more efficiently. Aside from high-power batteries, energy storage facilities will be the key technology, as well as fuels such as hydrogen and methane, which will be gained by way of renewable energies. Energies for electricity and transportation will be gained from methane hydrates. And what about nuclear fusion? Well, it also will not be available in 2050 – maybe in 2100.

Energy Trade and WTO Rules: Reflexions on Sovereignty over Natural Resources, Export Restrictions and Freedom of Transit

Mireille Cossy

Introduction

"WTO and energy" has become a fashionable topic. Various key energy-exporting or transit countries have recently acceded to the WTO, bringing with them a substantial part of energy trade, and others are currently negotiating their accession. Unbundling of vertically integrated state-owned companies and technological developments have created room for private operators, which has boosted negotiations on energy services. More recently, the interface between trade and climate policies, as well as concerns surrounding energy security have also contributed to raise the profile of energy-related issues in the WTO.

As compared to other economic sectors, the energy industry is "special" in several respects. With an estimated value of US$6 trillion a year (about a tenth of the world economic output), energy is one of the biggest markets in the world.[1] It is also one of the most politicised industries which plays an undisputed role in shaping international politics. Energy resources are scarce and their uneven geographical distribution gives raise to tensions between "have" and "have not". They are often situated in remote locations, and their transport over long distances requires expensive infrastructure (pipelines, LNG stations), whose construction and laying out raise important political stakes. The way we produce and consume energy is being put in question by climatic threats. And the surging demand for modern renewable energy technologies is giving rise to a fierce race between the main producers and exporters of these technologies to gain market shares, which may have WTO implications.

[1] "The Power and the Glory – A Special Report on Energy", The Economist, June 2008.

M. Cossy (✉)
WTO, Centre William Rappard, Rue de Lausanne 154, CH-1211 Geneva 21, Switzerland
e-mail: Mireille.Cossy@wto.org

C. Herrmann and J.P. Terhechte (eds.), *European Yearbook of International Economic Law (EYIEL), Vol. 3 (2012)*, European Yearbook of International Economic Law 3, DOI 10.1007/978-3-642-23309-8_9, © Springer-Verlag Berlin Heidelberg 2012

There is no specific Agreement on Energy in the WTO, but a number of different disciplines which have governed international trade in goods for the last 60 years are directly relevant for trade in energy goods and materials. The national treatment obligation prohibits discrimination, in terms or taxes or other regulation, between imported and domestic products. Similarly, according to the most-favoured-nation obligation, energy goods and materials cannot be discriminated against on the basis of their origin or destination. The GATT also prohibits quantitative restrictions on imports and exports, and establishes the principle of freedom of transit. Other important disciplines deal, *inter alia*, with state-trading enterprises, trade-distorting subsidies, labelling, mandatory and voluntary standards. The GATT also contains exception provisions. Of particular relevance in this context is GATT Articles XX (b) and XX(g), which allow, respectively, Members to take measures "necessary to protect human, animal and plant life and health" and measures "relating to the protection of exhaustible natural resources". And, under Article XXI, Members can take action relating to fissionable materials, which means, in essence, that most transactions relating to nuclear energy are likely to fall outside the scope of WTO. Services trade is an important component of energy trade and, since 1995, the General Agreement on Trade in Service (GATS) applies to energy services supplied through four different modes.[2]

However, WTO rules do not offer a fully appropriate framework to address all the specificities of the energy industry and there are some areas where these rules might usefully be clarified or further developed. This process has started already in the context of the negotiations which are taking place under the aegis of the Doha Development Agenda (DDA). Moreover, several countries which have jointed the WTO over the last 10 years have undertaken so-called "WTO+" obligations which are energy-related.

This contribution will focus on three topics which we feel are particularly important in the broad interface between the energy sector and the multilateral trading system. We shall first discuss the implications of WTO obligations for States' regulation of their natural resources. The second and third topics will deal with, respectively, the application (and non-application) of WTO disciplines on export restrictions and transit. This will include a discussion on how these two issues have been dealt with in accession negotiations, as well as the proposals currently under consideration in the DDA negotiations.

---

[2] For a review of the various WTO provisions relevant for energy trade, see Marceau, The WTO in the Emerging Energy Governance Debate, Global Trade and Customs Journal 5 (2010) 3, pp. 83–93, and World Trade Organization, World Trade Report 2010 – Trade in Natural Resources, 2010.

The Regulation of Natural Resources Under WTO Law

The principle of States' sovereignty over living and non-living natural resources situated on their land territories and in their territorial seas was assumed early on in public international law. As a corollary, States have the exclusive right to explore and exploit underground natural resources, such as oil and gas deposits, situated in the subsoil of territories they own.

WTO rules do not address the issue of sovereignty over natural resources and no WTO provision regulates ownership of natural resources. As stated in the World Trade Report 2010, "[t]here is no provision that speaks directly to the issue of ownership of natural resources or the allocation of natural resources between states and foreign investors".[3] Nevertheless, natural resources are subject to WTO agreements regulating trade in goods when they are marketed, whether in raw form or processed. Furthermore, a number of services subject to the disciplines of the General Agreement on Trade in Services (GATS) are closely related to natural resources. This "proximity" raises the question of the potential impact that WTO obligations may have on the regulation of natural resources.

Natural Resources in Their "Natural State"

The question of the status of natural resources "in their natural state" under trade agreements arose in the context of the North American Free Trade Agreement (NAFTA) with a controversy over whether NAFTA obligations could oblige Canada to export bulk water to the United States. At the time, the controversy was settled with a "joint statement" whereby the governments of Canada, Mexico and the United States declared that "the NAFTA creates no rights to the natural water resources of any Party to the Agreement". The three signatories further agreed that

> unless water, in any form, has entered into commerce and become a good or product, it is not covered by the provisions of any trade agreement, including the NAFTA. And nothing in the NAFTA would oblige any NAFTA Party to either exploit its water for commercial use, or to begin exporting water in any form. Water in its natural state in lakes, rivers, reservoirs, aquifers, waterbasins and the like is not a good or product, is not traded, and therefore is not and has never been subject to the terms of any trade agreement.[4]

This interpretation was supported by various commentators who argued that water and other natural resources in their "natural state" (trees, animals, ores, etc)

---

[3] World Trade Organization, World Trade Report 2010 – Trade in Natural Resources, 2010, p. 179.

[4] See for instance, Government of Canada, Water Exports and the NAFTA, available at: http://dsp-psd.pwgsc.gc.ca/Collection-R/LoPBdP/BP/prb0041-e.htm.

are not covered by WTO rules until they are extracted and marketed. As a consequence, nothing in the WTO can be read to oblige a State to exploit and export its natural resources.[5]

However, a recent WTO dispute obliges to qualify this view because it shows that, in certain circumstances, natural resources "in their natural states" may be found to be covered by WTO rules. One of the issues at stake in the *US – Softwood Lumber IV* dispute between Canada and the United States was whether the rights to harvest trees on government land that the Canadian government had granted to certain lumber harvesters against a low remuneration could be considered to be a prohibited subsidy under the Agreement on Subsidies and Countervailing Measures (SCM Agreement). Canada argued that standing trees, as opposed to trees after they had been cut down, were not "goods" provided by the government, but represented only intangible rights to harvest trees. Hence, as explained by the Appellate Body, the question at stake was whether the term 'goods' in Article 1.1 of the SCM Agreement[6] "captures trees *before they are harvested*, that is, standing timber attached to the land (but severable from it) and incapable of being traded across borders as such".[7]

The Appellate Body noted that the terms goods "includes items that are tangible and capable of being possessed" and that "... the ordinary meaning of the term 'goods' in the English version of Article 1.1(a)(1)(iii) of the *SCM Agreement* should not be read so as to exclude tangible items of property, like trees, that are severable from land". It concluded that

> ... nothing in the text of Article 1.1(a)(1)(iii), its context, or the object and purpose of the *SCM Agreement*, leads us to the view that tangible items—such as standing, unfelled trees—that are not both tradable as such and subject to tariff classification, should be excluded, as Canada suggests, from the coverage of the term "goods" as it appears in that Article. It follows that we agree with the Panel that standing timber—trees—are 'goods' within the meaning of Article 1.1(a)(1)(iii) of the *SCM Agreement*.[8]

In the view of the Appellate Body, the fact that the Canadian government granted a right to enter onto government lands, to cut standing timber and to enjoy exclusive rights over the timber that was harvested amounted to providing the standing timber itself. Hence, what was crucial, according to the Appellate Body, was the "consequence of the transaction".

---

[5] See, for instance, Cossy, Le statut de l'eau en droit international économique, in: Boisson de Chazournes/Salman (eds.), *Les ressources en eau et le droit international*, 2005, pp. 169–208; Brown Weiss, Water Transfers and International Trade Law, in: Brown Weiss/Boisson de Chazournes/Bernasconi-Osterwalder (eds.), *Fresh Water and International Economic Law*, 2005, pp. 61–89.

[6] Article 1.1(a)(1)(iii) provides that "... a subsidy shall be deemed to exist if: ... a government provides goods or services other than general infrastructure, or purchases goods".

[7] Report of the Appellate Body, United States – Final Countervailing Duty Determination With Respect To Certain Softwood Lumber From Canada, WT/DS257/AB/R / DSR 2004:II, 587 (hereinafter US – Softwood Lumber IV), para. 57.

[8] US – Softwood Lumber IV, para. 67.

Rights over felled trees or logs crystallize as a natural and inevitable consequence of the harvesters' exercise of their harvesting rights. Indeed, as the Panel indicated, the evidence suggests that making available timber is the *raison d'être* of the stumpage arrangements. Accordingly, like the Panel, we believe that, by granting a right to harvest standing timber, governments provide that standing timber to timber harvesters.[9]

The Appellate Body's conclusions in this case show that, in certain circumstances, WTO rules apply to natural resources "in their natural state". At the same time, the Appellate Body carefully qualified its findings. First, it noted that "goods" in Article 1.1 of the SCM Agreement and "products" in Article II of the GATT 1994 "are different words that need not necessarily bear the same meanings in the different contexts in which they are used". Hence, these findings, made under the SCM Agreement, may not necessarily be transposed under other agreements, for instance to determine when a natural resource becomes a "product" subject to GATT obligations. Second, and more importantly, in the *US – Softwood Lumber IV* dispute, the main concern of the Appellate Body was to prevent the circumvention of subsidy disciplines "in cases of financial contributions granted in a form other than money, such as through the provision of standing timber for the sole purpose of severing it from land and processing it". In this case, the Appellate Body sanctioned the fact that harvesting rights, i.e. entitlements with an economic value, had been granted on standing trees. And, "[b]y granting a right to harvest, the provincial governments put particular stands of timber at the disposal of timber harvesters and allow those enterprises, exclusively, to make use of those resources".[10] In other words, the Canadian government granted rights to standing trees so that these trees could be cut down and sold: the real object of the arrangement was the right to sell felled trees (not the intangible right to cut down trees), and, consequently, the right to harvest trees amounted to receiving the cut trees themselves.

In this case, the fact that trees, although still "in their natural state", had been explicitly and deliberately given a commercial value, motivated the decision to consider them as "goods" for the purpose of the SCM Agreement. While we cannot exclude at this stage other situations where natural resources could be found subject to WTO obligations before they are harvested or extracted, we can conclude that natural resources in their "natural state" which are not the object of any kind of economic transaction, because, for instance, there is a policy objective to protect them (total prohibition to harvest certain species of trees or to extract hydrocarbons in certain protected areas, for instance) would not fall under WTO disciplines. It also means that WTO rules should not interfere with Members' decisions as to whether or not exploiting a natural resource.

---

[9] Id., para. 75.

[10] Id., paras. 63–64, 75.

Ownership of Natural Resources and Services Trade

Services may relate to natural resources in many different ways, from management and protection, to exploration, exploitation, testing, transport, brokering and commercialization.[11] The negotiations on energy services involve a range of activities all along the energy supply chain, for example: services incidental to mining (e.g., site preparation, rig installation, drilling, well testing, etc.); services incidental to energy distribution; pipeline transportation of fuels; bulk storage services of liquids and gases; wholesale trade services of solid, liquid and gaseous fuels and related products; retailing services of fuel oil, bottled gas, coal, and woods; etc. Hence, the question arises as to whether obligations undertaken under the General Agreement on Trade in Services (GATS) may affect government's right to regulate ownership of and access to the natural resources concerned.

The issue of ownership of natural resources has come up in the services negotiations. In this context, Members have consistently stressed that natural resources were under the sovereignty of each government and that the question of access to, or ownership of natural resources was not on the negotiating table. For instance, in the negotiations on energy services, the United States recalled that "[i]n a large number of countries, including our own, many natural resources are held in trust for the public. The United States recognizes this, and is not proposing to address issues of ownership of natural resources". Japan proposed "to exclude discussions on the issue of the public ownership of natural resources". According to Norway, "[t]he question of public ownership of natural resources falls outside these negotiations". Cuba indicated that "[. . .] ownership of, rights of access to and use of natural energy resources are issues that should not be addressed in these negotiations". For Indonesia, "[o]bligations arising from international economic co-operation must be based on the principle of mutual benefit, as well as on international law, and should not impair the inherent right of all peoples to enjoy and utilize fully and freely their natural wealth and resources".[12] Also, the eleven Members who signed the collective request on energy services clarified that the request "does not extend to the ownership of energy resources, which remains under the full sovereignty and sovereign rights of each Member, and is outside of the scope of GATS negotiations".[13] Similarly, in the discussions on environmental

---

[11] World Trade Organization, World Trade Report 2010 – Trade in Natural Resources, 2010, p. 162.

[12] These statements are found in WTO documents S/CSS/W/24 (United States), S/CSS/W/42/Suppl. 3 (Japan), S/CSS/W/59 (Norway), S/CSS/W144 (Cuba) and S/CSC/W/42/Rev.2 (Indonesia).

[13] For more information on the collective request and the energy services negotiations, see Cossy, Energy Services Under the General Agreement on Trade in Services (GATS), in: Selivanova (ed.) *Energy Trade in WTO and Beyond: Current International Disciplines and Future Challenges*, Kluwer Law International BV, The Netherlands, 2011.

services, a group of Members stated that it "fully respects [. . .] that WTO Members have the right to regulate access to natural resources".[14]

The GATS itself is silent on this issue.[15] However, the argument could be made that GATS obligations cannot provide a basis for claiming ownership or control over a natural resource on which a service is performed. The reason is that the GATS applies to trade in <u>services</u>, while the production of goods on a company's own account, i.e., performed by an entity which owns the raw material, is deemed not to be a service. Hence, the fact that a firm has a proprietary title on the resource should mean ipso facto that, with regard to the processing of this resource, it is not a service supplier within the meaning of the GATS, but it is the producer of a good.[16] This means that commitments undertaken under the GATS are relevant, for instance, for oilfield services companies, i.e. companies providing services to other firms in relation to the exploration, development and production of oil and gas, and which do not have a proprietary title over the resource. However, the GATS would normally not apply to companies processing a resource they own. Similarly, entities transporting their own oil are not service suppliers are performing an in-house activity and, therefore, are not regarded as services suppliers. On the other hand, an entity transporting oil belonging to another entity, and being paid for that activity, is a service supplier under the GATS.[17]

Restricting Exports of Energy Products

Export Restrictions and WTO Rules

Article XI of the GATT lays down the fundamental principle of the prohibition of quantitative restrictions on imports and exports.[18] This prohibition is seen as one of

---

[14] Communication from Australia, The European Communities, Hong Kong China, Japan, New Zealand, The Separate Customs Territory of Taiwan, Penghu, Kinmen and Matsu, and the United States, Joint report on informal discussion on environmental services in the context of the DDA, TN/S/W/28, 11th February, 2005.

[15] Unlike the GATT, the GATS does not contain an exception for measures relating to the protection of "exhaustible natural resources". For more on this point, see World Trade Organization, World Trade Report 2010 – Trade in Natural Resources, 2010, p. 169.

[16] Cossy, Energy Services Under the General Agreement on Trade in Services (GATS), in: Selivanova (ed.) *Energy Trade in WTO and Beyond: Current International Disciplines and Future Challenges*, Kluwer Law International BV, The Netherlands, 2011. See also Background Note on Energy Services, Note by the Secretariat, S/C/W/311, 10th January, 2010, para. 77.

[17] Cossy, Energy Transport and Transit in the WTO, in: Pauwelyn (ed.), *Global Challenges at the Intersection of Trade, Energy and the Environment*, Center for Economic Policy Research (CEPR), 2010.

[18] Art. XI:1 states that: "No prohibition or restrictions other than duties or other charges, whether made effective through quotas, import or export licences or other measures, shall be instituted or maintained by any contracting party on the importation of any product of the territory of any

the cornerstones of the GATT system because quantitative restrictions are considered to have distorting trade effects and to lack transparency. Under Art. XI, Members are allowed, however, to levy "duties, taxes or other charges" on imported or exported products. As explained by a dispute Panel, the idea is that, when it comes to protection at the border, "tariffs are the preferred and acceptable form" because "quantitative restrictions impose absolute limits on imports, while tariffs do not".[19] However, the symmetry between imported and exported products is imperfect because the disciplines are more stringent for the former than for the latter.

Firstly, the prohibition of quantitative restrictions on exports is subject to the Article XI:2(a) exception which allows export prohibitions or restrictions "temporarily applied to prevent or relieve critical shortages of foodstuffs or other products essential to the exporting" Member. This exception has never been applied in any GATT/WTO dispute settlement proceedings so far. While energy products, such as oil and gas, could arguably be considered "essential" to the exporting Members, the condition that restrictions be applied "temporarily" might make it difficult to invoke this exception to justify long-term export restrictions as a form of management of natural resources.

Secondly, while GATT Article II requires that other duties and charges on the importation be bound in tariff schedules, there is no such requirement for export taxes. As a consequence, it is generally understood that Article XI does not prevent WTO Members from applying export taxes.[20] In practice, few export taxes have been bound in tariff schedules and there is very little transparency in this field.

The asymmetry between disciplines applying, respectively, to import and export measures is due to the fact that, at the end of World War II, the drafters of the GATT wanted to set up a framework for international trade so as to prevent the spiral of import restrictions which had affected trade policy in the 1930s. The main concern was to fight import protectionism and to guarantee that import markets would remain open.

Yet, when it comes to international trade in natural resources, export restrictions, either via export quota, taxes, licences, tend to be more prevalent than import restrictions. Countries richly endowed in natural resources may be tempted to tax the export of these resources for various reasons, in particular because they allow to keep down domestic prices: domestic processing industries can buy the raw material on more favourable terms and thus benefit from a competitive advantage *vis-à-vis* their foreign competitors which have to buy necessary inputs at higher

---

contracting party or the on exportation or sale for export of any product destined for the territory of any other contracting party".

[19] Report of the Panel, Turkey – Textiles and Clothing, WT/DS34/R, 31st May, 1999, paras. 9.63–9.65.

[20] World Trade Organization, World Trade Report 2010 – Trade in Natural Resources, 2010, p. 166. In this context, an important question is to what extent a prohibitive export tax could be likened to a quantitative restriction, and thus be found to be incompatible with GATT Art. XI:1.

international prices. Restricting the export of raw material may also serve indirectly as a means to attract foreign direct investment as foreign companies producing value-added goods cannot find needed inputs at competitive prices on international markets. As a corollary, importing countries, whether developed or developing, tend to maintain lower tariff protection in the natural resources sector than for overall merchandise trade.[21] The WTO World Trade Report estimates that between 5% and 10% of world trade in fuels and mining is covered by export taxes; moreover, these products are subject to other types of export restrictions, such as non-automatic licensing, quotas and outright prohibitions.[22]

While the vast majority of GATT/WTO disputes under GATT Article XI have dealt with import restrictions, the issue of export restrictions might prove more contentious in the future. A case in point is the ongoing dispute launched by the European Union, Mexico and the United States against China regarding export measures related to various raw materials. The complainants argue, *inter alia*, that measures such as export quotas that China imposes on the export of nine raw materials, including bauxite, coke, magnesium, manganese, zinc, etc., are contrary to GATT Art. XI.[23] The result of this dispute will be important because it could set the tone for future disputes involving export restrictions on natural resources, including for energy products.[24] Moreover, references to the WTO being used to challenge export restrictions on key inputs appear more frequently. For instance, in a recent report addressing its trade strategy for raw materials, the European Commission indicated that it "has continued to tackle barriers primarily through dialogue, but when no progress was registered has been ready to use other tools, including WTO dispute settlement".[25]

Export Restrictions vs. Production Restrictions

Can a restriction on the production of a natural resource be considered to amount to a restriction on the export of that resource and, thus, be found contrary to GATT Article XI? The question is far from being merely theoretical. A broad

---

[21] Tariff protection is lowest in the mining and fuel sectors. See World Trade Organization, World Trade Report 2010 – Trade in Natural Resources, 2010, p. 114.

[22] Id., pp. 117, 119.

[23] China – Measures Related to the Exportation of Various Raw Materials, WT/DS394, –395 and –398. A panel was established in December 2009 to examine these claims and its conclusions were not known at the time of writing this contribution.

[24] This dispute may be indirectly relevant for the energy sector as some of the raw materials at stake are being used by the renewable energy industry, in particular in the wind sector.

[25] Commission Communication, Tackling The Challenges in Commodity Markets and on Raw Materials, COM(2011) 25 final, 2nd February, 2011.

interpretation of GATT Art. XI covering production limitations might allow to challenge, for instance, oil production quota, such as those fixed by OPEC.

The possibility to challenge OPEC practices in the WTO was debated in the United States. In December 2006, Congressman DeFazio, noting that eight of the twelve OPEC countries were also WTO Members, sent a letter to Pres. Bush, urging him to "file a case against OPEC at the WTO for illegal market manipulation and price fixing".[26] In the same vein, Senator F. Lautenberg issued a report some in 2004, concluding that OPEC's practices were in violation of WTO rules and that a case against the WTO Members of OPEC "could have immediate, large and lasting benefits to the US consumer and economy by driving down oil and gas prices".[27] Both the Lautenberg report and the DeFazio letter argue, in essence, that OPEC's production quotas are contrary to GATT Article XI because they de facto restrict exports. Indeed, according to economic theory, production limitations and export restrictions have similar effects: ". . . like an export restriction, a production quota in the exporting country lowers the supply in international markets and increases the world price, thus shifting the rent from the importing to the exporting country".[28]

Case-law related to GATT Art. XI indicates that the interpretation of key terms, such as "prohibition" and "restrictions" tends to be rather broad as it includes not only blanket prohibitions or precise numerical limitations, but also brings under the scope of this provision measures that indirectly affect quantities of goods exported.[29] Nevertheless, most commentators consider that Article XI does not go as far as covering limitations on production per se and, hence, "[t]here are no obligations imposed on Members to extract and produce energy resources".[30] This

---

[26] See "DeFazio Urges Action Against OPEC Price Fixing", 15th December, 2006, available at: http://www.defazio.house.gov/index.php?option=com_content&view=article&id=225:defazio-urges-action-against-opec-price-fixing&catid=57.

[27] Lautenberg, Busting Up the Cartel: The WTO Case Against OPEC, July 2004, available at: http://lautenberg.senate.gov/documents/foreign/OPEC%20Memo.pdf.

[28] World Trade Organization, World Trade Report 2010 – Trade in Natural Resources, 2010, p. 185.

[29] In Colombia – Ports of Entry, the fact that Colombia limited the number of ports through which goods could enter the country was found to be contrary to GATT Art. XI, even though there was no limit on the quantity of goods which could be imported through these ports. See Report of the Panel, WT/DS366/R, and the case-law quoted therein, paras. 7.233–7.240

[30] See Marceau, The WTO in the Emerging Energy Governance Debate, Global Trade and Customs Journal 5 (2010) 3, pp. 83–93. In the same sense, see also Broome, Conflicting Obligations for Oil Exporting Nations: Satisfying Membership Requirements of Both OPEC and the WTO, The George Washington International Law Review 38 (2006), pp. 409–436; Crosby, Background to WTO Rules and Production/Trade Restrictions in the Field of Energy, in: Pauwelyn (ed.), Global Challenges at the Intersection of Trade, Energy and the Environment, 2010, pp. 83–86. For a different view, see Desta, The Organization of Petroleum Exporting Countries, the World Trade Organization, and Regional Trade Agreements, Journal of World Trade 37 (2003) 3, pp. 523–551. This author argues that OPEC minimum export price requirements could be contrary to GATT Art. XI.

is also the view of the WTO World Trade Report which concludes that "based on the language of this provision, it has been generally understood that production restrictions are not covered by Article XI and thus would be permissible".[31] Moreover, WTO obligations must be interpreted in the light of other relevant international instruments, among which, for instance, UN Resolution 1803 (XVII) on "Permanent Sovereignty Over Natural Resources", whose preamble recommends that "that the sovereign right of every State to dispose of its wealth and its natural resources should be respected". The Energy Charter Treaty could also be relevant, in particular its Article 18 ("Sovereignty over energy resources") which reasserts "state sovereignty and sovereign rights over energy resources" and guarantees, inter alia, that "[e]ach state continues to hold in particular the rights to decide the geographical areas within its Area to be made available for exploration and development of its energy resources, the optimalization of their recovery and the rate at which they may be depleted or otherwise exploited . . .".

Applying Art. XI to production restrictions might have far-reaching consequences. It would mean that countries could be obliged to exploit and export their natural resources, the ultimate effect being that the GATT would be turned into some kind of resource-sharing agreement by indirectly granting importing countries a "right to buy" natural resources situated in other countries. Needless to say that this would have a serious impact on Members' sovereignty over their natural resources.[32]

Strengthening GATT Disciplines on Export Restrictions

A Recurrent Concern

In the GATT/WTO history, strengthening the disciplines on export restrictions has been a recurrent concern for countries relying on imports of raw materials, but the various attempts to do so have invariably raised heated controversies. Countries in favour of more stringent disciplines argued that export restrictions represent a form of trade protection, or indirect subsidization, because, by allowing domestic firms access to cheap supplies, they give them an undue advantage over foreign firms which must pay higher world market prices for their inputs. On the other hand,

---

[31] World Trade Organization, World Trade Report 2010 – Trade in Natural Resources, 2010, p. 166.

[32] This view seems to be shared by the US government. When asked, during a 2004 press conference, whether he thought that it could be "theoretically possible to use the WTO to get at OPEC", R. Zoellick, then US Trade Representative, replied: "Under WTO rules in general there's no apparent basis to be able to compel people to sell things. . . . It would be like somebody coming to the United States and saying . . . we must dig up more of this metal or that metal or produce more of this or that product." Press conference, US Trade Representative R. Zoellick and Bahraini Minister of Finance and National Economy Abdulla Hassan Saif, 27th May, 2004.

countries endowed in natural resources invoke the need to protect and manage the resources over the long-term; they also argue that export duties on raw material are justified by the fact that countries importing raw material tend to impose higher tariffs on products processed from this raw material (this is known as "tariff escalation"), thus disadvantaging exports of their own manufactured goods.

For instance, discussions regarding export restrictions already took place in 1973 against the backdrop of the oil crisis. A Note by the then GATT Secretariat may now sound premonitory:

> It is not known whether the recent spreading of export restrictions is the beginning of a trend or a temporary phenomenon. However, whatever the future, it is now possible to visualize concretely situations in which export restrictions could be a major factor in world commerce. Historically, international economic organization has been based on the assumption that free trade could be achieved by giving all nations the right to sell abroad; in the future, the right to buy from other countries might have to be added in some areas.[33]

However, no concrete action ensued from this work. During the Uruguay Round (1986–1992), attempts were made to discuss export restrictions and other measures affecting trade in energy products in the Negotiating Group on Natural Resources-Based Products. The United States proposed to address various measures affecting trade in energy products, in particular dual pricing, export restrictions and trade distortions arising from government ownership and control in resource-based industries.[34] However, there was strong opposition to including energy goods in the discussion. Similarly, proposals to discuss broader issues, such as access to supplies, were flatly turned down.

> As regards access to supply, several delegations maintained that this question was outside the scope of negotiations in the Uruguay Round. A number of other delegations pointed out that restrictions of access to supplies distorted production and trade patterns, and that attention will have to be given not only to the interests of natural-resource-rich countries but also to the interests of natural resource have-nots. Another delegation made the point that, even though liberalization of market access was the avowed objective, the objective might not be attained unless importing countries could be given some assurances on matters of access to supplies and on trade practices.[35]

Hence, the Uruguay Round did not produce new disciplines regarding export restrictions on raw materials, but efforts were pursued on other fronts, inside and outside the WTO.

Efforts to better disciplines export measures have been made in some preferential trade agreements (PTAs) where they have proved more successful. For instance, the North American Free Trade Agreement, (NAFTA) between Canada, Mexico

---

[33] GATT and Export Restrictions, Technical Note by the Secretariat, MTN/3B/9, 1st May, 1974.

[34] Negotiating Group on Natural Resource-Based Products, Natural Resource-Based Products: Two-Tier Pricing Issues, Submission from the United States, MTN.GNG/NG3/W/13, 8th June, 1988.

[35] Negotiating Group on Natural Resource-Based Products, Meeting of 29th April, 1987, Note by the Secretariat, MTN.GNG/NG3/2, para. 6.

and the United States, explicitly prohibits export duties, taxes or other charges "unless such duty, tax or charge is adopted or maintained on: (a) exports of any such good to the territory of all other Parties; and (b) any such good when destined for domestic consumption" (Article 314). The same prohibition is contained in Chap. 6 which deals specifically with energy and petrochemicals. Similar disciplines are contained in other PTAs signed by the United States, such as US–Singapore or US–Australia.[36] The recent free trade agreement between the EU and the Republic of Korea also includes disciplines on export taxes.[37]

The Energy Charter Treaty does not go much beyond the WTO when it comes to export restrictions. Under the ECT, Parties which are WTO Members remain bound by their WTO obligations in this regard. However, ECT Parties which are not yet WTO Members "endeavour not to" increase customs duties or charges imposed in connection with importation or exportation above applied levels.

"WTO+" Disciplines in Accession Negotiations

The issue of export measures, in particular export duties, also arises in accession negotiations where WTO Members have been able to impose specific export-related disciplines on countries wishing to join the WTO. In some cases, the acceding Member is only asked to reiterate existing WTO obligations and undertake some transparency obligations. For instance, Croatia confirmed that

> ... after accession to the WTO, [it] would apply export duties only in accordance with the provisions of the WTO Agreement and published in the Official Gazette 'Narodne Novine'. Changes in the application of such measures, their level and scope would also be published in the Official Gazette 'Narodne Novine'. The Working Party took note of this commitment.[38]

Other countries that have recently joined the WTO have been requested to undertake more binding commitments, including an exhaustive list of product subject to export taxes (with indication of the bound rate) and/or a timetable for reduction of those duties.

For instance, China undertook, in its Accession Protocol, to eliminate "all taxes and charges applied to exports", except for a list of some 80 goods listed in an annex

---

[36] For instance, Art. 2.11 of US – Australia stipulates that "Neither Party may adopt or maintain any duty, tax, or other charge on the export of any good to the territory of the other Party, unless such duty, tax, or charge is adopted or maintained on any such good when destined for consumption in its territory".

[37] Art. 2.11, entitled "Duties, Taxes or Other Fees and Charges on Exports", stipulates that "Neither Party may maintain or institute any duties, taxes or other fees and charges imposed on, or in connection with, the exportation of goods to the other Party, or any internal taxes, fees and charges on goods exported to the other Party that are in excess of those imposed on like goods destined for internal sale".

[38] Report of the Working Party on the Accession of Croatia to the World Trade Organization, WT/ACC/HRV/59, 29th June, 2000, para. 101.

to the Protocol. With respect to the latter, China further confirmed that "the tariff levels ... are maximum levels which will not be exceeded" and that "it would not increase the presently applied rates, except under exceptional circumstances".[39] In its Accession Protocol, China undertook further obligations regarding export quotas and other export measures.[40] These obligations are at stake in the dispute brought by the European Union, Mexico and the United States regarding the alleged export restrictions implemented by China on the export of various raw materials.[41]

The case of Ukraine is also interesting because it shows that, even in the context of accession negotiations, the imposition of more stringent disciplines on export measures remains a controversial topic among WTO Members. The Working Party Report indicates that Ukraine was requested to "continue phasing out its export duties so that these would be eliminated by the date of Ukraine's accession to the WTO, and thereby allowing Ukraine to commit not to apply export duties as a Member of the WTO". Ukraine also agreed to apply export duties only to certain goods listed in its Working Party Report and to reduce them in accordance to a binding schedule. Ukraine further confirmed that it would not increase export duties, nor apply measures having an equivalent effect, unless justified under the exceptions of GATT 1994. Finally, Ukraine confirmed that the current export duties would be published in the Official Gazette and that, from the date of its accession to the WTO, it would not apply any obligatory minimum export prices.

However, the additional export-related obligations undertaken by Ukraine seem to have been questioned by some Members as the Report indicates that "some developing country Members, on the contrary, had a very positive view of export duties as a developmental instrument. Other Members noted that the imposition of export tariffs was not inconsistent with WTO rules. In reply, the representative of Ukraine stated that export duties per se were consistent with the WTO Agreements, but he acknowledged that high export duties could act as trade barriers and hence needed reduction. ... Ukraine recognized the negative impact the export duties had on investment and bilateral trade." These diverging views regarding the desirability of more stringent disciplines on export measures presumably prompted Members to state, in the same Report, that "the Working Party agreed that these commitments do not constitute a reinterpretation of GATT 1994, nor affect the rights and obligations of other members in respect of provisions on the application of export duties, that are measures in accordance with GATT 1994."[42]

---

[39] Protocol on the Accession of the People's Republic of China, WT/L/432, 23rd November, 2001.

[40] Report of the Working Party on the Accession of China, WT/ACC/CHN/49, 1st October, 2001.

[41] China – Measures Related to the Exportation of Various Raw Materials, WT/DS394, -395 and -398. The panel report was still pending at the time this contribution was written.

[42] Report of the Working Party on the Accession of Ukraine to the World Trade Organization, WT/ACC/UKR/152, 25th January, 2008, paras. 229–230, 240.

Export Restrictions in the DDA Negotiations

The issue of export restrictions has made a come-back in the DDA negotiations where it is addressed from two different – and complementary – angles. Unsurprisingly, it remains highly controversial among WTO Members.

In 2006, the European Union tabled an ambitious proposal for a "WTO Agreement on Export Taxes"[43] whose main objective was a general prohibition on export duties and taxes. Pursuant to this proposal, developed countries would not be allowed to maintain export taxes. Developing and least-developed countries would be allowed to maintain export taxes "for a limited number of products" and "at low levels" under certain conditions: (i) export taxes must be necessary to ensure financial stability, facilitate economic diversification, etc. and not adversely affect international trade.[44] Moreover, any remaining export taxes would have to be applied on a MFN basis and bound in Members' schedules. The EU also proposed that remaining export taxes should be subject to future negotiations with a view to eliminating them, and advocated notification and consultation procedures for new export taxes or increases in existing ones. This proposal was met with stiff resistance and obliged the EU to water down its ambitions. A new 2008 proposal left out substantive disciplines and focused on transparency and predictability.[45] With respect to transparency, the EU proposed that existing transparency provisions, in particular notification obligations, be made operational: introduction and modification of export taxes should be notified. In order to ensure predictability, the EU text further proposed that export taxes should be scheduled and bound at levels to be negotiated.

Other proposals focused on increasing transparency in the field of export measures, rather than disciplining the measures *per se*. For instance, Japan proposed an Agreement to enhance transparency on export restrictions. This proposed Agreement, which is modelled on the WTO Agreement on Import Licensing, would contain procedures for publication of relevant rules and administrative measures in relation to export restrictions ("export licensing"), notification procedures to a Committee and publication of relevant statistics, such as domestic production.[46]

---

[43] Communication from the European Communities, Negotiating Proposal on Export Taxes, TN/MA/W/11/Add.6, 27th April, 2006.

[44] Art. 3.1 of the EC proposed text reads: "Export taxes may be maintained and listed in Members' schedules for a limited number of products, at low levels and only in so far as: a) they are necessary, in conjunction with domestic measures, to maintain financial stability, to satisfy fiscal needs, or to facilitate economic diversification and avoid excessive dependence on the export of primary products; and b) they do not adversely affect international trade by limiting the availability of goods to WTO Members in general or by raising world market prices of any goods beyond the prices that would prevail in the absence of such measures, or otherwise cause serious prejudice to the interests of developing country Members".

[45] Communication from the European Communities, Revised Submission on Export Taxes, TN/MA/W/101, 17th January, 2008.

[46] Communication from Japan, Text-Based Proposal for Negotiation on Enhanced Transparency on Export Restrictions, TN/MA/W/15/Add.4, 18th April, 2006.

In subsequent negotiations, the original Japanese proposal has received support from several other Members and was redrafted into a "Protocol on Transparency in Export Licensing" which includes detailed notification requirements, possibility for Members to request information regarding, *inter alia*, the administration of measures on export licensing, the export licences recently granted and measures taken in conjunction with export licensing.[47] This draft Protocol is contained nearly in extenso in the 4th Revised Draft of NAMA negotiations, issued in December 2008.[48]

Transit of Energy Products

The Principle of Freedom of Transit in the GATT[49]

In its Article V, the GATT establishes the principle of the freedom of transit for all goods. This provision, which is based on the 1921 Barcelona Convention and Statute on Freedom of Transit, has attracted very limited attention so far in the GATT/WTO. However, energy-related concerns have contributed to drag it out of oblivion.

Pursuant to Article V, goods are in transit when the passage across a country "is a portion of a journey beginning and terminating beyond the frontier" of the country across whose territory the traffic passes (Art. V:1). This provision further establishes that "there shall be freedom of transit through the territory of each contracting party, via the routes most convenient for international transit, for traffic in transit to or from the territory of other contracting parties. No distinction shall be made which is based on the flag of vessels, the place of origin, departure, entry, exit or destination, or on any circumstances relating to the ownership of goods, or vessels or of other means of transport" (Art. V:2). Countries must not subject transit traffic to "unnecessary delays or restrictions" and are not allowed to levy customs or transit duties on goods in transit. Transportation charges or charges commensurate with administrative expenses entailed by transit or with the cost of the services rendered may be levied. Charges and regulations imposed on traffic in transit must be "reasonable" having regard to the conditions of traffic. Transit countries are bound by the MFN obligation with respect to goods in transit and

---

[47] The last version is contained in Communication from Chile; Costa Rica; Japan; Republic of Korea; the Separate Customs Territory of Taiwan, Penghu, Kinmen and Matsu; Ukraine and the United States, Enhanced Transparency on Export Licensing, TN/MA/W/15/Add.4/Rev.7, 23rd November, 2010.

[48] TN/MA/W/103/Rev.3, p. 53.

[49] The content of this section builds on Cossy, Energy Transport and Transit in the WTO, in: Pauwelyn (ed.), *Global Challenges at the Intersection of Trade, Energy and the Environment*, Center for Economic Policy Research (CEPR), 2010.

cannot discriminate among WTO Members. Finally, it should be recalled that the obligations contained in GATT Article V apply only to WTO Members: goods traded between two WTO Members and transiting through a non-Member are not covered. For instance, oil and gas transiting through most of Central Asian countries are currently not subject to GATT transit disciplines as several of these countries are not yet WTO Members. However, most of them are currently negotiating their accession and transit issues are high on the agenda in these negotiations.

GATT Article V applies to all goods, and is, therefore, relevant for energy goods, including oil, gas and electricity.[50] However, the transportation of energy goods has characteristics different than those of other goods, which raises specific challenges when it comes to applying GATT Article V to energy transit.

First, some argue that GATT transit disciplines do not apply to fixed infrastructures, such as electricity grids or oil and gas pipelines, but cover only mobile modes of transport. Art. V does not seem to provide a textual basis for this view, though. This provision does not spell out all possible modes of transport, but refers instead more generally to "vessels" and "other modes of transport"; in fact, the only mode of transport excluded from the scope of the transit obligation (aircraft in transit) is explicitly mentioned in paragraph 7 of Art. V. While it is true that fixed infrastructures, such as pipelines and power grids, are not themselves in transit, the goods they transport are in transit and, thus, are covered by Article V: they fall under the broad definition of "traffic in transit" (para. 1). Hence, nothing in the text of GATT Article V seems to support a reading excluding transit through fixed infrastructure. The wish to exclude fixed infrastructure appears to stem from concerns that pipelines are somehow "different" from other modes of transport, in particular because they have limited available capacity, raise specific security and financial concerns, and also because they are often privately-owned. Concerns related to the different nature of transport via fixed infrastructure should nevertheless not be sufficient to justify an altogether exclusion of such modes of transport from the scope of Art. V. However, the specificities of grid-bound energy transport would have to be taken into account in the application of GATT Art. V. For instance, the concept of "most convenient" routes may have to go beyond mere geographical considerations in order to take into account the problem of limited available pipeline capacity.[51]

Article V:5 contains an MFN obligation with respect to charges, regulations and formalities imposed on transit goods and it might be argued that Article V:2 entails a form of national treatment obligation, which may be of limited usefulness in practice, i.e. requirements not to discriminate between foreign and national goods in transit. However, there is no requirement to treat goods in transit like goods

---

[50] There has been a long and still unsettled controversy as to whether electricity is a good or a service. The majority view seems to consider it as a good.

[51] See Azaria, Energy Transit Under the Energy Charter Treaty and the General Agreement on Tariffs and Trade, Journal of Energy & Natural Resources Law 27 (2009) 4, pp. 559–595.

imported to, or exported from, the domestic market, or like goods transported within the domestic market. Hence, goods in transit could be made subject to higher standards with respect to, for instance, environmental, safety and other traffic regulation, subject to the requirement that, as stipulated in Art. V:4, these remain "reasonable, having regard to the conditions of transit".

Transportation networks in the energy sector are often in the hands of powerful companies, whether public or private, which often are de facto, if not de jure, in a monopoly situation and, hence, can significantly influence the transit of energy goods. On the other hand, like other WTO provisions, Article V imposes obligations on WTO Members and it is unclear whether energy companies them- selves can be obliged to comply with GATT transit disciplines.[52] However, while WTO disciplines do not apply to non-state actors, there are cases in the WTO agreements where Members undertake that certain types of commercial entities, e.g. those with special privileges, comply with WTO standards (see, for instance, GATT Article XVII on state-trading enterprises and GATS Article VIII on monopolies and exclusive suppliers). Nothing, then, would prevent Members from including a similar disciplines in relation to transit.

Finally, the obligation to ensure freedom of transit through the "most convenient routes" means that the duty to grant free transit does not extend to all routes.[53] It also implies that transit must be granted through existing routes and, consequently, that Members are not obliged to build or allow the construction of new transit infrastructure.

There has been little practical experience in the GATT/WTO history with GATT Article V so far. This provision has only recently been applied in the dispute *Colombia – Indicative Prices and Restrictions on Ports of Entry*, and the Panel adopted a broad interpretation of the transit obligation. The Panel concluded, inter alia, that Article V:2, required that "goods from all Members must be ensured an identical level of access and equal conditions when proceeding in international transit."[54] As discussed by Azaria, the requirement to provide an "identical level of access"

---

[52] Note that the Panel in Korea – Various Measures on Beef described the legal status of Art. XVII:1(a) in the GATT framework in the following terms: "Article XVII.1(a) establishes the general obligation on state trading enterprises to undertake their activities in accordance with the GATT principles of non-discrimination. *The Panel considers that this general principle of non-discrimination includes at least the provisions of Articles I and III of GATT.*" (Report of the Panel, Korea – Various Measures on Beef, WT/DS161 and –/169, emphasis added, finding not reviewed by the Appellate Body). The question arises whether this finding might be broadened to include other GATT obligations, such as Art. V, or, at least, the non-discrimination obligations contained in Art. V.

[53] WTO, Article V of the GATT 1994 – Scope and Application, Note by the Secretariat, TN/TF/W/ 2, 12th January, 2005.

[54] Report of the Panel, Colombia – Indicative Prices and Restrictions on Ports, WT/DS366/R, circulated on 27th April, 2009. For a discussion of the possible consequences of applying the Panel's findings in this case to energy transit through fixed infrastructure, see Azaria, Energy Transit Under the Energy Charter Treaty and the General Agreement on Tariffs and Trade, Journal of Energy & Natural Resources Law, Vol. 27 No 4, 2009, pp. 559–595.

may be problematic in the case of fixed infrastructure because it may amount to granting a mandatory third-party access (TPA) to such infrastructure, something that not even the Energy Charter Treaty, nor its Draft Protocol on Transit have been able to do.[55] Hence, we would agree with this author that, in case of fixed infrastructure, the concept of "identical level of access" could only refer to the establishment of procedural rules, such as transparency requirements, granting owners of goods "identical possibilities to access the infrastructure".[56]

It is interesting to compare GATT Article V with the corresponding provision of the Energy Charter Treaty, i.e. Article 7, entitled "Transit". First, Article 7 of the ECT contains a more precise definition of transit and explicitly covers grid-bound energy transport, including high-pressure gas transmission pipelines, high-voltage electricity transmission grids and lines, crude oil transmission pipelines, and other facilities, such as pipelines for coal and oil products and port facilities. Paragraph 3 of Article 7 contains a form of national treatment obligation whereby each Party must treat energy materials and products in transit no less favourably than such materials and products when they are imported to or exported from its own territory. Thirdly, the transit provision of the ECT contains an obligation to allow the building of new capacity, i.e., "not to place obstacles in the way of new capacity being established" if transit cannot be achieved on commercial terms through existing capacity. Contracting Parties are nevertheless not obliged to permit the construction of new facilities if they demonstrate that such new capacity would endanger the security or efficiency of their energy systems, including the security of supply (Article 7(5)). Under paragraph 6, Parties are prohibited from interrupting or reduce transit flows when a transit-related dispute is pending. Finally, Article 7(7) contains a specific conciliation mechanism for disputes related to transit, providing, inter alia, for the appointment of an independent conciliator whose task will be to make recommendations in order to solve the dispute and who can fix interim transit tariffs for until the resolution of the dispute.

To conclude, Article 7 of the Energy Charter Treaty is much better equipped than GATT Art. V to deal with the specificities of energy transit, which entitles the Energy Charter Secretariat to claim that "Article 7 already represents the most elaborate set of multilateral legal obligations in existence dealing specifically with energy transit flows".[57] On the other hand, the DDA negotiations provide an opportunity to bridge the gap. Several proposals made in the Negotiating Group

---

[55] The article on third-party access in the draft Transit Protocol provides that owners or operators of transport facilities shall "negotiate in good faith with any other Contracting Parties or Entities of Contracting Parties requesting access to and use of Available Capacity for Transit". Hence, it grants negotiating rights to private parties, but does not ensure third-party access per se.

[56] Azaria, Energy Transit Under the Energy Charter Treaty and the General Agreement on Tariffs and Trade, Journal of Energy & Natural Resources Law, Vol. 27 No 4, 2009, p. 572.

[57] Energy Charter Secretariat, The Energy Charter Treaty – A Reader's Guide, available at: http://www.encharter.org/index.php?id=20.

on Trade Facilitation aim at addressing some of the weaknesses of GATT Article V identified above (see section below Transit Issues in the DDA Negotiations).

Transit Issues in WTO Accession Negotiations

The main "WTO+" obligations in relation to transport and transit of energy have been undertaken by Ukraine, which acceded to the WTO in 2008. Ukraine is a key transit country for gas coming from Russia and flowing to the European market and, unsurprisingly, its accession to the WTO was seen as an opportunity to strengthen disciplines for energy transit. Transit-related issues arise in two respects. First, in the Working Party Report, Ukraine confirmed that it

> would apply all its laws, regulations and other measures governing transit of goods (including energy), such as those governing charges for transportation of goods in transit, in conformity with the provisions of Article V of the GATT 1994 and other relevant provisions of the WTO Agreement.[58]

The specific reference to energy arguably aims at ensuring that Article V disciplines will apply to transport of gas irrespective of the means of transport, i.e. including transport through fixed infrastructure.

Second, in its GATS schedule, Ukraine has undertaken full market access and national treatment commitments, on modes 1–3, for pipeline transportation of fuels.[59] Ukraine also undertook an "additional commitment" for this sector, which reads as follows:

> Ukraine commits itself to provide full transparency in the formulation, adoption and application of measures affecting access to and trade in services of pipeline transportation.
>
> Ukraine undertakes to ensure adherence to the principles of non-discriminatory treatment in access to and use of pipeline networks under its jurisdiction, within the technical capacities of these networks, with regard to the origin, destination or ownership of product transported, without imposing any unjustified delays, restrictions or charges, as well as without discriminatory pricing based on the differences in origin, destination or ownership.[60]

---

[58] Report of the Working Party on the Accession of Ukraine to the World Trade Organization, WT/ACC/UKR/152, para. 367 (emphasis added).

[59] The 1991 United Nations Central Product Classification, which is being used by WTO Members for scheduling their specific commitments, defines pipeline transportation of fuels as follows: "transportation via pipeline of crude or refined petroleum and petroleum products and of natural gas" (CPC 7131). For basic information on key GATS concepts, see WTO Secretariat, The General Agreement on Trade in Services – An Introduction, 2006, available at: http://www.wto.org/english/tratop_e/serv_e/serv_e.htm.

[60] Ukraine – Schedule of Specific Commitments, GATS/SC/144, 10th March, 2008.

So far, Ukraine is the only Member which has listed such an additional commitment for pipeline transportation. Although it does not refer to "transit", this GATS commitment is meant to be read together with the transit obligation in GATT Art. V.

The first part of Ukraine's additional commitment goes further than the GATS transparency disciplines contained in Article III. For instance, the requirement to provide full transparency in the "formulation" of measures appears to go further than the notification requirement of GATS Article III:3 which only obliges Members to inform the Council for Trade in Services "of the introduction" of any new measures which "significantly affect trade in services". The reference to the "formulation" of measures might imply an obligation to provide information while the measure is still in the preparation phase. Moreover, Ukraine undertakes to provide information not only with respect to "trade in services", but also with respect to "measures affecting access to" pipeline transportation: the latter appears to be broader as it could arguably include information which any entity wishing to use a pipeline for the purpose of transporting its goods, such as available capacity, may wish to obtain, even though it is not a pipeline transportation service supplier stricto sensu.

The second sentence breaks new grounds as it appears to introduce a non-discriminatory third-party access obligation to Ukraine's pipelines. Leaving aside the question of how such an obligation will be eventually implemented in practice, this GATS additional commitment raises an interesting systemic issue in the WTO system as we are here on the dividing line between trade in goods and trade in services: obligations are included in a services schedule, but they appear to aim primarily at providing minimum access guarantees for the goods transported, rather than for the suppliers of pipeline transportation services. However, as I argued elsewhere, the GATS protects suppliers of services, in this case suppliers of pipelines transportation services. A company transporting its own goods is performing an in-house activity, but is not supplying a service. Therefore, while this additional commitment could arguably be invoked by entities transporting energy goods owned by other entities (and thus performing a transportation service) in order to access to and use a pipeline, it should not cover companies transporting their own goods, because these ought not be regarded as services suppliers and, thus, fall outside the scope of the GATS.[61] In any case, the relationship between the GATT transit obligation and GATS commitments on transportation services would need to be further clarified, beyond the case of energy and fixed infrastructure, as questions may also arise with respect to other modes of transport.

---

[61] Cossy, Energy Services Under the General Agreement on Trade in Services (GATS), in: Selivanova (ed.) *Energy Trade in WTO and Beyond: Current International Disciplines and Future Challenges*, Kluwer Law International BV, The Netherlands, 2011.

Transit Issues in the DDA Negotiations

Proposals to strengthen GATT Article V have been made at an early stage in the DDA negotiations and are being considered in the Negotiating Group on Trade Facilitation. Energy-related concerns clearly underpin several proposals.

In 2002, the European Communities proposed to consider several issues that may lead to possible clarifications or improvement of this provision. One of these issues reflects the concern to ensure non-discrimination between modes of transport in relation to transit procedures and to ensure that goods transiting via fixed infrastructure be covered. In this regard, the EC notes that

> [i]n addition to "classic" modes of transit such as air, road, rail or boat, it should be noted that the carriage e.g. of oil and gas and other products via pipelines or other means, may also fall within the scope of transit. WTO Members may wish to evaluate whether freedom of transit for such goods is effective and whether there is any need or scope for reassessing GATT Article V to take account of the special nature of this form of transit.[62]

A few years later, several Members tabled a proposal which also addresses the scope of GATT Article V and the specificities of transit of energy goods. First, these Members propose a definition of "traffic in transit" which would clarify, *inter alia*, that "goods in transit" includes "those moved via fixed infrastructure, *inter alia* pipelines and electricity grids". It would be further clarified that "[m]eans of transport shall be deemed to be traffic in transit also if they carry exclusively goods in transit, even if the means of transport are not themselves in transit ....".[63] This text would put an end to the controversy mentioned above, i.e. whether goods transiting through fixed infrastructure also benefit from the transit obligations contained in GATT Article V.

The same Members further propose to include an obligation whereby "[e]ach Member undertakes that if it grants to any enterprise, formally or in effect, exclusive or special privileges, such enterprise shall, in its regulations, formalities, fees and charges – including transportation charges –, on or in connection with traffic in transit, act in a manner consistent with the provisions on traffic in transit of this Agreement and otherwise solely in accordance with commercial considerations".[64]

---

[62] Communication from the European Communities, WTO Trade Facilitation – Strengthening WTO Rules on GATT Article V on Freedom of Transit, G/C/W/422, 30th September, 2002. The EC also notes "the need to better clarify the interface between the freedom of transit for third country vehicles and vessels guaranteed by GATT Article V and the fact that, under the GATS, the right to provide a transport service in or across the territory of a third country depends on specific commitments having been made by that third country".

[63] Proposal by The Former Yugoslav Republic of Macedonia, Mongolia, Switzerland and Swaziland, Transit – Third Revision of Textual Proposal, TN/TF/W/133/Rev.3, 26th June, 2009, para. 1.

[64] Id., para. 2.

This text seems to be based on GATT Article XVII ("State Trading Enterprises")[65] and aims at ensuring that disciplines regulating freedom of transit are not circumvented by state or private enterprises with special privileges or monopolies affecting freedom in transit. As noted by the sponsors of the proposal, at the time of drafting GATT Article V, most infrastructure relevant for transit was government-owned.[66] However, the situation has changed, with the privatization of infrastructure such as railways, ports or airports, and, in the energy sector, companies are frequently granted a monopoly or other types of exclusive rights over transportation infrastructures, like a pipeline or an electricity grid.

A third element worth mentioning is the proposal to include a form of national treatment between goods in transit, on the one hand, and goods imported/exported by the transit country: "[w]ith respect to all [laws, regulations, formalities], fees and charges, including transportation charges imposed on or in connection with transit, each Member shall accord to traffic in transit to or from the territory of any Member, treatment no less favourable than that accorded to its own export or import traffic. This principle refers to like products being transported on the same route under like conditions."[67]

The latest version of the "Draft Consolidated Negotiated Text" produced by the Negotiating Group on Trade Facilitation includes an article 11, entitled "Freedom of Transit", which takes on board a number of these proposals, although in a heavily bracketed manner.[68] First the text would state that goods subject to GATT Article V would include those moved "via fixed infrastructure, inter alia pipelines and electricity grids", thus dispelling any doubt in this regard. The text would further clarify that

> [f]or greater certainty, nothing in Article V of the GATT 1994 or this Agreement shall be construed to require a Member:
> (a) to build infrastructure of any kind in its territory, or to permit the building of infrastructure by others, in order to facilitate the transit of goods;

---

[65] Art. XVII(1) reads as follows: (a) Each contracting party undertakes that if it establishes or maintains a State enterprise, wherever located, or grants to any enterprise, formally or in effect, exclusive or special privileges,* such enterprise shall, in its purchases or sales involving either imports or exports, act in a manner consistent with the general principles of non-discriminatory treatment prescribed in this Agreement for governmental measures affecting imports or exports by private traders. (b) The provisions of subparagraph (a) of this paragraph shall be understood to require that such enterprises shall, having due regard to the other provisions of this Agreement, make any such purchases or sales solely in accordance with commercial considerations,* including price, quality, availability, marketability, transportation and other conditions of purchase or sale, and shall afford the enterprises of the other contracting parties adequate opportunity, in accordance with customary business practice, to compete for participation in such purchases or sales.

[66] Negotiating Group on Trade Facilitation, Summary Minutes of the Meeting Held from 13th–17th October, 2008, TN/TF/M/26, para. 16.

[67] Proposal by The Former Yugoslav Republic of Macedonia, Mongolia, Switzerland and Swaziland, Transit – Third Revision of Textual Proposal, TN/TF/W/133/Rev.3, 26th June, 2009, para. 6.

[68] Negotiating Group on Trade Facilitation, Draft Consolidated Negotiating Text – Revision, TN/TF/W/165/Rev.7, 25th February, 2011. The text is reproduced here without brackets.

(b) to provide access to any infrastructure for transit unless such infrastructure is open to general use by third parties. For the purpose of this Agreement, the term "general use by third parties" does not include access to infrastructure granted on a contractual basis.

Sub-paragraph (a) would confirm that GATS Article V does not entail an obligation to build new infrastructure, which shows that WTO Members are not in a position to accept an obligation similar to Article 7(4) of the ECT whereby Parties undertake to promote the development of their network ("shall not place obstacles in the way of new capacity being established") in the event existing facilities do not allow to achieve transit on commercial term. Sub-paragraph (b) could be relevant for energy transport facilities like pipelines, where access is often granted on a contractual basis by the owners of the facility. This provision would, as a minimum, exclude any form of third-party access obligation with respect to privately-owned infrastructure like pipelines.

Another interesting provision, which reflects the proposal mentioned above, would require that Member governments oblige state enterprises or other enterprises to comply with the WTO transit obligation.[69] Finally, it is also proposed to introduce a form of national treatment to ensure that goods in transit are treated no less favourably than imported/exported goods and/or goods in domestic traffic.[70] These two provisions would echo similar obligations contained in, respectively, paragraphs (6) and (3) of Article 7 of the ECT.

The proposals highlighted in this section remain under negotiations and it is impossible to predict at this stage what the final agreement will look like. However, the very fact that these issues are being discussed confirms that WTO transit disciplines are relevant for energy trade and, should there sufficient political will by Members, could be further strengthened in order to better take into account the specificities of this sector.

Conclusion

The energy landscape is undergoing a period of turbulences and fundamental socio-economic choices will have to be made in a near future. Lack of reliable and affordable primary energy supply is a factor of economic instability, social unrest

---

[69] The current draft reads as follows (Art. 11.2): "Each Member undertakes that if it establishes or maintains a State enterprise or if an enterprise has, formally or in effect, exclusive or special privileges, such enterprise shall, in its regulations, formalities [fees] and charges – including transportation charges –, on or in connection with traffic in transit, comply with the provisions on traffic in transit of this Agreement and otherwise act solely in accordance with commercial considerations".

[70] The current draft reads as follows (Art. 11.5): "With respect to all regulations and formalities imposed on or in connection with traffic in transit, including charges for transportation, traffic regulations, safety regulations and environmental regulations, Members shall accord to traffic in transit treatment no less favourable than that accorded to export or import traffic/domestic traffic/traffic which is not in transit. This principle refers to like products being transported on the same route under like conditions".

and may even degenerate into armed conflicts. There are mounting tensions over diminishing resources, in particular as developing countries are claiming an increasing share of these resources to support their economic growth. The promotion of energy efficiency and the development of cleaner energy sources are becoming unavoidable if we want to respond to the threats posed by climate change.

As stated by its Director General, Pascal Lamy, the WTO can make an important contribution to the complex energy chessboard. More predictable and transparent trade rules could benefit both energy-importing and energy-exporting countries, and, beyond them, companies engaged in energy trade, as well as consumers.[71] This statement echoed the conclusions of the World Energy Council that "governments must maintain open energy markets, seek ways to expand international co-operation, and apply measures affecting energy trade, investment, and movement of persons that are fully consistent" with the GATT and other WTO agreements.[72]

On the other hand, the set of WTO rules is not always appropriate to address all the specificities of the energy sector. The dichotomy between disciplines for goods and services, the lack of a comprehensive investment regime, the focus on import measures are some of the weaknesses affecting the application of WTO rules to energy trade.

While the Appellate Body decision on *US – Softwood Lumber IV* obliges us to qualify the statement that WTO rules do not apply to natural resources in their "natural state", this decision should not affect Members' decision as to whether exploiting a natural resource. This dispute indicates that natural resources in their "natural state" which are not the object of any kind of economic transaction, because, for instance, there is an explicit policy objective to protect them (total prohibition to harvest certain species of trees or to extract hydrocarbons in certain protected areas, for instance) would not fall under WTO disciplines. Moreover, in the services negotiations, Members have consistently stressed that natural resources were under the sovereignty of each government and that the question of access to, or ownership of natural resources was not on the negotiating table. Furthermore, the GATS applies to trade in services, i.e. to service suppliers which do not normally own the raw material in relation to which they provide services. Hence, it should not be possible to use the GATS as a basis for claiming any type of ownership or access right to natural resources.

GATT disciplines for export restrictions are weaker than those for import restrictions, which may prove to be problematic as the former tend to be more prevalent than the latter when it comes to trade in natural resources, including energy resources. In the past, the various attempts to strengthen these disciplines have proved difficult. Nevertheless, "WTO+" obligations have been undertaken in this regard by countries which have acceded to the WTO over the last 15 years, and the DDA negotiations also offer an opportunity to revisit this issue.

---

[71] Pascal Lamy, Speech at the 20th World Energy Congress, November 2007, available at: http://www.wto.org/english/news_e/sppl_e/sppl80_e.htm.

[72] World Energy Council, Trade and Investment Rules for Energy, 2009.

The principle of freedom of transit established in GATT Art. V is of key importance in the energy sector. It might be desirable, however, to clarify and reinforce the current provisions in order to better serve transit of energy goods. Here again, several proposals, which appear to be directly motivated by energy-related concerns, are being considered in the DDA negotiations.

While there is no sign that a WTO "Agreement on Energy" will emerge in a near future, WTO rules can develop incrementally through negotiations, in order to better address the specificities of energy trade and case-law will also contribute to the clarification of existing disciplines.

Acknowledgments Views and opinions expressed in this paper are personal and cannot be attributed to WTO Members or the WTO Secretariat. I want to thank Gabrielle Marceau for her useful comments on this paper.

The Energy Charter and the International Energy Governance*

Yulia Selivanova

Introduction

The Energy Charter Treaty is unique as a multilateral treaty,[1] indeed it is the only international legally binding agreement specific to the energy sector.

The Energy Charter process started after the break-up of the Berlin wall. There was a need for energy resources in Western Europe and need of the former Soviet Republics for investments to exploit their resources. Therefore the discussions on how to develop energy cooperation in the region started. For energy producing countries in the territory of the former Soviet Union export of energy was the major source of revenue. To secure the capital inflow they needed to upgrade their energy infrastructure and technology.

The European Energy Charter Declaration signed in 1991 was initiated by the Prime Minister of the Netherlands Lubbers in reaction to the collapse of the USSR.[2]

The views expressed in this chapter are strictly personal and should not be attributed to the Secretariat or the Contracting Parties of the Energy Charter Treaty.

*First published in Yulia Selivanova (ed.) "Regulation of Energy in International Trade Law: WTO, NAFTA and Energy Charter", Kluwer Law International, 2011.

[1] Bamberger/Linehan/Waelde, The Energy Charter Treaty in 2000: In a New Phase, in: Roggenkamp (ed.), *Energy Law in Europe*, 2000.

[2] The Final Act of the European Charter Conference describes best the beginning of the process: 'During the meeting of the European Council in Dublin in June 1990, the Prime Minister of the Netherlands suggested that economic recovery in Eastern Europe and the then Union of Soviet Socialist Republics could be catalysed and accelerated by cooperation in the energy sector. This suggestion was welcomed by the Council, which invited the Commission of the European Communities to study how best to implement such cooperation. In February 1991 the Commission proposed the concept of a European Energy Charter. Following discussions of the Commission's

Y. Selivanova (✉)
Energy Charter Secretariat, Brussels, Belgium
e-mail: yulia.selivanova@encharter.org

C. Herrmann and J.P. Terhechte (eds.), *European Yearbook of International Economic Law (EYIEL), Vol. 3 (2012)*, European Yearbook of International Economic Law 3, DOI 10.1007/978-3-642-23309-8_10, © Springer-Verlag Berlin Heidelberg 2012

The document, not being a binding agreement but rather a declaration of common principles between signing states, emphasized two sets of objectives: safeguarding the energy supply security of the West and providing necessary capital and technology for exploration of the energy resources of the East. Thereby the Energy Charter process contributed to development of the economies in transition.[3] The broader objective of the Energy Charter process was to serve as a political and legal foundation for East-West cooperation.

The European Energy Charter Declaration represents a political commitment to cooperation in the energy sector, based on common objectives and principles such as development of open and efficient energy markets; creation of conditions that will stimulate the flow of private investments and the participation of private enterprises; non-discrimination among participants; respect for state sovereignty over natural resources; recognition of the importance of environmentally sound and energy-efficient policies.[4]

The European Energy Charter Declaration also emphasized the need for the establishment of an appropriate international legal framework for energy cooperation between participants. Whereas the declaration was a political document, it gave impetus for creation of a legally binding international framework – consequently, the Energy Charter Treaty (ECT) was signed in December 1994.[5] Article 2 of the ECT sets forth its purpose 'to promote long-term cooperation in the energy field, based on complementarities and mutual benefits', Article 3 imposes an obligation 'to work to promote access to international markets on commercial terms, and generally to develop an open and competitive market, for Energy Materials and Products'.[6] Through its mandatory unique framework, the ECT 'increases

---

proposal in the Council of the European Communities, the European Communities invited other countries of Western and Eastern Europe, the Union of Soviet Socialist Republics and the non-European members of the Organisation for Economic Co-operation and Development to attend a conference in Brussels in July 1991 to launch negotiations on the European Energy Charter. A number of other countries and international organizations were invited to attend the European Energy Charter Conference as observers.' See The Energy Charter Secretariat, The Energy Charter Treaty and Related Documents. A Legal Framework for International Energy Cooperation, p. 25, available at: www.encharter.org/fileadmin/user_upload/document/EN.pdf (last visited on 15th August, 2010).

[3] Bamberger/Linehan/Waelde, The Energy Charter Treaty in 2000: In a New Phase, in: Roggenkamp (ed.), *Energy Law in Europe*, 2000, p. 2.

[4] Energy Charter Secretariat, The Energy Charter Treaty. A Reader's Guide, 2002, p. 8.

[5] Negotiations on the ECT started in 1992 and could be successfully concluded after a period of three years. The ECT was signed in Lisbon on 17th December, 1994, and entered into force on 16th April, 1998.

[6] The role of the European Energy Charter declaration is significant as it should be taken into account in interpreting the ECT, since the ECT's preamble makes clear that the Treaty is intended to provide the basis for implementing the principles contained in the Charter; Bamberger/Linehan/ Waelde, The Energy Charter Treaty in 2000: In a New Phase, in: Roggenkamp (ed.), *Energy Law in Europe*, 2000, p. 3.

confidence by investors and the financial community and promotes investment and trade flow among members'.[7]

The ECT contains a unique set of rights and obligations of a 'hard law' nature, enforceable in legally binding arbitration or through GATT-type dispute resolution.[8] Those lie in investment protection, trade, transit provisions of the Treaty. Furthermore, the ECT contains 'soft law' provisions on energy efficiency and environmental aspects,[9] competition, technology transfer and access to capital.

The ECT is the only multilateral intergovernmental agreement in energy field that has legally binding rules backed up by a dispute settlement mechanism. It is also the first binding multilateral agreement in the promotion and protection of foreign investment in the energy field. Finally, it is the first multilateral instrument that sets forth detailed principles of energy transit.[10]

The importance of the ECT's role is accentuated by the fact that it is the only forum that is open to all countries along the energy chain: producers, consumers and transit states; industrialized, transition and developing economies. The Energy Charter process gained a global dimension: Japan, Mongolia as well as Central Asian states of Kazakhstan, Kyrgyzstan, Tajikistan, Turkmenistan and Uzbekistan are Contracting Parties of the ECT. The Treaty has been signed and acceded by 51 states. Furthermore, the United States,[11] Canada, China, Algeria, Venezuela and many Middle East energy producing states have observer status.[12]

It is important to note what the ECT does not do: the ECT does not prescribe the structure of domestic energy sector, ownership of energy companies or oblige member countries to open up their energy sector to foreign investors. One of the remarkable features of the Treaty is its provision confirming the principle of national sovereignty over energy resources in Article 18. ECT Contracting Parties

---

[7] Sussman, The Energy Charter Treaty's Investor Protection Provisions: Potential to Foster Solutions to Global Warming and Promote Sustainable Development, Oil, Gas & Energy Law Intelligence 6 (2008) 3, p. 2.

[8] Bamberger, *The Energy Charter Treaty. A Description of Its Provisions*, 1995.

[9] The Protocol on Energy Efficiency and Related Environmental Aspects entered into force simultaneously with the Treaty on 16th April, 1998.

[10] Selivanova, Managing the Patchwork of Agreements in Trade and Investment, in: Goldthau/Witte (eds.), *Global Energy Governance: The New Rules of the Game*, 2010, pp. 49–72.

[11] United States actively participated in the ECT negotiations but decided not to join the Treaty for the following reported reasons: investment protection under the ECT is not as strong as in the bilateral agreements concluded by the United States; there is a potential conflict between the ECT's unconditional provision of the MFN and the Jackson-Vanik Amendment to the 1970 U.S. Trade Act; it would be difficult to ensure that the ECT is implemented on a sub-federal level. Furthermore, it was reported that the US did not become a party to the treaty because it was not clear how to bind the States at the pre-investment stage which relates to resources access conditions, Sussman, The Energy Charter Treaty's Investor Protection Provisions: Potential to Foster Solutions to Global Warming and Promote Sustainable Development, Oil, Gas & Energy Law Intelligence 6 (2008) 3, p. 7.

[12] Lists of ECT's members and observers are available at: www.encharter.org/index.php?id=61 (last visited on 15th August, 2010).

are free to develop their energy resources in a manner and in accordance with national policy objectives. The states are free to decide the extent to which they will open their energy sector to foreign investments. Lastly, the ECT does not impose mandatory third-party access to energy infrastructure.

ECT Key Provisions and Disciplines

Sovereignty over Natural Resources

The ECT is the only international treaty that explicitly proclaims state sovereignty over countries' resources.[13] Its Contracting Parties recognize state sovereignty and sovereign rights over energy resources. These must be however exercised in accordance with and subject to the rules of international law. Contracting Parties are free to choose the governing system of property ownership of energy resources. Furthermore, each state can freely decide the geographical areas to be made available for exploration and development of its energy resources, the optimization of their recovery and the rate at which they may be depleted or otherwise exploited, to specify and enjoy any taxes, royalties or other payments for such exploration and exploitation. It is also the right of resource owning states to regulate the environmental and safety aspects of such exploration and development. At the same time the Contracting Parties undertake to facilitate access to energy resources, *inter alia*, by allocating in a non-discriminatory manner on the basis of published criteria authorizations, licenses, concessions and contracts to prospect and explore for or to exploit or extract energy resources. The latter provision was perceived sometimes with apprehension by resource owning states, as it could arguably be interpreted as to impose foreign access to energy resources.

The ECT Trade Framework

A distinctive feature of the Energy Charter Treaty is that it provides a set of rules that covers the entire energy chain, including not only investments in production

---

[13] However, before the ECT was negotiated, the UN General Assembly Resolution 626 (VII) of 21st December, 1952 recommended all Member States "to refrain from acts direct and indirect, designed to impede the exercise of the sovereignty of any state over its natural resources", – see General Assembly Resolution 626 (VII), www.un.org/documents/ga/res/7/ares7.htm (last visited on 15th August, 2010). Later General Assembly resolution 1803 (XVII) of 14th December, 1962 on "Permanent sovereignty over natural resources" recognized that "The right of peoples and nations to permanent sovereignty over their natural wealth and resources must be exercised in the interest of their national development and of the well-being of the people of the State concerned."

and generation but also the terms under which energy can be traded and transported across various national jurisdictions to international markets.

The ECT trade framework is based on the rules of the multilateral trade system as set forth in GATT and other WTO Agreements.[14] Non-derogation from WTO rules is the cornerstone of the ECT trade regime.[15]

Through 'WTO by reference' approach, the ECT applies the rules of the WTO to trade of Contracting Parties that are not members of the WTO,[16] both in those countries' relations with WTO members and in their relations with one another. The ECT therefore has the effect of treating those of its members, which are not members of the WTO, as if they were WTO members – in the framework of energy related trade.[17]

The trade provisions of the ECT cover a wide range of energy materials and products including coal, natural gas, oil, petroleum and petroleum products, electricity, charcoal and nuclear energy. Interestingly, the list does not include renewable energies.[18] This may be explained by the fact that at the time when the Treaty was negotiated – in the beginning of 1990s – development of renewable energies was just starting. Arguably, the Treaty could still play a major role for the renewable energy sector, since most types of renewable energies are used for electricity generation and electrical energy is included in the ECT list of Energy Materials and Products covered by the Treaty.

Trade Amendment

Since the ECT was negotiated at the same time as the WTO Agreements, it first contained reference only to GATT. It was then amended to take into account relevant changes in the multilateral trade rules that resulted from the Uruguay Round. The Trade Amendment,[19] apart from incorporating relevant WTO rules,[20] contained several essential additions to the ECT trade regime.

---

[14] Annex EQ I.

[15] Art. 4 provides: "Nothing in this Treaty shall derogate, as between particular Contracting Parties which are parties to the GATT, from the provisions of the GATT and Related Instruments as they are applied between those Contracting Parties."

[16] As of August 2011, this was relevant for seven member countries of the Energy Charter Treaty that are not yet members of the WTO.

[17] Energy Charter Secretariat, The Energy Charter Treaty. A Reader's Guide, 2002, p. 13.

[18] The covered energy products are listed in Annex EM I.

[19] The Trade Amendment entered into force on 21st January, 2010.

[20] Not all WTO rules are applicable under the ECT (See Annexes G and W). It was decided for instance not to incorporate provisions of the WTO General Agreement on Trade in Services (GATS). However, trade in services is indirectly addressed by the ECT, in particular through the ECT provisions on investment.

The trade provisions of the ECT originally only applied to trade in energy materials and products. The Trade Amendment extended the ECT trade rules to energy-related equipment. As a result, the ECT trade regime now covers more than seventy categories of items of energy-related equipment, such as pipelines, fittings, turbines, nuclear reactors, power masts, furnaces, platforms, transformers, pumps, etc.[21] This is a significant enlargement of the scope of the ECT as it ensures access to equipment on a non-discriminatory basis, both in terms of most-favoured nation treatment and national treatment.

Furthermore, the Trade Amendment foresees a facilitated procedure for moving to bound tariff regime for the covered products, if the ECT members decide to create such a regime.[22] Before such regime is created, the ECT contains only 'best endeavour' obligation with respect to tariffs on covered products.[23] In annual reviews, the Energy Charter Conference has to examine the possibility of moving to bound tariffs regime.[24] Under the Amendment, for such a change only a Conference decision by unanimous vote is required without the need to go through a formal Treaty amendment procedure.

Amendments to the WTO Agreement insofar as they amend or relate to the ECT trade provisions apply automatically under the Trade Amendment – unless a Contracting Party requests the Energy Charter Conference to disapply or modify such amendment.[25]

The ECT trade obligations are applicable not only to government bodies administering trade policies but also to energy monopolies. The Amendment provides that if any Contracting Party establishes, maintains or authorizes, formally or in effect, a monopoly of the importation or exportation of any Energy Material or Product or in respect of Energy-Related Equipment, such monopoly shall not operate so as to afford protection on the average in excess of the amount of protection permitted by the standstill obligation provided for in Article 29(6) or (7).[26]

---

[21] Annex EQ I.

[22] The possibility to move to a future legally binding commitment for agreed items which are presently subject to the best endeavours commitment is foreseen by paras. (6) and (7) of amended Art. 29.

[23] However, any increase of import duties is subject to a notification obligation and consultation procedure (Art. 29(5)).

[24] Items subject to a legally binding tariff commitment will be listed in Annexes EM II and EQ II, both of which are empty until the Conference decides otherwise. In case of a respective decision of the Conference, Contracting Parties may not increase any customs duty or charge of any kind imposed on or in connection with importation or exportation of respective Energy Materials and Products or Energy-Related Equipment above the rates applied on the date of the decision by the Charter Conference to list the particular item in the relevant Annex.

[25] In this case, the Energy Charter Conference shall take the decision by a three-fourths majority of the Contracting Parties and determine the date of the disapplication or modification of such amendment. Such a request to the Conference can be made within six months of the circulation of a notification from the Secretariat that the amendment has taken effect under the WTO Agreement. Annex W (B)(10)(b).

[26] Annex W (B)(4)(iv).

Trade Disputes

In respect of trade-related disputes, the Treaty provides for a dispute resolution mechanism[27] that is based on the GATT/WTO panel model.[28] It applies only in cases where at least one of the disputing parties is not a member of the WTO.[29]

As a general rule, dispute settlement under Article 29(7) is a substitute for state-to-state arbitration under Article 27 and investor-to-state arbitration under Article 26. Nevertheless, if both parties to a dispute agree they could submit a trade-related dispute (including a dispute on trade-related investment matters (TRIMs)) to arbitration under Article 27.[30] Moreover, Article 29 does not exclude that foreign investors may bring actions relating to TRIMs under Article 26.[31] There are two main differences between the ECT and the WTO dispute settlement system. The ECT panel's report is subject to adoption by the Charter Conference by a vote of three-fourth of those present and voting, provided that at least a simple majority of all CPs to the Treaty supports the decision. This is different from the WTO procedures, where panel reports are automatically adopted unless disapproved by consensus. Therefore, the Treaty retains an element of political decision-making.[32] The second difference lies in the absence of the appellate body under the ECT.

The Trade Amendment specifies that the ECT Panels resolving trade disputes shall be guided by the interpretations given to the WTO Agreement within the framework of the WTO Agreement. They cannot question the compatibility with Article 5 or 29 of practices applied by any Contracting Party which is a member of the WTO to other members of the WTO and which have not been taken by those other members to dispute resolution under the WTO Agreement. However, in the absence of a relevant interpretation of the WTO Agreement adopted by the Ministerial Conference or the General Council of the WTO concerning provisions applicable under Article 29(2)(a), the Charter Conference may adopt an interpretation.[33]

---

[27] Annex D.

[28] Art. 29(7).

[29] Disputes between two WTO members that are also ECT members are to be resolved in the WTO dispute settlement forum.

[30] Art. 28.

[31] See Art. 5 and 10(11).

[32] Energy Charter Secretariat, The Energy Charter Treaty. A Reader's Guide, 2002, p. 56.

[33] Annex W(B)(1).

Transit

The Charter promotes development of trade in energy by, *inter alia*, facilitating access to transport infrastructure for international transit purposes in order to improve security of energy supply. Transit regime is perceived as an important tool for guaranteeing energy security.[34] Indeed, energy products (and hydrocarbons in particular) are transported over increasingly large distances from producers to consumers. In the case of natural gas, most of which is transported by pipeline, this often involves crossing different national borders. Bilateral disputes over energy transit can have adverse implications for energy security of the whole region, underlining the importance of multilaterally accepted standards to promote reliability of cross-border energy flows.

It was felt that general provisions on transit contained in GATT were not sufficiently detailed because transit transactions in the energy sector are becoming more and more complex. This is especially true with respect to transit fees for access to transit pipelines.[35] Congestions management and construction of new infrastructure in case of need were not addressed by international rules. More elaborate provisions were thus thought to be needed in addition to GATT Article V to ensure transit on reasonable terms based on the balance between the sovereign interests of states and the need for security and stability of transit.[36]

The Treaty addresses in a detailed manner the important strategic issue of energy transit. Although ECT provisions on transit essentially reiterate the principle of freedom of transit contained in Article V GATT, they are more detailed and oriented towards energy-related transit issues. Similarly to GATT Article V, current Treaty transit provisions contained in Article 7 oblige participating states to take the necessary measures to facilitate transit of energy, consistent with the principle of freedom of transit, and to secure established energy flows. Article 7 has been commented upon as 'the most significant instance in the ECT of a 'GATT-plus' trade provision creating new forms of rights and obligations'.[37]

Indeed, the ECT transit regime contains several elements that are absent in a more general GATT framework. For instance, the ECT members are under obligation not to obstruct creation of new capacity if transit cannot be carried out

---

[34] See Declaration adopted by the Energy Charter Conference, 17th December, 2001. The Conference has declared that strengthening energy supply security throughout the Energy Charter's constituency is a priority for the cooperation in the Charter process. In this context the conference linked supply security to transit and the adoption of the draft Transit Protocol. See Azaria Energy Transit under the Energy Charter Treaty and the General Agreement on Tariffs and Trade, Journal of Energy and Natural Resources Law 27 (2009) 4, pp. 559–596.

[35] Energy Charter Secretariat, The Energy Charter Treaty. A Reader's Guide, 2002, p. 29.

[36] Ibid.

[37] Bamberger, *The Energy Charter Treaty. A Description of Its Provisions*, 1995, p. 13.

through existing infrastructure due to lack of capacity.[38] Transit countries are also under an obligation not to interrupt or reduce existing transit flows, even if they have disputes with another country concerning this transit.[39] There is a special conciliation procedure foreseen for resolution of transit disputes.[40]

The Transit Protocol to the ECT, the negotiations of which are pending, would elaborate in more detail some specific aspects of energy transit, such as conditions for access to networks and methodologies for calculation of transit tariffs.

The speedy resolution of disputes is of a particular importance in transit matters, because such disputes have a potential to undermine energy supply security in large territories. The typical dispute resolution mechanisms are too lengthy to resolve disputes in a reasonable amount of time. Article 7(7) gives the ECT members the possibility to invoke a conciliation mechanism concerning transit disputes. As compared to regular dispute settlement procedures under Article 27, conciliation might have the advantage of being faster and less formal. There are however unresolved issues of Article 7(7) interpretation, which might impede the use of the conciliation provision by the ECT Member States.

The ECT Investment Framework[41]

The need for stability in the relationship between investors and host governments is particularly acute in the energy sector, where projects tend to be long-term and highly capital-intensive. The perceived degree of political risks in the host country considerably affects the decision of foreign companies whether to make an investment in the first place or not, and what level of return it would require.[42] The goal of the investment protection regime is to 'create a 'level playing field' for investments in the energy sector and to minimize the non-commercial risks associated with such investments'.[43] By reducing the political risks that foreign investors face in the host country, the ECT seeks to boost investor confidence and to contribute to an increase in international investment flows. The ECT's investment provisions build upon the content of bilateral investment treaties as they have developed during the last half-century.[44]

---

[38] Art. 7(4) of the ECT.

[39] Art. 7(6) of the ECT.

[40] Art. 7(7) of the ECT. See L. Ehring & Y. Selivanova "Energy Transit" in Y. Selivanova (ed.) "Regulation of Energy in International Trade Law: WTO, NAFTA and Energy Charter", Kluwer Law International (2011).

[41] The ECT's principal investment provisions are contained in Part III of the Treaty.

[42] Energy Charter Secretariat, The Energy Charter Treaty. A Reader's Guide, 2002, p. 19.

[43] Hober, Investment Arbitration and the Energy Charter Treaty, Journal of International Dispute Settlement, 1 (2010) 1, pp. 153–190 (155).

[44] Ibid.

The Energy Charter Treaty takes a balanced approach to investors' access to resources. On the one hand, the Treaty is explicit in confirming national sovereignty over energy resources: each member country is free to decide how, and to what extent, its national and sovereign energy resources will be developed,[45] and also the extent to which its energy sector will be opened to foreign investments.[46] On the other hand, there is a requirement that rules on the exploration, development and acquisition of resources are publicly available, non-discriminatory and transparent.

The scope of the investment protection of the ECT is determined by the definitions of 'Investment' and 'Economic Activity in the Energy Sector'.[47] The ECT's definition of an 'investment' is broad, non-exhaustive and 'asset-based'.[48] 'Investment' means every kind of asset, owned or controlled directly or indirectly by an investor.[49] The Treaty mentions – in a non-exclusive list – tangible and intangible, moveable and immovable property; shares, stocks, or other forms of equity participation in a company; bonds and other debt of a company; claims to money and claims to performance pursuant to a contract having an economic value associated with an investment; intellectual property; returns; any right conferred by law, contract or license. Changes in the form of investments do not affect their character as investments. The definition also covers assets that are indirectly owned or controlled by the investor (e.g., assets owned by a holding company). 'Control' covers both equity interests of the investor and the ability to exercise substantial influence over the company.

The term Investment refers to any investment 'associated with an Economic Activity in the Energy Sector'.[50] The latter means an economic activity concerning the exploration, extraction, refining, production, storage, land transport, transmission, distribution, trade, marketing, or sale of energy materials and products.[51] However fuel wood, charcoal, and the distribution of heat to multiple premises are excluded from the definition for investment purposes. Bamberger observes that the extension of the definition of 'Investment' to investments 'associated with' an 'Economic Activity in the Energy Sector' 'attenuates the sectoral restriction of the Treaty's protections and dispute resolution mechanisms':

---

[45] See Art. 18 of the ECT and s. II.A above.

[46] Mernier, The Rules of Energy Trade, Speech of at the World Energy Council, 12th November, 2007.

[47] Art. 1(5)(6) of the ECT. The definition sets forth that the term "Investment" refers to any investment "associated with an Economic Activity in the Energy Sector", which is related to the definition of 'Energy Materials and Products'.

[48] Energy Charter Secretariat, The Energy Charter Treaty. A Reader's Guide, 2002, p. 20.

[49] According to Art. 1(6).

[50] Art. 1(5).

[51] Annex EM lists those 'Energy Materials and Products' that are covered by the Treaty. These include nuclear energy (e.g., uranium, other radioactive chemical elements, heavy water), coal, natural gas, petroleum, petroleum products, and electrical energy.

[I]t can provide a basis for claiming coverage, for example, with respect to otherwise uncovered petrochemical facilities within an oil refinery complex, or maritime transportation that is 'associated with' a covered on-land investment'.[52]

The ECT members undertake to encourage and create stable, equitable, favourable and transparent conditions for investors to make investments.[53] Such conditions include a commitment to accord at all times to investments of investors of other CPs fair and equitable treatment.[54] The Treaty provides that investments 'shall also enjoy the most constant protection and security'; and in no way be impaired in their management, maintenance, use, enjoyment or disposal by 'unreasonable or discriminatory measures'.[55] Moreover, it is a violation of a Contracting Party's obligations under the ECT to breach an investment agreement: 'Each Contracting Party shall observe any obligations it has entered into with an Investor or an Investment of an Investor of any other Contracting Party'.[56]

The investment disciplines of the ECT are divided in those applied to 'pre-investment' stage[57] and applied to 'post-investment'. While negotiating the ECT, it was initially intended to extend the principle of non-discrimination to the making of an investment. As a result, foreign investors would have been on equal legal footing with their domestic competitors in the host country when applying for an investment authorization or any other kind of permission necessary for their establishment.[58] However it was impossible to reach the necessary agreement to apply the 'national treatment' standard on a legally binding basis to the 'pre-investment' stage. That led to deferral of this subject to a 'second-phase' negotiation of a 'Supplementary Treaty', mandated by the ECT, and encompassing issues of

---

[52] Bamberger/Linehan/Waelde, The Energy Charter Treaty in 2000: In a New Phase, in: Roggenkamp (ed.), *Energy Law in Europe*, 2000, p. 5.

[53] According to Art. 10(1).

[54] Hober notes in this respect: "This standard of 'fair and equitable treatment' is derived from international law, and has, through its frequent application by tribunals in BIT and NAFTA arbitrations, become an important principle of investment protection. Although certain principles have developed in arbitral practice (good faith, protection of legitimate expectations, due process, proportionality, etc.), the exact scope and meaning of fair and equitable treatment is not easily described in general terms ... tribunals applying the principle of fair and equitable treatment have found it to include principles such as the protection of legitimate investor expectations with respect to the maintenance of a stable and predictable business and legal environment by the host government, the principle of transparency, the good-faith and abuse of rights principles, due process, proportionality and the prohibition on arbitrariness. References to the prohibition on arbitrariness and requirements of transparency are frequently made within the general framework of due process, which must be observed by courts and authorities of the host state", Hober, Investment Arbitration and the Energy Charter Treaty, Journal of International Dispute Settlement, 1 (2010) 1, p. 4.

[55] Art. 10(1).

[56] Bamberger/Linehan/Waelde, The Energy Charter Treaty in 2000: In a New Phase, in: Roggenkamp (ed.), *Energy Law in Europe*, 2000, p. 6.

[57] The stage of "making investments" and the issue of access conditions.

[58] Energy Charter Secretariat, The Energy Charter Treaty. A Reader's Guide, 2002, p. 22.

privatization and demonopolization.[59] At present, the Treaty establishes a 'soft' pre-investment regime characterized by 'best efforts' obligations.[60] The ECT members also undertook to endeavour not to introduce new restrictions for foreign investors concerning the making of an investment ('standstill'), and to progressively reduce remaining restrictions ('rollback').[61]

As a result, the legally binding obligation to grant non-discriminatory treatment applies only to investments already made (so-called 'post-establishment' or 'post-investment' phase). In the 'post-investment' stage, host states are obliged to grant to investments of investors[62] from other ECT members treatment at least as favourable as that they accord to the investments of their own investors or of investors of other countries, that is, the better of national treatment or Most-Favoured Nation (MFN) treatment.[63] This standard applies not only to the investments of investors of other Contracting Parties, but also to 'their related activities including management, maintenance, use, enjoyment or disposal'.[64]

An interesting feature of the ECT investment regime is that not only state is responsible for government action that discriminates against foreign investors, it

---

[59] Bamberger/Linehan/Waelde, The Energy Charter Treaty in 2000: In a New Phase, in: Roggenkamp (ed.), *Energy Law in Europe*, 2000, p. 3. Art. 10(4) provides for negotiations on the extension of the non-discrimination principle to the pre-establishment phase. These negotiations began in 1995. Although negotiators had come close to a final agreement, a number of political issues could not be resolved. The basic structure of the draft "Supplementary Treaty" consisted of two components:

(1) An obligation of CPs to grant foreign investors national treatment and most favoured nation treatment concerning their establishment in the host country. According to Understanding Nr. 10 to the ECT, this includes the issues of privatization and de-monopolization.

(2) The right of each CP to launch individual exceptions to this commitment ("top-down approach"). The "Supplementary Treaty" would also have considerable significance in the context of privatization. Foreign investors who would like to participate in tender procedures and the subsequent sale of state assets would be protected against discrimination.

[60] Bamberger/Linehan/Waelde, The Energy Charter Treaty in 2000: In a New Phase, in: Roggenkamp (ed.), *Energy Law in Europe*, 2000, p. 4.

[61] "Blue Book" contains all exceptions to the principle of non-discrimination that member countries/signatories have reported concerning the making of a foreign investment in the energy sector. The exceptions are regularly reviewed in the ECT Investment Group, either through individual country examinations or horizontal reviews (e.g., concerning existing authorization procedures, screening mechanisms, restrictions on land ownership, etc). See Energy Charter Secretariat, The Energy Charter Treaty. A Reader's Guide, 2002, p. 24.

[62] In Art. 1(7), "Investors" are defined simply as natural persons having the citizenship or nationality of or permanently residing in a Contracting Party "in accordance with its applicable law", and as companies or other entities organized "in accordance with the [applicable] law". The ECT recognizes a right to deny the advantages of the investment provisions in two cases: (1) so-called "mailbox companies" (i.e., a company that has no substantial business activities in the country where it is organized); (2) if the denying CP does not maintain diplomatic relations with the third country, or adopts or maintains measures that prohibit or restrict transactions with investors of that state.

[63] Art. 10(7).

[64] Ibid.

also makes states responsible for actions of state trading enterprises they establish.[65]

Expropriation

Investment is protected against nationalization and confiscation. According to Article 13, investments may only be expropriated if certain conditions are fulfilled. The only exceptions are permitted when expropriation is in the public interest, non-discriminatory and is carried out under due process of law. Such expropriation has to be accompanied by prompt, adequate and effective compensation (with interest to the date of payment) that amounts to fair market value immediately before the expropriation or impending expropriation became known in such a way as to affect the investment's value.

In many case, expropriation in energy sector does not involve the direct taking of assets of an investor by the state, but rather takes more sophisticated forms such as change of tax regime, environmental regulation or similar policies that result in the loss of profit from an investment activity. The expropriation article could be construed to cover expropriation by exorbitant regulation, for example, in environmental matters.[66] Moreover, it also covers, in spite of the very restrictive treatment of tax matters in the Treaty, confiscatory taxation.[67] Regardless of whether an expropriation is 'lawful' or 'unlawful', the investor is entitled to prompt, adequate and effective compensation.[68]

Compensation for Losses

The Treaty also provides for the compensation for other losses such as those caused by armed conflict, war, state of national emergency, civil disturbance or similar

---

[65] The ECT contains provisions on responsibility of state enterprises to conduct their activities consistently with obligations under investment provisions of the Treaty (Art. 22(1)).

[66] Hober notes in this respect: "The significance of the protection against expropriation is not primarily the protection against outright takings of investments by the host state, but rather the protections against "measures having equivalent effect to nationalisation or expropriation", i.e. various forms of indirect or creeping expropriation such as exorbitant regulations or confiscatory taxation that undermines the operation or enjoyment of the investment", Hober, Investment Arbitration and the Energy Charter Treaty, Journal of International Dispute Settlement, 1 (2010) 1, p. 161.

[67] Bamberger/Linehan/Waelde, The Energy Charter Treaty in 2000: In a New Phase, in: Roggenkamp (ed.), *Energy Law in Europe*, 2000, p. 9.

[68] Hober states in this respect: "In the first case, compensation is a precondition for the lawfulness of the expropriation, and, in the latter case, compensation is equivalent to damages for the loss suffered by the investor as a result of the unlawful expropriation", Hober, Investment Arbitration and the Energy Charter Treaty, Journal of International Dispute Settlement, 1 (2010) 1, p. 161.

event.[69] This provision is of considerable importance for foreign investors who are concerned that the host country has not yet reached a satisfactory level of political stability, resulting in the risk of internal armed conflicts or even wars with other countries.[70]

In the above circumstances, the host state is obliged to grant the better of national and MFN treatment as regards restitution, indemnification, compensation or other settlement. An obligation to compensate foreign investors therefore only exists if the host country decides to compensate its own investors or investors of any third state (i.e., granting of national treatment/MFN treatment).

There is however an absolute obligation to compensate foreign investors in particular circumstances. For instance, foreign investors shall receive prompt, adequate and effective restitution or compensation from the host government if they suffer a loss resulting from the requisitioning of the investment, or unwarranted destruction of the investment by the authorities or forces of the host government.[71]

Transfer of Payments

A considerable disincentive for investors is the risk of not being able to transfer capital connected to their investment to another country.[72] This risk is especially acute in countries with high inflation, long delays in transfer systems, widely fluctuating exchange rates, or poor foreign exchange reserves. Therefore, the ECT members are under obligation to guarantee the free transfer of investment-related funds, both into and out of the host country, without delay and in a freely convertible currency.[73]

Key Personnel

The ECT permits foreign investors to employ key personnel of their choice, regardless of nationality, so long as such personnel has the required work and residence permits. The Treaty requires the host country, subject to its laws and regulations, to examine in good faith requests by the foreign investor concerning the entry and temporary stay of employed key personnel to be engaged in activities connected with the making or development, management, maintenance, use,

---

[69] Art. 12 of ECT.

[70] Energy Charter Secretariat, The Energy Charter Treaty. A Reader's Guide, 2002, p. 24.

[71] Ibid.

[72] Ibid.

[73] Art. 14(1) containing a non-exclusive list of transfers mentions initial and additional capital, returns, payments under a contract, unspent earnings and other remuneration of personnel, proceeds from sale or liquidation, dispute settlement proceeds, and compensation of expropriation.

enjoyment or disposal of relevant investments. This includes, for instance, advice or technical services by energy experts.[74]

Individual Investment Contracts

In the energy sector most major investments are made on the basis of an individual contract between the investor and the state. Under the ECT, a breach of an individual investment contract by the host country becomes a violation of the Treaty itself: 'Each Contracting Party shall observe any obligations it has entered into with an Investor or an Investment of an Investor of any other Contracting Party'.[75] As a result, the foreign investor and its home country may invoke the dispute settlement mechanism of the Treaty.

Dispute Settlement

The strength of the ECT is that rights and obligations it creates for its members can be enforced through a fully-fledged system of international dispute resolution that is accessible not only to the ECT members' governments but also to investors. Private recourse to the dispute resolution under the ECT is especially important, considering that governments would often be reluctant to pursue a dispute that affects interests of a particular entity with another state that has leverage in any area of their bilateral relations.

The Energy Charter Treaty contains a comprehensive system for settling disputes on matters covered by the Treaty. There are two basic forms of binding dispute settlement under the ECT. The first one is the state-state arbitration[76] applicable to disputes arising out of application and interpretation of almost all provisions of the ECT (except for competition and environmental issues). The second is the investor-state arbitration for investment disputes.[77] Dispute settlement provisions make a significant contribution to investor confidence and to a more reliable investment environment.

Moreover, there are special provisions, based on the WTO model, for the resolution of inter-state trade[78] issues. The Treaty also offers a conciliation

---

[74] Art. 11, see Energy Charter Secretariat, The Energy Charter Treaty. A Reader's Guide, 2002, p. 28.

[75] Art. 10(1). Under Art. 26 and 27, Contracting Parties may opt out of application of the ECT dispute settlement to breaches of this obligation (see Art. 26(3)(c) and 27(2)). Australia, Hungary and Norway have opted out of the application of this provision.

[76] Art. 27.

[77] Art. 26.

[78] Art. 29, Annex D.

procedure for transit disputes.[79] The latter derogates from the otherwise applicable general provisions on state-to-state dispute settlement. For the competition[80] and environment[81] related disputes, the ECT provides for 'softer' and less formal dispute resolution mechanisms.

Investor-to-State Disputes

Based on the model of bilateral investment agreements, Article 26 grants foreign investors the right to sue the host country in case of 'an alleged breach of an obligation of the host State under Part III of the Treaty', that is, the provisions relating to investment promotion and protection.

According to Article 26(1), disputes shall be settled, if possible, amicably. Both sides have a period of three months for consultations. If consultations/negotiations fail, the foreign investor has three options where to submit the dispute for resolution: (1) to the domestic courts or administrative tribunals of the host state to the dispute; (2) to any applicable, previously agreed dispute settlement procedure – e.g., an arrangement under bilateral investment treaties; (3) to international arbitration.[82]

If foreign investors choose to submit a dispute to international arbitration, they have the choice between three alternative arbitration procedures[83]: (1) the International Centre for the Settlement of Investment Disputes, Washington, D.C.[84]; (2) a sole arbitrator or an ad hoc arbitration tribunal established under the UNCITRAL Arbitration Rules; or (3) the Arbitration Institute of the Stockholm Chamber of Commerce.[85]

Regardless of which of the three above-mentioned basic options for international arbitration is chosen, the dispute shall be decided in accordance with the provisions of the Treaty and the rules and principles of international law.[86] The award is binding and final and may include interest.[87]

---

[79] Art. 7.

[80] Art. 6.

[81] Art. 19.

[82] Art. 26(2).

[83] Art. 26(4).

[84] This option is available if both the home state of the investor and the host state are parties to the ICSID Convention. Alternatively, the foreign investor may invoke the ICSID Additional Facility Rules for the Administration of Proceedings by the Centre. These arbitration rules are applicable where only either the home state of the investor or the host state – but not both – is a party to the ICSID Convention.

[85] Art. 26(3)(b). The Treaty permits Contracting Parties listed in Annex ID to decline giving their unconditional consent to the submission of a dispute to international arbitration where the investor has previously submitted the dispute to another dispute resolution forum.

[86] Art. 26(6).

[87] Art. 26(8). Pursuant to Art. 26(5)(b), an investor-state arbitration shall, at the request of any party to the dispute, be held in a state that is a party to the United Nations Convention on the

State-State Disputes

In addition to investor-state dispute settlement, Article 27 of the ECT provides for inter-state arbitration. In comparison with investor-to-state disputes under Article 26, the scope of inter-state disputes is wider. It is not limited to investment disputes but applies to the application and interpretation of the Treaty as a whole. However, for various kinds of inter-state dispute resolution (e.g., trade disputes), the ECT contains specific rules that derogate from the general provision of Article 27.[88]

According to Article 27(2), disputes have to be submitted to an ad hoc tribunal, subject to certain exceptions. For such disputes, the UNCITRAL rules shall apply, unless there is an agreement to the contrary between the Contracting Parties.

Energy Efficiency

The Treaty requires that each Contracting Party strive to minimize, in an economically efficient manner, harmful environmental impacts resulting from all operations within the energy cycle in its area.[89] After the Kyoto Protocol, the energy efficiency acquired major importance as a tool in achieving the reduction in green house gases (GHG) emissions. The Protocol on Energy Efficiency and Related Environmental Aspects (PEEREA) expands and makes the ECT provisions on energy efficiency more concrete. It is the first time that all well-known principles of energy efficiency have been incorporated into a multilateral agreement between so many countries.

As a basis for the development of energy efficiency policies and greater international and institutional cooperation, the Protocol promotes the principles of 'full-cost', 'cost-effectiveness', and 'sustainable development'. Moreover, the Protocol enhances the policy framework that will support greater energy efficiency: the introduction of market mechanisms, price formation reflecting real energy and environmental costs, cost-effective energy policies, transparency of regulatory frameworks, dissemination and transfer of technologies, and promotion of investments.[90] Sectoral policies, such as housing, industrial, transport and infrastructure policies should integrate energy efficiency issues. The Protocol explicitly

---

Recognition and Enforcement of Foreign Arbitral Awards. This Convention requires state parties to recognize and enforce within their courts arbitral awards rendered in foreign states. This provision permits the investor to ensure that such states are obliged to enforce the award. Moreover, the ICSID Convention already requires that its parties recognize and enforce ICSID arbitral awards. Therefore, if this option is chosen, the ICSID awards will generally be enforceable in a large number of states even if the New York Convention is, for some reason, inapplicable.

[88] See discussion in s. II.B.2 above and Art. 27(9).

[89] Art. 19.

[90] Protocol on Energy Efficiency and Related Environmental Aspects (PEEREA), Art. 3, available at: www.encharter.org/fileadmin/user_upload/document/EN.pdf (last visited on 15th August, 2010).

requests third party financing, access to private capital markets and the use of fiscal and financial incentives to energy users.

The PEEREA obliges the participants to formulate policies for improving energy efficiency and reducing adverse negative environmental impact of energy production and use. The ECT members are required to develop energy efficiency strategies and legislation as well as monitor their implementation. The Protocol requires the establishment of specialized energy efficiency bodies at appropriate levels to initiate and implement policies.

The emphasis in the work on energy efficiency is not on legal obligations but rather on practical implementation of a political commitment to improve energy efficiency. This is promoted through policy discussions based on analysis and exchange of experience between the member countries, invited independent experts and other international organizations. The PEEREA process consists of a series of energy efficiency peer reviews and recommendations for states on improvement of energy efficiency strategies. The PEEREA provides a mechanism for international co-operation and exchange of experience and ideas between countries in the area of energy efficiency.

Through the implementation of PEEREA, the Energy Charter provides its member countries with a choice of good practices and a forum in which to share experiences and policy advice on energy efficiency issues. Within this forum, particular attention is paid to such aspects of a national energy efficiency strategy as taxation, pricing policy in the energy sector, environmentally-related subsidies and other mechanisms for financing energy efficiency objectives.

For the resolution of the environmental disputes, the ECT contains a special 'soft law' procedure in case if arrangements for the consideration of such disputes are not available in other appropriate international fora.[91] The Charter Conference shall, at the request of one or more Contracting Parties, review disputes concerning the application or interpretation of the respective obligations. The Conference acts as a consultative body that may make recommendations to the parties in dispute on how to settle the case.

Transfer of Technology

One of the main necessities of the resource-endowed countries that became the ECT members has been development of state-of-the-art energy technologies. Indeed such technology is necessary in order to make use of energy resources in a cost-efficient, technologically sound and environmentally friendly manner.[92] The Treaty contains 'soft law' provisions aimed to achieve this goal.

---

[91] Art. 19(2).

[92] Energy Charter Secretariat, The Energy Charter Treaty. A Reader's Guide, 2002, p. 36.

According to Article 8(1), CPs agree to promote access to and transfer of energy technology on a commercial and non-discriminatory basis. Article 8 does not however impose a mandatory technology transfer. Article 8 is a 'best efforts' clause concerning the encouragement of technology transfer. Moreover, the CPs undertook to eliminate existing and create no new obstacles to the transfer of technology.

Competition

The ECT members aim at alleviating market distortions and barriers to competition.[93] They also have to enforce laws as are necessary and appropriate to address unilateral and concerted anti-competitive conduct.[94] The ECT also requires experienced Contracting Parties to provide other Contracting Parties with technical assistance on the development and implementation of competition rules. There is a special information and consultation procedure concerning disputes on competition issues.[95]

Article 6(5) deals with the settlement of competition disputes. Article 6(5) reflects the fact that the ECT does not establish a common competition regime between Contracting Parties. Rather, the ECT confirms the applicability of their domestic competition rules. Consequently, Article 6(5) establishes a mutual information and consultation mechanism in respect of the interpretation and application of national competition laws.

If a CP considers that any specified anti-competitive conduct carried out in the territory of another CP is adversely affecting an important interest concerning the alleviation of market distortions and barriers to competition, it may notify the other Contracting Party and request that the latter's competition authorities initiate appropriate enforcement action. The notified Contracting Party or its competition authorities may consult with the competition authorities of the notifying Contracting Party before deciding on an eventual enforcement action with respect to the alleged anti-competitive conduct.

Access to Capital

Open capital markets are of special importance for investment projects in energy field, especially when the host county's financial market is too weak or too small to

---

[93] Art. 6(1).

[94] Art. 6(2).

[95] Art. 6(5).

guarantee foreign companies unlimited access.[96] CPs acknowledge the importance of open capital markets in encouraging the flow of capital to finance energy trade and investment.[97] Each CP undertook to endeavour to promote conditions for access to its capital market by companies and nationals of other CPs for the purpose of such financing on a non-discriminatory basis. Under Article 9(2), a CP may adopt or maintain programmes relating to the promotion of trade or investment abroad (e. g., public loans, grants, insurance and guarantees). Such programmes shall apply to energy trade and investment with/in other CPs.

State Trading Enterprises

Considering that so-called state enterprises often have a dominant or even monopolistic position and consequently play a major role in the energy sector, it was important to address this issue through the ECT. The Treaty contains various obligations of CPs with regard to the conduct of their state enterprises, although it does not create direct obligations of these companies themselves.[98]

The ECT members have to ensure that their state enterprises respect the investment-related Treaty provisions when they sell or otherwise provide goods and services.[99] The Treaty prohibits discrimination of foreign investors by state trading enterprises. State enterprises are obliged, for instance, to supply natural gas or electricity to foreign investors at prices no higher than those charged to domestic companies.[100]

ECT members undertook not to encourage or require its state enterprises to conduct its activities in a manner inconsistent with any other obligation of that Contracting Party under the Treaty. For instance, this would apply to state enterprises that operate transit pipelines.[101] ECT Member States cannot encourage or require such an enterprise to charge higher transit fees from foreign pipeline users than from domestic users for a comparable operation.

In addition, when the ECT state establishes and entrusts enterprises or other entities with regulatory, administrative or other governmental authority, it has to ensure such entities exercise their authority consistent with the Treaty obligations.[102] The provision primarily aims to prohibit discrimination against

---

[96] Energy Charter Secretariat, The Energy Charter Treaty. A Reader's Guide, 2002, p. 37.

[97] Art. 9(1).

[98] Energy Charter Secretariat, The Energy Charter Treaty. A Reader's Guide, 2002, p. 39.

[99] Art. 22(1).

[100] Energy Charter Secretariat, The Energy Charter Treaty. A Reader's Guide, 2002, p. 41.

[101] Energy Charter Secretariat, The Energy Charter Treaty. A Reader's Guide, 2002, p. 41. Similar obligation exists with respect to enterprise, agency or other organization to which an ECT Member State grants exclusive or special privileges.

[102] Art. 22(3).

foreign energy companies (e.g., as regards the application of official tariff rates, or the adoption of energy-related regulations and administrative decrees).[103]

Finally, and more generally, the ECT members are prohibited from encouraging or requiring any enterprise, agency or other organization to which they grant exclusive or special privileges to conduct they activities contrary to the Treaty obligations.[104]

The ECT and Current Challenges of International Energy Governance

Criticism of the ECT

Over the past several years, the ECT has been facing criticism that the Treaty does not fully reflect the modern realities of the energy world. Such criticism came from some key stakeholders, most notably from Russia[105] that stopped provisional application of the Treaty from 19 October 2009. Considering that the Treaty was negotiated almost two decades ago and energy markets have evolved drastically since then, some of the criticism may seem justified. A large part of the criticism is however not fair. The present section aims at dealing with both sets of arguments.

Firstly, it has been argued that the ECT is unbalanced and leans towards protecting the interests of energy consuming states more than interests of energy producing or transit states. Indeed, the ECT was negotiated at the time when energy producing states in the territory of the former Soviet Union were in a particularly vulnerable position – both politically and economically.[106] This fact did not result however in an unbalanced set of disciplines as many would argue.

---

[103] Energy Charter Secretariat, The Energy Charter Treaty. A Reader's Guide, 2002, p. 41.

[104] Art. 22(4).

[105] At the tenth anniversary session of the Energy Charter Conference in December 2001, Valery A. Yazev, member of the Russian Duma, expressed Russia's disappointment in the ECT for its failure to live up to these expectations: "Regrettably, the dynamic of the 'post-treaty' period is not bright. The Protocol on Hydrocarbons was not developed. The Protocol on Emergency-Situations was not developed. The Supplementary Treaty was not concluded. Negotiations on the development of a Protocol on Electricity always postponed. Negotiations on the Protocol on Transit that are most important for Russia appear close to a dead end." Speech of the Russian State Duma Delegate Mr. Valery A. Yazev at the occasion of the ten-year anniversary session of the Energy Charter Conference on the 17th December, 2001, para. 5, unpublished, cited from van Agt, Tabula Russia. Escape from the Energy Charter Treaty, Briefing Paper, Clingendael International Energy Program, September 2009, p. 11.

[106] Arguably, interests of regional energy producing states have changed now from those of the early nineties when the ECT was negotiated and countries like Russia were in a weak negotiating position. These interests are now claimed to be best served by state control and strong "national champions" to compete with international oil and gas companies. See van Agt, Tabula Russia.

The ECT is the only international treaty that stipulates that states have the sovereignty over their energy resources.[107] They are free to decide the way and pace at which they develop and exploit their resources, the fiscal regime as well as ownership and structure of the sector.

As far as trade in energy materials and products is concerned there is a symmetry between obligations on exporters' and importers' side, which, considering the energy dependence of ECT's importing states made from the outset the position of exporters stronger. Indeed even before acceding to the WTO they could benefit from the MFN and national treatment of their exports in the territory of their import markets. At the same time, export duties on energy materials and products remained unbound.

Furthermore, the argument of unbalanced character of the ECT to the detriment of the energy producers may stem from the high level of investment protection. This is erroneous however as the major producing states are in dire need of capital and technologies to explore more energy fields in more remote areas with severe weather conditions. The ECT sets forth only best endeavour obligations on the pre-investment stage, so it is in the discretion of the energy owning states to decide the conditions on which they open their energy resources to exploration and development. Once the foreign investor has been granted the investment contract it is only fair to grant the protection against discriminatory treatment and unlawful expropriation. In the end, the host states are the beneficiaries of the predictable investment regime as it enables capital inflows in their energy sector. Of course there are times when this need is less obvious – when the oil prices peak. In times of the crisis however, when demand is soaring, the competition for capital is tight and the argument may change direction.

Secondly, the Treaty was criticized for ambiguity of some of its key provisions. For instance, it is unclear in what circumstances conciliation mechanism of Article 7 can be used and what form of non-discriminatory treatment is required by Article 7(3) of the ECT. Reportedly, these were the very issues that caused major dissatisfaction of the Russian government.[108] Moreover, there is a great deal of misperception concerning the content of obligations contained in the Treaty, even in those instances where the obligations are quite clear. Most notable example relates to the misperception that the ECT requires mandatory third-party access, a thorny issue for companies like Gazprom. In fact, the opposite is true – in the Understanding to

---

Escape from the Energy Charter Treaty, Briefing Paper, Clingendael International Energy Program, September 2009, p. 11.

[107] Art. 18, see discussion in s. II.1 above.

[108] Other examples of misperceptions, cited by Konoplyanik, are that "the ECT opens access to the Gazprom transportation system at the discounted domestic transportation tariffs", the claim that the ECT "obliges Russia to open access to its energy resources", or it requests unbundling of Gazprom", or "requests cancellation of long-term gas export contracts", etc. Konoplyanik, Common Russia-EU Energy Space: The New EU-Russia Partnership Agreement, Acquis Communautaire and the Energy Charter, Journal of Energy & Natural Resources Law 27 (2009), p. 278.

the ECT it is specified that the provisions of the Treaty 'do not ... oblige any Contracting Party to introduce mandatory third party access'.[109]

Thirdly, the Energy Charter process faced major difficulties because of the lack of progress in the negotiations of the Transit Protocol. Although it is true that the ECT already has very important provisions on transit, the core issues – most importantly those related to setting transit tariffs, congestion management and construction of new infrastructure – needed further elaboration. The aim of the Transit Protocol negotiations has been to specify general rules applicable to transit contained in Article 7 of the ECT. These negotiations were initiated upon the request of Russia and were reportedly a precondition for Russia's ratification of the ECT. A decade's long negotiation that did not result in completion of the agreement was a discouraging signal on a lack of political will to move on the outstanding issues.

Fourthly, since the ECT was negotiated in the beginning of the 1990s, some key issues that figure prominently on the current energy agenda were not addressed by the Treaty's negotiators. Some other issues, although addressed, were so controversial that it was impossible to reach consensus in order to include them in the Treaty. Most notable issue from the latter category is the binding commitment regarding non-discrimination in the stage of making investments. Although this issue continued to be subject of the negotiations on the so-called Supplementary Treaty, it was impossible to move forward to the conclusion of the agreement on pre-investment. Another issue that was not addressed by the Treaty is linked to the climate impact of energy production, distribution and use. Although the ECT recalls in its Preamble the United Nations Framework Convention on Climate Change and has soft law provisions on energy efficiency and environmental aspects,[110] the Treaty does not set any binding disciplines with respect to mitigation of harmful effect of energy production and consumption or promotion of cleaner methods thereof.[111] The climate change mitigation is directly linked to energy security. As the energy demand is growing energy consuming countries are at the

---

[109] The ECT Understanding IV.1(b)(i). For example, a long-standing opponent of ECT ratification, the former member and then the Chairman of the Energy Committee, and currently the Deputy Chairman of the Russian State Duma, Valery Yazev, contended for a long time that the ECT provides for mandatory third party access (MTPA) to the energy infrastructure. See Konoplyanik, Common Russia-EU Energy Space: The New EU-Russia Partnership Agreement, Acquis Communautaire and the Energy Charter, Journal of Energy & Natural Resources Law 27 (2009), p. 278.

[110] See Art. 19 and Protocol on Energy Efficiency and Environmental Aspects.

[111] Remarkably, the Treaty does not even include renewable energies in the list of energy products and materials covered by the Treaty. It may be argued that this omission is mitigated by the fact that electrical energy is covered by the Treaty and since the large share of renewable energy is geared towards producing electricity, the Treaty's provisions do indeed cover renewable energy to some extent. This example is however illustrative of the fact that the agenda of energy negotiations may have looked very different two decades ago than it does now. Indeed any serious attempt to negotiate an energy-specific Treaty in the twenty-first century would need to address renewable energies explicitly.

same time pressured to reduce their GHG emissions. The producing countries are consequently facing uncertainties in terms of the future demand growth, which makes investment decisions ever more difficult.

Finally, it has been claimed that the ECT does not possess the adequate tools to force its member countries to comply with its provisions, neither has it instruments to effectively prevent and resolve emergency situations in the energy field.[112] The ECT contains a comprehensive set of mechanisms to settle energy disputes both between states and between investors and states. Such dispute settlement has been effectively used – it has a proven record of over twenty cases of investor-state arbitration. It is true however that such dispute settlement proceedings usually take a substantial amount of time, thus being inefficient for resolving the emergency situations. As far as the state-to-state dispute settlement is concerned it remains at the discretion of the states concerned to make use of it. The fact that there has been no use of such mechanism foreseen by Article 27 may lead to several conclusions. Apart from the unlikely proposition that no state-to-state dispute has ever arisen (it is well known there have been a few such disputes), one possible reason is that the ECT states found other venues to solve the problems – mostly through negotiations and especially WTO accession negotiations of the energy-endowed states of the region.[113]

Most of the criticism the ECT faced stemmed from Russia, the main energy producer that signed the Treaty in 1994 but failed to ratify it amid objections on the part of the Russian parliament and important stakeholders, most notably Gazprom.

The ECT and Russia's Initiatives

After the gas crisis of January 2009,[114] the President of Russia Dmitry Medvedev made critical statements regarding the Energy Charter, in fact blaming the Treaty

---

[112] Konoplyanik, Energy Charter Plus – Russia to Take the Lead Role in Modernizing ECT?, Oil, Gas & Energy Law Intelligence 7 (2009) 4, p. 2. These criticisms were mainly voiced by Russia who in fact proposed in course of the ECT negotiations in the beginning of 1990s to develop a protocol on emergencies in the energy field of cross-border character aimed at securing non-interrupted transit.

[113] Although the coverage of the WTO with respect to energy is less than comprehensive, it has been reported that WTO members bring a wide range of energy-related issues to the negotiations table – many of them not covered by existing WTO disciplines.

[114] From Russia's perspective, the interruption was not due to Russia's failure to put the gas into the transportation system, but unsanctioned take-off of gas by Ukraine. Having subsidized deliveries to Ukraine for years, Russia wanted to obtain market price for its natural gas, which Ukraine simply could not afford to pay. See Doeh/Nappert/Popov, Russia and the Energy Charter Treaty: Common Interests or Irreconcilable Differences?, International Energy and Taxation Law Review 2006.

for not being effective in preventing and resolving the crisis.[115] Furthermore, he questioned the ability of the ECT to cope with problems gas trade had faced.[116] The transit crisis that happened in 2009 between Russia and Ukraine had drastic consequences as it lead to the stop of gas deliveries to some of the European countries in the middle of cold winter. It also damaged irreversibly the reputation of Russia as a reliable gas supplier to Europe. The claim that the ECT was not effective may not be fair however as Russia did not want to use the conciliation mechanism readily available under the ECT either in 2009 or during the similar crisis situation in January 2006. At the same time, it may be true that such crisis situations necessitate an emergency response to resolve them within much shorter period of time than possibly the Charter conciliation could do. The fact remains however that Russia did not even give a fair consideration to the use of the ECT conciliation.

Later, the Russian President stated that the ECT was not working and proposed the creation of a new legal framework of international energy governance.[117] This proposal came shortly after the signing of the declaration between the EU and Ukraine on the modernization of Ukraine's gas transit system,[118] which according

---

[115] See http://www.chile.mid.ru/2009/bull_015.html. Statement of Russian President Dmitry Medvedev of 20th January, 2009 said: "We should consider what international agreements – multilateral international agreements – are able to provide for the interests of sellers, transit countries, and consumers. Why do I mention this? Everyone knows about the so-called "Energy Charter", which was developed to a large extent with a view to protecting the interests of consumers – which is not a bad thing. One should not forget, though, that sellers are equally parties in any contractual relations and their interests should also be protected to the same extent as the interests of transit states. To make this protection effective, one needs new international mechanisms. I believe, we could think about either amending the existing version of the Energy Charter (if other member-countries agree to that) or developing a new multilateral instrument, which would fully correspond to these objectives, and which would address both procedural, technological and legal issues related to guarantees of payment for the gas supplied, performance by transit states of their functions and prevention of such problems, which, unfortunately were created by Ukraine late last year. I consider that both the Government of the Russian Federation and JSC "Gazprom" (as our main supplier of gas) ought to think about what mechanism to this effect could be appropriately developed and proposed to all members of the international community. I view this as our special task in the energy area by virtue of Russia being the largest energy producer in the world."

[116] "Did this Energy Charter help in the course of the recent gas conflict? Procedures which are provided by this charter did not work, incentives did not work either, the Energy Charter Treaty was not used. This means that we need another basis for downplaying such conflicts", http://www.rian.ru:economy/20090605/173397916.html (last visited on 15th August, 2010).

[117] In his speech in Helsinki on 20th April, 2009, Russia's President stated: "The existing bilateral arrangements and multilateral legally binding norms governing international energy relations have failed to prevent and resolve conflict situations. This makes it necessary to efficiently improve the legal framework of world trade in energy resources."

[118] The text of the joint declaration signed during Joint EU-Ukraine International Investment Conference on the Modernisation of Ukraine's Gas Transit System is available at: http://www.eeas.europa.eu/energy/events/eu_ukraine_2009/joint_declaration_en.pdf (last visited on 15th August, 2010).

to some commentators 'Russia saw as an attempt to sideline Russia in modernizing Ukraine's energy sector and the transit gas pipeline system that carries Russian gas to Europe'.[119]

During his state visit on the 20 April 2009 to Finland, President Dmitry Medvedev launched his proposal on a 'Conceptual approach to the new legal framework for energy cooperation' (the Concept or Conceptual Approach).[120] The Conceptual Approach reiterates that existing bilateral and multilateral legally binding norms of international energy relations turned out to be incapable to prevent and resolve conflict situations. This prompts the necessity of improving the legal basis of the world trade in energy resources. It is necessary to create a new universal international legally binding agreement, the document states, which would attract – unlike the existing system based on the Energy Charter – the participation and joint responsibility of the main energy producing (exporting), transit as well as consuming (importing) states.[121] This document must encompass all global aspects of energy cooperation.

Such new system of energy governance, in view of Russia, should be universal (meaning the possibility of its application to any states), open (allowing accession of third states), broad (encompassing all aspects of energy cooperation), non-discriminatory (not imbalanced in favour of some participants versus others). The framework also has to be effective – i.e., include the mechanism of enforcement. Finally, the Concept stresses that such a system should not contradict the existing obligations stemming from other international documents.

The main principles of energy cooperation would include absolute state sovereignty over national energy resources; ensuring non-discriminatory access to international energy markets, developing open competitive markets; coverage of all types of energy and related products and equipment; transparency of all market segments; non-discriminatory investment promotion and protection, including new investments into all energy chain links; promotion of mutual exchange of energy business assets within investment activities; non-discriminatory access to technology and technology transfer; possibility of non-interrupted delivery of energy products to international markets including through transit systems; ensuring physical security of energy infrastructure; development of early warning mechanisms of crisis situations; encouragement of scientific and technological cooperation.

---

[119] Bovt, Energy Dialogue: A Restart?, 28th April, 2009, available at: http://www.eu-russiacentre. org/our-publications/column/energy-dialogue-restart.html (last visited on 15th August, 2010).

[120] Konceptual'nyj podchod k novoj pravovoj baze mezhdunarodnovo sotrudnichestva v sfere energetiki (celi I principy), President of Russia, Official Web Portal, 21st April, 2009, available at: http://www.kremlin.ru/eng/text/docs/2009/04/215305.shtml (last visited on 15th August 2010).

[121] The Concept states that "existing bilateral arrangements and multilateral legally binding norms … have failed to prevent and resolve conflict situations." This refers implicitly to conflicts with Ukraine and inability not only of the ECT but also Bilateral Investment and Trade agreements (BITs) and even the WTO to prevent the crisis. See the commentary by van Agt, Tabula Russia. Escape from the Energy Charter Treaty, Briefing Paper, Clingendael International Energy Program, September 2009, p. 13.

Furthermore, the Concept contains a special annex describing elements of the transit agreement that sets out the obligations of transit countries to ensure an uninterrupted flow of energy resources through their territory. This is 'unequivocally designed to put Ukraine's gas transit system under more strict control by some supranational bodies, where Russia hopes to have a more or less decisive vote'.[122] The procedure of management of emergency situations is an indispensable part of the transit agreement. The agreement would define principles of setting transit tariffs (including transparency, cost reflectiveness, non-discrimination and comfortable tax regime); non-interruption of transit flow; system of solving emergency situations. Remarkably, the Concept proposes the establishment of an international commission for the management of emergency situations in transit but does not seem to aim at setting binding legal regime in this respect. Commentators viewed it as an evidence of 'Russia's difficulty in combining within a single non-discriminatory legal regime its offensive transit interest towards Ukraine, Belarus and beyond, with its defensive transit interest towards Central Asian and Caspian oil and gas exporters who depend on transit through Russia itself'.[123]

Despite the criticism of the Energy Charter, the Russian government imported major principles from the ECT to be included in the Concept. Indeed, such principles as state sovereignty over national energy resources; development of open competitive markets; non-discriminatory investment protection; non-interrupted delivery of energy products to international markets – are all core principles shared by the ECT.

Despite the fact that all types of energy and related products should be covered by the new framework, the list of products and materials contained as an annex to the Concept copies the list of products and materials covered by the ECT. Consequently, it has the same shortcoming as the ECT – it completely omits any mention of the renewable energy. Although renewables, understandably, may not be specifically on the radar screen of the Russian government, for the sake of fairness the system of energy governance that claims to be universal and encompassing major aspects of energy should include the renewable energy in its scope. The Concept generally seems to ignore the necessity (and the reality) of the transition to sustainable energy future or climate change as a global energy security issue. Such transition is however directly related to energy security and poses cross-border challenges that broad policy frameworks can best accommodate.[124]

Some observers note that the Concept does not share the importance that the 2006 G8 St Petersburg Principles attach to open and competitive energy markets. This reflects the trend towards public private partnerships and a reassertion of

---

[122] Bovt, Energy Dialogue: A Restart?, 28th April, 2009, available at: http://www.eu-russiacentre. org/our-publications/column/energy-dialogue-restart.html.

[123] van Agt, Tabula Russia. Escape from the Energy Charter Treaty, Briefing Paper, Clingendael International Energy Program, September 2009, p. 14.

[124] Ibid., p. 26.

government control over open and competitive energy markets that disenables the free energy trade.

Shortly after presenting the Concept, the Russian government took a decision to stop provisional application of the ECT, and respective notification was sent to the depositary declaring that Russia did not intend to become a party to the ECT.[125]

Russia's withdrawal from the ECT was not well received in the Russian circles and abroad. It was reported that the decision was purely political and went in contradiction to the expert assessment of benefits and drawbacks of the withdrawal made by the key Russian ministries and agencies. Indeed Russia itself would benefit from the international legally binding framework on investment protection and transit as its ability to attract necessary investment and technology seems contingent on adherence to principles of law. Moreover, Russia has an interest in diversification of export markets and investment protection also for its own energy sector investment's abroad.[126]

The question is what the ECT rules stand for now, that its major stakeholder dismissed adherence to them.

The ECT consolidates the unique legal governance structure in energy sphere and the Treaty's provisions set an important standard in international law.[127] Considering the fact that over 50 states across Eurasia are parties of the Energy Charter process,[128] it is inconceivable to lay foundations of a new international legally binding instrument that would cover all essential issues in energy trade and investment and that would include all key players in the field but would contain disciplines that contradict the ECT. Moreover, the momentum that existed when the ECT was negotiated is not present at the moment, when governments tend to pursue very different and contradicting policy objectives and finding a compromise in the energy negotiations seems ever more difficult.[129]

---

[125] On 20th August, 2009 the Russian Federation officially informed the Depository that it did not intend to become a Contracting Party to the Energy Charter Treaty and the Protocol on Energy Efficiency and Related Environmental Aspects. In accordance with Art. 45(3(a)) of the Energy Charter Treaty, such notification results in Russia's termination of its provisional application of the ECT and the PEEREA upon expiration of sixty calendar days from the date on which the notification is received by the Depository. Therefore, the last day of Russia's provisional application of the Energy Charter Treaty and the PEEREA was 18th October, 2009.

[126] van Agt, Tabula Russia. Escape from the Energy Charter Treaty, Briefing Paper, Clingendael International Energy Program, September 2009, p. 12.

[127] Ibid., p. 2.

[128] Forty-six of them have actually ratified the ECT.

[129] It has been commented, "the window of political opportunity is much narrower than it was in the early 1990s ... The euphoria and expectation of changes on both sides were so high that they opened a broad window of political opportunity for negotiations aimed at creating common rules of the game and a level playing field, particularly in energy, in a broader Europe. Today, this window is likely to have narrowed dramatically", Konoplyanik, Common Russia-EU Energy Space: The New EU-Russia Partnership Agreement, Acquis Communautaire and the Energy Charter, Journal of Energy & Natural Resources Law 27 (2009), p. 274.

The commentators have been thus sceptical regarding the proposition of Russia that a new legal framework should be put in place.[130] It was commented that it would be difficult to reach an agreement in a broader constituency on the very same issues on which Russia and EU could not agree among themselves.[131] At the same time, 'energy markets still require Russia's integration into a consensual multilateral governance system'.[132] Russia's proposals should be therefore carefully considered. What are the most efficient ways to accommodate legitimate concerns voiced by Russia and integrate it in the multilateral system of energy governance?

The best way to proceed seems to be through the discussion of Russia's proposals in the Energy Charter forum, as modernization of the Treaty and its adaptation to the changing realities of the energy world have already been addressed by the ECT states.[133] In fact, while the ECT members considered that

---

[130] Van Agt commented: "Replacing [the ECT] with a new legal framework to accommodate Russia appears frivolous and difficult in substance", van Agt, Tabula Russia. Escape from the Energy Charter Treaty, Briefing Paper, Clingendael International Energy Program, September 2009, p. 2. So far, there has been no top-level reaction from either the US or European leaders. For Europe, the ECT is too important to abandon it in favour of some vague proposals. Ibid. See also comments by Konoplyanik, Energy Charter Plus – Russia to Take the Lead Role in Modernizing ECT?, Oil, Gas & Energy Law Intelligence 7 (2009) 4, p. 1: "The truth is that initiatives on creating a new system in place of the ECT proposed by Russia did not enthuse potential partners. To the contrary, Brussels and some individual EU members declared that abolishment of the Energy Charter is out of the question." Konoplyanik pointed out negative consequences of potential withdrawal of Russia from the ECT. He argued that there was no reasonable benefit from such a withdrawal from the provisional application. Such withdrawal would not make any difference for the ongoing arbitration at the UNCITRAL on Yukos case brought by the latter's minority shareholders against the Russian government (as reportedly the case had been the key motivation behind the decision to stop the provisional application of the Treaty). Not only the cessation of provisional application would have no effect on the Yukos case, under the terms of such application Russia would remain bound by the investment protection regime of the ECT for another twenty years.

[131] "If Russia and the EU have failed so far to reach any large scale agreement in the energy sphere, why would it be viable to anticipate that it could be reached with a larger number of participants, including those who openly confront each other (the US and Venezuela)? It is very doubtful that Russia could quickly find strong supporters for its proposal. Nor is it clear who could eventually become supporters of such a sweeping reform of the whole international energy framework. Also, it could be asked why it is impossible in the eyes of the Russian leadership to amend and improve the existing documents instead of announcing them all as dead", Bovt, Energy Dialogue: A Restart?, 28th April, 2009, available at: http://www.eu-russiacentre.org/our-publications/column/energy-dialogue-restart.html.

[132] Ibid., p. 2. Most of the issues listed in Medvedev's New Legal Framework have been the subject of intensive EU-Russian energy dialogue in recent years in negotiations over the new Partnership Agreement as well as the ECT itself. They have not been resolved so far and, more importantly, are seen differently by Moscow and the EU. For instance, Russia has continuously complained that Europe discriminates against its companies investing in the EU, while it itself has put forward some severe restrictions on foreign investments into its "strategic spheres".

[133] The ECT countries recognized in Rome statement of the Energy Charter Conference of 9 Dec. 2009 that "the Energy Charter Process must reflect new developments and challenges in international energy markets and respond to broader changes across its constituency. This could entail

the principles and rules of the Treaty 'remain valid and should continue to apply as a tool to address the major challenges we face today in the energy sector', they recognized 'the need to improve legally binding rules governing international energy relations, investment and trade'. The discussions that take place in the Energy Charter's Strategy Group created in 2007 can be used to reflect on the elements of the Concept. There are indications that such an option is considered possible by Russia as well.[134]

Indeed it is more efficient to adopt an existing treaty to the present circumstances than to start a new negotiating process without the guarantee of its successful completion. Energy markets are constantly evolving. It is impossible to foresee all the trends in such development with maximum accuracy that is needed in order to create a legal framework that would stay acute for a long period of time. The effective international legal framework needs therefore to contain certain flexibilities in order to be adopted both to changes in energy market and internal circumstances in its member states. The Treaty amendments are not the only instruments that could be used to adapt the ECT to the realities of the changing world. The Energy Charter framework contains a number of different instruments of a possible adaptation such as protocols elaborating the Treaty, guidelines, recommendations, policy coordination, model agreements and declarations. Negotiations and implementation become more complex as the instruments become more binding.[135] The ECT indeed contains the necessary elements of the global energy treaty, and the core principles contained in the Energy Charter remain acute for the present energy world.

---

consultations, possibly leading to negotiations on the preparation of practical proposals on how the Energy Charter Process could be modernized, whilst remaining universal, comprehensive and equal in character, and to strengthen common implementation mechanisms as appropriate to be effective and efficient." The Road Map for the Modernisation of the Energy Charter Process was adopted 24 November 2010 by the Energy Charter Conference.

[134] President Medvedev admitted, as one of the options, "we could think about ... amending the existing version of the Energy Charter (if other member-countries agree to that)." The President of the European Commission Jose Manuel Barroso announced at a summit with President Dmitry Medvedev in Khabarovsk in May 2009 the EU's consent to improve the Energy Charter process and its instruments. "We are open to discussion of the proposals put forward by Russia but building on the existing agreements ... without destroying, without putting under pressure the system that already exists", Barroso said; see "EU Will Not Abandon Energy Charter Rejected by Russia: Barroso", EU Business, 22nd May, 2009, available at: http://www.eubusiness.com/news-eu/1242973023.48/ (last visited on 15th August, 2010).

[135] Konoplyanik, Common Russia-EU Energy Space: The New EU-Russia Partnership Agreement, Acquis Communautaire and the Energy Charter, Journal of Energy & Natural Resources Law 27 (2009), p. 287.

Conclusions: The ECT in the International Energy Governance

Increasing reliance on internationally traded energy, considerations of security of supply/demand and need of investment require predictability and transparency that could be achieved most effectively through a multilateral legal framework. Efforts to regulate energy relations on the bilateral level are not likely to be effective. For instance, problems in energy cross-border trade are often linked to transit. Transit relations involve at least three states, but often energy flow has to cross several transit countries to reach its consumer market. Therefore the most effective way to deal with cross-border energy flows is to address the issue at a multilateral level. The same holds true for other aspects of energy production and trade. Multilateral investment rules for energy sector are desirable because they would create a transparent and predictable framework. The uniform rules would provide a more balanced and efficient framework for international cooperation than what is offered by bilateral agreements. Moreover, considering the strategic geo-political significance of energy, international governance system of international energy markets based on legal rules is increasingly important for overall international security.[136]

The international rules and disciplines that apply to energy trade are thus of great strategic significance.[137] At the same time energy markets and trade are constantly evolving, so it is a real challenge to negotiate multilateral rules for energy trade.[138]

The regulation of the international energy sector has to take into account the difference of energy from other internationally traded commodity. Efforts to regulate the international energy sector in the same way as any other internationally traded commodity are likely to face difficulties. Energy is different, because it is a finite non-renewable resource that is vital to economic and social development. Moreover, the energy resources are under the sovereign control of a relatively small number of resource-owning countries.[139] This means that there is an irreducible

---

[136] US Senator Lugar stated: "The absence of a collective energy security strategy will lead to greater fragmentation among European nations and across the Atlantic. This fragmentation will not be exclusive to energy policy; it may also detrimentally impact on our ability to act upon shared security and economic issues." See "Lugar Calls for Trans-Atlantic Energy Security Strategy", Senator Lugar's speech to the U.S.-Ukraine Energy Dialogue Series, 15th April, 2008. On Lugar's Energy Initiative see http://lugar.senate.gov/energy/press/speech/ukraine.cfm (last visited on 15th August, 2010).

[137] Sussman notes: "With the increasing globalization of the world's economy, the interdependence of the energy sector, and the long term and highly capital intensive nature of energy projects, multilateral rules for international cooperation are needed. The ECT was negotiated to meet that need", Sussman, The Energy Charter Treaty's Investor Protection Provisions: Potential to Foster Solutions to Global Warming and Promote Sustainable Development, Oil, Gas & Energy Law Intelligence 6 (2008) 3, p. 3.

[138] Mernier, The Rules of Energy Trade, Speech of at the World Energy Council, 12th November, 2007.

[139] Decisions on depletion policy – on whether and how fast national resources are to be developed – are matters for resource-owning governments. International regulation is not likely to succeed if

political element to international energy trade. Negotiations in the energy sphere among so many parties having divergent interests are complex and politically sensitive.[140]

Most importantly, the system would need to address the concerns of different stakeholders – both energy-importing as well as energy-exporting states. To balance opposing interests is difficult to achieve. It is necessary to look at the principles and interests that are shared by countries along the energy value chain, including both producers and consumers.[141] In this respect, the decisions of G8 Summits in 2006 and 2007 directly supported the principles of the Energy Charter.[142]

The Energy Charter was a result of a multilateral compromise of almost 20 years ago and consequently reflects realities of that time.[143] It could be argued that the ECT framework is not as complete as desirable and that more detailed rules on transit (such as those contained in the draft Transit Protocol) as well as pre-investment rules are needed. The value of the Treaty should not however be underestimated. The Energy Charter Treaty has a unique role as the only energy-specific multilateral agreement that covers all major aspects of international energy turnover: trade, transit, investment and energy efficiency.

The ECT provides a useful value added to existing general WTO framework that covers much larger constituency. The cornerstone of the ECT is non-derogation from the WTO. Both ECT and WTO frameworks complement each other, creating synergies without unnecessary duplications.

---

it tries to infringe in a binding way on these national prerogatives. This was the experience during the preceding rounds of trade negotiations. Mernier, The Rules of Energy Trade, Speech of at the World Energy Council, 12th November, 2007. See UN Resolution No. 1803 of 18th December, 1962 on permanent sovereignty over natural resources.

[140] Bamberger/Linehan/Waelde, The Energy Charter Treaty in 2000: In a New Phase, in: Roggenkamp (ed.), *Energy Law in Europe*, 2000, p. 3.

[141] Mernier, The Rules of Energy Trade, Speech of at the World Energy Council, 12th November, 2007.

[142] van Agt, Tabula Russia. Escape from the Energy Charter Treaty, Briefing Paper, Clingendael International Energy Program, September 2009, p. 8. In 2006 leaders of G8 adopted the Energy Security Declaration which "support[ed] the principles of the Energy Charter and the efforts of participating countries to improve international energy cooperation" and committed to the following principles: "open, transparent, efficient and competitive markets for energy production, supply, use, transmission and transit services as a key to global energy security; transparent, equitable, stable and effective legal regulatory frameworks, including the obligation to uphold contracts, to generate sufficient, sustainable international investments upstream and downstream." G8, Global Energy Security (Russia 2006), see "Global Energy Security", Official Website of the G8 Presidency of the Russian Federation in 2006, 16th July, 2006, retrieved at: http://en.g8russia.ru/docs, (last visited on 15th August, 2010). See also G8 Summit 2007 Heiligendamm, Growth and Responsibility in the World Economy.

[143] Konoplyanik, Common Russia-EU Energy Space: The New EU-Russia Partnership Agreement, Acquis Communautaire and the Energy Charter, Journal of Energy & Natural Resources Law 27 (2009), p. 262.

The investment framework[144] and more elaborate transit rules are valuable features of the ECT that have not been negotiated in a detailed manner within the WTO. Considering that the WTO agreements do not deal with investment policy,[145] and only prohibit those investment measures that are inconsistent with obligations of national treatment and prohibition of quantitative restrictions, the investment provisions of the ECT provide important addition to the WTO framework.[146]

Moreover, due to its investment protection rules, the ECT could play an important role in fostering greenhouse gas mitigation and sustainable development.[147] This protection is reinforced by the dispute settlement provisions of the ECT including both state-state and investor-state arbitration – the ECT provisions can therefore be enforced by private entities through binding dispute settlement.[148] The ECT's dispute settlement system is unique both for the broad scope of covered issues (investment, trade, transit) and the number of countries having subscribed to it.[149]

Finally, the Charter process contributes to the dialogue between different groups of players: consuming, producing, transit countries at all stages of economic development. From this point of view the ECT has a distinctive role – no other energy-related organization provides common platform for the development and implementation of

---

[144] The tribunal stated in Plama case that the ECT is the "first multilateral treaty to provide as a general rule the settlement of investor-state disputes by international arbitration" and provides "a covered investor an almost unprecedented remedy for its claims against a host state." *Plama Consortium vs. Republics of Bulgaria*, 44 I.L.M. 721 (ICSID 2005), 739, 742. Sussman, The Energy Charter Treaty's Investor Protection Provisions: Potential to Foster Solutions to Global Warming and Promote Sustainable Development, Oil, Gas & Energy Law Intelligence 6 (2008) 3, p. 3.

[145] Except to a limited extent through GATS.

[146] Selivanova, Managing the Patchwork of Agreements in Trade and Investment, in: Goldthau/ Witte (eds.), *Global Energy Governance: The New Rules of the Game*, 2010, p. 7.

[147] Sussman argues that while increased investments in GHG mitigation projects will be necessary, the ECT could make such investments more attractive: "Accession to the ECT would contribute significantly to the attractiveness of investment in the developing countries and should serve to reduce the cost of such investment." Sussman, The Energy Charter Treaty's Investor Protection Provisions: Potential to Foster Solutions to Global Warming and Promote Sustainable Development, Oil, Gas & Energy Law Intelligence 6 (2008) 3, p. 9. This is because clean energy projects are based largely on local support schemes and governmental incentives and require that those be maintained in the same form as when the investment is made. The ECT creates rights for investors in cases where host countries decide to change incentives or subsidies in violation of the investment protection rules of the ECT (See *Nykomb Synergies Tech. Holding AB vs. The Republic of Latvia*, Arb. Inst. Of the SCC, Case No. 118/2001 (2003), pp. 31–32). Sussman contends that the ECT investment provisions are broad enough to cover many if not all of the currently known GHG mitigation measures including nuclear energy, coal gasification and carbon sequestration.

[148] Bamberger/Linehan/Waelde, The Energy Charter Treaty in 2000: In a New Phase, in: Roggenkamp (ed.), *Energy Law in Europe*, 2000, p. 1.

[149] Energy Charter Secretariat, The Energy Charter Treaty. A Reader's Guide, 2002, p. 53. Art. 26 (3)(c) grants CPs the right not to give their unconditional consent to international arbitration in respect of disputes of alleged breaches of the obligations under an individual investment contract. Three ECT members – Australia, Hungary, Norway – have opted for this.

binding disciplines among these different groups of stakeholders. The Energy Charter forum has to be effectively used to attract a larger number of countries across the whole energy production, distribution and consumption chain that would benefit from adherence to legally binding rules the Treaty establishes. In parallel to geographical expansion, the Energy Charter stakeholders have to conduct the evaluation of issues that need further reflection both in the Energy Charter forum and, possibly, the Energy Charter Treaty if the status quo does not suit major players. As the recent years have shown, all current multilateral governance systems[150] face criticism of not being able to coop with the current challenges, and the critical reassessment of stakes is therefore necessary.[151]

References

Azaria, D. 'Energy Transit under the Energy Charter Treaty and the General Agreement on Tariffs and Trade' (November 2009). *Journal of Energy & Natural Resources Law*, available at <www.ibanet.org/Publications/publications_JERL_November_2009.aspx>, 15 December 2010.

Bamberger, C. 'Adjudicatory Aspects of Transit Dispute Conciliation under the Energy Charter Treaty'. *Transnational Dispute Management*, 4, no. 1 (May 2006).

Bamberger, C., J. Linehan & T. Wälde, 'The Energy Charter Treaty in 2000: In a New Phase'. In M.M. Roggenkamp (ed.), *Energy Law in Europe* (Oxford: Oxford University Press, December 2000).

Belyi. A.V. & S. Nappert. 'A New Charter: Myth or Realty?'. *Oil, Gas & Energy Law Intelligence*, 2 (2009).

Belyi, A.V. 'A Russian Perspective on the Energy Charter Treaty (ARI)'. (2009), available at <www.offnews.info/verArticulo.php? pageNum_rsRelacionadas=44&totalRows_rsRelacionadas=441&contenidoID=15585>, 16 December 2010.

Bilder, G. 'Why Should Mercosur Associate to the Energy Charter Treaty?'. *Oil, Gas & Energy Law Intelligence*, 2, no. 5 (December 2004), 1–4.

Clark, B. 'Transit and the Energy Charter Treaty: Rhetoric and Reality' *Web Journal of Current Legal Issues* (1998), available at <//webjcli.ncl.ac.uk/1998/issue5/clark5.html>, 15 December 2010.

Coop, G. 'Long-Term Energy Sale Contracts and Market Liberalisation in New EU Member States'. *International Energy Law & Taxation Review*, no. 2 (2006): 64–71.

Coop, G. 'Liquefied Natural Gas Projects and Investment Protection under the Energy Charter Treaty'. *International Energy Law Review*, no. 2 (2008): 29–36.

Coop, G. 'Energy Charter Treaty and the European Union: Is Conflict Inevitable?' *Journal of Energy & Natural Resources Law*, 27, no. 3 (2009): 404–419.

---

[150] Be it in relation to trade, finance or energy.

[151] Van Agt comments: "Energy policy frameworks, and their legal architecture, have to evolve beyond their current limits to successfully tackle an imposing range of energy security, climate and social economic challenges. The WTO inspired multilateral energy governance system, in which the Energy Charter serves as a figure head for the energy sector, is re-evaluated actively by its stakeholders", van Agt, Tabula Russia. Escape from the Energy Charter Treaty, Briefing Paper, Clingendael International Energy Program, September 2009, p. 8.

Doeh, D., A. Popov & S. Nappert. 'Russia and the Energy Charter Treaty: Common Interests or Irreconcilable Differences?'. *Oil, Gas & Energy Law Intelligence*, 5 no. 2 (April 2007): 1–5.

Flynn, C. 'Russian Roulette: the ECT, Transit and Western European Energy Security'. *Oil, Gas & Energy Law Intelligence*, 4 no. 4 (November 2006).

Frasl, I. 'The Trade Rules of GATT and Related Instruments and the Energy Charter Treaty'. In T. Wälde (ed.), *The Energy Charter Treaty: An East-West Gateway for Investment and Trade* (London, The. Hague, Boston: Kluwer Law International, 1996).

Goodwin, P., et al. 'The Energy Charter Treaty – Recent Developments'. *Japan Dispute Avoidance Newsletter,* No. 90 (February 2010), available at <www.herbertsmith.com>, 16 December 2010.

Hober, K. & S. Nappert. 'Provisional Application and the Energy Charter Treaty: The Russian Doll Provisions'. *International Arbitration Law Review*, 10, no. 3 (2007): 53–57.

Hober, K. 'Investment Arbitration and the Energy Charter Treaty' *Journal of International Dispute Settlement*, 1, no. 1 (2010): 153–190.

Hodges, P. & M. Weiniger. 'Energy Charter Treaty Ruling Clarifies Effect of Russia's "Provisional application" accepting Jurisdiction to Hear Yukos' Claim' Herbert Smith E-Bulletin (4 December 2009).

Konoplyanik, A. 'Energy Charter Protocol on Transit: On the Way to Agreement – What Kind of Treatment Will Be Accorded to Russian Gas in EU Countries?'. *Oil, Gas & Energy Law Journal*, 2, no. 1 (February 2004),.

Konoplyanik, A. 'Transit Protocol Progress'. *Oil, Gas & Energy Law Intelligence*, 2, no. 5 (December 2004).

Konoplyanik, A. 'Russia-EU Summit: WTO, the Energy Charter and the Issue of Energy Transit'. *International Energy Law & Taxation Review*, no. 2 (2005): 30–35.

Konoplyanik, A. 'Russian Gas to Europe: From Long-Term Contracts, on Border Trade and Destination Clauses to . . .?'. *Journal of Energy & Natural Resources Law*, 23 (2005).

Konoplyanik, A. 'Russia-EU, G-8, ECT and Transit Protocol'. *Russian CIS Energy & Mining Law Journal*, 4 (2006).

Konoplyanik, A. 'Russian – Ukrainian Gas Dispute: Prices, Pricing and ECT'. *Oil, Gas & Energy Law Journal*, Vol. 4, no. 4 (2006).

Konoplyanik, A. & T. Wälde. 'Energy Charter Treaty and Its Role in International Energy'. *Journal of Energy & Natural Resources Law*, Vol. 24, no. 4 (2006).

Konoplyanik, A. 'Energy Charter and the Russian Initiative – Future Prospects of the Legal Base of International Cooperation'. *Oil, Gas & Energy Law Intelligence*, 2 (2009).

Konoplyanik, A. 'Energy Charter Plus – Russia to Take the Lead Role in Modernizing ECT?'. *Oil, Gas & Energy Law Intelligence*, 7, no. 4 (2009).

Konoplyanik, A. 'A Common Russia-EU Energy Space: The New EU-Russia Partnership Agreement, Acquis Communautaire and the Energy Charter'. *Journal of Energy & Natural Resources Law*, 27, no. 2 (2009): 258–291.

Konoplyanik, A. 'Gas Transit in Eurasia: Transit Issues between Russia and the European Union and the Role of the Energy Charter'. *Journal of Energy and Natural Resources Law*, 27, no. 3 (2009): 445–486.

Liesen, R. 'Transit under the 1994 Energy Charter Treaty'. *Journal of Energy & Natural Resources Law*, 17 (1999).

Marcinkeviciute, E. 'Energy Charter Treaty Transit Protocol: European Gas Market Liberalisation and its Effect on the European-Russian Gas Trade'. *Texas Journal of Oil, Gas & Energy Law*, 5 (August 2009): 109–129.

Mernier, A. 'Setting the Rules of Energy Trade'. In *Fundamentals of the Global Oil and Gas Industry 2008*. The official publication of the 19th World Petroleum Congress.

Nappert, S. 'EU-Russia Relations in the Energy Field: The Continuing Role of International Law'. *Oil, Gas & Energy Law Intelligence*, Vol. 7, no. 2 (2009).

Roche, P., S. Abraham & S. Petit. 'Russia's Withdrawal from the Energy Charter Treaty' (August 2009), available at <www.nortonrose.com/knowledge/publications/2009/pub22691.aspx? lang=en-gb>, 1 March 2010.

Selivanova, Y. 'Managing the Patchwork of Agreements in Trade and Investment'. In A. Goldthau & M.J. Witte (eds), *Global Energy Governance: The New Rules of the Game* (Berlin: Global Public Policy Institute, Washington, D.C.: Brookings Institution Press, 2010), 49–72.

Shore, L. 'The Jurisdiction Problem in Energy Charter Treaty Claims'. *International Arbitration Law Review*, 10, no. 3 (2007): 58–64.

Shtilkind, T.I. 'Energy Charter Treaty: A Critical Russian Perspective' *Oil, Gas & Energy Law Intelligence*, 3, no. 1 (March 2005).

Sussman, E. 'The Energy Charter Treaty Affords Investor Protection and Right to Arbitration'. *Oil, Gas & Energy Law Intelligence*, Vol. 4, no. 4 (October 2006).

Wearn, P. 'Transit Provisions of the Energy Charter Treaty and the Energy Charter Protocol on Transit'. *Journal of Energy & Natural Resources Law*, 2, no. 2 (2002): 172–191.

Wearn, P.K. 'European Energy Security and Cooperation: The Energy Charter Treaty and Its Protocol on Transit'. *Oil, Gas & Energy Law Intelligence*, 2, no. 5 (December 2004): 16–22.

The Impact of International Investment Agreements on Energy Regulation

Markus Krajewski

Introduction

International energy law and international investment law share much of a common history: Some of the first expropriation cases which were adjudicated by arbitration tribunals on the basis of international law concerned the expropriation of foreign investments relating to the production of oil.[1] Tensions and disputes between energy investors and host state governments continued to remain on the agenda of investment arbitration tribunals throughout the decades and form a prominent part of the case law of these judicial bodies.[2] More than a third of all investment disputes adjudicated under ICSID can be classified as energy-related disputes.[3]

---

[1] *Saudi Arabia vs. Arabian American Oil Company (Aramco)*, ILM 27 (1958), p. 117, and the so-called "Libyan cases" which originated in the nationalisation of foreign investors in the oil sector after 1971. On the latter see Lowenfeld, *International Economic Law*, (2nd ed.) 2008, pp. 496–503. The International Court of Justice (ICJ) was seized with a dispute concerning the expropriation of oil production already in 1951, but declined jurisdiction, ICJ, *Anglo-Iranian Oil Co. (United Kingdom vs. Iran)*, ICJ Reports 1952, p. 93.

[2] See most recently the commencement of proceedings in *Türkiye Petrolleri Anonim Ortaklığı vs. Republic of Kazakhstan*, ICSID Case No. ARB/11/2, registered 14th January, 2011 and *Nova Scotia Power Incorporated vs. Bolivarian Republic of Venezuela*, ICSID Case No. ARB(AF)/11/1, registered on 26th January, 2011 and *National Gas S.A.E. vs. Arab Republic of Egypt*, ICSID Case No. ARB/11/7, registered on 22nd March, 2011.

[3] According to ICSID statistics of 2011, 25% of the cases concerned oil, gas and mining while 14% concerned electric power and other energy, see ICSID, The ICSID Caseload – Statistics, 2011, p. 12. It should, however, be noted that the majority of energy-related investment disputes do not evolve around regulatory issues which are the focus of the present contribution. In fact, most of the cases identified as "energy-related" by the ICSID Secretariat are not special to the energy sector. They address general economic and fiscal policies or breaches of investment contracts which

M. Krajewski (✉)
Fachbereich Rechtswissenschaft, Friedrich-Alexander-Universität Erlangen-Nürnberg,
Schillerstraße 1, 91054 Erlangen, Germany
e-mail: markus.krajewski@jura.uni-erlangen.de

C. Herrmann and J.P. Terhechte (eds.), *European Yearbook of International Economic Law (EYIEL), Vol. 3 (2012)*, European Yearbook of International Economic Law 3, DOI 10.1007/978-3-642-23309-8_11, © Springer-Verlag Berlin Heidelberg 2012

By and large, the most often discussed and analysed question of the relationship between energy investment and international law concerns the protection of the investor against political and systemic risks arising out of the contentious nature of energy production.[4] Given the traditional focus of the debate on oil and gas production this is not surprising: In the petroleum producing sector, the interests of the state and of the investor are often antagonistic and interdependent at the same time. While the state claims sovereignty over the natural resources to be found in its territory and therefore controls their exploitation the investor disposes of the capacity (capital, know-how, etc.) to actually drill for, refine and transport oil and gas. Long-term concession agreements have been the typical legal instrument to manage this division of labour and interests.[5] More often than not, conflicts concerning energy-related investment evolved around ownership and the distribution of profits arising from the production of oil and gas.

In more recent times, disputes also concerned other sectors of the energy business including power generation and carbon-related energy investments and focused partly on regulatory aspects. In particular, disputes about investments in energy (electricity and gas) distribution to end users as well as cases arising out of environmental regulation of power generation show that international energy investment law cannot be reduced to the legal aspects of the protection of oil and gas production against the exercise of territorial sovereignty. Nevertheless, the discourse on energy investment law so far focussed predominantly on the bargain between the investor's capital and know-how and the host country's territorial sovereignty. In particular, the "pursuit of stability"[6] for energy investment through various legal tools stood at the centre of the debate. In this context, objectives and goals of energy policy and regulation have not been analysed much. As with most investment law research the focus has been on the protection of the rights and interests of the investor.

The present contribution adopts a different perspective: It will analyse the impact of international investment law, in particular of investment agreements on domestic energy regulation. This chapter therefore contributes to general debate on

---

affect investments in the energy sector as much as investments in any other sector. Only few energy-related investment disputes can be classified as regulatory disputes. For examples, see section "Areas of Contention" below.

[4] Cameron, *International Energy Investment Law – The Pursuit of Stability*, 2010, pp. 3–7; Wälde, International Energy Investment, Energy Law Journal 17 (1996), pp. 191–215, Joffé et al., Expropriation of oil and gas investments: Historical, legal and economic perspectives in a new age of resource nationalism, Journal of World Energy Law & Business 2 (2009), pp. 3–23.

[5] Sornarajah, *The International Law on Foreign Investment*, (2nd ed.) 2004, p. 40; Vielleville/ Vasani, Sovereignty Over Natural Resources Versus Rights Under Investment Contracts: Which One Prevails?, Transnational Dispute Management 5 (2003), p. 9; World Energy Council, *Trade and Investment Rules for Energy*, 2009, p. 16.

[6] See the subtitle of Cameron, *International Energy Investment Law – The Pursuit of Stability*, 2010.

investment law and regulatory autonomy[7] using the specificities of the energy sector as a case study. The analysis is developed in four steps: The next section summarises in a nutshell contemporary objectives of and regulatory approaches to energy policy ("Objectives and Policies of Energy Regulation"). This overview can only be very sketchy, but it provides the framework of the ensuing analysis of the relationship between energy regulation and investment law. The subsequent section turns to the "Economic Background and Historic Development of International Energy Investment Law". It will be shown that the current state of energy investment law is the result of a paradigm shift in the approach to energy investment in the 1980s. Based on this, section "International Investment Agreements as Instruments to Protect Energy Investment" will provide an overview of the main elements of international investment law and their functions regarding energy-related investments. Bringing the regulatory concerns identified in section II together with the standards of international investment law will enable us to see contentious issues which might result in conflicts ("Areas of Contention"). These areas of conflict will be illustrated with reference to selected energy-related state-investor disputes which have been adjudicated recently. The contribution concludes with a summary of its main findings ("Conclusion").

Objectives and Policies of Energy Regulation

The regulation of energy production, distribution and consumption is a key element of national economic law and policy. Developed economies depend on energy as the most important input for industrial production while developing countries rely on energy as a basis of their social and economic development.[8] Access to energy is fundamental for the livelihoods of citizens throughout the world.[9] The aims and objectives of national energy policies differ from country to country and depend in particular on the endowment with energy resources. Policy choices, consumer interests, patterns of industrialisation and energy-related accidents and catastrophes

---

[7] Tienhaara, *The Expropriation of Environmental Governance – Protecting Foreign Investors at the Expense of Public Policy*, 2009; Tung, Foreign Investors vs sovereign states: towards a global framework, BIT by BIT, in: Lewis/Frankel (eds.), *International Economic Law and National Autonomy*, 2010, pp. 243 et seq. (257–268). On a more theoretical notion see Schneiderman, *Constitutionalizing Economic Globalization – Investment Rules and Democracy's Promise*, 2008. For a review of these issues with regards to German BITs see Krajewski/Ceyssens, Internationaler Investitionsschutz und innerstaatliche Regulierung – Eine Untersuchung anhand der bilateralen Investitionsabkommen Deutschlands, Archiv des Völkerrechts 2007, pp. 180–216.

[8] Commission Communication, Energy 2020 – A strategy for competitive, sustainable and secure energy, COM(2010) 639 final, p. 2.

[9] Goldemberg, Development and Energy, in: Bradbrook/Ottinger (eds.), *Energy Law and Sustainable Development*, IUCN Environmental Policy and Law Paper No. 47, p. 1; International Energy Agency, Energy Poverty: How to make modern energy access universal, 2010, pp. 8 et seq.

shape the over-all architecture as well as the specific instruments of energy regulation in different countries. Despite the obvious variety in energy policies, some common regulatory concerns or policy objectives exist. At the risk of oversimplification three sets of regulatory objectives can be identified: Securing sufficient and continuous supply of energy, assuring universal and affordable (universal) access to energy and aligning energy production and consumption with the objectives of sustainability and environmental protection, in particular with regards to climate change.

Security and Sufficiency of Energy Supply

Ensuring secure and sufficient energy supply for industries and citizens is normally the most important energy policy objective. In the EU, Article 194 para 1 TFEU holds that the EU's energy policy shall aim, inter alia, to "ensure security of energy supply in the Union". According to the European Commission's most recent energy policy strategy paper, EU energy policy "has evolved around the common objective to ensure the uninterrupted physical availability of energy products and services on the market".[10] Similarly, in the United States assuring "abundant supplies of energy" to consumers has traditionally been considered one of the main objectives of US energy policy.[11] Comparable objectives can be found in other countries: For example, the Indian Energy Policy of 2006 considers ensuring energy security and meeting the growing energy demand through increased production, diversification and developing alternatives as major objective.[12]

Countries have traditionally employed different policies to achieve sufficiency and stability of energy supply. Some have sought to exercise control over the production of energy at home by nationalizing (parts of) the energy sector. Others have relied on incentives to stimulate diversity of sources in order to reduce the dependence on a single supplier or single energy source. An important instrument in this context is the use of international law. For example, the Energy Charter Treaty[13] aimed among other things at ensuring the stability of the delivery of oil and gas from Eastern Europe and Central Asia to Western European countries.

---

[10] Commission Communication, Energy 2020 – A strategy for competitive, sustainable and secure energy, COM(2010) 639 final, p. 2.

[11] Davies, Energy Policy Today and Tomorrow – Towards Sustainability, Journal of Law, Resources and Environmental Law 29 (2009), p. 74.

[12] Badrinarayana, India's Integrated Energy Policy: A Source of Economic Nirvana or Environmental Disaster? Environmental Law Reporter, 40 (2010) 7, p. 10707.

[13] See below III.

Universal and Affordable Access to Energy

Most states do not confine themselves to ensuring that the overall amount of energy produced or imported is sufficient, but focus on the distribution side as well. Ensuring that as many households and businesses as possible have affordable access to energy is therefore another central energy policy element. The European Commission considers the provision of energy "at a price which is affordable for all consumers (private and industrial)" as a key element of energy objectives at the EU level.[14] Article 3 of the EU's Directive on the internal market for electricity requires the EU Member States "ensure that all household customers, and, where Member States deem it appropriate, small enterprises (...) enjoy universal service, that is the right to be supplied with electricity of a specified quality within their territory at reasonable, easily and clearly comparable, transparent and non-discriminatory prices".[15] While the notion of "universal access" seems to be a concept which originated in the European context, ensuring access is an important policy objective in other countries as well. In the United States emphasis is placed on reasonable and competitive prices.[16] Access to energy is also a key policy objective in developing countries where large parts of the population often lack sufficient cooking, heating and lightening energy.[17] The International Energy Association considers access to energy as an important element of eradicating poverty and reaching the Millennium Development Goals (MDGs).[18] The Asian Development Bank even regards universal access to energy as a key objective of the 2009 Energy Policy.[19]

Again, countries have used different strategies to achieve universal and affordable access. Public ownership of energy companies or at least of the national grid are tools which have been employed by numerous countries at different times. Other states have relied on instruments of competition law based on the assumption that competitive market prices will enable as many citizens as possible to access energy. Further instruments which have been used include price control (price capping or ad hoc price control) or the administrative determination of the price.[20]

---

[14] Commission Communication, Energy 2020 – A strategy for competitive, sustainable and secure energy, COM(2010) 639 final, p. 2.

[15] Directive 2009/72/EC, OJ [2009] L 211/55.

[16] Davies, Energy Policy Today and Tomorrow – Towards Sustainability, Journal of Law, Resources and Environmental Law 29 (2009), p. 74.

[17] Bhattacharyya, Investments to promote electricity supply in India: regulatory and governance challenges and options, Journal of World Energy Law and Business 2008, p. 204.

[18] International Energy Agency, *Energy Poverty: How to make modern energy access universal*, 2010, p. 16.

[19] Asian Development Bank, Energy Policy 2009, available at: http://www.adb.org/Documents/Policies/Energy-Policy/Energy-Policy-2009.asp.

[20] Agarwal, Energy Price Regulation in India: The Case of Natural Gas Sector, United States Association for Energy Economics (USAEE) – International Association for Energy Economics (IAEE) Working Paper 10-040, February 2010, available at: http://ssrn.com/abstract=1548435.

Sustainability and Environmental Protection

While ensuring sufficiency and (universal) access can be seen as traditional regulatory objectives of energy policy, the environmental impact of energy production and consumption became an aspect for energy regulation in more recent times. Nowadays, its importance cannot be underestimated. The challenges related to climate change can only be addressed if the amount of carbon-based energy is reduced in favour of renewable energy production.[21] Environmental energy regulation is an issue for developed and developing countries alike.[22] The environmental impact of energy concerns both its production side as well as its consumption. Environmental energy regulation targeting energy production concerns air pollution and the disposal of waste produced in the context of energy generation, including nuclear waste.[23] Recently, governments aimed at increasing the share of renewable energy production in order to reduce the negative environmental effects of carbon- and nuclear-based energy production. The consumption side is addressed through measures aimed at energy efficiency[24] which do not only serve environmental objectives. The European Commission highlighted the multi-dimensional scope of energy efficiency in its 2010 energy strategy by stating: "Energy efficiency is the most cost effective way to reduce emissions, improve energy security and competitiveness, make energy consumption more affordable for consumers as well as create employment, including in export industries."[25]

Economic Background and Historic Development of International Energy Investment Law

Elements and Scope of International Energy Investment

There is no agreed definition of international energy investment.[26] For the purposes of the present contribution, energy investment shall not be restricted to the exploitation of raw materials, but will refer to investments in the entire energy chain

---

[21] UNCTAD, World Investment Report 2010 – Investing in a low-carbon economy, 2010, p. 101.

[22] For reference to India see Badrinarayana, India's Integrated Energy Policy: A Source of Economic Nirvana or Environmental Disaster? Environmental Law Reporter, 40 (2010) 7, p. 10709.

[23] Davies, Energy Policy Today and Tomorrow – Towards Sustainability, Journal of Law, Resources and Environmental Law 29 (2009), p. 76.

[24] Ottinger/Zalcman, Legal measures to promote renewable and energy efficiency resources, in: Bradbrook/Ottinger (eds), *Energy Law and Sustainable Development*, IUCN Environmental Policy and Law Paper No. 47, pp. 80 et seq.

[25] Commission Communication, Energy 2020 – A strategy for competitive, sustainable and secure energy, COM(2010) 639 final, p. 6.

[26] See e.g. World Energy Council, Trade and Investment Rules for Energy, 2009, p. 17.

including energy production and generation (production of raw materials, refinement and/or transformation) as well as transportation and distribution of energy.[27] Understood in this manner, a number of activities fall under the heading of energy investment many of which have already been the subject of investment disputes: Oil and gas production,[28] the transportation of oil and gas through pipelines,[29] coal mining,[30] coal-based power generation, including coal supply[31] and the building of transmission lines and distribution of electricity.[32]

It is difficult to gain a clear appreciation of the size and contents of international energy investment understood in this way, because international foreign trade and investment statistics do not consider "energy" as a distinct group. For example, the sectoral classification used by UNCTAD in the World Investment Report contains energy related investments in the subcategories "mining, quarrying and petroleum" which is part of the primary sector, "coke, petroleum products and nuclear fuel" which is part of manufacturing and "electricity, gas and water" which is an element of the services sector.[33] Similarly, international trade statistics record trade in "fuels and mining products" which include oil and gas as part of merchandise trade[34] while transnational trade in electricity is not recorded separately possibly due to its limited practical importance.

Based on this sectoral description it can be estimated that energy-related investments amounts to roughly 10% of the total FDI inward stock, a figure which has not changed much between 1990 and 2008.[35] This figure may come as a surprise given the high share of energy-related investor-state disputes.[36] However, energy-related investments are usually large projects requiring a significant amount

---

[27] UNCTAD, World Investment Report 2008: Transnational Corporations and the Infrastructure Challenge, 2008, p. 90 regarding electricity.

[28] *Türkiye Petrolleri Anonim Ortaklığı vs. Republic of Kazakhstan*, ICSID Case No. ARB/11/2, registered 14th January, 2011.

[29] *Ioannis Kardassopoulos and Ron Fuchs vs. Georgia*, ICSID Case No. ARB/05/18 and ARB/07/15, Award of 3rd March, 2010 and *National Gas S.A.E. vs. Arab Republic of Egypt*, ICSID Case No. ARB/11/7, registered on 22nd March, 2011.

[30] *Thai-Lao Lignite and Hongsa Lignite (Lao) vs. Lao People's Democratic Republic*, UNCITRAL Ad hoc arbitration, Arbitral Award of 4th November, 2009, available at: http://www.iareporter.com/downloads/20110306.

[31] *Nova Scotia Power Incorporated vs. Bolivarian Republic of Venezuela*, ICSID Case No. ARB (AF)/11/1, registered on 26th January, 2011.

[32] *TECO Guatemala Holdings, LLC vs. Republic of Guatemala*, ICSID Case No. ARB/10/23, registered on 23rd November, 2010.

[33] UNCTAD, World Investment Report 2010 – Investing in a low-carbon economy, 2010, p. 10.

[34] WTO, International Trade Statistics 2010, p. 43.

[35] Calculations based on UNCTAD, World Investment Report 2010, Annex table 21. Estimated world inward FDI stock, by sector and industry, 1990 and 2008, available at: http://www.unctad.org/sections/dite_dir/docs/wir2010_anxtab_21.pdf.

[36] See fn. 3.

of capital input and often implemented by large multinational corporations. This may explain why the energy sector accounts for a third of all investor-state disputes, but for only about 10% of global investment.

In absolute terms, energy investment has been on the rise in the last decades in the same manner as FDI in general. In 2009, world energy investment declined as the financial and economic crisis of 2008/2009 caused energy consumption to fall on a global level for the first time since 1981.[37] As a consequence of lower demand in energy, oil and gas producing companies engaged in drilling fewer wells and delayed or cancelled exploration projects. Furthermore, the tougher financial environment due to the crisis also restrained energy investment related activities which is not surprising for an industry which depends heavily on capital input.[38] The International Energy Agency (IEA) assumes, however, that energy consumption and production will reach normal levels again as soon as the results of the crisis have been overcome.[39] Furthermore, it is expected that the global demand for energy and hence the need for foreign investment in energy will raise in the coming years and decades due to an increased energy demand in particular in China and India.[40] Apart from the impact of general economic and financial developments energy investment can also be affected by singular events such as the Gulf of Mexico oil spill in mid-2010 or the nuclear catastrophe in Fukushima in early 2011.

Cycles of Cooperation and Confrontation – The Development of International Energy Investment Law

Over the last decades international investment law practice has been shaped by different paradigms. Energy investment during colonial times was largely part of the exploitation of the resources of the colonies by the imperial powers. The need for an international legal regime protecting such investments was minimal as they were protected by the imperial state[41] or through "gunboat diplomacy".[42] In strict legal terms the investment activity took place within the same jurisdiction and was not even an "international" investment in the formal sense. It was only after de-colonisation that foreign investment became an issue of international law.

While in some cases and countries, traditional concession agreements continued to be used as instruments of sharing profits between foreign investors and the host

---

[37] International Energy Agency, World Energy Outlook 2009, p. 42; UNCTAD, World Investment Report 2010 – Investing in a low-carbon economy, 2010, p. 10.

[38] UNCTAD, World Investment Report 2010 – Investing in a low-carbon economy, 2010, p. 10.

[39] International Energy Agency, World Energy Outlook 2009, p. 42.

[40] Bressand, Foreign Direct Investment in the Oil and Gas Sector – Recent Trends and Strategic Drivers, Yearbook on International Investment Law and Policy 2008/09, p. 125.

[41] Sornarajah, The International Law on Foreign Investment, (2nd ed.) 2004, p. 19.

[42] Subedi, International Investment Law – Reconciling Policy and Principle, 2008, pp. 11–12.

state, more often than not the newly independent states were reluctant if not hostile towards investment by companies based in the former imperial states, in particular if the investment concerned the extraction of minerals, oil and gas. Claims of territorial sovereignty over natural resources led to a wave of nationalisations and expropriations in the 1970s, in particular in the Middle East and Africa.[43] This development was further intensified and politically accompanied by activities of the United Nations including the General Assembly's Resolution on Permanent Sovereignty of Natural Resources of 1962[44] and the attempts to establish a New International Economic Order culminating in the 1974 Charter of Economic Rights and Duties of States.[45] The creation of the Organisation of Petroleum Exporting Countries (OPEC) can also be seen in this context.[46] At the domestic level, many countries established national oil companies charged with the production of oil on behalf of the producing state.[47] Investment disputes arising out of nationalisation were solved by and large on the basis of customary international law or "internationalised" concession agreements.

This overall picture changed remarkably at the end of the 1980s: A new concept of the role of the state with respect to the economy in general and energy investment in particular paved the way for a retreat from active governmental control in many countries. This in turn gave rise to a new wave of foreign investment in energy by private international oil companies.[48] At the same time, investment in other energy industries such as electricity and gas gained importance.[49] The reasons for this shift are manifold: The ideological victory of neoliberal politics in many countries,[50] the breakdown of communist regimes in Eastern Europe and Central Asia,[51] a decline of the oil price in the mid-1980s[52] and the emergence of a new general paradigm regarding the respective role of the state and the market have contributed to this

---

[43] Wälde, International Energy Investment, Energy Law Journal 17 (1996), p. 191; Cameron, *International Energy Investment Law – The Pursuit of Stability*, 2010, p. 7.

[44] A/RES/1803(XVII), 14th December, 1962. See Subedi, *International Investment Law – Reconciling Policy and Principle*, 2008, pp. 21 et seq.

[45] A/RES/29/3281, 12th December, 1974; see also Redgwell, International Regulation of Energy Activities, in: Roggenkamp et al. (eds.), *Energy Law in Europe*, (2nd ed.) 2007, p. 140.

[46] Joffé et al., Expropriation of oil and gas investments: Historical, legal and economic perspectives in a new age of resource nationalism, Journal of World Energy Law & Business 2 (2009), p. 5.

[47] Wälde, International Energy Investment, Energy Law Journal 17 (1996), p. 195.

[48] Joffé et al., Expropriation of oil and gas investments: Historical, legal and economic perspectives in a new age of resource nationalism, Journal of World Energy Law & Business 2 (2009), p. 6.

[49] Cameron, *International Energy Investment Law – The Pursuit of Stability*, 2010, p. 6.

[50] Wälde, International Energy Investment, Energy Law Journal 17 (1996), pp. 195 et seq.

[51] Cameron, *International Energy Investment Law – The Pursuit of Stability*, 2010, p. 6.

[52] Joffé et al., Expropriation of oil and gas investments: Historical, legal and economic perspectives in a new age of resource nationalism, Journal of World Energy Law & Business 2 (2009), p. 5.

cycle of cooperation between foreign investors and host state governments. In this context, a revival of concession agreements or the development of new forms of public private partnership shaped the contents of international investment law. Furthermore, bilateral investment agreements became an important element of the legal framework of energy investment.

The pendulum swung back again in the late 1990s and early 2000s, most prominently manifested by the raise to power of new governments in Venezuela, Ecuador and Bolivia with populist political programmes and national redistribution policies. This movement resulted in a new wave of de facto nationalisations and state dominance in the economy influenced the shape of international investment law.[53] A main focus of this policy was the energy sector ("energetic populism").[54] The development culminated in the termination of the ICSID agreement by Ecuador and Bolivia in 2007 and 2009 respectively.[55] In addition to this ideologically motivated shift, a significant increase in the oil price prompted a number of governments of oil-producing countries to reconsider their options and press for a renegotiation of arrangements agreed upon in different circumstances. There are, however, signs that this new wave lost its momentum towards the end of the first decade of the twenty-first century giving raise to yet another policy cycle which may again see more attempts to attract private foreign investment in the energy sector.[56] It should be no surprise that the latest policy shifts relating to energy investment resulted in a substantial number of energy-related investor-state disputes as many investors increasingly relied on the guarantees of bilateral investment treaties in order to secure the economic value of their investments.

Sources of International Energy Investment Law in the Twenty-First Century

International energy investment law is not a distinct and coherent body of international law. It consists of a variety of different legal sources which contain some core principles despite their heterogeneity. The most important sources of contemporary international energy investment law are bilateral investment treaties (BITs). BITs are international agreements in which each state party guarantees certain rights and remedies to investors of the other party. The relative importance of these

---

[53] Bressand, Foreign Direct Investment in the Oil and Gas Sector – Recent Trends and Strategic Drivers, Yearbook on International Investment Law and Policy 2008/09, pp. 158 et seq.

[54] De Sá Ribeiro, Sovereignty over Natural Resources Investment Law and Expropriation: The Case of Bolivia and Brazil, Journal of World Energy Law & Business 2 (2009), p. 129.

[55] Nowrot, International Investment Law and the Republic of Ecuador: From Arbitral Bilateralism to Judicial Regionalism, in: Tietje/Kraft/Lehmann (eds.), *Beiträge zum Transnationalen Wirtschaftsrecht*, 2010, pp. 5 et seq.

[56] Cameron, *International Energy Investment Law – The Pursuit of Stability*, 2010, p. 6.

agreements increased remarkably during the two last decades. While the total number of BITs amounted to about 400 in the 1980s, there are currently (as of 2010) 2750 BITs in force.[57] Most BITs have a comparable content[58] which includes international protection standards for foreign investors against expropriation and other negative interferences of the host state government. Many of these agreements provide for clauses on investor-state dispute settlement which usually gives the investor the right to claim an alleged violation of a BIT before an international arbitration tribunal which will then render a binding award. The increased incorporation of such a dispute settlement tool in BITs has been viewed as the major improvement from the perspective of foreign investors. The practical importance of this instrument is illustrated by the growing number of cases adjudicated by the International Centre for Settlement of Disputes (ICSID). By May 2011, the ICSID secretariat registered 126 pending cases and recorded 221 settled cases since 1972.[59]

Next to bilateral investment treaties are regional integration agreements or free trade agreements with an investment chapter. One example is NAFTA Chapter 11 which contains a full set of investment protection rules similar to many BITs.[60] The most important regional agreement relating directly to energy investment is the Energy Charter Treaty, a multilateral agreement concluded by 51 European and Central Asian states as well as the European Union.[61] The Energy Charter Treaty aims at promoting and securing energy-related investment in the territories of the member states. It contains similar protection standards as the bilateral investment agreements. In addition, the Energy Charter Treaty addresses trade liberalisation and rules on energy transit.[62] Other regional trade agreements also contain investment provisions[63], though some of them are less ambitious than NAFTA or the Energy Charter Treaty.[64]

Apart from public international law agreements, international energy investment law in a broader sense also includes the body of state-investor contracts, in particular concession agreements, which are concluded between a foreign investor

---

[57] UNCTAD, World Investment Report 2010 – Investing in a low-carbon economy, 2010, p. 81.

[58] Already in 1995 Dolzer and Stevens note a "homogeneity in the form and substance of most BITs", see Dolzer/Stevens, *Bilateral Investment Treaties*, 1995, p. 2.

[59] Information taken from ICSID, List of cases, available at http://icsid.worldbank.org/ICSID/FrontServlet (last visited on 19th May, 2011).

[60] Cameron, *International Energy Investment Law – The Pursuit of Stability*, 2010, pp. 164 et seq.

[61] For a comprehensive analysis of the Energy Charter Treaty see the contribution by Carsten Nowak in this volume.

[62] Bamberger/Wälde, The Energy Charter Treaty, in: Roggenkamp et al. (eds.), *Energy Law in Europe*, (2nd ed.) 2007, pp. 149 et seq.

[63] World Energy Council, Trade and Investment Rules for Energy, 2009, pp. 16–17.

[64] It should also be noted that the recent EU Free Trade Agreements concluded with Korea and with Colombia and Peru do not contain investment protection chapters, but clauses which require of review of investment protection and policies.

and the government of the host state.[65] These contracts are governed by the domestic legal order of the host state or by a legal order the parties agreed upon.[66] Consequently, they are national law instruments and are not considered part of public international law. There are, however, attempts to "internationalise" these contracts. While it is difficult to achieve this through a choice of law clause in the contract, international investment agreements can incorporate investor-state contracts: Some investment tribunals and academic commentators held that rights arising from state-investor contracts can be protected through bilateral investment agreements, in particular through so-called umbrella clauses.[67] Consequently, the violation of a concession agreement would be covered by bilateral or regional investment agreements. Importantly, this would allow investors to challenge the violation of those contracts through investor-state arbitration on the basis of the investment agreement whereas breaches of contracts between the investor and the state would normally be dealt with through commercial arbitration.[68] State-investor contracts in the field of energy investment often also contain so-called stabilization clauses which oblige the host government not to change its domestic law to the detriment of the investor. These obligations tend to "freeze" regulatory options of the government and are therefore particularly problematic from the perspective of preserving regulatory autonomy.[69]

International Investment Agreements as Instruments to Protect Energy Investment

As mentioned in the previous section, international investment agreements are the most important public international law instruments to protect energy investment. It is neither possible nor necessary for the present contribution to summarise all substantial and procedural features of these agreements. For the purposes of the research question of this contribution it suffices to discuss those standards of international investment agreements which have the largest impact on regulatory issues. These include the notion of indirect or regulatory expropriation, the standard of fair and equitable treatment and the so-called umbrella clause.

---

[65] Dolzer/Schreuer, *Principles of International Investment Law*, 2008, p. 72.

[66] Cameron, *International Energy Investment Law – The Pursuit of Stability*, 2010, p. 67.

[67] See below IV. 3. for a discussion of this issue.

[68] Dolzer/Schreuer, *Principles of International Investment Law*, 2008, p. 155.

[69] Howse, Freezing government policy: Stabilization clauses in investment contracts, Investment Treaty News (2011) 1, p. 3.

Protection Against Expropriation

The protection against expropriation – understood as the outright taking of property by the state – has been the main focus of international investment law throughout the twentieth century.[70] Most investment agreements contain provisions which stipulate that investments may only be expropriated or nationalised for the public benefit and only against compensation.[71] Such compensation must normally be paid promptly, in a freely transferrable currency and be equivalent to the value of the investment.[72] However, the last few decades have not seen many formal expropriations. Even the "expropriations" of foreign oil companies by the Bolivian Government in 2006 cannot be classified in this sense as they forced the foreign investors to renegotiate their contracts, but did not formally dispossess them.[73] Today, expropriation usually occurs in indirect forms.[74]

Investment agreements usually also subject indirect expropriations or measures the effect of which would be tantamount to an expropriation to compensation. However, the exact contours of indirect expropriation remain unclear and con-tested.[75] The language referring to indirect expropriations in investment treaties also varies: The term seems to be used interchangeably with expressions such as *de facto*, creeping, regulatory or disguised expropriation.[76] Despite this incoherent terminology, it can be argued that the term "creeping" expropriation has a distinct meaning and usually refers to a series of acts which have an effect similar to that of an expropriation if considered as a whole.[77] "Regulatory" expropriation denotes regulatory measures which generally aim (or are said to aim) at public interests but which deprive the investor of the commercial value of the investment. Regulatory expropriation is therefore a notion of international investment law which makes the potential for conflict between investors' rights and regulatory autonomy clearly

---

[70] Reinisch, Expropriation, in: Muchlinski/Schreuer/Ortino (eds.), *The Oxford Handbook on International Investment Law*, 2009, p. 408.

[71] Dolzer/Schreuer, *Principles of International Investment Law*, 2008, p. 91.

[72] See, e.g., Art. 13(1) Energy Charter Treaty, OJ [1998] L 69/26.

[73] De Sá Ribeiro, Sovereignty over Natural Resources Investment Law and Expropriation: The Case of Bolivia and Brazil, Journal of World Energy Law & Business 2 (2009), p. 133.

[74] OECD, "Indirect Expropriation" and the "Right to Regulate" in International Investment Law, Working Papers on International Investment 2/2004, p. 2.

[75] *Técnicas Medioambientales Tecmed S.A vs. The United Mexican States*, ICSID Case No. ARB (AF)/00/2, Award of 29th May, 2003, para. 114; Dolzer, The Impact of International Investment Treaties on Domestic Administrative Law, NYU Journal on International Law and Politics 2005, p. 959.

[76] Reinisch, Expropriation, in: Muchlinski/Schreuer/Ortino (eds.), *The Oxford Handbook on International Investment Law*, 2009, p. 422.

[77] *Compañia del Desarrollo de Santa Elena S.A. vs. Republic of Costa Rica*, ICSID Case No. ARB/ 96/1, Award of 17th February, 2000, para. 76. See also *Técnicas Medioambientales Tecmed S.A vs. The United Mexican States*, ICSID Case No. ARB (AF)/00/2, Award of 29th May, 2003, para. 114.

visible. The problem of regulatory expropriation has been especially relevant in the context of environmental measures.[78]

Arbitral tribunals have struggled to delineate legitimate or *bona fide* regulation for health, environmental or other public policy purposes which would not trigger compensation from regulatory measures with unjustifiably detrimental effects on the investor which would require compensation. Generally, there is agreement on the principles: On the one hand, states enjoy a sovereign right to regulate.[79] An investor cannot expect to be protected against all changes in the law which would have a detrimental impact on the investment.[80] On the other hand, states may not arbitrarily use regulatory measures to factually deprive the investor of his or her investment. However, the problem is – as often – to find the exact line in the sand ("line of demarcation"[81]) which distinguishes one from the other.

Traditionally, investment agreements have not attempted to define the line between regulatory expropriation and non-compensable forms of regulation. Instead, it was left to investment tribunals to develop the distinguishing features of the two. Recent treaty practice shows a reaction of the "legislator", i.e. the state parties to an investment agreement, as some states included definitions of expropriation in their investment agreements. However, these definitions do not seek to amend or rectify the jurisprudence of the investment tribunals but to codify it and therefore provide legal clarity and predictability.[82]

Investment tribunals and other international judiciary bodies have employed different methods to determine what amounts to an indirect expropriation.[83] The most often used approach has been a reference to the degree or the extent of the

---

[78] Reinisch, Expropriation, in: Muchlinski/Schreuer/Ortino (eds.), *The Oxford Handbook on International Investment Law*, 2009, p. 436.

[79] Sornarajah, *The International Law on Foreign Investment*, (2nd ed.) 2004, p. 97; Dolzer/ Schreuer, *Principles of International Investment Law*, 2008, p. 89; Subedi, *International Investment Law – Reconciling Policy and Principle*, 2008, p. 121.

[80] *Marvin Roy Feldman Karpa vs. United Mexican States*, ICSID Case No. ARB(AF)/99/1, Award of 16th December, 2002, paras. 103, 105.

[81] Dolzer/Stevens, *Bilateral Investment Treaties*, 1995, p. 99.

[82] For example new Model BIT of the United States contains an Annex on Expropriation which states: "The determination of whether an action or series of actions by a Party, in a specific fact situation, constitutes an indirect expropriation, requires a case-by-case, fact-based inquiry that considers, among other factors: (i) the economic impact of the government action, although the fact that an action or series of actions by a Party has an adverse effect on the economic value of an investment, standing alone, does not establish that an indirect expropriation has occurred; (ii) the extent to which the government action interferes with distinct, reasonable, investment-backed expectations; and (iii) the character of the government action. Except in rare circumstances, non-discriminatory regulatory actions by a Party that are designed and applied to protect legitimate public welfare objectives, such as public health, safety and the environment, do not constitute indirect expropriations."

[83] For a summary of relevant case law see OECD, "Indirect Expropriation" and the "Right to Regulate" in International Investment Law, Working Papers on International Investment 2/2004, pp.10 et seq.

interference with the investor's rights.[84] While the underlying rationale of this approach is appropriate it remains a crude criterion which needs further refinement. Some tribunals have accepted the view that regulatory measures would not amount to indirect expropriation if they are applied in a non-discriminatory manner and serve a public policy goal ("police power" exemption).[85] Other tribunals have, however, firmly rejected the view that the pursuit of public goals alone could justify non-compensation. In this respect, the tribunal in *Santa Elena/Costa Rica* case may have summarised the view of the majority of arbitration tribunals: "Expropriatory environmental measures – no matter how laudable and beneficial to society as a whole – are, in this respect, similar to any other expropriatory measures that a state may take in order to implement its policies: where property is expropriated, even for environmental purposes, whether domestic or international, the state's obligation to pay compensation remains."[86]

In *Azurix/Argentina*, the tribunal cited this passage with approval and added "the issue is not so much whether the measure concerned is legitimate and serves a public purpose, but whether it is a measure that, being legitimate and serving a public purpose, should give rise to a compensation claim".[87] Indirect expropriation therefore depends predominantly on the degree of interference and the effects of the measure,[88] but not on its purpose or intent.

Based on the foregoing, it is safe to assume that measures taken for regulatory purposes in the energy sector can amount to indirect or regulatory expropriations if they adversely affect the investor's assets in such a way that it deprives the investor of the value of the investment. Most likely, a tribunal would not consider the regulatory purpose of such a measure when assessing whether the state has to compensate the investor. However, it should be noted that investment tribunals have recently been reluctant to characterise measures as indirect or regulatory expropriations. Instead, they have assessed regulatory interferences with the investment in the context of the fair and equitable treatment standard.

---

[84] Pope and Talbot/Canada, NAFTA Interim Award, 26th June, 2000, para. 102, S.D. Myers/ Canada, NAFTA Partial Award, 13th November, 2000, para. 282; *Técnicas Medioambientales Tecmed S.A. vs. The United Mexican States*, ICSID Case No. ARB (AF)/00/2, Award of 29th May, 2003, para. 115.

[85] *Methanex vs. USA*, NAFTA Arbitration Under UNCITRAL Rules, Award of 3rd August, 2005, Part IV.D., para. 7, available at: http://www.state.gov/documents/organization/51052.pdf; *Saluka Investments B.V. vs. Czech Republic*, UNCITRAL Arbitration, Partial Award of 17th March, 2006, para. 262, available at: http://www.pca-cpa.org/showpage.asp?pag_id=1149.

[86] *Compañia del Desarrollo de Santa Elena S.A. vs. Republic of Costa Rica*, ICSID Case No. ARB/ 96/1, Award of 17th February, 2000, para. 72.

[87] *Azurix Corp. vs. Argentine Republic*, ICSID Case No. ARB/01/12, Award of 14th July, 2006, para. 310.

[88] Reinisch, Expropriation, in: Muchlinski/Schreuer/Ortino (eds.), *The Oxford Handbook on International Investment Law*, 2009, pp. 438 et seq.

Fair and Equitable Treatment

As a classical standard of investment protection, most investment treaties contain the requirement to afford the investor fair and equitable treatment.[89] This provision is increasingly used in investment arbitrations. Already in 2005, *Rudolf Dolzer* observed: "[H]ardly any lawsuit based on international investment treaty is filed these days without invocation of the relevant treaty clause requiring fair and equitable treatment".[90] This statement is still valid today. Many investment tribunals seem to shy away from declaring a particular government measure as an expropriation, because the measure has not yet reached a certain degree of interference, but often declare these measures to be violations of the fair and equitable treatment standard. The latter has hence sometimes been referred to as "expropriation light".[91]

Despite its frequent use in recent arbitration practice, the contours of the fair and equitable treatment standard still remain vague.[92] While some commentators have suggested that the term could be interpreted starting with its ordinary meaning,[93] most investment tribunals have approached the issue based on the object and purpose of the principle and on precedent. Based on this the contents of fair and equitable treatment can be divided into different categories of governmental behaviour which would amount to a violation of this principle.

The first and most important category[94] concerns the violation of legitimate expectations of the investor.[95] Legitimate expectations can be based on the legal framework in general[96] or on the behaviour of officials and agencies such as

---

[89] See Art. 10(1) of the Energy Charter Treaty and Art. 2(2) of the German Model BIT of 2009.

[90] Dolzer, Fair and Equitable Treatment: A Key Standard in Investment Treaties, International Lawyer 39 (2005), p. 87.

[91] Yannaca-Small, Fair and Equitable Treatment Standard: Recent Developments, in: Reinisch (ed.), *Standards of Investment Protection*, p. 112.

[92] Muchlinski, *Multinational Enterprises and the Law*, (2nd ed.) 2007, p. 635; Costamagna, Investor' Rights and State Regulatory Autonomy: the Role of the Legitimate Expectation Principle in the CMS v. Argentina case, Transnational Dispute Management 3 (2006) 2, p. 5.

[93] Dolzer, Fair and Equitable Treatment: A Key Standard in Investment Treaties, International Lawyer 39 (2005), p. 88; Muchlinski, "Caveat Investor"? The Relevance of the Conduct of the Investor under the Fair and Equitable Treatment Standard, International & Comparative Law Quarterly 2006, pp. 531 et seq.

[94] The investor's legitimate expectations are the "dominant element" of the fair and equitable treatment according to standard according to the tribunal in *Saluka Investments B.V. vs. Czech Republic*, UNCITRAL Arbitration, Partial Award of 17th March, 2006, para. 304, available at: http://www.pca-cpa.org/showpage.asp?pag_id=1149.

[95] Fietta, Expropriation and the "Fair and Equitable" Standard – The Developing Role of the Investors "Expectations" in International Investment Arbitration, Journal of International Arbitration 2006, p. 385.

[96] Dolzer/Schreuer, *Principles of International Investment Law*, 2008, p. 134; *CMS Gas Transmission Company vs. Argentine Republic*, ICSID Case No. ARB/01/8, Award of 12th May, 2005, para. 277.

specific promises or presentations about a particular legal or factual situation.[97] An investor does not have to expect sudden or fundamental changes of the law relevant to the respective investment. However, it has also been held that the fair and equitable treatment principle does not include a guarantee that the circumstances of the investment remain unchanged.[98] Furthermore, legitimate expectations must be based on information available to the investor at the time the investment was made.[99] In other words, an investor can base his or her expectations on the law as it stands at that time, but future developments are not relevant in this context.

A second fundamental element of the fair and equitable standard relates to the stability, predictability and consistency of the legal and business environment.[100] The tribunal in *CMS/Argentina* stated that a "stable legal and business environment is an essential element of FET [fair and equitable treatment]".[101] In this context, reference is often made to the object and purpose of investment treaties. Based on the preambles of these agreements which frequently refer to the intention to create favourable conditions for investments,[102] tribunals have concluded that guaranteeing a stable and predictable investment climate is one of the central purposes of these agreements. Legitimate expectations and the protection of a stable and predictable legal and business environment are closely linked as they both relate to the investment framework which the investor can legitimately expect.[103]

In addition to the notions of legitimate investor expectations and stable and predictable investment environment, tribunals have also considered requirements of judicial and administrative due process[104] as an element of the fair and equitable treatment standard at least if the violation of due process would amount to a

---

[97] *Metalclad Corporation vs. United Mexican States*, ICSID Case No. ARB(AF)/97/1, Award of 30th August, 2000, paras. 85 et seq.

[98] *Saluka Investments B.V. vs. Czech Republic*, UNCITRAL Arbitration, Partial Award of 17th March, 2006, para. 305.

[99] *AES Summit Generation Limited and AES-Tisza Erömü Kft. vs. Republic of Hungary*, ICSID Case No. ARB/07/22, Award of 23th September, 2010, para. 9.3.8.; Dolzer, The Impact of International Investment Treaties on Domestic Administrative Law, NYU Journal on International Law and Politics 2005, p. 968.

[100] Dolzer, Fair and Equitable Treatment: A Key Standard in Investment Treaties, International Lawyer 39 (2005), p. 105.

[101] *CMS Gas Transmission Company vs. Argentine Republic*, ICSID Case No. ARB/01/8, Award of 12th May, 2005, para. 274, explanation in brackets by this author.

[102] See, e.g., the preamble of the German Model BIT.

[103] See also Dolzer/Schreuer, *Principles of International Investment Law*, 2008, p. 133, who treat transparency, stability and legitimate expectations as elements of one category.

[104] Muchlinski, "Caveat Investor"? The Relevance of the Conduct of the Investor under the Fair and Equitable Treatment Standard, International & Comparative Law Quarterly 2006, p. 530; Mayeda, Playing Fair: The Meaning of Fair and Equitable Treatment in Bilateral Investment Treaties, Journal of World Trade 2007, p. 286; Dolzer/Schreuer, *Principles of International Investment Law*, 2008, p. 142.

"manifest failure of natural justice".[105] Furthermore, the prohibition of arbitrariness and discrimination, in particular "grossly unfair, unjust or idiosyncratic" behaviour[106] can be a violation of fair and equitable treatment. Finally, notions of transparency and proportionality can also be an element of fair and equitable treatment. In one particular far reaching statement, the *Tecmed* tribunal held that the host state must act "totally transparently in its relations with the foreign investor".[107]

The aforementioned elements of the fair and equitable treatment standards prompted some commentators to conclude that fair and equitable treatment is akin to the principles of good governance or of administrative law standards.[108] The proponents of the notion of Global Administrative Law have used the tribunals' interpretation of fair and equitable treatment as a key element of this new approach to public international law.[109] Indeed, the similarities of the standards for government behaviour under the fair and equitable treatment standard and basic constitutional and administrative law principles are striking. Nevertheless, tensions between the requirements of this standard and governmental regulations may arise if the fair and equitable treatment standard inhibits necessary adjustments and changes in the legal framework which the investor did not expect or which are seen as irrational or unjustifiable by the investment tribunals. As *Dolzer* and *Schreuer* conclude: Fair and equitable treatment "will narrow down the discretionary space of the host state."[110]

Umbrella Clauses

Another typical element of investment treaties which is of relevance for the present analysis are so-called "umbrella clauses". While the scope and wording of these clauses differ, they usually require the host state to fulfil "any other obligations" it may have entered into with regard to investments protected under the respective

---

[105] *Waste Management, Inc. vs. United Mexican States*, ICSID Case No. ARB(AF)/00/3, Award of 30th April, 2004, ILM 43 (2004), p. 967, para. 98.

[106] *Waste Management, Inc. vs. United Mexican States*, ICSID Case No. ARB(AF)/00/3, Award of 30th April, 2004, ILM 43 (2004), p. 967, para. 98.

[107] *Técnicas Medioambientales Tecmed, S.A. vs. United Mexican States*, ICSID Case No. ARB (AF)/00/2, Award of 29th May, 2003, para. 154.

[108] Dolzer, The Impact of International Investment Treaties on Domestic Administrative Law, NYU Journal on International Law and Politics 2005, p. 970.

[109] Kingsbury/Schill, Investor-State Arbitration as Governance: Fair and Equitable Treatment, Proportionality and the Emerging Global Administrative Law, NYU School of Law, Public Law & Legal Theory Research Paper, Working Paper No. 09-46, 2009. See also Van Harten/Loughlin, Investment Treaty Arbitration as a Species of Global Administrative Law, European Journal of International Law 2006, pp. 148 et seq.

[110] Dolzer/Schreuer, *Principles of International Investment Law*, 2008, p. 149.

treaty.[111] Umbrella clauses are nowadays a common element of investment agreements.[112] The most important issue concerning the umbrella clause is whether it covers obligations under state-investor contracts, such as concession agreements.[113] If this is the case, an investor may not only challenge direct violations of the principles of international investment agreements, but also breaches of investment contracts in an investor-state dispute settlement proceeding.

Investment tribunals have reached different decisions in this context[114]: According to the "conventional"[115] approach (sometimes called "expansive"[116] view) investor-state contracts constitute obligations which the host state entered into with regard to investments of the investor. These contracts are therefore protected by an umbrella clause. A prominent example of this approach is the decision of the tribunals in *Noble Ventures/Romania*.[117] Other tribunals have adopted a similar understanding of the umbrella clause, but declined jurisdiction due to forum choice clauses in the investment contracts with exclusive jurisdiction in domestic courts. The investment tribunals therefore felt they lacked jurisdiction to hear contract claims.[118]

According to the "narrow"[119] view the conclusion of a contract between the investor and the state or the violation thereof should not be covered by an umbrella clause. The leading case of this approach is *SGS/Pakistan:* The tribunal based its findings inter alia on the view that a broader interpretation of the umbrella clause would lead to unwanted results as it would open the floodgates for contractual claims in state-investor dispute settlement proceedings.[120] It has also pointed out that a broad interpretation of the umbrella clause would make other provisions of a BIT superfluous, because all these provisions would be already covered by the

---

[111] See e.g. Art. 10(1) of the Energy Charter Treaty and Art. 7(2) of the German Model BIT.

[112] OECD, *International Investment Law: Understanding Concepts and Tracking Innovations*, 2008, p.101.

[113] Dolzer/Schreuer, *Principles of International Investment Law*, 2008, p. 153.

[114] For a recent overview see Potts, Stabilizing the Role of Umbrella Clauses in Bilateral Investment Treaties: Intent, Reliance, and Internationalization, Virginia Journal of International Law 51 (2011), pp. 1011 et seq.

[115] Dolzer/Schreuer, *Principles of International Investment Law*, 2008, p. 155.

[116] Potts, Stabilizing the Role of Umbrella Clauses in Bilateral Investment Treaties: Intent, Reliance, and Internationalization, Virginia Journal of International Law 51 (2011), p. 1019.

[117] *Noble Ventures, Inc. vs. Romania*, ICSID Case No. ARB/01/11, Award of 12th October, 2005, para. 54. See also *CMS Gas Transmission Company vs. Argentine Republic*, ICSID Case No. ARB/01/8, Award of 12th May, 2005, paras. 296 et seq. and *MTD Equity Sdn. Bhd. and MTD Chile S.A. vs. Republic of Chile*, ICSID Case No. ARB/01/7, Award of 25th May, 2004, paras. 179 et seq.

[118] See e.g. *Bureau Veritas, Inspection, Valuation, Assessment and Control, BIVAC B.V. vs. Republic of Paraguay*, ICSID Case No. ARB/07/9, registered 11th April, 2007, paras. 141 et seq.

[119] Potts, Stabilizing the Role of Umbrella Clauses in Bilateral Investment Treaties: Intent, Reliance, and Internationalization, Virginia Journal of International Law 51 (2011), p. 1012.

[120] *SGS Société Générale de Surveillance S.A. vs. Islamic Republic of Pakistan*, ICSID Case No. ARB/01/13, Decision on Jurisdiction, 29th January, 2004, paras. 166 et seq.

protection of all other legal obligations incorporated by the umbrella clause.[121] While some tribunals have followed this approach others held that the umbrella clause would only cover measures of the state acting under sovereign power.[122] Hence, the interference of the host state with the contract on the basis of public authority (*acta iure imperii*) would fall within the scope of the investment agreement, while contractual breaches (*acta iure gestiones*), such as the non-payment of fees by the state, would not be covered.

The foregoing shows that there is no coherent approach in the current case law of the arbitral tribunals regarding the umbrella clause. As one commentator notes "the legal status of umbrella clauses is in a state of disarray. The current jurisprudence provides little predictive power for current and future investors concerning the redress of contractual breaches."[123] One might add that the lack of legal clarity is not only problematic from the perspective of the investor but also from the perspective of the host state.

The scope of the umbrella clause is of specific concern in the context of energy regulation, because energy-related investments are usually large-scale projects which require elaborate and detailed contracts (usually concessions) between the state and the investor. Often they contain a regulatory framework specific to the project and encompass commercial aspects as well as elements of public power (administrative contracts). In light of the complexity of these contracts and the various legal fields they address it is of great importance to the investor and the host state which forum will hear their respective claims in case a conflict arises.

Areas of Contention

The preceding sections of this contribution already indicated potential areas of conflict between the protection of (energy-related) investment through international investment agreements and the objectives and instruments of the regulation of energy production and consumption. In what follows, three specific areas of contention will be identified. They relate to the traditional issue of economic sovereignty and ownership, to price controls as a typical element of energy regulation and to the modern form of environmental regulation through standards.

---

[121] *El Paso Energy International Company vs. Argentine Republic*, ICSID Case No. ARB/03/15, Decision on Jurisdiction, 27th April, 2006, para. 76.

[122] Dolzer/Schreuer, *Principles of International Investment Law*, 2008, p. 159 with references.

[123] Potts, Stabilizing the Role of Umbrella Clauses in Bilateral Investment Treaties: Intent, Reliance, and Internationalization, Virginia Journal of International Law 51 (2011), p. 1045.

Ownership and Economic Sovereignty

The production of energy depends to a large degree on the extraction of raw materials (oil, gas, coal). Foreign direct investment in this context may therefore clash with claims of territorial sovereignty and control over these natural resources by the host state. While resentments against the exploitation of raw materials by foreign investors and the objective to benefit from these resources resulted in expropriations and nationalisations in the past,[124] recent moves towards greater involvement and participation of the host state have stopped short of the formal transfer of ownership.[125] It seems that host states have no intention to fight the battles of the past again and to use nationalisation as an element of national energy policy. As a consequence, outright clashes over ownership and sovereignty will not feature prominently in future conflicts between investors and host state governments.

The reasons for this reduced potential for conflict are diverse: They include a generally more liberal (or at least relaxed) attitude of many host states towards foreign direct investment even if the states are governed by socialist regimes. Furthermore, many governments have realised that they can reach their policy goals through lesser forms of intervention. Lastly, the remarkable increase of investment agreements and state-investor dispute settlement proceedings make it unlikely if not impossible for a government to directly expropriate a foreign investor in order to regain full control of a particular extractive business without having to pay a substantive amount of compensation. While governments may also have to compensate investors for indirect compensations or violations of other provisions of investment treaties, the risk to lose a case which involves a clear and obvious expropriation seems substantially higher than losing a case based on indirect forms of interference with the investment.

The legal regime addressing the issue of ownership is also very clear and based on two fundamental principles which are no longer contested: States enjoy the right to expropriate investors and regain ownership of extractive industries as part of their territorial and economic sovereignty.[126] Such expropriation – while in principle legal – must pursue public interests, be administered in a non-discriminatory and non-arbitrary manner and requires prompt, effective and fair compensation.[127]

---

[124] For a discussion of the reasons of resentments see Sornarajah, *The International Law on Foreign Investment*, (2nd ed.) 2004, pp. 77 et seq.

[125] See the Bolivian example as described by De Sá Ribeiro, Sovereignty over Natural Resources Investment Law and Expropriation: The case of Bolivia and Brazil, Journal of World Energy Law & Business 2 (2009), pp. 133 et seq.

[126] Sornarajah, *The International Law on Foreign Investment*, (2nd ed.) 2004, p. 97; Dolzer/Schreuer, *Principles of International Investment Law*, 2008, p. 89; Subedi, *International Investment Law – Reconciling Policy and Principle*, 2008, p. 121.

[127] Vielleville/Vasani, Sovereignty Over Natural Resources Versus Rights Under Investment Contracts: Which One Prevails?, Transnational Dispute Management 5 (2003), p. 11.

While details such as methods of calculating the fair value of an investment or questions about legal remedies may depend on the circumstances and the contents of a specific investment agreement, the fundamental principles are clear and provide host states and investors with sufficient legal clarity.

Price Controls

As shown in section "Objectives and Policies of Energy Regulation" the control of prices is traditionally a central policy tool of energy regulation. It has been used for various purposes including social, economic and ideological or populist reasons. Price controls and administrative price setting are often an important element of guaranteeing (universal) access to energy, because they enable even consumers who could not afford a market price access to energy. Price regulations can also be an instrument of competition policy, e.g. if the regulator deems that energy suppliers abuse their dominant positions by demanding uncompetitive, high prices or because energy suppliers have agreed on a price cartel. Lastly, price controls have been used to limit the "profit" of a foreign investor or to ensure the political support of the urban population in developing countries, because they sometimes benefit from price controls more than the poor rural population who often physically lack access to energy.

Price regulations can come under the scrutiny of investment law in a number of different situations. Theoretically and in extreme cases, price regulations could be so restrictive that they amount to an indirect expropriation. For example, if the government imposes unreasonably low prices without subsidising the energy supply or allowing the supplier to meet his or her costs in another manner, the investor may no longer enjoy any substantive rights of commercial value. However, this does not seem to be a typical situation. More often, the imposition of price regulations and the administrative determination of prices becomes an issue under the fair and equitable treatment standard.

In the well-known case of *CMS Gas/Argentina*[128] price regulation of the gas market imposed after the Argentinian financial crisis of 1999–2002 was a central issue. Argentina had adopted far reaching economic reforms including the privatisation of many public utilities in the late 1980s. In the mid-1990s, CMS Gas, a US company, acquired 29% of the shares of the privatised gas transportation company TGN.[129] According to the licence granted to TGN and corresponding regulations, the gas tariffs were to be calculated in US dollars and then converted

---

[128] *CMS Gas Transmission Company vs. Argentine Republic*, ICSID Case No. ARB/01/8, Award of 12th May, 2005.

[129] For a summary of the facts see also Costamagna, Investor' Rights and State Regulatory Autonomy: the Role of the Legitimate Expectation Principle in the CMS v. Argentina case, Transnational Dispute Management 3 (2006) 2, p. 2.

into pesos at a conversion rate which would be adjusted every 6 months based on the US Producer Price Index. As a first reaction to the serious economic crisis Argentina was facing, the government suspended the adjustment of the prices for some time and after a worsening of the crisis in 2002 abandoned it totally. Attempts to renegotiate the licences after the crisis proved to be unsuccessful. The ICSID tribunal seized with the matter by the investor ruled that Argentina violated the fair and equitable treatment standard of the US-Argentina bilateral investment agreement, but rejected the claim of expropriation and also rejected Argentina's general defence under the doctrine on necessity.

The tribunal recalled that "a stable legal and business environment is an essential element of fair and equitable treatment".[130] It went on to state that the decision to terminate the dollar adjustment transformed the legal and business environment of the investment entirely. Furthermore, the tribunal noted that the respective guarantees were crucial for the investment decision.[131] Even though the tribunal conceded that the legal system must not be frozen at all times, it held that the change of the price regulation was a breach of the fair and equitable treatment standard.[132] The tribunal did not further explain its findings and only cited approvingly two rulings of earlier tribunals.[133] As a defence Argentina invoked specifically the right to regulate public services. It argued that the transportation and the distribution of gas had to take into account particular needs of social importance and that the regulation of tariffs was subject to the discretionary power of the government which had to take social and other public considerations into account.[134] The tribunal did not engage in a discussion of these arguments. In fact, the tribunal explicitly rejected the idea that the purpose or intention of the government when imposing the respective measures should be of any relevance.[135]

The *CMS Gas* tribunal displayed a deplorable lack of sensitivity with regards to regulatory issues of energy distribution. Its main argument seems to have been that the state promised the investor that the particular price mechanism would not be changed and that the investor could therefore rely on whatever promises were made. It may well be that the argument of Argentina was a flawed one,

---

[130] *CMS Gas Transmission Company vs. Argentine Republic*, ICSID Case No. ARB/01/8, Award of 12th May, 2005, para. 273.

[131] *CMS Gas Transmission Company vs. Argentine Republic*, ICSID Case No. ARB/01/8, Award of 12th May, 2005, para. 275.

[132] *CMS Gas Transmission Company vs. Argentine Republic*, ICSID Case No. ARB/01/8, Award of 12th May, 2005, para. 281. Upheld by the Decision of the ad hoc Committee on the Application for Annulment of the Argentine Republic, 25th September, 2007, paras. 84–85.

[133] *CMS Gas Transmission Company vs. Argentine Republic*, ICSID Case No. ARB/01/8, Award of 12th May, 2005, paras. 278 et seq.

[134] *CMS Gas Transmission Company vs. Argentine Republic*, ICSID Case No. ARB/01/8, Award of 12th May, 2005, para. 93.

[135] *CMS Gas Transmission Company vs. Argentine Republic*, ICSID Case No. ARB/01/8, Award of 12th May, 2005, para. 280.

because – allegedly – consumer prices were artificially low due to the intervention.[136] Yet, it is disappointing that the tribunal did not engage in a serious assessment and evaluation of the view that the Argentinian measures aimed at regulating a public service.[137]

A similar approach, albeit with a different result, was employed by the investment tribunal in *AES Summit/Hungary*.[138] The arbitration which took place on the basis of the Energy Charter Treaty concerned the reintroduction of administrative pricing for distribution of electricity to the consumers. AES, a UK based investor, purchased the majority of shares of a company operating four power stations as part of the Hungarian privatization programme for state-owned power stations. The pricing system was based on administrative pricing until 2004 when a new system was established. However, after a political debate about energy prices, Hungary reintroduced the system of administrative price fixing about 2 years after its abolishment.

Again, the investor claimed the violation of a number of standards, but the tribunal rejected them all. Regarding the fair and equitable treatment standard the tribunal first held that the investor could not have legitimately expected that administrative prices would never again be adopted. In particular, the tribunal pointed out that government officials did not claim after the termination of the price administration that regulated prices would never again be introduced.[139] The tribunal also rejected the claim that Hungary failed to provide a stable legal and business framework with essentially similar arguments.[140] The tribunal then assessed whether the introduction of administrative pricing was a violation of the principles of due process, arbitrariness and transparency. It discussed the various steps which led to the reintroduction at great length and concluded that AES was not led to believe that administrative price setting had been abandoned for all times.[141] However, like the *CMS Gas* tribunal the *AES Summit* tribunal also does not place great importance on the regulatory purpose of the measure.

Based on a comparison of the two decisions it can be concluded that price controls which could have been anticipated and which were imposed in a non-discriminatory, non-arbitrary and rational manner do not violate the standards of

---

[136] *CMS Gas Transmission Company vs. Argentine Republic*, ICSID Case No. ARB/01/8, Award of 12th May, 2005, para. 72.

[137] For a similar critique see Mayeda, Playing Fair: The Meaning of Fair and Equitable Treatment in Bilateral Investment Treaties, Journal of World Trade 2007, p. 279.

[138] *AES Summit Generation Limited and AES-Tisza Erömü Kft. vs. Republic of Hungary*, ICSID Case No. ARB/07/22, Award of 23rd September, 2010, annulment proceedings pending since 28th January, 2011.

[139] *AES Summit Generation Limited and AES-Tisza Erömü Kft. vs. Republic of Hungary*, ICSID Case No. ARB/07/22, Award of 23rd September, 2010, para. 9.3.18.

[140] *AES Summit Generation Limited and AES-Tisza Erömü Kft. vs. Republic of Hungary*, ICSID Case No. ARB/07/22, Award of 23rd September, 2010, para. 9.3.37.

[141] *AES Summit Generation Limited and AES-Tisza Erömü Kft. vs. Republic of Hungary*, ICSID Case No. ARB/07/22, Award of 23rd September, 2010, paras. 9.3.43 et seq.

protection of an investment agreement. International investment law, however, seems blind vis-à-vis concerns of social regulation. This may have serious implications for the legitimacy of the current system of investment protection based on investment agreements and investor-state arbitration.

Environmental Regulation

The impact of international investment agreements on environmental regulation is one of the most contentious issues of the contemporary discourse on international investment law.[142] Product standards, land use and zoning regulations and the disposal of hazardous waste have been subject to prominent state-investor arbitration proceedings. In light of the importance of the energy sector for the achievement of environmental policy goals the protection of energy-related investment projects is bound to affect environmental regulation of these investments.

A recent case which has been settled without arbitration – *Vattenfall/Germany* – can be used as an example of how environmental regulation could clash with international investment law.[143] The case concerned the construction of a coal-based power plant in the city of Hamburg in Germany. The investor Vattenfall, a Swedish utility company owned 100% by the Swedish government, claimed that the issuance of administrative permits to build and operate the plant was delayed and that the permits did not fulfil promises made by a previous government of Hamburg. In particular, the permits concerned immission control regulations and water usage. Vattenfall claimed a violation of Article 10 (1) of the Energy Charter Treaty (fair and equitable treatment) and of Art. 13 of the Energy Charter Treaty (expropriation without compensation).[144]

As the case was essentially settled without a formal ruling it is unknown whether Germany made any compensatory payments or agreed to other compensations.

---

[142] Viñuales, Foreign investment and the environment in international law: an ambiguous relationship, British Yearbook of International Law 80 (2010), pp. 244–332 and Fauchald, International Investment Law and Environmental Protection, Yearbook of International Environmental Law 17 (2006), pp. 3–47; Miles, International Investment Law and Climate Change: Issues in the Transition to a Low Carbon World, presented at the Inaugural Conference of the Society of International Economic Law, July 2008, p. 3, available at: http://papers.ssrn.com/sol3/papers.cfm?abstract_id=1154588.

[143] *Vattenfall AB, Vattenfall Europe AG, Vattenfall Europe Generation AG vs. Federal Republic of Germany*, ICSID Case No. ARB/09/6, parties' settlement agreement rendered on 11th March, 2011. For an analysis see also Bernasconi, Background paper on Vattenfall v. Germany Arbitration, 2009 International Institute for Sustainable Development (IISD), 2009, available at: http://www.iisd.org/pdf/2009/background_vattenfall_vs_germany.pdf.

[144] *Vattenfall AB, Vattenfall Europe AG, Vattenfall Europe Generation AG vs. Federal Republic of Germany*, ICSID Case No. ARB/09/6, Request for Arbitration, 30th March, 2009, on file with author.

In any event, the case shows that issues of environmental regulation could come under the scrutiny of an investment tribunal which would then have to decide whether a particular regulation is consistent with the standards of international investment law. This poses certain risks on governments aiming to regulate energy investments from an environmental perspective. These risks may in turn then lead to the phenomenon of "regulatory chill"[145] which relates to a situation in which a government imposes fewer restrictions on an investor in order to avoid any conflicts with international law even if international law might allow stricter regulation.

Conclusion

The international legal issues evolving around energy-related foreign direct investments reflect the different interests of the host state and the foreign investor in this context. The law aims at a balance between legitimate regulatory concerns and the exercise of territorial sovereignty through the state on the one hand and the interests of the investor regarding legal stability and profit-maximisation on the other hand. In the past, conflicts often arose due to expropriations and nationalisations of the investor or because of general unstable legal conditions. The practical relevance of direct forms of expropriation is declining nowadays which is why there has been hardly any state investor dispute settlement practice concerning direct expropriation recently.

The focus has clearly shifted to the regulatory side of the picture these days. Disputes between host states and energy investors now mostly concern indirect expropriations, fair and equitable treatment and umbrella clauses. This raises the question whether the legal instruments and institutions of international investment law can adequately deal with the conflicts arising in this context. Traditionally, international investment law aimed at the protection and promotion of foreign investment. This was based on the assumption that the host state would voluntarily reduce its sovereign right to interfere with economic activities of foreign investors in order to provide with a stable investment climate which would attract the inflow and capital and know-how. Normative concepts such as "legitimate expectations" and "stable legal and business environment" directly flow from this function of international investment law.

If, however, governmental interference with economic activities of foreign investors is not based on classic notions of (territorial) sovereignty and self-determination, but on social and environmental concerns, the standards of investment law may need

---

[145] Tienhaara, *The Expropriation of Environmental Governance – Protecting Foreign Investors at the Expense of Public Policy*, 2009, p. 25; Miles, International Investment Law and Climate Change: Issues in the Transition to a Low Carbon World, presented at the Inaugural Conference of the Society of International Economic Law, July 2008, p. 22, available at: http://papers.ssrn.com/sol3/papers.cfm?abstract_id=1154588.

to be revisited. It could be necessary that regulatory intentions and policy goals are taken into account when assessing governmental activities. It may also become necessary that investment tribunals consider social and environmental objectives more seriously when they seek to strike a balance between the interests of the state and the investor. In this context, energy regulation could be an important area to test such new approaches. After all, the classical doctrines of international investment law were also developed in this field.

Acknowledgments I would like to thank Franceso Costamagna and Rhea Hoffmann for very helpful comments. Unless noted otherwise all decisions of investment arbitration tribunals cited in this contribution are available from the website of the International Centre for Settlement of Investment Disputes (ICSID) at http://icsid.worldbank.org/ICSID/Index.jsp or from the website Investment Treaty Arbitration at http://ita.law.uvic.ca.

Regulating Energy Supranationally: EU Energy Policy

Ludwig Gramlich

Introduction: "Energy is the Lifeblood of Our Society"

In November 2010, the European Commission published a "communication" on "Energy 2020" intended to inform the other main EU institutions about its "strategy for competitive, sustainable and secure energy".[1] Although the authors of this document stated that "a common EU energy policy has evolved around the common objective to ensure the uninterrupted physical availability of energy products and services on the market, at a price which is affordable for all consumers (private and industrial), while contributing to the EU's wider social and climate goals" and that "the central goals for energy policy (security of supply, competitiveness, and sustainability) are now laid down in the Lisbon Treaty"[2] – i.e. Art. 194 of the Treaty on the functioning of the European Union (TFEU)[3] – they were in serious doubt whether "the existing strategy was likely to achieve all the 2020 targets", and they thought it "wholly inadequate to the longer term challenges". So since "EU energy and climate goals have been incorporated into the Europe 2020 Strategy for smart, sustainable and inclusive growth,[4] adopted by the European Council in June 2010, and into its flagship initiative 'Resource efficient Europe'[5]", the "urgent task" for

---

[1] Commission Communication, Energy 2020 – A Strategy for Competitive, Sustainable and Secure Energy, 10th November, 2010, COM(2010) 639 final.

[2] Op. cit., p. 2, referring to the Treaty of Lisbon amending the Treaty on European Union and the Treaty establishing the European Community of 13th December, 2007, OJ [2007] C 306/1.

[3] On this provision, see below, at D.I.2.

[4] Commission Communication, Europe 2020 – A Strategy for Smart, Sustainable and Inclusive Growth, 3rd March, COM(2010) 2020 final.

[5] For an indicative roadmap of October 2010, see http://ec.europa.eu/governance/impact/planned_ia/docs/2011_ env_003_resource_efficient_europe_en.pdf.

L. Gramlich (✉)
TU Chemnitz, Thüringer Weg 7, 09126 Chemnitz, Germany
e-mail: prof.gramlich@wirtschaft.tu-chemnitz.de

C. Herrmann and J.P. Terhechte (eds.), *European Yearbook of International Economic Law (EYIEL), Vol. 3 (2012)*, European Yearbook of International Economic Law 3, DOI 10.1007/978-3-642-23309-8_12, © Springer-Verlag Berlin Heidelberg 2012

the EU should be "to agree the tools which will make the necessary shift possible and thus ensure that Europe can emerge from recession on a more competitive, secure and sustainable path".[6]

Some major findings of the communication were:

The internal energy market is still fragmented and has not achieved its potential for transparency, accessibility and choice".[7] "The EU is the level at which energy policy should be developed. Decisions on energy policy taken by one Member State inevitably have an impact on other Member States. The optimum energy mix, including the swift development of renewables, needs a continental market at least. Energy is the market sector where the greatest economic efficiencies can be made on a pan-European scale".[8] "In international energy affairs, the EU could be much stronger and effective if it took charge of its common interest and ambition. Despite accounting for one fifth of the world's energy use, the EU continues to have less influence on international energy markets than its economic weight would suggest.[9]

Thus, the conclusion drawn from these insights was:

We urgently need far-reaching changes in energy production, use and supply.

Consequently, the EU new energy strategy should focus "*on five priorities:*

1. Achieving an energy efficient Europe;
2. Building a truly pan-European integrated energy market;
3. Empowering consumers and achieving the highest level of safety and security;
4. Extending Europe's leadership in energy technology and innovation;
5. Strengthening the external dimension of the EU energy market".[10]

The following study tries to analyze more deeply whether the strategy change proposed by the European Commission is appropriate and, in particular, if there is indeed a (political) need as well as a solid legal basis to go on shaping a genuine common energy policy at the European (supranational) level. After having discussed specific aspects of the energy sector, especially its main segments and the (actual and probable future) distribution of resources (B.), I shall look more closely at major (international and European) developments within the last decades before the actual legal framework at EU level will be dealt with in details, including its international law context (C., D.). Finally, I shall sketch the relationship between EU energy policy and Member States' policies (E.) and, finally, draw some general conclusions (F.).

---

[6] Commission Communication, Energy 2020 – A Strategy for Competitive, Sustainable and Secure Energy, 10th November, 2010, COM(2010) 639 final, p. 3.

[7] Ibid.

[8] Commission Communication, Energy 2020 – A Strategy for Competitive, Sustainable and Secure Energy, 10th November, 2010, COM(2010) 639 final, p. 4.

[9] Ibid.

[10] Commission Communication, Energy 2020 – A Strategy for Competitive, Sustainable and Secure Energy, 10th November, 2010, COM(2010) 639 final, p. 6.

Fundamental Facts About Energy and the Energy Sector

Basic Aspects

Energy originates from four fundamental forces of physics: gravity, electromagnetism, weak and strong nuclear force. These forces generate commercial energy in six familiar forms: mechanical, chemical, thermal, radiant, nuclear and electrical. In any system, energy can be turned from one form into another. Energy scarcity becomes a problem because of the second "law" of thermodynamics which requires that when energy is converted, it is reduced in quality and in its ability to do work.

Energy resources are still often publicly owned[11] and considered basic wealth to a society. As such they are usually taxed – sometimes quite heavily.[12] Although most economists favour markets and private ownership for the allocation of goods and services they do not deny that markets may fail and that then government might (or should) step in. One such case is a decreasing-cost industry. For example, the electricity industry's huge capital costs and economies of scale had marked it a "natural monopoly" for many years.[13] But actual or alleged problems with government ownership and regulation, along with technical changes in electricity generation, have led to moves toward deregulation and privatization. With the first development, institutional arrangements or governance structures (including spot purchases, long-term contracts, and vertical integration) in markets are likely to evolve.[14] Next, energy production, transport, and consumption produce a variety of pollutants often affecting others besides their producers. Because of these negative externalities, private markets will not allocate energy efficiently, and governments have stepped in to respond.[15]

Energy was and is often produced in a technically complex industry. Uranium, e.g., requires sophisticated processing, natural gas is transported through complicated pipeline networks with computer systems to monitor and measure its location. With the "information (technology) revolution", even more technical choices influence how energy firms are organized and how they function. Finally, energy is – and will remain – a global business with many large national and multi- or transnational

---

[11] To be distinguished from State sovereignty over natural resources; cf. below, at fn. 86.

[12] Cf., e.g., National Research Council (ed.), *Energy Taxation: An Analysis of Selected Taxes*, 1980; Dahl, *International Energy Markets. Understanding Prices, Policies, and Profits*, 2004, pp. 65 et seq.; Toder, Energy Taxation: Principles and Interests, 2006, available at: http://www.urban.org/UploadedPDF/1001077_energy_ taxation.pdf.

[13] Cf., e.g., Schumacher, *Innovationsregulierung im Recht der netzgebundenen Elektrizitätswirtschaft*, 2009, pp. 128 et seq.; Dahl, *International Energy Markets. Understanding Prices, Policies, and Profits*, 2004, pp. 81 et seq.

[14] Cf. Zylka, *Marktaufsicht im Stromhandel*, 2010, pp. 29 et seq.

[15] Schumacher, *Innovationsregulierung im Recht der netzgebundenen Elektrizitätswirtschaft*, 2009, pp. 91 et seq.; Dahl, *International Energy Markets. Understanding Prices, Policies, and Profits*, 2004, pp. 199 et seq.

enterprises involved in its production, transportation, storage, and distribution.[16] So it is also quite important to develop a corporate culture that is compatible with the national cultures in every place where the company does business.[17]

Status Quo and Perspectives

World energy consumption has doubled since 1970, and energy demand continues to rise in virtually all regions of the world, particularly in China and India.[18] However, the pattern of the increase if addressed in terms of per capita consumption, total national consumption increase or in terms of percentage increase looks very different, and the major challenge to the global energy system will be changing the present unsustainable patterns of energy, especially oil use in industrialized countries. Thus, policies for containing and eventually reducing fossil fuel consumption in the developed world seem to be a prerequisite for global moderation.

In EU-27, oil is still the most important fuel followed by natural gas and solid fuels (coal, lignite, peat) while nuclear reached a share of 1/7 of total energy consumption. Renewable energy sources (biomass, hydro, wind, solar, geothermal) have steadily increased their contribution but their share is still below 10%. Energy in its various forms is consumed in all parts of the economy, the greatest parts of final energy being used in transport, industry and households. EU import dependency stands close to 50%, it is particularly high for oil and (in a minor degree) for natural gas.[19]

Legal Developments in the Energy Sector Relating to Europe

Overview

Energy policy in Europe and at a (Western) European level can be traced back to the first (European) supranational organization, the European Coal and Steel Community (ECSC) founded soon after the end of World War Two.[20] But also

---

[16] To name but a few: BP (www.bp.com), Exxon Mobil Corp. (www.exxon.com) or Shell (www.shell.com).

[17] Cf. more details, cf. Dahl, *International Energy Markets. Understanding Prices, Policies, and Profits*, 2004, pp. 499 et seq.

[18] For details, see the IEA's World Energy Outlook (edition 2010), available at: http://www.worldenergyoutlook.org, and U.S. Energy Information Administration, International Energy Outlook, July 2010, available at: http://www.eia.gov/oiaf/ieo/index.html.

[19] Cf. Commission Staff Working Document, Annex to the Green Paper "A European Strategy for Sustainable, Competitive and Secure Energy", SEC(2006) 317/2; European Central Bank, Energy Markets and the Euro Area Market Economy, 2010, pp. 12 et seq.

[20] Treaty of 18th April, 1951; see below, at II.1.

one of the Rome Treaties of 1957 was focusing on energy issues – i.e. the peaceful use of atomic energy – whereas the aims and tasks of the (then) European Economic Community (EEC)[21] were hardly dealing with that topic at all. From its very beginnings, the European Atomic Energy Community (EAEC)[22] has been cooperating closely with the International Atomic Energy Agency (IAEA).[23] Broader international aspects of energy policy were highlighted by the first "oil crisis" in the early 1970s, at least a particular aspect became evident, i.e. the need for security of supply from foreign, energy-producing (developing) countries for many industrialized (Western) states. So, within the framework of the OECD, a new institution, the International Energy Agency (IEA),[24] was established. In the 1980s, energy issues became a prominent topic also in East-West relations and, after the end of the "cold war", finally led to the conclusion of the Energy Charter treaty.[25] The last two decades – starting with the Rio summit on environment and development 1992[26] – have been characterized by tendencies of growing convergence between energy policy and environmental policy, as shown by the various international approaches to cope with climate change (caused by human activities [mis]using energy).

Developments in the Context of European (Economic) Integration

European Coal and Steel Community

The ECSC Treaty was signed in Paris on April 18, 1951 and brought France, Germany, Italy and the Benelux countries together in a "Community" (art. 1) with the purpose of organizing free movement of coal and steel and free access to sources of production. The idea of pooling Franco-German coal and steel production was not only an economic choice but also a political one, as these two raw materials were the basis of the industry and power of the two countries the underlying political objective being to strengthen Franco-German solidarity, banish the specter of war and open the way to European integration (ECSC Treaty, Preamble).[27]

---

[21] Treaty of 25th March, 1957; for more details, see below, at II.3.

[22] Treaty of 25th March, 1957; see below, at II.2.

[23] http://www.iaea.org. On its objections and functions, see Art. 2, 3 of the IAEA Statute; also see the Agreement of 14th September, 1973 between IAEA and EAEC/Member States, available at: http://www.iaea.org/Publications/Documents/Infcircs/Others/inf193.shtml.

[24] http://www.iea.org; see also below, at III.1.

[25] http://www.encharter.org; see also below, at III.2.

[26] See, e.g., Beyerlin, Rio-Konferenz 1992: Beginn einer neuen globalen Umweltrechtsordnung?, Zeitschrift für ausländisches öffentliches Recht und Völkerrecht 54 (1994), pp. 124 et seq.

[27] On the quite dominant political motives of the first European Community see, e.g., Uertz, Von der Montanunion zur EU, in: Buchstab/Uertz (eds.), Nationale Identität im vereinten Europa,

The aim of that Treaty was to contribute, through a common market for "coal and steel" (art. 81), to economic expansion, growth of employment and a rising standard of living (art. 2 par. 1). Thus, the institutions of the new organization – a High Authority, an Assembly, a Council of Ministers and a Court of Justice (art. 7) – had to ensure an orderly supply to the common market by ensuring equal access to the sources of production, the establishment of the lowest prices and improved working conditions, and all of this had to be accompanied by growth in international trade and modernization of production (art. 3). In the light of the establishment of the common market, the Treaty introduced the free movement of products without customs duties or taxes, and it prohibited discriminatory measures or practices, subsidies, aids granted by States or special charges imposed by States and restrictive practices (art. 4).

The High Authority (later on: the Commission, according to the Merger Treaty[28]) was the independent collegiate executive with the task of achieving the objectives laid down by the Treaty and acting in the general interest of the Community. It was a truly supranational body with power of decision supervising the modernization and improvement of production, the supply of products under identical conditions, the development of a common export policy and the improvement of working conditions in the coal and steel industries. The High Authority took decisions, made recommendations and delivered opinions (art. 14). It was assisted by a Consultative Committee made up of representatives of producers, workers, consumers and dealers (arts. 18, 19).

With regard to production, the ECSC played a mainly indirect, subsidiary role through cooperation with governments and intervention in relation to prices and commercial policy (art. 57). However, in the event of any decline in demand or shortage, it could take direct action by imposing quotas with the aim of limiting production in an organized manner or, for shortages, by drawing up production programs establishing consumption priorities, determining how resources should be allocated and setting export levels (arts. 58, 59).

In relation to price fixing, the Treaty prohibited practices which discriminated according to price, unfair competitive practices and discriminatory practices involving the application of dissimilar conditions to comparable transactions (art. 60). These rules also applied to transport. Furthermore, in certain circumstances, such as a manifest crisis, the High Authority could fix maximum or minimum prices either within the Community or in relation to the export market (art. 61).

So as to ensure that free competition was respected, the High Authority had to be informed of any action by Member States which was liable to endanger it (art. 67). Furthermore, the ECSC Treaty dealt specifically with the three cases which could distort competition: agreements, concentrations and the abuse of dominant

---

2006, pp. 30 et seq., also available at: http://www.kas.de/upload/Publikationen/montanunion-zur-eu.pdf.

[28] Treaty establishing a Single Council and a Single Commission of the European Communities of 8th April, 1965, OJ [1967] 152/1.

positions. Agreements or associations between undertakings could be cancelled by the High Authority if they directly or indirectly prevented, restricted or distorted normal competition (arts. 65, 66).

The treaty also dealt with the commercial policy of the ECSC towards third countries. Although the powers of national governments remained in place, a number of competences were transferred to the Community such as setting maximum and minimum rates for customs duties and supervising the granting of import and export licenses, as well as the right to be kept informed of commercial agreements relating to coal and steel (arts. 71 et seq.). Furthermore, the power of the High Authority prevailed in the fields of dumping, the use by undertakings outside the jurisdiction of the Community of means of competition contrary to the Treaty and substantial increases in imports which could seriously threaten Community production (art. 74).

Its validity period being limited to 50 years (art. 97), the Treaty expired on 23 July 2002.[29]

European Atomic Energy Community

To tackle the general shortage of "conventional" energy (like, e.g. coal) in the 1950s, the six States finally establishing this other new international organization (Belgium, France, Germany, Italy, Luxembourg and the Netherlands) looked to nuclear energy as a means of achieving energy independence. Since the costs of investing in nuclear energy could not be met by individual States, the founding States joined together to form Euratom.[30]

In the preamble of the EAEC Treaty, the signatories described themselves as:

– recognizing that nuclear energy represents an essential resource for the development and invigoration of industry and will permit the advancement of the cause of peace . . .,
– resolved to create the conditions necessary for the development of a powerful nuclear industry which will provide extensive energy resources, lead to the modernization of technical processes and contribute, through its many other applications, to the prosperity of their peoples,
– anxious to create the conditions of safety necessary to eliminate hazards to the life and health of the public,
– desiring to associate other countries with their work and to cooperate with international organizations concerned with the peaceful development of atomic energy.

According to its art. 1, the general objective of the treaty is to contribute to the formation and development of Europe's nuclear industries, so that all Member States can benefit from the development of atomic energy, and to ensure security of

---

[29] Cf. Grunwald, *Das Energierecht der Europäischen Gemeinschaften*, 2003, pp. 181 et seq.

[30] Cf. Schroeder, Die Euratom – auf dem Weg zu einer Umweltgemeinschaft, Deutsches Verwaltungsblatt 1995, p. 322; id., Der Euratom-Vertrag, Juristische Arbeitsblätter 27 (1995), p. 728.

supply. At the same time, the treaty guarantees high safety standards for the public and prevents nuclear materials intended principally for civilian use from being diverted to military use. The powers of Euratom's institutions – the same ones as in the E(E)C[31] – are strictly limited to peaceful civil uses of nuclear energy.

The objective of the Euratom Treaty is to pool the nuclear industries of Member States. In this context, it applies only to certain entities (Member States, physical persons, and public or private undertakings or institutions, art. 87) which carry out some or all of their activities in an area covered by the Treaty, i.e. special fissile materials, source materials and the ores from which source materials are extracted (arts. 92, 197).

According to the Treaty, the specific tasks of Euratom are, in particular[32]:

– To facilitate investment and ensure the establishment of the basic installations necessary for the development of nuclear energy in the EU (arts. 2 lit. c], 40 et seq.). The Commission regularly publishes nuclear illustrative programs[33] indicating, in particular, nuclear energy production targets and the investment required for their attainment. Persons and undertakings engaged in the industrial activities listed in Annex II to the treaty are required to notify the Commission of any investment projects (arts. 41, 42);
– To ensure that all users in the EU receive a regular and equitable supply of ores and nuclear fuels. In this context, the treaty prohibits all practices designed to secure a privileged position for certain users (art. 52 par. 2) and establishes an Agency – the Euratom Supply Agency having legal personality and financial autonomy and being supervised by the Commission, which issues directives to it and possesses a right of veto over its decisions (arts. 53, 54) – with a right of option on ores, source materials and special fissile materials produced in the territories of Member States and an exclusive right to conclude contracts relating to the supply of ores, source materials and special fissile materials coming from inside the Community or from outside (arts. 57 et seq., 64 et seq.);
– To make certain that civil nuclear materials are not diverted to other (particularly military) purposes.

The Euratom safeguards (arts. 77 et seq.) are applied in conjunction with those of the IAEA under tripartite agreements concluded between the Member States, the Community and the IAEA. Thus, this task is related to the one obliging the EAEC

---

[31] Schroeder, Der Euratom-Vertrag, Juristische Arbeitsblätter 27 (1995), p. 728.

[32] Cf. also, especially referring to Art. 31, 32, ECJ Case C-221/88, *Busseni*, [1990] ECR I-495; Trüe, EU-Kompetenzen für Energierecht, Gesundheitsschutz und Umweltschutz nach dem Verfassungsentwurf, Juristenzeitung 59 (2004), pp. 780 and 782; Kahl, Die Kompetenzen der EU in der Energiepolitik nach Lissabon, Europarecht 44 (2009), pp. 615 and 619; also ECJ, Case C-115/08, *Land Oberösterreich vs. ČEZ as*, [2009] ECR I-10265, paras. 100 et seq.

[33] Cf., e.g., Commission Communication "Nuclear Illustrative Programme" of 10th January, 2007, COM(2006) 844 final; also see http://ec.europa.eu/energy/strategies/2008/doc/2008_11_ser2/ nuclear_illustrative_programme _pinc_updt_communication.pdf.

institutions to foster progress in the peaceful uses of nuclear energy by working with other countries and international organizations. More details on external relations of Euratom are laid down in arts. 101 et seq. of the EAEC Treaty.

Contrary to the case of the E(E)C Treaty,[34] no major changes have ever been made to the Euratom Treaty, which remained in force after Nov. 30, 2009.[35] The European Atomic Energy Community has not been merged with the (new) European Union (EU)[36] and therefore retains a separate legal personality (arts. 184, 185), while continuously sharing the same institutions. Of course, the Treaty amending the EU and EC Treaties[37] changed certain provisions of the Euratom Treaty via protocol on transitional provisions[38] but these modifications were limited to adaptations to take account of the new rules established by the Lisbon Treaty, particularly in the institutional and financial fields.

Energy-Related Provisions in European Community Law from the Treaty of Rome to the Lisbon Treaty

Although the EEC was interested in some issues of energy policy from the very beginning and the Commission presented a report on a "common energy policy" as early as 1962,[39] E(E)C primary law was silent on these issues for a long time. So, quite similar to the development in the field of environmental law,[40] relevant provisions were at first based upon the broad enabling clause which originally was laid down in art. 235 of the EEC Treaty and later on in art. 308 EC now having become – in a modified version – art. 352 TFEU.[41] The Maastricht agreement[42] added a new field of activity to art. 3 par. 1 (lit. u]) of the (renamed) EC Treaty, putting together three rather different spheres like energy, civil protection and tourism but without transferring explicit complementary powers to the European

---

[34] See more closely below, at D.I.

[35] Consolidated Version of the Treaty establishing the European Atomic Energy Community of 30th March, 2010, OJ [2010] C 84/1.

[36] Kahl, Die Kompetenzen der EU in der Energiepolitik nach Lissabon, Europarecht 44 (2009), p. 616.

[37] Treaty of Lisbon amending the Treaty on European Union and the Treaty establishing the European Community of 13th December, 2007, OJ [2007] C 306/1.

[38] Treaty of Lisbon amending the Treaty on European Union and the Treaty establishing the European Community of 13th December, 2007, OJ [2007] C 306/1, pp. 159 et seq.; cf. Kahl, Die Kompetenzen der EU in der Energiepolitik nach Lissabon, Europarecht 44 (2009), p. 616.

[39] Cf. Nettesheim, Das Energiekapitel im Vertrag von Lissabon, Juristenzeitung 65 (2010), p. 19.

[40] Cf. Schweitzer/Hummer, *Europarecht*, (5th ed.) 1996, p. 478; Scherer/Heselhaus, Umweltrecht, in: Dauses (ed.), *Handbuch des EU-Wirtschaftsrechts*, 2010, O. para. 9.

[41] Nettesheim, Das Energiekapitel im Vertrag von Lissabon, Juristenzeitung 65 (2010), p. 19.

[42] Treaty on European Union of 7th February, 1992, OJ [1992] C 191/1.

level.[43] Nevertheless, the scope of supranational European energy policy grew steadily till the 1960s, and there has been a really rapid increase since the end of the last century.[44] In order to implement that, the EC bodies used various legislative competences of an indirect nature, i.e. not specifically dealing with energy issues, but at least being related thereto. In particular, relevant secondary legislation was based upon arts. 95 (harmonization for completing a single [internal] market), 154 et seq. (trans-European networks [TEN] also in the area of energy infrastructures) and 175 (environment) of the EC Treaty (Amsterdam version[45]). Some other EC regulations, directives, decisions or recommendations in this area referred to arts. 166 et seq. (research and technological development[46]). On the other hand, common commercial policy powers (art. 133 of the EC Treaty) were extended to external energy policy issues,[47] even if (or maybe: because) arts. 101 et seq. of the Euratom Treaty would not apply to topics outside of nuclear energy.

No specific provision of the EC Treaty was mentioned in the recitals of the Commission decision on establishing the European Regulators Group for Electricity and Gas (ERGEG).[48] The regulation[49] replacing ERGEG by a new Community body (art. 2 par. 1) named ACER – Agency for the Cooperation of Energy Regulators (art. 1 par. 1) – referred once again ("in particular") to art. 95 of the EC Treaty because the agency's main tasks should be "to fill the regulatory gap at Community level and to contribute to the effective functioning of the internal markets in electricity and natural gas" (recital 5).[50]

---

[43] Cf. Kahl, Die Kompetenzen der EU in der Energiepolitik nach Lissabon, Europarecht 44 (2009), p. 604; Nettesheim, Das Energiekapitel im Vertrag von Lissabon, Juristenzeitung 65 (2010), p. 20.

[44] Hobe, Energiepolitik, Europarecht 44 (2009), Supplement 1, pp. 220 et seq.; Kahl, Die Kompetenzen der EU in der Energiepolitik nach Lissabon, Europarecht 44 (2009), p. 605.

[45] Treaty of Amsterdam amending the Treaty on European Union, the Treaties establishing the European Communities and certain related acts of 2nd October, 1997, OJ [1997] C 340/1; cf. Streinz, Der Vertrag von Amsterdam, Juristische Ausbildung 20 (1998), pp. 59 et seq.; Hilf/Pache, Der Vertrag von Amsterdam, Neue Juristische Wochenschrift 51 (1998), pp. 706, 712.

[46] Cf. Trüe, EU-Kompetenzen für Energierecht, Gesundheitsschutz und Umweltschutz nach dem Verfassungsentwurf, Juristenzeitung 59 (2004), p. 799; for more details see Grunwald, *Das Energierecht der Europäischen Gemeinschaften*, 2003, pp. 25 et seq.; Schumacher, *Innovationsregulierung im Recht der netzgebundenen Elektrizitätswirtschaft*, 2009, pp. 200 et seq.

[47] Cf. Kahl, Die Kompetenzen der EU in der Energiepolitik nach Lissabon, Europarecht 44 (2009), p. 603.

[48] Decision 2003/796/EC, OJ [2003] L 296/34; cf. Britz, Vom Europäischen Verwaltungsverbund zum Regulierungsverbund?, Europarecht 41 (2006), pp. 62, 64 et seq.; Holznagel/Schumacher, Europäischer Regulierer für den Telekommunikations- und Energiewirtschaftssektor?, Deutsches Verwaltungsblatt 2007, pp. 411 and 416; Schumacher, *Innovationsregulierung im Recht der netzgebundenen Elektrizitätswirtschaft*, 2009, pp. 345 et seq.

[49] Regulation (EC) No. 713/2009, OJ [2009] L 211/1.

[50] http://ec.europa.eu/energy/gas_electricity/acer/acer_en.htm; also Bundesnetzagentur (Federal Net Agency, FNA), Entwurf des Vorhabenplans für das Jahr 2011, OJ FNA 2010, pp. 4315 et seq (4327).

International Organizations and Legal Instruments with Relevance for Energy Policy in Europe

International Energy Agency

The IEA was founded (by a decision of the OECD Council[51]) during the oil crisis of 1973–1974, so its initial role was quite naturally to co-ordinate measures in times of oil supply emergencies and was only later on expanded to include natural gas and electricity. The Agency's mandate (art. 6) has also been broadened to incorporate the "three E's" of balanced energy policy making: energy security, economic development and environmental protection. The IEA is an autonomous agency linked with the OECD, but not all OECD members participate in the Agency's work.[52] The IEA decision also provides for accession by the EC (now EU) after this organization will have become an OECD member in conformity with its own provisions (art. 3 of the 1994 Council decision). Till then, the relationship between IEA and EU (i.e. the Commission and/or the European External Action Service, Art. 27 par. 3 of the EU Treaty[53]) will be based upon art. 13 of the OECD convention of 1961 and Additional Protocol No 1[54]

Current IEA work focuses on diversification of energy sources, renewable energy, climate change policies, market reform, energy efficiency, development and deployment of clean energy technologies, energy technology collaboration and outreach to the rest of the world, especially major consumers and producers of energy like China, India, Russia and the OPEC countries.[55]

(European) Energy Charter

The Energy Charter Treaty of December 1994 as well as some related legal documents[56] are the results of a process the political foundation of which was provided for by the "European Energy Charter" being the concluding document of a conference at The Hague adopted by representatives of Western states (including

---

[51] OECD Decision establishing an International Energy Agency of the Organisation of 15th November, 1974, Bundesgesetzblatt (Federal Official Journal) 1995 II, pp. 739 et seq.

[52] List of Member countries available at: http://www.iea.org/country/index.asp.

[53] Complemented by Decision 2010/427/EU, OJ [2010] L 201/30.

[54] For a survey on cooperation, see http://ec.europa.eu/energy/international/organisations/iea_en. htm; on the first IEA review of EU energy policy cf. Press Release of 4th September, 2008, IP/08/1293.

[55] Cf. http://www.iea.org/about/ems.asp. On the International Renewable Energy Agency (IRENA), the statute of which was signed at Bonn in early 2009, cf. http://www.irena.org; on EU membership, see Press Release of 23rd November, 2009, IP/09/1804; also Bundestags-Drucksache 17/3885, 25th October, 2010.

[56] http://www.encharter.org/index.php?id=7.

Canada and the U.S.) as well as members of the former Soviet Bloc. This "declaration" of December 1991[57] – a major element of the (then) Conference on Security and Cooperation in Europe[58] – was aiming at the promotion of "a new model for energy co-operation in the long term in Europe and globally within the framework of a market economy and based upon mutual assistance and the principle of non-discrimination". The preamble also mentioned the "support from the European Community, particularly through completion of its internal energy market". The declaration is focusing on "objectives" (title I), "implementation" (II) and "specific agreements" (III). The desire of the signatories of this document – not eligible for registration under art. 102 of the UN Charter – is to improve the "security of energy supply" as well as to maximise "the efficiency of production, conversion, transport, distribution and use of energy, to enhance safety and to minimize environmental problems, on an acceptable economic basis". However, its objectives were stated and their implementation should take place only within "the framework of State sovereignty and sovereign resources over energy resources" (Preamble).

The treaty concluded some year later[59] established the fundamental "legal framework in order to promote long-term cooperation in the energy field, based on complementarities and mutual benefits", in accordance with the objectives (and principles) of the Energy Charter mentioned before (art. 2). The "contracting parties" (art. 1 par. 2) – including the European Community as well as Euratom[60] – agree to be bound by duties in the fields of "commerce" (arts. 3 et seq.) and the promotion and protection of "investment" (art. 1 par. 6). So, without derogating from the provisions of GATT and related (WTO) instruments (art. 4),[61] they consent to work together in order "to promote access to international markets on commercial terms" (art. 3), "and generally to develop an open and competitive market, for Energy Materials and Products" (art.1 par. 4), e.g. by alleviating "market distortions and barriers to competition in Economic Activity in the Energy Sector"[62] (art. 6 par. 1). Part III of the treaty (arts. 10 et seq.) provides for broad guarantees for foreign "investors" (art. 1 par. 7) including minimum standards like "fair and equitable treatment", "most constant protection and security" and prohibition of "unreasonable

---

[57] Energy Charter Secretariat, The Energy Charter Treaty and Related Documents, 2004, pp. 213 et seq., available at: http://www.encharter.org/index.php?id=29.

[58] http://www.osce.org/who.

[59] On 16th and 17th December 1994; see Energy Charter Secretariat, The Energy Charter Treaty and Related Documents, 2004, pp. 39 et seq.

[60] On membership, see http://www.encharter.org/index.php?id=61&L=1%5C%5C%5C%5C% 5C%5C%5C%5 C%5C.

[61] On Art. 7 of the ECT's transit provision, cf. Azaria, Energy Transit under the Energy Charter Treaty and the General Agreement on Tariff and Trade, Journal of Energy and Natural Resources Law 2009, pp. 559 et seq.

[62] As defined in Art. 1(5) and understanding No. 2 to this provision.

or discriminatory measures",[63] national as well as most-favoured nation treatment and efficient judicial redress before national courts. The settlement of disputes between an investor and a contracting party is not attributed solely to courts of the host state. The investor may choose to submit it to resolution by international conciliation or arbitration instead, and in this case, the other (State) party is bound to give its unconditional consent (art. 26).[64] Miscellaneous provisions are dealing with "environmental aspects" (art. 19), but are also restating the content and limits of "sovereignty over energy resources" (art. 18).

The Council and Commission decision on the conclusion, by the European Communities, of the Energy Charter Treaty and the Energy Charter Protocol on energy efficiency and related environmental aspects[65] was having regard to the ECSC, in particular, art. 95 thereof, then to the EC Treaty (Maastricht version[66]), in particular, art. 54 par. 2, the last sentence of art. 57 par. 2, arts. 66, 73c par. 2, 87, 99, 100a, 113, 130s par. 1 and 235, in conjunction with the second sentence of art. 228 par. 2 and the second subparagraph of art. 228 par. 3 thereof, and also to the Euratom Treaty, in particular, art. 101 par. 2 thereof.[67] The reasons for this approval (at supranational level) may be found in the following phrases of recitals 4–6:

"the principles and objectives of the Energy Charter Treaty are of fundamental importance to Europe's future, allowing the members of the Commonwealth of Independent States and the countries of Central and Eastern Europe to develop their energy potential, while helping to improve security of supply; . . . the principles and objectives of the Energy Charter Protocol will help to provide greater protection for the environment, notably by promoting energy efficiency; . . . it is necessary to consolidate the initiative and the central role of the European Communities, by enabling the latter to participate fully in the implementation of the Energy Charter Treaty and the Energy Charter Protocol".

Thus, ratifying the Energy Charter Treaty and the Energy Charter Protocol would "help attain the objectives of the European Communities". The last recital does clarify, however, that, "where the decisions to be taken by the Energy Charter Conference" (art. 34 of the treaty) "concern areas of mixed competence, the European Communities and the Member States are to cooperate with a view to achieving a common position, in accordance with the jurisprudence of the Court of Justice of the European Communities".

---

[63] On these widely used terms see, e.g., Montt, *State Liability in Investment Treaty Arbitration*, 2009, pp. 293 et seq.; Heiskanen, Arbitrary and Unreasonable Measures, in: Reinisch (ed.), *Standards of Investment Protection*, 2008, pp. 87 et seq.; Yannaca-Small, Fair and Equitable Treatment Standard: Recent Developments, in: Reinisch (ed.), *Standards of Investment Protection*, 2008, pp. 111 et seq.; Moss, Full Protection and Security, in: Reinisch (ed.), *Standards of Investment Protection*, 2008, pp. 131 et seq.

[64] Cf. Krajewski, *Wirtschaftsvölkerrecht*, (2nd ed.) 2009, p. 176.

[65] Decision 98/1817EC, OJ [1998] L 69/1; see also Decision 2001/595/EC, OJ [2001] L 209/32.

[66] Supra, at fn. 32.

[67] Decision 98/171/EC, OJ [1998] L 69/1, recitals 1-3.

Energy Community (Treaty)

An Energy Community was created by treaty (for 10 years, at least, art. 97) between the (then) EC on the one hand and some Southeast European States (two of them later on becoming members of the EU[68] which conforms to the treaty's intention also to prepare accession) in late 2005.[69] Since that date, new parties joined this treaty (like Moldavia), others are in the process of joining.[70] The Energy Community's main task is to create a legal and economic framework in relation to "Network Energy", i.e. electricity and gas sectors falling within the scope of directives 2003/54/EC and 2003/55/EC[71] (art. 2 para. 2). According to art. 2 para. 1 of the Community treaty, a "stable regulatory and market framework" should be capable of "attracting investment in gas networks, power generation, and transmission and distribution networks, so that all Parties have access to the stable and continuous energy supply that is essential for economic development and social stability" (lit. a]). The establishment of a single regulatory space for trade in "Network Energy" would also be "necessary to match the geographic extent of the concerned product markets" (lit. b]), and it could "enhance the security of supply" of this space "by providing a stable investment climate by which connections to Caspian, North African and Middle East gas reserves can be developed, and indigenous sources of energy such as natural gas, coal and hydropower can be exploited" (lit. c]). Moreover, the Community intends "to improve the environmental situation in relation to Network Energy and related energy efficiency, foster the use of renewable energy, and set out the conditions for energy trade in the single regulatory space" (lit. d]), and, finally, it wants to "develop Network Energy market competition on a broader geographic scale and exploit economics of scale" lit. e]). Art. 5 of the treaty requires that the Energy Community should follow the "acquis communautaire" described in Title II (arts. 9 et seq.) which is referring not only to energy (arts. 10, 11), but also to environment, competition, renewables and to "compliance with generally applicable standards of the EC" (arts. 21–23), and includes the adaptation and evolution of that acquis (arts. 24, 25). Two other important titles of the treaty are focusing on a "mechanism for operation of network energy markets" (arts. 26 et seq.) and "the creation of a single energy market" (arts. 40 et seq.), respectively. All obligations under the Community treaty are without prejudice to existing legal duties of its parties under WTO law (art. 102).[72]

---

[68] On this change of status (of Bulgaria and Romania) see Art. 99 of the Community Treaty.

[69] See Decision 2006/500/EC, OJ [2006] L 198/15; text of the Treaty ibid., pp. 18 et seq.

[70] On the first enlargement see http://www.energy-community.org/portal/page/portal/ENC_HOME/ENERGY_ COMMUNITY/Milestones.

[71] Directive 2003/54/EC, OJ [2003] L 176/37; Directive 2003/54/EC, OJ [2003] L 176/57. On these "second generation" directives, cf. also below, at D.II.2.a).

[72] See below, at 4.

Institutions of the Energy Community are empowered either to take "measures" (Ministerial Council, art. 47, and Permanent High-Level Group, art. 53) or issue "recommendations" (Regulatory Board, art. 58). In this body, the EU is represented by the Commission and ERGEG (now ACER[73]), art. 59, and the latter group (agency) must be consulted before the EU position in the board will be taken.

The Council decision on the conclusion by the EC of the Energy Community Treaty[74] refers "in particular" to arts. 47 para. 2, 55, 83, 89, 95, 133 and 175, in conjunction with the first sentence of the first subparagraph of art. 300 para. 2 and the second subparagraph of art. 300 para. 3 of the EC Treaty. These references are clearly resembling the parallel ones in the Energy Charter Treaty decision,[75] but there are slight divergencies as well.

World Trade Organization (WTO) and Energy

When the rules of the GATT 1947[76] were negotiated within the broader context of the "Havana Charter",[77] regulating or even liberalising trade in energy was not a political priority. This industry sector was dominated by state run monopolies and thus governed by strict territorial allocation. Moreover, international trade in energy products and resources was heavily concentrated, cartelised and controlled by a few "multinational" enterprises. Therefore, till now neither the GATT nor the WTO[78] have been dealing with energy as a distinct sector. Evidently it was felt that general rules, including the disciplines on state trading (e.g. art. XVII GATT),[79] would be sufficient to address the relevant issues. Also, no special agreement has been concluded on trade in energy within the framework of WTO law.[80] On the other hand, WTO rules are applicable to all forms of trade, they apply to trade in energy products or services, too, and can be enforced through the WTO dispute settlement mechanism[81] like rules related to other issues falling within the scope of application

---

[73] Supra, at II.3.

[74] Decision 2006/500/EC, OJ [2006] L 198/15, Art. 4(7).

[75] See Decision 98/171/EC, OJ [1998] L 69/1.

[76] http://www.fd.uc.pt/CI/CEE/OI/OMC.GATT/GATT-1947-ingles.htm; cf. Neugärtner, GATT 1947, in: Hilf/Oeter (eds.), *WTO-Recht*, (2nd ed.) 2010, § 3, pp. 81 et seq.

[77] http://www.worldtradelaw.net/misc/havana.pdf.

[78] Agreement establishing the World Trade Organization of 15 April 1994, OJ [1994] L 336/3.

[79] Cf.   http://www.worldenergy.org/publications/trade_and_investment_rules_for_energy/ii._promoting_energyre lated_investments/2592.asp

[80] Cottier/Malumfashi/Matteotti-Berkutova/Nartova/de Sépubus/Bigdeli, Energy in WTO law and policy, p. 1, available at: http://www.wto.org/english/res_e/publications_e/wtr10_forum_e/wtr10_ 7may10_e.pdf; for a detailed analysis, cf. Selivanova, The WTO and Energy, August 2007, pp. 22 et seq., available at: http://ictsd.org/downloads/2008/05/the20wto20and20energy.pdf.

[81] Cf. Annex II to the establishing the World Trade Organization of 15th April, 1994, OJ [1994] L 336/3; Yang/Mercurio/Li, *WTO Dispute Settlement Understanding*, 2005.

of WTO law. However, a few WTO members undertook limited commitments (under arts. XVI, XVII GATS) in three energy-related sectors: services incidental to mining and to energy distribution, and pipeline transportation of fuels.[82] Energy-related activities which are not exclusive to the energy industry are covered by other services sectors, such as transport, distribution, construction, consulting, and engineering. One exemption to most-favoured nation (MFN) treatment (i.e. non-discrimination, art. II GATS) has been made in pipeline transportation of fuels.

Energy services are included in the services negotiations (under art. XIX GATS) which started in early 2000.[83] Annex B attached to a report of the chairman of the Council for Trade in Services delivered to the Trade Negotiations Committee in November 2005,[84] provides a compilation of "sectoral and modal objectives" as identified individually or by groups of (WTO) members. Regarding energy services, these objectives include "scope of commitments", "regulatory issues and additional commitments" (art. XVIII GATS) and also "scheduling issues to be addressed" stating that the (current) absence of a specific energy services section should not prevent the scheduling of commitments as the relevant "guidelines" do only require "a sufficiently detailed definition to avoid any ambiguity as to the scope of the commitment".[85] As to the scope of commitments, the annex refers to the oil and gas sector only, pointing to, e.g., "exploration services, services incidental to mining, technical testing and analysis, and toll refining services", but on the other hand, it explicitly excludes negotiations in respect of "ownership of natural resources".[86] A collective request presented after the Hongkong ministerial conference in December 2005 tried to identify 12 types of activities relevant to the energy industry, belonging to three main sectors, namely business services, construction and distribution. A particular emphasis was placed upon the third mode (of four) of supply, i.e. a foreign company setting up subsidiaries or branches to provide services in another country. The request was neutral with respect to energy source, technology and whether offered onshore or offshore.[87]

Thus, the current status of energy under WTO is bound to change since privatisation and liberalisation of the sector led to market reform which resulted

---

[82] Cf. Selivanova, The WTO and Energy, August 2007, p. 17, available at: http://ictsd.org/downloads/2008/05/the20wto20and20energy.pdf.

[83] Cf, e.g., Lamy, Doha Round will benefit energy trade, available at: http://www.wto.org/english/news_e/sppl_e/sppl80_e.thm; Marceau, The WTO in the emerging energy governance debate, available at: http://www.wto.org/english/res_e/publications_e/wtr10_marceau_e.htm.

[84] WTO Doc. TN/S/23, 28th November, 2005, pp. 11 et seq. (17).

[85] WTO Doc. S/L/92, 28th March, 2001 (adopted by the Council for Trade in Services on 23rd March, 2001), p. 8 (no. 24); cf. Cottier/Malumfashi/Matteotti-Berkutova/Nartova/de Sépubus/Bigdeli, Energy in WTO law and policy, pp. 9 et seq, available at: http://www.wto.org/english/res_e/publications_e/wtr10_forum_e/wtr10 _7may10_e.pdf.

[86] As noted before (at fn. 11), this reservation may be misleading since it seems first of all a public law issue whether (and how far as well as when) States set up rules permitting private property rights in respect for (certain) natural resources.

[87] See http://www.wto.org/english/tratop_e/serv_e/energy_e/energy_e.htm.

in a conceptual separation of goods and services trade. For example, oil and solid fuels such as coal clearly fall within the category of goods; they are easily stored and traded across State borders. But also natural gas can be traded either via pipelines or after being liquefied for the purposes of transportation to remote regions or for storage. So today production of energy goods comes within the scope of GATT, whereas energy-related services, including transmission and distribution, fall under the scope of GATS. Looking at electricity, however, issues are more complex. It qualifies as a good under WTO/GATT law for a rather formal reason since it has been defined as such in the Harmonized System Nomenclature on the codification of commodities[88] and being classified under code 2716. The same is true for the Energy Charter Treaty[89] and for EU law as well since the European Court of Justice explicitly recognized in the "Almelo" case[90] that the rules on the free circulation of goods of the E(E)C Treaty (arts. 28 et seq.) also applied to electricity.

Current EU Legal Framework

EU Primary Law

Introduction

Before the status and structures of European energy law after Lisbon will be looked at more closely, it seems necessary to point rather shortly to some more areas of global concern which are relevant also for the (new) EU since the organization itself acceded to international legal instruments and thus is not only obliged to fulfil the obligations deriving therefrom in good faith but each institution of the Union (as well as its member states) is also bound by internal law (art. 216 para. 2 TFEU) to ordinarily perform these duties.[91] So, energy is addressed by a number of multilateral environmental agreements, in particular those relating to climate change, including the U.N. Framework Convention on Climate Change[92] and its Kyoto Protocol.[93] Another possible policy tool might be "green" public procurement if

---

[88] See the 2007 version, available at: http://www.wcoomd.org/files/1.%20Public%20files/ PDFandDocuments/ HarmonizedSystem/2007/0527_2007E.pdf.

[89] See supra, at 2.

[90] ECJ Case C-393/92, *Gemeente Almelo vs. Energiebedrijf Ijsselmij NV*, [1994] ECR I-1477, para. 28.

[91] Kahl, Die Kompetenzen der EU in der Energiepolitik nach Lissabon, Europarecht 44 (2009), pp. 613 et seq.; Nettesheim, Das Energiekapitel im Vertrag von Lissabon, Juristenzeitung 65 (2010), p. 21.

[92] Adopted on 9th May, 1992, see http://unfccc.int/resource/docs/convkp/conveng.pdf.

[93] Adopted on 11th December, 1997, see http://unfccc.int/resource/docs/convkp/kpeng.pdf.

and insofar it would be implemented in conformity with the EU's obligations under the "plurilateral" WTO Government Procurement Agreement.[94] Promotion of renewable energies might lead to conflicts with WTO rules on (or better: against) subsidies[95] and, at least at the level of Member State legislation,[96] even more with the EU State aid regime. And finally, while export (or import) restrictions would hardly be legitimate under art. XI GATT, there is controversy whether (energy) production control measures would violate disciplines of WTO law.[97]

The New Energy Provision of the TFEU

Title XXI on "energy" of Part III of the TFEU, consists of a sole provision. At first look, that may be rather surprising since the provisions immediately preceding art. 194 and relating to "environment" (title XX) are much broader and more complex. And although the energy sector would at least in parts include "services of general economic interest" (art. 14 TFEU)[98] and, moreover, its central importance for most human and especially industrial and commercial activities might hardly be doubted, there is no clause similar to that laid down in art. 11 TFEU (related to environmental protection) in order to ensure that energy policy requirements must be integrated in the definition or at least implementation of other EU policies and activities.[99]

The text of art. 194 TFEU is nearly identical to that of art. III-256 of the Treaty establishing a Constitution for Europe[100] which did not come into force. This earlier version was inserted as the last section (10) of chapter III ("Policies in Other Areas") of title III ("The Policies and Functioning of the Union") of that treaty, after a longer section (9) on "Research and Technological Development and

---

[94] OJ [1994] L 336/273; cf. Cottier/Malumfashi/Matteotti-Berkutova/Nartova/de Sépubus/Bigdeli, Energy in WTO law and policy, pp. 19 et seq.

[95] Cf. Cottier/Malumfashi/Matteotti-Berkutova/Nartova/de Sépubus/Bigdeli, Energy in WTO law and policy, pp. 11 et sq.; Selivanova, The WTO and Energy, August 2007, pp. 23 et seq.

[96] Because Art. 107 TFEU is not applicable to EU subsidies; cf. Schweitzer/Hummer, *Europarecht*, (5th ed.) 1996, p. 398.

[97] Cf. Lamy, Doha Round will benefit energy trade, available at: http://www.wto.org/english/news_e/sppl_e/sppl80_e.thm; Cottier/Malumfashi/Matteotti-Berkutova/Nartova/de Sépubus/Bigdeli, Energy in WTO law and policy, pp. 16 et seq.; Selivanova, The WTO and Energy, August 2007, pp. 15 et seq.

[98] Cf. Knauff, Die Daseinsvorsorge im Vertrag von Lissabon, Eurparecht 45 (2010), pp. 730 et seq.; also Koenig/Kühling/Rasbach, Versorgungssicherheit im Wettbewerb, Zeitschrift für Neues Energierecht 2003, pp. 3 et seq.; Ruffert, Völkerrechtliche Impulse und Rahmen des Europäischen Verfassungsrechts, in: Fehling/Ruffert (eds.), *Regulierungsrecht*, 2010, § 3 No. 74 et seq.

[99] Kahl, Die Kompetenzen der EU in der Energiepolitik nach Lissabon, Europarecht 44 (2009), pp. 601 et seq., might not agree with this argument.

[100] OJ [2004] C 310, pp. 1 et seq.; for more details, see Trüe, EU-Kompetenzen für Energierecht, Gesundheitsschutz und Umweltschutz nach dem Verfassungsentwurf, Juristenzeitung 59 (2004), pp. 786 et seq.; Kahl, Die Kompetenzen der EU in der Energiepolitik nach Lissabon, Europarecht 44 (2009), pp. 605 et seq.

Space". Section 8 on "Trans-European Networks"[101] was copied from arts. 154–156 of the EC Treaty and has now become title XVI of the TFEU's Part III. So, the EU shall go on contributing to the "establishment and development of trans-European networks in the areas of transport, telecommunications and energy infrastructures" (art. 170 para. 1) in order to help the objectives of a functioning internal market (art. 26) as well as strengthened economic, social and territorial cohesion (art. 174) and "to enable citizens of the Union, economic operators and regional and local communities to derive full benefit from the setting-up of an area without internal frontiers". EU action shall take place "within the framework of a system of open and competitive markets" and "aim at promoting the interconnection and interoperability of national networks as well as access to such networks" (art. 170 para. 2 TFEU).

After the publication of the (draft) "constitution for Europe", but before the conclusion of the Lisbon Treaty, the Commission presented a "Green Paper" on "a European Strategy for Sustainable, Competitive and Secure Energy",[102] followed by a "Communication" about "An Energy Policy for Europe".[103] This latter document explained the (then) three main objectives of EU energy policy as follows:

Sustainability, related to "(i) developing competitive renewable sources of energy and other low carbon energy sources and carriers, particularly alternative transport fuels, (ii) curbing energy demand within Europe, and (iii) leading global efforts to halt climate change and improve local air quality";

Competitiveness, which would mean: "(i) ensuring that energy market opening brings benefits to consumers and to the economy as a whole, while stimulating investment in clean energy production and energy efficiency, (ii) mitigating the impact of higher international energy prices on the EU economy and its citizens and (iii) keeping Europe at the cutting edge of energy technologies";

Security of supply, referring to the task of "tackling the EU's rising dependence on imported energy through (i) an integrated approach – reducing demand, diversifying the EU's energy mix with greater use of competitive indigenous and renewable energy, and diversifying sources and routes of supply of imported energy, (ii) creating the framework which will stimulate adequate investments to meet growing energy demand, (iii) better equipping the EU to cope with emergencies, (iv) improving the conditions for European companies seeking access to global resources, and (v) making sure that all citizens and business have access to energy".

Although their order was modified, these objectives are (although much shorter) repeated in art. 194 para. 1 according to which the EU policy on energy shall aim, "in a spirit of solidarity between Member States, to

---

[101] Cf. http://ec.europa.eu/energy/infrastructure/tent_e/ten_e_en.htm.

[102] COM(2006) 105 final, 8th March 2006; also Nettesheim, Das Energiekapitel im Vertrag von Lissabon, Juristenzeitung 65 (2010), p. 25.

[103] COM(2007) 1 final, 10th January 2007.

(a) Ensure the functioning of the energy market,
(b) Ensure security of energy supply in the Union,
(c) Promote energy efficiency and energy saving and the development of new and renewable forms of energy".

A fourth objective mentioned in art. 194 para. 1 – to "promote the interconnection of energy networks" – was also dealt with in the "Green Paper" already,[104] as one of the "core areas" for completing the internal electricity and gas markets should be "a priority interconnection plan" which was presented to the public in late 2006 (listing up five important aspects).[105] The communication on energy policy reiterated this view, but also pointed to the objective of energy security.[106] Moreover, it explained what was meant by insisting on "solidarity between Member States" by requiring the set up of "effective mechanisms ... in the event of an energy crisis" thereby complementing the earlier statement that "rapid" solidarity was needed towards a country "facing difficulties following damages to its essential infrastructure".[107]

EU energy policy must be not only implemented "with regard for the need to preserve and improve the environment" in general (art. 194 para. 1), but a specific issue thereof is explicitly linked to the implementation of environmental objectives: Art. 192 para. 2 subpara. 1 lit. c) TFEU authorizes the Council acting unanimously in accordance with a special legislative procedure (art. 289 para. 2) and after consulting the European Parliament, the Economic and Social Committee (ESC) and the Committee of the Regions (CoR), to adopt "measures significantly affecting a Member State's choice between different energy sources and the general structure of its energy supply".[108] On the contrary, such decision does not extend to a Member State's right "to determine the conditions for exploiting its energy resources", since art. 194 para. 2 subpara. 2 TFEU does not allow any prejudice to that (sovereign) right, too.[109]

---

[104] Op.cit. (fn. 102), pp. 6 et seq.

[105] COM(2006) 846 final, 10th January 2007; also Kahl, Die Kompetenzen der EU in der Energiepolitik nach Lissabon, Europarecht 44 (2009), pp. 608 et seq.

[106] Op.cit. (fn. 103), pp. 10 et seq; comments by Nettesheim, Das Energiekapitel im Vertrag von Lissabon, Juristenzeitung 65 (2010), p. 25.

[107] Op. cit. (fn. 103); cf. also Hobe, Energiepolitik, Europarecht 44 (2009), Supplement 1, pp. 226 et seq.; Nettesheim, Das Energiekapitel im Vertrag von Lissabon, Juristenzeitung 65 (2010), pp. 22 et seq.; Kahl, Die Kompetenzen der EU in der Energiepolitik nach Lissabon, Europarecht 44 (2009), pp. 607 et seq. and 613 (pointing also to Art. 122(1) TFEU).

[108] Cf. Nettesheim, Das Energiekapitel im Vertrag von Lissabon, Juristenzeitung 65 (2010), p. 23; Kahl, Die Kompetenzen der EU in der Energiepolitik nach Lissabon, Europarecht 44 (2009), pp. 610 et seq.; earlier already Trüe, EU-Kompetenzen für Energierecht, Gesundheitsschutz und Umweltschutz nach dem Verfassungsentwurf, Juristenzeitung 59 (2004), p. 781.

[109] Cf. Kahl, Die Kompetenzen der EU in der Energiepolitik nach Lissabon, Europarecht 44 (2009), pp. 611, 618 et seq.

Like other "principal areas", as for example "internal market", "economic, social and territorial cohesion", "environment" or "trans-European networks" (art. 4 para. 2 lits. a], c], e], h] TFEU), "energy", too, belongs to those competences which are shared between EU and member States (lit. i]).[110] Since art. 4 para. 1 does restrict this type of attribution of powers to competences which do not relate to the areas referred to in art. 3 (or art. 6), the exclusive competences of the Union regarding "common commercial policy" (art. 3 para. 1 lit. e]), "establishing of the competition rules for the functioning of the internal market" (lit. b]) and in the field of concluding international agreements as described in art. 3 para. 2 are not affected by the provisions of art. 4. Although "climate change" and "utilisation of natural resources" are energy-related topics at least, they were inserted (or – looking at the second one – remained) part of the provisions on "environment" (art. 191 para. 1, third and fourth sentence TFEU). Anyway, the increased "Europeanization" of energy policy will probably lead to quite difficult issues as there would be three (or even more) provisions which could be used for the basis of EU secondary legislation but since the relevant legislative procedures are rather different, clear and sharp distinctions must be drawn between EU actions founded on art. 194, on art. 191 or on art. 114 TFEU.[111] Another question might arise from the fact that more stringent (protective) measures of Member States are explicitly permitted (if they conform to certain conditions) under art. 114 (paras. 4 et seq.) and 193 TFEU, while art. 194 does not deal with this problem.

As far as EU institutions plan to take measures "necessary to achieve the objectives" in art. 194 para. 1, i.e. that their aim and purpose is exclusively or at least essentially related to energy policy, the right way to follow would be the ordinary legislative procedure (art. 294 TFEU). If those measures were, however, "primarily of a fiscal nature",[112] the Council has to act unanimously with a special legislative procedure (upon a Commission proposal as in each other case), but the Parliament (as well as the committees, i.e. ESC and CoR) would merely be consulted (art. 194 para. 3).[113]

---

[110] Nettesheim, Das Energiekapitel im Vertrag von Lissabon, Juristenzeitung 65 (2010), pp. 21, 22; Kahl, Die Kompetenzen der EU in der Energiepolitik nach Lissabon, Europarecht 44 (2009), p. 607.

[111] Kahl, Die Kompetenzen der EU in der Energiepolitik nach Lissabon, Europarecht 44 (2009), pp. 616 et seq.; Nettesheim, Das Energiekapitel im Vertrag von Lissabon, Juristenzeitung 65 (2010), p. 24.

[112] Cf. Kahl, Die Kompetenzen der EU in der Energiepolitik nach Lissabon, Europarecht 44 (2009), p. 612.

[113] For a recent analysis of Union competences see also Schneider, *EU-Kompetenzen einer Europäischen Energiepolitik*, 2010.

EU Secondary Legislation

EU Policy on Energy Since the "Green Paper" of 2006

In early 2007 the EU Commission proposed a new energy policy[114] as a first resolute step towards becoming a low-energy economy, whilst making the energy we do consume more secure, competitive and sustainable. A common policy would be the most effective way to tackle today's energy challenges, which are shared by all Member States. This policy put energy back at the heart of EU action, the position it occupied when the European venture first got under way with the ECSC and the Euratom Treaties. The aims of the policy are supported by market-based tools (mainly taxes, subsidies and the CO_2 emissions trading scheme), by developing energy technologies (especially technologies for energy efficiency and renewable or low-carbon energy) and by Community financial instruments. In 2008, the Commission published a five-point "EU Energy Security and Solidarity Action Plan" focusing on "infrastructure needs and the diversification of energy supplies, external energy relations, oil and gas stocks and crisis response mechanisms, energy efficiency, and making the best use of the EU's indigenous energy resources".[115] In order to remedy the effects of the financial and energy crises which affected the European economy in 2008, a regulation enacted in the summer of 2009[116] established a European Energy Programme for Recovery (EEPR) as a key element of an "Economic Recovery Plan"[117] to fund projects in three main areas, i.e. gas and electricity infrastructures, offshore wind energy, and carbon capture and storage. The Commission received 87 applications, and it decided to grant financial assistance to 58 projects, mainly in the first area.[118]

In the spring of 2007, the Commission launched a discussion by publishing another "Green Paper", this time on advancing the use of "market-based instruments for environment and related policy purposes",[119] in particular within the context of the review of the energy taxation directive. In the same year, its "European strategic energy technology plan" aimed at steps towards a "low carbon

---

[114] See already supra, at fn. 103.

[115] COM(2008) 781 final, 13th November, 2008; cf. further the Green Paper "Towards a Secure, Sustainable and Competitive European Energy Network", COM(2008) 782 final, also of 13th November, 2008.

[116] Regulation (EC) No. 663/2009, OJ [2009] L 200/31; modified by Regulation (EU) No. 1233/2010, OJ [2010] L 346/5.

[117] COM(2008) 800 final, 26th November, 2008; also Presidency Conclusions, European Council, 11th and 12th December, 2008, see http://register.consilium.europa.eu/pdf/en/08/st17/st17271-re01.en08.pdf.

[118] Cf. COM(2010) 191 final, 27th April, 2010.

[119] COM(2007) 140 final, 28th March, 2007.

future"[120] was presented. Two years later, this EU body proposed various European industrial initiatives pointing to several possible forms of public funding, like income generated by the future emission allowance trading scheme, Community programs (EEPR or the Intelligent Energy – Europe programme[121]) and, finally, lending by the European Investment Bank.[122] Intelligent Energy – Europe is part of the Competitiveness and Innovation Framework Programme (CIP) 2007–2013 established by a decision of Parliament and Council.[123]

"20 20 by 2020" is the short title of a communication on "Europe's climate change opportunity". In this document of January 2008,[124] the Commission elaborated on the challenge for the European economy to adapt to the "demands of a low-emission economy with secure energy supplies". Respecting the principles set up by the European Council in 2007, Commission proposals were, in particular, aimed at updating the Emissions Trading System (ETS),[125] establishing an EU framework for national commitments to cover the remaining emissions, fostering renewable as well as more energy efficiency, shaping rules for carbon capture storage (CCS),[126] but without forgetting to take regard of the particular needs of energy-intensive industries.

On 17 November 2010, the Commission adopted a communication on "Energy infrastructure priorities for 2020 and beyond".[127] A completely new infrastructure policy based upon a European vision would be needed to deliver the energy infrastructures for the next two decades including changes of the current practice of the TEN-E.[128] A "blueprint for an integrated European energy network" was based upon a new method (for strategic planning) and would include the following steps:

Identifying an energy infrastructure map leading towards a European "smart supergrid" interconnecting networks at continental level,

---

[120] COM(2007) 723 final, 22nd November, 2007. On carbon capture storage cf. Maslaton/Wolf (eds.), *CCS und Recht*, 2009.

[121] Cf. list of 15 energy projects for European economic recovery, Press Release, MEMO/09/542, 9th December, 2009, and above, at fn. 116, 117.

[122] COM(2009) 519 final, 7th October, 2009.

[123] OJ [2006] 310/15.

[124] COM(2008) 30 final, 23rd January, 2008; also COM(2008) 772 final, 13th November, 2008 („Energy efficiency: delivering the 20 % target").

[125] See http://ec.europa.eu/clima/policies/ets/index_en.htm.

[126] Cf. also COM(2009) 519 final, 7th October, 2009 ("Investing in the Development of Low Carbon Technologies – SET-Plan") and accompanying impact documents, SEC(2009)1295 – 1297.

[127] COM(2010) 677 final, 17th November, 2010; cf. also Bundesnetzagentur (Federal Net Agency, FNA), Entwurf des Vorhabenplans für das Jahr 2011, OJ FNA 2010, p. 4325.

[128] For an Implementation Report relating to the period 2002–2006 see COM(2008) 770 final, 13th November, 2008.

Focussing on a limited number of European priorities to be implemented till 2020"
to meet the long-term objectives and where European action is most wanted",
Identifying concrete "projects of European interest"[129] necessary to implement
these priorities in a flexible manner and building on regional cooperation so as
to respond to changing market conditions and technology development, and
Supporting the implementation of those projects through new tools, such as
"improved regional cooperation, permitting procedures, better methods and information for decision makers and citizens and innovative financial instruments.

In order to speed up implementation, the Commission also described in its
communication (four) elements of a complementary "toolbox".[130]

Selected Important Topics of EU Energy Policy

Internal Energy Market

To create a genuine, competitive international market also for energy is one of the
EU's priority objectives. It would be a strategic tool by giving, on the one hand,
European consumers a choice between different enterprises supplying energy, in
particular electricity and gas, at reasonable prices, and, on the other hand, by
making those markets accessible for all suppliers of energy, especially small ones
and those investing in renewables. Another market-related issue would be the
setting up of an adequate framework within which the mechanism for CO_2 emission
trading could function properly. Of course, a crucial condition for implementing an
internal energy market will be the existence of a reliable and coherent energy
network in Europe, i.e. adequate infrastructure investment. Then, a truly integrated
European market would also contribute to more diversification and thus to greater
security of supply.

To reach these goals, a lot of legal instruments, mainly directives, were enacted
during the last years (and often later modified thus setting up a "second" and even
"third" generation of relevant legal provisions). A first very important issue –
focusing on making markets (within the EU) more competitive – are "common
rules" for the internal market(s) in "natural gas" and "electricity", respectively.
Two (EP and Council) directives of July 2009[131] were repealing former ones

---

[129] See below, at 2.a); also Commission call for proposals, see http://ec.europa.eu/energy/infra-
structure/grants/doc/2011/2011_ten_e_call.pdf.

[130] Op.cit. (fn. 126), pp. 14 et seq.

[131] Directive 2009/72/EC, OJ [2009] L 211/55, and Directive 2009/73/EC, OJ [2009] L 211/94; on
implementation issues also Bundesnetzagentur (Federal Net Agency, FNA), Entwurf des
Vorhabenplans für das Jahr 2011, OJ FNA 2010, pp. 4327 et seq.

(enacted in 2003[132]), which had replaced legal acts of 1996[133] and 1998,[134] and those were an improvement as well as an extension of specific directives getting legal force in 1990 (concerning a Community procedure to prices charged to industrial end-users[135]) and 1991 (on the transit of natural gas through grids[136]). Although the 2003 directives were deemed to have made a signification contribution towards the creation of an internal market in each of both areas, fully open markets enabling all consumers to freely choose their suppliers and all suppliers freely to deliver to their customers had not yet been achieved.[137] There were remaining obstacles to the sale of electricity and gas on equal terms and without discrimination or disadvantages within the Union. In particular, non-discriminatory network access and an equally effective level of regulatory supervision in each Member State (or even the whole EEA) did not exist in 2009. So, the "third generation" legal framework tried to further develop cross-border connections in order to secure the supply of all energy sources at the most competitive prices to consumers and industry within the EU. Moreover, by effectively separating networks from activities of generation and supply (effective unbundling), the legal acts aimed at managing the inherent risk of discrimination not only in the operation of the network but also in the incentives for vertically integrated undertakings to invest adequately in their networks. To preserve the interests of the shareholders of those enterprises as far as possible, Member States were reserved the choice between various modes of "ownership unbundling" or setting up either a system or a transmission operator which must be independent from supply and generation interests.[138] Another fundamental provision of both new directives is the respect for public service requirements (art. 3), i.e. a universal service and common minimum standards following therefrom. And last but not least, consumer interests are at the heart of the directives, and quality of service should thus a central responsibility of both electricity and (natural) gas undertakings (annex I).

Although based upon art. 175 para. 1 (not on art. 95) EC, the EP and Council directive establishing a scheme for greenhouse gas emission allowance trading[139]

---

[132] See already above, at fn. 71; cf., e.g., Lecheler/Gundel, Ein weiterer Schritt zur Vollendung des Binnenmarktes – Die Beschleunigungs-Rechtsakte für den Binnenmarkt für Strom und Gas, Europäische Zeitschrift für Wirtschaftsrecht 2003, pp. 621 et seq.

[133] Directive 96/92/EC, OJ [1997] L 27/20.

[134] Directive 98/30/EC, OJ [1998] L 204/1.

[135] Directive 90/377/EEC, OJ [1990] L 185/16.

[136] Directive 91/296/EEC, OJ [1991] L 147/37.

[137] Cf. Commission Report on the "Progress in creating the internal gas and electricity market", COM(2008) 192 final, 15th April, 2008.

[138] Cf. Pießkalla, Die Kommissionsvorschläge zum „full ownership unbundling" des Strom- und Gasversorgungssektors im Lichte der Eigentumsneutralität des EG-Vertrags (Art. 295 EG), Europäische Zeitschrift für Wirtschaftsrecht 2008, pp. 199 et seq.

[139] Directive 2003/87/EC, OJ [2003] L 275/32.

which was extended and improved later on[140] is aiming at the reduction of those emissions "in a cost-effective and economically efficient manner" and thus sets up fully harmonized conditions of allocation within the Union as well as – in order to avoid distortions of competition – harmonized rules on new entrants so as to ensure that all Member States adopt the same approach. The original legal act already stated explicitly that Community provisions relating to allocation of allowances by the Member States would be necessary to contribute to preserving the integrity of the internal market.

A first EP and Council decision laying down a series of guidelines for trans-European energy networks[141] was replaced 7 years later (in 2003) by a second one[142] in order to incorporate new priorities stemming from the creation of a more open and competitive internal energy market ("first generation" directives). Conforming to this actualization, energy infrastructure should be constructed and maintained so as to enable the internal market efficiently, but without detracting from strategic and, where appropriate, universal service criteria. EC financial aid for construction and maintenance should therefore remain highly exceptional whereas private financing or financing by the economic operators concerned would be encouraged (art. 8 – "effects on competition"). The guidelines to be established by Community action (art. 5) should identify projects of common interest (art. 6, annex II), including those which have priorities (arts. 4, 7 and annex I). The 2003 decision was repealed by a legal act of the same character. The later one (of 2006)[143] not only took account of the alterations set up by the "second generation" of internal market directives but also laid down provisions related to a new category of top priority "projects of European interest" (art. 8 et seq., annex I) for each of which a European coordinator might be appointed. Based upon art. 156 ECT (now: art. 172 TFEU), Parliament and Council enacted in late 2009 a regulation putting up general rules of the granting of Community financial aid (for "projects of common interest" only, art. 2) in the field of trans-European networks as provided for in art. 171 para. 1 tir. 3 TFEU. EU aid might take one or several of the following forms: co-financing of studies related to projects, temporary subsidies on the interest on loans granted by financial bodies, contributions towards premiums for loan guarantees from financial institutions, direct grants to investments, but only in duly justified cases, and risk-capital participation for investment funds or comparable financial undertakings (art. 3 para. 1).[144]

Two EP and Council regulations of 2005[145] and 2009, respectively, were dealing with conditions for access to the natural gas transmission networks. Both of them

---

[140] Directive 2029/29/EC, OJ [2009] L 140/63.

[141] Directive 1254/96/EC, OJ [1996] L 161/147.

[142] Directive 1229/2003/EC, OJ [2003] L 176/11.

[143] Directive 1364/2006/EC, OJ [2006] L 262/1.

[144] Directive 67/2010/EC, OJ [2010] L 27/20.

[145] Directive 1775/2005/EC, OJ [2005] L 289/1.

aimed, according to art. 1 para. 1, at setting up non-discriminatory rules for access conditions to natural gas "transmission" (art. 2 para. 1 no 1) systems taking into account the specificities of national and regional markets with a view to the proper functioning of the internal gas market and were including provisions on the setting up of harmonized principles for tariffs (art. 3), or the methodologies underlying their calculation, for access to the network (art. 4), the establishment of third party access services and harmonized principles for "capacity" (art. 2 para. 2 no. 3) allocation and "congestion management" (no. 5), the determination of transparency requirements (art. 6), balancing rules and imbalance charges (art. 7) and facilitating capacity trading (art. 8). As a part of the "third" reform package of summer 2009, the second regulation[146] added (in art. 1) two more objectives, namely setting non-discriminatory rules for access conditions to LNG facilities and storage facilities taking into account the special characteristics of national and regional markets, and facilitating the emergence of a well-functioning and transparent wholesale market with a high level of security of supply in gas and providing mechanisms to harmonize the network access rules for cross-border exchanges in gas. The new legal act intends to ensure optimal management of the gas transmission network in the EU by a European Network of Transmission System Operators for Gas (ENTSO for Gas) which should be established in the course of a rather complex procedure in which draft statutes for cooperation put up by system operators will be reviewed by the Agency (ACER) as well as the Commission before they may finally be adopted and ENTSO for Gas be established by the operators (arts. 4, 5). A main task of this network will be to elaborate network "codes" in a number of areas, reaching from network security and reliability rules to energy efficiency regarding gas networks (art. 6–8), in close cooperation with the Commission and ACER and monitored by this agency (art. 9).

A parallel development took place in the electricity sector where ENTSO for Electricity will soon be established. The 2009 regulation[147] replacing a first one of 2003[148] aims at setting fair rules for cross-border exchanges in electricity which will include the establishment of a compensation mechanism for those "cross-border flows" (art. 2 para. 2 lit. b), the setting of harmonized principles for cross-border transmission charges and the allocation of available capacities of interconnections between national transmission systems as well as facilitating the emergence of a well-functioning and transparent wholesale market with a high level of security of supply (art. 1). The Commission is authorized to adopt guidelines (art. 18) relating to the inter-transmission system operator compensation mechanism in accordance with the principles set out in arts. 13, 14.

---

[146] Directive 715/2009/EC, OJ [2009] L 211/36.

[147] Directive 714/2009/EC, OJ [2009] L 211/15.

[148] Regulation (EC) No. 1228/2003, OJ [2003] L 176/1.

At last, directives on coordinating laws and procedures on public procurement are also relevant for entities operating in the energy sector,[149] and a Council directive of 2003 had as its prominent objective the restructuring of the Community framework for the taxation of energy products and electricity.[150] Having regard in particular to art. 93 EC (now: art. 113 TFEU), the directive was also motivated by reducing the existing different national levels of taxation, since the absence of Community provisions imposing a minimum rate of taxation on electricity and energy products other than mineral oil might adversely affect the proper functiong of the internal market (recitals 2–6).

In December 2010, the Commission presented a proposal for a regulation on "energy market integrity and transparency".[151] The development during the last 10 years of power exchange and standardized OTC contracts attracting a wide range of actors such as generators and suppliers, large energy users, pure traders or financial institutions, should be consolidated by creating sufficient confidence of all relevant actors in the integrity of these wholesale energy markets. So, rules should be enacted which clearly prohibit market abuse (including insider information and market manipulation) on wholesale markets in electrity, natural gas and related products. Those rules should be consistent with the provisions of the Market Abuse Directive,[152] and would not apply to financial instruments already covered by that legal instrument.

Energy Efficiency

Core policy orientations concerning this topic were set out in two communications of 2006[153] and 2008[154] the first one proposing an "Action Plan for Energy Efficiency" to realize its potential, the second one intended to explain how the 20% target (i.e. cutting the annual consumption of primary energy within the EU by that percentage by 2020) might be delivered.

An EP and Council directive enacted in 2004[155] dealt with promoting cogeneration based on a useful heat demand in the internal energy market. According to art. 1, the legal act which applies to "cogeneration" (art. 3 lit. a) and cogeneration

---

[149] Directive 2004/17/EC, OJ [2004] L 134/1; Directive 92/13/EEC, OJ [1992] L 76/14, as amended; on the relationship between regulation and public procurement cf. Ruffert, Völkerrechtliche Impulse und Rahmen des Europäischen Verfassungsrechts, in: Fehling/Ruffert (eds.), *Regulierungsrecht*, 2010, No. 46 et seq.

[150] Directive 2003/96/EC, OJ [2003] L 283/51.

[151] COM(2010)726 final, 8th December, 2010.

[152] Directive 2003/6/EC, OJ [2003] L 96/16; Zylka, *Marktaufsicht im Stromhandel*, 2010, pp. 112 et seq.; Bundestags-Drucksache 17/4322, 21st December, 2010.

[153] COM(2006) 545 final, 19th October, 2006.

[154] COM(2008) 772 final, 13th November, 2008.

[155] Directive 2004/8/EC, OJ [2004] L 52/50.

technologies listed in annex I (art. 2) aims at increasing energy efficiency and improving security of supply by creating a framework for promotion and development of "high efficiency cogeneration" (art. 3 lits. h, i) of heat and power based on "useful heat" (art. 3 lit. b) demand and primary energy savings in the internal market, taking into account the specific national circumstances especially concerning climatic and economic conditions. Although the directive intended to take measures to ensure that the potential for use of cogeneration would be better exploited, it was based, in particular, on art. 175 para. 1 EC Treaty. For the purpose of determining the efficiency of cogeneration in accordance with annex III (and art. 4) of the directive, a Commission decision later on established harmonized efficiency reference values for separate production of electricity and heat.[156]

Repealing an earlier Council directive of 1993,[157] an EP and Council legal instrument of 2006 "on energy end-use efficiency and energy services"[158] applied to energy and other companies, final customers as well as to the armed forces (art. 2) in order to enhance the cost-effective improvement of energy end-use efficiency (art. 3 lits. b, c) in the EU Member States by providing the necessary indicative targets (arts. 4, 5) as well as mechanisms, institutions and institutional, financial and legal frameworks (arts. 6–13) to remove existing market barriers and imperfections that impede the efficient end use of "energy" (art. 3 lit. a), and, moreover, by creating the conditions for the development and promotion of a market for "energy services" (art. 3 lit. e) and for the delivery of other "energy efficiency improvement measurers" (art. 3 lit. h) to final customers (art. 1).

In 2009, an EP and Council directive establishing a framework for the setting of ecodesign requirements for energy-using products[159] was not only substantially amended, but also recast in the interests of (legal) clarity.[160] The explicit purpose of this directive which does not apply to means of transport for persons or goods (art. 1 para. 3) is also ensuring the free movement of such products within the internal market (art. 1 para. 1, art. 6). All "energy-related products" (art. 2 no. 1) covered by implementing measures must fulfill certain requirements (art. 5: CE marking, EC declaration of conformity) to be placed on the market and/or to be put into service (art. 3, referring to definitions in art. 2 nos. 4, 5). The directive would thereby contribute to sustainable development by both increasing energy efficiency and the level of protection of the environment (art. 1 para. 2).

Complementary to the ecodesign directive, two other legal acts are focusing on labeling. As early as 1992, the Council enacted a directive "on the indication by labeling and standard product information of the consumption of energy and other

---

[156] Directive 2007/74/EC, OJ [2007] L 32/183.

[157] Directive 93/76/EEC, OJ [1993] L 237/28.

[158] Directive 2006/32/EC, OJ [2006] L 114/64, transformed in Germany by Federal Act of 4th November, 2010, Federal Official Journal part I, pp. 1483 et seq.

[159] Directive 2005/32/EC, OJ [2005] L 191/29.

[160] Directive 2009/125/EC, OJ [2009] L 285/10.

resources by household appliances"[161] which was amended more than once and finally recast in 2010.[162] Two years before, an EP and Council directive adopted a somewhat parallel regulation "on a Community energy-efficiency labeling program for office equipment"[163] since the most cost-effective measure for this field would be a voluntary "Energy Star" labeling program. The 2010 directive would also, by providing for more relevant details, further the aims of regulation 765/2008/EC containing general provision on market surveillance relating to the marketing of products.[164] It is meant to establish a framework not only for the harmonization of national measures for end-user information (arts. 4 et seq.) on the consumption of energy and "other essential resources" (art. 2 lit. c) during use but also for "supplementary information" (art. 2 lit. d) concerning new "energy-related products" (art. 1 para. 2, art. 2 lit. a) other than those mentioned in art. 1 para. 3, thereby enabling end-users to choose more efficient products (art. 1 para. 1). Core information requirements (art. 4) refer to labels and "fiches", i.e. a standard table for information related to a product (art. 2 lit. b) as well as to mentioning the energy efficiency class of a product.

At the same day as the new labeling directive, also an EP and Council directive "on the energy performance of buildings" was published.[165] This legal act, too, was a new amended version of a former one (of 2002[166]) and takes first of all account of the fact that buildings are a main cause of energy consumption within the EU, so its reduction and the use of "energy from renewable sources" (art. 2 no. 6) in the buildings sector would constitute important measures to diminish the Union's energy dependency as well as its greenhouse gas emissions. In order to improve the energy performance of buildings within the Union, the directive lays down, in particular, requirements as regards the common general framework for a methodology (art. 3, annex I) for calculating the integrated energy performance of "buildings" (art. 2 no. 1) and "building units" (art. 2 no. 8), the application of minimum requirements (arts. 4 et seq.) to the "energy performance" (art. 2 no. 4) of new buildings as well as of existing ones in the case of "major renovation" (art. 2 no. 10), national plans (art. 9) for increasing the number of "nearly-zero energy buildings" (art. 2 no. 2), energy certification for buildings (arts. 11 et seq.) and independent control systems for "energy performance certificates" (art. 2 no. 12) and inspections reports (art. 18).[167]

---

[161] Directive 92/75/EEC, OJ [1992] L 297/16.

[162] Directive 2010/30/EU, OJ [2010] L 153/1.

[163] Directive 2008/106/EC, OJ [2008] L 39/1.

[164] Directive 2010/31/EU, OJ [2010] L 153/13.

[165] Directive 2010/31/EU, OJ [2010] L 153/13.

[166] Directive 2002/91/EC, OJ [2003] L 1/65.

[167] For a general survey, cf. also Britz/Eifert/Reimer, *Energieeffizienzrecht*, 2010; also Bundestags-Drucksache 17/3341, 20th December, 2010.

Renewable Energies

In 1997 the Commission published a White Paper on renewable energy[168] which announced a target to double the Union's renewable energy share to 12% by 2010. The renewable energy policy to be founded on the need to address sustainability concerns surrounding climate change and air pollution would improve the security of Europe's energy supply and develop Europe's competitiveness and industrial and technological innovation. The White Paper also announced a renewable energy strategy and action plan. A key element of this plan was the establishment of European legislation to provide a stable policy framework and clarify the expected development of renewable energy in each Member State. The two key pieces of legislation (directives 2001/77/EC[169] and 2003/30/EC[170]) set indicative 2010 targets for all Member States and required actions to improve the growth, development and access of renewable energy. In addition, a Biomass Action Plan was adopted in 2005[171] to focus attention on the specific need for Member States to develop Europe's biomass resources.

Reports issued in 2007 (and 2009[172]) as well as the Renewable Energy Roadmap[173] highlighted the slow progress Member States were making and the likelihood that the EU as a whole would fail to reach its 2010 target, mainly because of the merely indicative nature of the national targets and the uncertain investment environment provided by the existing legal framework. The Commission therefore proposed a new, more rigorous package of rules to drive forward the development of renewable energy and more solid, legally binding targets for 2020, and in spring 2009, a new Renewable Energy directive was enacted amending and subsequently repealing the directives of 2001 and 2003.[174] The directive establishes a common framework for the promotion of "energy from renewable sources" (art. 2 para. 2 lit. a), sets mandatory national targets (art. 3, annex I) for the overall share of energy from those sources in "gross final consumption of energy" (art. 2 para. 2 lit. f), and for their share in transport (art. 5 para. 5, annex III; art. 21). Moreover, it lays down rules relating to statistical transfers between Member States (art. 6) and joint projects also with third countries (arts. 7–10), "guarantees of origin" (art. 2 para. 2 lit. j, art. 15), administrative procedures (art. 13), information and training (art. 14), and access to the electricity grid for energy from renewable sources (arts. 16). Not the least, the legal act sets up (in arts. 17–20) sustainability criteria for "biofuels" (art. 2 para. 2 lit. i) and

---

[168] COM(97) 599 final, 26th November, 1997.

[169] Directive 2001/77/EC, OJ [2001] L 283/33.

[170] Directive 2003/30/EC, OJ [2003] L 123/42.

[171] COM(2005) 628 final, 7th December, 2005; cf. also the "EU Strategy on Biofuels", COM (2006) 34 final, 8th February, 2006.

[172] COM(2009) 192 final, 24th April, 2009.

[173] COM(2006) 848 final, 10th January, 2007.

[174] Directive 2009/28/EC, OJ [2009] L 140/16.

"bioliquids" (lit. h). By decision of June 30, 2009,[175] the Commission then established a template for National Renewable Energy Action Plans under the directive.

At the end, it might be appropriate to point to two more Commission communications dealing with specific issues, namely "support of electricity from renewable energy sources"[176] and "Offshore Wind Energy" where the EU body required actions "needed to deliver on the Energy Policy Objectives for 2020 and beyond".[177]

European and Member States' Energy Policies – The German Example

The German National Renewable Energy Action Plan (as of July 2010)[178] might be a good example to show how supranational and national energy policies are interdependent. As the German government was working on a new overall national strategy for energy supply until 2050 defining key points of future German energy policy, the data and statements of the National Action Plan (NAP) have to be reviewed or even modified since the government adopted its new strategy in September 2010.[179] In the NAP, the share of renewable energy in gross final energy consumption was estimated to be 19.6% in 2020, i.e. reaching a higher value than the directive's binding national target of 18%.[180]

In fact, most measures and instruments necessary to achieve this national target were already enacted: In the electricity sector, the revised Renewable Energy Act[181] is the crucial basis for further development in the production of those energies. This also applies to the production of combined power and heating/cooling where the EEG is supplemented by a specific Act[182] and by emissions trading. In the heating/cooling sector, the main package of measures includes a

---

[175] Decision 2009/548/EC, OJ [2009] L 182/33.

[176] COM(2005) 627 final, 7th December, 2005.

[177] COM(2008) 768 final, 13th November, 2008.

[178] Adopted on 4th August, 2010; http://www.bmu.de/files/pdfs/allgemein/application/pdf/nationaler_aktionsplan_ee.pdf.

[179] Energiekonzept für eine umweltschonende, zuverlässige und bezahlbare Energieversorgung, 28th September, 2010, see http://www.bmwi.de/BMWi/Redaktion/PDF/Publikationen/energiekonzept-2010,property=pdf,bereich=bmwi,sprache=de,rwb=true.pdf.

[180] Directive 2009/28/EC, OJ [2009] L 140/16, Art. 3(1) and annex I.

[181] Gesetz für den Vorrang Erneuerbarer Energien (EEG) of 25th October, 2008 (Federal Official Journal part I, pp. 2074 et seq.), as amended.

[182] At the end of 2010, the Kraft-Wärme-Kopplungsgesetz of 2002 was modified in 2008 and did not, as originally planned, expire at the end of 2011.

Market Incentive Program,[183] the Renewable Energies Heat Act,[184] support programs by public financial institutions[185] and the Energy Savings Ordinance.[186] In the transports sector, compliance with the sustainability criteria for biofuels plays a major role. EU law obligations were implemented by the Biofuels Sustainability Ordinance[187] and in the field of power generation by the Biomass Power Sustainability Ordinance.[188] In order to fully transform the new Renewable Energy Directive into national law, the Federal Diet currently (January 2011) debates on a "European Law Adaptation Act for Renewable Energy"[189] providing for some further adjustments and specifications for existing instruments and schemes for the promotion of renewable energies. This EAG EE includes the implementation of the role model function of renewable energy use and increased energy efficiency in public buildings, a rule on the use of certificates of origin as well as defining the basis for the issuance and recognition thereof, moreover improvement of grid connection conditions and adjustment of energy statistics.

In addition to measures taken at national level, a number of other efforts to promote the development of renewable energy have taken place at regional and local level,[190] according to the distribution of legislative and administrative powers within the Federal Republic.[191]

Conclusion

Finally, I would like to come back to "Energy 2020", i.e. the Commission communication referred to at the start of this paper.[192] The EU body rightly states there that the Union is "on the threshold of an unprecedented period of energy policy".[193] But

---

[183] Several guidelines are available at: http://www.bmu.de/erneuerbare_energien/downloads/doc/43273.php.

[184] Gesetz zur Förderung Erneuerbarer Energien im Wärmebereich of 7th August, 2008 (Federal Official Journal part I, pp. 1658 et seq.), as amended.

[185] For a short survey, cf. http://www.iwr.de/foerderung/bund.html.

[186] Verordnung über energiesparenden Wärmeschutz und energiesparende Anlagetechnik bei Gebäuden, Version of 29th April, 2009 (Federal Offical Journal part I, pp. 954 et seq.).

[187] Verordnung über Anforderungen an eine nachhaltige Herstellung von Biokraftstoffen of 30th September, 2009 (Federal Official Journal part I, pp. 3182 et seq.), as amended.

[188] Verordnung über Anforderungen an eine nachhaltige Herstellung von flüssiger Biomasse zur Stromerzeugung of 23rd July, 2009 (Federal Official Journal part I, pp. 2174 et seq.), as amended.

[189] Europarechtsanpassungsgesetz Erneuerbare Energien (EAG EE), proposal by the Federal Government of 8th November, 2010, Bundestags-Drucksache 17/3629.

[190] Cf. some examples in NREAP, adopted on 4th August, 2010; http://www.bmu.de/files/pdfs/allgemein/application/pdf/nationaler_aktionsplan_ee.pdf.

[191] There are only various specific energy- and/or environment-related legislative powers a the federal level, according to arts. 30, 70 et seq. of the German Basic Law (Grundgesetz).

[192] Supra, fn. 1.

[193] Op. cit. (fn. 1), p. 20.

is it really true that "Member States have agreed" that the great challenges ahead "will be tackled most effectively by policies and action at EU level,[194] by 'Europeanizing' energy policy" which will include "directing EU public funding support towards priorities that markets fail to meet and that bring the most European value"? Of course, a new (EU) strategy must – and will – "ensure better leadership and coordination at the European level, both for internal action and in relations with external partners". And for sure, it seems also necessary "to look beyond the timescale of the present strategy to ensure that the EU is well prepared for the 2050 objective of a secure, competitive and low-carbon energy system" and to outline a roadmap for the longer term. But although the European Parliament has continuously supported ambitious energy and climate change objectives (till 2020),[195] will the majority of the people within the EU be informed about the risks and challenges as early and as clearly as possible, will the ordinary citizen be asked whether he would be ready to follow the road leading to quite fundamental changes in normal day life? To quote once more the Commission's initial statement: "The well-being of our people ... depends on safe, secure, sustainable and affordable energy".[196] So, democratic principles would require informed consent of the whole people since it might be neither sufficient nor the proper way to restrict public participation to persons immediately concerned. European programs, projects and actions – especially relating to (energy) infrastructure – must be based on democratic legitimacy – or they will fail at last and hardly reach the end of the "rocky road to a real transition",[197] i.e. to necessary radical social and mental changes of most human beings in the post "peak oil" era.

---

[194] Including regional initiatives for issues of common interest for two or more States see COM (2010) 721 final, 7th December, 2010.

[195] See, e.g., Press Release, 25th November, 2010, http://www.europarl.europa.eu/en/pressroom/content/20101125IPR00549/html/Climate-EU-should-move-to-30-emissions-reduction-target-say-MEPs.

[196] Op. cit. (fn. 1), p. 2.

[197] Chatterton/Cutler, The Rocky Road to a Real Transition, April 2008, available at: http://sparror.cubecinema.com/stuffit/trapese/rocky-road-a5-web.pdf.

The Energy Community of South East Europe

Carsten Nowak

Introduction

The Energy Community of South-East Europe,[1] established in order to extend
the European Union's internal energy market to South East Europe, is a roughly
5-year-old European Community which was – at least in parts – consciously
modelled on the European Coal and Steel Community,[2] the basis or forerunner of
today's European Union (EU). This still rather young Energy Community is based
on the Energy Community Treaty[3] which was signed in Athens on 25 October 2005
and entered into force on 1 July 2006. The Energy Community Treaty is the first
legally binding multilateral treaty between the Western Balkans after the terrible
wars and conflicts of the 1990s. It creates a legal framework for an integrated
regional energy market between the EU and several countries of South East Europe
– the largest internal market for electricity and gas in the world. The purpose is to
create an integrated energy market allowing for cross-border energy trade, to
provide energy interconnections also to the Middle East, central Asia and the
Caspian region, to enhance the security of energy supply, to attract investment in
power generation and networks and to improve the environmental situation in

---

[1] Hereinafter: 'ECSEE' or simply 'Energy Community'.

[2] See EC's Press Release IP/05/1346 of 25th October, 2005. The Treaty establishing the European
Coal and Steel Community, which was signed on 18th April, 1951, entered into force on 23rd July,
1952 and expired 50 years later on 23rd July, 2002; with first overviews see van Raalte, The Treaty
Constituting the European Coal and Steel Community, ICLQ 1 (1952), pp. 78 et seq.; Vernon, The
Schuman Plan – Sovereign Powers of the European Coal and Steel Community, AJIL 47 (1953),
pp. 183 et seq.

[3] Published in OJ [2006] L 198/18.

C. Nowak (✉)
FB Rechtswissenschaften, Europa-Universität Viadrina Frankfurt (Oder), Postfach 1786, 15207
Frankfurt/Oder, Germany
e-mail: cnowak@europa-uni.de

relation with energy supply. Thereby leading to an extraterritorial extension of the *acquis communautaire* regarding electricity, gas, renewables, environment and competition beyond the EU's borders, this Treaty is simultaneously a very good example for what is usually called 'regional-multilateral integration', 'neo-functionalism', 'regionalisation', 'regional cooperation', 'system transformation', 'europeanisation', 'pre-accession or enlargement strategy', 'foreign or external energy policy' and/or 'external governance'.[4]

The genesis of this multilateral Treaty, which consists of a preamble and 12 titles including 105 articles[5] followed by four annexes,[6] is closely connected with the intense engagement of the EU in its South Eastern neighbourhood which was, at the beginning, predominantly characterized by the *Stability Pact for South Eastern Europe* as well as by the *Stabilisation and Association Process* (SAP) aiming to

---

[4] For more on this, see Bozhilova, Energy security and regional cooperation in South-East Europe, Journal of Balkan and Near Eastern Studies 11 (2009), pp. 293 et seq.; Deitz/Stirton/Wright, South East Europe's electricity sector: Attractions, obstacles and challenges of Europeanisation, Utilities Policy 17 (2009), pp. 4 et seq.; Emerson, Recalibrating EU Policy towards the Western Balkans, CEPS Policy Brief No. 175/October 2008, p. 1 (7), available at: http://www.ceps.eu; Fischer/Lippert, Mehr Gleise – Energieaußenpolitik und Nachbarschaftspolitik der EU, Osteuropa 2009, pp. 53 et seq.; Hofer, *Die Europäische Union als Regelexporteur – Die Europäisierung der Energiepolitik in Bulgarien, Serbien und der Ukraine*, 2008, pp. 95 et seq.; Hofer, Neo-functionalism reloaded – The Energy Community of Southeast Europe, Paper for the 9th Annual Kokkalis Graduate Student Workshop Harvard University, pp. 1 et seq., available at: http://www.hks. harvard.edu/kokkalis/ GSW9/Hofer_paper.pdf; Lavenex, EU external governance in 'wider Europe', JEPP 2004, pp. 680 et seq.; Monastiriotis, Quo Vadis Southeast Europa? – EU Accession, Regional Cooperation and the Need for a Balkan Development Strategy, Hellenic Observatory Papers on Greece and Southeast Europe No 10/January 2008, pp. 1 et seq.; Bauer/Pitschel, Regionalisierung und Dezentralisierung in Mittel- und Südosteuropa 1997–2007, PVS 2009, pp. 130 et seq.; Renner, The Energy Community of Southeast Europe: A neo-functionalist project of regional integration, European Integration online Papers 13 (2009), pp. 1 et seq.; Sergi/Qerimi, The process of EU enlargement towards south-eastern Europe: current challenges and perspectives, South-East Europe Review (2007) 2, pp. 57 et seq.; Solioz/Stubbs, Emergent regional co-operation in South East Europe: towards 'open regionalism'?, Southeast European and Black Sea Studies 9 (2009), pp. 1 et seq.; Youngs, Europe's External Energy Policy: Between Geopolitics and the Market, Centre for European Policy Studies (CEPS) Working Document No 278/November 2007, pp. 1 et seq., available at: http://www.ceps.be.

[5] Title I (principles): Articles 1–8; Title II (extension of the acquis communautaire): Articles 9–25; Title III (mechanism for operation of network energy markets): Articles 26–39; Title IV (creation of a single energy market): Articles 40–46; Title V (institutions of the Energy Community): Articles 47–75; Title VI (decision-making process): Articles 76–88; Title VII (implementation of decisions and dispute settlement): Articles 89–93; Title VIII (interpretation): Article 94; Title IX (participants and observers): Articles 95 and 96; Title X (duration): Articles 97–99; Title XI (revision and accession): Article 100; Title XII (final and transitional provisions): Articles 101–105.

[6] Annex I regarding the timetable for the implementation of the EC Directives No. 2003/54 and 2003/55 and the Regulation (EC) No. 1228/2003 of 26 June 2003); Annex II regarding the timetable for the implementation of the acquis on environment; Annex III regarding Articles 81, 82 and 87 of the EC Treaty (since the Treaty of Lisbon, which entered into force on 1st December, 2009, Articles 101, 102 and 107 of the Treaty on the Functioning of the European Union; consolidated version of this Treaty in: OJ [2010] C 83/47); Annex IV regarding contributions to the budget).

ensure or to promote economic, political and social development of the Western Balkans on the basis of bilateral agreements and partnerships (pp. 407 et seq.). The divers objectives of the Energy Community Treaty, which differentiates between Parties, Participants and Observers (pp. 413 et seq.), and the different tasks or activities of this Community are extensive and ambitious (pp. 416 et seq.). The institutional and organisational structures of the Energy Community are to a certain extent similar to those existing within the EU, even if there are several significant differences especially in the fields of decision-making, implementation and dispute settlement (pp. 429 et seq.). Finally, some recent and actual developments concerning the Energy Community are worth to be mentioned (pp. 438 et seq.).

Genesis and Background of the Energy Community

During the 1990s, South East Europe experienced and witnessed the collapse of communist regimes in the region as well as several wars and conflicts, which created a politically and economically unstable climate and deeply affected the social and economic life of people in this region. As a consequence, stability, security and prosperity in South East Europe became important priorities of the EU.[7] The *Royaumont Process of Stability and Good Neighbourliness in South-East Europe* launched in December 1995 under the French EU Term-Presidency, subsequently followed by the adoption of the so called 'Regional Approach', was the first real EU initiative aimed at stabilizing the Western Balkans.[8] Additionally, the latter countries decided to be part of the *South-East European Cooperation Process* (SEECP) that – as a new forum for diplomatic and practical dialogue among Albania, Bosnia and Herzegovina, Bulgaria, Greece, the Former Yugoslav

---

[7] See Anastasakis, The EU's political conditionality in the Western Balkans: towards a more pragmatic approach, Southeast European and Black Sea Studies 8 (2008), pp. 365 et seq.; Becker, The European Union and the western Balkans, South-East Europe Review (2008) 1, pp. 7 et seq.; Renner, The Energy Community of Southeast Europe: A neo-functionalist project of regional integration, European Integration online Papers 13 (2009), pp. 1 et seq. (4 et seq.); Wittkowsky, Der Stabilitätspakt für Südosteuropa und die „führende Rolle" der Europäischen Union, Aus Politik und Zeitgeschichte 29–30 (2000), pp. 3 et seq.

[8] For more on this and on the 'Regional Approach', see Bechev, Carrot, sticks and norms: the EU and regional cooperation in Southeast Europe, Journal of Southern Europe and the Balkans 8 (2006), pp. 27 et seq. (31 et seq.); Elbasani, EU enlargement in the Western Balkans: strategies of borrowing and inventing, Journal of Southern Europe and the Balkans 10 (2008), pp. 293 et seq. (295 et seq.); Sadakata, The Balkans between the EU and NATO: focusing on the Former Yugoslavia, Romanian Journal of European Affairs 6 (2006), pp. 38 et seq. (40); Türkes/Gökgöz, The European Union's Strategy towards the Western Balkans: Exclusion or Integration, East European Politics and Societies 20 (2006), pp. 659 et seq. (674 et seq.); Tzifakis, EU's region-building and boundary-drawing policies: the European approach to the Southern Mediterranean and the Western Balkans, Journal of Southern Europe and the Balkans 9 (2007), pp. 47 et seq. (57 et seq.).

Republic of Macedonia, Moldova, Romania, Serbia, Croatia, Montenegro and Turkey – was launched in Sofia in July 1996.[9]

In order to demonstrate its ability to promote post-conflict stabilization and reconstruction in this region immediately and to achieve a significant contribution to the economic, political and social development of the Western Balkans, the international community, following the above mentioned lead of the EU,[10] initiated the *Stability Pact for South Eastern Europe* in 1999, bringing together approximately 40 partner countries and organizations including the countries of the South East European region, the EU Member States, the European Commission, Canada, Japan, Norway, Russia,[11] Switzerland, Turkey, USA as well as several international organizations (UN, OSCE, Council of Europe, UNHCR, NATO and OECD), some international financial institutions (World Bank, International Monetary Fund, European Bank for Reconstruction and Development, European Investment Bank and Council of Europe Development Bank) and some regional initiatives (Organization for Economic Cooperation in the Black Sea Region, Central-European Initiative, Initiative for Cooperation in South-Eastern Europe etc.). The Stability Pact for South Eastern Europe, set up by the international community in Cologne on 10 June 1999, was not an international organization,[12] but a political declaration of commitment, a comprehensive conflict-prevention strategy and a regional policy

---

[9] This initiative was launched during a meeting of the Ministers of Foreign Affairs of South-East European countries, which decided to start a long-term process of multilateral cooperation among participating states in several fields (strengthening stability, security and good-neighbourly relations; economic development; humanitarian, social and cultural issues; justice, combat against organized crime, drug and arms trafficking, and terrorism).

[10] For more on the EU's first initiatives in this context, see Friis/Murphy, 'Turbo-charged negotiations': the EU and the Stability Pact for South Eastern Europe, Journal of European Public Policy 2000, pp. 767 et seq.; Türkes/Gökgöz, The European Union's Strategy towards the Western Balkans: Exclusion or Integration, East European Politics and Societies 20 (2006), pp. 659 et seq. (674 et seq.); Wittkowsky, South-eastern Europe and the European Union – promoting stability through integration?, South-East Europe Review for Labour and Social Affairs 2000 (1), pp. 79 et seq. (81).

[11] The participation of Russia within the Stability Pact for South Eastern Europe did at the end not lead to its membership within the Energy Community, although Russia is – inter alia with regard to energy issues – very important for the EU as well as for the Western Balkans. For more on the important energy relations between the EU and Russia, see Hadfield, EU-Russia Energy Relations: Aggregation and Aggravation, Journal of Contemporary European Studies 16 (2008), pp. 231 et seq.

[12] Later, the Regional Table, the central consultative body of the Stability Pact for South Eastern Europe, agreed to transform this Pact into an organizational form called Regional Cooperation Council (RCC) giving greater scope for regional ownership; for more on this see Anastasakis, The EU's political conditionality in the Western Balkans: towards a more pragmatic approach, Southeast European and Black Sea Studies 8 (2008), p. 365 (369); Andreev, Sub-regional cooperation and the expanding EU: the Balkans and the Black Sea Area in a comparative perspective, Journal of Balkan and Near Eastern Studies 11 (2009), pp. 83 et seq. (102 et seq.); Solioz, Rethinking south-eastern Europe through a pan-European perspective, South-East Europe Review (2007) 2, pp. 67 et seq. (78); Solioz/Stubbs, Emergent regional co-operation in South East Europe: towards 'open regionalism'?, Southeast European and Black Sea Studies 9 (2009), pp. 1 et seq. (8).

framework in order to stimulate regional cooperation,[13] to support the countries in that region in their efforts to foster peace, democracy, respect for human rights and economic prosperity, to create the political conditions for effective international assistance to the region by coordinating donors as well as to achieve stability and growth in the region as a whole.[14]

Nearly at the same time, the EU started the *Stabilisation and Association Process* (SAP)[15] which – accompanied by the establishment of the European Agency for

---

[13] On various co-operative efforts undertaken by South Eastern European governments after the end of the 'Cold War' see Segell, New Hopes for South Eastern Europe, Journal of European Area Studies 10 (2002), pp. 229 et seq.

[14] On the different objectives, activities, principles, difficulties and significance of this Stability Pact see Altmann, Schemes of Regional Co-operation in Southeast Europe, Southeast European and Black Sea Studies 3 (2003), pp. 126 et seq. (141 et seq.); Axt, Der Stabilitätspakt für Südosteuropa: politischer Aktionismus oder langfristig tragfähiges Konzept?, Südosteuropa 48 (1999), pp. 401 et seq.; Bartlett/Samardžija, The Reconstruction of South East Europe, the Stability Pact and the Role of the EU: an Overview, MOCT-Most 2000, pp. 245 et seq.; Bechev, Carrot, sticks and norms: the EU and regional cooperation in Southeast Europe, Journal of Southern Europe and the Balkans 8 (2006), pp. 27 et seq. (34 et seq.); Biermann, Stabilitätspakt und EU-Balkanpolitik: Von der Stabilisierung zur Integration?, integration 2002, pp. 210 et seq.; Busek, Zukunft des Stabilitätspakts – Das Engagement der Europäer in Südosteuropa, Internationale Politik 57 (2002), pp. 25 et seq.; Cremona, Creating the New Europe: the Stability Pact for South Eastern Europe, The Cambridge Yearbook of European Legal Studies 2 (1999), pp. 463 et seq.; Elbasani, EU enlargement in the Western Balkans: strategies of borrowing and inventing, Journal of Southern Europe and the Balkans 10 (2008), pp. 293 et seq. (297 et seq.); Emerson, On the Forming and Reforming of Stability Pacts: from the Balkans to the Caucasus, CEPS Policy Brief No. 4/May 2001, pp. 1 et seq., available at: http://www.ceps.eu.

[15] See in particular the Commission Communication of 26th May, 1999, COM(1999) 235 final; for more on the SAP and its narrow relation to the Stability Pact for South Eastern Europe see Bartlett/ Samardžija, The Reconstruction of South East Europe, the Stability Pact and the Role of the EU: an Overview, MOCT-Most 2000, pp. 245 et seq.; Bechev, Carrot, sticks and norms: the EU and regional cooperation in Southeast Europe, Journal of Southern Europe and the Balkans 8 (2006), pp. 27 et seq. (37 et seq.); Bretherton/Vogler, *The European Union as a Global Actor*, (2nd ed.) 2006, pp. 144 et seq.; Busek, South Eastern Europe: On the Way to Political and Economic Integration within the EU, The Analyst – Central and Eastern European Review 4 (2007), pp. 5 et seq.; Calic, EU Enlargement and Common Foreign and Security Policy in the Western Balkans, Südosteuropa Mitteilungen 2007, pp. 12 et seq.; Cameron/Kintis, Southeastern Europe and the European Union, Southeast European and Black Sea Studies 1 (2001), pp. 94 et seq. (99 et seq.); Chandler, The EU's promotion of democracy in the Balkans, in: Laïdi (ed.), *EU Foreign Policy in a Globalized World – Normative power and social preferences*, 2008, pp. 68 et seq.; Elbasani, EU enlargement in the Western Balkans: strategies of borrowing and inventing, Journal of Southern Europe and the Balkans 10 (2008), pp. 293 et seq. (297 et seq.); Friis/Murphy, 'Turbo-charged negotiations': the EU and the Stability Pact for South Eastern Europe, Journal of European Public Policy 2000, pp. 767 et seq.; Hoffmeister, Die Beziehungen der Europäischen Union zu den Staaten des Westbalkans, in: Kadelbach (ed.), *Die Außenbeziehungen der Europäischen Union*, 2006, pp. 125 et seq.; Kotios, Southeastern Europe and the Euro Area – The Euroization Debate, Eastern European Economics 40 (2002), pp. 24 et seq.; Renner, The Energy Community of Southeast Europe: A neo-functionalist project of regional integration, European Integration online Papers 13 (2009), pp. 1 et seq. (5); Sadakata, The Balkans between the EU and NATO: focusing on the Former Yugoslavia, Romanian Journal of European Affairs 6 (2006), pp. 38 et seq. (40 et seq.); Stewart, EU Democracy Promotion in the Western Balkans, in: Jünemann/Knodt (eds.), *European*

Reconstruction[16] – subsequently served as a programmatic platform for the set-up of bilateral contractual relations between the EC and its Member States, of the one part, and Croatia, Macedonia, Albania, Bosnia and Herzegovina, Montenegro, Serbia and Kosovo as defined by resolution 1244 of the UN Security Council, of the other part. Indeed, since a couple of years the South Eastern European countries are connected to the EU by individual 'Accession Partnerships'[17] or at least 'European Partnerships'[18] which are based on Council Regulation (EC) No 533/2004 of 22 March 2004 on the establishment of European partnerships in the framework of the stabilisation and association process.[19] Core elements of these bilateral partnerships are some preparatory (trade-related) 'Interim Agreements'[20] as well as several 'Stabilisation and Association Agreements'[21] aiming particularly to support the efforts of the Western Balkans to strengthen democracy and the rule of law, to contribute to political, economic and institutional stability in these States, to provide an appropriate framework for political dialogue, allowing the development of close political relations between the Parties and to foster regional cooperation in all fields covered by the agreements in question.[22]

External Democracy Promotion, 2007, pp. 231 et seq.; Theofanis, The European Union, the Enlargement and the South-Eastern Europe, Romanian Journal of European Affairs 5 (2005), pp. 51 et seq.; Türkes/Gökgöz, The European Union's Strategy towards the Western Balkans: Exclusion or Integration, East European Politics and Societies 20 (2006), pp. 659 et seq. (677 et seq.).

[16] See Regulation (EC) No. 2667/2000, OJ [2000] L 306/7.

[17] See Council Decision 2008/119/EC of 12th February, 2008, OJ [2008] L 42/51; as well as Council Decision 2008/212/EC of 18th February, 2008, OJ [2008] L 80/32.

[18] See Council Decision 2008/210/EC of 18th February, 2008, OJ [2008] L 80/1; Council Decision 2008/211/EC of 18th February, 2008, OJ [2008] L 80/18; Council Decision 2008/213/EC of 18th February, 2008, OJ [2008] L 80/46; and Council Decision 2007/49/EC of 22nd January, 2007, OJ [2007] L 20/16.

[19] OJ [2004] L 86/1; amended by Regulation (EC) No. 269/2006, OJ [2006] L 47/1.

[20] See, for example, the Interim Agreement on trade and trade-related matters between the European Community, of the one part, and the Republic of Montenegro, of the other part, OJ [2007] L 345/2 and the Interim Agreement on trade and trade-related matters between the European Community, of the one part, and Bosnia and Herzegovina, of the other part, OJ [2008] L 233/6.

[21] See, for example, the Stabilisation and Association Agreement between the European Communities and their Member States, of the one part, and the former Yugoslav Republic of Macedonia, of the other part, OJ [2004] L 84/13, the Stabilisation and Association Agreement between the European Communities and their Member States, of the one part, and the Republic of Croatia, of the other part, OJ [2005] L 26/3, and the Stabilisation and Association Agreement between the European Communities and their Member States, of the one part, and the Republic of Albania, of the other part, OJ [2009] L 107/166.

[22] The 'fields' regularly covered by the Stabilisation and Association Agreements (beyond 'political dialogue', 'regional cooperation' and some 'institutional, general and final provisions') are: free movement of goods, movement of workers, establishment, supply of services, current payments and movement of capital, investment promotion and protection; approximation of laws and law enforcement, competition, justice and home affairs and financial cooperation; for more on this, with further references, see Emerson, Recalibrating EU Policy towards the Western Balkans, CEPS Policy Brief No. 175/October 2008, pp. 1 et seq. (2 et seq.), available

The above mentioned years of war and conflict significantly damaged electricity generation and transmission infrastructure in the Western Balkans.[23] Since the energy sector – in particular security of energy supply as well as a proper balance between energy supply and demand – is vital to economic growth, development, social stability and well-being, industrialization and the prosperity of the region, the European Commission already brought forward proposals for the creation of a regional electricity market in South-East Europe in March 2002. Subsequently, the 'Athens Memorandum',[24] which outlined the principles and the institutional necessities for regional electricity market development in South-East Europe, was signed at the Athens Ministerial in November 2002 by Albania, Bosnia and Herzegovina, Bulgaria, Croatia, Greece, Romania, Turkey, Federal Republic of Yugoslavia, Former Yugoslav Republic of Macedonia and some observers[25] with the European Commission and the above mentioned Stability Pact acting as donors. Under the Athens Memorandum, which was extended to natural gas in 2003,[26] a South-East Europe Regional Energy Market was envisioned, to form part of the EU's internal energy market. Thus, the extended Athens memorandum demanded the liberalization of the electricity and gas sectors, the setting up of national regulatory authorities independent of the energy industry, the unbundling of the vertically integrated national electricity and gas companies and the establishment of transmission system operators.

Moreover, the European Council in Thessaloniki on 21 June 2003 endorsed the 'Thessaloniki Agenda for the Western Balkans: moving towards European integration', which aimed to further strengthen the privileged relations between the EU

---

at: http://www.ceps.eu; Nowak, Legal Arrangements for the Promotion and Protection of Foreign Investments Within the Framework of the EU Association Policy and European Neighbourhood Policy, in: Bungenberg/Griebel/Hindelang (eds.), *International Investment Law and EU Law*, 2011, pp. 105 et seq. (112 et seq.).

[23] For more on this, see Altmann, Südosteuropa und die Sicherung der Energieversorgung der EU, SWP-Studie 1/2007, pp. 1 et seq. (13). For an interesting overview regarding the development of the generation of electricity in several South East European countries during 1995–2004 see Hooper/Medvedev, Electrifying integration: Electricity production and the South East Europe regional energy market, Utilities Policy 17 (2009), pp. 24 et seq.

[24] Memorandum of Understanding on the Regional Electricity Market in South East Europe and its Integration into the European Union Internal Electricity Market, "Athens Memorandum – 2002", available at: http://www.seerecon.org/infrastructure/sectors/energy/documents/mou-rem-see.pdf.

[25] Austria, Hungary, Italy, Moldova and Slovenia.

[26] Memorandum of Understanding on the Regional Electricity Market in South East Europe and its Integration into the European Community Internal Electricity Market, "Athens Memorandum – 2003", signed by Albania, Bosnia and Herzegovina, Bulgaria, Croatia, Romania, Turkey, the State Union of Serbia and Montenegro, Former Yugoslav Republic of Macedonia, The United Nations Interim Administration Mission in Kosovo (UNMIK) pursuant to UN Security Council Resolution 1244, the European Community, the Special Coordinator of the Stability Pact, some political participants to the process (Greece, Italy and Austria) and some observers (Hungary, Moldova and Slovenia).

and the Western Balkans[27] and in which the EU encouraged the countries of the region to adopt a legally binding South-East European energy market agreement. Consequently, the above mentioned Athens Memorandum did set up a number of institutions, which collectively are known as the 'Athens Process'.[28] In 2004, the Athens Forum meeting decided to name this process 'Energy Community' and paved the way for the opening of negotiations in order to conclude a legally binding agreement.[29] Meeting in Athens on 14 December 2004, Ministers and representatives from the – at that time – 25 EU Member States and 11 countries of South East Europe, including Turkey, agreed on the basic principles contained in a text of a Treaty to formally establish an Energy Community between them.[30] Finally, the Athens Process resulted in the Energy Community Treaty which was signed in Athens on 25 October 2005 by the EC, the Republic of Albania, the Republic of Bulgaria, Bosnia and Herzegovina, the Republic of Croatia, the former Yugoslav Republic of Macedonia, the Republic of Montenegro, Romania, the

---

[27] At the EU Thessaloniki summit on 21st June, 2003, the EU made the promise or proclamation that South-East European countries could join the Union provided they bring themselves up to EU standards; for more on this and on recent developments regarding the different accession perspectives of the Western Balkan countries see Balázs, Issues of European Integration for the Western Balkans, The Analyst – Central and Eastern European Review (2007) 4, pp. 13 et seq., available at: http://www.ceeol.com; Belloni, European integration and the Western Balkans: lessons, prospects and obstacles, Journal of Balkan and Near Eastern Studies 11 (2009), pp. 313 et seq.; Busek, South Eastern Europe: On the Way to Political and Economic Integration within the EU, The Analyst – Central and Eastern European Review (2007) 4, pp. 5 et seq., available at: http://www.ceeol.com; Djurović/Radović, Lobbying for a faster integration track for the western Balkans region, SEER Journal for Labour and Social Affairs in Eastern Europe 2010, pp. 217 et seq.; Phinnemore, Beyond 25 – the changing face of EU enlargement: commitment, conditionality and the Constitutional Treaty, Journal of Southern Europe and the Balkans 8 (2006), pp. 7 et seq. (12 et seq.); Pridham, Securing fragile democracies in the Balkans: the European dimension, Romanian Journal of European Affairs 8 (2008), pp. 56 et seq. (63 et seq.); Timmins/Jović, Introduction: The Next Wave of Enlargement: The European Union and Southeast Europe after 2004, Journal of Southern Europe and the Balkans 8 (2006), pp. 1 et seq.; Türkes/Gökgöz, The European Union's Strategy towards the Western Balkans: Exclusion or Integration, East European Politics and Societies 20 (2006), pp. 659 et seq. (681 et seq.).

[28] For more on this, see Renner, The Energy Community of Southeast Europe: A neo-functionalist project of regional integration, European Integration online Papers 13 (2009), pp. 1 et seq. (9 et seq.); Röhm-Malcotti, Natural Gas on the Balkan. The role of an integrated market for energy for the economic and political stability of the countries of South East Europe with particular view to natural gas and the Energy Community of South East Europe (ECSEE) initiative, Centre Européen de Recherche Internationale et Stratégique (CERIS), Research Papers No. 3, 2005, pp. 1 et seq. (34 et seq.).

[29] With first annotations from that time, see for example Röhm-Malcotti, Natural Gas on the Balkan. The role of an integrated market for energy for the economic and political stability of the countries of South East Europe with particular view to natural gas and the Energy Community of South East Europe (ECSEE) initiative, Centre Européen de Recherche Internationale et Stratégique (CERIS), Research Papers No. 3, 2005, pp. 28 et seq.; Walendy, Stabilität durchs Netz? – Die Energiegemeinschaft Südosteuropa, Osteuropa 2004, pp. 263 et seq.

[30] See EC's Press Release IP/04/1473 of 14th December, 2004.

Republic of Serbia and the UN Interim Administration Mission in Kosovo pursuant to the UN Security Council Resolution 1244.[31] Following the ratification and notification process,[32] the Energy Community Treaty, which was approved by the European Council on 29 May 2006[33] and published in the Official Journal of the EU on 20 July 2006,[34] entered into force on 1 July 2006. Without prejudice to Article 98 of the Energy Community Treaty, giving any Party the right to withdraw from this Treaty by giving 6 months notice addressed to the Secretariat,[35] this Treaty is concluded for a period of 10 years from the date of entry into force, while the Ministerial Council,[36] acting by unanimity, may decide to extend its duration.[37]

Countries, Institutions and Other Actors Involved in the Energy Community

A great number of countries, institutions and other actors are in fact involved in the Energy Community for South East Europe. While some of them belong to the so called 'Parties' (I) or to the smaller group of 'Observers' (II), others are 'Participants' (III) or simply 'Donors' (IV).

Parties

Several provisions laid down in the Treaty establishing the Energy Community are addressed to *Parties,*[38] whereas some other provisions are addressed to *Contracting Parties*[39] or to *Adhering Parties.*[40] Therefore, it is expedient and useful that already

---

[31] Turkey participated in the Athens process but in the end did not sign this Treaty.

[32] The EU, Albania, Bulgaria, Croatia, the former Yugoslav Republic of Macedonia, Romania and UNMIK on behalf of Kosovo had brought the ratification process to a conclusion by July 2006; the three remaining Contracting Parties (Bosnia and Herzegovina, Montenegro and Serbia) ratified the Treaty in December 2006.

[33] See Council Decision 2006/500/EC of 29th May, 2006, OJ [2006] L 198/15.

[34] OJ [2006] L 198/18.

[35] For more on this important institution, see section pp. 433 et seq.) below.

[36] For more on this powerful institution, see pp. 429 et seq.) below.

[37] See Article 97 of the Energy Community Treaty with the further clarification that, if no such decision is taken, this Treaty may continue to apply between those Parties who voted in favour of extension, provided that their number amounts to at least two thirds of the Parties to the Energy Community.

[38] See, for example, Articles 1, 6, 8, 14, 29 and 41 of this Treaty.

[39] See, for example, Articles 10, 12, 18, 20 and 22 of this Treaty.

[40] See, for example, Articles 9, 26, 36 and 40 of this Treaty.

the preamble of the Treaty establishing the Energy Community declares what was meant by these three different terms in general, at least on 25 October 2005 when the Treaty was signed. According to this preamble, the group of Adhering Parties consists of the Republic of Albania, the Republic of Bulgaria, Bosnia and Herzegovina, the Republic of Croatia, the former Yugoslav Republic of Macedonia, the Republic of Montenegro, Romania and the Republic of Serbia, which all signed the Treaty on 25 October 2005. These Parties, together with the UN Interim Administration in Kosovo pursuant to the UN Security Council Resolution 1244, not an Adhering Party, are also 'Contracting Parties'. Finally, the preamble in question makes sufficiently clear that the broadest term 'Parties' includes all Contracting Parties as well as the European Community.

In the last years and months following the entry into force of the Treaty establishing the Energy Community, a couple of important changes occurred with regard to the circle of Parties: With the entering into force of the Treaty of Lisbon[41] the European Community, which signed the Energy Community Treaty on 25 October 2005, ceased to exist. According to the last sentence of Article 1(3) TEU in its consolidated version of the Treaty of Lisbon,[42] the European Union, uniting 27 Member States, shall replace and succeed the European Community. Therefore, the Energy Community Treaty is now legally binding for the European Union which, since more than three years, also covers Bulgaria and Romania originally belonging to the Adhering Parties. On 1 January 2007, Bulgaria and Romania joined the European Union and their former status (Adhering Parties) was – as provided for in Article 99 of the Energy Community Treaty – changed to that of a Participant.[43] Moldova, which originally did not belong to the Parties, joined the Energy Community on 1 May 2010. Whilst Moldova became a full fledged member as of 1 May 2010, Ukraine officially acceded the Energy Community on 1 February 2011. Thus, the Energy Community Treaty, at present, is legally binding for the EU, representing 27 Member States, as well as for Albania, Bosnia and Herzegovina, Croatia, Kosovo (via UNMIK), Republic of Macedonia, Moldova, Montenegro, Serbia and Ukraine. Negotiations with Turkey upon accession to the Energy Community are ongoing.[44] Norway has also applied to join the Energy Community,

---

[41] Treaty of Lisbon amending the Treaty on European Union (TEU) and the Treaty establishing the European Community (TEC), signed at Lisbon on 13th December, 2007, OJ [2007] C 306/1; for more on this Treaty, which entered into force on 1st December, 2009, see with further references Nowak, *Europarecht nach Lissabon*, 2011, pp. 51 et seq.

[42] For this consolidated version of the TEU see OJ [2010] C 83/13.

[43] For the concrete meaning of the term Participant in this context, see p. 415 below.

[44] Following a decision taken by the Ministerial Council of the Energy Community, on 15th July, 2008, the Council of the EU mandated the European Commission to carry out accession negotiations not only with Ukraine and Moldova, but also with Turkey, see EC's Press Release IP/08/1783 of 26th November, 2008. The European Commission opened negotiations with Turkey upon accession to the Energy Community on 9th September, 2009, see EC's Press Release IP/09/1299 of 10th September, 2009. For more on Turkey's great importance inter alia regarding energy supply to the EU, see Bozhilova, Energy security and regional cooperation in South-East Europe,

but for the moment this country is – like Turkey and Georgia – still only 'observer'[45] in the following sense.

Observers

Beyond numerous Treaty provisions only addressed to the Parties mentioned above, Article 96(1) of the Energy Community Treaty provides for an observer status for the benefit of neighbouring third countries. Once accepted as an Observer, such a third country may attend the meetings of the Ministerial Council, the Permanent High-Level Group, the Regulatory Board and the Fora, without participating in the discussions.[46]

Participants

Upon accession of an Adhering Party to the EU, that party shall become a Partici-pant as provided for in Article 95 of the Energy Community Treaty.[47] According to this provision, any Member State of the European Union may obtain the status of a 'Participant'. A country with such a status has the right to take part in all the institutional meetings of the Energy Community.[48] As of April 2008, the group of Participants to the Treaty establishing the Energy Community amounts to 14 and comprises Austria, Bulgaria, Cyprus, Czech Republic, France, Germany, Greece, Hungary, Italy, the Netherlands, Romania, Slovakia, Slovenia and the United Kingdom.

Journal of Balkan and Near Eastern Studies 11 (2009), pp. 293 et seq. (309); Carper/Staddon, Alternating currents: EU expansion, Bulgarian capitulation and disruptions in the electricity sector of South-east Europe, Journal of Balkan and Near Eastern Studies 11 (2009), pp. 179 et seq. (189 et seq.); Roberts, The Turkish Gate – Energy Transit and Security Issues, Centre for European Policy Studies (CEPS), EU-Turkey Working Papers No. 10/October 2004, pp. 1 et seq., available at: http://www.ceps.be; Altmann, Vertrag mit einer wichtigen Transitregion: Energiegemeinschaft EU-Südosteuropa, Jahrbuch Internationale Politik 2008, pp. 322 et seq. (326).

[45] Norway and Ukraine, together with Moldova and Turkey, joined the Energy Community as Observers on 17th November, 2006, see EC's Press Release IP/06/2006 of 17th November, 2006. Upon reasoned request by Georgia, the Ministerial Council decided in accordance with the relevant provisions of the Energy Community Treaty to accept Georgia as an Observer to the Energy Community in December 2007.

[46] See Art. 96(2) of the Energy Community Treaty; for more on the above mentioned institutions of the Energy Community, see pp. 429 et seq. below.

[47] See Art. 99 of the Energy Community Treaty.

[48] See Art. 95 of the Energy Community Treaty.

Donors

'Donors' are institutions, organisations or government agencies for development wishing to contribute to the success of the Energy Community. Since the entry into force of the Treaty establishing the Energy Community, the following donors particularly support the reform process of the Energy Community: Canadian International Development Agency (CIDA), European Agency for Reconstruction (EAR), European Bank for Reconstruction and Development (EBRD), European Investment Bank (EIB), European Commission, KfW Bankengruppe, World Bank and United States Agency for International Development (USAID).

This 'donors community' is especially involved in the activities of the Energy Community Fora.[49] In addition to the financial support, the donors give recommendations and guidance on priority policy issues. Moreover, they conduct and finance in-depth studies for the benefit of the process in question and take part to various Energy Community workshops. Finally, these donors meet to discuss and to coordinate their actions several times per year.

Main Objectives and Activities of the Energy Community

The objectives of the Treaty establishing the Energy Community as well as the different tasks and activities of this Community are extensive and ambitious. Article 2(1) of the Energy Community Treaty states that the task of this Community shall be to organise the relations between the Parties and to create a legal and economic framework in relation to Network Energy[50] in order

– to create a stable regulatory and market framework capable of attracting investment in gas networks, power generation, and transmission and distribution networks, so that all Parties have access to the stable and continuous energy supply that is essential for economic development and social stability;

---

[49] For more on these Fora, see pp. 432 et seq. below.

[50] According to the second paragraph of this provision, 'Network Energy' shall include the electricity and gas sectors within the scope of the two following EC Directives: Directive 2003/54/EC, OJ [2003] L 176/37; Directive 2003/55/EC, OJ [2003] L 176/57; for relevant replacements see section D.I.1) below. Furthermore, see Art. 1(2) of the Decision No. 2008/03/MC-EnC of the Ministerial Council of the Energy Community concerning the implementation to the oil sector provisions of the Treaty and the creation of an Energy Community Oil Forum, available at: http://www.energy-community.org., according to which Network Energy as mentioned in Art. 2(2) of the Energy Community Treaty shall be understood as to include the oil sector, i.e. supply, trade, processing and transmission of crude oil and petroleum products falling within the scope of European Community Directive 2006/67/EC and the related pipe-lines, refineries and import/export facilities.

- to create a single regulatory space for trade in Network Energy that is necessary to match the geographic extent of the concerned product markets;
- to enhance the security of supply of the single regulatory space by providing a stable investment climate in which connections to Caspian, North African and Middle East gas reserves can be developed, and indigenous sources of energy such as natural gas, coal and hydropower can be exploited;
- to improve the environmental situation in relation to Network Energy and related energy efficiency, foster the use of renewable energy, and set out the conditions for energy trade in the single regulatory space; (and)
- to develop Network Energy market competition on a broader geographic scale and exploit economies of scale.

For the purposes mentioned above, the *activities* of the Energy Community, which are coordinated by the European Commission,[51] in particular include the extension or implementation of the acquis communautaire on energy, environment, competition and renewables as well as compliance with certain 'Generally Applicable Standards' of the EU (I), the setting up of a mechanism for the operation of Network Energy Markets (II) and, last but not least, the creation of a single energy market (III). Insofar, the Energy Community Treaty establishes a three-tier structure which may be described as the Treaty's concentric circles.

Implementation of the Acquis Communautaire on Energy, Environment, Competition and Renewables Including 'Generally Applicable Standards'

In order to reach its objectives provided for in Article 2 of the Treaty establishing the Energy Community, the activities of this Community shall, first of all, include the implementation by the Contracting Parties of the acquis communautaire on energy (1), environment (2), competition (3) and renewables (4) as described in Title II (Articles 9–25) of the Energy Community Treaty.[52] In this context and in relation to the additional obligation of the Contracting Parties to comply with certain 'Generally Applicable Standards' of the EU (5), the term 'Contracting Parties' does not refer to the EU and its Member States.[53]

---

[51] See Art. 4 of the Energy Community Treaty.

[52] For more on this, see also Deitz/Stirton/Wright, South East Europe's electricity sector: Attractions, obstacles and challenges of Europeanisation, Utilities Policy 17 (2009), pp. 4 et seq. (8 et seq.); Mihajlov, A Treaty for a Southeast European Energy Community, in: Stec/Baraj (eds.), *Energy and environmental challenges to security*, 2009, pp. 73 et seq. (75 et seq.).

[53] See Art. 9 of the Energy Community Treaty according to which the provisions of and the measures taken under this Title – that is Title II (Art. 9–25) – shall apply only to the territories of the Adhering Parties, and to the territory under the jurisdiction of the UN Interim Administration in Kosovo. For the concrete meaning of the terms 'Adhering Parties' and 'Contracting Parties' see pp. 413 et seq. above.

Implementation of the Acquis Communautaire on Energy

According to Article 3 lit. b and Article 10 of the Treaty establishing the
Energy Community, the Contracting Parties are obliged to implement the acquis
communautaire on energy as described in Article 11. The latter provision clarifies
that, for the purpose of this Treaty, the acquis communautaire on energy shall mean

- Directive 2003/54/EC of the European Parliament and of the Council of 26 June
  2003 concerning common rules for the internal market in electricity and
  repealing Directive 96/92/EC,[54]
- Directive 2003/55/EC of the European Parliament and of the Council of 26 June
  2003 concerning common rules for the internal market in natural gas and
  repealing Directive 98/30/EC[55] and
- Regulation (EC) No 1228/2003 of the European Parliament and of the Council
  of 26 June 2003 on conditions for access to the network for cross-border
  exchanges in electricity,[56]

establishing a new regulatory framework for the internal markets for electricity and
gas, that is to be transposed to the region of South East Europe. The timetable for
the implementation of the above mentioned acquis communautaire on energy[57] is
provided for in Annex I of the Treaty establishing the Energy Community.
According to this annex, the implementation of the acquis communautaire on
energy should have been completed by 1 July 2007. Moreover, the markets for
non-household customers should have been liberalized by 1 January 2008 – for all
customers by 1 January 2015.[58] The aforementioned acquis communautaire on

---

[54] OJ [2003] L 176/37.

[55] OJ [2003] L 176/57.

[56] OJ [2003] L 176/1.

[57] For more details on the three aformentioned legal acts, adopted for the benefit of progressing
liberalisiation of the EU's internal energy market, see Adetoro, Liberalisation of the Energy
Sector – Is It Reserved for Countries with Overcapacity?, European Energy and Environmental
Law Review 2009, pp. 185 et seq.; Eising, Policy Learning in Embedded Negotiations: Explaining
EU Electricity Liberalization, International Organization 56 (2002), pp. 85 et seq.; Lecheler/
Gundel, Ein weiterer Schritt zur Vollendung des Energie-Binnenmarktes: Die Beschleunigungs-
Rechtsakte für den Binnenmarkt für Strom und Gas, Europäische Zeitschrift für Wirtschaftsrecht
2003, pp. 621 et seq.; Szydlo, Regulatory Exemptions for New Gas Infrastructure – A Key
Challenge for European Energy Policy, European Energy and Environmental Law Review 2009,
pp. 254 et seq.

[58] See No. 2 of Annex I according to which each Contracting Party must ensure that the eligible
customers within the meaning of the Directives 2003/54/EC and 2003/55/EC are, from 1st
January, 2008, all non-household costumers, and from 1st January, 2015, all costumers.

energy not only obliges members of the Energy Community to undertake substantial reforms,[59] but is also of significant importance to Turkey.[60]

This acquis is by no means static, as illustrated firstly by the fact that the Energy Community Ministerial Council already in December 2007 decided to extend the acquis communautaire on energy to Regulation (EC) No 1775/2005,[61] to Directive 2005/89/EC[62] as well as to Directive 2004/67/EC[63] and agreed to implement these two Directives prior to 31 December 2009. Thus, on 27 June 2008 in Brussels, the Energy Community Ministerial Council had an exchange of views concerning the security of supply status in the region and stressed the importance for the Contracting Parties to implement Directive 2005/89/EC concerning measures to safeguard security of electricity supply and Directive 2004/67/EC concerning measures to safeguard security of natural gas supply before 31 December 2009.[64] Secondly, Art 1(2) of the Decision No 2008/03/MC-EnC of the Ministerial Council of the Energy Community concerning the implementation to the oil sector provisions of the Treaty and the creation of an Energy Community Oil Forum[65] must be pointed out in this context. According to this provision, Network Energy as

---

[59] See International Energy Agency, Energy in the Western Balkans – The Path to Reform and Reconstruction, 2008, pp. 119 et seq.; and ABS Energy Research, Electricity Deregulation Report Global 2006, 2006, pp. 108 et seq., available at: http://www.absenergyresearch.com; as well as Diaconu/Oprescu/Pittman, Electricity reform in Romania, Utilities Policy 17 (2009), pp. 114 et seq.; Ganev, Bulgarian electricity market restructuring, Utilities Policy 17 (2009), pp. 65 et seq.; Heidenhain/Pravda, Das Energierecht in der EU und in der Tschechischen Republik, Wirtschaft und Recht in Osteuropa 2004, pp. 321 et seq.; Hofer, *Die Europäische Union als Regelexporteur – Die Europäisierung der Energiepolitik in Bulgarien, Serbien und der Ukraine*, 2008, pp. 67 et seq.; Jednak/Kragulj/Bulajic/Pittman, Electricity reform in Serbia, Utilities Policy 17 (2009), pp. 125 et seq.; Scholl, Electricity reform in Bosnia and Herzegovina, Utilities Policy 17 (2009), pp. 49 et seq.; Silva/Klytchnikova/Radevic, Poverty and environmental impacts of electricity price reforms in Montenegro, Utilities Policy 17 (2009), pp. 102 et seq.; Pollitt, Evaluating the evidence on electricity reform: Lessons for the South East Europe (SEE) market, Utilities Policy 17 (2009), pp. 13 et seq.; Taleski, Electricity reform in the Republic of Macedonia, Utilities Policy 17 (2009), pp. 88 et seq.; Tiede/Schirmer, Das moldawische Energierecht unter dem aktuellen Einfluss des Europarechts, Wirtschaft und Recht in Osteuropa 2008, pp. 358 et seq.; Vailati, Electricity transmission in the energy community of South East Europe, Utilities Policy 17 (2009), pp. 34 et seq.

[60] See Bagdadioglu/Odyakmaz, Turkish electricity reform, Utilities Policy 17 (2009), pp. 144 et seq.; Işik, Turkey's Energy Prospects in the EU-Turkey Context, Centre for European Policy Studies (CEPS), EU-Turkey Working Papers No. 9/October 2004, pp. 1 et seq., available at the CEPS website, http://www.ceps.be; Toksoz, Turkey's energy market – issues in reform, Journal of Southern Europe and the Balkans 4 (2002), pp. 47 et seq.

[61] Regulation (EC) No. 1775/2005, OJ [2005] L 289/1.

[62] Directive 2005/89/EC, OJ [2006] L 33/22.

[63] Directive 2004/67/EC, OJ [2004] L 127/92.

[64] See EC's Press Release IP/08/1051 of 27th June, 2008. The Ministerial Council already decided in December 2007 to extend the acquis on energy to Directive 2005/89/EC and agreed to implement these two Directives prior to 31st December, 2009.

[65] Available at: http://www.energy-community.org.

mentioned in Article 2(2) of the Energy Community Treaty shall be understood as to include the oil sector, i.e. supply, trade, processing and transmission of crude oil and petroleum products falling within the scope of European Community Directive 2006/67/EC[66] and the related pipe-lines, refineries and import/export facilities. Thirdly, the dynamic nature of the acquis communautaire on energy is emphasised by the (third) energy liberalisation package which entered into force in September 2009. This ambitious legislative package[67] contains two directives on development of the internal market in electricity[68] and natural gas[69] as well as three regulations on access to the electricity network,[70] on the internal market for natural gas[71] and on the establishment of an Agency for the Cooperation of Energy Regulators.[72] All of them are to be implemented by the EU-States into national law by March 2011.

Article 25 of the Energy Community Treaty insofar anticipates and allows for the thereby evident dynamic of the acquis communautaire on energy and the thus arising need for adaption among the state parties of the Western Balkans as this provision stipulates, that the Energy Community may take measures to implement amendments to the acquis communautaire on energy, in line with the evolution of EU law. Those measures already have been adopted. Based on the Energy Community Council decisions D/2009/05/MC-EnC of 18 December 2009 and D/2010/02/MC-EnC of 24 September 2010 the acquis communautaire on energy was newly defined[73] and extended to three EU Directives in the area of energy end-use efficiency and energy services,[74] energy performance of buildings[75] and

---

[66] Directive 2006/67/EC, OJ [2006] L 217/8.

[67] For a good overview, see for example Gundel/Germelmann, Kein Schlussstein für die Liberalisierung der Energiemärkte: Das Dritte Binnenmarktpaket, Europäische Zeitschrift für Wirtschaftsrecht 2009, pp. 763 et seq.; Kühling/Pisal, Das Dritte Energiebinnenmarktpaket – Herausforderungen für den deutschen Gesetzgeber, Recht der Energiewirtschaft 2010, pp. 161 et seq.; Ludwigs, Die Energierechtsgesetzgebung der EU zwischen Binnenmarkt und Klimaschutz, Zeitschrift für Gesetzgebung 2010, pp. 213 et seq. (222); Petersen, Restructuring the Electricity Sector in the EU and in Russia, European Energy and Environmental Law Review 2009, pp. 171 et seq.; Zimmermann/Talus, Regulation of Electricity Markets at the EU Level, European Energy and Environmental Law Review 2008, pp. 12 et seq.

[68] Directive 2009/72/EC, OJ [2009] L 211/55.

[69] Directive 2009/73/EC, OJ [2009] L 211/94.

[70] Regulation (EC) No. 714/2009, OJ [2009] L 211/15.

[71] Regulation (EC) No. 715/2009, OJ [2009] L 211/36.

[72] Regulation (EC) No. 713/2009, OJ [2009] L 211/1.

[73] See Recommendation No. 2010/02/MC-EnC of the Ministerial Council of the Energy Community on the implementation of amendments to the acquis communautaire on energy, available at: http://www.energy-community.org, according to which each Contracting Party should implement the acquis on energy defined in Art. 11 of the Energy Community Treaty as amended and replaced by the following pieces of EU law: Directive 2009/72/EC, OJ [2009] L 211/55, Directive 2009/73/EC, OJ [2009] L 211/94, Regulation (EC) No. 714/2009, OJ [2009] L 211/15 and Regulation (EC) No. 715/2009, OJ [2009] L 211/36.

[74] Directive 2006/32/EC, OJ [2006] L 114/64.

[75] Directive 2010/31/EU, OJ [2010] L 153/13.

labelling.[76] In this context, the implementation deadlines vary from 31 December 2011 to January 2017.

Implementation of the Acquis Communautaire on Environment

The Treaty establishing the Energy Community seeks, inter alia, to improve the environmental situation in relation to network energy.[77] Therefore, Article 12 of this Treaty provides that each Contracting Party shall also implement the acquis communautaire on environment in compliance with the timetable for the implementation of those measures set out in annex II of this Treaty. This annex clarifies in conjunction with Article 16 of the Energy Community Treaty that the obligation to implement the acquis communautaire on environment within clear deadlines only covers.

- Council Directive 85/337/EEC of 27 June 1985 on the assessment of the effects of certain public and private projects on the environment,[78] as amended by Directive 97/11/EC[79] and Directive 2003/35/EC[80] (to be implemented on the entry into force of the Energy Community Treaty[81]);
- Council Directive 1999/32/EC of 26 April 1999 relating to a reduction in the sulphur content of certain liquid fuels and amending Directive 93/12/ECC[82] (to be implemented by 31 December 2011[83]);
- Directive 2001/80/EC of the European Parliament and of the Council of 23 October 2001 on the limitation of emissions of certain pollutants into the air from large combustion plants[84] (to be implemented by 31 December 2017[85]);
- Article 4(2) of Council Directive 79/409/EEC of 2 April 1979 on the conservation of wild birds[86] (to be implemented on the entry into force of the Energy Community Treaty[87]).

---

[76] Directive 2010/30/EU, OJ [2010] L 153/1.

[77] See Art. 2(1)(d) of the Energy Community Treaty; on environmental problems in the Western Balkans see Moomaw, Environmental Sustainability and Collaboration in South Eastern Europe, Southeast European and Black Sea Studies 6 (2006), pp. 307 et seq.

[78] OJ [1985] L 175/40.

[79] Directive 97/11/EC, OJ [1997] L 73/5.

[80] Directive 2003/35/EC, OJ [2003] L 156/17.

[81] See No. 1 of annex II.

[82] OJ [1999] L 121/13.

[83] See No. 2 of annex II.

[84] OJ [2001] L 309/1.

[85] See No. 3 of annex II.

[86] OJ [1979] L 103/1.

[87] See No. 4 of annex II.

The different deadlines provided for in annex II do not apply for Article 13 and Article 14 of the Energy Community Treaty, according to which each Contracting Party shall additionally endeavour to accede to the Kyoto Protocol and to implement Council Directive 96/61/EC of 24 September 1996 concerning integrated pollution prevention and control.[88] Moreover, Article 17 of the Energy Community Treaty states that the provisions of and the measures taken under this chapter[89] shall only apply to 'Network Energy' within the meaning of Article 2(2) of this Treaty.[90]

Implementation of the Acquis Communautaire on Competition

Core elements of European Competition Law are the far-reaching prohibition clauses laid down in Articles 101(1), 102 and 107 of the Treaty on the Functioning of the EU (TFEU)[91] which – due to the Lisbon Treaty[92] – recently have replaced the rather identical competition rules formerly provided for in Articles 81(1), 82 and 87 of the Treaty establishing the EC. Thus, Article 18(1) of the Treaty establishing the Energy Community follows these prohibition clauses by declaring the following to be incompatible with the proper functioning of this Treaty, insofar as they may affect trade of Network Energy between the Contracting Parties:

– All agreements between undertakings, decisions by associations of undertakings and concerted practices which have as their object or effect the prevention, restriction or distortion of competition,
– Abuse by one or more undertakings of a dominant position in the market between the Contracting Parties as a whole or in a substantial part thereof,
– Any public aid which distorts or threatens to distort competition by favouring certain undertakings or certain energy resources.

---

[88] OJ [1996] L 257/26.

[89] That is chapter III (Art. 12–17) of the Energy Community Treaty regarding the acquis on environment.

[90] According to this provision 'Network Energy' shall include the electricity and gas sectors falling within the scope of the EC Directives 2003/54/EC, OJ [2003] L 176/37, and 2003/55/EC, OJ [2003] L 176/57; for relevant replacements see section D.I.1) above; for a relevant extension see Art. 1(2) of the Decision No. 2008/03/MC-EnC of the Ministerial Council of the Energy Community concerning the implementation to the oil sector provisions of the Treaty and the creation of an Energy Community Oil Forum, available at: http://www.energy-community.org, according to which Network Energy as mentioned in Art. 2(2) of the Energy Community Treaty shall be understood as to include the oil sector, i.e. supply, trade, processing and transmission of crude oil and petroleum products falling within the scope of European Community Directive 2006/67/EC and the related pipe-lines, refineries and import/export facilities.

[91] For the consolidated version of the TFEU see OJ [2010] C 83/47.

[92] Treaty of Lisbon amending the Treaty on European Union (TEU) and the Treaty establishing the European Community (TEC), signed at Lisbon on 13th December, 2007, OJ [2007] C 306/1; for more on this Treaty, which entered into force on 1st December, 2009, see with further references Nowak, *Europarecht nach Lissabon*, 2011, pp. 51 et seq.

These prohibition clauses have to be interpreted in the light of the relevant jurisprudence of the Court of Justice of the EU and the relevant decision-making practice of the European Commission in the scope of EU Competition Law, since Article 18(2) of the Energy Community Treaty states that any practice contrary to the first paragraph of this provision shall be assessed on the basis of criteria arising from the application of the rules of Articles 81, 82 and 87 of the Treaty establishing the EC (now: Articles 101, 102 and 107 TFEU). Further important elements of EU Competition Law are the rules of Article 106(1) and (2) TFEU (ex Article 86[1] and [2] of the Treaty establishing the EC). Therefore, Article 19 of the Energy Community Treaty provides, with regard to public undertakings and undertakings to which special or exclusive rights have been granted, that each Contracting Party shall ensure that as from six months following the date of entry into force of this Treaty, the principles of the Treaty establishing the EC (now: Treaty on the Functioning of the EU), in particular Article 86(1) and (2) thereof (now: Article 106[1] and [2] TFEU) are upheld.

Implementation of the Acquis Communautaire on Renewables

The first sentence of Article 20 of the Treaty establishing the Energy Community states that each Contracting Party shall finally provide to the European Commission within one year of the date of entry into force of this Treaty a plan to implement the two following Directives which belong to the acquis communautaire on renewables:

- Directive 2001/77/EC of the European Parliament and of the Council of 27 September 2001 on the promotion of electricity produced from renewable energy sources in the internal electricity market[93]; (and)
- Directive 2003/30/EC the European Parliament and of the Council of 8 May 2003 on the promotion of the use of biofuels or other renewable fuels for transport.[94]

Subsequently, the European Commission shall present the plan of each Contracting Party to the Ministerial Council[95] for adoption. Pursuant to Article 25 of the Energy Community Treaty, the Energy Community may take further measures to implement amendments to the acquis communautaire on renewables, in line with the evolution of EU law.[96]

---

[93] OJ [2001] L 283/33.

[94] OJ [2003] L 123/42.

[95] For more on this institution, see pp. 429 et seq. below.

[96] For recent and actual developments in EU law concerning renewable energy, see Directive 2009/28/EC, OJ [2009] L 140/16; as well as Behrens, The Role of Renewables in the Interaction between Climate Change Policy and Energy Security in Europe, Journal of Renewable Energy Law and Policy 2010, pp. 5 et seq.; Frenz/Kane, Die neue europäische Energiepolitik, Natur und

Compliance with Generally Applicable Standards of the EU

The above mentioned duties to implement the aquis communautaire on energy, environment, competition and renewables are accompanied by the obligation of the Contracting Parties to comply with certain 'Generally Applicable Standards' of the EU related to Network Energy. In order to clarify this additional obligation, Article 23 of the Energy Community states that the term 'Generally Applicable Standards' refers to any technical system standard that is applied within the EC,[97] and is necessary for operating network systems safely and efficiently, including aspects of transmission, cross-border connections, modulation and general technical system security standards issued where applicable via the European Committee for Standardization (CEN), the European Committee for Electrotechnical Standardization (Cenelec) and similar normation bodies or as issued by the Union for the Coordination of Transmission of Electricity (UCTE) and the European Association for the Streamlining of Energy Exchanges (Easeegas) for common rule setting and business practices. As regards the procedural aspect, Article 21 and 22 of the Energy Community Treaty provide for a three-stage procedure in order to ensure the required compliance with 'Generally Applicable Standards' of the EU. Firstly, the Secretariat[98] shall, within one year of the date of entry into force of this Treaty, draw up a list of these standards, to be submitted to the Ministerial Council[99] for adoption.[100] Secondly, the Ministerial Council has to adopt such a list. Thirdly, the Contracting Parties shall, within one year of the adoption of the list, adopt development plans to bring their Network Energy sectors into line with the Generally Applicable Standards of the EU mentioned above.[101]

Setting up of a Mechanism for the Operation of Network Energy Markets

The activities of the Energy Community also include the setting-up of a specific regulatory framework permitting the efficient operation of Network Energy markets

---

Recht 2010, pp. 464 et seq. (472 et seq.); Kahl, Alte und neue Kompetenzprobleme im EG-Umweltrecht – Die geplante Richtlinie zur Förderung erneuerbarer Energien, Neue Zeitschrift für Verwaltungsrecht 2009, pp. 265 et seq.; Lowe, Regulating Renewable Energy in the European Union, Journal of Renewable Energy Law and Policy 2010, pp. 17 et seq.

[97] Now the EU, due to the entry into force of the Treaty of Lisbon amending the Treaty on European Union (TEU) and the Treaty establishing the European Community (TEC), signed at Lisbon on 13th December, 2007, OJ [2007] C 306/1.

[98] For more on this institution, see pp. 433 et seq. below.

[99] For more on this institution, see pp. 429 et seq. below.

[100] See Art. 21 of the Energy Community Treaty.

[101] See Art. 22 of the Energy Community Treaty.

across the territories of the Contracting Parties and part of the territory of the EU, and including the creation of a single mechanism for the cross-border transmission and/or transportation of Network Energy, and the supervision of unilateral safeguard measures, as further described in Title III (Articles 26–39) of the Treaty establishing the Energy Community. Contrary to Article 9 of the Energy Community Treaty regarding the geographic scope of the provisions of Title II dealing with the extension of the acquis communautaire on energy, environment, competition and renewables as well as with Generally Applicable Standards of the EU,[102] the provisions of and the measures taken under Title III regarding the mechanism for the operation of Network Energy markets shall apply to the territories of the (remaining) Adhering Parties,[103] to the territory of the United Nations Interim Administration Mission in Kosovo, to the territories of Austria, Greece, Hungary, Italy and Slovenia[104] and to the territories of Bulgaria and Romania[105] earlier belonging to the Adhering Parties. The measures which the Energy Community shall or may take under Title III of the Treaty establishing this Community are divers (1). Additionally, the Energy Community Treaty empowers the above mentioned Parties to take safeguard measures in the event of a sudden crisis on the Network Energy market in the territory of the Party concerned (2).

Relevant Measures of the Energy Community

In order to create a stable mechanism for long-distance transportation of network Energy, Article 28 of the Energy Community Treaty first of all states that this Community shall take additional measures establishing a single mechanism for the cross-border transmission and/or transportation of Network Energy. The important aspect of security of supply is the central subject of Article 29 of the Energy Community Treaty. Although this provision does not imply a necessity to change energy policies or purchasing practices,[106] the Parties concerned are requested to adopt – within one year of the date of entry into force of this Treaty – security of supply statements describing in particular diversity of supply, technological security and geographic origin of imported fuels. They have subsequently to be communicated to the Secretariat and shall be updated every 2 years. Moreover, the Energy Community shall promote High-Levels of provision of network Energy to all its citizens within the limits of the public service obligations contained in the

---

[102] For the geographic scope of Title II, see fn. 53 above.

[103] For the concrete meaning of the term 'Adhering Parties', see pp. 413 et seq. above.

[104] See Art. 26 in conjunction with the first sentence of Art. 27 of the Energy Community Treaty.

[105] In this context, see the second sentence of Art. 27 of the Energy Community Treaty which states: 'Upon accession to the European Union of an Adhering Party, the provisions of and the measures taken under this Title shall, without any further formalities, also apply to the territory of that new Member State.'

[106] See Art. 30 of the Energy Community Treaty.

relevant acquis communautaire on energy. For this purpose, the Energy Community may, on the basis of Article 32 of the Energy Community Treaty, take measures to allow for the universal provision of electricity, to foster effective demand management policies and to ensure fair competition. These measures may be accompanied by recommendations which the Energy Community may make in order to support effective reform of the Network Energy sectors of the Parties, including, inter alia, to increase the level of payment for energy by all costumers, and to foster the affordability of Network Energy prices to consumers.[107] Additionally, the Energy Community may take measures concerning compatibility of market designs for the operation of Network Energy markets, as well as measures concerning mutual recognition of licences and measures fostering free establishment of Network Energy companies.[108] Finally, the Energy Community may adopt measures to foster development in the areas of renewable energy sources and energy efficiency, taking account of their advantages for security of supply, environment protection, social cohesion and regional development.[109]

Safeguard Measures in the Event of a Sudden Crisis

In the event of a sudden crisis on the Network Energy market in the territory of a Party referred to in Article 26 and Article 27 of the Treaty establishing the Energy Community, where the physical safety or security of persons, or Network Energy apparatus or installations or system integrity is threatened in this territory, the concerned Party may temporarily take necessary safeguard measures on the basis of Article 36 of the Energy Community Treaty. In such a case the Party concerned has to act cautiously, since those safeguard measures shall cause the least possible disturbance in the functioning of the Network Energy market of the Parties.[110] Additionally, Article 38 of the Energy Community Treaty requests the Party concerned to notify such safeguard measures without delay to the Secretariat, which shall immediately inform the other Parties. Following such a notification, the Energy Community may decide that the safeguard measures taken by the Party concerned do not comply with the relevant provisions (in particular Article 37 of the Energy Community Treaty), and request the Party concerned to put an end to, or modify, those safeguard measures.

---

[107] See Art. 33 of the Energy Community Treaty.

[108] See Art. 34 of the Energy Community Treaty.

[109] See Art. 35 of the Energy Community Treaty.

[110] See Art. 37 of the Energy Community Treaty which additionally clarifies that such safeguard measures shall not be wider in scope than is strictly necessary to remedy the sudden difficulties which have arisen and that they shall not distort competition or adversely affect trade in a manner which is at variance with the common interest.

The Creation of a Single Energy Market

The activities of the Energy Community finally also include the creation of a single market in Network Energy without internal frontiers, including the coordination of mutual assistance in case of serious disturbance to the energy networks or external disruption, and which may include the achievement of a common external energy trade policy, as further described in Title IV (Articles 40–46) of the Treaty establishing the Energy Community. Contrary to Article 9 of the Energy Community Treaty regarding the geographic scope of the provisions of Title II as well as to Article 26 and Article 27 of this Treaty regarding the geographic scope of the provisions of Title III, the provisions of and the measures taken under Title IV shall apply to the territories of all Contracting Parties including the EU.[111] These provisions and measures concern the internal dimension of the single energy market (1), the external energy trade policy (2) and the topic of mutual assistance in the event of disruption of Network Energy supply (3).

Internal Dimension of the Single Energy Market

The two Treaty provisions specifically regarding the internal energy market (Article 41 and Article 42 of the Energy Community Treaty) are characterized in particular by a prohibition clause, which is in parts similar to Article 30 and Article 34 TFEU, as well as an empowerment to take certain measures with the aim of creating a single energy market without frontiers for Network Energy. Pursuant to Article 41(1) of the Energy Community Treaty, customs duties – even those of a fiscal nature – as well as quantitative restrictions on the import and export of network Energy and all measures having equivalent effect shall be prohibited between the parties. Pursuant to the first sentence of Article 94 of the Energy Community Treaty, the former provision has to be interpreted in conformity with the relevant case law of the Court of Justice of the European Union.[112] This obligation also includes Article 41(2) of the Energy Community Treaty, according to which the prohibition clause contained in the first paragraph shall – similarly to Article 36 TFEU – not preclude quantitative restrictions or measures having equivalent effect, justified on grounds of public policy or public security, the protection of health and life of humans, animals or plants, or the protection of industrial and commercial property, as long as such restrictions or

---

[111] See Art. 40 of the Energy Community Treaty.

[112] According to the first sentence of Art. 94 of the Energy Community Treaty, the institutions (of this Community) shall interpret any term or other concept used in this Treaty that is derived from European Community Law (due to the entry into force of the Lisbon Treaty – now EU law) in conformity with the case law of the European Court of Justice or the Court of First Instance of the European Communities; for the new names of these courts, see Art. 19(1) TEU in its consolidated version of the Treaty of Lisbon, OJ [2010] C 83/13.

measures do not constitute a means of arbitrary discrimination or a disguised restriction on trade between the Parties.

The EU Economic Law illustrates adequately, that prohibition clauses ("negative integration") of the aforementioned kind do not suffice to ensure the smooth functioning of the internal market. Rather, the adoption of secondary acts ("positive integration") is required. The legislator of the Union is for example empowered by Articles 46, 48, 50 and 59 TFEU to take such measures regarding the internal market. The fact that Article 42(1) of the Energy Community Treaty authorizes this Community to take measures with the aim of creating a single market without frontiers for Network Energy is to be welcomed for this reasons. However, this basis for authority is rather restricted, since Article 42(2) of the Energy Community Treaty excludes fiscal measures, measures relating to the free movement of persons and measures relating to the rights and interests of employed persons from its scope.

External Energy Trade Policy

The external dimension of the internal energy market ultimately forms the core subject matter of Article 43 of the Treaty establishing the Energy Community, according to which this Community may additionally take measures necessary for the regulation of imports and exports of network Energy to and from third countries with a view to ensuring equivalent access to and from third country markets in respect of basic environmental standards or to ensure the safe operation of the internal energy market.

Mutual Assistance in the Event of Disruption of Network Energy Supply

The smooth functioning of the single energy market, its establishment being one of the principal activities of the Energy Community, eventually requires an effective mechanism in order to quickly and effectively react to a sudden disruption of the Network Energy Supply with cross-border effects. Therefore, Article 44 of the Energy Community Treaty first of all demands that, in the event of disruption of Network Energy supply affecting a Party and involving another Party or a third country, the Parties shall seek an expeditious resolution in accordance with the provisions of this Chapter. This refers, first of all, to Article 45 of this Treaty according to which the Ministerial Council,[113] upon request of the party directly affected by the disruption of Network Energy supply, shall meet and may take the necessary measures in response to the disruption in question. Article 46 of the Energy Community Treaty allows and obliges the Ministerial Council to – within 1 year of the date of entry into force of this Treaty – adopt a Procedural Act for the

---

[113] For the details concerning this institution, see pp. 429 et seq. below.

operation of the mutual assistance obligation under this Chapter, which may include the conferral of powers to take interim measures to the Permanent High-Level Group.[114]

Institutions of the Energy Community, Decision-Making and Dispute Settlement

With regard to the institutional design of the Energy Community,[115] the Treaty establishing this Community does not only contain several provisions regarding the main tasks and the composition of the relevant institutions (I), but also some provisions concerning the decision-making process (II) and further provisions dealing with the implementation of decisions as well as with an interesting dispute settlement mechanism (III).

Institutions of the Energy Community

Title V of the Treaty establishing the Energy Community (Articles 47–75) is mainly dealing with the institutions of this Community. These institutions, partially supported by the European Commission,[116] are the Ministerial Council (1), the Permanent High-Level Group (2), the Regulatory Board (3), two Electricity and Gas Fora (4) and the Secretariat (5).

Ministerial Council

The Ministerial Council is the most important and powerful institution of the Energy Community insofar as it is the principal decision-making body and shall ensure that the objectives set out in the Energy Community Treaty are attained; therefore, it shall provide general policy guidelines, take measures[117] and adopt

---

[114] For the details concerning this institution, see p. 431 below.

[115] For a brief introduction to the institutional framework of the Energy Community, also see Goudriaan/Spenn, The Energy Treaty institutions – a glaring democratic and social deficit, South-East Europe Review (2006) 2, pp. 87 et seq.; Nowak, Multilaterale und bilaterale Elemente der EU-Assoziations-, Partnerschafts- und Nachbarschaftspolitik, Europarecht 44 (2010), pp. 746 et seq. (767 et seq.); Renner, The Energy Community of Southeast Europe: A neo-functionalist project of regional integration, European Integration online Papers 13 (2009), pp. 1 et seq. (10 et seq.).

[116] See, for example, Art. 4, 53 lit. f and 61 of the Energy Community Treaty.

[117] For the different forms of such measures see pp. 434 et seq. below.

Procedural Acts[118] which may include the conferral, under precise conditions, of specific tasks, powers and obligations to carry out the policy of the Energy Community on the Permanent High-Level Group, the Regulatory Board or the Secretariat.[119] Additionally, the Ministerial Council may decide on the acceptance of observers[120] as well as on Energy Community Treaty amendments, on the implementation of other parts of the acquis communautaire, on the extension of this Treaty to other energy products and carriers or other essential network infrastructures and on the accession of a new Party to the Energy Community.[121] Moreover, the Ministerial Council shall adopt the budget of the Energy Community by Procedural Act every 2 years.[122] Finally, the Ministerial Council plays an important role within the Energy Community's dispute settlement mechanism[123] and submits annual reports on the activities of the Energy Community to the European Parliament and to the Parliaments of the Adhering Parties and Participants.[124]

The Ministerial Council, which consists of one representative of each Contracting Party and two representatives of the EU,[125] shall – according to the third sentence of Article 50 of the Energy Community Treaty – meet at least once every six months. Following a decision in December 2009, the Ministerial Council, empowered under Article 49 of the Energy Community Treaty to adopt its internal rules of procedure,[126] now meets once a year. The Presidency of this Council, which shall be assisted by one representative of the EU and one representative of the incoming Presidency as Vice-Presidents,[127] is held in turn by each Contracting Party for a term of twelve months in the order decided by a Procedural Act of the Ministerial Council.

---

[118] In this context, see in particular Art. 86(1) of the Energy Community Treaty, according to which a Procedural Act shall regulate organizational, budgetary and transparency issues of the Energy Community, including the delegation of power from the Ministerial Council to the Permanent High-Level Group, the Regulatory Board or the Secretariat, and shall have binding force on the institutions of the Energy Community, and, if the Procedural Act so provides, on the Parties; for the meaning of the term 'Parties' see pp. 413 et seq. above.

[119] See Art. 47 of the Energy Community Treaty.

[120] See Art. 96(1) of the Energy Community Treaty.

[121] See Art. 100 of the Energy Community Treaty.

[122] See Art. 74(1) of the Energy Community Treaty.

[123] For more on this, see p. 437 below.

[124] See Art. 52 of the Energy Community Treaty; for the meaning of the terms 'Adhering Parties' and 'Participants', see pp. 413 et seq. above.

[125] See Art. 48 of the Energy Community Treaty with the further clarification that one non-voting representative of each Participant may participate in the meetings of this Council.

[126] In this context, see Procedural Act No. 2006–01 on Internal Rules of Procedures of Ministerial Council of Energy Community, available at: http://www.energy-community.org.

[127] See Art. 51 of the Energy Community Treaty.

Permanent High-Level-Group

The second important institution of the Energy Community is the Permanent High-Level Group established, firstly, to prepare the work of the Ministerial Council.[128] In this respect, the Permanent High-Level Group slightly resembles the so-called *Conseil des Représentants Permanents* (COREPER)[129] which supports the Council of the EU within the institutional framework of the EU.[130] Secondly, the Permanent High-Level Group gives assent to technical assistance requests made by international donor organisations, international financial institutions and bilateral donors, reports to the Ministerial Council on progress made toward achievement of the objectives of the Energy Community Treaty, takes measures, if so empowered by the Ministerial Council, adopts Procedural Acts, not involving the conferral of tasks, powers or obligations on other institutions of the Energy Community, and discusses the development of the acquis communautaire described in Title II[131] on the basis of a report that the European Commission shall submit on a regular basis.[132] Like the Ministerial Council, also the Permanent High-Level Group consists of one representative of each Contracting Party and two representatives of the EU.[133] Like the Ministerial Council under Article 49 of the Energy Community Treaty, also the Permanent High-Level Group is empowered by Article 55 of this Treaty to adopt its internal rules of procedure.[134]

Regulatory Board

The Regulatory Board of the Energy Community may also adopt Procedural Acts and may take measures, if so empowered by the Ministerial Council, shall issue recommendations on cross-border disputes involving two or more Regulators, upon request of any of them, and shall advise the Ministerial Council or the Permanent High-Level Group on the details of statutory, technical and regulatory rules.[135]

---

[128] See Art. 53 lit. a of the Energy Community Treaty.

[129] Cf. Goudriaan/Spenn, The Energy Treaty institutions – a glaring democratic and social deficit, South-East Europe Review (2006) 2, pp. 87 et seq. (88).

[130] For more on this, see Lewis, Informal Integration and the supranational construction of the Council, Journal of European Public Policy 2003, pp. 996 et seq. (999 et seq.).

[131] For more on Title II of the Energy Community Treaty concerning the extension of the acquis communautaire on energy, environment, competition and renewable, see pp. 417 et seq. above.

[132] See Art. 53 lit b-f of the Energy Community Treaty.

[133] See Art. 54 of the Energy Community Treaty with the further clarification that one non-voting representative of each Participant may participate in its meetings. For more on the Presidency of the Permanent High-Level Group, see Art. 56 and Art. 57 of this Treaty.

[134] In this context, see Procedural Act No. 2006/01/PHLG of 17th October, 2006 on the adoption of Internal Rules of Procedures, available at: http://www.energy-community.org.

[135] See Art. 58 of the Energy Community Treaty.

Therefore, the Regulatory Board, which shall meet in Athens,[136] consists, first of all, of one representative of the energy regulator of each Contracting Party, pursuant to the relevant parts of the acquis communautaire on energy.[137] The EU, on the other side, is represented by the European Commission, assisted by one regulator of each Participant, and one representative of the European Regulators Group for Electricity and Gas (ERGEG).[138] Moreover, the Regulatory Board, also empowered to adopt its internal rules of procedure by Procedural Act,[139] shall elect a president for a term determined by this Board.[140]

Fora: Electricity Forum, Gas Forum and New Fora

Article 63 of the Energy Community Treaty states that two Fora, composed of representatives of all interested stakeholders, including industry, regulators, industry representative groups and consumers, shall advise the Energy Community. One of these Fora, the Electricity Forum, shall meet in Athens, whereas the Gas Forum shall meet at a place to be determined by a Procedural Act of the Ministerial Council.[141] These two Fora, both chaired by a representative of the EU,[142] particularly may adopt conclusions to be forwarded to the Permanent High-Level Group.[143]

Following an intense debate on the lacking social dimension of the Treaty establishing the Energy Community,[144] discussions on the possible establishment of a new Forum on social issues began to unfold already in 2007. These discussions finally led to the signature of a Memorandum of Understanding on the social dimension of the Energy Community,[145] which was signed in Vienna on 18 October

---

[136] See Art. 62 of the Energy Community Treaty.

[137] See the first sentence of Art. 59 of the Energy Community Treaty; for more on the acquis communautaire on energy, see pp. 418 et seq. above.

[138] See the second sentence of Art. 59 of the Energy Community Treaty.

[139] See Art. 60 of the Energy Community Treaty in conjunction with Procedural Act No. 2007/01/ECRB on the adoption of Internal Rules of Procedure of the ECRB, available at: http://www.energy-community.org.

[140] See Art. 61 of the Energy Community Treaty with the further clarification that the European Commission shall act as Vice-President.

[141] See Art. 66 of the Energy Community Treaty. Originally, the Gas Forum's seat in the pre-version of the Energy Community Treaty was supposed to be in Istanbul, see Goudriaan/Spenn, The Energy Treaty institutions – a glaring democratic and social deficit, South-East Europe Review (2006) 2, pp. 87 et seq. (89). But this changed since Turkey, still being only an Observer, did not sign this Treaty, see pp. 407 et seq. above.

[142] See Art. 64 of the Energy Community Treaty.

[143] See Art. 65 of the Energy Community Treaty.

[144] For more on this, see Goudriaan/Spenn, The Energy Treaty institutions – a glaring democratic and social deficit, South-East Europe Review (2006) 2, pp. 87 et seq. (92).

[145] Available at: http://www.energy-community.org.

2007.[146] The main provisions of that *Memorandum of Understanding on Social Issues* aim at strengthening social dialogue in the gas and electricity sector and reinforcing the social dimension of the Energy Community Treaty.[147] The signatories of the abovementioned Memorandum of Understanding, inter alia, agreed to assess the need for a Social Forum for the consideration of the social impacts of energy market reform. At the following Ministerial Council, the Secretariat presented a paper proposing the establishment of the Social Forum. The first Social Forum took place in November 2008. The main task of this Forum, which convenes annually, is to review the implementation of the principles laid down in the Memorandum of Understanding on Social Issues.[148] Finally, in June 2008, the Secretariat presented a *Working Paper on Developing Oil Dimension* to the attention of the Ministerial Council.[149] Half a year later, at its December 2008 meeting, the Ministerial Council decided to implement certain provisions of the Energy Community Treaty on the oil sector and to establish the Oil Forum.[150] The first Energy Community Oil Forum took place on 24–25 September 2009. This rather new Forum advises the Energy Community on matters related to the oil sector and meets annually in Belgrade, Serbia.

Secretariat

The Secretariat, seated in Vienna,[151] administers the day-to day activities of the Energy Community. First of all, it provides administrative support to the Ministerial Council, the Permanent High-Level Group, the Regulatory Board the Fora and the donors.[152] Furthermore, the Secretariat reviews the proper implementation by the Parties of their obligations under the Energy Community Treaty, and submits

---

[146] See EC's Press Release IP/07/1559, 18th October, 2007.

[147] For more on this, see Deitz/Stirton/Wright, South East Europe's electricity sector: Attractions, obstacles and challenges of Europeanisation, Utilities Policy 17 (2009), pp. 4 et seq. (10).

[148] For the actual objectives and activities within this social dimension of the Energy Community see pp. 11 et seq. of the Energy Community Work Programme 2010–2011, which has been adopted by the Ministerial Council of the Energy Community on 26th June, 2009 at its meeting in Sarajevo.

[149] For activities of the Ministerial Council to further explore the possibility to develop an Energy Community Oil Dimension with two main components (first, the establishment of an Oil Forum which should allow discussing and promoting regional oil infrastructure projects and the development of the oil markets in the region, second, the oil dimension should allow implementing the EU legislation in relation with the oil sector) see EC's Press Release IP/08/1051 of 27th June, 2008.

[150] See Decision No. 2008/03/MC-EnC of the Ministerial Council of the Energy Community concerning the implementation to the oil sector provisions of the Treaty and the creation of an Energy Community Oil Forum, available at: http://www.energy-community.org.

[151] See Art. 72 of the Energy Community Treaty.

[152] See Art. 67 lit. a and lit. c of the Energy Community Treaty; additionally, see Art. 71 of this Treaty, according to which the Director of the Secretariat or a nominated alternate shall assist at the Ministerial Council, the Permanent High-Level Group, the Regulatory Board and the Fora.

yearly progress reports to the Ministerial Council. Moreover, the Secretariat reviews and assists in the coordination by the European Commission of the donors' activity in the territories of the Contracting Parties,[153] and is responsible for ensuring that the Energy Community's budget – to which all Parties contribute – is correctly spent and accounted for. Finally, the Secretariat shall carry out other tasks conferred on it under this Treaty[154] or by a Procedural Act of the Ministerial Council, excluding the power to take measures, and adopt Procedural Acts.[155] The Secretariat, which also prepares conferences,[156] consists of a Director, to be appointed by a Procedural Act of the Ministerial Council,[157] and such staff as the Energy Community may require.[158] Both, the director and the staff, shall act impartially and promote the interests of the Energy Community.[159] Consequently, the first sentence of Article 70 of the Energy Community Treaty states that in the performance of their duties the Director and the stuff shall not seek or receive instructions from any Party to this Treaty.

Decision-making Process

Title VI (Articles 76–88) of the Treaty establishing the Energy Community sets out the decision-making rules of this Community. This Title consists of general provisions (1), provisions concerning 'Measures' and different Titles (2) and provisions concerning 'Procedural Acts' (3).

General Provisions

The Ministerial Council is allowed to take 'Measures'.[160] If so empowered by this Council, the Permanent High-Level Group and the Regulatory Board may also take those measures.[161] Such measures may take the form of a legally binding

---

[153] See Art. 67 lit. b and lit. c of the Energy Community Treaty.

[154] See, for example, Art. 21, the last sentence of Art. 29 and Art. 75 of the Energy Community Treaty.

[155] See Art. 67 lit. d and lit. e of the Energy Community Treaty.

[156] For example the high level conference on investments for the Energy Community on 28th September, 2007 in Athens, see EC's Press Releases IP/07/1415 and IP/07/1423 of 28th September, 2007.

[157] See Art. 69 of the Energy Community Treaty.

[158] See Art. 68 of the Energy Community Treaty.

[159] See the second sentence of Art. 70 of the Energy Community Treaty.

[160] See Art. 47 lit. b of the Energy Community Treaty.

[161] See Art. 53 lit. d and Art. 58 lit. c of the Energy Community Treaty.

'Decision'[162] or of a 'Recommendation' that has no binding force.[163] Finally, the general provisions clarify that each party generally shall have one vote[164] and the above mentioned institutions may act only if two third of the Parties are represented.[165]

Measures Under Different Titles

Following the above mentioned general provisions, Title VI of the Energy Community Treaty distinguishes between measures under Title II (a), measures under Title III (b) and measures under Title IV (c).

Measures Under Title II

Title II of the Energy Community Treaty, mainly regarding the extension of the acquis communautaire on energy, environment, competition and renewables,[166] empowers the Energy Community to take Measures.[167] These measures are referred to in the first sentence of Article 79 of the Energy Community Treaty according to which the Ministerial Council, the Permanent High-Level Group or the Regulatory Board shall take Measures under Title II on a proposal from the European Commission.[168] In this context, each Contracting Party represented in the Ministerial Council, in the Permanent High-Level Group or in the Regulatory Board shall have one vote,[169] while the three institutions mentioned above shall act by a majority of the votes cast.[170] This waiver of the requirement for unanimity justifies the assertion that the decision-making process within the framework of the Energy Community is at least partly consistent with the idea of institutional supranationality.

---

[162] See Art. 76(2) of the Energy Community Treaty, according to which a Decision is legally binding in its entirety upon those to whom it is addressed.

[163] See Art. 76(3) of the Energy Community Treaty with the further clarification that the Parties – at least – shall use their best endeavours to carry out such Recommendations. For the relevance of such recommendations, inter alia, see Art. 33 of this Treaty.

[164] See Art. 77 of the Energy Community Treaty.

[165] See Art. 78 of the Energy Community Treaty with the further clarification that abstentions in a vote from Parties shall not count as votes cast.

[166] For more on all this, see pp. 416 et seq. above.

[167] See, in particular, Art. 24 and Art. 25 of the Energy Community Treaty.

[168] Additionally, see the second sentence of this provision according to which the European Commission may alter or withdraw its proposal at any time during the procedure leading to adoption of the Measures.

[169] See Art. 80 of the Energy Community Treaty.

[170] See Art. 81 of the Energy Community Treaty.

Measures under Title III

Title III of the Energy Community Treaty, mainly regarding the mechanism for operation of Network energy Markets including safeguard measures,[171] also empowers the Energy Community to take measures.[172] These measures are referred to in Article 82 of the Energy Community Treaty according to which the Ministerial Council, the Permanent High-Level Group or the Regulatory Board shall take Measures under Title III not on proposal from the European Commission, but on a proposal from a Party or the Secretariat. In doing so, the Ministerial Council, the Permanent High-Level Group or the Regulatory Board shall act by a two third majority of the votes cast, including a positive vote of the EU.[173]

Measures under Title IV

Finally, Title IV of the Energy Community Treaty, regarding the creation of a single energy market,[174] empowers the Energy Community to take measures.[175] These measures are referred to in Article 84 and Article 85 of the Energy Community Treaty according to which the Ministerial Council, the Permanent High-Level Group or the Regulatory Board shall take Measures under Title VI on a proposal from a Party and by unanimity. Therefore, the abovementioned idea of the institutional supranationality would be inapt at this point.

Procedural Acts

According to several provisions enshrined in the Treaty establishing the Energy Community, the Ministerial Council, the Permanent High-Level-Group and the Regulatory Board are also empowered to adopt 'Procedural Acts'.[176] Those acts regulate organizational, budgetary and transparency issues of the Energy Community, including the delegation of power from the Ministerial Council to the Permanent High-Level Group, the Regulatory Board or the Secretariat, and have binding force on the institutions of the Energy Community, and, if the Procedural Act in question so provides, to the Parties.[177] Save as provided in Article 88 of the Energy Community Treaty, Procedural Acts shall be adopted in compliance with the

---

[171] For more on all this, see pp. 424 et seq. above.

[172] See, in particular, Art. 28, 32, 34 and 35 of the Energy Community Treaty.

[173] See Art. 83 of the Energy Community Treaty.

[174] For more on all this, see pp. 427 et seq. above.

[175] See, in particular, Art. 42, 43 and 45 of the Energy Community Treaty.

[176] See, for example, Art. 46, 49, 55, 60, 66, 69, 73, 74 and 75 of the Energy Community Treaty.

[177] See Art. 86 of the Energy Community Treaty.

decision-making process set out in the third chapter of Title VI.[178] This means, that the adoption of a Procedural Act generally requires a proposal from a Party or the Secretariat and a two third majority of the votes cast, including a positive vote of the EU.[179]

Implementation of Decisions and Dispute Settlement

Pursuant to Article 89 of the Treaty establishing the Energy Community the Parties shall implement Decisions addressed to them in their domestic legal system within the period specified in the Decision. Furthermore, Articles 90–93 create a dispute settlement mechanism which bears certain resemblance to the EU's infringement procedure without, however, providing for a judicial decision in the last instance. Under these rules, a Party to the Treaty, the Secretariat or the Regulatory Board – upon complaint by private bodies or on its own motion – may bring a case of non-compliance by a Party with Energy Community law to the attention of the Ministerial Council.[180] Subsequently, the Ministerial Council may determine the existence of a breach by a Party of its obligations by way of a decision.[181] In this context, the Ministerial Council shall decide by a simple majority, if the breach relates to Title II, by a two third majority, if the breach relates to Title III, or by unanimity, if the breach relates to Title IV.[182] In cases of serious and persistent breaches, certain rights deriving from the application of the Energy Community Treaty to the Party concerned, including voting rights, may be suspended by the Ministerial Council.[183] When adopting the above mentioned decisions referred to in Article 91 and Article 92 of the Energy Community Treaty, the Ministerial Council shall act without taking into account the vote of the representative of the Party concerned.[184]

On 27 June 2008, the Ministerial Council of the Energy Community adopted more detailed and partially innovative rules on dispute settlement[185] which, in particular, structure the procedure and further define the roles and rights of all actors within the dispute settlement procedure.[186]

---

[178] For the decision-making process set out there see p. 436 above.

[179] For relevant exceptions to these rules, see Article 88 of the Energy Community Treaty.

[180] See Art. 90(1) of the Energy Community Treaty.

[181] See Art. 91(1) of the Energy Community Treaty.

[182] For the main contents of the Titles II-IV see pp. 416 et seq. above.

[183] See Art. 92(1) of the Energy Community Treaty.

[184] See Art. 93 of the Energy Community Treaty.

[185] See EC's Press Release IP/08/1051 of 27th June, 2008.

[186] See Procedural Act No. 2008/01/MC-EnC of the Ministerial Council of the Energy Community of 27th June, 2008 on the Rules of Procedure for Dispute Settlement under the Treaty; available at: http://www.energy-community.org/pls/portal/docs/2969193.pdf.

Conclusion and Outlook

Firstly, the Treaty establishing the Energy Community illustrates the increasing relevance and importance of energy policy issues for the EU.[187] Secondly, this Treaty is a sector specific prototype of how the EU exports its own rules and structures to neighbouring countries[188] by creating real prospects of EU-member-ship[189] at the same time. Insofar as the Energy Community Treaty involves legally binding compliance with the acquis communautaire in the sectors in question for all parties, both for existing EU law and for further adaptations,[190] it follows the model of the European Economic Area, but just for the sectors in question.[191] Its sector specific approach, its limited duration,[192] its institutional design[193] and its potential to generate certain spill-over effects[194] resembles to a certain degree the European Coal and Steel Community on which the Energy Community Treaty has consciously been modelled on. While limited in scope to the electricity and gas sectors, and partially to the oil sector, the Energy Community Treaty represents a significant systematic development for EU policy in the Balkans insofar as it jumps ahead of the bilateralism of the SAA process[195] by being multilateral between the EU and all the Western Balkans at the same time.[196]

Thus, the Energy Community process is part of a rather new multilateral approach of the EU, which is equally apparent in the so-called European Neighbourhood Policy (ENP). The ENP, established as an independent policy

---

[187] For more on this, see Inotai, Towards a Common Energy Policy in the European Union?, Romanian Journal of European Affairs 8 (2008), pp. 5 et seq.; Fischer/Lippert, Mehr Gleise – Energieaußenpolitik und Nachbarschaftspolitik der EU, Osteuropa 2009, pp. 53 et seq.; Frenz/Kane, Die neue europäische Energiepolitik, Natur und Recht 2010, pp. 464 et seq.; Geden, Die Energie- und Klimapolitik der EU – zwischen Implementierung und strategischer Neuorientierung, integration 2008, pp. 353 et seq.; Kahl, Die Kompetenzen der EU in der Energiepolitik nach Lissabon, Europarecht 44 (2009), pp. 601 et seq.; Nowak, *Europarecht nach Lissabon*, 2011, pp. 250 et seq.

[188] In a similar way, see Renner, The Energy Community of Southeast Europe: A neo-functionalist project of regional integration, European Integration online Papers 13 (2009), pp. 1 et seq. (12).

[189] With further references, see fn. 27 above.

[190] See pp. 416 et seq. above.

[191] See Emerson, Recalibrating EU Policy towards the Western Balkans, CEPS Policy Brief No. 175/October 2008, pp. 1 et seq. (7), available at: http://www.ceps.eu.

[192] See section B above.

[193] See section E above.

[194] For the recent establishment of the 'Oil Dimension' see sections D.I. and E.I.4); for the additional 'Social Dimension' of the Energy Community, especially based on the 2007 Memorandum of Understanding on Social Issues see pp. 432 et seq.).

[195] For more on this, see pp. 407 et seq. above.

[196] See Emerson, Recalibrating EU Policy towards the Western Balkans, CEPS Policy Brief No. 175/October 2008, pp. 1 et seq. (7), available at: http://www.ceps.eu.

field in 2003/2004,[197] is a serious offer for the creation and development of privileged relationships regarding exclusively Algeria, Armenia, Azerbaijan, Belarus, Egypt, Georgia, Israel, Jordan, Lebanon, Libya, Moldova, Morocco, Palestinian National authority, Syria, Tunisia and Ukraine.[198] The primary aim of the ENP is to prevent the emergence of new dividing lines between the EU, due to the eastern European Expansion now enlarged to 27 Member States, and the aforementioned EU neighbours, and rather strengthen prosperity, stability and security of the involved players.[199] Core elements of the ENP are numerous Association Agreements, Cooperation Agreements and Partnership Agreements,[200] whose bilateral regulatory approach has recently been enhanced by two new forms of multilateral cooperation, which partly overlap with the Energy Community. On the one hand, this regards the so-called *Union for the Mediterranean*,[201] which serves a complementary multilateralisation of bilateral contractual relationships within the framework of the southern ENP-dimension next to the simultaneous

---

[197] See the Commission Communication "European Neighbourhood Policy – Strategy Paper" of 12th May, 2004, COM(2004) 373 final.

[198] For the voluminous literature on the European Neighbourhood Policy see Andreev, The future of European neighbourhood policy and the role of regional cooperation in the Black Sea area, Southeast European and Black Sea Studies 8 (2008), pp. 93 et seq.; Balfour, The Challenges of the European Neighbourhood Policy, The International Spectator 40 (2005), pp. 7 et seq.; Bechev/ Nicolaidis, Whither the European neighbourhood policy? – Scenarios for a special relationship, EurView 2008, pp. 23 et seq.; Duta, European Neighbourhood Policy and Its Main Components, Romanian Journal of International Affairs 10 (2005), pp. 229 et seq.; Edwards, The Construction of Ambiguity and the Limits of Attraction: Europe and its Neighbourhood Policy, Journal of European Integration 30 (2008), pp. 45 et seq.; Emerson, European Neighbourhood Policy: Strategy or Placebo?, CEPS Working Document No. 215/November 2004, pp. 1 et seq.; Lippert, The Neighbourhood Policy of the European Union, Intereconomics 2007, pp. 180 et seq.; Magen, The Shadow of Enlargement: Can the European Neighbourhood Policy Achieve Compliance, Columbia Journal of European Law 2006, pp. 383 et seq.; Nowak, *Europarecht nach Lissabon*, 2011, pp. 265 et seq.; Ott, Is second best still good enough? – The European Neighbourhood Policy as an alternative to EU accession, Maastricht Journal of European and Comparative Law 2006, pp. 377 et seq.; Parmentier, The reception of EU neighbourhood policy, in: Laïdi (ed.), *EU Foreign Policy in a Globalized World – Normative power and social preferences*, 2008, pp. 103 et seq.; Sasse, The European Neighbourhood Policy: Conditionality Revisited for the EU's Eastern Neighbours, Europa-Asia Studies 60 (2008), pp. 295 et seq.; Smits, The Outsiders: The European Neighbourhood Policy, International Affairs 81 (2005), pp. 757 et seq.; *van Vooren*, A case study of "soft law" in EU external relations: The European Neighbourhood Policy, European Law Review 34 (2009), pp. 696 et seq.

[199] For more on the backgrounds and objectives of the ENP see the Commission Communications "European Neighbourhood Policy – Strategy Paper" of 12th May, 2004, COM(2004) 373 final, and "A Strong European Neighbourhood Policy" of 5th December, 2007, COM(2007) 774 final.

[200] For more on this, see with further references Nowak, Legal Arrangements for the Promotion and Protection of Foreign Investments Within the Framework of the EU Association Policy and European Neighbourhood Policy, in: Bungenberg/Griebel/Hindelang (eds.), *International Investment Law and EU Law*, 2011, pp. 105 et seq. (118 et seq.).

[201] See, in particular, the Commission Communication "Barcelona Process: Union for the Mediterranean" of 20th May, 2008, COM(2008) 319 final.

development of the traditional EU Mediterranean Policy[202] and Euro-Mediterranean Partnership.[203] Next to the European Commission and the 27 member states of the EU, Albania, Algeria, Bosnia and Herzegovina, Croatia, Egypt, Israel, Jordan, Lebanon, Mauritania, Monaco, Montenegro, Morocco, the Palestinian National Authority, Syria, Tunisia and Turkey have joined this Union Mediterranean in order to tackle some acutely ambitious goals and projects within the framework of this multilateral partnership.[204]

The fact that four states that are also Contracting Parties of the Energy Community participate in the Union for the Mediterranean[205] shows, that there are common elements among the aforementioned forms of multilateral cooperation. It further illustrates that the boundaries between the association and enlargement policy related to the states of the Western Balkans, on the one hand, and the ENP, on the other hand, are overlapping. The same holds true for the second new form of multilateral cooperation within the framework of the ENP, namely the so-called *Eastern Partnership* created on 7 May 2009.[206] This Partnership, based on an initiative by Poland and Sweden, was originated by the Joint Declaration of the Prague Eastern Partnership Summit on 7 May 2009 during the Czech presidency. The declaration was adopted (in the presence of the President of the European Council, the President of the European Commission and the Secretary General of the Council of the European Union) by the heads of state or government of the EU

---

[202] For more on this, see Martinez, European Union's exportation of democratic norms – The Case of North Africa, in: Laïdi (ed.), *EU Foreign Policy in a Globalized World – Normative power and social preferences*, 2008, pp. 118 et seq.; Pace, The Ugly duckling of Europe: The Mediterranean in the Foreign Policy of the European Union, Journal of European Area Studies 10 (2002), pp. 189 et seq.; Youngs, European Approaches to Security in the Mediterranean, Middle East Journal 57 (2003), pp. 414 et seq.

[203] For more on this see Bicchi, 'Our size fits all': normative power Europe and the Mediterranean, Journal of European Public Policy 13 (2006), pp. 286 et seq.; Tzifakis, EU's region-building and boundary-drawing policies: the European approach to the Southern Mediterranean and the Western Balkans, Journal of Southern Europe and the Balkans 9 (2007), pp. 47 et seq.

[204] The respective Joint Declaration of 13th July, 2008 aims at a Middle East Zone free of weapons of mass destruction, the establishment of a Free Trade Area and strengthening of regional cooperation. Moreover, the declaration explicitly lists the following (priority) initiatives: De-pollution of the Mediterranean Sea, the development of Maritime and Land Highways, the establishment of a Joint Civil Protection programme on prevention, preparation and response to disasters, as well as certain energy, education and Business Development initatives. In addition, a visionary plan for solar energy has already been established under the umbrella of the Union of the Mediterranean, entailing the foundation of the widely noticed *Desertec*-Project on 13th July, 2009.

[205] This refers to Albania, Crotia, Bosnia and Herzegovina as well as Montenegro.

[206] For more on this new Partnership, see Nowak, Multilaterale und bilaterale Elemente der EU-Assoziations-, Partnerschafts- und Nachbarschaftspolitik, Europarecht 44 (2010), pp. 746 et seq. (759 et seq.); Pop, Balkan's model to underpin EU's Eastern Partnership, available at: http://euobserver.com/15/26766?print=1; Schäfer, The Eastern Partnership – 'ENP Plus' for Europe's Eastern neighbours", CA Perspectives 4 (2009), pp. 1 et seq.; Tiede/Schirmer, Die Östliche Partnerschaft der Europäischen Union im Rahmen des Gemeinschaftsrechts, Osteuropa-Recht 55 (2009), pp. 184 et seq.

Member States as well as by the representatives of Armenia, Azerbaijan, Belarus, Georgia and the Republic Moldova and Ukraine. According to the declaration, the Eastern Partnership shall primarily create a new impetus for the strengthening and development of already existing political and economic relations between the participating actors. The fact that two states which have recently joined the Energy Community also participate in the *Eastern Partnership*[207] shows that the boundaries between those two forms of multilateral cooperation are equally overlapping. Insofar it cannot be ruled out that also in the future further states already associated with the EU within the framework of the ENP will join the Energy Community.

Acknowledgments The author would like to thank *Songül Seker* (Universität Siegen) and *Lena Borth* (Europa-Universität Viadrina) for helpful support.

---

[207] Whilst Moldova became a full fledged member of the Energy Community as of 1st May, 2010, Ukraine officially acceded the Energy Community on 1st February, 2011; for the actual 'observer status' of Georgia, see pp. 413 et seq. above.

Part II
Regional Integration

The European Union and Regional Trade Agreements

Colin M. Brown

Introduction

This contribution is intended to provide an overview of recent activities in the European Union (EU) as regards Free Trade Agreements (FTAs).[1] Rather than focus on one particular FTA, this contribution provides an overview of the most salient activities of the EU in this domain.[2]

In general terms, it can be noted that the EU remains particularly active in the negotiation of FTAs. This can be seen, both in the significant activity in opening negotiations, negotiating and concluding agreements but also in the policy documents adopted during the period examined. This contribution first examines the statements made in the Commission's Communications on future EU trade and investment policy and thereafter provides an overview of various agreements.

Overall Policy Developments

On 9 November 2010 the European Commission adopted a Communication setting out its vision of the EU's future trade policy during the mandate of the current Commission (i.e. until 2015).[3] This Communication, entitled "Trade, growth and

---

[1] This contribution focuses on developments during 2010 up until May 2011.

[2] For an overview of the EU-Korea FTA see Brown, The European Union and Regional Trade Agreements: A Case Study of the EU-Korea FTA, in: Herrmann/Terhechte (eds.), *European Yearbook of International Economic Law (2011)*, 2011, p. 297.

[3] Commission Communication, Trade, Growth and World Affairs: Trade Policy as a Core Component of the EU's 2020 Strategy, 9th November, 2010, COM(2010) 612 final.

C.M. Brown (✉)
European Commission, DG Trade, Brussels, Belgium
e-mail: colin.brown@ec.europa.eu

C. Herrmann and J.P. Terhechte (eds.), *European Yearbook of International Economic*   445
Law (EYIEL), Vol. 3 (2012), European Yearbook of International Economic Law 3,
DOI 10.1007/978-3-642-23309-8_14, © Springer-Verlag Berlin Heidelberg 2012

world affairs: Trade policy as a core component of the EU's 2020 Strategy" succeeds and builds upon the previous "Global Europe" Communication.[4] Under the heading "Completing the ongoing Free Trade Agreements (FTA) Negotiating Agenda" it states

> The Global Europe agenda of an ambitious new generation of bilateral trade agreements with important trading partners is a tough undertaking. Some emerging economies already represent a significant and increasing share of world trade. In framing our level of ambition, we will continue to take account of the differing levels of development of our trading partners.
>
> But this agenda is the right course for Europe to follow, and it has started to bring results.
>
> This is a significant and highly challenging agenda, not least because these new trade agreements go beyond import tariffs, whose importance has diminished, addressing regulatory barriers in goods, services and investment, intellectual property rights, government procurement, the protection of innovation, sustainable development (i.e. decent work, labour standards and environmental protection) and other important issues.
>
> But the benefits should be substantial. On the assumption that all these ongoing negotiations are successfully concluded:
>
> – About half of the EU's external trade will be covered by free trade agreements;
> – The average tariff faced by EU exports would fall by around one half (to about 1.7%) and the average EU import tariff by nearly a fifth (to 1.3%)23;
> – Taken together, these various FTAs should, as part of future trade policy's contribution to growth, add up to 0.5% to EU GDP in the longer run.
>
> We have successfully concluded FTA negotiations with Korea, as well as with Peru, Colombia and Central America. Talks with the Gulf countries, India, Canada, and Singapore are at an advanced stage. We reopened important negotiations with the MERCOSUR region. Completing our current agenda of competitiveness-driven FTAs remains a priority. We should make good use of fast-growing regional trade in East Asia and pursue our strategic economic interests in that region, inter alia by linking into the rapidly growing network of free trade areas in that region. We will therefore seek to expand and conclude bilateral negotiations with ASEAN countries, beginning with Malaysia and Vietnam, and to deepen our trade and investment relations with the Far East.
>
> In parallel, and to help establish an area of shared prosperity with Europe's neighbourhood, we will continue to pursue Deep and Comprehensive Free Trade Agreements (DCFTAs) within the respective frameworks of the Eastern Partnership and the Euro-Mediterranean Partnership, offering the prospect to countries in the region of participating in the internal market once the conditions are met. This remains a powerful agent of change via regulatory convergence and the removal of tariff and other barriers, carried out in parallel with the negotiation of Association Agreements, to provide economic integration in a context of political association.
>
> Concluding this agenda, in short, would greatly improve the way in which we do business with the rest of the world.[5]

This view expressed herein by the Commission continue to place the negotiation and application of bilateral agreements at the heart of the EU's trade policy. This is

---

[4] Commission Communication, Global Europe: Competing in the World, 4th October, 2006, COM (2006) 567 final.

[5] Ibid., p. 9.

not seen as an alternative track to the Doha Development Negotiations in the WTO. The same Communication refers to the Doha Round as "our top priority".[6]

The Council of the European Union responded by adopting its own policy document in the form of Council Conclusions. These Conclusions also give prominence to bilateral agreements. They state that the EU should[7]

> Make progress in relation to on-going regional and bilateral trade negotiations in both our neighbourhood and further afield, with a view to achieving ambitious, comprehensive and balanced outcomes, which add value to our multilateral commitments; and maintain a focus on competitiveness-driven FTAs with fast growing emerging economies;

With the entry into force of the Treaty of Lisbon, the European Parliament has become a key player in EU trade policy. It will also react to the Commission's Communication. At the time of writing, it was preparing its Own Initiative Report. The draft of the report available to the author at the time of writing stated, as regards FTAs[8]:

> Parliament sees Free Trade Agreements (FTAs) as a second-best but necessary solution
>
> 11. Reiterates that all new FTAs concluded by the EU should be WTO-compatible, comprehensive, ambitious, lead to real reciprocal market access and go beyond both existing multilateral commitments and those expected to result from a successful conclusion of the DDA; welcomes the progress made in some negotiations; at the same time regrets that most of the negotiations have not been concluded yet; asks the Commission to analyse what could be done or changed in order to conclude outstanding FTA negotiations better and faster; asks the Commission to analyse the possibility of including WTO dispute settlement mechanisms in bilateral Free Trade Agreements; asks the Commission to reduce the spaghetti-bowl effect, e.g. by negotiating multilateral rules of origin;
>
> 12. Reminds the Commission to carry out a better evaluation of European interests before deciding on future FTA partners and negotiation mandates; reminds the Commission and the Council to take seriously into account Parliament's views when deciding about the mandates;

As is very clear, while none of these documents suggest that the EU's FTAs should be given priority over the efforts to reach an agreement in the WTO's Doha Development Agenda there is a clear expectation that FTAs remain as one of the main planks for future EU trade policy.

The entry into force of the Treaty of Lisbon, in addition to changing the institutional set-up for the conduct of trade policy also brought changes to EU competence. The most significant such change was the addition of an explicit competence for foreign direct investment. This is understood, at least by the Commission, to mean that the EU has exclusive competence (i.e. excluding the ability of the Member States to adopt legally binding acts) for provisions both on

---

[6] Ibid.

[7] Point 12 of the Council Conclusions on the EU's trade policy of 21st December, 2010, available at: http://www.consilium.europa.eu/uedocs/cms_data/ docs/pressdata/en/misc/118657.pdf.

[8] Points 11 and 12 of the Draft Report, available at: http://www.europarl.europa.eu/sides/ getDoc.do?pubRef=-//EP//NONSGML+COMPARL+PE-460. 634 + 01 + DOC + PDF + V0// EN&language = EN.

market access and investment protection. Given the fact that investment protection is not included in the WTO negotiations, the sole vector for the EU to develop the competence for investment is through the negotiation of bilateral agreements. Indeed, the EU has already been negotiating chapters on market access for investment in FTAs. In its Communication on the EU's future investment policy, which was adopted before the Communication on the future trade policy, the Commission took the view that investment protection provisions should be included in FTAs. It stated[9]:

> In the short term, the prospects for realising the integration of investment into the common commercial policy arise in ongoing trade negotiations, where the Union has so far only focused on market access for investors. The latest generation of competitiveness-driven Free Trade Agreements (FTAs) is precisely inspired by the objective of unleashing the economic potential of the world's important growth markets to EU trade and investment. The Union has an interest in broadening the scope of negotiations to the complete investment area. In some cases, we could also respond to a request from our negotiating partners themselves. In the EU-Canada negotiations towards a Comprehensive Economic and Trade Agreement, our partner has expressed an interest in an agreement that would cover investment protection. Other ongoing negotiations in which investment protection should be considered include the EU-India negotiations towards a Broad-based Trade and Investment Agreement, the EU Singapore negotiations towards a Free Trade Agreement, and the EU-Mercosur trade negotiations.
>
> In the short to medium term, the Union should also consider under which circumstances it may be desirable to pursue stand-alone investment agreements. China, which is characterised by a high proportion of greenfield investments, including from the EU, may be one candidate for a stand-alone investment agreement, in which the protection of all kinds of assets including intellectual property rights should be covered. The Commission will explore the desirability and feasibility of such an investment agreement with China, and report to the Council and the European Parliament. Russia also presents particular opportunities and challenges to European investors. The negotiation with Russia of investment including investment protection should be further considered and discussed, for example in the context of a comprehensive agreement, such as the agreement that would replace the Partnership and Cooperation Agreement.
>
> A further legal argument for incorporating investment commitments into trade agreements relates to the fact that trade agreements, when they comply with relevant WTO rules on economic integration, are sheltered from the WTO obligation of most-favoured nation treatment, which requires WTO members to immediately and unconditionally extend the most favourable treatment to the rest of the membership. In other words, only if offered inside a trade agreement, preferential treatment, for example on investment market access, can remain preferential. This is most relevant for FDI in services sectors, given that the General Agreement on Trade in Services (GATS) addresses the supply of services through a commercial presence, which is essentially FDI.

This policy development, which has been broadly welcomed by the other EU institutions, will lead to the EU concluding FTAs covering the entire spectrum of trade and investment activity. As such, the extension of the EU's competence is

---

[9] Commission Communication, Towards a Comprehensive European International Investment Policy, 7th July, 2010, COM(2010) 343 final, available at: http://trade.ec.europa.eu/doclib/docs/2010/july/tradoc_146307.pdf.

clearly an important step which will have major implications for the shape of the EU's future FTAs. At the timing of writing, negotiations have not been completed on any EU agreement including investment protection. The countries mentioned in the Communication are likely to be among the first group of countries with which the EU will negotiate agreements including investment protection.

These important developments show the direction of the EU's FTA policy over the next years. That translates into continuing to place a relatively high importance on FTA negotiations and a further extension of the scope of such agreements so as to cover all areas of trade and investment.

Developments in Particular Negotiations

While there have been significant developments in the overall policy objectives of the EU significant progress has been made on a number of negotiations.

Korea

Undoubtedly the most important recent development was the signature and agreement on provisional application of the EU-Korea FTA. This agreement is the most significant trade agreement to be concluded by the EU since the conclusion of the Uruguay Round creating the World Trade Organisation. The Council of the European Union authorised its signature and provisional application of the agreement on 16 September 2010 and the agreement was actually signed on 6 October 2010.[10] It will be provisionally applied from 1 July 2011.

This date was eventually decided after discussions between the EU Member States. Importantly, choosing this date permitted the European Parliament to vote on the agreement before the agreement was provisionally applied. Article 218 of the Treaty on the Functioning of the European Union (TFEU) which sets out the procedures for the ratification of agreements by the European Union permits the Council to decide to provisionally apply an agreement in the same decision in which it decides to authorise the signature of the agreement. Since the Council authorises the signature of the agreement and then the agreement is sent to the European Parliament for its consent, the Parliament felt particularly concerned that should the agreement be provisionally applied before it had given its views, its ability to exercise its right to refuse to give consent could be effectively undermined. This element was a factor in the decision to have the agreement only be provisionally applied from 1 July 2011. On 17 February 2011 the European Parliament gave its

---

[10] See Decision 2011/265/EU, OJ [2011] L 127/1.

consent to the agreement. This was followed by the Korean Parliament on 5 May 2011. These approvals clear the way for the agreement to be provisionally applied. It is only provisionally applied because, for the EU, it is considered a mixed agreement, and hence ratification by the Member States is also required.

The signature of the Agreement, and the consent granted by the European Parliament were also accompanied by the adoption of a regulation setting out the procedures in the EU for applying the bilateral safeguard provisions of the Agreement. This most importantly sets out the procedures in the EU for investigations and the imposition of safeguard measures in the event the conditions for applying safeguard measures are met. It was considered necessary that this regulation be in place before the agreement was provisionally applied and indeed one of the conditions for the provisional application to be approved in the EU (imposed by the Council) was that the safeguard regulation should have entered into force by the time the agreement was applied. The regulation needed to be adopted by the Council and European Parliament on the basis of the ordinary legislative procedure (see Article 294 TFEU). It was the first major piece of trade legislation adopted subsequent to the entry into force of the Treaty of Lisbon.

Political agreement on the regulation was reached in December 2010. The Council formally approved the regulation on 11 April 2011. The Parliament had approved it on 17 February 2011, at the same time as it gave its consent to the agreement itself.

The most significant change to the regulation as proposed by the European Commission was the addition of the possibility for EU industry to lodge a complaint, which, if it satisfies on a *prima facie* basis the requirements of the regulation, would require the Commission to open an investigation. This is the first safeguard regulation in the EU which provides for that possibility.

The vote in the Parliament was also accompanied by a Statement by the Commission and a Joint Declaration by the Commission and the Parliament.[11] In the latter document, the two institutions agreed that if the Parliament adopts a recommendation to initiate a safeguard investigation, then the Commission will carefully examine whether the conditions for *ex officio* opening of investigations are fulfilled. If that is not the case, then it will report back to the European Parliament. The Commission' Statement involved a number of commitments on implementation of the safeguards regulation, but more broadly on other elements of the FTA such as monitoring of the sustainable development requirements of the FTA and the status of the processing zones on the Korean peninsula. It accompanies another Commission statement, associated with the Decision approving the signature of the agreement, in which the Commission sets out a number of commitments as regards the implementation of the Agreement.[12]

---

[11] Available at: http://www.europarl.europa.eu/sides/getDoc.do?type=TA&reference=P7-TA-2011-0061&language=EN (last visited on 14th May, 2011).

[12] See OJ [2011] L 127/4.

With the completion of these legislative developments, the path is now clear for the most ambitious FTA in the history of the EU to be applied.

Andean Community and Central America

Early in 2011 the European Commission initialled agreements with Columbia and Peru and with a number of Central American countries.

The so-called MultiParty Trade Agreement with Columbia and Peru was initialled on 13 April 2011. This agreement was in the first place intended to be with all four countries of the Andean Community. However, Bolivia and Ecuador decided not to complete negotiations on the agreement with the EU at this time. The name of the agreement is intended to signal that the agreement is not with the Andean Community as such and these countries could later accede to the agreement.

The agreement itself includes the main elements expected in an FTA – liberalisation of trade in goods and services.[13] It also includes provisions of establishment outside the services field, significant disciplines and commitments on government procurement, intellectual property, subsidies and competition. The agreement also contains an effective dispute settlement system, and a mediation mechanism, which is designed to promote the settlement of disputes without having recourse to formal dispute settlement. Of particular importance are the provisions of the agreement dealing with sustainable development, which require adherence to certain core International Labour Organisation conventions and which prevent the parties from lowering or failing to properly implement their environmental standards. The agreement also provides for technical assistance and capacity building to ensure that the maximum benefits of the agreement are garnered by Columbia and Peru.

The agreement with the Central American countries was initialled on 22 March 2011. This is an agreement between Costa Rica, El Salvador, Guatemala, Honduras, Nicaragua, Panama on the one side and the EU on the other. Rather than being an FTA, it is an Association Agreement which includes an FTA or a trade pillar. In terms of substance, the agreement is broadly similar to the Multi-Party agreement with Columbia and Peru.[14]

---

[13] The text of the agreement as initialled is available at: http://trade.ec.europa.eu/doclib/press/index.cfm?id=691 (last visited on 14th May, 2011).

[14] The full text of the agreement is available at: http://trade.ec.europa.eu/doclib/press/index.cfm?id=689 (last visited on 14th May, 2011).

Canada

Negotiations on a new agreement were launched in May 2009 after earlier efforts to upgrade the bilateral trade relationship had failed to produce results. The agreement currently being negotiated goes by the name of Comprehensive Economic and Trade Agreement (CETA). It is one of the agreements which may include provisions on investment protection. One of the key issues is the extent to which the Canadian provinces also take on obligations.

India

Negotiations between the EU and India have been underway since June 2007. This agreement may also include provisions on investment protection. At the time of writing a number of outstanding issues remained to be resolved before there could be conclusion of the negotiations.

ASEAN

Negotiations with ASEAN as a whole were initiated in April 2007. However, progress at a regional level was elusive, and in 2009 the parties agreed to pause their negotiations. Since then the EU has started negotiations with Singapore and Malaysia, in March and October 2010 respectively. It is envisaged that further negotiations on a bilateral basis may start with other countries member of ASEAN. It is possible that the agreement with Singapore will include provisions on investment protection.

MERCOSUR

The EU started negotiations with MERCOSUR in 1999. While some progress was made, these negotiations were put on hold for some time because the parties considered that they needed to know the results of the Doha Development Agenda in the WTO before commitments could be exchanged. Negotiations were re-launched in May 2010. At the time of writing exchanges of offers had yet to take place.

Libya

The EU had been negotiating an FTA with Libya, and while far from complete some progress had been made. In the light of events in Libya in early 2011 negotiations have been suspended.

Gulf Co-Operation Council

Negotiations with the Gulf Co-Operation Council started in the early 1990s. Significant progress was made, but then negotiations were suspended since agreement on a small number of outstanding issues was problematic. Consultations on these issues are ongoing.

Ukraine

The EU has been negotiating an extensive Association Agreement with Ukraine since February 2008. Subjects for negotiation include an FTA and substantial approximation of legislation between Ukraine and the EU.

African, Caribbean and Pacific (ACP) Countries

This large group of countries has for a long time benefited from preferential access to the EU market. Under a number of conventions, this has been a unilateral preference. This has been accompanied by a waiver from Article I GATT.[15] However, upon the expiry of the trade regime of the Cotonou Agreement at the end of 2007 the unilateral trade preferences have been replaced by FTAs. These FTAs obviate the need for a waiver from the WTO.

These FTAs take the form of so-called Economic Partnership Agreements (EPAs). These agreements typically combine an FTA with a framework for technical assistance. The EU grants duty and quota free access to all imports from these countries and does not expect similar liberalisation on the part of the ACP countries.

Rather than undertake negotiations with each of the countries individually, negotiations with six regions have taken place. In principle, agreements have been signed with all countries who have wished to conclude negotiations on such

---

[15] The Waiver granted for the so-called Lomé Convention featured prominently in the WTO disputes over bananas.

agreements.[16] The most comprehensive such agreement is with the Cariforum countries (Antigua and Barbuda, The Bahamas, Barbados, Belize, Dominica, Grenada, Guyana, Haiti, Jamaica, Saint Lucia, Saint Vincent and the Grenadines, Saint Kitts and Nevis, Surinam, Trinidad and Tobago and the Dominican Republic). The Economic Partnership Agreement between the CARIFORUM States and the European Union was signed in October 2008.[17] This agreement has been in provisional application since 29 December 2008. It is a comprehensive FTA, and includes commitments on trade in good, services, establishment, intellectual property etc.[18]

Where such comprehensive EPAs were not available, the EU often completed negotiations on so-called "interim" EPAs which included only provisions on goods, and did not necessarily have a complete regional coverage. In the Pacific, Papua New Guinea and Fiji have both signed such an interim agreement, and it is in application between Papua New Guinea and the EU. Such negotiations also took place with a grouping of Southern Africa Development Corporation (SADC) countries and led to the text of an interim EPA. This agreement has been signed by Botswana, Lesotho, Swaziland and Mozambique but not by Namibia, which is also a member of the group. South Africa has also been involved in the negotiations of this group but has not initialled such an agreement (it has a pre-existing FTA with the EU). A similar agreement has been negotiated with the Eastern African Community (Kenya, Uganda, Tanzania, Rwanda, Burundi). It has been initialled, but not signed. There is also such an agreement with the countries of Eastern and Southern Africa (Mauritius, Seychelles, Zimbabwe and Madagascar, Zambia and Comoros). This agreement has been signed by Mauritius, Seychelles, Zimbabwe and Madagascar and initialled by Zambia and Comoros. In the Central African region there is an interim agreement with Cameroon which was signed in January 2009. In West Africa, interim EPAs were negotiated with Ivory Coast and Ghana. Ivory Coast has signed but Ghana has only initialled. In all cases, negotiations are continuing on regional and comprehensive EPAs, at various stages of advancement. All countries which have at least initialled such an agreement benefit from the EPA Market Access Regulation (Council Regulation 1528/2007) which provides duty and quota free access to the EU market and serves as a transitional mechanism as these countries move from initialling to signature to full ratification of the agreement.

---

[16] All least developed countries have duty and quota free access to the EU's market on the basis of the Everything But Arms scheme included in the EU's Generalised System of Preferences; see Art. 9 of Regulation (EC) No. 732/2008, OJ [2008] L 211/1. The existence of this regime lessens the need for such countries to accede to an EPA.

[17] Economic Partnership Agreement between the CARIFORUM States and the European Community and its Member States of 15th October, 2008, OJ [2008] L 289/I/3.

[18] For a comprehensive analysis see Imana/Zampetti, *The CARIFORUM-EU Economic Partnership Agreement: A Practitioners' Analysis*, forthcoming.

Conclusions

This overview has demonstrated that FTAS play a key role in the EU's trade policy. The general set-up of EU trade policy, as expressed in the Commission's Communication and the reactions of the Parliament and Council illustrate the central place of FTAs in the EU's policy, and the extension of EU competence to include investment and particularly investment protection will bring a new dimension to EU FTA activity.

The approval of the EU-Korea FTA and the safeguard regulation which accompanies it is a path-setting development which will in procedural terms set the context for future EU agreements.

Furthermore, as surveyed in this overview, the EU's ongoing FTA activities are both ambitious and comprehensive and are attracting even more interest. For example Spurred on, undoubtedly by the EU-Korea agreement, Japan is seeking to engage the EU in negotiations on an FTA. Taken together, all of this activity is likely to fulfil the expectations in the Commission's Communication and add in a tangible manner to growth in EU GDP.

International Economic Law in North America: Recent Developments in Dispute Resolution Under Regional Economic Agreements

Patrick C. Reed

Introduction

This chapter reviews legal developments in regional economic integration in North America, including Central America and the Caribbean, by examining recent dispute resolution decisions under international economic agreements in the region. The chapter finds that these recent decisions represent a modest body of case law. The agreements providing for regional integration in North America are intergovernmental as opposed to supranational, and the region has no centralized or unified adjudicatory body analogous to the European Court of Justice.[1] The dispute resolution processes are used sparingly, resulting in a small number of decided cases, most of which are investment disputes addressed in investor-state arbitrations. Most of the recent decisions make sound contributions to international economic law, and they belie the stereotype that investor-state arbitrations tend to be biased in favor of business interests.[2] But some decisions do not go as far as might be hoped in

---

[1] Cf. Clarkson, Integration and Disintegration in North America: The Rise and Fall of International Economic Law in One Region, in: Herrmann/Terhechte (eds.), *European Yearbook of International Economic Law (2011)*, pp. 327 et seq. (340) (in last year's survey for this yearbook, characterizing NAFTA as having little or no "self-sustaining capacity to generate transnational economic norms" or "offset the power of the dominant member while boosting that of smaller ones, as they do in Europe.").

[2] E.g., id. (contending that NAFTA's "investor-state dispute settlement panels favoured the strong (transnational investors) over the periphery's weaker governments.") (according to Clarkson, somehow Canada is a weaker periphery country); Editorial, The Secret Trade Courts, New York Times, 27th September, 2004, p. 26 ("the arbitration process . . . is often one-sided, favoring well-heeled corporations . . ..").

P.C. Reed (✉)
Department of Business Law, Baruch College, City University of New York, New York, NY, USA

Center for Global Affairs, New York University, New York, NY, USA
e-mail: pcr@simonswiskin.com

C. Herrmann and J.P. Terhechte (eds.), *European Yearbook of International Economic Law (EYIEL), Vol. 3 (2012)*, European Yearbook of International Economic Law 3, DOI 10.1007/978-3-642-23309-8_15, © Springer-Verlag Berlin Heidelberg 2012

promoting stability and predictability in the law, the classic goal for dispute resolution in international economic institutions.[3] These disappointing decisions are a minority of the total. They suffer from questionable reasoning or from inconsistency with other decisions on identical issues. Other decisions, while apparently correct under existing law, reveal gaps in the availability of dispute resolution in the regional agreements.

Focusing on dispute resolution in this year's survey reflects an absence of recent developments in negotiation or approval of new agreements on international economic matters in North America. Professor Dunoff's contribution to the first issue of this yearbook 2 years ago gave an overview of the most important of initiatives for economic integration in the region.[4] These include four existing plurilateral treaty instruments: the North American Free Trade Agreement (NAFTA), the Central America – Dominican Republic – United States Free Trade Agreement (CAFTA-DR), the Central American Common Market, and the CARICOM Single Market. Dunoff also discussed the proposed Free Trade Agreement of the Americas (FTAA) and efforts to create an Economic Union under the auspices of the Organization of Eastern Caribbean States. In addition to these plurilateral institutions, one should not overlook a number of bilateral investment treaties between states in the North American region.[5]

Dunoff observed that "States in North America, Central America, and the Caribbean have engaged in numerous efforts at regional integration."[6] But he concluded that NAFTA "has proved to be politically contentious," "the efforts among smaller economies ... are still in their formative stages," and the proposed FTAA "has run aground."[7] If the FTAA had run aground as of 2008, 2 years later it is a sunken ship that has disappeared from the radar screen.[8] Meanwhile, even an international agreement that had progressed to the point of being negotiated and

---

[3] E.g., Jackson, *Sovereignty, the WTO, and Changing Fundamentals of International Law*, 2006, p. 89 ("the procedures of rule application, which often center on a dispute settlement procedure, should be designed to promote as much as possible the stability and predictability of the rule system."); cf. WTO Dispute Settlement Understanding, Art. 3(2) ("dispute settlement ... is a central element in providing security and predictability").

[4] Dunoff, North American Regional Economic Integration: Recent Trends and Developments, in: Herrmann/Terhechte (eds.), *European Yearbook of International Economic Law* (2010), p. 297.

[5] Canada has bilateral investment treaties in force with Costa Rica, Panama, and Trinidad and Tobago. The United States has bilateral investment treaties in force with Grenada, Panama, and Trinidad and Tobago. Mexico has bilateral investment treaties with Panama and Trinidad and Tobago.

[6] Dunoff, North American Regional Economic Integration: Recent Trends and Developments, in: Herrmann/Terhechte (eds.), *European Yearbook of International Economic Law* (2010), pp. 297 et seq. (311).

[7] Id.

[8] See Declaration of Commitment of Port of Spain, Fifth Summit of the Americas, 19th April, 2009 (no mention of FTAA); cf. U.S. Trade Representative, 2009 Trade Policy Agenda, March 2009, p. 122 (reporting that FTAA negotiations have remained suspended since 2005) with U.S. Trade Representative, 2010 Trade Policy Agenda, March 2010 (no mention of FTAA).

signed in 2007 – the preferential trade agreement between the United States and Panama – remains unapproved in the United States and has been pending before Congress with no action taken in 2008, 2009, or 2010. The Obama Administration has not negotiated any new preferential trade agreements.

As regards dispute resolution, not only does each of the existing international agreements in the region create separate institutions, but also individual agreements have multiple dispute resolution processes. In the NAFTA, the three dispute settlement processes in international economic matters are investor-state arbitrations under chapter 11, binational panel review in antidumping and countervailing duty cases under chapter 19, and state-to-state dispute settlement under chapter 20.[9] The CAFTA-DR provides for investor-state arbitrations under chapter 10 and state-to-state dispute settlement under chapter 20. Each BIT provides for investor-state arbitration.

The first section of this chapter examines investor-state arbitrations. As indicated below, these cases comprise the largest category of dispute resolution decisions during the time period this chapter covers. The second section of the chapter examines binational panel review under NAFTA chapter 19. The third section examines state-to-state dispute settlement.

Investor-State Investment Disputes

Overview

NAFTA chapter 11 governs transborder investment among Canada, Mexico, and the United States and establishes an international arbitral process for settlement of disputes between one NAFTA party and an investor of another NAFTA party. CAFTA-DR chapter 10 does the same for Costa Rica, El Salvador, Guatemala, Honduras, Guatemala, the Dominican Republic, and the United States. NAFTA chapter 11 and CAFTA-DR chapter 10 both follow the model of bilateral investment treaties.

Since the previous contributions to this yearbook have not analyzed investment disputes in detail, this chapter will include investment disputes since the end of 2007.[10] From November 2007 though December 2010, six reported final decisions have been issued in investment disputes under NAFTA chapter 11, one has been issued under the Canada-Costa Rica bilateral investment treaty, and one has been issued under the US-Grenada bilateral investment treaty. In addition, one case has

---

[9] NAFTA's Side Agreements on Environmental Matters and Labor Matters also have their own dispute settlement processes, which are outside the scope of this chapter.

[10] For a summary of NAFTA chapter 11 cases through 2004, see Hufbauer/Schott, *NAFTA Revisited: Achievements and Challenges*, 2005, pp. 224–235.

been resolved under the arbitration clause of an investor-state contract. There have also been two investment disputes under the CAFTA-DR resulting in interim rulings on jurisdiction and related threshold issues.[11]

Two decided cases present threshold issues of the jurisdiction of the arbitral tribunal. Cases that reach the merits address the substantive obligations to provide national treatment (NAFTA Article 1102), to provide "treatment in accordance with [customary] international law, including fair and equitable treatment" (NAFTA Article 1105(1)), not to impose enumerated "performance requirements" (NAFTA Article 1106), and not to "expropriate an investment . . . or take a measure tantamount to . . . expropriation" without compensation (NAFTA Article 1110). One case considered the measure of damages for a denial of fair and equitable treatment. Two cases presented the issue of whether a state could interpose the affirmative defense that its measures constituted justified countermeasures. Two related cases considered, first, the interpretation of an investor-state contract and, second, the effect of the first arbitral award for purposes of collateral estoppel in a later investment treaty arbitration. These jurisdictional and substantive issues will be analyzed below, taking the respective issues seriatim.

Jurisdiction

Canadian Cattlemen for Fair Trade v. United States.[12] In *Canadian Cattlemen,* a group of Canadian cattle producers challenged a U.S. prohibition on importation of live cattle from Canada that was imposed because of an outbreak of "mad cow" disease (BSE). The U.S. government objected to the jurisdiction of the tribunal because the claimants did not own any business operations in the territory of United States and, instead, only owned investments located entirely in Canadian territory.

Despite the fundamental nature of this issue, the tribunal found that "the provisions of NAFTA Chapter Eleven [are] less clear and consistent than one might hope for in a treaty so long negotiated and so closely scrutinized and debated."[13] Under NAFTA article 1101, the scope of chapter 11 extends to measures of a Party relating to "(a) investors of another Party; (b) investments of investors of another Party in the territory of the Party; and (c) with respect to

---

[11] SCID, ARB/09/12, *Pac Rim Cayman LLC vs. El Salvador*, Decision on the Respondent's Preliminary Objections, 2nd August, 2010; ICSID, ARB/07/23, *Railroad Development Corp. vs. Guatemala*, Second Decision on Objections to Jurisdiction, 18th May, 2010; ISCID, ARB/07/23, *Railroad Development Corp. vs. Guatemala*, Decision on Objection to Jurisdiction, 17th November, 2008.

[12] NAFTA, *Canadian Cattlemen for Fair Trade vs. United States*, Award on Jurisdiction, 28th January, 2008.

[13] Id. & 110.

Articles 1106 [performance requirements] and 1114 [environmental measures], all investments in the territory of the Party."[14] The ambiguity, as the tribunal observed, is that clause (a) does not expressly limit the term "investors of another Party" to investors who own investments in the territory of the Party imposing the measure being challenged. To resolve the ambiguity, the tribunal turned to the definition of "investor of a Party," which defines investor as one that "seeks to make, is making or has made an investment."[15] The tribunal then read this definition in conjunction with clauses (b) and (c), which "explicitly limit Chapter Eleven's coverage to investments in the territory of the Party whose measure is at issue ...."[16] On this basis, the tribunal concluded that Chapter 11 is "applicable only to investors of one NAFTA Party who seek to make, are making, or have made, an investment in another NAFTA Party."[17] The tribunal lacked jurisdiction.

Canadian Cattlemen illustrates an unsuccessful attempt to shoehorn a trade dispute into the investment dispute procedures. While the tribunal's decision is undoubtedly correct, it appears to have been hasty in suggesting that the dispute could have been heard as a state-to-state claim under NAFTA chapter 20. The claimant's substantive argument was that the U.S. embargo on imports of cattle from Canada was irrational because cattle in the United States and Canada essentially comprise a single herd. As a practical matter, it seems unlikely that the Canadian government would be willing to espouse such a theory in a state-to-state dispute against the United States, since Canada would probably want to retain the power to impose a public health embargo against imports from the United States. Therefore, as a practical matter, it does not appear that NAFTA provides any forum for adjudicating the merits of the Canadian cattlemen's legal theory, whether or not it has any merit. Judicial review in U.S. courts would have been an option, although the chances of success seem limited.

Anderson v. Costa Rica.[18] *Anderson* arose under the bilateral investment treaty between Canada and Costa Rica. A group of Canadian individuals had deposited money in an enterprise in Costa Rica that held itself out as being engaged in foreign-exchange trading and other financial transactions. In fact, the enterprise was perpetrating a fraudulent Ponzi scheme of which the Canadian depositors were victims. The Costa Rican government ultimately intervened and closed the enterprise, but the Canadian depositors lost their money. The Canadians brought a claim against the Costa Rican government alleging that their losses "had been caused by various actions or omissions of the government of Costa Rica in violation of the Canada-Costa Rica BIT."[19]

---

[14] NAFTA, Art. 1101(1).

[15] NAFTA, Art. 1139.

[16] Canadian Cattlemen ¶ 126.

[17] Id. ¶ 127.

[18] ICSID, ARB(AF)/07/3, *Anderson vs. Costa Rica*, 19th May, 2010.

[19] Id. ¶ 28.

The bilateral investment treaty defined the term "investment" as "any kind of asset owned ... by an investor of one Contracting Party in the territory of the other Contracting Party *in accordance with the latter's laws*."[20] The tribunal noted that not all BITs contain an "in accordance with ... laws" provision and saw its presence in this BIT as "a clear indication of the importance that [the contracting parties] attached to the legality of investments made by investors of the other Party and their intention that their laws with respect to investments be strictly followed."[21] The relevance of this requirement was that the fraudulent enterprise was not operated in accordance with the laws of Costa Rica, since it was engaged in financial intermediation without any authorization from the Central Bank or other governmental regulatory body, as required by Costa Rican law. As a result, the tribunal held that the Canadian claimants' deposits did not meet the definitional requirement of being "assets ... owned ... in accordance with [Costa Rican] laws" and, therefore, dismissed the case for lack of jurisdiction.

According to the tribunal, the BIT promotes the fundamental policy interest of assuring respect for host-country law "by requiring investments under the BIT to be owned and controlled according to law."[22] Furthermore, "prudent investment practice requires that any investor exercise due diligence before committing funds to any particular investment proposal," but in this case "it is clear that the Claimants did not exercise the kind of due diligence that reasonable investors would have undertaken to assure themselves that their deposits in the ... scheme were in accordance with the laws of Costa Rica."[23]

This commentator feels that the tribunal's decision is unpersuasive. The Canadian investors had not violated Costa Rican law themselves. Their fundamental claim was that the Costa Rican government did not adequately enforce the regulatory laws that are supposed protect the public against financial frauds. The *Anderson* tribunal seems to be saying that victims of transnational Ponzi schemes, rather than having a right to adequate enforcement of such laws, need to exercise due diligence to assure themselves that they are not being defrauded. If the investors had done so, of course the dispute over the host government's allegedly inadequate enforcement would never have arisen. A better interpretation would have been that the jurisdictional limitation to investments in accordance with Costa Rican law was intended to bar claims in which the investor itself had violated the law.[24] The denial of jurisdiction suggests that the parties to the BIT intended that a dispute of the kind presented in *Anderson* should be resolved in a state-to-state claim outside the BIT.

---

[20] Id. ¶ 46 (quoting Canada-Costa Rica BIT, Art. I(g)) (italics added).

[21] & 53.

[22] Id. ¶ 58.

[23] Id.

[24] *Cf.* North Carolina, *Webb vs. Fulchire*, 25 N.C. (3 Ired.) 483 (1843) (ruling, in the context of enforceability of an illegal contract, that "the artless fool, who seems to have been alike bereft of his senses and his money, is not to be deemed a partaker in the same crime, in pari delicto, with the juggling knave, who gulled and fleeced him.").

This conclusion seems unlikely, in this commentator's view. It seems more likely that disputes relating to injuries resulting from allegedly inadequate enforcement of the host government's financial regulatory laws should be heard under the investor-state procedures.[25]

National Treatment

Archer Daniels Midland Co. v. Mexico and Corn Products International, Inc. v. Mexico.[26] Archer Daniels Midland (hereinafter ADM) and Corn Products International (hereinafter CPI) are twin cases relating to a Mexican tax on soft drinks sweetened with high fructose corn syrup. The tax imposed a significantly higher excise tax on soft drinks sweetened with high fructose corn syrup than on soft drinks sweetened with sugar. Mexico enacted the tax in the aftermath of an economic crisis in its sugar industry. The economic crisis, in turn, resulted largely if not entirely from U.S. restrictions on imports of sugar from Mexico, which Mexico contended were themselves in violation of NAFTA.

The issue in the *ADM* and *CPI* cases was the lawfulness of Mexico's tax, and the tribunals in both cases found that it violated the national treatment obligation in NAFTA.[27] Under this provision, "[e]ach Party shall accord to investors of another Party treatment no less favorable than it accords, *in like circumstances*, to investments of its own investors with respect to the ... operation ... of investments."[28] Both tribunals held that U.S.-owned subsidiaries in Mexico that blended and sold U.S.-origin high fructose corn syrup were "in like circumstances" to Mexican-owned enterprises that produced and sold sugar. The tribunals explained that the issue was not strictly speaking whether high fructose corn syrup and sugar were "like products." But high fructose corn syrup and sugar were perfect substitutes for each other as the sweetener in soft drinks, and a WTO case had already held that high fructose corn syrup and sugar were "like products" under GATT article III(2).[29] Therefore, the NAFTA tribunals held that

---

[25] Whether the investors would prevail on the merits is another question. There is authority for finding host state liability under international law for egregiously inadequate enforcement of criminal laws. *Janes (USA) vs. Mexico*, Rep. Int'l Arb. Awards 4 (1926), p. 82.

[26] NAFTA/ICSID, No. ARB(AF)/04/05, *Archer Daniels Midland Co. vs. Mexico*, Award, 21st November, 2007; NAFTA/ICSID, ARB(AF)/04/01, *Corn Products International, Inc. vs. Mexico*, Decision on Responsibility, 15th January, 2008. In addition to these two cases, a third NAFTA case, *Cargill Inc. vs. Mexico* (filed 2005, apparently decided in 2009), challenged the same Mexican taxes, but the Award and all papers in the case after the notice of intent to arbitrate are confidential.

[27] *ADM vs. Mexico*, ¶¶ 193–213; *CPI vs. Mexico*, ¶¶ 109–143.

[28] NAFTA, Art. 1102(2) (italics added).

[29] Report of the Panel, Mexico – Tax Measures on Soft Drinks and Other Beverages, WT/DS308/R, 7th October, 2005, *aff'd*, AB-2005-10, WT/DS308/R/AB, 6th March, 2006) (cited in ADM v. Mexico, ¶ 212, and CPI v. Mexico, ¶¶ 121–122).

the firms producing the respective like products were "in like circumstances" within the meaning of NAFTA article 1102. And since the tax on the soft drinks sweetened with high fructose corn syrup was significantly higher than that on soft drinks sweetened with sugar, Mexico had treated the U.S.-owned firms producing high fructose corn syrup less favorably than the Mexican-owned firms producing sugar, in violation of NAFTA article 1102.[30]

Fair and Equitable Treatment

The Debate Over The Legal Standard. A continuing controversy surrounds the legal standard for determining whether a host country government has given an investment "fair and equitable treatment." The three NAFTA parties adopted an interpretation in 2001 under which fair and equitable treatment means "the customary international law minimum standard of treatment of aliens" and does not require treatment in addition to or beyond that minimum standard.[31] Therefore, the controversy focuses on what the minimum standard of treatment of aliens in customary international law is.

One position is that the standard remains essentially as stated in the 1926 international arbitral decision in *Neer v. Mexico*,[32] in which the tribunal ruled that a host state violates international law when "the treatment of an alien ... amount[s] to an outrage, to bad faith, to wilful neglect of duty, or an insufficiency of governmental action so far short of international standards that every reasonable and impartial man would readily recognize its insufficiency."[33] A contemporaneous decision of the same tribunal, *Chattin v. Mexico*,[34] restated the "insufficiency of governmental action" branch of the *Neer* standard as "insufficiency of action apparent to any unbiased man" or "manifestly inadequate government action."[35]

---

[30] In another national treatment claim, the NAFTA tribunal in *Merrill & Ring Forestry LP vs. Canada*, 30th March, 2010) held that timber companies operating on Canadian federal land in British Columbia were not "in like circumstances" to timber companies operating on provincial land. Although the federal regulatory regime was allegedly more onerous than the corresponding provincial regime, there was no violation of national treatment because all timber companies operating on federal land were treated equally. The decision properly reflects that, in federal systems such as those found in all three NAFTA parties, national treatment does not require federal measures to be consistent with state or provincial measures on the same subject.

[31] The 2001 interpretation is quoted in, e.g., NAFTA, *Chemtura Corp. vs. Canada*, Award, 2nd August, 2010, ¶ 118.

[32] 4 Rep. Int'l Arb. Awards 4 (1926), p. 60.

[33] Id., p. 61–62.

[34] 4 Rep. Int'l Arb. Awards (1927), p. 282.

[35] Id., pp. 287–288 (ruling that the host state had violated international law where a criminal defendant was not fully informed of the charges against him, the proceeding was unduly delayed, and the hearings in open court lasted only five minutes and were conducted with a lack of seriousness).

The *Neer* and *Chattin* standards appear to be similar to the concept of "arbitrariness" that International Court of Justice described in the 1989 *ELSI* case as "a wilful disregard of due process of law, an act which shocks, or at least surprises, a sense of judicial propriety."[36]

The alternative to the *Neer* standard is a higher, more probing, and more detailed level of scrutiny by the arbitral tribunal over the government action, going beyond merely assessing whether the action was an outrage, bad faith, wilful neglect, or manifestly inadequate.[37] In support of this alternative higher standard, it is urged that customary international law inevitably must have evolved since the 1920s and that the numerous bilateral investment treaties setting out a "fair and equitable treatment" obligation reflect the contemporary standard of customary international law.

Chemtura Corp. v. Canada.[38] In *Chemtura*, the investor was a pesticide manufacturer that challenged the decision of the responsible Canadian federal regulatory agency to terminate the registration, and thereby ban the continued use or sale, of a pesticide known as lindane. It was not disputed that the Canadian agency had the legal authority to terminate a pesticide registration or that lindane, which had been in use since the 1930s, was increasingly considered to create health and environmental risks under contemporary regulatory standards.

The manufacturer claimed that the process leading to termination of the registration denied it fair and equitable treatment. The *Chemtura* tribunal did not articulate any applicable legal standard for fair and equitable treatment of aliens under customary international law. Instead, it said that "the assessment of the facts is an integral part of [the tribunal's] review" and that application of the legal standard "must be conducted in concreto."[39]

In substance, the tribunal decided that the legal standard was immaterial because the factual evidence did not substantiate the investor's claim of a lack of fair and equitable treatment under any standard. The investor's principal claims were that the agency's decision to review lindane's registration was made in bad faith, that its review process was scientifically and procedurally flawed, and that the decision to terminate the registration had been a foregone conclusion when the review began. After receiving testimony from agency officials and reviewing the documentary record, the tribunal ruled that "the evidence . . . does not establish that [the agency] acted in bad faith or in breach of due process standards."[40] The tribunal also

---

[36] ICJ Case, *Elettronica Sicula S.p.A. (ELSI) (United States vs. Italy)*, 1989, p. 76 (¶ 128).

[37] In one case, for example, the investor argued that the standard of customary international law includes good faith, fairness, transparency, protection against arbitrariness and abuse of rights, protection of legitimate expectations, and a secure legal environment. NAFTA, *Merrill & Ring Forestry LP vs. Canada*, Claimant's Memorial, 13th February, 2008.

[38] NAFTA, *Chemtura Corp. vs. Canada*, Award, 2nd August, 2010.

[39] Id. & 123.

[40] Id. & 162.

considered additional claims by the investor of lack of fair and equitable treatment, but likewise found that they were unproved.[41]

Glamis Gold Ltd. v. United States.[42] The dispute in *Glamis Gold* arose from U.S. federal and California state measures affecting a proposed gold mine that the Canadian investor, Glamis, planned to construct on federal public land in southeastern California. The project was located in an area subject to a complex regulatory landscape under federal and California laws, including federal mining, land management, and environmental protection legislation, and state mining and environmental protection legislation. In addition, the area held religious, cultural, and historical significance to a Native American tribe, making it subject to federal and state legislation on historic preservation and protection of Native American culture.

Glamis submitted its proposed plan of operation for the mine to the U.S. Interior Department in December 1994, with revisions in 1996 and 1997. The Interior Department, in the closing days of the Clinton Administration, denied the plan of operations in January 2001, based largely on an Interior Department legal opinion issued in 1999. Then, in October 2002, the Bush Administration Interior Department rescinded the denial and reopened the review. Meanwhile, in late 2002 and early 2003, California adopted new state legislation and regulations that would require a reclamation technique known as complete backfilling, or filling in a mine pit, at the end of the expected duration of the project.

The investor claimed that the federal and state measures denied it fair and equitable treatment under NAFTA article 1105. The tribunal undertook a lengthy examination of the applicable standard of law. After reviewing pertinent authorities, it concluded that customary international law on fair and equitable treatment remains fundamentally the same as the 1926 *Neer* standard. The tribunal summarized this standard as establishing that "a violation of the customary international law minimum standard of treatment ... requires an act that is sufficiently egregious and shocking ... as to fall below accepted international standards ...."[43] The "egregious and shocking" act could be "a gross denial of justice, manifest arbitrariness, blatant unfairness, a complete lack of due process, evident discrimination, or a manifest lack of reasons ...."[44] The tribunal said that although customary international law had undoubtedly evolved since the 1920s, the

---

[41] In addition to the fair and equitable treatment claim in *Chemtura*, the investor claimed that Canada violated the most-favored-nation treatment clause in NAFTA article 1102. The theory was that Canada was also a party to sixteen bilateral investment treaties whose fair and equitable treatment clauses were more favorable to non-NAFTA investors, since the clauses were not subject to the 2001 NAFTA interpretive note. The tribunal rejected this argument, finding "no facts ... that would even come close to ... a breach of the [fair and equitable treatment] standard" and no evidence that Canada's conduct "was in breach of such hypothetical additional measure of protection allegedly afforded by an imported [fair and equitable treatment] clause." Id. & 236.

[42] NAFTA, *Glamis Gold Ltd. vs. United States*, Award, 8th June, 2009.

[43] Id. ¶¶ 22 & 616.

[44] Id. ¶¶ 22 & 616.

evolution was limited to a change in what procedural failures would be considered egregious and shocking.

The tribunal found that the U.S. and California measures did not constitute a denial of fair and equitable treatment under this standard. The action raising the most difficult question was the 1999 legal opinion by the Interior Department and the 2001 denial based on it. The tribunal acknowledged that the legal opinion "represented a significant change from settled practice"[45] – "a decades-old rule and century old regime upon which Claimant had based reasonable expectations."[46] At the same time, it "was a reasoned, complicated legal opinion on an issue of first impression," in that no previous mining project had been "'found to have a significant, unavoidable adverse impact to cultural resources and Native American sacred sites.'"[47]

The issue, the tribunal said, was "whether a lengthy, reasoned legal opinion violates customary international law because it changes, in an arguably dramatic way, a previous law or prior legal interpretation upon which an investor has based its reasonable, investment-related expectations."[48] The tribunal said no. The Interior Department opinion was not arbitrary since it was a legal opinion prepared by the legal office of the responsible agency; it did not exhibit a manifest lack of reasons and instead set out the factual and legal analysis on which it was based; and it did not exhibit blatant unfairness to the investor or discriminate against this particular investor, since it was an opinion of general applicability. Further, the opinion did not upset the investor's reasonable expectation because "the federal government did not make any specific commitments to induce Claimant to persevere with its mining claims" and "did not guarantee Claimant approval of its claims [or] offer Claimant any benefits to pursuing such claims ...."[49] Finally, the legal opinion did not show a complete lack of due process even though it was arguable that, as a matter of U.S. administrative law, the Interior Department should have initiated a formal proceeding to amend its regulations and promulgate the revised standard. The tribunal ruled that any procedural shortcoming was rectified by the 2002 decision to rescind the denial, leading the tribunal to conclude that "domestic channels" afforded "a process that does not evidence 'a complete lack of due process.'"[50]

The tribunal also rejected the argument that the government denied fair and equitable treatment because consideration of the project was unreasonably delayed. It ruled that even though "the review efforts were perhaps somewhat more

---

[45] Id. ¶ 759.

[46] Id. ¶ 761.

[47] Id. ¶ 760 (quoting U.S. Counter-Memorial).

[48] Id. ¶ 761.

[49] Id. ¶ 767.

[50] Id. ¶ 771.

protracted than is customary," nevertheless "this was a particularly complicated, contested issue in which numerous parties took an interest."[51]

Merrill & Ring Forestry LP v. Canada.[52] In *Merrill*, a U.S.-owned timber company operating in British Columbia challenged measures adopted under the Canadian regulatory program for log exports. Under that program, if a potential log exporter wishes to export unprocessed logs from British Columbia, British Columbian log processors have an opportunity, or right of first refusal, to buy the logs at "fair market value." If a British Columbian log processor offers to buy the logs at fair market value, the program administrator denies an export permit for the logs. The program administrator has the authority to determine whether an offer is at fair market value or not. In this determination, the administrator invariably follows the recommendations of a group called the Federal Timber Export Advisory Committee, which is composed of members of the British Columbian timber industry plus one Canadian government official. This Committee's policy is that "fair market value" can be as much as 5% below the current domestic market price and does not take the price in export markets into consideration at all.

Like the *Glamis Gold* tribunal, the *Merrill* tribunal discussed at length the legal standard for assessing fair and equitable treatment. The tribunal said that *Neer* and similar cases in the 1920s "dealt with due process [and] may be described as the first track of the evolution of the so-called minimum standard of justice," a track that "became a part of the international law of human rights, applicable to aliens and nationals alike."[53] In international human rights law, the tribunal said, the concept of an international minimum standard of treatment was outmoded and that "what mattered now was 'fair treatment' to nationals and foreigners alike."[54] At the same time, state practice was "seen as being inconsistent with the ... concept of an 'international minimum standard,'" and showed "even less support of the standard referred to in the *Neer* case."[55] The Tribunal concluded that "[n]o general rule of customary international law can be found which applies the *Neer* standard, beyond the strict confines of personal safety, denial of justice and due process."[56]

The tribunal then identified what it called "a second track [of customary international law] concerned specifically with the treatment of aliens in relation to business, trade and investments."[57] On this track, the tribunal found a "much more liberal" standard under which states espoused their citizens' international claims of economic injury "with an open mind, and without requiring a showing of

---

[51] Id. ¶ 774.

[52] NAFTA, *Merrill & Ring Forestry LP vs. Canada*, Award, 31st March, 2010.

[53] Id. ¶ 201.

[54] Id. ¶ 202.

[55] Id. ¶ 204.

[56] Id.

[57] Id. ¶ 205

'outrageous' treatment before doing so."[58] The tribunal found that "[s]tate practice with respect to ... the treatment of aliens in relation to business, trade and investment ... has generally endorsed an open and non-restricted approach to the applicable standard to the treatment of aliens under international law."[59]

Based on this analysis, the tribunal said that "the outcome of this changing reality" is a "requirement that aliens be treated fairly and equitably in relation to business, trade and investment" and establishes a standard that "protects against all ... acts or behavior that might infringe a sense of fairness, equity or reasonableness."[60] As a result, according to the tribunal, "today's minimum standard is broader than that defined in the *Neer* case" and requires "fair and equitable treatment of alien investors within the confines of reasonableness."[61] In effect, the tribunal seems to be saying that NAFTA's reference to "international law including fair and equitable treatment" reflects that customary international law requires the treatment of alien investors to be fair and equitable, as opposed to not being manifestly inadequate.

In applying its legal standard to the facts, the tribunal posited "two different scenarios" for evaluating the reasonableness of the challenged Canadian measures. Under the "first scenario," the "threshold ... is a comparatively low one ...."[62] In contrast, "[t]he second scenario ... is based on the view that ... a state's wrongful conduct or behavior must be sufficiently serious as to be readily distinguishable from an ordinary effect of otherwise acceptable regulatory measures."[63] The tribunal said that several aspects of the log export regime might be considered unreasonable under the "first scenario." In particular, it was "facially troubling" that the Advisory Committee charged with making the invariably adopted recommendations about fair market value was "heavily weighted in favor of the local industry that is the beneficiary of the regulation."[64] In contrast, under the so-called "second scenario" of reasonableness, the tribunal noted that six of seven industry representatives who seemed potentially biased were actually probably not biased, the committee followed conflict-of-interest rules to exclude members who had business relationships with a processor making an offer, and the committee appeared to follow a transparent process for monitoring actual market prices. Thus, the tribunal felt that the committee probably was not "operated in a sufficiently non-transparent, arbitrary and unfair manner such that it ... contravenes the ... minimum standard ... under the second scenario."[65]

---

[58] Id.

[59] Id. ¶ 209.

[60] Id. ¶ 210.

[61] Id. ¶ 213.

[62] Id. ¶ 219.

[63] Id.

[64] Id. ¶ 227.

[65] Id. ¶ 239.

Ultimately, the tribunal reached the surprising decision that it was unnecessary to choose between the "first scenario" and the "second scenario" and decide whether or not the Canadian measure violated the "fair and equitable treatment" obligation. This was because, in the tribunal's view, the investor had failed to prove its monetary damages. A later section of this chapter will discuss the tribunal's reasoning on damages.

Commentary on the Three Decisions. In *Chemtura,* the investor apparently had a weak case for lack of fair and equitable treatment, and the tribunal's decision appears to be sound. As a result, however, the decision contributes little to advancing the understanding of fair and equitable treatment.

The *Glamis Gold* and *Merrill* tribunals adopted entirely different interpretations of "fair and equitable treatment." In this commentator's view, *Glamis Gold* is much more persuasive. *Glamis Gold* focused carefully on identifying a legal standard that the three NAFTA states accepted as customary international law, and it found that the United States, Canada, and Mexico all had endorsed the *Neer* standard. *Merrill* did make a valid observation that the *Neer* standard appears to have lain dormant from the 1920s until the 1990s, when interest in "fair and equitable treatment" clauses of BITs developed. It is also apparently correct that the *Neer* standard was never applied to economic injuries. But the reference in *Merrill* to an "open and non-restricted" approach to international economic claims appears to refer to the wide variety of interests that were the subject of expropriation claims. These cases do not offer clear guidance on the standard applicable to non-expropriation claims. Nor do they support the *Merrill* tribunal's "reasonableness" standard, which the tribunal appears to have created from thin air. In fact, the tribunal's inability to choose between the "two scenarios" for assessing reasonableness seems to underscore that "reasonableness" is not an established legal standard.[66]

Ultimately, the shortcoming in *Merrill* is that "reasonableness" is, in oversimplified terms, the same standard of judicial review that domestic courts apply in adjudicating the lawfulness of agency actions, at least in the United States.[67] There is no indication in NAFTA chapter 11 that the three state parties intended investor-state arbitration to serve as a substitute for judicial review of administrative decisions in domestic courts. On the contrary, as Professor Sornarajah observed even before *Glamis Gold* and *Merrill* were decided, the

---

[66] Cf. Sornarajah, *The International Law on Foreign Investment,* (2nd ed.) 2004, p. 339 ("Despite brave assertions that the law on the subject of state responsibility has evolved, there has been little demonstration as to ... what the content of the law is. ... [T]he extent of protection [BITs] create is a matter of uncertainty because of the paucity of jurisprudence and the difficulty of identifying the content of these standards.").

[67] E.g., Davis, *Administrative Law Treatise, Vol. 5,* (2nd ed.) 1985, p. 332; Strauss, *Administrative Justice in the United States,* (2nd ed.) 2002, pp. 335–336; see generally id., pp. 335–386 (scope of judicial review in U.S. administrative law).

NAFTA states' decision to adopt the 2001 interpretive note on fair and equitable treatment teaches that "states will not permit intrusive supervision of their regulatory mechanisms by international tribunals on the pretext of inquiring into the fairness of the use of regulation," except where "there is such a gross violation of procedural norms that shocks the sense of justice."[68] According to *Chattin v. Mexico*, the 1927 companion to *Neer*, the *Neer* standard reflects that "it is a matter of the greatest political and international delicacy for one country to disacknowledge the judicial decision of a court of another country."[69] By analogy, the same "political and international delicacy" applies to an international tribunal's scrutiny of a country's administrative adjudications.

Performance Requirements

Merrill & Ring Forestry LP v. Canada.[70] The investor in *Merrill* claimed that the Canadian regulatory regime constituted an illegal performance requirement under NAFTA article 1106. As noted above, the regime required a particular economic performance by giving local timber processors a right of first refusal on the timber being offered for export, thereby restricting the investor's ability to export. But the tribunal denied the claim. It ruled that the specific kinds of performance requirements prohibited in NAFTA do not include the Canadian measure in issue. The Canadian measure requiring *sale* to a domestic customer exercising the right of first refusal was not, for example, a requirement "to export a given level or percentage of goods," "to achieve a given level or percentage of domestic content," "to *purchase* ... goods produced or services provided in its territory, or to *purchase* goods or services from persons in its territory," or "to *restrict* sales of goods ... in its territory ...."[71]

The tribunal was correct that the Canadian log regime does not establish any illegal performance requirement under the particular definition set out in NAFTA article 1106. Still, the investor was undoubtedly correct that it distorts the free market and could be considered a performance requirement in a more generic sense. In fact, the Canadian regime appears to violate GATT article XI as a "restriction[] ... maintained ... on ... the sale for exportation of [a] product destined for the territory of any other contracting party."[72] It also appears to violate the WTO

---

[68] Sornarajah, *The International Law on Foreign Investment*, (2nd ed.) 2004, p. 339.

[69] *Chattin vs. Mexico*, 4 Rep. Int'l Arb. Awards (1927), pp. 282, 288 (citation omitted).

[70] NAFTA, *Merrill & Ring Forestry LP vs. Canada*, Award, 31st March, 2010.

[71] NAFTA, Art. 1106(1)(a), (b), (c) & (e).

[72] GATT, Art. XI(1).

agreement on trade-related investment measures as measures that restrict "the exportation or sale for export by an enterprise of products, ... specified ... in terms of ... value of products."[73] But since NAFTA chapter 11 does not incorporate WTO standards, a NAFTA investor-state arbitration lacks jurisdiction to address a WTO violation.

ADM v. Mexico and CPI v. Mexico.[74] In the twin cases relating to the discriminatory Mexican taxes on soft drinks, both investors claimed that the Mexican tax constituted an illegal performance requirement. In *CPI*, however, the investor failed to elaborate the claim after stating it in its notice of arbitration, and therefore the tribunal dismissed the claim. In *ADM*, in contrast, the investor specified and the tribunal accepted an argument that the parties and the tribunal in *CPI* overlooked entirely. The illegal performance requirement consisted in giving Mexican soft drink producers a tax incentive to purchase sugar, all of which was domestically produced, instead of high fructose corn syrup, all of which was imported. As a result, the Mexican tax on its face was inconsistent with NAFTA article 1106(3) by requiring the Mexican soft drink producers "to achieve a given ... percentage of domestic content" (namely, 100% of the sweetener) and a "preference to goods produced in [Mexican] territory" (namely, Mexican sugar).[75] Even though this performance requirement was imposed on the Mexican soft drink producers instead of the U.S. investor (ADM's Mexican subsidiary), the tribunal interpreted the NAFTA prohibition to extend to performance requirements imposed on Mexican companies operating in Mexico. This was because, under article 1101(1)(c), NAFTA chapter 11 applies to host country measures "relating to ... with respect to Article 1106 and 1114, *all* investments in the territory of the Party," not simply those of another NAFTA party. The tribunal concluded that "all investments" included investments by Mexican companies in Mexico.

In this commentator's view, however, the *ADM* decision is questionable. The tribunal's analysis was correct up to the point that it ruled that article 1101(1)(c), which governs the scope of chapter 11, does by its terms cover investments by Mexican investors in Mexico. But the tribunal overlooked that article 1106(3) is limited to performance requirements "in connection with an investment in its territory of an investor of a Party or of a non-Party."[76] This language suggests that NAFTA prohibits performance requirements imposed on foreign investors, whether from NAFTA parties or elsewhere, but not on domestic investors in the home country.

---

[73] WTO Agreement on Trade-Related Investment Measures, Annex ¶ 2(c).

[74] NAFTA/ICSID, No. ARB(AF)/04/05, *Archer Daniels Midland Co. vs. Mexico*, Award, 21st November, 2007; NAFTA/ICSID, ARB(AF)/04/01, *Corn Products International, Inc. vs. Mexico*, Decision on Responsibility, 15th January, 2008.

[75] NAFTA, Art. 1106(3)(a) & (b).

[76] NAFTA, Art. 1106(3).

Expropriation and Measures Tantamount to Expropriation

Glamis Gold v. United States.[77] In *Glamis Gold*, the investor claimed that the Interior Department's denial of the plan of operation for the mining project and the California measures requiring complete backfilling of the exhausted mine pits both were measures tantamount to expropriation of an investment within the meaning of NAFTA article 1110. As a threshold matter, it was undisputed that the "investment" in issue was the proposed mining project in California. Under applicable U.S. mining law, the investor unquestionably possessed a legally protected property interest in the mining claim.

Having identified the investment in issue, the tribunal stated that the legal standard for determining whether a measure is tantamount to an expropriation "often ... involves two questions: the severity of the economic impact and the duration of that impact."[78] The legal standard was also said to involve whether the property was "impaired to such an extent that it must be seen as being 'taken,'" or whether "the Claimant was radically deprived of the economical use and enjoyment of its investments, as if the rights related thereto ... ceased to exist."[79] The tribunal then rejected, first, the investor's claim that the Interior Department's denial of the plan of operations was tantamount to an expropriation. The reason was that the denial "was quickly reversed and therefore of short duration."[80] Next, the tribunal considered the California legislation and regulations. The investor asserted that the project originally had a value of approximately \$49 million, but a value of negative \$8.9 million after the adoption of the backfilling measures. The tribunal reviewed the investor's values and supporting methodology in detail, but ultimately disagreed with the calculation in a number of details. Even after giving Glamis the benefit of the doubt on disputed calculations, the tribunal found that the value of the project was unquestionably positive. Therefore, the tribunal "conclude[d] that the California backfilling measures did not result in a radical diminution in the value of the Imperial Project."[81]

Merrill & Ring Forestry LP v. Canada.[82] In the "tantamount to expropriation" claim in *Merrill*, the investor argued that the expropriated investment consisted in its intangible "interest in realizing the fair market value for its logs on the international market."[83] The tribunal ruled that "the right to access the international market is a fundamental aspect of the [investor's] log export business" that would

---

[77] NAFTA, *Glamis Gold Ltd. vs. United States*, Award, 8th June, 2009.

[78] Id. ¶ 356.

[79] Id. ¶ 357 (citations omitted).

[80] Id. & 360. It was implicit that denial of the plan of operation would have been an expropriation if it had not been reversed.

[81] Id. & 366.

[82] NAFTA, *Merrill & Ring Forestry LP vs. Canada*, Award, 31st March, 2010.

[83] Id. ¶ 140.

qualify for protection under NAFTA if it were "impeded or prohibited."[84] In contrast, however, "the protection against expropriation does not, and cannot, guarantee [that] exports will be made at a certain price."[85] Moreover, "no argument has been made about the company operating at a loss as a consequence of government measures."[86] Accordingly, the tribunal ruled that administration of the Canadian log export regime did not constitute a measure tantamount to an expropriation.

Chemtura Corporation v. Canada.[87] In *Chemtura*, the parties agreed that for a measure to be tantamount to an expropriation, "the measure must amount to a substantial deprivation of the Claimant's investment."[88] The parties agreed further that the allegedly expropriated investment was the entire Canadian company. In other words, the investment was not the company's ability to continue to manufacture and sell the pesticide in issue. This was because the Canadian government had the power under the applicable regulatory laws to cancel the product's registration. Defining the investment as the company as a whole instead of the single prohibited product was fatal to the investor's claim. The tribunal found that "the sales from lindane products were a relatively small part of the overall sales of Chemtura Canada at all times" and that the company "remained operational and its yearly sales, although reduced in [the year lindane was banned], continued in a ascending trend [in the following years]."[89] Therefore, the measure prohibiting lindane did not amount to a "substantial deprivation" of the investment in the company.

AbitibiBowater Inc. v. Canada. In *AbitibiBowater*, the investor challenged legislation enacted by the provincial government of Newfoundland and Labrador that expropriated the investor's pulp and paper mills and related assets in the province. But the dispute did not even proceed to arbitration. Instead, after the investor filed a notice of intent to arbitrate in April 2009, the parties reached a negotiated settlement in August 2010. Under the settlement, the Canadian government paid the investor an amount that the government itself said "represents the fair market value of the company's expropriated assets."[90]

Commentary on the Four Expropriation Cases. AbitibiBower is apparently the first instance under NAFTA of a direct expropriation of an investment, as opposed to a measure tantamount to expropriation. The outcome is instructive. It suggests that the legal standards on expropriations in NAFTA article 1110 are so clear and well established that the parties were able to reach a negotiated settlement without the need for arbitration. The decisions on measures tantamount to expropriation in *Glamis Gold, Merrill,* and *Chemtura* are all eminently sound, in this commentator's

---

[84] Id. ¶ 143.

[85] Id. ¶ 144.

[86] Id. ¶ 148.

[87] NAFTA, *Chemtura Corp. vs. Canada*, Award, 2nd August, 2010.

[88] Id. ¶ 242.

[89] Id. ¶¶ 263–264.

[90] News Release, Foreign Affairs and International Trade Canada, Statement on AbitibiBowater Settlement, 24th August, 2010).

view. The decisions plainly avoid finding that a measure causing a decrease in profits could be tantamount to expropriation.

Countermeasures as a Defense

The two related cases of Mexico's tax on beverages containing high fructose corn syrup, *CPI* and *ADM*,[91] presented the issue of whether the tax constituted a justifiable countermeasure under international law. In support of its countermeasures defense, Mexico alleged that the United States had violated the provisions of NAFTA governing the staged reduction of U.S. duties on sugar imported from Mexico, triggering an economic crisis in the Mexican sugar industry. In addition, Mexico alleged that the United States had stymied Mexico's attempt to initiate state-to-state dispute resolution procedures under NAFTA chapter 20. Mexico claimed that, under the circumstances, it had enacted the discriminatory tax on soft drinks sweetened with high fructose corn syrup as a justified counter-measure in retaliation against the alleged U.S. violation.

In *CPI v. Mexico*, the tribunal dismissed Mexico's defense on the ground that one of the requirements in international law for a valid countermeasure is that is must be "directed against the State which has committed the alleged prior wrongful act,"[92] namely, in this case, the United States. The discriminatory tax affecting U.S. investors did not meet this requirement, the tribunal ruled. On the contrary, it ruled categorically that "the doctrine of countermeasures ... is not applicable to claims under Chapter XI of the NAFTA" because "[t]hose claims are brought by investors, not by States," since "[a] central purpose of Chapter XI ... was to remove such claims from the inter-State plane and to assure that investors could assert rights directly against a host State."[93] This conclusion, said the tribunal, was based on the language of chapter XI that "confer[s] substantive rights directly upon investors."[94] Therefore, "an investor which brings a claim is seeking to enforce what it asserts are its own rights under the treaty and not exercising a power to enforce rights which are actually those of the State."[95]

In *ADM v. Mexico*, the tribunal also dismissed Mexico's countermeasures defense. But before considering whether NAFTA chapter 11 creates independent rights for investors, the tribunal ruled that the defense failed because Mexico "has neither proved that the Tax was enacted in response to the alleged U.S. breaches nor that the measure was intended to induce compliance by the United States with its

---

[91] NAFTA/ICSID, No. ARB(AF)/04/05, *Archer Daniels Midland Co. vs. Mexico*, Award, 21st November, 2007; NAFTA/ICSID, ARB(AF)/04/01, *Corn Products International, Inc. vs. Mexico*, Decision on Responsibility, 15th January, 2008.

[92] *CPI vs. Mexico*, ¶ 163.

[93] Id. ¶ 161.

[94] Id. ¶ 169.

[95] Id. ¶ 174.

NAFTA obligations."[96] Based on the debate in the Mexican legislature, the tribunal found that the tax on soft drinks sweetened with high fructose corn syrup was simply intended to help the Mexican sugar industry in the economic crisis triggered by the alleged U.S. violations of NAFTA. On the issue of individual rights for investors, the majority of the tribunal ruled that "Chapter Eleven sets forth substantive obligations which remain inter-State, without accruing individual rights for [investors]."[97] The majority concluded that NAFTA Chapter 11 "does not provide individual substantive rights for investors"[98] because the substantive obligations regarding investments are set out in Section A of chapter 11 and "remain interstate,"[99] whereas Section B of chapter 11 governing investor-state arbitration is only "a procedural right to trigger arbitration against the Host state."[100] The third member of the tribunal filed a concurring opinion in which he concluded that chapter 11 does create substantive rights for investors.

The tribunals' respective analyses of the countermeasures defense represent another example in which NAFTA tribunals adopt inconsistent reasoning. In this commentator's view, the position of the *CPI* panel and the concurring arbitrator in *ADM* is more persuasive.

Measure of Damages for Violation of Fair and Equitable Treatment

As noted above, the tribunal in *Merrill & Ring Forestry v. Canada* denied the investor's claim without deciding whether Canada violated the fair and equitable treatment standard. This was because "damages have not been proven to the satisfaction of the Tribunal."[101]

Merrill urged that its damages were equal to its lost "export premiums," that is, the higher prices exporters would receive if they could sell their logs in export markets instead of the domestic British Columbian market. For past sales, Merrill calculated the export premiums based on actual past sales and on the actual prices obtained in export and local sales. It estimated future losses by projecting the past losses into the future, taking into account the company's projected future harvest plan. And it also claimed damages based on its increased costs of operating under the Canadian log export regime.

The tribunal's fundamental concern about past damages was "whether, in the absence of affected contractual rights, it is possible to identify an intangible interest which could be affected by the measures complained of."[102] Since Merrill had not

---

[96] *ADM vs. Mexico*, ¶ 151.

[97] Id. ¶ 168.

[98] Id. ¶ 171.

[99] Id. ¶ 173.

[100] Id.

[101] NAFTA, *Merrill & Ring Forestry LP v. Canada*, Award, 31st March, 2010, & 266.

[102] Id. ¶ 257.

entered into any contracts for the export of logs, damages could not be based on the difference between the contract price and the lower price at which the exporter was compelled to sell the logs. Instead, the tribunal characterized Merrill's intangible interest as "an uncertain expectation" of earning profits that "does not appear to provide a solid enough ground on which to construct a legitimately affected interest."[103] A further problem was that, if the Canadian regulatory regime did not exist, prices in a hypothetical free market would be different from those in the regulated market as it existed. Export prices would be expected to fall and the local prices would be expected to rise, thereby decreasing the export premium, and therefore the tribunal felt that it "cannot conclude with any certainty that the Investor would have achieved any 'export premiums' for past sales."[104]

As for future sales, the tribunal found that future damages would be even more uncertain than the past and "will be characterized more by speculation than by educated guesses,"[105] thereby precluding recovery. Finally, the tribunal disallowed Merrill's claim for its increased cost of operating under the regime because there is "a cost of compliance ... [in] every regulatory regime" and "[c]ompensation for such costs ... is not possible."[106]

In this commentator's view, the *Merrill* tribunal's analysis of past damages was erroneous. The investor had the legally protected right to receive fair and equitable treatment in government measures affecting its investment. The damage analysis should have started from the assumption that the Canadian measure violated this obligation. Rather than being an uncertain expectation of profits, the injury was that the investor's access to the international market was distorted because unfair and inequitable government measures diverted potential sales into the local market at a reduced price. As stated in the section of the award on the expropriation claim, the log export regime impaired Merrill's "interest in realizing the fair market value for its logs on the international market."[107] This loss is analogous to impairment of market access in WTO cases, where there are abundant decisions quantifying the nullification or impairment in situations that are surely as uncertain as Merrill's lost export premiums.[108] Viewed in this light, Merrill's methodology for calculating its lost export premiums in past sales appears to be reasonable.[109]

---

[103] Id. ¶ 258.

[104] Id. ¶ 262.

[105] Id. ¶ 264.

[106] Id. ¶ 265.

[107] Id. ¶ 140.

[108] E.g., Recourse to Arbitration by the United States Under Article 22.6 of the DSU, United States – Measures Affecting the Cross-border Supply of Gambling and Betting Services, WT/DS285/ARB, 21st December, 2007 (calculating Antigua's lost revenue from internet gambling on horseracing in the United States as $21 million).

[109] This commentator also finds puzzling the *Merrill* tribunal's statement that since past damages were limited to the three-year limitations period for NAFTA chapter 11 claims, the short time period made the investor's damages more uncertain. In this commentator's view, a short period of lost market access should make the proof of damages easier.

The tribunal's decision does, nevertheless, perhaps illustrate a fundamental conceptual flaw in bilateral investment treaties of using monetary damages as the chosen remedy.[110] While monetary damages are suitable for expropriations, they can be much harder to apply to non-expropriation claims. But given that monetary damages are the chosen remedy, the *Merrill* tribunal should not have required an unrealistic level of proof. *Merrill* seems to allow a host country to violate its fair and equitable treatment obligations with impunity – particularly by distorting the market so completely that it obscures what free market prices would be.

The *Merrill* tribunal's denial of damages for the increased cost of compliance with the Canadian regime was contrary to the earlier NAFTA decision in *Pope & Talbot v. Canada*, in which the damages awarded were precisely for the increased costs imposed by the denial of fair and equitable treatment.[111] Contrary to the *Merrill* tribunal's view, the damages the investor suffered were not the ordinary cost of compliance with any regulatory regime, but the increased costs resulting from denial of fair and equitable treatment.

The commentator agrees with the *Merrill* tribunal that the investor should not be able to recover damages for future sales. The denial of fair and equitable treatment had occurred during a specific period in the past, and the resulting injury was reduced prices on sales during the same time period. Future damages would have to be linked to a showing of future violations.

Interpretation of Investor-State Contract and Collateral Estoppel Effect of Arbitral Award

In *RSM Production Corp. v. Grenada*,[112] a U.S. corporation in the oil and gas industry alleged that Grenada violated a written agreement with the corporation by refusing to grant an exploration license that would permit the corporation to search for oil and gas deposits in a designated area in the waters off Grenada. Under the agreement, RSM was required to apply for the exploration license "as soon as possible but in no event later than ninety (90) days" after July 4, 1999, the effective date of the agreement. But on July 18, 1999, RSM suspended the 90-day period by invoking the agreement's force majeure provision. The justification for force majeure was that the designated exploration area was the subject of maritime boundary disputes that Grenada was having with Venezuela and Trinidad and

---

[110] See van Harten/Loughlin, Investment Treaty Arbitration as a Species of Global Administrative Law, EJIL 17 (2006), p. 121 (passim & 131–133) (identifying monetary damages as a key feature of investment treaty arbitration).

[111] NAFTA, *Pope & Talbot Inc. vs. Canada*, Award on Damages, 31st May, 2002.

[112] ICSID, ARB/05/14, *RSM Production Corp. vs. Grenada*, 13th March, 2009.

Tobago, respectively. It was not until nearly 5 years later that RSM notified Grenada of the end of force majeure, first on January 12, 2004 (but in a letter not addressed to the correct individual designated in the agreement) and again in a letter dated February 27, 2004. RSM then submitted its application for the exploration license by letter that was dated April 13, 2004, and received on April 14, 2004. Grenada denied the exploration license on April 27, 2004 and terminated the agreement on July 5, 2004.

The 1999 RSM-Grenada agreement, which was governed by the law of Grenada, included a choice-of-forum clause specifying ICSID arbitration. The tribunal held that Grenada did not violate the agreement and, instead, had acted within its rights by denying the exploration license and terminating the agreement because RSM had not submitted the license application within the required 90-day period. The tribunal ruled that the 14 days between July 4 and July 18, 1999 counted toward the 90-day period and that the 90-day period restarted on January 12, 2004, not allowing RSM to benefit from its own error in addressing the letter. Therefore, the 90-day period expired on March 28, 2004, or 16 days before RSM submitted the license application. Furthermore, the tribunal ruled as a matter of contractual interpretation under the law of Grenada that the 90-day period was "a 'condition precedent' of the Agreement in the legal sense that RSM's failure to act timeously within the ninety-day period relieves Grenada from a correlative obligation to proceed with further performance of its substantive obligations under the Agreement . . . and also entitles Grenada to terminate the Agreement . . .."[113]

Shortly after the decision in *RSM*, the corporation's shareholders and RSM began a new ICSID arbitration against Grenada entitled *Grynberg v. Grenada*[114] (hereinafter, for convenience, *RSM-II*). In *RSM-II* the investors alleged that Grenada's denial of the exploration license to RSM and cancellation of the 1999 RSM-Grenada contract violated the US-Grenada bilateral investment treaty, including constituting an illegal expropriation and a denial of fair and equitable treatment. The *RSM-II* tribunal, however, granted Grenada's request to dismiss the arbitration because it was barred by the doctrine of collateral estoppel as a result of *RSM-I*. In doing so, the tribunal invoked ICSID Arbitration Rule 41(5), newly adopted in 2006, that allows a tribunal to order the expeditious dismissal of a claim that is "manifestly without merit."[115]

The tribunal ruled that "the doctrine of collateral estoppel is now well established as a general principle of law applicable in the international courts and tribunals such as this one."[116] Among the findings of the *RSM-I* tribunal that were

---

[113] Id. ¶ 377.

[114] ICSID, ARB/10/6, *Grynberg vs. Grenada*, 10th December, 2010. The Grynberg family members were the shareholders of RSM.

[115] Id. ¶ 2.1.1 (quoting ICSID Rule 41(5)).

[116] Id. ¶ 7.1.2. Under collateral estoppel, "a finding concerning a right, question or fact may not be re-litigated (and, thus, is binding on a subsequent tribunal), if, in a prior proceeding: (a) it was distinctly put in issue; (b) the court or tribunal actually decided it; and (c) the resolution of the question was necessary to resolving the claims before that court or tribunal." Id. ¶ 7.1.1.

binding on the *RSM-II* tribunal under collateral estoppel were that "Grenada did not breach any of its obligations to RSM under the [1999] Agreement in failing to issue an exploration license to RSM, such obligation having lapsed on 28 March 2004," and that "[t]he Agreement was lawfully terminated by Grenada on 5 July 2004 so that Grenada thereafter had no further substantive contractual obligations to RSM."[117] The *RSM-II* tribunal then concluded that "an essential predicate to the success of each of Claimants' claims [under the BIT] is an ability for the Tribunal to relitigate and decide in Claimants' favor conclusions of fact or law concerning the parties' contractual rights that have already been distinctly put in issue and distinctly determined by the Prior Tribunal."[118] And since "the Tribunal has concluded ... that it cannot properly revisit those conclusions, the Tribunal finds that each of Claimant's claims is manifestly without legal merit."[119] In addition to dismissing the claim, the tribunal ordered the claimants to pay Grenada nearly $300,000 for its legal and other costs.

Binational Panels Under NAFTA Chapter 19

NAFTA Chapter 19 establishes a process of binational panel review of administrative determinations under the NAFTA parties' antidumping and countervailing duty statutes. Binational panel reviews are a substitute for judicial review of the administrative determinations in domestic courts. NAFTA includes, however, a choice-of-law provision that directs the binational panel to apply each country's domestic laws – "the relevant statutes, legislative history, regulations, administrative practice, and judicial precedents"[120] – as well as the same standard of judicial review that a domestic court would apply.[121]

In *Stainless Steel Sheet and Strip in Coils from Mexico*,[122] the binational panel considered the legality of an antidumping determination in which the responsible U.S. agency, the Commerce Department, used the practice of so-called "zeroing" in calculating the dumping margin in the administrative review stage of an antidumping proceeding. Under zeroing, if the export price is higher than the normal value, the dumping margin is treated as zero instead of a negative number for purposes of calculating the weighted-average dumping margin. The WTO Appellate Body has ruled that zeroing violates the WTO Antidumping Agreement, first in 2001 in a case against the European Communities and later in 2006 in a case against the United

---

[117] Id. ¶ 7.1.8.

[118] Id. ¶ 7.2.1.

[119] Id.

[120] NAFTA, Art. 1902.2.

[121] Id. Art. 1902.3.

[122] NAFTA, No. USA-MEX-2007-1904-01, Stainless Steel Sheet and Strip In Coils From Mexico: 2004/2005 Antidumping Review, 14th April, 2010.

States.[123] Within the United States, however, the Commerce Department has continued to use zeroing in administrative reviews, including in the contested determination in *Stainless Steel Sheet and Strip*. The U.S. Court of Appeals for the Federal Circuit, the federal appellate court that exercises judicial review under the antidumping statute, sustained the Commerce Department's use of zeroing in administrative reviews. The court held in its 2004 decision in *Timken Co. v. United States*,[124] that zeroing represents a reasonable interpretation of an ambiguous statute. The Federal Circuit adhered to *Timken* in 2007 in *Corus Staal BV v. United States*,[125] despite the 2006 WTO decision against the United States.

Stainless Steel Sheet and Strip produced a split decision. In seeking to apply the applicable U.S. judicial precedents, the three majority panelists saw what they interpreted as "two competing lines of cases ... at the Federal Circuit."[126] This led the majority to feel that "[i]t is open to this Panel to follow either of the competing lines of authority."[127] One line of cases apparently "recognized the relevance of WTO jurisprudence to judicial review"[128] The other line of cases "appear to have signaled a retrenchment on the part of [the U.S.] courts to rely on the reasoning of international tribunals in the process of judicial review."[129] The majority then ruled that the *Timken* decision sustaining zeroing was factually distinguishable because it had been issued before the 2006 WTO decision that rejected zeroing in cases against the United States. For these reasons, the majority chose to rely on the Federal Circuit cases containing language that supports WTO-consistent interpretations of U.S. statutes. The majority remanded the case to the Commerce Department for recalculation of the dumping margin without zeroing. Two panelists dissented strongly, urging that the panel should have followed the Federal Circuit decisions in *Timken* and *Corus* sustaining zeroing.

---

[123] Report of the Appellate Body, AB-2006-2, United States – Laws, Regulations and Methodology for Calculating Dumping Margins ("Zeroing"), WT/DS294/AB/R, 18th April, 2006; Report of the Appellate Body, European Communities – Anti-Dumping Duties on Imports of Cotton-Type Bed Linen from India, WT/DS141/AB/R, 12th March, 2001.

[124] Fed. Cir., 354 F.3d 1334 (2004), *cert. denied sub nom. Koyo Seiko Co. vs. United States*, 543 U.S. 976 (2004).

[125] Fed. Cir., 502 F.3d 1370 (2007); *accord, Fed. Cir., Corus Staal BV vs. U.S. Department of Commerce*, 395 F.3d 1343 (2005), *cert. denied*, 546 U.S.1089 (2006).

[126] NAFTA, No. USA-MEX-2007-1904-01, Stainless Steel Sheet and Strip In Coils From Mexico: 2004/2005 Antidumping Review, 14th April, 2010, p. 20 (Majority Decision).

[127] Id., p. 22.

[128] Id., p. 20; see also id., p. 14 ("The Federal Circuit has confirmed that statutes must be interpreted consistently with international obligations, absent contrary indications in the statutory language or its legislative history.") (citing Fed. Cir., *Federal Mogul Corp. vs. United States*, 63 F.3d 1572 (1995)).

[129] Id., p. 22. These cases, which include *Timken* and *Corus*, originate with Fed. Cir,, *Suramerica de Aleaciones Laminadas, C.A. vs. United States*, 966 F.2d 660 (1992).

In this commentator's view, the majority was completely wrong. First, the majority erred by failing to follow *Timken* and *Corus*. This commentator does disagree with the Federal Circuit's reasoning and regrets its inconsistency with WTO decisions, but at the same time recognizes that *Timken* and *Corus* remain binding precedents until the Federal Circuit overrules them.[130] Even if other Federal Circuit decisions contain language that seems to be inconsistent, the holdings of the other cases do not specifically address zeroing.

Second, the majority was wrong that there are two competing lines of cases in the Federal Circuit. The Federal Circuit precedents can all be reconciled with careful analysis of the holdings of the cases. In one case recognizing the relevance of WTO jurisprudence, *Allegheny Ludlum Corp. v. United States*,[131] the Federal Circuit overruled a Commerce Department interpretation that the court found to be contrary to the unambiguous U.S. statute, and the court said that inconsistency of the agency's interpretation with a WTO decision provided "additional support" for the decision. Judicial review in U.S. administrative law makes a fundamental distinction between statutory provisions that the court finds "unambiguous" and those it finds "silent or ambiguous."[132] Therefore, *Allegheny Ludlum* does not support overturning the agency's interpretation where, as in *Timken*, the court found the relevant statutory language ambiguous. In other cases recognizing the relevance of WTO jurisprudence, the Federal Circuit has sustained the agency's interpretation of an ambiguous U.S. statute and ruled that WTO consistency supports the conclusion that the agency's interpretation is permissible.[133] In contrast, as this commentator's previous research found, "no [U.S.] court has held that an agency interpretation [of an ambiguous U.S. statute] is impermissible solely because is it inconsistent with a WTO panel or Appellate Body decision."[134] Instead, U.S. courts uniformly hold that "inconsistency with a WTO decision is not sufficient by itself to require reversing an agency's interpretation of an ambiguous statute."[135] Thus, U.S. judicial precedent does not support the majority opinion because the U.S. antidumping statute is ambiguous with respect to zeroing (as *Timken* held) and the Commerce Department was not relying on WTO consistency in support of its interpretation.

---

[130] In fact, the Federal Circuit again upheld zeroing and reaffirmed *Timken* and *Corus* in January 2011. Fed. Cir., App. No. 2010-1128, *SKF USA Inc. vs. United States*, 7th January, 2011.

[131] Fed. Cir., 367 F.3d 1339 (2004), p. 1348.

[132] See S.Ct.U.S., *Chevron U.S.A., Inc. vs. Natural Resources Defense Council*, 467 U.S. 837 (1984); Strauss, Administrative Justice in the United States, (2nd ed.) 2002, pp. 349–375.

[133] Fed. Cir., *Luigi Bormioli Corp. vs. United States*, 304 F.3d 1362 (Fed. Cir. 2002); Fed. Cir., *Federal Mogul Corp. vs. United States*, 63 F.3d 1572 (1995).

[134] Reed, Relationship of WTO Obligations to U.S. International Trade Law: Internationalist Vision Meets Domestic Reality, Geo. J. Int'l L. 38 (2006) 1, pp. 209 et seq. (233).

[135] Id., p. 234; see also Davies, Connecting or Compartmentalizing the WTO and United States Legal Systems? The Role of the Charming Betsy Doctrine, JIEL 10 (2007) 1, p. 117 (reaching much the same conclusions as this commentator based on a different analysis).

The majority opinion seriously undermines the idea in NAFTA chapter 19 that binational panel review is supposed to replicate domestic judicial review, including adhering to applicable judicial precedents.

State-to-State Disputes

No decisions have been issued in state-to-state disputes under the international economic agreements in the North American region during the period of time this chapter covers.[136] A development warranting mention, however, is that the United States requested consultations with Guatemala in July 2010 about Guatemala's alleged failures to enforce its labor laws adequately, as required by CAFTA-DR.[137] Despite the significance of the case for international economic law, unfortunately no subsequent information about the consultations was available publicly when this chapter went to press. At a minimum, the request for consultations reflects that the dispute resolution processes under international economic agreements in North and Central America are not limited to investment and trade complaints by business interests.

Conclusion

This chapter concludes by offering this commentator's summary report card on the disputes surveyed here. In this commentator's view, *Glamis Gold*, *Chemtura*, *CPI*, and *RSM-I&II* are sound. So are the rulings in *ADM* on national treatment and in *Merrill* on national treatment and expropriation. *Merrill* is correct on the performance requirements claim as the law exists, but reveals a peculiar substantive discrepancy between the NAFTA and WTO rules on performance requirements, as well as the jurisdictional anomaly that NAFTA tribunals cannot consider WTO

---

[136] In the long unresolved state-to-state dispute between Mexico the United States over the U.S. failure to implement the NAFTA provisions allowing Mexican truckers to operate in the United States, Mexico ended nearly a decade of forbearance by imposing retaliatory import duties on $2.4 billion of U.S. imports into Mexico in early 2009 and expanded the retaliatory duties to $2.5 billion in August 2010. See Powell, "Trucking Dispute rolls toward dead end – A collision of interests blocks search for agreement – Trucks: Trade war has escalated", Houston Chronicle, 22nd August, 2010; see also NAFTA, No. USA-MEX-98-2008-01, *Cross-Border Trucking Services*, 6th February 6, 2001 (finding the United States in violation).

[137] CAFTA-DR, Art. 16.2(1)(a) ("A Party shall not fail to effectively enforce its labor laws, through a sustained or recurring course of action or inaction, in a manner affecting trade between the Parties …."); see also Letter from U.S. Trade Rep. & Sec. of Labor to Guatemalan Officials, 31st July, 2010; USTR Press Release, USTR Kirk Announces Labor Rights Trade Enforcement Case Against Guatemala, 30th July, 2010.

violations. *Merrill* is flawed on the legal standard for fair and equitable treatment and the proof of damages. *Canadian Cattlemen* is correct under existing law, but reveals the jurisdictional anomaly of having difference procedures for trade disputes and investment disputes. It is disappointing and confusing to see the inconsistent reasoning on fair and equitable treatment in *Glamis Gold* and *Merrill* and on countermeasures and performance requirements in *ADM* and *CPI*.[138] *Anderson* seems unpersuasive, but if correct reveals an odd jurisdictional anomaly of barring investors' claims for inadequate host country enforcement of financial regulatory laws. The majority opinion in the binational panel decision in *Stainless Steel Sheet and Strip in Coils from Mexico* is seriously flawed, in this commentator's opinion.

With the possible exception of *ADM* and *CPI*, the investment disputes considered here do not reveal an institutional bias in favor of business interests in international arbitral tribunals. *RSM-I&II* reflect that a small developing country like Grenada can not only defend itself against a multinational enterprise, but even inflict a crushing defeat. *Chemtura* and *Glamis Gold* create the impression that investor-state arbitration might not offer any advantage over domestic judicial review for foreign investors aggrieved by government regulatory actions, and indeed that domestic judicial review might well offer plaintiffs better chances of success.[139] *ADM* and *CPI* illustrate that the substantive rules on foreign investment do insulate foreign businesses if a host country reacts to domestic economic problems by introducing discriminatory measures.[140] *ADM* and *CPI* also reveal that NAFTA did not have an adequate safeguard or other mechanism for handling the broader problem of the economic difficulties experienced in Mexico's sugar industry, particularly to the extent a U.S. violation of NAFTA may have caused the problem.

Acknowledgment The author wishes to express his appreciation to Professor Claire R. Kelly for her comments on an earlier draft.

---

[138] Cf. Stiglitz, Regulating Multinational Corporations: Toward Principles of Cross-Border Legal Frameworks in a Globalized World Balancing Rights with Responsibilities, Am. U. Int'l L. Rev. 23 (2008), pp. 451 et seq. (456) (criticizing international investment law on the ground that "[d]ifferent arbitration panels have interpreted the same words [in BITs] differently, creating a high level of uncertainty, among both governments and investors, about exactly what BITs can accomplish.").

[139] Cf. van Harten/Loughlin, Investment Treaty Arbitration as a Species of Global Administrative Law, EJIL 17 (2006), pp. 121 et seq. (150) (identifying "the justification for removing such regulatory disputes from the jurisdiction of domestic courts" as an issue inviting further inquiry).

[140] Cf. Stiglitz, Regulating Multinational Corporations: Toward Principles of Cross-Border Legal Frameworks in a Globalized World Balancing Rights with Responsibilities, Am. U. Int'l L. Rev. 23 (2008), pp. 451 et seq. (548–49) (favoring national treatment obligations, despite criticizing existing BITs in many other respects).

The Rule of Law and the Implementation of an Economic Acquis Communautaire in Sub Saharan Africa: Legal Challenges for the East African Community

Teresa Thorp

Background

Headquartered in Arusha, Tanzania, the East African Community (EAC) is a regional intergovernmental organisation. The EAC brings together five Partner States: Burundi, Kenya, Rwanda, Tanzania and Uganda. Governed by the EAC Treaty, which entered into force on 7 July 2000, Kenya, Tanzania and Uganda officially launched the EAC on 15 January 2001. Burundi and Rwanda became full EAC Partner States with effect from 1 July 2007.

By virtue of Article 5(2) of the EAC Treaty (as amended on 14 December 2006 and 20 August 2007), EAC Partner States undertake to establish a Customs Union, a Common Market, subsequently a Monetary Union and ultimately a Political Federation among themselves. EAC Partner States aim to strengthen and regulate industrial, commercial, infrastructural, cultural, social, political and other relations to accelerate harmonious and balanced development and sustained expansion of economic activities and to share the benefit of these endeavours on an equitable basis. Various protocols, acts and regulations reinforce the EAC Treaty framework.

In March 2004, EAC Partner States signed the EAC Customs Union Protocol, which came into effect in January 2005; but it was not until 5 years later that a "fully fledged" Customs Union entered into force on 1 January 2010. At the 11th Ordinary Summit held on 20 November 2009, the EAC Heads of State signed and approved the EAC Common Market Protocol. Pursuant to a directive made at the November 2009 Summit, the Heads of State directed the Council of Ministers to oversee and approve the institutional arrangements that will support the

T. Thorp (✉)
Insight International, Watford, UK
e-mail: teresa.thorp@insight-int.org

C. Herrmann and J.P. Terhechte (eds.), *European Yearbook of International Economic Law (EYIEL), Vol. 3 (2012)*, European Yearbook of International Economic Law 3, DOI 10.1007/978-3-642-23309-8_16, © Springer-Verlag Berlin Heidelberg 2012

management of the EAC Common Market and urged Partner States to ratify the EAC Common Market Protocol to enable it to start operating on 1 July 2010.[1] By 30 April 2010, all five Partner States had ratified the EAC Common Market Protocol.[2] In tandem with the ratification process, Partner States endeavoured to ensure the enactment of relevant enabling legislation to give effect to the EAC Common Market Protocol by 21 August 2010.[3] These deadlines were perhaps too ambitious and somewhat scuppered by juggling several other policy directives simultaneously.

From a strategic policy perspective, the EAC Development Strategy 2006–2010 supports the EAC's economic *acquis communautaire* and facilitates its implementation in a systematic way. Yet, the EAC Development Strategy gives little attention to the legal approximation of the Common Market Protocol. What mechanisms have EAC Partner States instituted to give legal effect to the provisions of the Common Market Protocol and what mechanisms will be instituted going into 2011? These were the questions asked of Partner States in the process of drafting this paper. This article presents the results of that research. It evaluates the substantive content of the EAC's economic *acquis communautaire*; and assesses the processes each Partner State is undertaking to set up the necessary administrative and judicial bodies to approximate their national laws with the regional framework.

Structure of the Paper

This paper unfolds in two parts. Part one considers the character and scope of the economic *acquis communautaire* of the East African Community within the context of multilayered governance. It examines the meaning of *acquis communautaire* and then moves on to analyse the East African Community's economic *acquis communautaire* in a much broader way. It does this by evaluating the economic *acquis communautaire* of the EAC Customs Union and then that of the EAC Common Market. Having determined the character and scope of the EAC's

---

[1] EAC Secretariat Press Release, Burundi Ratifies EAC Common Market Protocol, available at: http://www.eac.int/news/index.php?option=com_content&view=article&id=231:burundi-ratifies-eac-common-market-protocol&catid=48:eac-latest&Itemid=69 (last visited on 22nd January, 2011).

[2] EAC Secretariat Press Release, Council Chairperson Assures Community on Ratification of Common Market Protocol, available at: http://www.eac.int/news/index.php?option=com_content&view=article&id=226:ratification-of-common-market-protocol&catid=48:eac-latest&Itemid=69 (last visited on 22nd January, 2011).

[3] Communiqué of the 11th Ordinary Summit of EAC Heads of State, 20th November, 2009, EAC Secretariat, para 6.

economic *acquis communautaire* in part one of the paper, part two turns to the question of approximation. The analysis juxtaposes the approximation methods used at an EAC wide level with those used within Partner States. It does this by examining three main questions. First, what are the practical arrangements instituted to facilitate approximation? Second, what national rules of law have Partner States enacted to domesticate the EAC Common Market Protocol and transpose its economic acquis into their respective legal systems? Third, how will Partner States enforce EAC economic law governing the EAC common market? In concluding, the paper puts forward a series of recommendations, which aim to present a constructive way of advancing the process of incorporating the economic *acquis communautaire* of the East African Community within a new common market and, by extension, within Sub-Saharan Africa as a whole.

Character and Scope of the EAC's Economic Acquis Communautaire

The Evolving Nature of the EAC's Acquis Communautaire

Defining precisely what is meant by the East African Community's *acquis communautaire* is a necessary first step to incorporate the economic *acquis communautaire* of the East African Community (hereinafter referred to as the EAC) within a new common market. Definition is needed for legal approximation: EAC Partner States "undertake to approximate their national laws and to harmonise their policies and systems, for the purposes of implementing the EAC Common Market Protocol".[4] Approximation is essential to advancing economic partnership agreements; and advancement of the acquis is central to any future accession negotiations, say with the Democratic Republic of the Congo, Sudan, Ethiopia and other pending constitutional reforms in the Horn of Africa.

At this point in time, EAC law does not define the term *acquis communautaire*. The term is not defined in the 1999 Treaty for the Establishment of the EAC (hereinafter referred to as the EAC Treaty) or within any other Protocol or Annex.[5]

---

[4] EAC Common Market Protocol, Art. 47, para. 1. In the European Union, Member States are obliged to "align national laws, rules and procedures in order to give effect to the entire body of EAC law contained in the EAC's *acquis communautaire*". European Commission Guide to the Approximation of European Union Environmental Legislation, a revised and updated version of SEC(97) 1608 of 25th August, 1997, available at: http://ec.europa.eu/environment/archives/guide/part1.htm (last visited on 22nd January, 2011).

[5] Treaty for the Establishment of the East African Community, 30th November, 1999, entered into force on 7th July, 2000 in accordance with Art. 152, UNTS I-37437, Volume 2144, No 37437, available at: http://untreaty.un.org/unts/144078_158780/8/5/1975.pdf or http://treaties.un.org/doc/Publication/UNTS/Volume%202144/v2144.pdf (last visited on 22nd January 2011).

Similarly, in Europe where there exists a more recent regional economic community, neither the Treaty on European Union nor any other Treaties define the term *acquis communautaire*.[6] Contrary to the EAC's position, however, the Treaty on European Union uses the term *acquis communautaire*. The Treaty on European Union provides that "the Union shall maintain and build on the *acquis communautaire*".[7] The European Union's interpretation infers that *acquis communautaire* encompasses the "body of common rights and obligations which bind all the Member States together within the European Union".[8] Analogous in function but stemming from completely different origins, *acquis communautaire* in the EAC context, and as used here, refers to the body of common rights and obligations that bind together all EAC Partner States. Yet, what precisely are those common rights and obligations that constitute the EAC's *acquis communautaire*?

In returning to Europe, the European Council has made a number of varying statements that set out the scope of "Europe's" *acquis communautaire*. For the European Council, the European Union's *acquis communautaire* constitutes "the content, principles and political objectives of European Union Treaties, including the Treaty of Amsterdam; legislation adopted in implementation of the Treaties and Court of Justice case law; declarations and resolutions adopted within the European Union framework; joint actions, common positions, declarations, conclusions and other acts within the framework of common foreign and security policy; joint actions, common positions, signed conventions, resolutions, declarations and other acts concluded within the framework of justice and home affairs; international agreements concluded by the European Community, and those concluded by Member States with each other in the area of Community activities".[9] For transparency purposes, the European Community publishes a directory of community

---

[6] The Treaty of Amsterdam amending the Treaty on European Union, Art. 2, The Treaties Establishing the European Communities and Related Acts, signed on 2nd October, 1997, entered into force on 1st May, 1999, OJ [1997] C 340/1. Treaty on the Functioning of the European Union (Treaty of Lisbon), signed on 13th December, 2007, entered into force on 1st December, 2009, OJ [2007] C 306/1. Consolidated versions of the Treaty on European Union and the Treaty on the Functioning of the European Union, Art. 20, OJ [2008] C 115/1, see http://eur-lex.europa.eu/en/treaties/index.htm#founding (last visited on 22nd January, 2011).

[7] The Treaty Establishing the European Economic Community (Treaty of Rome), signed in Rome on 25th March, 1957, entered into force on 1st January, 1958. Art. B, fifth indent, of the Treaty on European Union (Treaty of Maastricht), signed on 7th February, 1992, entered into force on 1st November, 1993; OJ [1992] C 191/1, see: http://eur-lex.europa.eu/en/treaties/index.htm#founding (last visited on 22nd January 2011).

[8] EU Glossary, see http://europa.eu/scadplus/glossary/community_acquis_en.htm (last visited on 22nd January 2011).

[9] Legal Questions of Enlargement, European Parliament Briefing No. 23, http://www.europarl.europa.eu/enlargement/briefings/23a2_en.htm#F11 (last visited on 22nd January, 2011). Cf. Statement by President-in-Office of the Council at the 31st March, 1998 conference on EU accession by the Czech Republic, para. 19. Identical statements were made at the openings of accession negotiations with Poland, Hungary, Estonia and Slovenia.

legislation in force, which groups Europe's *acquis communautaire* by 20 themes.[10] Whereas, for accession purposes, the European Union refers to 35 chapters.[11] Observably, the *acquis communautaire* of the European Union is continually evolving and constantly in a state of flux.

In a similar vein, the *acquis communautaire* of other regional economic communities constitute legal systems that are continually evolving and constantly in a state of flux. Throughout Sub Saharan Africa, the situation is no different. The *acquis communautaire* of the EAC (East African Community), COMESA (Common Market for Eastern and Southern Africa), ECOWAS (Economic Community of West African States) and SADC (Southern African Development Community) is continually evolving. Nascent national rules of law require constant attention in order to give effect to the substantive and procedural aspects of law governing each respective regional economic community, accessions to the community and future mergers between communities.

Before readily comparing the European Union's construction of *acquis communautaire* to that of the EAC, or to any other regional economic community, a consideration of the first principles that shape a regional economic community as a system of law, as an *acquis communautaire*, is worthwhile. One must appreciate the rule of EAC law before one applies it.

For the purposes of explanation, an introductory reference is made to the work of modern legal positivists of the Anglo-American predilection. Citing Hart, "law is a union of primary and secondary social rules". Primary laws govern substantive conduct. Secondary laws govern procedure whereby procedural governance incorporates the rule of recognition, the rule of change and the rule of adjudication.[12] The rule of recognition gives certainty to the law by comprehending what is law. The rule of change provides for a dynamic process that incorporates creating new laws and amending or repealing existing laws. The rule of adjudication confers credibility on the rule of law by prescribing a remedy in the case of breach.

For Dworkin, procedural process may go broader and deeper still. Principles and policies may not necessarily be prescribed as a rule but they may still be integral to a system of law. Principles of fairness and equity, for instance, may derive from due process and may, by extension, be part of an *acquis communautaire*.[13]

---

[10] Legislation in force as of 1st May, 2010; Directory of Community legislation in force: Chapter 01 General, financial and institutional matters (number of acts: 1111); Chapter 05 Freedom of movement for workers and social policy (number of acts: 482); Chapter 06 Right of establishment and freedom to provide services (number of acts: 245); and Chapter 10 Economic and monetary policy and free movement of capital (number of acts: 423). http://eur-lex.europa.eu/en/legis/20100501/index.htm (last visited on 22nd January, 2011).

[11] Commission, Enlargement Process, How does a country join the EU?, available at: http://ec.europa.eu/enlargement/enlargement_process/accession_process/how_does_a_country_join_the_eu/negotiations_croatia_turkey/index_en.htm#3 (last visited on 22nd January, 2011).

[12] Hart, *The Concept of Law*, (2nd ed.) 1997.

[13] Dworkin, *Law's Empire*, 1998.

Raz pointed out that there may be multiple procedural processes within a single system; and so is true of the interactions between the EAC *acquis communautaire* and other systems of law in Sub Saharan Africa.[14] When a regional *acquis communautaire* comes into play, a dynamic multilayered system of governance and proxy constitutionalism evolves. This is not to say, in any shape or form, that the law of the EAC is a self-contained body of law. It is not. The law of the EAC exists within a much broader dialectic context that interacts with national, regional and international law.

Correspondingly, the challenge of legal harmonisation that is endemic in regional economic integration manifests at national, regional and international levels. To give an example, the *acquis communautaire* of the EAC constitutes a legal system that governs the substantive and procedural laws of the EAC. Yet, to legitimize the *acquis communautaire* of the EAC as a system of law, it needs to align with the broader prevailing body of international law and that of the African Economic Community. In tandem, it needs to be "internalized" within the primary and secondary rules, principles, policies and processes of Partner States.

At the international level, the EAC Treaty provides that Partner States shall honour their multinational commitments.[15] While the EAC's task is to put its objectives and aspirations at the centre of its decision-making processes, the EAC *acquis communautaire* is not to be read in clinical isolation from obligations it makes in public international law.[16]

On the African continent, the EAC regards consolidation as a stepping-stone towards attaining the objectives of the 1991 Treaty Establishing the African Economic Community (hereinafter referred to as the Treaty Establishing the AEC).[17] By co-ordinating and harmonizing economic, social, cultural and development policies with the view to raising the standard of living of African peoples and fostering peace, the Treaty Establishing the AEC aims to establish an African Economic Community on a continental scale over a period not exceeding 34 years.[18]

Harmonisation of an African-wide *acquis communautaire* exists in a different but interrelated plane to incorporating a regional *acquis communautaire* at a local level. The Protocol to the Treaty Establishing the African Economic Community Relating to the Pan-African Parliament 2001 establishes a Pan-African Parliament to facilitate the effective implementation of an all-African regional economic

---

[14] Raz, *The Concept of a Legal System: An Introduction to the Theory of a Legal System*, (2nd ed.) 1980.

[15] Art. 130(1) EAC Treaty, International Organisations and Development Partners.

[16] Report of the Appellate Body, United States – Standards for Reformulated and WTO Conventional Gasoline (Complainant: Venezuela), WT/DS2/AB/R, 29th April, 1996, pp. 15–16.

[17] Art. 130(2) EAC Treaty, International Organisations and Development Partners.

[18] The Treaty Establishing the African Economic Community, 3rd June, 1991, entered into force on 12th May, 1994; Art. 2, 3, 4, and 6, available at: http://www.africa-union.org/root/au/Documents/Treaties/treaties.htm (last visited on 22nd January, 2011).

community. To guide this process, the Protocol provides for the promotion, co-ordination and harmonisation of the *acquis communautaire*, i.e., laws, policies, measures, programmes and activities of Member States and of the Africa Regional Economic Communities, with that of the African Union.[19]

The African Union itself emerges from the Constitutive Act of the African Union of 2000 (hereinafter referred to as the Constitutive Act of the AU) with its aim being to achieve even greater unity, solidarity and accelerate integration.[20] The Constitutive Act of the AU provides that the Constitutive Act has precedence over and supersedes any inconsistent provision in the Treaty establishing the AEC.[21]

Some may claim that the aims and aspirations of the AU are an unattainable panacea. The discussion that follows will show clearly that they are not. There are simply a number of challenges to be addressed along the way. For starters, the Durban Summit and First Assembly of the Heads of State of the African Union launched the African Union on 9 July 2002.

To harmonise the *acquis communautaire* at an all-African wide level and gradually achieve the objectives of the Constitutive Act of the AU, the Constitutive Act of the AU delegates the responsibility for coordinating and harmonising policies between the existing and future Regional Economic Communities to the African Union.[22] The Constitutive Act of the AU makes provision for specialized technical committees. A committee on Trade, Customs and Immigration, for instance, is responsible to the Executive Council and, amongst other tasks within its field of competence, ensures the coordination and harmonisation of projects and programmes of the African Union.[23] Incorporation of the economic *acquis communautaire* of the EAC in a new Common Market therefore needs to align with this much broader multi-levelled structure.

In terms of attentive care to incorporating an *acquis communautaire* at the regional level, the EAC applies some substantive and procedural principles but shies away from others. This is illustrative in the EAC's attempts to reconcile bottom up perspectives with the top down.

---

[19] Protocol to the Treaty Establishing the African Economic Community Relating to the Pan-African Parliament, adopted on 2nd March, 2001 entered into force on 14th December, 2003, (Art. 2, Established the Pan-African Parliament; Art. 3, Objectives include facilitating effective implementation of policies and objectives of the OAU/AEC and African Union and cooperation among Regional Economic Communities and their Parliamentary fora; Art. 11 Functions and Powers, para. 3, 7), available at: http://www.africa-union.org/root/au/Documents/Treaties/treaties.htm (last visited on 22nd January, 2011).

[20] Constitutive Act of the African Union, adopted on 11th July, 2000, entered into force on 26th May, 2001; Art. 2 established the African Union; Art. 3 Objectives, available at: http://www.africa-union.org/root/au/Documents/Treaties/treaties.htm; or http://www.africa-union.org/root/au/AboutAU/Constitutive_Act_en.htm#Article33 (last visited on 22nd January, 2011).

[21] Art. 33(2) Constitutive Act of the AU.

[22] Art. 3(1) Constitutive Act of the AU.

[23] Art. 14(1)(c), Art. 15(1)(c) Constitutive Act of the AU.

From a bottom up perspective, rationalisation of economic law at a national level steps up in prominence as the EAC makes its tentative moves through the various stages of regional integration (from a Free Trade Area to a Customs Union to a Common Market to Political Federation). Historically, an earlier formation of the EAC made direct provision for the supremacy of an economic *acquis communautaire*. By virtue of the Treaty for East African Co-operation of 1967, "a Common Market Tribunal was to make binding decisions over disputes arising out of the Treaty".[24] No longer was an East African Community to operate a *de facto*. Instead, it was to consolidate a *de jure* regional economic community, one that was advancing at a far faster pace than the European Union. Despite best intentions, a number of internal and external factors led to a standstill and the EAC of 1967 collapsed in 1977. Similar political factors reappear from time to time to haunt the current integration process.

The 1999 EAC Treaty again provided for supremacy of EAC law over like national law in areas of EAC competency: "community organs, institutions and laws shall take precedence over similar national ones on matters pertaining to the implementation of this Treaty".[25] Even so, at a local level, supremacy of EAC law is under pressure yet again.

In certain quarters, there is political pressure not to cede any more sovereign rights to the Community. Likewise, there is still the challenge of ascertaining and making transparent the mechanisms Partner States will institute to give effect to the new Common Market Protocol, which was scheduled for 21 August 2010.[26]

What is fundamentally different to the recipe for advancement this time round is the occasioning of a parallel advancement in multi-layered governance at the international level, within the WTO for instance, within the African Union and within other near-by Regional Economic Communities. For epicureans, the benefits of taking attentive care to prepare a classic lasagna recipe are outweighing those of serving a bland knotted mass of spaghetti. Antidotes must move on.

From a top down perspective, socio economic and political pressures are equally prevalent. (A Tripartite Memorandum of Understanding (MoU) came into force on 19 January 2011; and negotiations for the EAC-COMESA-SADC FTA were launched in June 2011), investigating a SACU-EAC Free Trade Area is another example; investigating a SACU-EAC Free Trade Area is another.[27] Advancing EAC relations with ECOWAS is also imminent.

Reconciliation of these two perspectives, the top-down and the bottom-up, is vital. As Barog, the engineer in charge of the Kalka Shimla Railway build in India

---

[24] Green, The Treaty for East African Co-Operation: A Summary and Interpretation, The Journal of Modern African Studies 5 (1967) 3, pp. 414–419.

[25] Art. 8(4) EAC Treaty, General Undertaking as to Implementation.

[26] Art. 8(4) EAC Treaty, "Community organs, institutions and laws shall take precedence over similar national ones on matters pertaining to the implementation of this Treaty".

[27] A Tripartite Memorandum of Understanding (MoU) came into force on 19 January 2011; and negotiations for the EAC-COMESA-SADC FTA were launched in June 2011.

demonstrated, there is always the possibility that when one seeks efficiency in building a tunnel by digging from the two ends that those two ends may not end up meeting at all. To avoid such misfortune, reaching common ground on the *acquis communautaire* of a Common Market from a Sub Saharan African perspective, and notably an African Union perspective, is therefore necessary to harmonise Common Markets emerging within the underlying substructure, that of regional economic communities.

As this agenda plays out, the EAC, like all other Regional Economic Communities in Sub Saharan Africa, confronts the need to balance two priorities. The first priority is the legal rationalization of the relationships between the African Economic Community and the underlying Regional Economic Communities. The second priority is for EAC Partner States to follow through on commitments undertaken to approximate their national laws with the entire body of EAC law as contained in the EAC *acquis communautaire*. For completeness, that *acquis communautaire* comprises the following:

(a) The content, principles and political objectives of the EAC Treaty, including the EAC Treaty. (Nomenclature of the EAC Treaty interprets the EAC Treaty as the Treaty establishing the East African Community and any annexes and protocols thereto)[28];
(b) Judgments of the East African Court of Justice (hereinafter referred to as the EACJ) in ensuring adherence to law in the interpretation and application of and compliance with the EAC Treaty[29];
(c) Act's of the Community[30];
(d) Regulations, directives, decisions and actions relating to the EAC framework; and
(e) Relevant principles of international law.

More recently, there has been an evolution in two main bodies of the EAC's economic *acquis communautaire*. First, there has been an evolution in the laws governing the EAC Customs Union. The EAC Customs Union establishes a Free Trade Area between Partner States (zero tariffs and, with the exception of Rules of Origin, no other major policy restrictions on trade between Partner States) and an identical rate of tariff levied on goods imported from third countries, countries outside the EAC, i.e., a Common External Tariff or CET. Second, there has been an evolution in the laws governing the EAC's Common Market. The EAC's Common Market incorporates and builds on the EAC Customs Union by integrating the Partner States' markets into a single market in which there is the free mobility of labour, capital and intellect to produce goods and services. The Protocol on the Establishment of the EAC Common Market (hereinafter referred to as the EAC

---

[28] Art. 1 EAC Treaty, Interpretation.

[29] Art. 23 EAC Treaty, Role of the Court.

[30] Art. 62 EAC Treaty, Acts of the Community.

Common Market Protocol) extends to five freedoms (the free movement of goods, persons, labour, services and capital) and two rights (the rights of establishment and residence).[31]

The next two sub-sections evaluate the character and scope of the economic *acquis communautaire* of the EAC Customs Union and the EAC Common Market in a far broader way, but not by any means in an exhaustive way. The task, however, is an indispensable one. It aims to set up the framework within which to assess the challenge of approximation (for that assessment, go straight to part two, entitled, "Approximation of the EAC's Economic Acquis Communautaire").

The Acquis Communautaire of the EAC Customs Union

The EAC's "fully-fledged" Customs Union entered into force on 1 January 2010 following a 5-year transition period. The "fully-fledged" legal framework derives from:

(a) Relevant provisions of the EAC Treaty, the Protocol on the EAC Customs Union and Annexes to the Protocol (of note the EAC Common External Tariff, the Programme for the Elimination of Internal Tariffs, Rules of Origin, and Safeguard Measures);
(b) Applicable judgments made by the EACJ;
(c) Acts of the Community enacted by the East African Legislative Assembly, including the East African Community Customs Management Act 2004, revised edition 2009 (2004), which provides for the management and administration of EAC customs;
(d) Regulations and directives made by the Council, including the EAC Customs Management Regulations of 2006, which provide implementing regulations for transitional measures and the gradual elimination of internal tariffs; and
(e) Relevant principles of international law.[32]

At a multilateral level, the EAC's Customs Union has legal cover under the WTO's Enabling Clause.[33] The Enabling Clause provides for an exception to

---

[31] Art. 2 EAC Common Market Protocol, Establishment of the East African Community Common Market.

[32] Art. 39 EAC Customs Union Protocol, Customs Law of the Community.

[33] WTO Decision, Differential and More Favourable Treatment Reciprocity and Fuller Participation of Developing Countries, L/4903, 28th November, 1979, available at: http://www.wto.org/english/docs_e/legal_e/enabling_e.pdf (last visited on 22nd January, 2011). The WTO refers to the EAC's Customs Union having legal cover under the WTO Enabling Clause (date of signature was 30th November, 1999, date of notification 9th October, 2000, and entry into force on 7th July, 2000), http://rtais.wto.org/UI/PublicAllRTAList.aspx (last visited on 22nd January, 2011). WTO notifications show that only the EAC Treaty was communicated in 2000 (WTO, East African Community Communication from the Parties, Committee on Trade and Development,

Article I Most Favoured Nation (hereinafter referred to as MFN) obligations of the General Agreement (the General Agreement on Tariffs and Trade, hereinafter the GATT) under certain conditions.[34] If the contracting parties meet the relevant conditions, they have the option to accord differential and more favourable treatment to developing countries and treat like products differently irrespective of their origin and without according such treatment to other contracting parties.[35]

Exemptions are more restrictive when the Enabling Clause applies to regional arrangements. The Enabling Clause covers "regional or global arrangement[s] entered into amongst less-developed contracting parties for the mutual reduction or elimination of tariffs and, in accordance with criteria or conditions which may be prescribed by the Contracting Parties, for the mutual reduction or elimination of non-tariff measures, on products imported from one another". Nothing in this clause restricts regional or global arrangements extending to Free Trade Area's (hereinafter referred to as FTA's) or Customs Unions. The regional or global arrangement must provide for the mutual reduction or elimination of tariffs and non-tariff measures. Except under exceptional conditions, once a tariff is bound it is not to be increased.

There is no reference within the Enabling Clause to other Contracting Parties intervening in the decision-making process of parties to the regional arrangement in setting their mutual tariff reduction or elimination; that is left to the parties to the regional or global arrangement to work out. In terms of non-tariff measures, the Contracting Parties may prescribe criteria or conditions on the reduction or elimination of non-tariff measures; but this is not obligatory and prescription is optional.

Another aspect that could bamboozle is whether the word "prescribe" means recommend or oblige. In the context of the Enabling Clause's object and purpose, and pursuant to the WTO's development agenda, the Contracting Parties are to rest more on the side of flexibility; if not, they would defeat the object and purpose of the Enabling Clause and render its effect manifestly absurd or unreasonable.[36] Paragraph 6 of the Enabling Clause provides further support for this interpretation: the Contracting Parties are to "[have] regard to the special economic difficulties and the particular development, financial and trade needs of the least-developed

---

WT/COMTD/25, 11th October, 2000). The Protocol on the Establishment of the East African Customs Union was communicated in 2006 (WTO, East African Community Communication from the Parties Addendum, Committee on Trade and Development, WT/COMTD/25/Add.1, 1st November, 2006).

[34] General Agreement on Tariffs and Trade 1994, 15th April, 1994, Marrakesh Agreement Establishing the World Trade Organization, Annex 1A, The Legal Texts: The Results of the Uruguay Round of Multilateral Trade Negotiations 17 (1999), 1867 U.N.T.S. 187, 33 I.L.M. 1153 (1994) [hereinafter GATT].

[35] Report of the Appellate Body, European Communities – Regime for the Importation, Sale and Distribution of Bananas, WT/DS27/AB/R, 25th September, 1997.

[36] See also Report of the Appellate Body, European Communities – Conditions for the Granting of Tariff Preferences to Developing Countries, AB-2004-1, WT/DS246/AB/R, 20th April, 2004, para. 114.

countries, the developed countries shall exercise the utmost restraint in seeking any concessions or contributions for commitments made by them to reduce or remove tariffs and other barriers to the trade of such countries, and the least-developed countries shall not be expected to make concessions or contributions that are inconsistent with the recognition of their particular situation and problems".[37]

Whether "least-developed" countries can equate to "less-developed" or "developing" contracting parties is something altogether different. As an exception to GATT Article I, the Enabling Clause only applies in a regional context to arrangements amongst "less-developed contracting parties". If WTO members had sought to qualify "less-developed" as "developing" they may have perhaps drafted the Enabling Clause as such; but they did not.

Another well-documented problem arises. There is no clear determination of developing countries within the WTO. Instead, countries may simply proclaim themselves as developing; and this may be contended by other WTO Members.

While the WTO generally refers to the UN to define LDC's, the UN itself frequently uses the term "LDC" interchangeably to refer to either "least-developing countries" or "less-developing countries". Clearly, the Enabling Clause makes no explicit provision for regional trade arrangements between developed and developing countries. It is not clear, however, as to whether the provision for "less-developed contracting parties" extends to "developing", "less-developing" and "least-developing" contracting parties. The Enabling Clause distinguishes the "least developed among the developing". At times it contrasts the "developed" with the "less-developed" and, at other times, it contrasts the "developed" with the "developing". However, the term "less-developed" is not necessarily one and the same thing as "developing". The terms are therefore not necessarily interchangeable. Arguably, the WTO needs to turn to the UN to segment developing country members into three tiers of developing countries: the "least-developed", the "less-developed" and the "developing". Going forward, more robust segmentation of *common but differentiated responsibilities* is needed to successfully conclude a number of multilateral negotiations, including those in trade and climate change.

Back to the EAC context, the UN lists Burundi, Rwanda, Tanzania and Uganda as least developed countries; but not Kenya.[38] Considering the WTO has already declared that the Enabling Clause provides cover to the EAC's regional arrangement, then this declaration may infer the Enabling Clause extends to all developing countries party to a regional arrangement amongst themselves. By extension, mutual reduction implies that developing country members may not have to reduce or eliminate tariffs and non-tariff measures by anymore than the reductions undertaken by LDCs.

---

[37] WTO Decision, Differential and More Favourable Treatment Reciprocity and Fuller Participation of Developing Countries, L/4903, 28th November, 1979, available at: http://www.wto.org/english/docs_e/legal_e/enabling_e.pdf (last visited on 23rd January, 2011).

[38] For the UN's Current List of Least Developed Countries, see http://www.unohrlls.org/en/ldc/related/62 (last visited on 23rd January, 2011).

In the future, if the EAC is not deemed covered by the Enabling Clause, it would still remain open for the Contracting Parties to consider on an *ad hoc* basis, under the GATT provisions for joint action, any proposal for differential and more favourable treatment to give legal cover to EAC flexibilities. Long standing practice of the WTO declaring the EAC to have legal cover under the Enabling Clause may be all that suffices.

Alternatively, Regional Trade Agreements may obtain legal cover for goods under GATT Article XXIV; but in comparison to the Enabling Clause, GATT Article XXIV conditions are far more stringent. A lot has been written on GATT Article XXIV.[39] Various views have been expressed about incorporating even greater flexibilities for developing countries. One popular view is to amend Article XXIV to account for development but that is not the view taken here. As in the case of defining *common but differentiated responsibilities* what is required first in terms of *special but differentiated treatment* is clarification on existing disciplines and procedures.

It is also important to recall that GATT Article XXIV sets a minimum standard of best practice for FTA's, Customs Unions and Interim Arrangements in goods; and is therefore a critical step to forming a Common Market. Instead of contesting the provisions of the Enabling Clause, LDC spokespersons could do far better by aiming to graduate from the Enabling Clause and obtain cover under GATT Article XXIV. To reap the benefits of a "fully fledged" customs union, the EAC itself is aiming to comply with the GATT in its entirety. The Partner States have constantly, and throughout, embraced their WTO commitments and continually made honest endeavours to ensure consistency with their international obligations.

To be consistent with GATT Article XXIV, FTA's, Customs Unions and Interim Agreements leading to the formation of a FTA or Customs Union, must satisfy *inter alia* the provisions of paragraphs 5–8 of that article.[40] In other words, there are to be no higher or more restrictive barriers for third parties.[41] An interim agreement shall include a plan and schedule for the formation of a FTA or customs union within a reasonable period of time (qualified by the Understanding on the Interpretation of GATT Article XXIV, paragraph 3, to exceed 10 years only in exceptional cases).[42] Any modification to schedules, such as, an increase in a bound rate of duty, or tariff negotiations, shall be consistent with GATT Article XXVIII (Modification of Schedules) and procedure and compensatory adjustments shall take due account of compensation already afforded by the union.[43] There is an obligation for the parties deciding to enter into a FTA, Customs Union, or interim agreement leading to the formation of a FTA or Customs Union, to notify the other Contracting

---

[39] Bartels/Ortino (eds.), *Regional Trade Agreements and the WTO Legal System*, 2006.

[40] WTO, Understanding on the Interpretation of Article XXIV of the General Agreement on Tariffs and Trade 1994.

[41] Art. XXIV.5(a),(b) GATT.

[42] Art. XXIV.5(c) GATT.

[43] Art. XXIV.6 GATT.

Members promptly. In addition, a working party is to examine the agreement for consistency with the GATT and the Understanding on the GATT's Interpretation. The working party shall submit its findings to the Council for Trade in Goods.[44] Substantially all the trade shall be covered by the liberalization between the constituent territories in products originating in such territories in the case of a FTA; whereas, in the case of a Customs Union, substantially all the trade shall be covered by the liberalization between the constituent territories of the union or at least with respect to substantially all the trade in products originating in such territories.[45]

As a result, SADC's Free Trade Area and the Southern African Customs Union (SACU), which have legal cover under GATT Article XXIV,[46] face much heavier burdens than those facing the EAC, which is covered under the Enabling Clause. (Of course it is important to point out that SADC may not yet have a fully operational Free Trade Area, for instance, due to the treatment of certain sensitive products). SADC and SACU are prohibited from creating new obstacles for third parties; they must meet timetable obligations, adhere to correct procedure for modifying concessions, meet the obligations of notification and transparency; and meet the relevant infamous provision on covering substantially all the trade.[47]

In addition, pursuant to Article XXIV, paragraph 12 of the GATT, each party to the Regional Trade Agreement in goods is obligated to take reasonable measures for regional and local governments and authorities within its territories to observe the provisions of the GATT.[48] The provision is not a presumption. Instead, it clearly provides for the domestication of regionalism and the need for Contracting Parties to the WTO to incorporate the economic *acquis communautaire* of the GATT, including but not limited to Article XXIV, into their local jurisdictions.

Within the confines of GATT Article XXIV, two main exceptions may be cited. The first relates to the emergence of powerful developing country coalitions. The second relates to provisions that would otherwise undermine the object and purpose of the WTO Treaty series.

Although consensus is always preferable due to potential repercussions in other forums, paragraph 10 of GATT Article XXIV provides that contracting parties may approve exceptions to [GATT Article XXIV] paragraphs 5–9 inclusive by a two-thirds majority provided the proposals lead to the formation of a FTA or Customs

---

[44] GATT XXIV.7 and its Understanding on the Interpretation of Article XXIV GATT 1994. See also WTO, Transparency Mechanism for Regional Trade Agreements General Council Decision of 14 December 2006, WT/L/671, 18th December, 2006.

[45] Art. XXIV.8 GATT.

[46] Southern African Development Community (SADC), Free Trade Agreement, notified to the WTO under GATT Article XXIV, date of notification 2 August 2004; http://rtais.wto.org/UI/PublicShowRTAIDCard.aspx?rtaid=45; last visited 24 October 2011.

[47] WTO, RTA Database, available at: http://rtais.wto.org/UI/PublicAllRTAList.aspx (last visited on 23rd January, 2011).

[48] Art. XXIV.12 GATT.

Union in the sense of Article XXIV. (There is no derogation from incorporation of the GATT's economic *acquis communautaire*).

Obtaining a majority is unlikely to be an insurmountable task. As at 23 July 2008, the WTO had 153 members, so two-thirds of that is 102. Even the G77 (now with 130 developing country members) is more than ready to pronounce on WTO developments.[49] As another example, again while not all WTO members, the ACP Group of States with 79 members is not far off attaining a two-thirds majority. Further, the European Union with its 27 members is unlikely to want the European Commission to create a fiasco by undermining the Cotonou Accord's development provisions and its own member's trade and political relations with Africa, the Caribbean and the Pacific.

Paragraph 11 of GATT Article XXIV is also of note. It provides special provisions for India and Pakistan due to the exceptional circumstances in which they established as independent States, the fact that they have long constituted an economic unit and pending the establishment of their mutual trade relations on a definitive basis. Neither India nor Pakistan is on the United Nations Least Developed Country list. Arguably, exceptional circumstances existed in the establishment of the five EAC Partner States as independent States and they have long constituted an economic unit. "Organised [Western facilitated] cooperation between them started with the construction of the Kenya-Uganda railway (1897–1901), followed by the establishment of a customs collection centre in 1900, the East African Currency Board (1905), the Court of Appeal for Eastern Africa (1909), East African Governors' Conference (1926), the East African Income Tax Board (1940), and the Joint Economic Council in 1940".[50] Further, the EAC aims to do much more than establish mutual trade relations: it aims to form a political federation.

While perhaps only indirectly applicable to the EAC's Customs Union, the existence of these derogations strengthen the argument that exceptions may be made within the Doha negotiations without any need to amend Article XXIV of the GATT. Interpretative effect may be far more useful than substantive redrafting of Article XXIV. In addition, while the Doha Ministerial Declaration, supported by the Hong Kong Ministerial Declaration, provides for the agreement and clarification on disciplines and procedures for regional trade agreements and the taking into account of developmental aspects of regional trade agreements in negotiations, it does not relax Article XXIV for the majority of the WTO's

---

[49] The G77 established from the Joint Declaration of the Seventy-Seven Countries at the end of the first session of the United Nations Conference on Trade and Development on 15th June, 1964, see: http://www.g77.org/doc/index.html (last visited on 23rd January, 2011). See also, Position paper of the Group of 77 and China on strengthening the role of the UN in global economic governance, 2nd June, 2010.

[50] EAC Secretariat (Authors: Mugisa/Onyango/Mugoya), An Evaluation of the Implementation and Impact of the East African Community Customs Union, Final Report, March 2009, p. 1.

membership, i.e., developing countries.[51] Logically, too many exceptions would undermine the rule and render it useless.

What is important, however, is that the evolution of an EAC-COMESA-SADC FTA is likely to require conformity to, and cover under Article XXIV of the GATT, or the evolution of a more specific rule at the multilateral level to give effect to Regional Trade Agreement's incorporating developing countries. Tabling a more specific rule could be argued on the above basis, for example, by extending the unequal and discriminatory treatment provided solely to India and Pakistan by virtue of Article XXIV.11 to other developing countries, i.e., by maintaining GATT Article XXIV as a principle rule and by establishing a special rule of interpretation. It is easy to forget that GATT Article XXIV was a hard won battle. Tinkering with it now may do more harm than good.

Any such special rule of interpretation may take a leaf out of the EAC's approach to addressing variances. Article 1 of the EAC Treaty interprets the "principle of asymmetry" to mean the principle that addresses variances in the implementation of measures in an economic integration process for the purposes of achieving a common objective. Partial adaptation, as applied in the EAC, guides the EAC's transitional roadmap by taking into account the development stages of each Partner State. An extension of the principle of asymmetry could perhaps, but not necessarily, be used to recognise the benefits of regional integration of less developing and developing countries for the broader benefit of the multilateral community.

In any event, the EAC's legal framework embodies the major constituents of a Customs Union pursuant to the GATT. In sum, the framework incorporates the following:

(a) A programme for the elimination of internal tariffs (FTA);
(b) A common external policy and common external tariff to third parties;
(c) A collective administration of the Customs Union;
(d) A common tariff nomenclature and valuation method for tradable goods;
(e) A programme for the elimination of non-tariff barriers to ensure trade facilitation;
(f) The duty free quota free circulation of tradable goods within the EAC Customs Union;
(g) Common Sanitary and Phytosanitary measures (SPS) and food standards for regulating the import of goods from third parties;
(h) The deployment of IT systems (Raddex, electronic cargo tracking systems, etc.);
(i) Economic reform of tax and administrative policies; and
(j) A uniform application of Customs laws and regulations.

---

[51] WTO, Ministerial Declaration, Ministerial Conference Fourth Session, 9th–14th November, 2001, WT/MIN(01)/DEC/1, 14th November, 2001, para. 29. WTO, Doha Work Programme, Ministerial Declaration, Ministerial Conference Sixth Session, 13th – 18th December, 2005, WT/MIN(05)/DEC, 18th December, 2005, Annex D.

Fundamental to the operation of the Customs Union is the effective application of the Common External Tariff (hereinafter referred to as CET). Subject to sensitive products, the EAC's CET has a three-band tariff structure: (i) raw materials and capital goods 0%; (ii) intermediate goods 10%; and (iii) finished goods 25%. Some concerns continue about the variances and increases in special concessions and exemptions. Yet overall, intra-EAC and extra-EAC trade has benefited from the CET at the expense of third party imports.[52]

Rules of Origin raise an all-together more complex challenge in incorporating the EAC's economic *acquis communautaire* in Partner States jurisdictions. By their very nature, Customs Unions do not theoretically apply preferential rules of origin within the Union. Goods traded within the Customs Union are to circulate free of hindrances. With no customs taxes, e.g., tariffs on internal trade, there is no need for a Partner State to incur the transaction cost of facilitating a reduction or exemption. There is therefore no need to authenticate whether an EAC product is genuinely eligible for preferential reductions or exemptions from customs duties.

In several EAC Partner States, however, modalities for collection and accounting for customs revenue are not yet in place. Local and foreign products are not often easy to distinguish. So while the EAC Customs Union aims to enhance integration within the EAC through trade liberalisation, Partner States are somewhat restricted by the ongoing burden of administering Rules of Origin. Notwithstanding, the EAC does have its own Rules of Origin. The EAC's Rules of Origin show that the originating status of the good is the EAC and that substantial transformation has occurred. What is needed now is for Partner States to provide a more harmonised approach to interpretation, application and enforcement. Over time, incorporation of the EAC's economic *acquis communautaire* will help to consolidate the aims of the EAC customs union to encourage more value add in the region, and improve competitiveness in global markets, by trading goods on the basis of free circulation.

For now, complications are emerging from the tangle of Rules of Origin negotiated, or to be negotiated, in bilateral and regional agreements. Constraints on accounting for intermediate inputs will become even more challenging within EAC-COMESA-SADC Tripartite arrangements. The prospect of trade deflection, re-routing goods through countries that do not have the same level of preferences, may become even more prevalent. In some respects, these are foregone conclusions and necessary interim tradeoffs if Africa is to forge an African Economic Community at the continental level. In the interim, Partner States need to give attention to convergent liberal rules of origin regimes in order to resolve potential distortions and increased operating costs for national authorities and businesses. In moving towards an EAC-COMESA-SADC Customs Union, Partner States need to reflect on liberalizing not only tariffs but also rules of origin in order to ensure that a protectionist fortress does not consolidate in sub-Saharan Africa.

---

[52] EAC Secretariat (Authors: Mugisa/Onyango/Mugoya), An Evaluation of the Implementation and Impact of the East African Community Customs Union, Final Report, March 2009.

Besides, several countries, like Uganda, are largely dependent on import substitution and see rules of origin as a tool to combat fraud. Due to issues of poor accounting, overlapping Regional Trade Agreements and fraud, EAC Rules of Origin will therefore continue to prevail in the foreseeable future, even in a "fully fledged Customs Union".[53]

While the tendency to adopt complicated Rules of Origin that extend well beyond the simple task of authentication of origin or substantial transformation in a Partner State may be suitable to more sophisticated trading blocks, and even neighbouring ones, it does not foster development or the integration of small-scale operators into global trade. To help ensure that rules of origin do not counteract the benefits of trade and investment liberalisation too much, the EAC provides for two mechanisms: an EAC Certificate of Origin; and an EAC Simplified Certificate of Origin for small-scale cross border trades. The EAC's endeavours to simplify rules of origin versus some other regional economic community's far more restrictive approaches will be an ongoing challenge in terms of negotiating and incorporating the *acquis communautaire* of EAC-COMESA-SADC economic partnerships into local trade.

Overall, EAC Partner States still need to work on the treatment of sensitive products within an EAC context but especially in terms of relations with main foreign trading partners. Transitions in revenue generation (from over dependence on trade taxes to other forms of taxation, e.g., consumption taxes, which have an initial disproportionate effect on the poor) are yet to be properly affected and necessitate robust institutions and mechanisms to support employment. All EAC Partner States have prior experience in regional integration but effort and capacity building is still required to conform to the main constituents of the Customs Union and, in particular, to streamline Rules of Origin. All these issues relate to the approximation of the EAC's economic *acquis communautaire* and are prerequisites to a well-functioning Common Market and a consolidated rule of law in sub-Saharan Africa.

The Acquis Communautaire of the EAC Common Market

To recap, a Common Market is generally equivalent to a customs union plus the free mobility of labour, capital and intellect to produce goods and services. The Protocol for the Establishment of the EAC Common Market (hereinafter referred to as the EAC Common Market Protocol) governs the *acquis communautaire* of the EAC Common Market. In governing the economic *acquis communautaire* of the EAC Common Market, the EAC Common Market Protocol provides for five

---

[53] Njau, EAC Fully Fledged Customs Union: Implications for Private Sector, EABC Briefing Paper, January 2010, available at: http://www.kepsa.or.ke/pdfs/EAC_Briefing_Paper_Jan_2010. pdf (last visited on 23rd January, 2011).

freedoms (the free movement of goods, persons, labour, services and capital) and two rights (the rights of establishment and residence).[54]

While the economic *acquis communautaire* of the EAC Common Market codifies the five freedoms and two rights aforementioned, it is equally important to take cognisance of the EAC's *acquis communautaire* as a whole. The EAC Common Market Protocol provides for a far more extended array of economic and plurilateral cooperation encompassing the Protection of Cross-Border Investments; Economic and Monetary Policy Co-ordination; Financial Sector Policy Co-ordination; Harmonisation of Tax Policies and Laws; Prohibited Business Practices; Prohibited Subsidies; Public Procurement; Consumer Protection; Co-ordination of Trade Relations; Co-ordination of Transport Policies; Harmonisation of Social Policies; Environmental Management; Cooperation in Statistics; Research and Technological Development; Co-operation in Intellectual Property Rights; Co-operation in Industrial Development; and Co-operation in Agriculture and Food Security.[55] These supplementary areas of co-operation remain relevant to the analysis of the EAC's economic *acquis communautaire*. They certainly warrant further examination; but due to the confines of this article, I only delimit the five freedoms and two rights in the following section with the view being to set out the character and scope of the framework parameters of the Common Market prior to assessing the practical implementation, transposition and enforcement thereof.

Free Movement of Goods

Part C, Article 6, of the EAC Common Market Protocol, governs the *acquis communautaire* of the Free Movement of Goods between the EAC Partner States. The body of law governing the Free Movement of Goods encompasses the Customs Law of the Community as specified in Article 39 of the EAC Customs Union Protocol; and additional provisions for Technical Barriers to Trade (TBT), Sanitary and Phytosanitary Measures (SPS) and other instruments.[56]

To recall, the EAC's Customs Union derives from:

(a) Relevant provisions of the EAC Treaty, the Protocol on the EAC Customs Union and Annexes to the Protocol (key among them being on the EAC Common External Tariff, the Programme for the Elimination of Internal Tariffs, Rules of Origin, and Safeguard Measures);
(b) Applicable judgments made by the EACJ;

---

[54] Art. 2 EAC Common Market Protocol, Establishment of the East African Community Common Market.

[55] Art. 29–45 EAC Common Market Protocol, Part H, Other Areas of Co-Operation in the Common Market.

[56] Art. 6(1) EAC Common Market Protocol, the full provisions on the Free Movement of Goods are covered by Art. 6 EAC Common Market Protocol, Part C.

(c) Acts of the Community enacted by the Legislative Assembly, including the East African Community Customs Management Act 2004, revised edition 2009 (2004), which provides for the management and administration of EAC customs;

(d) Regulations and directives made by the Council, including the EAC Customs Management Regulations of 2006, which provide implementing regulations for transitional measures and the gradual elimination of internal tariffs; and

(e) Relevant principles of international law.[57]

In addition, the EAC Common Market Protocol provides that the free movement of goods shall be governed by:

(a) The East African Community Protocol on Standardisation, Quality Assurance, Metrology and Testing;

(b) The East African Community Standardisation, Quality Assurance, Metrology and Testing Act, 2006;

(c) The provisions of the Common Market Protocol;

(d) Protocols that may be concluded in the areas of cooperation on sanitary and phyto-sanitary and technical barriers to trade; and

(e) Any other instruments relevant to the free movement of goods.[58]

Issues pertaining to the Customs Union have been discussed earlier. Further work is required in all Partner States in terms of standards.

Free Movement of Services

Unlike Article XXIV of the WTO's GATT, Article V of the WTO's General Agreement on Trade in Services (hereinafter referred to as the WTO's General Agreement on Trade in Services (GATS)) explicitly provides flexibility for developing countries in Economic Integration Agreements. Article V, subparagraph 3 (a) provides for three mandatory provisions where developing countries are parties to an Economic Integration Agreement liberalizing trade in services. First, flexibility shall be provided in terms of substantial sectoral coverage (considering the number of sectors, volume of trade and modes of supply while not providing for the *a priori* exclusion of any mode of supply). Second, and in particular, flexibility is to be given to developing country parties in absenting or eliminating substantially all discrimination in the sense of Article XVII (National Treatment) between or among the parties in the sectors inscribed in a Members Schedule to meet substantial sectoral coverage above. Operationally, this is to be done through providing flexibility to "eliminate existing discriminatory measures and/or through the prohibition of new or more discriminatory measures either at the entry into force of that

---

[57] Art. 39 EAC Customs Union Protocol, Customs Law of the Community.

[58] Art. 6(2) EAC Common Market Protocol.

Economic Integration Agreement in services or on the basis of a reasonable time frame, except for measures permitted under Articles XI, XII, XIV, and XIV bis". In providing flexible treatment, consideration may be given to the relationship of the agreement to a wider process of economic integration or trade liberalization among the countries concerned. Third, the obligation for flexibility shall be in accord with the level of development of the countries concerned, both overall and in individual sectors and subsectors, i.e., a form of partial adaptation.

The priority is to move progressively towards inscribing substantial sectoral coverage in accord with the parties' level of development. In particular, flexibility is to be given to progressively eliminate discrimination and prohibit new or discriminatory measures between services and service providers with respect to sectors inscribed in a Members Schedule, subject to any conditions and qualifications set out therein.

In addition, in the case of economic integration agreements in services involving only developing countries, an optional provision exists to grant more favourable treatment to any juridical persons owned or controlled by natural persons of the parties to such an agreement, whether it provides substantive business operations in the territory or not.[59] One opinion is that a juridical person of a developed country member constituted under the laws of one of the developing country members shall be entitled to the same favourable treatment provided it engages in substantive business operations in the economic territory. While that opinion is debatable, from a policy perspective such treatment would be inconsistent with providing flexibility for economic integration agreements in services involving only developing countries. Further, pursuant to GATS Article V.6, a juridical person constituted under the laws of a party to an economic integration agreement in services is only entitled to treatment in that Economic Integration Agreement in services (excluding the treatment provided exclusively to developing country members) provided it engages in substantive business operations in the territory of the parties to such agreement.[60] In terms of North–South Regional Trade Agreement's, there is no provision stipulating that developing country members have to provide substantive business operations in a developed country member in order to benefit from an Economic Integration Agreement in services.

Some doubt also persists as to whether there is to be an elimination of existing discriminatory measures and prohibition of new or more discriminatory measures, in the sense of *Article XVII*. Alternatively, is there to be an elimination of existing discriminatory measures or prohibition of new or more discriminatory measures, in the sense of *Article XVII*? The eventual objective and purpose of the article seems to be to eliminate discrimination in the inscribed sectors. A fundamental question

---

[59] General Agreement on Trade in Services, 15th April, 1994, Marrakesh Agreement Establishing the World Trade Organization, Annex 1B, The Legal Texts: The Results of the Uruguay Round of Multilateral Trade Negotiations 284 (1999), 1869 U.N.T.S. 183; 33 I.L.M. 1167 (1994) [hereinafter GATS]; GATS, Art. V.3(b) and V.6.

[60] Art. V.6 GATS.

therefore is surely whether the measure concerned modifies the conditions of competition in favour of services or service suppliers of the Member compared to like services or service suppliers of any other Member. In the case where there are different levels of development, then those differences could perhaps be reflected in terms of the principle of asymmetry, i.e., variances in measures or partial adaptation of the *acquis communautaire*. There is nothing to enforce the EAC, or any other developing country, to jeopardise its regional integration agenda by opening up too rapidly and without all the attendant regulatory and competitive reforms in place: that would simply result in another EU-type financial crisis in which contagion would hurt all parties.

Other doubts exist in terms of what constitutes a reasonable timeframe.[61] A reference may be made to the Understanding on the Interpretation of Article XXIV of the GATT 1994, paragraph 3, which provides for a 10 year transition period in exceptional cases. Recall, however, that goods are not services. All the accompanying regulatory and competitive reforms needed for services liberalisation and implementing a strategic services marketing mix are far more resource pressing than the reforms demanded for liberalising goods.

By extension, the WTO's provisions governing the EAC's developments in services integration allow for a lesser coverage of services sectors and flexibility in terms of eliminating discrimination between services and service suppliers. Engaging in trade negotiations, say in terms of EAC-EC Economic Partnership Agreements, on the basis of a positive list approach (rather than a negative list approach) would clearly foster better governance and help provide for an overall balance of rights and obligations for both EAC and EC persons. Further, the flexibility provided for EAC Partner States as developing countries in GATS Article IV, Increasing Participation of Developing Countries, and GATS Article XIX, Negotiation of Specific Commitments both in specific sectors and overall, is not excluded by virtue of entering into an Economic Integration Agreement in services.

An economic integration agreement under the GATS obliges the EAC Partner States to notify the Council for Trade in Services promptly of any such agreement. In addition, the EAC Partner States shall report periodically on its implementation. While helpful, it is nonetheless optional, for the Council for Trade in Services to establish a working party to examine the agreement.[62]

At the EAC level, Part F, Articles 16–23 of the EAC Common Market Protocol, and Annex V thereto (the EAC Common Market Schedule of Commitments on the Progressive Liberalisation of Services), govern the Free Movement of Services. In defining trade in services between EAC Partner States, the EAC Common Market Protocol adopts the language and structure of the GATS.[63]

---

[61] WTO, Compendium of issues related to Regional Trade Agreements, Background Note by the Secretariat, Revision, Negotiating Group on Rules, TN/RL/W/8/Rev.1, 1st August, 2002.

[62] Art. V:7 GATS, Economic Integration.

[63] Art. I.2 GATS.

The free movement of services shall cover the supply of services: (a) from the territory of a Partner State into the territory of another Partner State; (b) in the territory of a Partner State to service consumers from another Partner State; (c) by a service supplier of a Partner State, through commercial presence of the service supplier in the territory of another Partner State; and (d) by the presence of a service supplier, who is a citizen of a Partner State, in the territory of another Partner State."[64] Similar to the GATS, these four modes of supply correspond to cross-border supply, consumption abroad, commercial presence and presence of natural persons.

Likewise, in terms of exceptions, the EAC Common Market protocol adopts the substance of the GATS and excludes services "in the exercise of governmental authority which are not provided on a commercial basis or in competition with one or more service suppliers".[65] Further, the definition of services includes "services normally provided for remuneration, in so far as they are not governed by the provisions relating to free movement of goods, capital and persons.[66]

MFN transparency (trade without discrimination between foreign services and service suppliers of the other Partner States), applies to treatment one Partner State accords to like services and service suppliers of other Partner States or to any third party or customs territory.[67] National Treatment obligations provide for the absence of all discriminatory measures that modify the conditions of competition in favour of services or service suppliers of the Partner State compared to like services or service suppliers of the other Partner States.[68] Partner States must notify the EAC Council on the entry into force of the protocol of all measures affecting the free movement of services and shall promptly inform the EAC Council of any changes.[69]

In terms of domestic regulation, EAC Partner States may regulate services in accord with national policy objectives. However, there is to be no inconsistency with commitments taken under the EAC Common Market Protocol and they must not constitute barriers to trade. Application of all measures is to be in a "reasonable, objective and impartial manner".[70]

General exceptions apply to the following: public morals; public order; the protection of human, animal, plant life or health; laws that are designed to prevent deception and fraud, protect privacy and safety; a derogation from National Treatment for imposition or collection of direct taxes and a derogation from MFN as the result of an agreement of the avoidance on double taxation, provided there is no arbitrary, unjustifiable discrimination or disguised restriction on trade in services between Partner States where like conditions prevail.[71] Protection of essential security issues is also provided for by virtue of a number of special security exceptions.[72]

---

[64] Art. 16(2) EAC Common Market Protocol, Free Movement of Services.

[65] Art. I.3 GATS; Art. 16(7)(a) EAC Common Market Protocol, Free Movement of Services.

[66] Art. 16(7)(b) EAC Common Market Protocol, Free Movement of Services.

[67] Art. 18 EAC Common Market Protocol, Most Favoured Nation Treatment.

[68] Art. 17 EAC Common Market Protocol, National Treatment.

[69] Art. 19 EAC Common Market Protocol, Notification.

[70] Art. 20 EAC Common Market Protocol, Domestic Regulation.

[71] Art. 21 EAC Common Market Protocol, General Exceptions to Trade in Services.

[72] Art. 22 EAC Common Market Protocol, Security Exceptions on Trade in Services.

On reviewing the EAC's Schedule of Service Commitments set out in Annex V to the EAC Common Market Protocol, it would seem that the EAC has used a traditional GATS positive list approach to scheduling market access and national treatment commitments, however, this is not stipulated. Market access in terms of services is not defined in the EAC Common Market Protocol and there is no reference to the meaning and application of market access in the schedules. For completeness, an interpretative note from the EAC Secretariat would give coherence to the links between the substantive core of the EAC's agreement on trade in services, (that embodied in the EAC Common Market Protocol) and Annex V thereto.[73]

Going forward, the Partner States have agreed to open services further. The EAC Council is obliged to issue directives on modalities for Partner States to undertake additional commitments following the entry into force of the EAC Common Market Protocol.[74] Just when those directives will be made is yet to be announced.

Free Movement of Persons and Workers

The EAC Common Market Protocol acknowledges the Free Movement of Persons and Workers as fundamental rights of EAC citizens.[75] Part D, Articles 7–12, of the EAC Common Market Protocol, Annex I EAC Common Market (Free Movement of Persons) Regulations, and Annex II EAC Common Market (Free Movement of Workers) Regulations, govern the EAC's provisions on the Free Movement of Persons and Workers.[76] The two regulations set out implementing guidelines to ensure uniformity among Partner States on the Free Movement of Persons and Workers.

Free Movement of Persons. The EAC Common Market Protocol permits EAC citizens to enter each other's territories without a visa, freely circulate and leave without the imposition of restrictions.[77] While national laws guarantee EAC citizens protection in other Partner States, they are not exempt from prosecution

---

[73] East African Community, The East African Community Common Market, Schedule Of Commitments On The Progressive Liberalisation Of Services, Annex V, EAC Secretariat, November 2009. For a WTO reference see: WTO, Trade in Services, Guidelines for the Scheduling of Specific Commitments Under the General Agreement on Trade in Services (GATS), S/L/92 (Scheduling Guidelines), adopted by the Council for Trade in Services on 23rd March, 2001.

[74] Art. 23(2)(3) EAC Common Market Protocol, Implementation of the Free Movement of Services.

[75] Art. 7(1), 10(1) EAC Common Market Protocol.

[76] EAC Common Market (Free Movement of Persons) Regulations, Annex I EAC Common Market Protocol, EAC Secretariat, November 2009; EAC Common Market (Free Movement of Workers) Regulations, Annex II EAC Common Market Protocol, EAC Secretariat, November 2009.

[77] Art. 7(2) EAC Common Market Protocol.

for crimes committed and Partner States maintain the right to impose limitations for the purposes of public policy, security or public health.[78] Partner States are to notify any such limitations to other Partner States.

The East African Community Common Market (Free Movement of Persons) Regulations, Annex I to the Common Market Protocol, apply to visitors, those seeking medical attention, persons in transit, students, interns or those participating in industrial training, and any other lawful purpose other than to work or be self-employed.[79] To comply, EAC citizens who seek to enter, transit or exit another Partner State must present immigration officers with a valid national travel document or national identity card and declare all information relating to entry and exit.[80] The Partner States are obliged to establish a common standard system of issuing national identity cards.[81] Travel documents shall also be standardized through a common system. Using electronic national identity cards as travel documents is optional.[82]

EAC citizens will have a 6-month right of sojourn, subject to renewal. Immigration authorities will issue a 6-month pass without charge.[83]

The Partner States are obliged to advise and consult the EAC Council on border management, including easing border crossings for EAC citizens, manning the border posts 24 h, and harmonizing immigration procedures.[84] EAC citizens may also be required to register their presence with national competent authorities.[85]

Free Movement of Workers. In terms of labour markets, the EAC *acquis communautaire* guarantees the move, stay and exit of workers, spouses of workers and children of workers. The right to work is subject to conforming to one of the categories of workers scheduled by the respective Partner State. The East African Community Common Market (Free Movement of Workers) Regulations (Annex II to the EAC Common Market Protocol) set out the schedules.

Citizens of Partner States are guaranteed the right to move freely for the purposes of employment. The right to work entitles EAC citizens to be accompanied by their spouse, children and dependants. Their spouse and, subject

---

[78] Art. 7(4)(5)(6) EAC Common Market Protocol.

[79] The East African Community Common Market (Free Movement of Persons) Regulations, Annex I to the Common Market Protocol, Regulation 4, Scope of Application. Regulation 7, Limitations.

[80] The East African Community Common Market (Free Movement of Persons) Regulations, Annex I to the Common Market Protocol, Regulation 5, Entry, Stay and Exit, para. 2.

[81] Art. 8 EAC Common Market Protocol, Standard Identification System.

[82] Art. 9 EAC Common Market Protocol, Travel Documents.

[83] The East African Community Common Market (Free Movement of Persons) Regulations, Annex I to the Common Market Protocol, Regulation 5, Entry, Stay and Exit.

[84] The East African Community Common Market (Free Movement of Persons) Regulations, Annex I to the Common Market Protocol, Regulation 8, Border Management.

[85] The East African Community Common Market (Free Movement of Persons) Regulations, Annex I to the Common Market Protocol, Regulation 9, Registration.

to age limits imposed by national law, their children and dependants, shall be entitled to work or engage in any economic activities as a self-employed person.[86]

Discrimination on the basis of nationality, remuneration or other conditions of work and employment, is prohibited.[87] Workers shall be entitled to enjoy social security benefits and employment assistance as accorded to workers of the Host Partner State.[88] In terms of social security benefits, implementation shall be on the basis of the Council issuing directives and making regulations.[89]

Labour movement is confined to private sector endeavours unless the laws of Partner States provide for entry to the public service.[90] Other limitations may be made subject to notification to other Partner States on the basis of public policy, public security or health.[91]

EAC citizens who seek to enter, transit or exit another Partner State for the purpose of employment must present immigration officers with a valid national travel document or national identity card and declare all information relating to entry and exit.[92] In addition, they must present immigration officers with a contract of employment.[93] Immigration authorities will then issue a 6-month pass for the purposes of completing the formalities needed to obtain a work permit. Six-month passes will also be provided to a spouse, children and worker's dependants subject to completing the formalities needed to obtain a dependant pass.[94] There shall be no fee for the passes.[95]

As to the requirements for a work permit, detailed procedure is set out in the implementing regulations.[96] The formalities governing work permits may, however, be in question with respect to full labour market integration. Arguably, the EAC's aspirations for a full labour market integration should consider the

---

[86] Art. 10(5) EAC Common Market Protocol, Free Movement of Workers; Art. 13, para 3 (a) and Art. 13, para 4 EAC Common Market Protocol, Right of Establishment.

[87] Art. 10 EAC Common Market Protocol, Free Movement of Workers; Art 13, para 3 (a) and Art 13, para 4.

[88] Art. 10 EAC Common Market Protocol, Free Movement of Workers.

[89] Art. 10(4) EAC Common Market Protocol, Free Movement of Workers.

[90] Art. 10(10) EAC Common Market Protocol, Free Movement of Workers.

[91] Art. 10(11)(12) EAC Common Market Protocol, Free Movement of Workers.

[92] The East African Community Common Market (Free Movement of Workers) Regulations, Annex II to the Common Market Protocol, Regulation 5, Entry, Stay and Exit, para. 2.

[93] The East African Community Common Market (Free Movement of Workers) Regulations, Annex II to the Common Market Protocol, Regulation 5, Entry, Stay and Exit, para. 2(c) and 3.

[94] The East African Community Common Market (Free Movement of Workers) Regulations, Annex II to the Common Market Protocol, Regulation 5, Entry, Stay and Exit, paras. 4–6. The inclusion of worker's dependant's is further provided for by virtue of the EAC Common Market Protocol, Art. 13, Right of Establishment, para. 4.

[95] The East African Community Common Market (Free Movement of Workers) Regulations, Annex II to the Common Market Protocol, Regulation 5, Entry, Stay and Exit, para. 6.

[96] The East African Community Common Market (Free Movement of Workers) Regulations, Annex II to the Common Market Protocol, Regulation 6, Procedure for Acquiring Work Permit.

requirements concerning work permits and be notified to the WTO's Council for Trade in Services.[97]

EAC Partner States are also working on the harmonisation and mutual recognition of academic and professional qualifications. Partner States shall conclude provisions on the harmonisation and mutual recognition of academic and professional qualifications in accordance with Annexes to the EAC Common Market Protocol.[98] Whereas, the harmonisation of labour policies, laws and programmes to facilitate the free movement of workers shall be in accordance with directives and regulations issued by the Council.[99]

The EAC Common Market Protocol (Free Movement of Workers Regulations) place additional obligations on the Secretariat. The Secretariat is responsible for monitoring the EAC labour market by carrying out surveys, maintaining a labour force database and submitting regular reports, including analysis and recommendations, to the Council.[100]

Free Movement of Capital

Removal of restrictions on the free movement of capital is part of the EAC's overall plan to move progressively to an integrated financial system and economic and monetary union. The nomenclature of capital, and related payments and transfers, provided for in the EAC Common Market Protocol cover: (a) direct investments; (b) equity and portfolio investments; (c) bank and credit transactions; (d) payment of interest on loans and amortisation; (e) dividends and other income on investments; (f) repatriation of proceeds from the sale of assets; and (g) other transfers and payments relating to investment flows.[101]

By virtue of Part B, Articles 24–28 of the EAC Common Market Protocol and Annex VI thereto (Schedule on the Removal of Restriction on the Free Movement of Capital), the EAC *acquis communautaire* makes provision for the progressive liberalisation of capital movements save in four exceptional circumstances. Alternatively, Partner States may invoke the safeguard clause.

The four main permitted exceptions to liberalising capital movements include: (i) prudential supervision; (ii) public policy considerations; (iii) money laundering; and (iv) financial sanctions agreed to by the Partner States.[102] The exceptions are

---

[97] Art. V bis GATS, Labour Markets Integration Agreement.

[98] Art. 11 EAC Common Market Protocol, Harmonisation and Mutual Recognition of Academic and Professional Qualifications.

[99] Art. 12 EAC Common Market Protocol, Harmonisation of Labour Policies, Laws and Programmes.

[100] The East African Community Common Market (Free Movement of Workers) Regulations, Annex II to the Common Market Protocol, Regulation 14, Monitoring of the Labour Market.

[101] Art. 28 EAC Common Market Protocol, Capital and Related Payments and Transfers.

[102] Art. 25 EAC Common Market Protocol, General Exceptions.

subject to furnished proof that the action was "appropriate, reasonable and justified". In addition, Partner States are obligated to notify the Secretariat and Partner States.

In terms of safeguards, there are three situations where Partner States may adopt safeguard measures subject to conditions.[103] First, Partner States may adopt safeguard measures where the movement of capital leads to disturbances in the functioning of the financial markets in a Partner State. Second, Partner States may adopt safeguard measures where a competent authority of a Partner State makes an intervention in the foreign exchange market, which seriously distorts the conditions of competition. Here, the other Partner States may take, for a strictly limited period, necessary measures in order to counter the consequences of the intervention. Third, Partner States may adopt safeguard measures where there is a balance of payments difficulty or serious threat thereof.

In accord with the EAC Common Market Protocol, the safeguard:

(a) Must be non-discriminatory among Partner States in favour of third parties;
(b) Must seek to minimize commercial, economic or financial injury to other Partner States;
(c) Must not exceed what is necessary to deal with the circumstances;
(d) Must be temporary and phased out progressively;
(e) Shall not be adopted or maintained for the purpose of protecting a particular sector or to contravene the EAC Common Market Protocol;
(f) Shall be notified to the Secretariat and to the other Partner States.[104]

In the event of a safeguard being imposed, the Council is mandated to establish procedures for periodic consultations including, where possible and desirable, prior consultations with the objective of making recommendations to the concerned Partner State for the removal of the safeguard measures. These consultations shall address compliance with the conditions under which the safeguard was applied and, in particular, the progressive phase out thereof.[105]

Partner States have agreed to specific transition periods. Annex VI to the EAC Common Market Protocol (the EAC Common Market Schedule on the Removal of Restrictions on the Free Movement of Capital) sets out a defined roadmap for implementation. To illustrate, one example has been extracted from the schedules. Kenya, Rwanda and Uganda have no existing restrictions on the purchase of foreign security locally by non-residents. Tanzania will phase out the restriction on non-residents to participate only in the stock market up to 60% of shares of primary or secondary issues by 31 December 2015. While, in Burundi a financial market development plan is at its inception stage. The capital market does not yet exist

---

[103] Art. 26 EAC Common Market Protocol, Safeguard Measures, and Art. 27 EAC Common Market Protocol, Conditions for Application of the Safeguard Measures.

[104] Art. 27 EAC Common Market Protocol, Conditions for Application of the Safeguard Measures.

[105] Art. 27(6) EAC Common Market Protocol, Conditions for Application of the Safeguard Measures.

in Burundi and therefore there are no specific regulations in this area, i.e., on the purchase of foreign security locally by non-residents.

Rights of Establishment and Residence

Part E, Articles 13–15, of the EAC Common Market Protocol provide for the rights of establishment and residence. Two implementing regulations supplement these rights. Annex III to the EAC Common Market Protocol sets out the EAC Common Market (Right of Establishment) Regulations; and Annex IV to the Protocol sets out the EAC Common Market (Right of Residence) Regulations.

The right of establishment is guaranteed to nationals of other Partner States. The right of residence is guaranteed to EAC citizens provided they have been admitted in another Partner State under the provisions governing the freedom or work or the right to establishment.[106]

Right of Establishment. The right of establishment extends to nationals, i.e., natural persons and legal persons (defined as companies and firms). EAC nationals are entitled to pursue economic activities as a self-employed person; and they are also entitled to set up and manage economic undertakings in the territory of Partner States.[107]

In terms of self-employment, the EAC Common Market (Right of Establishment) Regulations provide that self-employed persons must apply for a work permit within 30 working days from the date of entry into the territory of the host Partner State. If the application is successful, then the respective Partner State will issue a work permit for an initial period of up to 2 years. Self-employed persons must obtain a special pass of entitlement to engage in an economic activity for the period stated in the pass. Obtaining the special pass is a prerequisite to establishment. The self-employed may not establish without having been issued with a special pass.

Right of Residence. The EAC Treaty does not automatically provide for the right to residence. Special rules relating to residence prevail.

Once admitted, a worker or self-employed person may apply for residence. Partner States are obliged to issue residence permits to citizens of other Partner States qualifying for the right of residence.[108] In other words, while the EAC Common Market Protocol confers residence status to members of Partner States that residence is subject to a residence permit. In addition to the residence permit, the Partner State may also demand an alien identification document.[109]

---

[106] Art. 13(1)(5) EAC Common Market Protocol, Right of Establishment; and Art. 14 EAC Common Market Protocol, Right of Residence.

[107] Art. 13(3)(a),(4),(5) EAC Common Market Protocol, Right of Establishment.

[108] Art. 14(3) EAC Common Market Protocol, Right of Residence.

[109] EAC Common Market Protocol, Annex IV, EAC Common Market (Right of Residence) Regulations, Regulation 5, Basis for Residence.

As provided in the EAC Common Market (Right of Residence) Regulations, workers or self-employed persons must apply for a residence permit within 30 working days from the date of entry into the territory of the host Partner State. A residence permit is issued on the basis of the worker or self-employed person holding a work permit and the duration of residence shall be equivalent to the duration of the work permit. In addition, the worker or self-employed person must maintain their common standard travel document and the duration of the residence permit shall not exceed the duration of the validity of the common standard travel document.

The Common Market Protocol only applies to temporary residence. As provided for by the EAC Common Market Protocol: "permanent residence shall be governed by the national policies and laws of the Partner States".[110]

Family. Akin to the right to work, the right to establishment entitles self-employed EAC citizens to be accompanied by their spouse, children and dependants; and guarantees the right of residence for the spouse, child and dependant of a worker or self-employed person.[111] A spouse and, subject to age limits imposed by national law, children and dependants, shall be entitled to work or engage in any economic activities as a self-employed person.[112] The right to residence also covers spouses, children and dependants and they must hold a dependant's pass.

Non-discrimination. Partner States are to remove restrictions on the right of establishment that are imposed on the nationality of companies, firms and self employed persons; and there are to be no new restrictions on the right of establishment otherwise than provided by the EAC Common Market Protocol.[113] Once established, companies and firms "established in accordance with the national laws of a Partner State and having their registered office, central administration or principal place of business and which undertake substantial economic activities in the Partner State shall, for purposes of establishment, be accorded non discriminatory treatment in other Partner States".[114]

In terms of companies and firms undertaking economic activity in other Partner States, "the Partner States shall mutually recognize the relevant experience obtained, requirements met, licenses and certificates granted to a company or firm in the other Partner States".[115] Whereas, for the self-employed, they will eventually

---

[110] Art. 14(7) EAC Common Market Protocol, Right of Residence.

[111] Art. 14(4) EAC Common Market Protocol, Right of Establishment; Art. 14(2) EAC Common Market Protocol, Right of Residence.

[112] Art. 10(5) EAC Common Market Protocol, Free Movement of Workers; Art. 13(3)(a),(4) EAC Common Market Protocol, Right of Establishment.

[113] Art. 13(5) EAC Common Market Protocol, Right of Establishment.

[114] Art. 13(6) EAC Common Market Protocol, Right of Establishment.

[115] Art. 13(7) EAC Common Market Protocol, Right of Establishment.

benefit from the harmonisation and mutual recognition of academic and professional qualifications, which shall be concluded by Partner States in accordance with Annexes to the EAC Common Market Protocol.[116] The self-employed will also benefit from the opportunity to join a social security scheme in another Partner State.[117]

Limitations. Partner States may only maintain limitations on the right of establishment and the right of residence on the grounds of public policy, public security or public health; and subject to notification to other Partner States.[118] In terms of the right of establishment and the right of residence, the Partner States maintain jurisdiction over access to and use of land and premises. National policies and laws of the Partner States will still govern the use of land and premises.[119]

Incorporation. There are specific provisions relating to incorporating the *acquis communautaire* of the right of establishment in Partner States jurisdictions. Partner States are obliged to remove obstacles in the form of administrative procedures and practices that result from earlier accords entered into with Partner States. For example, Partner States shall progressively remove obstacles resulting from national laws that restrict the right of establishment; ensure the protection of already established workers; coordinate the approximation of safeguard measures for the protection of companies and firms; and ensure that the right of establishment is not restricted by prohibited subsidies or state aid.[120] Incorporating the *acquis communautaire* of the right of residence will also require significant changes, such as to immigration.

While the EAC Treaty provides that EAC law is supreme, and therefore seemingly prevails over domestic law, practical application, transposition of the EAC acquis and enforcement determine the EAC's credibility. In other words, legal approximation is required to give effect to the EAC's *acquis communautaire*. Not only is legal approximation (practical implementation, transposition and enforcement) required but it is also required on a timely basis. At the time of drafting this article, the agreed deadlines (operation of the EAC Common Market Protocol on 1 July 2010 and completion of the approximation of national laws by 21 August 2010) were fast approaching. Predictions that success in incorporating the *acquis communautaire* of the EAC into Partner States jurisdictions would weigh heavy on whether there would be economic, social and cultural cohesion at the local level turned out to be correct.

With elections in several countries in 2010, efforts leant towards more pressing national issues. In June 2010, Nkurunziza of Burundi was re-elected. In August

---

[116] Art. 11 EAC Common Market Protocol, Harmonisation and Mutual Recognition of Academic and Professional Qualifications.

[117] Art. 13(3)(b) EAC Common Market Protocol, Right of Establishment.

[118] Art. 13(8)(9) EAC Common Market Protocol, Right of Establishment; Art. 14(4)(5) EAC Common Market Protocol – Right of Residence.

[119] Art. 14(1)(2) EAC Common Market Protocol, Access to and Use of Land and Premises.

[120] Art. 13(11) EAC Common Market Protocol, Right of Establishment.

2010, President Kagame of Rwanda won a new term and in October 2010 President Kikwete of Tanzania was re-elected. Kenyans approved a new constitution by referendum on 4 August 2010, which sets limits on presidential powers and devolves certain responsibilities to the regions. (President Kibaki began his second five-year term in December 2007). Uganda's presidential and parliamentary elections were scheduled for February 2011 (President Museveni was re-elected on 20 February 2011). Going into 2011, work was still required to complete the approximation of national laws.

Approximation of the EAC's Economic Acquis Communautaire

Incorporating the economic *acquis communautaire* of the EAC in a new common market raises fundamental questions with respect to legal approximation: practical implementation, transposition and enforcement. First, what national institutions and supporting regulatory and judicial bodies have oversight for implementation of the EAC economic *acquis communautaire* and how do they function? Second, what national rules of law have been enacted to domesticate the EAC's Common Market Protocol and transpose its economic *acquis communautaire* into Partner States legal systems? Third, how will Partner States enforce EAC economic law governing the EAC common market? Part two of this paper addresses each of these questions concerning the approximation of the EAC's economic *acquis communautaire* in turn.

Practical Implementation

The EAC Mandate Governing the Approximation Process

As demonstrated, the EAC Common Market Protocol subsequently expands the EAC's policy competencies from goods to the free mobility of labour, capital and intellect to produce both goods and services, the rights of establishment and residence, and social and cultural dynamics. The responsibility for implementing this body of EAC Law rests firmly with the EAC's Ministerial Council, the policy organ of the EAC. Pursuant to Article 50 of the EAC Common Market Protocol, the Council shall establish a framework for monitoring and evaluating the implementation of the EAC Common Market Protocol; ensure that the operations of the Common Market conform to the EAC Common Market Protocol; and evaluate implementation and take any appropriate measures to remedy delay. The Secretariat, as the executive organ of the Community, has day-to-day operational oversight.

The EAC Council consists of responsible Ministers of each Partner State. As the policy organ of the Community, the Council's mandate is twofold: first is to promote, monitor and keep under constant review the programmes of the Community; and, second, is to ensure the Community's proper functioning and development.[121] The Council's functions are extensive. In accord with the EAC Treaty, the Council makes policy decisions; initiates and submits Bills to the East African Legislative Assembly; makes regulations, issues directives, takes decisions, makes recommendations and gives opinions; considers the budget of the Community; considers measures that should be taken by Partner States in order to promote the attainment of the Community's objectives; makes rules and regulations pertaining to staff and finance of the EAC; submits annual progress reports to the Summit, which consists of Heads of State or Government of the Partner States; implements the decisions and directives of the Summit as may be addressed to it; endeavours to resolve matters that may be referred to it; and exercises such other powers and performs such other functions as are vested in or conferred on it by the EAC Treaty.[122]

For the purposes of implementing the EAC Common Market Protocol, the EAC Council is tasked with issuing directives for the Partner States to implement their undertakings to approximate their national laws and to harmonise their policies and systems.[123] Directives issued by the Council are to be published in the Community Gazette.[124]

While the EAC Common Market Protocol provides for the approximation of laws, it does not provide a comprehensive roadmap for legal approximation. Notwithstanding, the Council and the Summit directed that legal approximation be done by 21 August 2010. The target was ambitious: the scope of the *acquis communautaire* and the number of laws to be harmonized was extensive. As at early December 2010, no other directive had been issued with respect to incorporating the EAC's economic *acquis communautaire* into Partner States jurisdictions. On 13 December 2010, Hon. Hafsa Mossi (Chairperson of the EAC Council of Ministers), gave assurance that the approximation and harmonisation of laws and policies to *operationalise* the protocol were ongoing.[125]

Effort is required to develop a comprehensive inventory of the EAC's economic *acquis communautaire*, compare it with current national policy and laws and propose strategic and regulatory measures to facilitate approximation. All countries have now established national task forces to audit their national laws and ascertain where they conflict with the Common Market Protocol. The EAC reported in

---

[121] Art. 13 EAC Treaty, Membership of the Council; Art. 14(1)(2) EAC Treaty, Functions of the Council.

[122] Art. 14 EAC Treaty, Functions of the Council.

[123] Art. 47(1)(2) EAC Common Market Protocol.

[124] Art. 14(5) EAC Treaty.

[125] EAC Press Release, Review of Laws for Common Market On, Council Chair tells EALA, Hon. Hafsa Mossi Assures House after Members Query Pace of Approximation and Harmonization of Laws and Policies to Operationalize Protocol East African Community Headquarters, 13th December, 2010, available at: http://www.eac.int/about-eac/eacnews/530.html?task=view (last visited on 17th January, 2011).

December 2010 that delays had been due to "unforeseen logistical problems" but that the "report of Kenya's Task Force on the Review of Domestic Laws had been submitted to Kenya's Attorney General for further action; and in Tanzania and Uganda similar Task Forces were at advanced stages of review and consultation."[126]

The EAC Secretariat has facilitated interrelated work on the harmonisation of laws at a Community wide level. To support Partner States in incorporating the *acquis communautaire*, the EAC Secretariat commissioned a study to prioritise the harmonisation of commercial laws that have an impact on the common market. The phase of identification and review of commercial laws was finalized July 2010 and has since moved to the phase of drafting bills. The entire work programme feeds into the work of the EAC's Committee on the Approximation of Laws, which has launched a sub-project on the harmonisation of commercial laws. The sub-project will include model bills for consideration by the Community's legislative organ, the East African Legislative Assembly (hereinafter referred to as the EALA). As at end April 2010, "45 pieces of legislation on trading, business registrations, investment, insurance and banking had been identified".[127]

It should however be recalled that the five freedoms (the free movement of goods, persons, labour, services and capital) and the two rights (the rights of establishment and residence) are the cornerstone of the EAC's economic *acquis communautaire*. While of course other matters, such as, competition policy, intellectual property, social and cultural laws, are also integral to the common market, immediate work is required to audit and approximate laws relating to the five freedoms and two rights.

Recall also that the EAC Common Market Protocol will be implemented progressively and in accordance with schedules approved by the Council.[128] Work needs to be done to develop and approve such schedules. Attention to the laws that influence the free movement of goods, i.e., have a bearing on cross border transactions, etc. is a priority, as approximation will complete the "fully-fledged" Customs Union.

As to the free movement of services, progressive implementation will need to be undertaken hand in hand with a comprehensive competition policy and the appropriate regulatory reforms. While Kenya and Tanzania have more tested competition laws, Burundi, Rwanda and Uganda are expediting the process of incorporation.[129] Sitting above these local reforms is the EAC's Competition Act 2006, which promotes and

---

[126] Ibid.

[127] EAC Secretariat Press Release, Meeting on Approximation of National Laws in the EAC Context Held in Nairobi, 18th February, 2010; Council Chairperson Assures Community on Ratification of Common Market Protocol, 29th April, 2010.

[128] Art. 76(2) EAC Treaty, Establishment of a Common Market.

[129] Muwanga, "East Africa: EAC Competition Law Imposes $100,000 Fine", East African Business Week, 21st December, 2009, see http://allafrica.com/stories/200912211204.html (last visited 23rd January, 2011).

protects competition in the Community, provides for consumer welfare and establishes the EAC Competition Authority. The EAC's Sectoral Council on Trade, Industry, Finance and Investment has adopted the EAC Competition Regulations and referred the regulations to the Sectoral Council of Legal and Judicial Affairs for legal input. The EAC's Competition Regulations will facilitate the implementation of the EAC's Competition Act. The EAC is nearing the stage where it can put the EAC Competition Act into effect and establish the East African Competition Authority. As part of this process, Partner States will need to co-ordinate not only the application and enforcement of competition policy between the activities of the EAC's Competition Authority and Partner States but also the co-ordination of the Common Market and associated sectoral reforms. Subject to the Treaty, the Council's competency extends to, but is not limited to, establishing the relevant sectoral committees.

To give effect to its policy mandate, the Council shall also give directions to the Partner States and to all other EAC organs and institutions excluding the Summit, Court and the Assembly.[130] The Council shall also make regulations, issue directives, take decisions, make recommendations and give opinions. Any directive issued on legal approximation will be binding on all Partner States and all other organs and institutions of the EAC excluding the Summit, the Court and the Assembly.[131] The Council may also request advisory opinions from the East African Court of Justice (hereinafter referred to as EACJ) and did just this with respect to variable geometry, i.e., progressive multi-speed incorporation of the *acquis communautaire*.[132]

Responding to a request from the Council of Ministers, the EACJ's 2008 Advisory Opinion deals with the issue of progressive and flexible implementation of the *acquis communautaire*. On the one hand, the EAC Treaty provides for the operational principle of variable geometry: flexibility in the progression of integration activities, projects and programmes; and differentiation in terms of the speed at which Partner States incorporate the *acquis communautaire*.[133] On the other hand, decisions of the Summit and Council are to be made by consensus.[134] One of the salient features of the EAC is its consensual policy decision-making process, subject to a protocol on decision-making.[135]

In comparison with how EAC law may interact with law in other regions of the world, the EACJ made reference to the application of the principle of variable geometry in EU law. Not every Member State of the EU has to take part in every

---

[130] Art. 14(3)(c) EAC Treaty, Functions of the Council.

[131] Art. 16 EAC Treaty, Effects of Regulations, Directives, Decisions and Recommendations of the Council.

[132] Art. 14(4) EAC Treaty, Functions of the Council.

[133] Advisory Opinion of the East African Court of Justice, EACJ, In The Matter Of A Request By The Council Of Ministers Of The East African Community For An Advisory Opinion; Application No. 1 of 2008, East African Court of Justice at Arusha, First Instance Division, para. 2.7.2; Art. 1, Art. 7(1)(e) EAC Treaty.

[134] Art. 12(3), 15(4) EAC Treaty.

[135] Art. 15(4)(5) EAC Treaty, Meetings of the Council.

policy area. Some belong to the Schengen acquis on border controls, others don't. Some use the euro, some don't. The danger, however, is that a smorgasbord approach to the EAC's *acquis communautaire*, rather than a fixed menu or one *à la carte*, would detract from the EAC's core integration process and serve to weaken and fragment the community. Integration that proceeds between a couple of Partner States at a faster pace, rather than simultaneously, could mean that some Partner States may not be party to core decisions that would impact them at a later date. In effect, decision-making would be by majority rather than by consensus.

The EACJ distinguished consensus from variable geometry. Consensus is a decision making tool used in the Summit and Council. Conversely, variable geometry is a strategy for implementation.

While not going as far as Kenya's submission to categorise the EAC *acquis communautaire* as mandatory or optional, whereby no Partner State shall derogate from mandatory provisions but may derogate from optional provisions by the application of variable geometry, the EACJ did agree that the principle of variable geometry is an exception and not the rule. The Court went on to suggest that Partner States may wish to consider the "core" versus "periphery" distinction made by the European Union but elaborated no further.

The request by the Council and the EACJ's response served to enhance the Court's role as the Community's judicial organ, an organ that was proactive and dynamic in interpreting Community law. As a result of the EACJ's advisory opinion, simultaneous implementation of the EAC *acquis communautaire* is impractical in some circumstances and the principle of variable geometry is in harmony with the requirement for consensus in decision-making. The principle of variable geometry can apply to guide the common market integration process, the requirement for consensus in decision-making notwithstanding. Consensus in decision-making does not imply unanimity of the Partner States.

In any event, Partner States are expected to act in good faith to approximate their municipal laws with those of the EAC's economic *acquis communautaire*. Directives may be issued when Partner States have not performed their obligations. As of now all Partner States seem to be doing something to approximate, reform or revise their laws (not necessarily with an impetus on aligning with the EAC Common Market Protocol *per se* but to modernize their laws); and not necessarily simultaneously but at different speeds.

More detailed strategic planning would assist to align this entire approximation process. While still contentious, the principle of variable geometry does not necessarily necessitate an amendment to the EAC Treaty to put the principle into operation. Operation will not happen unless project plans and roadmaps are in place and it is the Council that is in the right position to approve and amend such schedules based on decision-making priorities that should be agreed by consensus.

In distinguishing the "mandatory" *acquis communautaire* from the "optional", the "essential" is surely to implement the "fully fledged Customs Union", i.e., align border legislation of the Customs Union and Common Market with the WTO, WCO and revised Kyoto Convention; improve rules of origin in line with the EAC Customs Union (Rules of Origin) Rules (Annex III to the EAC Customs Union

Protocol); and improve revenue collection. At the same time, some Partner States are starting to address implementation plans across the broader spectrum covered by the EAC Common Market Protocol, including the free movement of persons, labour, services (and its associated competition issues), capital and the rights of establishment and residence. Here, the Partner States could reach consensus on core policy decisions while modifying strategic implementation to one that is EAC *à la carte*. The peril for those on the frontiers of implementation, however, will be whether they will be able to quarantine the core from the periphery.

Institutional Arrangements

Besides the institutional arrangements aforementioned, the EAC Treaty mandates the EAC Ministerial Council to establish Sectoral Councils to deal with matters arising under the Treaty. Decisions of the Sectoral Councils are deemed decisions of Council.[136] The EAC Treaty also charges the Council with establishing Sectoral Committees.[137] Committee decisions are not deemed Council decisions.

Sectoral Council. The EAC's Sectoral Council on Legal and Judicial Affairs (spearheaded by the Attorneys General of Partner States) plays a pivotal role in incorporating the EAC's economic acquis communautaire at a national level. The Council convenes to address legal and judicial issues pertaining to regional integration. It often reviews the implementation status of previous decisions made by the Council. At its ninth meeting in March 2010, the Sectoral Council considered, among others, the draft EAC Customs Management Regulations 2009, the draft EAC Competition Regulations 2009 and the report of the Sub-Committee on Approximation National Laws.

Sectoral Committee. At the regional level, the EAC has established a "Sub-committee on the Approximation of National Laws in the EAC Context". Subject to decisions made by the Sectoral Council on Legal and Judicial Affairs, the Chairpersons of the Law Reform Commissions co-ordinate the activities of the "Sub-committee on the Approximation of National Laws in the EAC Context" and receive and consider its reports.[138] As its name implies, the sub-committee's task is to assist Partner States to "approximate" national laws of Partner States with those of the EAC legal acquis. Guided by the EAC Council's approved schedules, the sub-committee is responsible for the roadmap, implementation plan and delivery of the legal approximation programme and shall meet as often as necessary to discharge its functions properly.

---

[136] Art. 14(3)(i) EAC Treaty, Functions of the Council.

[137] Art. 14(3)(j) EAC Treaty, Functions of the Council.

[138] Note, however, that the Art. 17 EAC Treaty, Composition of the Co-ordination Committee, and Art. 18 Functions of the Co-ordination Committee, provides for the responsible Permanent Secretaries of Partner States sitting as the EAC Co-ordination Committee to co-ordinate committee activities (not those of sub-committees) and receive and consider their reports.

Task Force. At an operational level a Task Force, established by the Sub-Committee on the Approximation of National Laws in the EAC Context, supports the process of harmonisation of laws in the East African Community. The Task Force is supported by representation from the Partner States' Law Reform Commissions, Offices of the First Parliamentary Counsel, Coordinating Ministries and line Sectoral Departments. Its role is to carry out the technical work regarding the approximation of laws. The task force is therefore charged with: identifying priority areas for the approximation and harmonisation of municipal laws; facilitating exchange of information between the Law Reform Commissions; establishing synergy with other institutions and bodies engaged in law reform programmes; preparing working papers for the Sub-Committee on Approximation of National Laws in the EAC Context; and preparing draft tripartite instruments (COMESA-EAC-SADC). The task force undertakes research on laws to be approximated, and policies to be harmonised, at a national level and makes recommendations for the enactment of an EAC law or for amendments or repeal of national laws to conform to global trends or best practices. On approval by the relevant Sectoral Councils, a recommendation from the task force becomes a directive to the Partner States to implement.

EAC Secretariat. The EAC Secretariat, the executive organ of the EAC and guardian of the EAC Common Market Protocol, supports the institutional arrangements governing the incorporation of the EAC *acquis communautaire*. The Secretariat plays a pivotal role in a number of areas. Article 71 of the EAC Treaty sets out the responsibilities of the Secretariat to include the following: "initiating, receiving and submitting recommendations to the Council and forwarding of Bills to the Assembly through the Co-ordination Committee; initiating studies and research; planning, managing, implementing and monitoring Community programmes; using its initiative to inform the Community of any matter that appears to merit examination; co-ordination and harmonisation of policies and strategies; general promotion and dissemination of information to stakeholders and the general public; submitting reports to the Council through the Co-ordination Committee; general administration and financial management; mobilization of development funds; budget submission to the Council; implementation of Summit and Council decisions; organization and record keeping of the institutions meetings excluding those of the Court and Assembly".[139] Note that Article 71 (1) (a) of the EAC Treaty, which provides for the Secretariat "to initiate, receive and submit recommendations to the Council and forward Bills to the Assembly through the Co-ordination Committee", is not correct. The EAC Secretariat informs that Article 71 (1) (a) is a drafting error, which has been identified for amendment. The Secretariat will only forward Bills to the Assembly through the Council. With respect to the economic *acquis communautaire*, the Secretariat's efforts will increasingly focus on issues of conformity and implementation.

---

[139] Art. 71 EAC Treaty, Functions of the Secretariat.

Co-ordinating Ministries. The establishment of co-ordinating Ministries by the Partner States ensued from the implementation of a decision by the Heads of State during their Summit held in Dar es Salaam in May 2005. The Summit directed that all East African States should each create a Ministry of East African Cooperation to deal with EAC issues, pursuant to Article 8 paragraph 3 of the EAC Treaty. The establishment of EAC co-ordinating ministries in each Partner State represents a cornerstone in institutional reform. In doing so, the Partner States extended the Community's principle of subsidiarity to facilitate a far broader multi-level participation of national stakeholders in the process of economic integration.

The Government of Burundi co-ordinates EAC integration and respect of the EAC Treaty through its Ministry of EAC Affairs (Ministère des Affaires de la Communauté Est Africaine).[140] Burundi has made hefty reforms in implementing the economic *acquis communautaire*, including incorporating customs legislation; introducing a VAT regime and setting up the Burundi Revenue Authority; setting up the Burundi Investment Promotion Agency; and harmonisation of the investment code and competition laws with those of the other EAC Partner States.[141]

Kenya first established a Ministry to focus on EAC integration in 2004. In 2006, that Ministry was renamed the Ministry of East African Community.[142] For 2009/2010, the Ministry has set itself the task to review and speed up its approach on the Harmonisation of Municipal laws into the EAC context.[143]

The Government of Rwanda established the Ministry of East African Community (MINEAC) in 2008 and tasked it with the coordination of activities related to the integration of Rwanda into the East African Community.[144] Integration is a key pillar of Rwanda's Vision 2020, its Economic Development and Poverty Reduction Strategy and its EAC Development Strategy for 2006–2010. Under its coordination and facilitation of EAC activities programme, the Ministry is tasked with ensuring that EAC legal instruments relevant to Rwanda are approximated.

---

[140] Burundi, Ministère des Affaires de la Communauté Est Africaine, see http://www.eac.bi (last visited on 23rd January, 2011).

[141] EAC Press Release, Burundi Ratifies EAC Common Market Protocol, EAC Secretariat, 30th April, 2010; see:
http://www.eac.int/news/index.php?option=com_content&view=article&id=231:burundi-ratifies-eac-common-market-protocol&catid=48:eac-latest&Itemid=69 (last visited 23rd January, 2011); see also: Study of the impact of Burundi's membership of the East African Community (EAC) Common Market and preparation of a negotiating strategy, Final report, Prepared for the East African Community and Deutsche Gesellschaft für Technische Zusammenarbeit (GTZ) GmbH Eschborn, Germany at the request of the EAC-GTZ programme "Strengthening the Integration Process in the EAC Region", May 2008.

[142] Kenya, Ministry of East African Community, see http://www.meac.go.ke (last visited on 23rd January, 2011).

[143] Kenya, Ministry of East African Community, Annual Work Plan 2009/10; http://www.meac.go.ke/index.php?option=com_docman&task=cat_view&gid=1&Itemid=2 (last visited on 23rd January, 2011).

[144] Rwanda Ministry of East African Community (MINEAC), see http://www.mineac.gov.rw (last visited on 23rd January, 2011).

Tanzania established the Ministry of East African Cooperation in 2006 with a view to enhancing the effective participation of Tanzania and accelerating the region's integration process.[145] Like several of the EAC integration ministries, it has a focus on delivering to its stakeholders through its customer care charter.

In 2007, Uganda's Ministry of East African Community Affairs became a fully-fledged Ministry tasked with promoting Uganda's interests in the pursuit of a politically united EAC.[146] Amongst other strategic leadership, co-ordination, relationship, communication and monitoring mandates, the Ministry's task is to harmonize EAC policies and programmes.

In terms of practical implementation of the EAC economic acquis communautaire, each Partner State has taken strides in establishing or extending the competence of EAC supporting regulatory and judicial bodies. Ministries of EAC Affairs, Ministries of Justice, Attorney General's chambers, Law Reform Commissions, and the judiciaries all function through the Sectoral Council on Legal and Judicial Affairs (spearheaded by Attorneys General), the Sub-Committee on Approximation of laws (spearheaded by chairpersons of the Law Reform Commissions) and the Sub-Committee on Judicial Education (composed of judges and registrars from all the Partner States). The EAC's private sector development strategy fosters institutional interactions with the private sector.

There remains a requirement for a single contact point in each co-ordinating Ministry, updated websites in plain English and the local language, and help guides, particularly in Kiswahili. In addition, it would be useful to establish an integrated approach to facilitating trade and investment to external markets. An EAC Trade and Investment Commission, perhaps operating under similar lines to the recently established South Pacific Trade and Invest Commissions, could be tasked with practical implementation of the economic acquis communautaire by facilitating successful connections for exporters, investors and stakeholder organisations.

While the EAC Summit directed the finalization of the institutional arrangements that will support the implementation of the East African Common Market by April 2011,[147] all these implementation activities come at a cost. Partner States need to set priorities and make some commitment to an EAC Development Fund.

---

[145] The Ministry of East African Cooperation was established Vide Government Notice No. 1 of January, 2006, see http://www.meac.go.tz (last visited on 23rd January, 2011).

[146] Uganda's Ministry of East African Community Affairs, see http://www.meaca.go.ug (last visited on 23rd January, 2011); for an Overview of the Ministry of East Africa Community Affairs (MEACA), presented by the Permanent Secretary, Ms. Edith N. Mwanje at Kampala International University on 8th May, 2010, see http://www.mak.ac.ug/documents/eac/MEACAOverview.ppt (last visited on 23rd January 2011).

[147] Communiqué of the 12th Ordinary Summit of EAC Heads of State Theme: "EAC: A Second Decade Of Higher Achievements", 3rd December, 2010, EAC Secretariat, para. 12.

Transposition

Domestication of EAC Law

Partner States discussed the issue as to how they engage with the EAC Secretariat on the domestication of laws in detail at one of the Sub-committee on the Approximation of National Laws meetings in February 2010. It was resolved that since all Partner States domesticated the EAC Treaty, all Treaty provisions are enforceable in the five Partner States, including Article 8, paragraph 4, of the Treaty which requires that EAC organs, institutions and laws take precedence over similar national ones. The meeting concluded that there was no need to amend national laws domesticating the EAC Treaty to provide expressly that EAC organs, institutions and laws take precedence over similar national ones as EAC law is self-executing. In other words, the EAC Treaty, and by extension, the EAC Common Market Protocol, have direct effect in Partner States. Individuals may therefore invoke an EAC Community provision irrespective as to whether it has been transposed into national law.

In practice, most Partner States approach the approximation of laws through the enactment of municipal laws to align with commitments made at the EAC wide level and at tripartite and African Union levels of cooperation. Interpretative methods of enforcement and pro-EAC interpretation by local courts could supplement these efforts but, with the exception of Customs laws, there is some way to go yet before the EAC's economic *acquis communautaire* will be self-executing at a local level.

Even then, that is not to say that the EAC's economic *acquis communautaire* will have immediate applicability it its entirety. The EAC Treaty's reference to the establishment of a common market, and the principle of variable geometry, aforementioned, provide for progressive implementation. Transitory inconsistency will therefore exist in most Partner States. In other words, direct applicability of the EAC Common Market Protocol will be rejected where the Partner States have used their margin of discretion and agreed with other Partner States not to implement a specific provision just yet.

As a result, any discussion on the incorporation of the economic *acquis communautaire* of the Common Market must define the *acquis communautaire* applicable by Partner State. As with the request for the EACJ to provide an Advisory Opinion with respect to variable geometry, the Council could make a request to the EACJ for an Advisory Opinion as to what minimum provisions will have direct effect. It would then be for Partner States to continue the approximation process and communicate to their citizens their rights and obligations, those that apply community wide and those additional engagements undertaken by individual Partner States.

In many respects, the question of supremacy of law charters unknown territory for the EAC. The EAC's economic *acquis communautaire* is supreme between the parties to the EAC Treaty but not all the time. When the EAC as a body corporate or a Partner State enters into binding arrangements with other Members of the WTO, those that are not party to the EAC, then WTO law may prevail. Every treaty in force is binding upon the parties to it and must be performed by them in good faith; this is the rule of "pacta sunt servanda".[148] As aforementioned, this provision is mirrored in GATT Article XXIV whereby each contracting party shall take reasonable measures to observe GATT law by the regional and local governments and authorities within its territories.[149] In tandem, other members of the WTO have an obligation to interpret WTO agreements so as to account for special and differential treatment and development. Further, unless an internal provision is of fundamental importance or a peremptory norm of general international law ("jus cogens") then Partner States may not invoke a provision of its internal law as justification for its failure to perform a treaty.[150] The EAC's aims are not only to incorporate WTO law within Partner States but also to incorporate WTO plus provisions. There is no contravention here.

However, to recall pursuant to Articles 8 paragraphs 4 and 5 of the EAC Treaty: "Community organs, institutions and laws shall take precedence over similar national ones on matters pertaining to the implementation of the Treaty; and the Partner States undertake to make the necessary legal instruments to confer precedence of Community organs, institutions and laws over similar national ones". Arguably, in a common market, national constitutions governing national organs, institutions and laws, and being the supreme law of the Partner States, are not "similar" to Community organs, institutions and laws. Albeit, at what point in the progress towards a political federation will community law be a proxy substitute for national constitutions? Answer: probably not until a regional constitution evolves.

In the meantime, while EAC Partner States seem to have a firm position as to how to resolve any emerging conflict of laws between WTO law and EAC law, some confusion persists regarding the interrelationships between the laws of the African Union and EAC law; and EAC law and Partner State law. To illustrate, the EAC Treaty provides that all rules and orders made by the Summit, and all regulations and directives made or given by the Council, under the Treaty shall come into force on the date of publication in the Official Community Gazette unless otherwise provided therein.[151] The cover extends to Acts of the Community, as the Heads of State must assent to every Bill.[152] Furthermore, if the relevant provision is not to come into force on publication in the EAC Gazette then it is for the order,

---

[148] Vienna Convention on the Law of Treaties 1969, done at Vienna on 23rd May, 1969, entered into force on 27th January, 1980, Art. 26, United Nations, Treaty Series, Vol. 1155, p. 331.

[149] Art. XXIV(12) GATT.

[150] Vienna Convention on the Law of Treaties 1969, done at Vienna on 23rd May, 1969, entered into force on 27th January, 1980, Art. 27, Internal Law and Observance of Treaties, United Nations, Treaty Series, Vol. 1155, p. 331.

[151] Art. 11(8) EAC Treaty, Functions of the Summit; Art. 14(5) EAC Treaty, Functions of the Council.

[152] Art. 62(1) EAC Treaty, Acts of the Community.

i.e., the Gazette notice, to "otherwise provide therein" by making it clear that a particular provision may not apply to a specific Partner State at that point in time. Even so, there is still the prospect of a conflict of laws arising, say when one Partner State views that publication must be in its local Gazette and not the Community Gazette. (The matter is discussed further below with respect to Kenya, which has now agreed to revise that requirement with the view that though published in the EAC Gazette a relevant provision must still be published in the Kenyan Gazette).

Despite the vagueness on some elements of incorporating the economic *acquis communautaire* of the Common Market into Partner States domestic regimes, all Partner States have nevertheless made a solid commitment to domesticate the economic *acquis communautaire* of the EAC; and the incorporation process has been accommodating of different procedural processes in each Partner State. It is now important to make that approach visible and transparent.

What national rules of law have been enacted to domesticate the EAC Treaty and its economic acquis?

Any examination of the domestication of EAC law must consider a Partner States constitutional framework and then work progressively through an assessment of how it has incorporated the EAC Treaty and all its implementing appurtenances. Starting with Burundi, the brief overview below highlights some of the findings.

Burundi's Constitution of 2005 provides that the President of the Republic guarantees the respect of treaties and international accords by virtue of the rule of law; but that any international Peace Treaty or Treaty of Commerce (Trade), treaties relative to international organisation, treaties engaging state finance, and those that concern the people of Burundi, must be ratified by virtue of a domestic law.[153] To date, Burundi has been vigilant in pursuing the process of harmonisation. Burundi has ratified domestic laws governing its Treaty Accession to the EAC.[154] It has given effect to the 2007 EAC Treaty amendments.[155] It has

---

[153] Constitution of the Republique du Burundi, 18th March, 2005, Art. 95, 290; Loi No 1/010 du 18 mars 2005 portant promulgation de la Constitution de la Republique du Burundi, http://www.accpuf.org/images/pdf/cm/burundi/constitution-du-burundi-180305.pdf. Constitution de Burundi, 1st June, 1998, available at: http://www.unhcr.org/refworld/docid/452d025f4.html. The Acte Constitutionnel de Transition replaced the Constitution of Burundi dated 9th March, 1992. For La Cour constitutionnelle du Burundi see: http://www.accpuf.org/index.php?option=com_content&task=view&id=48&Itemid=76 (last visited on 23rd January, 2011).

[154] Loi n° 1/08 du 30 Juin 2007 portant ratification par la République du Burundi du Traité d'adhésion du Burundi à la Communauté Est Africaine, signé à Kampala, le 18th June 2007.

[155] Loi n° 1/05 du février 2008 portant ratification par la République du Burundi des amendements du Traité portant Création de la Communauté Est Africaine tels que signés par les Chefs d'Etat des pays membres de la Communauté Est-Africaine le 20th August 2007 à Arusha en République Unie de Tanzanie.

given effect to the application of the Common External Tariff of the Customs Union[156]; and ratified the Common Market Protocol.[157]

Kenya's 2005 Draft Constitution, which was soundly defeated, set out Kenya's sources of law including, but not limited to, the laws of the EAC and international law, to the extent that they are consistent with the National Constitution.[158] Interestingly, there is no such reference in the current revision. By 2008 all such references had been removed. Kenya's 2008 revised Constitution provided for the supremacy of Kenyan law over any other law and made no specific reference to the ratification of treaty's or the position of EAC law.[159] By the time the proposed constitutional reforms went to public referendum, on the 4 August 2010, there had been further reflection and modification to account for international law. The referendum held on 4 August 2010 led to over 67% of Kenyan voters approving the proposed constitutional reforms and the enactment of the constitution on 27 August 2010.

As a result of the new enactment, Kenya's Constitution is the supreme law of the Republic while the general rules of international law form part of the law of Kenya and any treaty or convention ratified by Kenya forms part of the law of Kenya under the Constitution.[160] In consideration that treaty's and conventions now form part of the law of Kenya, the question arises as to how treaty law will be interpreted at a domestic level and by whom.

Kenyan courts addressed these issues in the infamous 2007 Nyong'o case. The High Court of Kenya found that it, and no other Kenyan Court, had jurisdiction to determine issues touching on the EAC Treaty or amendment thereof.[161] When

---

[156] Loi n° 1/10 du 30 June 2009 portant Application du Taux Extérieur Commun "TEC" de la Communauté Est Africaine.

[157] Loi N°1/10 du 30 avril 2010 Portant Ratification par la République du Burundi du Protocole Portant création du Marché Commun de la Communauté Est Africaine et ses six Annexes déjà négociés, signé à Arusha, République Unie de Tanzanie, le 20 November 2009.

[158] The Proposed New Constitution of Kenya, 2005 Draft, Chapter 1 para. 3. Special Issue, Kenya Gazette Supplement No. 63; Republic of Kenya, Kenya Gazette Supplement, 22nd August, 2005; The Proposed New Constitution of Kenya, Drafted and Published by the Attorney-General Pursuant to Section 27 of the Constitution of Kenya Review Act. For a copy go to African Network of Constitutional Lawyers, http://www.ancl-radc.org.za/en/kenya (last visited on 23rd January, 2011).

[159] The Constitution of Kenya, Laws of Kenya, (Revised ed.) 2008, published by the National Council for Law Reporting with the Authority of the Attorney General, issued from Kenya's State Law Office as being the latest version, dated 24th May, 2010, Chapter 1 para. 3. A subsequent version of the Constitution of Kenya and all surrounding government communication apparatus was officially backdated to 6th May, 2010, and subject to a referendum on 4th August, 2010.

[160] The Constitution of Kenya, 2010, published by the Attorney-General in accordance with Sec. 34 of the Constitution of Kenya Review Act, 2008 (No. 9 of 2008), http://www.parliament.go.ke (last visited on 18th January, 2011).

[161] Peter Anyang' Nyong'o & 10 Others vs. Attorney General & Another [2007] eKLR, Case number Petition 49 of 2007, delivered 19th March, 2007, see www.kenyalaw.org (last visited on 23rd January, 2011).

before the EACJ, the first respondent, the Attorney General of Kenya, was of the view that the only person that had *locus standi* as the protector of Kenya's public interest was the Attorney General of the Republic of Kenya and that the EACJ had no jurisdiction.[162] The EACJ disagreed and proceeded to determine whether Kenya's election rules governing the election of members to the East African Legislative Assembly were inconsistent with Article 50 of the EAC Treaty. Kenya's rules were found to be inconsistent and, in a retaliatory standoff, Kenya wielded its influence to amend the EAC Treaty.[163]

In terms of the transposition of the EAC's economic *acquis communautaire*, which is the issue of analysis here, Kenya is of the view that such laws "can only come into force after publication in the Kenya Gazette" as opposed to the EAC Gazette.[164] Though published in the EAC Gazette a relevant provision must still be published in the Kenyan Gazette. Notwithstanding this stance, Kenya has made a number of endeavours to not only contribute to and benefit from Community rights but to cede to its legal obligations through the Community's jurisdiction. Kenya has enacted the Treaty for the Establishment of East African Community Act 2000 and it has implemented the EAC's Customs Management Act. Work on the Kenyan Constitution led to a successful outcome and recognition of ratified treaties and conventions as forming part of Kenyan law under the Constitution. Although the Constitution gives no reference to the EAC, it could be deduced that Kenya would acknowledge the EAC as a sovereign regional body, by virtue of Treaty ratification; but it may not.

In practice, Kenyan's are actively engaged in domesticating EAC law. As gazetted in March 2010, Kenya's Minister for East Africa Community appointed a Task Force on the EAC Common Market Legal Reforms to be in force for a period of 45 days with effect from 23rd February, 2010. "The Task Force [was] engaged in: (i) fully interpreting the EAC Common Market Protocol and its Annexes in the context of existing Kenyan laws; (ii) fully understanding the implication of the EAC Common Market Protocol for Kenyans, Government and Private Sector Operations; and (iii) undertaking a thorough audit for the EAC Common Market Protocol and its Annexes with a view of recommending necessary reforms in Government operations".[165]

Extensions of time ensued. The report of the task force was with the Attorney General's office for further action by December 2010. At the time of writing, the

---

[162] EAC Judgment No. 1 of 2006, *Prof. Peter Anyang' Nyong'o and Others vs. Attorney General of Kenya and Others* [Nyong'o II], 30th March, 2007, http://www.eacj.org/docs/judgements/EACJ_Reference_No_1_2006.pdf (last visited on 23rd January, 2011).

[163] *Peter Anyang' Nyong'o & 10 Others vs. Attorney General & Another* [2007] eKLR; Case number Petition 49 of 2007; delivered 19th March 2007, see www.kenyalaw.org (last visited on 23rd January, 2011).

[164] EAC Secretariat Press Release, Meeting on Approximation of National Laws in the EAC Context Held in Nairobi, 18th February, 2010.

[165] Gazette Notice No. 2915, Ministry of East African Community, Appointment, dated 19th March, 2010, A. J. Kingi, Minister for East African Community, http://www.kenyalaw.org/KenyaGazette/view_gazette.php?title=3256 (last visited on 23rd January, 2011).

task force had identified the need to harmonise a raft of national laws with the EAC Common Market Protocol. While Kenya's Statute Law (Miscellaneous Amendments) Bill 2009 is likely to make minor changes to legislation, some of the changes required for the Common Market require substantive legislative changes. Proposals have been made to amend Kenya's Immigration Act to provide for residence permits; and the Employment Act may be amended to comply with the free movement of workers.

Rwanda has also established a High Level Task Force to assist with its approximation process. Constitutionally, the President of Rwanda ratifies international treaties. "Peace treaties and treaties or agreements relating to commerce and international organizations and those which commit state finances, modify provisions of laws already adopted by Parliament or relate to the status of persons, can only be ratified after authorisation by Parliament".[166] The EAC Treaty may be invoked directly in Rwanda's national courts as it has been conclusively adopted in accordance with the provisions of the law and published in the official gazette. Article 190 of the Constitution provides further that such treaty "shall be more binding than organic laws and ordinary laws except in the case of non compliance by one of parties" [official English version]. Rwanda's monist approach to incorporation mirrors provisions in the French Constitution, which provide that "Treaties or agreements duly ratified or approved shall, upon publication, prevail over Acts of Parliament, subject, with respect to each agreement or treaty, to its application by the other party".[167] The official French version of Rwanda's Constitution is more akin to this later interpretation.

Rwanda's Presidential decree N° 24/01 of 28 June 2007 supported the accession of Rwanda to the EAC and the ratification of the EAC Treaty; and Law n° 29/2007 of 27 June 2007 authorised the accession.[168] The ensuing Treaty amendments were ratified by the Presidential decree n° 55/01 of 31 December 2007.[169]

---

[166] Title X. International Treaties and Agreements, Art. 189, amended by the Amendment of 2nd December, 2003 (O.G n° special of 2nd December, 2003, p. 11), amended by the Amendment of 8th December, 2005 (O.G n° special of 8th December 2005), amended by the Amendment of 13th August, 2008 (O.G n° special of 13th August, 2008); N.B. Amended articles have been incorporated in the text of the Constitution of the Republic of Rwanda on 4th June, 2003.

[167] The French Constitution of 1958, Art. 55, adopted on 4th October, 1958, Journal Officiel de la République Française, http://www.legifrance.gouv.fr/jopdf/common/jo_pdf.jsp?numJO=0&dateJO=19581005&pageDebut=09151 (last visited on 23rd January, 2011).

[168] Arrête Présidentiel N° 24/01 Du 28/06/2007 Portant Ratification du Traité d'Adhésion de la République du Rwanda à la Communauté d'Afrique de l'Est, Signé à Kampala en date du 18 Juin 2007; J.O. N° Spécial du 28 Juin 2007; Date de Promulgation: 2007-06-28; Date de Publication: 2007-06-28; Status : en vigueur. Loi n° 29/2007 du 27/06/2007 Autorisant la Ratification du Traité d'Adhésion de la République du Rwanda à la Communauté d'Afrique de l'Est, signé à Kampala, en Ouganda, en date du 18 juin 2007, J.O. N° spécial du 28 juin 2007; date de promulgation: 2007-06-27; date de publication: 2007-06-28; Status : en vigueur.

[169] Arrêté présidentiel n° 55/01 du 31/12/2007 Portant Ratification de l'Amendement au Traité relatif à la Création de la Communauté d'Afrique de l'Est, signé à Arusha en date du 20 août 2007;

Rwanda's customs laws apply uniformly with those of the EAC and EAC customs law takes precedence over any inconsistencies. The EAC Management Act and the EAC Common External Tariff have therefore replaced earlier laws. Rwanda has made other amendments to account for consumption tax (VAT) and enacted a revised Investment Code. It has also abrogated its law providing for a special tax on sugar, as it was discriminatory.[170] Like other Partner States, substantial progress is required to incorporate other aspects of the economic *acquis communautaire* of the Common Market.

Tanzania is a unitary republic based on multiparty parliamentary democracy with state power exercised by the Government of the United Republic of Tanzania (URT) and the Revolutionary Government of Zanzibar. The EAC Treaty is implemented through the normal national legislative process.[171]

Jurisdictional matters, however, may be considered "Union", "Non-Union Tanzania" or "Non-Union Zanzibar". The "Union government" has authority over all union matters in the URT and governs Tanganyika (frequently referred to as "mainland Tanzania"). "Non-union" matters are under the exclusive domain of either the Union government or the Revolutionary Government of Zanzibar. The Revolutionary Government of Zanzibar governs Zanzibar. The Union government and the Revolutionary Government of Zanzibar have independent executive, legislative and judiciary organs. Legislative power therefore resides in two parliaments.

Tanzania's three-tiered legal system unites the jurisdictions of indigenous law, Islamic law, and British common law. Indigenous law and common law are practiced in the main on mainland Tanzania.

Zanzibar's court structure comprises a High Court, Kadhis Courts and the Magistrates court. It shares a Court of Appeal with mainland Tanzania.

Sharia law is not uncommon in the region – Kenya for instance has Kadhis' Courts – but it is a heated subject albeit jurisdiction is typically limited to personal status, marriage, divorce and inheritance and all parties must profess the Muslim faith. Islamic law is predominant in Zanzibar and regulates private matters, such as family law and issues of succession. The extent of redress of social and environmental issues in Zanzibar's Islamic Court system, and that of other Partner States, however, will need to be treated sensitively in incorporating these issues from the EAC Common Market Protocol into municipal law. Article 39 of the EAC

J.O. N°8 du 15/04/2008 n.b. Les amendements sont inclus dans le texte constitutif de l'EAC. Date de promulgation: 2007-12-31; date de publication: 2008-04-15; Status : en vigueur.

[170] Law No. 72/2008 of 31st December, 2008 determining the entry into force of the East African Community Customs Management Act of 1st January, 2005, amendments to EAC CET 2007 Version; Law No. 75/2008 of 31st December, 2008, modifying and complementing law No. 26/2006 of 27th May, 2006, determining and establishing consumption tax on some imported and locally manufactured products; Law No. 71/2008 of 31st December, 2008 repealing law No. 41/2002 of 31st December, 2002, establishing special tax on imported sugar.

[171] Report by the Secretariat, Trade Policy Review East African Community, Annex 2 Tanzania, WT/TPR/S/171, 20th September, 2006, p. A2-143.

Common Market Protocol, for instance, provides for the Harmonisation of Social Policies.

A common law approach applies to the settlement of most international trade and commercial disputes. Specificities pertaining to international trade, however, are vague. Equivocal arrangements manifest in a multitude of challenges, three of which are highlighted below.

First, Tanzania's constitution does not define the scope of non-union matters. Constitutionally, international trade is a "union" matter but the Constitution does not define the parameters of trade.[172] Zanzibar has its own "non-union" policies for investment, competition, intellectual property, export promotion and sectoral strategies, such as agriculture, tourism, communications, transport, finance and land. Whereas tourism services, for instance, frequently involve trade in services. Tariff and non-tariff instruments need to be reviewed to ensure alignment with those of the Union, the EAC and the WTO. Likewise, it is sometimes unclear as to how Zanzibar should work within the EAC and SADC. In terms of regional integration, the treaty process is a URT obligation but with Zanzibar participation. There is a common obligation but a different partition of powers. At a fiscal level, there are tax and revenue generation ambiguities.

Second, Zanzibar's legal and institutional framework for trade is extremely fragile. Ad hoc arrangements exist but there is no transparent enabling framework by which to deal with union matters. The supporting framework is therefore totally confusing and unwieldy to those that need it most, i.e., the traders. Discriminatory incentives have at times favoured foreign investors over local investors. The trading environment could hardly be said to be conducive to local investment. In reality, it restrains local investors from benefiting from the positive flow through benefits of international trade, namely growth and poverty reduction. At the institutional level, there is no link between "porter industries" (agriculture, infrastructure, education...) and trade. Similar dynamics of major aid-funded programmes supporting local farmers to improve production and yield but without any consideration as to how to market these crops is endemic throughout sub-Saharan Africa. Increasing yield over and above consumption may be a measure of economic success but in practical terms may only result in surplus and waste unless secure markets can be found within the region, let alone within the target markets of Europe and the US. Attempts to find a market, such as the way and manner by

---

[172] The 1977 Constitution amended by 14 amendments provides for a distinction between union and non-union matters. Trade related Union matters are provided for by Art. 4(3) of the Union Constitution; Art. 64; Art. 98; First Schedule to the Constitution; Second Schedule; Union matters by practice; and Union matters by judicial interpretation. Fiscal, Monetary Policy, Foreign Affairs, Foreign Trade, External Borrowing, Civil Aviation in relation to tourism and air transport, Exclusive Economic Zones and Petroleum and Natural Gas are typically union matters. Non-union trade related matters, those within Zanzibar's jurisdiction include inland revenue (e.g., VAT and hotel levies, but not income tax, corporation tax or customs duty), Intellectual Property, Investment, Tourism Services, Agriculture, Environment and Conservation, Fisheries regulation, Land, Education, Labour, Commercial Law and certain aspects of Dispute Resolution.

which farmers are supported to export offshore, may be questionable. Yet, these issues are not only isolated to agriculture.

Third, Zanzibar's company and commercial laws have historically differed from those on the mainland. The approximation of commercial laws at a EAC wide level is helping to resolve some of these tensions.

Intellectual Property is another example where more work is required in terms of union integration. The WTO's Trade Related Aspects of Intellectual Property Agreement, TRIPS, is not a union matter so laws are not harmonized and the question of exhaustion of rights remains.

Notwithstanding, Tanzania is of the view that since all Partner States have domesticated the Treaty that all the provisions of the EAC Treaty shall have effect in Partner States. In Tanzania, The Treaty for the Establishment of East African Community Act, 2001 – (Act No. 4), enacted 2001, gives effect to the EAC Treaty by incorporating the EAC Treaty in its entirety as a Schedule to the Act.[173] In particular, section 8 (1) of the Act provides that any Act of the EAC shall, from the date of its publication of the Act in the Official Gazette of the Community, have the force of law in the United Republic.

Turning to Uganda, Uganda's 1995 Constitution, as amended, provides for the supremacy of Ugandan law over any other law. "If any other law or any custom is inconsistent with any of the provisions of this Constitution, the Constitution shall prevail, and that other law or custom shall, to the extent of the inconsistency, be void".[174] While the Constitution (Amendment) (No. 2) Act, 2005 provides for regional government, regional government does not encompass the EAC's *acquis communautaire* and is limited to the formation of regional government by two or more districts within Uganda.

In terms of transposition of the EAC acquis, the Ugandan East African Community Act of 2002 gives the EAC Treaty the force of law in Uganda and recognises all remedies and procedures under the EAC Treaty. For the purposes of constitutional alignment, Section 11 of the East African Community Act 2002 obliges the Minister responsible for regional co-operation to cause a copy of any amendment or modification to be laid before Parliament.

Uganda's East African Community Act 2002 provides that any Acts of the Community shall, from the date of publication of that Act in the Official Gazette of the Community and subject to orders scheduling operation as provided in that Act, have the force of law in Uganda.[175] Akin to other Partner States, the EAC Customs Management Act 2004 and the EAC Customs Management Regulations 2006 also have the force of law in Uganda.

---

[173] The Treaty for the Establishment of East African Community Act, 2001 – (Act No. 4), enacted 2001; see http://www.parliament.go.tz/Polis/PAMS/Docs/4-2001.pdf (last visited on 23rd January, 2011).

[174] Constitution of the Republic of Uganda 1995, Chapter 1(2)(2), Supremacy of the Constitution.

[175] Sec. 9 East African Community Act 2002.

As shown in East Africa, there can be no knee-jerk assumption that former francophone administrations will adopt a traditional monist approach to incorporation and that former common law countries will adopt a dualist approach. Further, the issue of supremacy of Community law and direct effect of the *acquis communautaire* have been shown to be two different but related issues, both are relevant and addressed in more detail below.

Incorporating the full body of the economic *acquis communautaire* of the Common Market into Partner States municipal jurisdictions entails a far more extensive and consuming process than that of incorporating the acquis of the EAC Customs Union, which was neatly governed by harmonised EAC Acts and Regulations. As previously mentioned, the free movement of services, for instance, requires not only the transposition of agreed schedules and all the concomitant amendments, repeals and enactment of entirely new laws but also the necessary institutional and regulatory frameworks.

National Law Reform Commissions have a key role to play in these efforts. The Law Reform Commission of Kenya, Tanzania and Uganda have already been engaged in a project to approximate the municipal laws of the EAC countries with participation from Burundi and Rwanda. The Rwandan Senate endorsed the establishment of the Rwanda Law Reform Commission in November 2009; and the Law Reform Commission will be tasked with co-ordinating and approximating laws at the EAC level.[176] Some mechanism such as that adopted by the Organisation pour l'Harmonisation du Droit des Affaires en Afrique may be equally helpful.

In the interim, Partner States will have to rely on the Customs Management Act and its implementing regulations before enacting the necessary laws to incorporate the Common Market Protocol within municipal jurisdictions. While Partner States grapple with the legislative and technical aspects of approximation of the EAC's economic *acquis communautaire* both in terms of completing implementation of the Customs Management Act, e.g., the appellate process remains sketchy in some Partner States, and in terms of aligning with the EAC Common Market Protocol, local firms will need to get ready to reap the benefits from the expanded regional market.

In sum, most Partner States have been attempting to achieve legal and regulatory reform by fast-tracking and simplifying existing company and commercial laws rather than systematically controlling the flow of the approximation of EAC laws that go through the policy and law-making machinery of government and will speed up regional integration. Interests of the international community often herald an impetus on commercial reform but this frequently manifests in a myriad of disconnected debt and equity donor programmes launched by an array of un-coordinated international bodies. Many of these reforms have therefore been ad hoc and

---

[176] Uganda Law Reform Commission, see http://www.ulrc.go.ug/reps&pubs/reps_&Bills.php; Law Reform Commission of Tanzania, see http://www.lrct.or.tz; Kenya Law Reform Commission, see http://www.klrc.go.ke (last visited on 23rd January, 2011).

piecemeal in nature. They have focused on eliminating specific bottlenecks of concern to foreign rather than local investors. While important, they have sidelined efforts to incorporate a collective EAC economic *acquis communautaire* within Partner States. The harmonisation process therefore remains encumbered by a conflict of interests, legal pluralism and a kaleidoscope of social and cultural dynamics. Notwithstanding, all Partner States recognise the need for a robust regional legal system and are wading their way through the challenges in order to advance the benefits of economic integration and offer certainty to investors (foreign and local alike); but to what extent are Partner States enforcing these endeavours in practice?

Enforcement

Dispute Settlement under the Common Market

Established by virtue of Article 9, paragraph 1(e) of the EAC Treaty, and formally inaugurated on 30 November 2001, the East African Court of Justice (EACJ) is another medium for advancing the region's integration agenda and the incorporation of the economic *acquis communautaire* into Partner States domestic laws. The EACJ could play a pivotal role in the harmonisation process but, as will be shown, parallel dispute settlement mechanisms and the imbalance of powers between the EAC's executive, legislature and judiciary, sometimes marginalise the courts competence.

To put dispute settlement in context, Partner States are to settle any dispute arising from the interpretation or application of the EAC Common Market Protocol in accordance with the EAC Treaty.[177] As the judicial body of the EAC, the East African Court of Justice (EACJ) ensures the "adherence to law in the interpretation and application of and compliance with [the EAC] Treaty".[178]

Recall by definition that the EAC Treaty extends to incorporate not only the body of the EAC Treaty but also to any annexes and protocols thereto. The substantive law of the economic *acquis communautaire*, which governs the EAC Customs Union Protocol and EAC Common Market Protocol, would therefore seem to come within the Court's competence.

In terms of customs disputes, EAC Customs Union (Dispute Settlement Mechanism) Regulations aim to facilitate the settlement of these disputes amongst Partner States pursuant to Article 41 of the EAC Customs Union Protocol. While the EAC Customs Union Protocol recognises the EACJ, it also establishes the EAC Committee on Trade Remedies as a new dispute resolution body.

---

[177] Art. 54 EAC Common Market Protocol, provides for the settlement of disputes pertaining to the Common Market.

[178] Art. 23 EAC Treaty, Role of the Court.

The EAC's Committee on Trade Remedies handles matters pertaining to trade disputes, i.e., rules of origin, anti-dumping measures, subsidies and countervailing measures, safeguard measures, dispute settlement provided for under the EAC Customs Union (Dispute Settlement Mechanism) Regulations and any other matter referred to the Committee by Council.[179] The principle of *lex specialis derogat generali* applies and the more specific rules pertaining to adjudication by the EAC Committee on Trade Remedies replace what would otherwise come under the EACJ's jurisdiction. The special does not set aside general treaty provisions but it does step in to replace the general.[180] In some ways therefore, the EAC's Committee on Trade Remedies sidelines the EACJ.

The Registrar of the EACJ has been particularly vocal on this matter. In his words: "the ousting of the jurisdiction of the East African Court of Justice is contradictory and illegal" and as a result "there has been no single case on the customs union and no transparency from the committee".[181]

Under scrutiny, there has been no redress or assurance of conformity with the Customs Union elements of the free movement of goods, i.e., trade disputes. Whether a Partner State may invoke Article 28, paragraph 2, of the EAC Treaty and claim that decisions of the EAC's Committee on Trade Remedies are *ultra vires*, unlawful or infringe the EAC Treaty remains to be seen. In any event, such a position would be likely to be strongly contested: subject to EAC regulations, the EAC's Committee on Trade Remedies shall determine its own procedure and its decisions are final.[182] In other words, the EACJ does not even act as an appellate division on customs elements governing the free movement of goods.

In parallel with the competence given to the EAC Committee on Trade Remedies, which addresses trade disputes, other mandates under the EAC Customs Management Act 2004 (revised edition 2009) are given to the [EAC] Directorate of Customs [currently Trade and Customs], the Commissioner responsible for customs in each Partner State, national courts and tax tribunals. To explicate, the EAC Directorate responsible for customs is responsible for coordinating and monitoring compliance and enforcement of the Customs Law of the Community.[183] However,

---

[179] Art. 24 EAC Customs Union Protocol, East African Community Committee on Trade Remedies. See Annex IX to the EAC Customs Union Protocol, East African Community Customs Union (Dispute Settlement Mechanism) Regulations.

[180] United Nations, Fragmentation of International Law: Difficulties arising from the Diversification and Expansion of International Law, Report of the Study Group of the International Law Commission, 1st May – 9th June and 3rd July – 11th August, 2006, finalized by Martti Koskenniemi, General Assembly Distr., A/CN.4/L.682, 13th April, 2006.

[181] Ruhangisa, Registrar, East African Court of Justice The Role of the East African Court of Justice in the Realization of the Customs Union and Common Market, A Paper for Presentation During the Inter-Parliamentary Relations Seminar, (Nanyuki – V –) to be held at Burundi National Assembly, 27th–31st January, 2010.

[182] Art. 24(5)(6) EAC Customs Union Protocol, East African Community Committee on Trade Remedies.

[183] Sec. 3 and 4 EAC Customs Management Act 2004 (revised edition 2009), Part II.

the Directorate has no enforcement powers. Instead, commissioners within the Partner States may settle cases under the EAC Customs Management Act.[184] Sub-ordinate courts may hear and determine proceedings under the Act.[185] Orders issued by the Commissioners may be reviewed and, if not satisfied, an appeal may be made to tax tribunals or shall lie to the High Court of that Partner State if a tax tribunal is not established. No such appeal may be made to the EACJ.[186] In addition, a number of more specific regulations supplement enforcement.[187]

While the EAC Directorate responsible for customs has no enforcement powers *per se* it may, through the Secretary General of the EAC, seek explanation from a Partner State when it considers a possible infringement has occurred. If the Directorate is not satisfied then it may refer the matter to Council and subsequently to the EACJ. To date, the Directorate has been reluctant to follow this route even when there have been infringements. The situation regarding exemptions is illustrative.[188]

Dispute settlement under the Common Market Protocol takes a similar approach. There too there is a watering down of the powers of the EACJ. Article 54 of the EAC Common Market Protocol provides for the settlement of disputes in accord with the Treaty. Further, Partner States guarantee the right of redress to any person whose rights and liberties, as recognised by the EAC Common Market Protocol, have been infringed; and the competent judicial, administrative or legislative authority or any other competent authority, shall rule on the rights of the person who is seeking redress.[189] The determination of "competent authority" is unclear and, as under the Customs Management Act, power could be devolved further away from the EACJ and even from the national courts. Devolution may not be all-together a bad thing. Decisions could be made closer to the people.

For completeness, it is important to mention that there are some safety nets. Article 34 of the EAC Treaty, for example, provides for Preliminary Rulings of National Courts. "Where a question is raised before any court or tribunal of a Partner State concerning the interpretation or application of the provisions of this Treaty or the validity of the regulations, directives, decisions or actions of the Community, that court or tribunal shall, if it considers that a ruling on the question

---

[184] Sec. 219(1) EAC Customs Management Act 2004 (revised edition 2009), Part XVII, Settlement of Cases by the Commissioner.

[185] Sec. 220(1) EAC Customs Management Act 2004 (revised edition 2009), Part XIX, Legal Proceedings.

[186] Sec. 229, 230, 231, 252 EAC Customs Management Act 2004 (revised edition 2009), Part XX Appeals.

[187] EAC Customs Management (Working Arrangements Between the Directorate and the Customs) Regulations, 2009; in exercise of the powers conferred by Sec. 4(3) and 251(1) of the East African Community Customs Management Act, 2004, the Council of Ministers made these Regulations 27th February, 2009. As at 24th May, 2010, the official regulations did not include Part III, Enforcement of Customs Law and Trade Facilitation.

[188] Art. 29 EAC Treaty.

[189] Art. 54(2) EAC Treaty, Settlement of Disputes.

is necessary to enable it to give judgment, request the [EACJ] to give a preliminary ruling on the question". Discretion remains with the national judge.

While the Community has spurned a "trigger happy" litigious culture at the regional level, it still has other mechanisms at its disposal that may be more in line with a culture that seeks social atonement rather than confrontation and discredit.[190] The EAC Treaty makes provision for the EACJ to establish itself as an arbitration tribunal. Whereas, the 2008 EACJ Rules of Procedure provide for Alternative Dispute Resolution and guidelines for mediation.[191]

The EACJ is empowered to hear and determine any matter arising from an arbitration clause contained in a contract or agreement provided: (i) the Community or any of its institutions is a party; and (ii) that the contract or agreement confers such jurisdiction on the EACJ. In terms of commercial contracts or agreements, the EACJ is empowered to hear and determine any matter arising from an arbitration clause contained in a commercial contract or agreement in which the parties have conferred jurisdiction on the EACJ.

The EACJ is further empowered to hear and determine any matter arising from a dispute between Partner States regarding the EAC Treaty provided the Partner States concerned submit a *special agreement* constructed between themselves to the EACJ.[192] This provision is carried over into the Arbitration Rules of the EACJ.

The term *special agreement* is not, however, defined. Nonetheless, it could be interpreted that consent of the Partner States to submit to the jurisdiction of the EACJ as an arbitration tribunal would be a cornerstone to any arbitration award.

While the EACJ's rules of arbitration have existed since 2004, the arbitration process has not been utilized; or, if it has been utilized, then there has been no dispute to lead the Court to publish the findings thereof. In practice, many arbitration cases from the region are still taken offshore. London's Court of International Arbitration is a frequent destination.

Establishing credibility is a problem. The choice of forum may stem in part from the fact that the EACJ's jurisdiction is "almost unknown" to stakeholders rather than an overt attempt not to legitimise Community wide enforcement mechanisms.[193]

Taken ensemble, however, these issues flag a far wider concern as to just how effective EAC enforcement mechanisms may be and whether EAC law will evolve as a harmonised *acquis communautaire* that takes precedence over similar national laws. One approach that may aid the EACJ to attain credibility could be if the private sector itself decides to recognise the EACJ as a regional arbitration tribunal rather than continually take its disputes to Europe.

---

[190] Idowu/Oke, Theories of Law and Morality: Perspectives from Contemporary African Jurisprudence, In-Spire Journal of Law, Politics and Societies 3 (2008) 2.

[191] EAC; EAC Gazette; Volume AT 1 – No. ... Arusha; 30th December, 2008 [official citation].

[192] Art. 32 EAC Treaty, Arbitration Clauses and Special Agreements.

[193] Nsekela, The Role Of The East African Court Of Justice In The Integration Process, A Paper for Presentation During the 3 rd East African Community Media Summit, 21st – 22nd August, 2009.

To summarise this section, all Partner States are committed to implementing the EAC Customs Management Act and supporting regulations; but there is still some divergence between enforcement at regional versus national levels. Issues arise particularly in terms of consolidating the trade and investment regime versus revenue maximisation. Commissioners themselves approach customs reviews in an inconsistent fashion and their discretionary powers vary enormously between different Partner States. Complicated overlays and a lack of awareness in the business community hinder enforcement and dispute settlement. The free movement of goods aside, the development of enforcement mechanisms for the other dimensions of the Common Market are some way off but some insights may be gleaned from the lessons learnt by other regional economic communities. Albeit that the EAC needs to develop its own unique enforcement mechanisms and body of jurisprudence, reference to the European Court of Justice and similar courts is a useful one: they illustrate the workings of legal procedure at a regional level. Yet, the test of enforcement of the EAC's economic *acquis communautaire* will certainly not be to what extent the East African Court of Justice mirrors the European Court of Justice; but rather as to how effective the EACJ is in interpreting and enforcing EAC Community law. It is down to the degree of transparency, conformity and compliance by Partner States to mark the degree of effectiveness and legitimacy of the EAC's enforcement mechanisms.

Effective Enforcement Mechanisms

The effectiveness of EAC mechanisms to govern the EAC's economic *acquis communautaire* links to, and derives from, three seminal principles: the rule of law, economic human rights and the separation of powers. In parallel with the International Covenant on Economic, Social and Cultural Rights, the EAC's Common Market Protocol embodies economic, social and cultural rights.[194] Yet, rights are effective so long as they are governed by a rule of law and equitably enforced; whereas, equitable enforcement infers an effective remedy and a fair and public hearing by an independent and impartial tribunal.

The right of access to an effective remedy by the competent national tribunals, and the right to an effective judiciary, is embodied in the Universal Declaration of Human Rights.[195] By extension, the African Charter on Human and Peoples' Rights provides for the right for an individual to have his or her cause heard before the competent national organs.[196] Integrity, impartiality and independence of the

---

[194] International Covenant on Economic, Social and Cultural Rights, G.A. res. 2200A (XXI), 21 U. N. GAOR Supp. (No. 16) at 49, U.N. Doc. A/6316 (1966), 993 U.N.T.S. 3, entered into force 3rd January, 1976.

[195] Art. 8, 10 Universal Declaration of Human Rights, G.A. res. 217A (III), U.N. Doc A/810 at 71 (1948).

[196] Art. 7 African [Banjul] Charter on Human and Peoples' Rights, adopted 27th June, 1981, OAU Doc. CAB/LEG/67/3 rev. 5, 21 I.L.M. 58 (1982), entered into force on 21st October, 1986.

EAC judiciary are well enshrined in Article 24 of the EAC Treaty. The right to an effective remedy, the right of access to an impartial and independent tribunal and the right to a fair trial constitute guarantees that the EAC's *acquis communautaire* is governed by the rule of law.

To solidify this process, the EAC's National Human Rights Commissions are drafting an EAC Bill of Rights with mechanisms for enforcement. A draft bill resulting from the third meeting of the EAC's National Human Rights Commissions, held on the 1 June 2010, is being presented to stakeholders for discussion and input.[197]

At this stage, the draft EAC Bill of Rights recognizes the importance of developing common standards to protect and uphold human rights in East Africa; and to provide for a minimum standard of equal treatment in the free movement of goods, persons, labour, services and capital and the rights of establishment and residence. Variable geometry, as applicable to the EAC's economic *acquis communautaire*, should likewise have its parameters set within the context of economic human rights and in the quality of defined common standards.

At the centre of the economic rights issue, however, is the broader multilayered issue of governance. Incorporating an economic *acquis communautaire* extends to the rule of law as a regional body of law, economic rights as a minimum standard of equality before the law and an effective balance of powers between the executive, legislature and judiciary. The EAC recognises these interrelationships. Complemented by a proposed Protocol on Good Governance, the EAC Bill of Rights will put the EAC's Framework for Good Governance, Human Rights and Equal Opportunities into effect. While the Protocol will be a crucial complement to the EAC's entire *acquis communautaire* there are still a number of challenges.

Good governance at the EAC level infers that those whom are governed by the EAC's *acquis communautaire* have the right to access an effective remedy before the competent regional tribunals and, in many instances, EAC law is to have direct effect within local jurisdictions. Yet, the remedy is only effective in as much as it is delivered timely and justly: *justice delayed is justice denied*. Arguably, effective enforcement also needs to address the cost implications. By extension, legal protection should also encompass the right to legal aid for those who would otherwise be denied access to justice.

As illustrated, the effectiveness of EAC Treaty enforcement derives from economic human rights and the rule of law. However, to be free to exercise their role and ensure the adherence to law in the interpretation, application of and compliance with the EAC Treaty, the judiciary needs to be independent from other arms of government. The EACJ needs to operate independently. While fostering good relations between the executive, legislature and judiciary is healthy, there needs

---

[197] East African Community Brief to UN Member States on "The EAC Peace, Security and Good Governance Initiatives and Strategies for a Sustainable Integration", 18th October, 2010, http://www.un.org/africa/osaa/speeches/EAC_Presentation_18Oct2010.pdf (last visited on 21st January, 2011).

to be an unequivocal separation of powers between the executive, legislature, and judiciary.

Under scrutiny, the EAC Treaty unamended provides for a defined balance of powers between the Community's policy, executive, legislative and judicial organs. The Council of Ministers (EAC Council), supported by the Co-ordination Committee and Sectoral Committees, is the Community's policy organ; the EAC Secretariat is the executive organ; the East African Legislative Assembly is the legislative organ; and the East African Court of Justice is the judicial organ. The EACJ reinforced this balance of powers when it concluded in *Calist Mwatela, Lydia Wanyoto Mutende, Isaac Abraham Sepetu vs East African Community* that the Council does not have exclusive competence on the initiation of Bills.[198] The Council and EALA Members can initiate proposals for Bills.

On 27 November 2006, the issue of the separation of powers arose again when the EACJ issued an interim order in the Nyong'o I ruling. Having the effect of a Court decision and precedence over decisions of a national court on a similar matter, the interim order prevented nine Kenyan nominees being sworn in as members of the EALA. The grounds presented were that Kenyan law might be in conflict with Article 50 of the EAC Treaty, which sets out the procedure for electing Members to the Assembly.[199] Rather than follow judicial procedure, the Summit responded by calling an emergency meeting on the 14 December 2006 and subsequently amended the EAC Treaty, deposited instruments of ratification and published the amendments in the EAC Gazette.[200]

In Nyong'o II, the EACJ's judgment of 30 March 2007 founded on the substantive issues of the case. The Court concluded that the requirement for Partner States to elect members of the Assembly (by virtue of Article 50 of the EAC Treaty), required some form of voting process. Constructing a list of nominees that excluded representation by the people was inconsistent with the EAC Treaty. Kenya was entitled to elect but not selectively appoint members of the Assembly.

While fair elections are a seemingly lucid element of good governance, it should be recalled that the dynamics of the executive being able to wield unbridled power has long been endemic in Kenya and was the catalyst to recent constitutional reforms. In response, Kenya's 2010 Constitution provides for a more balanced

---

[198] EACJ Judgment, Application No. 1 of 2005, *Calist Mwatela, Lydia Wanyoto Mutende, Isaac Abraham Sepetu vs. East African Community*, see http://www.eacj.org/judgments.php (last visited on 24th May, 2010).

[199] EAC Ruling, No. 1 of 2006, *Prof. Peter Anyang' Nyong'o and Others vs. Attorney General of Kenya and Others* [Nyong'o I]; 27th November, 2006, see http://www.eacj.org/docs/rulings/EACJ_rulling_on_injunction_ref_No1_2006.pdf (last visited on 23rd January, 2011).

[200] EAC Judgment, No. 1 of 2006, *Prof. Peter Anyang' Nyong'o and Others vs. Attorney General of Kenya and Others* [Nyong'o II], 30th March, 2007, see http://www.eacj.org/docs/judgements/EACJ_Reference_No_1_2006.pdf (last visited on 23rd January, 2011); EAC Judgment, No. 3 of 2007, *East African Law Society and Others vs. Attorney General of Kenya and Others* [Nyong'o III]; 8th September, 2008, http://www.eacj.org/docs/judgements/E_A__Law_Society__4_Others_vs__A_G__Kenya__3_Others_.pdf (last visited on 23rd January, 2011).

separation of powers. The President will account to Parliament but not be a Member of Parliament or hold any other state office. There will be an independent and impartial judiciary with appointment subject to nomination by a newly empowered Judicial Service Commission rather than appointment, remuneration, promotion and removal from office controlled by the executive.[201] The legislature will be more independent.

Even so, the consequences of Nyong'o II are illustrative of the recurring struggles for change. These challenges are outlined below.

As to the resulting amendments to the EAC Treaty, the Summit communicated the reconstitution of the EACJ by establishing two divisions. There is now a Court of First Instance and an Appellate Division with powers over the Court of First Instance (by virtue of an amendment to Article 24 of the EAC Treaty).

Note that the EAC Treaty, Article 27, paragraph 2, Jurisdiction of the Court, provides for the Court to have appellate, human rights and other jurisdiction to be determined by the Council at a suitable subsequent date and subject to a protocol to operationalise the extended jurisdiction. However, Article 27 was not amended. Effort has been made to introduce the Protocol. A decision was made in November 2004 to extend the Courts jurisdiction to an appellate process and human rights jurisdiction. The Protocol to Operationalise the Extended Jurisdiction has been drafted and sent to Partner States for their inputs and comments. Once the consultation process is concluded, the Protocol will be presented to the Sectoral Council on Legal and Judicial Affairs for legal inputs and then to Council for adoption. In the interim, there is need to strengthen the EACJ by facilitating the Judge President to be resident in Arusha in order to expedite matters of administration of justice.

Amongst other amendments, the Emergency Summit of 2006 also directed a review of the administration of justice and the procedure for the removal of Judges from office to include all possible reasons even those outside of the Treaty. A judge of the EACJ may now be removed for "moral turpitude", which escapes precise definition and can be determined by any Partner State (amendment to Article 26 of the EAC Treaty).

The Summit also amended the Court's jurisdiction so as not to apply to jurisdiction conferred by the Treaty on organs of the Partner States (amendments to Articles 27 and 30 of the EAC Treaty). Article 27, paragraph 1, revised, now stipulates that the Courts jurisdiction over the interpretation and application of the Treaty "shall not include the application of any such interpretation to jurisdiction conferred by the Treaty on organs of Partner States". Disquiet is mounting as to whether the executive and legislative organs of the Community may now exercise unfettered power. Further, the amendment undermines the founding principle of supremacy of EAC Law.

Article 30, as amended, adds two new provisions. Where reference is made by a legal or natural person, proceedings "shall be instituted within 2 months of the

---

[201] See Sec. 104 Constitution of Kenya, (Revised ed.) 2008, Remuneration of certain officers, Laws of Kenya, http://www.kenyalaw.org/update/index.php (last visited on 23rd January, 2011).

enactment, publication, directive, decision or action complained of, or in the absence thereof, of the day in which it came to the knowledge of the complainant, as the case may be".[202] Prompt justice averts delayed justice. However, in an EAC operating environment where there is already a good degree of poor transparency, and often retrospective transparency, the rights of legal and natural persons could, in effect, be greatly limited. Considering current processes, most cases are unlikely to be instituted within 2 months. Further, the EACJ's jurisdiction in terms of legal and natural persons is excluded where an Act, regulation, directive, decision or action under the EAC Treaty has been reserved to an institution of a Partner State.[203]

As to the implications of the aforementioned, the EACJ in Nyong'o III concluded that the amendment process was inconsistent with the "spirit and intendment" of the Treaty.[204] The amendments did not convey people centred or market driven cooperation.

In Nyong'o III, the EACJ was of the view that amending Article 26 of the EAC Treaty to remove judges of the Court for all possible reasons as determined by Partner States and, by extension, by representatives of the Partner States in the executive and legislature, infringed Article 38, paragraph 2, of the EAC Treaty. Under the EAC Treaty unamended, Article 38 paragraph 2 of the EAC Treaty provided for the acceptance of judgments of the Court whereby the Partner States were obliged to refrain from any action that might be detrimental to the resolution of the dispute or might aggravate the dispute. Dismissing a judge for his or her findings would surely be detrimental to effective enforcement of the *acquis communautaire*.

Nonetheless, the EACJ declined to invalidate the amendments. Instead, the Court held that the involvement of the people of the EAC in the Treaty amendment process shall have prospective application.

The Court, however, was not immune to the ramifications of Nyong'o III and expressed unequivocal concern about the chipping away of the *acquis communautaire*. Of note was the Court's "strong recommendation" in Nyong'o III to revisit the amendments. In particular, Article 27 and 30 of the EAC Treaty undermine the doctrine of supremacy; the role of the EACJ in interpreting, applying and ensuring compliance with the EAC Treaty; and that decisions of the EACJ have precedence over national decisions and preliminary rulings of the Court (EAC Treaty Articles 23, 33(2) and 34). The Court also issued another "strong recommendation" that the amendment pertaining to the automatic removal and suspension of judges be reviewed at the earliest opportunity possible.

For now, the EAC Treaty as amended sets forth a new partisan balance of power that weakens the effectiveness of enforcement and, in turn, weakens integration. On the one hand, the actions taken by Kenya at a municipal level have subsequently demonstrated prompt recognition of the Court's judgments in Nyong'o I, II and III.

---

[202] Art. 30(2) EAC Treaty.

[203] Art. 30(3) EAC Treaty.

[204] Ibid., Nyong'o III.

However, on the other hand, and in the heat of the moment, the Council and Summit have seemingly colluded with perhaps the unintentional effect of undermining economic human rights, the rule of law and the separation of powers (aspirations that they themselves had tabled for the EAC). On reflection, it is without doubt, however, that with prudence the Partner States could address and resolve these issues promptly for their mutual benefit.

Partner States are still politically committed to domesticate the Common Market Protocol: they are continuing to facilitate incorporation of the *acquis communautaire* and compliance procedures. However, there is no clear momentum for the EAC to enforce Council Directives upon Partner States.

Regulations, Directives, Decisions and Recommendations of the Council are binding on the Partner States.[205] However, many directives of the Council and those of the Sectoral Council on Legal and Judicial Affairs regarding harmonisation may remain unimplemented. Missing the 21 August 2010 deadline by which to incorporate the EAC *acquis communautaire* of the Common Market into Partner States municipal jurisdictions is an example. The undertaking was just too ambitious and not anchored by national obligations.

Where a directive amounts to a misuse or abuse of power, Partner States may refer it to the Court for a determination that it is *ultra vires;* but giving effect to that determination is now likely to be usurped by the recent Treaty amendments.[206] While idealistic efforts to speed up the integration process through the issue of unattainable directives and decrees may not be an abuse of power they do undermine the credibility of the Community's good work.

As another alternative, the EAC Treaty provides that where a directive, ruling, opinion, order or a decree of the EACJ is issued it shall be considered a "judgment" and Partner States are obliged to implement it without delay.[207] However, the new amendments prevail and the organs of Partner States may decide whether or not to comply. As a consequence, the EACJ, as the judicial body of the community no longer has an opportunity to play an effective role in the integration process, neither in terms of giving the Common Market Protocol its interpretative value nor in terms of sequencing integration. Its role in the harmonisation of laws could and should be influential in contributing to the jurisprudence of the Community; but until Partner States revisit the EAC Treaty amendments the EACJ, and effective enforcement of the EAC's *acquis communautaire*, will sit on the periphery.

Historically, the EACJ was tasked with ensuring adherence to the EAC *acquis communautaire* in the interpretation, application and compliance with the EAC Treaty.[208] The Court's jurisdiction extended to interpretation and application of the

---

[205] Art. 16 EAC Treaty, Effects of Regulations, Directives, Decisions and Recommendations of the Council.

[206] Art. 28 EAC Treaty, Reference by Partner States.

[207] Art. 1 EAC Treaty, Interpretation; Art. 38(3) EAC Treaty, Acceptance of Judgments of the Court.

[208] Art. 23 EAC Treaty, Role of the Court.

Treaty and Partner States were obligated to conclude a protocol to put its extended jurisdiction into operation, such as that of appellate jurisdiction.[209] Subject to procedure, Partner States, the Secretary General, Legal and Natural Persons, and disputes between the Community and its employees, could be referred to the EACJ.[210] Legal and natural persons were able to refer for determination by the Court, the legality of any Act, regulation, directive, decision or action of a Partner State on the grounds that it was unlawful or infringed the provisions of the EAC Treaty.[211] By virtually stripping the EACJ of the competencies it was set up to execute, collective actions of the EAC have altered the Community's balance of powers by introducing punitive action against the judiciary; whereas, on the Court's side, and in the face of adversity, the EACJ has stood on its principles of integrity, impartiality and independence.

Enforcement of Community Law in Partner States is fundamental to the success of the integration process. To succeed with regional integration, however, Partner States must be prepared to cede a degree of sovereignty to the Community. Giving legitimacy to the EAC is a hard won frontier struggle. A conflict of interests sometimes emerges between Community law and that of the national order. Partner States need to resolve these differences for the mutual benefit and the equitable advancement of integration in the spirit of human rights, the rule of law and a well-governed balance of powers. In doing so, the Community needs to return to its original aims and aspirations and advance the interests East African's economic, social and cultural development.

Partner States could consider three immediate actions by which to advance the approximation of the EAC's economic *acquis communautaire*. All three actions relate to questions of good governance. First, revisit the amendments to the EAC Treaty at the earliest opportunity possible. East African's must be guaranteed an effective remedy before competent national and regional tribunals that are empowered by the tenants of integrity, impartiality and independence. Second, Council needs to issue realistic and attainable directives setting out the substantive and procedural aspects of scheduling required to incorporate the EAC's economic *acquis communautaire* into municipal jurisdictions. Third, laws relating to implementation of the EAC Common Market Protocol need to be enacted by the Legislative Assembly so that they become binding on all Partner States.

---

[209] Art. 27 EAC Treaty, Jurisdiction of the Court.

[210] Art. 28 EAC Treaty, Reference by Partner States; Art. 29 EAC Treaty, Reference by the Secretary General; Art. 30 EAC Treaty, Reference by Legal and Natural Persons; Art. 9(2) EAC Treaty, Establishment of the Organs and Institutions of the Community.

[211] Art. 28 EAC Treaty, Reference by Partner States; Art. 29 EAC Treaty, Reference by the Secretary General; Art. 30 EAC Treaty, Reference by Legal and Natural Persons; Art. 9(2) EAC Treaty, Establishment of the Organs and Institutions of the Community.

Conclusion

The free movement of goods, services, workers, persons and capital and the rights of establishment and residence facilitate the opportunity to leverage the advantages created by a larger, more cohesive, market. One fear though is that bigger economies and big business will swallow up the smaller economies and fledging small businesses and thereby distort competition in intra-community trade. As demonstrated by Nyong'o III, this fear will only come to fruition if the process is not properly controlled and if the Community loses its fundamental objectives. To recall, those fundamental objectives focus on widening and deepening cooperation.

To achieve the desired outcomes, regional integration has influenced the changing dynamics of economic law and of the *acquis communautaire* as a whole within the EAC. Extensive legal reform in the Partner States, notably in the areas of the free movements and rights of establishment and residence, is necessary to give effect to the aims and aspirations of the community.

Driven in large by intra-regional dynamism, these reforms need to leverage foreign policy objectives made at a regional level to attain the objectives of the EAC and strengthen the aims and aspirations of the East African Community at the grassroots level. Reforms in the rule of economic law are fundamental. Such changes have played, and will continue to play, an important role in gearing the legal systems of East Africa towards a new, more openly competitive environment, one that will favour investment, advance growth and sustainable development.

The process of incorporating the *acquis communautaire* into Partner States jurisdictions is time consuming, complex and frequently fraught with conflicting agendas and demands for reforms in both substantive and procedural law. Going forward, efforts towards legal approximation will need to be reconciled at the national, regional and international levels as a matter of priority to procure just outcomes. The requirement is for legitimacy rather than veto; prescription rather than proscription; legal surety rather than ambiguity; and methodical order rather than mayhem. The force of rash words spoken in the heat of the moment could be felt for years, whereas a soft answer may turn away wrath. If East Africans, and sub-Saharan Africa in general, are sincere about regional integration and advancing good governance through the effective enforcement of economic human rights, the separation of powers and the rule of law, they must invest to attain all the attendant benefits of a "fully-fledged" economic *acquis communautaire*. As Ronald Dworkin reminded us earlier this year: *justice is for hedgehogs*.

Acknowledgments This paper is the final version of a paper prepared for the 2010 Society of International Economic Law Conference in Barcelona. I am grateful for inputs received, questionnaires completed and interviews conducted with the EAC Secretariat, Partner States and other stakeholders.

Part III
Institutions

The Doha Development Agenda at a Crossroads: What Are the Remaining Obstacles to the Conclusion of the Round – Part III?

Edwini Kessie

Introduction

Following the inability of countries to resolve the outstanding negotiating issues in 2010, there was the widespread expectation that the modalities for agriculture and NAMA would be agreed before the summer of 2011, paving the way for the conclusion of the Doha Round in December 2011 when the WTO is scheduled to hold its Eighth Ministerial Conference. The view that the Round had to be concluded in 2011 was primarily because of the belief that it would be difficult to get the United States to engage in an election year (2012), meaning that the only possibility would be in 2013 and beyond.[1] With the possibility that Members would lose interest and abandon the negotiations, the year started with a flurry of meetings. The initial signs were encouraging, as all the key players engaged bilaterally and plurilaterally to resolve the outstanding issues.[2] The progress made in these negotiations led to the belief that revised texts could probably be produced before the Easter break, with the remaining issues resolved before the Ministerial meeting in December 2011. In his statement to the Trade Negotiations Committee (TNC) on 2 February 2011, DG Lamy observed that "the change of gear and approach is detectable in both legs of the negotiating process, i.e. in the Negotiating Groups as well as in the bilateral and plurilateral consultations".[3] The progress made was

---

[1] Sutherland, The Tragedy of Trade Blindness, available at: http://www.project-syndicate.org/commentary/sutherland2/English.

[2] See, for example, the statement by the United States Trade Representative, Ron Kirk, at the Plenary Session of APEC Ministers regarding the Doha Round of World Trade Organization Talks in Big Sky, Montana, on 19th May, 2011.

[3] http://www.wto.org/english/news_e/news11_e/tnc_dg_stat_02feb11_e.htm.

E. Kessie (✉)
WTO, Centre William Rappard, Rue de Lausanne 154, 1211 Geneva 21, Switzerland
e-mail: edwini.kessie@wto.org

C. Herrmann and J.P. Terhechte (eds.), *European Yearbook of International Economic Law (EYIEL), Vol. 3 (2012)*, European Yearbook of International Economic Law 3, DOI 10.1007/978-3-642-23309-8_17, © Springer-Verlag Berlin Heidelberg 2012

evident in the genuine search for compromises. Members focused, *inter alia*, on textual proposals to bridge differences and remove square-bracketed texts.

With the global economic recovery strongly underway, there was the momentum to conclude the negotiations and give a further boost to the global economy. The comparison of the Round to a low hanging fruit by DG Lamy was very apt, as it would not cost a great deal to conclude but deliver significant benefits for all countries and in the process strengthen the world economy. According to the Peterson Institute, a successfully concluded Doha Round could deliver about US\$ 300 billion in additional world output, boosting markets and growth opportunities. These benefits are expected to increase over time and strengthen the global economy. The OECD also postulates that an agreement on trade facilitation could potentially reduce trade transaction costs by 9%, through more transparent and predictable border procedures. A 1% reduction in worldwide trade transaction costs could generate US\$ 43 billion in worldwide welfare gains, of which 65% would accrue to developing countries. According to former Director-General Peter Sutherland, failure to conclude the Round could cost the global economy \$700 billion in additional income.[4]

Notwithstanding these forecasts, it had become clear by March 2011 that the negotiations were in trouble. In a statement to the TNC on 29 March, DG Lamy warned Members about the risk of failure and urged them to "reflect on the costs of non-Round to the world economy as well as to the development prospects of Members, in particular the smaller and least-developed which are more dependent on an improved set of global trade rules".[5] The sense of optimism was replaced with doom, as some WTO Members questioned whether it was even necessary to produce revised texts considering the continuing gaps in Members' positions on the key issues, including whether or not participation in sectoral agreements and when the special safeguard mechanism could be activated by developing countries in cases of import surges. The revised texts and reports of the Chairpersons were eventually circulated, but they were quite disappointing as overall they did not bridge the existing gaps in Members' positions on the most contentious issues. In a statement accompanying the texts, DG Lamy stated that "we are confronted with a clear political gap which, as things stand, under the NAMA framework currently on the table, and from what I have heard in my consultations, is not bridgeable ... This

---

[4] http://www.project-syndicate.org/commentary/sutherland2/English.

[5] http://www.wto.org/english/news_e/news11_e/tnc_dg_infstat_29mar11_e.htm. See further DG Lamy's statement to the World Bank's Development Committee and the IMF's International Monetary and Financial Committee in Washington on 16th April, 2011: "The WTO system is today in danger of not being able to conclude the Doha Development Round we started ten years ago. The optimism with which we started this year with has all but evaporated. WTO members have stalled on the last hurdles of the WTO Doha Round trade negotiations, i.e. industrial tariff reductions for developed and emerging economies. It is high time governments rise above narrow vested interests and consider the consequences of weakening the multilateral trading system which has so successfully helped resist protectionism during the crisis", available at: http://www.wto.org/english/news_e/news11_e/dgpl1_16apr11_e.htm.

is a grave situation for the Round and for all of the efforts and aspirations it embodies. It is our reality, however, and we must face it squarely in order to try to find a way forward together".[6]

In the aftermath of the circulation of the texts and reports, various commentators expressed the view that the Doha Round was dead and that the WTO should own up to that reality. A number of reasons were given as to why it would be difficult to break the impasse.[7] For some observers, the Round was a knee-jerk response to the slumping global economy made worse by the events of 11 September 2001 and that Members had not shown any interest right from the beginning to adopt further trade and economic reforms to ensure sustainable growth and development. It was this lack of commitment that has made Members reluctant to overcome their differences which in economic terms do not amount to much. For others, the Doha Round is simply too ambitious both in its coverage and the commitments expected from Members. With 153 Members at very different levels of economic development, it was impossible to agree on market openings and tighter regulatory mechanisms which limit their policy options and may not always be in conformity with their national development goals.

The single undertaking approach, under which nothing in the DDA negotiations is agreed until everything is agreed, was also blamed for the impasse in the negotiations. The argument has been advanced that flexibility is needed and that where a critical mass of countries are prepared to move forward, they should be allowed to do so and not wait for the consent of other Members. Other observers also point out that the negotiating agenda gives too much emphasis to classic issues such as tariffs and subsidies and less prominence to emerging issues such as export restrictions and energy insecurity. Others also point out that the WTO's classification system of countries is obsolete and does not reflect the current trends in the global economy where certain developing countries are beginning to play a larger role and could probably offer more commitments in the negotiations.

Regardless of the reasons for the impasse in the negotiations, most WTO Members, particularly the least-developed and low-income developing countries have indicated that they would like to see the Round concluded as it would offer them the opportunity to increase and diversify their exports and enable them to use trade to achieve sustainable growth and development. At the TNC meeting on 29 April, several of them refused to concede that the Doha Round was dead. They rather exhorted the major trading powers to overcome their differences and find solutions to the intractable issues. They pointed out that unlike them, they had limited options and that it was important for the key players to look beyond their narrow interests and consider the impact the collapse of the negotiations would have on them.

---

[6] TN/C/13, 21st April, 2011, pp. 1–2.

[7] DG Lamy's statement to the TNC on 29th April, 2011, available at: http://www.wto.org/english/news_e/news11_e/tnc_dg_infstat_29apr11_e.htm.

With the exhibited determination of Members not to jettison the Round and continue searching for compromises, DG Lamy called for a reality check and said that he would be consulting Members on the way forward and report back to the TNC at its meeting scheduled for 31 May 2011. He said that it was evident that if progress had to be made, an entirely new approach was needed. Members agreed with him that the "business as usual" approach would not work as Members would continue to insist on their negotiating positions without making any attempts to forge compromises. This approach would not produce the intended results and would only undermine the credibility of the WTO. He also said that the "stopping and starting from scratch" approach would not work either as Members would be throwing away 10 years of hard work, which has produced far-reaching results in many areas. There was no guarantee that even if the current Round was abandoned and commenced afresh, Members would be able to reach a result. He further said that the "drifting away" approach would also not work either as the difficult issues in respect of which consensus has evaded the WTO membership would not simply disappear. A conscious effort had to be made to resolve them.[8]

The critical question confronting Members is what the next steps should be. There is the growing view that the level of ambition needs to be adjusted and that it is impossible as this stage to believe that a comprehensive result can be obtained in all the negotiating areas. Proponents of this view argue that the WTO should salvage what is possible from the agreements reached thus far and conclude the Round on that basis. The former United States Trade Representative, Ms. Susan Schwab, shares the view that WTO should focus on a limited number of issues and abandon the Doha Round.[9] The so-called "Plan B" is supported by many developing countries, particularly the least-developed among them, who are seeking a package covering issues of importance to them, including duty-free quota-free access, a waiver to enhance their participation in services trade, trade facilitation and a few others.[10] The position of developed countries is quite nuanced. While some of them could support a package for developing countries, particularly the least-developed among them, they may be hesitant to do so if it would jeopardize the chances of reviving the Round. Dismembering the Round by agreeing

---

[8] Ibid.

[9] Schwab, "Why the Negotiations Are Doomed and What We Should Do about It", Foreign Affairs, May-June 2011. See further: http://drezner.foreignpolicy.com/posts/2011/05/11/what_next_for_world_trade.

[10] Bridges Weekly Trade News Digest, 27th April, 2011, p. 3. Apart from trade facilitation and DFQF, other candidates for a possible „deliverables" package include fisheries subsides, environmental goods and services, clarification of the interface between specific trade obligations in multilateral environment agreements and WTO rules, information exchange between MEA secretariats and relevant WTOP Committees, elimination of all forms of export subsidies, cotton subsidies, dispute settlement improvements, tighter disciplines on non-tariff barriers on manufactured products, LDC waiver in services, non-tariff barriers and RTA transparency mechanism.

selectively to certain agreements could make the search for compromises more difficult at a later stage and could hasten the Round's death.

The jury is still out on what WTO Members would do after admitting that none of the three approaches outlined by DG Lamy is a viable option and with divergent views on a possible "deliverables" package in December 2011. As stated by the USTR, Mr. Ron Kirk, while Members could repeat their commitment to concluding the Round, it rang "increasing hollow" and that they needed to do more, but the key question is what could be done?[11] It is clear that WTO Members do not have clear answers and that the consultations being carried out by the DG would determine the way forward. In the meantime, WTO Members have been at pains to shore up the credibility of the institution by stressing on its other functions particularly the effective dispute settlement mechanism and the monitoring of Members' trade policies. Put it differently, the WTO transcends the Doha negotiations and the difficulties in the negotiations should not be exploited to undermine the effectiveness of the institution as a whole. While it is true that WTO has other important functions, failure to conclude the Round would undermine the confidence of least-developed countries in the organization and negatively affect its public perception, especially the time and resources spent on the negotiations. As noted by Peter Sutherland, "to pretend that the Doha Round's failure would not have negative and lasting effects for the WTO betrays a profound lack of understanding of the risks we run, as well as of the Round's vital importance for weaker and smaller states".[12]

Remaining Issues in the Various Negotiating Areas

Agriculture

As noted in the earlier articles, while considerable progress has been made on the domestic support and export competition pillars, there are a number of difficult issues remaining under the market access pillar. In his latest report to the TNC, Chairman David Walker affirmed this view.[13] He said that since assuming the chairmanship of the Special Session of the Committee on Agriculture in April 2009, work had proceeded mainly on four levels, namely (i) consultations with Members on the issues that are bracketed in the 6 December 2008 draft modalities text and other related texts; (ii) the development of "templates" for the presentation of data which would form the basis for the development of modalities and eventually Members' schedules of commitments; (iii) substantive discussion of data

---

[11] Supra note 2.

[12] Sutherland, The Tragedy of Trade Blindness, available at: http://www.project-syndicate.org/commentary/sutherland2/English.

[13] TN/AG/26, 21st April, 2011, p. 9.

requirements and the submission and verification of data; and (iv) identification of ambivalent technical provisions in the draft modalities text and clarification thereof.

Market Access Pillar

With respect to sensitive products, it would be recalled under the draft modalities text, it is foreseen that developed countries would be able to designate 4% of their tariff lines as sensitive and make lesser cuts on the selected products. Where a Member has 30% of a Member's tariff lines fall in the highest band, then that country would be entitled to designate a further 2% of its tariff lines. Canada and Japan are pressing for further flexibilities, but other Members remain opposed. The Chairman reported that Members' positions on this issue had not evolved.[14] Regarding special products, it is envisaged that developing countries would be able to designate 12% of their tariff lines as special products on the basis of food security, rural development and livelihood security. Five percent of the tariff lines would not be subjected to any cuts at all, while for the remaining tariff lines the average cut shall not exceed 11%. There has not been any significant movement on this issue, as some Members continue to have reservations about the proposed numbers in the text. Some believe that the numbers are too high and could affect export opportunities.[15]

With respect to the special safeguard mechanism, the Chairman reported that that notwithstanding technical contributions from Members on a range of issues, including seasonality, price and volume cross-check, price-based SSM flexibilities, flexibilities for SVEs and pro-rating, there has not been any significant progress in narrowing the differences in Members' positions. In fact, he had advised the Special Session in October 2010 that the stage of useful analytical discussion had appeared to have been exhausted and what was needed was "problem solving engagement among members to design a mechanism capable of being used to address cases of disruptive import surges, while not disrupting demand-induced trade". He further noted that no compromise proposals had been submitted to the Special Session for its consideration.[16]

On tropical and diversification products, the Chairman reported significant progress following the agreement on bananas between the European Union, ACP states and Latin American suppliers in December 2009. The communications by the parties contained proposed modalities for tariff reductions on bananas to be made by the European Union as well as treatment of tropical products and preference

---

[14] Ibid., p. 3, paras. 14–15.

[15] Ibid., p. 4, paras. 26–28.

[16] Ibid., p. 4, paras. 35–36.

erosion. Certain Members have sought clarification as to how the proposed modalities would affect their interests.[17] With respect to tariff capping, it had been proposed that developed-country Members should only be able to impose a tariff in excess of 100% only on products designated as sensitive. Japan and some other Members are strongly opposed to this proposal and their positions have not evolved. There is also disagreement on the payment options, should this exception be allowed.[18]

On whether it should be possible for new tariff quotas to be created, there has not been any significant change in Members' positions with some insisting that it would be a retrograde step if it were to be allowed. The Chairman reported that Members' positions have not evolved, but that there was a general willingness to continue technical discussions of the issue on a "without prejudice" basis. Regarding tariff simplification, it had been proposed that no tariff shall be bound in a form more complex than the current binding and that all simplified bound tariffs should not amount to any increase over the original more complex tariff. It is also being proposed that all bound tariffs or at least 90% of a developed country's tariffs should be expressed as simple *ad valorem* tariffs. The Chairman reported that work was continuing among Members but no definitive text has emerged.[19]

Domestic Support Pillar

The Chairman reported that there has not been any significant movement on the cotton issue, with some Members opposed to the language in the draft modalities text, which would require deeper cuts to cotton subsidies. He said that while there have been consultations at the political level, it appears that had not spurred the tabling of new technical or substantive contributions. He stated, however, that all the Members involved in the consultations were committed to finding a solution that would address the issue of cotton "ambitiously, expeditiously and specifically" consistent with the Hong Kong Ministerial Declaration. He suggested that a solution could probably be found to the cotton issue only when the broad contours on agreement on agriculture and more generally the Round are in place.[20] With respect to product-specific limits under the Blue Box, he suggested that a political decision had to be made regarding the bracketed numbers (i.e. 110 or 120) in paragraph 42 of the draft modalities text.[21]

---

[17] Ibid., p. 5, paras. 40–43.

[18] Ibid., p. 3, paras. 16–17.

[19] Ibid., p. 3, para. 25.

[20] Ibid., p. 2, paras. 8–11.

[21] Ibid., para. 11.

Export Competition Pillar

The Chairman did not report on any specific issues under the export competition pillar. In the past, some concerns had been expressed about a number of issues, including the monetization of food aid and whether the monopoly powers of agricultural state trading enterprises should be prohibited or disciplined. It could probably be inferred that considerable progress has been made on these issues and that they are not deal breakers.

NAMA

As noted in previous articles, considerable progress has been made in the NAMA negotiations, with broad agreement on a number of issues, including the formula, the co-efficients to be used by developed and developing countries, the treatment of unbound tariffs and flexibilities for countries which have bound less than 35% of their tariff lines. For the most part of 2010 and 2011, work in the Negotiating Group on Market Access has focused on non-tariff barriers, flexibilities for certain developing-country Members and sectorals. With respect to NTBs, the Chairman pointed out that work was advanced and that there were encouraging signs of agreements emerging on the horizontal mechanism, textile labeling and transparency. He noted that there was a "significant potential NTB-package within reach which would, *inter alia*, constitute a series of improvements to the functioning of the TBT Agreement, create stimuli for legislators to privilege the reference to international standards and to diminish the tendency to deviate from international standards". He added that there were still some issues to be clarified and that future work would focus on these outstanding issues.[22]

With respect to flexibilities for certain developing-country Members, the chairman reported that there were continuing differences among Members on the proposals submitted by the requesting developing-country Members. In that regard, he reported that there had been no progress on the flexibilities being sought by South Africa, Argentina, Venezuela and Kenya. He also alluded to specific requests of SVEs, Maldives and the disproportionately affected Members such as Bangladesh and Sri Lanka.[23]

Regarding sectorals, the Chairman stated that since negotiations had been taking place among Members bilaterally and plurilaterally, he had nothing significant to report on.[24] However, in his report to the TNC, DG Lamy elaborated on his

---

[22] TN/MA/W/103/Rev.3/Add1, 21st April, 2011, p. 3, para. 3.

[23] Ibid., pp. 1–2, paras. 2(ii)–(viii).

[24] Ibid., p. 1, para. 2(i).

consultations with seven Members on the issue.[25] He recalled that sectoral negotiations were being pursued to achieve the overall objective of reducing or eliminating tariffs, as appropriate, with participation not being mandatory and the results extended to all WTO Members on an MFN basis. He noted that the fundamental issue in the negotiations was whether certain developing-country Members, including Brazil, China and India had to participate in some sectoral agreements.[26] In that regard, the consultations had focused on "sectoral priorities, views on the product basket approach and or other possible approaches, details on the products requested and offered the respective contribution of formula cuts and sectorals to the overall NAMA level of ambition, as well as possible trade-offs within NAMA and across other areas of the negotiation".[27]

From the consultations, it appeared that all the participating countries were prepared to participate in one or more sectorals, depending on the specifics of the treatment and how sensitivities on specific tariff lines were accommodated. As regards the "product basket approach", DG Lamy noted that different views had been expressed on the number of baskets to be used, products to be assigned to each basket and the treatment to be given to products within each basket. With respect to treatment, he said that while some Members envisaged the elimination or substantial reduction of tariffs on the bulk of products within the chosen sectors, others were adamant and not prepared to reduce the tariffs on the bulk of their products to zero. If tariffs on chemicals, industrial machinery, electric and electronic products were brought down to zero, developed and developing countries participating in the sectorals would effectively be applying a coefficient of 4 and 8, respectively, instead of 8 and 20–22 envisaged in the draft modalities.[28] Where there was the greatest gulf between the countries was the role of sectorals in achieving an appropriate level of ambition in the negotiations. From the perspective of certain developed Members, the objective of sectorals was "to rebalance the disparity in contribution between developed and emerging economies and to achieve, if not equalization, a harmonization of their tariffs".[29] This view is rejected by emerging economies who insist that effect has to be given to the Doha mandate which envisaged special and differential treatment for developing countries and recognised that there would be less than full reciprocity in the negotiations. They believe that the NAMA draft modalities text strikes a careful balance between the interests of developed and developing countries, especially considering that it had already been agreed that participation in sectorals would not be mandatory.

---

[25] The countries are Australia, Brazil, China, the European Union, India, Japan and the United States.

[26] Proponents are seeking commitments in the following sectors: chemicals, industrial machinery, electronics and electrical products, enhanced health care, forest products, raw materials, gems and jewellery.

[27] TN/C/14, 21st April, 2011, p. 1, para. 4.

[28] Ibid., p. 2, para. 11.

[29] Ibid., p. 2, para. 12.

In his concluding remarks, DG Lamy noted that there was a fundamental gap in expectations in sectorals, which could not be bridged through adjustments in the architecture of sectorals. There was a political gap, which appeared to be unbridgeable judging by the representations of the countries involved in the consultations.[30]

Services

As noted in previous articles, one of the main issues in the services negotiations is the quality of offers on the table. The scope and breadth of some offers are very limited and do not in certain instances match current access conditions in some countries. Some Members have placed excessive limitations on their offers and others are unwilling to remove current restrictions in their schedules. Generally, developed countries would like developing countries to provide greater access, particularly under modes 1 and 3, in sectors of interest to their services providers, particularly financial services, telecommunications and professional services, while developing countries would like to see greater commitments in mode 4 and the implementation of specific measures which would enhance their participation in services trade. The negotiations on domestic regulations and GATS rules have also been proceeding at a glacial pace.

In his report to the TNC, the Chairman of the Services negotiations reaffirmed that there had been limited progress in the market access negotiations since the July 2008 signalling conference, at which Members undertook to improve the quality of their offers if progress was made in other areas of the DDA. He noted that for developed countries, the "remaining gaps between offers or signals and bilateral and plurilateral requests or applied regimes were still substantial, and that they had difficulty in obtaining clarity from recipient Members about real difficulties faced in meeting requests".[31] Developing countries also saw an imbalance in the market access negotiations to the extent that special and differential treatment had not been taken into account in requests made, and sectors of export interest had not figured prominently in tabled offers.[32] The assessment of the Chairman is borne out by the reports of the coordinators of the plurilateral request/offer groups which showed significant gaps in the positions of Members in almost all the 18 sectors where improved offers are being sought.[33]

---

[30] Ibid., pp. 2–3, paras. 13–14.

[31] TN/S/36, 21st April, 2011, p. 2, para. 5.

[32] Ibid., p. 2, para. 6.

[33] Accounting services; air transport services; architecture, engineering and integrated engineering services; audiovisual services, computer-related services; construction services; distribution services; energy services; environmental services; financial services; legal services; logistics and related services; maritime transport services; postal and courier services, including Express Delivery; private education services:; services related to agriculture; telecommunication services and tourism services.

As alluded to the Chairman in previous reports, progress in the Services market access negotiations are dependent on developments in other areas of the DDA negotiations, particularly the market access negotiations in agriculture and NAMA. Currently, developing countries appear to be of the view that developed countries are not offering much in agriculture and NAMA, especially considering the obligations they will have to assume in these areas. They believe that the exchange rate is not right and are likely to hold out until they see improvement in the offers of developed countries.

On domestic regulation, the Chairman noted that the recent intensification of negotiations had produced notable progress towards the adoption of a revised draft text, but there were still important gaps to be filled. He noted that there were paragraphs in the draft text on which agreement had been reached on an *ad referendum* basis; paragraphs where there had been no agreement but language proposals reduced to a single alternative with brackets, in addition to the Chairman's March 2009 text; and paragraphs where there was limited progress and multiple alternatives and language options remain".[34] He also said that there was no agreement on whether a normative standard in the form of a "necessity test" should be incorporated into the disciplines.[35]

Regarding GATS rules, the Chairman said that the report of the Chairperson of the Working Party on GATS Rules indicated that there had not been any significant progress in all the three areas, namely subsidies, emergency safeguards and government procurement. He noted that the proponents had not managed to convince the Membership of the need for new disciplines in these areas. The divergences over the objectives and expected outcomes of the negotiations were so wide preventing the move to text-based negotiations. With respect to emergency safeguards (ESM), he reported that some Members had indicated their preparedness to continue discussions on ESM-related statistics. Regarding government procurement, he said that Members were interested in continuing discussions on the economic importance of procurement in services as well as the proposal for an annex to the GATS dealing with the subject. On subsidies, Members wanted to enhance their understanding of the trade distortive effects of subsidies and consider whether any multilateral disciplines were necessary.[36]

With respect to the LDC waiver, the Chairman reported that constructive discussions had taken place on the textual proposal by the LDC Group, but there were divergent views on whether the waiver should be restricted to only market access measures or also cover additional measures. Greater clarity has also been sought by some Members on the rules of origin for services and service suppliers

---

[34] Ibid., p. 11, para. 75.

[35] Ibid.

[36] Ibid., p. 12, paras. 79–82.

benefitting from preferences. Further work was required to bridge the differences in Members' positions.[37]

Development

It will be recalled that pursuant to paragraph 44 of the Doha Ministerial Declaration, developing countries tabled 88 agreement-specific proposals with a view to making current special and differential treatment (SDT) provisions more precise and legally enforceable. Developing countries have long insisted that the hortatory character of SDT provisions has meant that they are not implemented by developed countries, thus defeating the purpose for which they were inserted into the multilateral trade agreements. In his report, the Chairman of the Special Session of the Committee on Trade and Development said that work on the six remaining Category I proposals had proceeded on the basis of the last language circulated in May 2010, but it had not been possible to bridge the divergent positions of Members on the proposals.[38] Regarding the 28 proposals agreed to in principle by Members on an *ad referendum* basis, he said that there was a shared understanding what remained was their formal adoption by the membership at an opportune time. With respect to the Category II proposals, he said that there had not been any progress and this was partly due to the slow progress in the overall DDA negotiations.[39]

With respect to the monitoring mechanism, the Chairman reported that good progress had been made in the consultations on the basis of the fourth revision of the text circulated by his predecessor. There was now convergence on the scope, functions and operations of the monitoring mechanism. There was also an agreement to review the mechanism 3 years after its entry into force and thereafter whenever it is deemed necessary. He cautioned, however, that there were still differences in Members' views on the language of the preamble, the review procedure and the status of recommendations made within the framework of the mechanism.[40]

Rules

In his report to the TNC, the Chairman of the Negotiating Group on Rules noted that while some progress had been recorded, there were still significant gaps in

---

[37] Ibid., p. 12, para. 83.

[38] TN/CTD/26, 21st April, 2011, p. 3.

[39] Ibid.

[40] Ibid.

Members' positions on a broad range of issues in the three relevant areas, namely antidumping, horizontal subsidies and fisheries subsidies.[41] As regards the negotiations on anti-dumping, he said that while he had chosen to present a revised text, it should not be construed to mean that significant progress had been made in the negotiations. He said that as in the 2008 Chair text, the major "political" issues had not yet been settled and they remained square-bracketed in the revised text.[42] Work in the last 2 years had succeeded in throwing useful light on Members' proposals and positions on some of the key issues under negotiation and clarified the parameters of certain provisions in the Antidumping Agreement.[43]

Most of the proposed changes are not controversial and would enhance the transparent application of the rules. The Chairman noted that the most divisive issue in the negotiations was the practice of "zeroing". Some Members of the view that it should be completely forbidden irrespective of the comparison methodology used and in respect of all proceedings, while others were of the view that it should be authorized in all contexts. Others had a more nuanced view and indicated their preparedness to engage in further technical discussions to consider its applicability in certain contexts such as targeted dumping.[44] Another contentious issue is whether it should be made mandatory for investigating authorities to separate and distinguish the effects of dumped imports and other factors and conduct a quantitative as opposed to a qualitative analysis of non-attribution.[45]

There is also disagreement on whether the lesser duty rule should be made mandatory, so that countries would be obliged to impose a lesser duty if that would be sufficient to remove the injury caused to the relevant domestic injury.[46] Views also differ on whether or not detailed rules are required to determine the circumstances under which producers who are related to exporters or importers or who are themselves importers may be excluded when establishing the relevant domestic industry in a country.[47] Another divisive issue is whether it is necessary to have a robust public interest clause which would require representations of domestic interested parties to be taken into account when deciding whether to impose an antidumping duty.[48] There is also no convergence on the need for dedicated rules on anti-circumvention. Some Members are advocating for new investigations upon

---

[41] TN/RL/W/254, 21st April, 2011, p. 1.

[42] Ibid. It would be recalled that among the difficult issues previously identified include zeroing, causation of injury, material retardation, the exclusion of related producers, product under consideration, information requests to affiliated parties, public interest and lesser duty, anti-circumvention, sunset reviews, third country dumping, special and differential treatment and technical assistance.

[43] Ibid.

[44] Ibid., p. 6.

[45] Ibid., p. 8.

[46] Ibid., p. 19.

[47] Ibid., p. 9.

[48] Ibid., p. 19.

its occurrence, while others prefer the harmonization of procedures used by Members.[49] There are divergent views on the scope of sunset reviews. Some Members have proposed that antidumping measures should automatically lapse after 5 years without any possibility of extension, while others are vehemently opposed to the idea of automatic termination.[50] There is also disagreement on the flexibilities to be provided to investigating authorities from developing countries and whether a trade remedies facility should be set up to build the capacity of developing countries to have recourse to such remedies.[51]

It is clear from the foregoing that there are significant gaps in Members' positions on numerous issues and that further intensive work would be required to narrow the differences.

Regarding horizontal subsidies, the Chairperson said that he had decided not to present a revised text but rather submit a report, as there was not any sufficient basis for him to do so. Notwithstanding intensive consultations over the last 2 years, there had been no signs of convergence on the bracketed issues as contained in the 2008 Chair text. On the unbracketed text, there were relatively a small number of issues but these had proved to be very controversial. Furthermore, the Negotiating Group has not had the time to discuss new proposals that had been submitted by Members or discuss the transposition of the possible changes in antidumping provisions into their counterpart CVD Provisions.[52] Among the unresolved bracketed issues is whether new disciplines are needed to regulate certain loans and loan guarantees provided government financial institutions that do not operate on an independent, commercial basis, and that benefit from long-term government support to state enterprises unable to obtain financing from commercial lender.[53] There is also no agreement on the proposal that a developing country should be deemed to have attained export competitiveness only when it has attained a market share of 3.25% over a 5 year rolling period instead of the current two consecutive calendar years.[54]

There are differences of view on the proposal by Brazil to amend item (j) and the first paragraph of the Illustrative List of Export Subsidies (Annex I), so that in determining the existence of a benefit in connection with a prohibited export subsidy account is taken of the benefit to the recipient instead of the current language of the cost to government.[55] Likewise, there is also no consensus on the proposal that any changes to the OECD's Arrangement on Officially Supported

---

[49] Ibid., p. 21.

[50] Ibid., p. 23.

[51] Ibid., pp. 27–28.

[52] Ibid., p. 37.

[53] Ibid., pp. 37–38.

[54] Ibid., pp. 38–39.

[55] Ibid., pp. 39–40.

Export Credits should be reviewed and adopted by the WTO before it can be used as a benchmark.[56]

With respect to unbracketed language, the Chairman highlighted the proposed amendment to footnote 6 which would prevent any item in the Illustrative List of Export Subsidies from being read in an *a contrario* sense to establish when a measure is not an export subsidy.[57] Another difficult issue is the proposal by the European Union for benchmarks to be introduced to determine the specificity of subsidies conferred through the provision of goods and services at regulated prices.[58] Other controversial issues referred to by the Chairman included the definition of a "benefit", pass-through and subsidy allocation.[59] The Chairman provided a summary of the status of the five new proposals that have been submitted by Members since the circulation of the 2008 text. They dealt with (i) export financing benchmarks for developing Members; (ii) countervail procedures; (iii) tax and duty rebate schemes; (iv) phase-out period for developing Members graduating from Annex VII; and (v) the presumption of serious prejudice.[60]

With respect to fisheries subsidies, the Chairman said that because there had not been any significant developments since the circulation of the last text, he thought it best to present a report instead of a revised text. In that context, he noted that "there is too little convergence on even the technical issues, and indeed virtually none of the core substantive issues, for there to be anything to put into a bottom-up, convergence legal text, and there are no fisheries subsidies disciplines already in existence to which we could refer or revert".[61] The Chairman said it was regrettable that significant progress had not been made in the negotiations, considering the proliferation of proposals in the last 2 years by Members and the logic for reaching an agreement, which could "help bring about a situation where profitability and economic and environmental stability are mutually reinforcing, contributing to sustainable wealth creation".[62]

With respect to horizontal issues and proposals, the Chairman noted whereas there is broad agreement on prohibiting subsidies which contribute to overcapacity and over-fishing, there was no agreement on how a prohibition of any given type of subsidy should be framed.[63] In that regard, whereas some Members supported a broad and strict prohibition of fisheries subsidies (top-down approach), subject to narrowly defined exceptions, other Members favoured a more conditional approach

---

[56] Ibid., pp. 40–41.

[57] Ibid., p. 41.

[58] Ibid.

[59] Ibid., p. 41–42.

[60] Ibid., pp. 42–44.

[61] Ibid., p. 46.

[62] Ibid., pp. 48–49.

[63] Ibid., p. 49.

to prohibition insisting that there is no confirmed *a priori* link between subsidies and overcapacity or overfishing and that the problems could be attributed to Illegal, Unreported and Unregulated ("IUU"). These Members maintain that a prohibition should be upheld only when a subsidy has been proven to have caused overcapacity or overfishing, or only where there was no fisheries management in place or inadequate management.[64] There is also disagreement on whether certain types of subsidies benefitting artisanal or small-scale fisheries should be exempted from prohibition only in developing countries or in all countries.[65] There is also no consensus on the *de minimis* general exception, under which there would be a higher threshold for developing countries, possibly differentiated according to their size and/or share off global capture.[66]

As regards specific subsidies being considered for prohibition, the Chairman reported that there was broad support for the elimination of subsidies for transfer of vessels, subsidies to Illegal, Unreported and Unregulated vessels, and subsidies for onward transfer by a payer government of foreign access rights acquired under fisheries access agreements, but that there were differences in view as to whether the following subsidies should be prohibited: subsidies for vessel construction, repair and modification, subsidies for operating costs of vessels and of in-or-near port processing activities, subsidies for certain infrastructure, income support, price support for products of marine wild capture fishing, subsidies that support destructive fishing practices, subsidies in respect of overfished fisheries.[67]

Regarding special and differential treatment for developing countries, particularly least-developed countries, the Chairman said that there was broad support for differential treatment considering the importance of the fisheries sector in the alleviation of poverty and its contribution to the realization of certain development-related objectives. There were, however, some concerns as to which exemptions should be granted, and whether developing countries with a small share of global wild fish capture should be treated the same way as LDCs. There was also the concern that there was the possibility of other Members teaming up with LDCs to circumvent their obligations.[68] With respect to technical assistance, whereas there was the recognition that developing countries should be provided with technical assistance to implement their obligations, there were different visions as to what would be involved, and how it would be structured and implemented.[69]

Finally with respect to fisheries management, the Chairman reported that the contribution of fisheries management to resolving the problem of overfishing and overcapacity is recognised by all Members, but there was disagreement as to

---

[64] Ibid., p. 49–50.

[65] Ibid., p. 50.

[66] Ibid.

[67] Ibid., pp. 51–55.

[68] Ibid., pp. 55–62.

[69] Ibid., pp. 63–64.

whether effective fisheries management *per se* could combat the pressure of overfishing and overcapacity caused by the provision of subsidies. The differences in view have influenced the proposals submitted by Members.[70] There was broad agreement on the mandatory elements of fisheries management, but there was disagreement as to the degree to which the new disciplines should be differentiated for different categories of Members and/or in respect of different kinds of fisheries.[71] There is also no agreement on what role Regional Fisheries Management Organizations should have in management conditionalities.[72] Whereas there is broad agreement that the new disciplines should contain enhanced notification and surveillance provisions beyond those in the existing Subsidies Agreement, there is no consensus on issues such as the forum for notifications, periodicity of notifications, the nature of information to be notified.[73]

Overall, it is clear from the Chairman's report that further intensive work is needed to bridge Members' position on the broad array of issues. As noted by the Chairman, "[i]n order for the negotiations to make significant progress, ... negotiators will have to focus more on ...[the] incontrovertible realities no matter how inconvenient, and less on protecting their short-term defensive interests".[74] He adds that unless this happens, there are no "great prospects for the fisheries subsidies negotiations."[75]

Regarding regional trade agreements (RTAs), the Chairman reported good progress in the negotiations over the transparency mechanism, but said that no definitive decision had been reached on the draft text. As regards the systemic issues, he said that there has been greater focus on the definition of "substantially all the trade" and special and differential treatment for developing countries in the context of Article XXIV of the GATT 1994. However, Members had suggested varying approaches to resolving these issues. Whereas some had called for a forward-looking, post-Doha work programme, others had insisted that the Doha mandate is clear and that an outcome on the development-related aspects of RTAs was required. Given the opposing views, the Chairman cautioned members that unless they adopted a pragmatic, flexible and less doctrinaire approach to the negotiations, it would be difficult to resolve the impasse in the negotiations.[76]

---

[70] Ibid., p. 64.

[71] Ibid., p. 65.

[72] Ibid.

[73] Ibid., pp. 66–67.

[74] Ibid., p. 49.

[75] Ibid.

[76] TN/RL/W/253, 21st April, 2011.

Trade Facilitation

It would be recalled that the mandate in the trade facilitation negotiations is to clarify and improve Articles V, VIII and X of the GATT 1994. Although the negotiations only started in October 2004, considerable progress has been made leading to the speculation that they could become a candidate for early harvest. Progress in the negotiations could be attributed to the acceptance by all countries, including least-developed countries that it was in their own interest to adopt trade facilitation measures to simplify trade rules and reduce red tape which increase the cost of doing business and in the process scare away foreign direct investment. Another reason why the negotiations have progressed well is the understanding that implementation of any resulting obligations would be linked to the capacity of a country to do so. This guarantee has encouraged developing countries to be very forthcoming in the negotiations.

The Chairman did not present a report but a draft consolidated negotiating text. The text has two sections; the first section contains the substantive obligations of Members, while the second section contains special and differential treatment provisions for least-developed and developing countries.[77] The substantive obligations spelt out cover, *inter alia*, the publication and dissemination of information through various mediums, including the internet and enquiry points; consultations with other Members and affording them the opportunity to comment on draft regulations before their implementation, issuance of advance rulings; due process and appellate review procedures; fees and charges which can be charged in connection with importation and exportation; release and clearance of goods; consularization; formalities connected with importation and exportation; freedom of transit; border agency co-operation and institutional arrangements.[78]

The provisions in second section affirm the principle that implementation would depend on the capacity of countries. For LDCs, the draft text makes it clear they would only be required to undertake commitments to the extent consistent with their individual development, financial and trade needs or their administrative and institutional capabilities. The text distinguishes among three categories of obligations depending on its complexity. Category A commitments are provisions which developing and least-developed countries would be expected to implement following the entry into force of the agreement. Category B obligations are those which developing and least-developed countries would be expected to implement after a transitional period, while Category C obligations are those which they would be expected to implement after a transitional period and upon the furnishing of technical and financial assistance. While there is broad agreement that the classification of measures is going to be done individually by least-developed and developing countries, there are differences in view as to when the notification should be

---

[77] TN/TF/W/165/Rev.8, 21st April, 2011.

[78] Ibid., pp. 3–29.

made following the entry into force of the agreement. For provisions falling under categories B and C, developing and least-developed countries would be required to submit implementation plans, although it is envisaged that they could subsequently request for a delay in the implementation of the obligations and also for provisions to be switched from one category to another.[79]

The draft text contains extensive provisions on technical assistance, financial assistance and capacity building. It is stated that the provision of technical and financial assistance and capacity building by developed country members and relevant international organizations is a precondition for the acquisition of implementation capacity by developing and least-developed countries. It is further provided that "in cases where technical assistance and capacity building is not provided or lacks the requisite effectiveness, developing country and least-developed country members are not bound to implement the provisions notified under Category C."[80] The language is square-bracketed suggesting differences in the views of Members. While there is broad agreement that there should be a moratorium before recourse could be made to the WTO dispute settlement system, there are differences in view as to the number of years during which an action cannot be brought after the entry into force of a particular provision in any of the categories. Members are encouraged, however, to provide adequate opportunity for consultations with respect to any issue relating to the implementation of the agreement.[81]

While substantive progress has been made in the negotiations, there are still significant gaps in Members' positions on certain issues. It is evident that progress in other areas of the DDA negotiations would help a great deal in pushing Members closer to an agreement.

TRIPS – Multilateral System of Notification and Registration of Geographical Indications (GI) for Wines and Spirits

It would be recalled that the main issues in the negotiations for a Register of GIs are whether participation in the system should be mandatory, and whether the registration of a GI should create a rebuttable presumption that it would be protected in other WTO Members, except in a country that has lodged a reservation within a specified period.

In his report,[82] the Chairman of the Special Session of the Council for Trade-Related Aspects of Intellectual Property annexed a draft composite text which

---

[79] Ibid., pp. 30–35.

[80] Ibid., p. 35.

[81] Ibid., pp. 34–35.

[82] TN/IP/21, 21st April, 2011.

reflects the current state of negotiations on the six elements identified by him, namely (i) notification; (ii) registration; (iii) legal effects/consequences of registration; (iv) fees and costs; (v) special and differential treatment; and (vi) participation.[83] The Chairman makes it clear from the outset that the text is not agreed and that Members could revert to any issue at any time.[84] In fact, most of the language is bracketed and alternatives are provided. With respect to participation, the text provides that participation in the system is voluntary. However, it goes on to provide alternative formulations. One option reaffirms that participation would be voluntary, while another provides that each WTO member shall consult the Register before making any decision about registration.[85] With respect to notification of a GI, the text offers two alternatives, namely whether it is only the participating countries which should make a notification to the WTO or should the obligation be complied with by all WTO Members? The text contains detailed information to be furnished by the notifying Member.[86]

As regards registration, it is foreseen that it is the WTO Secretariat shall oversee the process.[87] There are differences of view on whether the Secretariat should automatically register any notification or whether it should be satisfied that the formalities and documents submitted are in order before proceeding with registration.[88] With respect to legal effects and consequences of registration, there is no consensus on whether Members shall merely consult the database or take its information into account when making decisions regarding registration and/or protection of trademarks and GIs in accordance with its laws and regulations and domestic procedures.[89] Likewise, there are variations in Members' positions regarding the effects of registration. Broadly speaking, registration shall have the following rebuttable effects in domestic administrative or legal proceedings involving the GI in the participating countries: (i) it shall be considered *prima facie* evidence of the interested parties who could enforce the GI protection; (ii) it would be presumed that the registered GI satisfies the definition in Article 22.1 of the TRIPS Agreement; and (iii) that the GI is protected in the country of origin. The text provides grounds where a participating Member may refuse protection of a GI in accordance with its domestic laws. It also specifies that decisions of administrative or judicial bodies shall only have territorial effect.[90] Regarding fees and costs,

---

[83] Ibid., p. 3.

[84] Draft Composite Text, JOB/IP/3/Rev1, 20th April, 2011.

[85] Ibid., Sec. A, p. A-3.

[86] Ibid., Sec. B, pp. A-3-A4.

[87] Ibid., Sec. C, p. A-5.

[88] Ibid., Sec. D, pp. A-5-A6.

[89] Ibid., Sec. E, pp. A-7-A8.

[90] Ibid., p. A-8.

it is provided that registration should be subject to the payment of the requisite fee and that the user-pays principle shall be applicable.[91]

With respect to special and differential treatment, it is being proposed that the section on legal effects and consequences of registration would not be applicable for a number of years after the entry into force of the agreement. There is also the provision that they would be exempted from the payment of registration fees.[92] On the section on technical assistance, it is foreseen that developed countries would provide effective technical assistance as well as financial assistance to developing and least-developed countries to facilitate their participation in the system as well as the implementation thereof.[93]

As reiterated by the Chairman, there is still a long way to go before an agreement can be reached on the various elements. Progress in the negotiations would depend on movement on the other TRIPS issues being considered outside the Special Session and in the DDA in general.[94]

Trade and Environment

It would be recalled that paragraph 31(i) provides for negotiations on the relationship between existing WTO rules and specific trade obligations (STOs) set out in multilateral trade agreements (MEAs). It further provides that the negotiations would be limited in scope to the applicability of the relevant WTO rules among the parties to the MEAs in question. Paragraph 31(ii) mandates Members to draw up procedures for regular information exchange between MEA Secretariats and the relevant WTO Committees, and the criteria for the granting of observer status. Paragraph 31(iii) provides for negotiations aimed at reducing or, as appropriate, eliminating tariff and non-tariff barriers on environmental goods and services.

In his report, the Chairman of the Special Session of the Committee on Trade and Environment said that good progress had been made in the negotiations enabling him to table a draft Ministerial Decision on paragraphs 31(i) and 31(ii). He underlined, however, that the text was not agreed and that its purpose was only to

---

[91] Ibid.

[92] Ibid.

[93] Ibid., p. A-9.

[94] The other TRIPs issues being considered are whether the additional protection offered to wines and spirits should be extended to other products. While useful technical work has been done such the use of trademarks systems to protect GIs, there are still significant gaps in the position of Members. The other issue is the interface between the TRIPS Agreement and the Convention on Biological Diversity. While there is broad support for the key principles of prior informed consent and equitable sharing of benefits, there are still significant gaps in Members positions, particularly as regards the need for a specific disclosure mechanism for genetic resources and traditional knowledge. The issue of "roll-back" is being considered in the agriculture negotiations.

capture progress made in the negotiations.[95] The text contains a number of square brackets indicating the differences of views among Members on the key issues. With regard to paragraph 31(i), the Chairman states that the draft Decision reflects the understanding that a specific trade obligation (STO) in a multilateral environment agreement (MEA) enjoins a party to take or refrain from taking a particular trade action. However, there is no consensus on the necessity of providing an exhaustive definition of an STO. The draft Decision seeks to promote coordination at the national level in the negotiation and implementation of STOs in MEAs and the sharing of domestic experiences in the Committee on Trade and Environment.[96]

With respect to collaboration between the WTO Secretariat and MEA Secretariats, the draft Decision reiterates the Chairman's proposals in Annex II of his March 2010 to the TNC. It is foreseen that there would be regular information exchange sessions with MEA Secretariats and access to each other's non-confidential documents. It is not yet decided whether information exchanges should only take place in the Committee on Trade and Environment or also in other WTO bodies.[97] The draft Decision also addresses the issue of observer status in the CTE by putting forward different formulations to be worked further on by Members.[98] It also foresees the provision of effective technical assistance to developing countries to facilitate the implementation of STOs in MEAs.[99] There is the also the proposal for the establishment of a group of experts on trade and environment to give advice on certain issues to developing countries.[100] With respect to dispute settlement, the Decision invites members who are parties to a dispute regarding the relationship between existing WTO rules and an STO, to seek the advice of experts on the MEA in question. It is further provided that the CTE shall encourage the disputing parties to agree or request the Panel to utilize the procedures in Article 13 DSU to seek advice and information in relation to the MEA in question.[101]

The Chair's Report on paragraph 31(iii) covers four main elements, namely (i) preambular language; (ii) coverage; (iii) treatment of tariffs and non-tariff barriers, including special and differential treatment, and (iv) cross-cutting and development elements.[102] With respect to the preambular language, the Chairman states that Members agree that a successful outcome of the negotiations under Paragraph 31 (iii) should deliver a triple-win in terms of trade, environment and development for

---

[95] The Chairman stated that "everything is conditional in the deepest sense and requires further engagement and deliberations in open-ended session, consistent with the bottom-up, member-driven process, and our customary negotiating principles of inclusiveness and transparency": TN/TE/20, 21st April, 2011.

[96] TN/TE/20, 21st April, 2011, p. 5.

[97] Ibid.

[98] Ibid.

[99] Ibid.

[100] Ibid., p. 6.

[101] Ibid.

[102] Ibid., p. 3.

WTO Members. First, the negotiations can benefit the environment by improving countries' ability to obtain high quality environmental goods at low cost or by enhancing the ability to increase production, exports and trade in environmentally beneficial products. This can directly improve the quality of life for citizens in all countries by providing a cleaner environment and better access to safe water, sanitation or clean energy. The liberalization of trade in environmental goods and services can be beneficial for development by assisting developing countries in obtaining the tools needed to address key environmental priorities as part of their on-going development strategies. Finally, trade wins because these products become less costly and efficient producers of such technologies can find new markets. In addition, liberalizing trade in environmental goods will encourage the use of environmental technologies, which can in turn stimulate innovation and technology transfer.[103]

Regarding coverage, the Chairman recalled that several proposals have been put forward by Members with a view to establishing an "environmentally credible universe of products to which the treatment modalities could apply". He identified this issue as the one on which Members' positions were far apart.[104] Based on the proposals of Members, the Chairman's report advocates a hybrid approach covering the following elements: (i) an agreed core list[105] which would comprise a targeted set of environmental goods on which all Members would take commitments; (ii) a complementary self-selected list: developed countries would individually select a number of environmental products for tariff elimination and developing countries are encouraged to participate; (iii) as a complement to the common core list and complementary lists, products would be identified through a request/offer process,

---

[103] Ibid.

[104] One proposal focuses on identifying environmental goods on the basis of environmental projects, with broad criteria for designating such projects decided by the CTE using the six broad categories under which goods have been classified, namely (i) air pollution control; (ii) renewable energy, (iii) waste management and water treatment; (iv) environmental technologies, (v) carbon capture and storage and (vi) others. Another proposal advocates a request and offer process that would permit each member to designate its own list of environmental goods and assume liberalization commitments on that basis. Another proposal also envisages two lists – one for developed countries and the other for developing countries, with both being self-selected from the reference universe and on the understanding that list of developed countries would cover more products. There are other variations of this proposal, with some Members urging a common core list of products that could deliver an ambitious and significant outcome, and supplemented by a complementary list on which consensus could not be reached and from which Members would have to self-select a certain percentage to apply the treatment modalities. Another proposal advocates for a core common list to be supplemented by a development list covering products of interest to developing countries which tariffs would be eliminated or reduced significantly.

[105] A group of Members identified, on an illustrative and starting-point basis, 26 tariff lines drawn from the reference universe. Preliminary discussions showed that some of the goods included in this set could be considered by the membership as clear environmental goods, as long as they can be specifically identified in the HS classification by an ex-out or otherwise. See Annex II.B of the text.

the outcome of which would be multilateralised in accordance with the MFN principle; and (iv) environmental projects could be used to identify lines for inclusion in the common core list, the complementary self-selected list or the request-offer list or by unilateral liberalization if used in environmental projects.[106] The Report contains further details on each of the elements.[107]

With respect to treatment, the Chairman said that the modalities would depend on the final structure of the agreement. However, proposals for options include a reduction of tariffs to zero for certain products or a reduction including 0 for X and a 50% cut after formula application and elimination of tariffs within a defined time-frame. There are also proposals for eliminating and disciplining non-tariff barriers to safeguard the integrity of commitments and promote transparency.[108]

Regarding special and differential treatment, it is envisaged that developing countries would be able to exempt some products from tariff cuts, make lesser reductions and be given longer transitional periods to implement their obligations. Additional flexibilities are envisaged for least-developed countries.[109] With respect to the cross-cutting elements, the Chairman singled out the work being pursued in the Special Session of the Council for Trade in Servicers on environmental services. He said that one option would be to draft textual elements cross-referring to the work there on enhanced commitments on environmental services. Another option would be to associate the enhanced commitments on environmental services with environmental goods in the reference universe or categories or to an agreed set of environmental goods. With respect to environmental technologies, he said that there was a general understanding that it should be an integral part of an outcome.[110]

It is clear from the Chairman's report that Members are no closer to an agreement and that further intensified work would be needed to bridge the gaps in their positions.

Dispute Settlement

It would be recalled that the mandate given by Ministers was to improve and clarify the DSU on the basis of work done thus far, as well as any additional proposals by Members. Given the strategic importance of the dispute settlement system, the negotiations were excluded from the "single undertaking" and given a shorter time-frame. They were supposed to have been concluded in May 2003, but they are still

---

[106] TN/TE/20, 21st April, 2011, p. 15.

[107] Ibid., pp. 15–19.

[108] Ibid., p. 4.

[109] Ibid., p. 4.

[110] Ibid., p. 4.

dragging on. It has been suggested that WTO Members are satisfied with the operation of the DSU and as such they are not in a hurry to introduce changes which may undermine its effectiveness. It has also been surmised that Members have made a linkage with the other negotiations under the DDA and that the difficulties in agriculture and NAMA have also affected the tempo of the DSU negotiations.

In his report to the TNC, the Chairman noted that the July 2008 draft text[111] circulated by him had brought greater focus to the discussion and provided a unified basis for further work.[112] He mentioned that the Special session was close to an understanding on draft legal text on sequencing between Article 21.5 and Article 22.2 of the DSU. There were also key points of convergence on post-retaliation and Members had also undertaken constructive work on third-party rights, time savings and various aspects of effective compliance. Progress had also been made on certain aspects of flexibility and Member-control over the DSU process. In that context, work was advanced on a draft legal text on the suspension of panel proceedings.[113] The Chairman cautioned, however, that there were still divergent positions on a number of issues, including panel composition, remand authority for the Appellate Body, mutually agreed solutions, strictly confidential information, transparency and *amicus curiae* briefs.[114] He also mentioned that no progress has been made on developing country interests, including special and differential treatment in the DSU process.[115] Some developing countries are seeking enhanced third party rights, a dispute settlement fund, the award of legal costs and enhanced remedies, including retroactive remedies and collective retaliation.

As noted by the Chairman, there are a significant number of issues to be resolved and that a successful conclusion to the negotiations would require additional flexibility in Members' positions.[116]

Concluding Remarks

It is clear from the foregoing that while progress has been made across all the negotiating areas in recent months, it has not been enough to bridge the gaps in Members' negotiating positions, particularly in agriculture and NAMA. Members appear to be exhausted from 10 years of grueling negotiations and do not want to continue negotiating with the expectation that they would be able to bridge their

---

[111] JOB(08)/81, 18th July, 2008.

[112] TN/DS/25, 21st April, 2011, p. 1.

[113] Ibid.

[114] Ibid.

[115] Ibid.

[116] Ibid., pp. 1–2.

existing differences at some point in the future. As previously stated, the "business as usual" approach would not work, so also is the "drifting away" approach. Against this background, Members have been considering a "Plan B" under which they would like to salvage agreements on issues that have been reached in the various negotiating areas, particularly those of interest to least-developed countries such as duty-free, quota-free access for their products with simplified rules of origin and the implementation of modalities to enhance their participation in services trade.

While several Members have spoken in favour of this effort, it cannot be assumed that it attracts the support of all the membership. Some Members would be concerned that such a step would hasten the death of the Doha Round and undermine the single undertaking approach, under which nothing is agreed until everything is agreed. Should the package contemplated be smaller and benefit only least-developed countries, the chances of an such an agreement being accepted would be quite high. The reality, however, is that it may be extremely difficult to agree on a package which would only benefit least-developed countries considering the inter-connectedness of countries and cross ownership of companies operating in least-developed countries and elsewhere. Should the package be substantial and benefit other Members, it would be extremely difficult to get an agreement, as certain countries may not want to lose their leveraging power to extract concessions from countries which may benefit from the issues included in the package.

The jury is still out on whether WTO Members will choose a dignified exit by agreeing on a package of measures in favour of developing countries, particularly least-developed countries and claim to have delivered on the development dimension of the Doha Round or whether they will prefer to lose everything which would do an incalculable damage to the credibility of the organization, which has done so much to strengthen the global economy for the past six decades. It appears from recent consultations that it would be difficult for Members to agree on any package in December. Efforts are still on-going, but the pronouncements of the key players seem to indicate that nothing substantial can be expected at the Ministerial meeting. It appears Members are no longer keen on classifying issues according to their degree of ripeness and bearing in mind who the beneficiaries would be.

The WTO is at a critical juncture since its creation in 1995. Its usefulness became evident during the global financial crisis. Its monitoring mechanism was widely credited for restraining WTO Members from adopting protectionist policies and abiding by their commitments. The Doha Round holds great promise for all countries, particularly the least-developed countries, which have been operating at the periphery of the multilateral trading system. A successful Round would reduce the current distortions in the system and offer them an opportunity to anchor their development plans on trade. There is still a window of opportunity for WTO Members to demonstrate their faith in the organization and the multilateral trading system by harvesting the agreements that have already been reached on a number of issues and work intensively to bridge their differences on the remaining issues between now and the December ministerial meeting and thereafter. All WTO members have a stake in a strong, vibrant multilateral trading system and should look beyond their narrow trade interests and make the necessary compromises which would strengthen the system for the benefit of all countries.

Acknowledgments The views expressed in this paper are those of the author and should not in any way be attributed to the WTO. Helpful comments were provided by Kofi Amenyah and Kofi Kusi Achampong.

WTO Dispute Settlement: Current Cases

Andreas Krallmann

Nine panel reports and one Appellate Body report were published in 2010, many of which touched upon systemically and politically important questions.

Some of the recent decisions were important from a *political* point of view:

China won its first two cases as a complainant against the two traditional main users of the dispute settlement system, i.e. the USA and the EU. This is a clear signal that the dispute settlement system does not only work in favour of the developed countries that have considerable experience in using the system but serves all members of the WTO.

In summer 2010, more than 5 years after a panel had been established against the EU, the panel issued its report in *EC and Certain Member States – Large Civil Aircraft ('the Airbus case')* dealing with EU member states' support for the Airbus company. A decision in the sister case which deals with the corresponding support measures by the USA for its manufacturer Boeing will follow suit in 2011. Thus, the picture of government support for large civil aircraft will only be completed once both cases – and maybe both appeals – have been decided.

Some of the decisions which will be presented in more detail in this chapter have important implications on *WTO jurisprudence*. As pointed out in some detail in last year's contribution, the Appellate Body (hereafter *AB*) and panel rulings are of paramount importance in understanding WTO law.[1]

The views expressed in this article are those of the author and should not in any way be attributed to the German government.

[1] Krallmann, WTO Dispute Settlement – The Establishment of *'Binding Guidance'* by the Appellate Body in *US Stainless Steel* and Recent Dispute Settlement Rulings, in: Herrmann/ Terhechte (eds.), *European Yearbook of International Economic Law (2011)*, pp. 417 et seq. (420–429).

A. Krallmann (✉)
Permanent Mission of Germany to the Office of the United Nations and Other International Organisations in Geneva, 28 C, Chemin du Petit-Saconnex, 1209 Geneva, Switzerland
e-mail: andreas.krallmann@web.de

C. Herrmann and J.P. Terhechte (eds.), *European Yearbook of International Economic Law (EYIEL), Vol. 3 (2012)*, European Yearbook of International Economic Law 3, DOI 10.1007/978-3-642-23309-8_18, © Springer-Verlag Berlin Heidelberg 2012

For the very first time in history of WTO dispute settlement the panel in *USA – Tyres (China)* had to rule on a safeguard measure which was not based on the multilateral WTO Safeguards Agreement but on the transitional product-specific safeguard mechanism under Paragraph 16 of the Chinese Protocol of Accession.

In another case involving CHN, *USA – Anti-Dumping and Countervailing Duties (CHN)*, the panel had to decide how benchmarks could be determined for the comparison of loans provided in renminbi by Chinese state-owned commercial banks. In allowing the USA to compare these Chinese loans with other external loans in a different currency, the panel arguably has set an important standard for the determination of benchmarks in the future. The case also had to decide whether the USA was allowed to apply anti-dumping and countervailing duties cumulatively on the same products. In addition, it defined when an entity providing financial benefits has to be classified as a 'public body' within the meaning of Article 1 of the SCM Agreement.

In the *EC – IT Products* case the panel was faced with the task of clarifying the scope of the plurilateral IT Agreement and the question whether it should take a dynamic approach when interpreting the terms of the agreement or whether it could ignore the drastic change of IT products' characteristics since the parties entered into the IT Agreement in 1996.

Both the outcome of the *Airbus* ruling and its appeal could influence the definition of 'general infrastructure' which is exempted from the disciplines of the SCM Agreement. The panel also elaborated on the requirement of Article 3 of the SCM Agreement that a prohibited export subsidy needs to be conditional or dependent upon actual or anticipated export performance.

The *Thailand – Cigarettes (Philippines)* decision was the second decision in the 15 year history of WTO dispute settlement to ever have interpreted the Customs Valuation Agreement. Furthermore, *Australia – Apples* and *US – Poultry (China)* involved sanitary and phytosanitary measures and the question of how members have to justify such restricting measures.

Also significant was the sheer volume of the single cases published: in the biggest single case ever in WTO history, the *Airbus* panel report with an unprecedented volume of more than 1,000 pages exceeded by far the length of any prior panel proceeding, both in volume and time. Furthermore, the panel decisions *EC – IT Products* and *Australia – Apples* encompassed more than 500 pages each. Summing it up in an unconventional way: The pile of the 10 decisions of 2010 weighs 10 kg.

The Appellate Body issued only one report in 2010 upon Australia's appeal in a phytosanitary case. The AB would have at least issued one more ruling in 2010 if the Airbus appeal had been concluded within the foreseen 90 day period. Due to the complexity and volume of the *Airbus* case, a decision could, however, not be made within that 90 day time-limit. Not only was it impossible to issue the report in the Airbus case, the complex appeal also caused a serious backlog for other cases. Due to the AB's current workload the AB could not take on further appeals in other cases.[2] In practice, parties to a dispute asked the membership to agree to postpone the deadline for appeal to some point in the future when the AB will have the capacity to work on these cases. Thus, a couple of cases are lined up for their 'slots' at the AB.

With regard to the EU, note should be taken that the '*European Communities*' were replaced by the '*European Union*'. The Council of the European Union and the European Commission informed the WTO and its members that due to the Lisbon Treaty coming into force of, 'the European Union will exercise all rights and assume all obligations of the European Community, including its status in the Organisation'.[3] Regarding the rights and obligations of the single EU member states versus the EU, and the question whether individual EU member states can be proper respondents in a WTO case, the *Airbus* panel recalled that the single member states of the EU are also members of the WTO in their own right. The panel clarified that the fact that the member states may choose to defend their interests before a panel separately from the EU delegation is a matter within their discretion. In practice, representatives of EU member states appear before the panels and the AB but it is the EU delegation that submits oral and written submissions on behalf of the EU and its member states. The panel concluded that no matter what responsibility the EU delegation bears 'does not diminish [the EU member states'] rights and obligations as WTO members, but is rather an internal matter concerning the relations between the European Communities and its member states'.[4]

This chapter will provide an overview of the main factual aspects of the 10 cases published in 2010 and selected systemic implications of the findings will be sketched out.[5]

Panel Australia – Measures Affecting the Importation of Apples from New Zealand (DS 367)

Facts of the Case

The case dealt with an Australian phytosanitary import ban on apples from New Zealand due to the alleged danger of spreading three distinct pests. The Australian ban had been in place for nearly 90 years. Pests are defined by the International Plant

---

[2] WT/DS371/7, WT/DS397/6 and WT/DS399/5.

[3] WT/L/779; this chapter will therefore refer to the EU unless the reference to EC is part of the official name of a case.

[4] Report of the Panel, European Communities and Certain Member States – Measures Affecting Trade in Large Civil Aircraft, WT/DS316/R, paras. 7.173–7.176.

[5] The extensive use of references by way of footnotes referring to the relevant passages of the single reports should enable and encourage the reader to deepen his or her understanding of the decisions by quickly and precisely allowing the reader to find his or her areas of particular interest. Throughout the chapter, language is taken from the respective decisions. Quotes with inverted commas, however, are reserved for special terms and longer quotes.

Protection Convention as 'any species, strain, or biotype of plant, animal or pathogenic agent injurious to plants or plant products.'[6] The three pests at issue were fire blight, European canker and apple leafcurling midge. Fire blight is a plant disease caused by a bacterium which infects flowers, young leaves, stems and fruits. European canker is a plant disease caused by a certain fungus. The primary symptom is the production of cankers on limbs and trunks. Apple leafcurling midge is a small fly which lays eggs on apple leaves. These eggs hatch to produce larvae and at a later stage these larvae find a pupation site on the ground. The spread of this disease happens through a mixture of adult flight and transportation of infected apple trees.[7]

The Australian authority carried out a pest risk analysis on the importation of apples from New Zealand, assessing the likelihood of a transfer of the pests from an infected apple to a susceptible Australian host plant. Australia used a semi-quantitative approach that combined a quantitative estimation of the probability of entry and spread of the pest with a qualitative assessment of the consequences.[8] Australia tried to provide a high level of protection 'aimed at reducing risk to a very low level, but not zero'.[9] The panel examined whether Australia's import ban could be justified according to the Agreement on the Application of Sanitary and Phytosanitary Measures, the SPS Agreement. The panel was assisted by independent scientists which is not exceptional in complicated SPS-related matters in which scientific evidence needs to be assessed frequently.

Important Aspects of the Findings

At the outset, Australia criticised the choice of the external assisting experts who advised the panel during the proceedings. In Australia's view, there should *inter alia* have been two independent experts for each of the pests involved. The panel dealt with the concern as a matter of 'due process' which can be understood as the right to a fair hearing.[10] According to the working procedures for panel proceedings it is up to the panel to decide how many experts it chooses to advise the panel. The

---

[6] Report of the Panel, Australia – Measures Affecting the Importation of Apples from New Zealand, WT/DS 367/R, para. 2.116.

[7] Report of the Panel, Australia – Measures Affecting the Importation of Apples from New Zealand, WT/DS367/R, paras. 2.1, 2.9, 2.21–2.24 and 2.30.

[8] Report of the Panel, Australia – Measures Affecting the Importation of Apples from New Zealand, WT/DS367/R, paras. 2.26, 2.45 and 2.63.

[9] Report of the Panel, Australia – Measures Affecting the Importation of Apples from New Zealand, WT/DS367/R, para. 2.59.

[10] Report of the Panel, Australia – Measures Affecting the Importation of Apples from New Zealand, WT/DS367/R, para. 7.5.

panel found no error in consulting only one expert on each of the pests and admitted that it had difficulties in finding suitable experts on apple leafcurling midge at all.[11]

The panel answered the threshold question to an SPS case, i.e. whether the measures in question constitute SPS measures within the meaning of Annex A(1), to the positive.[12]

New Zealand successfully argued that the Australian risk assessment was no proper risk assessment within the meaning of Article 5.1 of the SPS Agreement. Article 5.1 stipulates that a sanitary or phytosanitary measure needs to be based on an appropriate risk assessment, taking into account risk assessment techniques developed by the relevant international organisations.

The panel assessed the single steps and assumptions that underlay the Australian risk assessment. Most of the assumptions needed for the calculation of the probability of importation of the pests which formed the basis of the risk assessment could not be supported by adequate scientific evidence. For example, the Australian scientific evidence did not properly take into account New Zealand's climatic conditions when determining the frequency of apple infections with European canker and the spread of apple leafcurling midge in Australia.[13] When looking at the scientific basis of the Australian risk assessment concerning apple leafcurling midge, the panel identified the scientific basis, verified whether it came from a respected and qualified source and assessed whether Australia's reasoning was objective. Referring to the AB in *Canada/US – Continued Suspension* it reviewed 'whether the particular conclusions drawn by [the restricting member] find sufficient support in the scientific evidence relied upon'.[14]

The panel found that Australia's assessment of the likelihood of entry, establishment and spread of the three pests in question was not objective.[15] The panel also agreed with New Zealand that Australia generally overestimated the likelihood of negligible events, thereby 'turning what are often the remotest of possibilities into events that are assessed as occurring with some frequency'.[16]

---

[11] Report of the Panel, Australia – Measures Affecting the Importation of Apples from New Zealand, WT/DS367/R, para. 7.13, 7.21. and 7.36.

[12] Report of the Panel, Australia – Measures Affecting the Importation of Apples from New Zealand, WT/DS367/R, paras. 7.172 and 7.187.

[13] Report of the Panel, Australia – Measures Affecting the Importation of Apples from New Zealand, WT/DS367/R, para. 7.544 for European canker and para. 7.854 for apple leafcurling midge.

[14] Report of the Panel, Australia – Measures Affecting the Importation of Apples from New Zealand, WT/DS367/R, para. 7.790.

[15] Report of the Panel, Australia – Measures Affecting the Importation of Apples from New Zealand, WT/DS367/R, paras. 7.446–7.448 and 7.471–7.472 for fire blight, 7.747–7.749 for European canker, paras. 7.868–7.871, 7.885 for apple leafcurling midge.

[16] Report of the Panel, Australia – Measures Affecting the Importation of Apples from New Zealand, WT/DS367/R, paras. 7.508 and 7.780–7.781; the panel did, however, not side with some of New Zealand's claims against Australia's risk assessment like the alleged overestimation of the projected volume of trade, cf. para. 7.507.

Therefore, the panel held that there was no proper risk assessment within the meaning of Article 5.1 and paragraph 4 of Annex A of the SPS Agreement. Consequently, the panel decided that Australia's requirements concerning the pests were inconsistent with Articles 5.1, 5.2 and 2.2 of the SPS Agreement since they failed to adequately take into account the available scientific evidence.[17]

New Zealand, however, failed to establish a violation of Article 5.5 of the SPS Agreement. New Zealand tried to argue that two pests of Japanese pears posed a similar risk to Australia but that the Japanese pears were treated more favourably. The panel followed the guidelines of previous jurisprudence on Article 5.5 of the SPS-Agreement which involves the application of a three step test. The first requirement is that the situations identified by the claimant are different but comparable. The panel found that the pests which affect certain Japanese pears were comparable to the pests in this case.[18] New Zealand could, however, not establish the second element necessary, i.e. the existence of arbitrary or unjustifiable distinctions in the risk assessment of the comparable pests. The panel did not have sufficient evidence to compare the risks and, in one case, decided that the risk of the comparable pest was lower.[19]

Some of the Australian measures were also found to be more trade-restrictive than required and thus in breach of Article 5.6 of the SPS Agreement. Article 5.6 of the SPS Agreement requires a three-pronged test, (1) whether an alternative measure is technically and economically feasible, (2) whether this alternative measure achieves the member's appropriate level of protection and (3) whether it is significantly less restrictive.[20] Concerning the import ban of apples to avoid the spread of fire blight and European canker, New Zealand successfully established that a mere restriction of imports of apple fruit that are mature and symptomless would suffice and would be less trade-distortive. Similarly, with regard to the avoidance of the spread of apple leafcurling midge, the panel agreed with New Zealand that a requirement to inspect a 600-fruit sample of each imported lot would meet the aforementioned three requirements.[21]

---

[17] Report of the Panel, Australia – Measures Affecting the Importation of Apples from New Zealand, WT/DS367/R, para. 7.510 for fire blight, paras. 7.778–7.779 for European canker, paras 7.886–7.887 for apple leafcurling midge. The panel further found in para. 7.905 that general measures which were based on the risk assessment, like orchard inspections, were also in breach of Art. 5 of the SPS Agreement.

[18] Report of the Panel, Australia – Measures Affecting the Importation of Apples from New Zealand, WT/DS367/R, para. 7.954 and 7.960.

[19] Report of the Panel, Australia – Measures Affecting the Importation of Apples from New Zealand, WT/DS367/R, paras. 7.1043 and 7.1088. Consequentially, there was no violation of Article 2.3 of the SPS Agreement either, para. 7.1095.

[20] Report of the Panel, Australia – Measures Affecting the Importation of Apples from New Zealand, WT/DS367/R, para. 7.1098.

[21] Report of the Panel, Australia – Measures Affecting the Importation of Apples from New Zealand, WT/DS367/R, para. 7.1266 for fire blight and European canker, para. 7.1364 for apple leafcurling midge. New Zealand failed, however, to establish alternatives for certain general measures, para. 7.1403.

AB Australia – Measures Affecting the Importation of Apples from New Zealand (DS 367)

Upon Australia's appeal, the AB largely confirmed the panel's findings.[22]

The AB agreed with the panel that the Australian measures in question were *SPS measures*. It recalled that the concept of a 'measure' within WTO dispute settlement is wide and could include 'any act or omission attributable to a WTO member'. To be categorised as an *SPS measure* according to Annex (A)1 of the SPS Agreement, a measure must have 'a clear and objective relationship...' to 'the specific purposes enumerated in Annex (1)(a) of the SPS-Agreement'.[23] The AB did not agree with Australia that during such an assessment a distinction should be drawn between 'ancillary' and 'principal' measures. Since the panel had assessed whether the Australian measures individually met the requirements of Annex A(1), the AB consequently found that the panel correctly categorised the measures in question as SPS measures.[24]

The AB also sided with New Zealand that Australia neither applied a proper risk assessment as required by Article 5.1 of the SPS Agreement nor sufficiently took into account the available evidence according to Article 5.2 of the SPS Agreement.[25] The AB recalled its definition of risk assessment which it defined as 'a process characterized by systematic disciplined and objective enquiry and analysis, that is, a mode of studying and sorting out facts'. Whether a risk assessment is a proper one has to 'be determined by assessing the relationship between the conclusions of the risk assessor and the relevant available scientific evidence'.[26] The AB further recalled that a panel should verify if the scientific basis of the risk assessment comes from a respected and qualified source and is considered reputable science, while the correctness of the scientific views expressed need not necessarily be accepted by the wider scientific community. The reasoning of the risk assessor needs to be objective and must be supported by the underlying scientific basis.[27]

---

[22] New Zealand's other appeal on a jurisdictional question was partly successful: The AB found that the panel erred in not assessing the New Zealand's claim under Article 8 of the SPS Agreement and Annex C(1)a but held that Australia did not violate the aforementioned stipulations, cf. Report of the Appellate Body, Australia – Measures Affecting the Importation of Apples from New Zealand, WT/DS367/AB/R, paras. 426 and 441.

[23] Report of the Appellate Body, Australia – Measures Affecting the Importation of Apples from New Zealand, WT/DS367/AB/R, paras. 171 and 173.

[24] Report of the Appellate Body, Australia – Measures Affecting the Importation of Apples from New Zealand, WT/DS367/AB/R, paras. 181 and 183.

[25] Report of the Appellate Body, Australia – Measures Affecting the Importation of Apples from New Zealand, WT/DS367/AB/R, para. 261.

[26] Report of the Appellate Body, Australia – Measures Affecting the Importation of Apples from New Zealand, WT/DS367/AB/R, paras. 207–208.

[27] Report of the Appellate Body, Australia – Measures Affecting the Importation of Apples from New Zealand, WT/DS367/AB/R, paras. 214 and 220.

The AB found that the panel did not err in reviewing the intermediate conclusions of the Australian risk assessment and that it correctly assessed whether the reasoning of the Australian risk assessment revealed an objective link between the scientific evidence and the conclusions reached.[28] The AB affirmed the panel's finding that the errors of the Australian risk assessment were too numerous and serious and thus inconsistent with Article 5.1 of the SPS Agreement.[29]

The AB found, however, in Australia's favour that the panel interpreted and applied Article 5.6 of the SPS Agreement in the wrong way. When the panel decided whether or not Australia could have applied the above mentioned alternative measures regarding fire blight and apple leafcurling midge which New Zealand had proposed, the panel failed to assess correctly whether these alternatives would achieve the appropriate level of protection. The AB therefore reversed the finding that these Australian measures were in breach of Article 5.6 of the SPS Agreement.[30]

Panel United States – Definitive Anti-Dumping and Countervailing Duties on Certain Products from China (DS 379)

Facts of the Case

The USA had imposed both definitive anti-dumping and countervailing duties on four different categories of goods from CHN. The goods in questions were certain steel pipes and tubes, laminated woven sacks and off-the-road tyres. Common underlying feature in all these investigations was that some Chinese state-owned enterprises provided the basic materials for the production or that an enterprise which purchased the basic material from a state-owned enterprise provided for them. In addition, state-owned commercial banks provided preferential loans for the producers of three of the four products in question. Furthermore, the producers of tyres were given land-use rights by the Chinese government. The USA imposed countervailing duties of up to more than 600% and anti-dumping duties of up to 264%. In determining the amount of the subsidies the USA decided that private

---

[28] Report of the Appellate Body, Australia – Measures Affecting the Importation of Apples from New Zealand, WT/DS367/AB/R, paras. 230 and 248.

[29] Report of the Appellate Body, Australia – Measures Affecting the Importation of Apples from New Zealand, WT/DS367/AB/R, paras. 258–259.

[30] Report of the Appellate Body, Australia – Measures Affecting the Importation of Apples from New Zealand, WT/DS367/AB/R, para. 359; the Appellate Body tried to complete the legal analysis with the correct legal standard on the basis of uncontested facts before it but could not do so, cf. paras. 385 and 402.

prices in China and the interest rates charged by Chinese banks could not serve as appropriate benchmarks.

China claimed that the imposed measures were in violation of the Anti-Dumping Agreement and the SCM Agreement. China criticised the imposition of 'double remedies', i.e. applying anti-dumping and countervailing duties cumulatively. According to China, the USA should in general be prevented from applying cumulatively both forms of sanctions on the same products at the same time.[31]

The case therefore touches upon the systemically important question whether a member needs to restrict itself to either anti-dumping sanctions or countervailing duties when faced with products that are both dumped and subsidised. Furthermore, it had to define the meaning of the term 'public body' in Article 1 of the SCM Agreement since the panel had to decide whether the Chinese state-owned banks and enterprises had to be qualified as governmental bodies within the meaning of the SCM Agreement. It also raised the significant question how the relevant benchmarks for the comparison of interest rates for commercial loans should be established in a case involving China and its state-owned commercial banks.

Important Aspects of the Findings

To qualify a measure as a subsidy within the meaning of the SCM Agreement, there must be a financial contribution from a member which transfers a benefit to the recipient producer. Furthermore, the subsidy needs to be specific.[32] China's argument that its state-owned enterprises and commercial banks were no *'public bodies'* according to Article 1.1 lit. a (1) of the SCM Agreement was not successful. The panel chose a broad reading of the term 'public body' and held that it covers 'any entity which [is] controlled by a government'.[33] The term is 'not limited to government agencies and other entities vested with and exercising governmental authority'.[34] Otherwise members could easily hide behind the private nature of such entities, even if these entities are run deliberately to provide trade-distorting

---

[31] Report of the Panel, United States – Definitive Anti-Dumping and Countervailing Duties on Certain Products from China, WT/DS379/R, paras. 2.1–2.18.

[32] Report of the Panel, United States – Definitive Anti-Dumping and Countervailing Duties on Certain Products from China, WT/DS379/R, para. 9.30.

[33] Report of the Panel, United States – Definitive Anti-Dumping and Countervailing Duties on Certain Products from China, WT/DS379/R, paras. 8.94, 8.79 and 8.67.

[34] Report of the Panel, United States – Definitive Anti-Dumping and Countervailing Duties on Certain Products from China, WT/DS379/R, para. 8.73.

subsidies.[35] In other words, the decisive criterion is the question of *control* of the respective government. The panel held that the USA could indeed conclude that the state-owned enterprises and commercial banks in question were public bodies since that finding was based on sufficient evidence that these entities were controlled by the Chinese government. [36]

The USA further did not err in claiming that the preferential loans of Chinese state-owned commercial banks to Chinese tyre producers were *de iure* specific. In order to be specific, Article 2.1 of the SCM Agreement requires the subsidies to be limited to 'certain enterprises' but does not define how narrow the term needs to be interpreted.[37] The panel decided that Article 2.1 lit. a of the SCM Agreement does not require the grantor to identify explicitly both 'certain enterprises that are and [...] certain enterprises that are not eligible for the subsidy'.[38] After analysing China's Five-Year Plans and the subsidiary central government-level instruments and practice of the banks, the subsidies to the tyres industry appeared to be *de iure* specific in the eyes of the panel.[39]

When assessing whether the Chinese loans which were provided by state-owned commercial banks were subsidies, the USA regarded the lending rates in China as distorted and not suitable to serve as market benchmarks. It therefore chose external benchmarks to compare the lending rates. China was of the opinion that the US rejection of Chinese interest rates as benchmarks and the use of external benchmarks constituted a violation of Article 14 lit. b of the SCM Agreement.[40] Accordingly, the panel answered the general question whether the rejection of in-country interest rates as benchmark was permissible by interpreting the general guidelines Article 14 of the SCM Agreement provides to an investigating author-ity.[41] While the four sub-paragraphs of Article 14 of the SCM Agreement give some flexibility to the precise methodology of the comparison, the chapeau of Article 14 of the SCM Agreement establishes the general principle that a comparison has to take place with the commercial market terms. Thus, an investigating authority needs a 'commercial' loan which is 'comparable' to the loan in question. To qualify as a comparable loan, the panel demanded a benchmark loan that was established

---

[35] Report of the Panel, United States – Definitive Anti-Dumping and Countervailing Duties on Certain Products from China, WT/DS379/R, para. 8.82.

[36] Report of the Panel, United States – Definitive Anti-Dumping and Countervailing Duties on Certain Products from China, WT/DS379/R, paras. 8.138 and 8.143.

[37] Report of the Panel, United States – Definitive Anti-Dumping and Countervailing Duties on Certain Products from China, WT/DS379/R, para. 9.33.

[38] Report of the Panel, United States – Definitive Anti-Dumping and Countervailing Duties on Certain Products from China, WT/DS379/R, para. 9.42.

[39] Report of the Panel, United States – Definitive Anti-Dumping and Countervailing Duties on Certain Products from China, WT/DS379/R, paras. 9.95 and 9.105–9.107.

[40] Report of the Panel, United States – Definitive Anti-Dumping and Countervailing Duties on Certain Products from China, WT/DS379/R, paras. 10.84–10.85.

[41] Report of the Panel, United States – Definitive Anti-Dumping and Countervailing Duties on Certain Products from China, WT/DS379/R, paras. 10.105 and 10.107.

around the same time with the same structure, similar maturity, similar size and should be denoted in the same currency.[42] However, currency differences between the loan in question and the benchmark loan would not pose an insurmountable hurdle like China argued.[43] Yet, the benchmark loan needs to be one that the borrower 'could actually obtain on the market'.[44] The panel elaborated that in the process of finding a suitable benchmark some 'degree of approximation will be inevitable' and that Article 14 lit. b of the SCM Agreement allows the use of proxies.[45] China's interpretation of Article 14 of the SCM Agreement to allow only comparisons with renminbi-denominated loans was found to be overly formalistic since it would unduly limit the investigating authority's obligation to find a suitable benchmark. China's argument would mean that if all loans in a given country were made by its government, the investigating authority would have no choice but to compare one government loan with another government loan of that same government. Such a comparison would be circular.[46] Consequently, the US investigating authority's finding that other Chinese rates were distorted and not suitable as benchmarks was found to be no violation of Article 14 of the SCM Agreement.[47]

The panel sided with China that the USA violated Articles 1.1 and 14 of the SCM Agreement on not having determined the precise role of Chinese trading companies which purchased inputs from state-owned companies and sold them on to the producers of the goods in question.[48] In this regard, however, the panel could have violated its duty laid down in Articles 6 and 11 of the Understanding on Rules and Procedures Governing the Settlement of Disputes (hereafter 'DSU') to objectively assess the case before it. The panel stated that it had some doubts on whether this particular claim was properly before it. However, it disregarded its doubts because the USA had presented full rebuttals to China's arguments concerning this claim and assessed the claim.[49] It remains to be seen how the Appellate Body views this question of jurisdiction.

---

[42] Report of the Panel, United States – Definitive Anti-Dumping and Countervailing Duties on Certain Products from China, WT/DS379/R, para. 10.112.

[43] Report of the Panel, United States – Definitive Anti-Dumping and Countervailing Duties on Certain Products from China, WT/DS379/R, para. 10.120.

[44] Report of the Panel, United States – Definitive Anti-Dumping and Countervailing Duties on Certain Products from China, WT/DS379/R, paras. 10.107–10.113.

[45] Report of the Panel, United States – Definitive Anti-Dumping and Countervailing Duties on Certain Products from China, WT/DS379/R, para. 10.117.

[46] Report of the Panel, United States – Definitive Anti-Dumping and Countervailing Duties on Certain Products from China, WT/DS379/R, paras. 10.120–10.121.

[47] Report of the Panel, United States – Definitive Anti-Dumping and Countervailing Duties on Certain Products from China, WT/DS379/R, paras. 10.147–10.148.

[48] Report of the Panel, United States – Definitive Anti-Dumping and Countervailing Duties on Certain Products from China, WT/DS379/R, paras. 12.52, 12.57 and 12.58.

[49] Report of the Panel, United States – Definitive Anti-Dumping and Countervailing Duties on Certain Products from China, WT/DS379/R, para. 12.31.

The panel held that China's *as such claim* concerning the double remedy of applying anti-dumping and countervailing duties simultaneously was outside its terms of reference for procedural reasons.[50] The panel, therefore, did not decide whether the general rule of applying a double remedy was inconsistent with the WTO Agreements but assessed whether the specific application of the double remedy in this case was inconsistent. Although the panel decided only on the specific instances of the applied double remedies in this specific case, the reasoning of the panel nevertheless shows that the panel might not have seen a general problem in applying anti-dumping and countervailing duties simultaneously.

At the outset, the panel and the USA agreed with China that there may be a risk of a double remedy 'if countervailing duties are simultaneously applied to imports of the same good' since 'the subsidy is likely to be 'offset' more than once, i.e. once through the anti-dumping duty, and again at least partially through the countervailing duty'.[51] China argued that the parallel levy of the US anti-dumping duty offset the subsidies the Chinese companies had received with the effect that there remained no subsidy which could be offset through the imposition of additional countervailing duties.[52] The panel, however, could not see that this would violate Article 19.4 of the SCM Agreement which limits the amount of countervailing duties to 'the amount of the subsidy found to exist'. The panel interpreted this stipulation to be 'oblivious to any potential concurrent imposition of anti-dumping duties'. Even if the '*effect*' of the anti-dumping duty may have been to offset the subsidy, it would not have any effect on the *existence* of the subsidy which 'depends on the existence of a financial contribution and of a benefit'. Thus, 'the narrowly-crafted discipline in Article 19.4 of the SCM Agreement does not address situations of 'double remedies".[53] Nor could such a general prohibition of double remedies be derived from Article VI:5 of the GATT 1994 which precisely addresses the question of double remedies. However, Article VI:5 of the GATT 1994 limits the prohibition of double remedies only to cases of 'export subsidization'. Thus, Article VI.5 of the GATT 1994 does not apply to other subsidies except export subsidies.[54] The US double remedy was therefore not found to be in violation of the WTO Agreements.

---

[50] Report of the Panel, United States – Definitive Anti-Dumping and Countervailing Duties on Certain Products from China, WT/DS379/R, paras. 14.36, 14.39 and 14.43.

[51] Report of the Panel, United States – Definitive Anti-Dumping and Countervailing Duties on Certain Products from China, WT/DS379/R, paras. 14.70–14.71.

[52] Report of the Panel, United States – Definitive Anti-Dumping and Countervailing Duties on Certain Products from China, WT/DS379/R, para. 14.110.

[53] Report of the Panel, United States – Definitive Anti-Dumping and Countervailing Duties on Certain Products from China, WT/DS379/R, para. 14.112.

[54] Report of the Panel, United States – Definitive Anti-Dumping and Countervailing Duties on Certain Products from China, WT/DS379/R, paras. 14.116–14.118.

Panel *Thailand – Customs and Fiscal Measures on Cigarettes from the Philippines* (DS 371)

Facts of the Case

The dispute arose about Philip Morris Thailand's importation of cigarettes manufactured in the Philippines by another Philip Morris subsidiary, the Philip Morris Philippines.[55] The Philippines claimed that Thai Customs improperly rejected the transaction values of its cigarette imports and incorrectly applied the so called deductive valuation method. Furthermore, Thai Customs were accused of having disclosed confidential information to the public. The Philippines also argued that imported cigarettes were taxed in excess of domestic cigarettes.[56]

The only Thai domestic manufacturer of cigarettes is an organisation of the Thai government.[57]

The case was only the second case in WTO dispute settlement history to interpret the Customs Valuation Agreement.[58]

Important Aspects of the Findings

According to Article 1 of the Customs Valuation Agreement the starting point for the determination of the customs value is the transaction value of a good. Like the panel in *Colombia – Ports of Entry*, the panel recalled that if a customs authority rejects the transaction value, another valuation method of the Customs Valuation Agreement needs to be used by observing the sequential order of the methods set out in Articles 2, 3, 5–7 of the Customs Valuation Agreement.[59] Article 1.2 lit. a of the Customs Valuation Agreement stipulates that the fact alone, that buyer and seller are related as in the current case, is not sufficient for not accepting the declared transaction value. Instead, in cases of doubt the customs authorities are

---

[55] Report of the Panel, Thailand – Customs and Fiscal Measures on Cigarettes from the Philippines, WT/DS371/R, paras. 7.77–7.78.

[56] Report of the Panel, Thailand – Customs and Fiscal Measures on Cigarettes from the Philippines, WT/DS371/R, paras. 7.1–7.4.

[57] Report of the Panel, Thailand – Customs and Fiscal Measures on Cigarettes from the Philippines, WT/DS371/R, para. 7.585.

[58] The first case that dealt with the Customs Valuation Agreement was the Panel Columbia – Ports of entry. For a short overview, cf., Krallmann, WTO Dispute Settlement – The Establishment of '*Binding Guidance*' by the Appellate Body in *US Stainless Steel* and Recent Dispute Settlement Rulings, in: Herrmann/Terhechte (eds.), *European Yearbook of International Economic Law (2011)*, pp. 417 et seq. (436–438).

[59] Report of the Panel, Thailand – Customs and Fiscal Measures on Cigarettes from the Philippines, WT/DS371/R, para. 7.154

required to examine the case based on the given information. The Customs Valuation Agreement tries to strike a balance between customs' need to address cases of doubt and protecting the legitimate interests of the traders. The panel derived from this provision that the customs authorities have to ensure that importers are given an opportunity to provide information that the relationship between buyer and seller did not influence the price. Importers are then responsible for providing the necessary information to the customs authority. Having received such information, the customs authorities must examine the case, which involves a critical review of the information before them.[60]

The panel held that Thailand failed to examine the circumstances of the sales in question.[61] Furthermore, Thai customs failed to communicate its grounds for thinking that the relationship between Philip Morris Thailand and Philip Morris Philippines influenced the declared transaction costs which meant a violation of Articles 1.2 lit. a and 16 of the Customs Valuation Agreement.[62] In addition, Thailand violated Article 7 of the Customs Valuation Agreement by not consulting the importer when deciding that sales allowances, provincial taxes and transportation costs would not be deducted; the absence of that information meant that the deductive valuation method was inconsistent with Article 7.1 of the Customs Valuation Agreement.[63]

Not surprisingly, the panel also held that the disclosure of c.i.f. prices, certain transaction values and certain import volumes by Thailand was a breach of the protection of confidential information laid out in Article 10 of the Customs Valuation Agreement.[64] The panel defined confidential information as one that 'is not in the public domain and if its disclosure would be likely *inter alia* to be of significant competitive advantage to a competitor..., to have a significant adverse effect upon the party who submitted the information [...]'.[65]

Concerning the alleged violations of the GATT 1994, the panel held that Thailand acted inconsistently with Article III:2, first sentence of the GATT 1994 in two ways. Firstly, Thailand imposed a higher VAT on the cigarettes from the

---

[60] Report of the Panel, Thailand – Customs and Fiscal Measures on Cigarettes from the Philippines, WT/DS371/R, paras. 7.171–7.172.

[61] Report of the Panel, Thailand – Customs and Fiscal Measures on Cigarettes from the Philippines, WT/DS371/R, para. 7.195.

[62] Report of the Panel, Thailand – Customs and Fiscal Measures on Cigarettes from the Philippines, WT/DS371/R, paras. 7.223 and 7.266.

[63] Report of the Panel, Thailand – Customs and Fiscal Measures on Cigarettes from the Philippines, WT/DS371/R, paras. 7.332 and 7.365. Cf., for the violation of Article 7.3 of the Customs Valuation Agreement, para. 7.397.

[64] Report of the Panel, Thailand – Customs and Fiscal Measures on Cigarettes from the Philippines, WT/DS371/R, paras. 7.411 and 7.405.

[65] Report of the Panel, Thailand – Customs and Fiscal Measures on Cigarettes from the Philippines, WT/DS371/R, para. 7.408.

Philippines and, secondly, it only excluded domestic cigarettes' resale from the VAT obligations automatically.

In its assessment of Article III:2 of the GATT 1994 the panel followed the well-established likeness test of the AB to find out whether Thai cigarettes could be considered as 'like' cigarettes.[66] In a second step it assessed whether the imported cigarettes were subject to a higher VAT duty than domestic ones. The panel defined VAT as a 'tax assessed at each step in the production of a commodity, based on the value added at each step by the difference between the commodity's production cost and its selling price. A value added tax [therefore] effectively acts as a sales tax on the ultimate consumer'.[67] The panel furthermore recalled that even the smallest amount of excess of the levy would be sufficient for the tax to fulfil the criterion 'in excess'.[68] The panel found that the Thai authorities systematically established the wrong marketing costs (selling expenses and profits) for cigarettes from the Philippines which resulted in an artificial increase of the retail price. This retail price formed the basis of the final VAT liability and consequently led to taxation in excess of domestically produced cigarettes.[69] Another breach of Article III.2, first sentence of the GATT 1994 was found because the Thai regime *de iure* exempted the resale of domestic cigarettes of VAT whereas no automatic offset existed for the resale of imported cigarettes.[70]

Panel United States – Anti-Dumping Measures on Polyethylene Retail Carrier Bags from Thailand (DS383)

The case was yet another zeroing case brought against the USA. Zeroing is a methodology applied when calculating the margins of anti-dumping duties which artificially increases the margins.[71] This time the USA applied the zeroing

---

[66] Report of the Panel, Thailand – Customs and Fiscal Measures on Cigarettes from the Philippines, WT/DS371/R, para. 7.433.

[67] Report of the Panel, Thailand – Customs and Fiscal Measures on Cigarettes from the Philippines, WT/DS371/R, para. 7.454.

[68] Report of the Panel, Thailand – Customs and Fiscal Measures on Cigarettes from the Philippines, WT/DS371/R, para. 7.479.

[69] Report of the Panel, Thailand – Customs and Fiscal Measures on Cigarettes from the Philippines, WT/DS371/R, paras. 7.546 and 7.555. The panel's definition of marketing costs can be found in para. 7.499.

[70] Report of the Panel, Thailand – Customs and Fiscal Measures on Cigarettes from the Philippines, WT/DS371/R, para. 7.637: only if the reseller satisfied certain administrative requirements, the liability could be offset. If a reseller failed, however, to meet these burdens, he remained subject to VAT. This "potential liability" discriminated imported cigarettes.

[71] Cf., for a description of the zeroing methodology and the related problems, Krallmann, WTO Dispute Settlement – The Establishment of 'Binding Guidance' by the Appellate Body in US

methodology in determining final dumping margins for Thai exporters of plastic bags.[72] In light of numerous decisions of panels and the AB which condemn the zeroing methodology, it was no surprise that the panel ruled in favour of Thailand.

The peculiarity here was, however, that the whole case and even the details of the implementation seem to have been orchestrated by the parties from the very outset of the case. The parties' agreement on procedures in the dispute reveals that the USA had promised not to object to Thailand's request for the establishment of the panel and that it agreed on the length of the reasonable period of time for the implementation of the report even before the panel had been established.[73]

Thailand initiated the case and claimed that the use of the zeroing methodology was inconsistent with Article 2.4.2, first sentence of the Anti-Dumping Agreement. The USA did not object to the establishment of the panel when Thailand asked the Dispute Settlement Body for the first time[74] although they could have easily done so and would have avoided the establishment of a panel at that stage.[75] The USA also acknowledged that the Thai description of the use of zeroing in the case was accurate and did not contest the legal claim.[76]

Notwithstanding the USA not contesting the violation of the Anti-Dumping Agreement, the panel held that Article 11 of the DSU obliged it to make an 'objective assessment' of its own which meant that Thailand still had to make a *prima facie* case of the alleged violation.[77] The panel was, however, satisfied that Thailand had demonstrated that the USA had used the zeroing methodology and that the present case was 'identical in all material aspects to those addressed by the Appellate Body in *Softwood Lumber V*'. Thus, the USA was found to have violated Article 2.4.2 of the Anti-Dumping Agreement.[78]

Stainless Steel and Recent Dispute Settlement Rulings, in: Herrmann/Terhechte (eds.), *European Yearbook of International Economic Law (2011)*, p. 417, (438–443).

[72] Report of the Panel, United States – Anti-Dumping Measures on Polyethylene Retail Carrier Bags from Thailand, WT/DS383/R, para. 3.1.

[73] WT/DS383/4.

[74] Report of the Panel, United States – Anti-Dumping Measures on Polyethylene Retail Carrier Bags from Thailand, WT/DS383/R, para. 1.1.

[75] Cf. Article 6.1 of the DSU.

[76] Report of the Panel, United States – Anti-Dumping Measures on Polyethylene Retail Carrier Bags from Thailand, WT/DS383/R, paras. 3.3. and 7.1.

[77] Report of the Panel, United States – Anti-Dumping Measures on Polyethylene Retail Carrier Bags from Thailand, WT/DS383/R, paras. 7.5 and 7.7.

[78] Report of the Panel, United States – Anti-Dumping Measures on Polyethylene Retail Carrier Bags from Thailand, WT/DS383/R, paras. 7.10 and 7.24.

Panel United States – Measures Affecting Imports of Certain Passenger Vehicle and Light Truck Tyres from China (DS 399)

Facts of the Case

The USA in 2009 determined that its tyre industry suffered market disruptions caused by rapidly increasing imports of Chinese tyres. As a consequence, as of September 2009 the USA imposed additional duties on certain imported tyres from China for a period of 3 years. The safeguard measure meant an extra 35% ad valorem duty in the first, a 30% duty in the second and a 25% duty in the third year on Chinese tyres. This safeguard measure was not based on the multilateral WTO Safeguards Agreement but the transitional product-specific safeguard mechanism under Paragraph 16 of the Chinese Accession Protocol. Thus, the panel for the first time in WTO jurisprudence was called upon to interpret this product-specific safeguard mechanism.[79] Paragraph 16 of China's Protocol of Accession provides the possibility for the other members 'to withdraw concessions or otherwise to limit imports' if Chinese products enter another member's territory 'in such increased quantities or under such conditions as to cause or threaten to cause market disruption'.[80] China was of the view that the conditions of Article 16 of its Protocol of Accession were not met.

Important Aspects of the Findings

The panel rejected all Chinese claims and held that the US safeguard measure was consistent with Paragraph 16 of the Chinese Protocol of Accession. China argued that there had been no rapidly increasing imports any more, since in 2008 – which was the most recent data the USA relied upon – there was a *decline in the rate of increase*.[81] The panel did not agree. According to the panel, an investigating authority is not required 'to focus on the movements in imports during the most recent past', nor 'does a decline in the rate of increase necessarily preclude a finding that imports are increasing rapidly'.[82] The panel continued that the latest increase of

---

[79] Report of the Panel, United States – Measures Affecting Imports of Certain Passenger Vehicle and Light Truck Tyres from China, WT/DS399/R, paras. 2.1, 2.2 and 7.3.

[80] Cf. the Protocol's wording in Report of the Panel United States – Measures Affecting Imports of Certain Passenger Vehicle and Light Truck Tyres from China, WT/DS399/R, paras. 7.26 and 7.382.

[81] Report of the Panel, United States – Measures Affecting Imports of Certain Passenger Vehicle and Light Truck Tyres from China, WT/DS399/R, paras. 7.38 and 7.87.

[82] Report of the Panel, United States – Measures Affecting Imports of Certain Passenger Vehicle and Light Truck Tyres from China, WT/DS399/R, paras. 7.90 and 7.92.

Chinese imports of 10.8% was not – as China had claimed – just a 'modest increase'.[83] In fact, there was an increase of tyres imported from China in relation to the domestic production year after year.[84] The absolute volume of tyre imports from China rose every year during the period of investigation and so did the percentage of imported tyres from China: In 2005, the imports grew by 42.7% compared to the previous year, in 2006 the growth was 29.9%, in 2007 there was a plus of 53.7% and in 2008 the imports of Chinese tyres still increased by 10.8%.[85]

In an *as such claim*, China also attacked the domestic US law which implemented the special safeguard mechanism of the Chinese Protocol of Accession. However, the panel found the domestic law, the so called Section 421, to implement the Protocol's stipulations correctly. The panel decided that the US formulation *'contributes significantly'* to the material injury could be equalled with the Protocol's prerequisite of 'a significant cause'.[86]

Furthermore, China's argument that the decline in the domestic US market was not caused by the Chinese imports was rejected. The panel found that the data the USA had used in its determination allowed the conclusion that there was an overall coincidence between the upward movement in Chinese tyre imports and the downward movement in the US tyre industry.[87] During the period of investigation, the US industry's market share fell every year, the US production and the industry's capacity declined; the number of production-related workers in this section fell by 14%, the wages paid decreased by 12.5%.[88] In the same vein, China could not establish that the downward trend of US industry was caused by other factors which were non-attributable to the Chinese imports. For example, China attempted to make the US business strategy accountable because US industry voluntarily gave up the production of the low-end tyre market.[89] Furthermore, though the imports of Chinese tyres which were produced and imported by US companies accounted for 23.5% of all Chinese imports, they were not held responsible for the US market

---

[83] Report of the Panel, United States – Measures Affecting Imports of Certain Passenger Vehicle and Light Truck Tyres from China, WT/DS399/R, para. 7.93.

[84] Report of the Panel, United States – Measures Affecting Imports of Certain Passenger Vehicle and Light Truck Tyres from China, WT/DS399/R, para. 7.98.

[85] Report of the Panel, United States – Measures Affecting Imports of Certain Passenger Vehicle and Light Truck Tyres from China, WT/DS399/R, paras. 7.83

[86] Report of the Panel, United States – Measures Affecting Imports of Certain Passenger Vehicle and Light Truck Tyres from China, WT/DS399/R, paras. 7.139, 7.146 and 7.160.

[87] Report of the Panel, United States – Measures Affecting Imports of Certain Passenger Vehicle and Light Truck Tyres from China, WT/DS399/R, paras. 7.236, 7.238 and 7.260.

[88] Report of the Panel, United States – Measures Affecting Imports of Certain Passenger Vehicle and Light Truck Tyres from China, WT/DS399/R, para. 7.234.

[89] Report of the Panel, United States – Measures Affecting Imports of Certain Passenger Vehicle and Light Truck Tyres from China, WT/DS399/R, para. 7.312.

disruption.[90] The panel also declined to hold that the adverse effect on US industry was caused by the effects of the fall in demand during the 2008 recession.[91]

In completing its analysis of Paragraph 16 of the Chinese Protocol of Accession, the panel held that the US neither had to explain why it chose a 3 year application period for the safeguard measure, nor was there an obligation on the US to exactly quantify the injury to its tyre industry.[92]

Panel United States – Certain Measures Affecting Imports of Poultry from China (DS 392)

Facts of the Case

China's first case against the USA involved a factually rather complicated SPS measure taken by the USA. The measure prohibited certain imports of poultry that were processed in China: The US Congress enacted budget allocation legislation which prohibited the US administration from using funds allocated by the US Congress for the purpose of establishing or implementing a rule which permitted the importation of certain poultry products from China. The Act was motivated by serious concerns of the US Congress about contaminated foods from China.[93] Although the measure looked like a purely monetary measure concerning the activities of certain parts of the US administration, it effectively functioned as the US Congress' way to control certain SPS matters, meaning that poultry exports from China could not commence.[94]

---

[90] Report of the Panel, United States – Measures Affecting Imports of Certain Passenger Vehicle and Light Truck Tyres from China, WT/DS399/R, para. 7.315.

[91] Report of the Panel, United States – Measures Affecting Imports of Certain Passenger Vehicle and Light Truck Tyres from China, WT/DS399/R, para. 7.354.

[92] Report of the Panel, United States – Measures Affecting Imports of Certain Passenger Vehicle and Light Truck Tyres from China, WT/DS399/R, para. 7.414.

[93] Report of the Panel, United States – Certain Measures Affecting Imports of Poultry from China, WT/DS392/R, paras. 2.1–2.2.

[94] Report of the Panel, United States – Certain Measures Affecting Imports of Poultry from China, WT/DS392/R, paras. 7.119 and 7.123.

The US administration authorises poultry imports on a country-by-country basis. Interested countries have to make a request for a determination of *eligibility*. The administration will then assess an applicant country's poultry system whether it is equivalent to that of the USA. If the system is equivalent, the USA will then publish a rule allowing for the importation of poultry from that country. Subsequently, annual reviews are being conducted to see whether the safety standards continue to be equivalent, cf. paras. 2.6–2.7.

China initially requested an equivalence determination in 2004. The US administration found a number of deficiencies by the end of 2004 and conducted a second audit in 2005. In 2005 the final report on China was issued. The administration proposed to add China to the list of countries

Important Aspects of the Findings

China won its first case against the USA because the panel sided with China that the USA was in breach of its obligations under the SPS Agreement.

At the outset, the panel decided that it could rule on the measure though the measure had already expired in September 2009. The panel held that China would otherwise be deprived of any meaningful review of the measure. Like previous panels it decided that it should be possible to rule upon expired measures if the repealed measure could easily be re-imposed by the defendant. The panel also recalled the AB's argumentation in *Chile – Price Bands* according to which a complainant should not have to face a 'moving target scenario'.[95]

The panel clarified that the SPS Agreement is *lex specialis* to the GATT 1994 if a measure is found to be an SPS measure within the meaning of Annex A of the SPS Agreement.[96]

The panel reviewed the previous panels' approaches to the definition of an SPS measure.[97] It held that in order to assess whether the monetary stipulation of the law in question was an SPS measure, the panel had to 'encompass an holistic examination of the measure, including, both its form and nature'. It examined 'whether it serves one of the purposes set forth in Annex A(1)(a) through (d) and whether it is of the type listed in the second part of Annex A'.[98] Although the US law only appropriated funds for a certain part of the US administration it was, in the panel's view, enacted for the purposes of protecting human and animal life and health.[99]

---

eligible for the export of *poultry provided that the poultry products processed in certified establishments in China came from poultry slaughtered in the USA or other countries eligible to export poultry to the USA*, cf. paras. 2.17–2.18.

On 20 December 2007, the US administration requested the annual certification of eligibility. Only six days later, a law was enacted which restricted the use of funds to establish or implement any rule allowing poultry imports from China; the law, however, expired in September 2008. In March 2008, i.e. nearly two years after the USA's first request, China provided information on its certified establishments to the USA. In July 2008 China was included as eligible to export processed poultry products but at the same time eligibility was suspended for animal health reasons. In February 2009, China enacted a new food safety law. In March 2009 the US Congress enacted legislation which – like the US law enacted by the end of 2007 – restricted the use of funds to establish or implement any rule allowing for the importation of poultry products from China. The law expired at the end of September 2009, cf. paras. 2.23–2.29.

[95] Report of the Panel, United States – Certain Measures Affecting Imports of Poultry from China, WT/DS392/R, paras. 7.55–7.56.

[96] Report of the Panel, United States – Certain Measures Affecting Imports of Poultry from China, WT/DS392/R, para. 7.67. Cf., furthermore, the wording of Art. 2.4 of the SPS Agreement.

[97] Report of the Panel, United States – Certain Measures Affecting Imports of Poultry from China, WT/DS392/R, paras. 7.84 et seq.

[98] Report of the Panel, United States – Certain Measures Affecting Imports of Poultry from China, WT/DS392/R, paras. 7.101–7.102.

[99] Report of the Panel, United States – Certain Measures Affecting Imports of Poultry from China, WT/DS392/R, paras. 7.107 and 7.115.

The fact that the measure was an appropriations bill did not prevent it from being excluded from the scope of the SPS Agreement. In the panel's view the law did affect international trade since its effect was that poultry exports from China to the USA could not commence.[100]

After having taken the hurdle of qualifying the measure as an SPS measure, the panel also rejected the US argument that the law in question was part of the on-going equivalence proceeding and that, therefore, Article 4 of the SPS Agreement would be the only applicable provision of the SPS Agreement.[101] The panel held that the US ban was a 'substantive SPS measure in its own right' and thus subject to the obligations under Articles 5 and 2 of the SPS Agreement.[102]

The panel found that the USA was in breach of Articles 5.1 and 5.2 of the SPS Agreement because the USA had not presented any evidence of a risk assessment in respect of the US law. The panel recalled that the requirement of conducting a risk assessment cannot be 'satisfied merely by a general discussion of the disease sought to be avoided' but 'must address the specific risk at issue'.[103] Since the law was not based on a risk assessment it was deemed to be inconsistent with Article 5.1 and 5.2 of the SPS Agreement.[104]

The importation of poultry from China on the one hand and other countries on the other was found to be a different but comparable situation. The panel decided that the different level of protection that the US applied to both situations was arbitrary or unjustifiable and meant a discrimination of Chinese imports. Conse-quentially, the USA was also in breach of 5.5 of the SPS Agreement.[105] The US was also found to be in breach of Article 2.3 of the SPS Agreement because a violation of the more specific Article 5.5 of the SPS Agreement necessarily implies a violation of the basic violation of Article 2.3 of the SPS Agreement.[106]

The US conduct also meant a violation of the fundamental most-favoured nation principle which is protected by Article I:1 of the GATT 1994. The panel stated that even if the Chinese poultry production provided equivalent food safety standards

---

[100] Report of the Panel, United States – Certain Measures Affecting Imports of Poultry from China, WT/DS392/R, paras. 7.119 and 7.123.

[101] Report of the Panel, United States – Certain Measures Affecting Imports of Poultry from China, WT/DS392/R, paras. 7.125 et seq.

[102] Report of the Panel, United States – Certain Measures Affecting Imports of Poultry from China, WT/DS392/R, para. 7.154.

[103] Report of the Panel, United States – Certain Measures Affecting Imports of Poultry from China, WT/DS392/R, para. 7.179.

[104] Report of the Panel, United States – Certain Measures Affecting Imports of Poultry from China, WT/DS392/R, paras. 7.191–7.192.

[105] Report of the Panel, United States – Certain Measures Affecting Imports of Poultry from China, WT/DS392/R, para. 7.294

[106] Report of the Panel, United States – Certain Measures Affecting Imports of Poultry from China, WT/DS392/R, para. 7.318.

compared with those of the USA, the funding prohibition would in effect make Chinese exports to the USA impossible. However, no other country was affected by the provision which meant that China was denied the advantage of exporting to the USA.[107] Furthermore, the prohibition of Chinese imports also meant a violation of Article XI:1 of the GATT 1994.[108] Neither the violation of Article I:1 of the GATT 1994 nor the one of Article XI:1 of the GATT 1994 could be justified under Article XX of the GATT 1994. Article XX lit. b of the GATT 1994 allows for exceptions if they are necessary to protect human health. However, according to the SPS Agreement's preamble it is the Agreement's purpose to elaborate rules for the application of the provisions of the GATT 1994, in particular, Article XX lit. b of the GATT 1994. The SPS Agreement is, thus, explaining in detail how to apply Article XX lit. b of the GATT 1994. Due to the inconsistencies with the SPS Agreement the US measure could therefore not be justified.[109]

Panel European Communities and its Member States – Tariff Treatment of Certain Information Technology Products (DS 375–377)

Facts of the Case

The USA, Japan and Taiwan initiated proceedings against the EU because they accused the EU of levying tax for certain information technology products although the bilateral Information Technology Agreement required the EU to grant duty-free treatment to these goods. The goods in dispute were flat panel display devices, set-top boxes with a communication function and multifunctional digital machines.[110] According to an estimation of the US Trade Representative global exports of these three goods amounted to US-$ 70 billion.[111]

The legal question was whether the EU practice was inconsistent with Article II:1 lit. a and b of the GATT 1994 because the tariffs imposed on these three product groups were in excess of the concession the EU had made in its WTO schedule.

---

[107] Report of the Panel, United States – Certain Measures Affecting Imports of Poultry from China, WT/DS392/R, paras. 7.439–7.441.

[108] Report of the Panel, United States – Certain Measures Affecting Imports of Poultry from China, WT/DS392/R, para. 7.457.

[109] Report of the Panel, United States – Certain Measures Affecting Imports of Poultry from China, WT/DS392/R, paras. 7.470, 7.471 and 7.483.

[110] Report of the Panel, European Communities and its Member States – Tariff Treatment of Certain Information Technology Products, WT/DS375/R, para. 2.1.

[111] http://dex-dwds.appspot.com/www.ustr.gov/sites/default/files/uploads/speeches/2008/asset_upload_file683_14917.pdf, p. 1.

In 1996, 29 members of the WTO had adopted the bilateral "Ministerial Declaration on Trade in Information Technology Products", the ITA. Therein, members agreed to bind and eliminate customs duties within the meaning of Article II:1 lit. b of the GATT 1994 for the goods listed in the ITA. The ITA includes two different lists: One is a product classification with tariff codes as classified in the Harmonized System (HS) which is the common tariff nomenclature. The second list is the so-called narrative description in Attachment B of the ITA which specifies and describes certain products without reference to the HS code.[112]

Before the panel, the complaining parties argued that the technologically advanced products in question, which were not in existence at the time the ITA was concluded, were covered by the ITA. The EU, on the contrary, argued that these new technologies would not fall under the scope of its old concessions in the ITA since they were different to the goods listed in the 1996 agreement.

Important Aspects of the Findings

At the outset, the panel assessed whether flat panel display devices were covered by the EU concession. The EU applied a 14% ad valorem duty on certain monitors which are capable of receiving signals from sources other than an automatic data-processing machine or are fitted with certain connectors.[113] The EU ITA commitment mentions flat panel monitors twice, once in the section where tariff codes are listed and once in the narrative description.

The complainants argued that the flat panel monitors in question were covered by the description 'flat panel display devices (including LCD, [...], Plasma, [...] and other technologies)' in the narrative part of the EU concession and also by a certain HS Code in the first part of the EU ITA concession.

According to the EU, the flat panel monitors in dispute were 'new multifunctional products for which there [was] no specific heading. Thus, these monitors [in the EU's view] had to be classified on a case-by-case basis, considering their specific characteristics'.[114]

The panel had to decide whether the monitors in question fell under the wording of the EU commitments. Crucial for the panel's interpretation was the headnote to the narrative part of the ITA which read '[w]ith respect to any product described

---

[112] Report of the Panel, European Communities and its Member States – Tariff Treatment of Certain Information Technology Products, WT/DS375/R, paras. 7.1–7.7.

[113] Report of the Panel, European Communities and its Member States – Tariff Treatment of Certain Information Technology Products, WT/DS375/R, paras. 7.235 and 7.288–7.291.

[114] Report of the Panel, European Communities and its Member States – Tariff Treatment of Certain Information Technology Products, WT/DS375/R, paras. 7.119–7.120.

[...] to the extent not specifically provided for in this Schedule, the customs duties [...] shall be [...] eliminated [...], *wherever the product is classified'*. After this headnote follows the above mentioned description for flat panel display devices.[115] Since flat panel devices were mentioned not only in the first part by means of a certain tariff code but also in the narrative part of the EU commitments, the panel had to decide whether the narrower HS definition of flat panel devices in the first part of the EU commitment was exhaustive.

The panel held that the participants to the ITA agreed to implement their commitments through a *dual approach*, i.e. eliminating tariffs for products classified in tariff codes and for products specified and described in the narrative part.[116] The panel interpreted the phrase 'wherever the product is classified' to be 'open-ended'. Therefore, the tariff codes were not found to exhaust the product descriptions and limit the scope of product coverage.[117]

Accordingly, the panel did not only have to look at the specific tariff code in question to assess whether the flat panel products in question were covered but had to interpret the narrative description of the EU commitment as well. Contrary to the EU argumentation the panel chose a broad interpretation of the term 'flat panel display devices' which included devices that are able to reproduce signals from sources other than automatic data-processing machines. The wording was found not to imply any limitation on the type of connector sockets either.[118]

The EU furthermore argued without success that the technology in question had been subject to major changes in the last years and that today's monitors were fundamentally different from monitors which were traded at the time the ITA was concluded. Therefore, in the EU's view, the ITA 'was not expected to cover every new product that may come along in the rapidly developing converging information technology sector'.[119]

The panel, however, categorised the EU commitment on flat panel monitor devices as a generic term which covered a wide range of products. It made clear that the EU could have chosen a precise or even exclusive term to limit the scope of coverage for monitors. Since it had not done so, the panel could not read such qualifications into the commitment of the EU.[120]

---

[115] Report of the Panel, European Communities and its Member States – Tariff Treatment of Certain Information Technology Products, WT/DS375/R, paras. 7.320–7.321.

[116] Report of the Panel, European Communities and its Member States – Tariff Treatment of Certain Information Technology Products, WT/DS375/R, para. 7.403.

[117] Report of the Panel, European Communities and its Member States – Tariff Treatment of Certain Information Technology Products, WT/DS375/R, paras. 7.337, 7.338 and 7.489.

[118] Report of the Panel, European Communities and its Member States – Tariff Treatment of Certain Information Technology Products, WT/DS375/R, paras. 7.471 and 7.598.

[119] Report of the Panel, European Communities and its Member States – Tariff Treatment of Certain Information Technology Products, WT/DS375/R, paras. 7.362 and 7.587.

[120] Report of the Panel, European Communities and its Member States – Tariff Treatment of Certain Information Technology Products, WT/DS375/R, paras. 7.592–7.593.

Thus, the EU violated Article II:1 lit. a and b of the GATT 1994 by not extending duty-free treatment to all monitors that were covered by the ITA's schedule but setting a duty rate of 14% for certain monitors.[121]

Similarly, the panel assessed whether set-top boxes were subject to the duty-free commitment of the EU. The question before the panel was if the EU concession 'set top boxes which have a communication function' encompassed also electronic devices that achieve their interactive communication function via WLAN, ISDN or Ethernet and if devices which additionally contain recording functionality, e.g. a hard drive, were covered too.[122] The panel found again that the tariff codes did not delimit the particular products but that the EU concession was defined by the narrative product description in the Annex.[123] It therefore interpreted the narrative description which reads as follows: 'Set top boxes which have a communication function: a microprocessor based device incorporating a modem for gaining access to the Internet and having a function of interactive information exchange'.[124] The panel chose a wide interpretation of the term modem, saying that 'the term modem should not be interpreted in an overly narrow or technical sense, but should be informed by the clear emphasis on functionality'.[125] The panel further recalled that it was neither desirable nor possible to consider the relevance of the state of technology of the time when the concession was made.[126] The panel interpreted the EU concession to include set top boxes which are microprocessor-based, incorporate a modem and are capable of gaining access to the internet and handling two-way interactivity or information exchange.[127] Accordingly, the panel held that set top boxes which achieve their interactive communication via WLAN, ISDN or Ethernet were covered by the EU concession.[128] With respect to the recording function the panel stated that the definition of set top boxes was not limited to products that only have a communication function but added that additional

---

[121] Report of the Panel, European Communities and its Member States – Tariff Treatment of Certain Information Technology Products, WT/DS375/R, paras. 7.598, 7.737, 7.739, 7.745 and 7.757. Please note that the EU did not impose duties on all monitors that fell within the definition but on some which was sufficient to find a violation.

[122] Report of the Panel, European Communities and its Member States – Tariff Treatment of Certain Information Technology Products, WT/DS375/R, paras. 7.825 and 7.841.

[123] Report of the Panel, European Communities and its Member States – Tariff Treatment of Certain Information Technology Products, WT/DS375/R, paras. 7.835 and 7.837.

[124] Report of the Panel, European Communities and its Member States – Tariff Treatment of Certain Information Technology Products, WT/DS375/R, para. 7.838.

[125] Report of the Panel, European Communities and its Member States – Tariff Treatment of Certain Information Technology Products, WT/DS375/R, paras. 7.882 and 7.910.

[126] Report of the Panel, European Communities and its Member States – Tariff Treatment of Certain Information Technology Products, WT/DS375/R, para. 7.946.

[127] Report of the Panel, European Communities and its Member States – Tariff Treatment of Certain Information Technology Products, WT/DS375/R, para. 7.952.

[128] Report of the Panel, European Communities and its Member States – Tariff Treatment of Certain Information Technology Products, WT/DS375/R, para. 7.979.

features, 'at a certain point', could make the product lose its character as a set top box. Here, a case-by-case analysis of the objective characteristics would have to be undertaken to see whether the product lost the essential character of a set top box.[129] Thus, the panel found that the EU had imposed a tariff of 13.9% or 14% on at least some set top boxes which fell within the scope of the EU definition and thus was in breach of Article II:1 lit. a of the GATT 1994.[130]

The third product group involved multifunctional digital machines capable of connecting to an automatic data processing machine or a network which perform two or more of the following functions: printing, copying or facsimile transmission.[131] The panel reached the conclusion that the 6% tax levy for some of the products was a violation of Article II:1 lit. b of the GATT 1994 because the EU had promised duty-free import for those machines. The panel held that some of the products the complainants referred to fell under the scope of the EU concession but it remained vague at defining which of the products exactly.[132] This leaves some ambiguity as how to exactly implement the ruling.

European Communities and Certain Member States – Measures Affecting Trade in Large Civil Aircraft (DS 316)

Facts of the Case

In summer 2010, more than 5 years after the US request for the establishment of a panel, the Airbus panel issued its more than 1,000 page report. The dispute assessed whether European support measures for large civil aircrafts weighing more than 15 tons, with turbofan engines carried under low-set wings and with a transport capacity of 100 or more passengers were subsidies within the meaning of the SCM Agreement. Presently, Boeing and Airbus form a duopoly in the global market of large civil aircrafts. The development of these aircrafts requires significant up-front investments over 3–5 years.[133] Since its establishment in 1970, the French, German, British and Spanish governments had entered into member state financing agreements to fund the development of the Airbus models A300, A310,

---

[129] Report of the Panel, European Communities and its Member States – Tariff Treatment of Certain Information Technology Products, WT/DS375/R, para. 7.981.

[130] Report of the Panel, European Communities and its Member States – Tariff Treatment of Certain Information Technology Products, WT/DS375/R, paras. 7.986–7.988.

[131] Report of the Panel, European Communities and its Member States – Tariff Treatment of Certain Information Technology Products, WT/DS375/R, para. 7.1131.

[132] Report of the Panel, European Communities and its Member States – Tariff Treatment of Certain Information Technology Products, WT/DS375/R, paras. 7.1487, 7.1489 and 7.1491.

[133] Report of the Panel, European Communities and Certain Member States – Measures Affecting Trade in Large Civil Aircraft, WT/DS316/R, paras. 2.1, 2.2. and 7.367–7.368.

A320, A330, A340 and A380. The proportion of development costs financed through member state finance had decreased from close to 100% in the beginning down to a maximum of one-third of the costs after the conclusion of a bilateral agreement between the EU and the USA in 1992.[134] The disbursement of the challenged member state financing was detailed in the respective contractual frameworks with member states. Airbus was 'required to reimburse all funding contributions, plus any interest at the agreed rate, exclusively from revenues generated by deliveries of the [. . .] model that is financed'. Additionally, some of the contracts included the obligation to make 'royalty payments on a per-aircraft basis [. . .] on deliveries made *in excess* of the number needed to secure repayment of the disbursed principal plus any interest'. This means that the member states could actually make a profit if a model sold better than projected. On the other hand, member states were provided no guarantee of repayment if Airbus failed to sell the number of deliveries needed to reimburse the full amount obtained from member states, i.e. there was no security by a lien on Airbus' assets or a guarantee by a third party.[135]

The USA claimed that, thereby, Great Britain, France, Germany and Spain illegally subsidised Airbus whereas the EU brought parallel proceedings against the USA for its subsidies for Boeing. Since the Airbus panel against the EU was established earlier than the Boeing panel, the Airbus panel was the first to deliver its ruling. Both cases are clearly interconnected which comes as no surprise since in 1992 the USA and the EU concluded a bilateral agreement on the modalities of support for their respective producers. This agreement restricted government support measures to a maximum of 33% of the development costs.[136] However, in 1994 the USA terminated that bilateral agreement and went for litigation before the WTO against the EU member state financing. Thus, the Airbus and the Boeing cases represent two sides of the same coin and should be be read together to get the full picture of the dispute.

Important Aspects of the Findings

As a first preliminary issue, the EU argued that since some of the alleged support measures were granted prior to the coming into force of the SCM Agreement in 1995, they were outside the temporal scope of the proceedings as reflected in the non-retroactivity principle of Article 28 of the VCLT. The panel disagreed.

---

[134] Report of the Panel, European Communities and Certain Member States – Measures Affecting Trade in Large Civil Aircraft, WT/DS316/R, para. 7.369.

[135] Report of the Panel, European Communities and Certain Member States – Measures Affecting Trade in Large Civil Aircraft, WT/DS316/R, paras. 7.372–7.374.

[136] Report of the Panel, European Communities and Certain Member States – Measures Affecting Trade in Large Civil Aircraft, WT/DS316/R, paras. 2.1 and 7.369.

According to the panel, the SCM Agreement considered subsidies granted prior to 1995 to be relevant to the serious prejudice determination and, therefore, potentially to give rise to adverse effects under Article 5 of the SCM Agreement.[137]

Furthermore, the EU could not evade the allegations by interpreting the bilateral 1992 agreement with the USA as a waiver to the US rights under the WTO Agreements. The panel held that a member could not waive its rights under the WTO Agreements by means of a bilateral agreement that entered into force prior to the existence of the WTO Agreements. Additionally, the panel did not interpret the language of the 1992 agreement between the EU and the US to imply that both the USA and the EU would be barred from challenging support measures to large civil aircraft prior to 1992.[138] The panel also dismissed the EU argument that its early member state finance for the A320 and A330/A340 had to be assessed in light of the Tokyo Round Subsidies Code instead of measuring them against the standard of the SCM Agreement which came into force in 1995 only.[139]

The EU also argued that a subsidy could only cause adverse effects pursuant to Article 5 of the SCM Agreement if the USA could show that the support still, i.e. *presently,* conferred a benefit on Airbus as the recipient. The EU argued that due to several restructuring measures of the Airbus company and a series of fair market transactions involving changes in the ownership, subsidies which may have existed at some point in time in the past would have been extinguished. The panel, however, also rejected this line of thought. Today's Airbus SAS was considered to be the same producer as the former consortium *Airbus Industrie*.[140] Article 5 of the SCM Agreement would not require the claimant 'to establish that the benefit to the recipient is current or continuing in order to establish that [. . .] the subsidy has caused adverse effects to the complaining member's interest'.[141] In the panel's view, the wording of Article 1.1 of the SCM Agreement suggests that the financial contribution and the benefit to the recipient came into existence at the same time but the provision does not suggest a concept or a requirement of a *'continuing benefit'*.[142]

---

[137] Report of the Panel, European Communities and Certain Member States – Measures Affecting Trade in Large Civil Aircraft, WT/DS316/R, para. 7.64.

[138] Report of the Panel, European Communities and Certain Member States – Measures Affecting Trade in Large Civil Aircraft, WT/DS316/R, paras. 7.91 and 7.93.

[139] Report of the Panel, European Communities and Certain Member States – Measures Affecting Trade in Large Civil Aircraft, WT/DS316/R, para. 7.325.

[140] Report of the Panel, European Communities and Certain Member States – Measures Affecting Trade in Large Civil Aircraft, WT/DS316/R, para. 7.286; for a description of Airbus' corporate structure, cf. pp. 360 et seq.

[141] Report of the Panel, European Communities and Certain Member States – Measures Affecting Trade in Large Civil Aircraft, WT/DS316/R, paras. 7.221, 7.214 and 7.216.

[142] Report of the Panel, European Communities and Certain Member States – Measures Affecting Trade in Large Civil Aircraft, WT/DS316/R, para. 7.218; the panel clarified that the EU argument had to be distinguished from the causation analysis which assesses the effects of the subsidy in question. Art. 5 of the SCM Agreement would, however, not require the claimant to establish that

The USA failed to prove that member state financing of France, Germany, Great Britain and Spain for the current development of the Airbus A350 existed at the time the panel was established. Accordingly, the claim against the support for the A350 was dismissed.[143]

The member state financing for other Airbus models, though, was found to be a subsidy. The panel analysed whether the funds were provided on 'terms that are more advantageous than those that would have been available to the recipient on the market'.[144] The panel declined to use the conditions that the USA and the EU agreed upon in their bilateral 1992 agreement as the relevant benchmark for the comparison.[145] The question that the panel asked itself was 'whether the rate of return obtained by the relevant EC member state governments when providing [... member state financing] is less than the rate of return that would be asked by a market-based lender for financing on the same or similar terms and conditions'.[146] The panel found that the contracts constituted a transfer of funds at below market interest rates to Airbus.[147]

The USA, however, failed to demonstrate that the EU ran a uniform programme of member state financing 'for the development of each and every new' Airbus model at below-market interest rates.[148] The panel was not convinced that the USA had met the high evidentiary burden of establishing the existence of such a uniform unwritten programme which applied to all Airbus models. The panel emphasised the differences in the member state financing for the different Airbus models in the past and was not convinced that future member state financing would necessarily involve loans with non-commercial interest rates.[149]

---

the benefit to the recipient is current or continuing in order to demonstrate that the subsidy has caused adverse effects to the complaining member's interests, cf. paras. 7.221–7.222; in an alternative finding the panel also assessed whether the benefit was extinguished by subsequent sales recipient/recipient's shares for market value, cf. paras. 7.224 et seq.

[143] Report of the Panel, European Communities and Certain Member States – Measures Affecting Trade in Large Civil Aircraft, WT/DS316/R, para. 7.314.

[144] Report of the Panel, European Communities and Certain Member States – Measures Affecting Trade in Large Civil Aircraft, WT/DS316/R, para. 7.382.

[145] Report of the Panel, European Communities and Certain Member States – Measures Affecting Trade in Large Civil Aircraft, WT/DS316/R, para. 7.389.

[146] Report of the Panel, European Communities and Certain Member States – Measures Affecting Trade in Large Civil Aircraft, WT/DS316/R, paras. 7.401 and 7.482.

[147] Report of the Panel, European Communities and Certain Member States – Measures Affecting Trade in Large Civil Aircraft, WT/DS316/R, para. 7.497.

[148] Report of the Panel, European Communities and Certain Member States – Measures Affecting Trade in Large Civil Aircraft, WT/DS316/R, para. 7.514.

[149] Report of the Panel, European Communities and Certain Member States – Measures Affecting Trade in Large Civil Aircraft, WT/DS316/R, paras. 7.575–7.581.

Some of the member state financing contracts, namely the Spanish, German and British for the A380, were not only found to be actionable subsidies within the meaning of the SCM Agreement but also prohibited export subsidies.[150] Export subsidies are defined by Article 3 of the SCM Agreement as being 'contingent, in law or fact, whether solely or as one of several other conditions, upon export performance'. The panel examined whether the provision of the loans was 'conditional or dependent upon actual or anticipated export performance.' The panel assessed whether the subsidy was 'granted *because* of actual or anticipated export performance'.[151] The panel looked into the different contracts and concluded that the respective governments expected that Airbus as a 'global company operating in a global market' would sell 'much if not most of its production in export markets'.[152] Thus, according to the panel, some member state governments 'anticipated exportation or export earnings'.[153] The panel held that, in some instances, exports could not be replaced with domestic sales in order to achieve the number of projected sales which were necessary to repay the loans.[154]

The USA, however, failed to establish that 12 loans by the European Investment Bank (EIB) to Airbus were actionable subsidies. The 12 loans were subsidies within the meaning of the SCM Agreement[155] but in light of the EIB's overall lending activities they were not found to be specific.[156]

The panel looked also into certain infrastructure projects that were realised in the territory of the four EU member states. There was disagreement between the parties whether these infrastructure projects were 'general infrastructure' for which the disciplines of the SCM Agreement do not apply. The panel thus had to clarify the meaning of the term 'general infrastructure' in detail for the very first time.[157] The panel understood the term 'general infrastructure' as 'infrastructure that is not

---

[150] Report of the Panel, European Communities and Certain Member States – Measures Affecting Trade in Large Civil Aircraft, WT/DS316/R, para. 7.689.

[151] Report of the Panel, European Communities and Certain Member States – Measures Affecting Trade in Large Civil Aircraft, WT/DS316/R, para. 7.648.

[152] Report of the Panel, European Communities and Certain Member States – Measures Affecting Trade in Large Civil Aircraft, WT/DS316/R, paras. 7.652, 7.656 and 7.659.

[153] Report of the Panel, European Communities and Certain Member States – Measures Affecting Trade in Large Civil Aircraft, WT/DS316/R, paras. 7.654 and 7.660.

[154] Report of the Panel, European Communities and Certain Member States – Measures Affecting Trade in Large Civil Aircraft, WT/DS316/R, para. 7.678.

[155] Report of the Panel, European Communities and Certain Member States – Measures Affecting Trade in Large Civil Aircraft, WT/DS316/R, para. 7.888.

[156] Report of the Panel, European Communities and Certain Member States – Measures Affecting Trade in Large Civil Aircraft, WT/DS316/R, paras. 7.1004–7.1008.

[157] Report of the Panel, European Communities and Certain Member States – Measures Affecting Trade in Large Civil Aircraft, WT/DS316/R, paras. 7.1034–7.1035.

provided to or for the advantage of only a single entity or limited group of entities, but rather is available to all or nearly all entities'. However, the panel found it 'difficult if not impossible to define the concept [...] in the abstract'.[158] It argued that there would be no infrastructure 'which is inherently general per se'. Instead, the determination needs to be made on a 'case-by-case basis, taking into account the existence or absence of *de jure* or *de facto* limitations on access or use, and any other factors that tend to demonstrate that the infrastructure was or was not provided to or for the use of only a single entity or a limited group of entities'. If infrastructure was not general per se it would also follow that infrastructure 'may be general within the meaning of Article 1.1(a)(1)(iii) at some point in time, but not at another'.[159] Applying this standard, the panel found that the provision of some German, French and Spanish infrastructure was no general infrastructure but a specific subsidy to Airbus.[160]

Furthermore, the panel found that certain transfers of the German government's ownership shares in Deutsche Airbus to the Daimler Group, which were part of the government's decision to restructure Deutsche Airbus in the late 1980s, were subsidies to Airbus.[161] Similarly, several capital contributions to French Aérospatiale made by the French government and Crédit Lyonnais in the 1980s and 1990s were found to be specific subsidies because these investment decisions were found to be inconsistent with the 'usual investment practice of private investors in France'.[162] The panel continued that some European, Spanish, British and German research and development programmes constituted a specific subsidy to Airbus, too.[163] However, the US claim that in 1998 the German government had subsidised Airbus by a debt forgiveness of DM 7.7 billion was not successful since the USA failed to establish that there had been a benefit to Deutsche Airbus.[164]

---

[158] Report of the Panel, European Communities – Definitive Anti-Dumping Measures on Certain Iron or Steel Fasteners from China, WT/DS397/R, para. 7.1037.

[159] Report of the Panel, European Communities – Definitive Anti-Dumping Measures on Certain Iron or Steel Fasteners from China, WT/DS397/R, paras. 7.1039–7.1044. The panel rejected the EU interpretation that Art. 2.2 of the SCM Agreement should be read to mean that "only a subsidy that is limited to certain enterprises within a designated geographical region within the jurisdiction of the granting authority" should be regarded as specific, cf. paras. 7.1224 et seq.

[160] Report of the Panel, European Communities – Definitive Anti-Dumping Measures on Certain Iron or Steel Fasteners from China, WT/DS397/R, para. 7.1244.

[161] Report of the Panel, European Communities – Definitive Anti-Dumping Measures on Certain Iron or Steel Fasteners from China, WT/DS397/R, paras. 7.1245–7.1302.

[162] Report of the Panel, European Communities – Definitive Anti-Dumping Measures on Certain Iron or Steel Fasteners from China, WT/DS397/R, paras. 7.1380 and 7.1414.

[163] Report of the Panel, European Communities – Definitive Anti-Dumping Measures on Certain Iron or Steel Fasteners from China, WT/DS397/R, para. 7.1608.

[164] Report of the Panel, European Communities – Definitive Anti-Dumping Measures on Certain Iron or Steel Fasteners from China, WT/DS397/R, paras. 7.1304–7.1322.

The last part of the decision was devoted to the question whether the subsidies caused adverse effects to the US industry within the meaning of Articles 5 and 6 of the SCM Agreement. The parties did not agree whether there should be a single product comparison between all Airbus and all Boeing large civil aircraft in the different markets or if, for the purposes of the determination of adverse effects, there should be a distinction between the different 'families' of aircraft. The panel started by explaining that the two relevant questions would be what the subsidised product was and what could be identified as the like product for the purposes of the adverse effects analysis.[165] The panel concluded that since there was no requirement in the SCM Agreement to group products according to certain characteristics the USA could frame its case 'as it chooses'.[166] Furthermore, in the panel's view, all Airbus aircraft share particular characteristics and there would be no obvious reason to choose one among them to divide the large civil aircraft into different segments.[167] Therefore, the relevant like product for the analysis of adverse effects was found to be all Boeing large civil aircraft.[168] The panel concluded that the EU subsidies had enabled Airbus to develop and place on the market large civil aircraft that it could otherwise not have launched and that these subsidies caused lost sales for Boeing *but for* these subsidies. The subsidies were found to have caused serious prejudice to the US interests in the form of displacement of US imports in the EU market according to Article 6.3 lit. a of the SCM Agreement, displacement of US exports in third markets according to Article 6.3 lit. b of the SCM Agreement and lost sales in the US market according to Article 6.3 lit. c of the SCM Agreement.[169] However, the USA failed to demonstrate that there was a threat of material injury to the US industry.[170]

It remains to be seen whether the AB shares the panel's reasoning, e.g. on issues like the role of the 1992 agreement, the continuity of benefit and export subsidies. The AB decision will be very significant, both from a political and a legal point of view.

---

[165] Report of the Panel, European Communities – Definitive Anti-Dumping Measures on Certain Iron or Steel Fasteners from China, WT/DS397/R, para. 7.1650.

[166] Report of the Panel, European Communities – Definitive Anti-Dumping Measures on Certain Iron or Steel Fasteners from China, WT/DS397/R, para. 7.1662.

[167] Report of the Panel, European Communities – Definitive Anti-Dumping Measures on Certain Iron or Steel Fasteners from China, WT/DS397/R, para. 7.1664.

[168] Report of the Panel, European Communities – Definitive Anti-Dumping Measures on Certain Iron or Steel Fasteners from China, WT/DS397/R, para. 7.1680.

[169] Report of the Panel, European Communities – Definitive Anti-Dumping Measures on Certain Iron or Steel Fasteners from China, WT/DS397/R, para. 7.2025.

[170] Report of the Panel, European Communities – Definitive Anti-Dumping Measures on Certain Iron or Steel Fasteners from China, WT/DS397/R, para. 7.2186.

Panel European Communities – Definitive Anti-Dumping Measures on Certain Iron or Steel Fasteners from China (DS 397)

Facts of the Case

In its first case against the EU, China targeted certain aspects of the European anti-dumping policy. One part of China's claim involved the concrete imposition of definitive anti-dumping duties on imports of certain iron or steel fasteners originating in China. The other aspect concerned the general claim that part of the legal regime of the EU anti-dumping law violated WTO law. Under certain conditions, an EU provision allowed for the imposition of a single, country-wide duty rate for all Chinese producers instead of applying individual duties for each and every Chinese producer.[171]

Article 9(5) of the EU Basic Anti-Dumping Regulation stipulated that the EU had to specify the anti-dumping duty for each supplier unless it was either impracticable to specify the duty for each supplier *or* in cases of Article 2(7) lit. a of the Basic Anti-Dumping Regulation, e.g. where the normal value is determined on the basis of analogue country prices.

If the exporter was located in a non-market economy WTO member like China, exporters could still try to demonstrate that for their specific situation market economy conditions prevailed. The test which the EU applied in this regard was the so called market economy test. If exporters succeeded in proving that market economy conditions prevailed for their enterprises, these producers were treated like a producer in a market-economy. This market economy test, however, was not in dispute here. The parties instead argued whether the so called individual treatment test in that EU provision was consistent with the WTO Agreements.

If exporters failed the aforementioned market economy test, a producer could still apply for individual treatment: if an enterprise satisfied the so called individual treatment test which included *inter alia* the requirement to be wholly or partially owned by foreign firms and that its terms of sale were freely determined, the EU would still specify an individual rate for that producer. Exporters who did not satisfy cumulatively the five criteria set out in Article 9.5 of the Basic Anti-Dumping Regulation and, therefore, failed the individual treatment test, were subject to a country-wide duty rate.[172]

---

[171] Report of the Panel, European Communities – Definitive Anti-Dumping Measures on Certain Iron or Steel Fasteners from China, WT/DS397/R, paras. 2.1 and 7.48.

[172] Report of the Panel, European Communities – Definitive Anti-Dumping Measures on Certain Iron or Steel Fasteners from China, WT/DS397/R, paras. 7.47–7.50.

China challenged this provision in general and its application in the fasteners investigations, i.e. that Chinese producers who failed the individual treatment test were not subject to individual anti-dumping duties but country-wide ones.[173]

Important Aspects of the Findings

The panel first assessed whether Article 9(5) of the European Basic Anti-Dumping Regulation was WTO consistent and sided with China that it was not. The panel held that although Article 9(5) of the Basic Anti-Dumping Regulation on the surface does not mention dumping margins, the provision necessarily determined whether the EU would calculate an individual dumping margin for a producer. The panel found this provision of the EU anti-dumping regime to be key to the decision whether an individual or country-wide margin calculation of the duty was undertaken.[174] The question whether or not an individual margin of dumping had to be determined is addressed in Article 6.10 of the Anti-Dumping Agreement. The panel interpreted Article 6.10 of the Anti-Dumping Agreement to lay down the rule that an investigating authority has to calculate an individual dumping margin for each known exporter or producer. The sole exception which Article 6.10 of the Anti-Dumping Agreement allows is sampling, i.e. where the number of producers or product types is 'so large' as to make it impracticable for the investigating authority to calculate individual margins. In these exceptional cases investigating authorities are allowed to rely on statistically valid samples or on the largest percentage of the volume of exports to determine a country-wide margin.[175] The panel, therefore, found that Article 9(5) of the Basic Anti-Dumping Regulation was inconsistent with Article 6.10 of the Anti-Dumping Agreement.[176] The EU further-more failed to justify its provision by arguing that there would be a presumption in non-market economies that the state is in control and should therefore be seen as the producer. The panel, in contrast, did see no legal basis for such an assumption in the Anti-Dumping Agreement. According to the panel 'it would seriously undermine the logic of Article 6.10 which requires ... individual margins'.[177] It remains to

---

[173] Report of the Panel, European Communities – Definitive Anti-Dumping Measures on Certain Iron or Steel Fasteners from China, WT/DS397/R, para. 7.84.

[174] Report of the Panel, European Communities – Definitive Anti-Dumping Measures on Certain Iron or Steel Fasteners from China, WT/DS397/R, paras. 7.71–7.77.

[175] Report of the Panel, European Communities – Definitive Anti-Dumping Measures on Certain Iron or Steel Fasteners from China, WT/DS397/R, paras. 7.84–7.90.

[176] Report of the Panel, European Communities – Definitive Anti-Dumping Measures on Certain Iron or Steel Fasteners from China, WT/DS397/R, para. 7.98.

[177] Report of the Panel, European Communities – Definitive Anti-Dumping Measures on Certain Iron or Steel Fasteners from China, WT/DS397/R, paras. 7.96–7.97.

be seen whether the panel's assessment would withstand the Appellate Body's review on a possible appeal of this question.

In the same vein, the panel concluded that there was a violation of Article 9.2 of the Anti-Dumping Agreement. The provision would require the investigating authority to *name* the individual exporters unless the number of producers is so large that this would be impracticable. The panel read the exception in Article 9.2 of the Anti-Dumping Agreement in parallel with the requirements of Article 6.10, meaning that it contained no basis for the imposition of a single country-wide anti-dumping duty in cases of non-market economies.[178]

Furthermore, the EU methodology was found to violate the most favoured nation principle embodied in Article I:1 of the GATT 1994 since Chinese producers did not have the advantage of getting individual margins. The panel held that imports from non-market economies could only be treated differently to the extent the WTO Agreements allowed such a different treatment. According to the panel the EU had not demonstrated that there was a relevant difference in the nature of imports stemming from non-market economies which justified a different treatment.[179]

Concerning the definitive anti-dumping duties on the imports of certain iron and steel fasteners originating in China, the panel logically followed that the EU was in breach of its WTO obligations by basing its country-wide margins on Article 9(5) of its Basic Anti-Dumping Regulation which the panel had just found to be inconsistent.[180] The other allegations made by China received a mixed result. The panel shared some of China's concerns like an improper assessment of whether the EU industry suffered injury[181] and the disclosure of confidential information.[182] However, most allegations failed.

China had accused the EU of acting inconsistently with Article 2.1 and 2.6 of the Anti-Dumping Agreement by defining the scope of the 'product under consideration' to include standard and special fasteners though both categories showed differences in characteristics and use.[183] The panel recalled that the Anti-Dumping Agreement does not provide for a definition of the product under consideration. It held that the very fact that members agreed on a definition of the like product showed that they were able to define the terms of the Anti-Dumping Agreement

---

[178] Report of the Panel, European Communities – Definitive Anti-Dumping Measures on Certain Iron or Steel Fasteners from China, WT/DS397/R, para. 7.112.

[179] Report of the Panel, European Communities – Definitive Anti-Dumping Measures on Certain Iron or Steel Fasteners from China, WT/DS397/R, paras. 7.124–7.125.

[180] Report of the Panel, European Communities – Definitive Anti-Dumping Measures on Certain Iron or Steel Fasteners from China, WT/DS397/R, para. 7.148.

[181] Report of the Panel, European Communities – Definitive Anti-Dumping Measures on Certain Iron or Steel Fasteners from China, WT/DS397/R, para. 7.438.

[182] Report of the Panel, European Communities – Definitive Anti-Dumping Measures on Certain Iron or Steel Fasteners from China, WT/DS397/R, para. 7.561.

[183] Report of the Panel, European Communities – Definitive Anti-Dumping Measures on Certain Iron or Steel Fasteners from China, WT/DS397/R, para. 7.246.

carefully. The failure to provide a definition for the product under consideration was thus found to be intentional. The panel concluded that it would be 'absurd' to follow China's argumentation and impose the definition of a 'like product' from Article 2.6 of the Anti-Dumping Agreement onto the undefined term 'product under consideration'.[184] In the light of previous panels having decided this very question in the past in the same way, the panel criticised that China neither addressed these rulings nor tried to distinguish the current case from the previous ones.[185] The panel, furthermore, held *inter alia* that China failed to demonstrate that the EU did not undertake an objective examination of price undercutting[186] and that the EU examination of the impact of dumped imports on the EU industry was inconsistent with Article 3.1 and 3.4 of the Anti-Dumping Agreement.[187]

---

[184] Report of the Panel, European Communities – Definitive Anti-Dumping Measures on Certain Iron or Steel Fasteners from China, WT/DS397/R, paras. 7.260 and 7.271.

[185] Report of the Panel, European Communities – Definitive Anti-Dumping Measures on Certain Iron or Steel Fasteners from China, WT/DS397/R, para. 7.273.

[186] Report of the Panel, European Communities – Definitive Anti-Dumping Measures on Certain Iron or Steel Fasteners from China, WT/DS397/R, para. 7.335.

[187] Report of the Panel, European Communities – Definitive Anti-Dumping Measures on Certain Iron or Steel Fasteners from China, WT/DS397/R, para. 7.411.

The World Customs Organization and its Role in the System of World Trade: An Overview

Hans-Michael Wolffgang and Christopher Dallimore

Introduction

This series of contributions to the European Yearbook of International Economic Law examines the activities of the World Customs Organization and explains their significance for world trade.

The first contribution aims to introduce the reader to the field of customs and the World Customs Organization (hereinafter "WCO"). It is divided into five sections: the first briefly describes the development of customs and its importance to world trade. The second section deals with the creation of the WCO and outlines its structure, instruments and overall strategic policy. This is followed by an examination of its three core activities. The fourth section examines the way the WCO interacts with other international organizations. The conclusion summarizes the main points of the previous sections, underlines the relevance of customs to world trade and points to future subjects of investigation.

Functions of Customs Administrations

Customs is one of the most ancient governmental institutions whose origins date back 3,000 years.[1] Historically, the term "customs" refers to the practice of

---

[1] For a detailed history of customs see generally Asakura, *World History of the Customs and Tariffs*, 2002.

H.-M. Wolffgang (✉)
Universität Münster, Rechtswiss. Fakultät, Universitätsstr. 14-16, 48143 Münster, Germany
e-mail: michael@wolffgang.de

C. Dallimore
Dpt. of Customs and Excise, Rechtswiss. Fakultät Universitätsstr, 14-16, 48143 Münster, Germany
e-mail: dallimore@wwu.de

C. Herrmann and J.P. Terhechte (eds.), *European Yearbook of International Economic Law (EYIEL), Vol. 3 (2012)*, European Yearbook of International Economic Law 3, DOI 10.1007/978-3-642-23309-8_19, © Springer-Verlag Berlin Heidelberg 2012

collecting fees (referred to as a "duty" or "toll") from travellers for the use of transportation routes such as highways, bridges or waterways in accordance with tariff tables as a means of raising revenue for the state or ruler.[2] Over time, customs authorities came to perform three core functions: the collection of revenue, enforcement of laws and the facilitation of trade.

The rise of the nation state in the nineteenth century saw the creation of national customs authorities as executive agencies under the control of the treasury or ministry of finance. Customs authorities therefore became closely associated with national sovereignty: as one writer points out, "[c]ustoms [...] is often the first window through which the world views a country".[3] This brings to mind the symbol of the portcullis – the former badge of UK Customs – which signified the twin aims of security and freedom.[4]

Nowadays, the core functions of customs authorities are essentially the same although the emphasis has shifted in response to global events.[5] As a result of the GATT trade rounds, revenue collection has greatly declined in industrialized countries. However, developing countries (DCs) are still heavily dependent on customs receipts. The enforcement function has become increasingly complex with administrations enforcing a multitude of laws at the border.[6] Owing to their strategic position and the special powers at their disposal,[7] customs authorities are also well-positioned to perform a vital role in foreign relations, especially concerning the enforcement of unilateral or multilateral trade policy measures.[8]

---

[2] Wolffgang, Emerging Issues in European Customs Law, World Customs Journal, 1 (2007) 1, pp. 3–4, available at: http://www.worldcustomsjournal.org/media/wcj/-2007/1/Emerging_issues_in_European_customs_law.pdf.

[3] See McLinden, Integrity in Customs, Legal Framework for Customs Operations and Enforcement Issues, in: de Wulf/Sokol (eds.), *Customs Modernization Handbook*, 2005, p. 68, available at: http://siteresources.worldbank.org/INTEXPCOMNET/Resources/Customs_Modernization_Handbook.pdf.

[4] On the symbolic meaning of the portcullis, see: The Portcullis, House of Commons Information Office, Factsheet 9, General Series, Revised August 2010, available at: http://www.parliament.uk/documents/commons-information-office/g09.pdf.

[5] According to one internationally agreed definition of customs' functions, customs enforces the law, collects duties and taxes, clears goods promptly and ensure compliance. See the Introduction to the Revised International Convention on the Simplification and Harmonization of Customs Procedures, available at: http://www.wcoomd.org/Kyoto_New/Content/content.html.

[6] See Mikuriya, Legal Framework for Customs Operations and Enforcement Issues, in: de Wulf/Sokol (eds.), *Customs Modernization Handbook*, 2005, p. 62 with further references, available at: http://siteresources.worldbank.org/INTEXPCOMNET/Resources/Customs_Modernization_Handbook.pdf.

[7] For an overview of the powers and constitutional position of US Customs (CBP) see Dallimore, *Securing the Supply Chain: Does the Container Security Initiative Comply with WTO Law?*, 2008, pp. 99–102 with further references, available at: http://miami.uni-muenster.de/servlets/DerivateServlet/Derivate-4781/diss_dallimore.PDF.

[8] See generally Bhala, Fighting Bad Guys with International Trade Law, University of California at Davis Law Review 31 (1997) 1, with reference to US legislation. On the role of trade

As always, the facilitation of trade must be balanced with the need to protect the public.[9] When performing their tasks customs administrations must comply with the international obligations that bind their governments (most notably those of the WTO).[10]

Customs and the Globalization of Trade

From the perspective of international trade, customs has a Jekyll and Hyde character insofar as it plays an instrumental role in both protectionism and trade facilitation.[11] Historically, the potential of customs to divide nations can be seen from the French tariff of 1667[12] as well as the "Smoot-Hawley" Tariff Act of 1930.[13] In both cases, legislators ratcheted up tariffs on imports as a means of protecting domestic industry and thereby triggered border warfare with their trading partners. In both cases, trade conflict was a prelude to full-blown war.

After the Second World War, the Allied Powers under the leadership of the United States sought to ensure world peace through the creation of the multilateral trading system. Owing to its direct impact on trade flows,[14] it was essential to integrate national customs administrations into this system.[15] At European level, the national powers of customs authorities have been largely harmonized through

---

sanctions see United Nations, A More Secure World: Our Shared Responsibility, Report of the Secretary-General's High-Level Panel on Threats, Challenges and Change, 2004, p. 55, paras. 178 et seq, full report available at: http://www.un.org/secureworld/report3.pdf.

[9] The Great Council of Ragusa (today known as Dubrovnik) passed a Decree in 1377 imposing a quarantine period of 30 days for ships and passengers entering the city. See Gensini et al., The Concept of Quarantine in History: From Plague to SARS in: Journal of Infection 49 (2004), pp. 257–259, available at: http://www.birdflubook.com/resources/0Gensini257.pdf.

[10] Cf. Art. 31 and 32 of the Vienna Convention on the Law of Treaties 1969.

[11] As one writer points out: "When a government enforces conditions or exactions on entry into its jurisdiction, a frontier becomes a barrier": see I.C. and R.G.H., Western Union, The World Today 5 (1949) 4, pp. 170 et seq. (179), available at: http://www.jstor.org/stable/40392221 (subscription only).

[12] For details on the French tariff see Asakura, *World History of the Customs and Tariffs*, 2002, pp. 193–194.

[13] The Tariff Act 1930, P.L. 71-361.

[14] For an investigation into the importance of customs procedures for world trade as well as the methodology of measuring trade facilitation, see Creskoff, Trade Facilitation: An Often Overlooked Engine of Trade Expansion, Global Trade and Customs Journal 3 (2008) 1, pp. 1 et seq.

[15] On the *tension* between global governance and global sovereignty, see generally, Morais, The Quest for International Standards: Global Governance vs. Sovereignty, University of Kansas Law Review 50 (2002), pp. 779 et seq. (787).

legislation and decisions of the European Court of Justice.[16] At international level, the various agreements of the WCO and WTO have developed legally-binding global standards for customs administrations.[17] Nowadays, the only area where states can claim exclusive jurisdiction over customs matters is national security, which has proved an enduring bone of contention in international trading relations.[18]

For much of the late twentieth century, customs policy was determined by the need to facilitate trade. The advent of containerization in the 1950s, just-in-time delivery techniques and the division of labour saw the world economy surge forward. By the year 2000, world trade was booming, borne on the "international supply chain", an edifice of complex trading relationships and low-cost (primarily maritime) transportation. In light of increased trade flows, customs administrations were compelled to rethink their approach to customs enforcement.[19] The result was greater reliance on the private sector and the utilization of information technology.[20]

On the 11th of September 2001, the perception of globalization as a benevolent force changed with the destruction of the World Trade Centre in New York by two airliners –. The international supply chain came to be seen as a security risk because it offered terrorists a realistic means of smuggling Weapons of Mass Destruction (WMD) around the world.[21] 9/11 therefore heralded a new era of "supply chain security" whereby states introduced unilateral security measures to prevent the

---

[16] For an overview of national jurisdiction in European customs law see Lux, *Guide to Community Customs Legislation*, (2nd ed.) 2002, pp. 32-36.

[17] Many provisions of the GATT directly relate to customs matters including Art. I (MFN principle); Art. II (schedule of concessions); Art. V (freedom of transit); Art. VI (anti-dumping and countervailing duties); Art. VII (valuation for customs purposes); Art. VIII (fees and formalities connected with import and export), Art. XI (abolition of quantitative restrictions) and Art. XXVIIIbis (tariff negotiations). Concerning the conventions of the WCO see Gottschlich, The World Wide Development of International Customs Law, International Business Law Journal 7 (1988), pp. 947 et seq. (954–956).

[18] See generally on Art. XXI GATT, Hahn, Vital Interests and the Law of GATT: An Analysis of GATT's Security Exception, Michigan Journal of International Law 12 (1991), pp. 558 et seq., Schloemann/Ohlhoff, Constitutionalization and Dispute Settlement in the WTO: National Security as an Issue of Competence, American Journal of International Law 93 (1999), pp. 424 et seq.

[19] For an overview of the challenges of globalization from a customs perspective, see Gordhan, Customs in the 21st Century, World Customs Journal 1 (2007) 1, pp. 49–52, available at: http://www.worldcustomsjournal.org/media/wcj/-2007/1/Customs_in_the_21st_century.pdf.

[20] See the North American Free Trade Agreement Implementation Act 1993, Public Law No: 103-182, (H.R. 3450), Title VI (Customs Modernization). This legislation has been described as "the most sweeping regulatory reform legislation since the U.S. Customs Service was organized in 1789." See "Everything Changed 1989 – 2003", US Customs Today, February 2003, available at: http://www.cbp.gov/xp/CustomsToday/2003/February/everything.xml.

[21] See generally Flynn, *America the Vulnerable*, 2004; Gerencser et al., Port Security Wargame, Implications for U.S. Supply Chains, 2002, available at: http://www.boozallen.com/media/file/128648.pdf.

potential proliferation of WMD by means of shipping containers.[22] Owing to their function as border enforcement agencies, customs administrations were to play the leading role in developing and enforcing such measures.[23]

The World Customs Organization

The WCO was created in 1950 as "The Customs Co-operation Council", in order to deal specifically with customs matters. It is an international organization with legal capacity,[24] and has 177 member states with the European Union having a status equal to membership.[25]

Founding

Like other international organizations relating to trade and foreign relations, the preamble of the CCC Convention reflects the immediate post-war circumstances of its creation.[26] In 1947, the war-time destruction had left the countries of Europe almost wholly dependent on American imports and financial assistance.[27] The creation of a European customs union (i.e. "the complete renunciation of duties

---

[22] The Container Security Initiative (CSI) was announced by the former U.S. Customs Commissioner in 2002; see Robert C. Bonner, U.S. Customs Commissioner, Remarks before the Centre for Strategic and International Studies, 17th January, 2002, available at: http://www.cbp.gov/xp/cgov/newsroom/speeches_statements/archives/2002/jan172002.xml.

[23] See generally Mikuriya, The Customs Response to the 21st Century, Global Trade and Customs Journal 2 (2007) 2, p. 21. On the changing role of customs in relation to security and facilitation, see also Widdowson, The Changing Role of Customs: Evolution or Revolution?" World Customs Journal 1 (2007) 1, pp. 31 et seq, available at: http://www.worldcustomsjournal.org/media/wcj/-2007/1/The_changing_role_of_Customs_evolution_or_revolution.pdf.

[24] Art. II, Section 2, Annex to the Founding Convention.

[25] A list of member states is available on the WCO Website at: http://www.wcoomd.org/files/1.%20Public%20files/PDFandDocuments/About%20Us/Members_table_174_EN.pdf. The European Union joined the World Customs Organization following a resolution by the WCO Council on 30th June, 2007: see Commission Proposal for a Council Decision on the accession of the European Communities to the World Customs Organisation and the exercise of rights and obligations akin to membership ad interim Brussels, 14th May, 2007, COM(2007) 252 final.

[26] For an overview of its creation see Asakura, *World History of the Customs and Tariffs*, 2002, pp. 287 et seq.

[27] Anon, Reflections on the Marshall Offer, The World Today 3 (1947) 8, pp. 336 et seq., available at: http://www.jstor.org/pss/40392042. See also D.K.M.K., The World Today 3 (1947) 4, pp. 155 et seq. (161), available at: http://www.jstor.org/stable/40392010 (both subscription only).

on products passing frontiers within the Union"[28]) was considered an essential component of economic recovery because it would serve to enlarge the trading areas of the respective countries, thereby increasing their self-reliance.[29] The political will for the creation of a customs union was provided by the "urgency of post-war co-operation".[30]

The Committee for Economic Co-operation set up the European Customs Union Study Group on the 12th of September 1947 to examine this undertaking.[31] It soon became clear, however, that creating a customs union would be exceedingly complex owing to the political ramifications of economic integration[32] and it was decided to concentrate on promoting customs co-operation instead. With the entry into force of the Convention Establishing a Customs Co-operation Council in 1952 (hereinafter "The Founding Convention),[33] the Study Group was replaced by the Customs Co-operation Council (hereinafter "CCC").[34] The inaugural session of the CCC took place on the 26th of January 1953 with the representatives of 17 European countries.[35]

Over the next 40 years, the membership of the CCC steadily increased and (in 1994) the organization adopted the informal name "World Customs Organization". This new name reflected its development into a multilateral organization as well as the changed circumstances of world trade.[36] On official documents,

---

[28] See I.C. and R.G.H., Western Union, The World Today 5 (1949) 4, pp. 170 et seq. (179), available at: http://www.jstor.org/stable/40392221 (subscription only).

[29] Anon, Notes of the Month: Steps Towards European Co-operation, The World Today 4 (1948) 3, available at: http://www.jstor.org/stable/40392093 (both subscription only).

[30] Schokking/Anderson, Observations on the European Integration Process, The Journal of Conflict Resolution 4 (1960) 4, pp. 389 et seq. (391), available at: http://www.jstor.org/stable172723 (subscription only).

[31] See Art. 6 of the Convention for European Economic Co-operation 1948; Robertson, Different Approaches to European Unity, The American Journal of Comparative 3 (1954) 4, pp. 502 et seq. (508-509), available at: http://www.jstor.org/pss/837596 (subscription only).

[32] The major difficulty lay in the pre-requisite of "a common political authority with an importance perhaps equal to or greater than that of the national Governments or the constituent countries." Quoted from A.N.O., Reflections on the Marshall Offer, The World Today 3 (1947) 8, pp. 336 et seq. (345), available at: http://www.jstor.org/stable/40392042. The difficulties in creating a customs union were confirmed by the planned Franco-Italian customs union. See A.C., Franco-Italian Customs Union, The World Today 4 (1948) 11, pp. 481 et seq. (482), available at: http://www.jstor.org/stable/40392074 (both subscription only).

[33] Signed in Brussels on 15th December, 1950, entered into force on 4th November, 1952: see United Nations Treaty Collection, Vol. 157, I-2052.

[34] Gottschlich, The World Wide Development of International Customs Law, International Business Law Journal 7 (1988), pp. 947 et seq. (952 et seq.)

[35] An overview of the creation of the WCO and historical milestones, is available at the WCO website: http://www.wcoomd.org/home_about_us_auhistory.htm.

[36] See Asakura, World History of the Customs and Tariffs, 2002, p. 290, pointing out that the CCC was the second largest international organization next to the WTO and that by the end of the 1980s its membership had increased to 102.

however, the organization is still referred to by its original name ("The Customs Co-operation Council").

Organization

The functions, activities and institutional arrangements of the WCO are governed by Founding Convention of 1950 as well as other more modern instruments. It has a complex hierarchy of working bodies which deal with all customs-related aspects of world trade. The WCO is considered a "member-driven" organization and its official mission is to "improve the effectiveness and efficiency of its Member Customs administrations across the globe".[37]

The WCO is financed mainly by the contributions of its member states. In this respect, the largest contributors are the United States, Japan and the European Union. Other sources of revenue include the proceeds from its various activities including publications and seminars.[38]

Working Bodies and Instruments

The working bodies of the WCO have been established by the Founding Convention and Resolutions of the Council. The Terms of Reference for the Working Bodies of the WCO[39] describes their functions, key deliverables and operational practices. Owing to the sensitivity of certain issues, it is important that the working bodies keep to their terms of reference and follow transparent practices.[40] The following describes the most important working bodies and instruments of the WCO.

---

[37] See World Customs Organization, Mission, Objective, Activities, 2009/2010, p. 2, available at: http://www.wcoomd.org/files/1.%20Public%20files/PDFandDocuments/About%20Us/DEPL%20OMD%20UK%20A4.pdf.

[38] However, the European Union and its 27 Member States together constitute the largest contributor, accounting for 32.76% of the WCO's budget. In 2009, the total budget of the WCO amounted to 15,016,603.75 Euros. See Sonnenfeld, Warum sind die Mitgliedstaaten der Europäischen Union noch „selbständige" Mitglieder bei der WZO?, Außenwirtschaftliche Praxis (2009) 10, pp. 145–146.

[39] Terms of Reference of WCO Working Bodies, August 2010, available at: http://www.wcoomd.org/files/1.%20Public%20files/PDFandDocuments/About%20Us/Terms%20Reference%20WB%20E_Rev20090513.pdf.

[40] E.g. the SECURE Working Group set up in 2008 to examine intellectual property issues was disbanded after members complained about its terms of reference. See Speech by Kunio Mikuriya, WCO, Strengthening the Fight against Counterfeiting and Piracy, 3rd Pan-European Intellectual Property Summit, 4th and 5th December, 2008, available at http://www.wcoomd.org/speeches/?v=1&lid=1&cid=10.

The Council

The Customs Co-operation Council was established by Art. I of the Founding Convention and is the most important working body of the WCO. According to Art. VII, it is required to meet at least twice a year.[41]

The core tasks of the Council are contained in Art. III of the Founding Convention and include co-operation in customs matters; legislation; dispute resolution and information dissemination. A more detailed description is provided in its terms of reference.[42] The Council is assisted in its tasks by the Permanent Technical Committee and General Secretariat.[43] According to Art. XI of the Founding Convention, the Council appoints a Secretary-General and Deputy and determines their functions and duties. It also elects a chairperson and vice-chairperson from among the delegates who are responsible for the organization of meetings.

The contracting parties have the right to nominate one delegate (usually the Directors-General of its customs administration) as well as one or more deputies and advisors. In addition, the representatives of non-member governments, international organizations and NGOs may be admitted as observers. This ensures participation by a broad range of interested parties.[44] Levels of participation are high, ranging from 85 to 90% of members.[45]

The voting rights of delegates at Council Sessions are regulated in Article VIII of the Founding Convention. Accordingly, each member has one vote and decisions are taken by two-thirds majority of the members present and entitled to vote. The Council can only decide on a matter if more than half of the members entitled to vote on that matter are present.

The majority of WCO members are developing countries (DCs) or least-developed countries (LDCs). Capacity building therefore features prominently in the activities of the WCO, although certain policies have proved controversial with

---

[41] Art. VII, Founding Convention. However, these two meetings are held concurrently in June. See WCO, Terms of Reference for the Council, Terms of Reference for WCO Working Bodies, August 2010, para. 5.

[42] See WCO, Terms of Reference for the Council, Terms of Reference for WCO Working Bodies, August 2010, para. 5.

[43] Article V, Founding Convention. Nowadays, it is also assisted by the Policy Commission and Finance Committee: see WCO, Terms of Reference for the Council, Terms of Reference for WCO Working Bodies, August 2010, para. 5.

[44] According to the authors' estimation, the First Session of the Capacity Building Committee held in Brussels on the 22nd November, 2010 was attended by 106 Heads of Delegation, 50 alternative representatives, 49 advisors, 16 representatives of capacity building bodies, eleven university representatives, 54 observers and two other invitees. See WCO, Report of the Capacity Building Committee, Doc. No. HC0008E19, 22nd November, 2010, available at: http://www.wcoomd.org/files/1.%20Public%20files/PDFandDocuments/Capacity%20Building/HC0008E1.pdf.

[45] See Matsudaira, Trade Facilitation, Customs and the World Customs Organization: Introduction to the WCO Trade Facilitation Instruments, Global Trade and Customs Journal 2 (2007) 6, pp. 243 et seq. (250), Chart 3C.

developing member states (e.g. certain aspects of the enforcement of intellectual property rights).[46]

Committees[47]

The working bodies deal with many different aspects of customs policy. Of particular importance for the functioning of the WCO are the Policy Commission, the Permanent Technical Committee, the Audit Committee and the Private Sector Consultative Group. Unlike the Council, these bodies have a restricted membership.

The **Policy Commission** was created in 1978 as a "dynamic steering group to the Council". It is chaired by the Chairperson of the Council and consists of 17 members elected by the Council for a two-year period. The Policy Commission is essentially an advisory body which deals with broad policy questions. It initiates "policies, practices and procedures of the WCO with the objective of assisting the Council to achieve the broad aims of its activities". It can make recommendations, undertake further research or request the Secretary-General to take action.

The **Audit Committee** oversees the performance of the WCO working bodies and advises the Council, Policy Commission and Secretary General concerning *inter alia* the implementation of the strategic plan, budget allocation and programme management including risk mitigation. It meets annually and its key deliverables are to review and approve plans for internal and external audits, provide reports on reviewed audit findings and recommendations for the Council and Policy Commission.

The **Permanent Technical Committee** (hereinafter "PTC") was established by Art. 5 of the Founding Convention in order to assist the Council discharge its functions. The PTC meets at least four times a year and according to Art. X (a) it consists of representatives of Council members specialized in technical customs matters. According to its terms of reference, the PTC performs a wide range of functions relating to the enhancement of customs co-operation, information technology, trade facilitation and capacity-building. When performing its functions the PTC can establish committees and collaborate with international organizations, governmental bodies and the private sector.

---

[46] See Speech by Kunio Mikuriya, WCO, "Strengthening the Fight against Counterfeiting and Piracy", 3rd Pan-European Intellectual Property Summit, 4th and 5th December, 2008, available at: http://www.wcoomd.org/speeches/?v=1&lid=1&cid=10. At the same time, developing countries are strongly involved in the fight against counterfeit medicines. See Address by French President Jacques Chirac at the World Customs Organization Council Session, 24th June, 2010, available at: http://www.wcoomd.org/files/1.%20Public%20files/PDFandDocuments/Highlights/Discours_Jacques_Chirac_Conseil_2010.pdf.

[47] The following descriptions of the Policy Commission, audit Committee and Permanent Technical Committee were summarized from the Terms of Reference for the Policy Commission, in: Terms of Reference for WCO Working Bodies, August 2010.

The **Private Sector Consultative Group** (hereinafter "PSCG") was set up in 2005 to advise the High Level Strategic Group and Secretary-General on the SAFE Framework of Standards. It consists of members of the private sector engaged in and affected by the trade security and facilitation measures of the WCO. A broad range of businesses are represented in terms of size and geographic location. Although the activities of the PSCG mainly relate to all issues concerning the Framework of Standards its terms of reference also extend to similar or related Framework implementation concerns as expressed by trade.[48]

Instruments

The Council issues five types of instrument: Conventions, Recommendations, Resolutions, Declarations and Opinions.[49] The Founding Convention only refers to the first two types of instrument but does define them.

Of these instruments, only a convention is legally-binding on the members[50] although the WCO lacks a formal enforceability mechanism (despite the fact that provisions of the Founding Convention refer to such a function).[51] Recommendations on Customs Technique are proposed by the PTC and approved by the Council. They are issued in relation to a wide range of subjects and are "[o]ne of the most practical instruments for securing the highest degree of harmonization".[52] Recommendations also produce an informal binding effect insofar as the WCO makes clear that the adoption of a recommendation entails an implicit commitment to implement its provisions as far as possible.[53] In addition, Art. III (e) of the Founding Convention authorizes the Council to issue recommendations for the

---

[48] Summarized from the PSCG's website. Terms of reference available at: http://www.wcopscg. org/what_we_do.html.

[49] For an overview of each see Matsudaira, Trade Facilitation, Customs and the World Customs Organization: Introduction to the WCO Trade Facilitation Instruments, Global Trade and Customs Journal 2 (2007) 6, pp. 243 et seq. (251).

[50] A convention is a source of international law according to Art. 38 a. of the Statute of the International Court of Justice; according to Art. 31 of the Vienna Convention on the Law of Treaties, states are obliged to perform their obligations under treaties in good faith (see e.g. Art. III of the HS Convention).

[51] See Article III (e) and Article IX of the Founding Convention. Concerning the possibility of establishing such a body see Rovetta, The European Community Joins the World Customs Organization: Time to Create a WCO Dispute Settlement Mechanism?, Global Trade and Customs Journal 3 (2008) 1, pp. 51 et seq. (51–52).

[52] See WCO, The Nature of WCO Recommendations and the Procedure for their Acceptance, 21st July, 1995, p.1, available at: http://www.wcoomd.org/files/1.%20Public%20files/ PDFandDocuments/Recommendations/Recommendations_General.pdf; Gottschlich, The World Wide Development of International Customs Law, International Business Law Journal 7 (1988), pp. 947 et seq. (950 et seq.).

[53] However, they do not have the same force as a treaty: see WCO, The Nature of WCO Recommendations and the Procedure for their Acceptance, 21st July, 1995, p.1.

settlement of a dispute which can be accepted as binding by the disputants.[54] Resolutions refer to unilateral action to be taken by the WCO[55] and take the form of decisions (legally-binding) or recommendations (non-binding). They are approved by the Council. Declarations contain principles of fundamental importance; they are addressed to WCO members and are non-prescriptive. Opinions are similarly non-binding and usually provide advice on how to implement a certain instrument (e.g. methods of customs valuation).

The instruments at the WCO's disposal provide a range of prescriptive and nonprescriptive options when tackling customs subjects. A convention is appropriate if there is the political will to create global standards. On the other hand, nonprescriptive instruments will be suitable if there is an obvious need for global standards but the subject is very sensitive (e.g. the Revised Arusha Declaration on Integrity in Customs)[56] or where prompt guidelines are needed for a highly complex subject (e.g. the SAFE Framework of Standards).[57]

WCO Fields of Activity

The overarching aims of the WCO are laid down in the preamble to the Founding Convention. They are to "secure the highest degree of harmony and uniformity in their Customs systems"; to "study the problems inherent in the development and improvement of Customs technique and Customs legislation in connection therewith". Traditionally, its major fields of activity have been the harmonization of nomenclature and customs valuation as well as the simplification of customs formalities.[58]

---

[54] However, this possibility does not appear to have been utilized: see e.g. the WCO's webpage "WCO Council Recommendations Related to Customs Procedures and Facilitation", which does not refer to any Recommendations issued in respect of dispute settlement, available at: http://www.wcoomd.org/home_pfoverviewboxes_tools_and_instruments_pfrecommendationslist.htm.

[55] Matsudaira, Trade Facilitation, Customs and the World Customs Organization: Introduction to the WCO Trade Facilitation Instruments, Global Trade and Customs Journal, 2 (2007) 6, pp. 243 et seq. (251).

[56] See McLinden, Integrity in Customs, Legal Framework for Customs Operations and Enforcement Issues, in: de Wulf/Sokol (eds.), *Customs Modernization Handbook*, 2005, pp. 72–74 (explaining the non-prescriptive approach).

[57] See SAFE Framework of Standards to Secure and Facilitate Global Trade, 2007, available at: http://www.wcoomd.org/files/1.%20Public%20files/PDFandDocuments/SAFE%20Framework_EN_2007_for_publication.pdf. The legal status of the SAFE Framework is uncertain: the foreword to the Framework refers to it as a "unique international instrument". However, it is non-prescriptive and arguably resembles a Declaration.

[58] As referred to in the Preamble and Art. III(e) of the Founding Convention. The Convention on Nomenclature for the Classification of Goods in Customs Tariffs and the Convention on the Valuation of Goods for Customs Purposes were signed on the same day as the Founding Convention, namely the 15th December, 1950.

The WCO also issues a Strategic Plan for a three-year period which elaborates its activities in greater detail.[59] This has been complemented by the strategic policy document "Customs in the 21st Century" which provides a blueprint for the development of "a new strategic perspective and policies that will shape the role of Customs in the 21st century".[60] It reflects the changed conditions of international trade following 9/11 and the global economic crisis.

The following provides an overview of the WCO's activities relating to harmonization and simplification. Nowadays, however, the WCO's activities go much further to include security and enforcement, partnerships and co-operation as well as modernization and capacity building.[61]

The Harmonization of Nomenclature

Arguably the greatest achievement of the WCO has been to create a harmonized system of nomenclature that nowadays forms the foundation of international trade. Historically, countries applied customs duties using their own tariff schedules[62] and the lack of harmonization in classifying products presented a considerable barrier to trade.[63] The policy of the GATT 1947 to reduce tariffs required Contracting Parties to agree on a common basis for their tariff schedules in order to ensure their tariff concessions under Article II.[64]

---

[59] Prepared by the Secretariat and submitted to the Policy Commission for review. The plan is then submitted to the Council which finalizes and adopts it. See Terms of Reference for the Policy Commission, in: Terms of Reference for WCO Working Bodies, para. 4(d).

[60] See Resolution of the Customs Co-operation Council on the Role of Customs in the 21st Century, June 2008, available at: http://www.wcoomd.org/files/1.%20Public%20files/ PDFandDocuments/Resolutions/Role%20of%20Customs%20in%20the%2021st%20Century% 20_June%202008_.pdf; see also World Customs Organization, Customs in the 21st Century: Enhancing Growth and Development through Trade and Facilitation and Border Security, June 2008, para. 2, available at: http://www.wcoomd.org/files/1.%20Public%20files/ PDFandDocuments/Annex%20II%20-%20Customs%20in%20the%2021st%20Century.pdf.

[61] See World Customs Organization, Mission, Objective, Activities, 2009/2010, p. 3, available at: http://www.wcoomd.org/files/1.%20Public%20files/PDFandDocuments/About%20Us/DEPL %20OMD%20UK%20A4.pdf.

[62] The first tariff table dates back to A.D. 136 and was issued by Palmyra in Syria. Reproduced in Asakura, *World History of the Customs and Tariffs*, 2002, pp. 70–73.

[63] For example, it hindered the introduction of electronic data processing and consistent analysis of trade data. See Wind, HS 2007: What's It All About? Global Trade and Customs Journal 2 (2007) 2, p. 80; Chaplin, An Introduction to the Harmonized System, North Carolina Journal of International Law and Commercial Regulation 12 (1987), pp. 417 et seq. (423 et seq.).

[64] See e.g., Report of the Panel, European Communities – Customs Classification of Certain Computer Equipment, WT/DS62/R, 5th February, 1998, p. 53, para. 6.36.

The Convention on Nomenclature for the Classification of Goods in Customs Tariffs 1950[65] aimed to simplify international customs tariff regulations and facilitate the comparison of trade statistics. Article III (b) provided for the creation of a Nomenclature Committee whose functions included the collection of information concerning the application of nomenclature, study of classification procedures and the preparation of explanatory notes on the interpretation and application of nomenclature. The Convention had 52 signatories and was applied by over 150 countries and territories.[66]

This 1950 Convention was superseded by the WCO's International Convention on the Harmonized Commodity Description and Coding System 1983 (hereinafter "HS Convention"), which reflected greater knowledge of the effects of different product classification systems on trade.[67] The HS Convention established a uniform 6-digit multi-purpose nomenclature for their tariff schedules and trade statistics whilst giving countries the freedom to add further sub-divisions in reflection of national requirements.[68] Article 6 of the HS Convention sets up a Harmonized System Committee whose functions are similar to those of the Nomenclature Committee.[69] However, it also prepares recommendations to ensure uniformity in the interpretation and application of the Harmonized System (Art. 7 (c)). As of June 2010, 137 states and the European Union had signed the HS Convention.[70]

Customs Valuation

Art. VII:2 (a) of the GATT lays down fundamental principles for calculating customs value whilst leaving the actual method of customs valuation to the contracting parties. The different methods of customs valuation used by countries can also constitute a significant barrier to trade. For example, GATT members

---

[65] Concluded in Brussels on 15th December, 1950. It entered into force on the 11th September, 1959. See United Nations Treaty Series, Vol. 347, I-4994.

[66] Gottschlich, The World Wide Development of International Customs Law, International Business Law Journal 7 (1988), pp. 947 et seq. (955 et seq.)

[67] Concluded in Brussels on 14th June, 1983. It entered into force on the 1st of January, 1988. See United Nations Treaty Series, Vol. 1503, I-25910.

[68] For example, the Combined Nomenclature of the European Union consists of the 8 digits: the HS nomenclature with 2 additional digits indentifying the CN subheadings. See Regulation (EEC) No. 2658/87, OJ [1987] L 256/1.

[69] The HS Committee is also assisted by a Sub-Committee, which reviews the HS under its general guidance and proposes amendments. See WCO, Terms of Reference for the Harmonized System Review Sub-Committee, Terms of Reference for WCO Working Bodies, August 2010.

[70] A list of signatories is available at the WCO's website: http://www.wcoomd.org/files/1.%20Public%20files/PDFandDocuments/HarmonizedSystem/Countries_applying_HS_Eng_20100626. pdf.

could maximise the taxable value of the goods thereby frustrating the tariff concessions granted during trade rounds.[71]

The first attempt to create an international standard for customs valuation was in the Convention on the Valuation of Goods for Customs Purposes of 1950 which was administered by the Customs Co-operation Council.[72] However, despite having almost 100 signatories, it failed to establish a global standard largely because it was difficult to apply in practice and the USA (the world's largest trading power) declined to adopt it.[73]

The Tokyo Round resulted in a new agreement on customs valuation, namely the Agreement on the Implementation of Article VII. With the creation of the WTO in 1995, the "single package approach" ensured its application by all 153 members thereby establishing a truly global standard for customs valuation. Article 18:2 of the Agreement established a Technical Committee on Customs Valuation at the WCO in order to ensure "at the technical level, uniformity in interpretation and application of this Agreement."[74] This body issues advisory opinions, commentaries and explanatory notes on the valuation of imported goods.[75] Disputes relating to customs valuation are to be settled by the WTO's Dispute Settlement Body with the assistance of the Technical Committee.[76]

Customs valuation remains a highly contentious subject owing to the opposing interests of customs and trade, different methods of valuations, correct definitions of terms[77] and complexities of transactions. For this reason, the instruments of the WCO Technical Committee on Customs Valuation are of great practical importance in realizing the aims of the WTO Customs Valuation Agreement.

---

[71] Art. II of the GATT states: "No contracting party shall alter its method of determining dutiable value or of converting currencies so as to impair the value of any of the concessions provided for in the appropriate Schedule annexed to this Agreement."

[72] Concluded in Brussels on 15th December, 1950. It entered into force on 28th July, 1953. See United Nations Treaty Series Vol. 171, I-2234.

[73] See Witte/Wolffgang (eds.), *Lehrbuch des Europäischen Zollrechts*, (6th ed.) 2009, pp. 377, 378 et seq.

[74] The individual functions of the Technical Committee are listed in paras. 2 (a) – (g), Annex II of the Customs Valuation Agreement 1994.

[75] These are issued in the WCO Customs Value Compendium, which includes the instruments of the WCO Technical Committee on Customs Valuation, an Index of Valuation Rulings and Conclusions from Member administrations. The Compendium is updated annually, available at (subscription only): http://bookshop.wcoomdpublications.org/catalogsearch/result/?q=WCO%20Customs%20Valuation%20Compendium.

[76] See Art. 19 of the WTO Customs Valuation Agreement 1994.

[77] See e.g., Art. 37 of Annex 23 of the Implementing Provisions to the Community Customs Code, under Art. 31(1) no.(2) which requires customs administrations to apply "reasonable flexibility" when applying the valuation methods.

The Simplification of Customs Formalities

The simplification of customs formalities represents another fundamental function of the WCO. The term "customs formalities" refers to "all the operations which must be carried out by the persons concerned and by the Customs in order to comply with the Customs law".[78] There is a wealth of evidence showing that customs formalities have a major impact on trade facilitation, especially with regard to developing countries.[79] Simplifying customs formalities reduces the time taken to transport goods and thereby the costs of import and export[80]; eliminating interruptions to transit also enhances security by reducing the opportunities for corruption and pilfering.

The Revised International Convention on the Simplification and Harmonization of Customs Procedures

In 1973 the Customs Co-operation Council adopted the International Convention on the Simplification and Harmonization of Customs Procedures (the "Kyoto Convention").[81] It aimed to simplify and harmonize the parties' customs procedures with a view to effectively contributing to the development of international trade and of other international exchanges. Although 62 parties had signed the Convention by 2004, it was considered unsatisfactory because parties could select and qualify their obligations and it was quickly overtaken by developments in global trade.

The Kyoto Convention was superseded by the Revised Kyoto Convention ("RKC"), which was adopted in 1999 and entered into force in 2006.[82] It consists of a general annex and 10 specific annexes, the former containing core principles for procedures and practices to be uniformly applied by customs administrations. The provisions improve the transparency and predictability of customs procedures

---

[78] See Chapter 2, General Annex of the Revised International Convention on the Simplification and Harmonization of Customs Procedures.

[79] The need for simplifying formalities is also reflected in Article VIII of the GATT. The importance of this subject for development is underlined by Goal 8: A Global Partnership for Development of the Millenium Goals, which refers *inter alia* to the further development of "an open, rule-based, predictable, non-discriminatory trading and financial system.", available at: http://www.undp.org/mdg/goal8.shtml.

[80] For a statistical overview of these aspects see the World Bank, Doing Business: Trading Across Borders website, which compares data from 183 countries. For example, as of June 2010 the time required for export ranged from five to 80 days and the related cost per container from $ 450 to $3, 280. Statistics available at: http://www.doingbusiness.org/data/exploretopics/trading-across-borders.

[81] Concluded on 25th September, 1974. It entered into force on the 25th September, 1974. See United Nations Treaty Series, Vol. 950, I-13561.

[82] The text of the RKC is available at: http://www.wcoomd.org/Kyoto_New/Content/content.html.

by requiring easy access to customs rules and regulations. Thereby, they accord with Articles V, VIII and X of the GATT.

The RKC differs from its predecessor in two respects: first, it takes account of new developments in international trade (e.g. application of information technology and new philosophies on customs controls) and second, signatories must accept the provisions of the general annex without reservation.[83] This approach ensures a minimum standard of simplification and harmonization. According to the WCO, implementation of the RKC "will provide international commerce with the predictability and efficiency that modern trade requires."[84]

There are currently 72 contracting parties although the WCO anticipates that all members will accede to the Convention.[85] The RKC is administered by a Management Committee which meets annually and recommends updates to the Convention.

The Framework of Standards to Secure and Facilitate Global Trade

As a result of 9/11, the WCO was mandated by world leaders at the G8 Summit 2002 to seek produce a global set of standards to ensure the security of the supply chain.[86] The WCO passed a Resolution in 2004 setting up a High Level Strategic Group to prepare a framework for the facilitation and security of global trade within 12 months.[87]

In accordance with the Resolution, the WCO Council adopted the Framework of Standards to Facilitate and Secure Global Trade in June 2005.[88] The aim of the framework is to create harmonized standards for security and trade facilitation. Developing countries are to be assisted in implementing the security standards through capacity-building measures in conjunction with the Columbus

---

[83] Art. 12(1), (2) and Art. 13(1)-(3) RKC. However, the signatories can choose which provisions of the specific annexes to apply.

[84] See WCO, Revised Kyoto Convention: Your Questions Answered, February 2006, p. 4, available at: http://www.wcoomd.org/files/1.%20Public%20files/PDFandDocuments/Procedures%20and%20Facilitation/kyoto_yourquestionsanswered.pdf.

[85] WCO, Revised Kyoto Convention: Your Questions Answered, February 2006, p. 7.

[86] See Cooperative G8 Action on Transport Security, issued at the Kananaskis Summit, 26th and 27th June, 2002, available at: http://www.canadainternational.gc.ca/g8/summit-sommet/2002/transport_security-securite_transport.aspx?lang=eng.

[87] WCO, Resolution of the Customs and Co-operation Council on Security and Facilitation of the International Supply Chain, June 2004, paragraph A (3), available at: http://www.wcoomd.org/files/1.%20Public%20files/PDFandDocuments/Resolutions/Global_Security-Facilitation_Measures_Int_Trade_Supply_Chain.pdf.

[88] See Resolution of the Customs Co-operation Council on the Framework of Standards to Secure and Facilitate Global Trade, June 2005, available at: http://www.wcoomd.org/files/1.%20Public%20files/PDFandDocuments/Conventions/Framework%20of%20Standards%20to%20Secure%20and%20Facilitate%20Global%20Tra%C3%A2%E2%82%AC%C2%A6.pdf.

Programme.[89] The Framework does not form part of the RKC but facilitates its implementation.[90]

The Framework of Standards also provides for the mutual recognition of security measures. This is very important because security requirements such as advanced submission of cargo data can be very onerous on importers and could potentially constitute a barrier to trade.[91]

The SAFE Framework is administered by the SAFE Working Group. To date, 163 countries have expressed their intention to implement it.[92]

Co-operation with Other International Organizations

Despite its European origins, the Customs Co-operation Council was conceived as a multilateral institution in the field of customs. Article IX of the Founding Convention provides that the Council is to establish relations with the United Nations and other inter-governmental or international organizations. In addition, it may make arrangements necessary to facilitate consultation and co-operation with non-governmental organizations interested in matters within its competence.

Effective co-operation with other international organizations that have links to customs is important in order to achieve a coherent customs policy at international level.[93] The main committee responsible for liaison with international organizations is the PTC, which may "co-operate, promote joint projects, and

---

[89] Resolution of the Customs Co-operation Council on the Framework of Standards to Secure and Facilitate Global Trade, June 2006, p. 3, para. (4), available at: http://www.wcoomd.org/files/1.% 20Public%20files/PDFandDocuments/Enforcement/FSSecure_FGT_062006.pdf. See also WCO, Business Case for the Columbus Programme, July 2008, pp. 12 et seq, available at: http://www. wcoomd.org/files/1.%20Public%20files/PDFandDocuments/Capacity%20Building/columbus/ columbus_pg_bc.pdf.

[90] WCO, Revised Kyoto Convention: Your Questions Answered, February 2006, p. 9.

[91] For an investigation of the economic impacts of US supply chain security see generally Carluer, *Global Logistic Chain Security: Economic Impacts of the US 100% Container Scanning Law*, 2008.

[92] A list of the countries that have expressed such an intention is available at the WCO website: http://www.wcoomd.org/files/1.%20Public%20files/PDFandDocuments/Enforcement/ FOS_bil_04.pdf.

[93] Concerning the topic of coherence, see Art. II:5 of the WTO Agreement and the Ministerial Declaration on the Contribution of the World Trade Organization to Achieving Greater Coherence in Global Economic Policymaking, available at: http://www.wto.org/english/docs_e/legal_e/32-dchor_e.htm. The WTO has stated that the concept of "coherence" in the latter document extends beyond co-operation with the IMF and World Bank to embrace co-operation with other international organizations.

share information and experiences with international, governmental and non-governmental organizations."[94]

The following provides examples of co-operation with the WTO, the United Nations and the World Bank as well as other organizations.[95]

Examples of International Co-operation

There has been a long co-operation between the WCO and WTO and its predecessor in the fields of customs valuation, nomenclature and trade facilitation, with the latter[96] becoming an increasingly important area of co-operation between the two organizations.[97] The WTO negotiations on trade facilitation focus on Articles V, VII and X which directly affect customs matters. Therefore, it is important to avoid conflicts and duplications with the international standards of the RKC. It is expected that the WTO will deal with higher level aspects, leaving implementation to the WCO.[98]

The WCO co-operates with a large number of UN agencies[99] including the United Nations Economic Commission for Europe in relation to data exchange. The WCO also co-operates with the United Nations Conference on Trade and Development (UNCTAD) in the field of trade facilitation.[100] It also collaborates with

---

[94] See WCO, Terms of Reference for the Permanent Technical Committee, para. 5, Terms of Reference for WCO Working Bodies, August 2010.

[95] See the comments of Clarke, Report of the Capacity Building Committee, Document No. HC0008E1a, 22nd November, 2010, p. 10, para. 74 referring to postal, telecommunications, tourism institutions, UNICEF, UNCTAD, WTO, World Bank, International Monetary Fund, UNODC and more as having links with customs.

[96] Doha Work Programme: Decision adopted by the WTO General Council on 1st August, 2004, WT/L/579, 2nd August, 2004, expressly states that the work of the WCO in this area is to be taken into account.

[97] Concerning the framework of WTO negotiations on trade facilitation see Doha Work Programme, Annex D Modalities for Negotiations on Trade Facilitation, WT/L/579, 2nd August, 2004.

[98] See Lux/Malone, A Place for Customs in the WTO: A Practical Look at the Doha Facilitation Negotiations, Global Trade and Customs Journal 1 (2006) 1, pp. 39 et seq. (39, 42–43, 47), concerning the role of the RKC. The authors point out that the advantage of such an agreement would be that it is legally binding and enforceable under WTO rules.

[99] A list of co-operations with UN agencies can be viewed at: http://www.wcoomd.org/home_pfoverviewboxes_international_cooperation_pfunagencies.htm.

[100] See the comments of Clarke, Report of the Capacity Building Committee, Document No. HC0008E1a, 22nd November 2010, p. 9, para. 65 and p. 10, para. 74, underlining the important role of customs in the realization of the UN Millenium Goals and pointing out room for greater collaboration.

other international organizations in implementing the UN's global anti-terrorism strategy.[101]

The World Bank has supported many projects relating to customs reform and modernization over the past 20 years[102] and has set up the Customs and Border Management Practice group, which advises on customs and trade matters.[103] It has entered into a number of joint projects with the WCO concerning customs modernization projects.[104]

In the field of education and training, the WCO has established a long-standing co-operation with the International Network of Customs Universities. The two organizations have produced the PICARD Professional Standards for customs senior and middle management which are being used by universities and other educational establishments in their customs programmes.[105] Further collaboration between the two organizations includes the annual PICARD conference and the World Customs Journal.[106]

Certain projects of the WCO involve co-operation with several international organizations. Examples include the Harmonized System, which was developed with the UN Statistical Division, the WTO and the International Chambers of Commerce; the Framework of Standards which incorporates the standards of other international organizations[107] and needs assessments for capacity building, which are conducted by the WTO, World Bank and WCO.[108] In addition, the WCO is a prime mover in the fight against counterfeiting and piracy and collaborates with

---

[101] E.g., the International Maritime Organization and the International Civil Aviation Organization (ICAO): see WCO News, No. 53, June 2007, pp. 31–32, available at: http://wcoomdpublications. org/downloadable/download/sample/sample_id/17/.

[102] See Engelschalk/Le, Two Decades of World Bank Lending for Customs Reform: Trends in Project Design, Project Implementation and Lessons Learned, in: de Wulf/Sokol (eds.), *Customs Modernization Handbook*, 2005, pp. 128 et seq., available at: http://siteresources.worldbank.org/ INTEXPCOMNET/Resources/Customs_Modernization_Handbook.pdf.

[103] The webpage of the Group is available at: http://go.worldbank.org/8R9I8R6KJ0.

[104] See e.g., WCO Press Release, World Bank and WCO agree to launch major Customs capacity building initiative, 18th October, 2010, available at: http://www.wcoomd.org/press/? v=1&lid=1&cid=7&id=234.

[105] See Introduction to the WCO's PICARD Professional Standards, available at: http://incu.org/ PICARD_standards.html.

[106] The World Customs Journal and information on the annual PICARD conference is available at: http://www.incu.org.

[107] See WCO SAFE Framework of Standards, 2007, p. 37, para. 5.2. Referring to the security requirements and standards set by e.g. the International Maritime Organization (IMO), UN Economic Commission for Europe (UNECE), and International Civil Aviation Organization (ICAO).

[108] See generally, WCO News, No. 54, October 2007, p. 46, available at: http://wcoomdpublications. org/downloadable/download/sample/sample_id/18/.

other international organizations in this field through the Global Congress Steering Group.[109]

Conclusion

It has been said that customs is as old as trade itself[110] and admittedly this contribution has barely scratched the surface of this historical profession. Nevertheless, it is possible to draw the following general conclusions about customs and the WCO on the basis of this overview.

Concerning customs generally, the following statements can be made:

- It is a general principle that a state's economic prosperity depends on its ability to participate in international trade.[111]
- Customs is of *fundamental importance* to international trade because international trade takes place *subject to* customs regulations.[112]
- Customs has been largely harmonized through legally-binding conventions. However, exceptionally, customs administrations can still act unilaterally to protect the state's national security interests.
- The primary role of all customs administrations in the twenty-first century is to facilitate trade whilst safeguarding national security.[113]
- Customs administrations must respond to the conditions of international trade. As a result, its operations and fields of activities are constantly expanding.

As the only international organization specializing in customs matters, the World Customs Organization:

- is a major source of harmonized standards for international trade. Examples include the HS Convention, the RKC and the Framework of Standards.

---

[109] The group consists of the WCO, the International Criminal Police Organization (INTERPOL), the World Intellectual Property Organization (WIPO), the International Chamber of Commerce (ICC) and the International Trademark Association (INTA). See website at: http://www.ccapcongress.net/steering%20group.htm.

[110] See Asakura, *World History of the Customs and Tariffs*, 2002, p. 11.

[111] See de Wulf, Strategy for Customs Modernization, in: de Wulf/Sokol (eds.), *Customs Modernization Handbook*, 2005, p. 3, available at: http://siteresources.worldbank.org/INTEXPCOMNET/Resources/Customs_Modernization_Handbook.pdf.

[112] For example, the INCO terms governing the seller's obligations with regard to the delivery of the goods are a major part of any international sales contract. The data transmission requirements of the United States also require consideration by the contractual parties.

[113] See WCO, Customs in the 21st Century, Enhancing Growth and Development through Trade Facilitation and Border Security, June 2008, Annex II to Doc. No. SC0090 E1a, p. 2, para. 1 (referring to the demands for "effective security and control of international supply chains" and "greater facilitation of trade" as "contradictory").

- is a prime-mover of customs-related initiatives at international level. This can be seen in relation to supply chain security and the enforcement of intellectual property rights.
- adopts a member-driven organization which sets standards and helps its members implement them. This can be seen from the Columbus Programme to implement the Framework of Standards and the PICARD programme for the training of customs managers.
- largely consists of DCs and LDCs. Capacity development therefore plays a major role in its activities. This can be seen from the creation of the Capacity Building Committee in 2010.
- co-operates closely with other international organizations in creating a coherent policy for international trade. In this respect, it is playing an important role in the negotiations of a trade facilitation agreement at the WTO.

Each year on the 26th of January, the WCO celebrates the International Customs Day to signify the first official meeting of the Customs Co-operation Council. According to tradition, the Secretary-General of the WCO chooses a theme for the year. For 2011, Kunio Mikuriya has chosen the theme "Knowledge, a catalyst for Customs excellence" in recognition of the fact that "in our changing world, knowledge is a critical resource".[114] It is the authors' hope that these contributions will promote awareness within the academic community of the immense impact that customs has on international trade.[115]

---

[114] Speech by Kunio Mikuriya, Secretary General, WCO, 26th January, 2011, available at: http://www.wcoomd.org/speeches/default.aspx?lid=1&id=250.

[115] The World Customs Journal published by the International Network of Customs Universities under the auspices of the World Customs Organization: www.incu.org. The Department of Customs and Excise at the University of Münster under the directorship of Prof. Dr. Hans-Michael Wolffgang, also runs the Master of Customs Administration (MCA), a customs-specific postgraduate course: http://www.uni-muenster-mca.de.

Recent Reforms of the Finances of the International Monetary Fund: An Overview

Bernhard Steinki and Wolfgang Bergthaler

Introduction

Under its charter,[1] the International Monetary Fund (the "IMF") – with its near universal membership of 187 countries – is charged with "oversee[ing] the international monetary system.[2]" One of its key purposes is "to give confidence to members by making the general resources of the Fund temporarily available to them under adequate safeguards, thus providing them with opportunity to correct

---

The views expressed herein are those of the authors and should not be attributed to the IMF, its Executive Board, or IMF management. This chapter reflects the status as of April 2011.

[1] The IMF's charter is the IMF's Articles of Agreement (the "IMF's Articles"), which were adopted at the United Nations Monetary and Financial Conference, Bretton Woods, New Hampshire, 22nd July, 1944 and entered into force on 27th December, 1945. The IMF's Articles were amended effective 28th July, 1969, by the modifications approved by the Board of Governors in Resolution No. 23–5, adopted 31st May, 1968 ("First Amendment"); amended effective 1st April, 1978, by the modifications approved by the Board of Governors in Resolution No. 31–4, adopted 30th April, 1976 ("Second Amendment"); amended effective 11th November, 1992, by the modifications approved by the Board of Governors in Resolution No. 45–3, adopted 28th June, 1990 ("Third Amendment"); amended effective 10th August, 2009, by the modifications approved by the Board of Governors in Resolution No. 52–4, adopted 23rd September, 1997 ("Fourth Amendment"); amended effective 18th February, 2011 by the modifications approved by the Board of Governors in Resolution No. 63–3, adopted 5th May, 2008 ("Fifth Amendment"); and amended effective 3rd March, 2011 by the modifications approved by the Board of Governors in Resolution No. 63–2, adopted 28th April, 2008 ("Sixth Amendment"). The IMF's Articles are available at: http://www.imf.org/external/pubs/ft/aa/index.htm.

[2] See: Art. IV, Sec. 1 and 3(a) of the IMF's Articles of Agreement.

B. Steinki (✉) • W. Bergthaler
Legal Department, International Monetary Fund, 700 19th Street NW, Washington, DC 20431, USA
e-mail: bsteinki@imf.org; wbergthaler@imf.org

C. Herrmann and J.P. Terhechte (eds.), *European Yearbook of International Economic Law (EYIEL), Vol. 3 (2012)*, European Yearbook of International Economic Law 3, DOI 10.1007/978-3-642-23309-8_20, © Springer-Verlag Berlin Heidelberg 2012

maladjustments in their balance of payments without resorting to measures destructive of national or international prosperity."[3]

The primary source for IMF lending is the quota subscriptions of its members, which are held in the General Resources Account ("GRA") of the General Department of the IMF. Quota resources can be supplemented by borrowing. A secondary and separate source of financing for IMF members is the Special Drawing Rights ("SDR") Department, which administers the special drawing rights, a reserve asset created by the IMF in 1969. Third, the IMF administers contributor resources for the benefit of low income members on concessional terms (in particular, the Poverty Reduction and Growth Trust ("PRGT")). As a financial institution, the IMF covers its administrative expenses from its own resources and operations; it does not receive annual budget contributions from its members.

Two developments in recent years revealed the need for reforms in the finances of the IMF. The sharp decline in outstanding IMF lending from 2003 to 2007 pointed to weaknesses in its income model, as generating income to defray the IMF's administrative expenses was not sustainable in a low-lending environment without the IMF incurring losses. The IMF's response was the endorsement of a new income model in April 2008, which has been implemented since. The global financial crises that started in the fall of 2008 exposed the second challenge in the IMF's finances, namely the need to considerably increase the IMF's financing capacity for it to be in a position to meet the financing needs of its members. With the decisive backing of its membership, the IMF responded with the adoption and implementation of a comprehensive set of measures to increase the IMF's financing capacity.

This chapter summarizes the measures taken by the IMF to reform its income model and to improve its financing capacity.[4] It also touches on related developments, in particular IMF governance reform, which is inextricably linked to the financing reform through the link of quota share and voting power in the IMF, and the reform of the IMF financing facilities, i.e., the modalities through which the IMF provides financing to its members, which also influence the size of the IMF.

---

[3] Art. I(v) of the IMF's Articles.

[4] It may be helpful to briefly describe the IMF's organs to better understand the IMF's decision making process: The highest decision-making body of the IMF is the Board of Governors, consisting of one Governor per member (i.e. currently 187 Governors). Responsible for conducting the business of the IMF is the Executive Board, consisting of 24 Executive Directors, which also exercises all the powers delegated to it by the Board of Governors. The Managing Director conducts, under the direction of the Executive Board, the ordinary business of the IMF. See, Art. XII of the IMF's Articles. The International Monetary and Financial Committee (IMFC) is an advisory committee of the Board of Governors at ministerial level that reflects in its composition the Executive Board. See for more background: Gianviti, Decision Making in the International Monetary Fund, in: *Current Developments in Monetary and Financial Law, Volume 1*, 1999, pp. 31–67.

A New Income Model

The need for a new income model became obvious following the sharp drop in outstanding IMF credit from 2003 onwards.[5] The resulting loss in lending income meant that without additional income sources or significant cuts in its administrative expenses, the IMF would run the risk of losses (which indeed materialized in FY 2008[6]).

Under the old income model, the setting of the margin for the basic rate of charge (i.e., the IMF's interest rate) on outstanding financing from the IMF was the main tool to generate the income needed to cover the IMF's administrative expenses. The basic rate of charge consists of the SDR interest rate, which corresponds to the refinancing cost of the IMF,[7] plus a margin, expressed in basis points, that is added to the SDR interest rate. Taking into account the IMF's other, non-lending income sources, the margin was calculated to generate sufficient income to cover both the administrative expenses of the IMF and to generate a targeted amount of net income that could be placed to reserves. With decreasing levels of IMF lending in the years before the 2008 global financial crises, this system became unsustainable as its continued application would have resulted in excessively high IMF interest rates.

Not only was the old income model unsustainable in a low credit environment, it was also considered unfair as it placed the financial burden of funding the various activities of the institution (i.e., lending and non-lending activities) primarily on its borrowing members, which in a situation of highly concentrated IMF credit meant that effectively a few members were bearing the costs for all IMF activities.

The IMF has additional income sources besides lending. In particular, it has the authority to transfer currencies from the GRA equivalent to its reserves to the IMF's Investment Account ("IA")[8] as a means for the IMF to generate income to meet its administrative expenses. The IA was established and funded in 2006 as part of the IMF's response to its income problem.[9] The investment authority of the IA,

---

[5] Outstanding IMF credit decreased from its historical peak in September 2003 at SDR 70 billion to just about SDR 5.8 billion in March 2008. As of end February 2011, IMF outstanding credit again amounted to about SDR 61.4 billion. Information on total IMF Credit Outstanding for all IMF members from 1984–2011 is available at: http://www.imf.org/external/np/fin/tad/extcred1.aspx; see also a historical overview of IMF credit outstanding since 1947 at: http://www.imf.org/external/about/lending.htm.

[6] Press Release No. 07/82, IMF Executive Board Reviews Fund's Income Position and Leaves Rate of Charge Unchanged for FY 2008, available at: http://www.imf.org/external/np/sec/pr/2007/pr0782.htm. IMF, Review of the Fund's Income Position for FY 2008 and FY 2009, 2008, available at: www.imf.org/external/np/pp/eng/2008/041408.pdf.

[7] The rate of remuneration the IMF pays to members whose quota subscription payments it uses for its financing operations shall be not more than, nor less than four-fifths of, the SDR interest rate; see Art. V, Sec. 9(b) IMF's Articles.

[8] See: Art. XII, Sec. 6(f) of the IMF's Articles.

[9] IMF, Establishment of the Investment Account, 2006, available at: www.imf.org/external/np/pp/eng/2006/041406i.pdf; Press Release No. 06/90, IMF Executive Board Reviews Fund's Income

however, was limited to marketable obligations of members and international financial organizations, thereby constraining the amount of income that could be generated from investment activities.[10] Moreover, the size of the IA was too small to generate, even under an expanded investment authority, the income needed to fund the IMF's administrative expenses in a sustainable way.

The Endorsement of a New Income Model

In April 2008, the IMF Executive Board endorsed a new income model. It was the outcome of a 2-year process that had started in May 2006 with the establishment of the Committee of Eminent Persons to Study Sustainable Long-Term Financing of the IMF Running Cost (the "Committee").[11] The new income model[12] has the following key components:[13]

– A separate "endowment portfolio" in the IA funded with the profits from the limited sale of 403.3 metric tons of the IMF's gold holdings to increase the contribution of investment income to the administrative expenses of the IMF.
– An expansion of the IMF's investment authority through an amendment of the IMF's Articles to broaden the range of instruments in which the IMF may invest. Such an expansion of the IMF's investment authority would enable the IMF to

---

Position, Sets Rate of Charge for FY 2007 and Approves Establishment of an Investment Account, available at: http://www.imf.org/external/np/sec/pr/2006/pr0690.htm. The IMF had the authority to establish the IA since the entry into force of the Second Amendment but only exercised it in 2006.

[10] Former Art. XII, Sec. 6(f)(iii) of the IMF's Articles prior to the Fifth Amendment in the context of the new income model.

[11] The Committee was chaired by Andrew Crockett, and included Mohamed A. El-Erian, Alan Greenspan, Tito Mboweni, Guillermo Ortiz, Hamad Al-Sayari, Jean-Claude Trichet, and Zhou Xiaochuan.

[12] See: Report of the Managing Director to the International Monetary and Financial Committee on a New Income and Expenditure Framework for the International Monetary Fund, 2008, available at: www.imf.org/external/np/pp/eng/2008/040908b.pdf. Press Release No. 08/74, IMF Managing Director Strauss-Kahn Applauds Executive Board's Landmark Agreement on Fund's New Income and Expenditure Framework, available at: http://www.imf.org/external/np/sec/pr/2008/pr0874. htm; Press Release No. 08/101, IMF Board of Governors Approves Key Element of IMF's New Income Model, available at: http://www.imf.org/external/np/sec/pr/2008/pr08101.htm.

[13] The Committee made two additional proposals: (i) it proposed an amendment to the country contribution policy for the IMF's capacity building activities (i.e., technical assistance and training). While the IMF developed and implemented this amendment to the country contribution policy for technical assistance and training, its application for IMF technical assistance has been delayed and for IMF training has been suspended since January 2010; see: IMF Country Contribution Policy for Capacity Building, available at: http://www.imf.org/external/np/ta/2008/ capacity.htm. (ii) the Committee also proposed the investment of quota resources; this proposal did not receive the necessary support by the membership to make it a viable component of the new income model.

generate higher investment income and to adapt its investment strategy over time without the need for further amendments of the IMF's Articles.

- A new framework for setting the margin for the rate of charge, which should cover the IMF's intermediation costs and the build-up of reserves.
- Resumption of the reimbursement of the GRA for the administrative expenses of the PRGT[14] (i.e., the IMF's main lending vehicle for lending to low-income countries) in the financial year in which the IMF adopts a decision authorizing the gold sales, with the safeguard that the IMF should temporarily suspend reimbursement if the resources of the PRGT are likely to be insufficient to support anticipated demand for PRGT assistance and the is unable to obtain additional subsidy resources.

Implementation of the New Income Model

Amendment of the IMF's Articles (the Fifth Amendment)

Implementing the new income model included an amendment to the IMF's Articles, (i) to expand the investment authority of the IA and (ii) to facilitate the transfer of all profits from the agreed sale of gold to the IA to fund the endowment.[15] The IMF Board of Governors approved an amendment of the IMF's Articles to implement these changes on May 5, 2008.[16] The amendment entered into force on February 18, 2011 after the requisite majorities of the IMF membership[17] had accepted the

---

[14] Under the PRGT framework, in principle, the GRA is reimbursed from the PRGT's Reserve Account for the expenses incurred by the IMF in the administration of the PRGT. Reimbursement has been often suspended leading to a negative impact on GRA income. See Decision No. 8760-(87/176), 18th December, 1987, as amended at IMF, Selected Decisions and Selected Documents of the International Monetary Fund, 34th issue, 2010, p. 462, available at: http://www.imf.org/external/pubs/ft/sd/index.asp?decision=8760-(87/176).

[15] The IMF's Articles normally limit the amount of currencies that can be transferred from the GRA to the IA to the total amount of its general and special reserve at the time of the transfer; see: Art. XII, Sec. 5(f)(ii) of the IMF's Articles. To ensure that all gold profits can be transferred to the IA to fund the endowment, irrespective of the level of the IMF's reserves, an amendment to Art. XII, Sec. 5(f)(ii) of the IMF's Articles was required.

[16] Board of Governors Resolution No. 63–3 effective 5th May, 2008, available at: http://www.imf.org/external/pubs/ft/sd/index.asp?decision=63-3; IMF, Report of the Managing Director to the International Monetary and Financial Committee on a New Income and Expenditure Framework for the International Monetary Fund, 2008, available at: www.imf.org/external/np/pp/eng/2008/040908b.pdf. Press Release No. 08/101, IMF Board of Governors Approves Key Element of IMF's New Income Model, available at: http://www.imf.org/external/np/sec/pr/2008/pr08101.htm.

[17] In accordance with Art. XXVIII(a) of the IMF's Articles, once the IMF certifies by formal communication that 3/5 of IMF members having 85% of the total voting power have accepted a proposed amendment, an amendment enters into force for all IMF members. See for further detail: Acceptances of the Proposed Amendments of the Articles of Agreement, available at: http://www.imf.org/external/np/sec/misc/consents.htm#a2.

amendment.[18] The expansion of the IMF's investment authority enables the IMF Executive Board (with a 70% majority of the total voting power) to adapt its investment strategy over time without the need for further amendments to the IMF's Articles. The new rules and regulations for investment are currently in preparation and the IMF Executive Board is expected to adopt them in the coming months.

Gold Sales

In September of 2009 the IMF took the decision to sell all its gold holdings acquired after the Second Amendment, a total of 403.3 metric tons or about one-eighth of the IMF's total gold holdings.[19] The decision required an 85% majority of the total voting power, and became possible after the U.S. Congress had authorized the Executive Director for the U.S. (who exercises over 16% of the IMF's total voting power) to vote in favor of the gold sales.[20] The gold sales took place from October 2009 through December 2010. In the first months, sales were limited to official sector buyers, and a total of 212 metric tons of gold was sold during this period.[21] On-market sales started in February 2010 and were completed by December of 2010.[22] Following the entry into force of the Fifth Amendment on February 18, 2011, consistent with the provisions of the amendment, the profits of the gold sales were transferred to the IA while the book value of the gold is retained in the GRA. The bulk of the profits are expected to be used consistent with the new income model to fund an endowment to generate income for the administrative expenses of the IMF.

As gold profits, however, were higher than assumed in 2008 when the new income model was adopted, agreement was reached in July 2009 in the context of discussions to finance assistance to low-income countries members that up to

---

[18] Press Release No. 11/52, IMF's Broader Investment Mandate Takes Effect, available at: http://www.imf.org/external/np/sec/pr/2011/pr1152.htm.

[19] Press Release No. 09/310, IMF Executive Board Approves Limited Sales of Gold to Finance the Fund's New Income Model and to Boost Concessional Lending Capacity, available at: http://www.imf.org/external/np/sec/pr/2009/pr09310.htm.

[20] IMF, U.S. Congress Vote Marks Big Step For IMF Reform, Funding, 2009, available at: http://www.imf.org/external/pubs/ft/survey/so/2009/new061809a.htm.

[21] Press Release No. 10/44, IMF to Begin On-Market Sales of Gold, available at: http://www.imf.org/external/np/sec/pr/2010/pr1044.htm; Press Release No. 09/381, IMF Announces Sale of 200 metric tons of Gold to the Reserve Bank of India, available at: http://www.imf.org/external/np/sec/pr/2009/pr09381.htm; Press Release No. 09/413, IMF Announces Sale of 2 Metric Tons of Gold to the Bank of Mauritius, available at http://www.imf.org/external/np/sec/pr/2009/pr09413.htm; Press Release No. 09/431, IMF Announces Sale of 10 Metric Tons of Gold to the Central Bank of Sri Lanka, available at: http://www.imf.org/external/np/sec/pr/2009/pr09431.htm.

[22] Press Release No. 10/509, IMF Concludes Gold Sales, available at: http://www.imf.org/external/np/sec/pr/2010/pr10509.htm.

SDR 0.7 billion of the profits would be made available for subsidy contributions to the IMF's main Trust for low income countries ("LICs") financing, the PRGT.[23] In April 2011, the IMF Executive Board held a preliminary discussion on the use of the remaining windfall profits from the IMF's gold sales.[24]

New Rules for Setting the Margin for Basic Rate of Charge and PRGT Reimbursement

As an immediate response to its income problem, the rule for setting the margin was amended in 2006 with effect for FY 2007 by allowing, in exceptional circumstances, for flexibility in setting the rate of charge in an environment of projected income shortfalls.[25] Since the endorsement of the new income model in 2008, the IMF has relied on the exceptional circumstance clause in its rule for setting the margin for the rate of charge[26] for FY2009–2011 but it has been guided by the principles of the new framework, namely that the margin should be set in such a way that it covers the intermediation cost for IMF financing and the build-up of precautionary balances.[27] A new rule for setting the margin is expected to be adopted in the coming months.

As regards the reimbursement of the GRA for the administration of the PRGT, it was decided in 2009 – as part of the LIC financing package – that the suspension of the reimbursement will continue until FY 2012, in view of the insufficient subsidy resources in the PRGT to support anticipated demand.[28]

---

[23] PIN No. 09/94, IMF Reforms Financial Facilities for Low-Income Countries, available at: http://www.imf.org/external/np/sec/pn/2009/pn0994.htm. Press Release No. 09/268, IMF Announces Unprecedented Increase in Financial Support to Low-Income Countries, available at: http://www.imf.org/external/np/sec/pr/2009/pr09268.htm. See also section on Increasing the IMF Financing Capacity For Its Low-Income Members below.

[24] IMF, Use of Gold Sale Profits – Initial Considerations and Options, 2011, available at: http://www.imf.org/external/np/pp/eng/2011/031611.pdf; PIN No. 11/48, IMF Executive Board Considers Use of Gold Sale Profits, available at: http://www.imf.org/external/np/sec/pn/2011/pn1148.htm.

[25] Specifically, see Rule I-6(4) of the IMF's Rules and Regulations. IMF, Review of the Fund's Income Position for FY2006 and FY2007, 2006, available at: www.imf.org/external/np/pp/eng/2006/041206.pdf; Press Release No. 06/90, IMF Executive Board Reviews Fund's Income Position, Sets Rate of Charge for FY 2007 and Approves Establishment of an Investment Account, available at: http://www.imf.org/external/np/sec/pr/2006/pr0690.htm.

[26] See Rule I-6(4) of the IMF's Rules and Regulations.

[27] IMF, The Fund's Income Position for FY 2010 – Midyear Review, 2009, available at: www.imf.org/external/np/pp/eng/2009/120709.pdf.

[28] See PIN No. 09/94, IMF Reforms Financial Facilities for Low-Income Countries, available at: http://www.imf.org/external/np/sec/pn/2009/pn0994.htm.

Conclusion

While the IMF's immediate income situation has improved significantly with the increased lending in response to the global financial crisis, the new income model provides the IMF with a much improved long-term income framework, in particular when outstanding lending decreases to more normal pre-crisis levels. The successful completion of the gold sales program has provided the IMF with an important new source of income from the investment of the profits under the IMF's expanded investment authority.

Increasing the Financing Capacity of the IMF

Prior to the outbreak of the global financial crisis in the fall of 2008, the IMF's outstanding lending was very low and conversely IMF liquidity looked more than comfortable.[29] The Thirteenth General Review of Quotas was completed in January 2008 with no proposed increase in members' quotas.[30] Only a few months later, the global financial crisis changed the landscape completely and the IMF was suddenly confronted with unprecedented demand for its financing.[31]

In principle, an increase in the IMF's financing capacity can be achieved in two ways: Either by an increase in the IMF members' quotas (i.e., the IMF's own resources) or through borrowing by the IMF. In addressing the challenge, the IMF adopted a multi-pronged and sequenced strategy, including both borrowing and a general quota increase.

Following the recommendations of the Heads of State and Government of the Group of Twenty Industrialized and Emerging Market Economies ("G-20") at their meeting in London in April 2009,[32] the International Monetary and Financial Committee ("IMFC"), the ministerial level advisory body of the IMF, endorsed the following measures[33]:

---

[29] At end-September 2008, prior to any crises related GRA lending, lendable IMF resources stood at about US$255 billion (see below).

[30] See Board of Governors Resolution No. 63–1 effective 28th January, 2010 in: IMF, Selected Decisions and Selected Documents of the International Monetary Fund, 34th issue, 2010, p. 17, available at: http://www.imf.org/external/pubs/ft/sd/index.asp?decision=63-1.

[31] See IMF Lending arrangements for IMF members as of March 31, 2011 at: http://www.imf.org/external/np/fin/tad/extarr11.aspx?memberKey1=ZZZZ&date1key=2020-02-28. See the world map of IMF lending at http://www.imf.org/external/np/exr/map/lending/index.htm.

[32] Communiqué of the Heads of State and Government of the Group of Twenty Industrialized and Emerging Market Economies, The Global Plan for Recovery and Reform, 2nd April, 2009, available at: http://www.g20.org/Documents/final-communique.pdf.

[33] Communiqué of the International Monetary and Financial Committee of the Board of Governors of the International Monetary Fund, 25th April, 2009, see: http://www.imf.org/external/np/sec/pr/2009/pr09139.htm.

– Immediate IMF borrowing from members or their institutions of US\$250 billion.
– An expansion of the New Arrangements to Borrow ("NAB"), the IMF's standing credit facility, by up to US\$500 billion, into which the bilateral borrowing would be incorporated.
– Advancement of the Fourteenth General Review of Quotas by 2 years.
– A general SDR allocation equivalent to US\$250 billion.[34]

The bilateral borrowing agreements ensured immediate additional liquidity. The expansion of the NAB required more time as it needed to be negotiated with the then 26 participants and 13 new participants and required high majorities of participants' consent to become effective. The general SDR allocation could also be implemented with little delay while quota reform was the most complex challenge as it involved sensitive discussions on the relative voting power of members in the IMF. The general quota increase was inextricably linked to a longstanding governance reform debate in the IMF that is dominated by the issue of adequate representation of members in the IMF and could therefore only be solved as a package of quota and governance reform.

Basic Financial Structure of the IMF and Its Financing Capacity

The primary source for IMF financing is the quota subscription payments of members held in the GRA. Each IMF member is assigned a quota expressed in SDRs, the IMF's unit of account.[35] Total approved quotas currently amount to SDR 238.4 billion.[36] The quotas of individual members range from SDR 42.1 billion in the case of the United States, the IMF member with the largest quota, to SDR 1.8 million in the case of Tuvalu, the IMF's member with the smallest quota.[37]

Members normally pay 75% of their quota subscription in their own currency and the rest in the currency of other members specified by the IMF or in SDRs.[38] Balances of a member's currency are held by the IMF with the central bank of the

---

[34] See more below under the General and Special SDR Allocations.

[35] Art. III, Sec. 1 of the IMF's Articles. Quotas are subject to periodic reviews, at least every five years, but can also be changed on an ad-hoc basis (Art. III, Sec. 2 of the IMF's Articles). Any change in quotas must be adopted by the Board of Governors with an 85% majority of the total voting power.

[36] Following the entry into force of the Sixth Amendment on 3rd March, 2011, ad hoc quota increases for 54 eligible members under the 2008 quota and voice reform will become effective, once those members have consented to, and paid for, their increases. See Reform of IMF Quotas and Voices, available at: http://www.imf.org/external/np/exr/ib/2008/040108.htm.

[37] For individual IMF member country quota information, see: http://www.imf.org/external/np/sec/memdir/members.htm.

[38] Art. III, Sec. 3(a) of the IMF's Articles.

members, the so-called designated depository.[39] In place of any part of the member's currency not needed for IMF operations and transactions, the IMF accepts non-negotiable and non-interest bearing promissory notes, subject to maintaining minimum cash balance of one-quarter of 1% of quota.[40]

The GRA Financing Mechanism

The IMF uses quota resources for its financing operations as follows: A member requesting IMF financing purchases the currency of another member in exchange for its own currency. As a result, the IMF's holdings of the currency of the member receiving IMF financing increases while the IMF's holdings of the currency of the member whose currency is sold decrease.

A member whose currency is sold by the IMF and whose currency is not a freely usable currency[41] is obliged, at the request of the purchasing member, to convert its currency into a freely usable currency of its choice.[42] This conversion obligation is imposed by the IMF's Articles because the purchasing member is normally in need of currencies that it can effectively use for international payments. Therefore, for IMF financing to be effective, the purchasing IMF member is given the right to request a freely usable currency. As not all IMF members are in a position to exchange their currency into a freely usable currency because of their balance of payments and reserve position, the IMF only draws on those members for its GRA financing transactions that are in a strong balance of payments and reserve position.[43] These members are included in the so-called Financial Transactions Plan ("FTP"), which is normally established quarterly and identifies the maximum amount of use of a member's currency by the IMF in its GRA lending and

---

[39] Art. XIII, Sec. 2(a) of the IMF's Articles provides: "(a) Each member shall designate its central bank as a depository for all the IMF's holdings of its currency, or if it has no central bank it shall designate such other institution as may be acceptable to the Fund." In addition, Art. V, Sec. 1 of the IMF's Articles stipulates that "Each member shall deal with the IMF only through its Treasury, central bank, stabilization fund, or other similar fiscal agency, and the IMF shall deal only with or through the same agencies." When a country joins the IMF it designates the fiscal agency for its dealings with the IMF.

[40] Art. III, Sec. 4 of the IMF's Articles and Rule E-1 of the IMF's Rules and Regulations.

[41] Art. XXX(f) of the IMF's Articles defines the term "freely usable currency" as follows: "A freely usable currency means a member's currency that the IMF determines (i) is, in fact, widely used to make payments and transfers for international transactions, and (ii) is widely traded in the principal exchange markets. Currently, the euro, Japanese yen, pound sterling and the U.S. dollar are considered freely usable currencies. See Executive Board Decision No. 11857-(98/130), 17th December, 1998, see: IMF, Selected Decisions and Selected Documents of the International Monetary Fund, 34th issue, 2010, p. 782.

[42] Art. V, Sec. 3(e)(i) and (ii) of the IMF's Articles.

[43] Art. V, Sec. 3(d) of the IMF's Articles.

repayment operations during the plan period.[44] FTP members have standing arrangements with the IMF under which they have indicated which freely usable currency they are willing to provide in purchase transactions of their currencies.

The member whose currency is sold by the IMF establishes a liquid (remunerated) creditor position in the GRA for the amount by which the IMF's holdings of its currency are below the member's quota ("reserve tranche position").[45] Conversely, the purchasing member who provides its own currency establishes a debtor position for the amount of the purchase, which is subject to interest ("charges" in the IMF's terminology).[46] The IMF's currency holdings in the GRA are maintained in terms of the SDR. This implies that if a member's currency appreciates vis-à-vis the SDR, the currency holdings are adjusted downward while up-ward adjustments are required if a member's currency depreciates vis-a-vis the SDR. Such adjustments arise at the time of use of a member's currency in an operation or transaction between the IMF and another member and at the end of the IMF's financial year (end-April), at which time resulting payments from or to the IMF are made, or at such other times as the IMF may decide or the member may request.[47] The maintenance of value rule implies a de facto SDR denomination of members' creditor and debtor position in the GRA.

When members repay their IMF credit, the reverse transactions take place as follows: A debtor member repurchases the IMF's holdings of its currency with balances of another member's currency specified by the IMF. The effect is that the IMF's holdings of the debtor member's currency subject to charges are reduced while the holdings of the member's currency with whose currency the repurchase was made are increased, thus reducing the remunerated reserve tranche position of that member by the amount of the repurchase.

The repurchasing member can effectively repay the IMF with a freely usable currency as the member whose currency is selected for repurchase, is under the obligation to accept a freely usable currency of its choice and convert it into its own currency for credit to the IMF's account with the designated depository of the member.[48] As a practical matter, most IMF members who participate in the FTP provide and receive US dollar and euro in purchase and repurchase transactions but the conversions take place outside of the IMF's accounts.

---

[44] Currently there are 52 members on the Financial Transactions Plan. The most recent published version of the FTP can be obtained at http://www.imf.org/cgi-shl/create_x.pl?ftp+2010.

[45] The amount by which holdings are below quota is called the reserve tranche. It forms part of a members reserve assets as a member has the right to make purchases for the amount of its reserve position upon representation of balance of payments need (see Art. XXX(c) of the IMF's Articles). The reserve tranche is remunerated, except for a small portion (Art. V, Sec. 9(a) and (b) of the IMF's Articles).

[46] Art. V, Sec. 8(b) of the IMF's Articles.

[47] Art. V, Sec. 11 of the IMF's Articles.

[48] Art. V, Sec. 7(j)(i) of the IMF's Articles.

IMF Financing Capacity

The IMF measures its financing capacity in terms of the 1-year Forward Commitment Capacity ("FCC"). The FCC measures the IMF's capacity to make new financial resources available to members from the GRA over the next 12 months.[49] The FCC is defined as the IMF's stock of usable resources[50] less undrawn balances under existing arrangements, plus projected repurchases during the coming 12 months, less repayments of borrowing due 1-year forward, less a prudential balance intended to safeguard the liquidity of creditors' claims and to take account of any erosion of the IMF's resource base.[51] Modifications to the FCC definition will be required going forward to fully reflect the up to 6 months activation period under the NAB, which is shorter than the normal 1-year FCC.[52]

IMF Borrowing

The IMF has the authority to replenish its currency holdings in the GRA through borrowing.[53] The IMF has relied on this authority to borrow under bilateral borrowing agreements in a number of instances in the past when the IMF's current and prospective liquidity was regarded inadequate, in particular when the time and size of a general quota increase was uncertain, and to finance newly established facilities.[54] The IMF also has two standing multilateral borrowing arrangements, the NAB and the General Arrangements to Borrow ("GAB").

---

[49] See more on the *Forward Commitment Capacity* at http://www.imf.org/cgi-shl/create_x.pl?liq.

[50] Usable resources consist of: (i) IMF holdings of the currencies of members considered by the IMF Executive Board to have a sufficiently strong balance of payments and reserve position for them to be included in the FTP for the financing of the IMF's operations and transactions; (ii) IMF holdings of SDRs; and (iii) unused amounts available under currently active bilateral loan and note purchase agreements, and unused amounts available under the New Arrangements to Borrow or the General Arrangements to Borrow when these have been activated.

[51] The prudential balance is calculated as 20 percent of the quotas of members included in the FTP, amounts made available under bilateral loan and note purchase agreements, and any amounts activated under the NAB or the GAB. At end-September 2008, prior to any crises related GRA lending, lendable IMF resources stood at about US$255 billion, of which US$199 billion available to cover potential new lending commitments under the FCC in addition to US$54 billion under the NAB, the IMF's primary borrowing mechanism. IMF, Review of the Adequacy of and Options for Supplementing Fund, 2009, available at: www.imf.org/external/np/pp/eng/2009/011209.pdf. See more on the IMF's Financial Resources and Liquidity Position at http://www.imf.org/external/np/tre/liquid/2009/0909.htm.

[52] See IMF Financial Activities, updated 7th April, 2011, available at: http://www.imf.org/external/np/tre/activity/2011/040711.htm.

[53] Art. VII, Sec. 1 of the IMF's Articles.

[54] Examples include the Oil facilities in 1974–75, the Supplementary Financing Facility in 1979–81, and the enlarged access policy of 1981–86; see IMF, Financial Organization and Operations of the IMF, No. 45, (6th ed.) 2001, p. 77.

Bilateral Borrowing as the Immediate Crisis Response

Bilateral borrowing started with a landmark US$100 billion loan agreement with Japan that was signed on February 13, 2009.[55] To date, 20 countries or central banks have agreed bilateral borrowing agreements with the IMF equivalent to a volume of about US$300 billion.[56] The key financial terms of these borrowing agreements are identical, in particular the maturities of drawings (3 months but automatically renewable to match maturities of IMF financing), the interest rate (i.e., SDR interest rate), and the repayment regime. Differences exist with respect to the currencies borrowed, the denomination of the overall commitment, any weekly and monthly limits for drawings, the right of lenders to request early repayment of outstanding loan balances in case of balance of payments need, the period for drawings (effectively between 2 and 5 years) and the modalities for extending the period for drawings. Following IMF members' preferences and domestic legal requirements, some agreements were entered between the member and the IMF, other agreements were entered between the respective members' central banks and the IMF.[57]

A number of IMF members indicated that it would be preferable for them to provide financing to the IMF by purchasing promissory notes instead of providing a loan. In response, IMF staff developed, and the Executive Board endorsed, a Notes Purchase Agreement ("NPA") framework.[58] The framework consists of a model NPA and General Terms and Conditions for IMF Series A and Series B Notes that provide the basis for individual agreements with specific members, which are approved by the IMF Executive Board.[59] The key financial terms of IMF notes regarding maturity, interest rate, denomination, right to encashment are identical to claims under bilateral borrowing. Notes are freely transferable to other eligible holders in the official sector. These include all IMF members, their central banks,

---

[55] Press Release No. 09/32, IMF Signs US$100 Billion Borrowing Agreement with Japan, available at http://www.imf.org/external/np/sec/pr/2009/pr0932.htm.

[56] See links to all borrowing agreements and the related press releases in "Bolstering the IMF's Lending Capacity", available at: http://www.imf.org/external/np/exr/faq/contribution.htm. To date, counterparties of the IMF's borrowing agreements include the Government of Japan, Norges Bank, the Government of Canada, the Government of France, the Government of the United Kingdom, Deutsche Bundesbank, Spain, De Nederlandsche Bank NV, Danmarks Nationalbank, Banca d'Italia, Banco de Portugal, Central Bank of Malta, National Bank of Belgium, Slovak Republic, Oesterreichische Nationalbank, Bank of Finland, Sveriges Riksbank, Czech National Bank, and Bank of Slovenia.

[57] In this regard, it should be noted that Art. VII, Sec. 1 of the IMF's Articles requires the member's consent if the IMF borrows a member's currency from source other than the member, including its central bank.

[58] See Press Release No. 09/248, IMF Approves Framework for Issuing Notes to the Official Sector, available at: http://www.imf.org/external/np/sec/pr/2009/pr09248.htm.

[59] IMF, A Framework for the Fund's Issuance of Notes to the Official Sector, 2009, available at: http://www.imf.org/external/np/pp/eng/2009/061709B.pdf.

the fiscal agency of a member, and official institutions that are prescribed holders of SDRs. Transfers to other official entities are permitted with consent from the IMF, but transfers to the private sector are not permitted. To date the IMF has concluded NPAs with the People's Bank of China, Federal Republic of Brazil, and Reserve Bank of India in a total amount of SDR 70 billion.[60] As bilateral borrowing was understood to bridge the period until the expanded and amended NAB would be effective, the borrowing and note purchase agreements provide that NAB participants have the option to cancel their bilateral borrowing agreements upon effectiveness of the expanded NAB and to fold any outstanding claims under bilateral loan and note purchase agreements into the NAB.[61]

Expanded and More Flexible New Arrangements to Borrow

As mentioned above, the IMF has two main standing credit arrangements, the GAB and the NAB. The GAB, which has 11 participants (i.e., members or their central banks), was originally established in 1962 to provide a source for additional resource in case of a need for IMF financing by G-10 members.[62] The NAB, which until the recent reform (effective March 11, 2011) had 26 participants with total credit commitments of SDR 34 billion (about US\$ 52 billion), was established in response to the 1995 Mexican crisis and became effective in 1998.[63] The purpose of the (old) NAB was to provide "supplementary resources to the IMF when these are needed to forestall or cope with an impairment of the international monetary system or to deal with an exceptional situation that poses a threat to the stability of that system.[64]" The NAB has been renewed twice for additional 5 year periods, most recently in November 2007 for the period November 2008 through 2013.[65] In relation to the GAB, the NAB is the credit facility of first resort. The cumulative commitment of participants under the (old) NAB and the GAB was SDR 34 billion

---

[60] See all press releases and agreements in "Bolstering the IMF's Lending Capacity", available at: http://www.imf.org/external/np/exr/faq/contribution.htm.

[61] See: IMF, Proposed Decision to Modify the New Arrangements to Borrow, 2010, available at: http://www.imf.org/external/np/pp/eng/2010/032510c.pdf.

[62] Decision No. 1289-(62/1), 5th January, 1962, as amended; see IMF, Selected Decisions and Selected Documents of the International Monetary Fund, 34th issue, 2010, p. 470, available at: http://www.imf.org/external/pubs/ft/sd/index.asp?decision=1289-(62/1). There is an associated arrangement with Saudi Arabia for an additional SDR 1.5 billion, see: http://www.imf.org/external/np/exr/facts/gabnab.htm.

[63] For commitments of the 26 participants under old NAB, see Annex to Decision No. 11428-(97/6), 27th January, 1997 in IMF, Selected Decisions and Selected Documents of the International Monetary Fund, 34th issue, 2010, p. 486, available at: http://www.imf.org/external/pubs/ft/sd/index.asp?decision=11428-(97/6) ("NAB Decision (old)").

[64] See preamble to the NAB Decision (old).

[65] See Press Release No. 07/270, IMF Executive Board Approves Renewal of Standing Borrowing Arrangements, available at: http://www.imf.org/external/np/sec/pr/2007/pr07270.htm.

as drawings under the NAB counted towards a participant's commitment under the GAB and vice versa.[66]

The 2008 global financial crises revealed that the maximum financing capacity of the NAB of SDR 34 billion was too small for the NAB to provide an effective backstop for quota resources in crises situations. In addition to its size, other reforms were required to make the NAB a more effective crisis tool. In particular, limitations under the NAB regarding its use for specific IMF arrangements had to be eliminated, for example to allow use for NAB resources for drawings under any GRA arrangements including the new IMF facilities such as Flexible Credit Line ("FCL") or Precautionary Credit Line ("PCL") arrangements.[67] The activation procedures were also too cumbersome, in particular each use of NAB resources required a multi-stage consultation and decision-making process subject to high voting majorities. Moreover, new participants could only be admitted at the time of renewal of the NAB, which prevented an increase in the NAB credit arrangements through the admission of new participants in response to the crisis as the next renewal was only scheduled for 2013.[68]

Following the call from the G-20 and the endorsement by the IMFC, on April 12, 2010 the IMF Executive Board adopted the decisions to expand the NAB and make it more flexible.[69] The reform, which became effective on March 11, 2011,[70] has the following key elements[71]:

---

[66] Paragraph 21 of NAB Decision (old).

[67] See more below under Influence Of The Reform Of The IMF Lending Toolkit.

[68] Paragraphs 6 A and B, 7A(a), 7A(b), and 7A(g),(h) and (i) of NAB Decision (old).

[69] IMF, Proposed Decision to Modify the New Arrangements to Borrow, 2010, available at: http://www.imf.org/external/np/pp/eng/2010/032510c.pdf. The provisions of the amended and enlarged NAB may be found in the before-mentioned paper and are referred to as "NAB Decision (new)" throughout the chapter.

[70] The NAB reform was adopted on 12th April, 2010. Its effectiveness required the consent of participants representing 85 percent of total credit arrangements to the amendments of the NAB to make it more flexible (Paragraph 15(a) of the NAB Decision (new)), and the consent of participants representing 85 percent of total credit arrangements of participants, including the consent of each participant whose credit arrangement is changed (i.e., 22 participants), for the increases in credit arrangements of current participants (Paragraph 5(b) of the NAB Decision (old)). As both the effectiveness of the amendments and the increases in credit arrangements were linked, the effectiveness of the NAB reform effectively required the consent of the 22 participants whose credit arrangements were changed, which represent 96 percent of the total voting power. Moreover, for the NAB to be operational for drawings, the adherence to the modified NAB of new participants representing at least 70 percent of the proposed total credit arrangements of new participants was required (Paragraph 24 of the NAB Decision (new)). For many members, consent to the NAB reform required legislative approval, in particular budgetary authorization. See Consents and Adherences to the Proposed Expansion of the Fund's New Arrangements to Borrow (NAB), available at: http://www.imf.org/external/np/fin/misc/nab.htm.

[71] Press Release No. 11/74, Major Expansion of IMF Borrowing Arrangements Takes Effect, Boosting Resources for Crisis Resolution, available at: http://www.imf.org/external/np/sec/pr/2011/pr1174.htm.

- The NAB was amended to allow for adherence of new participants outside of a renewal decision. Specifically, the number of NAB participants was increased from 26 to 39. Credit arrangements of current participants were increased so that together with the credit arrangements of new participants total credit arrangements will be increased from SDR 34 billion to SDR 367.5 billion, representing a major increase in the resources available for the IMF's lending to its members.[72]
- The amended NAB is available for all GRA financing.
- Regarding activation, the loan-by-loan activation is replaced by a general activation for activation periods. An activation period can be for up to 6 months and will establish the maximum amount of NAB resources that can be committed during the period. Also, there is now a uniform activation standard, eliminating the differentiation under the old NAB between activation for NAB participants and activation for other lenders.[73] Once activated, all arrangements and purchases approved during an activation period can be funded with calls on NAB participants. Specific calls will be made in accordance with quarterly Resources Mobilization Plan that will indicate for each participant the maximum amount of calls under its credit arrangement during a quarterly period.

The NAB reforms entered into effect on March 11, 2011[74] and the NAB was first activated on April 1, 2011 for a 6-month period and a maximum amount of SDR 211 billion.[75]

---

[72] Press Release No. 10/145, IMF Executive Board Approves Major Expansion of Fund's Borrowing Arrangements to Boost Resources for Crisis Resolution, available at: http://www.imf.org/external/np/sec/pr/2010/pr10145.htm.

[73] The NAB can be activated "when the Fund's resources available for the purpose of providing financing to members from the General Resources Account need to be supplemented in order to forestall or cope with an impairment of the international monetary system"; see Paragraph 5(a) NAB Decision (new). Under paragraphs 6A and B of the NAB Decision (old), the standard required for activation differed whether the NAB was activated for NAB participants or non-NAB participants: While for the former the standard was "to forestall or cope with an impairment of the international monetary system", the latter required "existence of an exceptional situation associate with balance of payments problems of members of a character or aggregate size that could threaten the stability of the international monetary system."

[74] Press Release No. 11/74, Major Expansion of IMF Borrowing Arrangements Takes Effect, Boosting Resources for Crisis Resolution, available at: http://www.imf.org/external/np/sec/pr/2011/pr1174.htm.

[75] Press Release No. 11/109, IMF Activates Expanded Borrowing Arrangements, available at: http://www.imf.org/external/np/sec/pr/2011/pr11109.htm. See: IMF Financial Activities, updated 7th April, 2011, available at: http://www.imf.org/external/np/tre/activity/2011/040711.htm.

Doubling of IMF Quotas – Completion of the 14th General Review of Quotas

Increasing IMF quotas was added to the crises response reform agenda.[76] While not expressly covered by the G-20 Communiqué of the April 2009 London summit, the IMFC at its April 2009 meeting, which generally endorsed the G-20 conclusions, noted that "the IMF is, and shall remain, a quota based institution" and urged "a prompt start to the Fourteenth General Review of Quotas so that it is completed by January 2011", thereby advancing the deadline for the completion of the quota review by 2^{77} years.[78] At its October 2009 meeting the IMFC emphasized that "[i]n the context of this review, the Fund should examine the appropriate size and composition of its resources needed to safeguard its long-term ability to meet members' needs, consistent with the Fund's status as a quota-based institution" and recognized "that the distribution of quota shares should reflect the relative weights of the Fund's members in the world economy, which have changed substantially in view of the strong growth in dynamic emerging market and developing countries." It supported "a shift in quota share to dynamic emerging market and developing countries of at least 5% from over-represented countries to under-represented countries using the current quota formula as the basis to work from" and committed to "protecting the voting share of the poorest members."[79]

---

[76] Quota reform has been at the center of the discussions for the last few years: Starting in September 2006, the IMF approved a first set of initial ad hoc increases in quotas for a small group of the most under-represented countries comprising China, Korea, Mexico and Turkey; see Press Release, IMF Executive Board Recommends Quota and Related Governance Reforms, available at: http://www.imf.org/external/np/sec/pr/2006/pr06189.htm. Following up in April 2008, as part of the IMF's broader quota and voice reform, the IMF Board of Governors approved increases in the quotas of 54 members that were underrepresented under the newly adopted quota formula and requested that the IMF Executive Board recommend further realignments of members' quota shares in the context of future general quota reviews, beginning with the Fourteenth General Review, to ensure that they continue to reflect members' relative positions in the world economy; see Board of Governors Resolution No. 63–2, adopted 28th April, 2008; IMF, Selected Decisions and Selected Documents of the International Monetary Fund, 34th issue, 2010, p. 18, available at: http://www.imf.org/external/pubs/ft/sd/index.asp?decision=DN3.

[77] As discussed above, quota reviews are required at intervals of five years under the IMF's Articles.

[78] Communiqué of the International Monetary and Financial Committee of the Board of Governors of the International Monetary Fund, 25th April, 2009, available at: http://www.imf.org/external/np/sec/pr/2009/pr09139.htm.

[79] Communiqué of the International Monetary and Financial Committee of the Board of Governors of the International Monetary Fund, 4th October, 2009, available at: http://www.imf.org/external/np/sec/pr/2009/pr09347.htm.

Size of the IMF

At the core of a general quota review is the question on the adequate size of the IMF. The adequacy of quota resources is assessed relative to a number of economic indicators on the global economy, in particular: GDP, trade and financial flows, and domestic and international asset and liability positions. With no general quota increase since 1998, the size of the IMF had shrunk substantially relative to the global economy as measured by these indicators and to members' potential financing needs. Based on the above-mentioned indicators, a quota increase between 80% and 315% was indicated. Access and financing scenarios on potential need for IMF resources indicated magnitudes of SDR 580 to SDR 675 billion in a tail event far exceeding current quota levels.[80]

Reform of the IMF Lending Toolkit

The discussion on the appropriate size of the IMF has to be also seen against the new lending instruments, such as the FCL, that were created in response to the global financial crises. The IMF traditionally provides financing to its members to address their balance of payments problems through outright purchases or over a period of time under arrangements, such as Stand-By or Extended Fund Facility arrangements.[81] Financing in the GRA is typically subject to policy conditionality[82] and other safeguards – such as program design, access limits,[83] phasing and

---

[80] For a more detailed analysis see IMF, Fourteenth General Review of Quotas-The Size of the Fund – Initial Considerations, 2010, available at: https://www.imf.org/external/np/pp/eng/2010/031210.pdf.

[81] Art. V, 3(b)(ii) of the IMF's Articles. Commonly, financial assistance is provided through an IMF arrangement which is a decision of the IMF that gives an IMF member the assurance that the IMF stands ready to provide SDRs or usable currencies during a specified period and up to a specified amount, in accordance with the agreed terms; see Art. XXX(b) of the IMF's Articles. The member's economic program underlying an IMF arrangement is formulated by the country in consultation with the IMF and is presented to the IMF's Executive Board in a Letter of Intent ("LOI"), typically, together with a Memorandum of Economic and Financial Policies ("MEFP"), and a Technical Memorandum of Understanding ("TMU"). See more on the nature of IMF arrangements: Leckow, The Stand-By Arrangement: Its Legal Nature and Principal Features, in: *Current Developments in Monetary and Financial Law, Volume 2*, 2003, pp. 33–49.

[82] More on IMF conditionality see: Leckow, Conditionality in the International Monetary Fund, in: *Current Developments in Monetary and Financial Law, Volume 3*, 2005, pp. 53–64.

[83] Access limits are intended to balance the need to provide members with confidence regarding the scale of possible IMF financing with the need to preserve IMF liquidity and the revolving character of IMF resources. The amount of financing a member can obtain from the IMF (its access limit) is a multiple of the member's quota. See: IMF, Review of Limits on Access to Financing in the Credit Tranches and Under the Extended Fund Facility, and Overall Access Limits Under the General Resources Account, 2008, available at: www.imf.org/external/np/pp/eng/2008/090208E.pdf.

reviews,[84] policy on repurchases,[85] and charges and surcharges[86] – that aim to preserve the revolving nature of GRA lending.[87] The IMF's GRA lending toolkit is organized around two broad criteria: (i) the nature of the balance of payments problem and (ii) the strength of the member's fundamentals and policies. The comprehensive reform of the GRA toolkit in April 2009[88] among other things[89] created the new Flexible Credit Line[90] and doubled annual and cumulative

---

[84] See: Relationship between Performance criteria and phasing purchases under Fund arrangements – o perational guidelines, see: Decision No. 7925-(85/38), 8th March, 1995, as amended in IMF, Selected Decisions and Selected Documents of the International Monetary Fund, 34th issue, 2010, p. 334, available at: http://www.imf.org/external/pubs/ft/sd/index.asp?decision=EBM/09/29.

[85] See: Repurchase, Decision No. 5703-(78/39), 22nd March, 1978, as amended in: IMF, Selected Decisions and Selected Documents of the International Monetary Fund, 34th issue, 2010, p. 424, available at: http://www.imf.org/external/pubs/ft/sd/index.asp?decision=EBM/09/29.

[86] All GRA arrangements are subject to the IMF's market-related interest rate, known as the "rate of charge" and large loans (above certain limits) carry a surcharge; see I-Rules of the IMF's Rules and Regulations at http://www.imf.org/external/pubs/ft/bl/blcon.htm. See also: SDR Interest Rate, Rate of Remuneration, Rate of Charge and Burden Sharing Adjustments 2010, available at: http://www.imf.org/cgi-shl/create_x.pl?bur: and Decision No. 12346-(00/117), 28th November, 2000, as amended in: IMF, Selected Decisions and Selected Documents of the International Monetary Fund, 34th issue, 2010, p. 428, available at: http://www.imf.org/external/pubs/ft/sd/index.asp?decision=12346-(00/117). Further, a commitment fee is charged on IMF arrangements which are precautionary (i.e., under which the member has not yet drawn) which are refundable in case the member draws. See: Rule I-8 of the IMF's Rules and Regulations. A new system of surcharges and commitment fees is in place since 2009. See: IMF, GRA Lending Toolkit and Conditionality: Reform Proposals, 2009, available at: www.imf.org/external/np/pp/eng/2009/031309a.pdf; IMF, The Acting Chair's Summing Up – GRA Lending Toolkit and Conditionality – Reform Proposals March 24, 2009 in IMF, Selected Decisions and Selected Documents of the International Monetary Fund, 34th issue, 2010, p. 292, available at: http://www.imf.org/external/pubs/ft/sd/index.asp?decision=EBM/09/29.

[87] Art. V, Sec. 3(a) of the IMF's Articles.

[88] See for further background: IMF, Review of Fund Facilities – Analytical Basis for Fund Lending and Reform Options, 2009, available at: http://www.imf.org/external/np/pp/eng/2009/020609a.pdf; IMF, Review of the Fund's Financing Role in Member Countries, 2008, available at: http://www.imf.org/external/np/pp/eng/2008/082808.pdf.

[89] Also, the IMF eliminated certain recently infrequently used facilities, which were repealed by Decision No. 14282-(09/29), adopted 24th March, 2009. These are the Short-Term Liquidity Facility, Decision No. 14184-(08/93), adopted 29th October, 2008, Supplemental Reserve Facility, Decision No. 11627-(97/123), adopted 17th December, 1997, as amended, and Compensatory Financing Facility, Decision No. 8955-(88/126), adopted 23rd August, 1988, as amended in: IMF, Selected Decisions and Selected Documents of the International Monetary Fund, 34th issue, 2010, p. 296, available at: http://www.imf.org/external/pubs/ft/sd/index.asp?decision=EBM/09/29. See, IMF, GRA Lending Toolkit and Conditionality: Reform Proposals, 2009, available at: http://www.imf.org/external/np/pp/eng/2009/031309A.pdf.

[90] See, IMF, GRA Lending Toolkit and Conditionality: Reform Proposals, 2009, available at: http://www.imf.org/external/np/pp/eng/2009/031309A.pdf; see PIN No. 09/40, IMF Overhauls Nonconcessional Lending Facilities and Conditionality, 2009, available at: http://www.imf.org/external/np/sec/pn/2009/pn0940.htm.

normal[91] access limits.[92] The FCL was designed to meet the increased demand for crisis-prevention and crisis-mitigation financing from countries with robust policy frameworks and strong track records in economic performance. It replaced traditional ex-post conditionality with a set of ex-ante qualification criteria and reviews (the latter, depending on the length of the FCL arrangement), signaling that IMF resources would be available in large amounts to members meeting these criteria to ensure that the IMF is well-equipped to fully meet the needs of its membership in the context of the global financial crisis. The FCL was fine-tuned in 2010 and made more flexible in the application of its duration and the reviews, and by removing the implicit access limit of 1,000% of quota.[93] In addition to the FCL, the Precautionary Credit Line was created in 2010.[94] The PCL's objective is to provide effective crisis prevention to members with sound fundamentals, policies, and institutional policy frameworks but moderate vulnerabilities that do not qualify for FCL financing. For the PCL, the qualification criteria aim at establishing confidence that the member will take appropriate measures to reduce remaining vulnerabilities and respond appropriately to shocks despite the absence of intensive ex post conditionality. An additional key requirement for PCL qualification is that a member does not face an actual balance of payments need at the time of approval of the arrangement. The PCL requires ex post conditionality.

Both the FCL and PCL and the doubling of normal access limits can lead to potentially significant commitments of IMF resources. Three FCL and one PCL arrangements are currently effective for a total amount of about SDR 68 billion.[95]

---

[91] Subject to four criteria, the IMF is prepared to make resources available to members in excess of normal access limits. See: Access Policy, Summing-up 02/94, 6th September, 2002, as amended in: IMF, Selected Decisions and Selected Documents of the International Monetary Fund, 34th issue, 2010, p. 392, available at: http://www.imf.org/external/pubs/ft/sd/index.asp?decision=EBM/02/94.

[92] Normal access limits in the GRA were doubled to 200% of quota annually and 600% of quota cumulatively; see IMF, GRA Lending Toolkit and Conditionality: Reform Proposals, 2009, available at: http://www.imf.org/external/np/pp/eng/2009/031309A.pdf and PIN No. 09/40, IMF Overhauls Nonconcessional Lending Facilities and Conditionality, available at: http://www.imf.org/external/np/sec/pn/2009/pn0940.htm.

[93] IMF, The Fund's Mandate – The Future Financing Role: Revised Reform Proposals, 2010, available at: www.imf.org/external/np/pp/eng/2010/082510.pdf.

[94] IMF, The Fund's Mandate – The Future Financing Role: Revised Reform Proposal, 2010, available at: http://www.imf.org/external/np/pp/eng/2010/082510.pdf.

[95] Currently, Mexico (SDR 47 billion), Colombia (SDR 2.3 billion), and Poland (SDR 19 billion) have a FCL arrangement. See: IMF, Colombia: Staff Report Arrangement Under the Flexible Credit Line, 2011, available at: http://www.imf.org/external/pubs/ft/scr/2010/cr10156.pdf; IMF, Staff Report Mexico: Arrangement Under the Flexible Credit Line, 2011, available at: http://www.imf.org/external/pubs/ft/scr/2011/cr1111.pdf; IMF, Staff Report Republic of Poland: Arrangement Under the Flexible Credit Line, 2011, available at: http://www.imf.org/external/pubs/ft/scr/2011/cr1124.pdf. Macedonia (total of SDR 412 million over two years) has a PCL arrangement. See: IMF, Staff Report for the 2010 Article IV and Arrangement under the Precautionary Credit Line, 2011, available at: http://www.imf.org/external/pubs/ft/scr/2011/cr1142.pdf.

Offering such high-access facilities of crises prevention financing requires commensurate IMF resources to ensure IMF liquidity in case purchases are made under such arrangements.

Quotas and Voting in the IMF

As mentioned earlier, quotas largely determine the voting power in the IMF.[96] The advancement of the 14th General Review of Quotas was critical to some members in part as only increases in quotas that change the relative quota share of members can shift the voting power in the decision making bodies of the IMF, while resources provided by members under borrowing agreements do not result in additional voting power. The willingness of many members to provide the IMF with resources under bilateral borrowing agreements and to adhere to the NAB (or increase their NAB credit arrangements) was clearly linked to an expected increase in IMF quotas that would shift quota share and with it voting power to dynamic emerging market and developing members.

Governance Reform

The quota discussion was inextricably linked to the discussion on IMF governance reform[97] and it became soon clear that the completion of the 14th General Review

---

[96] Quota is the main component that determines voting power in the IMF (i.e., one vote per SDR 100,000 in quota). A minimum of votes is distributed to all members in the form of basic votes pursuant to Art. XII, Sec. 5(a) of the IMF's Articles. The Sixth Amendment to the IMF's Articles (Voice and Participation Amendment), which entered into force on 3rd March, 2011 essentially tripled basic votes to approximately 742 votes (from a fixed number of 250 basic votes under the former Art. XII, Sec. 5(a) of the IMF's Articles), once all eligible members have paid their ad hoc quota increases under the 2008 reform. In addition, this amendment also ensures that basic votes can no longer be eroded by quota increases, by allocating a fix percentage of total votes (i.e., 5.502%) that will be divided among the IMF membership equally as basic votes – assuming there are no fractional votes. The Sixth Amendment was adopted by the Board of Governors Resolution No. 63–2 effective 28th April, 2008 and entered into force on 3rd March, 2011. Acceptance of the Proposed Amendments of the Articles of Agreement at http://www.imf.org/external/np/sec/misc/consents.htm#a2. See: IMF, Reform of Quota and Voice in the International Monetary Fund – Report of the Executive Board to the Board of Governors, 2008, available at: www.imf.org/external/np/pp/eng/2008/032108.pdf. For background see: IMF, Proposed Amendment of the Articles of Agreement Regarding Basic Votes – Preliminary Considerations, 2006, available at: www.imf.org/external/np/pp/eng/2006/122206a.pdf.

[97] The discussion on IMF governance reform started with an assessment report by the IMF's Independent Evaluations Office. See: IEO, Governance of the IMF An Evaluation, 2008, available at: http://www.ieo-imf.org/eval/complete/pdf/05212008/CG_main.pdf. In response to this report, the Managing Director requested an eminent committee to review IMF governance. A report authored by the eminent committee headed by Mr. Trevor Manuel followed in 2009. Press Release

of Quotas could only happen in the context of a broader quota and governance reform. Picking up from previous Communiqués, in April 2010, the IMFC pledged to complete the quota review before January 2011, in line with the parameters agreed by the IMFC in October 2009, and in parallel to deliver on other governance reforms.[98]

In October 2010, the IMFC reiterated its previous calls on quota reform and reemphasized that quota and governance reforms are critical to institutional legitimacy and effectiveness.[99] The key[100] issues in the governance debate[101] were (i) ministerial engagement and oversight, (ii) Executive Board composition, size, and decision making and (iii) selection of the management and staff diversity.[102] Only with progress on at least some of these issues, the necessary majority for completion of the 14th General Review of Quotas could be secured.

Quota Formula and Other Issues

Shifts in quota share are politically very difficult as they require a Board of Governors resolution adopted by an 85% majority of total voting power, i.e., very broad consensus in the IMF membership.[103] In addition to the question of the overall size of a general quota increase, a quota review is typically dominated by two issues: (i) how to determine the relative position of a member in the world economy, and

---

No. 09/88, IMF Managing Director Dominique Strauss-Kahn Welcomes Experts' Report on Fund Decision Making, available at: http://www.imf.org/external/np/sec/pr/2009/pr0988.htm. Its report was published in 2009: Committee on IMF Governance Reform, 2009, available at: http://www.imf.org/external/np/omd/2009/govref/032409.pdf. See also: IMF, IMF Governance – Summary of Issues and Reform Options, 2009, available at: http://www.imf.org/external/np/pp/eng/2009/070109.pdf; IMF, IMF Governance Reform, 2010, available at: www.imf.org/external/np/pp/eng/2010/070710.pdf; PIN No. 10/108, IMF Executive Board Discusses IMF Governance Reform, available at: http://www.imf.org/external/pp/longres.aspx?id=4464.

[98] Communiqué of the International Monetary and Financial Committee of the Board of Governors of the International Monetary Fund, 24th April, 2010, available at: http://www.imf.org/external/np/sec/pr/2010/pr10166.htm.

[99] Communiqué of the International Monetary and Financial Committee of the Board of Governors of the International Monetary Fund, 9th October, 2010, available at: http://www.imf.org/external/np/sec/pr/2010/pr10379.htm.

[100] Other issues include the strengthening of ministerial involvement in the IMF's decision making, double majorities, or the delineation of responsibilities among IMF organs.

[101] For further background, see, Hagan, Reforming the Fund in International Monetary and Financial Law. The Global Crisis, 2011, pp. 40–68.

[102] IMF, Executive Board Progress Report to the IMFC: The Reform of Fund Governance, 2010, available at: http://www.imf.org/external/np/pp/eng/2010/042110a.pdf; IMF, IMF Governance Reform, 2010, available at: www.imf.org/external/np/pp/eng/2010/070710.pdf; PIN No. 10/108, IMF Executive Board Discusses IMF Governance Reform, available at: http://www.imf.org/external/np/sec/pn/2010/pn10108.htm.

[103] Art. III, Sec. 2(c) of the IMF's Articles.

(ii) how to distribute the quota increase in a manner that ensures that the actual quotas of members more closely reflect their relative positions in the world economy.

The first issue requires agreement on a quota formula to arrive at the calculated quota share for each member on the basis of relevant economic criteria. The current quota formula was agreed in 2008 and formed the basis for the 2008 quota and voice reform that recently entered into effect.[104] It should be noted that there is no agreement among members on what indicators should be used in calculating a member's relative position in the world economy. The current quota formula was the result of considerable debate and represented a difficult compromise between members with very different views on the relative importance of the various elements of the formula.

The second challenge is how to bring members' actual quotas in line with their calculated quota share under the quota formula. Most members are either over- or underrepresented in relation to their calculated quota and the question is to what extent this deviation should be narrowed for each member in the context of a general quota review. If additional quota is allocated based on actual quota shares, this leaves intact the relative quota share and with it the relative voting power of members in the decision making bodies of the IMF. If, on the other hand, quota increases are used to reduce over and underrepresentation in the IMF based on the calculated quota, they result in "winners" and "losers" in terms of voting power. Because of the special majority requirement of 85% of the total voting power, changes in relative quota shares have in the past been only gradual, leading to significant over- and underrepresentation based on the quota formula.[105]

Implementation

In December 2010, the IMF Executive Board reached agreement on a comprehensive package of quota and governance reform that was endorsed by the IMF Board of Governors.[106]

---

[104] The current quota formula was agreed upon in April 2008. IMF, Reform of Quota and Voice in the International Monetary Fund – Report of the Executive Board to the Board of Governors, 2008, see http://www.imf.org/external/pp/longres.aspx?id=4235. The current quota formula is a weighted average of GDP (weight of 50 percent), openness (30 percent), economic variability (15 percent), and international reserves (5 percent). For this purpose, GDP is measured as a blend of GDP based on market exchange rates (weight of 60 percent) and on PPP exchange rates (40 percent). The formula also includes a "compression factor" that reduces the dispersion in calculated quota shares across members

[105] See Tables in IMF, Fourteenth General Review of Quotas – Realigning Quota Shares: Initial Considerations, 2010, available at: https://www.imf.org/external/np/pp/eng/2010/030410a.pdf.

[106] See: Board of Governors Resolution No. 66–2 effective 15th December, 2010, in IMF, IMF Quota and Governance Reform Elements of an Agreement, 2010, available at: www.imf.org/external/np/pp/eng/2010/103110.pdf.

As regards quota, agreement was reached on a doubling of IMF quotas from SDR 238.4 billion as agreed under the 2008 reform to a total of SDR 476.8 billion with a corresponding reduction in NAB credit arrangements, with details to be determined during the review of the NAB to be completed by mid-November 2011. It was further agreed to review the quota formula by January 2013 and to move forward the target for completion of the Fifteenth General Review of Quotas to January 2014. Once effective, the quota reform will result in an unprecedented shift of over 6% in quota share to dynamic emerging and developing countries and from over to underrepresented countries while fully protecting the quota share of the IMF's poorest members.

With respect to governance reform,[107] the Board of Governors approved[108] a proposed amendment of the IMF's Articles to move to an all-elected Executive Board, i.e., to eliminate the category of appointed Executive Directors at the Executive Board.[109] This is a far reaching reform as the right of the members with the five larges quotas to appoint their own Executive Director has been an important feature of the governance structure of the IMF. The move to an all elected Board is expected to eventually facilitate the consolidation of chairs of European Executive Directors in the IMF, as EU members that are among the five largest IMF members would no longer have to appoint their own Executive Directors but could join constituencies. The Board of Governors Resolution that approved the proposed amendment also contains a clause that the Board of Governors takes note of the commitment to reduce the number of Executive Directors representing advanced European countries by two no later than the first regular election of Executive Directors after the entry into force of the proposed amendment on an all elected Executive Board and members having no less than 70% of total quotas have

---

[107] The Sixth Amendment together with Board of Governors Resolution No. 66–2 effective 15th December, 2010, in IMF, IMF Quota and Governance Reform Elements of an Agreement, 2010, available at: www.imf.org/external/np/pp/eng/2010/103110.pdf, introduced the option for the appointment of a Second Alternate Executive Director for constituencies of seven or more starting with the 2012 regular election of Executive Directors.

[108] IMF, IMF Quota and Governance Reform Elements of an Agreement, 2010, available at: www.imf.org/external/np/pp/eng/2010/103110.pdf. Press Release No. 10/418, IMF Executive Board Approves Major Overhaul of Quotas and Governance, available at: http://www.imf.org/external/np/sec/pr/2010/pr10418.htm; Press Release No. 10/477, IMF Board of Governors Approves Major Quota and Governance Reforms, available at: http://www.imf.org/external/np/sec/pr/2010/pr10477.htm.

[109] Under the current Art. XII, Sec. 3(b)(i) of the IMF's Articles, the five members with the largest quotas each have the right and obligation to appoint their own Executive Director at the IMF Executive Board. The remaining 19 Executive Directors are elected at an interval of two years. The Proposed Amendment on the Reform of the Executive Board was adopted by the Board of Governors Resolution No. 66–2 effective 15th December, 2010. See: IMF, IMF Quota and Governance Reform Elements of an Agreement, 2010, available at: www.imf.org/external/np/pp/eng/2010/103110.pdf. Pursuant to Art. XXVII(a) of the IMF's Articles, it will enter into force for all members, once the IMF certifies that 3/5 of members representing 85% of the total voting power have accepted the amendment.

consented in writing to the increases in their quotas under the 14th General Review of Quotas.

The 2010 quota and governance reform will take some time to become effective. In particular the proposed amendment needs to be accepted by the membership with the required majorities under the IMF's Articles (a process which may require parliamentary approval in certain IMF members[110]), and the effectiveness of the quota increase is conditioned on the entry into force of the proposed amendment on an all elected Executive Board and the consent of members having no less than 70% of total quotas.[111] The IMF membership committed to implement these steps by the IMF Annual Meetings in 2012.

The General and Special SDR Allocations

The G-20 summit in April 2009 called for a general SDR allocation equivalent to US$ 250 billion[112] and the rapid ratification of the Fourth Amendment to the IMF's Articles. Both measures were endorsed by the IMFC[113] and paved the way for the first general SDR allocation in over 30 years and the entry into forth of the Fourth Amendment.

Origins of SDR

The SDR was created by the IMF in 1969 to support the Bretton Woods fixed exchange rate system (First Amendment). In recognition of the inherent constraints on the supply of reserve assets (gold and the U.S. dollar) under the Bretton Woods system of fixed exchange rates, the SDR was introduced in order to establish a mechanism for the deliberate creation of reserve assets in order to supplement existing reserve assets, and thereby support the expansion of world trade and financial development.[114]

---

[110] See Art. XXVIII of the IMF's Articles.

[111] The Sixth Amendment, which was another condition precedent for the entry into effect of the quota increases under the 14th General Review of Quotas, entered into force on 3rd March, 2011.

[112] G-20 Communiqué of 2nd April, 2009, see: http://www.g20.org/Documents/final-communique.pdf.

[113] IMFC Communiqué of 25th April, 2009, see: http://www.imf.org/external/np/sec/pr/2009/pr09139.htm.

[114] The "Triffin dilemma" is sometimes invoked to suggest that accommodating demand for reserves would lead to dollar debt creation that could reach magnitudes that challenge sustainability. However, Triffin was principally concerned with the dollar's convertibility into gold, supplies of which were growing only slowly. With the dollar no longer tied to gold, demand for reserve assets can in principle be met entirely through the capital account (simultaneous

The resources of the SDR Department are held separately from the assets of all other accounts owned or administered by the IMF.[115] SDR holdings are part of IMF members' reserve assets. While participation in the SDR Department is not required for IMF members, all current IMF members are also participants in the SDR Department.[116] Other SDR holders include the IMF (which holds SDRs in the GRA) and some 15 international organizations prescribed by the IMF ("prescribed holders").[117] Private sector holdings of SDRs are not allowed.

SDR Valuation and SDR Interest Rate

The valuation of the SDR is reviewed regularly, under current policies every 5 years.[118] Under the current valuation rules the SDR is a basket of currencies consisting of the U.S. dollar, euro, yen, and pound sterling.[119] The SDR interest rate is established on a weekly on the basis of for 3-month interest rates in the money markets of the SDR basket currencies.[120] The last review of the SDR valuation and the SDR interest rate were completed in November 2010, and the revised SDR basket became effective on January 1, 2011.[121]

---

creation of claims and obligations with non-residents), with a balanced current account. That does not mean an unsustainable current account, or debt burden, could not arise. See: IMF, Reserve Accumulation and International Monetary Stability, 2010, available at: http://www.imf.org/external/np/pp/eng/2010/041310.pdf.

[115] Art. XVI, Sec. 1 and 2 of the IMF's Articles.

[116] See allocations per IMF members at http://www.imf.org/external/np/tre/sdr/proposal/2009/0709.htm.

[117] Under Art. XVII, Sec. 3(i) of the IMF's Articles, the IMF may prescribe as holders non-members, members that are non-participants (in the SDR Department), institutions that perform functions of a central bank for more than one member, and other officials entities as "prescribed holders."

[118] Art. XV, Sec. 2 of the IMF's Articles.

[119] Under the current valuation rules, the SDR basket comprises the four currencies that are issued by IMF members (or by monetary unions that include IMF members), whose exports of goods and services during the five-year period ending 12 months before the effective date of the revision had the largest value, and that have been determined by the IMF to be freely usable currencies in accordance with Art. XXX (f). Decision No. 12281-(00/98), adopted 11th October, 2000 in: IMF, Selected Decisions and Selected Documents of the International Monetary Fund, 34th issue, 2010, p. 709, available at: http://www.imf.org/external/pubs/ft/sd/index.asp?decision=8160-(85/186). IMF, Review of the Method of Valuation of the SDR, 2010, available at: www.imf.org/external/np/pp/eng/2010/102610.pdf; Press Release No. 10/434, IMF Determines New Currency Weights for SDR Valuation Basket, available at: http://www.imf.org/external/np/sec/pr/2010/pr10434.htm.

[120] Rule T-1(c) of the IMF's Rules and Regulations.

[121] IMF, Review of the Method of Valuation of the SDR, 2010, available at: www.imf.org/external/np/pp/eng/2010/102610.pdf; Press Release No. 10/434, IMF Determines New Currency Weights for SDR Valuation Basket, available at: http://www.imf.org/external/np/sec/pr/2010/pr10434.htm.

Functioning of the SDR Department

The basic structure and operation of the SDR Department is as follows: The allocation of SDRs to members leads to a financial position in the SDR Department that is characterized by (i) the allocation, which is like a liability from the perspective of the participant, and (ii) corresponding SDR holdings, which one can consider the asset side. The SDR Department pays interest on SDR holdings at the SDR interest rate and participants have to pay interest (in the terminology of the IMF's Articles "charges") at the SDR interest rate on their SDR allocation.[122] For SDR Department participants that never use their SDRs, both interest and charges cancel each other out.[123] The main transaction in the SDR Department is the transfer of SDR holdings between participants in exchange for freely usable currencies. There are no requirements on minimum holdings, i.e. participants can reduce their SDR holdings to zero. The IMF has the power to introduce reconstitution requirements where members would have to bring the SDR holding to levels prescribed[124] by the IMF, and such reconstitution regime was in place until 1981.[125]

The IMF ensures the liquidity of the SDR in two ways, (i) through a designation mechanism[126]; and (ii) through voluntary exchanges between members and prescribed holders ("transactions by agreement") in a market managed by the IMF. For more than two decades, the SDR market has effectively functioned through voluntary trading arrangements. Under these arrangements a number of members and one prescribed holder have volunteered to buy or sell SDRs within limits defined by their respective arrangements. In view of the expected increase in the volume of transactions following the 2009 SDR allocations (see below), the number and size of the voluntary arrangements has been expanded to ensure continued liquidity of the voluntary SDR market.

In the event that there is insufficient capacity under the voluntary trading arrangements, the IMF can activate the designation mechanism.[127] Under this mechanism, participants with sufficiently strong external positions can be designated by the IMF to exchange SDRs into freely usable currencies (subject to maximum limits). This arrangement serves as a backstop to guarantee the liquidity

---

[122] Rule T-1 of the IMF's Rules and Regulations.

[123] Rule O-10 of the IMF's Rules and Regulations.

[124] Art. XIX, Sec. 2(c) and 6 of the IMF's Articles.

[125] See Decision No. 6832-(81/65), 22nd April, 1981, in: IMF, Selected Decisions and Selected Documents of the International Monetary Fund, 34th issue, 2010, p. 749, available at: www.imf.org/.../Selected_decisions_and_selected_documents_of_the_International_Monetary_Fund_Thirty-fourth.pdf. See more on the reconstitution requirement in IMF, Proposal for a General Allocation of SDRs, 2009, available at http://www.imf.org/external/np/sec/pr/2009/pr09264.htm or Annex II of IMF, Guidance Note for Fund Staff on the Treatment and Use of SDR Allocations, 2009, available at: www.imf.org/external/np/pp/eng/2009/082809.pdf.

[126] Art. XIX, Sec. 3(a) of the IMF's Articles.

[127] Art. XIX, Sec. 4 of the IMF's Articles.

and the reserve asset character of the SDR. The reserve asset character of SDRs derives from the commitment of IMF members to hold and accept SDRs and to honor the obligations underlying the operation of the SDR system.

In addition to the above mentioned exchange of SDRs into freely usable currencies, members can use their SDR for a number of operations expressly authorized under the Articles or on the basis of Executive Board decisions, including in operations involving the IMF, such as the payment of charges (i.e., interest) on and repayment of IMF financing, or payment of the reserve asset portion of a quota increase.[128]

General SDR Allocations

Under the IMF's Articles, the IMF may allocate SDRs to members in proportion to their IMF quotas.[129] Allocations are done for so-called basic periods. The purpose of a general SDR allocation is to meet the long-term global need to supplement existing reserve assets, while promoting the attainment of the IMF's purposes and avoiding economic stagnation and deflation, as well as excess demand and inflation.[130] General allocations have been rare and to date have only been made three times.[131]

The third general allocation was approved on August 7, 2009 for an amount of SDR 161.2 billion and took place on August 28, 2009.[132] The allocation increased

---

[128] See for instance: Payment of reserve asset portion of a quota increase (Art. III, Section 3(a) of the IMF's Articles); the payment of charges (Art. V, Sec. 8 of the IMF's Articles); purchases (Art. V, Sec. 3(f) of the IMF's Articles) and repurchase (Art. V, Sec. 7(i) of the IMF's Articles) transactions under IMF arrangements. The IMF may prescribe other operations with a 70% majority of the total voting power for the use of SDRs under Art. XIX, Sec. 2(c) of the IMF's Articles and in practice has done this for additional use (Decision No. 6000-(79/1), adopted 28th December, 1978, as amended), loans (Decision No. 6001-(97/1), adopted 28th December, 1978), pledges (Decision No. 6053-(79/34), adopted 26th February, 1979), transfers as security for the performance of financial obligations (Decision No. 6054-(79/34), adopted 26th February, 1979), swap operations (Decision No. 6336-(79/178), adopted 28th November, 1979, forward operations (Decision No. 6337-(79/178), adopted 28th November, 1979), donations (Decision No. 6437-(80/37), adopted 5th March, 1980) in: IMF, Selected Decisions and Selected Documents of the International Monetary Fund, 34th issue, 2010, pp. 733, 734, 736, 738, 740, 741, and 742 at www.imf.org/.../Selected_decisions_and_selected_documents_of_the_International_Monetary_Fund_Thirty-fourth.pdf.

[129] Art. XVIII, Sec. 2 of the IMF's Articles.

[130] Art. XVIII, Sec. 1(a) of the IMF's Articles.

[131] The first allocation was for a total amount of SDR 9.3 billion, distributed in 1970–72 during the first basic period in yearly installments. The second allocation, for SDR 12.1 billion, was distributed in 1979–81 during the third basic period in yearly installments.

[132] The general allocation was endorsed by the Executive Board and approved by the Board of Governors. IMF, Allocation of Special Drawing Rights for the Ninth Basic Period: Draft

simultaneously members' SDR holdings and their cumulative SDR allocations by about 74.13% of their quota. While a large part of the SDR allocation went to industrialized countries, about USD100 billion of the combined allocations went to emerging market and developing countries, of which over USD 18 billion to low-income countries.[133]

Special SDR Allocation (the "Fourth Amendment")

A proposal for a special one-time allocation of SDRs was approved by the IMF's Board of Governors in September 1997[134] through the Fourth Amendment of the IMF's Articles. Its intent was to enable all members of the IMF to participate in the SDR system on an equitable basis and to correct for the fact that countries that joined the IMF after 1981 – more than one-fifth of the current IMF membership – had never received an SDR allocation. The Fourth Amendment became effective for all members on August 10, 2009 when the IMF certified that three-fifths of the IMF membership representing 85% of the total voting power had accepted it.[135] The special allocation was implemented on September 9, 2009. It increased members' cumulative SDR allocations by SDR 21.5 billion using a common benchmark ratio as described in the amendment.[136]

As a result of the Fourth Amendment, prospective IMF members will be entitled to receive an SDR allocation upon joining the IMF, provided that they become members of the SDR Department within 3 months of joining the IMF.

Executive Board Decision and Managing Director Report to the Board of Governors, 2009, available at: http://www.imf.org/external/np/pp/eng/2009/071609.pdf. See, in this regard: Press Releases No. 09/264, IMF Executive Board Backs US$250 Billion SDR Allocation to Boost Global Liquidity, available at: http://www.imf.org/external/np/sec/pr/2009/pr09264.htm and No. 09/283, IMF Governors Formally Approve US$250 Billion General SDR Allocation, available at: http://www.imf.org/external/np/sec/pr/2009/pr09283.htm.

[133] Press Release No. 09/264, IMF Executive Board Backs US$250 Billion SDR Allocation to Boost Global Liquidity, available at: http://www.imf.org/external/np/sec/pr/2009/pr09264.htm.

[134] The Fourth Amendment became effective 10th August, 2009, by the modifications approved by the Board of Governors in Resolution No. 52–4, adopted 23rd September, 1997. See: IMF Summary Proceedings 1997 – Part 4 of 4, available at: www.imf.org/external/pubs/ft/summary/52/pdf/part4.pdf; see Press Release 97/45, IMF Board of Governors Approves SDR Amendment, available at: http://www.imf.org/external/np/sec/pr/1997/pr9745.htm.

[135] See Press Release No. 09/283, IMF Governors Formally Approve US$250 Billion General SDR Allocation, available at: http://www.imf.org/external/np/sec/pr/2009/pr09283.htm. The Fourth Amendment amended Art. XV of the IMF's Articles, and introduced Schedule M into the IMF's Articles.

[136] See allocations per IMF members at http://www.imf.org/external/np/tre/sdr/proposal/2009/0709.htm.

Outlook

Recently, there has been renewed interest in the SDR and its role in the international monetary system. Long-standing proposal, some of which date back more than 30 years, have been put back on the agenda for discussion.[137] Regarding the SDR valuation, support has been expressed for inclusion of the Chinese Renmimbi in the SDR basket.

Increasing the IMF Financing Capacity for Low-Income Members

As part of its response to the global financial crises, the IMF also recognized that the crisis had a particularly devastating effect on its poorest members,[138] the so-called LICs.[139] While eligible to use the general resource of the IMF, this group of IMF members typically receives financing on concessional from a special trust that is administered by the IMF and funded with loan and subsidy resources contributed by members and also contributions from the IMF derived from certain IMF gold sales.[140] In accordance with Article V, Section 12(f)(ii) of the IMF's Articles, any excess of proceeds of gold sales held by the IMF before the Second Amendment of the IMF's Articles may be transferred to the Special Disbursement Account and can be made available on special terms to developing members for balance of payments assistance in difficult circumstances, and for this purpose the IMF may take into account the level of per capital income. The main vehicle in this regard is the PRGT in which the IMF as a trustee administers contributor resources and certain of its resources from the Special Disbursement Account for the benefit of low income members.[141]

---

[137] IMF, Reserve Accumulation and International Monetary Stability, 2010, available at: http://www.imf.org/external/np/pp/eng/2010/041310.pdf. IMF, Enhancing International Monetary Stability – A Role for the SDR?, 2011, available at: http://www.imf.org/external/np/pp/eng/2011/010711.pdf. See: Towards a more stable international monetary system, IMF conference in March 2011; see the Managing Director's remarks at: www.imf.org/external/np/seminars/eng/2011/ims/pdf/invitation.pdf.

[138] In 2010, the IMF Executive Board modified the eligibility criteria for the PRGT, see IMF Reviews Eligibility for Using Concessional Financing Resources, available at: http://www.imf.org/external/np/sec/pn/2010/pn1016.htm.

[139] See: The Impact of the Financial Crisis on Low-Income Countries, available at: http://www.imf.org/external/np/speeches/2009/030309.htm.

[140] Under Art. V, Sec. 2(b) of the IMF's Articles, the IMF has the authority to perform financial and technical services, including the administration of resources contributed by members that are consistent with the purposes of the IMF.

[141] The PRGT was established in 1987; see Decision No. 8759-(87/176), 18th December, 1987 at IMF, Selected Decisions and Selected Documents of the International Monetary Fund, 34th issue, 2010, p. 163. Other initiatives for the benefit of low income countries include HIPC or MDRI: The Highly Indebted Poor Countries (HIPC) Initiative was launched in 1996 by the IMF and World

In April 2008, in response to a call from the G-20,[142] the IMF agreed to increase concessional resources available to LICs to meet projected demand of about US$17 billion through 2014.[143] New loan and subsidy resources to facilitate this increase will come from a number of different sources, including use of up to SDR 0.7 billion of resources linked to the 2009/2010 gold sales.[144] To allow for the better mobilization of loan resources, the IMF adjusted the framework for PRGT financing, in particular to allow for the lending to the loan account of the PRGT through Note Purchase Agreement and to enhance the reserve asset status of claims on the Trust.

In addition to increasing the financing capacity of the PRGT, the IMF decided to amend the facilities under the PRGT in 2009.[145] Specifically, the PRGT facilities were made more flexible and tailored to the increasingly diverse need of LICs. All facilities[146] place a strong emphasis on poverty alleviation and growth. Country-

---

Bank, with the aim of providing debt relief to eligible low-income members that face an unsustainable debt burden. See: IMF/World Bank, The HIPC Initiative: Delivering Debt Relief to Poor Countries, 1999, available at: http://www.imf.org/external/np/hipc/art0299.pdf. The Multilateral Debt Relief Initiative (MDRI) followed an initiative by the G-8 to provide 100 percent cancellation of debt owed by HIPCs to the Fund. See: IMF, The Multilateral Debt Relief Initiative (G-8 Proposal) and Its Implications for the Fund – Further Considerations: Supplemental Information, 2005, available at: http://www.imf.org/external/np/pp/eng/2005/110105.pdf; IMF, The Multilateral Debt Relief Initiative (G-8 Proposal) and Its Implications for the Fund – Further Considerations – Supplement on Financing Arrangements, 2005, available at: http://www.imf.org/external/np/pp/eng/2005/110105s.htm.

[142] G-20 Communiqué of 2nd April, 2009, see: http://www.g20.org/Documents/final-communique.pdf.

[143] See Press Release No. 09/286, IMF Announces Unprecedented Increase in Financial Support to Low-Income Countries, available at: http://www.imf.org/external/np/sec/pr/2009/pr09268.htm.

[144] The strategy for subsidy financing would involve the use of windfall profits arising from gold sales at an average price in excess of U.S. dollar 850 per ounce in the first instance. To the extent that the realized windfall profits fall short of the required contribution, the difference will be generated through investment income from the gold endowment. This strategy would provide some flexibility on how the resources would be generated, and allow the IMF to preserve the corpus of the gold sales proceeds and thus the Fund's ability to implement the new income model. See: PIN No. 09/94, IMF Reforms Financial Facilities for Low-Income Countries, available at: http://www.imf.org/external/np/sec/pn/2009/pn0994.htm. See also: IMF, Use of Gold Sale Profits – Initial Considerations and Options, 2011, available at: http://www.imf.org/external/np/pp/eng/2011/031611.pdf; PIN No. 11/48, IMF Executive Board Considers Use of Gold Sale Profits, available at: http://www.imf.org/external/np/sec/pn/2011/pn1148.htm.

[145] IMF, A New Architecture of Facilities for Low-Income Countries, 2009, available at: www.imf.org/external/np/pp/eng/2009/062609.pdf.

[146] The revised instruments are: The Extended Credit Facility ("ECF"), the successor to the Poverty Reduction and Growth Facility ("PRGF"), allows the IMF to provide sustained program engagement and financing for countries facing protracted balance of payments difficulties. The Standby Credit Facility ("SCF") – similar to the Stand-By Arrangement – provides financial assistance and policy support to LICs with shorter-term or episodic financing needs emanating from a range of sources. It also allows for precautionary use, in cases where there is a potential rather than an actual financing need. The Rapid Credit Facility ("RCF") provides a limited amount of financing in response to urgent needs, with reduced conditionality particularly appropriate to the transitory nature of the financing need or instances in which policy implementation capacity is constrained. The Exogenous Shocks Facility ("ESF") has been eliminated.

owned poverty reduction strategies will remain the basis of sustained program relationships with the IMF under the Extended Credit Facility. PRGT-supported programs will include specific targets to safeguard social and other priority spending, wherever possible.

Conclusion

The IMF has taken decisive measures to address weaknesses in its income model and to improve its financing capacity in view of increased needs from the membership against the backdrop of the global financial crisis.

The necessary reforms included three amendments to the IMF's Articles (which had before only been amended four times in over 50 years), an overhaul of the lending frameworks in the GRA and the PRGT, unprecedented borrowing by the IMF, and the first SDR allocations in nearly 30 years. All these reforms occurred against the backdrop of an unprecedented crisis, the global financial crisis, which for the first time in many years required even members with advanced economies to turn to the IMF for financial assistance.

In the coming months, the IMF will continue work on the new investment mandate under its expanded investment authority. In particular, it will need to decide on the various portfolios in the investment account, including in particular the appropriate investment strategy for the endowment portfolio in which gold profits are to be invested.

With significantly increased levels of IMF lending, the adequacy of IMF reserves will require further analysis. The IMF has recently adopted a new indicative target for its precautionary balances of SDR 15 billion and a minimum floor of SDR 10 billion.

Looking forward, it is crucial that the membership takes the necessary measures to make the 2010 Quota and Voice reform effective. This will require for many members parliamentary approval to accept the proposed amendment of the IMF's Articles on the reform of the Executive Board and to consent to the proposed quota increases, including by the United States whose acceptance of the proposed amendment is critical as it is only with its acceptance that the proposed amendment and the quota increases under the 14th General Review, which are conditioned on the entry into force of the proposed amendment, can become effective. It remains to be seen whether the effectiveness target for the 2010 quota and voice reform (i.e., IMF Annual Meetings in 2012) will be met.

The Role of the Emerging Countries in the G20: Agenda-Setter, Veto Player or Spectator?

Katharina Gnath and Claudia Schmucker

The Stellar Rise of the G20

Sometimes it takes a crisis to change. The upgrade of the G20[1] to the level of the heads of state and government was one of the major institutional outcomes of the recent global financial and economic crisis. The development depicts a dramatic turnaround: In 2007, the G8 invited large emerging countries within the "Heiligendamm Process" on a restricted number of topics. A year later, the G20 convened for the first time at leaders' level, thereby making emerging countries such as China, India and Brazil permanent members of an informal gathering at highest political level.[2] In 2009, it's member established the G20 as the "premier forum of global economic coordination",[3] and South Korea was the first emerging country holding the presidency for a G20 leaders' meeting in 2010.

With the fading of the immediate crisis experience, the G20 finds itself at a crucial stage in its development from a temporary crisis management mechanism to a long-term global economic steering committee. If the forum does not want to fall into oblivion as quickly as it rose to prominence, it is decisive to ensure a high level of commitment by all its members. For that it is important to develop a common agenda of cross regional reach that bridges fault lines among the different G20 countries' interests and priorities and to meaningfully incorporate emerging

---

[1] The G20 members are Argentina, Australia, Brazil, Canada, China, France, Germany, India, Indonesia, Italy, Japan, Mexico, Russia, Saudi-Arabia, South Africa, South Korea, Turkey, the UK, and the US. The 20th member is the European Union.

[2] They were only members of the "Finance G20" that met since 1999.

[3] G20, Leaders Statment: the Pittsburgh Summit, 24th & 25th September, 2009 available at www.g20.org/documents/pittsburgh-summit-leaders-statement_150909.pdf. last visited on 18th oct 2011.

K. Gnath • C. Schmucker (✉)
Deutsche Gesellschaft für Auswärtige Politik e.V., Rauchstraße 17/18, 10787 Berlin, Germany
e-mail: gnath@dgap.org; schmucker@dgap.org

C. Herrmann and J.P. Terhechte (eds.), *European Yearbook of International Economic Law (EYIEL), Vol. 3 (2012)*, European Yearbook of International Economic Law 3, DOI 10.1007/978-3-642-23309-8_21, © Springer-Verlag Berlin Heidelberg 2012

countries on a long-term basis into the forum that now stands at the apex of global economic governance.

So far, there is little consensus on the role of emerging countries in the newly upgraded G20. The forum is still new, and practices and preferences have not fully developed on all aspects of the forum's work.[4] More importantly, the debate on the role of emerging countries has up to now been dominated by generalisations that cloud the underlying factors shaping the role of individual emerging countries: On the one hand, commentators cite the hopes and goals of the G20 to systematically include newly emerged economies into global governance structures to better reflect the shift of power in the world economy.[5] For instance, the new G20-summits are seen as an "opportunity of a less western-centred view of the difficulties of the world economy" in a forum in which emerging countries out-number the G8 members by a margin of 2:1.[6] Other authors have been more pessimistic on the emerging countries' role in the G20, arguing that the numerical advantage and the shift in rhetoric towards emerging countries do not translate into actual policy outcomes. It has been criticized that, so far the G20 agenda was still dominated by the G8-members' preferences, and emerging countries were merely spectators in the negotiations, rubber-stamping genuine G8-policies and thereby giving them a broader basis of legitimacy and support.[7]

The aim of the article is to refine previous cursory assessments on the role of emerging countries in the new G20 by systematically assessing the preferences of G20 members based on official statements, Press coverage and interviews and comparing them with G20 outcomes. The article identifies a number of key themes of the upgraded G20 and summarises their outcomes in past summit meetings 2008–2010. In a second step, we analyse the preferences of the United States and European member states as a proxy for G8 positions[8], which are juxtaposed with

---

[4] Assessments of the emerging countries' role in and towards the G8 are more advanced, see e.g., Cooper/Antkiewicz (eds.), *Emerging Powers in Global Governance: Lessons from the Heiligendamm Process*, 2008.

[5] See "After the G20", Financial Times, 13th November, 2010, p. 16. See also Zhang, G20 and Global Governance: Challenges and Impacts, in: Fues/Wolff (eds.), *G20 and Global Development: How can the new summit architecture promote pro-poor growth and sustainability*, 2010, p. 63, available at: http://www.die-gdi.de/CMS-Home page/openwebcms3.nsf/(ynDK_contentByKey)/ANES-8A5CS9/$FILE/E-Publication_G20.pdf.

[6] Malloch-Brown, "How the G20 glasshouse is under attack", Financial Times, 12th November 2010, p. 11.

[7] For a similar assessment of developing countries in the G20 group of finance ministers, see Martinez-Diaz, The G20 after Eight Years: How Effective a Vehicle for Developing-Country Influence? Brookings Global Economy and Development Working Paper No. 12, 2007; Pisani-Ferry, "The G20 agenda sounds a lot like that of the G7", The Economist, 29th June, 2010, available at: http://www.economist.com/economics/by-invitation/guest-contributions/g20_agenda_sounds_lot_g7 (last visited on 6th October, 2010).

[8] We use the term G8 as proxy for industrialized countries while technically being a member of the G8 group of countries. Russia is left out of analysis as it is not a full member of the group in questions of economical and financial policy. It is acknowledged that G8 members can also differ

preferences of China, India and Brazil as representatives of emerging countries within the G20. In a last step, the article assesses emerging countries' role in the G20, analysing whether they have agenda-setting or veto power, or whether they take a back-seat role among the G20 countries, being a spectator at the sidelines of the discussions.

We argue that all the emerging countries are interested in participating as equal and permanent members in G20. However,due to often heterogeneous preferences they do not generally act as block in G20 discussions. when comparing preferences of the emerging countries with the out comes of the G20 summits, the article finds that they are not mere spectators, instead they have a certain agenda setting power when they are able to forge coalation or hold a presidency.

Key G20 Issues: Mapping Outcomes and Preferences

Being an informal forum, the upgraded G20 does not have a clear-cut remit or agenda. The G20 at leaders' level was initially established to achieve an internationally coordinated response to the global financial crisis: At the first G20 summits in 2008 and 2009, the main focus was on crisis management. Subsequent G20 summits in 2010 have, furthermore, dealt with issues of global financial regulation and macroeconomic policy more broadly, as well as with the reform of important international financial institutions, Added development to G20's Agenda.

Early G20 Initiatives: Crisis Management and First Rescue Packages

At the G20 summit in London in April 2009, the G20 countries pledged 1.1 trillion US-Dollar (USD) for the IMF and other multilateral organisations, consisting of 750 billion USD in direct aid and 250 billion USD in Special Drawing Rights for the IMF, as well as 100 billion USD for multilateral development banks to increase lending. The aim was to dampen the immediate repercussions of the financial crisis. Furthermore, the IMF created two new credit lines for countries that were affected by the financial crisis: The so called Flexible Credit Line (FCL) was introduced in 2009 for high-performing countries to strengthen their economic position. In 2010, the Precautionary Credit Line (PCL) was established for countries facing moderate vulnerabilities not (yet) meeting the high FCL qualification standards. The new

---

in their positions and strategies. Disagreements among them are highlighted in the description of policy stances below.

credit lines were part of the G20's vision for an improved "global financial safety net" – a network of insurance and loan instruments that countries could draw on to cope with volatility and contagion in the face of a crisis.[9]

Moreover, many countries around the world introduced national stimulus packages in response to the crisis. Almost 90% of the global measures originated in G20 countries and were introduced after the first G20 summit in Washington, DC, in late 2008 and early 2009. Most of the stimuli were a mix of tax breaks, guarantees and actual spending. The biggest rescue packages (relative to GDP) were initiated by China, Saudi Arabia and the United States: In 2009, the US introduced the American Recovery and Reinvestment Act (ARRA) worth 800 billion USD. In addition, the Troubled Asset Relief Program (TARP) of 700 billion USD was established to support the troubled US banking sector. Germany introduced two stimuli packages in 2008 and 2009, which amounted to 82 billion USD (1.6% of GDP). On the part of the emerging countries under investigation, China initiated a 586 billion USD (13.9% of GDP) stimulus package to boost domestic demand. Measures included spending on infrastructure, health care in rural areas and low-rent housing. Furthermore, nine specific industries received direct tax cuts. India introduced a fiscal stimulus package worth 4.1 billion USD in December 2008 (0.3% of GDP). The programme focused on labour-intensive and export-oriented sectors. Lastly, Brazil set up a fiscal rescue package of 3.6 billion USD (0.2% of GDP), which focused specifically on the automobile sector that accounts for 5% of Brazil's economy.[10]

The first G20 leaders' summits dealing with the immediate effects of the financial crisis saw a largely unified front of industrialised and emerging countries. All members supported the increased funding for international financial institutions and believed in the need for national stimuli packages. While some G20 members – most prominently Germany – were reluctant to introduce more flexible credit for fear of provoking moral hazard, especially emerging countries were in favour of the new IMF credit lines.[11] The G20 agreed – under the chairmanship of South Korea – on the extension of PCL and FCL at the summit in Seoul.

---

[9] Goretti/Joshi, "A Step Closer to a Stronger Global Financial Safety Net", IMF Survey Magazine, 30th August, 2010, available at: http://www.imf.org/external/pubs/ft/survey/so/2010/pol083010a. htm (last visited on 15th February, 2011).

[10] Khatiwada, Stimulus Packages to Counter Global Economic Crisis: A Review, International Institute for Labour Studies Discussion Paper No. 196, 2009, pp. 10 and 27–32, available at: http:// www.ilo.org/public/libdoc/ilo/2009/109B09_49_engl.pdf (last visited on 11th January 2011); Yang, Country Fact Sheet – China, in: Pohlmann/Reichert/Schillinger (eds.), *The G-20: a "Global Economic Government" in the Making?*, International Policy Analysis, Friedrich Ebert Foundation, 2010, p. 22, available at: http://library.fes.de/pdf-files/id/ipa/07284.pdf.

[11] See, e.g., the BRIC countries joint communiqué, available at: http://www.reuters.com/article/idUSLE470008 20090314 (last visited on 21st January, 2011).

Paying for the Crisis: Financial Levies and Taxes

The debate before the June 2010 summit in Toronto was dominated by the question of how the financial sector could adequately share the costs of the financial crisis. Several measures were discussed at the G20 level, including the introduction of an international bank levy, or a financial tax (either in form of a financial transaction tax or a financial activity tax). The G20 members did not reach a consensus at the leaders' meeting in Toronto beyond a vague statement on a "fair and substantial contribution" on the part of the financial sector.[12] While the declaration gave green light to G20 countries wanting to implement a bank levy unilaterally, it made clear that not all of the G20 countries needed to pursue the same approach. Following the Toronto statement, bank levies were no longer part of the G20 discussions at Seoul. Instead, the supporters of the bank levy pursued individual tracks.[13] Similarly, the introduction of a financial tax proved too contentious and did not even find its way onto the final agenda of Toronto. It was subsequently ignored altogether at Seoul.

Whereas the European G20 members (Germany, France and United Kingdom), Japan and the United States supported a financial levy,[14] other industrialised countries and emerging economies were opposed to it: At the G20 summit in Toronto, host Canada stressed that its banking sector was already sufficiently regulated and that it had survived the financial crisis relatively unharmed. Large emerging countries such as China, India, Brazil and G20 chair South Korea were also critical: China and India stressed that their banks had not been at the root of the financial crisis and should therefore not be "punished". Their financial sectors were rather seen as source for future growth that should not be burdened unnecessarily. Brazil aligned with the Canadian position that there had not been a need to bail out its banks during the financial crisis and that there was therefore no need to impose a levy.[15] Opposition towards a financial tax proved to be stronger and there was not even a majority among the industrialised G20 members in favour of it: While Germany, France and the United Kingdom supported the financial tax, the US – who had supported a G20 bank levy – and Canada vehemently opposed it. Large emerging countries were very critical: India and Brazil were against the proposals which they saw mainly as a means for the heavily indebted EU countries to increase the tax revenue.

---

[12] G20, The G-20 Toronto Summit Declaration, 26th and 27th June, 2010, p. 5, available at: http://www.g20.org/ Documents/g20_declaration_en.pdf.

[13] Germany, France, and the United Kingdom pushed for an EU-wide bank levy. US President Obama initiated a national bank levy for lenders with assets exceeding 50 billion USD. Obama eventually gave up the levy in return for Congress support for the Dodd Frank Act on financial regulation.

[14] The introduction of a coordinated levy was also endorsed by the former IMF Managing Director Dominique Strauss-Kahn at the 2010 spring meeting of the IMF and the World Bank.

[15] "India cold to global bank tax proposal as G20 meet", Financial Express, 27th June, 2010, available at: http://www.financialexpress.com/news/india-cold-to-global-bank-tax-proposal-as-g20-meet-opens/638907/ (last visited on 10th January, 2011); Jones, "G20 waffles on bank tax", The Globe and Mail, 3rd June, 2010, available at: http://www.theglobeandmail.com/news/world/g8-g20/economy/g20-waffles-on-bank-tax/article1590440/ (last visited on 7th September, 2010).

Given the unanimity requirement in the G20, an issue is pushed off the agenda if there is a considerable opposition in form of several G20 members forming an issue-specific coalition. In the case of the financial levies and taxes, no one coalition was able to dominate the agenda and therefore put a joint measure thru despite being in the interest of a number of G8 members. The example shows that in their unanimous opposition and their alliance with some G8 countries, emerging countries were able to veto the issues at the G20.

Making the Financial System More Financial Regulation and Basel III

Since the G20 was upgraded to the leaders' level, international financial regulatory reform has been another key topic of the forum. At the London summit in April 2009, the heads of states and governments announced that no financial market, product or actor should remain unregulated in the future. In Toronto, stricter financial regulation was high on the political agenda – although the leaders merely took stock of the progress of the Basel Committee of Banking Supervision (BCBS). The BCBS was mandated to present its proposals until the Seoul summit in November 2010 at which the G20 unanimously endorsed the reform package.[16] "Basel III" includes a stronger definition of key capital (core tier one). In addition, the new key capital ratio will rise from 2% (Basel II) up to 7%, including a new capital buffer of 2.5%. Basel III also introduces a new leverage ratio for banks. G20 members were tasked to gradually phase in the new rules, starting in January 2013 until January 2019.

Especially the US and the EU were strong supporters of regulatory reforms given their internationally connected banking sector: For example, US Treasury Secretary Timothy Geithner called Basel III a "major milestone in the process of global financial reform": Raising the capital requirement reduced the risk of future crisis significantly.[17] And Michel Barnier, EU Commissioner for Internal Markets and Services, stressed: "We are learning the lessons of the crisis in requiring better capitalisation for our banks and larger liquidity cushions, two essential elements for stronger stability in our financial system."[18]

---

[16] G20, The Seoul Summit Leaders' Declaration, 11th and 12th November, 2010, available at: http://media.seoulsummit.kr/contents/dlobo/E1._Seoul_Summit_Leaders_Declaration.pdf (last visited on 1st February, 2011).

[17] Geithner, Written Testimony, House Financial Services Committee, Washington, DC, 22nd September, 2010, available at: http://financialservices.house.gov/Media/file/hearings/111/Treasury_Testimony092210.pdf (last visited on 1st February, 2011).

[18] Barnier cited in: "EU welcomes Basel III global banking rules", Business & Leadership, 13th September, 2010, available at: http://www.businessandleadership.com/leadership/item/25567-eu-welcomes-basel-iii/ (last visited on 15th February, 2011).

All G20 member states – including China, India and Brazil who had also been admitted to the BCBS[19] – agreed on the proposed regulations by the Basel Banking Committee and subsequently endorsed them at the G20 summit. The Chinese government supported the idea that risky speculations with futures trading had to be backed up with more and better capital as required by Basel III. However, China stressed that the new capital standards would have a limited impact on Chinese banks, as the average key capital ratio in 2010 was already at 9% and core capital accounted for 80% of the total capital.[20] Similarly, India supported the idea of Basel III but stressed that its banks fulfilled much of the higher capital ratios: In June 2010, the average capital to risk-weighted assets ratio of Indian banks was 13.4% and core tier one capital accounted for 9%.[21] Lastly, Brazil also strongly supported Basel III, as it had already implemented most of the issues.

Stronger financial regulation was largely undisputed among the G20 countries – even though the push for reform came mainly from G8 countries given their large international financial sectors. Particularly the US and the EU were engaged in the discussions at the BCBS to find a common language on regulatory reform. China, India, Brazil and the other emerging countries did not attach the same priority to the issue – their main concern being solid economic growth instead of financial regulation.[22] Yet, they went along with the proposals, as they were not strongly affected by it.

Subsequent Concerns: Framework for Growth and Macro-Economic Imbalances

At the 2009 Pittsburgh summit, the G20 launched the "Framework for Strong, Sustainable, and Balanced Growth". Initially, the framework served to coordinate countries' exit strategies out of their economic stimulus measures. G20 countries agreed to the Canadian proposal according to which industrialised countries would

---

[19] In addition to India, Brazil and Australia, Korea Mexico and Russia were invited to join BCBS in March 2009

[20] Ning/Bo, "CBRS sees little impact from Basel III on bank", China Daily, 19th September, 2010, http://www.chinadaily.com.cn/business/2010-09/19/content_11322145.htm (last visited on 16th February, 2011).

[21] Gorawantschy et al., G20-Gipfel in Toronto: Im Zeichen wachsenden Selbstbewusstseins – Indien, KAS Länderbericht, Konrad Adenauer Foundation, p. 3, available at: http://www.kas.de/wf/doc/kas_20147-544-1-30.pdf (last visited on 16th February, 2011); Barman/Sokhi, "Proposed Basel III rules not to impact Indian banks much", Daily News & Analysis, 8th September, 2010, available at: http://www.dnaindia.com/money/report_proposed-basel-iii-rules-not-to-impact-indian-banks-much_1434990 (last visited on 16th February, 2011).

[22] Ku/Armstrong, "Asia regulators say G20 reform driven by U.S., Europe", Reuters, 29th November, 2010, available at: http://www.reuters.com/article/2010/11/29/asia-regulation-idUSL3E6MT0GO20101129 (last visited on 1st February, 2011).

halve their fiscal deficits by 2013 and stabilise or reduce their debt-to-GDP ratios by 2016.[23] In a further step, the IMF was tasked with assisting the "Mutual Assessment Process" in the form of providing analysis, coherent and mutual compatibility of 610 members policy frameworks and with issuing policy recommendations[24]. In February 2011 the G20 finance ministers agreed on a set of indicative guidelines to help global imbalances; public debts and fiscal deficits; private saving rates and private debt; and the external imbalance composed of the trade balance and net income news, taking consideration of exchange rates, fiscal monetary and other policies[25] Seven systemic G20 countries[26] will now be assed according to these indicators.

The coordination of individual growth strategies became more controversial among the G20 over the course of 2010, as countries' recovery paths and economic strengths diverged more and more: Germany and China have been seeing considerable economic growth and a constant increase in current account surpluses, while countries like the US have continuously registered high budget and trade deficits with relatively low growth rates. In the run-up to the Seoul summit, the two sides clashed over the viability of strengthening domestic demand in export countries as a solution to the imbalances. Furthermore, at the G20 ministerial meeting in Gyeongju in October 2010, Timothy Geithner's call to restrict current account surpluses and deficits (to a maximum of 4% of GDP) ran into heavy criticism by export countries such as China (5.2% projected current account surplus for 2010), but also Germany (6.1%) and Japan.[27] The German government rejected the US' calls as flawed approach and denounced them as a step towards a planned economy. In contrast, Germany was adamant that large national public debts posed a severe problem for the international community and that exit from the stimuli programmes was to be preferred to publically boosting domestic demand through further debt.

China has supported the G20 Framework for Strong, Sustainable and Balanced Growth. Yet, "global imbalances" are understood to be an issue of uneven global development, rather than merely a problem of trade deficits and surpluses.[28] Similarly, the most important issue for India in the context of the Framework has been to secure global economic growth. India has sided with the US in rejecting an

---

[23] G20, G-20 Toronto Summit Declaration, 26th and 27th June, 2010, available at: http://www.g20.org/Documents/g20_declaration_en.pdf (last visited on 1st February 2011).

[24] The International Monetary Fund, The G20 Mutual Assessment Process and the role of the fund, 2nd December 2009.

[25] G20, Meeting of finance Ministers and Central Bank Governors, Communique, Paris, 18th to 19th February, 2011.

[26] United States, China, Germany, France, United Kingdom, Japan and India.

[27] China (People's republic of China) Current Account Balance Statistics, Economy Watch, www.economicwatch.com/economic-stastics/china/current_account_balance_percentage_GDP/. last visited on 19th oct 2011.

[28] See Xue/Zhang, National Perspectives on Global Leadership: China, NPGL Soundings: November 2010, available at: http://www.cigionline.org/publications/2010/11/national-perspectives-global-leadership-china (last visited on 21st January, 2011).

early exit from the stimuli programmes for fear of a double dip recession. According to Prime Minister Manmohan Singh, the recovery was still too fragile – especially in the Eurozone – and that industrialised countries still needed to strengthen domestic demand. With respect to global imbalances, India has opposed caps on individual countries' current account balances.[29] Similarly, Brazil has been opposed to terminating the economic stimulus measures swiftly at the expense of growth: The Brazilian Minister of Finance Guido Mantega stated that emerging countries should not be burdened by the global recovery, and advanced exporting countries should not make a severe, "draconian, exaggerated fiscal adjustment" at the expense of emerging countries.[30]

The latest conflict over the pertinence of countries' exchange rate and monetary policy stance also falls within the context of global imbalances. In the run-up to the 2010 summit in Seoul, the frustration over the low external value of the renminbi grew within the US administration: According to the US' view, China's exchange rate policy increased the costs of American exports and prevented a fast recovery – and thus a reduction of the trade deficits – of the US economy. Even though China's currency re-valued faster in the weeks prior to the summit, the Chinese government cautioned against too high expectations of a swift currency revaluation. China considered its monetary policy as a domestic affair and did not want the G20 to infringe on its sovereignty on this issue. In particular, it rejected pressures (especially by the US) to be bound by nominal targets within the G20 framework or to revaluate quickly against the USD, citing internal reasons for a slow pace of revaluation.[31] In return, China and other emerging countries blamed the United States for its loose monetary policy, which was leading to large capital inflows and to upward pressures on their local currencies. Germany joined the critics of the US' loose monetary policy[32]: The Federal Reserve Bank's buying of bonds worth 600 billion USD (quantitative easing or "QE2") was perceived as holding the dollar artificially down. In September 2010, the Brazilian finance

---

[29] Chatterjee, "PM Economy Lesson for G20 Leaders", The Telegraph, 28th June, 2010, available at: http://www.telegraphindia.com/1100628/jsp/nation/story_12619325.jsp (last visited on 21st January, 2011); "India to oppose cap on current a/c balances-source", Reuters, 21st October 2010, available at: http://www.reuters.com/article/2010/10/21/g20-india-idUSTOE69K03U20101021 (last visited on 1st February, 2011).

[30] Mantega cited in: Landau, National Perspectives on Global Leadership: Brazil, NPGL Soundings: June 2010, available at: http://www.cigionline.org/publications/2010/6/national-perspectives-global-leadership-brazil (last visited on 21st January, 2011).

[31] Böhme et al., G20-Gipfel in Toronto: Im Zeichen wachsenden Selbstbewusstseins, KAS Länderbericht, Konrad Adenauer Foundation, p. 5, available at: http://www.kas.de/wf/doc/kas_20147-544-1-30.pdf; see also Yang, Country Fact Sheet – China, in: Pohlmann/Reichert/Schillinger (eds.), The G-20: a "Global Economic Government" in the Making?, International Policy Analysis, Friedrich Ebert Foundation, 2010, p. 23, available at: http://library.fes.de/pdf-files/id/ipa/07284.pdf.

[32] E.g., "Brüderle: Lockere Geldpolitik der USA ist falsch", Reuters, 23rd October, 2010, available at: http://de.reuters.com/article/topNews/idDEBEE69M03F20101023 (last visited on 21st January, 2011).

minister Guido Mantega coined the term "currency war" before imposing controls on foreign portfolio investments, citing upward pressures on the real as main reason.[33]

What began as a bilateral dispute on adequate exchange rate policies between the US and China developed over the course of 2010 into a larger question on global capital flows and appropriate growth strategies, in which the G20 countries stood at odds with each other in a complex set-up of interests and alliances. Especially on currency policy, emerging countries such as China – but also Brazil – were vocal in their opposition to US' demands. Whereas Germany actively opposed the US-proposed cap on current account deficits and surpluses together with China, the alliance between "surplus" and "deficit" countries within the G20 was rather circumstantial and uneasy: German Chancellor Angela Merkel made clear that "the German surplus is different from the Chinese one in the sense that it is due to the quality and competitiveness of German products, not on currency manipulation."[34] In sum, whereas emerging countries were not able to shift the agenda to focus on uneven global development, they could successfully veto proposals by industrialised countries – in this case the US's call for quantitative caps – successfully in the context of the G20, especially as G8 members did not present a united front.

Emerging Countries' Main Concern: Reform of International Financial Institutions

One of the upgraded G20's main objectives was to reform international financial institutions – in particular the IMF – to acknowledge and reflect the change in the international economic balance of power in favour of emerging countries. A first round of quota reforms was initiated in 2008. With a procedural ploy to block the election of the new Executive Board, the US administration jump-started the reform discussions at the IMF in August 2010: The US maintained that if there was no compromise on reshuffling seats in favour of emerging countries, the practice of having twenty-four members on the IMF Executive Board – four more than provided for in the IMF's Articles of Agreement – would be discontinued. This would hurt precisely some of the big emerging countries such as Brazil or Argentina whose presence and influence should be strengthened within the framework of multilateral financial institutions.

---

[33] Wheatley/Leahy, "Trade war looming, warns Brazil", Financial Times, 9th January, 2011, available at: http://www.ft.com/cms/s/0/6316eb4a-1c34-11e0-9b56-00144feab49a.html#axzz1-BOgiojnd (last visited on 18th January, 2011).

[34] Quoted in Mistral: National Perspectives on Global Leadership: France, NPGL Soundings: November 2010, available at: http://www.cigionline.org/publications/2010/11/national-perspectives-global-leadership-france (last visited on 21st January, 2011).

In October 2010, the G20 finance ministers agreed under the South Korean chairmanship in Gyeongju on a reform package that was subsequently endorsed at the Leaders' summit in Seoul and at the IMF Executive Board. At the centre of the IMF reform package stands a quota shift by more than 6% in favour of large emerging countries. China will become the third-largest shareholder after the US and Japan. It will relegate Germany – which reduced its quota share to just under 6% – to the fourth position among the ten most powerful shareholders at the IMF that now also include Russia, India, and Brazil. Furthermore, the Fund's capital stock was doubled to 755.7 billion USD at current exchange rates.[35] Most remarkably, the G20 agreed on reforming the composition of the IMF Executive Board. In the future, advanced European countries will give up two of their currently eight seats. The Board's size was kept at twenty-four seats (in contrast to the US' preference to reduce it to its regular size of twenty members).

The United States argued that by holding on to all of its seats, Europe was denying emerging countries the opportunity to play a bigger role in the IMF.[36] Having been close to political exodus before the financial crisis, fundamental governance reform was seen as vital for the Fund's effectiveness and legitimacy, as it would help ensure that emerging countries – especially China – would not abandon the Fund for alternative regional or national arrangements in the future. In addition, the US hoped that by supporting emerging countries' demands, it would receive greater support on several vital policy issues at the IMF in the future. All emerging countries strongly supported the reform of the IMF and international financial institutions. For China, the issue of IMF reform held the highest priority on the G20's agenda: China required the fast implementation of the voting rights reform as a first step of overall reform and more senior management posts for staff members from emerging countries.[37] Similarly, India voiced the need to quickly progress IMF reforms on many occasions in the context of G20 preparations.[38] Brazil had previously criticised the lack of emerging countries' influence over the

---

[35] Each IMF member country is assigned a quota, based broadly on its relative position in the world economy. The quota determines its maximum financial commitment to the IMF, its access to IMF financing, and its voting power in the Fund. See also Meeting of Finance Ministers and Central Bank Governors, Communiqué, Gyeongju, 23rd October, 2010, available at: http://www.g20.utoronto.ca/2010/g20finance101023.pdf (last visited on 25th October, 2010); IMF Press Release No. 10/418, IMF Executive Board Approves Major Overhaul of Quotas and Governance, 5th November, 2010, available at: http://www.imf.org/external/np/sec/pr/2010/pr10418.htm (last visited on 9th November, 2010).

[36] While many commentators and policy makers outside the US also made this argument, the US was clear in the reform process.

[37] E.g., Xue/Zhang, National Perspectives on Global Leadership: China, NPGL Soundings: November 2010, available at: http://www.cigionline.org/publications/2010/11/national-perspectives-global-leadership-china (last visited on 21st January, 2011).

[38] E.g., Lee, "G20 urged to speed up IMF reform", Korea Times, 1st September, 2010, available at: http://www.koreatimes.co.kr/www/news/biz/2010/10/123_72401.html (last visited on 16th February, 2011).

IMF's lending decisions in the face of unequal voting power.[39] The three emerging countries under investigation have used the G20 forum to call for a stronger voice in international institutions.[40]

Thus, advanced European countries were confronted with an alliance of policymakers from the US, emerging countries, and the IMF itself to reduce their presence at the Executive Board. And while European member states did not fully embrace the reform process for fear of losing influence, they eventually acknowledged the changing tides and agreed to institutional reforms of the Fund. The fact that emerging countries got a seat at the G20 table made parallel reform in the IMF more necessary in the medium-term. In the short-run, however, the US' veto power and its strategy to use the blocking power to advance the reform momentum were vital elements to spur reforms of the executive board.

Expanding the Agenda: Development Concerns

The Seoul summit 2010 under the South Korean presidency saw a stronger focus on global development of the official agenda than the first leaders' summits and the previous G20 ministerial meetings.[41] In contrast to the G8, where the issue of development has mainly consisted in a pledging exercise, the South Korean G20 presidency shifted the focus on principles of development, mainly in the areas of growth, investment in infrastructure, trade and human resource development. The Seoul summit agreed on a "Development Consensus for Shared Growth", stating that there was no single formula for development success.

The shift toward development was strongly supported by emerging and developing countries. While it has not been China's primary concern, the country has called for more attention on the developing world and for promoting global development in the context of the G20.[42] Out of the three emerging countries under investigation, India has been keenest on shifting the G20's agenda towards

---

[39] Nogueira Batista, "Europe must make way for a modern IMF", Financial Times, 23rd September, 2010, available at: http://www.ft.com/cms/s/0/8b57a684-c744-11df-aeb1-00144feab49a.html (last visited on 1st October, 2010).

[40] E.g., the BRIC countries joint communiqué, 14th March, 2009, available at: http://www.reuters.com/article/idUSLE47000820090314 (last visited on 21st January, 2011).

[41] Elsinger/Gnath, G8 und G20: Eine neue Agenda für Sicherheit und Entwicklung, in: Braml et al. (eds.), *Einsatz für den Frieden. Sicherheit und Entwicklung in Räumen begrenzter Staatlichkeit*, Jahrbuch Internationale Politik Vol. 28, 2010, pp. 344–350.

[42] Xue/Zhang, National Perspectives on Global Leadership: China, NPGL Soundings: November 2010, available at: http://www.cigionline.org/publications/2010/11/national-perspectives-global-leadership-china (last visited on 21st January, 2011); see also Yang, Country Fact Sheet – China, in: Pohlmann/Reichert/Schillinger (eds.), *The G-20: a "Global Economic Government" in the Making?*, International Policy Analysis, Friedrich Ebert Foundation, 2010, p. 23, available at: http://library.fes.de/pdf-files/id/ipa/07284.pdf.

development, both as an individual agenda item, as well as through a refocusing of existing topics. For example, Prime Minister Singh advised that macroeconomic imbalances and the challenge of inter-country divergences "become an opportunity to deal with a more fundamental imbalance which is the development gap between the rich and poor countries."[43] While the emerging countries were able to introduce a developmental perspective into some of the key issues, it was due to the 2010 host South Korea – who saw itself as a bridge between the industrialised and the developing world – that development was included as individual item on the official agenda. Given the informality of the forum with no fixed topical mandate, the role of the presidency can, thus, be a powerful tool to refocus the agenda towards non-G8 concerns. Other emerging countries will have the chance in years to come with Mexico following France at the helm in 2012.

Conclusion: Assessing the Role of the Emerging Countries

The article has examined the role of emerging countries in the new G20 with a particular focus on the question whether they have acted as agenda setters, VETO players or mere spectators. The G7 countries were hit hardest by the financial crisis measured in terms of output loss. In contrast, emerging and developing countries were not immediately affected by the global disruptions that followed the Lehman collapse in 2008. They felt the medium-term effects of the economic crisis, but their banking systems remained largely stable.[44] As such, China and India managed to sustain a considerable growth rate – though lower than before the crisis. Similarly, Brazil was comparatively well prepared to counter the crisis having stabilised economic fundamentals (inflation rate, foreign debt repayment and foreign reserves) in the wake of the previous crisis. Moreover, its financial sector was relatively stable, with low liabilities abroad. Emerging countries have also come out of the crisis as growth motors: This trend has been strengthened in 2010, where growth figures for high-income countries at 3%, whereas the emerging countries of the G20 and the remaining developing countries are projected to grow at 7.1% – Asian emerging countries even at 9.3%.[45]

---

[43] Singh cited in Bhattachariee, "PM claims 'some credit' for development focus", Financial Express, 14th November, 2010, available at: http://www.financialexpress.com/news/pm-claims-some-credit-for-development-focus/710805/0 (last visited on 1st February, 2011).

[44] Persaud, The locus of financial regulation: home versus host, ICRIER, available at: http://www.icrier.org/pdf/Avinash%20Persaud-%20Session%201-Paper.pdf (last visited on 16th February, 2011).

[45] Sachs, "Die neuen Schwergewichte", Handelsblatt, 16th December, 2010, available at: http://www.handelsblatt.com/meinung/gastbeitraege/geopolitik-die-neuen-schwergewichte;2713339 (last visited on 1st February, 2011).

The establishment of the G20 and its initial key objective to prevent disintegration of the international economy was therefore mainly in the interest of the G8 countries that dominated the agenda of the G20 summits in the first two years. The emerging countries were altogether less affected by the financial crisis and showed therefore different priorities and preferences: Their interest has focused less on regulatory change and more on a reform of the international institutions. China's willingness to go along with the initial G20 agenda was underpinned by its interest in consolidating the G20 as an alternative forum to the G8 in order to secure influence for emerging countries in global economic governance. As such, it did not want to be seen as blocking major decisions: Besides its dispute with the US over its currency policy, the country has taken a back seat in the G20 discussions. Similar to China, India's participation in the G20 did not arise from its direct concerns with the immediate crisis but is rather seen as a means to be present at a key global forum. However, India still sees the UN as the major platform for international cooperation.[46] Therefore, India has not been a strong proponent of any particular position – with the exception of IMF reform. Brazil was one of the earliest advocates of an upgrade for the G20 of Finance Ministers, with a view to diminishing the influence of the G8 and abolishing the unpopular "Heiligendamm Process". However, Brazil distanced itself from the process and did not participate in the Gyeongju ministerial meeting.

While the emerging countries share some general preferences – especially with regard to their increased voice in global economic governance –, a joint G20 stance is difficult to achieve: Given their different general economic policy traditions and the diverse economic challenges they face, emerging countries vary considerably in their preferences on a range of G20 policies (e.g. on exchange rate policy or financial supervision) – much more so than the European countries or the G8 members within the G20.

Summing up, the analysis of the summit outcomes and members' preferences of the first two years of the new G20 suggests that emerging countries have not been able to influence (and shift) the formal agenda of the leaders' G20 single-handedly. However, while the United States and the European G20 members as the proxies for the industrialized countries have dominated the agenda of the first G20 summits, they have not necessary acted in concert. The "cacophony" of G8 voices has given emerging countries room to manoeuvre at the G20: Big emerging countries have not been mere spectators at the G20. Their leeway to shape outcomes has so far largely depended on the ability to strike coalitions among each other and with G8 countries, such as on IMF reform or financial taxes and levies.

The key question for the G20 is whether it can deliver on its pledge to become the premier forum for international economic coordination in the long run. The G20 is per definition (and volition) a more heterogeneous forum than the G8 ever was. However, for the survival and legitimacy of the G20 it is important that the forum

---

[46] International monetary fund, World Economic Outlook update, 25, January, 2011.

does not slide into empty promises and vague compromises. This will only be possible if the newly-involved emerging countries remain engaged in the process and the G20 does not develop hard fault lines along the G8/emerging country divide. It is encouraging that such fault lines have not hardened among G20 members so far. Including agenda items that are of immediate relevance for emerging countries will ensure their continued interest in the forum. This could include topics such as development or commodity markets. It is therefore important for the future presidencies to strike the right balance of topics for G20 countries – whether they are industrialised or emerging.

Addressing Global Policy Challenges: The G20 Way in 2010 and Beyond

Raymond Ritter*

Introduction

In the wake of the global financial crisis, the Group of Twenty (G20),[1] bringing together systemically important advanced and emerging countries, gained significantly in prominence. While up until 2008 G20 members had convened only at the level of finance ministers and central bank governors, G20 Leaders met for the first time in Washington in November 2008 after then U.S. President G.W. Bush had participated in parts of an extraordinary meeting – scheduled at short notice – of G20 ministers and governors on 11 October 2008. In the following year, Leaders convened in London and then in Pittsburgh where they designated the G20 to be the 'premier' forum for international policy cooperation. Another two G20 meetings at Leaders' level took place in 2010 in Toronto and Seoul, respectively.

The G20 Leaders' forum has played an important role both during the financial crisis as well as in its aftermath. It initially served as an effective global crisis committee, allowing members to coordinate their respective policy responses. In the post-crisis period, the G20 Leaders' forum performed the role of a committee

---

* The author would like to thank Frank Moss, Marcel Fratzscher and Regine Wölfinger (all ECB) for their helpful comments. The views expressed in this paper are those of the author and do not necessarily reflect the views of the European Central Bank.

[1] Members of the G20 are: Argentina, Australia, Brazil, Canada, China, France, Germany, India, Indonesia, Italy, Japan, Mexico, Russia, Saudi Arabia, South Africa, Republic of Korea, Turkey, the UK and the United States as well as the European Union. At meetings of finance ministers and central bank governors, the EU is represented by the ECB, the European Commission and the rotating EU Presidency, whereas at meetings at the level of Leaders the President of the European Commission and the President of the European Council participate.

R. Ritter* (✉)
European Central Bank, International Policy Analysis Division, Kaiserstr. 29, 60311 Frankfurt am Main, Germany
e-mail: raymond.ritter@ecb.europa.eu

C. Herrmann and J.P. Terhechte (eds.), *European Yearbook of International Economic Law (EYIEL), Vol. 3 (2012)*, European Yearbook of International Economic Law 3, DOI 10.1007/978-3-642-23309-8_22, © Springer-Verlag Berlin Heidelberg 2012

for global policy cooperation, which facilitated agreement on collective action to address various key policy challenges. Since their first meeting, G20 leaders have taken on an increasingly broad range of issues that include macroeconomic policy cooperation, financial sector reform, reform of the international financial institutions, fighting protectionism, development and poverty, and energy.

This paper reviews the main achievements of the two G20 Summits that were held in 2010 and subsequently sets out the main priorities of the 2011 French G20 Presidency. Some concluding observations are provided at the end.

Achievements During the 2010 Korean G20 Presidency

The first G20 Summit in 2010 took place in June in Toronto as Canada had been chosen to host the G8 Summit in that year. Korea served as co-chair of this Summit, jointly with Canada, given the Asian country's role as chair in 2010 of the forum of G20 finance ministers and central bank governors. The second G20 Summit in 2010 was held in Seoul in November. Both summits were also attended by five non-members[2] as well as the heads of several international institutions and bodies.[3]

The Toronto Summit of June 2010

At the Toronto Summit on 26–27 June 2010 – the fourth such meeting in this format and the first Summit in the G20's new capacity as the premier forum for international economic cooperation – Leaders emphasised the achievements so far in addressing the global economic crisis, while pointing to the remaining serious challenges.[4]

This was the first summit since the outbreak of the crisis, which did not result in many concrete outcomes, but which mainly took stock of work in progress. Progress is being made on the G20 Framework, on the fiscal exit strategy, on financial sector reform and on the financing and governance of international

---

[2] These were the prime minister of Ethiopia and chairman of the New Partnership for Africa's Development (NEPAD), the president of Malawi and Leader of the African Union, the prime minister of Vietnam and chairman of the Association of South-East Asian Nations (ASEAN) and the prime minister of Spain. Moreover, the prime minister of the Netherlands was present at the first Summit in Toronto, while the prime minister of Singapore attended the one in Seoul.

[3] The Financial Stability Board (FSB), the International Labour Organisation (ILO), the International Monetary Fund (IMF), the OECD, the United Nations, the World Bank and the World Trade Organisation (WTO).

[4] See the G20 Toronto Declaration at http://www.g20.org/Documents/g20_declaration_en.pdf.

financial institutions. But on all of these matters the Toronto Summit did not provide important breakthroughs.

The G20 Framework for Strong, Sustainable and Balanced Growth

Following up on their Pittsburgh Summit in 2009, Leaders completed the first stage of the G20 Framework's Mutual Assessment Process, in which the collective consistency of members' policy frameworks and global prospects under alternative policy scenarios was assessed.

Leaders at their Pittsburgh Summit had committed to work together to ensure that global growth is strong, sustainable and balanced. To that end, they had launched the Framework for Strong, Sustainable and Balanced Growth, through which G20 members (i) agree on shared policy objectives, (ii) assess the implications of national policy frameworks for global growth and (iii) agree on policy actions to meet the common objectives. Leaders had also committed to set up a cooperative G20-led process of mutual assessment of their progress towards meeting their objectives, the co-called Mutual Assessment Process or MAP. The IMF, World Bank, OECD, ILO and other international institutions were asked to support this process and provide technical assistance. Moreover, a G20 Framework Working Group, chaired by Canada and India, had been set up to provide guidance to international institutions on their technical support.[5]

In their assessment reports prepared for the Toronto Summit, IMF[6] and World Bank[7] staff highlighted that collective action by G20 members would result in substantial benefits for the global economy. More specifically, in their upside scenario of collaborative policy actions, they had found a significant increase in global output by up to USD 4 trillion and employment gains in the order of 52 million jobs. Also, 90 million people would be lifted out of poverty and global growth would be more balanced if G20 members were to take collective action.

To sustain the global recovery and to reach the objectives of the G20 Framework, Leaders committed to taking a number of actions relating to the areas of fiscal, structural and exchange rate policies differentiated according to G20 advanced and emerging countries having a current account surplus and deficit (see summary Table 1 below).

---

[5] Guidance is also provided by G20 finance ministers and central bank governors (see the annex to the Washington communiqué of 23rd April, 2010 at: http://www.g20.org/Documents/201004_communique_WashingtonDC.pdf).

[6] IMF staff, drawing on submissions by G20 members and considering key economic and financial developments, had calculated a baseline scenario and developed two alternative scenarios – an upside and a downside one – to identify the benefits of collective action (see http://www.imf.org/external/np/g20/pdf/062710a.pdf).

[7] See the assessment by World Bank staff at: http://siteresources.worldbank.org/DEC/Resources/G20Framework&MAP-WBReport-TorontoSummit-2.pdf.

Table 1 Policy commitments within the G20 Framework for Strong, Sustainable and Balanced Growth

	Current account surplus	Current account deficit
All countries	• Structural reforms to increase and sustain growth	
	• Reduce reliance on external demand	
	• Focus more on domestic sources of growth	
Advanced countries	• Follow through on fiscal stimulus and communicate growth-friendly fiscal consolidation plans	
	• Structural reforms to increase domestic demand	• Boost national savings
		• Maintain open markets
		• Enhance export competitiveness
Emerging countries	• Strengthen social safety nets	
	• Increase infrastructure spending	
	• Enhance exchange rate flexibility to reflect underlying economic fundamentals	

Concerning fiscal policy, differing views between notably the United States and European countries on the appropriate timing and phasing of fiscal consolidation led Leaders to agree on a not so ambitious aim for advanced countries to at least halve their deficits by 2013 and stabilise or reduce government debt-to-GDP ratios by 2016. An exemption from this commitment was granted to Japan, with Leaders welcoming the consolidation plans by the Japanese authorities.

With regard to exchange rates, the Declaration contains more detailed and explicit language than in the past. Emerging surplus economies pledge to "*enhance exchange rate flexibility to reflect underlying economic fundamentals*" and subscribe to the finding that "*market-oriented exchange rates that reflect underlying economic fundamentals contribute to global economic stability.*"

On the way forward, Leaders underlined that the afore-mentioned measures will be implemented at the national level and will be tailored to individual country circumstances. They agreed that the second stage of the Mutual Assessment Process will be conducted at the country and European level. Moreover, they tasked their finance ministers and central bank governors to elaborate on policy measures and to report to the Seoul Summit, on the occasion of which a comprehensive action plan will be announced.

International Financial Institutions

As far as reforms of the IMF are concerned, Leaders followed up on the commitments made at their Summit in London in April 2009. At that meeting, they had agreed to treble resources available to the Fund from USD 250 billion to USD 750 billion *inter alia* through immediate bilateral financing of USD 250 billion, which should subsequently be incorporated into an expanded New Arrangements to Borrow (NAB)[8] of up to USD 500 billion. In the area of IMF

---

[8] The New Arrangements to Borrow are credit arrangements between the IMF and a number of its members that provide supplementary resources to the Fund.

governance reform, Leaders had committed to implement the 2008 IMF quota and voice reforms and agreed to complete the next quota review by January 2011.

At their Toronto Summit, Leaders underscored their resolve to ensure ratification of the 2008 reforms and expansion of the NAB (in annex 3 of the Declaration, it is noted that those G20 members that have not yet formally accepted the reforms to the expanded NAB pledge to do so by the next meeting of G20 finance ministers and central bank governors). Moreover, they called for an acceleration of the substantial work still needed for the IMF to complete the next quota reform by the Seoul Summit and in parallel deliver on other governance reforms. Further, they recalled their earlier commitment to open, transparent and merit-based selection processes for the heads and senior leadership of all the IFIs and pledged to strengthen the selection processes in the lead up to the Seoul Summit in the context of broader reform.

As regards strengthening global financial safety nets, Leaders tasked their ministers and governors to prepare policy options for consideration at the Seoul Summit. Moreover, they called on the IMF to make rapid progress in reviewing its lending instruments and enhancing its surveillance to focus on systemic risks.

Financial Sector Reform

Leaders pledged to act together to achieve the commitments to reform the financial sector, made in the three previous summits, by the agreed timeframes, and identified some key pillars of the G20 financial regulatory reform agenda, including a new capital framework, effective supervision, addressing systemically important financial institutions (SIFIs), and transparent international assessments and peer reviews.

- Regarding the new capital framework, Leaders refrained from actively stepping into the ongoing Basel process but emphasised their resolve to reach agreement by the time of the Seoul Summit.
- Leaders agreed to strengthen financial market infrastructure by accelerating the implementation of measures to improve transparency and regulatory oversight of hedge funds, credit rating agencies and OTC derivatives and re-emphasised the importance of achieving a single set of high quality global accounting standards.
- With regard to the area of effective supervision as well as the treatment of SIFIs, Leaders called upon the FSB to develop concrete policy recommendations.
- As to transparent international assessments and peer reviews, Leaders re-confirmed their commitment to the IMF/WB Financial Sector Assessment Programs and pledged to support robust and transparent peer review through the FSB.
- Concerning the specific modalities as to how the financial sector should make a fair and substantial contribution towards paying for any burdens associated with government interventions to repair the financial system, Leaders as expected did not reach a common view.

Fighting Protectionism and Promoting Trade and Investment

Leaders renewed their commitment not to hinder investment and trade in goods and services and reiterated their support for bringing the WTO Doha Development Round to a conclusion as soon as possible.

The Seoul Summit of November 2010

At their second Summit in 2010 in Seoul on 11–12 November, Leaders underlined the importance of international policy cooperation in containing the global economic crisis and committed to continue to work closely together, while noting that uneven growth and widening global imbalances carry the risk of triggering unilateral policy actions.[9]

Reflecting the post-crisis situation, the Seoul Summit was not expected to take urgent or important decisions, but rather to endorse the outcomes of a number of important work streams that had been delivered in time for this summit, notably: (1) the Seoul Action Plan with concrete policy commitments in five policy areas aimed at delivering strong, sustainable and balanced growth; (2) a reform of IMF quotas and governance; (3) key building blocks for the transformation of the financial system to address the root causes of the crisis (including the Basel Committee work); and (4) a display of the awareness that the G20, as the premier forum for international economic cooperation, also has to reach out to the non-represented large group of developing and low-income countries.

The G20 Framework for Strong, Sustainable and Balanced Growth

Leaders underlined that the "*unprecedented and highly coordinated fiscal and monetary stimulus worked to bring back the global economy from the edge of a depression*". They emphasised that, given remaining downside risks, strengthened collaborative policy actions can further safeguard the recovery and lay the foundation for the shared objectives of strong, sustainable and balanced growth.[10]

To move closer to these objectives, they agreed on the Seoul Action Plan, which sets out actions in five policy areas (additional country-specific policy commitments are contained in an annex[11]):

---

[9] See the G20 Seoul Declaration at: http://www.g20.org/Documents2010/11/seoulsummit_declaration.pdf.

[10] Leaders' discussions were based on assessments provided *inter alia* by IMF staff (see http://www.imf.org/external/np/g20/pdf/111210.pdf) and World Bank staff (see http://siteresources.worldbank.org/DEC/Resources/G20-Report-Seoul.pdf).

[11] See http://www.g20.org/Documents2010/11/seoulsummit_annexes.pdf.

- Monetary and exchange rate policies: Leaders reaffirmed *"central banks' commitment to price stability, thereby contributing to the recovery and sustainable growth"*. As regards exchange rate matters, they pledged to move toward more market-determined exchange rate systems and enhance exchange rate flexibility to reflect underlying economic fundamentals and refrain from competitive devaluation of currencies. Also, advanced G20 economies committed to be vigilant against excess volatility and disorderly movements in exchange rates. Moreover, Leaders agreed that emerging economies under specific conditions (adequate reserves, overvalued flexible exchange rates, strong capital inflows) may resort to macro-prudential measures (capital controls are note mentioned).
- Fiscal policies: The Declaration repeats the language of the Gyeongju communiqué of finance ministers and central bank governors of 23 October 2010, saying that *"advanced economies will formulate and implement clear, credible, ambitious and growth-friendly medium-term fiscal consolidation plans in line with the Toronto commitment, differentiated according to national circumstances"*.
- Financial reforms: Leaders pledged to implement global standards that have been already agreed, thereby ensuring a level playing field and avoiding fragmentation and regulatory arbitrage.
- Structural reforms: They agreed to implement a range of structural reforms to boost and sustain global demand, foster job creation, contribute to global rebalancing, and increase the growth potential of their economies.
- Trade and development policies: Leaders committed to free trade and investment and recognized the importance of a prompt conclusion of the Doha negotiations.

With the re-emergence of global imbalances posing a major risk to the global outlook, Leaders pledged to strengthen multilateral cooperation to promote external sustainability. More specifically, there was agreement to refine the Mutual Assessment Process (MAP) beyond Seoul and to establish a procedure for assessing persistently large imbalances, to be assessed against indicative guidelines. These guidelines, which are still to be developed by ministers and governors, are to be composed of a range of indicators that should facilitate timely identification of imbalances. In this way also, differences in views among G20 members on how to move forward could be reconciled. Most notably, an earlier proposal by US Secretary of the Treasury T. Geithner, circulated ahead of the 23 October 2010 meeting of G20 finance ministers and central bank governors in Gyeongju, whereby G20 members should aim to reduce their external imbalances below a specified share of GDP over the next few years, did not command support.[12]

Going forward, Ministers and Governors are to review progress in the first half of 2011, and the IMF was asked to subsequently make an assessment of the progress towards external sustainability. At the same time, an explicit commitment was

---

[12] See Geithner's letter at: http://online.wsj.com/public/resources/documents/GeithnerG20Letter.pdf.

made to monitor the implementation of the policy commitments put forward by G20 members to aim at strong, sustainable and balanced growth.

Reform of International Financial Institutions

In the area of IMF governance, Leaders welcomed the agreement by finance ministers and central bank governors at their Gyeongju meeting (the Leaders' Declaration contains the same language as the communiqué of ministers and governors of 23 October 2010). This agreement, which was reached only a few days after the meeting of the International Monetary and Financial Committee (IMFC), the Fund's policy steering committee, marked a breakthrough in the very difficult negotiations held since 2009. It contains a number of important elements:

- G20 members agreed on shifts in IMF quota shares to dynamic emerging market and developing countries and to under-represented countries of over 6%. Following implementation of this agreement, the 10 largest members of the IMF will be the United States, Japan, the four BRIC countries Brazil, Russia, India, China and the four European countries France, Germany, Italy and the UK.
- Members also settled on a doubling of quotas with a corresponding rollback of the New Arrangements to Borrow. This agreement is meant to ensure that the Fund remains a quota-based institution; it is also necessary to achieve the aforementioned further shift in quota shares from advanced to dynamic emerging and developing countries.
- Members committed to a comprehensive review of the quota formula by January 2013 and a completion of the next general quota review by January 2014.
- G20 members agreed to two fewer advanced European chairs on the IMF Executive Board as well as to a move to an all-elected Board. Agreement in this area was the result of difficult negotiations, in the course of which European countries had faced the charge of being overrepresented on the Fund Board. Advanced European countries, i.e., EU member states and European non-EU countries, which hold close to 8.2 positions on the IMF Executive Board, will have to decide how to meet this commitment by the end of 2012.[13]

Moreover, Leaders reiterated the urgency of concluding the 2008 IMF quota and voice reforms, which in the meantime have been endorsed by a majority of the IMF membership.[14]

---

[13] The 8.2 Executive Director positions currently held by advanced European countries are calculated as follows: Each ED position for Germany, France, United Kingdom, Belgium, Netherlands, Italy, and Switzerland is counted as 1, adding up to 7; in addition, given rotation schemes in their constituencies, advanced European countries hold the ED position in the Nordic chair 85% of the time (=0.85) and Spain one third of the time (=0.33) in its constituency with Mexico, Venezuela and others.

[14] These reforms which entered into force on 3rd March, 2011 result in a significant shift in the representation of dynamic economies and enhance the voice and participation of low-income countries.

Leaders also called for a strengthening of IMF surveillance and welcomed the Fund's work to conduct spillover assessments of the impact of policies of systemically important countries. In a pilot project, the Fund intends to examine five economies, namely China, the euro area, Japan, the United Kingdom and the United States. Further, Leaders expressed their appreciation for the Fund's recent decision to make financial stability assessments under the Financial Sector Assessment Program (FSAP) a regular and mandatory part of Article IV consultations for members with systemically important financial sectors. Twenty-five such countries have been identified, including eleven in the EU (Austria, Belgium, France, Germany, Italy, Ireland, Luxembourg, the Netherlands, Spain, Sweden, and the United Kingdom).

Regarding global financial safety nets, Leaders observed that these mechanisms can help countries cope with financial volatility by reducing economic disruptions from sudden swings in capital flows and the perceived need for excessive reserve accumulation. They welcomed the changes in the Fund's toolkit, i.e. the enhancement of the Flexible Credit Line and the creation of the Precautionary Credit Line,[15] and called for ways to improve collaboration between Regional Financing Arrangements (RFAs) and the IMF as well as to enhance the capability of RFAs for crisis prevention.

Financial Sector Reforms

Leaders endorsed the various work streams underway in the FSB, BCBS and other bodies.[16] As in previous summits, follow-up work in several areas with precise delivery dates addressed to specific groupings of international institutions and bodies was commanded, with most of the time the request that the output be first discussed by G20 finance ministers and central bank governors.

– Leaders endorsed the agreement by the BCBS on the new capital and liquidity framework (Basel III). They committed to adopt and implement fully the new standards *"within the agreed timeframe that is consistent with economic recovery and financial stability"* and agreed that the new framework will be implemented starting on 1 January 1 2013 and fully phased in by 1 January 1 2019.

---

[15] As part of the measures to support countries during the financial crisis, the IMF had undertaken a number of significant changes to its lending toolkit. In this context, programme access and the duration of the Fund's Flexible Credit Line (FCL) – a precautionary lending facility introduced in 2009 for top-performing countries with strong policy track records, which entails only ex ante conditionality – were modified in August 2010. The August 2010 lending reform also saw the creation of a new Precautionary Credit Line (PCL). The PCL is designed for Fund members with sound policies which nonetheless do not meet the FCL's high qualification requirements, thus being available to a wider Fund membership.

[16] See the letter by the FSB chairman to G20 Leaders (http://www.financialstabilityboard.org/publications/r_101109.pdf) as well as the FSB report on progress in the implementation of the G20 recommendations for strengthening financial stability (http://www.financialstabilityboard.org/publications/r_101111b.pdf).

- They also endorsed the policy framework, work processes, and timelines proposed by the FSB to reduce the moral hazard risks posed by systemically important financial institutions (SIFIs) and address the too-big-to-fail problem.[17] Among the key issues, Leaders identified a resolution framework, a requirement that SIFIs and initially in particular financial institutions that are globally systemic (G-SIFIs) should have higher loss absorbency capacity, and other requirements including liquidity surcharges and levies. Leaders agreed that G-SIFIs should be subject to a sustained process of mandatory international recovery and resolution planning.
- Leaders underscored the importance of enhancing international assessment and peer review processes to ensure consistency in implementation of standards and principles across countries.
- They recommitted to strengthening regulation and supervision of hedge funds, OTC derivatives and credit rating agencies and reaffirmed the importance of fully implementing the FSB's standards for sound compensation.
- Leaders also underscored the importance of achieving a single set of global accounting standards and called on the IASB and the FASB to complete their convergence project by the end of 2011.
- The issue of levies and taxes on financial institutions, which the European Council at its meeting on 28–29 October 2010 had identified as an important area for further work, does not figure prominently in the Declaration.

Going forward, Leaders identified the following areas for future work: (i) macroprudential policy frameworks, including tools to mitigate the impact of excessive capital flows; (ii) regulatory reform issues pertaining specifically to emerging and developing countries; (iii) regulation and supervision of shadow banking; (iv) regulation and supervision of commodity derivatives markets; and (v) improving market integrity and efficiency.

Fighting Protectionism and Promoting Trade and Investment

Leaders underscored the important role of free trade and investment for the global recovery and identified the year 2011 as "*critical window of opportunity*" for the WTO Doha Development Round.

Consultation and Outreach

Leaders pledged to increase their efforts to conduct G20 consultation activities in a more systematic way, building on partnerships with international organizations, in particular the UN, regional bodies, civil society, trade unions and academia.

---

[17] See the FSB policy framework for addressing SIFIs (http://www.financialstabilityboard.org/publications/r_101111a.pdf).

The Seoul summit provided also some clarification on the issue of meeting attendance. Leaders reached a broad consensus on a set of principles for non-member invitations to summits, including that invitations will be extended to no more than five non-member invitees, of which at least two will be countries in Africa.

The increased focus on Africa can be derived also implicitly from the Seoul Development Consensus for Shared Growth and the Multi-Year Action Plan on Development, which are attached to the communiqué and which focus on developing and low income countries. In this context, there is an explicit call to evaluate the impact of regulatory regimes on trade finance (which is important for developing and low-income countries). The Leaders' Declaration contains also a commitment to support the regional integration efforts of African leaders.

The Way Forward: Priorities of the 2011 French G20 Presidency

There are several important policy issues and workstreams that are on the agenda of the French G20 Presidency for 2011. Further progress will have to be made on processes that were initiated earlier and require follow-up work such as the G20 Framework, the financial regulatory reform agenda as well as development issues. Moreover, a number of new items have been added to the agenda, including the reform of the international monetary system as well as commodity issues.[18]

As was agreed at the Toronto Summit, Leaders will hold one summit meeting annually going forward and are to convene in November 2011 under the chairmanship of France[19] (which is also holding the G7/G8 chair in 2011).

The G20 Framework for Strong, Sustainable and Balanced Growth

In their follow-up to the Seoul Summit, finance ministers and central bank governors at their first meeting under French chairmanship in February 2011 in Paris made progress on the design elements of the Mutual Assessment Process of

---

[18] See e.g. the press conference by the French President on 24th January, 2011 (available at: http://www.g20-g8.com/g8-g20/g20/english/for-the-press/speeches/adress-by-mr-nicolas-sarkozy-to-present-the.1021.html) and his address on 18th February, 2011, to G20 finance ministers and Central Bank governors (http://www.g20-g8.com/g8-g20/g20/english/for-the-press/speeches/nicolas-sarkozy-s-speech-to-the-g20-ministers.971.html).

[19] Invitations to the Summit in Cannes have been issued to five non-members, namely to Ethiopia as the current chair of the New Partnership for Africa's Development (NEPAD); Singapore, representing the 27-member Global Governance Group (3G); Spain; the United Arab Emirates, the current chair of the Gulf Cooperation Council; and Equatorial Guinea, the current chair of the African Union.

the G20 Framework.[20] They agreed on a set of indicators to be assessed to identify persistently large current account imbalances. These indicators pertain to the public sector (public debt and fiscal deficits), the private sector (private savings rate and private debt) and the external sector ("*the external imbalance composed of the trade balance and net investment income flows and transfers, taking due consideration of exchange rate, fiscal, monetary and other policies*"). Further work will focus on the operationalization of these indicators as well as the design of indicative guidelines against which the indicators will be assessed. Ultimately, corrective policy measures could be identified where needed and endorsed by G20 Leaders at their Summit in Cannes.

Financial Regulatory Agenda

The G20 will need to take forward the various items on the financial regulatory agenda, including the timely and consistent implementation of the new capital and liquidity framework as well as the design of a consistent framework for all systemically important financial institutions. Other issues where progress needs to be made relate *inter alia* to implementation of agreed remuneration standards, identification of non-cooperative jurisdictions and work on regulation of the shadow banking system.

International Monetary System

One key priority of the French G20 Presidency pertains to the reform of the international monetary system, or IMS, which can be understood to be the global framework for cross-border monetary transactions.[21] More specifically, the French Presidency aims to address vulnerabilities of the IMS and to improve its functioning. To that end, a G20 working group, co-chaired by Germany and Mexico, has been set up to pursue work in two areas. The first area relates to cross-border capital flows and possible ways to cope with undesirable volatility. International cooperation in this field is clearly desirable so as to avoid a proliferation of disorderly capital management measures. Hence, a framework of principles and best practices would be conducive to rendering individual countries' measures more efficient and the overall system more resilient. The second area pertains to the management of

---

[20] See the communiqué of G20 finance ministers and central governors of 18th and 19th February, 2011, at: http://www.g20.org/Documents2011/02/COMMUNIQUE-G20_MGM%20_18-19_February_2011.pdf.

[21] For an in-depth assessment of the IMS and its functioning, see e.g. ECB, The financial crisis and the strengthening of global policy cooperation, ECB Monthly Bulletin, January 2011, pp. 87–97.

global liquidity, including global financial safety nets and the role of the SDR. With regard to financial safety nets, views differ on whether and how the IMF's lending role should be enhanced and how to develop further collaboration between the Fund and regional reserve pools. Given that these various issues are complex and difficult in nature, it is not clear whether agreement will be reached already in 2011.

Commodity Issues

Another priority, which France intends to pursue, is to reduce volatility in commodity prices. To that end, the aim is to devise common rules to regulate financial commodity markets and to improve their transparency. To address food shortages in poor countries, it is suggested to devise inter alia a code of conduct to exempt food aid from export restrictions.

Development

Development issues continue to figure on the agenda of the G20 in 2011. Among the topics are the identification of infrastructure projects and their financing as well as more generally the mobilisation of official development assistance and innovative financing.

Concluding Observations

The upgrading of the G20 and its elevation to the Leaders' level in 2008 were very symbolic signs of the changed world as previously only the G7/G8 had met at the level of heads of state or government. A group of emerging economies was now recognised as being important for solving the global crisis.

These far-reaching changes in global governance reflect also a significant strengthening of informal intergovernmental policy cooperation that takes place outside the structures of existing international financial institutions. Rather, the IFIs are invited to meetings of the G20 and are assigned work in various areas. At the same time, it is worth emphasising that it was the informal G20 Leaders' forum that gave the impetus to a strengthening of the governance and finances of the IFIs. As far as the FSB is concerned, it is de facto practising accountability vis-à-vis the G20 as it, unlike the Bretton Woods institutions, has no prime decision-making body.

Looking at the track record of the G20 Leaders' forum so far, this informal grouping has been instrumental in providing high-level political impetus for crisis containment, crisis management as well as future crisis prevention. Leaders went beyond what the ministers and governors had prepared in their meetings and provided three types of value added, namely (i) taking urgent decisions, (ii) putting deadlines for delivery of certain actions and (iii) keeping up the momentum of ongoing work. The ability of the Leaders' forum to serve as consensus-building mechanism has been clearly confirmed. In this respect, G20 members have exhibited an exemplary degree of collective responsibility during the financial crisis as well as in the immediate post-crisis period.

Going forward, what will be important is to ensure that G20 cohesion will be sustained so that this group continues to operate as an effective 'premier' forum for international economic cooperation. It is hence highly welcome that G20 Leaders, most recently at their Seoul Summit in November 2010, underlined the importance of continued international policy cooperation to address the root causes of the financial crisis and to lay the foundations for sound global economic growth. In this respect, it will also be critical for G20 members to make further progress on implementing the agreements reached in the different policy areas and to lead by example in living up to the commitments made.

Part IV
Book Reviews

Thomas Cottier, Olga Nartova and Sadeq Z. Bigdeli (eds.), International Trade Regulation and the Mitigation of Climate Change

Cambridge University Press, 2009
ISBN 978-0-521-76619-7

David Freestone, Charlotte Streck (eds.), Legal Aspects of Carbon Trading – Kyoto, Copenhagen and Beyond

Oxford University Press, 2009
ISBN 978-0-19-95-956593-1

Roland Ismer

I

The volume eds. by *Thomas Cottier*, *Olga Nartova* and *Sadeq Z. Bigdeli* comprises twenty scholarly articles, which were originally presented at a conference in Geneva in 2007. The contributors are a group of distinguished attorneys at law, academics and civil servants, mostly coming from a legal background. This timely book explores avenues for post-Kyoto climate change mitigation efforts. While it reveals the underlying tensions between the imperatives of trade law and policy on the one hand and climate policy on the other, it also stresses the possibilities for the mutual strengthening of the two regimes. The book comes in six parts:

Part I lays the groundwork by briefly discussing climate science, political, international law and trade law foundations. In the first article, *Thomas Stocker* briefly introduces the climate science basics and points out that even a two-degree warming target cannot be considered absolutely safe. He concludes by calling for long-term mitigation measures rather than short-term fixes and by pointing out that, in addition to these mitigation measures, adaptation will also be necessary. *José Romero* and *Karine Siegwart* show that sustainable development is among the objectives of the WTO Agreement and that the UNFCCC as well as the Kyoto Protocol contain provisions seeking to minimize adverse implications on trade, so that "so far" the two regimes have not come into conflict. They list potential tensions

R. Ismer (✉)
Universität Erlanger-Hamburg, Lange Gasse 20, 90403 Hamburg, Germany
e-mail: Roland.Ismer@wiso.uni-erlanger.de

C. Herrmann and J.P. Terhechte (eds.), *European Yearbook of International Economic Law (EYIEL), Vol. 3 (2012)*, European Yearbook of International Economic Law 3, DOI 10.1007/978-3-642-23309-8_23, © Springer-Verlag Berlin Heidelberg 2012

between trade law and tools addressing climate change, ranging from the carbon market to the Global Environment Facility (GEF) and other finance mechanisms. *Thomas Cottier* and *Sofya Matteotti-Berkutova* then examine whether the "common concern of mankind" can justly be described as an evolving principle of international environmental law, which limits the exercise of sovereignty without consent by the respective State. They cautiously answer the question in the affirmative, stating that "sovereignty must be exercised within the global responsibilities set out principally in the Climate Change Convention as well as in the Rio Declaration and other relevant instruments" (p. 39). After explaining responsibilities emanating from the concept, they sketch the implications of common concerns for world trade law: while multilateral rules generally concretize the role of common concerns for justification of unilateral measures aimed at protecting them, such rules may themselves need to evolve in parallel to the evolution of the principle. In the last contribution to Part I, which is also by far the longest article in the book, *Robert Howse* and *Antonia L. Eliason* provide an overview of WTO legal issues with respect to carbon markets, schemes for the promotion of renewable energy as well as energy efficiency. Regarding carbon markets, they not only pre-empt the current debate on fraudulent transactions in the European emissions trading scheme, but also draw attention to the subsidies issues from free allocation and propose that GATS applies to trade in emission allowances and to the CDM. Moreover, they discuss the legality of trade restrictions for products from non-Kyoto countries, carbon taxes levied at the border and the application of cap-and-trade regulatory requirements to imports as well as issues surrounding the Clean Development Mechanism. With respect to renewable energy, it seems noteworthy that, in general, they do not consider such promotion schemes as a violation of the SCM.

Part II deals in more detail with trade in goods. *Donald Regan* revisits the long-running dispute on whether process or production methods (PPM) that leave no trace in the product can nevertheless make products "unlike". He argues that distinctions based on such PPMs can comply with GATT obligations regardless of Article XX GATT. Furthermore, in his view, regulatory purpose needs to be taken into account for assessing whether there is less favourable treatment. In the following article, *Daniel C. Crosby* contradicts him on both counts. In line with more conventional WTO wisdom, he favours dealing with PPMs in the framework of the narrower Article XX GATT, which also shifts the burden of proof to the country taking the unilateral measure. *Arthur E. Appleton* then examines whether private climate change standards and labeling schemes fall under the Agreement on Technical Barriers to Trade (TBT). He comes to the conclusion that, despite some legal uncertainty, such schemes generally fall outside the TBT.

Part III is devoted to trade in renewable energy sources. In what is arguably the most innovative contribution of the volume, *Sadeq Z. Bigdeli* deals with the question whether WTO rules on subsidies constrain policies for promoting renewables, especially through subsidization? He favours a wide definition of a subsidy and in particular of price support, which in his view also comprise price regulations (e.g. by way of feed-in tariffs) which confer benefit. He then shows that subsidies exist regarding biofuels as well as renewable electricity trade, that these subsidies may be specific and that these subsidies may cause adverse effects. He thus deems that new rules are necessary for renewable promotion in the SCM, a view that is shared by *Gary S. Horlick* in his short comment. In the last contribution of Part III, *Simonetta Zarrilli* and *Jennifer Burnett* examine the certification of biofuels. After providing an overview of certification schemes, they explain the ambiguous effect of certification schemes on world trade and in particular on developing countries. While they see concerns regarding the implementation of certification schemes, transparency as well as the costs for developing country certification, they also recognize that certification may make biofuels more acceptable on the market and thus increase trade. They then explore the legal issues of applicability of the TBT to non-product related processes and production methods (NPR-PPMs), likeness of differently produced bio-fuels, as well as less favourable treatment and Article XX GATT, before finally calling for an appropriately designed certification scheme for biofuels.

Part IV focuses on trade in services. *Panagiotis Delimatsis* and *Despina Mavromati* examine trade in renewable energy certificates (RECs). After giving some background on trade in financial services under GATS and on RECs, they lament the absence of a separate entry for energy-related services in the service classification list. Moreover, they find that Member States have already undertaken commitments in financial services and other sectors that impact on the energy sector, so that they propose a unified approach to trading of energy-related services and trading of related financial instruments. Under the somewhat misleading title "Assessment of GATS' impact on climate change mitigation", *Olga Nartova* deals with the challenges facing environmental services in the Doha negotiations. She begins by discussing different negotiation proposals for the classification of environmental services, before describing the benefits of and obstacles to liberalization of trade in environmental goods and services (EGS) as well as stressing the importance of an integrated negotiation approach for both goods and services. *Rudolf Adlung* names the highly diverse economic activities with respect to the environment, high degree of government involvement, frequent lack of competitive pressures on the recipients of environmental services and the absence of environmental standards as reasons why compared, e.g. to the telecoms sector there have been relatively little GATS' commitments to environmental services. As a potential way to proceed, he proposes Additional Commitments consisting of the development, implementation and enforcement of pertinent standards.

Part V deals with technology transfer, investment and procurement. *Felix Bloch* presents the rules on technology transfer contained in the UNFCC and the Kyoto Protocol. In his view, the rules can be interpreted in a mutually supportive way with the obligations under the Agreement on Trade Related Intellectual Property Rights (TRIPS), whereas under the chapeau of Article XX GATT, the justification may depend on the non-discriminatory nature of technology transfer. *Stefan Rechsteiner*, *Christa Pfister* and *Fabian Martens* examine conflicts between the CDM and the Agreement on Trade Related Investment Measures (TRIMS). They identify national legislation on local content requirements as the most likely conflict.

In addition to discussing the paper by Rechsteiner et al., *Jakob D. Werksman* draws attention to further areas of concern, where CDM investors may challenge both governments under international investment agreements and the CDM executive board. In her paper on "green" procurement policies and in particular on renewable procurement by the European Union, *Garba I. Malumfashi*, who also discusses some aspects of EU law, proposes that such procurement can be in accordance with the WTO Agreement on Government Procurement (GPA) as it may be considered a necessary measure under the exception. Also on government procurement, *Geert van Calster* highlights particular concerns: After a short reminder that sustainable development was not meant to be limited to environmental concerns, he tends to the view that procurement based on green NPR-PPMs does not fall under Article VI.1 GPA and favours a narrow interpretation of the requirement that there be no unnecessary obstacles to trade. He also considers standardization efforts by private organizations as being not a priori excluded from government procurement criteria. Finally, he stresses that more thought should be devoted to some kind of international minimum harmonization.

Part VI reflects upon institutional challenges and upon future negotiations. *Mireille Cossy* and *Gabrielle Marceau* examine coordination with other international actors and legal sources. After stressing that "the real challenge of the WTO will be to ensure that this non-hegemonic attitude is maintained", in particular with respect to other international organisations (p. 373), they explain the general basis for co-operation with intergovernmental and non-governmental organizations. Then they focus on the impact of non-WTO rules on the WTO dispute settlement procedures, which they rightly identify as both influencing the interpretation of WTO rules and providing the factual background for such rules, and on the use of standards developed by other international organizations. After briefly naming the pertinent issues at the Doha negotiations, they finally stress that WTO law limits should be less binding than the political will by governments. In the final contribution to the volume, *Thomas Cottier* and *Dora Baracol-Pinhāo* assess the main proposals made in the framework of the Doha negotiations with respect to EGS and present the environmental area initiative as an alternative approach that would allow a significant reduction in the complexity of the negotiations.

The volume covers a wide range of topics and assembles highly reputable contributors. It offers a good overview of the interface between climate change mitigation and world trade law, which will remain highly relevant for years to come. While it might be criticized that the fact that the volume consists of twenty distinct papers rather than being a single authored volume sometimes leads to some redundancies and while the book might have further profited from a brief introduction summing up the main findings and laying out the concept of the volume as well as from additional cross-referencing, such minor points cannot but underline how well the book succeeds in reflecting the plethora of issues, approaches and scholarly views in this ever expanding legal field. The book constitutes an impressive collection of scholarship which will be a valuable reference point, both in the design phase of future unilateral and multilateral measures and when such measures reach the litigation stage.

II

The volume eds. by David Freestone/Charlotte Streck assembles 28 scholarly articles, which are arranged in eight parts, with a length of 15–30 pages each as well as a brief summary and outlook. Taken together, the contributions provide a comprehensive and concise overview of emissions trading schemes in CO_2 and other greenhouse gases (in the book and in the following simply referred to as carbon markets) that have evolved after the adoption of the Kyoto Protocol. The articles cover the field in its whole complexity: after a valuable introductory chapter, it starts with general issues – such as the legal nature and ownership of allowances under the Kyoto Protocol and under EU ETS as well as accounting for emissions allowances and linking of schemes – followed by an analysis of the Kyoto Mechanisms (International Emissions Trading, Joint Implementation and, reflecting its practical importance, the Clean Development Mechanism), as well as regional (i.e. EU level), national and subnational schemes, before finally discussing post-Kyoto options.

In Part I, *David Freestone* gives an overview of the legal and institutional framework governing international efforts aimed at mitigating climate change. His contribution ranges from the evolution of the UNFCCC and the Kyoto Protocol to their implementation and to carbon contracting. He also briefly describes the publicly financed climate change funds and their governance. He finishes with a short depiction of the Bali Roadmap. He thus manages to provide the context to the later chapters, where the challenges posed by carbon markets are picked up again and elaborated in more detail.

Part II is devoted to general issues of carbon markets. First, *Matthieu Wemaere*, *Charlotte Streck* and *Thiago Chagas* examine the legal nature and characteristics of tradable units in the different carbon markets. They convincingly distinguish between emission "rights" under international law on the one hand, which merely serve as an instrument for fulfillment of the obligation not to emit more than the respective emissions target and where consequently there cannot be banking, and emissions allowances under domestic systems involving private individuals on the other. They rightly deplore the persisting heterogeneity of approaches regarding the latter (of which some EU Member States lately have become painfully aware through their substantial losses from VAT fraud) and call for more precisely defined rights. *Allan Cook* then deals with accounting for emissions schemes under International Financial Reporting Standards, a problem that has become ever more pressing with the advent of the possibility of banking emissions allowances. His proposal that in order to avoid the need for a rewrite of accounting rules, the free allocation of allowances be considered as a conditional liability rather than a grant, as they most likely have to be surrendered. However, one might object that with banking, it is not clear whether such probability statement is still true. *Marie Clair Cordonnier Segger* and *Markus Gehring* examine trade and investment implications of carbon trading for sustainable development and call for both more technology transfer and more international legal coherence in order to avoid 'climate chaos'. *Michael Mehling* discusses legal issues arising from linking of emissions trading schemes, to which high political hopes have been attached. He identifies the different legal instruments that could be employed for creating the link (unilateral, reciprocal unilateral, bilateral or multilateral) and explains some aspects of the regulatory framework with which a linking of schemes would have to comply. Despite the impeccable legal analysis, the recent travails of the common European currency may reduce the political will to engage in cross-jurisdictional linking, not least because the selling of allowances under one scheme and the purchase of allowances in the other achieves an indirect, albeit less visible form of linking anyway. In the last article of Part II, *Jolene Lin* analyzes the intriguing role of private actors, who are of tremendous importance given the aim of carbon markets of harnessing market forces both with respect to providing a highly efficient aggregation mechanism of decentralized knowledge and with respect to incentives to actually ensure real world implementation. She places particular emphasis on legal and regulatory risks faced by private actors on international and domestic emissions trading schemes, among them (lack of) judicial review, challenges by local stakeholders as well as administrative delays.

Part III deals with the flexible mechanisms under the Kyoto Protocol, which are of enormous practical and theoretical importance as they raise intriguing questions of supranational administrative law. *Sander Simonetti* and *Rutger de Witt Wijnen* explain international emissions trading under the Kyoto Protocol. They devote particular attention to green investment schemes, under which some or all of the revenue from the sale of Assigned Amount Units (AAU) is earmarked for greening activities in the seller country. They explain the legal forms that the greening can take, namely public international law treaties and private law contracts, and explore some of the legal issues created thereby. In the next contribution, which might have been better placed in Part VII, *Jelmer Hoogzaad* and *Charlotte Streck* argue that Joint Implementation (JI) has been neglected unjustifiably. While (not least due to its "prompt start") the Clean Development Mechanism (CDM) has given rise to more projects and has attracted far more attention, the probable future assumption of emissions caps by emerging economies implies that JI should become far more important, as CDM can only take place in countries without such caps. They suggest reforms to JI to facilitate this process. *Anthony Hobley* and *Carly Roberts* give a short overview of JI in practice and present major differences between CDM and JI – among them the greater heterogeneity between the regimes in different JI host countries – before discussing risks of JI projects and giving practical guidance on JI contracting. *Maria Netto* and *Kai-Uwe Barani Schmidt* give an overview of CDM by focusing on the different actors involved and in particular on the UNFCCC secretariat, on the work beyond the individual projects (accreditation of designated operational entities and approval of methodologies) as well as the different steps a CDM project has to go through. In the following article, *Matthias Krey* and *Heike Santen* analyse why CDM, despite the large emissions reduction achieved, became the object of severe criticism from stakeholders. They consider that in spite of the aim of transparency, uncertainty "is an immanent feature of the current structures and procedures of rule making" which extends to all stages of the project. *Axel Michaelowa* tackles changes in additionality definitions and regulatory practice over time. Since CDM projects take place in countries without emissions caps, additionality lies at the heart of the CDM in order to assess whether the project is useful from an emissions reduction perspective: the granting of CERs appears appropriate only where the emissions reductions in investments would not have happened anyway. The contribution explains how the definition of additionality has evolved over time. Given the enormous financial implications of decisions by the CDM administration, independent oversight of these decisions becomes a necessity. While considerable attention has been paid to the question whether private actors can seek judicial review of decisions by the CDM Executive Board that harm their commercial interests, *Christina Voigt* examines the opposite question of whether there should be a possibility that such decisions can also be attacked for lack of environmental integrity. She answers in the affirmative and proposes a judicial review process within the UNFCCC/Kyoto framework; however, she does not fully clarify who should be given standing in such disputes. The final two contributions of Part III deal with primary and secondary carbon contracting generally (and might thus have been better placed in Part II). *Martijn Wilder* and *Louisa Fitz-Gerald* first give advice to be heeded in carbon contracting, which urgently needs to take into account the regulatory framework of carbon trading. After describing different contracting approaches, they draw attention to the interplay between international and domestic laws and to specific risks in carbon contracting. Andrew Hedges then considers the secondary market. He begins with design elements for the creation of a successful secondary market, before moving on to market structures for emissions trading in the EU. He then presents issues arising from the coexistence, interplay and integration of primary and secondary markets.

Part IV contains the contributions on the European Union Emissions Trading Scheme (EU ETS), which represents by far the largest carbon market in operation to date. *Markus Pohlmann* commences with an overview of EU ETS, where he describes the cornerstones of the scheme, but also inherent tensions between subsidiarity and centralization/harmonization. He also explains linking of EU ETS to other schemes and lists lessons learned in the operation of the scheme. *Navraj Singh Galeigh* studies the European Court of Justice case law regarding EU ETS. He comes to the conclusion that through formalistic and restrictive decisions, in particular with respect to admissibility of challenges to Commission decisions on national allocation plans, the court has made a significant contribution to legal certainty.

Part V examines national and subnational schemes. *K Russell LaMotte, David M Wlliamson* and *Lauren A Hopkins* give an overview of legal issues surrounding emissions trading in the US both at the national and subnational level, ranging from property rights to taxation and linkages as well as constitutional limits to subnational schemes. *Kyle W Danish* discusses policy design issues and legal problems of offsets in the proposals for a cap and trade programme in the US. *Martijn Wilder* and *Louisa Fitz-Gerald* present the initiatives by the then Rudd government aiming at implementing a very ambitious nationwide carbon trading scheme as well as complementing measures and issues raised by voluntary carbon markets in Australia. *Gray E Taylor* and *Michael R Barrett* describe national and subnational (province level) mitigation initiatives in Canada. Finally, *Christopher Tung* gives an introduction to carbon law and practice in China, which is very interesting both given that China is the world's biggest host country of CDM and the calls for China to make emission reduction commitments.

In the only paper in Part VI, *Michelle Passero* leaves the confines of carbon markets set up by governments and introduces voluntary carbon markets. They allow a transfer of GHG reductions from one private party to another, who is under no obligation to surrender such offsets, but nevertheless for ethical or publicity reasons chooses to reduce the carbon footprint. She cautions against excessive government involvement in such markets, but indicates at the same time some scope for helpful interventions.

Part VII, which is entitled "Post-Kyoto: Moving towards Copenhagen" and which in the meantime without loss of substance might well be replaced by something like "Post-Kyoto and Post-Copenhagen" sketches options for the future. *Murray Ward* opens the part with a proposal for elements of a future global climate change deal. He is adamant that quantitative targets are necessary, but have to be complemented by the 'bigger picture', such as adaption, technology deployment and capacity building. *Jos Cozijnsen* and *Michael J Coren* consider offsets from project-based mechanisms such as JI and the CDM indispensable as a transitional measure. For they offer a limited link between domestic emissions trading schemes and offset mechanisms can lower the costs of mitigation targets in developed countries while at the same time direct mitigation investment to developing countries. In order to secure the latter, they call for the retention of a reformed CDM possibly complemented by credits for nationally appropriate mitigation actions and for reduced emissions from deforestation and degradation (REDD). *Christiana Figueres* and *Charlotte Streck* develop a post-2012 vision for the CDM. They appeal for maintaining environmental integrity and sufficient demand for CERs as well as improved governance. While they reject purely private sectoral approaches, they are more open towards government-led sectoral approaches. In order to effectively tackle tropical deforestation, *Robert O'Sullivan* and *Rick Saines* propose the extension of carbon markets to include REDD, initially at project level and then at national level. *Claybourne Fox Clarke* and *Thiago Chagas* discuss policy options for international measures aimed at reducing emissions from aviation. Such measures could take place under the auspices of the International Civil Aviation Organisation or, which the authors prefer given the former's failure to make significant progress, the UNFCCC/Kyoto-Successor. Mitigation in the airline sector could also take on the form of an inclusion in a national scheme or the pursuit of a sectoral approach.

As can be seen from the summary of contents, the book covers a wide range of topics, on which it contains a wealth of information. It is characterized by a mixture of innovative and survey-style contributions. It contains both a highly readable description of current practice and legal foundations of carbon markets on the one hand and future policy options on the other, both of which are highly relevant. For in such a fast moving regulatory environment, in which major decisions will have to be taken soon, balanced and careful analysis of future options is required to assess the impact on future developments for current investment decisions. The book is up to date, even though some concrete proposals have in the meantime been demoted to a mere remote and uncertain prospect. In short: The book is a true must-have for scholars, policy makers and practitioners interested in carbon markets.

Santiago Montt, State Liability in Investment Treaty Arbitration. Global Constitutional and Administrative Law in the BIT Generation
Hart Publishing, 2009
ISBN 978-1-84113-856-5

August Reinisch

This book is a revised version of a JSD dissertation submitted at Yale Law School in which the author, a Chilean lawyer, intends to link his own administrative law background with investment arbitration in the so-called BIT generation. The outcome is a fascinating and intellectually stimulating perspective on various salient issues of investment arbitration, focusing on two of the core protection standards in modern investment law, the law on expropriation and fair and equitable treatment.

Before actually turning *medias in res*, the author provides some lengthy introductory chapters providing his 'framework of analysis'. He first intends to correct some 'distorted' views on the Latin American approach to state responsibility, and in particular on the Calvo doctrine and clause; then he presents his own theory on the increasing popularity of BITs and finally he addresses legitimacy issues arising in a world of decentralized international investment arbitration. Though it is initially not wholly clear how these three preludes interact and relate to the main themes of expropriation and fair and equitable treatment, they offer most interesting insights and are based on a highly knowledgeable treatment by Santiago Montt.

Chapter 1 portrays the development of the Calvo doctrine which, as the author insists, is usually wrongly attributed to Carlos Calvo, being a creation of the Chilean jurist Andres Bello. In Mr. Montt's opinion this Latin American doctrine was primarily aimed at fending off unjustified exercises of 'diplomatic protection', which often appeared in the appalling form of gunboat diplomacy. Though this view is probably correct, it cannot really be regarded as particularly new. Also his interpretation of the Calvo clause, as a contractual renunciation of diplomatic protection freely entered into by foreign investors, does not appear very revolutionary. More interesting is his statement that during the height of the NIEO debate, the Calvo

A. Reinisch (✉)
Rechtswiss. Fakultät, Universität Wien, Schottenbastei 10-16, Stiege 2, 5. Stock, 1010 Vienna, Austria
e-mail: august.reinisch@univie.ac.at

C. Herrmann and J.P. Terhechte (eds.), *European Yearbook of International Economic Law (EYIEL), Vol. 3 (2012)*, European Yearbook of International Economic Law 3, DOI 10.1007/978-3-642-23309-8_24, © Springer-Verlag Berlin Heidelberg 2012

doctrine was in fact opportunistically used in order to justify expropriation without compensation (p. 57).

In his second preliminary chapter on the emergence of the BIT generation, Mr. Montt takes issue with the prominent view that the proliferation of BITs was the result of a prisoner's dilemma among developing countries competing against each other to attract FDI (p. 85). In fact, he does not really question that there are collective action problems; rather his point is that investment receiving countries may not necessarily be worse off with than without BITs. Montt's 'virtual network theory' claims that the BIT bargain of trading sovereignty for credibility to attract FDI was made 'under essential conditions of uncertainty' (p. 123) and that what developing countries would receive in exchange for more investment need not necessarily be the intrusive 'BITs-as-gunboat-arbitration' control by investment panels unbound. Rather, he sees the potential for a balanced development of investment arbitration into a nuanced 'experiment in global governance' if it grows into what the author calls 'BITs-as-developed-countries-constitutional-law-and-no-more' review (p. 123).

It is this concluding thought which is further explored in Chapter 3, entitled 'Trading off Sovereignty for Credibility: Questions of Legitimacy in the BIT Generation'. Montt discusses various points of criticism that have been raised against investment arbitration, among them the fact that arbitrators assume the role of constitutional law judges second-guessing national policy choices; that their interpretations cannot be overturned 'by proper amendment' (p. 138); that their interpretations of similar standards often lack coherence (p. 140), etc. He seems disillusioned about the legitimating force of various potential 'sources of legitimacy': the idea of 'consent legitimacy' stressing the fact that states have agreed to investor state arbitration in treaties is dismissed as too formalistic (pp. 141–144); 'output legitimacy' in the sense that BITs would increase FDI inflows is empirically questioned (p. 145); 'exit legitimacy' provided by the option of exiting the BIT system appears not feasible in practice (pp. 145–146); 'rule of law legitimacy' in the sense that a pre-established set of rules is applied by independent adjudicators is 'severely compromised by the extremely broad and vague nature of the treaties' main clauses' (p. 147). Clearly, indeterminacy is a main challenge to any rule of law concept based on the predictability of outcomes. Nevertheless, Montt remains modestly optimistic about the future development of investment arbitration as long as it avoided some 'excesses of current BIT jurisprudence' (p. 161).

The Second Part of Santiago Montt's book is devoted to analysing some of these 'excessive' interpretations, in particular with regard to two core standards of investment protection, the guarantee against expropriation without compensation and the fair and equitable treatment (FET) standard. Before actually discussing these two BIT standards, the author sets the scene for his state liability perspective. As the book's title suggests, state liability is Montt's main focus and the aim is to show under what conditions states normally become liable to citizens for their regulatory activity and to compare such domestic law liability with the outcomes of investor state arbitration. Chapter 4, entitled 'Property Rights v the Public Interest: A Comparative Approach to a Global Puzzle', thus focuses on principles developed in major Western legal traditions with regard to a duty to compensate property owners for interferences with their rights. Based on a comparative analysis of mostly property rights interference law, Montt concludes that while only the full destruction of property rights leads to compensation, 'non-destructive interferences' are normally permitted without compensation 'unless the state acted in an illegal, irrational, unequal, or disproportionate manner' (p. 229).

Chapter 5 then analyses the expropriation case-law of investment tribunals against this background. Montt concentrates on the identification of when an indirect expropriation takes place and outlines the development of the substantial deprivation doctrine in investment arbitration. He states that in spite of some initial fears that tribunals might significantly broaden the scope of compensable expropriations as compared to domestic constitutional jurisprudence, the overall trend has been one of adjudicatory restraint. Tribunals have generally displayed a high level of 'deference towards the regulatory state' (p. 289). Thus, Montt finds that states are unlikely to be exposed to excessive liability claims following their regulatory activities under the expropriation clauses contained in BITs. Therefore he concludes that the 'general adjudicative tension between the private and the public interest has been transferred from the expropriatory clause to the FET clause' (Ibid.).

The latter is the central focus of Chapter 6, entitled 'Controlling Arbitrariness through the Fair and Equitable Treatment Standard'. Montt starts this chapter by challenging the idea of FET as an autonomous standard – widely adhered to in non-NAFTA cases decided on the basis of BITs which do not contain an express reference to the international minimum standard and/or to general international law. While he is right in pointing out that pursuant to principles of systemic interpretation – based on Article 31(3)(c) Vienna Convention on the Law of Treaties – treaty terms should be interpreted taking into account 'relevant rules of international law applicable between the parties', he fails to convince the reader why the treaty terms 'fair and equitable treatment' should be regarded as no more than the international minimum standard. Granted, this would be a 'methodological constraint over arbitral tribunals' discretion' (p. 308), but that does not make the underlying assumption more convincing. Also Montt's later reliance on Thomas Wälde's statement that investor-state arbitration would be the main advantage of an investment treaty (p. 370) cannot overcome doubts about FET interpretations that would amount to 'simply repeat[ing] the principles and rules of [general international law]' (Ibid). The most interesting part of Chapter 6 is found in the author's attempt to embed the existing FET jurisprudence with its topoi 'due process', 'arbitrariness', 'lack of proportionality', 'legitimate expectations', etc. into a Global Administrative Law (GAL) approach. Montt sees a danger in the practice of investment tribunals to interpret FET in a hyper-autonomous fashion, unrestrained not only by the international minimum standard, but also by domestic law. This development might ultimately lead to what he has initially termed the intrusive 'BITs-as-gunboat-arbitration'. In contrast, Montt demands that FET interpretation and application be moderated in a twofold way: first, FET issues should always be decided taking into account the domestic law of the host state; second the international minimum standard, concretised through comparative law, should be applied in a non-intrusive way. His GAL approach is at times technical and overly-complex, but it provides a thoughtful new look at many issues surrounding the actual content of the FET standard.

In an excellent conclusion the different strands of the present work are brought together. Montt insists that the open-textured standards as such do not pose any threat to sovereignty and democratic self-determination, but that 'an unrestrained international investment jurisprudence' may do so (p. 370). The author reasserts, however, his opinion that a constrained investment arbitration may avoid the dangers of 'BITs-as-gunboat-arbitration'. The two major types of restraint he explained already in the FET chapter are more reliance on the domestic law of host countries and a moderate scrutiny under international law principles ascertained by a comparative approach that avoids decisions based on 'subjective impressions' (p. 373). With an optimistic outlook Montt concludes that a balanced body of investment law constitutes a goal that can and must be demanded from the BIT generation (p. 374).

This monograph contains a wealth of information, reflecting thorough research done by an author often looking beyond conventional wisdoms and looking for original sources. This is also reflected by extensive Spanish and French language sources which are often quoted at length (pp. 37, 43, 44, 47, 57, 371). However, sometimes an English translation, at least in the footnotes, would have been helpful. It is a pity that a number of typos ('Rechtsstaat' is sometimes correctly spelled p. 139, p. 367, often not 'Rechsstaat', p. 297; 'biding' instead of 'binding' on p. 144, 'apropriation' instead of 'appropriation' on p. 183, etc.) have not been eliminated in the final version of this book.

The critique Montt applies to the outcome of some arbitrations appears from time to time unbalanced. Some sweeping statements are irritating, for instance Montt's repeated assertion that FET corresponds to the international minimum standard – as expressed in the NAFTA Free Trade Commission interpretation of 2001 – and that the competing view that FET is an autonomous standard would be 'erroneous' (p. 138) or 'incorrect' (p. 152, footnote 150).

Equally, some points of criticism raised against investment arbitration would have won credibility had they been formulated in a more moderate fashion. For instance, Montt's assertion that 'many of the key BITs clauses have been applied in dissimilar and even contradictory ways, without clear justification in different textual formulations in treaties' (p. 140) may echo well often-heard allegations of incoherence and inconsistency. However, they miss the fact that in spite of the *ad hoc* character of investment arbitration, its outcomes are remarkably coherent and the often discussed inconsistencies concerning, for instance, the existence of a state of necessity, the scope of MFN clauses, the meaning of umbrella clauses, etc., are the exceptions rather than the rule.

On the whole, however, *State Liability in Investment Treaty Arbitration* provides a thought-provoking new outlook on familiar issues in international investment law. It is well written and contains a lucid analysis of some of the core problems concerning the actual application of the expropriation and FET standards in practice.

Thomas Gerassimos Riedel, Rechtsbeziehungen zwischen dem Internationalen Währungsfonds und der Welthandelsorganisation

Nomos, 2008
ISBN 978-3-8329-3703-4

Christoph Ohler

In July 2008, when this PhD thesis was published, only few people imagined the magnitude of the financial turmoil that would befall the western hemisphere and trigger a deep and long-lasting recession. Also in July 2008, most commentators were sceptical when asked whether there was at all a future for the old Bretton Woods System, in particular the IMF and its lending policy. Many countries, which only some years ago were dependent on support from the IMF, had announced to repay their facilities and stop co-operating with the Washington based international organisation, a fact which the author mentions shortly (p. 98). But, when the financial crisis hit Iceland, to name only one country affected, the IMF was back in business – which it is now eagerly defending. In the future, the question will be if the IMF can establish itself successfully as a global macroeconomic supervisor watching out to warn against the rise of systemic risks and global imbalances. It is the same logic when political leaders and academia discuss the role the various international fora around the G20 process will play and how they should be put into effective co-operation rather than left in isolated co-existence. Maybe, the biggest flaw of the past was that we (and not only they) all concentrated on our undoubtedly relevant but, narrow mandate (or academic interests), thereby neglecting the complex interplay between trade and finance. This is also the field where the mandate of WTO and IMF could be mutually strengthened in the future.

Riedels dissertation, as it is clear from its date of publication, could not anticipate these developments. Rather, the book starts by looking at the role of the IMF as one of the Bretton Woods "triplets" next to the World Bank (IBRD) and the ITO (pp. 37 et seq.). As the history of international economic law demonstrates, good ideas are not sufficient to make a system work. It took until 1995 that the IMF got its "younger twin" in the form of the WTO. It is worthwhile, as Riedel does in the middle of his work (pp. 141 et seq.), to compare the constitutional basis of both

C. Ohler (✉)
Rechtswissenschaftliche Fakultät, Friedrich-Schiller-Universität Jena, 07737 Jena, Germany
e-mail: christoph.ohler@recht.uni-jena.de

C. Herrmann and J.P. Terhechte (eds.), *European Yearbook of International Economic Law (EYIEL), Vol. 3 (2012)*, European Yearbook of International Economic Law 3, DOI 10.1007/978-3-642-23309-8_25, © Springer-Verlag Berlin Heidelberg 2012

institutions to find out which constructive elements they have in common and which they have not. While the WTO is an organisation on the basis of "one member, one vote", voting shares (and effective power) in the IMF depend largely on the quota subscribed by a member. Those quota are calculated primarily on the basis of national GDP and other economic factors. This is the reason why the IMF was and is dominated by the U.S. It will also remain dominated by this country after the "Quota and Voice Reform", an agreement on the realignment of voting shares in favour of emerging markets members that entered into force on 3 March 2011. This distribution of powers however, contributed to a relatively effective decision making process. In contrast to that, the negotiation procedures under WTO law are based on equal voting and reciprocity which makes it extremely difficult to find a compromise among the more than 150 members of the organisation. Even more stunning is the difference between treaty wording and treaty reality with reference to both institutions. Whereas the Articles of Agreement of the IMF are still highly technical and hardly readable, political practice of the IMF evolved far beyond the legal text. This made the institution a powerful (and sometimes heavily criticised) reformer in many economies that could urge for market economy standards and good governance at the same time. Admittedly, this could only become the case where a country was dependent on financial support from the IMF, whereas on a daily basis the Articles of Agreement provide no mechanism other than peer pressure to react on economic imbalances of a country. The discussion whether this is still adequate goes vividly on as it is demonstrated by the meeting of G-20 Finance Ministers and Central Bank Governors in Paris on 18–19 February 2011 and the high-ranking "Palais-Royal-Initiative" of 8 February 2011 under the chair of Michel Camdessus, Alexandre Lamfalussy and Tommaso Padoa-Schioppa. In comparison to such revival of the IMF, the ways and means of the WTO seem to be rather limited. The WTO started in 1995 with high expectations to liberalise world trade as it is clearly and positively reflected in its underlying agreements but, underwent within less than one decade a rapid process of disillusionment. Today, the global trade organisation is in the state of a political stalemate with members unable to close the current Doha-Round. It remains to be seen whether the promises of the G-20 to promote further trade liberalisation under the auspices of the WTO will turn out to be realistic.

Riedel describes the organs and their functioning of both institutions, explains the role of secondary law and illustrates the respective mandates. He discusses the legal nature of the stand-by-arrangements by the IMF and concludes that they are unilateral declarations and not agreements (pp. 92 et seq.). His remarks on conditionality are short but, they reflect the dominating view that this legal practice does not violate international law. With regard to the WTO the author discusses the perspectives of multilateralism and bilateralism within the organisation stressing the ever growing importance of regional integration agreements. Very shortly he analyses the rationale of the various trade agreements and of the dispute settlement procedure. In the second part of his book the author discusses the fields and forms of co-operation between the IMF and WTO. This is the place where he explains for the first time the importance of free movement of payments for international trade relations and the problem of current account deficits. In practice, the IMF tends to consent to national measures to reduce a current account deficit even if this has a negative impact on trade relations. As there exists a broad spectrum of measures that are fit to reduce a current account deficit (e.g. currency depreciations, exchange control regulations, direct and indirect trade restrictions) the Fund may not even have been informed about the measure as the author explains (p. 161). Both situations may give rise to conflicts with WTO law, in particular the GATT, even if this agreement permits in Article XII trade restrictions to safeguard the balance of payments. From a procedural point of view, Article XV:1 GATT mandates the WTO to enter into a cooperation agreement with the IMF the purpose of which is to alleviate the exchange of information and to form a basis for mutual consultations. The agreement between both institutions was made in 1996 which Riedel qualifies as a form of secondary law. Under its provisions however, the problem was not resolved to what extent the findings of the IMF are binding for a panel or the Appellate Body within a dispute settlement procedure under the DSU. One would add that secondary law cannot amend primary law so that the answer to this question depends fully on the provisions of the GATT and the DSU. Riedel elaborates the functioning of Article XV:2 and XV:9 GATT, provisions that so far were discussed in one dispute settlement procedure only (Dominican Republic – Measures affecting the importation and internal sale of cigarettes). As he points out, the wording of Article XV:2 GATT is unclear ("the CONTRACTING PARTIES shall accept all findings"). In his view, this should be interpreted that Article XV:2 GATT can generally bind the DSB towards findings of the IMF but, that the independence of the panel and the Appellate Body may restrict the binding effect (p. 209). As regards the material rule of Article XV:9 GATT the author argues that it creates an exception from treaty obligations under the GATT (p. 175). In both cases one would like to read more (and more coherently) about the critical scope of application of these provisions. Riedel then describes conflicts in the field of trade subventions with respect to the SCM Agreement and the IMF Articles of Agreement. One of the most eminent topics in this respect is China's currency policy where the author argues that China does not violate anti-subvention law of the WTO. The thesis ends with several recommendations de lege ferenda for the improvement of the existing co-operation mechanism.

The author's reasoning is sober and precise at any time. The problems discussed in the book are well-chosen and clearly explained, exhibiting a good portion of legal craftsmanship. But, from time to time the reader wishes to get more in-depth-analysis. One would desire that the author had dared to focus much stronger on some of the questions he raises. This is underlined by the impression that the author's reasoning is sometimes a bit pointillist when he interrupts his line of thoughts to go into side-problems. While criticizing that, one should not forget to mention that academic works on the IMF were rare in recent years. Riedel's dissertation is a solid basis for further research on the future of the international financial architecture.

Jan-Frederik Belling, Die Jurisdiktion *rationae materiae* der ICSID-Schiedsgerichte. Unter besonderer Berücksichtigung des Investitionsbegriffes des Weltbankübereinkommens vom 18.03.1965

Duncker & Humblot, 2008
ISBN 978-3-428-12443-5

Christian J. Tams

Over the last decade, international investment law has become an increasingly relevant discipline. To some extent, the law's rise to prominence merely follows factual developments, namely the increased importance of foreign direct investment. Yet another factor would seem to be equally important: International law has accepted an increasingly broad notion of 'investment', and thereby included a heterogeneous range of economic transactions into the area of investment law and within the potential jurisdiction of investment tribunals. The study under review, a doctoral dissertation submitted by Jan-Frederik Belling, analyses this latter factor, and in so doing, helps us appreciate the surprising rise to prominence of a niche area of law whose future, a generation ago, seemed at best uncertain.

Belling's chosen topic, the notion of "investment" as mentioned in Article 25 of the ICSID Convention, is of fundamental relevance, and Belling deals with it in a principled manner. His discussion of arbitral practice is preceded by balanced, if overly detailed, overviews over the historical evolution of foreign investment (section B, pp. 24–77) and the main features of the ICSID system of dispute settlement (sections C and D, pp. 78–135). Section E introduces the various ways and means of establishing ICSID jurisdiction and in this sense continues to "set the stage"; beyond that, however, it provides a helpful analysis of how international investment treaties (on which the clear majority of ICSID proceedings are based) define the notion of investment (pp. 136–176). In this respect, Belling rightly notes the trend towards broad, liberal approaches, which blur the line between traditional forms of foreign direct investment and other forms of property. Section F contrasts this broad approach to that adopted in Article 25 of the ICSID Convention. Belling is at pains to stress that even though the provision eventually left the matter open,

C.J. Tams (✉)
Professor of International Law, University of Glasgow, Glasgow, G12 8QQ, U.K.

C. Herrmann and J.P. Terhechte (eds.), *European Yearbook of International Economic Law (EYIEL), Vol. 3 (2012)*, European Yearbook of International Economic Law 3, DOI 10.1007/978-3-642-23309-8_26, © Springer-Verlag Berlin Heidelberg 2012

the drafters spent considerable time seeking to define the notion of investment, and the decision to omit a definition was adopted against considerable opposition. Belling's analysis on this point presents a much more nuanced picture than the often-quoted passages from the Director's Report which simply restate that the Convention provided no definition. On the basis of his analysis, Belling strongly defends an "objective" understanding of the term "investment" in the sense of Article 25 of the ICSID Convention, which insists on its autonomous meaning and underlines that it was intended to limit the Centre's jurisdiction *ratione materiae.*

Arbitral practice indeed reflects this objective approach as a matter of principle; yet it also shows that it is easily undermined in practice, as the required "objective definition" of investment is rather vague. Belling's discussion of key decision, while stressing the need for an objective approach, brings this out rather clearly. His review shows that arbitral tribunals have not hesitated to exercise jurisdiction over claims based on minority shareholdings, promissory notes or construction contracts. In fact, these categories of transactions are now regularly subsumed under the notion of investment. This does not mean that Article 25 had completely lost its restricting potential. Cases such as *Joy Mining* and others clarify that "one-off" activities such as contracts for sale remain outside the scope of ICSID jurisdiction and do not enjoy the privileged protection that contemporary international law accords to investments. However, the trend towards a broader, more inclusive understanding of investment seems unabated. To give just one example, in the wake of Argentina's financial crisis, state bonds (which Belling does not cover) have become recognized as a new form of investment in the sense of Article 25 of the ICSID Convention and are addressed by ICSID tribunals. Rather than by embracing narrow definitions, those seeking to restrict the jurisdiction of ICSID tribunals (that is, notably States) seem to make use of other techniques: if recent practice is any guide, legality clauses in particular seem to be the new Achilles heel of investors who in the course of their investment have infringed legal standards; in addition, the requirement of foreign nationality continues to present a hurdle. Still, Belling should not be accused of re-enacting old debates of the past. Even if his approach at present is unlikely to gain mainstream acceptance, investment law – driven as it is, at present, by ad hoc arbitration – needs thorough studies like his. Having grown un-organically over a decade, the law may require some form of consolidation, and a return to the basics. Looked at from a distance, it is curious how little headway has been made in understanding the crucial notion of 'investment', and how much discussions still center on types of activities as opposed to a proper definition. Belling's study is a useful and necessary reminder that a more thorough approach is possible.